D0712940

Transitional Justice

Volume II
Country Studies

Transitional Justice includes:

Volume I: General Considerations
Volume II: Country Studies
Volume III: Laws, Rulings, and Reports

Transitional Justice

How Emerging Democracies Reckon with Former Regimes

Volume II

Country Studies

NEIL J. KRITZ
EDITOR

Foreword by
Nelson Mandela

UNITED STATES INSTITUTE OF PEACE PRESS
Washington, D.C.

The views expressed in this book are those of the authors alone. They do not necessarily reflect views of the United States Institute of Peace.

United States Institute of Peace
1550 M Street NW, Suite 700
Washington, DC 20005-1708

First published 1995

Printed in the United States of America

The paper used in this publication meets the minimum requirements of American National Standard for Information Sciences—Permanence of Paper for Printed Library Materials, ANSI Z39.48-1984.

Library of Congress Cataloging-in-Publications Data
Transitional justice : how emerging democracies reckon with former regimes / Neil J. Kritz, editor.
p. cm.
Includes bibliographical references and indexes.
Contents: v. 1. General considerations — v. 2. Country studies — v. 3. Laws, rulings, and reports.
ISBN 1-878379-47-X. — ISBN 1-878379-43-7 (pbk.)
1. Political crimes and offenses. 2. Crimes against humanity. 3. Political persecution. 4. Criminal justice, Administration of. I. Kritz, Neil J., 1959– .
K5250.T73 1995
345'.0231—dc20
[342.5231]
95-24363
CIP

Volume II: COUNTRY STUDIES

Summary of Contents

Volume II: Country Studies

Contents

FOREWORD

This important publication on transitional justice comes at a time when the world is grappling with the problems of governance, legitimacy, democracy, and human rights. In recent years, particularly during the past decade, there has been a remarkable movement in various regions of the world away from undemocratic and repressive rule towards the establishment of constitutional democracies.

In nearly all instances, the displaced regimes were characterized by massive violations of human rights and undemocratic systems of governance. In their attempt to combat real or perceived opposition, they exercised authority with very little regard to accountability.

Transition in these societies has therefore been accompanied by enormous challenges. While it has signified new hopes and aspirations, it has at the same time brought into sharp focus the difficult choices that these countries would have to make on their road to democracy and economic progress.

Ironically, the advent of democracy has also put the welcome endeavors for national consensus to a test. In South Africa, for instance, it has highlighted the deep divisions that have existed within society.

As all these countries recover from the trauma and wounds of the past, they have had to devise mechanisms not only for handling past human rights violations, but also to ensure that the dignity of victims, survivors, and relatives is restored. In the context of this relentless search for appropriate equilibria, profound issues of policy and law have emerged. They have arisen out of the question of how a country in transition should respond to allegations of gross human rights violations by individuals of either the predecessor or extant authority. The issue that has concerned the international community is the problem created by the incompatibility of such amnesties with a state's international obligations.

In so far as these volumes on *Transitional Justice* bring together under one roof the diverse experiences of transitional societies, they provide an impetus for the creation of an international community predicated on human dignity and justice. The variety as well as the richness of experiences contained in this publication will certainly be a useful guide not only to students and researchers in retrospective justice, but also in the popular endeavors to reorganize civil society.

My heartfelt congratulations to the United States Institute of Peace for this timely and well-organized publication.

Nelson Mandela
President of the Republic of South Africa

PREFACE

The movement from repressive regimes to democratic societies has become a worldwide phenomenon as humanity approaches the twenty-first century. The transitions in South Africa, Central and Eastern Europe, and large parts of Latin America provide inspiring recent examples of this trend. The legacy of past political repression, however, can be an emotional and practical burden, affecting the stability of many a transition. How can a new society peacefully integrate those former officials who were associated with a past of repression as well as those who were its victims? How can an emerging democracy respond to public demands for redress of the legitimate grievances of some without creating new injustices for others? From 1989 to 1992, I observed the practical import of these complex questions while negotiating the United Nations Peace Agreement for Cambodia. The ultimate success of Cambodia's effort to build a participatory political order will be at least partly determined by the way the country handles its own recent past of genocidal violence and revolutionary repression.

The national culture, the history of the former regime, and the political realities of the transition process all influence the approach adopted by any society emerging from a period of repression. A constant in each case, however, is the search for a political process that will achieve justice as well as social stability and reconciliation. The history of the last fifty years provides a wealth of positive examples of the transition process as well as some notable missteps and failures.

The United States Institute of Peace is exploring these challenging questions through an ongoing project entitled "Transitional Justice," under the direction of our Rule of Law Initiative. The present three-volume collection, *Transitional Justice: How Emerging Democracies Reckon with Former Regimes*, is a major outcome of that project. *Volume I: General Considerations* addresses legal, political, and philosophical perspectives. *Volume II: Country Studies* examines more than twenty transitions in the period from World War II to the present. *Volume III: Law, Rulings, and Reports* includes over 100 samples of legislation, constitutional provisions, judicial decisions, and reports of official commissions of inquiry, as well as relevant treaty excerpts.

This collection should become a standard reference for governments, private organizations, scholars, and other individuals dealing with these difficult issues. Some of the models of a transition process documented here may suggest approaches that would facilitate a just and peaceful transition; others might best be consigned to the history books. The United States Institute of Peace does not endorse any one approach, but offers these volumes in the belief that a comparative review can provide insights and examples for leaders in emerging democracies as they confront the challenges of transitional justice.

Richard H. Solomon
President
United States Institute of Peace

INTRODUCTION

When the communist world began its collapse in the late 1980s and the post–Cold War period opened, newly democratic nations, some with vibrant histories of democracy, others ruled only by tyrants, and a few enjoying the promise of new nationhood, looked to the democracies, especially the United States, for help in creating democratic institutions and the complex foundation of a citizenry of democrats so necessary to traverse the inevitable rough waters ahead. How, they asked, might we best inspire our people with the habits of democracy and establish legal institutions to propel and protect our new freedoms?

Without question, the new historical era offers the most exciting opportunity for durable peace since the end of the First World War. With that prospect in mind, the United States Institute of Peace responded in a variety of ways, among them by establishing a Rule of Law Initiative and directing all programs—grants, fellowships, in-house projects, education and training, and library and communications—to pay special attention to the integral relationship between the rule of law and international peace with justice and freedom. By creating the initiative, the Institute underscored law as a crucial component of both scholarship and practice in peacemaking and peacebuilding, based upon the following propositions:

- Although in practice imperfect, democracy is by nature peaceful: on the international plane, democracies generally do not wage war against each other.
- Democratic structures require governance under the rule of law, which includes separate and independent lawmaking and judicial branches of government and incorporates basic norms of human rights and civil rights.
- The rule *of* law—not simply rule *by* law—ensures a system governed by openness, security, and accountability such that citizens may enjoy trust in their institutions and among each other.

In designing the initiative, we were intrigued by the immediate problem of how new leaderships in former totalitarian countries would treat previous governments. People had been ruled on a daily basis by violence, terror, and division, whether for decades or a few years. Civil trust had been impossible, economic opportunity crushed, and congenial social relations hard. With democracy now in the air, there were penetrating cries for retaliation against old rulers and for revelations about the past. Amnesties were discussed as were prosecutions. Decisions about the personnel and activities of the earlier governments came to mark a critical phase of this era of democratization. The Western world watched, commented, in some instances sent experts to advise. If judgments lacked fairness and if truth was subverted by bias and propaganda, the democratic foundation would be built on sand. If prosecutions (or decisions not to prosecute) complied with due process standards and if reports protected individual rights, then the symbols, structures, and operations of the new state would be built upon justice and the start would be strong. In short, democracy would not be safe over time without a thorough and careful application of normative rules to ensure that justice was achieved upon a foundation of the rule of law.

We believed that, while each country's experience was not only dramatic but unique, their problems were not unique, in particular with respect to the treatment of former officials. We were confident that similar issues were being struggled with across the world and that studies from the recent past would hold lessons for today. We determined to create a set of first-rate readings on basic questions of "transitional justice," demonstrating that, despite the uniqueness of each society and its historical and political context, there are unifying themes common to nations moving from despotism to democracy and lessons that each nation might bring to others.

These volumes are a major compilation of carefully selected excerpts from studies as well as primary documents on transitional justice, a subject that is itself a defining theme of the second half of the twentieth century and is likely to endure well into the new millennium as suppressed ethnic, religious, and political disputes continue to be unleashed and the struggle for democracy continues. The readings show continuity of issues across continents and time, while demonstrating remarkable complexity: readers will find passages rich in legal, moral, political, and social content and, perhaps most tellingly, deep historical context.

This project proceeded from the belief that the collection, editing, and organization of the best existing material would be an important contribution to the field, facilitating comparative analysis of issues that many countries have previously viewed as unique to their own experience. The project began with a review of over 17,000 books and articles of possible relevance to the project. With the exception of Volume III, the search was mostly limited to English-language materials. We also consulted extensively with political scientists, historians, legal experts, psychologists, theologians, human rights activists, philosophers, and specialists on various countries for ideas and references in the literature. And above all, we read, edited, and structured the volumes as our findings developed.

These volumes are limited, as the subtitle indicates, to the way that emerging *democratic* societies address the legacy of their repression of their own people. This approach has excluded consideration of non-democratic successor states (for example, the transition from the Pahlavi to Khomeini regimes in Iran, or from Somoza to the Sandinistas in Nicaragua). It has also excluded most material on the transition policies of occupation authorities (such as post–World War II Japan). Lastly, although proper handling of the transitional justice issue is integral to the process of democratization, these two issues are conceptually distinct; the present study therefore does not examine democratization per se.

Each volume stands on its own, and each reinforces the others. *Volume I: General Considerations* provides a range of views on the broad issues entailed in transitional justice. Political, historical, legal, psychological, and moral perspectives are all included.

Volume II: Country Studies examines the handling of these nettlesome issues in twenty-one countries during the last fifty years. These case studies are arranged in chronological order: five countries that dealt with the issues of transitional justice in an immediate post–World War II context (Germany, France, Denmark, Belgium, and Italy); South Korea's democratic interlude in the 1960s (with a brief discussion of that country's subsequent return to these issues nearly three decades later); transitional justice in Southern Europe in the 1970s (Greece, Portugal, and Spain); emergence from dictatorships in the 1980s in Latin America (Argentina, Uruguay, Brazil, and Chile) and in Uganda; and, finally, selected post-communist transitions in the former Soviet bloc (Czechoslovakia, Germany, Hungary, Bulgaria, Albania, Russia, and Lithuania). Because few authors have examined the full range of transitional justice issues in any one country, most of these chapters weave together material from several sources. Often, various excerpts from the same source are interspersed throughout a country study to permit thematic organization of the material.

Volume III: Laws, Rulings, and Reports contains samples of primary documents from the transitions in twenty-eight countries. Among the more than one hundred documents included are legislative charters for "truth commissions" along with lengthy excerpts from their resulting reports, amnesty and purge laws and their evaluation by the judiciary, and detailed provisions for the rehabilitation of victims of the former regime. While some of these are official translations, most are unofficial translations that we commissioned or obtained from a variety of sources.

Except as indicated, the articles and documents reprint the original text. With each of the 224 individual selections included, we have generally adhered to the style, format, and footnote numbering of the original material. As a consequence, the style may vary from selection to selection.

Finally, it is important to point to a fact that too often is left unsaid: readers should know that while they are using these books, people in many other countries are studying them too. We hope these volumes raise the profile of scholarship on transitional justice; it is extraordinarily important for the success of democracy and a world with greater freedom.

Charles Duryea Smith
Former General Counsel and Director
Rule of Law Initiative
United States Institute of Peace

ACKNOWLEDGMENTS

The compilation and editing of these volumes—involving tracking down thousands of books, documents, and articles, extensive consultations and research, conceptualization of the major issues as well as historical analysis—would not have been possible without the assistance of a great many people. Space does not permit the recognition of everyone who gave of their time and knowledge, but I would like to express my heartfelt appreciation to the following individuals: John Herz, Guillermo O'Donnell, Herman Schwartz, and Ruti Teitel, who reviewed a draft of the volumes and provided valuable advice and perspective; Tim Phillips and Eric Nonacs of the Project on Justice in Times of Transition; Dwight Semler at the Center for the Study of Constitutionalism in Eastern Europe; Susan Scharf, Jocelyn Nieva, and especially Donald Gressett, who, serving in succession on the staff of the Institute's Rule of Law Initiative, each ably managed myriad tasks to keep this project on course; the Institute's capable Publications staff; Bob Schmitt, the Institute's computer guru, who solved numerous technical problems; and last but far from least, my wife Francesca, for her patience and support.

THE DILEMMAS OF TRANSITIONAL JUSTICE

In March 1992, some fifty participants from twenty-one countries gathered in Salzburg, Austria for a two-day conference organized by the New York-based Charter Seventy-Seven Foundation. The group included a Czech journalist, members of the Lithuanian and Uruguayan parliaments, a former president of Argentina, a Hungarian philosopher, a professor of history from Madrid, and a member of the Bulgarian Constitutional Court. The subject of the meeting was the one thing this diverse collection of individuals had in common: each came from a country which had suffered through a brutal and repressive regime, been liberated, and was obliged to cope with the legacy of that ousted system.

One major theme of the conference (and of the effort to compile the present three-volume collection, which had begun in 1991) was the extent to which the Central and Eastern Europeans and former Soviets who were just emerging from communist rule could learn any useful lessons from the Latin American transitions of the previous decade.

A fascinating undertone seemed to dominate the first day of the conference, as the assembled began to describe the experience of their respective nations. In words spoken and unspoken, in skeptical glances and general body language, the Latin Americans and Europeans seemed to be expressing the same thing to one another: the suffering of our people during the old regime and the difficulties resulting from our legacy is far worse than any hardship you endured. Ours is the greater pain; there is little we can learn from your experience.

There is, of course, some legitimacy to each point of view. On the one hand, communism was entrenched for forty-five years in East Germany, seventy years in Russia—so long that whole generations of the citizenry knew no other way of life. Though the most horrific and large-scale abuses of the Stalinist period had yielded to milder forms of repression in later years, the entire culture and fabric of their societies had been decimated during those decades; in dealing with the legacy of the old system, those in the former Soviet bloc had to reconstruct both government and the private sector virtually from scratch. On the other hand, though the military dictatorships which seized power in Argentina, Uruguay, Chile, and elsewhere in that region ruled for much shorter periods of time, the brutality with which they systematically tortured, killed, and caused large numbers of their citizens to "disappear" numbs in its detail. Numerous other contrasts exist between the legacy problems of Latin America and of post-communist Europe.

And yet. By day two of the proceedings, there was a gradual but palpable recognition that many of the details and dilemmas were not so different. How best, for example, to highlight the division between old and new government, so as to instill public confidence in the latter? This was a key issue for the participants from both regions. How should they handle those perceived as having served the old regime—as senior officials and architects of the system, as bureaucrats who implemented the old policies and may continue to be obstacles to reform, as members of the military or secret police, or as paid or volunteer collaborators with the secret police? In some countries of the former Warsaw Pact, more than half the population was potentially implicated in one of these categories. The challenge, as one participant put it, was to strike the proper balance between a whitewash on the one hand and a witch-hunt on the other. Could victims of the old regime be fairly compensated? For that matter, was it possible to achieve consensus as to *who* were the victims of a system that, by its design, affected everyone in society? Above all, how to achieve authentic reconciliation and prevent the future recurrence of abuses of the sort inflicted by the old regime?

Over lunch one day at that meeting, I described to Raul Alfonsín, the courageous former president of Argentina who returned his country from military junta to civilian democracy, the "transitional justice" project underway at the United States Institute of Peace and some of the questions emerging from our examination of transitions from repressive regimes to democracy from the Second World War to the present. I pointed out that there were intriguing parallels between the cases of Argentina and Greece. (1) In both cases, a military junta ruled the country for a period of seven years. The relatively short duration is relevant in determining whether there are people who have "clean hands" and who can bring pre-regime experience and training to the job in replacing those affiliated with the ousted regime—or whether, as in Russia, nearly every qualified person was a part of the system in which they grew up. (2) In both Greece and Argentina, the regime was driven by a virulent, right-wing, anti-communist ideology. (3) Both were characterized by human rights abuses on a massive scale, including extensive use of torture, which prompted gradually increasing international condemnation and ostracism of the country. (4) In both cases, the junta had promised economic improvement, but was faced with a faltering economy by the end of the seven-year rule. (5) Both regimes were finally forced to relinquish power immediately following a failed military venture (in Cyprus and the Falklands respectively).

In Greece, President Karamanlis assumed power from the junta and dealt with the issues of "transitional justice"—including prosecution of ousted officials, purging from governmental and quasi-governmental agencies those affiliated with the former regime, access to and use of the surveillance and interrogation records of the military police, and compensation and rehabilitation of victims—in an unusually firm and swift manner in 1974-75. Certainly there were important differences between the Greek and Argentine cases. Given the striking continuities, however, I asked President Alfonsín whether he had had any information on Greece and the Karamanlis program when formulating his own government's approach to these same issues nine years later. Alfonsín was intrigued by the parallels between the two cases, but confirmed that, as he and his advisors grappled with these difficult questions in the transition from repressive rule, they had no such information to draw upon; they "invented" their approach from nothing. They would probably not have followed the identical course as Greece, he assured me, but having material regarding the Greek experience on the table would have been extremely valuable in helping them to frame the issues and the options. President Alfonsín urged that we at the United States Institute of Peace pursue the present project so as to ease the transition process in future cases.

In countries undergoing the radical shift from repression to democracy, this question of transitional justice presents, in a very conspicuous manner, the first test for the establishment of real democracy and the rule of law—the very principles which will hopefully distinguish the new regime from the old. Strong political pressure for victor's justice in dealing with those who served the repressive regime, and the need to demonstrate a separation between the old and the new governments, may call for immediate and harsh retribution against a large number of individuals. New terms are created for the country or region in question—*denazification* in Germany after Hitler, *defascistization* in Italy, *dejuntafication*, *decommunization*—but they all express the same attempt of a liberated society to purge the remnants of its vilified recent past. If handled incorrectly, however, such action may deepen rather than heal the divisions within the nation. The temptation exists to compartmentalize, by viewing the need to "clean up old business" as unrelated to the democratization process. A vivid demonstration to the contrary, however, is the kangaroo trial and execution of former dictator Nicolae Ceausescu immediately following the fall of his government in Romania: with that one act seen on television around the world, the new government damaged its ability to move forward and the credibility of its interest in democracy and the rule of law—in the eyes of both other nations and its own citizens. Dealing firmly and aggressively with those who participated in, or benefitted from, the repression of the past is one way to demonstrate a clear break between the old regime and the new order. Adhering to the new government's pronounced commitments to principles of democracy and the rule of law, particularly in the tough cases, is another. The tension between the two is a theme which runs through each of the basic components of "transitional justice."

Criminal Sanctions

A basic question confronting all transitional governments, of course, is whether to undertake the prosecution of the leaders of the ousted regime or their henchmen for the abuses they inflicted upon the nation. Some will argue that trial and punishment of these people is not only essential to achieve some degree of justice, but that a public airing and condemnation of their crimes is the best way to draw a line between the old and new governments, lest the public perceives the new authorities as simply more of the same. Others will claim that these are simply show trials unbefitting a democracy, that they are manifestations of victor's justice, that the best way to rebuild and reconcile the nation is to leave the past behind by means of a blanket amnesty. In some cases, abuses have been committed both by the former government and by its opponents, and it can be argued that the best approach is to forgive the sins of both sides.

The debate recurs time and again. Following the death of Franco, the relatively peaceful Spanish transition was marked by such a mutual amnesty. In Greece, nearly twenty years after the conviction of junta leaders who had overseen the torture of hundreds, plans to release them from prison still prompted huge protests. In newly democratic Argentina and Chile, the prospect of trials for the gross violations of human rights that had occurred under the old regime provoked bald threats of military intervention and a return to the terror of the past. In post-apartheid South Africa, disagreements at the end of 1994 regarding amnesty were reported to threaten the stability of the new coalition government. International standards are evolving which help deal with this question; there is a growing consensus that, at least for the most heinous violations of human rights and international humanitarian law, a sweeping amnesty is impermissible.

When a decision is made to prosecute, the desire to use criminal sanctions against those who served the old regime may run directly counter to the development of a democratic legal order. The principles of *ex post facto* and *nulla poena sine lege*, for example, form one of the basic concepts of that legal order, barring the prosecution of anyone for an act which was not criminal at the time it was committed. At the very time that countries emerging from repressive regimes are committing themselves to these basic principles, the reality is that many of the acts that they desire to punish today were not crimes when they were committed under the former regime; they were often laudable and encouraged under the old system. In post-war France, for example, this issue was fiercely debated. Ultimately, thousands of people were prosecuted under a 1944 law establishing the new offense of "national indignity" for acts they had committed prior to the law's adoption. In the immediate post-communist period, largely owing to this same *ex post facto* dilemma, German officials initiated proceedings against Erich Mielke, the former head of East Germany's Stasi secret police, not for any abuses of the hated Stasi, but for a murder he had allegedly committed half a century earlier—based on evidence extracted by Nazi police. Although some sort of justice might have been served by this trial, the Mielke prosecution could not provide for East Germans the kind of catharsis that would be achieved through a public airing and trial of secret police wrongdoing.

Some of the worst abuses inflicted by former regimes *were* crimes under the old system, but they obviously were not prosecuted. If the statute of limitations for these crimes has already elapsed by the time of the transition, can the new authorities still hold the perpetrators accountable for their deeds? In both Hungary and the Czech Republic, post-communist legislators argued that since these crimes (particularly those committed to suppress dissent in 1956 and 1968 respectively) had not been prosecuted for wholly political reasons, it was legitimate to hold that the statute of limitations had not been in effect during the earlier period. Now, freed of political obstacles to justice, the statutory period for these crimes could begin anew, enabling the new authorities to prosecute these decades-old crimes. Legislation was adopted accordingly. In both countries, the matter was put to the newly created constitutional court for review. In a fascinating pair of rulings, each court handed down a decision which eloquently addressed the need to view this question of legacy and accountability in the context of the new democracy's commitment to the rule of law. On this basis—with plainly similar fact patterns—the Czech constitutional court upheld the re-running of the statute of limitations for the crimes of the old regime as a requirement of justice; the Hungarian court struck down the measure for violating the principle of the rule of law.

How widely should the net be cast in imposing sanctions on those who served the former regime? How high up the chain of command should superiors be responsible for abuses inflicted by their underlings? What standard of evidence is required to demonstrate that, rather than random events, these acts of persecution, corruption, and violence were designed, or at least condoned, by those at the top? Conversely, how far down the chain should soldiers or bureaucrats be held liable for following the orders of their superiors in facilitating these abuses? In dealing with the legacy of the former East Germany, several young border guards were prosecuted in 1991 for implementing shoot-to-kill orders that produced nearly 600 deaths of East Germans attempting to escape across the border. Many criticized the first of these trials for punishing the "small fry" at the end of the chain of responsibility who actually pulled the trigger, while leaving untouched the party leaders who had designed the repugnant system and given the orders. (In January 1995, seven former senior East German officials *were* eventually charged, in a 1,600-page indictment, with manslaughter and attempted manslaughter for their roles in developing and overseeing the system.) In Rwanda, after ousting a regime that organized genocidal killings of at least half a million people, if the new government were to undertake prosecution of every person who participated in this heinous butchery, some 30,000-100,000 Rwandan citizens could be placed in the dock—a situation that would be wholly unmanageable and extremely destabilizing to the transition. Moving the nation forward toward both justice and reconciliation plainly precludes an absolutist approach to the chain of responsibility.

In bringing those who served the former regime to account for their actions, what kind of deeds should be scrutinized? Should prosecution be limited to egregious violations of human rights? Should they be extended to charges of corruption and economic mismanagement? In Bulgaria, for instance, several former officials were convicted because of their role in specific foreign aid decisions that contributed to the country's economic ruin.

Should there be limits on the penalties imposed in these criminal cases? Some will argue that, even in those countries in which capital punishment is used, it should not be available in transitional purge trials. Given the high emotion and political pressures inherent in these trials, they suggest that use of the death penalty will further aggravate tensions within the society.

The temptation of victims of ghastly human rights violations under the old regime to make short shrift of the criminal procedural rights of those put in the dock for the crimes of that regime—to pay them back for the abuses they inflicted—is certainly understandable. Providing yesterday's dictators and torturers with the judicial guarantees and procedural protections that they never afforded their victims may be a source of short-term frustration during the transition, prompting cynicism of the sort expressed by an East German activist: "what we wanted was justice; what we got was the rule of law." Nonetheless, if these defendants are not afforded all the same rights granted to common defendants in a democratic order, the rule of law does not exist and the democratic foundation of the new system is arguably weakened.

Non-Criminal Sanctions

At least as great a challenge to the installation of democracy and the rule of law comes in the context of administrative penalties. Most frequently, the issue is that of purging from the public sector those who served the repressive regime. In post-war France, the process was called *epuration*; in the Czech and Slovak Federal Republic, *lustration*. A variety of effective arguments are made in favor of this process. The new democratic authorities must find ways to restore public confidence in the institutions of government. The public may reasonably be skeptical when told they will now be treated differently, if these institutions simply retain all their existing personnel. These, after all, are the same people who kept the engine of the repressive state operating; it is unlikely that many of them have undergone a sudden epiphany that has turned them into committed democrats. Even if they do not actively attempt to sabotage the changes undertaken by the new authorities, these people are set in the old ways and will serve as obstacles to the process of democratic reform. Finally, jobs in public service, whether as senior ministers or as clerks, should be granted first and foremost to those who have demonstrated loyalty to the democratic ideals of the new order.

Depending on the country, those perceived as having supported the old regime might include senior officials and architects of the system, bureaucrats who implemented the old policies and may continue to be obstacles to reform, members of the military or police, paid or volunteer collaborators with the secret police, or even simply party members. Perhaps the most difficult of these categories in one country after another is the vague description of "collaborators." In some emerging democracies, those who fit into one of these categories potentially comprise more than half the population.

On the other hand, particularly in those countries where the ousted regime was in power for many years, these people may be the only ones with the knowledge and experience to staff the ministries and the banks and the other institutions without which the national infrastructure would surely collapse. Practical considerations may make them indispensable.

How to undertake such a purge while rebuilding on the basis of democratic principles? These programs of administrative sanctions do not, as a rule, provide individuals with the same level of due process protections from which they would benefit in a criminal proceeding. Driven by the fact that they involve a large number of people, purges tend to be conducted in summary fashion. Beyond procedural considerations, the rule of law rejects collective punishment and discrimination on the basis of political opinion or affiliation. In establishing accountability, even in a non-criminal proceeding, the burden of proof should be on the authorities making the accusation, not on the accused to prove his or her innocence. When large numbers of people are removed from their places of employment purely because they had worked there under the old system or because of their membership in a political party, without any demonstration of individual wrongdoing, they may legitimately cry foul and question the democratic underpinnings of the new government. Rather than contributing to reconciliation and rebuilding, the result may be the creation of a substantial ostracized opposition that threatens the stability of the new system.

In much of the former communist bloc, the issue of lustration was a source of great controversy during the first years after the revolutions of 1989. In Poland, for example, only 38 percent of those polled in late 1991 supported creation of a system for disqualification of former communists, officials, and collaborators from public offices; a March 1992 poll showed an increase to 64 percent in favor of disqualification. Some observers suggested that the trend was related to the complex questions of privatization and redistribution of wealth: necessary austerity programs and wrenching efforts to overhaul the entire economic system result in many people becoming more impoverished, and the desire consequently grows to assign blame for society's ills. In addition, a perception exists that many former communist officials gave themselves "golden parachutes" as they exited their government posts, in the form of embezzled funds and property or controlling interests in the newly privatized companies; rather than being punished, in other words, the old guard had won once again.

The courts reflect an interesting problem relative to the purge process. On the one hand, the rule of law requires an independent judiciary insulated from political pressures. This generally means that judges are not easily removable from their posts. Even if judges were easily purged, it might take years to train a qualified class of new lawyers and judges to replace them on the bench. On the other hand, in most cases of transition from totalitarian or authoritarian regimes, the judiciary was severely compromised and was very much a part of the old system, implementing the repressive policies and wrapping them in the mantle of law. In post-war Germany, when victims of Nazi persecution were authorized to file claims for damages, some of them were stunned to find their claims assigned to the very same judge who had sentenced the claimants or their relatives in the first place. In order to enhance the power and independence of the judiciary as part of the democratization process in post-communist Poland, a law was enacted establishing the irremovability of judges. One consequence, subsequently recognized, was that many tainted communist judges thereby became entrenched in the "new" court system. An effort followed to create a system for the verification of judges based on their past activity and affiliation, and apply that system to both prospective new judges and those already in office.

In Ethiopia, it was proposed that all members of the former ruling party be denied the right to vote in elections. Such denial of suffrage based on previous party affiliation has occurred in other places, such as Norway after World War II. Other countries may attempt to ban the former ruling party and its successor parties. In Russia, President Boris Yeltsin's decree banning the Communist Party and seizing its assets was hotly debated and resulted in a closely watched case before the country's new constitutional court, which ultimately struck down half of the ban while leaving significant elements of it intact.

Once again, these efforts can rub against the intention to create a new, freer society wholly unlike the old regime. Administrative purge programs can easily be abused for purely political motives. In many cases, the old regime actually used the same methods, banning political parties, denying people a say in choosing their government. Citizens' rights to vote, to run for office, or to exercise their freedom of association are fundamental elements of a democracy. The balancing act for countries feeling their way through transitional justice is not an easy one.

Acknowledging the Past

In all cases of transition from a repressive regime, history has been controversial. Even after its ouster, the old guard will still have its defenders, who will deny that the evil acts of which it is accused ever took place, or will claim that they were actually perpetrated by others, or will suggest that they were justified by exigent circumstances. If left uncontested, these claims may undermine the new government and strengthen the hand of those determined to return the former regime to power. They will also add insult to the injury already inflicted on the victims.

Establishing a full, official accounting of the past is increasingly seen as an important element to a successful democratic transition. Criminal trials are one way in which the facts and figures of past abuses may be established. The establishment of a "truth commission," several variations of which are covered at length in each of the three volumes, is another. Following the initial phase of transition, this history may be reaffirmed in the long-term through national days of remembrance, the construction of museums and commemorative monuments, and the incorporation of this recent history into the curriculum of the nation's schools.

Compensation, Restitution, and Rehabilitation

In Russia, during the early stages of the transition from communist rule, there was no program to provide restitution of property or material compensation to victims. There was also initially no attempt to deal with recent abuses. Instead, efforts focused on restoring to victims of Stalinism their good names. On a case-by-case basis, hundreds of these victims were granted posthumous rehabilitation. While acknowledging the wrongs inflicted decades earlier, such an approach is, of course, far less costly to the new government—in both material and political terms—than compensation of recent victims.

In Chile, where the terms of the transition proscribed the criminal prosecution of former officials—and the sense of justice and catharsis which might be achieved thereby—the new democracy undertook instead one of the most comprehensive programs of compensation and rehabilitation of those described herein, encompassing life-long pensions for the survivors of those who died in General Pinochet's prisons, compensation for prison time and for lost income, educational benefits, a national network of medical and psychological services for victims and their families, and exemptions from military service.

More often than not, the legacy left by departing totalitarian or authoritarian regimes includes a weak economy and empty government coffers, depleted through corruption or mismanagement. The nascent democratic government must use its limited resources to turn the economy around, restructure the bureaucracy to restore public trust in government and better fulfill its basic functions, and invest in new present- and future-oriented programs (such as overhaul of the educational system where it was previously infused with the ideology of the old regime) to ensure the security of democracy. In this circumstance, many will ask, how much of its limited funds should the new democracy be obliged to allocate for victims' compensation, paying for the sins of the old guard? In addition, some will argue, since it is impossible to adequately compensate all victims for their loss, perhaps it is unjust to divert precious resources when the only result is to make some more whole than others.

To be sure, the parents whose daughter was tortured to death by the former regime, which then disposed of her body without a trace, or the man who spent a dozen years in prison for his political beliefs when he should have been completing his professional training, building his career, and watching his toddlers become young adults cannot be made whole for their loss. Nevertheless, compensation serves at least three functions in the process of national reconciliation. First, it aids the victims to manage the material aspect of their loss. Second, it constitutes an official acknowledgment of their pain by the nation. Both of these facilitate the societal reintegration of people who have long been made to suffer in silence. Third, it may deter the state from future abuses, by imposing a financial cost to such misdeeds. There is a growing consensus in international law that (a) the state is obligated to provide compensation to victims of egregious human rights abuses perpetrated by the government, and (b) if the regime which committed the acts in question does not provide compensation, the obligation carries over to the successor government.

Internationalization of the Issues

In our ever-smaller world, the handling of transitional justice has increasingly become a source of interplay between new successor governments and those outside the country. When the Czech and Slovak Federal Republic adopted its "lustration" law to screen and purge a range of former communist officials and collaborators, it became a major focus of international attention. The Council of Europe and the International Labor Organization each analyzed it, as did numerous foreign non-governmental organizations. Foreign attention is often welcome. The report of the Chadian "Commission of Inquiry into the Crimes and Misappropriations Committed by Ex-President Habré, his Accomplices and/or Accessories" begins with a map and profile of the country—obviously meant mostly for foreign consumption.

Foreign governments are forced to play a role in either providing refuge to those from the former regime or facilitating their exclusion or extradition for trial. Assisting in the tracing and return of assets which have been moved out of the country by the former leaders and their cohorts may also be appropriate. Some functions may be performed by wholly international bodies, such as the truth commission for El Salvador or the UN war crimes tribunal for Rwanda. Alternatively, foreign governments may play a part in advising, critiquing, or participating in the new leaders' plans with respect to such issues as amnesty, purging, and retraining for government personnel; the United States has arguably played such a role in Haiti.

These issues of transitional justice are highly charged flashpoints in many countries emerging from repression, with societal wounds still open and in need of treatment. Having recognized that the way in which these dilemmas are handled can directly affect the short- and long-term stability of the transition in many countries, foreign policy makers would be well-advised to keep this lens in focus as they monitor, anticipate, and respond to such transitions around the world.

Financing Transitional Justice

In theory, all victims of past repression are entitled to maximum compensation from a new government emerging from years of repression, but who is going to pay for it? High profile trials of former officials, particularly when they are looking farther back in time, can be expensive propositions, but justice done on the cheap is inadequate. Truth commissions, if they are to credibly research and create an unimpeachable historical record, need human, financial, and technical resources. Each of the aspects of transitional justice discussed above has a price tag attached—a serious problem for most emerging democracies struggling to rebuild their society anew. Most observers will agree, of course, that the long-term price of not dealing with these issues is greater still.

A recent Polish example drives home the point. A victim of human rights abuses under the old regime filed a successful lawsuit for damages from the government, resulting in an order to pay a huge sum to the plaintiff. Following a public outcry over holding the new, financially strapped government accountable for the sins of its communist predecessor, all the money was donated to charity.

If the transitional government cannot afford to pay for these efforts, foreign governmental or private funding is obviously an option. The truth commission for El Salvador received $1 million, some forty percent of its total budget, from the United States government. The commission in Uganda has received major infusions of funding from the Ford Foundation in the U.S. and Danita in Denmark. The Rwandan court system will hopefully receive foreign funding for the genocide trials it will undertake. In a lengthy bulletin produced "for NGOs and the media," the Special Prosecutor's Office created to investigate and prosecute crimes of the Mengistu regime in Ethiopia includes a section on "foreign support" which lists the contributions of six countries to the effort, ranging from a Canadian donation of $40,000 to $403,000 from Sweden. A recently established United Nations Voluntary Fund for Victims of Torture may also be of assistance in certain cases.

Some observers are wary of moving to foreign funding too quickly, particularly for victim compensation programs. If the national government is freed to allocate its resources and fiscal priorities without factoring in this issue, if it does not reach into its own coffers to acknowledge the victims of repression in a material sense, then the new regime may less effectively integrate the lessons of the past, and the sense that the state is paying its respect to the victims and restoring to them their dignity may be lessened—weakening both long-term democratization and rehabilitation.

The national resources so often embezzled by the leadership of totalitarian and authoritarian regimes—yet another issue facing emerging democracies—offers an interesting source of financing. Whether this entails efforts like that undertaken by the Philippine government to lay legal claim to millions of dollars worth of foreign assets and accounts controlled by Ferdinand and Imelda Marcos, or the efforts in Bulgaria and Albania to seize properties amassed by the former ruling clique and order them to reimburse the state millions of dollars, there is a certain sense of justice and balance to recapturing these ill-gotten gains and applying them directly to pay for other aspects of transitional justice. A curious variation on this was a legislative proposal in Poland to impose a special tax on communists, with a sliding scale based on one's position within the Communist Party hierarchy.

Particularly in countries emerging from communism or other centrally controlled economies, property restitution is not only a form of justice for victims, it is also a highly complex issue of economic conversion and privatization with obvious consequences for clarity of ownership and for business and investment opportunities in the emerging democracy. This may provide an additional incentive for foreign governments or businesses to help the restitution process along, including through subsidization.

As a rule, these are not problems that disappear quickly or easily. A half-century after the Second World War, the scars of Nazism are still felt in Germany. After the fall of the Berlin Wall and reunification, many acknowledged that the debate over decommunization was in many ways a shadow debate among East and West Germans over the success of denazification and was significantly colored by a desire to "do it better this time." The trials of Klaus Barbie and Paul Touvier for their crimes as part of the Vichy regime exposed still-raw nerves and soul-searching in France some fifty years after the facts in question. In Namibia, several years after the transition, officials claim that it is still too soon for an investigation and accounting of those who disappeared on both sides of the conflict, that such an effort would threaten Namibian stability; others argue that this past will haunt the country until it is dealt with. And in Cambodia, talk of bringing charges against leaders of the Khmer Rouge for the genocide they inflicted on their country twenty years ago will continue to affect the reconstruction process.

This is, of course, an ongoing process. A full accounting is yet to be written of transitional justice in countries such as South Africa, El Salvador, or Ethiopia. The current global trend from totalitarian and authoritarian systems to democratic ones will hopefully continue, producing new cases of transitional justice in the years to come. Through the publication of these volumes and the ongoing work of the United States Institute of Peace and others on this subject, one can hope that positive lessons will be derived from past experience, that future transitions will bolster their own stability by achieving justice and reconciliation through the rule of law.

Neil J. Kritz, Editor

1

GERMANY (AFTER NAZISM)

EDITOR'S INTRODUCTION

On January 30, 1933, Adolph Hitler became chancellor of Germany and proceeded to transform the existing Weimar Republic into a totalitarian dictatorship. In August 1934, Hitler promulgated a law that combined the offices of chancellor and president, declaring himself *führer* (leader) of Germany. He then mobilized the German economy for war and invaded Poland on September 1, 1939, ushering in World War II. France and Britain declared war on Germany two days later. After a long-fought war, Germany eventually surrendered to the Allies on May 7, 1945.

Hitler left behind a legacy of systematic killing and persecution virtually unparalleled in history. By the mid-1930s, the *Schutzstaffel* (SS) military and *Gestapo* police force implemented a sophisticated program of terror. Members of the judiciary, state bureaucracy, and army were obliged to pledge unconditional allegiance to Hitler. Any opposition to Hitler or his National Socialist ("Nazi") party was generally met by persecution, arrest, or death at the hands of the regime. The 1935 Nuremberg Laws formalized official anti-Semitism, making political, social, and economic discrimination against Jews mandatory. Jews were harassed, arrested, and sent to concentration camps. By the late 1930s, Hitler's notion of racial purity resulted in his "final solution"—the attempted annihilation of "undesirable" groups such as gypsies, Catholics, homosexuals, and primarily Jews. Concentration camps soon became facilities for forced labor and mass exterminations. The campaign was enforced in each of the countries occupied by the Germans. By 1945, six million Jews—three-fifths of the pre-war European population—had been killed.

The victorious powers divided Germany into separate American, British, French, and Soviet military occupation zones, reflecting the membership of the Allied Control Council. The partition was designed to be temporary, facilitating the demilitarization and denazification of the four zones and their eventual reunification into a democratic German state. In each zone, authorities arrested those who fell into one of several categories of participation in the Nazi system, totaling 245,000 by January 1947. The intensity of overall denazification efforts varied between the four zones.

In a major historical precedent, the Allied powers established the International Military Tribunal at Nuremberg to prosecute the principal Nazi leaders for war crimes, crimes against humanity, and crimes against peace; subsequent Nuremberg tribunals were created to conduct additional trials. From 1945 to 1949, approximately 200 defendants were tried before these various tribunals. Individual trials focused on particular sectors of German society which had played noteworthy roles in the atrocities, including not only the SS, police and government ministers, but jurists, industrialists, and doctors. At peak staffing in 1947, the Nuremberg proceedings required the services of nearly 900 allied employees and an equal number of Germans.

The onset of the Cold War quickly divided the Allied Control Council. The three Western powers unified their zones and, on May 8, 1949, created the Federal Republic of Germany (West Germany). Theodor Heuss was elected president and Konrad Adenauer was elected chancellor. In October 1949, the German Democratic Republic (East Germany) was proclaimed in the Soviet zone. The chapter which follows focuses primarily on efforts to deal with the Nazi legacy in the Federal Republic.

Efforts to prosecute Nazi personnel, purge them from participation in public life and provide compensation to victims, begun under the Allied occupation, continued for many years under the new West German government. In 1974, some 4,000 criminal cases were still in process. Concurrently, by 1951, the "131 Law" instituted a process of rehabilitation and reintegration of former Nazi public servants. Many of these processes are still ongoing today, as is German public discussion of the manner in which the Nazi legacy has been handled in that country.

The following documents related to transitional justice in Germany after Nazism can be found in Volume III of this collection:

- Charter of the International Military Tribunal and Excerpts from Tribunal Decisions
- Screening Questionnaire (*Fragebogen*)
- Act for Liberation from National Socialism and Militarism
- Act Repealing the Statute of Limitations for the Crimes of Genocide and Murder

The Potsdam Program

John H. Herz, "Denazification and Related Policies"[*]

In answer to a violent and ideological war that Hitler had forced on the world, Nazi Germany's enemies were not satisfied with victory but tried to extirpate all remnants of nazism and remake the country in their image. The principles that were to guide this remaking of a nation were laid down, to the extent they could still agree, by the "nations united for victory" at Potsdam in August 1945. These principles are usually summarized by listing four "d"s: denazification, demilitarization, decentralization, and decartelization; to the four, however, there should be added one overarching fifth one: democratization, a term that took on different coloration when interpreted by the Soviets and the Western Allies; hence the split of the country.

In the economic sphere, one of the foundations on which Hitler built his rule was perceived as the "excessive concentration of economic power" through big trusts and cartels; *decartelization* thus became one of the major objectives of Allied policy.... As far as the general economic structure and, in particular, industry, are concerned, it can be said that decartelization meant not revamping but the restoration of the structures that had existed before: a market, or "free enterprise," system freed from the regulatory constraints that nazism (with the special objective of organizing the economy for war) had imposed but otherwise sharing with the Western industrialized nations the corporate-capitalist features characteristic of all such economic systems....

Demilitarization was comprised of a program that not only was aimed at the destruction of whatever remained of the German war machinery but also the prohibition against forming any military or paramilitary organizations or associations that might "keep alive the military tradition in Germany" and the production of any arms. This policy, of course, was reversed with the rearmament of both Germanies in consequence of the cold war....

The aim of *decentralization*, as in the case of decartelization, was based on the—perhaps dubious—assumption that the centralization of power—in this case, political and governmental power—had been responsible for Germany's turn toward dictatorship and aggressiveness. Therefore, government and administration in a democratized Germany were to be "directed toward the decentralization of the political structure and the development of local responsibility."...

Denazification, finally, was meant not only to destroy every remnant of the Nazi party and affiliated organizations and institutions and to repeal all Nazi types of laws (including those providing for racial and similar kinds of discrimination), but also to remove all nonnominal Nazis from positions of influence and responsibility as well as to bring to justice all those who had participated in war crimes and atrocities.

---

[*] Excerpted from John H. Herz, "Denazification and Related Policies," in John H. Herz, ed., *From Dictatorship to Democracy: Coping with the Legacies of Authoritarianism and Totalitarianism*, Copyright © 1982 by John Herz (Greenwood Press, 1982), pp. 17-19, an imprint of Greenwood Publishing Group, Inc. Westport, CT. Reprinted with permission.

PROSECUTION OF NAZI CRIMINALITY

John H. Herz, "Denazification and Related Policies"[*]

[The Transfer of Jurisdiction from Allied to German Control]

In a declaration dated Moscow, November 1, 1943, the leaders of the Big Three had proclaimed their commitment to pursue the perpetrators of the holocaust and other atrocities "to the uttermost ends of the earth" in order that justice would be done.[3] Subsequently there was exerted common four-power action through the establishment of an International Military Tribunal (IMT) at Nuernberg. At Nuernberg some chief Nazi leaders were tried and, for the most part were convicted of crimes of aggression, war crimes, and crimes against humanity. In contrast to Japan, where only one major war-crimes trial was conducted, Nuernberg was followed by trials of generals, industrialists, diplomats, SS leaders, and other persons involved in Nazi types of crimes conducted by the occupying powers in their respective zones (as there were follow-up trials of Nazi criminals in countries that had been under Nazi occupation). Subsequently, the prosecution of Nazi criminality was left to the Germans. Intensive pressure was brought to bear on the occupation authorities (such as U.S. High Commissioner John McCloy) to parole most of the convicted persons, which they did, thus releasing, among others, top industrialists convicted of having exploited and ill-treated slave labor.[4]

The German authorities, like most Germans, confused the "sanctions" provided for in denazification procedures (such as fines and temporary detention) with criminal penalties and were inclined to consider Nazi criminality as having been dealt with either by those procedures or else by Allied trials and convictions.

Fritz Weinschenk, "Nazis Before German Courts: The West German War Crimes Trials"[†]

Gradually, the German judicial system revived and was given increasingly broader jurisdictional powers by the Allies, until the "Enabling Treaty" of March 30, 1955, by which the Federal Republic attained full

---

[*] Excerpted from John H. Herz, "Denazification and Related Policies," in John H. Herz, ed., *From Dictatorship to Democracy: Coping with the Legacies of Authoritarianism and Totalitarianism*, Copyright © 1982 by John Herz (Greenwood Press, 1982), p. 19, an imprint of Greenwood Publishing Group, Inc. Westport, CT. Reprinted with permission.

[3] [omitted]

[4] Although some of these, grown rich as a result of the West German economic miracle, agreed, for moral rather than nonadmitted legal reasons, to pay victims a small indemnification (a one-time 500 DM or such), one of them, Flick, head of a huge conglomerate and one of the richest men in the world, refused to pay a penny (see Benjamin B. Ferencz, *Less than Slaves—Jewish Forced Labor and the Quest for Compensation* [Cambridge, Mass., 1979]).

[†] Excerpted from Fritz Weinschenk, "Nazis Before German Courts: The West German War Crimes Trials," *International Lawyer*, vol. 10, no. 3 (Summer 1976), pp. 517-519, Copyright 1976 American Bar Association. Used by permission.

judicial powers free of Allied control, passed the prosecution of war crimes and crimes against humanity solely to the German courts, prosecutors, and police.[3]

German activities with respect to adjudication of World War II crimes up to the "Enabling Treaty" were hampered by lack of space, funding, personnel, and power. Prior to the currency reform of 1948, starvation and lack of living essentials were forbidding obstacles. Prosecutions, for the most part, were based on denunciations of Germans by other Germans or displaced persons. Nevertheless, in 1948/49 the number of prosecutions was quite substantial.[4] In those years, the lower courts tried cases, which thereafter reached the newly constituted German appellate courts, chiefly the German Federal Supreme Court, the "Bundesgerichtshof." A number of basic decisions endeavored to close the gaps left by the Allied Nuremberg judgments and made the law which was to govern the post-war German concept of war crimes and crimes against humanity.[5]

After the war, there arose a ground swell of German public opinion whose tenor was to disregard, forget, minimize, and rationalize. The Allies, so the argument ran, tried the vanquished as victors in Nuernberg, a "kangaroo court" whose outcome was predictable. The overwhelming mass of Germans, so ran the rationale, was "clean" and ignorant of the horrors that had been committed. What about the air raids on Dresden, Hamburg, Leipzig and Schweinfurt? At any rate, what was done had to be done in prosecution of the war effort against "partisans"—every nation adopts ruthlessness in wartime. It is, so went the rationalization, a legitimate part of the right of self-defense, of which the Allies were just as guilty as the Germans.

This conflict erupted into the legal sphere, and both sides found advocates. The first trials evolved around the murder of the storm-troop leader Roehm in 1934, the trials of the "Einsatzgruppen," the flying death squads in Poland, and the trials of certain military commanders who issued summary execution orders against members of the German armed forces in the last days before the surrender in 1945 for "cowardice before the enemy."

In these cases, the defense argued that by virtue of the enabling law of 1933 Hitler had become the supreme head of the German state. His orders ... had become the "law of the land"—rightly or wrongly—and beyond individual scrutiny or power of refusal. The individuals following these orders, therefore, acted—perhaps in error—at any rate, in pursuit of what they had to consider orders by "legal" authority. Both army and civil service had sworn allegiance to Hitler personally. Theirs was not to question or

---

[3] "Ueberleitungsvertrag," (*Transition Statute*) German Federal Gazette, vol. II, p. 405.

[4] Detailed statistics are contained in the report of the Minister of Justice, to the President of the Bundestag of February 26, 1965, rendered on the occasion of the debate concerning the statute of limitations.

[5] Thus, for a detailed definition of the illegality of the Nazi system, see the judgments of May 20, 1948, (St S 3/48), May 25, 1948 (St S 1/48) and November 9, 1948, (St S 71/48) of the Supreme Court of Appeals for the British zone. The decision of the BGH (Federal Supreme Court) in 3 St R 701/53 established clearly that the Jewish deportations had no relationship to the conduct of the war or military necessity. A detailed analysis of these decisions would transcend the scope of this article.

scrutinize, but to "follow orders to the end." There are a number of decisions to this effect.[6]

The overwhelming majority of the German legal establishment, including the highest court of the Federal Republic, the "Bundesgerichtshof," emphatically discarded this reasoning. A German writer of great reputation in this field, in discussing the legality of the "euthanasia orders" of Hitler, which ordered the "elimination" of "useless mouths" and "biological garbage," put it this way:

> ...even if they had not been secret, these laws would nevertheless have been illegal. They would have been a gross violation of the higher-ranking norms of natural law. One may dispute the Natural Law, its jurisdictional and substantive limitations as one wishes. We are, at any rate, all agreed, that laws commanding murder violate the Natural Law and are void.[7]

...The hardening of East-West conflicts, culminating in the Berlin airlift and the Korean action in 1950, brought about a change in Allied policy toward war crimes in Germany. Cautiously at first, but with accelerated tempo, the Allies began to grant pardons to high-ranking, heavily implicated Nazi functionaries. The desire to obtain German cooperation in the cold war was undoubtedly a consideration. The result was that these individuals were able to go free, protected from later German prosecution by the terms of the "Transfer Agreement" which barred German retrials of cases adjudicated by the Allies as "double jeopardy."

Public opinion, which believed the Nazi bigwigs to have been sufficiently prosecuted by the Allies, and which was tired of war, brutality and horror, was set against a repetitive recount of the horrors of the camps, the atrocities and slaughters in the German courtrooms. "Numerous deeply implicated criminals, who had not yet been discovered, began to breathe easier."[8]

John Dornberg, "Schizophrenic Germany"[*]

[The Establishment of a Central Coordinating Office]

Seventeen major war-crimes trials took place or started in Federal Republic in 1958. Of these, a half dozen cases brought out testimony that implicated—and eventually brought to court—nearly a dozen new defendants. The complexity and incongruity of Germany's accounting with its own past is demonstrated most effectively and dramatically by ... the trial

---

[6] OLG Kiel, SJ2 47,323.

[7] Prof. Dr. Juergen Baumann, "Rechtmaessigkeit von Mordbefehlep," 31NJW 1398 (1964).

[8] [NS-PROZESSE, Dr. Adalbert Rueckerl, editor, Karlsruhe, 1971, (hereinafter cited as "Rueckerl")], p. 20.

[*] Excerpted from John Dornberg, *Schizophrenic Germany* (The Macmillan Company, 1961), pp. 19-22, 24-29. Reprinted with permission of Sterling Lord Literistic, Inc. Copyright © 1961 by John Dornberg.

of SS guard Martin Sommer ... and the hearing of ten former "extermination squad" members....

Martin Sommer was ... accused of murdering fifty-three inmates of notorious Buchenwald concentration camp where he had been an SS guard.... Sommer's month in court would have gone into the record as just another concentration camp case had it not been for the startling testimony of one witness who said: "The wrong defendant is sitting here. There ought to be someone who will file charges against Dr. Hans Eisele. He killed more people in one week than Sommer murdered in his entire lifetime.

"Imagine," said the witness, Wilhelm Jellineck, for years a political prisoner at Buchenwald, "this doctor now has a practice in Munich. Women—mothers, sisters, daughters, and wives—go to him in confidence, unaware that perhaps it was he who murdered their brothers, husbands, sons, or fathers."

This testimony [was] typical of the manner in which many other Nazi sadists [were] exposed and eventually brought to trial as the result of evidence at someone else's hearing....

Of all the trials held in the significant postwar legal year of 1958, one stands out as most important in terms of its later impact on German attitudes toward the war-crimes problem. This was the "extermination squad" case in Ulm. It not only was the first German hearing in which there were a number of defendants, all linked to the same act, but it also set the stage for a new, more methodical approach in war-crimes prosecution.

Actually, the mass trial was the result of a bit of legal luck. Bernhard Fischer-Schweder, one of the SS men convicted in the case, had succeeded in "going underground" after the war to avoid prosecution. He would probably never have been detected had he not filed a suit in a labor court under his real name. This resulted in several news stories about his past and eventually his arrest and indictment in May, 1956.... [A thorough investigation] on the part of Stuttgart prosecutor Erich Nellmann ... turned up most of the Gestapo, SS, and SD agents who, together with Fischer-Schweder, had taken part in the mass murder of 5,502 Lithuanian Jews in the occupied country. Their squad, in turn, had been part of a larger special unit responsible for the liquidation of Jews and Communists in the Baltic countries. The area covered by the Tilsit squad was a border strip only twenty-five miles wide.

By the time the trial opened, only ten defendants remained to go to court. Three others had committed suicide after their arrests. The hearings lasted sixty days. The sentences, however, [ranged from four to fifteen years], far below the demands of the prosecution.... In explaining the verdicts and sentences, the presiding judge excused the light terms by saying they had been handed down in recognition of the collective guilt of the entire German people. But the main defendants, he said, "were really Hitler and his stooges Himmler and Heydrich who carried out the mass slaying of thousands of innocent people with premeditation and planning."

"Wherever absolute power reigns, absolute injustice is usually right there, too," the judge said. He added that the real importance of the trial lay in driving that point home to Germany's youth which, he hoped, would never again be led into temptation by such a "front man" as Hitler.

But despite the disappointments which the trial brought for Stuttgart's district attorney, the case proved conclusively that even after fifteen years it was still possible to gather reliable evidence with which Nazi crimes could be punished. For Erich Nellmann this was an important realization that eventually led to his public plea for establishment of a central board for the investigation of unsolved, unpunished war crimes.... There had been the virtual chain reaction of cases in 1958, new suspects popping up at almost every trial.... Wasn't it possible, many Germans asked themselves, that hundreds of Nazis could hide out and escape prosecution until time had expired for the filing of new charges?

[In October 1958], at a conference of the various state ministers of justice, the proposal for such a central agency was made by Nellmann's superior, the Baden-Wuerttemberg minister of justice, Dr. Wolfgang Haussmann. When the meeting ended, the project was under way. Dr. Haussmann promised to take over responsibility for organizing the agency and establishing it as well as laying out the principles under which it would operate. Its basic purpose would be to seek out those individuals who had committed crimes as Nazis but had not yet been prosecuted. The emphasis, Haussmann decreed, would be on crimes committed by Germans in occupied territories during the war. The agency was to operate with a relatively small staff. It was not designed to be a prosecuting instrument or a special judicial institution, but merely a central investigative body which would pass the results of its research on to district attorneys responsible for the individual cases.

On December 1, 1958, the agency, officially called "Center for Preparation and Coordination for the Prosecution of Concentration Camp and War Crimes," took up its work in the little city of Ludwigsburg, not far from Stuttgart [or "Central Office"].

District attorney Erwin Schuele, chief of the prosecution team in the Tilsit extermination squad case, was appointed to head the project. In addition to passing evidence to local law enforcement authorities, the agency was also established to serve as a central clearing board for Nazi trials. Local prosecutors [were] instructed to submit information to the center on cases already being processed. A central index of all such cases [was] set up at Ludwigsburg.

At a press conference following the opening of the center, Justice Minister Haussmann answered questions on why it had taken so long to establish such an agency. Haussmann explained that the occupation powers had retained jurisdiction over these cases for a good many years and when the Germans finally assumed responsibility, it was the general belief throughout Germany that practically all the cases had come to trial. Local prosecutors, Haussmann explained, just weren't in a position to obtain an overall picture of the situation. It was not until the major trials of 1958 ... that German judicial authorities realized how much work remained to be done....

Less than a year after he "went into business," Schuele produced results. On October 21, 1959—by then the agency had quadrupled in size—he announced that his investigations had led to the filing of charges against some two hundred individuals.... Most of the cases involve special extermination squads or concentration camp atrocities.

*Fritz Weinschenk, "Nazis Before German Courts: The West German War Crimes Trials"**

[The central office in Ludwigsburg] obtained personnel, logistic support, documentation, and jurisdictional authority from the several "Laender." Its task was and still is

> to collect the entire attainable material concerning Nazi crimes, to catalogue, and to evaluate the same:... to work out facts and events delimited by place, time, and probable perpetrator; and to establish which persons involved can still be prosecuted....[10]

Once the Central Office has initiated, conducted and concluded its preliminary investigation, the file, findings and exhibits are transmitted to the district attorney who has jurisdiction of the court-prosecution of the defendants. The function of the "Central Office" is comparable to that of the federal "special prosecutor" or similar special state prosecutors.

Starting off with a staff of fifty prosecutors and magistrates, and fifteen detectives, the jurisdiction of the Central Office was substantially enlarged in 1964 and 1965.[11] As a result of this intensification, the German courts adjudicated a total of 71 proceedings, during the years 1968 to 1970, more than one-third of the number of proceedings completed during the previous nine years.[12] From its inception to 1974, the Central Office investigated 3,000 cases, which resulted in 9,000 proceedings against individuals. With life-sentences in 108 cases, over 1,200,000 records and over 300,000 evidential documents were sifted, evaluated, stored and indexed.[13]...

Parallel to the work of the Ludwigsburg Central Office, however, the prosecutorial staffs, magistrates and courts of the several states are carrying on their own investigations, proceedings, and, of course, trials. In a recent broadcast, chief prosecutor Dr. Rueckerl stated that in 1974, approximately 4,000 persons were standing accused of Nazi crimes in the Federal Republic....

A critical evaluation of the published data, statistics and surveys emanating from West Germany and elsewhere leads to the conclusion that, by and large the core of the Nazi criminals has been prosecuted, in many instances successfully. After the responsible actors in command positions, the judicial apparatus has reached up to the "desk-murderers," the Eichmann-type bureaucrats, and down to the "squad-leaders," the rank and file—often

---

* Excerpted from Fritz Weinschenk, "Nazis Before German Courts: The West German War Crimes Trials," *International Lawyer*, vol. 10, no. 3 (Summer 1976), pp. 519-527, Copyright 1976 American Bar Association. Used by permission.

[10] Pamphlet: "Zentrale Stelle der Landesjustizverwaltungen," dated September 15, 1967, p. 3.

[11] Pamphlet, *supra*, p. 3-4.

[12] "Rueckerl," *supra*, Statistical Annex, p. 197.

[13] New York German-language weekly "Aufbau," June 28, 1974.

entire units. There are two classes of criminals who have escaped prosecution: the ideologists, and the foreign, non-German helpers of the Nazis, mostly those of Eastern European background. Various factors, aside from the passage of time, have combined to make their prosecution and conviction highly unlikely—ever....

Questions of Evidence and Procedure

...The crimes now being prosecuted in West Germany date back, for the most part, to a period from 1940 to 1945, or even earlier.

Although hard work, diligence, patience, skill and large-scale financing have produced remarkable results, the circle of witnesses, the available documentation, and thereby the chances of obtaining convictions are steadily shrinking....

In the investigation of Nazi crimes, especially in the East, the Ludwigsburg office has proceeded on a new basis: the systematic combing out of Nazi crimes by area, unit, and time. Proceeding on the theory that—where one proven crime took place, others of like nature must have taken place fairly closely in time and space, the Luwigsburg office commenced a systematic survey of the areas occupied by German troops during World War II. Prosecutor Rueckerl commented on the problems involved in this task as follows:

> The novel approach requires investigations broader in scope than one was used to up to then in individual cases. Countless persons must be questioned, and relevant archives must be researched to feel one's way to the identity of the perpetrators. All this requires, aside from energy and adaptability, a considerable measure of specialized historical know-how, from the investigator in charge.[18]

...Crimes against humanity, both in the preliminary and trial stages, require a vast amount of intensive preparation. The prosecutor's proof usually fills the shelves and file cabinets of several rooms—resembling the volume of evidence in an American anti-trust case or other similar large-scale litigation.

German criminal procedure usually regards the oral testimony of witnesses as less potent than documentation, for which no foundation need be laid. Rueckerl points out[20] that in Nazi-crimes trials there are no "neutral" witnesses: the only knowledgeable sources of oral evidence are either pursuers or victims. While witnesses from the ranks of SS or police have an obvious motive to minimize, distort, or falsify, the victims suffer from unavoidable trauma—no matter how objective they try to be—from psychic breakdowns, and from loss of memory caused by suppression of lived-

---

[18] "Rueckerl," *supra*, p. 25. Chance and accident are unfortunately often the handmaidens of justice. For example: In the case against the SS-leaders of a small branch-camp of Auschwitz, called "Guenter-Grube," wall murals painted by a prisoner on a whim of the SS had been painted over after the war, but were restored. This evidence was invaluable for purposes of credibility.

[20] "Rueckerl," *supra*, p. 26ff.

through scenes too horrible and painful to preserve. In addition, the remoteness of the events increases the unreliability of oral testimony. "It is, therefore, foreseeable that oral proof in Nazi trials will lose in weight more and more rapidly, and will sink to the level of insignificance within the foreseeable future," says Dr. Rueckerl.[21]

Evidence comes from many sources. The passion for documentation on the part of the Nazi perpetrators has left thousands of official records all over Europe. Such evidence has been and still is emanating from Poland, the Soviet Union, Israel, France, Belgium, Holland, Norway, Luxemburg, Czechoslovakia, Yugoslavia, Greece, the United States,... the Red Cross, the Documentation Center in Arolsen, and some unlikely sources, such as the business records of certain German firms. Individuals like Simon Wiesenthal deserve mention here.

...[I]t is an invariable practice of the defendants to attribute the crimes to deceased colleagues or superiors.[24]

On the average, the duration of a Nazi-crime proceeding, from its preliminary stage to judgement and through appeals, is from three to seven years. In some cases, difficulties of proof, delays of various kinds, changes in prosecutorial or defense personnel and consequent familiarization of new personnel with the tremendous amount of material, and other factors[25] prolong the proceeding even more. It is therefore not surprising that—more and more—the final resolution of these crimes is, in the words of Dr. Rueckerl, a "biological" one: death or incompetency of the defendants.[26]

The Defenses

Most of the defendants in the Nazi-crimes cases are accused of murder under section 211 of the German Penal Code. This section defines a "murderer" as one who

> kills a person out of lust, to satisfy his sexual urge, for avarice, or for other base motives, by stealth or cruelty or by any means endangering others, or to facilitate or hide another crime.[27]

Section 212 defines and punishes homicide under circumstances not amounting to murder under section 211. Nazis cannot be prosecuted under this section, since the statute of limitations on section 212 expired on May 8, 1960.[28] However, any procedural step by the prosecutor or magistrate within

---

21 "Rueckerl," *supra*, p. 27.

24 [omitted]

25 The danger of error in law and fact, the monotonous repetition of horrors for months and years, and the magnitude and quantity of the evidence pose great stresses for judges, jury, and counsel on both sides. Judges have taken their lives or have fallen ill, apparently because of the stress. *Aufbau, supra*, on January 3, 1975 reported the suicide of Judge Kupke in Frankfurt as a result of stress in the retrial of FASOLD and others.

26 "Rueckerl," *supra*, p. 33.

27 [Petters-Preisendanz, STRAFGESETZBUCH, Berlin, 1971], p. 378.

28 The statute of limitations for "accessories" or homicides under section 212 is fifteen years calculated from May 8, 1945. See the decision of the Bundesgerichtshof (Supreme Court) in

the time limit, such as the filing of a report or the opening of a file will toll the statute and will make continued prosecution possible, even though the statute has run.

For "211" cases, the prosecutor must therefore prove facts sufficient to convince the court that the defendant personally committed the acts alleged "for base motives," *i.e.*, out of racial hatred, or sadistic perversion.

Such proof is difficult. So-called desk-murderers, bureaucrats who ordered mass exterminations, are guilty of aggravated murder under Paragraph 211 only if it is clearly shown that they were actors, not mere conduits or transmitters. The defense of "respondeat superior," which has been paraphrased by the synonym "I only followed orders," led to dismissals against persons who—knowing of the criminal nature of the work they were doing—only passed on and followed orders without themselves engaging in heinous acts. "Follower of orders" would have been guilty under the accessory (*Beihilfe*) or homicide (*Totschlag*) statutes. Both of these crimes are beyond the statute of limitations.... It follows that in any case in which the prosecutor is unable to prove heinous, sadistic acts of the defendant, the judgement must be one of "not guilty."

Nevertheless, in many cases the high-up "desk-murderers" (or "headquarters murderers") of the Eichmann type have not escaped, since as "order givers" not takers, or conduits, they fit into the pattern of Paragraph 211.[29]

Besides pleading alibis as to time, place, and person (identification problems are—after thirty years—substantial), the defendants invariably raise the defense of *Notstand* (duress).[30] This defense is based on the widespread belief in the "iron discipline" of the SS, the Gestapo, and other organs, and "probability" that disobedience or refusal to carry out illegal orders would have had the immediate result of landing the dissenter among the ranks of the victims.

Indeed, this defense goes to certain bases in the the nature and make-up of the Nazi regime and its relationship to the German people. Disobedience to orders in violation of oath, duty and fealty is deeply repugnant to the German character, and the Nazis exploited this. The so-called betrayal of 1918 had been one of the most popular and productive themes of Hitler.

"People against Stoebner and others," 5 St R 100/69 (1970), and cases cited there. By decision of the Bundestag after a—at times acrimonious—debate, the statute of limitations for murder under section 211 has been extended to December 31, 1979. *See*: New York Herald Tribune, Paris edition, January 20, 1968, p. 3.

[Editors's note: The Bundestag eventurally eliminated the statute of limitations for Nazi murder cases.]

29 A compendium of twenty-two major trials as of summer 1967 shows that at least 18 were directed against defendants in "desk" jobs, among them an official of the Foreign Office (Rademacher), a supervisor of a Gestapo training school (Rosenbaum), an SS-chemist (Widmann), and other police and Gestapo officials...."*Zusammenstellung von Hauptverhandlungen wegen NS-Gewaltverbrechen*," Zentrale Stelle der Landesjustizverwaltungen, Ludwigsburg, July 26, 1967.

30 Paragraphs 52 and 54, Penal Code, to the effect that acts done under the influence of irresistible force or threats of unavoidable danger to life or limb, are a defense to a crime, and excuse the threatened actor. "Petters-Preisendanz," *supra*, pp. 194 ff., SCHWARZ-DREHER, THE GERMAN PENAL CODE, annot. 27th edition, Munich, 1965, comments to Par. 51 ff.

Even when the criminality of the regime and the inevitability of defeat of Germany became obvious beyond doubt, the opponents in key positions to uproot the regime were still unable to overcome their scruples. How, then, argues the defense, could the brain-washed SS-robots be expected to react differently?...

It is therefore not surprising that the defense of "moral, educational, and traditional" brainwashing throughout childhood and adulthood to the inviolability of orders, no matter what, and the "unthinkable" act and consequences of refusal, skilfully and almost consistently proffered by defense counsel, strung both prosecution and courts to the quick. Neither is it surprising to find that this question was examined in and out of court at great length, exhaustively both in quantity and quality, and in extreme detail.

It was proven that despite intensive defense efforts not one instance could be conclusively established where any German was punished—even moderately—for refusing or circumventing participation in atrocities.... In the so-called Lemberg case, in which the perpetrators of the killings of thousands of Jews in the Lemberg area were tried, an expert called by the court, Dr. Hans Buchheim, testified that his historical studies of all available sources had not turned up one court-martial, disciplinary proceeding, or even demotion in cases where individuals shirked from participating in atrocities.[32]

The Ludwigsburg Central Prosecutor, by painstaking examination,[33] found that of dozens of alleged cases in which individuals claimed duress in being forced to take part in atrocities, not one could be substantiated to any degree of certainty. The Ludwigsburg study concludes that:

> ...damages to life and limb as a certain or highly probable consequence of refusal to carry out a criminal order must be generally discounted ... the refusal to carry out an illegal command did not constitute a "present danger to life and limb" and therefore an objective state of duress did not exist....[34]

The German Supreme Court has consistently turned down this defense in many decisions.[35]...

A total of over 50,000 cases has now been disposed of. Despite some reports to the contrary, very few of the Nazis in responsible places have, as was pointed out, escaped adjudication in one form or another, either by the Germans, the Western Allies, or the judicial authorities of the "Eastern bloc."[37]

---

32 Testimony of Prof. Dr. Buchheim in the so-called *Lemberg* case, 12 Js 1464/61-K 55/65, vol. 256, p. 2 ff.: testimony given on April 5, 1966.

33 "Zum Problem des sog. Befehlsnotstandes im NSG-Verfahren" memorandum issued by the Ludwigsburg Central Office, dated February 29, 1964.

34 *Ibid*. p. 78.

35 BGH, 4 St R 156/51; BGH 4 St R 417/54, and see cases collected and commented by Hinrichsen, in "Ruecker," *supra*. pp. 136-7.

37 As an example, an analysis of the fate of the commanding echelon of the notorious "Einsatzgruppen," the flying death-unit of the SS, reveals that of 52 commanding personnel only a single individual has not been apprehended:

Under its own rules, West Germany is the proper jurisdiction for trying all persons accused of crimes committed within the German borders of 1938, the areas under direct German administration from 1939 to 1945, and crimes committed by Germans or foreigners under German command. Some incriminated individuals have sought cover in the Near East, Africa, South America and the United States and Canada. The authorities of the Federal Republic have taken steps in such cases to have these persons extradited or repatriated.

*Ingo Müller, "Hitler's Justice: The Courts of the Third Reich"**

[Status of "Accomplices"]

When the "Law Accompanying Introduction of the Law on Illegal Activities" went into effect on October 1, 1968, its Article 1, number 6 contained a depth charge. This apparently insignificant piece of legislation, which had been unanimously adopted by the Bundestag after very little debate, added a new paragraph to the Criminal Code. The new paragraph 50, section 2 read: "If particular qualities, relationships, or circumstances which establish the criminal quality of the actor (particularly those of a personal nature) are lacking in the case of an accomplice to said crime, then his sentence is to be reduced and reckoned according to the rules governing an attempt at such a crime."[28] Before this law took effect, the relevant paragraph 49, section 2 of the Criminal Code on accomplices to crimes had established that sentences were to "be based on the law applying to the act which he has knowingly helped to commit." An accomplice's sentence could be reduced, but reduction was not mandatory. The maximum penalty remained the same as for commission of the crime itself. In the case of murder, the penalty was life imprisonment, and thus, prior to alteration of the Criminal Code, the statutory limit for prosecution of an accomplice to murder was twenty years, reckoned from December 31, 1949. Now, however, the newly added paragraph 50, section 2 required that the sentence of an accomplice to murder with no ascertainable personal motives that would classify his act as murder had to be reduced—in this case, from a maximum

---

Executed: 7
Cases pending: 7
Died of other than penal causes: 15
Incompetent to stand trial: 2
Life sentences: 5
Prison terms: 6
Pardoned by the Allies: 9
Fate not established: 1
Total: 52

(taken from: Alfred Strelm: "Die Verbechen der Einsatzgruppen in der Sowjetunion," in "Rueckerl," *supra*. pp. 102-106.

* Reprinted by permission of the publishers of HILTER'S JUSTICE: THE COURTS OF THE THIRD REICH by Ingo Müller, Cambridge, Mass.: Harvard University Press, Copyright © 1991 by the President and Fellows of Harvard College, pp. 246-248, 250-252, 254, 256-257.

[28] *Bundesgesetzblatt* (1968), I, 503.

life sentence to a maximum of fifteen years. But since all offenses with a maximum sentence of fifteen years' imprisonment had already fallen under the statute of limitations on May 8, 1960, the net effect was to exclude from prosecution, retroactively and with one stroke, the crimes of all Nazi accomplices to murder. And according to established construction of the courts, only Hitler, Himmler, and the top echelon of Nazis were murderers; everyone else was an accomplice....

The consequences of this legislative "error" became evident on May 20, 1969, when the Fifth Criminal Panel of the Federal Supreme Court made a ruling of fundamental significance in the first trial of what had originally been planned as a major series in connection with the activities of the Third Reich Central Security Office. The judges ruled that the new passage of the Criminal Code placed beyond the reach of prosecution all the atrocities that had been conceived and planned there. Overturning the Kassel County Court's conviction of an official in charge of Jewish affairs at the Krakow Police Department, the court observed:

> As the first trial established,... [the accused] knew that the victims were being killed purely out of racial prejudice. He did not share this base motive, however, but was merely obeying orders as a police officer and member of the SS, although he had come to realize that the orders were criminal. According to the new version of paragraph 50, section 2 of the Criminal Code, acting as an accomplice to murder in this ... may now be punished only with a penitentiary sentence of three to fifteen years. Paragraph 67, section 1 of the Criminal Code further specifies that this offense may not be prosecuted after the statutory limit of fifteen years has elapsed. This period had already expired when the first court action concerning the accused in connection with these events took place... The charges against him are therefore dropped.[32]

The decision brought to a halt the largest series of trials against Nazi criminals ever planned in the Federal Republic, just as they were getting underway. Eleven public prosecutors and twenty-three police officers had sifted through 150,000 files and divided the material into three main categories: participation in the "final solution," leadership of special military units, and participation in mass executions. The names of 2,700 witnesses had been collected and preparations completed for eighteen trials involving 300 defendants.[33]

With its decision to stop the trial, the Federal Supreme Court gave a clear signal to other courts. Soon thereafter, the Berlin County Court also dropped charges against seven high-ranking officials of the Reich Central Security Office....

In another trial, high-ranking civil servants at the Reich Ministry of Justice were accused of ordering the transfer of thousands of inmates from prisons to the Gestapo or to concentration camps, where, as the Wiesbaden

---

[32] *Entscheidungen des Bundesgeichtshofes in Strafsachen*, vol. 22, pp. 375ff; also *Neue Juristische Wochenschrift* (1969), 1181.

[33] Report of the Federal Minister of Justice, *Bundestags-Drucksache*, vol. 4, p. 3124.

County Court established, they were "hanged, shot, bludgeoned, or beaten until death occurred." The trial ended with a decision that found Hitler, Himmler, and Minister of Justice Thierack guilty "as indirect perpetrators of the murders of at least 573 prisoners sent to concentration camps." The ministry officials who had ordered them handed over were found to be "unwitting tools" who had not understood what they were doing, and were acquitted. Supposedly the evidence had not shown "that while they were engaged in this activity, they knew of or considered as possible the intended or already effected killings of the prisoners." It was admittedly true that the Ministry's correspondence had frequently referred to the prisoners' "annihilation," but in the view of the Wiesbaden County Court, their "awareness that the word 'annihilation' was being used did not in and of itself ... represent a sufficient basis to conclude that the defendants knew or suspected the killings were taking place."[43]...

Just as high Nazi party officials had been classified as "followers" in the early de-Nazification hearings and all responsibility ascribed to those leaders who were already dead, so now in an analogous manner the courts began to construe their actions consistently as those of mere "accomplices."... In November 1964, a case appealed by public prosecutors came before the Federal Supreme Court: the acquittal of a defendant accused of murdering Jews. Alois Häfele, a former SS officer who had participated in the killing of more than 89,000 people in the Kulmhof (Chelmo) death camp, had helped to organize the camp, had supervised the cleaning and maintenance of the gas vans, and had personally pushed the victims into them. He had stripped the dead of their valuables for personal profit and had received 800 marks and special leave from Heinrich Himmler as a reward. For all this, the Bonn County Court had classified him as a mere "accomplice without the intentions of a perpetrator."[49] On November 25, 1964, the Federal Supreme Court rejected the appeal of the Office of Public Prosecutions and referred to its own "distinction between perpetration of a crime and the act of aiding and abetting.... A decisive influence on the course of action,... the high rank of the accused,... [and] his extremely active participation in carrying out the murder program" all presented no obstacle to classing him as only an accomplice in the Holocaust, since "this participation was not based on his own motives but was instead limited to the forms established by the criminal leadership."[50]...

Sentencing

When, as did happen, Nazi criminals were actually found guilty, the courts often imposed sentences that, in the words of Fritz Bauer, former prosecutor general of Hesse, came "close to making a mockery of the victims' suffering."[58]... The Nazi criminals would "receive minimum sentences for

---

[43] Cited in Jörg Friedrich, *Die kalte Amnestie* (Frankfurt: Fischer Taschenbuch, 1984), 237.

[49] *Justiz und NS-Verbrechen*, vol. 21, pp. 270ff. (no. 594b).

[50] Ibid., vol. 21, pp. 345ff. (no. 594c).

[58] Bauer, "Im Namen des Volkes," in Hammerschmidt, ed., *Zwanzig Jahre danach*, 308.

'aiding and abetting murder,' sentences that in the eyes of the public reduce participation in mass murder to an offense about as serious as grand larceny, or regularly receiving stolen goods."[59] One or two days in prison per proven murder was quite common in these trials, and this was by no means due solely to the astronomical numbers of victims.

On occasion, judges made use of paragraph 47 of the Military Criminal Code, which was in effect at the time the deeds were committed, although not when the trials were held. Section 2 of this paragraph ran: "If the guilt of the subordinate is small, then a sentence may be dispensed with." Indeed, this law applied only to the armed forces and not to the police, but if the police duty in question was considered equivalent to "service in the war," then courts treated it as military service.[60] Sometimes even participation in the mass murders in the eastern territories was regarded as "service in the war." In the Chelmo trial mentioned above, for instance, the Bonn County Court determined on March 30, 1963, that paragraph 47 might be invoked even in those cases "involving the mass annihilations of innocent Jews that had nothing to do with the conduct of the war and which were carried out in secrecy." The judges conceded that the defendant Mehring had participated "in the murder of at least 26,000 people," but argued—using paragraph 47—that the "discrepancy" between his guilt and the minimum sentence of three years would be "so crass" that imposing it "would represent an indefensible hardship." They therefore acquitted him of murder.[61] When the prosecution appealed the verdict, the Federal Supreme Court set it aside and instructed the Bonn County Court that it had been mistaken in its reckoning of the penalty: the minimum sentence was not three years, but only nine months.[62] In a new trial the County Court then reached a decision, on July 27, 1965, that even this greatly reduced sentence "would stand in such disproportion to the guilt that it would constitute an unjust and indefensible hardship. If the legal minimum penalty would lead to such a situation of hardship,... then no penalty should be imposed at all."[63]

John H. Herz, "Denazification and Related Policies"[*]

[Assessment of the Prosecution Effort]

[Prosecution] procedures have been beset by long delays, long, drawn-out trials, the unavailability of witnesses, illnesses (real or faked) of

---

[59] Cited in Richard Henkys, *Die nationalsozialistischen Gewaltverbrechen* (Stuttgart: Kreuz-Verlag, 1964), 346.

[60] *Bundesgerichtshof* (Az: StR 55/55); cited in Rückerl, *Die Strafverfolgung von NS-Verbrechen*, 144.

[61] *Justiz und NS-Verbrechen*, vol. 21, p. 271 (no. 594b).

[62] Ibid., vol. 21, pp. 345ff. (no. 594c).

[63] Ibid., vol. 21, pp. 266-267 (no. 594a).

[*] Excerpted from John H. Herz, "Denazification and Related Policies," in John H. Herz, ed., *From Dictatorship to Democracy: Coping with the Legacies of Authoritarianism and Totalitarianism*, Copyright © 1982 by John Herz (Greenwood Press, 1982), p. 20, an imprint of Greenwood Publishing Group, Inc. Westport, CT. Reprinted with permission.

defendants, and by the high incidence of prosecutors and/or courts indulging in leniency if not sympathy for (now usually aged) defendants. Thus, although the statute of limitations (twenty years in the case of murder) was twice prolonged and finally abrogated by the Bundestag, convictions have been few and episodic. In over one thousand cases tried during the ten years between 1959 and 1969, fewer than one hundred of those convicted received life sentences, and fewer than three hundred received limited terms. Twelve years later, for some 6,000 convictions, 157 life sentences were meted out. The failure of denazification procedures to remove former Nazis from judicial positions ... has borne the bitter fruit of biased or weak justice. Nazi military courts, for instance, imposed twenty-six thousand death verdicts (as contrasted with less than three hundred in World War I), but none of those judges or prosecutors was tried, and it is hardly surprising that post-Nazi judges have refused to convict members of the Nazi "People's Court" who, in meting out their blood "justice," denied to defendants even the minimal procedural safeguards then in effect.

*Fritz Weinschenk, "Nazis Before German Courts: The West German War Crimes Trials"**

Like the Allied proceedings after World War II, the German program has its obvious—and serious—drawbacks:

1. Heavily incriminated Nazi bigwigs, saved from the gallows and pardoned after relatively short prison terms, now prospering through pensions, booksales, and business connections, are testifying as immune witnesses in the trials of their own former subordinates, faced with long terms in prison;

2. Disparities in chance survival of evidence will tie one individual into an "aggravated murder" pattern, while his comrade—with the same assignment, the same unit, and—probably—the same degree of guilt—will walk away free, because the evidence as to him happened to be insufficient;

3. The trials have taken too long. Prosecutors and judges alike are caught in the cross-fire of cries of "too much" and "not enough." While voices within and without Germany demand an end to the dragging, increasingly fruitless proceedings against the remnants of the Third Reich,[40] others demand renewed efforts to rectify unrequited wrongs.[41] It is a tragedy, deeply disturbing to an objective observer bent on adherence to the notions of due process and fairness, that there is much merit on both sides of this controversy.

4. Many of the prosecutors and judges will rate the value of the trials as deterrent or pedagogic rehabilitation of the perpetrators to be nil. Anyone

---

* Excerpted from Fritz Weinschenk, "Nazis Before German Courts: The West German War Crimes Trials," *International Lawyer*, vol. 10, no. 3 (Summer 1976), pp. 528-529, Copyright 1976 American Bar Association. Used by permission.

[40] *See, for example,* report of New York Times correspondent Craig R. Whitney, "After 30 years, trials of Nazis drag on," New York Times, August 29, 1975, page 1, col. 4, quoted *supra*, footnote 23.

[41] [omitted]

who has read some of the "confessions" of the accused will be overcome by the curious admixture of unrequited hate, baseness, arrogance and moronic insensibility which affirms the validity of Hannah Arendt's often-quoted words "banality of evil."

These problems, however, cannot substantially derogate from this vast national undertaking. Apart from establishing the truth about the Nazi crimes beyond reasonable doubt through the orderly methods of judicial inquiry, these trials have served notice on the "true believers"—from one corner of the earth to another—who defile human dignity by their acts of insanity, that there now exist precedents for the adjudication of genocide, crimes against humanity, and violation of the human ethic, and that somewhere, sometime, it might be their turn.

THE PURGE OF NAZI PERSONNEL

The Purge Program Under the Military Government

John H. Herz, "Denazification and Related Policies"[*]

There is a German saying: *Regierung vergeht, Verwaltung besteht* (Governments come and go, bureaucracy remains). This proverb proved to be true when imperial Germany turned into Weimar republicanism. One of the sources of democratic weakness and of the eventual failure of Weimar republicanism was the continuance in office of an antidemocratic, authoritarian bureaucracy of the old Prussian type in all branches of government; cabinets changed from right to left and back again, but the spirit that had rendered Germany's a "subject culture" continued to pervade every realm of life....

The Allies and those "other Germans" who had survived unscathed the twelve years of the "Thousand-Year Reich" realized that to democratize Germany for the first time in its history, it would not be enough to replace the Nazi political and governmental top stratum with democrats; the old, authoritarian bureaucracy, too, which had enabled Hitler to establish totalitarian control and had cooperated by lending nazism its expertise, would have to be transformed.... The problem was how to replace Nazis and Nazi collaborators with knowledgeable democrats or at least with non-Nazis in all the major fields of government, politics, administration, judiciary, education, and cultural life. Who would make the decisions and how? It was an undertaking without precedent. It required skill, courage, and determination. If it was not to appear from the outset as "imposed by the enemy," the program had to be implemented by Germans themselves as early as possible; but to be able to do this, those Germans entrusted with the procedures had to be backed to the hilt by a military government determined

---

[*] Excerpted from John H. Herz, "Denazification and Related Policies," in John H. Herz, ed., *From Dictatorship to Democracy: Coping with the Legacies of Authoritarianism and Totalitarianism*, Copyright © 1982 by John Herz (Greenwood Press, 1982), pp. 22-26, an imprint of Greenwood Publishing Group, Inc. Westport, CT. Reprinted with permission.

to see it through. As we shall see, initial interest and support dissipated and subsequently vanished, and for this and other reasons, the task eventually failed. It should not, for this reason, be deprecated or vilified (as it often was and still is). It was a novel and a noble effort, and its failure brought no dishonor on those who had devoted themselves to it.

The Potsdam agreement on eliminating Nazis from positions of influence had been preceded by preparatory studies undertaken during the war. While the French were not yet a party to these efforts (they had not yet been accorded their own zone of occupation), the main effort was made by the two chief Western allies, the British and the Americans....

The first stage of the "revolution by procedure" under which was to be pursued the aim of "democratization through denazification" was inaugurated by MG (Military Government) as soon as the occupying powers moved into Germany.... But because the more detailed guidelines were not available when the troops moved into Germany, the most pressing and immediate tasks of administration (finding shelter for bombed-out people, transporting food, etc.) often meant the arbitrary selection or reconfirmation in office of persons upon recommendations of local clergy or similar trusted, usually conservative elements.[9] To the extent that initial measures determine subsequent events, these decisions were not without effect on the subsequent implementation of policy.

Although denazification directives were meant to be executed uniformly in the zones, implementation in practice was left to the different zonal administrations.... [T]he experiment in the U.S. zone was the most thorough and systematic one.... Because the British zone was comprised of Germany's industrial heart, the Ruhr, the restoration of a working economy and an efficient administration was given preference over the purge of Nazis and thus denazification procedures were more haphazard. In the French zone, too, things were different. Because the French were not as much interested in rebuilding a democratic Germany as they were in keeping Germany weak and in gaining influence in their zone, their interest in denazification was minor. Possibly, they were skeptical about the feasibility of efficient denazification in view of the disillusioning experience they had just had with épuration in France....[11]

Confusion reigned from the beginning of the occupation. MG had established Special Branches (SpBr) to deal with denazification. SpBr started by distributing questionnaires to administrators, teachers, and other members of the public services, which then were sent to those MG officers who supervised the respective branches. These officers, according to MG directives, were to automatically arrest and send to internment camps certain categories of persons, in particular holders of higher ranks in the party, members of organizations condemned as "criminal" at Nuernberg (SS, Gestapo, SD [Security Service]), higher rank bureaucrats; bureaucrats were to

---

[9] [omitted]

[11] More details on denazification in the British zone can be found in Justus Fürstenau, *Entnazifizierung, Ein Kapitel deutscher Nachkriegspolitik* (Neuwied, 1969), pp. 103-133; on denazification in the French zone, see the same source, pp. 134-147.

be dismissed from positions they might still hold and were to be employed only as "ordinary laborers." In other cases dismissal and/or internment was left to the discretion of the MG officers. The procedure was overly schematic (e.g., omitting at first business and other nongovernmental sectors, whose members, however, might have been more closely affiliated with the Nazis than many nominal holders of party positions);[12] at the same time, it was overly discretionary, allowing in some areas (e.g., that of financial administration...) a procedure that was tough in the extreme, whereas in others, frequently under the pressure of new German administrators afraid of the complete breakdown of their offices, there was great leniency, which permitted the retention in office of persons whose dismissal should have seemed mandatory.... During that first year, the number of interned persons in the U.S. zone rose to 100,000; there was a constant influx but also a considerable release of internees.... After less than a year, the military governors gave up and transferred primary responsibility for denazification to the Germans.

The Purge Program Under German Authority

John H. Herz, "Denazification and Related Policies"[*]

The overall problem confronting the Germans in this second phase of denazification was how to find among the masses of the population those who, because of their involvement with nazism, should not be allowed to obtain in the new successor system positions of influence from which they might impede democracy. In a population of tens of millions, this might have been possible if the authorities had started with individual offices and institutions (e.g., specific police and other administrative offices, individual schools, and university departments) where purges, although executed in a haphazard and arbitrary fashion, had begun during the preceding stage and then, with the aid of Germans who had proved themselves non-Nazi in these offices and institutions, find those most incriminated and thus liable to be purged.[13] Instead, the "Liberation Law" (Law for Liberation from National Socialism and Militarism, enacted by the Laenderrat for the three Laender of the U.S. zone, March 5, 1946) provided for the screening and categorizing of the entire adult population. This was an impossible task; it condemned the program to failure from the outset; many Germans meant it to fail.

Questionnaires were used again, but this time, everybody over 18 years of age had to fill out a *Fragebogen*, detailing previous occupation and activities, membership or office in specified Nazi organizations, and so on.

---

[12] A special law subsequently issued by zonal commander General Lucius Clay required dismissal of management personnel with Nazi affiliation but was generally circumvented, thus remaining without effect.

[*] Excerpted from John H. Herz, "Denazification and Related Policies," in John H. Herz, ed., *From Dictatorship to Democracy: Coping with the Legacies of Authoritarianism and Totalitarianism*, Copyright © 1982 by John Herz (Greenwood Press, 1982), pp. 26-27, an imprint of Greenwood Publishing Group, Inc. Westport, CT. Reprinted with permission.

[13] [omitted]

There were about 13 million people involved and few could avoid submitting questionnaires because the receipt of food-ration coupons was made dependent on handing them in.[14] Filling them out deceptively, that is, omitting incriminating statements, was possible, of course, and was resorted to by some in a shifting population who had come to the zone from elsewhere, especially the eastern territories, and whose backgrounds were thus rarely traceable. A whole system of authorities was empowered to deal with this immense number of cases. There were public prosecutors, who, on the basis of the questionnaires, were authorized to place each person either into the group (largest of all, about 9.5 million) of those "not chargeable," that is, unaffected by the law, or else into one of five categories: major offender, offender, lesser offender, follower (*Mitlaeufer*), exonerated.... After being so categorized by the prosecutor, the incriminated was dealt with by local boards (*Spruchkammern*) consisting of three or more members; they acted either in written or oral procedures; from their decisions, appeal could be taken to appeal boards. It was up to the "defendant" to prove that the preliminary categorization by the prosecutor was wrong.

John Dornberg, "Schizophrenic Germany"[*]

[Categories of Offenders]

The "major offender" group included persons guilty of crimes against victims or opponents of National Socialism; pillaging, deporting, or other acts of violence; mistreating prisoners of war, and those who had held leading positions in the Nazi party or any Nazi or militaristic organization. The group also encompassed those individuals whose positions in government had been so important that only leading Nazis could have held them, as well as persons who had lent great support to the Nazi régime or had profited from its support. Automatically classified as major offenders were all active members of the Gestapo, SD (security service), SS (elite guard), secret military police, border police, and those who had participated in concentration camp, hospital, or insane asylum atrocities.

Punishments prescribed for them included work camp sentences up to ten years and confiscation of all property and wealth except that needed for their daily minimum requirements. The proceeds from such property, the de-Nazification law decreed, would be used to make reparations payments to victims of the Hitler régime.

Other possible penalties were permanent ineligibility to hold public office, loss of any legal claim to pensions, and the right to vote or be elected. Major offenders were barred from active participation in political parties. In addition to these sanctions, they could also be denied membership in a labor

---

[14] An estimated 100,000 did go underground, however; they surfaced after an amnesty in late 1948.

[*] Excerpted from John Dornberg, *Schizophrenic Germany* (The Macmillan Company, 1961), pp. 12-14. Reprinted with permission of Sterling Lord Literistic, Inc. Copyright © 1961 by John Dornberg.

union or professional organization and barred, for at least ten years, from undertaking an independent economic effort, owning shares, or holding any type of employment other than that of a laborer. They could be banned from teaching, preaching, writing, editing, or commenting on the radio. They were subject to recruitment for labor to the public benefit.

Furthermore, major offenders could be deprived of all concessions and other licenses, including the right to own or drive an automobile.

For the next group, the "offenders," the punishments were essentially the same except that labor camp internment was limited to five years and economic restrictions were slated for a period of at least five, instead of ten, years. This second group, which included many more people than the first, of course, was divided into three classifications: "activists, militarists, and profiteers."

The "activists" included those who had taught Nazism, had been judges, had agitated against the churches, had written for or spoken publicly in behalf of the Nazi régime, had spied or informed on their fellow citizens, or had been active in the destruction of the trade union movement.

"Militarists" had attempted to bring German life in line with a policy or militaristic force, had advocated or been responsible for the domination of foreign people, their exploitation or displacement, or had promoted armament for these purposes. The group also included individuals who had participated in the bombardment of dwelling areas.

A "profiteer" was described as anyone who had obtained an office or important position because of his membership in the Nazi party, had received substantial donations from the party, or had profited from the political, religious, and racial persecution of others. Also classified as profiteers were persons who had made disproportionately high profits from the arms industry, had enriched themselves in an unfair manner in connection with the administration of occupied territories, or had escaped military service because of membership in the Nazi party.

According to the law, "minor offenders" were those who "belonged" to the first two groups but could be expected to fulfill their duties as citizens of a peaceful and democratic state. They were usually placed on two- to three-year probationary periods during which they were not allowed to operate business enterprises of more than ten employees and frequently were ordered to work as common laborers.

"Followers" were defined as "insignificant supporters of Nazism," including particularly those who had belonged to party organizations but had paid only membership dues and participated in such meetings at which attendance was obligatory.

People who had resisted the Nazi régime and suffered disadvantages as a result of it were classified by the boards as "exonerated."

John H. Herz, "Denazification and Related Policies"[*]

The defendant's task proved to be easier than one might have assumed. The largest number of offenders, those who had not incriminated themselves by furnishing information that might have placed them in the more serious categories of offenders or (what happened rarely) were not so accused by other persons, found themselves almost automatically categorized as *Mitlaeufer*; these people had a choice between appealing, whereupon they were in many cases completely exonerated, or paying their usually small fines, after which they were considered "denazified" and restored to full-fledged citizenship, employable (again) in all occupations and offices. In the small number of cases in which the incriminated had been placed in high categories, they subsequently tried to prove that they should have been placed in the *Mitlaeufer* category (or even be exonerated) or at worst judged "lesser offenders." In those cases (as also in the ones in which designated *Mitlaeufer* appealed to be exonerated), the local or appeal boards were presented with a rich array of whitewashing documents (popularly known as *Persilscheine*, after a well-known brand of German soap) obtained not only from friends but also from clergymen testifying to their loyal church attendance, from former employees testifying to their generous attitudes as employers, and so on.[15] On the other hand, there occurred what amounted to a "witness strike" observed by persons who might have incriminated the defendants. None of the defendants was ready to take the stand for his Nazi convictions anymore; they all claimed to have joined the party or its organizations for opportunistic reasons, to keep their jobs, and so on. While this was true in many cases involving small fry, one usually failed to differentiate between them and the big shots; all who could prove the barest of extenuating circumstances were classified followers, and the whole procedure soon became known as *Mitlaeuferfabrik* (followers' factory).

No wonder. The local boards, lay people[16] drawn (often reluctantly) from known non-Nazis (former trade unionists, members of the newly founded parries, and so on) soon became swamped. Sometimes the boards were difficult to establish; people were afraid of recrimination and revenge, found themselves intimidated by influential relatives or friends of the indicted, often ostracized by the public. They were badly paid and thus open to corruption; they became politically and socially more and more isolated, and in any event, they were buried beneath a mass of complex cases. After it was all over, they ran into difficulties in finding employment at a time when

---

[*] Excerpted from John H. Herz, "Denazification and Related Policies," in John H. Herz, ed., *From Dictatorship to Democracy: Coping with the Legacies of Authoritarianism and Totalitarianism*, Copyright © 1982 by John Herz (Greenwood Press, 1982), pp. 27-29, an imprint of Greenwood Publishing Group, Inc. Westport, CT. Reprinted with permission.

[15] Even the incriminated exchanged *Persilscheine*; for example, former Gestapo officers gave mutual assurance that they had always been courteous when questioning political opponents.

[16] Only the chairman of an appeal board had to be legally trained. That the whole system was not meant to be part of the judiciary but a separate administrative setup is also apparent from the designations given to the participants: respondents (not defendants), public prosecutors (not district attorneys), board members (not judges), and so on.

jobs were scarce, having been filled by those that they had "denazified." No wonder, therefore, that a law had to be passed under which persons could be drafted for board service; only a small number of members acted out of conviction and a feeling of duty. Expressing the attitude that typified the position of the churches, Cardinal Faulhaber forbade priests to become board members. Paster Niemöller similarly advised his Protestant colleagues.

The scandal of high party leaders, Gestapo officials, and others known as strongly involved in Nazi activities "getting away with murder" at one point provoked General Clay to threaten to resume MG responsibility for denazification, but nothing came of his threat. The political atmosphere had changed, not only in Germany but also in the United States. The developing cold war shifted the attention of the American public away from denazification and similar matters; it was now considered more important to build up the Western zones of Germany as fast as possible so that they could contribute to the strengthening of the emerging Western camp, which seemed to require the reinstatement of efficient administrators in their jobs, the rehiring of experienced managers who had proved capable of directing industrial enterprises, and so forth.

In contrast to the earlier phase of the second stage of denazification, the Americans now urged the Germans to terminate the program, and a number of measures were enacted to compel even those Germans (in the denazification ministries, e.g.) who had hoped for a meaningful conclusion to give in. The termination of the program was all the more significant because up to that time chiefly small cases had been dealt with, in particular those of internees whose cases were prosecuted in order to render them employable again, whereas most of the serious cases had not been dealt with (thus in Bavaria, in October 1947, there were still pending over one half million cases involving serious offenders). But a series of amnesties (for younger offenders, a Christmas amnesty, and so on) rendered most of those not in group I "not chargeable," and prosecutors, unable or unwilling to investigate each amnesty case according to its merits, ruled automatically that "no sufficient reasons" existed to suspect that a person, unless incriminated on the basis of his questionnaire, was a "major offender." Finally, amendments to the Liberation Law as well as the final amnesties of late 1947 and early 1948 allowed almost every case of even major offenders to be downgraded to the category of followership, which, in turn, rendered the offender eligible for amnesty. This meant that even a majority of those who had belonged to groups defined as criminal organizations (SS, Gestapo, and others) by the Nuernberg Tribunal were exonerated and, to the extent that they had been kept in military internment, released (later, when some of them were tried in war-crimes trials, such detainment under denazification rules was counted against their prison terms...).[17] By March 1948, the program was terminated for all practical purposes. On paper, that is, legally, cases could still be dealt

---

[17] In this way those who had committed real crimes had the best of both worlds: Denazification authorities proved unable (or unwilling) to ferret them out as criminals; once "denazified," they were considered by prosecution authorities and courts no longer subject to trial because of their denazification.

with until the early 1950s, when, upon the recommendation of the new West German government, all the Laender officially terminated the program.

The Results and the Impact of Denazification

As mentioned above, procedures in the two other Western occupation zones, the British and the French, were less comprehensive than those in the American zone. In the British zone,... the cancellation of proceedings plus acquittals amounted to about 40 percent of the cases, fines to over 35 percent, and prison sentences to 20 percent; however, not only prison sentences but also fines were in almost every case considered as having been "paid for" by previous internment. In the French zone, there had been little internment or the prohibition of employment. In the U.S. zone, final figures revealed that of three and a half million people processed by local boards, almost two and a half million were granted amnesty without trial; of the remainder, about 37 percent were exonerated; 51 percent were classified followers, 10.7 percent were classified lesser offenders, 2. 1 offenders, and 0. 1 major offenders; however by May 1948, appeal boards had downgraded all but 30 percent of those classified I, II, and II by the local boards, so that most of them had escaped, or could expect to escape, the higher categorizations. Of those convicted, the vast majority was merely fined; of those sentenced to labor camps, most had previous internment counted against such sentence; and of those held ineligible to hold public office or subject to other employment restrictions, such proscriptions were limited to short probation periods.

John Dornberg, "Schizophrenic Germany"[*]

State Department figures of May 1949, reveal that less than 10 percent of those individuals originally registered had been tried in de-Nazification courts. And of this small minority, only 1,600 had been classified as major offenders and 22,000 as offenders. The minor offender and follower category included more than 600,000.

The sentences—and they duplicate themselves in many instances—included 9,600 labor camp terms, 569,000 fines, 124,000 employment restrictions, 28,500 confiscations of property, and 23,000 bannings from public office. Appeals had reduced the sanctions in approximately 10 percent of the cases. Many Germans still feel today that important Nazis were allowed to go free or were sentenced to insignificant financial disadvantages or fines while thousands of unimportant fellow travelers were treated too severely.

---

[*] Excerpted from John Dornberg, *Schizophrenic Germany* (The Macmillan Company, 1961), pp. 15-16. Reprinted with permission of Sterling Lord Literistic, Inc. Copyright © 1961 by John Dornberg.

Rehabilitation and Reparations for Government Employees

*Arnold Brecht, "Personnel Management"**

[T]he law of March 5, 1946, stated explicitly that no person declared to be a lesser offender or "follower" could claim either reinstitution in public office or damages because of his removal (Art. 64). The final decision on his reappointment was left to the personnel management of the new democratic governments.

Consequently the individual *Länder* governments developed principles of their own about reappointment. Typical was the Bavarian ordinance of January 29, 1947,[11] which said (Art. 3) that an official removed from office may not be reinstated unless he not only fulfills professional requirements but also has the personal qualities for the job. These must include "the guarantee that he will cooperate positively in building up, and assuring permanent foundations to, a democratic form of government" and, in case he is to serve in the higher brackets, that he "owns the political, liberal and moral qualities which justify the expectation that he will contribute to the promotion of democracy in Germany." It was added (Art. 4) that, if removed by the military government, he could be reinstated only with its written consent.

These principles were perfect in theory. But in practice there prevailed a notable tendency not to go beyond the results of the judicial procedures in rejecting candidates for political reasons....

Ingo Müller, "Hitler's Justice: The Courts of the Third Reich"†

According to [a study entitled "Some Aspects of Re-Nazification in Bavaria" by the American commissioner for the State of Bavaria to the high commissioner], "the return of party members to positions of power and influence [is] proof of how little has changed."[13] For example in the district of Lower Bavaria/Upper Palatinate between November 1948 and March 1949, when government agencies were being reopened and new staff was being hired, it had been impossible to find jobs for fifty-eight former government employees who had not been Nazis. But during the same period, in the same district, sixty-nine former Nazi party members had been reemployed in some sector of public service.

...A stream of civil servants was pouring from the previously German-occupied territories and the Soviet zone of occupation to the east, and from Alsace-Lorraine and other occupied regions to the west, into the three western zones, which taken together did not cover even half the area of

---

* Excerpted from Arnold Brecht, "Personnel Management," in Edward H. Lithcfield et al., *Governing Postwar Germany* (Cornell University Press, 1953), p. 268.

11 This ordinance was declared invalid by the Bavarian Constitutional Court on April 24, 1950, because it had been passed by the cabinet only, but it was subsequently confirmed retroactively by the legislature on July 27, 1950.

† Reprinted by permission of the publishers of HILTER'S JUSTICE: THE COURTS OF THE THIRD REICH by Ingo Müller, Cambridge, Mass.: Harvard University Press, Copyright © 1991 by the President and Fellows of Harvard College, pp. 203-205, 261-262.

13 National Archives, Washington, D.C., RG 59, pp. 321ff.

the old "Greater German Reich" and all of these people were seeking employment. This resettling led to a concentration of (former) Nazis such as even the Third Reich had not known. Some government agencies had more party members working at them in 1948-1949 than they had had under Hitler.[15]

In order to create more room for ex-Nazi civil servants in the now overfilled agencies, the "outsiders" hired with limited contracts after 1945 were let go, especially the numerous people given preference by the De-Nazification Tribunals—people who had usually been victims of Nazi persecution and opponents of Fascism. Although they had often been promised further employment in government service, they had no legal claim to it. There was a general sense of relief at being rid of the unpopular "de-Nazifiers." Only a minority of them found other work quickly; two thirds remained dependent for a long time on welfare and unemployment benefits.[16]... The few experienced public servants without an incriminating past, who were needed so urgently, were now considered to have "incriminated" themselves by supporting de-Nazification; in the early years of the Federal Republic, this was a far worse stigma than having been a National Socialist.

...In the late forties, jurists were heatedly arguing the question of whether the German Reich had ceased to exist or whether it had continued after the unconditional surrender—a discussion which at first could seem somewhat macabre.... The seemingly absurd debate about the cessation or continued existence of the German Reich was not just an academic exercise, however. It had quite genuine relevance to the question of whether civil servants of the Reich still had a claim to their old status. At issue was whether these people had had their connections with the civil service permanently severed when the Allied forces of occupation had dismissed them, or whether they had merely been temporarily suspended....

[The "131 Law"]

In the debates of the Parliamentary Council, which was meeting to draft a new German constitution, the delegates—many of whom were high-level civil servants themselves in various ministries—could not agree on a policy for civil servants with an incriminating Nazi past. The first version prepared by the drafting committee had included the statement: "Any person who was a civil servant or government employee on May 8, 1945, cannot claim a right to reemployment on these grounds."[20] In the final debate, however, the council decided to postpone a solution to the problem, and Article 131 of the Basic Law (*Grundgesetz*), as it was eventually passed, directed future lawmakers "to regulate by federal law ... the rights of persons employed in the civil service as of May 8, 1945, including refugees and those expelled

---

15 Lutz Niethammer, "Zum Verhältnis von Reform und Rekonstruktion," in Wolf-Dieter Narr and Dietrich Thränhardt, eds., *Die Bundesrepublik Deutschland: Entstehung, Entwicklung, Struktur* (Köningstein/Taunus: Verlagsgruppe Athenäum, 1979), 33.

16 Lutz Niethammer, *Die Mitläuferfabrik: Die Entnazifizierung am Beispiel Bayerns* (Berlin: Deitz, 1982), 595.

20 Cited in Friedrich, *Die kalte Amnestie*, 273.

from their homes, who ceased to be employed there for reasons other than those covered by the civil service or salary laws and who until now have either not found employment at all or not at the former level."

When the Bundestag (Federal Parliament) met to discuss such a law, no mention at all was made of the reasons why the judges and civil servants had been dismissed. Instead, members of parties across the entire political spectrum spoke of the need to help those "admirable people"[21] who had "spent a lifetime in public service,"[22] so that "the group affected by Article 131 can feel they are recognized as valuable members of the state."[23] References were also made to the "reestablishment of a constitutional state," a task for which "the contribution of their knowledge, experience, and manpower" was needed.[24]

The statute referred to colloquially as "the 131 Law" was passed on May 11, 1951, effective retroactively as of April 1. In effect, it gave a foundation in law to the reintegration of Nazi officials in the civil service, a process that was by then complete in any case.[25] After an amendment was added in August 1953, the statute gave all public servants of the National Socialist state a legal claim to reemployment, and also the right to claim back pay for the time they had not been able to work.[26] The sole exceptions were agents of the Gestapo and civil servants who had been classed as "major offenders" in de-Nazification proceedings. In addition, the law required that at least 20 percent of employees in all departments of public administration be former Nazis; departments failing to meet this requirement would be fined an amount equal to the salaries thus "saved." These new legal claims and the quota system now meant that old party members had to be given first priority in hiring, and thus more than 90 percent of the Nazi officials dismissed after 1945 found their way back into public service. Since public funds were so limited and the civil service bureaucracy so overstaffed (by 1949 the German administrative regions, or *Länder*, were virtually bankrupt), for all practical purposes former membership in the Nazi party became a requirement for joining the civil service.*...

---

[21] Wackerzapp (CDU), cited ibid., 280.

[22] Heinemann (CDU), ibid.

[23] Menzel (SPD), ibid.

[24] Kleindienst (CDU), ibid.

[25] *Bundesgesetzblatt* (1951), I, 307.

[26] Ibid., 980.

* [Editor's note: Although there is general agreement on the negative consequences of the "131 Law," some observers ascribe benevolent motives to its origin, noting that it

> was designed to relieve the plight of former German civil servants who had lost their jobs through evacuation, expulsion, or flight from the eastern sections of Germany (or former Germany) or from Czechoslovakia or through discontinuance of public offices.... All this has been done, not just in favor of former Nazis, of course, but primarily in the interest of decent public servants put out of jobs through accidental circumstances and to relieve the financial burden arising from their claims for pensions or salaries.

Most of the people found guilty of Nazi crimes had been civil servants during the Third Reich, since the worst atrocities had been ordered by the government. A conviction on criminal charges has unpleasant consequences for a civil servant; in the case of Nazi criminals, according to paragraph 31 of the Criminal Code (now paragraph 45), a conviction carrying with it a penitentiary sentence automatically resulted in "disqualification for office." Those still active in the civil service were dismissed and lost all rights to a pension, while pension payments immediately ceased for civil servants already in retirement. This rule did not apply, however, to convictions handed down by "non-German" courts. In effect, that is to say, someone found guilty of murder by a court in another country had a legal right to reemployment in the German civil service, and in some circumstances even to back pay. The Nuremberg war crimes trials of Nazi leaders and related trials were counted as "non-German" convictions.

Nevertheless, a solution was also found for officials with convictions from German courts: since 1924, persons who leave the civil service have been able to transfer their previous pension insurance payments to a pension fund for non-civil service government employees.[1] Paragraph 141 of the old Civil Service Law prohibited such a transfer in the case of a criminal conviction, but on July 14, 1953, when this law was revised and passed as the Federal Civil Service Law (in essence, merely a de-Nazified version of the old one), this limiting clause was dropped. When a general reform of pension regulations took place in 1957, the transfer of money paid into pension funds was expressly permitted, regardless of the reasons for departure or dismissal from the civil service.[2] According to the new law, the government was not only permitted but even required to grant retroactive insurance to officials who had been denied their civil service pensions by court decisions[3] and furthermore, the "131 Law,"... at the same time contained the provision that they must receive a retroactive pension insurance transfer. As a result, such persons suffered not the slightest inconvenience, even if they had been convicted of murders numbering in the thousands. For those in the middle or upper echelons of the civil service, this transfer was even advantageous, because the pension as calculated according to the new law, was not only higher than their original one but also tax free. The Federal Social Court established a principle of "value-free social insurance"[4] guaranteeing the right to a pension transfer even in cases where an official had been found guilty of the worst crimes against humanity or the rule of law....

The courts were even generous in filling "gaps" in the careers of former Nazis that would have led to reduced pensions. In one case, the Federal Social Court reckoned as "equivalent" to a period of employment for pension

---

Excerpted from Arnold Brecht, "Personnel Management", in Edward H. Litchfield et al., *Governing Postwar Germany* (Cornell University Press, 1953), pp. 269-270.]

1 Decree of February 13, 1924; *Reichsgesetzblatt* (1924), I, 62.

2 Amended versions of Paragraphs 1232 RVO and 9 AVG; *Bundesgesetzblatt* (1957), I, 45 and 88.

3 Law of June 9, 1965; *Bundesgesetzblatt* (1965), I, 476.

4 Decision of November 24, 1965; *Entscheidungen des Bundessozialgerichts*, vol. 25, p. 106.

purposes the time a career Nazi party official had spent in prison after sentencing by a French military court.[6]

*John Dornberg, "Schizophrenic Germany"**

In particular, the [131] law covers those civil servants who worked for a government bureau or office which since has been dissolved; those who were employed in government bureaus outside the territorial limits of the Federal Republic; those in the state or local administration of the Protectorate of Bohemia and Moravia, employed in the state or local administration of a foreign country who were expelled because of their German origin; retired and inactive civil servants who were unable to receive their pensions and retirement benefits after May 8, 1945; professional soldiers of the former *Wehermacht* who were still on active duty or already retired and entitled to their pensions; the professional employees of the Reich Labor Service, and the dependents of individuals in all these groups and classifications.

This law has made it possible for thousands of ex-Nazis to reenter government service, the military, and other branches of public endeavor which fall under civil service regulations in Germany.... Those who have not been reemployed have been permitted to retire with the benefits they accrued during the Third Reich.... Germany today [1961]is faced with the strange dilemma of having to shell out millions annually, not only to the victims of Nazi persecution but to the persecutors as well. Those ex-Nazis who have failed to regain their civil service positions or to get on the retirement and pension dole have established powerful lobby groups with which they hope to change the "131 Law" so that they, too, will be included in its provisions....

Although there are distinct safety controls in the law, hundreds of big and small Nazis have successfully obtained pensions, returnee payments, POW compensation, and long-term loans under the provisions of the various programs. Generally it is up to the local courts and civil service disciplinary boards to make the decision. But if the circumstances are right, if an applicant has a good lawyer, he's as good as on the payroll....

In late summer of 1958 the Lower-Saxony council of the German Federation of Labor Unions published a shocking report about former high-ranking Nazis who had received pensions, government loans, or subsidies, or were back in public life.[5] Publication of the list set off a wave of protests, in and out of Germany, but with little result.

---

[6] Cited in Ulrich Vultejus, *Kampfanzug unter der Robe* (Hamburg: Buntbuch, 1984), 85.

* Excerpted from John Dornberg, *Schizophrenic Germany* (The Macmillan Company, 1961), pp. 41-42, 44. Reprinted with permission of Sterling Lord Literistic, Inc. Copyright © 1961 by John Dornberg.

[5] [omitted]

Judges and Jurists

Karl Loewenstein, "Justice"[*]

Prior to Potsdam, the famous JCS 1067 of 1945, dealing specifically with the part of Germany occupied by the United States forces, had directed the closing of all ordinary criminal, civil, and administrative courts except those previously re-established by American Military Government and the immediate abolition of all extraordinary courts and Nazi party courts.[2] Reopening of the ordinary courts was to be permitted only after the elimination of Nazi features and personnel and the establishment of appropriate controls, including the power to review and veto decisions. Both the Potsdam Declaration and JCS 1067 called for the abrogation of all peculiarly Nazi legislation....

Denazification of the Judiciary—Denazification, in the legal field, involved both purging German law of Nazi concepts and practices[38] and elimination of Nazi-tainted personnel from the legal services. A brief analysis of this fundamental issue of the occupation is indispensable for the present-day appraisal of the German judiciary. When the Nazis set out to revolutionize the *Rechtsstaat*, the new regime was accepted by the legal profession with no less approval or complacency than by other influential classes. Active nonconformists were expelled at once by the Law of April 7, 1933, misnamed the Law for the Restoration of the Professional Civil Service.[39] Aside from those ousted for racial or political reasons, only a handful of mostly older judges resigned voluntarily. On May 1, 1937, the Public Officials Act entered into force. While not explicitly requiring party membership for public officials, it suspended permanently over their heads the sword of dismissal for "political unreliability."[40] Consequently, the vast majority of the bench took out membership badges or otherwise demonstrated their allegiance to the party.[41]

Ingo Müller, "Hitler's Justice: The Courts of the Third Reich"[†]

[The Allied] Control Commission's Law 4 of November 30, 1945, stated: "To effect the reorganization of the judicial system all former members of the Nazi party who have been more than nominal participants in its activities

---

[*] Excerpted from Karl Loewenstein, "Justice," in Edward H. Lithcfield et al., *Governing Postwar Germany* (Cornell University Press, 1953), p. 236, 345.

[2] On the extraordinary courts, see Karl Loewenstein, "Law in the Third Reich," *Yale Law Journal*, XLV (1936), 808.

[38] For a full discussion of the denazification of law, see Karl Loewenstein, "Law and the Legislative Process in Occupied Germany," *Yale Law J.*, LVII (1948), 734 ff., 994 ff.

[39] *Gesetz zur Wiederherstellung des Berufsbeamtentums* in 1 RGB1. 175 (1933); see Karl Loewenstein, "Law in the Third Reich," *Yale Law J.*, XLV (1936), 779, 794.

[40] See *Berufsbeamtengesetz*, sec. 171 (Jan. 26, 1937) in 1 RGB1. 39 (1937).

[41] Automatically and irrespective of membership in the party, all judges were enrolled in the Civil Servants Association (*Reichsbeamtenbund*), an organization supervised by the party. No special organization for judges existed.

[†] Reprinted by permission of the publishers of HILTER'S JUSTICE: THE COURTS OF THE THIRD REICH by Ingo Müller, Cambridge, Mass.: Harvard University Press, Copyright © 1991 by the President and Fellows of Harvard College, pp. 202-203.

and all other persons who directly followed the punitive practices of the Hitler regime must be dismissed from appointments as judges and prosecutors and will not be admitted to these appointments."[7] It soon became evident, however, that such draconian de-Nazification measures would keep the German courts closed for good. In Westphalia, for example, 93 percent of court personnel had been members of either the Nazi party or one of its subsidiary organizations.[8] In the district of the Bamberg Court of Appeals, 302 out of 309 jurists had been in the party, and at the Petty Court in Schweinfurt the figure was a solid 100 percent.[9] In the American enclave of Bremen in the British Zone, the Americans found a grand total of two judges who could be considered to have an untainted record. One solution was to call back judges who had retired prior to 1933, and to employ attorneys on the bench part time. It soon became clear that these measures would not solve the problem. The British decided to treat all jurists who had joined the Nazi party after 1937 as having a clean slate, including former army judges who for a long time had not been allowed to join. When these steps also failed to produce a sufficient number of acceptable judges, they came up with the "piggy-back method": For every untainted judge, one with a bad record could also be employed. Even this restriction was lifted in June 1946, and every jurist could be considered for the bench who had been through de-Nazification.[10]

When the judges from the Weimar Republic were sent into retirement for the second time, their places were quickly taken by the bulk of Special Court judges and former SA members, who by this time had gone through the very liberal de-Nazification procedures. The de-Nazification commissions of the British Zone and the similar tribunals of the American Zone had begun with strong measures, but were soon classifying virtually everyone in either Category 4 ("followers") or Category 5 ("exonerated"). Other Allied authorities viewed with concern the "returning stream of Nazis to the German judiciary and judicial system" that resulted.[11] By 1948, 30 percent of the presiding judges and 80 to 90 percent of the assisting judges at the Country Courts in the British Zone were former party members.[12] The other western zones presented a similar picture.

A report from the American commissioner for the State of Bavaria to the high commissioner, John McCloy, entitled "Some Aspects of Re-Nazification in Bavaria," reveals that in 1949, 752 of 924 judges and public prosecutors were former Nazis, or 81 percent.

---

[7] *Official Gazette of the Control Council for Germany*, 2 (November 30, 1945), 27.

[8] Wenzlau, *Der Wiederaufbau der Justiz*, 103.

[9] Jörg Friedrich, *Die kalte Amnestie: NS-Täter in der Bundesrepublik* (Frankfort: Fischer Taschenbuch-Verlag, 1984), 40.

[10] Wenzlau, *Der Wiederaufbau der Justiz*, 103 and 130.

[11] [omitted]

[12] Bernhard Diestelkamp, "Rechts- und verfassungsgeschichtliche Probleme der Frühgeschichte der Bundesrepublik Deutschland," *Juristische Schulung* 21 (1981), 492.

*Karl Loewenstein, "Justice"**

Schematic tests for what constituted an "active" Nazi brought hardships, however, in numerous individual cases and left the cardinal issue, that of determining who among the rank and file of the lower judiciary was only a nominal Nazi, very much where it had been before—within the discretion of the military government officer in charge of denazification in the particular instance. Intensive experimentation failed to develop foolproof tests. The most convenient criterion, known as the "vintage" principle, proceeded from the belief that the earlier the date of entry, the greater the entrant's sympathy with the party. On the other hand, for many in American Military Government there was some truth in the contention of many early Nazis that their initial enthusiasm soon had paled and they had become anti-Nazis, though they had not risked leaving the party after their "conversion."...

When the appointive power in the judicial field was transferred from American Military Government to the ministers of justice at the end of 1945, it carried with it, implicitly, the responsibility of denazification.... The candidate for office had to submit a yard-long questionnaire or *Fragebogen*, that ubiquitous symbol of the "revolution by bureaucracy." A special *Fragebogen* existed for the legal profession, though it never revealed, in the case of a judge with an impeccable paper record, how he had behaved in office, in what decisions he had participated, or whether his opinions reflected subservience to the regime.

In fact, therefore, denazification of legal personnel shifted to the judicial class. The judges knew best who among them had "kowtowed" more than was necessary, who had gained unmerited recognition and promotion, who had been a "profiteer." But here entered a socio-psychological element which military government was unable to neutralize—the class solidarity of the judiciary, which, subconsciously or consciously, began to balance and outweigh what desire for political cleanliness may have existed. In fact, under the impact of the occupation, a national solidarity emerged, not merely in the civil service but among all classes, which tried to save as many colleagues as possible from the clutches of denazification.[49]...

The German Phase of Denazification—The strong undercurrent of tolerance towards the past sinners among the judiciary broke into the open with the deliberate transfer of responsibility for denazification to the Germans by the Law of the Liberation from National Socialism and Militarism of March 5, 1946.[50] This law contained in an appendix an elaborate list of positions and offices whose former holders were considered, on rebuttable presumption, to be either major offenders (Class I) or offenders (Class II). Class I included the top-ranking judicial and administrative officials, all judges and prosecutors of the *Volksgerichte*, and presidents and general prosecutors of the

---

* Excerpted from Karl Loewenstein, "Justice," in Edward H. Lithcfield et al., *Governing Postwar Germany* (Cornell University Press, 1953), pp. 247-249.

49 See Karl Loewenstein, "Denazification Report," *New York Times*, December 2, 1946, p. 1OE, col. 5.

50 For text, see MGR 24-500; Bavaria, GVB1. 197 (1946); Württemberg-Baden, RGB1. 75 (1946); Greater Hesse, GVB1. 57 (1946).

Oberlandesgerichte, appointed after December 31, 1938. In Class II were all members of the National Socialist party (NSDAP) who joined prior to May, 1937, judges and prosecutors of the *Sondergerichte*, presidents and chief prosecutors of the *Landgerichte*. All these positions, it can be definitely stated, could be held, at least after 1937, only by tested Nazis.

From these examples, it may be seen that the categories of primafacie disqualified legal officials were narrowly defined. The total number of persons in such offices, though it may run close to 2,000, is insignificant when compared with the number of legal officials who joined the party. The vast majority of all holders of judicial office were shoved by the denazification tribunals into minor categories. As a rule, the individual was classified as a follower or fully exonerated.

Ingo Müller, "Hitler's Justice: The Courts of the Third Reich"[*]

There could be no real question of recalling to active service those who had been leaders of the legal profession during the Nazi era. If they were still living, however, the new German government granted them pensions corresponding to their former high offices. Thus, for example, the jurists who at Nuremberg in 1947 had been tried by the Americans, found guilty, and removed from office received pensions covering even the time they had spent in prison.... Rothenberger, received 2,073 marks per month.[2] Only those few jurists with "political" posts were forced into retirement with a pension, however. Less prominent Nazi judges at high and even the highest levels were rehired within the judicial system, usually at a similar position, and often with a promotion or two.... Just as judges from the higher ranks of the courts and the legal bureaucracy moved into the West German judicial system, so did many of the others from the Special and Military Courts, judges from the People's Court and judges from the Race Law trials.... Dr. Hans Puvogel, author of the dissertation containing a plea for the "removal of inferior beings through killing," was named minister of justice in the state of Lower Saxony in 1976. When a judge drew public attention to the dissertation, disciplinary proceedings were not opened against Puvogel but against the judge! He was officially reprimanded, for by publishing the information he was guilty of failing to show the proper respect to his superior.... Seventeen of the judges who had handed down decisions in Race Law trials in Hamburg were still living after the war; of these seventeen, eleven found new positions in the judicial system.[28]...

In appointing Nazi jurists to new positions after the war, those responsible often showed a lack of tact. Günther Schultz, who as a member of the Sixth Criminal Panel of the Hamburg County Court in 1940-41 had

---

[*] Reprinted by permission of the publishers of HILTER'S JUSTICE: THE COURTS OF THE THIRD REICH by Ingo Müller, Cambridge, Mass.: Harvard University Press, Copyright © 1991 by the President and Fellows of Harvard College, pp. 208, 212-216, 270-273, 276-278, 283-284.

[2] Jörg Friedrich, *Die kalte Amnestie: NS-Täter in der Bundesrepublik* (Frankfurt: Fischer Taschenbuch-Verlag, 1984), 25-26.

[28] Hans Robinsohn, *Justiz als politische Verfolgung* (Stuttgart: Deutsche Verlags-Anstalt, 1977), 154.

participated in Race Law decisions, was a made a Court of Appeals judge in Hamm after the war. Then he of all people was named presiding judge of a board in Hamburg to hear the cases of war victims claiming damages; here he decided claims filed by the survivors of his own earlier trials, and by the relatives of those he had sentenced to death.[32]...

On September 8, 1961, the Law on Judges was amended to give all judges and public prosecutors who had "participated in the administration of criminal law from September 1, 1939, to May 9, 1945," the opportunity to resign from office by June 30, 1962, with no reduction in pension. Only 149 former jurists of the National Socialist era took advantage of it, however.[38] Most of them chose to remain in office even after this date, and several continued to exercise influence on the legal order of the young democracy from high positions....

Even as the German judicial system was being recreated in the old mold and the identical personnel was attempting to forge links with the past, the most comprehensive investigation of Nazi jurists ever undertaken was proceeding in Nuremberg. The third in the series of trials organized by the Americans in the wake of the main War Crimes Trial, known as "Case 3" or the "Altstoetter trial," was devoted to the jurists of the Third Reich. But just as in the other Nuremberg trials—the physicians' trial, the trial of Field Marshal Milch, the Pohl, Krupp, Flick, and I.G. Farben trials, the Reich Central Security Office trial, the special units, Wilhelmstrasse, and Armed Forces High Command trials—the main emphasis was placed on crimes committed against foreigners. The Americans had no particular interest in prosecuting crimes committed by Germans against other Germans, and this would also have gone beyond the international law justification of the proceedings. As in the eleven other trials, the charges leveled against the jurists concerned war crimes, organized crime, and crimes against humanity.

The sixteen defendants, "the embodiment of what passed for justice in the Third Reich" in the eyes of their accusers, stood in the dock as representatives of the entire system.... The highest official on trial was ... Franz Schlegelberger, former undersecretary in the Reich Ministry of Justice and acting minister.... The other defendants included [two undersecretaries; the] prosecutor general at the People's Court;... senior public prosecutors;... the vice-president of Nuremberg Special Court;... the presiding judge of one of its panels;... and two presiding judges of other Special Courts....

The main charges against the jurists were "judicial murder and other atrocities which they committed by destroying law and justice in Germany, and then by utilizing the empty forms of legal process for persecution, enslavement, and extermination on a vast scale."[3]

Schlegelberger, expressly recognized by the court as a "tragic figure," based his defense on the claim that he had remained at his post to prevent

---

[32] Michel Anders, *Die Sippe der Krähen* (Frankfurt: Eichborn, 1981), 46.

[38] Information provided by the West German government, *Bundestags-Drucksache* 10, no. 6566, p.23.

[3] [*Trials of War Criminals before the Nuremberg Military Tribunals* (Washington, D.C.: U.S. Government Printing Office, 1951), III], 32-33.

the worst from happening, and that only for this reason had he committed all the acts of which he stood accused. In the last analysis, however, this argument could be used not only by him and all the other jurists on trial to exonerate themselves, but also by every jurist, physician, official, and soldier who had any share in the crimes of the Third Reich.... [T]his line of defense ... in the end would have left Hitler as the sole culprit.

The court gave this hypothesis very careful and thorough study:

> Schlegelberger presented an interesting defense.... He feared that if he were to resign, a worse man would take his place.... Upon analysis this plausible claim of the defense squares neither with the truth, logic, or the circumstances.
>
> The evidence conclusively shows that in order to maintain the Ministry of Justice in the good graces of Hitler and to prevent its utter defeat by Himmler's police, Schlegelberger and the other defendants who joined in this claim of justification took over the dirty work which the leaders of the State demanded.... That their program of racial extermination under the guise of law failed to attain the proportions which were reached by the pogroms, deportations, and mass murders by the police is cold comfort to the survivors of the "judicial" process, and constitutes a poor excuse before this Tribunal....[4]

During the trial, 138 witnesses were heard and 2,093 pieces of evidence examined.... From the overwhelming mass of evidence, the court finally drew this conclusion: "Defendants are charged with crimes of such immensity that mere specific instances of criminality appear insignificant by comparison. The charge, in brief, is that of conscious participation in a nationwide government-organized system of cruelty and injustice, in violation of the laws of war and of humanity, and perpetrated in the name of law by the authority of the Ministry of Justice, and through the instrumentality of the courts. The dagger of the assassin was concealed beneath the robe of the jurist."[6] What was most shocking to the court, however, was not the various appalling crimes themselves (the previous trials had exposed the outrages of the Third Reich with sufficient clarity) but the fact that they had been committed under the cloak of legality.

The court gave the two undersecretaries ... and the Special Court judges ... life sentences in a penitentiary; four of the other defendants were acquitted, and the rest received prison sentences of five or six years. Although the Nuremberg trial could deal only with a limited number of examples—in the short time available, the prosecution could barely scratch the surface of Nazi crimes committed through the legal system—it has remained until today the most concerted effort to shed light on the role of the judiciary under the Nationalist Socialist dictatorship....

At the time of the Nuremberg jurists' trial, when the German criminal justice system had not even begun to think of bringing charges against judges for their actions in the Third Reich, an academic discussion got underway concerning the extent of their legal accountability.... An instance

---

[4] Ibid., 1086.

[6] *Trials of War Criminals before the Nuremberg Military Tribunals*, III, 984-985.

of perversion of justice was [claimed to be] a criminal offense only if a judge performed it "consciously" and against his own better knowledge—that is, with "direct intent."[26]... The majority of legal scholars and officials enthusiastically adopted this view—that a judge could be found guilty of murder, manslaughter, or false imprisonment only if it could be proved that he had knowingly broken the law....

Many Nazi criminals profited from the notion developed during these years that an "insufficient awareness of injustice" in connection with an act rendered its perpetrator innocent in the eyes of the law. As it turned out, the professional group to benefit most from this concept were precisely those who were supposed to embody an "awareness of justice" for the whole country. "There is no one today who can make head or tail of the split personality common among lawyers," wrote Fritz Bauer, prosecutor general of Hesse, in 1962. "In the de-Nazification files we read that they were opposed, to the last man. But then the minute prosecutors and judges are to be called to account for an excessive number of death sentences, they claim to have persecuted and killed with the clearest conscience, so that according to prevailing opinion we cannot accuse them of perversion of justice and manslaughter."[28]

The Kassel County Court, for example, did not believe that "conscious perversion of justice" could be proven on the part of the former Special Court judges there, who had sentenced the engineer Werner Holländer to death as a "dangerous habitual criminal" for carrying on a love affair. The County Court argued on behalf of Judge Kessler, author of the Holländer opinion and "probably the ablest jurist in Kassel" that his thinking was "imbued with the spirit of the saying 'Whatever benefits the people is just,' and he may have believed it was just retribution and in the interest of the *Volk* to find Holländer guilty and have him executed." Indeed, the court continued, Kessler may even have believed that this murderous perversion of justice represented "a high level of judicial achievement." The court cited, in the defendant's favor, the argument that in 1943 the former judges of the Special Court "were ardent, even fanatic Nazis," although this argument would have been used against other criminals of the era. Because of the judges' fanaticism, "the possibility of blindness to injustice, based on political delusions,... cannot be excluded." The verdict was therefore "not guilty."[29]...

In handing down decisions relating to their colleagues from the Third Reich, judges used phrases like these repeatedly, until they became part of their stock in trade. It did not stop there, however: after a series of acquittals, prosecutors and courts began using them in their orders to close an investigation on a case before it even came to trial. On September 3, 1964, the Karlsruhe Court of Appeals, for example, dropped charges against Wolfgang Fränkel, the federal prosecutor general who had entered pleas of nullity and

---

26 Radbruch, "Gesetzliches Unrecht und übergesetzliches Recht,"*Süddeutsche Juristenzeitung* (1946), 104; and "Urteilsanmerkung," *Süddeutsche Juristenzeitung* (1947), 634.

28 "Justiz als Symptom," in Helmut Hammerschmidt, ed, *Zwanzig Jahre danach: Eine deutsche Bilanz* (Munich: Desch, 1965), 227.

29 Printed in Klaus Moritz and Ernst Noam, eds., *NS-Verbrechen vor Gericht, 1945-1955* (Wiesbaden: Kommission für die Geschichte der Juden in Hessen, 1978), 308ff.

altered the prosecution's recommendation to the death penalty in at least fifty cases during the Third Reich. The court saw no "possibility of proving that the accused had ever so much as doubted the validity of the regulations in question ... during the war, much less recognized their invalidity."[35]

...Gerhard Meyer, the Social Democrat senator for justice in the West Berlin government, made a last attempt to bring to justice the 67 surviving judges and prosecutors from the 570 members of the People's Court. Investigations recommenced, but in 1983 Meyer's successor ... requested the public to be patient, since the inquiry was proving "extraordinarily difficult, extensive, and protracted." Still and all, after four years' work, prosecutors had managed to question two of the alleged perpetrators![44] When the inquiry began, most of those under investigation were in their eighties, and in the course of the next seven years half of them died. The Berlin Office of Public Prosecutions finally put an end to the macabre farce by closing the case on September 26, 1986.

The judicial system of the Third Reich remains an open chapter. The People's Court was the chief symbol of a system without justice and no doubt its most openly brutal institution, but it was only a part of that system. If its judges had been tried and found guilty, then it would have been impossible to acquit the numerous others who had handed down sentences on the Race Laws elsewhere or had presided at the Special and Military Courts. Conviction of a single judge of the Third Reich would have started an avalanche that would inevitably have engulfed the majority of postwar West German judges.... As the journalist Jörg Friedrich observed bitingly, "Judge Rehse of the People's Court could not have committed murder, for this would have meant that the West German judicial system had been established by murderers in the hundreds."[45]...

All too often, Nazi jurists could be acquitted only at the cost of declaring that the brutal laws and show trials of the Third Reich had been "legally perfectly sound." The acts of injustice had to be minimized and the victims of terror convicted for a second time, so to speak.

In one instance of this, the Wiesbaden County Court found in March 24, 1952, that the instructions issued by the Reich Ministry of Justice for transferring convicted Jewish, Russian, and Ukrainian criminals to the SS for "elimination through work" were not unlawful. The fact that all Jewish prisoners were included in this regulation, regardless of the length of their sentences, was considered by the court to be "unjust, certainly, but the tension between the legal norm ... and what would have been just had not yet reached an intolerable level." And so the Wiesbaden judge arrived at the conclusion that "depriving the Jewish prisoners of their liberty was therefore not objectively in violation of the law."[1]

---

[35]Cited in Friedrich Karl Kaul, *Geschichte des Reichsgerichts* (Glashütten/Taunus: Auvermann, 1971), IV, 221; see also *Braunbuch* (1968), 121.

[44] See P. von Feldmann, "Die Auseinandersetzung um das Ermittlungsverfahren gegen Richter und Staatsanwälte am Volksgerichtshof," *Kritische Justiz* 16 (1983), 306 and 310.

[45] Friedrich, *Freispruch für die Nazi-Justiz*, 457.

[1] *Justiz und NS-Verbrechen: Sammlung deutscher Strafurteile*, vol. 9, p. 367 (no. 310).

ASSESSMENT OF DENAZIFICATION

*John H. Herz, "Denazification and Related Policies"**

Denazification thus meant at best barring certain persons temporarily from positions of influence rather than providing for their definite or long-term ineligibility to serve in such positions. In the economic field, the same was true of the confiscations of properties, which were restored following the downgrading or the exoneration of owners; confiscations based on the verdicts of tribunals were extremely rare, notably, in the case of industrialists or other major owners; the latter seldom were placed in categories mandating the imposition of this penalty.[18]

Thus a process that had begun with wholesale incriminations turned in the direction of wholesale exemptions and then ended in wholesale exonerations. Denazification, in the end, meant not purge but rehabilitation.... It was not German society that was being "denazified" in the sense of being freed from Nazis and Nazi influence, but Mr. X, who would claim to have been "successfully denazified" in the sense of having been certified as being free from the taint of his previous Nazi connection.... Also, the failure to distinguish between what should have been considered administrative sanctions with penalties imposed after convictions in judicial trials led many to object to the violation of due process in procedures that seemed to convict for acts not legally established as crimes when the deeds were committed; it was not only Nazi sympathizers but also liberals believing in *Rechtsstaat* principles that raised such objections. Others came to believe that "punishment" (what little there was) was meted out for "political error" rather than for criminal or quasi-criminal action. And as procedures dragged on into a time when political life ... was being resumed, political considerations came to play a role; parties, especially the more rightist ones ... tried to attract the vote of the "victims" of denazification, in particular the masses of the small fry; but even social democrats and communists eventually found themselves swayed by such considerations. And the churches, afraid that "leftist radicalism" might prevail if too many conservative collaborators of nazism were eliminated, reiterated their early appeals for rehabilitation plus forgiveness.... Thus the reabsorption of the masses of the "denazified" into society proceeded apace. Denazification had been the instrument through which those who might have formed a cohort for the propagation of discontent and the promotion of antidemocratic leanings and activities were rendered "absorbable."

---

* Excerpted from John H. Herz, "Denazification and Related Policies," in John H. Herz, ed., *From Dictatorship to Democracy: Coping with the Legacies of Authoritarianism and Totalitarianism*, Copyright © 1982 by John Herz (Greenwood Press, 1982), pp. 29-34, an imprint of Greenwood Publishing Group, Inc. Westport, CT. Reprinted with permission.

18 For additional figures, see Conrad F. Latour and Thilo *Vogelsang, Okkupation und Wiederaufbau—Die Tätigkeit der Militärregierung in der amerikanischen Besatzungszone Deutschlands 1944-1947* (Stuttgart, 1973), p. 144. For a listing of certain especially scandalous whitewash cases, see my article ["The Fiasco of Denazification in Germany," *Political Science Quarterly* 63 (4), December 1958,] pp. 577 ff., 581-590, and Niethammer, *Entnazifizierung in Bayem*, pp. 547 ff., 580-599.

The result of both denazification and the prosecution (or nonprosecution) of Nazi criminality may be summed up as follows: The top elite of the Nazi regime, small in numbers, was eliminated (or eliminated itself, through suicide, flight abroad, and so on); most of the collaborationist elite, in administration, justice, education, the economy, remained in or reentered positions held under the Nazi regime.... Unlike France and Italy, Germany did not contain a group of young resisters ready to take over, and thus the older ones, in part Weimarians but for the most part those who had served the Nazi regime or at least had not resisted its rule, took over again.

This restoration of personnel also meant that real, that is, unreconstructed Nazis (and occasionally even Nazi criminals) were periodically discovered in office, even at the ministerial level, usually by mere accident; some of Adenauer's aides had to resign because such earlier activities had become public knowledge. Such disclosures have occurred for decades, as *vide* the notorious Filbinger case.[21] Revelation that such figures had succeeded in becoming members of the political elite of West Germany cannot help tarnishing a successor democracy's image—abroad and also at home.

On the other hand, it can hardly be said that the continuance of former Nazis in office has affected the functioning of the democratic system. It is true that under the occupation and thereafter, only a minority emerged that was genuinely committed to the values and the ideals of Western liberal democracy.[22]... They did not, therefore, constitute an effective counterelite that could have replaced the elite under the Nazi regime. The new-old elite had to be comprised of an alliance between minority democrats and former Nazis and collaborators who constituted a majority of officeholders and other leading groups.[23] How that alliance or, perhaps better, the concerted activities of both groups, has affected government and society can be illustrated from a few examples. In regard to the rebuilding of political parties,... we have mentioned the attempt of some new and revived ones to appeal to the rank and file of the denazified; they were more or less successful, but it can hardly be said that the influx of *Mitlaeufer* influenced the parties in their formulation of more or less democratic policies and attitudes. To be sure, there were also groups that tried to establish themselves as neo-Nazi parties, namely, the Socialist Reich party (SRP),

---

21 Filbinger, minister president of Württemberg-Baden and one of the leading lights of the CDU, in 1979 by pure coincidence (a writer had come across some World War II documents) was found to have been one of the Nazi military judges responsible for cruel verdicts and executions of German sailors. He had to resign, but it is characteristic of the general attitude of "forgiveness" that CSU leader and subsequent candidate for chancellor, Franz Joseph Strauss, inveighed not against Filbinger but against his uncoverer and those who insisted on Filbinger's abdication.

22 On this contrast between a democratic minority and a noncommittal majority in the West German bureaucracy, see my article "German Officialdom Revisited, Political Views and Attitudes of the West German Civil Service," *World Politics* 7 (1), October 1954, pp. 63-83.

23 See the conclusion of one of the most discerning American observers of the West German postwar scene: One had to admit, he said, that "denazification ... and the other punitive programs that had been justified in part as programs to change elites in Germany were a failure" (John Gimbel, *The American Occupation of Germany, Politics and the Military, 1945-1949* [Stanford, 1968], p. 253).

which was outawed by the Federal Constitutional Court, and the National Democratic party (NPD), which was not outlawed; this was perhaps all to the good because its rather small role in German political life has provided both an outet for the "incorrigibles" (*Unverbesserliche*) and an alternative to their penetration of other parties, which might have posed a threat to the stability of a democratic system.

As for the restoration of the bureaucracy, it has meant a return to (or a continuation of) traditional German authoritarianism....

In education (teachers are civil servants, as are university professors) the return of the denazified has ensured that efforts to present to youth a true picture of nazism and to replace the perverted values inculcated by Nazi indoctrination with democratic ones were condemned to failure. Nothing is more essential for the success of a successor democracy than presenting an accurate image of the predecessor regime. But for a long time teachers either continued to glorify the past or evaded the topic altogether. Such repression of the past,... a kind of "protective amnesia with respect to the Nazi years,"[25] characterized not only education but the pattern of behavior evinced by most groups in the postwar period. A prime prerequisite for the emergence of a democratic reaction to the Nazi legacy was awareness of the realities of the regime. Adults had to repress it, but the young were given no basic information on which to base a judgment. Only belatedly, when it had already become more or less "history," was instruction (in history as well as in other disciplines) extended to this subject matter.[26] On the other hand, a somewhat more positive picture emerges from the realm of the media, in particular the press, where early occupation policies proved more successful than in other areas in placing non-Nazis in leading positions; the success of this effort has given the public an example of what freedom of information means in contrast to indoctrination of the Nazi type. Liberal media policies and structures (subsequently developed in radio and TV) have proved a boon to democracy in Germany....

A more positive development has also taken place in regard to the military.... West German rearmament did not effect the revival of militarism ... in the sense of the military obtaining (as in the Prussianized old Reich) the highest prestige in the stratification system of society; nor did it conduce to the revival of traditional nationalism.... [C]are was taken to select officers, especially generals, who had not been involved with Hitlerite policies. In addition, the armed forces (*Bundeswehr*) were set up with the intention of preventing the emergence of the "Prussian" militaristic style of harsh discipline, blind obedience, and so forth and of inculcating the notion of the "citizen in uniform," who has his rights as well as his duties; a parliamentary "military ombudsman" is in charge of dealing with complaints made by soldiers. Moreover, in a system of conscription, a right of conscientious objection is constitutionally protected and rather broadly interpreted.... [T]he principle of civilian control over the military has been firmly set. Officers are

---

[25] Thomas Flanagan in *The Nation*, December 6, 1980, p. 613.

[26] [omitted]

now considered—and most consider themselves—technicians serving without the traditional *esprit de corps*.

...Perhaps the most beneficial factor in regard to the post-World War II legacy problem was the absence, during the crucial period of building democracy, of a *Reichswehr* and a central police. Demilitarization proved decisive. Had there been such elements, they would in all likelihood have remained unpurged, like the other strata (or like the military in Spain), and thus in a position to threaten a budding democratic structure.

The Reform of Education

Jutta-B. Lange-Quassowski, "Coming to Terms with the Nazi Past: Schools, Media and the Formation of Public Opinion"[*]

In terms of the *teaching of history*, it was of common concern to the Western Allies to alter the content of the discipline as well as its value orientation. One method of achieving this goal was the control of school textbooks. Because the Allies did not want to use books written by emigrés, preferring to encourage indigenous initiatives, they undertook a review of old textbooks. They excluded texts that contained glorifications of war, endorsements of war preparations, propaganda justifying the doctrines of nazism, racism, and hostility toward international organization. In the end, three history books were chosen for reprinting.[33] In 1946 principles to guide the writing of history books were formulated and issued. They centered on according priority to social and cultural history. In addition to presenting a realistic assessment of national history, European and world history would be taught with the goal of promoting international understanding.[34]

John Dornberg, "Schizophrenic Germany"[†]

The circumstances in the immediate postwar period are described pointedly in a report issued in 1948 by the Office of Military Government for Hesse.[1] The problem in Hesse was also that of almost every other area of Germany....

---

[*] Excerpted from Jutta-B. Lange-Quassowski, "Coming to Terms with the Nazi Past: Schools, Media and the Formation of Public Opinion," in John H. Herz, ed., *From Dictatorship to Democracy: Coping with the Legacies of Authoritarianism and Totalitarianism*, Copyright © 1982 by John Herz (Greenwood Press, 1982), p. 93, an imprint of Greenwood Publishing Group, Inc. Westport, CT. Reprinted with permission.

[33] Karl-Ernst Bungenstab, *Umerziehung zur Demokratie? Re-education-Politik im Bildungswesen der US-Zone, 1945-49* (Düsseldorf, 1970).

[34] Maria Halbritter, *Schulreformpolitik in der britischen Zone 1945-1949* (Weinheim, 1979).

[†] Excerpted from John Dornberg, *Schizophrenic Germany* (The Macmillan Company, 1961), pp. 193-196. Reprinted with permission of Sterling Lord Literistic, Inc. Copyright © 1961 by John Dornberg.

[1] *Hesse: A New German State*. Arranged by Dexter L. Freeman. Druck und Verlagshaus, Frankfurt am Main, 1948.

Finding books that were not tainted by militaristic and "master race" ideas was a problem ... in the first year of occupation. Under pressure to get the elementary, middle, and secondary schools back in operation on a de-Nazified basis, Military Government education personnel undertook an intensive program of screening textbooks and planning new teacher outlines. Quickly discovering that practically all the texts dating from the Hitler régime (even arithmetics) were full of Nazi propaganda, the educators turned their attention to books of pre-Hitler days and arranged for a few elementary readers and arithmetics to be reprinted intact for temporary emergency use in schools....

Responsible educators were agreed that any policy of importing U.S. manufactured texts and imposing them on the German schools would be unwise and even dangerous.... The alternative was clear: enough German manufactured books had to be dug up to get the schools started. In Hesse, German and Military Government educational authorities launched a book hunt that extended from musty school stockrooms to closed down publishing houses and private libraries, while higher authorities in OMGUS[2] set about rounding up all available copies of acceptable German textbooks which had found their way abroad. Meanwhile, in the fall of 1945, emergency paper allocations covered the printing of a quantity of new textbooks for distribution to grades one through eight.

...Hesse's shortage of textbooks was no more serious than the shortage of teachers who could pass de-Nazification screening tests. Military Government found that the instructors had become imbued with NSDAP dogmas even more than their impressionable pupils. Before education officers could give Hesse's school system a passably clean bill of health, 52 percent of the elementary and secondary school teachers had been banned from their classrooms, and of the remaining 48 percent, there were many borderline cases. The situation was not surprising when one took a glance at the notorious Nazi educational policy files....

In October, 1945, an American observer visited a fourth grade class in Wiesbaden and gleaned some startling information. From several children he learned, for instance, that World War II was started by Jewish money grabbers. And the only reason the United States had joined in the conflict, declared others in the class, was that Americans had become envious of the Germans' industriousness.

When the American visitor brought up the subject of concentration camps with the pupils, the teacher flushed with embarrassment. "You oughtn't discuss such matters," he said. "That's all past history."

In October, 1945, the schoolbells rang ... for the first time since the war ended and nearly 229,000 elementary pupils (in Hesse) trooped into the classrooms, representing approximately two thirds of all children between the ages of six and fourteen years. The sad part of it was that there was only 2,707 teachers for the 1,345 schoolhouses. In 1939, 5,748 teachers had been employed to teach approximately the same number of children. The postwar lack of non-Nazi teachers produced an average pupil-teacher ratio of 85 to 1, while in some localities, the ratio soared as high as 120 to 1. In rural schools one teacher generally taught all eight grades of the elementary schools eight hours a day, five days a week....The secondary schools were a little slower in getting started, chiefly because of de-Nazification troubles and building shortages.... In May [1946] the teaching staff totaled 1,129, more than 700 short of

---

[2] Office of Military Government, United States zone.

the number needed to permit normal operations. And, at the end of the year, the figure was still more than 450 below par.

*Jutta-B. Lange-Quassowski, "Coming to Terms with the Nazi Past: Schools, Media and the Formation of Public Opinion"**

[I]n the 1950s, when the production of German school texts was resumed on a large scale, a retrogressive development began. The cold war, anti-Communism, and Western integration favored an exculpatory ideology that sought to transfer a substantial part of the responsibility for the rise of national socialism to foreign nations. German national traditions were again emphasized. German fascism under the motto "Hitler was responsible for everything," was reduced to Hitlerism. He alone was made responsible for Nazi atrocities. The German people had nothing to do with his crimes.[37] During the 1950s, the Nazi regime was frequently not even mentioned. Instruction often ceased with the Bismarck period.

John Dornberg, "Schizophrenic Germany"†

Thousands of teachers [in 1961] are still trying to untangle their own murky notions about the twelve-year Reich and the turbulent political period preceding it.... [T]hey avoid the topic or circumvent it with brief and indefinite allusions. Many high—and middle—school students have been heard to say that teachers fear being ridiculed by their own pupils. To explain objectively Hitler's rise to power teachers would have to point out how the mass of the German people had been duped by the dictator. But they would appear ludicrous in front of their classes should a student happen to ask: "Teacher, what did you do during the period?"...

The official textbooks that are in use in German schools have met with considerably more criticism than the teaching plans and the efforts of individual teachers.... Although it would be unfair to generalize about all the books, there are certain generalities which do apply to them all. They are characterized by a relatively brief and superficial treatment of the period from World War I until the present. All the books tend to gloss over the injustices of the Hitler régime but become more detailed when they discuss the unfortunate lot of Germans in the occupation periods after the Second and First World Wars.... Although each book[11] makes at least some mention of the brutalities and atrocities committed by the Nazis, these are treated in

---

* Excerpted from Jutta-B. Lange-Quassowski, "Coming to Terms with the Nazi Past: Schools, Media and the Formation of Public Opinion," in John H. Herz, ed., *From Dictatorship to Democracy: Coping with the Legacies of Authoritarianism and Totalitarianism*, Copyright © 1982 by John Herz (Greenwood Press, 1982), p. 94, an imprint of Greenwood Publishing Group, Inc. Westport, CT. Reprinted with permission.

[37] Jürgen Redhardt, *NS-Zeit im Spiegel des Schulbuchs* (Frankfurt a.M., 1970).

† Excerpted from John Dornberg, *Schizophrenic Germany* (The Macmillan Company, 1961), pp. 204-207. Reprinted with permission of Sterling Lord Literistic, Inc. Copyright © 1961 by John Dornberg.

[11] The author examined twelve of the most widely used texts, ranging from *Volksschule* through *Gymnasium* level.

such generalities and so superficially that they leave no marked impression on the student whatever.

Jutta-B. Lange-Quassowski, "Coming to Terms with the Nazi Past: Schools, Media and the Formation of Public Opinion"[*]

In [late] 1959 the desecration of Jewish cemeteries and memorials for the victims of the National Socialist regime resulted in the decision to admit the past.[38] The curriculum was changed in the 1960s to reflect this decision even though analysts of school texts have concluded that the presentation of such events continues to be rather weak. However, in that decade genocide and war crimes and the physical and psychological terror exercised by the regime were called by name and portrayed without artifice. Nevertheless, the Third Reich was viewed as more of an "accident"; no attempt was made to explore its origins and its continuity with German history. The portrayal is still replete with personalization, psychologizing, and even attempts at exoneration. The image of the "decent German soldier" is contrasted to that of the abominable Nazi.

Regarding the 1970s, analysts have concluded that the presentation of the persecution of the Jews in the textbooks has changed in a positive way, both qualitatively and quantitatively. Along with school textbooks (and in part curricula) for instruction in history and politics, textbooks for religious instruction and German readers have been examined to ascertain their treatment of the holocaust. The findings with respect to all three fields indicate that as of the mid-1960s, information about the persecution and mass murder of the Jewish people had increased and that almost all textbooks published by the end of the 1970s contain correct and often satisfactory information.[39]

COMPENSATION FOR VICTIMS

John H. Herz, "Denazification and Related Policies"[†]

Here we have another, more positive aspect of the legacy problem: What to do about or for victims of regime persecution and criminality? Although the dead cannot be revived and the suffering of survivors cannot

---

* Excerpted from Jutta-B. Lange-Quassowski, "Coming to Terms with the Nazi Past: Schools, Media and the Formation of Public Opinion," in John H. Herz, ed., *From Dictatorship to Democracy: Coping with the Legacies of Authoritarianism and Totalitarianism*, Copyright © 1982 by John Herz (Greenwood Press, 1982), pp. 94-95, an imprint of Greenwood Publishing Group, Inc. Westport, CT. Reprinted with permission.

38 Harald Kästner, "Zur Behandlung des Nationalsozialismus im Unterricht," in *Aus Politik und Zeitgeschichte*, Beilage B 22/79, pp. 19-23.

39 Heinz Kremers, "Judentum und Holocaust im deutschen Schulunterricht," in *Aus Politik und Zeitgeschichte*, Beilage B 4/79, pp. 37-45.

† Excerpted from John H. Herz, "Denazification and Related Policies," in John H. Herz, ed., *From Dictatorship to Democracy: Coping with the Legacies of Authoritarianism and Totalitarianism*, Copyright © 1982 by John Herz (Greenwood Press, 1982), p. 21, an imprint of Greenwood Publishing Group, Inc. Westport, CT. Reprinted with permission.

be expiated by monetary means alone, the restitution of despoiled properties and indemnification for material losses can to some extent alleviate the conditions of the victims; and the expressed will to "make good" can serve as a sign of accepting responsibility for the evil done. In this respect the West German record, on the whole, is a favorable one. Considering itself (in contrast to the GDR and Austria) the legal successor to the Reich (including the phase of the "Third Reich") and thus liable to its obligations, the FRG embarked on a comprehensive program of restoring properties (restitution laws) and indemnifying for material damage (indemnification laws)....

In some other respects the successor democracy was less generous. Thus, in contrast to indemnifications for material damage, little compensation has been paid for the hell passed in concentration camps (less than the amount being paid to survivors residing in the GDR by the GDR), perhaps a reflection of "capitalist" standards of value that emphasize material rather than human loss. Also, courts and other authorities entrusted with the implementation of the legislation often failed to act generously in practice, whereas, generally, a spirit of generosity has governed the awarding of pensions to former Nazis and their heirs as well as compensation for the loss of their properties.[8] Thus an exonerated, prominent Nazi or his widow can live in comfort, in contrast to the heirs of resistance fighters murdered by the Nazis who have been denied compensation. Such a paradox reflects a more general failure to "rehabilitate" members of the Resistance. To many Germans the actions of the Resistance appeared (or still appear) as disloyalty rather than heroism.

In more formal, legal ways there was rehabilitation. Citizenship was restored to those who had lost it for racial or political reasons and wanted it restored. Doctoral and similar degrees were restored. Those convicted for political or racial reasons under nazism were, for the most part, rehabilitated.

Kurt Schwerin, "German Compensation for Victims of Nazi Persecution"[*]

Even during the War the governments-in-exile of occupied countries took steps to declare null and void the confiscatory acts of the Germans in those occupied territories. Immediately after the War, initial steps were taken to remedy the spoliation within Germany.[40] In the period 1947-49, the military governments enacted legislation, restricted, however, to the restitution of identifiable property. Law No. 59 of November 10, 1947, was enacted for the American Zone of Occupation, Law No. 59 of May 12, 1949, for the British Zone, and Decree No. 120 of November 10, 1947, for the French Zone.[41] For West Berlin, the Allied Government (*Kommandatura*) issued, in July, 1949, the Decree on Restitution of Identifiable Property.[42]...

---

[8] Enabling some of them to finance neo-Nazi activities.

[*] Excerpted from Kurt Schwerin, "German Compensation for Victims of Nazi Persecution," *Northwestern University Law Review*, vol. 67 (1972), pp. 489-520.

[40-42] [omitted]

The differences between the restitution laws in the various zones added to the complexity of the restitution proceedings.[46]...

Ultimately, the various decrees and regulations dealing with the loss of or damage to property under the Nazi regime were incorporated in the Federal Restitution Law of July 19, 1957, and its amendment of October 2, 1964.[48] Whereas, in the Restitution Law of 1957, the total sum for which the Federal Republic was liable had been limited to DM 1.5 billion, with the provision that all claims were to be satisfied up to at least fifty percent, the amendment of 1964 removed the ceiling and raised the quote to one hundred percent. It also provided a hardship fund of DM 800 million to cover the claims of those who did not file their applications in time.[49]

The First Compensation Laws and Agreements

The restitution laws already mentioned extended only to the restitution of, or compensation for, identifiable property. Special German legislation was enacted to carry the principle of compensation further: damage to life, health, liberty, property and possessions, damage to vocational and economic pursuits, losses suffered in jobs and professions and the loss to widows and orphans of their providers were all made compensable....

The lack of uniformity in the laws of *Länder* made standard, federal legislation imperative following the establishment in 1949 of the Federal Republic. In the Treaty on the Settlement of Problems Resulting from War and Occupation of 1952 and in the 1954 "Paris Protocol,"[54] the Federal Republic assumed responsibility for enactment of legislation to supplement that of the states, with the provision that the new laws be no less favorable to the persecuted than those then in force in the American Zone.

Meanwhile, in September, 1951, Chancellor Adenauer, before the Bundestag, reminded the world that

> unspeakable crimes were perpetrated in the name of the German people which impose upon them the obligation to make moral and material amends, both with regard to the individual damage which Jews have suffered and with regard to Jewish property for which there are no longer individual claimants.[55]

46-47 [omitted]

48 Bundes-Rückerstattungsgesetz: Bundesgesetz zur Regelung der rückerstattungsrechtlichen Geldverbindlichkeiten des Deutschen Reichs und gleichgestellter Rechtsträger (BRüG vom 19. Juli 1957, [1957] BGB1. I 734 und 2. Oktober 1964, [1964] BGB1. I 809. For an English translation of the 1957 law, see Institute of Jewish Affairs, World Jewish Congress, Federal Law on the Discharge of the Restitutionary Monetary Obligations of the German Reich and Assimilated Entities [Federal Restitution Law (BRüG)] (N. Robinson transl. 1957).

49 For a brief summary of the restitution laws, see H. van Dam, M. Hirsch & R. Loewenberg, [WIEDERGUTMACHUNGSGESETZE 91966)] at 254. *Cf.* Bentwich, [*Nazi Spoliation and German Restitution, 10 Leo Baeck Institute Yearbook* 223 (1965)]....

54 [1955] BGB1. II 431....

55 F. Shinnar, Bericht Eines Beauftragten: Die Deutsch-Israelischen Beziehungen 1951-66, at 28 (1967) [hereinafter cited as Shinnar]....

Adenauer promised early passage of federal compensation laws and expressed his readiness to discuss a settlement of the material indemnification problem with representatives of Jewish organizations and of the state of Israel. Shortly thereafter the Conference on Jewish Material Claims against Germany (Claims Conference), comprising twenty Jewish organizations, was established. The Conference supported Israel's claim concerning the integration in Israel of victims of the Nazis.... After difficult negotiations at the Hague, the Federal Republic and Israel concluded an agreement in Luxemburg on September 10, 1952.[57] The Federal Republic agreed to pay Israel compensation of DM 3 billion to assist in the integration of uprooted and destitute refugees from Germany and from lands formerly under German rule. This sum was earmarked chiefly for the purchase of goods and services to expand opportunities for the settlement and rehabilitation of such refugees in Israel. In compliance with Protocol No. 2, drawn up with the Claims Conference, the Federal Republic agreed to pay Israel for the benefit of the Claims Conference an additional DM 450 million.[58] This money transferred by Israel to the Claims Conference was to be used for the relief, rehabilitation and resettlement of Jewish victims of the Nazis ... living outside Israel at the time of the agreement.[59]...

The Federal Supplementary Law for the compensation of Victims of National Socialist Persecution (*Bundesergänzungs-gesetz zur Entschädigung für Opfer der national-sozialistischen Verfolgung*) was finally published September 18, 1953, to take effect on October 1 of that year.[64] This federal law was subsequently amended to expand the coverage and improve its provisions. The "Third Law to Amend the Federal Supplementary Law" was dated June 29, 1956, and is entitled "Federal Compensation Law: *Bundesentschädigungsgesetz—BEG*." The "Federal Compensation Terminal Law: *BEG-Schlussgesetz*" was passed in 1965.[65]

The Federal Compensation Law (BEG)

The BEG has ten parts. The first (paragraphs 1-14) deals with general provisions, and the second (paragraphs 15-141) with categories of damage. Part three (paragraphs 142-148) deals with special provisions for legal persons, institutions or associations, part four (paragraphs 149-166) with special groups of persecutees and part five with persons damaged because of their nationality. The last five parts (paragraphs 169-241) include provisions for the payment of claims, the mitigation of hardship, the distribution of the

---

57 [1953] BGB1. II 35. The agreement is known as the Luxemburg Agreement....

58 Protocol No. 2 (*The Hague Protocol No. 2*) between the Government of the Federal Republic of Germany and the Conference on Jewish Material Claims Against Germany of Sept. 10, 1952, [1953] BGB1. II 95-97.

59 *Id.*

64 [1953] BGB1. I 1387. H. van Dam, *et al.*, Das Bundes-Entschädigungsgesetz: Systematische Darstellung und Kritische Erläuterungern (1953); G. Blessin & H. Wilden, Bundes-Entschädigungsgesetze (1964).

65 [1956] BGB1. I 559; [1957] BGB1 I 1250.... The "Federal Compensation Terminal Law: BEG—Schlussgesetz" was dated September 14, 1965. [1965] BGB1. I 1315.

compensation load, the establishment of compensation authorities and procedures and "transitional and final provisions for the payment of claims, the mitigation of hardship, the distribution of the compensation load, the establishment of compensation authorities and procedures and "transitional and final provisions." The Federal Compensation Terminal Law (*BEG-Schlussgesetz*), enacted in 1965, has twelve articles. The first two amend the BEG, and the sixth replaces BEG part five. The principal provisions of the BEG, as amended by the Terminal Law, follow—some in translation, some summarized[66]—with references to related laws and decisions.

Basic Principles

A victim of the Nazi persecution (a persecutee) is defined as one who was oppressed because of political opposition to National Socialism, or because of race, religion or ideology, and who suffered in consequence loss of life, damage to limb or health, loss of liberty, property or possessions, or harm to vocational or economic pursuits. Treated on a par with persecutees, thus defined, are those persecuted by the Nazis because: 1) their consciences had prompted them to take the risk of opposing actively the regime's disregard of human dignity and destruction of life; 2) they adhered to artistic or scientific beliefs rejected by National Socialism; or 3) they were closely connected with a persecutee.[67]

Since Hitler's regime demanded complete adherence to its ideological aims in all areas of public and private life, the term "political opposition" is a broad one. It applies not only to membership in various political parties but also to a wide range of private activities which the authorities treated as political opposition. In their decisions the Federal Supreme Court and other courts have regarded as political opposition activities such as refusal to join the Nazi Party, refusal to display the swastika flag, refusal to show anti-Jewish signs, refusal to contribute to special party-controlled projects ... and listening to and disseminating foreign radio broadcasts.... Those who were themselves members of the Nazi Party, or who aided and abetted the National Socialist regime, are excluded from claiming compensation under the BEG.[69]

---

66 The translation is from Institute of Jewish Affairs, World Jewish Congress, The [West German] Federal Compensation Law and its Implementary Regulations (N. Robinson transl. 1957) [the law is hereinafter cited as BEG], with consideration to the amendments of the BEG which are translated by this writer.

For complete text, with commentary, of the BEG, the Schlussgesetz, and the implementary regulations, see Blessin-Giessler, Bundes-Entschädigungs-Schlussgesetz (1967) [hereinafter cited as Blessin & Giessler]....

67 BEG ¶ 1. Also regarded as a persecutee was 1) the survivor of a persecutee; 2) a damagee who, while committing an offense in combating the National Socialist oppressive regime or warding off persecution, was able to conceal the motive for the offense; 3) a damagee affected by the oppressive measures because he was mistakenly regarded as belonging to a group of persons persecuted for the reasons specified; and 4) a damagee who, as a close relative of the persecutee, was affected by the oppressive measures.

69 BEG ¶ 6. Compensation is also not payable for damages which, most certainly, would have been caused by another event. BEG ¶ 9. *Cf.* E.J. Cohn, *Causa Superviens*, in 1 Manual of German Law 108 (2d ed. 1968).

A second important aspect of the criteria for eligibility under the BEG is that law's principle of territoriality. A claim for compensation is tied to the claimant's residence in Germany.... A right of compensation also exists ... for repatriates within the meaning of the "Repatriates Law,"[71] for expellees and refugees from the Soviet Zone within the meaning of the "Federal Expellees' Law"[72] and for persecutees in displaced persons' camps and homeless aliens within the territory of the Federal Republic.

An expelled persecutee has a claim to compensation even if his affinity to the German "nation" ("German Folk") is based merely on his belonging to a German linguistic or cultural group; an explicit declaration of belonging to the German "nation" is not necessary for a claim to membership in a German linguistic or cultural group.[73]...

Categories of Damage

Loss of Life. A claim for loss of life exists if the persecutee has been killed or driven to his death by persecution. Two categories are recognized: death immediately or within eight months of the end of the persecution that caused death (paragraph 15) and death, resulting from harm to limb or health, more than eight months after the persecution (paragraph 41).[78] The distinction is of particular importance to stateless persons and refugees, who can claim compensation under paragraph 15 but not under paragraph 41.[79] Compensation for loss of life is payable in the form of an annuity, a lump-sum in case of remarriage or a capital indemnity.[80]

The courts have frequently interpreted the provisions concerning compensation for loss of life. Loss of life includes homicide, manslaughter and death as a result of damage to health inflicted on the victim individually, including that suffered in concentration camps. Loss of life, for purposes of the BEG, also includes death caused by a deterioration in health resulting from emigration or from living conditions detrimental to health—particularly conditions in tropical countries. In addition, compensation has been paid in cases of suicide prompted by persecution, including suicide

---

71 Law of Assistance to Repatriates: Gesetz über Hilfsmassnahmen für Heimkehrer (Heimkehrergesetz) June 19, 1950, [1950] BGB1. I 221; Law of Oct. 30, 1951, [1951] BGB1. I 875; Law of Aug. 17, 1953, [1953] BGB1. I 931. Repatriates within the meaning of this law are former German prisoners of war, or Germans who had been interned outside of the Federal Republic or Berlin....

72 [omitted]

73 Many Jewish expellees from the territories outside the German Reich could not claim belonging to the German "nation" ("German folk"), but they belonged to the German linguistic or cultural group. *Cf.* H. van Dam, M. Hirsch & R. Loewenberg, *supra* note 11, at 154. "Belonging to the German 'nation' ('German folk')" is an approximate translation of "*deutsche Volkszugehoerigkeit.*"

78-79 [omitted]

80 The annuity was computed on the basis of the maintenance payments that would be granted to survivors of a federal civil servant whose salary group was comparable to the economic position of the persecutee. The monthly minimum amount of the annuity, beginning on October 1, 1964, was DM 292 (about $95) for the widow or widower, with smaller amounts to orphans, grandchildren, or parents. *Cf.* BEG ¶¶ 16, 18-19. The monthly payments have been periodically increased....

caused by economic difficulties which the victim could not overcome in the country to which he immigrated. In all these latter cases, however, the claim to compensation presupposes some direct and specific act against the victim and an adequate chain of causation between the persecution and the victim's death.[81]...

Since claims by survivors are differentiated according to whether or not the victim died within eight months of the end of the persecution,[86] the definition of the term "end of the persecution" has been significant for many claimants. The Federal Supreme Court has held that the end of the persecution is not for all purposes May 8, 1945, the date of the collapse of the Nazi regime. Rather, the end of the persecution must be defined individually for each case, but must precede May 8, 1945, when, with the breakdown of National Socialism, persecution generally ended.[87]

Damage to Life and Health. A persecutee is entitled to compensation if he has suffered damage to limb or health that is more than insignificant. It is sufficient for recovery that there be a probable nexus between the damage to limb or health and the persecution of the victim. Damage is deemed insignificant if it does not entail, nor is likely to entail, lasting impairment of the persecutees' mental or physical faculties. In such cases compensation takes the form of medical care, annuity, capital indemnity, out-of-hospital allowance, retaining assistance and maintenance of survivors.[88]

...The person claiming compensation for damage to health had to agree to an examination by a consulting physician, appointed by the compensation authorities. Consulting physicians (*Vertrauensärzte*) have also been added to German diplomatic and consular missions abroad. Especially difficult problems have arisen from psychiatric and psychosomatic cases.[89]... Not only will temporary harms provide no basis for compensation; even in the case of permanent damage compensation is awarded only if, in subjective medical terms, the well-being of the injured person has been impaired....

Damage to Liberty.... A persecutee has a claim to compensation if at any time between January 30, 1933, and May 8, 1945, he was deprived of his liberty. Compensation is also available if the claimant was deprived of his liberty by a state other than Germany in flagrant disregard of the rule of law and 1) the deprivation was made possible by the fact that the claimant had lost German nationality or the protection of the Reich, or 2) the foreign

---

81, 86 [omitted]

87 [*Rechtsprechung zum Wiedergutmachungsrecht* [hereinafter cited as RzW]] 369-70 (1962). Blessin & Giessler, *supra* note 66, at 326. In view of the great difficulty of proving the exact date of persecution in many cases of damage to health, this ruling of the court is highly questionable. *Cf.* note 180 *infra*.

88 BEG ¶¶ 28-29, 31, 32. According to paragraphs 31-32, the annuity is based on an impairment of the earning power from 25 percent to 80 percent and more, and amounts to from 15 percent to not more than 70 percent of the salary to which the persecutee would have been entitled if he were classified as belonging to a comparable civil servants' group, according to his age on May 1, 1949. The monthly amount of the annuities is based on the persecutee's earning capacity and ranged from DM 147 to DM 365 (about $46 to $115), beginning October 1, 1964. The amounts have been periodically increased. On October 1, 1966, they ranged from DM 159 to DM 395 (about $50 to $123).

89 [omitted]

government was induced by the German authorities to effect the deprivation of liberty.[93]

Deprivation of liberty includes police or military detention, arrest by the National Socialist Party, custodial or penal imprisonment, detention in a concentration camp and forced stay in ghetto. A persecutee is also regarded as having been deprived of liberty if he lived or did forced labor under conditions resembling detention or did service in a penal or reform unit of the German armed forces.[94]

Restrictions of liberty giving a claim to compensation include having worn the Star of David and having lived "underground" under conditions unfit for a human being....

The compensation for deprivation or restriction is payable in the form of a capital indemnity of DM 150 for each full month of deprivation or restriction.[96]...

To claim compensation for detention in a concentration camp, the claimant must show that he was persecuted, or at the least a political opponent, of the Nazi regime, since criminals, the socially deranged and other so-called "undesirable elements" were also held in the camps.[98] A list of concentration camps, published in a regulation supplementing the BEG, shows no fewer than 902 individual camps and subsidiary camps.

...Forced labor under "conditions similar to detention,"... has been held also to require that the persecutee have lived under those conditions outside the place of work. This decision in particular has been criticized by observers who have pointed out that forced labor in itself is a life similar to detention.[102] Similar criticism has been aimed at judicial interpretation of the term "living underground under conditions unfit for a human being." The courts have held that living underground in itself does not entail necessarily such conditions, but that the persecutee, to qualify for compensation within the meaning of that phrase, must have lived like, or under conditions worse than a prisoner.[103]

Damage to Property. A persecutee has a claim for property damage if any object which belonged to him was destroyed, defaced or left to be looted within the territory of the Reich as of December 31, 1937[104] or in the Free City of Danzig. The loss must have followed because the claimant emigrated or fled Nazi oppression, was deprived of his liberty or lived "underground" or was expelled or deported in connection with his persecution.[105] The courts have held that a claim exists only if the damage was caused by "a direct action against the property" (*unmittelbare Einwirkung auf die Sachsubstanz*), or if the claimant were excluded from control of the property and the property

---

93 BEG ¶ 43(1)....

94 BEG ¶ 43, §§ 2, 3.

96 *Id.* at ¶¶ 45, 48.

98 RzW 262 (1954); RzW 17 (1957).

102-104 [omitted]

105 BEG ¶ 51.

turned over to a third party. An abandonment to looting means that the authorities of the state had withheld any protection from the property.[106]

Compensation is to be computed in Deutschmarks at the replacement cost of the property at the time of the decision, with due regard to the value of the object at the time of the damage. Compensation for a single claimant may not exceed DM 75,000.[107]

Damage to Possessions. The claim for damage to possessions parallels that for damage to property. No compensation is payable for losses totalling less than 500 Reichsmark. Impairment of a persecutee's use of his property or possessions is deemed equivalent to damage to possessions.[108] A claim for compensation also exists for expenses necessary to emigration or expulsion. As in the case of damage to property, compensation in these last-mentioned cases is not to exceed DM 75,000.[109]

Discriminatory Levies, Fines, Penalties and Costs. Compensation may be awarded for general discriminatory levies and for 1) losses through forced contracts,[110] 2) payments to the Deutsche Goldiskont-Bank to obtain an export license,[111] 3) payment of the Reich Flight Tax,[112] and 4) payment of surcharges for overdue payments, interest for default and bank charges and execution costs incurred in connection with payment of discriminatory levies.[113]...

Damage to Vocational and Economic Pursuits. Compensation is to be awarded if, in the course of persecution begun in the Reich as of December 31, 1937, or in Danzig, a claimant suffered significant damage to vocational or economic pursuits.[116] Such damage existed if the victim lost use of his earning power.[117]

A self-employed persecutee is entitled to assistance in resuming his former occupation, or one of equal standing, through the issuance of the requisite licenses, admissions and purchase permits. He also has a claim for interest-free loans or loans at a reduced rate, if he cannot otherwise raise the money to resume his self-employment or a comparable vocation. In normal circumstances, the maximum allowed is DM 30,000. Under "particular trying conditions" an additional interest-free loan of up to DM 20,000 is authorized and provision made for waiving its repayment.[118]...

---

106 Blessin & Giessler, *supra* note 66, at 459-60. W. Brunn & R. Hebenstreit, *supra* note 66, at 180. RzW 403 (1958); RzW 80 (1962); RzW 318-19 (1963); RzW 316 (1965)....

107 BEG ¶¶ 52, 55.

108 *Id.* at ¶ 56. In a number of decisions the courts have interpreted the term "possessions" to include inventions, patents, goodwill, business connections, and reversionary interests. Blessin & Giessler, *supra* note 66, at 473; RzW 83 (1957); RzW 32 (1959); RzW 510 (1963); RzW 266 (1965).

109 BEG ¶¶ 57-58.

110-111 [omitted]

112 Reich Flight Tax (Reichsfluchsteuer): A tax of 25 percent of the total property, with certain exemptions, was imposed on persons who transferred their residences to foreign countries....

113 Blessin & Giessler, *supra* note 66, at 498-500....

116 BEG ¶ 64.

117 *Id.* at ¶ 65.

118 *Id.* at ¶¶ 67-72.

A formerly self-employed persecutee may also recover for the period in which he was excluded from, or restricted in exercise of, his occupation. Here compensation takes the form of a capital indemnity or a pension. The capital indemnity is computed on the basis of three-fourths of the salary to which a comparable civil servant would have been entitled at the time of the persecutee's discharge. The indemnity will not be paid for any time beyond the date on which the victim of persecution has taken up an occupation which provided him an adequate subsistence. The claimant may elect an annuity in lieu of a capital indemnity. The annuity is payable for life—without regard to the size of the capital indemnity entitlement—provided that the persecutee has no adequate subsistence at the time of the compensatory decision. The annuity is based on two-thirds of the pension of a comparable civil servant. The maximum monthly annuity ranges from DM 600 up to March 1, 1957, to DM 1,000 beginning January 1, 1966. If the successful claimant has died after electing an annuity, his widow, until remarriage, and dependent children are entitled to a fraction of the annuity.[120]

A persecutee who was privately employed has a claim for damages if he suffered dismissal, forced premature retirement or transfer to a job with substantially lower pay. An eligible claimant is entitled to restoration to his former, or equivalent, employment, unless in the interim he has reached 65 or become unable to work. He is also entitled to either a capital indemnity or an annuity.... The provisions for widows and children are similar to those for self-employed occupations.[121]

A persecuted member of the public service may claim compensation, for the period before April, 1950,[122] for losses resulting from termination or dismissal from the service. Types of losses include discharge without pension, discharge with reduced pension, premature retirement or transfer to a lower-paying job.... For the period before April 1, 1950, a capital compensation is provided for civil servants, professional soldiers, employees and workmen, non-tenured professors and lecturers and employees of religious organizations and their survivors.[124]

A persecutee's vocational pursuits are also deemed compensably damaged if he has been excluded from vocational or pre-vocational training, has been compelled to interrupt that training or has been barred from employment despite its completion. The victim is entitled to a grant of DM 10,000. Children unable to begin or complete vocational or pre-vocational training because of the persecution of their parents are entitled to a grant of

---

[120] *Id.* at ¶¶ 74-76, 81-83, 85-86. In accord with the periodic increases of the civil servants' pensions, the annuity has been periodically increased. The election of an annuity consequently was more advantageous than a capital indemnity....

[121] BEG ¶¶ 89, 91, 95, 97-98. The maximum amounts of the annuity have been periodically increased. Blessin & Giessler, *supra* note 66, at 621.

[122] [omitted]

[124] *Id.* at ¶¶ 102-12. For the period after April 1, 1950, compensation is provided by the special law for the redress of damage to public servants....

up to DM 10,000 for the resumption of that training.[125] The maximum capital indemnity for damage to vocational pursuits is DM 40,000.[126]

Under the heading "Damage to Economic Pursuits" compensation is provided for loss of insurance, other than social insurance.... A claim for health insurance is provided for certain groups of persecutees.[129]

Special Provisions for Legal Persons, Institutions or Associations

Legal persons, institutions or associations ... have a claim for compensation if they have suffered damage by National Socialist oppressive measures. If such a legal person or institution has ceased to exist and there is no successor in right, the claim may be asserted by a successor in purpose or by a successor organization established under restitution legislation.[130]

This claim to compensation exists only with respect to damage to property and possessions....

Special Groups of Persecutees

...Under paragraph 150 a persecutee from an expulsion area who is not a resident of the Federal Republic has a claim for damage to limb and health, damage to liberty, payment of discriminatory levies and damage to vocational pursuits, if the persecutee belonged to the "German sphere of language and culture."[135]... In the case of persons who qualify as persecutees,[138] but for whom special-purpose funds are not otherwise provided, hardship mitigation payments are available. These "hardship" payments may take the form of grants for subsistence, medical care, the purchase or household goods, building a basis for self-sustenance, and for vocational training. For this purpose and for providing living quarters loans are also available.[139]

Many victims of Nazi persecution do not suit the requirements of BEG paragraph 4, or of any of the paragraphs just discussed. Among these victims are Belgian, Danish, Dutch or French nationals who were persecuted and damaged in their own countries. To meet their claims, a number of nations have concluded with the Federal Republic of Germany "global agreements" under which they receive funds for payment to individual claimants. The individuals have no direct claim against Germany, but rather must file their

---

125 *Id.* at ¶¶ 113-16, 119.

126 *Id.* at ¶ 123.

129 BEG ¶ 141a.

130 *Id.* at ¶ 142.

135 *Id. See also* H. van Dam, M. Hirsch & R. Loewenberg, *supra* note 11, at 153. The claimants under paragraph 150 of the BEG do not receive compensation for property damage (BEG ¶ 51, *see* note 105 *supra*), damage to possessions (BEG ¶ 56, *see* note 108 *supra*), or for damage to economic pursuits (BEG ¶ 127, *see* note 127 *supra*). They are also not compensated for imposed fines and penalties (BEG ¶ 61, *see* note 114 *supra*). Some expellees can claim compensation for damage to property and possessions under the Equalization of Burdens Law....

138 [omitted]

139 BEG ¶ 171.

claims in their own nations. The following countries have concluded agreements with West Germany:[140]

Luxemburg, July 11, 1959, (BGB1. 1960 II, 2077)	for DM 18 million
Norway, August 7, 1959, (BGB1. 1960 II, 1336)	" " 60 "
Denmark, August 24, 1959, (BGB1. 1960 II, 1933)	" " 16 "
Greece, March 18, 1960, (BGB1. 1961 II, 1596)	" " 115 "
Netherlands, April 8, 1960, (BGB1. 1963 II, 629)	" " 125 "
France, July 15, 1960, (BGB1. 1961 II, 1029)	" " 400 "
Belgium, September 28, 1960, (BGB1. 1961 II, 1037)	" " 80 "
Italy, June 2, 1961, (BGB1. 1963 II, 791)	" " 40 "
Switzerland, June 29, 1961, (BGB1. 1963 II, 155)	" " 10 "
Austria, November 27, 1961, (BGB1. 1962 II, 1041)	" " 101 "
Great Britain & Northern Ireland, June 9, 1961, (BGB1. 1964 II, 1032)	" " 11 "
Sweden, August 3, 1961, (BGB1. 1964 II, 1402)	" " 1 "
TOTAL	DM 977 million

Finally, for persecutees who do not meet requirements of any of the BEG sections already discussed—because of domicile, status or time limitations—and who are not covered by "global agreements"—such as refugees from the East-bloc countries—the BEG-Terminal Law provides grants from a special fund of DM 1.2 billion.[141]

Compensation Authorities and Procedures

The cost of compensation is borne by the Federal Government and the *Länder*.... Two groups of compensation authorities have been established, the compensation agencies of the *Länder* and the compensation courts. Applications for compensation must first be filed with the compensation offices; if a final settlement cannot be reached in agency proceedings, the claim is submitted to the compensation courts. Compensation divisions have been created on three levels of the regular court system: 1) the compensation chambers at the district courts (*Landgerichte*), and compensation senates at 2) the courts of appeal (*Oberlandesgerichte*), and 3) the Federal Supreme Court (*Bundesgerichtshof*).[143]

Detailed procedural regulations are found in concurrent and concluding paragraphs of the law. These cover points such as facts and evidence, presumption of death, jurisdiction of the compensation agencies, time limits for applications, appeals and representation by lawyers. Some of these regulations refer to, and some modify in favor of claimants, the standard rules of the Civil Procedure Code....

140-143 [omitted]

Before and After the Law

Opponents and Supporters

The drafting of the compensation law met considerable opposition. Fritz Schaeffer, Federal Minister of Finance and later Minister of Justice, repeatedly offered a financial rationale for his opposition to the legislation.... Certain anti-Semitic and nationalist groups, including the *Deutsche National- und Soldaten-Zeitung*, supported Schaeffer in his argument that indemnification would endanger the stability of the German mark—this despite the strong financial position of the Federal Republic by 1957.[147] Objections were also raised by the individual *Länder*, which had provided compensation laws before the Federal Government acted, and which originally were expected to bear the main financial burden. A compromise was finally reached under which the Federal Government assumed a substantial part of the outlay.[148]...

Successor Organizations and the United Restitution Organization

Organizations[155] were established to recover communal properties for which no private claimants appeared.... The United Restitution Organization (URO), established in 1949 as a legal aid organization for indigent claimants, represented until the end of 1968 about 300,000 victims of persecution with a total of more than 450,000 claims. The sums recovered by URO for claimants for compensation (as distinguished from restitution) up to that date amounted to $547 million.... Moreover, a department of the Claims Conference,[157] working closely with URO, had recovered smaller sums from German industrial corporations which used Jews as slave labor during the War. I.G. Farben paid DM 30 million, Krupp DM 10 million, Siemens DM 7 million, A.E.G. DM 5 million and Rheinmetall a lesser sum.[158]

...URO has twenty-seven offices and a number of correspondents in [sixteen countries].... In its peak period, 1958, URO employed a staff of 1,026 full-time and 106 part-time persons, of whom 223 were registered lawyers and 73 had legal qualifications. The staff was reduced gradually and in January, 1968, numbered 451 full-time and 94 part-time employees, including 110 lawyers and 47 persons with legal training.... The claimants represented by URO were living in all parts of the world. Each must be approached and seen personally in the country of his residence.... When the documents in support of a claim have been gathered, they are sent to the appropriate office in Germany. The German authorities and courts regularly turn to URO Headquarters for evidence. URO, through its research staff, has exercised an influence, often decisive, in favor of the victims of persecution, on every legal problem of compensation and restitution and legislation and administration.

---

[147] K. Grossman, [Die Ehrenschuld: Kurzgeschichte der Wiedergutmachung (1967)], at 62, 87-90, 165-166.

[148] *Id.* at 69....

[155-158] [omitted]

In addition, URO has been in the forefront in bringing test cases to the highest German courts in order to protect the interests of all claimants.[161]

The Effects of the Law

The network of compensation offices established in the *Länder* and in Berlin[162] and the German courts handled an avalanche of restitution and compensation cases. In 1966, for example, every eighth case before the Federal Supreme Court in Karlsruhe (*Bundesgerichtshof*) was a compensation case.[163] That the German authorities were interested in disseminating reliable information on compensation is shown by a number of meetings held outside Germany in which government officials explained the purpose and the workings of the compensation laws to thousands of claimants.[164] The handling of the flood of claims was facilitated by the provision in the law that former German lawyers whose qualifications were cancelled by the persecution might represent claimants,[165] and that the URO might represent indigent claimants.[166]

By July 1, 1971, total payments under the Federal Restitution Law, the Federal Compensation Law (BEG), the Luxemburg Agreement with Israel (DM 3.45 billion) and the global agreements (DM 1 billion) amounted to DM 40.91 billion. The Federal Government estimated that additional payments of some DM 11.5 billion would be made before 1975. This would represent a total outlay for indemnification of about DM 52.4 billion up to 1975. The estimate for annuity payments, beginning in 1976, amount to an additional DM 25-30 billion.[167]

Up to July 1, 1971, 703,050 claims were received under the Restitution Law and 587,290 were settled. On that date 115,760 claims (16.5%) were still pending. Under the Compensation Law 4,256,453 claims were received and 4,133,765 were settled, leaving, as of July 1, 1971, 122,688 (2.8%) pending.

A breakdown of the period September, 1965 to June 30, 1971, shows that, of the 1,000,506 claims settled during that period under the Compensation Law (BEG), 372,755 were approved, 245,018 were rejected, 23,894 were referred to other countries—probably under the global treaties—and 358,839 were "settled in other ways."[168]

Impressive though these figures are, it is both surprising and alarming that twenty-five years after the War many restitution and compensation

---

161 N. Bentwich, [The United Restitution Organisation 1948-68 (1968)].

162 BEG ¶ 184. Blessin & Giessler, *supra* note 66, at 839.

163 O. Küster, [Erfahrungen in der Deutschen Wiedergutmachung (1967), which is volumes 346-47 of the series: Recht und Staat in Geschichte und Gegenwart] at 12.

164-165 [omitted]

166 BEG ¶ 183....

167 These and the following figures are from the official German Federal Statistics, Bundes-Statistik: "Leistungen der öffentlichen Hand auf dem Gebiete der Wiedergutmachung," "Stand der Verfahren," (July 1, 1971); "Statistischer Bericht über Anträge und Entschädigungsleistungen nach dem Bundesentschädigungsgesetz (BEG)," (June 30, 1971).

168 "Settlement in other ways" includes withdrawal of applications, special agreements, and referral on the basis of special laws or of the global treaties....

cases are still pending. It is especially disturbing that some of these cases have been pending for more than twenty years. One could hardly suggest that an appeal to the Supreme Court is properly dealt with if years have passed between its filing and a decision.... [O]ne cannot now predict when the compensation work will finally end.[169]

The Working of the Law: Weaknesses and Accomplishments

Responsible observers have repeatedly criticized certain aspects of the compensation legislation, suggesting that it is inadequate for some categories of damage and for some groups of persecutees.[170]... [Some] maintain that damage to property and possessions receive unjustly favorable consideration, while damage to life and health are treated less generously.

A second source of unevenness is the law's principle of territoriality. This principle distinguishes between persecutees who have resided in Germany or are German citizens, persecutees from expulsion areas who are not residents of Germany and persecutees who are stateless persons or refugees within the meaning of the Geneva Convention.[173] Equally disadvantaged are persecutees who do not meet requirements of specified dates for residence, flight or expulsion. Each of these aspects of the law has the effect of producing unequal compensation for the victims of equal harm.

By contrast, one group of persecutees has been clearly favored. These are the former members of the German civil service, former officers of the German government, including judges, professors and teachers, and—in a limited way—officers and civil servants of the former Jewish communities. Compensation of these groups has been very generous, amounting basically to reinstatement in the position, salary or pension group which the claimant would have reached had the persecution not taken place.[174]

Quite apart from the inequalities written into the compensation law, further basis for criticism has been found in the law's administration. The compensation agencies and courts have been criticized for not keeping in mind the basic purpose of the law and for becoming entangled in casuistic search for petty problems and thus losing sight of ethical guidelines.

---

[169] RzW 439 (1970)....

[170] O. Küster, *supra* note [163], *passim*. Bentwich, *Nazi Spoliation*, *supra* note [49], at 217-18, 221; W. Schwarz, In den Wind Gesprochen: Glossen zur Wiedergutmachung des nationalsozialistischen Unrechts (1969)....

[173] BEG ¶¶ 4, 150; Terminal Law art. V, Sept. 14, 1965, [1965] BGB1. I 1315....

[174] Law Regulating the Redress of National Socialist Wrongs to Public Servants (Gesetz zur Regelung der Wiedergutmachung nationalsozialistischen Unrechts für Angehörige des öffentlichen Dienstes: BWGöD), Dec. 15, 1965, [1965] BGB1. I 2073. *See* note 76 *supra*; Blessin & Giessler, *supra* note 66, at 1015, 1035; O. Küster, *supra* note [163], at 18-19; Bentwich, *Nazi Spoliation*, *supra* note [49], at 221....

*Ingo Müller, "Hitler's Justice: The Courts of the Third Reich"**

According to the laws first passed after the war, victims of Nazi laws or crimes first had to prove that they were not "unworthy of reparations" before a pension or payments were granted.... The heirs of a Jewish businessman sentenced for a "racial sexual offense" were also told that he had been found "unworthy." Their application was rejected by the Reparations Office in Hamburg on the grounds that their relative, who died in 1943, had "committed adultery over a period of many years. [At that time] he could have incurred criminal penalties for it." The lawsuit over the family's application for reparations was ended only by a settlement reached at the County Court.[8]...

[The BEG covered] only those who had suffered discrimination or injury "because of their opposition to National Socialism or because of their race, creed, or ideology."[10] The wording of the law thus excluded large groups or victims from the very start, including the 350,000 people who had undergone forced sterilization and the families of all those murdered in the course of the euthanasia program. Applications for reparation payments filed by the former group were regularly turned down because sterilization was not a form of persecution but was performed purely for medical reasons," and because "the Law for Prevention of Hereditary Diseases was not unconstitutional as such."[11]

Other groups of those persecuted, tortured, or murdered by the Nazis were left empty-handed by the courts' and bureaucracies' extremely narrow interpretation of the law. In the case of the gypsies (Sinti and Roma tribes), for example, although they were actually sent to concentration camps and murdered for racial reasons, the official explanation given during the Third Reich was "prevention of crime."... Courts and officials in postwar West Germany willingly seized on this terminology, and as a result Sinti and Roma who had suffered persecution before March 1, 1943, had no legal claim to reparation payments.... Even as late as 1956, the Federal Supreme Court determined that "in spite of the occurrence of racial considerations, the measures taken were based not on race as such but rather on the gypsies' asocial characteristics."[13]

Minor acts of resistance to the regime during the Third Reich also gained neither recognition nor reparation after the war, since the courts did not recognize them as "opposition to National Socialism" and therefore refused to consider the often brutal sanctions imposed as "Nazi coercion." A typical case was that of Erna Brehm, a housemaid in the town of Calw. At the age of seventeen she had fallen in love with a young Polish auto mechanic

---

* Reprinted by permission of the publishers of HILTER'S JUSTICE: THE COURTS OF THE THIRD REICH by Ingo Müller, Cambridge, Mass.: Harvard University Press, Copyright © 1991 by the President and Fellows of Harvard College, pp. 262-265.

[8] Ibid., 161.

[10] Paragraphs 4ff. of the Federal [Compensation] Law of September 18, 1953; *Bundesgesetzblatt* (1953), I, 1387.

[11] Cited in Norbert Schmacke and Hans-Georg Güse, *Zwangssterilisiert* (Bremen: Brockkamp, 1984), 155.

[13] Decision of January 7, 1956; *Rechtsprechung zur Wiedergutmachung* (1956), 113.

named Marian Gawronsky, one of the more than ten million "foreign workers" brought into the "Old Reich" to replace the men at the front. When word of their love affair leaked out, the police arrested Erna Brehm and shaved her head in the middle of the market square as a public humiliation. The Stuttgart Special Court then sent her to prison for eight months for violating the ban on "associating with prisoners of war." After serving her sentence she was not released, but was sent to the Ravensbrück concentration camp; according to the order for preventive detention dated February 6, 1942, and signed by Reinhard Heydrich, her behavior endangered "the future and security of the *Volk* and the state." The young woman was not equal to the barbaric conditions at the camp, and after two years during which she wasted away to mere skin and bones and caught tuberculosis in both lungs, she returned to her parents with the notification that she was "unfit for further internment." Erna Brehm never recovered from this treatment; in 1947 she still weighed only about eighty pounds and suffered from the delusion that any government official she encountered was plotting her death.

Erna Brehm's application for a disability pension was rejected and her appeal against this decision was rejected by the Calw Petty Court on August 9, 1951, in a decision which also ordered her to pay all court costs.... Erna Brehm was imprisoned on political grounds; supposedly she had posed a threat to "the future and security of the *Volk* and the state," and while in the concentration camp she was forced to wear the red badge identifying political prisoners. After the war, however, the court refused in her case to recognize the "opposition to National Socialism" required by the [Compensation] Law. "Her youth alone," the court found, argued against the assumption "that her contact with the Pole [was] based on firm political convictions that were opposed to National Socialism." It thus assumed that Erna Brehm had been prosecuted not for "political reasons but rather for entirely personal ones." The fact that the Third Reich itself had treated her actions as a political offense was supposedly irrelevant.... Erna Brehm died on August 19, 1951, at the age of twenty-seven. Her parents' suit for reparations, which they continued after her death, was rejected by the Tübingen County Court.[14]

Kurt Schwerin, "German Compensation for Victims of Nazi Persecution"[*]

The provisions of the law for compensating death offer another instance where problems of narrow drafting and interpretation arise. To be compensated, a claimant must show an adequate causative link between persecution and death.[178] Additionally, the law differentiates between death during persecution or within eight months and death later traceable to

---

14 The case is documented in Dieter Galinski and Wolf Schmidt, eds., *Die Kriegsjahre in Deutschland, 1939-1945* (Hamburg: Verlag Erziehung und Wissenschaft, 1985), 121ff.

* Excerpted from Kurt Schwerin, "German Compensation for Victims of Nazi Persecution," *Northwestern University Law Review*, vol. 67 (1972), pp. 520, 522-523.

178 Blessin & Giessler, *supra* note 66, at 230, 325-26....

damage to limb or health. This distinction has been criticized because, for large groups of claimants, it provides no claim for death after a prolonged period of suffering.... [M]any persecutees died long after their liberation from incurable diseases contracted in the camps.[180]...

Of equal interest has been the basis of computation of the compensation rate for damage to life, to health and to vocational pursuits. This basis is arrived at by classifying a persecutee with the federal civil servant group of comparable economic position. The group in which a persecutee is classified is determined according to his economic and social position before the persecution. The results of this determination have invited a substantial amount of protracted litigation.[187]

Despite the inadequacies in the compensation law and the shortcomings of individual decisions, it must be borne in mind that the compensation effort as a whole has been a successful undertaking, of enormous proportions and of great historical and legal significance. The program has given financial aid to hundreds of thousands of victims of the Nazis....

Perhaps most important, for many thousands of refugees—many living in the United States, England, Latin America and Israel, and now of advanced years—the indemnification payments have meant the difference between abject poverty and a dignified life with modest security.

This does not mean that complete or even genuine restitution has been made. The persecutions by the Nazi regime were unparalleled and unique in their scope and inhumanity. They cannot be atoned and cannot be forgotten. However, from an historical and legal point of view, the compensation program and reparations constitute a unique operation.

How Germany Has Coped: Four Decades Later

Lutz R. Reuter, "Political and Moral Culture in West Germany: Four Decades of Democratic Reorganization and **Vergangenheitsauseinandersetzung***"*[*]

The twelve years of Nazi dictatorship in Germany and Europe overshadow centuries of German history; the Nazi rule is still the dominant paradigm for research and analysis of contemporary Germany.... [T]he *Historikerstreit* of 1986-1987 (the dispute among West German historians about how to interpret the Nazi past) clearly demonstrates that the (West)

---

180 In many such cases, of course, it was extremely difficult, if not impossible, to prove an adequate causation between the persecution and the death or permanent damage to health.... *See* Blessin & Giessler, *supra* note 66, at 377 *et seq.*; O. Küster, *supra* note [163], at 19-20.

187 BEG ¶¶ 18, 31, 67, 83. *See* notes 80, 88, 120 *supra* and accompanying text. Blessin & Giessler, *supra* note 66, at 352, 409, 555.

* Excerpted from Lutz R. Reuter, "Poltical and Moral Culture in West Germany: Four Decades of Democratic Reoganization and *Vergangenheitsauseinandersetzung*," in Kathy Harms, Lutz R. Reuter and Volker Dürr, eds. *Coping with the Past: Germany and Austria after 1945* (The University of Wisconsin Press, 1990), pp. 155-157, 175-179.

Germans of today have not yet reconciled themselves with their history from 1933 to 1945.[2]...

"[C]oping with the past" (*Auseinandersetzung mit er Vergangenheit*, not *Vergangenheitsbewältigung*, or "getting over history," which is impossible) after 1945 in Germany (and Austria) refers mainly to the period of National Socialism; hence, my focus is the question of origins, guilt, responsibility, and consequences....

Karl Jaspers [developed his] concept of guilt and method of "purification" as outlined in his famous lecture *The Question of German Guilt*.... To establish a common ground of communication and of ethical-political convictions in Germany among Germans, Jaspers first discussed the question of German guilt in a class at Heidelberg University in the winter semester of 1945/1946.[4] His demand was that Germans—whether guilty or innocent, at home or in exile, running with the pack, being silent observers of injustice, or opponents of the Nazi system—were indeed obligated by their human dignity to understand the question of German guilt and to draw their own conclusions.[5]...

The most impressive example of attempts at developing "guilt consciousness" was the Stuttgart Guilt Confession of October 1945.[68] The central sentence reads: "We have caused immeasurable suffering in various countries and peoples. Even if we fought against the awful ideology of National Socialism, we accuse ourselves of not confessing more courageously, not praying more devotedly, not believing more cheerfully, and not loving more urgently."

This and some other confession appeals—characterized by the spirit of solidarity, identification, and empathy—were supported by Protestant groups that had adapted to, partly collaborated with, or even resisted the Nazis, and by members just liberated from death camps, such as Martin Niemöller and Karl Barth. The Stuttgart Guilt Confession was not only a "penitence appeal" of a church to its members, it was a public declaration of deep moral guilt toward the public, especially toward the non-German members of the Ecumenical Movement present at Stuttgart in 1946. The reactions of congregations and the public were ambiguous; the majority of the Germans did not recognize the opportunity this gesture presented, nor the need for an analysis of personal guilt, or, in Jaspers' words, "purification by the loving struggle between individuals who maintain solidarity among

---

[2] Published, in 1986 and 1987, in a series in West German newspapers; see Jürgen Habermas, *Eine Art Schadensabwicklung* (Frankfurt, 1987) and "Historikerstreit": Die Dokumentation der Kontroverse um die Einzigartigkeit der national-sozialistischen Judenvernichtung (Munich and Zurich, 1987).

[4] Karl Jaspers, *The Question of German Guilt* (New York, 1947); Karl Jaspers, *Wohin treibt die Bundesrepublik?* (Munich, 1965); Karl Jaspers, *Antwort: Zur Kritik an meiner Schrift "Wohin treibt die Bundesrepublik?"* (Munich, 1967); Eugen Kogon, "Gericht und Gewissen" (April 1946) und "Das Recht auf politischen Irrtum" (July 1947), in *Kleine Bibliothek des Wissens und des Fortschritts*, vol. 4 (Frankfurt, 1964).
[Editor's note: An excerpted version of the Jaspers essay appears in Volume One of the present collection.]

[5] Cf. Jaspers, *Question*, pp. 7-25.

[68] Text published in Johannes Beckmann, ed., *Kirchliche Jahrbücher 1945-1948* (1950), p. 26.

themselves." A large majority believed that a one-sided confession of German guilt would only be used to justify expelling, slaughter, and rape of Germans in the eastern territories.[69] They misunderstood the Stuttgart Declaration as a confession of undifferentiated collective guilt and responsibility for all Nazi atrocities. In vain, Martin Niemöller tried repeatedly to distinguish between the crimes of the Nazi regime and the core of moral guilt: "We have let all these things happen without protest against these crimes and without supporting the victims.[70] We should not blame the Nazis—they will find their prosecutors and judges, we should blame ourselves and draw logical conclusions."[71]

Opportunities to publicly express guilt consciousness passed; other such opportunities were the adoption of the Basic Law in May 1949, and the constituent sessions of the state parliaments and the Bundestag between 1946 and 1949. Further statements, most notably those by Federal Chancellor Konrad Adenauer (September 1951), the leader of the opposition, Kurt Schumacher, and the Bundestag, in the context of legislation concerning material restitution in 1952, were all related to moral failure. They expressed abhorrence of the Nazi crimes, claimed the nonparticipation by the majority of the German people, and made reference to examples of individual support for victims. They omitted, however, the question of moral guilt consciousness and did not initiate public discussions on the question of "Why did we accept and not resist?" The same question characterizes the [statute of] limitation debates in 1965 and 1969. The experiences Germans had as main perpetrators, criminals, accessories, supporters, citizens running with the pack, soldiers, emigrants, and victims of the Third Reich were too varied. Only in single families, in small private circles, and among the intellectual, religious, and nonpartisan political elites, were questions of personal guilt, lack of courage, individual responsibility, or personal resistance discussed.

The dominating characteristic of the postwar decades was the repression of history *(Vergangenheitsverdrängung)*, especially in its focus on individual behavior. But today we have to admit that we do not know if and how a collective discussion on moral questions and individual responsibilities, or a "collective grief," could have taken place more successfully; also, it is questionable if there are any historical precedents.[72] But there are many examples of concealed criminal and moral guilt—the way

---

69 It is a significant reflection of that attitude that the hometown of Martin Niemöller, the Westphalian village of Lotte, rejected the motion for honorary citizenship because of Niemöller's signature on the *Stuttgart Guilt Confession*. See also Christoph Cobet, ed., *Deutschlands Erneuerung 1945-1950: Bibliographische Dokumentation* (Frankfurt, 1985).

70 Citation published in Walter Niemöller, *Neuanfang 1945: Zur Biographie Martin Niemöllers* (Gütersloh, 1967).

71 Letter of the Council of Evangelical Churches in Germany to the Allied Control Council and to the German State Governments, May 2, 1946; published in Friedrich Söhlmann, ed., *Wort zur Verantwortung der Kirche für das öffentliche Leben* (Freysa, 1945-1946).

72 Cf. Roman Herzog, "Nationalsozialismus," in *Evangelisches Staatslexikon*, ed. Hermann Kunst (Stuttgart, 2d ed. 1975), pp. 1597-1610.

of concealment and amnesty legislation were and are always easier and more common than guilt confessions.[73]

From today's standpoint, one should not oversimplify when judging the postwar behavior of the prewar generations. It was the end of a period of total absorption of the population in the Nazi party's ideological, political, societal, and military objectives, the absurdity of which was obvious to everyone, at least by 1945. The population was deeply alienated from the standards of civic life as a result of the lasting collective experience of the front line, the bombing raids, the concentration and death camps, the destruction of cities, social institutions, and means of production, and the millions of homeless, refugees, former inmates of death camps, and prisoners of war or displaced persons. It is difficult today to imagine the extent of daily poverty, the disorientation of the orphans, or the impact of the—understandably—numerous acts of revenge on Germans, especially in the eastern territories in Poland, Czechoslovakia, or the Soviet Zone of Occupation.

Thus, the failure by the broad majority to accept moral guilt had various "reasons" or explanations: the sociopsychological resistance in the society which had just stopped following the *Führer*, the contextual circumstances of suffering and revenge, the degeneration of the denazification process, the impunity of scientists and Nazis important to the occupying powers, and the international insistence on collective German guilt.[74]

The price of driving the past out of consciousness was and still is considerable. A subtle feeling of undifferentiated guilt persisted and intensified the Germans' sensitivity. It caused the alienation of important segments of the postwar generations. Tough critique of the Germans' incapability of confessing moral responsibility merged with the reproach of materialism, restauration, political apathy—and, partly, even into a fundamental critique of liberal democratic capitalism. Others in the postwar generation did not dare to ask more detailed questions about the role of their parents and grandparents during the Nazi regime—in order to maintain family peace.[75] And, finally, a small minority left the ground of reasonable

---

73 Cf. re-democratization in Greece, Spain, Portugal, and Argentina. For "coping with the past" in France after 1945, see Alfred Grosser, *Germany in Our Time: A Political History of the Postwar Years* (New York, 1985), p. 23; for Austria and the Waldheim affair, see Gerhard Botz, *The Waldheim Case: An Analysis of Austria's Nazi Past* (Boulder, 1988). See also Karl Gutkas, *Die Zweite Republik: Österreich 1945-1985* (Vienna, 1985) and Ernst Bruckmüler, *Nation Österreich: Sozialhistorische Aspekte ihrer Entwicklung* (Vienna, Cologne, and Graz, 1984); For Germany, see Geoffrey Hartman, ed., *Bitburg in Moral and Political Perspective* (Bloomington, 1985); for the United States, see Walter Laqueur, *The Terrible Secret: Suppression of the Truth about Hitler's "Final Solution"* (New York, 1985), David S. Wyman, *The Abandonment of the Jews: America and the Holocaust, 1941-1945* (New York, 1985), and Tom Bower, *The Paperclip Conspiracy: The Hunt for the Nazi Scientists* (Boston, 1987).

74 Cf. Karl Dietrich Erdmann, *Das Ende des Reichs und die Neubildung deutscher Staaten* (Gebhardt, *Handbuch der deutschen Geschichte*, vol. 22 [Munich, 2d ed. 1982]), p. 233.

75 See Sichrovsky, *Strangers* (New York, 1987), pp. 174-85, and Sichrovsky, *Schuldig geboren* (Cologne, 1987).

private or political behavior and opted for anarchism and brute violence toward the representatives of the "system."[76]

As Alexander and Margarete Mitscherlich have declared: "Common grief (*Trauerarbeit*) can only be achieved when we know what to detach from; only through the slow detachment from lost 'object relations'—to individuals or to ideals—can our relation to reality and the past be maintained in a reasonable manner. Without painful remembrance the old object relations remain unconsciously in effect."[77]... Attempts by participants in the *Historikerstreit* at comparing Nazi crimes to other historical events reflect the shortcomings of historical consciousness today.[78] The comparison of the Nazi atrocities with the bloody history of other peoples is hardly a reasonable and legitimate task of (German) historians that could offer new insights into human history—except when one is looking for precedents for "how to cope." The singularity of the Nazi crimes in terms of global history may be questionable, but a debate about this question among German historians hurts the victims' feelings. It is illegitimate and unreasonable; it aims at bringing relief for the Germans, even if only subconsciously.

Particularly those within the social and political elites—who missed the chance to come to terms with the Nazi past in a historical continuum based on historical and moral consciousness—are unable to accept calmly international debates on Nazi Germany and Germany today; such persons tend toward countercritique and counterreproaches.

Nevertheless, research on various aspects of National Socialism has progressed significantly during the last two decades,[79] and many attempts have been made at making this knowledge available to the public.... But the facts about Nazi-regime responsibilities of the postwar elites in politics, administration, jurisprudence, and economics—most of them retired in the meantime—remain shrouded in historical ignorance even today. The unspeakable role of the courts between 1933 and 1945 has not been completely explored, and the continuity of judicial personnel and jurisdiction (e.g., the unbelievable delay of Nazi-crime prosecution, depressing judicial rulings, improper trial procedures, blindness toward the criminals in the judges' robes) is the gloomiest example of West Germany's moral culture.[81] But the generational change in the courts should also be mentioned;

---

[76] Cf. Alexander and Margarete Mitscherlich, "Ihr endet bel der destruktiven Gleichgültigkeit: Brief an einen (fiktiven) Sohn" (1977), in Duve, *Aufbrüche*, pp. 267-70.

[77] Alexander and Margarete Mitscherlich, *Die Unfähigkeit zu trauern: Gundlagen kollektiven Verhaltens* (Munich, 1968), pp. 82-83.

[78] See *"Historikerstreit"*; Reinhard Kühnl, *Vergangenheit, die nicht vergeht: Die "Historiker Debatte." Darstellung, Dokumentation, Kritic* (Cologne, 1987); Ernst Nolte, *Das Vergehen der Vergangenheit: Antwort an meine Kritiker im sogenannten Historikerstreit* (Berlin, 1987); Rolf Kosiek, *Historikerstreit und Geschichtsrevision* (Tübingen, 1987); Eike Hennig, *Zum Historikerstreit: Was heißt und zu welchem Ende studiert man Faschismus?* (Frankfurt, 1988); Hans-Ulrich Wehler, *Entsorgung der deutschen Vergangenheit? Ein polemischer Essay zum "Historikerstreit"* (Munich, 1988): Immanuel Geis, *Die Habermas Kontroverse: Eine deutscher Streit* (Berlin, 1988).

[79] [omitted]

[81] Jörg Friedrich, *Die Kalte Amnestie: NS-Täter in der Bundesrepublik* (Frankfurt, 1984); Erwin Wilkens, "Nationalsozialistische Gewaltverbrechen," in Kunst, *Evangelisches Staatslexikon*, pp. 1612-16; Turner, *Big Business*.

significant attitudinal changes are reflected by judges active in political parties, unions, and civic action groups, participating in demonstrations and in political protest (e.g., "jurists against nuclear war,") or by verdicts concerning civil disobedience, political asylum, and human rights' cases.

Regional and local or day-to-day histories of Nazism are still young branches of the discipline. Teachers, students, and local initiatives try to gather information about these dimensions of history—often meeting with the resistance of the local power elites.[82] The research on Nazi medicine and the role of research, scholars, and their victims is still limited; some of the victims—e.g., homosexuals, mentally handicapped, victims of medical experiments—wait in vain, if still alive, for at least material restitution. The extent of the postwar generations' knowledge of Nazi history varies greatly and is still incomplete. Teachers of the first postwar generation, who wished to inform students about the Nazi past and blamed their parents and grandparents, often stand in direct conflict with the second postwar generation, which asks for a more positive image of national history and therefore questions whether National Socialism was really so bad, since so many had supported the Nazis.

But there is no doubt that at least a segment of the West German society has developed a collective memory. All federal presidents and chancellors have reminded the West German public of the atrocities of the Hitler regime, and the mass media have continuously reported on that issue during the postwar decades, especially since the late 1960s. The Auschwitz trial and the Holocaust movie, aired after some political struggle, initiated long and intensive discussions. Many people were outraged at the development of the Maidanek trial, its length (1976-1981), the disrespectful behavior of the lawyers, and the final sentence. This was the last death camp trial and, as such, much more important as a historical reminder for Germans than as a punishment for the perpetrators. Yet another important contribution to the development of historical consciousness over the last years was the speech by Federal President Richard von Weizsäcker on the occasion of the 40th anniversary of the end of World War II.[83] He referred to Jaspers' guilt concept, emphasizing the Germans' need to continue the discussion of individual moral guilt and to accept history as the basis of national identity and lasting German responsibility.

Although only a minority of the West Germans may have developed a moral consciousness, and most of them may still have an incomplete historical consciousness, younger Germans have been especially involved in reconciliation activities, motivated by moral obligations, historical reflections, or simply "bad conscience." In spite of all negative experiences pertaining to attitudes and behavior toward minorities in (West) Germany, there seems to be an increased awareness of minority rights and needs....

---

[82] Cf. high school competition of 1982 "Alltag im Nationalsozialismus" of the Hamburg based Körber Foundation; for instance, Anja Rosmus-Wenninger, *Widerstand und Verfolgung: Am Beispiel Passaus* (Passau, 1983).

[83] Richard von Weizsäcker, *Zum 40. Jahrestag des Krieges in Europa und der Nationalsozialistischen Gewaltherrschaft* (Ansprache zum 8. Mai 1985 in der Gedenkstunde im Plenarsaal des Deutschen Bundestages [Bonn, 1985]).

The restauration of synagogues, the rebuilding of Jewish schools and cultural centers, and the foundation of the small Jewish University affiliated with Heidelberg University, which graduated students in Judaism for the first time in 1987, are some of the attempts at developing a new positive relationship, particularly with those 30,000 Jews who decided to live as German Jews in Germany again.

Coping with the past after Hitler and the Nazis, after genocide and total war, could only be a sum of more or less successful attempts. A great majority of West Germans have accepted political guilt and have tried to come to terms with it by developing a democratic political culture.... Some West Germans tried to accept individual moral guilt and to renew the moral and spiritual platform of the (West) German society. The result of these attempts at reconciliation with the past are mixed.

2

FRANCE

EDITOR'S INTRODUCTION

In June 1940, the French government evacuated Paris to escape the advancing German army. Marshall Philippe Pétain, a World War I military hero, became prime minister and immediately signed an armistice agreement. Pétain's government established its capital in the city in Vichy. Increasingly, this government cooperated with—and at times surpassed—Nazi directives, enacting nearly sixty discriminatory laws and interning, torturing, or deporting hundreds of thousands of Jews, Communists, resistance members, Spanish exiles, and others.

The legitimacy and popularity of the Vichy government was relatively widespread at first, partly because it kept France out of World War II and maintained the existence of the French Empire. General Charles de Gaulle established an opposition movement in exile, but relatively few left France to join. A variety of anti-Vichy resistance groups did gradually organize within France, culminating in the establishment of the umbrella Counseil National de la Résistance (CNR). In November 1942, the Allies liberated the French territory of Algeria, which soon became the headquarters for de Gaulle and his Free French movement. On June 3, 1943, General de Gaulle formed the Comité Français de Libération National, which then became the Provisional Government of the French Republic.

France was liberated in December 1944. The punishment of those who collaborated with the Pétain government, however, began more than a year earlier. By mid-December 1943, over 550 individuals were interned in Algeria for collaboration with Vichy or related criminal acts. During the period shortly before and after the liberation of France, many resistance groups carried out their own purges, which included mass arrests, the shaving of heads of women accused of sexual relations with Germans, and summary executions. In the area surrounding Toulouse in southern France, for example, over 650 individuals were summarily executed, the majority of these before liberation. The resistance also conducted underground courts-martial and established an ad hoc court system to try collaborators.

This ad hoc approach was soon replaced by a more orderly system of purges and prosecutions which extended through most sectors of French society. As noted by Roy Macridis in the overview which follows, taking into account the unofficial as well as the legal action, more than 400,000 people were affected by the "Great Purge" in postwar France.

Nearly fifty years after the liberation of France, the problems of the purge still persist. A Committee of Children of the Deported was established in 1978 and has pressed for public access to still-sealed government files from that period—many of which are not scheduled to be available until at least the year 2000—and for the prosecution of war crimes. In late 1992, documents were smuggled out of the French National Archives and published in many newspapers revealing extensive French governmental participation in the internment of hundreds of thousands in France during World War II and in the round-up and deportation of 75,000 French Jews to Nazi death camps.

Following his extradition from Bolivia, Klaus Barbie, former Gestapo chief of Lyon, was tried in 1987 on charges of crimes against humanity and sentenced to life in prison. The trial, which received extensive media coverage, renewed debate regarding collaboration and resistance during wartime France. Paul Touvier, the former chief of military intelligence in Lyon, was sentenced to death after the war, went into hiding, and was pardoned in 1971 by President Pompidou, who urged the French people to "forget the time when they did not like each other." In March 1994, a new trial began of Touvier for crimes against humanity. Criminal cases against a handful of other significant Vichy officials are still under investigation.

OVERVIEW

*Roy C. Macridis, "France: From Vichy to the Fourth Republic"**

The Resistance, comprised of various groups within France and, by the end of 1942, virtually all French forces and territories outside the metropolis under de Gaulle, seemed to agree about the necessity of (1) doing away with every institutional aspect of the Vichy regime, of purging all those who worked *for* it and even *under* it;... (2) not only of preventing a return to the institutional arrangements of the Third Republic but of fashioning a *new* one. The Resistance, it is important to bear in mind, was as much *against* Vichy as it was *against* the Third Republic; (3) acquiring political power by wresting it from both the Vichy officials and cadres and from the political, business and financial elites of the Third Republic.

The "epuration"—the purges—can in fact be studied and interpreted not only as a power struggle pitting the Resistance as a whole against both Vichy and the Third Republic, but also as a power struggle that pitted Resistance groups (especially Gaullists and Communists) against each other.

The overall objectives of the Resistance groups were (a) social revolution involving the overhaul of economic and social structures ranging from drastic and revolutionary (Communists and their allies) to comprehensive (Gaullists and some of their allies) to moderate (other groups); (b) political overhaul to pave the way for a "people's democracy" (Communists and some of their allies) or for the restoration of a republic based on central authority of the state under strong executive leadership and the achievement of fundamental structural reforms—political and economic (Gaullists and their allies).... The implementation of the purge followed the logic of the political struggle.... Even when there was agreement about whom, what and how to purge, it often amounted to only a tactical and temporary agreement about the necessity to achieve different political and social goals....

[Distinguishing Qualities]

Without a careful comparison with "liberations" in other countries and the manner in which self-generated or imposed Nazi types of regimes were purged, we cannot say with certainty what was peculiar to or different about the French situation and purge.

The following list encompasses what appears to me to be germane to France.

1. Until 1942 (November 11) there was an occupied as well as an unoccupied part of France under the Vichy regime.... The nonoccupied part enjoyed internal sovereignty and in the beginning had considerable freedom

---

* Excerpted from Roy C. Macridis, "France: From Vichy to the Fourth Republic," in John H. Herz, ed., *From Dictatorship to Democracy: Coping with the Legacies of Authoritarianism and Totalitarianism*, Copyright © by John Herz (Greenwood Press, 1982), pp. 161-169, 172, 176-177, an imprint of Greenwood Publishing Group, Inc. Westport, CT. Reprinted with permission.

in its foreign policy in accordance with the decision reached at the Montoire meeting between Hitler and Petain.... As Paxton has argued, Vichy emerged as a genuine French product that was to continue for some time.[1]

2. Support for Vichy was widespread at first. It weakened somewhat with the outbreak of the Nazi-Soviet war, when French Communists retreated from their stance and discovered that Germany was the enemy of democracy and socialism. Public support began to decrease rapidly after November 11, 1942.... But the original strong support for Vichy led many to participate in what was a genuine French government.

3. If Vichy was a genuine product—a sovereign regime at least until 1942—so was the Resistance abroad. None of the exile groups from the other "occupied" countries developed what they claimed to be—"governments" controlling jurisdiction, manpower, and supply in substantial territories. The Gaullists had the time to prepare their plans, develop their organization and ultimately bring force to bear. There was no Resistance movement representing any other European country whose national forces in exile were so strong and so independent for so long before the Liberation that at some time or other, they made use of their own territory in order to impose their presence and eventually control the metropolis.

4. The importance of Petain as a symbolic figure should not be underestimated. No other Quisling regime was led by a person whom many French considered the most heroic figure of the nation—age, peasant virtues, military glory—all combined to make him venerable and anodyne. He symbolized a kind of France that many longed for.

5. To the extent that Vichy was a homemade product, many identified with it, "bet on it" or hedged their bets. To that extent the reprisals taken against Vichy can be considered drastic.[2]

[Legitimacy of Vichy]

On July 10, 1940, Petain was given the requisite votes to issue a new constitution: "The National Assembly ... gives all powers to the *Government of the Republic*, under the authority and the signature of Marshal Petain to promulgate through one or more laws a new constitution *of the French State*. It should guarantee the rights of the family, labor, and the nation. It will be ratified *by the nation* and will be applied by the assemblies that will be established."...

The legitimacy of the Vichy regime was widespread at first. It protected French interests; it kept France out of the war, it maintained by and large the integrity of the empire.... Petain personified "the state," and

---

1 Robert O. Paxton, *Vichy France: Old Guard and New Order 1940-1944* (New York, 1962).

2 There is no study of the intensity of the purge in psychological terms. Petain, Vichy, and "collaborationism" became in a sense scapegoats to relieve the French of their own guilt. In 1944 everybody, except some diehard ideologues or paid mercenaries, claimed to be a "resistant" looking for "collabos" everywhere only because they could not bear to look at themselves in the mirror.

in this sense his legitimacy was great among the "corps constitués": army, civil service, judiciary, prefects, mayors and others. Few failed to take the oath of allegiance; few defected to de Gaulle. Only a handful collaborated with the British. Petain symbolized legitimacy in his person and legality in the manner in which he had come to power. He, more than anyone else at the time, including de Gaulle, was a historic person with whom France could be identified. The Communists at first preached cooperation with the Germans and hence with the marshal.

Finally, de Gaulle and his Free French in a curious way legitimized the Vichy regime. The general and his forces provided a safety valve for Vichy. De Gaulle *offered an alternative,* which provided, unwittingly to be sure, a rationale for *attentisme,* or *opportunism,* or sitting on the fence. De Gaulle and Petain, it was argued, were *both* serving France. If Germany won, France would have some kind of place in the new order; if the British and later the "Anglo Saxons" and the Russians won ... well ... de Gaulle might share the fruits of victory.[5] Attentisme declined gradually after November 1942. So did support for the Vichy regime....

The "Anti-Vichy" State

The setting up of the "anti-Vichy" state within territories under the jurisdiction of Vichy began with the establishment of the Gaullist Free French movement in London and its implantation in Tchad and in Equatorial Africa in 1940; in France proper only after the entry of the Soviet Union into the war and the subsequent establishment of the National Liberation Committee. The two movements, seemingly separate at first, began to coordinate their efforts without ever reaching a common direction. Without the support of the metropolitan Resistance, de Gaulle lacked legitimacy; without de Gaulle, the metropolitan Resistance overwhelmingly dominated by the Communists, lacked political credibility and reliability....

In France beginning in June 1941 an organization of various Resistance groups—Combat, Libération, Franc-Tireurs, Organisation Civile et Militaire, and so on—was formed. Only in February 1943 did their Committee of Coordination become the *Conseil National de la Résistance*—comprised of the leaders of the various Resistance movements, the trade unions, the political parties, including the French Communist party, hostile to Vichy.

De Gaulle returned to Algiers on May 29, 1943, to form a new *Committee of National Liberation....* [T]he organization of the "anti-Vichy state" moved forward rapidly, and there developed a convergence and a coordination of the Gaullist and metropolitan Resistance.

On November 3, 1943, a Provisional Consultative Assembly was organized in Algiers. It consisted of 102 members from the "metropolitan Resistance" designated by the Conseil National de la Résistance (CNR); 21 from the extrametropolitan Resistance also selected by the CNR; 20 from

---

[5] The point is forcefully made by Robert Aron in *Histoire de la Libération* (Paris, 1962).

the parliamentarians: 5 Socialists, 5 Radicals, 3 Communists, and 7 from the center-right; and 12 local and municipal representatives. By the end of the year the structure of the anti-Vichy state had begun to emerge....

The Committee of National Liberation became the supreme authority of the "anti-Vichy" state. It was (a) the central French political organization and "government"; (b) in charge of the war effort on behalf of France; (c) the custodian of sovereignty everywhere outside the areas under the control of the enemy; (d) empowered to conduct foreign policy and to enter into treaties and agreements; (e) authorized to exercise its functions until the liberation of the national territory when in conformity with the laws of the republic, a provisional government would be instituted....

[Through a series of ordonnances issued between January and April 1944,] French territory was provisionally divided into "regional commissariats" (corresponding to regional prefects). The regional "commissaire" was composed of the representatives of the central authority who were appointed by decree. They constituted a provisional administrative corps and could be removed at any time by the central authority (the Ministry of the Interior). They were responsible for administering the territory, *for reestablishing republican legality*, and for providing for the security of the French and allied forces. Under certain circumstances they were empowered to (a) suspend all laws in force; (b) take all decisions to maintain order and so on; (c) remove all elected or appointed officials and replace them with interim appointments; (d) freeze all private accounts.

...For every liberated territory, a representative of the National Liberation Committee was empowered to exercise all administrative and regulatory powers on behalf of the committee.... [U]ntil a constitutional assembly could be convened, the municipal councils elected and in operation prior to September 1, 1939, were to be reconstituted.[6] All assemblies nominated by the "usurper" or created after September 1, 1939, were to be dissolved. Also, mayors and municipal councilors who cooperated with the usurper were to be dismissed.

In each department immediately after the Liberation, a "department Committee of Liberation" was to be established to assist the prefect. It was to consist of representatives of the Resistance organization, trade union organizations, and political parties directly affiliated with the CNR....

These then were the major political and military prescriptions and organizations:

1. The mandatory removal of all appointed or elected officials of government under Vichy—indeed, since September 1, 1939.

2. Detailed procedures were issued for the replacement of all governmental officials.

3. The growth—on paper—of the anti-Vichy state was gradual and comprehensive; it was comprised of the Resistance in the metropolis,

---

6 The Communist party was outlawed on September 26, 1939. See Jacques Fauvet, *Histoire du Parti Communiste Français* (Paris, 1964).

outside the metropolis, in the empire, and, of course, Gaullist organizations.

4. The National Committee of Resistance exercised the greatest weight in the appointment of local committees and departmental Committees of Liberation and in the Consultative Provisional Assembly. Through the *Commissaires de la République* and the civil and military representatives of the Committee of National Liberation, the "central authority" (de Gaulle) maintained a dominant position and an overall direction. The center was secure; the base remained politically explosive.

5. Political parties were represented within the Consultative Assembly. Virtually all parties under the Third Republic (except the parties that openly professed collaboration with the Nazis or Vichy) were given return tickets, but not the deputies who had voted for Petain on July 10, 1940.

6. Participation of the people in the fashioning of the new republican institutions was assured and enlarged by guaranteeing to women the right to vote.

The framework for dismantling and replacing "Vichy" was meticulously constructed, exceeding the preparations made by any other "Resistance movement" that I know of.

The Dismantling—The Great Purge

The dismantling of Vichy occurred by a process of physical elimination; dismissals and exclusion; the forfeiture of property and civil rights; nationalizations and state takeover of economic activities; judicial trial and sanctions. It affected individuals and "personnes morales," that is, associations and organizations. The major effort was made between June 1944 and the end of 1945. The major purge was completed by January 20, 1946, when de Gaulle left office. All—or virtually all—major legislative enactments were incorporated in "ordonnances" issued by the provisional government of General de Gaulle. It was a "big purge" that affected virtually every level of French society and every aspect of social and political life and every one of its institutions from the church to the Académie Française and from the press, the army, and the parliament to the schools, entertainment, sports, and so on.

The purge varied in intensity from one region to another and from month to month. The latter half of 1944 was the year of paroxysm—the year of the "insurrection." According to Robert Aron, during that year alone 40,000 French were killed by other French and about 150,000 were interned.... Aron estimates that aside from those who appeared before the High Court, the number of people exposed to the judicial procedures described above was close to 200,000. In addition, about 150,000 were interned for indeterminate periods of time—one to three years; at least 40,000 were assassinated or summarily executed. More than 7,000 death sentences were pronounced, and there were about 800 executions; 13,000 were sentenced to forced labor—2,750 for life. Precisely how many lost part or the whole of their property is not known. But internment, summary justice, military courts, and judicial courts accounted for about 350,000 "cases." Including assassination and summary executions of around 40,000, more than 400,000 Frenchmen were affected.[11] If their families are included, it is reasonable to say that a minimum of one and a half million persons were directly affected....

The purges accomplished at least two major objectives: (a) they seriously weakened the political class and discredited the political parties of the Third Republic (except the Communists and in part the Socialists); (b) they made room for new groups and new parties to occupy and move in—physically and politically. Only incidentally and by a process of negation did the purges reaffirm republican legality and legitimacy. A positive formulation and institutionalization of the new republic remained to be decided.

The purges of the press and the nationalization of key economic sectors struck another blow against the elites of the Third Republic in two of the most sensitive and central areas through which they had held and exercised power. The purges ushered in a new press with new men and women in charge and opened the doors to new recruits..., who affected the overall administration of the state. The same pattern of replacing high-ranking officers characterized the purged military corps.

Although the removal of the old elites had been sought jointly by *Gaullists and Communists*, their replacement was in effect controlled by de Gaulle. He was able to keep the commanding heights of the economy, the army, the police, the judiciary, and the administration away from the Communists. But he was unable to revise the republican constitution along the lines he advocated; the Communists did not succeed either. De Gaulle advocated a system that would have prescribed the independence of the executive branch and the state apparatus from the parliament and the parties. The Communists in essence favored a system that would have subordinated the state apparatus and even the parliament to the parties and to grass-roots committees. The proponents of a technocratic state clashed with the advocates of Communist populism under the leadership of an avant-garde party.... In retrospect, the Fourth Republic was a standoff between the Communist-led and the Gaullist-led Resistance forces in their struggle to take power and shape the new institutions.

The forces that had supported Vichy in alliance with many notables of the Third Republic rallied a number of times. As modernization accelerated and the war in Indochina came to an end, the "third force" began to disintegrate. The political forces that had supported Vichy attempted to make a comeback in 1956 by using the electoral showing of Pierre Poujade; between 1956 and 1958, when the war in Algeria intensified; by using the army in Algeria and a number of veterans organizations and the Independents. The spirit of Vichy came to an end in 1958—some say even as late as 1961 when de Gaulle put down the military uprising in

---

11 The vast majority were men—the "collaboration horizontale" varied in punishment depending on whether it was "pour le commerce" or for other more or less insidious reasons.

Algeria and proceeded to grant it independence on July 5, 1962. It was only then that the Gaullist "Resistance" and the Gaullist movement gained control of the state.

*Herbert R. Lottman, "The Purge: The Purification of French Collaborators After World War II"**

The punishment of persons known or suspected to have assisted the enemy is known as *épuration*, which can be translated as purge, or purification.... In recent years the postwar purge has had a bad press. Few Frenchmen now admit to personal experience of it. In the immediate postwar years some of the purged and their advocates published accounts of their ordeal (often privately printed). But the people who did the purging seldom wrote about their achievement, and official records have been secret until now. Some persons made it a point of honor not to speak of what they had seen or what they had done, while others apparently feared to admit participation in field courts martial, summary executions, and similar acts located in a twilight zone between legal and illegal.... Certainly this process of forgetting was helped along by successive amnesty laws. So that most of what we can know about the purge comes from those who felt themselves to be its victims. Necessarily the picture is one-sided.

...In the decade following the liberation the purge was often compared to the reign of terror during the French Revolution, and its excesses were described as atrocities of the sort usually attributed to the enemy in wartime. In one of these accounts a husband is killed, his wife is raped and then murdered, together with their eleven-year-old son (so that he cannot serve as a witness). A bound man is forced to look on while his virgin daughter is raped a dozen times.[6]... Torture often precedes execution in these accounts—e.g., an accused collaborator is stabbed in the eyes, his genitals are torn off, or he is made to lie on a bed of burning sawdust.[8]... Sex and sadism are combined in many hostile accounts of the purge.... Collaborators are forced to walk barefoot in a pit filled with broken glass, while the women among them must strip naked to serve their captors, and some are made to copulate with animals.[12] We are also told of women who help commit these atrocities—e.g., in the mountainous Auvergne region, two resistance women punish collaborators while dressed only in brassieres and panties.[13]...

Women shorn of their hair: This seems to have been the first act of purging nearly everywhere; it accompanies arrests, shootings, sometimes replaces them.... During the occupation some young and older women had been seen in the company of German soldiers; young women also took part in

---

* Excerpted from Herbert R. Lottman, *The Purge: The Purification of French Collaborators After World War II* (William Morrow and Company, Inc., 1986), pp. 15-17, 66-68. Copyright © 1986 by Herbert R. Lottman. By Permission of William Morrow & Company, Inc.

6 Maurice Bardèche, *Lettre à François Mauriac* (Paris, 1947), 111.

8 Jean Pleyber, "Les Travaux et les Jours," *Ecrits de Paris* (Paris), June 1950.

12 *Ecrits de Paris*, June 1952.

13 *Ibid.*, February 1951.

Militia activities. They could serve as informers against the resistance, against young men who refused compulsory labor in Germany—just as easily as men could. Some women appeared well fed, well dressed, flaunting and occasionally boasting of their liaisons with occupation soldiers or privileged collaborators. When liberation came, revenge was in the cards.... [One] writer describes a scene in flag-draped Libourne at the hour of liberation accompanied by rousing Patriotic songs. A summary court is set up at the town hall, where a prostitute denies having "fooled around" with Germans. "Her hair is sheared off all the same; she is stripped naked and forced to run to the pedestal which supported the statue of the first duke Decazes, a statue which the Germans removed to melt down the bronze." She is raised to the duke's place, to be jeered by assembled townspeople.[21]

Was there a national directive to shear the heads of female collaborators? Apparently not, and yet the act was carried out in every corner of France.... [A] *Sunday Express* correspondent speaking on the BBC French program described the scene at Nogent-le-Rotrou, on the road to Chartres, where he found three thousand people on the town square looking on as sixteen women, aged from twenty to sixty, were lined up to be shorn. As each rose from the barber's chair with a shaved head the crowd laughed, booed.... The correspondent concluded with a description of the bathing of these women in a tub before they were paraded through the streets....[22]

If shorn and stripped women served as expiatory objects, they had another and perhaps more immediately useful function: to sop up the anger that would otherwise have ended with bloodshed. At least one participant in the liberation fighting sensed this: Father Roger More, chaplain and member of the FTP resistance in the Savoie. When informed that some young women had been arrested and were to be sheared he told his partisans: "Let them do it." He felt that by allowing the shearing they'd be providing a firebreak—energies would be diverted from killing. "For a long time after that," he would later say, "women wearing turbans would no longer say hello to me. But blood didn't flow."[23] The scars lasted. Nearly four decades after the fact, in 1983, a woman was discovered living as a recluse in a town in the Auvergne. She had avoided public contact ever since her shearing at the liberation, hadn't been seen at all for thirty years, and had gradually sunk into madness.[24]

---

21 Jacques Chastenet, *Quatre fois vingt ans* (Paris, 1974), 368.

22 James Wellard, in *Voix de la Liberté*, V, 191f.

23 Abbé Roger More, *Totor chez les FTP* (Chambéry, 1974), 120ff. A similar conclusion is proposed by Peter Novick, *The Resistance Versus Vichy* (New York, 1968), 69.

24 *Le Monde* (Paris), October 22, 1983.

THE INITIAL PHASE

Herbert R. Lottman, "The Purge: The Purification of French Collaborators After World War II"[*]

As part of the Gaullist effort to coordinate mainland discussions, a Committee of Experts was created in Lyon in 1942, which soon took a more formal title, Comité Général d'Etudes (CGE)—literally, General Committee of Studies. Its mission was triple: to prepare immediate measures to be carried out when the Gaullists replaced the retreating Germans and Vichy; to suggest general policies for the new regime; finally, to draw up a list of persons to be appointed to key posts in postwar France.... Early in 1943 it made contact with Maurice Rolland, then thirty-nine, deputy prosecutor for Paris: Would he draw up, for the committee, a study of the judicial consequences of liberation?...

In their study of the purge to come the Rolland group paid particular attention to procedure. Collaboration, they felt, was a form of collusion with the enemy—a crime already covered by the penal code. Still, they recognized that some acts committed by collaborators were not crimes strictly speaking; for such acts a lesser sanction had to be found. They came up with the notion of *indignité nationale*—literally, unworthiness, to be punished by a range of sanctions including deprivation of civil rights and professional status.

Algiers

Charles De Gaulle had rallied the Free French around him from a base in London. But after the Allied takeover of North Africa in November 1942 the Gaullists were able to make their home on a parcel of liberated French territory. De Gaulle himself arrived in Algiers on May 30, 1943, and on June 3 the Comité Français de Libération Nationale (CFLN[†]) was founded; a year later it became the Provisional Government of the French Republic....

Before the year ended the Gaullists had unveiled an impressive arsenal of measures to be ready for liberation day.... In August the Gaullists established a purge commission to investigate elected officials and civil servants; it could also deal with lawyers, doctors, and those in press or radio work who had been involved with censorship.... In October 1943 the Gaullists issued a decree on another thorny subject which would have to be faced soon enough:... financial collaboration.... A number of these early purge measures could be applied at once, for as has been noted, some of those who had served Vichy were now within reach. Indeed, the purge of the administration of French Algeria after the November 1942 Allied takeover

---

[*] Excerpted from Herbert R. Lottman, *The Purge: The Purification of French Collaborators After World War II* (William Morrow and Company, Inc., 1986), pp. 41, 44-48. Copyright © 1986 by Herbert R. Lottman. By Permission of William Morrow & Company, Inc.

[†] [Editor's note: This committee is referred to in other excerpts in this chapter as the "CLN;" it is the same entity.]

had been severe.... A similar purge at the top was carried out in the neighboring protectorates of Tunisia and Morocco.[8]...

But of course the chief concern of the Free French was their nation across the Mediterranean, now and at the hour of liberation.... The decree containing the essence of the judicial purge was signed on June 26, 1944. A preamble circulated by the Justice Commissariat but not published argued that the Vichy government was not legitimate, and thus its orders did not excuse acts of collaboration. Crimes to be punished were those already defined in existing legislation; no new crime would be created. The only retroactivity would be in the direction of "benevolence and justice," since courts would be able to attenuate penalties. Finally, because there simply weren't enough courts for all the cases that would have to be heard, new courts would have to be set up so that justice could be meted out rapidly, "so that the Nation can proceed calmly to heal its wounds and rebuild".[11]...

In the view of the Gaullists, then, the key to the purge was to be found in existing legislation. This meant reference to a series of decrees issued by the Edouard Daladier government in July 1939 on the eve of the war, designated as Articles 75 to 83 of the penal code. Article 75, the principal authority for the trials to come, defined as a traitor punishable by death

> Any French person who bears arms against France;
> Any French person who engages in collusion with a foreign power for the purpose of encouraging it to wage war against France....
> Any French person who, in time of war, engages in collusion with a foreign power or with its agents for the purpose of assisting the acts of this power against France.

...Formal debate on the purge was scheduled by the Consultative Assembly for January 11, 1944. And it was lively. Communist delegate Fernand Grenier offered the example of a successful purge: the execution of a prosecuting attorney on mainland France three days after he had sent patriots to the guillotine.... Remembering these things later, de Gaulle [wrote] ... that the state of mind revealed by the Assembly debates had made it clear to him that it was not going to be easy, after the liberation of mainland France, "to contain vengeance and to leave it to justice to decide punishment."[15]

---

8 AN BB 30 1730.

11 AN BB 30 1729.

15 De Gaulle, *Mémoires de Guerre*, II, 155.

*Peter Novick, "The Resistance Versus Vichy: The Purge of Collaborators in Liberated France"**

[Retribution and Ad Hoc Justice]

[Before the liberation of France, the] principal agency upon which De Gaulle relied for the establishment of his authority and the maintenance of order was a new corps of "commissaires de la République"—eighteen "super-prefects", each with the responsibility for the administration of a region. These *commissaires*—together with the departmental prefects under them—were nominated by a special C.F.L.N. commission inside occupied France which acted on the advice of the metropolitan Resistance.... Among their duties, none was more important than the orderly management of the purge. Their enumerated tasks included the removal of compromised officials and the arrest of suspects. If it appeared desirable, they could organize courts martial to try collaborators. All of this, however, was to be accomplished in an orderly fashion. They were to bear in mind that the public was "just as anxious to see life return to its normal course as to see that traitors were punished"; they were reminded that "prolonged disorder would not only constitute a temptation for the Allied armies [to set up a military government] but would diminish the authority of the C.F.L.N. and compromise [the nation's] rebirth".[12]...

The arrogation of state authority by the Resistance was most frequently seen—and most tragic in its consequences—with respect to the purge. There were understandable reasons for this. The instructions of the C.N.R. to the C.D.L.'s [Comités Départmentaux de Libération], while stressing the importance of avoiding injustice due to hasty action, assigned these committees an important role in dealing with collaborators: this role frequently overlapped that of the [commissaires].[22]... [T]he habit learned in the underground days of personally settling accounts with collaborators and *miliciens* was not readily set aside after the Liberation.

At least four and a half thousand summary executions took place in France in the months following the Liberation.[23] The geographic incidence of summary executions is not known with any precision, but appears to have been very uneven.... Sometimes the executions followed drum-head trials [with even less a semblance of due process that the courts martial later established by the regional commissaires] which were held discreetly

---

* Excerpted from Peter Novick, *The Resistance Versus Vichy: The Purge of Collaborators in Liberated France* (Columbia University Press, 1968), pp. 65-66, 71-72,

[12] "Circulaire du Délégué Général du C.F.L.N." [May 9, 1944], reprinted in *Les Cahiers Politiques*, No.18 (February-March 1946), 23-26; cf. Commissariat àla Justice, *Instructions* (Algiers: 1944), pp. 5, 20-21. An insistence on orderly procedures was the invariable leitmotif of all Government instructions concerning the purge....

[22] *Cahiers du Témoignage Chrétien*, Vols. XXVI-XXVII (May 1944); Hostache, pp. 300, 465-70; Michel, *Courants*, pp. 335-37; United States, Office of Strategic Services, *Resolutions of the French National Council of Resistance* (Washington: 1944), pp. 51-53.

[23] [omitted]

(*pour éviter le spectacle*) but whose results were posted publicly afterwards.... (According to Government estimates, roughly one-quarter of the post-Liberation summary executions were preceded by a *de facto* trial.[26]) Sometimes a *milicien* was simply shot out of hand when his identity was discovered.... [M]any executions seem to have been committed for private gain; criminal elements sometimes infiltrated the F.F.I. or masqueraded as *résistants* to cover their lootings and murders. In other cases, partisan political advantage or revenge seems to have been the motive for assassinations. Most executions, however, were the result of either spontaneous and uncontrollable outrage, or frustration at the slowness of official justice.

*Herbert R. Lottman, "The Purge: The Purification of French Collaborators After World War II"**

On the grounds that the existing court system on the mainland had collaborated with Vichy, and because the Courts of Justice conceived by the Provisional Government to carry out the purge were not yet in place,... [c]ourts martial sprouted.... [A]s soon as it was securely established the Gaullist government did what it could to shut down these improvised courts, and to transfer defendants to the jurisdiction of the Courts of Justice. But ... in many ways courts martial composed of recognized officers of the FFI were an improvement over the revolutionary people's tribunals which had been created in a number of liberated towns. As they took power, the Regional Commissioners of the Republic often closed down these people's tribunals—and set up courts martial in their place.[1]...

A year later few Frenchmen would have accepted the quality of justice dealt out in the summer of 1944. But there were other questions to be asked. For example, would the collaborators handled so expeditiously by these courts have survived, in the absence of these courts, to stand trial in more tranquil jurisdictions?... "It is important ... to avoid letting the mob carry out its own justice on the pretext that legal justice isn't ready," explained Henry Ingrand, Commissioner of the Republic of the Auvergne region, to justify the setting up of a court martial in Vichy on September 5, 1944....

While the more official judicial purge was under way Justice Minister François de Menthon confided to members of the Consultative Assembly in a secret session of its Justice and Purge Committee in May 1945 that in addition to the sixteen hundred death sentences which until then had been ordered by the Courts of Justice there had been—"but I can't publish this, especially because of foreign opinion"—some one thousand victims of summary executions during the liberation, and about a thousand others

---

[26] J.O., A.N. Debates, November 9, 1951, p. 7835.

* Excerpted from Herbert R. Lottman, *The Purge: The Purification of French Collaborators After World War II* (William Morrow and Company, Inc., 1986), pp. 69-70, 74, 123-124. Copyright © 1986 by Herbert R. Lottman. By Permission of William Morrow & Company, Inc.

[1] Foulon, *Le Pouvoir en province*, 136.

sentenced to death and executed by special tribunals, courts martial, resistance courts, during the months of September and October 1944.[14]

But then in 1951, in response to a question by Jacques Isorni, the member of parliament who led the fight for amnesty, the Justice Ministry was able to give a more precise figure, which turned out to be lower. There had been 766 death sentences ordered and carried out by liberation courts martial "set up either by civil or military authorities."[15]...

[Establishing Order]

The chief instrument for punishing collaboration was going to be the Court of Justice, that new jurisdiction conceived during underground conferences of resistance jurists in mainland France and polished up by the Free French in Algiers. However unorthodox the new court might appear to traditionalists, however much it was criticized then and later—and it was easy enough to do that—the best minds of anti-Vichy France saw the Court of Justice as an improvement over frontier justice....

Ex-professor François de Menthon ... arrived in Paris from Algiers at the beginning of September 1944 to take over the Ministry of Justice on Place Vendéme. He saw resistance courts martial as a violation of the will of the Provisional Government, and although these temporary tribunals had been favored by the Interior Ministry, at no time did he accept them as *faits accomplis*, or ratify their findings.... [I]f to avoid disorder it was necessary to call expeditious measures into play then he would have preferred military tribunals staffed by genuine military judges.[2]

One problem faced by the new men at Justice was the absence, or the inadequacy, of liaison between Paris and the provinces.... [D]e Menthon turned to Maurice Rolland, head of the resistance jurists' task force which had helped put together the purge legislation. A new job was created for Rolland: inspector general of the magistrature. During the month of September he and three colleagues divided France among them, and then went off to establish the new courts in the provinces. Their first goal was to make sure that the purge was being carried out within the ranks of court personnel, and that capable people were available to replace the judges and prosecutors who had been purged. They also had to see that officials dismissed by Vichy got their jobs back, that persons jailed by Vichy for political offenses were all free.[4]

A more immediate concern of Rolland and his team was to close down ad hoc courts. In accordance with de Menthon's feelings, they accepted military tribunals as a stopgap until Courts of Justice could be set up. Often the Paris inspectors had to negotiate with local resistance chiefs, in some cases with veritable gang leaders, to persuade them to relinquish their

---

14 Minutes, May 24, 1945. Archives of the Assemblée, Nationale, Paris.

15 *JORF*, Assemblée Nationale, November 9, 1951, 7835.

2 Talk with François de Menthon.

4 Ministère de la Justice, Inspection des Services Judiciaires: Historique. Courtesy of Maurice Rolland.

courts martial. As Rolland saw it, the liberation government had to reestablish justice before the railroads—i.e., had to set up workable courts even before other essential services were in full operation.[5]

PURGE LAWS

*Peter Novick, "The Resistance Versus Vichy: The Purge of Collaborators in Liberated France"**

Resistance determination to see collaborators in the dock had more to do with a desire for *renversement* than with a desire for *renouvellement;* it responded to the thirst for retribution on the part of men who for years had been hunted down, imprisoned, and tortured by the followers of Pétain and the agents of Germany.

But side by side with this passionate longing was the attachment of *résistants* to those principles of justice and equity which distinguished them from the rulers of Nazi Germany and Vichy France.... The decrees of the Provisional Government concerning judicial action against collaborators had to reconcile the appeals of the heart with respect for the traditions of French justice.

The principle of *nullum crimen sine lege, nulla poene sine lege,* that laws enacted after the crime which they set out to punish are worse than no laws at all, is one common to all systems of jurisprudence. It would be hard to find a principle more fundamental not only to traditional conceptions of law, but to the layman's instincts of equity. The French Revolutionary Constitution of 1793 noted that the enactment of retroactive laws was the hallmark of tyranny;... article four of the French Penal Code stated (and states) that no offense, no misdemeanor, no crime can be punished by penalties that were enacted after the act was committed.

The widespread abhorrence of retroactive legislation is rooted in the proposition that if a man knows in advance the consequences of his acts—or at least whether or not they are legal—he may legitimately be held accountable for them; if not, not. In France, the overwhelming majority of the population believed Vichy to be the legal and legitimate government of France. They might support or oppose its policies (as they supported or opposed the policies of the Third Republic), they might hold various opinions on its degree of subservience to Nazi Germany, they might even, as a matter of conscience, disobey its laws and enter into an illegal existence. But if they followed this last course there was no doubt in their minds that what they were doing *was* illegal; conversely, those who obeyed that Government's commands had no doubt that they were following the only legal road....

---

5 Talk with Maurice Rolland.

* Excerpted from Peter Novick, *The Resistance Versus Vichy: The Purge of Collaborators in Liberated France* (Columbia University Press, 1968), pp. 140-143, 145-149 © Columbia University Press, New York. Reprinted with permission of the publisher.

But the Provisional Government could not accept this picture of realty; to do so would be to renounce any punishment of the men of Vichy.... Vichy was not the legal government; it was, in the language of hundreds of ordinances, "the *de facto* authority, calling itself 'Government of the French State'", or alternatively, "the usurper". Its orders, unlike those of a legal state, did not absolve the executant of responsibility; they were to be considered only as a form of *force majeure*—a mitigating circumstance if they could not be evaded or circumvented, no excuse at all if they could.

Not only was the Vichy Regime properly speaking (from July 11, 1940, on) declared illegal by the Provisional Government in Algiers, but this illegality was extended back to the formation of the Pétain cabinet under the Third Republic (June 17)....

Despite the breadth of the existing statutes, and the desire to avoid retroactivity, there was general agreement concerning the need to "interpret" some of the provisions of the prewar Code. Accordingly, legislation was enacted by the C.F.L.N. "to facilitate the Court's interpretation of [the [prewar] texts".[6]... Even with these "interpretations", however, the Penal Code was not a completely satisfactory instrument for performing the work which had to be accomplished. Its use would at the same time punish too few and too harshly. Minor collaborators might slip through the coarse mesh of the existing laws and thus continue to play a nefarious role in French public life; also, the penalties prescribed by the Penal Code were too rigidly severe to be appropriate or practical for dealing with "*les petits*"....

The problem, in any case, was not how to swell the prison population, or exhaust the ammunition of the firing squads, but how to build a France *pure et dure*. And to do this, penal sanctions were not necessarily required; rather

> all those who by their action or propaganda either indirectly aided the enemy or worked for the establishment in France of a political order inspired by Hitlerite doctrines ... [had to be] temporarily or permanently disqualified from exercising any public function in the largest sense, from participating, in any form, in political or public life.[11]

There was virtually unanimous agreement, from the right to the left of the Resistance spectrum, on the need to introduce a new measure which would at the same time be both an instrument of *renouvellement* and a *lex mitior*—substituting a lighter penalty for the harsh sanctions of the Penal Code.

[The "State" of National Indignity]

In response to demands from the metropolitan Resistance and from the Consultative Assembly the Government, on June 26, 1944, submitted to the

---

[6] J.O., A.C.P. Debates, July 27, 1944, pp. 147-54.

[11] C.G.E. *Questionnaire*, Michel, *Courants, loc. cit.*

Assembly a "Proposed Ordinance Instituting National Indignity".[12] In language almost identical with that suggested by an underground group, the draft defined "national indignity" as the "state entered into" by one who "directly or indirectly, voluntarily aided Germany or her allies, or harmed the unity of the nation or the liberty and equality of Frenchmen".[13]

The Government did its best to avoid frankly labelling the measure as retroactive. National indignity was called not a crime, but a "state" into which one entered by the performance of listed acts; one's presence in that "state" was to be "declared"—not by a frankly judicial body, but by a "jury d'honneur". In presenting the measure to the Assembly, Justice Commissioner François de Menthon maintained that if it had been a choice between presenting a retroactive law or no law at all he would have chosen the former course, but it had not been necessary.[14]

The conception did not survive the Assembly session at which the bill was discussed. Dumesnil de Gramont, *rapporteur* of the proposal, expressed the majority sentiment:

> Unless we distort the laws and make them say what was never in the minds of their authors, it is clear that there are a great many kinds of collaboration that aren't covered at all by the laws in force on June 16, 1940.... The government ... solution lacks both clarity and frankness.
>
> We believe, together with the Committee of Jurists of the Resistance, that it would be better to admit unambiguously that national indignity is a new offense, born of the extraordinary circumstances brought about by the defeat; and therefore we believe that there should be no hesitation in giving the penalty retroactive effect.[15]

With minor modifications resulting from the Assembly's deliberations, the Ordinance instituting national indignity was promulgated on August 26. The *exposé de motifs* is frank, clear and enlightening concerning the inspiration of the enactment.

> The criminal conduct of those who collaborated with the enemy did not always take the form of a specific act for which there could be provided a specific penalty ... under a strict interpretation of the law. Frequently it has been a question of antinational activity reprehensible in itself. Moreover, the disciplinary measures by which unworthy officials could be removed from the administration

---

12 J.O., A.C.P. Documents, No. 108.

13 Cf. "Rapport reçu de France", *Cahiers Français*, No. 51 (December 1943). Albert Colombini points out that the language of the Ordinance is very close to that employed in the Law of October 29, 1793, defining the competence of the Revolutionary Tribunal. ("Le Crime d'Indignité Nationale", *Les Lois Nouvelles*, 1946, p. 3 n. 1).

14 J.O., A.C.P. Debates, July 27, pp. 147-64.

15 *Ibid*. The Government advanced various other arguments by way of denial that it was introducing retroactive legislation. The most cogent was the contention of René Cassin and others that the introduction of national indignity represented the retroactive substitution of a lighter for a heavier penalty (*lex mitior*)—a practice specifically permitted under the French Codes.

> are not applicable to other sections of society. And it is as necessary to bar certain individuals from various elective, economic, and professional positions which give their incumbents political influence, as it is to eliminate others from the ranks of the administration.
>
> Any Frenchman who, even without having violated an existing penal law, has been guilty of activity defined as antinational, has degraded himself; he is an unworthy citizen whose rights must be restricted in so far as he has failed in his duties. Such a legal discrimination between citizens may appear serious, for all discriminatory measures are repugnant to democracy. But it is not contrary to the principle of equality before the law for the nation to distinguish between good and bad citizens in order to bar from positions of leadership and influence those among the French who have rejected the ideals and the interests of France during the most grievous trial in her history.

The definition of the acts constituting unworthy conduct was both broad and specific. It included any voluntary aid to the Axis after June 16, 1940, or any willful act of what might be termed *lèse-liberté-égalité-fraternité*. Among the enumerated specific acts, performance of which would carry a presumption of guilt, were:

1. having been a member of any of Pétain's cabinets;
2. having held an executive position in either Vichy's propaganda services or in the Commissariat for Jewish Affairs;
3. having been a member, even without active participation, of collaborationist organizations;[16]
4. having helped organize meetings or demonstrations in favor of collaboration;
5. having published writings or given lectures in favor of the enemy, collaboration with the enemy, racism, or totalitarian doctrines.

Performance of any of the enumerated acts did not automatically entail national degradation for life. The court was to take into account not only the importance and frequency of the acts, but also any pressure that might have been exerted on the individual.[17] If the extenuating circumstances were found, the penalty might be inflicted for a minimum of five years. Further, the court might suspend the penalty in the case of those who, subsequent to the acts charged against them, "rehabilitated" themselves, either by military action in the war against the Axis or by participation in the Resistance.[18] Finally, the courts could (and frequently

---

[16] [omitted]

[17] This last was not contained in the original Government proposal, but was added on the recommendation of the A.C.P.: one of the rare cases in these years when the Assembly proposed the softening of a Government proposal.

[18] The original provision called for "active participation"; this was altered in the Ordinance of December 26 to "sustained and effective active participation"; a measure of self-defense against the *septembristes*.

did) simply acquit an individual despite the fact that technically he came within the scope of the Ordinance (for example, by membership in a proscribed organization).

The list of disqualifications in the original Ordinance was consistent with the aim in view: barring the unworthy from positions of leadership and political influence. Among the disqualifications were: exclusion from the franchise and from eligibility to elective office; a ban on public employment; loss of rank in the armed forces (and of the right to wear decorations); exclusion from directing functions in semi-public corporations, banks, other financial institutions, as well as the press and radio industries; exclusion from office in trade-unions and professional associations; exclusion from the legal, teaching and (the regular exercise of the) journalistic professions; exclusion from such state-connected bodies as the Institut de France; a ban on keeping or bearing arms. None of these penalties could be parcelled out, but had to be applied *en bloc*. (Violating, or aiding and abetting the violation of any of these measures, was punishable by up to five years in prison.)

There were, in addition, two discretionary measures which could be added to this list. The first, contained in the original Ordinance, was a temporary ban on residence in a given area. The second was added by a modifying ordinance of September 30: confiscation of all or a part of the property of the *indigné*. A derivative consequence of national degradation, probably unintended by those who drafted the legislation, was the loss of pension rights, since a 1924 law had stipulated that pension payments are suspended during the term of sanctions involving the loss of civic rights. For a variety of reasons, complete and permanent loss of pension rights turned out to be the exception, not the rule.[19]

These, then, the laws: an "interpreted" Penal Code for the principal offenders; national indignity for the less guilty. But the large problem remained of how these laws were to be applied: what courts and what procedures would be best?...

---

19 First, under the 1924 Law, if the individual deprived of civic rights had a wife or minor children, they received that portion of the pension which they would have received in the event of his death. Second, while the *cours* and *chambres* could not remove individual consequences of national degradation, but had to apply or suspend the penalty *en bloc*, presidential pardons (which were numerous) could be selective, and were frequently used to reinstate pension rights. Finally, amnesties with retroactive effect intervened.

NEW COURTS

*Peter Novick, "The Resistance Versus Vichy: The Purge of Collaborators in Liberated France"**

The "cours de justice", set up by the Provisional Government as France was liberated, were miniature versions of the *cours d'assises*, the traditional French tribunals for felonies. There were principal courts in each of the twenty-seven districts of the *Cour d'Appel*, subsidiary courts in each *département*—and these in turn might be divided into sub-sections as the need arose (the Paris Court had seventeen subsections). Despite their basic resemblance to the Assize Courts, there were several significant modifications in the organization and procedures of the new jurisdictions.

The *cours de justice* retained the traditional French institution of the examining magistrate (*juge d'instruction*) who conducts a personal interrogation of the accused with a view to determining whether the Government should bring him to trial or drop the case. In the new courts, however, while the examining magistrate could recommend one course of action or the other, the final decision was taken out of his hands and put in those of the state prosecutor.[26]... It was (correctly) anticipated that the mutually reinforcing factors of a purge of the magistrature and the creation of over a hundred new jurisdictions would put a serious strain on the personnel resources of the French judiciary. All sections of opinion were extremely anxious that the collaboration trials be completed as quickly as possible.... Any step which could speed up the procedure without doing substantive violence to equity was clearly desirable.

At the same time, the Government was constantly aware that cases before the courts of justice could be politically explosive. Leaving the decision on prosecution to a judiciary which many suspected of being lukewarm toward the purge would risk outbursts of popular indignation if prominent collaborators were not indicted. Placing the decision in the hands of an official of the Ministry of Justice gave the Government a valuable instrument of control....

The *cours d'assises* had been composed of three judges and twelve lay jurors. The new *cours* ... were made up of a single judge (again, the question of availability of judicial personnel was determining) and four lay jurors.... The most significant change was not, however, in the size of the jury, but in the method of its selection.... The jury panels for the Courts of Justice were to be drawn up by a Commission consisting of a superior court magistrate and two delegates from the Liberation Committee in the area. The list was to include only those men and women (this last was an innovation) "who had never ceased to demonstrate their patriotic sentiments."[27]

---

* Excerpted from Peter Novick, *The Resistance Versus Vichy: The Purge of Collaborators in Liberated France* (Columbia University Press, 1968), pp. 151-156, © Columbia University Press, New York. Reprinted with permission of the publisher.

26 [omitted]

27 This of course implied that they should be, if not *résistants*, at least Resistance sympathizers. However, in addition to the traditional exclusion from juries of those whose

No feature of the new court system came in for more sustained or more bitter criticism. The more moderate critics observed that :

> the jurors thus designated were résistants, called to judge adversaries of the resistance. They were usually persons of good faith. But what impartiality could the accused expect from a deportee who had returned from Buchenwald or from a mother whose son had been shot by the *milice*?[28]

Many, however, went further. "Because of the manner of their composition, the juries ceased to be a guarantee of impartiality in favor of the accused, and became an infallible instrument of partisan vengeance."[29]...

In any event, these were the juries that deliberated on, these were the courts which judged, the cases of well over 100,000 Frenchmen. (The Courts which heard accusations of national indignity—called *chambres civiques*—were attached to them, and shared their organization and procedures in virtually every respect.[31])

The Ordinance of June 26, 1944, had established the jurisdictions competent to deal with collaboration, but had made no special provision for the trials of Pétain and his ministers.... [T]he trials of these men were intended to be the symbol of their rejection by the nation, and thus it was finally decided that a "High Court", which would symbolically represent the nation, would be preferable.... This new jurisdiction, the "Haute Cour de Justice", was established by the Ordinance of November 18, 1944. It had jurisdiction over the *chef d'Etat* (Pétain), the *chef du Gouvernement* (Laval), plus all cabinet and sub-cabinet officers and colonial governors who had participated in the "governments or pseudo-governments" sitting in France between June 17, 1940, and the Liberation....

The court was to be composed of twenty-seven members: three jurists who would preside, and twenty-four jurors chosen by the Consultative

---

personal relations with the accused might carry the presumption of impartiality either way, the Ordinances provided that no one could be a judge or juror in a given case who had previously dealt with the case as a participant in a "Resistance Tribunal."

28 Charpentier, *Au service*, p. 259.

29 Louis Rougier, "La France est-elle un Etat de Droit?" *Escrits de Paris*, February 1950, 87....

31 The name of the *chambres civiques*, but not their attributes, underwent two modifications during 1944. Called "jurys d'honneur" in the original Government bill submitted to the Assembly, they were changed to "sections speciales" (of the *cours de justice*) in the Ordinance of August 26, 1944. A month later, because of the unfortunate connotations of this phrase (it had been the name given by Vichy to extraordinary repressive tribunals), the name was changed to "chambres civiques", which they retained throughout their life. One minor difference between their procedure and that of the *cours de justice* was that they could receive cases not only from the government prosecutor, but also directly from the C.D.L.'s. The *chambres civiques* were not the only bodies which could sentence an individual to national degradation. While the *cours de justice* and the *Haute Cour* only heard cases in which the defendant was charged with a penal offense, national degradation was always automatically added to whatever penal sanctions they handed down. Even if a man appearing before one of these jurisdictions was found innocent of the penal offenses with which he was charged, he might be found guilty of national indignity and sentenced to national degradation.

Assembly. The Assembly was to draw up two lists: one of fifty senators and deputies holding office on September 1, 1939; the other of fifty men who had not been legislators at that time. Twelve names were to be chosen by lot from each list in order to make up a jury. The court's *commission d'instruction* was similarly mixed: five professional judges and six men chosen by the Assembly. The court thus constituted was to be completely sovereign. It could assign whatever penalty it wished—from death to national degradation—to any crime. There was no provision for appeal. (Presidential pardons were, however, applicable to High Court verdicts.) And, breaking with normal French procedure, verdicts pronounced *in absentia* were to be executed without a retrial.

*Herbert R. Lottman, "The Purge: The Purification of French Collaborators After World War II"**

These Courts of Justice satisfied no one. For strict legalists, the selection of jurors seemed shocking. Jurors were to be endorsed by resistance groups, so of course they would be resistance veterans who might themselves have suffered at the hands of the collaborators they were trying.[24] To that objection Pierre-Henri Teitgen, who replaced François de Menthon at Justice, replied that in any case collaboration "left none of us indifferent."[25]...

For the Communists [and Socialists], debating the issue in the Justice and Purge Committee of the Provisional Consultative Assembly ... justice seemed to be dragging its feet, while the guiltiest offenders weren't being touched. This was at the beginning of December 1944, and Minister de Menthon had to plead the material difficulties of getting the new courts underway.[26] They were dealing with a new kind of crime for which the previous experience of judges had not prepared them. And the number of cases they had to handle—over three hundred thousand were submitted to the liberation courts—was unprecedented. The continuing shortage of qualified personnel exacerbated the difficulties. In the end it would prove impossible to prepare cases against many of those who had been arrested, indicted, and brought into court.[27]...

But before the new courts had been in operation for more than a few weeks it became obvious that the very rules which had set them up were slowing them down. And dangerously, for the appeals procedure was cumbersome, creating a bottleneck at the top, while in the provinces impatient citizens demanded that justice be done.... Late in November 1944 Minister de Menthon called in his staff director, Zambeaux, who had been

---

* Excerpted from Herbert R. Lottman, *The Purge: The Purification of French Collaborators After World War II* (William Morrow and Company, Inc., 1986), pp. 129, 130-132. Copyright © 1986 by Herbert R. Lottman. By Permission of William Morrow & Company, Inc.

24 Garçon, *Code Pénal annoté*, 268.

25 Teitgen, *Le Cours de Justice*, 29.

26 Minutes of Commission de la Justice et de l'Epuration, November 24, December 1, 1944. Archives of the Assemblée Nationale.

27 Jean Bracquemond, "Intervention," *Libération de la France*, 803; Garçon, *Code Pénal annoté*, 266.

working on a revision of the decree to take account of difficulties that had arisen in its early application.... The earlier decree, as amended on September 14, provided for appeal via a court of procedural appeals; now such recourse was to be directed to a special section of each regional appeals court, and with a strict deadline for each step of the procedure. Appeal would be possible only in case of violations of the rights of the defense, but it could deal with the facts of the case as well as procedures, thus precluding the need for a new trial.[29] Zambeaux, with jurist René Cassin, wrote the new decree late into the night.... The decree was printed at once, rushed to a military airport at dawn for dispatch to the hot spots of the south.[30]

[The Trials]

If the Paris Court of Justice was not the first, it immediately stole the limelight. For many of accused collaborators brought into court in the early weeks were newspaper columnists whose names everyone knew. They were not the first to come to trial because they had symbolized collaboration by their public professions of faith in it, but for the more banal reason that it had been easy to collect evidence against them: their published articles. These articles became both their indictment and their sentence.[1]

In these trials ... juries took into account the notoriety of the author (the more famous he was, the more damage he had done), good faith (writers who had already been pro-German before the war might get off more lightly, for they obviously hadn't been opportunists), and the amount of money each collaborator had earned by serving as a spokesman for collaboration.[2]... In the view of the purgers, propaganda was a serious matter.

Peter Novick, "The Resistance Versus Vichy: The Purge of Collaborators in Liberated France"[*]

There was a potential seed of discontent in the different conception of the task of justice held by the metropolitan Resistance and by General de Gaulle. The Resistance wanted a sweeping, root-and-branch purge that would renew and renovate the country. All of De Gaulle's pronouncements, on the other hand, stressed the need to forgive and forget. "A tiny number of *malheureux*", "a handful of *misérables*": these were the phrases which the General used to describe those who should be tried. While the Resistance desired a surgical operation which would cut off diseased

---

[29] *JORF*, November 29, 1944, 1543.

[30] From Charles Zambeaux.

[1] Talk with Robert Vassart.

[2] René Floriot, *La Répression des faits de collaboration* (Paris, 1945), 5.

[*] Excerpted from Peter Novick, *The Resistance Versus Vichy: The Purge of Collaborators in Liberated France* (Columbia University Press, 1968), pp. 157-159, 161, 166, © Columbia University Press, New York. Reprinted with permission of the publisher.

members lest they continue to infect the body politic, De Gaulle's leitmotif was "France needs all her sons."[3]

This difference in the "quantitative" desires of De Gaulle and the Resistance was, however, much less important than what united them on this question. Both were agreed that the task of justice should be accomplished quickly, so that the positive work of reconstruction and renovation could be begun. Both were dedicated to the idea that justice should be proportionate: "*Nous frappons d'autant plus fort que les coupables seront plus haut*". For reasons largely beyond the control of the Provisional Government, these hopes were unfulfilled. The trials dragged on for years; disproportionate verdicts caused widespread disgust. The purge ended not with satisfaction at a job, albeit an unpleasant job, well done; not with reconciliation and the restoration of national unity—but with a universal sense of frustration and bitter disappointment....

The enormity of the task confronting the judicial authorities was clear—no one expected that it could be completed overnight. Less apparent were the many practical obstacles that had to be overcome. Transportation and communication had broken down. The police and the judiciary could not be an effective tool of repression until they themselves had been purged. Finally, there was the monumental task of establishing, amid this chaos, over two hundred new courts, each with an investigative and prosecuting staff. (At the height of their activity the *cours de justice* and *chambres civiques* employed almost half of the judicial personnel of the country.)

In the Paris area there were almost 4,000 arrests in the week following the Liberation; a week later the total had risen to between 6,000 and 7,000; by early October 10,000 persons were interned—most of them in the Vélodrome d'Hiver and the former Jewish concentration camp at Drancy. A total of 80,000 people were arrested throughout France in the wake of the Liberation.[5] Those arrested were held in "administrative internment", a security measure enacted by the Daladier Government shortly after the beginning of the war in 1939 and renewed by the Provisional Government.

---

3 *Mémoires de guerre* (Paris: 1954-59), III, 405, 421....

5 Henri Denis, *Le Comité Parisien de la Libération* (Paris: 1963), pp. 137, 239, *Figaro*, September 1, 1944; *New York Times*, September 17, 1944; *Combat*, October 23, 1944; *Carrefour*, January 6, 1945. The number of arrests in France was the lowest, relative to population, of all the occupied countries of Western Europe. In Denmark about 22,000 persons were arrested in the two days following the Liberation. (C.C. Givskov, "Danish 'Purge Laws'", *Journal of Criminal Law*, XXXIX [1948], 448.) In Norway there were 24,000 arrests. (Johs Andenoes, "La Répression de la Collaboration avec l'Ennemi en Norvège", *Revue de Droit Pénal et de Criminologie* [Brussels], XXVII, 7 [April 1947], 604.) In Belgium between 50,000 and 70,000 suspects were arrested in September 1944. The number detained declined to just under 40,000 by May 1, 1945, but after V-E Day, as a result of indignation at the first verified accounts of concentration camps from returning survivors, another 20,000 were arrested. (Henry L. Mason, *The Purge of Dutch Quislings: Emergency Justice in the Netherlands* [The Hague: 1952], p. 173 n. 12.) In Holland there were not only relatively more arrests than in France, but incredibly, more in absolute terms. Between 120,000 and 150,000 persons were arrested, 96,000 being the highest number detained at any given time (October 1945). By September 1946 there were still 62,000 detaines, exclusive of these already sentenced to prison terms. (Mason, p. 40; W.J. Ganshof van der Meersch, *Réflexions sur la répression des crimes contre la sûreté extérieure de l'Etat belge* [Brussels: 1946], p. 76-77.)

"Sifting commissions" were immediately established—five were at work in Paris within a week of the Liberation. The three-man commissions were made up of representatives of the Departmental Liberation Committees, the Ministry of Justice, and the police. They worked night and day; by the end of 1944 the number of those detained without having had a preliminary examination had been reduced to 5,000.[6]...

Once the trials began—and in Paris they began in late October—dissatisfaction centered not on delays, but on "incoherence". Some categories of collaborators, it was alleged, were punished too severely, while others were punished too lightly—or escaped altogether. The trend of verdicts was said to differ widely from one region to another. Even when the same court considered apparently identical cases, verdicts seemed almost capricious.... The Count de Puységur, "an obscure scribbler whose writings will never influence anyone", was sentenced to death[17]; Stephane Lauzanne, editor of the influential, German-subsidized *Le Matin*, was sentenced to twenty years' imprisonment. Captain Paul Chack, chairman of the "Committee for Anti-Bolshevik Action", was executed; Georges Albertini, secretary-general of the equally Germanophile (and much more important) Rassemblement National Populaire, was sentenced to five years' imprisonment.

Herbert R. Lottman, "The Purge: The Purification of French Collaborators After World War II"[*]

[Controversies Surrounding the Trials]

After the righteous anger of the first hours of liberation a reflux was not long in coming. There were too many establishment personalities prepared to plead the case for indulgence for it not to take root in the public mind. It will be easier to understand this if it is also remembered that the overwhelming majority of French men, and women had played no part in the occupation, neither in collaboration nor in resistance. The first vigorous challenge to purge justice came from an unimpeachable man, François Mauriac, one of the few members of the French Academy who had taken real risks during the German occupation. He had belonged to the underground writers' movement, the Comité National des Ecrivains, and even wrote a book for an underground publisher, Editions de Minuit. At the liberation he had a privileged platform on the front page of *Le Figaro*,

---

[6] J.O., A.C.P. Debates, December 27, 1944, pp. 604-07; Denis, pp. 138-39, 239-40; *Carrefour*, January 6, 1945. Many tragic errors had been made however.... A ... widespread problem was excessively long internments without real hearings. In one case a man was held in custody for more than two years before he was able to convince the authorities that they had confused him with another person of a similar name. (*Cahiers des Droits de l'Homme*, N.S., Nos. 44-48 [May 1948], 361-62.)

[17] *France* (London), November 24, 1944.

[*] Excerpted from Herbert R. Lottman, *The Purge: The Purification of French Collaborators After World War II* (William Morrow and Company, Inc., 1986), pp. 142-144. Copyright © 1986 by Herbert R. Lottman. By Permission of William Morrow & Company, Inc.

whose publication in the Vichy zone until November 1942 had not prevented its return to the newsstands under the liberation government. As early as September 8, 1944, just a fortnight after the liberation of Paris, Mauriac was warning of the dangers of slipshod justice. He did not wish to plead for the guilty, he said, "but only to recall that these men and women are accused of crimes, but that no court has yet convicted them of the offense or crime for which they are indicted." He was not looking for excuses or seeking to block strict justice; how could he, who had seen "Jewish children squeezed like poor lambs into freight trains?"[1]

Le Figaro was a venerable institution. *Combat* was a new Paris daily, a reincarnation of the underground sheet distributed during the occupation, published by a group of resistance writers the best known of whom was Albert Camus. In an unsigned editorial on *Combat*'s front page Camus called for swift and thorough justice.... Next day Mauriac called for "national reconciliation."[3]

"We don't agree with Mr. François Mauriac," announced Camus's unsigned reply to that. He conceded that frontier justice was uncalled for. But punishment was necessary despite whatever misgivings one might have....

So it would be a debate.... [According to Mauriac, it] was true that Frenchmen who had delivered other Frenchmen to the enemy should be shot, that those who served the enemy and got rich doing it should be punished.... But he decried the abuses of the purge, for example the detention of persons against whom no charges had been filed.[9] In an editorial entitled "The Lottery" he protested the inequality of sentences at the Courts of Justice, where "everything is chance and arbitrary."[10]

Albert Camus replied, agreeing that the courts were coming up with "absurd sentences" and "preposterous indulgences." He suggested that further purge laws were needed.[11] "What a pity," retorted Mauriac.... He blamed Camus for emitting judgments "from on high, from the heights, I imagine, of his future work."... In the same editorial Mauriac compared the purge to repression during the German occupation "to the extent that we too have forgotten charity."[12] "Mr. Mauriac has just published an article on 'misunderstanding charity' that I find neither just nor charitable," replied Camus, this time in a signed article which concluded: "We shall until the end refuse a divine charity which will deprive men of their justice."[13]

---

[1] F. Mauriac, *Le Baillon*, 24ff.

[3] F. Mauriac, *Le Baillon*, 87ff.

[9] *Le Figaro* (Paris), December 12, 1944, in *ibid.*, 171ff.

[10] *Le Figaro* (Paris), December 27, 1944.

[11] *Combat* (Paris), January 5, 1945.

[12] *Le Figaro* (Paris), January 7-8, 1945, in F. Mauriac, *Le Baillon*, 222ff.

[13] *Combat* (Paris), January 11, 1945.

Peter Novick, "The Resistance Versus Vichy: The Purge of Collaborators in Liberated France"[*]

On January 5, 1945, after two and a half months of experience with the *cour de justice* of Paris, Camus wrote resignedly:

> Now it is too late. Journalists who have not deserved it will still be condemned to death. Recruiting agents who have proved eloquent will still be partially acquitted, and weary of so lame a justice, the people will continue to intervene from time to time in affairs that should no longer be of their concern. A certain natural common sense will save us from the worst excesses; weariness and indifference will do the rest. One can get accustomed to anything, even to shame and to stupidity.... But we do not write this without bitterness and without sadness. A country which fails in its purge is ready to fail in its restoration. Nations bear the mark of their justice. Our country should be able to show the world something other than these disordered features. But clear thinking and human integrity cannot be learned. Lacking these, we shall have need of petty consolation. We can see that M. Mauriac is right; we shall have need of charity.[19†]

Camus' disgust with shockingly disproportionate verdicts was shared by his colleagues. *Franc-Tireur* wrote of "the grave risk that justice will become the object of the most dangerous kind of ridicule"[20] ; this view found many echoes in the press, the Resistance movements, and the Consultative Assembly.[21] Dissatisfaction with the trials was not confined to the ardent

---

* Excerpted from Peter Novick, *The Resistance Versus Vichy: The Purge of Collaborators in Liberated France* (Columbia University Press, 1968), p. 167, © Columbia University Press, New York. Reprinted with permission of the publisher.

19 Camus' capitulation to Mauriac was, for the moment at least, partially rhetorical. On January 11 he wrote of Mauriac's charity as constituting admirable morality but deplorable citizenship. Three years later, however, in a talk at a Dominican monastery, he announced that "regarding the fundamentals, and on the precise point of our controversy, François Mauriac, and not I, was right". (*Actuelles* [Paris: 1950], pp. 212-13.)

† [Editor's note: In August 1945, Camus went on to write:

> It is clear that henceforth the purge in France is not only lost, but discredited. The word "purge" was painful enough in itself; the thing has now become odious. The failure is complete.... Too many have shouted for death as if prison at hard labor was inconsequential ... too many have claimed that it was a return to The Terror when dishonor and denunciation were rewarded with a few years in prison.... In any case, we see ourselves impotent.... Today we can only attempt to prevent the most flagrant injustices from further poisoning an atmosphere which Frenchmen already find difficult to breathe.

Reprinted from Peter Novick, *The Resistance Versus Vichy: The Purge of Collaborators in Liberated France* (Columbia University Press, 1968), p. 158, © Columbia University Press, New York. Reprinted with permission of the publisher.]

20 January 3, 1945.

21 All sections of the non-Communist Resistance—even the most *enragé*—opposed particular sentences as being too harsh. The Communists, while they frequently drew invidious comparisons between severe sentences for the "lampistes" and over-indulgent ones for "les

and articulate editors of the Resistance and its representatives in the Assembly. Public opinion polls during the winter of 1944-45 showed broadly-based impatience and frustration with the course of justice. Verdicts were generally regarded as too slow in coming, often too lenient, and, above all, disproportionate.

*Herbert R. Lottman, "The Purge: The Purification of French Collaborators After World War II"**

It should be clear that from the moment of its inception there were people—and not only accused collaborators—who wished to see an early end to the Court of Justice. The decrees which had set up this special jurisdiction made it clear that it would cease to be competent to take on new cases after a certain deadline, which was eventually announced as November 1945. But ... even courts and Civic Chambers which were officially terminated were maintained in activity to hear cases that were already in the pipeline. (All other cases were to go to a Military Tribunal.)[2]...

Balance sheets of the Courts of Justice were being released almost from their inception, in part to show public opinion that the government was performing its duty to purge, and later to contest exaggerated reports of purge excesses.... In May of [1945] Justice Minister de Menthon appeared before the Justice and Purge Committee of the Consultative Assembly to announce that already there had been 17,300 trials and 1,598 death sentences. Civic Chambers had issued 17,500 sanctions of *indignité nationale*. Courts and chambers together were issuing sentences at the rate of 5,000 per month.[8]... [D]e Menthon's successor at Justice, Pierre-Henri Teitgen, [provided further] statistics in a speech he made in April 1946. In all, 108,338 cases had been investigated.... To those who complained that wartime France had ... done a better job, Teitgen responded: "The revolutionary tribunals of 1793 limited themselves to a total of 17,500 convictions. So that if you compare the number of sentences pronounced by the tribunals of 1793 and those of today's Courts of Justice, you can't say we didn't do much; you have to say that we did a great deal."... Later that year, speaking to the Consultative Assembly, Teitgen wound up a summary of purge achievements with a similar comparison: "You certainly think that in comparison with Robespierre, Danton, and the others, the Minister of Justice who stands before you is a child. Well, they were the children, if you judge by the figures!"[10]

---

grands responsables", never, to my knowledge, directly protested that a particular sentence was too harsh.

* Excerpted from Herbert R. Lottman, *The Purge: The Purification of French Collaborators After World War II* (William Morrow and Company, Inc., 1986), pp. 162-164, 182-183. Copyright © 1986 by Herbert R. Lottman. By Permission of William Morrow & Company, Inc.

2 *JORF*, July 30, 1949; *Le Monde* (Paris), July 31-August 1, 1949.

8 *Bulletin hebdomadaire d'informations judiciaires* (Ministère de la Justice), June 2, 1945.

10 *JORF*. Assemblée Nationale Constituante, August 7, 1946 (session of August 6), 3000ff.

...[Only a few years later,] the military tribunal which inherited the purge ... showed an indulgence suited to its time.... Thus when Horace de Carbuccia, publisher of *Gringoire*, a well-known collaboration newspaper, went before the Paris Military Tribunal after years of hiding in France and Switzerland, *L'Humanité* concluded its report of his trial with some irony: "... Horace de Carbuccia has finally been acquitted. What else could have been done with him? His editor Henri Béraud was sentenced to death. But that was ten years ago!"[12]... [A] new and slimmed-down court—three judges, seven jurors—was to sit in the mid-1950s to deal with collaborators already sentenced in absentia, and who were now willing to give themselves up. One predictable result was that, considering the time that had elapsed since the occupation, Vichy officials were now to receive lighter sentences or even acquittal on charges of the same level of seriousness as those which had carried a death sentence ... in 1944.

*Peter Novick, "The Resistance Versus Vichy: The Purge of Collaborators in Liberated France"**

The procedure for the selection of High Court juries provided for proportionality only on the panel of ninety-six; the twenty-four sitting jurors were chosen from this panel by lot. Thus, by the luck of the draw, a defendant might face a jury with a lenient (Radical-M.R.P.-Right) or severe (Communist-Socialist) majority.[46] Fluctuation in the political composition of High Court juries was simply one among many factors which added to the impression of "incoherence" in High Court verdicts.

In the spring of 1946, High Court verdicts ranged from death to suspended national degradation. The verdicts were, in fact, roughly proportional to the seriousness of the offense of the minister involved. Those receiving heavy sentences had generally been zealous collaborationists, and had been personally responsible for deportations or bloody repressions.... Those who got off lightly were those who had served briefly in the early days of Vichy in "technical ministries", and those who had used their influence to combat collaboration inside the regime....

The trials dragged on for years, with the High Court continuing to hear cases through the summer of 1949.... [In 1947] the procedure for the selection of High Court jurors was modified to make the juries themselves, as well as just the panels, proportional to voting strength in the Assembly....

In all, 108 cases fell within the Court's competence during its four-year history. Eight men died before the Court could act; in forty-two cases the Court decided not to prosecute. Of the remaining fifty-eight cases, sixteen were heard *in absentia*, forty-two in the presence of the accused. Of the

---

12 *L'Humanité* (Paris), October 20, 1955.

* Excerpted from Peter Novick, *The Resistance Versus Vichy: The Purge of Collaborators in Liberated France* (Columbia University Press, 1968), pp. 181, 184, 186-187, © Columbia University Press, New York. Reprinted with permission of the publisher.

46 As it happened, there was never a jury with a purely Communist majority (i.e., thirteen jurors plus the Communist vice-president).

latter eight cases resulted in death sentences (three of which were executed), seventeen in "peines privatives de liberté" of various sorts; there were fourteen sentences of national degradation, seven of which were suspended; three men were acquitted.[3]...

The *cours de justice* and *chambres civiques* finished the bulk of their work sooner than the High Court, although the last *cour de justice* did not cease operation until 1951. Most departmental *cours* and *chambres* were closed down in 1946 and their cases transferred to the principal courts at the seats of the judicial districts. These too were abolished in 1947, only the regional courts at Paris, Colmar, Toulouse, and Lyon remaining open. Eventually all were closed except the court at Paris; that jurisdiction finally stopped its work on January 31, 1951, and handed over its few remaining cases to the Military Tribunal of Paris. In all, the *cours de justice* and *chambres civiques* heard 124,751 cases. Death sentences in the presence of the accused totalled 2,853, of which 767 were carried out; 3,910 death sentences were handed down *in absentia*. There were 38,266 sentences involving "peines privatives de liberté": 2,702 sentences of life to hard labor; 10,637 terms of hard labor; 2,044 sentences to solitary confinement; 22,883 to terms of imprisonment. National degradation was visited upon 49,723 individuals: in 3,578 of these cases this was the principal penalty decreed by a *cour de justice*; the *chambres civiques* sentenced 46,145 individuals to national degradation, and in addition imposed the penalty and then immediately suspended it in 3,184 cases.[4]

Too harsh? Too lenient? Pointing to the experience of other western European countries is only begging the question, yet it is perhaps not without interest. There were, in absolute terms, more executions in France than anywhere else, though fewer relative to population than in Belgium.[5] (In Denmark, Holland, and Norway, the death penalty had been abolished for many years, and was reintroduced—temporarily—to deal with collaborators.) The 38,000 prison sentences in France meant that 94 out

---

[3] Law No. 54-288 of March 3, 1954, annulled that section of the ordinance setting up the High Court which provided for the execution of sentences pronounced *in abstentia*. As a result, a number of émigrés returned for retrial before a temporarily reconstituted High Court. In all cases the new trials resulted in acquittals, suspended sentences, or sentences already having expired (e.g., a sentence handed down in 1960 calling for ten years banishment as of 1945). See *Bilans Hebdomadaires*, No. 421 (June 24, 1954); Yves-Frédéric Jaffre, *Les Tribunaux d'exeception: 1940-1962* (Paris: 1962), pp. 145-46.

[4] Emile Garçon, *Code pénal annoté* (Paris: 1952-59), I, 266. Cf. J.O., A.N. Debates, December 12, 1951, p. 9100; July 12, 1952, p. 3939; October 21, 1952, p. 4248; March 23, 1954, p. 1213; Ministère de la Justice, *Compte général de l'administration de la justice civile et commerciale et de la justice criminelle: 1944 à 1947* (Melun: 1951), pp. 262-64; and Appendix E below.

[5] There were 25 executions in Norway. (Paul Sérant, *Les Vaincus de la libération* [Paris: 1964], p. 327.). As of the beginning of April 1948, 23 death sentences had been carried out in Denmark. (C.C. Givskof, "Danish 'Purge Laws'", *Journal of Criminal Law*, XXXIX [1948], 459-60.) In Holland, as of December 1950, 36 collaborators had been executed. (Henry L. Mason, *The Purge of Dutch Quislings: Emergency Justice in the Netherlands* [The Hague: 1952], p. 64.) In Belgium, 230 death sentences had been carried out as of December 1949. (Mason, p. 177 n. 20.) Considering that Belgium's population is one-fifth that of France, the relative incidence of executions in Belgium was, therefore higher.

of every 100,000 Frenchmen were imprisoned for collaboration. The 14,000 prison sentences in Denmark meant that 374 out of every 100,000 Danes were jailed for this offense; the 50,000 in Belgium, 596 out of every 100,000 Belgians; the 20,000 in Norway, 633 out of every 100,000 Norwegians.[6]

In France, as elsewhere, figures concerning trial verdicts do not accurately reflect the severity of the punishment actually meted out to collaborators; presidential pardons and commutations were widely employed to soften overly harsh verdicts and bring some order out of the chaos of postwar jurisprudence. The process of equalization was, of course, a one-way street, since while overly harsh penalties could be reduced, overly lenient ones could not be increased. The aim of scaling down verdicts in more or less identical cases to the lowest common denominator produced a result not unlike that of the amateur carpenter who tries to even out the legs of a table with a saw: the general level became lower and lower.

THE POLITICAL ARENA

Politicians

Herbert R. Lottman, "The Purge: The Purification of French Collaborators After World War II"[*]

[W]hen the Free French set up the Provisional Consultative Assembly in Algiers in September 1943, the form to be taken by the purge of the old parliament was already clear. For the new Assembly excluded from its ranks any member of the old parliament who had voted for Pétain in July 1940, at which time there had been 569 affirmative votes, to 80 nays. Nor would the Free French accept any member of a Vichy cabinet, anyone who had acted, written, spoken in favor of collaboration, who had accepted a position of authority, an advisory post, under Vichy. Those who had voted for Pétain in 1940 could purge themselves, however, if they had participated in the resistance and could get the Conseil National de la Résistance to say that they had.[2]

Peter Novick, "The Resistance Versus Vichy: The Purge of Collaborators in Liberated France"[†]

In early 1945, as the local and departmental elections approached, the Government slightly modified the list of activities entailing ineligibility

---

[6] André Boissarie, *La Répression* (Paris: 1949), p. 8, *Monde*, April 14, 1949; J.O., A.N. Debates, October 28, 1952, p. 4499; Sérant, *Vaincus*, p. 168.

[*] Excerpted from Herbert R. Lottman, *The Purge: The Purification of French Collaborators After World War II* (William Morrow and Company, Inc., 1986), pp. 184-185. Copyright © 1986 by Herbert R. Lottman. By Permission of William Morrow & Company, Inc.

[2] *JORF*. September 23, 1943, 140.

[†] Excerpted from Peter Novick, *The Resistance Versus Vichy: The Purge of Collaborators in Liberated France* (Columbia University Press, 1968), pp. 100-104, 112, © Columbia University Press, New York. Reprinted with permission of the publisher.

[for political office] and substantially altered the procedure for its suspension.[13] The revised list of actions which carried ineligibility included: having been a Vichy minister, having been removed from office by the administrative purge, having been fined for garnering illicit profits under the occupation, having been named a National or Departmental Councillor by Vichy, having voted full powers to Pétain on July 10, 1940, having retained a Vichy appointment to an executive position in the administration after Pierre Laval's return to office in April 1942. Collaborationist (or "unworthy") behavior in general was removed from the new list. Since the previous enactment, laws and a court system to deal with collaboration had been established, and anyone convicted of collaboration, or declared to be in a state of "national indignity" was automatically ineligible; there was thus no need to include these offenses in the new legislation on ineligibility.

As before, ineligibility might be suspended on grounds of Resistance activity. There were, however, various objections to the existing system, which gave this power to the Departmental Liberation Committees and the prefects. Members of Liberation Committees might themselves be local candidates, in which case a conflict of interest would be created. More than one prefect of C.D.L. might have jurisdiction over the case of a given individual, and return contradictory opinions. Finally, while in some departments ten or more suspensions had taken place, in seventeen there had been no prefectoral suspensions at all. It was decided to create a new, unified jurisdiction to consider the cases of all Vichy-appointed departmental and national councillors and all "yes-voting" senators and deputies whose cases had not previously been the basis of a prefectoral decision.

A "*Jury d'Honneur*" was created, consisting of the Vice-President of the Conseil d'Etat, the Chancellor of the Ordre de la Libération, and the President of the C.N.R.[14] It was a sovereign jurisdiction, no appeal from its decisions being permitted. The Jury made its decisions on the basis of dossiers compiled by the Ministry of the Interior, affidavits from local officials, Liberation Committees and Resistance groups, and depositions made by the individual concerned. All decisions, together with a brief indication of the reasons for the determination arrived at were published in the Journal Officiel.

Virtually all the cases considered by the Jury were completed by the end of 1945; in 1946 a number of cases were reconsidered on the basis of new evidence; in October 1946 the Jury disbanded. Under the Ordinance of April 6, electoral ineligibility applied only to the communal and departmental elections of April and May 1945. Further ordinances and laws extended

---

[13] Ordinance of April 6, 1945 (J.O., April 7, pp. 1914-15).

[14] René Cassin, Vice-President of the Conseil d'Etat, presided over the Jury. Neither Louis Saillant, President of the C.N.R., nor Admiral Thierry d'Argenlieu, Chancellor of the Ordre de la Libération, participated in the Jury's work; their seats were filled by their deputies: Maxime Blocq-Mascart (of the O.C.M.) and A. Postel-Vinay (also of the O.C.M., later head of the Banque d'Outre-mer), respectively.

ineligibility to all subsequent local and national elections through the general elections of 1951. (In 1953 an amnesty abolished the institution of ineligibility based on wartime conduct.)

Given the brevity of the explanations offered by the *Jury d'Honneur* for its decisions, it is extremely difficult to be precise concerning its criteria.... A phrase which frequently recurs in Jury decisions indicates that it set a particularly high standard for senators and deputies:

> The acts which [a certain deputy] performed in behalf of Frenchmen and the Resistance do not indicate that [degree of] participation in the struggle against the enemy which the nation had a right to expect from its elected representatives.[18]

...Almost all the full accounts accompanying a decision to suspend ineligibility stress the "active and effective participation in the struggle against the enemy and the usurper" demanded by the Ordinance; failure to satisfy this requirement, "in the strict sense", was offered as an explanation for leaving an otherwise eminently worthy individual ineligible.[21] This criterion was sometimes applied with incredible rigor.... While no hard-and-fast limiting date was adopted by the Jury, even the most active participation in the Resistance was rejected as grounds for suspension if it came very late in the day.[24]...

Despite the rigorous standards of the *Jury d'honneur*, almost a third of those whose cases came before it received a favorable decision. Out of 416 senators and deputies whose cases were considered by the Jury, 114 (27 per cent) were relieved of ineligibility;... out of 223 Vichy councillors, 79 (35 per cent) had their ineligibility suspended;[31] in all, out of 639 final decisions handed down by the Jury, 193 (33 per cent) were favorable. Taking into account prefectoral decisions, 172 out of 474 senators and deputies (36 per cent) and 280 out of 424 councillors (66 per cent) were relieved of ineligibility, making a grand total of 452 favorable decisions (51 per cent) out of 898 cases.[32]...

The parliamentary purge, which aimed at "renewing" French political life, had retired hundreds of prewar politicians; in relative terms it was more severe than the purge in any other area. And the French parliament *was* renewed; the overwhelming majority of postwar legislators were "new men."... There were undoubtedly men who would have been returned to the legislature if the *Jury d'Honneur*, or their party, had not excluded them. But the radical shift in political strength in the

---

[18] J.O., October 14, 1945, p. 6513.

[21] J.O., January 10, 1946, p. 252.

[24] J.O., December 15, 1945, p. 8298.

[31] [omitted]

[32] It should be reiterated that tens of thousands of men (probably including some prewar senators and deputies) automatically became ineligible following sentences by *cours de justice* and *chambres civiques*. There is no practical way of determining how many senators and deputies might have become ineligible in this way....

new Assemblies, and the dramatic success of Resistance candidates, indicated that more fundamental causes were at work.

Government Administration

*Herbert R. Lottman, "The Purge: The Purification of French Collaborators After World War II"**

The most comprehensive decree covering what was to become known as the administrative purge ... called for disciplinary sanctions against civil servants whatever their rank who had collaborated with the enemy, defining collaboration as "favoring the enterprises ... of the enemy ... opposing the war effort of France and its allies ... damaging constitutional institutions or fundamental freedoms ... having willingly obtained or sought to obtain material benefits" from Vichy laws.

Punishment could take a number of forms: dismissal with or without pension, transfer, demotion, suspension or retirement, temporary suspension. It could also mean temporary or permanent barring from a profession (employees of organizations receiving government support were included in the decree). For military personnel a sanction might call for a discharge with or without a pension. The only appeal was to the Council of State on the grounds that a decision went beyond the powers granted in the decree.[2]

If there was a priority, it was the purge of the police and judicial system, for these were the corps which had to arrest and punish everyone else.... By the end of 1944 there had been five thousand decisions to discharge, suspend, or arrest police officials, and commissioners and most of their deputies had been replaced. All police chiefs were dismissed. Most of them were arrested, and five were even sentenced to death.[4] The job of carrying out the cleansing of the court system fell to resistance jurist Maurice Rolland. He drew up his own guidelines: (1) The chiefs were responsible and had to be replaced unless they could prove that they had been active in the resistance; (2) their subordinates could remain on duty unless charges of collaboration were proved against them. In the court system the "chiefs" were, in each region, the presiding justice of the court of appeals and his prosecutor general. There were two thousand to three thousand other magistrates (the higher figure included justices of the peace). In uncertain cases, judges would be asked to take leave or to retire instead of being dismissed. When a prosecutor had not collaborated but through poor judgment had applied Vichy laws harshly, he was to be transferred. Indeed, the purgers were dealing with a whole corps of court officers who had gone about their normal business during the occupation, applying the law of the moment—Vichy's law—to deal with cases on their dockets. But some of these judges had nevertheless managed to sabotage

---

* Excerpted from Herbert R. Lottman, *The Purge: The Purification of French Collaborators After World War II* (William Morrow and Company, Inc., 1986), pp. 194-197, 203-205, 209-210.

[2] *JORF*, July 6, 1944 (Decree of June 27).

[4] C. Angeli and P. Gillet, *La Police dans la politique (1944-1954)*, (Paris, 1967), 137.

Vichy's law by slowing down the judicial process, dragging out trials so that the defendant would never reach a sentencing stage. In some cases anti-Vichy judges had managed to keep custody of defendants so that they would not be picked up by the Germans—this was done for Jews, for example. Sometimes the most patriotic act had been to try a Jew or a resistance fighter and to send him to jail to keep him out of German hands. Maurice Rolland himself, as a magistrate during the occupation, had been involved in such acts.[5]

In a final report on the purge of the courts, made to the Consultative Assembly on May 24, 1945, Justice Minister François de Menthon said that his ministry had examined 403 cases, heard 363 of them, and that represented 17 percent of all court officers on the rolls; there had been 237 suspensions. In addition to that, 97 magistrates who had served in special Vichy jurisdictions went before the purge commission of the Justice Ministry. It was found that many of the suspects had actually carried out their jobs in liaison with resistance groups—and such judges were of course exonerated. At the highest appeals court, 11 magistrates out of 61 were heard, and 6 of them were dismissed. Of 48 presiding judges and prosecutors of lower appeals courts serving in mainland France at the liberation, 34 had been brought up on charges; 15 in each category were sanctioned by various penalties. In the Paris Court of Appeals and city court system 32 magistrates were accused of collaboration; 9 were dismissed and 13 received lesser sanctions. There had been 203 sanctions in provincial courts, of which 64 were outright dismissals and 65 forced retirements. Within the ministry itself, all divisional directors and the inspector general of judiciary services had been dismissed with pension or forced to retire.[6]

The purge of the diplomatic corps ... began in North Africa, although in those days few French ambassadors came under Gaullist authority.... In liberated Paris in September 1944 de Gaulle appointed the president of the Conseil National de la Résistance, Georges Bidault, as Foreign Minister. And Bidault lost no time in setting up a purge commission within his ministry, presided over by an ambassador, Paul-Emile Naggiar; its members represented the Consultative Assembly, the CNR, and personnel of the ministry itself who had not collaborated.[8] It was decided that all personnel decisions made by Vichy would be considered null and void, notably early retirements, dismissals, suspensions—this to bring back the patriots who had refused Vichy, or who had been refused by Vichy. Vichy's recruitment examinations would also be voided, although candidates would have an opportunity to take new examinations. The only exceptional promotions would be for diplomats who had joined the Gaullists early, or who had performed significant acts of resistance.[9]...

---

[5] Talk with Maurice Rolland.

[6] *Bulletin hebdomadaire d'informations judiciaires* (Ministère de la Justice), June 2, 1945.

[8] Decree of October 3, 1944, Notes, Direction du Personnel, Dossier Epuration, Ministère des Relations Extérieures.

[9] Note from Secretary-General Raymond Brugère to Minister Bidault, October 4, 1944. Dossier Epuration, Ministère des Relations Extérieures.

In all, the Foreign Ministry purge commission was to examine 506 cases, recommending sanctions for about one person in six. Two thirds of all ambassadors heard were sanctioned, two fifths of embassy ministers, but only a fourth of counciliors, a fifth of the consuls general....

One of the biggest challenges to the purgers was France's educational system, which from Paris controlled 185,000 women and men in every French city and town, and in that most sensitive of areas: the young mind. Pétain had understood the importance of controlling that channel to French families, and an effective purge of Vichy required that professors, simple schoolteachers, and—importantly—their supervisors be above suspicion. As early as August 1943 a decree promulgated in Algiers called for a purge commission within the Education Ministry, and an investigation committee was set up that same December to deal with the volume of affairs that was expected. Each sector of the educational system was to get its own purge unit (a Conseil Académique d'Enquête), and then a higher body (Conseil Supérieur d'Enquête) would supervise procedures and deal with higher-ranking officers.[1]...

And it was the Counseil Supérieur d'Enquête which had the final word on the six thousand cases submitted to it. An objective examination of its case load suggests the difficulties it had to face. On one hand, complaints against teachers and professors often betrayed traces of personal or professional animosity. On the other, the purgers had to weigh errors of judgment, such as that of a teacher who had joined a collaborationist movement in order to obtain the performance of his verse play, the work of his life. Talented artists had accepted invitations to visit Germany, young women had associated with members of the occupation army (who occasionally claimed to be not German but Austrian, and anti-Nazi at that). Or during a ceremony a headmaster might pay homage to Pétain as victor of Verdun.[4] As of June 1945, 2,362 persons within the educational system had been subjected to inquiry; of this number 370 received reprimands, 359 were transferred, 110 demoted, 69 released for duties, 90 retired, 17 suspended definitively or for a given period from pension rights, 194 banned temporarily or permanently from teaching (this was often combined with other penalties), 18 stripped of the right to wear medals; finally, 59 were dismissed with pension, 259 without. Seven cases were turned over to the War Ministry, 114 to the Interior or Justice Ministry. In addition, 357 higher-ranking educational officers were punished, 18 of them banned from their profession.[5]...

[E]arly sanctions were harsh, as they were harsh in the courts. But the utilization of pardons and amnesties, especially after 1948, helped redeem the balance. When the Council of State voided a sanction the case was reconsidered; after the 1953 amnesty, which extended the deadline for appeals, five hundred cases were reexamined. Even after the deadline the Education Ministry accepted appeals, and there were many cases of

---

[1] AN, Inventaire, Versements du Ministère de l'Education Nationale 1958-1968.

[4] André Basdevant, "L'Epuration administrative," in *Libération de la France*, 798.

[5] AN F72 bis 689.

reintegration, reestablishment of pensions, voiding of demotions. This was more difficult in corps containing smaller numbers of persons, such as inspectors and university professors, easier for high schoolteachers, grade school instructors.[7]...

On the national level, in 1945 a public opinion poll asked whether the administrative purge seemed sufficient, insufficient, or too severe. Fourteen percent of the sample replied "sufficient," 65 percent "insufficient," 6 percent "too severe." Qualified replies accounted for another 3 percent, while 12 percent had no opinion.[26]

How many civil servants were affected by the purge, in all? Just as was true for the number of deaths, for other sanctions, exaggeration has confused the issue. To the charge that there had been 120,000 such sanctions, the government pointed out that if all government departments were included, as well as public corporations such as the railroads, the total was in fact 16,113.[27] In the national administration alone the purge as called for in the June 1944 decree had affected 11,343 persons.[28]

Dismissal without pension	4,052
Dismissal with pension	521
Forced retirement	841
Temporary or permanent suspension of pension	215
Temporary suspension of duties	1,024
Demotion in rank	36
Demotion in category	608
Automatic transfer	1,516
Warning	34
Reprimand	965
Delay in promotion	36
Ban on exercising profession	822
Withdrawal of medal	29

Those purged could appeal. First, through normal recourse to the Council of State, the final arbiter of administrative acts; later, thanks to parliamentary amnesty. Even a rapid review of decisions of the Council of State allows us to see how various governmental departments dealt with their black sheep, and to what extent their decisions stood up to scrutiny by more fastidious legal minds. The Council of State refused, for example, to accept sanctions against relatives of collaborators.... The council distinguished between cases of government officers whose duties had required regular contact with the Germans, and others who in the course of their work had not had to deal with the enemy. The accused had to be shown to have willingly and intentionally committed an act. And a distinction was made between participation in a group with the unambiguous name Collaboration, and simply joining the Pétainist

7 Basdevant, "L'Epuration administrative," 798.

26 *Bulletin d'informations de l'Institut Français d'Opinion Publique*, January 16, 1945.

27 *JORF*, Assemblée Nationale, January 26, 1951, 408; August 3, 1948, 5230.

28 *JORF*, Assemblée Nationale, January 26, 1951, 408.

veterans' group, Légion Française des Combattants, which could have seemed the patriotic thing to do.[32]

For a commander of municipal policemen in Paris to have repeated Radio Paris's collaborationist propaganda in talking to colleagues and subordinates justified a sanction, while simply going to hear a lecture by a collaborationist did not.[33] But the Council of State rejected punishment for a group of government officers on the vague charge that they had "served with zeal and admiration the Vichy government and thus can be considered to have favored the efforts of the enemy."[34]

Starting with an amnesty voted in 1947, administrative sanctions were softened. At this time, punishment by transfer (a minor sanction on the scale) was simply amnestied, although this did not give the official the right to return to his job, which often left the person in limbo. But it was the law of August 6, 1953 (to be discussed in its place), which finally wiped out all administrative sanctions.[35] It did not provide for automatic reintegration, but made that more possible. In fact its most immediate effect was to restore pensions. All sanctions previously ordered were stricken from the books, so that a "dismissed civil servant" became, simply, a "former civil servant."[36]

PURGE IN THE ECONOMIC SPHERE

*Herbert R. Lottman, "The Purge: The Purification of French Collaborators After World War II"**

What the national government really hoped to achieve is indicated by the October 16, 1944, decree on the purge of business and industry. The preamble provides a rationale: The economic recovery of the nation would be compromised by the presence of owners, managers, foremen, even workers or white-collar personnel who had collaborated with the enemy. But their prosecution in the courts was likely to take a long time. So it was essential to take immediate measures to purge this business community. Collaborators could be transferred to another job, or be suspended with or without salary, could be dismissed with or without indemnity, could even be banned from holding a position of responsibility in the company or profession involved. And none of these sanctions prevented the courts from sentencing the subject for collaboration crimes.

---

32 G. E. Lavau, "De quelques principes en matière d'épuration administrative," *La Semaine Juridique* (Paris), 1947, I, 584, 1-5.

33 *Recueil des arrêts du Conseil d'Etat*, 1949, 715.

34 *Ibid.*, 712

35 Basdevant, "L'Epuration Administrative," 797.

36 René Tunc, "La Loi D'Amnistie du 6 août 1953," *La Semaine Juridique* (Paris), 1953, II, 1123, 4.

* Excerpted from Herbert R. Lottman, *The Purge: The Purification of French Collaborators After World War II* (William Morrow and Company, Inc., 1986), pp. 214-215, 217, 221, 227-228.

Each region was to establish a Comité Régional Interprofessionnel d'Epuration, composed of court officers, representatives of Comités Départementaux de Libération, of labor and employee associations, middle-level staff, with a representative of employers too. These regional committees could set up separate sections in iron and steel, chemicals, transportation, banking, and other areas. The committees could recommend punishment, but the decision belonged to the Regional Commissioner of the Republic or, in the Paris region, to the prefect; appeal was possible to the Council of State. Finally, a National Interprofessional Purge Commission (CNIE) was established by the same decree. It was headed by a superior-court justice, sitting with two representatives of the CNR, representatives of the government, and the same mix of workers and management already provided for. The CNIE could take up a case on its own initiative or when the government or a regional committee sent it in. It could issue sanctions, subject only to Council of State review.[5]

There was another way to get at business profiteers, and where it would hurt most: taking back the money earned through collaboration. On October 18, 1944, the government issued detailed instructions for calculating the amount of profit made from trading with the enemy, and for getting the money back. "Independently of the penal action which must be applied to bad citizens," read the preamble, "the most elementary fiscal justice requires that the Treasury recover illicit proceeds earned over a period of four years of war and occupation." This measure covered two kinds of profiteering: dealing with the enemy and speculation (for example, profits made by violation of price regulations and rationing, or by taking advantage of enemy rules or requisitions). The confiscation of such profits was to be considered a fiscal measure, and did not rule out the possibility of later prosecution of the same offender for acts of collaboration.[6] In January 1945 the decree was modified to include, among other things, profits earned in connection with seized Jewish property. The same decree speeded up procedures in order to cope with the large number of cases to be dealt with—there were 12,906 on the docket.[7]...

Today it is possible to examine the long-secret files of the National Interprofessional Purge Commission. A first reaction may be surprise. For many very large corporations are cited in the CNIE files, yet the individuals called up for sanctions are not often owners or directors of these corporations. They are lower-level management, shop foremen, simple workers on the floor. Some of the major companies which supplied goods and services to the Germans were never punished except through lower-echelon personnel....

The purge of the nation's business class could never have been thorough, if only to keep the factories humming in the interests of economic recovery.[31] Jurists contested it; its most decisive sanction, confiscation, was

---

5 *JORF*, October 17, 1944, 965f.

6 Georges Capdevielle and Jean Nicolay, *La Confiscation des profits illicites* (Paris, 1944), 5ff.

7 *Le Monde* (Paris), January 10, 1945.

31 Baudot, "La Répression," 780.

seen by bar leader Jacques Charpentier as a return to "the worst traditions of tyranny." He called the purge committees "caricatures of courts," less concerned with justice than with politics; the punishment of a manufacturer could become "a factory revolution organized by discontented personnel against a boss on whom they were taking revenge."[32] Actually, the government was not using the purge to reform the economic and social system; such a tactic was rejected out of hand by Justice Minister Teitgen, who said that to do that would represent "an abominable abuse of power."[33]...

Apart from a few spectacular nationalizations it could not be said that the maximum demands of the resistance for moral reparation were being met. In the following years the industrial map of France changed less than any resistance ideologist could have imagined would be the case.... Purge procedures were slow, often focused on minor offenders. Appeals taken to the Council of State modified, mitigated decisions announced in the immediate wake of liberation. The Council of State stressed the limits of the purge of business and industry....

Roy C. Macridis, "France: From Vichy to the Fourth Republic"[*]

[Targeting Collaborators or Capitalists?]

What explains the relatively mild legislation and the even relatively milder rigor of its application? The answer is simple—*nationalizations*. The expression "la punition de coupables grace aux nationalisations" was a more frequent utterance of Gaullists than of Communists. But who were the guilty parties? Not necessarily "collaborationists." In fact the "guilty" were the economic elites of the Third Republic. The purpose of nationalization was to purge the society of the nefarious power they exercised. Thus the CNR in its program had insisted on "the return to the nation of the important means of production and monopolies, the fruits of our common labor, of sources of energy, of the mineral wealth, of the insurance companies and the large banks...." De Gaulle had stated that "the collectivity," that is, the state, "must take under its direction the great sources of the common wealth ... and must control certain other economic activities ... without excluding ... private initiative and a just profit."

For the Communists nationalization was an instrument of the class war; the elimination of the cause of nazism and fascism that they equated with the power of the trusts and the monopolies.... Even for the leaders of the MRP, "the Resistance has waged war against Germany and Vichy but

---

[32] Charpentier, *Au Service de la liberté*, 262.

[33] Foulon, *Le Pouvoir en province*, 171.

[*] Excerpted from Roy C. Macridis, "France: From Vichy to the Fourth Republic," in John H. Herz, ed., *From Dictatorship to Democracy: Coping with the Legacies of Authoritarianism and Totalitarianism*,

also against the capitalist regime which, despite everything else, is the fundamental reason for the defeat of 1940."[13]

The major political energy of all political parties and groups was directed against the tangible enemy—the capitalists and the capitalist regime—instead of against those businessmen and industrialists who had collaborated with the enemy or Vichy.

THE MEDIA AND THE ARTS

Roy C. Macridis, "France: From Vichy to the Fourth Republic"[*]

[Print Media]

On the eve of the war some 1,300 newspapers (dailies and weeklies) were published outside Paris. About 100 dailies were published in Paris, such as *Paris-Soir, Petit Parisien, Figaro, Le Temps, Matin, Intransigeant, Oeuvre, Populaire, and Humanité.*

Immediately after the occupation and the establishment of the Vichy regime, some 650 stopped publication or, to use the naval term the French used, were scuttled by their owners. About 600 were left—289 in the occupied zone (some 60 of them dailies) and 320 in the nonoccupied zone—50 dailies, notably *Le Temps,* which had been moved to the nonoccupied zone in Lyon. Some newspapers ... were published and circulated in a clandestine fashion. New Resistance papers were published:... Many of them appeared irregularly in mimeographed form.

In essence therefore the "purge" of the press involved the papers that had either continued *after* the armistice or had appeared *since....*

Studies and plans had been made in advance of the Liberation by a "Commission de la Presse, " established under Jean Parodi, de Gaulle's general delegate in metropolitan France, and by a homemade Resistance organization—the "*Fédération de la Presse clandestine*" comprised of most of the editors of clandestine papers....

For the purpose of the purges that followed, a newspaper was defined to include the name of the paper, the administrators responsible, as well as all those who worked as reporters, editors, and so on, and its office building and printing presses. One circular and two ordonnances issued by the provisional government—the first from Algiers and the other two from Paris (July 8, 1944, and September 30, 1944) provided the basic guidelines for purging the press.

---

13 Robert Aron, ibid.

* Excerpted from Roy C. Macridis, "France: From Vichy to the Fourth Republic," in John H. Herz, ed., *From Dictatorship to Democracy: Coping with the Legacies of Authoritarianism and Totalitarianism,* Copyright © by John Herz (Greenwood Press, 1982), pp. 172-173, an imprint of Greenwood Publishing Group, Inc. Westport, CT. Reprinted with permission.

*Herbert R. Lottman, "The Purge: The Purification of French Collaborators After World War II"**

[T]he principal directive was ... the decree of September 30, 1944, issued in liberated Paris.... First of all the new decree confirmed the ban [issued from Algeria before the Liberation] on all newspapers which had seen the light of day during the occupation, and on all papers existing before the June 1940 armistice which continued to appear a fortnight after that armistice in German-controlled French territory, or more than a fortnight after the Germans moved into the Vichy zone on November 11, 1942. Further, newspapers and periodicals which had been published by individuals under prosecution by the purge courts were also suspended until their cases were decided. Papers exclusively devoted to religious, literary, sports, scientific, or professional concerns which had published no collaboration propaganda could be authorized to reappear. The ban on a newspaper was to end if its owners or editors were not put on trial six months after the present decree took effect.[8] This cutoff proved too short, for the courts couldn't move that quickly; in February 1945 the ban was extended for a second six month period.[9] Another decree ordered a permanent ban on the use of the titles of collaboration newspapers; the preamble explained why: "Whatever the guilt of the publishers of these newspapers, the titles bear the memory of shame, of treason. They cannot be placed at the service of the nation after having been instruments of its servitude."[10]

The September 30 ban on collaborating newspapers was eventually to affect 900 different dailies, weeklies, and other periodicals, while 649 press companies were subjected to judicial seizure.[11] And a wholly new press was ready to take over—new titles, many born of the resistance such as *Combat, Libération, Franc-Tireur, Défense de la France,* or prewar papers which were felt to have gone through the war uncompromised, like *Le Progrés* in Lyon, *Le Figaro,* Socialist *Le Populaire,* Communist *L'Humanité*. New editors and reporters, many of whom arrived in a straight line from the underground, dominated the postwar scene, and in fact the law saw to the strict screening of the older generation. The September 30 decree excluded from the press not only those found guilty of treason but writers who had displayed "a weak patriotism or who had not maintained a sufficiently independent attitude with respect to the enemy."[12] The purification was to be carried out via a system of official press cards without which one couldn't get near a typewriter. This screening, more strict than that for any other profession, allowed one of the

---

* Excerpted from Herbert R. Lottman, *The Purge: The Purification of French Collaborators After World War II* (William Morrow and Company, Inc., 1986), pp. 230-236, 244-246, 250-258.

[8] *JORF*, October 1, 1945, 851.

[9] *JORF*, February 18, 1945, 851.

[10] *Ibid.*

[11] Ministère de l'Information, Les Séquestres de presse. AN 72 AJ 383.

[12] *JORF*, October 1, 1944, 851.

new journalists—Camus—to declare in *Combat* that "journalism is the only field in which the purge is total, because we carried out, in the insurrection, a total renewal of its personnel."[13]...

And the press purge got additional punch through a May 1945 decree calling for court prosecution of newspapers—and not only of their owners. It was "inadmissible," declared the decree's preamble, that the company which had published a paper serving enemy propaganda for four years could escape any form of sanction. To punish publishers, editors, didn't always prevent the newspaper company itself from pursuing its activity, with the accrued capital earned through its treason. Owners who had objected to the collaboration of their paper would be protected: In the event of confiscation, their shares would be indemnified. For in the event a newspaper was found guilty in court the penalty would be liquidation of the company, confiscation of its property. The same punishment applied to publishing houses, news and advertising agencies.[20] Paradoxically, the new procedure opened a breach in the September 1944 decree banning collaborationist newspapers, for now if a paper was acquitted in court it could recover its property and publish again; only its original title remained banned....

By the end of 1948, of 538 press and publishing enterprises brought to trial under the May 1945 decree, 115 had been convicted. Sixty-four were subjected to total confiscation, 51 to partial confiscation. Thirty were acquitted. Another 393 cases had been dismissed, and 35 remained on the docket in Paris. The right to pardon applied to corporations, often reducing the percentage of property seized, even allowing former owners to recover their papers. Indeed, the old press reborn soon became a threat to the new resistance press.[24]... At the time there was a fear that some of the prewar papers which had served the enemy would survive the purge intact, a prospect which [some] thought would be demoralizing for the country.[25] And then time would do its work. The longer it took to prosecute, the less urgent it seemed to ban a paper, to dissolve a company. The case of *L'Illustration* came to trial only in December 1949. Even then the magazine was dissolved, and 10 percent of its property was seized. But the dissolution was rescinded in June 1954, along with the ban on publication.[26]

Dealing with book publishers was no less of a problem; in a sense it was more of a problem. For a daily newspaper could be defined by its editorials. But often the same publisher who turned out collaboration propaganda and racist tracts did fine books by prestigious authors. Following the liberation these houses had not been shut down and some were busily engaged in publishing the work of resistance veterans. How to draw the line? Resistance writers themselves were confused. Could you put a big publisher out of business because he had collaborated if he was also

---

[13] *Combat* (Paris), October 11, 1944.

[20] *JORF*, May 6, 1945, 2571ff.

[24] Mottin, *Histoire de la presse*, 51ff.

[25] *Le Monde* (Paris), June 16, 1948.

[26] ZN C.J. 492 (L'Oeuvre): C.A. 4628.

your own publisher? Two of the most prominent imprints of occupied Paris, Gallimard and Denoël, happened to be the houses of prominent Communist resistance writers, Louis Aragon and Elsa Triolet; indeed, Aragon and Triolet were published by them during the German occupation.

In the underground resistance authors had worked within the framework of a Comité National des Ecrivains (CNE), the National Writers Committee, whose organ was the underground *Les Lettres Françaises*.... As with other professions, book publishing soon had a purge committee. Attached to the Ministry of Education, its membership included Jean Bruller, who [wrote] under the pseudonym Vercors.... Jean-Paul Sartre, who had been published by Gallimard during the occupation and whose plays were performed on the stage in German Paris, but who was a resistance man at heart, was also a member.[29] He and the other panel members complained that this purge committee had no legal status, no means to enforce sanctions. To protest their helplessness they announced their intention to suspend activity at the end of November 1944, after three months of work.... At the beginning of February 1945 the purge of publishers obtained more authority with the creation of a Consultative Commission for the Purge of Publishing, responsible for compiling cases and making recommendations for sanctions to the National Interprofessional Purge Commission (CNIE). Its chairman was Raymond Durand-Auzias, head of a lawbook-publishing house. Vercors remained a member, with resistance publisher Pierre Seghers, CNE member Henri Malherbe (a writer), and the veteran Catholic journalist and publisher Francisque Gay. Editors and lower-echelon staff of publishing houses, and the bookselling trade, were also represented.

Chairman Durand-Auzias understood how difficult their job was going to be. As he summed up the problem in March 1945 to the CNIE, a publishing company isn't only a business, so publishers couldn't be called to account only for their financial dealings with the enemy—as was happening in other professions. It was the books they published which defined their treason. "A treason quite hard to define in juridical terms ... and yet infinitely more serious in its consequences, immediate and long term, than the simple fact of having sold leather or cement to the enemy."...

No major publishing imprint, whether or not its owners or directors were indicted or convicted, disappeared from the bookstores. Publishers held on to their authors—to resistance authors too. And indeed few publishers received sanctions proportionate to the services they had rendered to the occupying forces in lending their names to the myth that all was normal in German Paris, that cultural life could go on as usual under Nazi rule.[32]...

---

29 *Les Lettres Françaises* (Paris), September 30, 1944.

32 Galtier-Boissière, *Mon Journal depuis la libération*, 218.

Writers and Artists

...A decree of May 30, 1945, which set up the procedure for the purge of men of letters, authors and composers, painters, illustrators, sculptors, and engravers explained in its preamble that public opinion "could not accept the fact that works which had as their object or effect to favor the purposes of the enemy or to oppose the war effort of France and its allies can continue to be a source of profit for their creator." So a procedure was established similar to that for other professions. "But if it seems desirable to subject these writers and artists to a ban or limitation of professional activity having the character both of public censure and a financial sanction, we must carefully avoid any system of repression affecting the right of free expression of thought." The decree set up separate purge committees for, on one hand, writers and composers, and on the other, painters, illustrators, sculptors, and engravers. Writers and composers were liable to a ban on works that were responsible for the sanction, as well as to a temporary ban on new works, contributing articles to the press, lecturing, broadcasting, receiving royalties. Artists were liable to a ban on exhibiting and selling works, selling material to the press, lecturing, broadcasting, receiving payment for work. In both cases sanctions were limited to two years, or for persons convicted by a purge court, for the length of the sentence, for a maximum of five years.[22]

The Comité National d'Epuration des Gens de Lettres, Auteurs et Compositeurs [had six members designated by various professional associations of writers and composers.]... The government appointed the chairman, Gérard Fréche, attorney general at the Paris Court of Appeals. Complaints were processed by three-member examining commissions, which called in an accused author to inform him or her of the charges pending, and then request a verbal or written defense. The accused writer could engage a lawyer. The examining commission passed the case up to a plenary meeting of the purge committee, which could accept the commission's recommendation or reopen the case.[23]

...In turn the committee would be called on for help by other agencies—e.g., the prefect of police of Paris, before issuing passports or visas to writers or lecturers, had to know if the applicants had been sanctioned.[25] Publishers, newspaper editors planning to assign stories, and authors' associations wishing to know if an author was allowed to receive royalties came to the committee for help. A professor in Scotland who was preparing an anthology of contemporary literature appealed to the committee, for he wanted to avoid including banned authors.[26] The French Cultural Services in New York forwarded a request for similar information from the U.S. Dramatists Guild.[27]

---

22 *JORF*, May 31, 1945, 3108.

23 AN F21 13

25 AN F21 13.

26 AN F21 22.

27 AN F21 13.

Of course the writers' purge committee had before it the CNE blacklist. It also disposed of batches of questionnaires which authors' societies had sent out to their memberships. The Société des Auteurs, Compositeurs et Editeurs de Musique, for example, had sent out a printed questionnaire asking members to certify on their honor that they were telling the truth; questions covered membership in collaborationist groups, personal relations with Germans, writing songs or scenarios serving German propaganda. Had the author enjoyed the right to use a private automobile during the occupation? (This was an indication of official favor.) Had he participated in broadcasts, performances, visits to Germany? Not surprisingly, members failed to confess to reprehensible behavior.[28]

It can be said that the committee's achievement hardly represented a bloodbath.... One reason for the slim results was the committee's decision not to hear the cases of authors subject to trial.[29] This shortened the list of candidates for purging considerably, and certainly eliminated the most notorious, for they were the ones most likely to be under indictment. Committee files show that when an author faced trial or even investigation by another body, the committee couldn't get its hands on the file anyway, and so it postponed or dropped the case....

Every significant organization of writers carried out its own purge, just as every organization of any kind was expected to do....

The purge of creative people was bound to be controversial, perhaps more so than the purge of any other category of private citizen. For one always risked the reproach that one was seeking to interfere with the free expression of ideas. A number of members of the Société des Auteurs, Compositeurs et Editeurs de Musique, among them the composer Arthur Honegger, objected to any purge based on the way their work had been utilized in propaganda media during the occupation, on the grounds that they had written music, and music had no political meaning. There had been a decision to refuse to pay royalties to these composers for music written for the pro-German newsreel agency France-Actualités. But the composers argued that the same music written for France-Actualités during the German occupation was now being employed by France-Libre-Actualités. "Thus, the music which accompanied Marshal Pétain on the screen today accompanies General de Gaulle.... We thus obtain the absurd result that the same music can be damned or glorious. The same music can receive royalties or not receive them."[13]

In fact the purgers usually judged composers not on the content of their music but on what nonmusical activities they had in their files....

Soon the banned writers were at work again, publishing under pseudonyms. Or writers in jail such as Charles Maurras and Henri Béraud were being reprinted in deluxe editions, even if their royalties went to the government. A body of literature was growing out of courtroom and prison experience—some of these books signed, some published with a signature

---

28 *Ibid.*

29 *Ibid.*

13 April 4, 1945. AN F21 18.

like "X." A few of these books were violent, clearly the work of unrepentant Fascists, anti-Semites.[19]

Painters and sculptors, like musicians, seldom inserted political messages into their works. But as individuals they may have participated in punishable activities, or had lent their famous names to collaborationist causes. Some had participated in German-sponsored cultural events. But the resistance had also had its artists. At the liberation a Front National des Arts under the chairmanship of Pablo Picasso submitted a list of artists to the Paris district attorney and the prefect of police, requesting their arrest and trial....

The same decree which created the writers' purge committee set up an artists' purge committee, as has been seen. The principal objects of investigation of this National Purge Committee of Painters, Illustrators, Sculptors and Engravers were those artists who had traveled to Nazi Germany during the occupation, although what they had actually done there remained a matter of debate.... In June 1946, twenty-three artists were sanctioned by the purge panel....

[Show Business]

The world of show business might seem to be a curious place to look for traitors. But in fact the stars of stage, screen, and the concert hall were much in evidence in the otherwise grim occupation years, and what they said and did had certain impact. Some of France's leading entertainers were compromised; theaters and movie companies served enemy propaganda.

The burden of organizing an orderly purge of the entertainment profession fell to a veteran theater man, Edouard Bourdet.... One of Delegate Bourdet's first acts was to order that in the weeks immediately following the liberation no one could take part in a theatrical performance without a temporary permit which was to be granted only after the appropriate union had received written assurance from the applicant that he or she had not collaborated....

Bourdet set up separate panels to handle the various components of the profession—for example, for theater managers, stage directors, performers.[3] Each smaller grouping had its own purge agency—e.g., there was a Purge Committee of the Union of Chorus Members.[4] The Ministry of Education drew up criteria for these temporary panels covering such offenses as the offer of one's services to the enemy, denouncing and persecuting fellow Frenchmen, joining paramilitary formations such as the Militia. Any of these offenses could be grounds for immediate dismissal. In other cases, such as membership in one of the pro-Fascist parties, or taking part in propaganda plays or films, "the sanction to apply will depend on the

---

[19] André Thérive, "La Littérature clandestine sous la IV République," *Ecrits de Paris* (Paris), January 1949, 53ff.

[3] September 6, 1944. AN F21 1.

[4] AN F21 1.

seriousness of the acts as well as on whether they were habitual or only isolated and accidental." Entertainers who had been forced to collaborate under pressure or whose collaboration was due to "momentary weakness" and who had atoned for their error "by acts of civic courage" could be excused. Sanctions ranged from a permanent ban on exercise of a profession down to a temporary ban—three months to three years.[5]...

And then the show business purge received consecration in a decree of October 13, 1944. It limited the ban on professional activity to one year, while punishing violations of the ban with a year of prison; the manager of a theater in which a banned performer or other member of the profession defied the ban would also be punished, and the theater closed down.[7] At first the Governmental Commission for the Purge of Entertainment was presided over by an actor, but he was soon replaced by a government attorney in order to give the proceedings judicial force. Some 140 sanctions were recommended during the life of this commission.[8]...

But the entertainment purge had only begun. On February 1, 1945, a new decree [established] a National Purge Committee of Dramatic and Musical Performers and Performing Musicians.... Headed by a court officer, it was composed of representatives of government and the entertainment world; the decree further provided that in individual hearings, a representative of the appropriate branch of activity would participate. Sanctions, limited to one year, could involve exclusion from work in a particular theater, a particular branch of the industry (theater, movies, radio, music), or from all professional activity. This last sanction also applied to persons convicted of *indignité nationale*, and for the duration of the sentence.[12]

One important task of the new purge body was to issue certificates requested by theaters, theatrical agencies, and other potential employers, to guarantee that a particular performer had been cleared. Even an applicant for a passport required such a certificate.[13] And now some of France's best-known entertainers were to undergo the process....

---

5 *Ibid.*

7 *JORF*, October 14, 1944, 937.

8 AN F21 1.

12 *JORF*, February 18, 1943.

13 AN F21 4.

THE FINAL PHASE

Herbert R. Lottman, "The Purge: The Purification of French Collaborators After World War II"[*]

The Punished

...By the mid-1970s the survey which had begun under the auspices of a Committee of History of the Second World War attached to the French Premier's office had been completed in fifty-three administrative districts, and the director of the survey, Marcel Baudot (then inspector general of French Archives), was able to announce a total of 5,009 summary executions for the years of occupation and through the early liberation months; if the same averages applied to the rest of France as had been observed in the fifty-three districts for which satisfactory data were available, the national total would be between 8,500 and 9,000 deaths.[33]

A decade later statistics were still to be sifted. The best estimate for summary executions, which includes executions following courts martial and other ad hoc jurisdictions, now approaches the ten thousand figure which de Gaulle had published back in 1959.[34]... At the time the last Court of Justice was shut down in 1951 the total number of cases tried was in fact 57,954, to which may be added the 69,797 cases dealt with by the Civic Chambers. The results were as follows:[37]

Death sentences in the presence of defendant	2,853
Death sentences in absentia	3,910
Death sentences carried out	767
Sentences to terms of hard labor for life	2,702
Sentences to lesser terms of hard labor	10,637
Sentences to solitary confinement	2,044
Sentences to prison	22,883
Indignité nationale as a main sentence by a Court of Justice	3,578
Indignité nationale by a Civic Chamber (of which sentences 3,184 were excused)	46,145

These are high figures—or low ones, depending on one's feelings about the resistance, about Vichy. In the view of Charles de Gaulle the death sentences actually carried out were as equitable as they could be, while sentences to prison were "on the whole equitable and moderate."[38]...

* Excerpted from Herbert R. Lottman, *The Purge: The Purification of French Collaborators After World War II* (William Morrow and Company, Inc., 1986), pp. 274-284.

33 *Ibid.*, 767f.

34 Talk with Marcel Baudot.

37 Garçon, *Code Pénal annoté*, 266.

38 De Gaulle, *Mémoires de Guerre*, III, 127.

[The Question of Amnesty]

In France the purge was still in full swing in 1946 when François Mauriac raised the issue of amnesty for certain forms of collaboration crime, certain categories of offenders. "There are informers, murderers, torturers ... for whom even the adversary of the death penalty I have always been couldn't imagine anything else but the supreme punishment," the Catholic writer declared in his column in *Le Figaro*. But, in addition to the totally innocent, there was "the crowd of the misled of all ages, and first of all the young people whose milieu condemned [them] to think and to believe what they thought and what they believed." Mauriac felt that it was the duty of Christians to raise the question of amnesty now.[1]... Mauriac appealed not only to Christian pity but to French history. "We must think of today's Dreyfuses, if they exist; it's for these living Dreyfuses that it would be generous to fight and to compromise ourselves."[2]

The amnesty law that was finally passed, on August 16, 1947, did seem to meet some of Mauriac's concerns. It covered minors under eighteen who had acted "without judgment" when they committed minor acts of collaboration, or who had joined a collaborationist movement. (Minors up to the age of twenty-one were covered by this amnesty if they had subsequently served in combat on the Free French side.) These amnesties were automatic. And then minors under eighteen who had been convicted of more serious acts of collaboration, minors up to twenty-one who had belonged to a collaborationist movement without having committed specific crimes, could apply for amnesty, which could be granted by decree. Civil servants who had received the lowest possible penalty in the administrative purge—transfer to another job—also benefitted from the 1947 amnesty. As in all amnesty law, the original crime was considered not to have occurred, and reference to it would be removed from court records.[3]...

In the first months of 1948 an opinion poll suggested that the mass of French men and women were hardly prepared to forgive or to forget. Should we let bygones be bygones? The large majority (63 percent) replied no (24 percent yes, 13 percent without an opinion). And 47 percent of respondents felt that the purge courts had not been sufficiently harsh (only 16 percent felt they had been too harsh, and 18 percent saw them as just right, with 19 percent being without an opinion)....[4]

A year later the French felt differently. The movement in favor of forgiving and forgetting had hardly become an avalanche, yet amnesty was now out in the open; Mauriac was no longer alone. In the pages of the MRP daily *L'Aube* Georges Bidault made the point that the purge had been necessary "in the name of law, in the name of the nation, and also for public tranquillity and national reconciliation."... It was for those who had

---

[1] March 7, 1946. François Maurice, *Journal*, V (Paris, 1953), 5ff.

[2] *Ibid.*, 44ff. (April 30, 1946).

[3] *JORF*, August 17, 1947; Henri Faucher, "Amnistie et Collaboration avec l'Ennemi," *La Semaine Juridique* (Paris), 1947, II, 658.

[4] *Sondages* (Paris), April 1, 1948.

resisted, Bidault argued, to say that the hour had come for forgetting what could be forgotten. Those collaborators who had neither killed nor denounced their fellows, those who had not been traitors but who had been led into error, could now be "reintegrated into the nation."

Not all resistance veterans could accept that. The Mouvement National Judiciaire, whose secretary-general was Maurice Rolland, now known as "the father of the judicial resistance," came out flatly against amnesty. It contested the notion that liberation justice had been exceptional.... The rights of the accused had not been violated by the liberation courts, so there was no reason to go beyond normal procedures for pardon now.[6] Daily *Combat* ... opened its columns to the debate, under the title "Clémence ou Réhabilitation?" The majority of those who contributed opinions favored pardons rather than any form of across-the-board amnesty....

President Auriol ... announced that except for traitors, informers, and torturers, convicted collaborators would recover their liberty and their civil rights.[9] A poll taken immediately after Auriol's speech (in May 1949) suggested that the French would follow him. Amnesty was now approved by 60 percent of the population (23 percent opposed it; 17 percent remained without an opinion).[10] But a broad amnesty still stuck in the throats of many opinion makers....

So it is no surprise that the first broad amnesty of the postwar had a painful birth. Many drafts, much argument within the cabinet, inside the majority parties.... [I]n autumn 1950 a bill was placed on the desks of French legislators, and discussion moved to the floor of the National Assembly.... A headline in *Le Populaire* spoke for the Socialists:

YES TO PARDONS THROUGH AMNESTY
NO TO WHITEWASHING COLLABOS

In fact the bill offered by Justice Minister René Mayer was a compromise between the two possibilities. The main beneficiaries would be persons sentenced by Civic Chambers for relatively minor offenses. Mayer gave the Assembly new data on the prison population: There had been 10,611 collaborators in prison on January 1, 1949, 6,402 on November 1 of that year, and a year later the number was down to 4,784. Of the present total, 539 persons were serving sentences of life at hard labor, 3,060 lesser terms of hard labor, 813 solitary confinement, 362 prison. Ten others waited for decisions on appeals from death sentences.[16]

The debate in the Assembly was bitter that fall.... Former Justice Minister Teitgen ... blamed the Communists (France was now a party to the cold war) for the excesses of the purge: That party, he said, had wished to utilize the purge for "political subversion," while the liberation

---

[6] *Le Monde* (Paris), April 14, 1949.

[9] *Le Monde* (Paris), May 31, 1949.

[10] Service de sondages et statistiques, in *Le Figaro* (Paris), June 21, 1949.

[16] *Le Populaire* (Paris), October 4, 1950.

government had sought to maintain legality. He agreed that amnesty was possible for lesser offenses; his party, the MRP, supported the government bill.[19] Privately, Teitgen felt that amnesty was a necessary remedy for the wide disparity of verdicts of the Courts of Justice.[20]...

Both the Socialists and the Communists voted against the amnesty when it came to a vote (at six o'clock one morning in December 1950). In his summing-up in behalf of the bill Minister Mayer promised: "Amnesty doesn't justify anything."[21] The bill passed. Among its chief provisions, this law of January 5, 1951, authorized early release for persons sentenced to prison terms of less than life. *Indignité nationale* would cease to be a criminal offense, and its effects would be limited to deprivation of civil rights, of certain professional activities, including work in the media. Some sentences would benefit from automatic amnesty: This applied to those who had been given fifteen years or less of *indignité,* to minors under twenty-one sentenced to five years or less of prison. Amnesty was also available—but on application only—to collaborators sentenced to minor terms of prison provided that they were not accused of denouncing or responsibility for torture, deportations to camps, or murder. A full amnesty was granted to resistance fighters whose acts had been intended "to serve the cause of the liberation of national territory."[22]

A "timid" law, defenders of the purged were to say. It helped those convicted of *indignité nationale,* but offered less relief to those still in prison.... And so the debate was taken up again.... For resistance veterans, a wider amnesty still represented "total rehabilitation" of traitors—so declared an organization of former camp victims.[27] They also feared that amnesty signified "liquidation of the Resistance," and called attention to provisions in a new bill which was before the Assembly which could prevent victims from naming the persons who had tortured them.[28] In fact this broader amnesty was the subject of six different bills, and fifteen days of parliamentary discussion stretched over a period of a year beginning July 1952.... [R]esistance veterans ... pointed to the experience of the other countries occupied by the Nazis, which had jailed more collaborators than France had.[31]... The final vote [on the bill] was 394 to 212, Communists and Socialists in the opposition.[33]

The law of August 6, 1953, as promulgated by President Auriol began by dealing with its critics:

> Article 1—The French Republic renders homage to the Resistance, whose combat within and without its frontiers saved the nation. It

---

19 *Ibid.,* 7475ff.

20 Talk with Pierre-Henri Teitgen.

21 *Le Monde* (Paris), December 6, 1950.

22 *JO,* Lois et Decrets, January 6, 1951; *Le Monde* (Paris), August 951, 16.

27 *Combat* (Paris), December 29, 1951.

28 *L'Humanité* (Paris), January 4, 1952.

31 *JO,* Assemblée Nationale, October 29, 1952, 4500f.

33 *Le Monde* (Paris), July 26-27, 1953.

> intends to dispense clemency today in fidelity to the spirit of the Resistance.
> Amnesty is not rehabilitation nor revenge, no more than it is criticism of those who in the name of the nation had the heavy task of judging and punishing.[34]

This 1953 amnesty, the final word in the Postwar Republic's disposal of collaboration crimes, dealt first of all with the matter of *indignité*. Those who had received this sentence—except as verdicts of the High Court—were now amnestied; High Court sentences to *indignité* could also be effaced, but only by special decree. Those convicted of trading with the enemy, if their sentences did not exceed five years of prison and a twenty-thousand-franc fine, also benefitted from the new measure. There was an automatic amnesty for persons sentenced to five years or less—High Court sentences excepted—although those who had been accused of murder, rape, or denunciation, or whose acts or statements had exposed others to torture, deportation to camp, or death, or who had cooperated with the enemy armed forces, police, or espionage agencies, were not covered. Collaborators sentenced to fifteen years or less (twenty years for war invalids, camp victims, decorated resistance fighters) could obtain amnesty on application. The pardon applied to convictions in absentia, even to cases not tried, as well as to prisoners originally sentenced to death but whose sentences were later commuted and reduced.

The 1953 amnesty also dealt with the administrative and professional purge. It did not give civil servants a right to return to their former posts, but made that possible, and restored the all-important right to a pension. The amnesty had among its consequences the removal of the penalty of confiscation of property, except when confiscation had represented reparation. Once again the law offered a protective umbrella to resistance veterans for acts which they had considered in the interests of the country. And Article 45 banned any future reference to amnestied convictions or penalties, which provision a jurist saw as unworkable—since it would make it impossible for convicted collaborators to make use of court records to appeal their own sentences.[35]

Indeed, the provision for elimination of all references to collaboration crime from the files of the convicted was to terrorize historians of the Second World War for years to come.

Peter Novick, "The Resistance Versus Vichy: The Purge of Collaborators in Liberated France"[*]

By the time that the ... amnesty bill was debated by the National Assembly in October 1952, the number of those still imprisoned for

---

[34] *JO*, Lois et Decrets, August 7, 1953, 6942.

[35] Tunc, "La Loi d'Amnistie," 1123.

[*] Excerpted from Peter Novick, *The Resistance Versus Vichy: The Purge of Collaborators in Liberated France* (Columbia University Press, 1968), p. 188, © Columbia University Press, New York. Reprinted with permission of the publisher.

collaboration was down to 1,500.[11]... By 1956, only sixty-two men remained in prison; by 1958, nineteen; in 1964, twenty years after the Liberation, there were none.[12]

ASSESSMENT OF THE PURGE

Herbert R. Lottman, "The Purge: The Purification of French Collaborators After World War II"[*]

Many public officials, many white-collar offenders slipped through the net, as did many unsavory criminals.... If present French law was not so protective, one could name members of the French elite, including respected authors and artists, famous journalists, statesmen, leaders in business and industry, who went unpurged, or whose purging did not stick.... And let it be recalled that a considerable number of lower-echelon civil servants, including policemen who, on order, had arrested political dissidents and Jews, as well as the middle-echelon civil servants who had kept the police departments and the prefectures running, escaped the purge undisturbed. At worst, they were transferred out of sight of their victims. Indeed, no one of any rank was seriously punished for his or her role in the roundup and deportation of Jews to Nazi camps.[17]...

When the first comprehensive amnesty was promulgated in January 1951 it contained a clause which allowed victims of the unofficial purge—families of victims of resistance executions, for example—to file claims for war reparations.[18] There were no notable claims.[19]

Peter Novick, "The Resistance Versus Vichy: The Purge of Collaborators in Liberated France"[†]

Frenchmen who agree on nothing else have joined in denouncing the purge, although, to be sure, for very different reasons. In the eyes of many *résistants* it was a series of timorous and half-hearted gestures which lost France her best chance for *renouvellement*. To others—mainly Vichyites—it was an orgy of vengeance and partisanship which deformed the Fourth Republic at birth.... The failure of the purge to satisfy either of these groups—or indeed, to satisfy anyone—was inevitable.... Even if the purge

---

[11] Memorandum from André Boissarie to General de Gaulle, October 15, 1957.

[12] J.O., A.N. Debates, October 6, 1956, p. 4048; May 15, 1958, p. 2330; *Express*, December 14-20, 1964, 27-28.

[*] Excerpted from Herbert R. Lottman, *The Purge: The Purification of French Collaborators After World War II* (William Morrow and Company, Inc., 1986), pp. 289-290. Copyright © 1986 by Herbert R. Lottman. By Permission of William Morrow & Company, Inc.

[17] From Serge Klarsfeld.

[18] *JO*, Lois et Decrets, January 6, 1951, 262.

[19] Talk with Pierre-Henri Teitgen.

[†] Excerpted from Peter Novick, *The Resistance Versus Vichy: The Purge of Collaborators in Liberated France* (Columbia University Press, 1968), pp. 188-190, © Columbia University Press, New York. Reprinted with permission of the publisher.

had progressed much more smoothly and serenely than it did, no one would have been—no one could have been—satisfied....

A third group, standing between *résistants* and *vichyssois*, speaks of the purge more in sorrow than in anger: they are the apostles of "reconciliation". Recognizing that a purge of some sort was inevitable after the Liberation, they blame the postwar regime for not having centered its attention on reconciling "les deux Frances" of 1940-44. They are deeply concerned over what they perceive to be a continuing malaise occasioned by the nation's failure to bind up its wartime wounds.

The wounds undeniably still exist: wartime antagonisms which divided Frenchmen have proved much more lasting than wartime alliances. But within a very few years, as new issues and new alignments appeared, these quarrels became more and more marginal to the political life of the nation.

3

DENMARK

EDITOR'S INTRODUCTION

Germany invaded Denmark on April 9, 1940. In order to avoid a complete Nazi takeover, the Danish government adopted a policy of appeasement and cooperation. In exchange, Germany permitted the Danish government to retain formal sovereignty over the country. In recognition of this relationship, all official communications with Germany were conducted through the Danish Ministry of Foreign Affairs. The Danes implemented a program of self-imposed censorship and prohibited political demonstrations. Some crimes were removed from the jurisdiction of Danish courts, which were not trusted by the Germans to mete out Nazi orders for punishments. After the German invasion of Russia in 1941, Germany required the Danish government to intern Danish Communists and outlaw their activities.

Gradually, as Nazi control grew tighter, nationalism and anti-Nazi sentiment grew in Denmark. The Resistance movement gained popular support, receiving supplies and coordination from Britain. Opposition to the Nazis took a variety of forms, from songfests to some 2,500 acts of armed sabotage to the nationwide rescue of nearly the entire Danish Jewish community of 7,000 from deportation. In August 1943, following demonstrations and mass strikes throughout the country, the German military responded with force, taking formal control of Denmark. Opposition groups continued to grow, many of them coming together to form the Danish Freedom Council in late 1943. Retribution for Resistance activities was often visited on the general population in the form of murders and bombings. Public gatherings of more than five people were banned, censorship was tightened, and large numbers of Danes were jailed at least temporarily. The Danish police force was disbanded and 2,000 of its members were deported to German concentration camps.

The cycle of violence and reprisals continued to escalate in 1944 and 1945. As it became apparent that Germany was losing the war, Danish politicians and the Resistance recognized a need for greater coordination. They decided on the formation of a post-war government to include nine members of the Resistance, nine politicians, and selected Danes who had served in exile, with former Prime Minister Vilhelm Buhl resuming that office. On May 4, 1945, the Germans capitulated to the Allies. The next day, a new government under Buhl was formed.

After liberation, attention focused on those Danes suspected of collaborating with the Nazis and betraying members of the Resistance. During the war, a "judicial committee" of the Danish Freedom Council had prepared draft laws to deal with the crimes of collaborators and the compensation of victims. An "apprehension committee" had compiled lists of suspected collaborators. The new government adopted legislation in 1945 under which anyone found guilty of collaboration received a minimum sentence of four years in prison and the loss of civil rights. For minor offenses, judges were granted more discretion. In total, 34,000 Danes were arrested for collaboration, 78 were sentenced to death, and 46 were actually executed. In June 1946, amendments to the laws allowed the revision of some of the initial, harsh sentences. This proved so controversial that the Resistance briefly occupied a prison holding collaborators, threatening to carry out its own sentences against them. Notwithstanding the controversy, the amendments remained in force.

The following document related to transitional justice in Denmark can be found in Volume III of this collection:

- Purge Laws

THE PURGE LAWS

Carl Christian Givskov, "The Danish Purge Laws"[*]

Before turning to the particular theme I shall briefly give some historical notes on the background for the Danish "Purge" laws. On April 9, 1940 the Germans invaded Denmark. They issued an appeal to the Danish people and promised not to meddle in interior Danish affairs. The King and the Danish Government also appealed to the people to keep peace and order and with dignity to submit to the occupation. In spite of their promise the German interference with the Danish internal relations and the plundering of the country—as in other occupied countries during the occupation—grew more and more violent. Shortly after the occupation the Germans tried to organize a "Danish" corps to fight for the Germans—the so-called Free-corps Denmark. They did actually succeed in getting a small number to enlist, partly in search of adventure, partly on account of political conviction. In August 1943 in various cities strikes broke out. The Germans would not stand for this and demanded severe reprisals against the "saboteurs". The Danish Government which until then, although reluctantly, had submitted to the German demands would no longer submit and on August 29, 1943, the Government withdrew. The German response was a military state of siege and internment of the Danish army and fleet. On October 1, 1943 the Germans commenced action against the Danish Jews. During the winter and spring, 1944, the resistance as well as the sabotage increased. The Germans responded by starting the so-called "clearing murders"; i.e. every time a German or a Danish collaborator was killed by the resistance movement, two or three of the best of the Danish compatriots were murdered by gangs supported by the Germans. At the same time the Germans began the so-called *Schalburgtage*, named after von Schalburg, one of the leaders of "Free-corps Denmark." It consisted in acts of terror such as blowing up of important Danish buildings. The resistance increased constantly and the Germans by and by grew afraid that the Danish police would lead the "rebellious action". The Germans therefore on September 19, 1944, removed the Danish police, interned the police-forces in Copenhagen and other greater towns and deported them to concentration camps in Germany. Now began the last and darkest period of the occupation. Deprived of the army, the Government and at last of the police, all the criminal elements in Denmark had a free hand. The Germans established gangs of murderers and organized an auxiliary police, the *Hipocorps*, which terrorized the people throughout the country. Murders, robberies, blowing up of buildings and trains filled with passengers were every day's occurrence.

In the evening of May 4, 1945 at 8:40, the Danish broadcasting from London sent the message of the German capitulation in Denmark. On May 5, 1945 the "purge" began and here we have arrived at the real theme.

---

[*] Reprinted from Carl Christian Givskov, "The Danish 'Purge Laws,'" *The Journal of Criminal Law and Criminology*, vol. XXXIX, No. 4 (Nov./Dec. 1948), pp. 447-460.

In the early morning of May 5, 1945, the Danish underground army swarmed out. People from all classes with armbands and weapons appeared. They had to do away with the traitors. All over the country arrest groups had been formed on the demand of the Danish "liberty-council" to lead the internments. Everything was planned, file cards were ready and according to these the arrests took place, cars for transport were on hand and men to man them. During that day and the following about 22,000 persons were interned (in Copenhagen and vicinity alone about 8,000 persons).

But did the Danish laws authorize these internments? No one must admit that the whole action was not backed by the laws. However everybody realized the necessity as well as the justification of the large majority of the internments. The common opinion—also among the majority of the Danish jurists—no doubt was, that the internments taking place were a continuation of the war and an inevitable consequence of the conditions which had prevailed in the country during the years of occupation. Immediately after the capitulation a Government was established. One of the first and most important tasks of this Government was to pass a penal law according to which persons who had been guilty of treacherous activity could be punished. Contrary to other occupied countries, Denmark had had no exile government which during the occupation could pass laws regulating these questions. The law was passed as Law No. 259 of June 1, 1945, named: "Supplement to the civil penal law concerning treason and treacherous activity" (in the following cited as law 259/45). On the same day another law was passed, No. 260 named: "Supplement to the law of procedure" (in the following cited as law 260/45) regulating certain special conditions in the treatment of criminal cases according to Law 259/45.

The two laws are both named supplements to former laws *viz.* the Civil Penal Law of 1930 and the Law of Procedure of 1919. This will show that it was not the intention to discontinue the established principles of the Danish laws. However the Laws 259/45 and 260/45 constitute a breach of former Danish principles of law.

[Punishment of Treason: Law 259/45]

The law (259/45) deviates in several particulars from the principles of the Danish penal law previously in force. The two more significant particulars undoubtedly are retroactivity and reestablishment of the death penalty.

In the law the principle of *nulla poena sine lege* is abandoned. This principle throughout the years was leading in the Danish penal legislation. The Danish Constitution did not, as the Norwegian, include any clause prohibiting the passing of retroactive penal laws. But the principle was approved of theoretically as well as practically by all Danish jurists as the foundation of just penal legislation. The penal law of 1930 provides in § 3-1 that later, more severe penal law must yield to former more lenient laws. Certainly it must be admitted, that the principle *nulla poena sine lege* in its full extent already was abandoned in § 1 of the penal law of 1930. It provides: "Punishment can only be charged in a case where the culpability is authorized by law or what is quite similar thereto." Hereby it is acknowledged that analogy from the penal law can be applied as to penal authority. Referring to this clause some of the Danish jurists proposed, that the new questions should be solved by analogy from the existent clauses in the penal law, especially chapter 12 about treason, etc. The Congress was of opinion that this would not be satisfactory and would lead to confusion and diversity in judgment which had to be avoided even if the price should be abandonment of fundamental principle.

The law is limited to acts committed from the occupation-day, April 9, 1940, until one year after the law had come into force. This last date was stipulated in order to punish the were-wolf organizations and their acts, which might occur when the occupation was over, but before full peace and order could be restored. After the passing of the law some prominent Danish jurists rather sharply attacked the retroactivity of the law and we have indeed to regret the breach of a principle stipulated throughout long years in Danish jurisprudence. We only have to hope that this special law shall form no precedent but be only a passing phenomenon created by the war and the hard conditions during the occupation. The law as applied is valid only to Danish citizens or persons living in Denmark at the time of committing the crime. It does not concern the war criminals. Their punishment having been passed to special tribunals chosen by the Allied Nations f.e. the Nurnberg Tribunal.[1]

The law (259/45) restores the death penalty in Danish civil penal law which had been abolished by the law of 1930, as to the civil law, but maintained in the military penal law. The general opinion shared by most of the Danish jurists was, that the death penalty had to be restored. The justification of restoring it may be discussed. The aim of punishment in the various penal theories is: 1) retaliation, 2) deterrence, 3) security or 4) reformation. The theory of retaliation in Denmark as a principle has long been given up. But as well as according to the theory of deterrence as that of security, there seems to be strong reasons for restoring the death penalty. It was meant to be a warning that such men and such acts were not to be tolerated in the future in Denmark. As to the security of the citizens it was found, too, that restoring the death penalty was needed. The persons to whom it was to be applied had committed crimes of such extraordinary and hitherto unknown character that the community was obliged to shield itself against their being free again either by amnesty or by escape, and enabled to commit new crimes. From the point of view of the reformation theory it must be admitted that by the death penalty no attempt can be made to improve, the condemned to make them good citizens again. The general opinion was that those persons were so raw and rugged in thoughts and manners that their "resocialisation" had to be considered vain. Whatever theoretically may be said about restoring the death penalty, no

---

[1] Later on a law has been passed (no. 395 of July 12, 1946) according to which the war criminals may be punished in Denmark.

doubt it was a public claim, which would have been very difficult if not impossible for the government not to answer.

The death penalty can only be applied when certain grave felonies have been committed. It is never the only penalty, but always facultative. Persons having been not over 18 years of age when their crime was committed cannot be sentenced to death. The cases in which death penalty can be applied are: 1) *high treason* with aggravating circumstances, 2) *arson*, by which people perished or were exposed to impending danger of life, 3) *murder* and man-slaughter, 4) *injury* and *transferring in helpless condition* to inforce evidence or confession (ill-treatment or torture), 5) *informing* leading to loss of life, severe damage of life or health, deportation or deprivation of freedom for a long time or such consequences might have been intended.

The other sorts of penalty known in Danish legislation are: prison, work-house, custody, custody of psychopaths, juvenile prison, arrest (custodia honesta) and fine. According to law (259/45) only prison and juvenile prison can be applied. Juvenile prison only when the perpetrator has not completed his 18th year at the time of committing the crime. According to the law prison shall be imposed from four years to life imprisonment. This very severe limit of penalty was explained during the proceedings in the congress to have been established because it was intended only to prosecute according to the law in serious cases of treason and treacherous activity. If in single cases extenuating circumstances should be present, § 3-3 of the law provides that the penalty may be reduced to one year of prison. In case of particular reasons for reducing the penalty it may be put down to 30 days of imprisonment.

During the proceedings under the law the clause providing a minimum penalty of four years of imprisonment was subject to criticism. It was maintained that this easily would lead to omitting prosecution (*nolle prosequi*) in the cases in which it might be perceived that the courts would not condemn to such a severe penalty as four years of imprisonment, especially if the court should find plausible reasons for a less severe punishment. If these cases were still prosecuted it was apprehended that the courts would discharge and thus several persons who deserved a minor penalty might be free. It was proposed to lower the limits of penalty considerably—to 30 days or possibly one year of imprisonment. However, the government insisted upon a severe limit of penalty, and the law was passed. It now happened that the prosecuting authority sued far more widely than primarily intended by the law according to the declarations in the congress. As the courts in many of those cases did not wish to apply the severe penalty, the clauses concerning extenuating circumstances were applied on a large scale to bring the penalty into reasonable proportion to the guilt and to avoid discharge. This occurred on a considerably larger scale than primarily intended. The development might have been avoided if the severe limits of penalty had not been maintained, but as it often happens the administration of justice in practice has corrected the apparent absurdities in the legislation.

Aggravating clauses stipulated that parole and probation was not to be applied. Furthermore, the sentence might stipulate that he who was found guilty might have his property, interests or income partly or entirely confiscated for the benefit of the Treasury. Properties belonging to the *Hipo-Schalburg* corps should be confiscated to the benefit of the Treasury.

Penal responsibility according to law (259/45) cannot be lost by prescription. One more difference from the common rules of the penal law, which stipulates a time of prescription from two to ten years according to the weight of the penalty deserved. By altering this common principle of law it was intended to: enable trespassers of these laws to avoid penal responsibility e.g., by hiding abroad for some years and to return without hindrance, later, to take up again their normal existence. It is stipulated that no applied sentence may be lost by prescription.

At last it was stipulated that he who has been found guilty of punishable acts according to the law shall be pronounced as unworthy of common confidence forever, or, under extenuating circumstances, for a certain time not less than five years to be fixed by the sentence. The loss of common confidence means loss, of most of the political and civil rights. This clause was strongly criticized and justly, too. It is maintained that thus the condemned after having suffered punishment were prevented from returning to normal social life. The fields left to them were practically only those of labourers and farmers. Thus their "resocialisation" within their vocational fields was prevented.

Law 259/45. Chapter 2, deals with the questions of the deeds which are to be punished according to the law. A more severe penalty is stipulated for those, who, for the purpose of furthering German interest or for other treasonous aims have undertaken an act which is punishable according to the penal law of 1930. It was more aggravating if the perpetrator, when committing the deed, was dressed in German uniform or was otherwise: indicated as belonging to the occupation power or cooperating organizations, or had given offense by profiting from the special conditions created by the occupation.

Furthermore, they are punished who recruited or enlisted in the German military service, who served in a corps working in connection with the occupation power against the legal authorities of Denmark or Danish citizens, or exercised police activity in this country. If the last mentioned activity had occurred after September 19, 1944—the date of internment of the Danish police—the penalty is especially severe: from 10 years of imprisonment to death.

The clause "German military services" has been subject to great discussions. The question was: how many of the various groups, more or less uniformed, working for the Germans, were covered by the clause "military service"? There was no doubt that persons enlisted in the German army may be as ordinary soldiers, SS. troops, Freecorps Denmark, Regiment Nordland or similar corps had enlisted for "German military service." The Germans, however, employed Danish citizens in corps, e.g., as guards, firemen, etc. It has been very difficult to decide if such service was to be named "German military service" or not. The prosecuting authority and the courts have considered being uniformed and armed as the deciding criterion.

The penal cases against those persons have given rise to discussions among Danish jurists. Some of them have maintained that persons enlisted before August 29, 1943—the date when the Danish Government withdrew—were not to be punished because law 259/45 § 1 provides that acts committed before this day are unpunishable if the perpetrator acted "according to law or order or instruction given by a legal Danish authority". The Danish government had until August 29, 1943—by compulsion—followed a cooperation policy. It is now maintained that the government should have expressed its view of persons enlisted to "German military service"—Freecorps Denmark and similar corps—in such a way that those persons might have been of opinion that they enlisted with the consent or even after instruction from the Danish government. Against this argument it is said they could not possibly forget the fact that the Danish government acted under force of special conditions during the occupation, that they could not ignore how the majority of their compatriots looked upon their activity in "German military service" and that most of them belonged to a nazi-infected group of the population, who absolutely cared nothing for what the Danish government did and said. It therefore was not possible to discharge them. Only in special cases of further extenuating circumstances, was it possible to do so. Such doubts and discussions clearly show the drawbacks of a retroactive penal law. They could have been avoided if the recognized principle, *nulla poena sine lege*, had been maintained.

Punishment, too, was stipulated for the public functionary who gave the occupation power uninvited but not unessential assistance; for "squealers" (*Stikkere*) i.e. persons who by information or in other ways have aided in some one's seizure. For those persons the penalty can amount to death if the information has led to one's 1) losing his life, 2) suffering severe damage of body or health, 3) being deported, 4) deprived of his freedom for a considerable period, or 5) even if such consequences were intended. Furthermore, persons are to be punished who have caused interference of the Germans or their collaborators with the Danish government or authorities. Also, persons are to be punished who applied to German authority or collaborating persons, to gain economic or other profits from the special conditions due to German interference with citizens; *e.g.*, persons who by application to the Germans, had obtained a post or business that had belonged to arrested or runaway Jews. It is also stipulated that the more grave cases of the so-called *Værnemageri*, (i.e. collaboration) with the occupation power chaser, furnisher, contractor and the like, may be punished if they have membership in a German friendly organization; have acted from political conviction; shown especially offensive initiative or otherwise have collaborated offensively with the occupation power. The law does not cover the other less grievous cases of *Værnemageri*.

Finally, a clause provides that he is to be punished who furthered German interest, or obtained economic gain or other profits, otherwise than by ordinary civil wage-work; by normal business or employment; who in word and deed has rendered, assistance to the occupation power or its collaborators. Moreover, he is punishable who has counteracted the war efforts of the Allied Nations, the Danish resistance movement, or has supported the press—or other nations which offensively helped the Germans.

[Procedure for Purge Cases: Law 260/45]

As above-mentioned Law, 260/45, is appended to Law 259/45 stipulating some special rules concerning procedure in these cases. Law 260/45 deviates in several important particulars from the ordinary Danish criminal procedure.

It is stipulated that prosecution according to law 259/45 is to be brought and decided in the first instance in the lower courts attended by jurors. These courts, which act as special courts, consist of a judge especially chosen for this task and two jurors. According to the ordinary Danish administration of justice most of the cases should have been brought before the superior courts attended by a jury. The alteration has been made in the interest of speed.

Further it is stipulated that sentences imposed in the special cases cannot be appealed by the condemned if the penalty does not exceed ten years of imprisonment or if the death penalty has been imposed, unless permission of appeal has been granted by a specially appointed Commission of Appeal. This too is contrary to Danish administration of justice, which always—except in case of small fines—grants the condemned the right of appeal to a superior court. The purpose is to speed procedure and to avoid superfluous and aimless appeals. As to the prosecuting authority there is no limitation of appeal. When appeal can be taken the case is dealt with in the superior courts attended by jurors. Here three judges and three ordinary citizens impose the sentence. Appeal of the cases to the supreme court as well by the condemned as by the prosecuting authority can be admitted only in rather special particulars and only with permission of the Ministry of Justice.

Another special clause provides that when there are strong reasons to believe a person has trespassed law 259/45, he must be arrested and kept in custody till the case is finally settled, or if he is condemned, till the beginning of the sentence. This also is contradictory to the ordinary Danish rules of justice. According to them an accused person can be arrested only if something rather special is pleaded. He may be expected 1) to try to shun the prosecution by flight, 2) to counteract the investigation, 3) to play upon witnesses, 4) to continue his criminal activity or 5) to have committed some rather serious crime claiming his immediate imprisonment. The judge determines if one or more of these reasons for arrest are at hand. According to law 260/45 nothing else has been left to the decision of the judge, than the question if there is sufficient reason for the charge. If so the accused must be arrested.

In contradiction to the ordinary rules, according to which the prosecuting authority in the lower courts is represented by the chief of police or his deputy as prosecuting attorneys, it is provided by law 260/45 that the Minister of Justice has to appoint a number of lawyers especially fitted for making the accusations. However this clause has been interpreted in such a way, that the accusation in the lower courts is made partly by the ordinary prosecutors, partly by lawyers especially appointed. In the Supreme Court and the superior courts the prosecution is conducted as ordinarily by State prosecutors and their assistants, supplemented by a number of especially appointed prosecutors.

A counsel for the defendant must always be appointed. Any lawyer may be appointed if he is found fit. If the defendant wishes to use a certain lawyer, he must be appointed, if he is found fit. The decisions of apprehension or of imprisonment by a lower court can be appealed to the superior courts in the ordinary way. Other decisions of the lower courts in these cases can not be appealed in order not to retard procedure.

If in a case according to law 259/45 sentence is passed by the supreme court or one of the superior courts resumption of the case can take place only if the Commission of Appeal allows it. Resumption of a sentence passed by the lower courts is not allowed. Here you must apply for appeal to the superior courts.

The Danish Constitution grants every citizen the right, if seized by the police, to be brought before a judge within 24 hours. This rule is applied also to persons accused of transgression of law 259/45. However this rule for a short time was suspended during the internments made by the resistance movement immediately after the liberation on May 5, 1945. But as fast as possible the interned also were brought before a judge, who decided the question of imprisonment or release. It must be considered encouraging that this rule, so important to secure the citizens against encroachment from the State, was applied again.

Penal Law for Collaboration in "Work and Trade:" Law 406/45

As above mentioned, law 259/45 was meant to punish the most grave cases of treasonous activity. However there is a certain number of persons not covered by this law, who ought to be punished for their activity and collaboration with the Germans. It is the so-called *Værnemagere,* i.e. persons who have collaborated offensively in work and trade with the occupation. To be sure law 259/45 § 15 established punishment of the most grave cases of *Værnemageri.* This rule especially combined with the very severe limit of punishment—imprisonment from four years to imprisonment for life—made a law on this particular question necessary. The bill was passed as No. 406 of August 28, 1945, a Supplement to Law No. 259/ of June 1, which is a Supplement to the Civil Penal Law on Treason and other Activity (in the following cited as law 406/45).

The law has punishment of the *Værnemagere* in view. Not all collaboration in work and trade with the occupation power is punishable. In fact it was absolutely necessary for the economy of the country to a certain degree to collaborate in work and trade with the Germans. More than mere collaboration in work and trade therefore is required. This is expressed by the word "offensively".

"Offensive collaboration" has been difficult to define and the law does not make any attempt to give a precise and clear definition. The law confines itself to quoting special cases which are to be taken into consideration, namely: 1) activity in getting commercial connection with the occupation power initiated, continued or extended, 2) change of commercial operations, 3) contribution of greater or quicker production in German interest, 4) invoking assistance of the occupation power to secure higher prices or bigger supplies, 5) prevention of admittance for the Danish authorities to industry or attainment of unreasonable profit. This is not an exhaustive repetition of "offensive collaboration" but only guiding examples.

The penalty according to law 406/45 is fixed at imprisonment of 30 days to 4 years. In addition to imprisonment fines may be charged as supplemental punishment and the net profit gained by the punishable act—eventually fixed by the court to an estimated amount—may be confiscated for the benefit of the Treasury. Furthermore the condemned may be found unworthy of common confidence or be deprived of certain political or civil rights.

To secure possible fines the property of an accused may be seized. Fines may be paid through life insurance or annuity. Gifts and the like which are rendered after the beginning of the punishable act may be invalidated and the claims of the fine may be executed upon the estate of a deceased condemned person.

The cases under law 406/45 are dealt with by the same courts as above mentioned. The rule that one condemned by a lower court cannot appeal to the superior court without special permission is not applicable in these cases. An accused who, with sufficient reason is charged of trespassing the law may (but not necessarily) be arrested.

Law 406/45 as well as law 259/45 is retroactive, punishing crimes committed after April 9, 1940. The reason for departure from the principle, *nulla poena sine lege*, is the same as mentioned in law 259/45.

In the interpretation of law 406/45 and its application one question has been very much discussed: is collaboration with the occupation power before August 29, 1943—the date of the withdrawing of the Danish government—unpunishable, because of the instruction which the government was said to have given for commercial trade with the occupation power? That commercial trade with Germany took place, was tolerated by the government and even was necessary for the entire country, is beyond doubt. A part of the trade and the profits gained by persons collaborating with Germany, therefore, were legitimate. But a part of the Danish population has been engaged in trade and other cooperation with the Germans in such a way and to such an extent, e.g., by persons manufacturing of war materials or constructions of German fortifications—that it was found quite reasonable to deprive them of their profits, and even to punish them otherwise. Here it must be taken in consideration, that the amounts which they have gained are not a result of normal trade with a foreign country, but are paid by the country and its citizens themselves, because the Germans caused the Danish National Bank to finance all those trades.

Other Purge Laws

In addition to the above-mentioned laws others have been passed aimed at calling to account persons who flinched from their duty to their country during the occupation, without actually punishing them. In this connection law No. 322 of July 7, 1945 establishes a special tribunal to deal with the smaller cases against public officials and to decide if they may be allowed to keep their offices or should be discharged with or without pension. Furthermore, Laws No. 330 of July 12, 1945, No. 499 of October 9, 1945 and No. 500 of October 9, 1945 all aim at drawing profits into the Treasury for the benefit of the population of the entire country.

Amendments

The often strong criticism of certain provisions in Law 259/45 has led to the appointment of a committee for further examination of the law and to move certain amendments to it. This has led to the rather unusual result that the Danish Congress in the midst of the "purge", with hundreds of cases settled according to law 259/45 and hundreds of cases pending, made important amendments to the law. They were passed as Law No. 356 of June 29, 1946 and were designated: "Amendments and Supplements to Law No. 259 of June 1 1945 to supplement the civil penal law on treasonous activity."

This law, cited as Law 356/46, extended the validity of Law 259/45 to two years after its coming in force, i.e., to June 1, 1947.

The criticism against the severe limit of penalty with its minimum of four years of imprisonment, together with the wide application by the courts of extenuating circumstances, has led to minimum penalty fixed at two years of imprisonment. Circumstances which are considered extenuating are cited. Only one of these rules will be especially emphasized, namely that it shall be considered extenuating to have enlisted to "German Military Service" before August 29, 1943 (the date of the withdrawing of the Danish government), and the penalty may be reduced to one year of imprisonment. In certain circumstances it may be reduced to 30 days.

To facilitate the "resocialisation" of the condemned it has been provided that release on probation can take place according to the rule of the civil penal law, however, only after the expiration of one year of the prison term. The depriving of common confidence cannot take place any more. Which of the political or civil rights the condemned has to be deprived of is now fixed in the sentence. Substantially it is the same he would lose by being deprived of common confidence. However, the rule about depriving of the right to get a trade license and the loss of public support has been repealed.

Another amendment makes the law less severe. It is a rule that penalty for service in a corps collaborating with the occupation power may be reduced to 1 year of imprisonment under extenuating circumstances.

The new law 356/46 fixes rules also, which are aggravating because the number of persons who can be prosecuted has been enlarged. It is fixed, e.g., that he may be punished who has been a member of the supreme direction of the Danish Nazi Party (D.N.S.A.P.) or other Nazi-organisations offensively collaborating with the occupation power, and contributing to, or omitting to counteract the collaboration of these organisations with the occupying power. He, too, may be punished, who has rendered assistance to the occupation power by propaganda or likewise. Here it is to be pointed out, that ordinary membership in the Danish Nazi Party is not to be punished, unless a member has committed other offensive acts.

Furthermore he is to be punished, who, as a pressman has worked at a publication for furthering German propaganda, or otherwise by writing or speaking public has been aiding German propaganda.

On the other hand the rule is maintained that he is unpunishable who has collaborated with the occupation power only by civil wage-work, normal business-activity or other normal trade-activity.

Conclusion

The purge is still going on. Most of the cases now are settled but a considerable number remain.

As of April 1, 1948 about 15,000 persons have been charged, 2,000 of them for transgression of Law 406/45.

About 1,000 persons have been discharged.

Forty-five persons have been condemned to death in the lower and superior courts, three persons at the supreme court. Of these, 23 have had their punishment changed to prison either by superior court or by pardon; 23 have been executed.

The purge laws apparently will have no lasting influence on the Danish normal legal system. They were meant as special legislation. But we must not forget that we have a retroactive penal law and this perhaps—under certain circumstances—may be a precedent. We hope it will not be so.

It is still impossible for us to judge if the purge in Denmark has succeeded. Certainly much might have been better, but largely the laws may be said to fulfill the claims that are made for them.

The future will [be] judge of the result.

4

BELGIUM

EDITOR'S INTRODUCTION

German troops invaded Belgium on May 10, 1940 and on May 28, King Leopold III surrendered. The German forces were welcomed by leaders of Belgian fascist parties such as the Rexist Party and the Flemish National League (VNV). By 1942, most government offices were heavily staffed by members of these two parties. The majority of the Belgian population, including many followers of the Rexists and VNV, refused to participate in this government. A government-in-exile was established, first in France and later in London, which functioned throughout the four-year occupation.

German authorities instituted strict economic control. They seized all food supplies and imposed a harsh system of rationing. In 1942, they began massive labor deportations of Belgians to work in German factories and deported many, particularly Jews, to concentration camps. Of the nearly 90,000 Jews living in Belgium before World War II, only some 20,000 survived.

Belgium was liberated in September 1944, after four years of brutal occupation in which large numbers of Belgians lost their lives. The government-in-exile, headed by Hubert Pierlot, immediately returned to Brussels. The Parliament which had been in existence before the German invasion was reinstated, excluding those legislators who had collaborated with the occupation regime. Leopold III and his family, who had been removed to Austria by the Germans in 1944, were freed by Allied forces in May 1945. However, the king's behavior and contact with Hitler during the war became a highly controversial political issue following Belgian liberation. A national referendum was held in March 1950 on the question of Leopold's prospective return from exile. The deep divisions reflected in the results, together with mass demonstrations and violence over the issue, resulted in his abdication in July 1951.

Even prior to liberation, the government-in-exile had adopted laws directed at those Belgians who participated in the four-year occupation. The new government expanded on these measures, adopting a two-pronged approach. Administrative proceedings were undertaken against the officials and staff of government agencies, resulting in the purge of many collaborators from their positions. In addition, a process of criminal investigation resulted in the deprivation of civil and political rights for some collaborators (without a full judicial proceeding) and the prosecution of others.

The article which follows examines the extent to which the pressures of politics and national reconstruction influenced this purge process.

THE CRIMINAL JUSTICE SYSTEM IN PERIODS OF TRANSITION

Luc Huyse, "The Criminal Justice System as a Political Actor in Regime Transitions: The Case of Belgium (1944-1950)"[*][1]

Societies which are struck by an acute political crisis of vast magnitude are like surfacing icebergs, abruptly showing their full size and complexity. Basic aspects of their functioning which are otherwise hard to observe appear with great clarity. Such episodes in the life of a society naturally create large opportunities for the social scientist. In the case of the sociologist of law, major political crises produce lab-like conditions for studying the linking between the legal system and the political and socio-economic order.

War, especially if accompanied by external conquest of the national territory and by the installation of a new regime, is one source of deep crisis. Revolution is another. War and revolution force societies to cope with traumatic transitions: the end of and, eventually, the restoration of national integrity, the fall and rise of regimes. For the last six decades Europe has witnessed several examples of transitions of that kind: the breakdown and restoration of democratic states in the thirties and the forties and, more recently in Southern and Eastern Europe, the termination of authoritarian systems and the process of the construction or reconstruction of a democratic regime.

The problem we want here to deal with is that of the role of the legal system, especially the criminal justice system, in transitional periods. The focus will be on one particular case: the redemocratization of Belgium (1944-1950) after the defeat of the Germans and their Belgian collaborators.

In Search of Literature

There exist two bodies of academic literature on the connection between the law and political development. The first may be grouped as political science publications on regime transitions.[2] The problem with these publications, however, is that they usually disregard the role of courts and their personnel in the rise and demise of regimes. By neglecting this issue, political science is one of the victims of the myth that judicial

---

* Reprinted from Luc Huyse, "The Criminal Justice System as a Political Actor in Regime Transitions: The Case of Belgium, (1940-1950)," *Recht der Werkelijkheid*, vol. 12, (1991), pp. 87-96.

1 [omitted]

2 Important works here are: Maier, C. (1975) Recasting Bourgeois Europe. Stabilization in France, Germany, and Italy in the Decade after World War I. Princeton: Princeton University Press; Linz, J. and Stepan, A. (eds.) (1978) The Breakdown of Democratic Regimes. Baltimore: The Johns Hopkins University Press; O'Donnell. G, Schmitter, P. and Whitehead, L. (eds.) (1982) Transitions from Authoritarian Rule: Southern Europe. Baltimore, The Johns Hopkins University Press.

activities are apolitical or nonpolitical by nature.[3] Another source is the socio-legal literature on the interlocking of politics and courts.[4] Many of these works look at the political functions that appellate courts fulfill through judicial review and judicial activism. This is an important, but narrow focus and it holds the risk of delivering a distorted picture of the links between the justice system and the political order. There is, with regard to our purpose, a second limitation: these books almost never deal with the effects of court decisions on regime transitions.[5] They study behavior of courts in situations which are not a direct threat to the survival of a political system, such as the fight for equal rights and the anti-war activism in the United States, and the domestic opposition of dissident writers in Eastern Europe. Adequate literature is thus scarce. This is not to say that political science and sociology of law publications are of no use at all to the study of the criminal justice system in regime crises. They certainly can be exploited as suppliers of key notions and relevant hypotheses.

Paths Toward Redemocratization

In a recent essay, A. Stepan differentiates several paths to redemocratization.[6] In three of these, warfare and foreign occupation play a vital part in the process of restoration: the return to democracy takes place after the defeat of an external conqueror. Stepan sees the events in Belgium, Norway, Denmark, the Netherlands, France, Italy and Greece, after WW II, as cases which fall into this broad category. The differences between these countries are linked to the answer to four crucial questions: (1) did the population perceive the leaders of the original regime as culpable for the conquest; (2) did the previous leaders collaborate with the occupier; (3) did a resistance movement unconnected to the defeated democratic leadership become a competing center of national identification and authority; and (4) did the occupation bring enduring changes in the social, economic, and political structures of the country. Stepan writes: "The

---

3 Shattuck, P. (1974) Law as Politics. 7/1 Comparative Politics 130.

4 A series of publications originated in the early seventies and was aimed at an understanding of the repression of the political unrest that shook the United States in the sixties: Balbus, I. (1973) The Dialectics of Legal Repression. Black Rebels before the American Criminal Courts. New York: Russell Sage Foundation; Becker,T. (ed.)(1971) Political Trials. Indianapolis: Bobbs-Merrill; Goodell, C. (1973) Political Prisoners in America. New York: Random House. Their major inspiration was Kirchheimer, O. (1961) Political Justice. The Use of Legal Procedure for Political Ends. Princeton: Princeton University Press. Also important are: Hannover, H. and E. (1966) Politische Justiz 1918-1933. Frankfurt: Fischer; Schubert, G. (1974) Judicial Policy Making. The Political Role of the Courts. Glenview: Scott and Foresman. Recent publications include: Christenson, R. (1986) Political Trials: Gordian Knots in the Law. New Brunswick: Transaction Books; Colton, D. and Graber, E. (1982) Teacher Strikes and the Courts. Lexington: Heath; Koch, H. (1989) In the name of the Volk: Political Justice in Hitler's Germany. London: Tauris; Jacob H. (1986) Law and Politics in the United States. Boston: Little and Brown; Waltman, J. and Holland, K. (eds.)(1988) The Political Role of Law Courts in Modern Democracies. London: MacMillan.

5 Two exceptions: Kircheimer, O. o.c.; Hannover H. and E. o.c.

6 Stepan, A. (1982) Paths toward Redemocratization: Theoretical and Comparative Considerations, in O'Donnell, Schmitter and Whitehead (eds) o.c. 64-84.

more the answer is in the negative for all questions, the more likely it is that the outcome after reconquest will be the restoration of the previous democratic system, with full legal continuities between the old and new democratic regimes."[7] According to Stepan the obvious cases that fit this path to redemocratization are the Netherlands, Belgium, Norway and Denmark. For reasons that fall outside the main argument of this article, I disagree with this author's interpretation of the conditions that guided Belgium's return to democracy. But he is right in stating that the ultimate outcome was "restoration with full legal continuities between the old and new democratic regimes".

Courts and the Return to Democracy

Redemocratization has not been an easy task in Belgium. The first nine months after the end of the occupation witnessed a continuing inability of the newly liberated country and its political institutions.[8] Democracy looked pale and vulnerable. But gradually things changed and a stable democracy was finally firmly established. How was this stability achieved?

A major trend in comparative politics defines stability as the "...long-term ability to make decisions and secure adherence to them without the use of naked force".[9] Stability thus has two components: an instrumental one, effectiveness (the ability "...to satisfy the basic functions of government as defined by the expectations of most members of a society"[10]) and an evaluative one, legitimacy (the capacity to secure loyalty and keep the conviction alive that the political institutions are trustworthy). The judicial system has a key role in the establishment of legitimacy as was demonstrated in two ways in post-war Belgium. Shortly after the liberation of the country the Supreme Court ('Hof van Cassatie') ruled that all the legislative measures taken by the Belgian government-in-exile had full legality, including those laws that dismantled the legal output of the authoritarian collaborationist order.[11] But another task of great importance was given to the criminal justice system: the trial and punishment of those who collaborated with the

---

[7] Idem, 66.

[8] See Huyse, L. and Dhondt, S. (1991). Onverwerkt verleden. Collaboratie en repressie in België—1942-1952 (The Undigested Past. Collaboration and Repression in Belgium). Leuven: Kritak.

[9] The definition is S.M. Lipset's taken from his chapter in Smelser, N. (1967) Sociology: An Introduction. New York: Wiley, (p. 442), but has been widely accepted.

[10] Lipset, S.M. (1959) Political Sociology, in Merton, R.K. Sociology Today. New York: Harper and Row, (p. 108).

[11] Germany imposed a military rule on occupied Belgium. The civil administration of the country thus remained in the hands of Belgians. But national and local administration were gradually taken over by members of three Germanophile movements (two Flemish: VNV and DeVlag, one Francophone: Rex). Most of the prewer holders of public positions were expelled from office.

occupying force so as to strip them of all remaining legitimacy. This latter process is the major focus of our article.[12]

The Purge of the Belgian Quislings

The political elite who in September 1944, returned to power had many reasons to organize the elimination of the collaborators as efficiently as possible. The legitimacy of the reinstated leadership partly depended on the speed and the thoroughness with which the unpatriotic governors of occupied Belgium and their following were expelled from the political and public fora.[13] But the returning elite also knew that its authority and legitimacy were challenged by a new and unquestioned power, the resistance movements. It had to avoid every political move which could push the resistants in the direction of revolutionary action.[14] Any suggestion of weakness in the government's handling of the collaborators would certainly have been a provocation in the eyes of the resistance movements.

The Belgian government-in-exile and its immediate successors developed two ways of dealing with the collaborators of the German invaders. Part of the punishment took place outside the criminal justice system. Trials without courts were held in many governmental departments and public agencies. They were aimed at examining the wartime behavior of civil servants and, eventually purging those who had endangered the integrity of the nation-state. Political control by the government was almost total here.

But the core of the operation against the collaborators was judicial. Manipulation of the criminal process for political purposes, here the granting of legitimacy to a restored elite, is a risky enterprise. It runs counter to the sacred principle of separation of powers and it creates precedents which can be turned against the political leadership. The consecutive governments therefore chose not to try to impose their will on the criminal justice system that traditionally is charged with adjudication, viz. the civil courts. Instead they turned to the military courts and made them competent for the trial of collaborators. This strategy opened several doors for political intervention, while keeping such intervention formally within the realms of legality. One opportunity was linked with the appointment of military personnel as judges: three of the five judges in every court were army officers. It was to be expected that

---

12 This mission was, as we will later explain in greater detail, not devoid of ambiguity since it sometimes collided with the hunt for effectiveness, the other face of political stability.

13 A complicating factor was that a large part of the collaborating population belonged to political movements (VNV in Flanders, REX in Francophone Belgium) that had won between 13% and 20% of the parliamentary seats in the prewar elections of 1936 end 1939. These movements had thus been for a long time redoubtable competitors for power. See: Brustein W. (1988) The Political Geography of Belgian Fascism: The Case of Rexism. 88/53 American Sociological Review 69-90.

14 See Warner, G. (1978) La crise politique Belge de novembre 1944: un coup d'état manqué? (The Political Crisis of November 1944 in Belgium: An Aborted Coup?). 79/798 Courrier Hebdomadaire du Crisp 2-26.

these non-professional judges would be easier targets for political pressure. Political use of the judicial process was also facilitated by what happened in the prosecutor's office. The Belgian military procedure involves the merger, in the hands of the prosecutor, of competences which in the civil procedure are spread over several judicial roles: to start an inquiry, to make an arrest and extend or terminate it, to write a search-warrant and execute it, to proceed against or discharge a suspect, to require a penalty. One former Prime Minister has, in Parliament, spoken of these prosecutors as "*...armés d'une pussiance comparable à celle d'un roi-nègre.*"[15] Unlike judges, prosecutors are members of a strict hierarchical organization in which guidelines move from top to bottom. Some of these guidelines may come from the head of the department of justice, a political figure. In sum, the prosecutors in the military courts had unusually large competences and were more vulnerable to political pressure. But there is more. The manpower of the military prosecuting office had to be increased tenfold.

Table 1
PROFESSIONAL ORIGIN OF NEWLY RECRUITED MILITARY PROSECUTORS*

Professional origin of all military prosecutors	Sept 1944	Oct-Dec 1944	Jan-March 1945	April-June 1945	after June 1945	total
Civil judge or prosector %	29%	8%	4%	1%		10
Advocate (practicing lawyer)	57%	80%	85%	89%	82%	78%
Other	14%	12%	11%	10%	18%	12%
Total	100%	100%	100%	100%	100%	100%
	(n=126)	(n=169)	(n=132)	(n=91)	(n=33)	(n=551)
Professional status of recruited advocates						
At least 8 years of practice	37%	20%	15%	21%	4%	19%
4-7 years of practice	29%	25%	15%	38%	37%	27%
Less than 4 years of practice	34%	55%	70%	41%	59%	54%
Total	100%	100%	100%	100%	100%	100%
	(n=71)	(n=135)	(n=113)	(n=81)	(n=27)	(n=427)

* Based on the decrees of appointment as published in the *Belgisch Staatsblad* (Official Gazette)

15 "...armed with an authority that resembled the omnipotence of an African king" (J. Pholien, Senate, April 9, 1946).

That was the only way to deal efficiently with the 405,000 files of Belgians suspected of unpatriotic behavior (7% of the adult population). At first, it was thought that the civil justice system would serve as a sufficient source for appointments. But this turned out to be a vast miscalculation as can be seen in Table 1. The share of practising prosecutors and professional judges in the consecutive waves of appointments sank from 29% in September 1944 to 1% in the Spring of 1945. The Minister of Justice then redirected his efforts and solicited members of the Bar. Their share in the recruitment figures rose quickly to a maximum of 89% in the second trimester of 1945. But in no time, as the second part of Table 1 tells us, the reserve of experienced advocates was exhausted and very young lawyers had to be recruited as prosecutors. This was an important development. Fidelity to legality and the rule of law, if it is imbued in the minds of members of the judiciary, is a strong safeguard against political and partisan use of the judicial process.[16] It is not clear where and how such fidelity originates. Abel and Lewis, dealing with this problem, write: "How much of this behavior can be attributed to the office—which is supposed to embody legality—and how much to the background or training of its occupant?"[17] But it seems plausible to hypothesize that men who have just left law school are badly equipped to offer resistance against political intrusion in their activities as prosecutors.

Criminalization of Political Acts

The trial and punishment of military collaborators and of informers were executed without much public or political debate. But the search for legitimacy made the restored elite very sensitive to what would happen to the political collaborators of the German occupation. These men and women were responsible for the expulsion of the old leadership and for the establishment of an authoritarian regime. The problem was that the prewar penal law did not cover the many forms of political action which only in the context of the total (psychological) warfare of World War II took a collaborationist dimension. Simple extension of the coverage of penal law was not self-evident, since part of the political behavior in question could be seen as falling under the constitutional right of freedom of opinion, freedom of speech or freedom of association. How could the rank-and-file of the VNV or REX movements, which in the thirties participated in the parliamentary game, be punished? Why was a man culpable of a crime, whose only political activity had been the subscription to a collaborationist journal? The Belgian government-in-exile answered these questions in a straightforward way: it stripped an extensive list of political actions of their political dimension by qualifying them as

---

16 Abel and Lewis write: "There is some evidence that professional identity strengthens the 'independence' of the judiciary and its willingness to defy or at least obstruct grossly illegal acts by the mere political branches" (Abel, R. and Lewis, P. (eds.) (1989) Lawyers in Society, Vol. 3, Comparative Theories, Berkeley: University of California Press. (p.482).

17 Ibidem, 482.

ordinary crimes. The result was that tens thousands of Belgians were punished for their political behavior during the occupation.

Decriminalization of Economic Collaboration

Legitimacy is only one of two dimensions of stability. Effectiveness is the other. According to the mainstream of political science publications, effectiveness is the capacity of a regime to satisfy the basic functions of government by making the economy grow.[18] This task was huge in a country, the industrial infrastructure of which was crippled by four years of German looting and several months of bombing by the allied forces. Providing food, clothing and coal to the population was for more than a year an almost impossible mission for the political leadership. Of crucial importance was the unconditional cooperation of the economic, financial and industrial elite. It was precisely at this point that the purge of the collaborators risked becoming counterproductive. More than 110,000 complaints had been received on the basis of Article 115 of the Penal Code that made economic collaboration punishable. Nearly 60,000 of these files referred to blue collar workers who had volunteered to work in Germany. They were not at the heart of the problem. The other suspects were commercial and industrial people. The opening of a file was a serious handicap for most of the involved commercial and industrial businesses: it meant seizure of the books and sometimes required sequestration of goods and assets. This considerably mortgaged the search for economic recovery. In May 1945, after nine months of hesitation, the socialist-led government edited a so-called interpretative law in which Article 115 of the Penal Code underwent a substantial reduction of its scope. The prosecutor had to prove now that the wartime behavior of a business man or of a plant manager was aimed at helping the German war machine. Completely in tune with Belgium's preference for delicately-balanced compromises, the government also ruled to dismiss all charges against the 60,000 blue collar workers. This double surgical operation, in fact, caused the decriminalization of much of the formerly punishable economic behavior: only 2% of all files resulted in a court case (against 43% for military collaboration, 33% for political collaborators and 18% for police informers).[19]

The Ambivalence of the Criminal Justice System

It is in the differential treatment of political collaboration on the one side and of economic collaboration on the other, that the political use of

---

18 "In the modern world, such effectiveness meant primarily constant economic development" (Lipset, S.M. (1963) Political Man. The Social Bases of Politics. New York: Doubleday. p.70) and from the same author: "In new states or postrevolutionary regimes ... effectiveness means one thing: economic development" (Political Sociology, in Smelser, N. o.c. 445).

19 The source is Gilissen, J. (1950-1951) Etude sur la Gilissen répression de l'incivisme. 1950-1951 Revue de Droit Pénal et de Criminilogie 513-628.

the criminal justice system is most visible. How exceptional is such a situation?

In socio-legal studies of criminal law and criminal justice strong arguments have been developed to support the proposition that, in Western Europe, the judicial reaction towards criminal behavior is ambivalent: property crimes (theft, burglary, larceny, robbery) and crimes of violence (various types of assault, theft with violence) have generally been prosecuted more rigidly than violations of certain other rules, especially rules in the area of economic regulation. Infringements of the second type (tax evasion and fraudulous foreign exchange transactions, price control violation, fraud in custom duties, but also violation of the building code, water pollution, etc.) are treated with rather different judicial and administrative procedures, which in many cases aim at decriminalization of the charges.[20] The specific handling of these latter crimes is linked with some of their characteristics: the victim is diffuse and abstract ('the economy', 'the state'); the legal grounds, on which prosecution is based, are challenged or are at least not deeply anchored in the legal consciousness of the justiciables[21] ; these offenses are proportionally, more to be found in the higher strata of the population. The last attribute has a central place in the argument: the differential treatment of white collar crime is theoretically linked with the legislators', judges' and administrators' resentment against a traditional criminal prosecution of holders of key positions in the social and economic order. A highly publicized trial and conviction of such persons and the imposition of imprisonment are considered by some groups in society to do more damage to the social order than the crime itself. The cautiousness, with which criminal law and the criminal court system then proceed, is to be seen as a sort of autocensorship in defense of the general interest. That is precisely what happened in the case of economic collaborators.[22]

But how can we reconcile this theory with the fate of the political collaborators? Political assistance to an occupying power has, as an offence, many of the characteristics which we attributed to economic collaboration. The victim, 'the integrity of the state', was diffuse. The legal grounds for prosecution and the procedural techniques which were used were challenged by the defendants and their lawyers. Their argument was that in the Belgian legal tradition, political crimes, if need be, have to be judged by a grand jury. Lastly, the offenders often belonged to the intellectual and administrative elite: teachers, journalists, writers, civil

---

20 The key reference here is Sutherland, E.H. (1949) White Collar Crime. New York: Holt, Rinehart and Winston.

21 See the publications of the Knowledge and Opinion about Law Research Group, esp. Podgorecki, A. et al. (1974) Knowledge and Opinion about Law. London: Martin Robinson.

22 Studies of the Dutch, French and Norwegian treatment of economic collaboration came to a similar conclusion. See Belinfante, A. (1978) In plaats van Bijltjesdag: de geschiedenis van de bijzonderr rechtspleging na de tweede wereldoorlog (The Trials of Dutch Collaborators). Assen: Van Gorcum; Rousso, H. (1987) Le syndrome de Vichy. Paris: Seuil; Aubert, V. (1964) Likhet og Rett, Oslo: Pax.

servants.[23] But political collaboration was prosecuted without the cautiousness which usually accompanies the handling of infringements with these three attributes. This problem suggests the need for an amendment to the 'ambivalence theory': the autocensorship which legislators, prosecutors and judges apply, only operates when applicable to men and women who belong to a totally unquestioned elite. In the eyes of the traditional elites, the Belgian leaders and members of the Germanophile movements had been dangerous competitors for a much longer time. Accordingly, there was no need for prudence and generosity.[24]

Political or Partisan Justice?

All political trials, writes Christenson, differ from ordinary trials because they address simultaneously a legal and a political agenda. But they are not equal in their ranking of that dual agenda. Partisan trials "...proceed according to a fully political agenda with only a facade of legality (although the legalism might be turgid)". The issue in all these trials is the same: "expediency in the use of power". A second category include those which operate under the rule of law: "They are fair trials despite their political agenda."[25]

In terms of formal legality the trials of Belgian collaborators fall into the second category. Every procedure was covered by law.[26] But the real conditions, as described earlier in this article, in which the criminal justice system worked made the dominance of the political agenda a constant possibility. Reality sometimes deviated from what the formal codes predicted. There is one vigorous illustration of this latent reality. Two thirds of those who were accused of political collaboration did not appear before the courts, but were registered on a very special list. Registration, which was planned as a sort of summary proceedings, implied the loss of a series of political and civil rights. It was the military prosecutor, and he alone, who decided in the first instance which persons were sent to the courts and who was put instead on the list. Tens of thousands of Belgians were registered. However, not the size of the group but the timing of the campaign is important. Almost 60% of all registrations were made between December 1945 and February 15th 1946, that is, in a period of two months. Finishing the remaining part of the operation took the prosecutors more than two years. The extreme speed with which the registration started is no coincidence. February 17th 1946, was the date of the first post-war

---

23 See for an empirical description of political collaboration: Huyse, L. and Dhondt, S. o.c.

24 The French and Dutch situation was different. In both these countries political collaboration was performed by persons who in the pre-war period either belonged to the traditional groups, or did not constitute a real political threat. As a consequence political collaborators were spared or were granted a general pardon shortly after the war. See Belinfante, A. o.c.; Rousso, H. o.c.

25 Christenson, R. o.c. 10-11.

26 Such a qualification would certainly not be accepted by many of those who were convicted. Their definition of the situation will be closer to what Christenson calls "victor's justice": a purely partisan trial of a defeated regime.

elections. In this electoral campaign the parties of the left fought a bitter battle with the catholic party, then in opposition. It was thought that most of the political collaborators were catholics. Preventing them from becoming candidates or having a vote could give the catholic party a serious handicap. The government, which was based on a coalition of left parties, put pressure on the prosecutors to deprive as many political collaborators as possible of their eligibility and of their right to vote. Once the elections were over, the tempo of the operation slowed down considerably. The story certainly suggests that the line between partisan justice and political justice under the rule of law was very thin indeed.

5

ITALY

EDITOR'S INTRODUCTION

Benito Mussolini, founder and head of the National Fascist Party (PNF), became prime minister of Italy in 1922. Although he was invited to form this government by King Victor Emmanuel III, Mussolini's movement of fascist paramilitary *squadristri* ("Blackshirts") had already gained control of most of the country through a campaign that included not only political rallies but murder and the violent seizure of towns. Over the next decade, Mussolini gained control over all parts of the government, including the parliament, the courts, and the army. By the mid-1930s, the fascist regime of *il Duce* (the leader), as Mussolini became known, instituted strict censorship of the press and banned opposition political parties. On average, the political police conducted 20,000 searches, arrests, interviews and seizures of literature each week. Political prisoners were often subjected to internal exile. Homosexuals, political dissenters, and intellectuals were especially subject to persecution. With the exception of the Catholic Church and its affiliates, no non-fascist organizations were permitted. Large state corporations were created to oversee all aspects of the economy. By the late 1930s, the regime became increasingly militaristic, imposing changes on Italian customs and attire. As Italy's alliance with Nazi Germany grew, a series of anti-Jewish laws were adopted, provoking strong protest within Italy.

In 1940, Mussolini entered World War II on the side of Hitler and the Axis powers. In July 1943, Allied forces landed in Italy. Mussolini was jailed and a new government was formed with Marshal Pietro Badoglio as prime minister. On September 3, Italy signed an armistice with the Allies, with an unconditional surrender announced on September 8. The German army occupied much of Italy, blocking the Allied and Italian forces. On September 12, 1943, the German military rescued Mussolini, who established a new government of the "Italian Social Republic," based in German-occupied Salò in northern Italy. This division of the country between Mussolini's Salò regime and the liberated *Regno del Sud* (Southern Kingdom) remained until the end of the war in 1945.

In late 1943, plans were announced in the south to purge and prosecute Fascists and their collaborators. When Rome was retaken from German forces in June 1944, a new government was formed, headed by Ivanoe Bonomi. Victor Emmanuel, compromised by his early relationship with Mussolini, transferred the monarchy to his son Humbert. In April 1945, during the final weeks of the war, Mussolini was captured and shot by members of the resistance, who hung his disfigured corpse upside down in Milan's central square for public display.

From the first stage of liberation through the post-war reconstruction of the country, the treatment of those who served Mussolini's regime became one of the most controversial issues within Italian society. Conservative parties and the church cautioned against severe, large-scale punishment of fascists and collaborators; the Communist and Socialist parties argued for harsher enforcement. The anti-fascist resistance groups who fought to liberate northern Italy from German control organized politically into a coalition called the Committee of National Liberation (CLN) and advocated the most comprehensive and punitive sanctions. A High Commission for Sanctions against Fascism was created. Its mandate had four parts: criminal prosecution, purge of the government, confiscation of ill-gotten profits, and confiscation of Fascist party property. By June 1946, after the processing of thousands of cases, an amnesty was adopted. Although some parts of the sanctions program continued and there was agitation for harsher measures—particularly in the north, where partisans continued to be dominant—the program was phased out after 1946.

The following document related to transitional justice in Italy can be found in Volume III of this collection:

- 1947 Constitution—Transitory and Final Provisions

CONTENDING WITH A FASCIST LEGACY

Giuseppe Di Palma, "Italy: Is There a Legacy and is it Fascist?"[*]

The scholar who wants to engage in a comparative study of the issues that successor democracies face concerning the legacies of the previous regime and democratic reconstruction may be guided by some discernible distinctions: (1) as to the nature of the previous regime, the distinction between authoritarian and totalitarian regimes; (2) as to the mode of its collapse, the distinctions between revolution, reform, or defeat; and (3) as to the agents who establish the successor democracy, the distinction between indigenous and occupation forces....

As to the nature of the previous regime, Fascist Italy was neither wholly totalitarian (compared to Germany-Austria) nor simply authoritarian ... but combined in an unresolved fashion elements of both. As to collapse, the generally accepted view that Fascism—like nazism in Germany-Austria, the Vichy regime in France, and military dictatorship in Japan—was overthrown through defeat in war is only partially correct. Mussolini's preemptive ouster designed to forestall defeat and the ensuing armed Resistance testify to the presence of domestic reformist and revolutionary elements.[1] Although the role of the Allied forces in dealing with the transition was important, it was not as salient in Italy as it was in Japan, Germany, and Austria. And the range of indigenous forces active in the Italian transition was broader than those in the other defeated countries. They ranged from a monarchy compromised by Fascism to the Communist party and the forces of the military-political machinery of the Resistance, thus reflecting a diversity that was surpassed only three decades later by the more peaceful and consensual Spanish transition.

If we add to these features, namely, the ambiguous character of Fascism and the diversity of the agents that were instrumental in the transition, the fact that the changeover was effected during a cold war that primarily reshaped anti-Fascist coalitions, we can say that the Italian transition was the most contentious of those triggered by World War II. Regardless of whether other solutions to the twin problem of the authoritarian legacy and democratic reconstruction could have been implemented, Italian political actors were widely divergent in their perceptions not only of what was desirable but also of what was possible and probable during those years.

As to the Fascist legacy, some of the domestic forces were of the opinion that defascistization had to and could be stopped quickly, as soon as a specific number of fascist institutions created by the dictatorship had

---

[*] Excerpted from Giuseppe Di Palma, "Italy: Is There a Legacy and is it Fascist?" in John H. Herz, ed., *From Dictatorship to Democracy: Coping with the Legacies of Authoritarianism and Totalitarianism*, Copyright © 1982 by John Herz (Greenwood Press, 1982), pp. 107-108, an imprint of Greenwood Publishing Group, Inc. Westport, CT. Reprinted with permission.

[1] Evolution/self-dissolution was the initial mode followed at the end of Franco's Spain and the Greek junta. Revolution initially marked the sudden end of the Portuguese dictatorship.

been abolished and top Fascist cadres had been purged or punished. Others believed that the process should be extended in order to reform or transform those pre-Fascist institutions and structures in which Fascism had found nurture and asylum. To be sure, this issue posed a dilemma to those grappling with legacy problems in the other defeated countries and, indeed, to other successor democracies.... But in the other defeated countries legacy as an issue of contention was partially defused by the much closer Allied supervision of defascistization, thus displacing the blame for doing too much (or too little) on the occupying forces.[2] In Italy the issue was complicated by the fact that domestic forces who were given some leeway in matters of defascistization included elements of the previous regime; yet the latter's new attitude toward Fascism was not considered sufficient by anti-Fascist forces either to absolve them from past responsibilities for the Fascist takeover and the war or to justify the termination of defascistization.[3]

The same contentiousness characterized democratic reconstruction. Indeed, reconstruction appeared to most domestic forces as the obverse of the legacy issue, another way of making Italy safe from dictatorship. But how much and in what way should the postwar democracy depart from the incipient democracy whose weaknesses had propelled Fascism to power? And what place should the Marxist left occupy in it?...

*Gianfranco Pasquino, "The Demise of the First Fascist Regime and Italy's Transition to Democracy: 1943-1948"**

[The Role of Fascism in Italian Society]

After almost twenty years of rule, Benito Mussolini was overthrown as head of Fascism and prime minister of the Italian government on 25 July 1943.... The formal demise of Fascism was the product of a vote taken by the Fascist Grand Council "calling for royal leadership and the rehabilitation of moribund state institutions."[1] This vote (by nineteen out of twenty-eight members) created the conditions under which the king could dismiss Mussolini as prime minister of Italy. Historically responsible for having appointed Mussolini in 1922, the king assumed responsibility for his dismissal as well. No single institution opposed the king's action and the immediate reaction of the population was one of enthusiasm as well as

---

2 In France, formally a victor, the issue of how to deal with Vichy was simplified by the fact that it was a short-lived and semicollaborationist regime partially imposed by the German occupation. Similar considerations also apply to Austria and more so to the Quisling type of regimes.

3 Thus there was less room in post-Fascist Italy for the evolution from within that marked Spain after Franco and might even have marked Portugal under Caetano.

* Excerpted from Gianfranco Pasquino, "The Demise of the First Fascist Regime and Italy's Transition to Democracy: 1943-1948," in Guillermo O'Donnell, Philippe C. Schmitter & Laurence Whitehead, eds., *Transitions from Authoritarian Rule: Southern Europe* (Johns Hopkins University Press, 1986), pp. 45-47.

1 C.F. Delzell, *Mussolini's Enemies: The Italian Anti-Fascist Resistance* (New York: Howard Fertig, 1974), pp. 231-32.

preoccupation: enthusiasm for the fall of Fascism, preoccupation regarding the continuation of the war.

Many issues were raised by this bloodless breakdown of a twenty-year-old regime and by the lack of organized reaction and opposition to it. The two most important ones are, of course, the nature of the regime (and its apparent weakness) and the determinants of its demise. The two are related, and their analysis will yield the elements necessary to explain the process of breakdown and to understand the subsequent transition to a democratic regime.

It has rightly been pointed out that the Fascist attempt to integrate Italian society into the state in a totalitarian way did not succeed.[2] Italian Fascism can thus be characterized as a failed totalitarian experiment; it allowed the persistence of a degree of limited pluralism which has been singled out as an important characteristic of authoritarian regimes.[3] The presence of the monarchy created what Mussolini dubbed, "the tragedy of the diarchy," whereby it was impossible for the Duce completely to "fascistize" the state.[4] The Italian form of limited pluralism was evident on the one hand in the existence of the monarchy and the preservation of its constitutional powers; the persistence of an army whose loyalty went to the king rather than to Mussolini or to Fascism; the continuity of a state apparatus already bureaucratic and authoritarian, but fragile and cumbersome; and on the other hand, in the inability of Fascism to create viable institutions of its own to replace or supersede the traditional institutions. The House of Corporations never really took hold (while the Royal Senate remained a respected body); the National Fascist party became more and more a bureaucratic organization, overstaffed and largely passive.[5] Ironically, the only body that could exercise real power and play an active role, the Fascist Grand Council, was the one that took the initiative in the ousting of Mussolini and, consequently, in the demise of Fascism (a connection of which most of its members were well aware).[6]

Not even in civil society had Fascism achieved hegemony. Landowners and industrialists acquired and enjoyed a free hand; protected from a working class deprived of its organizations, they made large profits both in peacetime and in wartime. Most important of all, through the concordat signed by Mussolini and the Lateran Pacts, the church was able to reacquire a legally sanctioned role in civil society. While the church never became an anti-Fascist institution, and in some instances was deeply

---

2 A. Aquarone, *L'organizzazione dello Stato totalitario* (Turin: Einaudi, 1965), p. 290.

3 Juan Linz's well-known definition is most appropriate to Italian Fascism: "Authoritarian regimes are political systems with limited, not responsible, political pluralism; without elaborate and guiding ideology (but with distinctive mentalities); without intensive nor extensive political mobilization (except some points in their development); and in which a leader (or occasionally a small group) exercise power within formally ill-defined limits but actually quite predictable ones." "An Authoritarian Regime: Spain," in *Cleavages, Ideologies, and Party Systems*, ed. E. Allardt and Y. Littunen (Helsinki: Academic Bookstore, 1964), p. 297.

4 [omitted]

5 Aquarone, *L'organizzazione dello Stato totalitario*, pp. 301-2.

6 For the composition and the functioning of the Grand Council, last convened 7 December 1939, see G. Binachi, *25 luglio. Crollo di un regime* (Milan: Mursia, 1963), pp. 519-26.

compromised with the regime, it prevented Fascism from achieving full hegemony over the minds of many Italians.[7]

Does this mean that Fascism never had the consent of the Italian population? On this point the debate is still rampant, and acrimonious.... The issue, of course, is whether that consent was a purely passive acquiescence to the existence of a regime that granted security and internal peace to most of its citizens, or whether it involved active support for the choices and the policies made and implemented by that regime.[8]

In order to arrive at a balanced assessment of a quantity and quality of consent Fascism received, one cannot refrain from pointing to one historical fact. Despite the persistence of anti-Fascist activities throughout the *ventennio* (twenty-year reign), the great majority of the population "did not demonstrate willingness to consider the regime as a mortal enemy which had to be overthrown at any cost or, even less, to run serious risks in order to achieve such a goal."[9] On the other hand, it is also true that Fascism never engaged in massive mobilization efforts after its phase of initial consolidation and, therefore, potential conflicts were largely avoided (with few exceptions such as a clash with the church and Catholic associations in 1931).

Expressions of support became, as in other authoritarian regimes, fundamentally ritualistic and symbolic, and oppositional activities never enjoyed widespread support.... Briefly, the most important conclusion to emerge so far is that Fascism never enjoyed full control over the Italian political system and its members. It was unable and unwilling to destroy and reshape all political and bureaucratic institutions (there was no *Gleichschaltung* as in Nazi Germany) and therefore was compelled to share power with the fundamentally monarchist state apparatus and with the church. It was unsuccessful in the creation of its own institutions, for example, the House of Corporations, the National Fascist party, the Fascist Syndicates. It exploited adroitly a pervasive climate of authoritarianism in Europe and the imperfect democratization of the previous Italian regime, but it proved unable to build large-scale support for its aims and goals. However, one should be cautious in concluding that Fascism was consequently and certainly doomed. Indeed, the debate on the determinants of the fall of Fascism remains lively and unresolved, for good reasons....

---

7 See R. A. Webster, *The Cross and the Fasces: Christian Democracy and Fascism in Italy* (Stanford: Stanford University Press, 1960); P. Scoppola and F. Traniello, eds., *I cattolici tra fascismo e democrazia* (Bologna: Il Mulino, 1975) and P. G. Zunino, *La questione cattolica nello sinistra italiana (1940-1945)* (Bologna: Il Mulino, 1976).

8 Specifically, R. De Felice, *Mussolini il duce. Gli anni del consenso (1929-1936)* (Turin: Einaudi, 1974); *Intervista sul fascismo* (Bari: Laterza, 1975); and G. Amendola, *Intervista sull'antifascismo* (Bari: Laterza, 1976).

9 Aquarone, *L'organizzazione dello Stato totalitario*, p. 310....

Giuseppe Di Palma, "Italy: Is There a Legacy and is it Fascist?"[*]

[A Preliminary Analysis of Defascistization]

[I]n Italy—much more than in the other defeated countries—the definition of what Fascism was, its disposition, and the reactions to that disposition became entangled with and cannot be understood outside the contentious issues associated with the transition. And because the evolution of the new democracy has also been affected by the outcome of contentiousness, the issue of legacy—or, if you wish, of antifascism as a collective value to be realized—has been a recurrent theme in Italian political life. For example, most of the literature on defascistization bemoans the fact that the machinery of defascistization failed to achieve significant results either in the prosecution of crime or in ridding the state apparatus of undesirable personnel.[33] Many accounts of the transition interpret defascistization as an aborted process, a missed opportunity to break significantly with the Fascist (and the pre-Fascist) past and finally fulfill the frustrated hopes of the Italian *Risorgimento*.[34]

That the machinery of defascistization achieved meager results (at least in terms of what many anti-Fascists not only of the left expected) is unquestionable. That this can be attributed, as some maintain, to political and bureaucratic conspiracies to restore the old state in a new guise is, however, a moralizing view that explains everything and nothing. To be sure, "conspiracies" existed galore; most compromised officials remained in office or were reinstated, and many of the most hideous Fascist crimes committed during the liberation were either not punished or condoned. Even making ample allowance for these interpretations the nature of both Fascism and the transition made it very difficult to achieve more radical results.[35]

Juan Linz has noted that in dealing with the legacy issue, democratic "regimes succeeding highly ideological and exclusionary totalitarian regimes ... face a less difficult situation than those succeeding amorphous authoritarian regimes."[36] The reason is twofold. First, it is difficult to

---

[*] Excerpted from Giuseppe Di Palma, "Italy: Is There a Legacy and is it Fascist?" in John H. Herz, ed., *From Dictatorship to Democracy: Coping with the Legacies of Authoritarianism and Totalitarianism*, Copyright © 1982 by John Herz (Greenwood Press, 1982), pp. 116-119, 121-122, an imprint of Greenwood Publishing Group, Inc. Westport, CT. Reprinted with permission.

33 See as examples of this literature Guido Quazza, *Resistenza e storia d'Italia* (Milan, 1976); Antonio Bevere, "Fascismo e antifascismo nella prassi dell'apparato statale," in *Fascismo e antifascismo nell'Italia repubblicana*, ed. Guido Quazza (Turin, 1976), chapter 2; Marcello Flores, "L'epurazione," in AA.VV., *L'Italia della liberazione*, pp. 413-467.

34 References to the liberation and the Resistance as a *Secondo Risorgimento* are common both in the literature and in political discourse.

35 As Achille Battaglia commented, "...it is not true that the judiciary consistently sabotaged antifascist laws, thus weakening the new regime. Within some limits, the very opposite is true; the fallacious interpretation and the lack of enforcement of the laws were born from the political weakness of antifascism." See Achille Battaglia, *I guidici e la politica* (Bari, 1962), p. 96.

36 Juan Linz, *The Breakdown of Democratic Regimes: Crisis, Breakdown and Reequilibration* (Baltimore, 1978), p. 35.

justify legally or even politically the retroactive prosecution of leaders and cadres of a regime that was not highly differentiated with respect to the larger society and to the past (especially one that enjoyed popular support). Second, it is difficult to identify objectively responsible persons and groups, the risk being of including too many (or too few). Aside from this, questions can be raised about the efficacy of using purges that could result in prejudicing loyalties against the new democratic order. In the Italian case, once the outer totalitarian layers were removed, there remained the more problematic task of dealing with the older, more deeply rooted, and more hidden authoritarian underpinnings. There are, in principle at least, two ways to resolve such predicaments.

The first is by the peaceful and consensual self-transformation of the authoritarian regime, which has the advantage of allowing former regime opponents as well as old regime cadres to legitimize one another without requiring the extensive punishment or banning of individuals and groups.[37] But in Italy, contrary to Spain after Franco, such an evolution proved impossible once the Fascist regime entered the war, and once the monarchy, despite its break with Fascism, proved incapable (because of its inability to pursue intelligent relegitimizing behavior) of asserting itself as a stable force in a consensual transition to democracy. In the second way, the agent of change charged with determining the course of the legacy issue is an occupying force. This way may prove to be deleterious by adding new to old injustices, especially when the occupier is motivated by vindictiveness or Jacobin zeal and has little knowledge of local reality. However, it may prove to be advantageous by relieving the domestic forces of the task of defascistization and thus preventing the sundering of the new regime. But Allied forces in Italy, after an initial attempt in the south, soon abandoned their dominant role in defascistization.

As the war dragged on, the Allies found it increasingly convenient to rely on local officials and notables, that is, on the existing political class, to administer the liberated territories and thus tended to soft-pedal initiatives toward rapid defascistization. When the CLN [Committee of National Liberation] entered the political arena, the Allies began to recognize that domestic interests were involved in this issue. Following the liberation of Rome, it became a standard feature of Allied rule in many liberated areas to apply Italian defascistization laws often through interim Italian courts while awaiting the installation of the Italian machinery. Also, the Allies showed more interest in the purging of state and local apparatuses than they did in the prosecution of Fascist crimes, which, contrary to their recognition of the international nature of Nazi and Japanese crimes, they considered entirely an Italian matter. When they stepped in, their action at times was dictated by the desire to render purges more effective, but more often their intervention was motivated by the need to curb apparent instances of retaliation. This was especially the case in the north, where, after liberation day, partisan tribunals and people's

---

37 Giuseppe de Palma, "Founding Coalitions in Southern Europe: Legitimacy and hegemony," *Government and Opposition*, 15 (Spring 1980), pp. 162-189.

courts, not recognized by the government and the CLNAI [the northern Committee of National Liberation], began to take the law into their own hands.[38]

What these aspects of the Allied role in defascistization indicate is that the British and the American authorities took a less punitive and a more armslength view of Italian Fascism than they did of Nazism. The smaller international role of Fascism, the fact that it had been far less cruel and dehumanizing than Nazism and that it had been overthrown by internal dissent, the opportunity to use repentant political and bureaucratic classes to rebuild a stable political order—all were factors suggesting a less harsh (and a less direct) treatment. But in choosing a low profile (and they probably could not have done otherwise), the Allies opened a Pandora's box, for the Italians were divided on the ostensibly lesser "evilness" of Fascism.

Had Fascism been, as Benedetto Croce and other pre-Fascist liberals have argued, merely a temporary but baleful sickness in the otherwise healthy body of pre-Fascist liberal Italy, normalization (and thus a return to liberal politics) via surgical removal would have been effective as well as legally and politically justifiable.[39] It would have been sanctioned by the lawful dismissal of Mussolini by the monarchy—a circumstance that alone would have reestablished the liberal state—and by the pact between the monarchy and the anti-Fascist parties. But Fascism was not an interlude, and the continuity of the state from pre-Fascism to Badoglio, apparent in many aspects, could not distance itself from Fascism to the extent implied in Croce's (and the monarchy's) arguments. What ought to be considered is not only the semiparliamentary fashion in which Mussolini was called to govern and did in fact govern until 1925 (Hitler, too, formally acceded to power by parliamentary means) but also the fact that even Mussolini's abolition of all residues of parliamentary life was never used by the party as a pretext for replacing the old state and its personnel. Instead, the party relied on legal institutions and codes (and constraints), some inherited from the past, that raised questions about the illegality of Fascism and the gap between the old state and the new regime. Of equal if not greater importance is the fact that, especially in the thirties, Fascism in Italy, far from being a mere repressive apparatus, enjoyed widespread although diluted "Bonapartest" support. All the questions raised doubts about the justice *and the sincerity* of retroactively punishing individuals and groups who had supported or benefited from Fascism.

Doubts remained despite the fact that the war had eroded that support, had resurrected the subversive face of Fascism, and had challenged the improvident philofascism of those who, perhaps hoping to constitutionalize it, had made possible Mussolini's assumption of power. Decisive in explaining these doubts is the fact that from the start, the control of defascistization was less in the hands of anti-Fascist forces,

---

38 All the points mentioned above are in Harris, *Allied Military Administration of Italy*, especially pp. 173, 224, 284.

39 For these remarks, see Gambino, *Storia del dopoguerra della liberazione*, pp. 73-77.

which, persecuted throughout the regime, would have been entitled to turn popular resentments of Fascism toward swift, extensive, and self-legitimizing popular justice, than it was in the hands of the old state apparatus. And that apparatus included a king who had been supreme commander of the armed forces at war, the heir to the crown who had been given command of one of the armies, and Marshal Badoglio who had earned his baton and the leadership of the joint chiefs of staff for masterminding the invasion of Ethiopia [under Mussolini]....

Like many Catholics and a few liberals, leftists had a view of Fascism that was radically different from Croce's. Rejecting the assertion that Fascism was an accident, they considered it a "revelation"—the visible perfection of the class-reactionary tendencies of the superficially liberal regime that preceded Fascism.... [A]fter the liberation of the north, laxity infected the entire [defascistization] apparatus, spilling over from the area of administrative purges to the more serious area of Fascist crimes. This caused a legitimate sense of injustice among anti-Fascist forces.[47] Nevertheless, the gadflylike pronouncements of the left (and they continued to be nothing more than pronouncements) catalyzed the resentments of those who assessed the defascistization process, at least in its purge aspect, as exceeding its limitations....

Despite defascistization, the old administrative class remained in place.[51] Judicial applications of the purge decrees and a final amnesty adopted in February 1948 resulted in the fact that "...most of the 1,879 civil servants who had been dismissed (for collaborating with the government of the north) and the 671 who had been compulsorily retired were reinstated.[52] Similarly, the whole process of confiscating the illicit gains of Fascist profiteers and of purging compromised business leaders came close to naught. As to Fascist criminals, the justified restraint shown in the early legal proceedings turned, as the war faded into the background, into a veritable travesty of prosecution and of [an earlier] amnesty.[53]...

---

47 Yet the law offered cause for laxity. For example, Article 2 of the July 1944 decree punished with death "members of the fascist government and fascist hierarchs guilty of having suppressed constitutional guarantees, destroyed popular liberties, created the fascist regime, compromised and betrayed the country, leading it to the present catastrophy." As Pavone comments, "no judge was able to find a single fascist who by his personal action could be deemed demonstrably responsible for that series of disasters." See Pavone, "La continuita dello stato," p. 244. Most of the heirarchs were executed on CLNAI instructions by partisan courts in the few days that followed the liberation.

51 My argument if it is not clear from the text is neither for nor against a deeper purge; it is with the mystifying nature of the process.

52 Harris, Allied Administration of Italy, p. 359. Data on the impact of purges are generic, scanty, and incomplete owing to the dispersion of archival material. See Flores, "L'epurazione," p. 442. There are also contradictions in the data reported at the time by the authorities in charge. See Pavone, "La continuita dello stato," p. 260. If the outcome of the purges was minimal, an equally important if poorly documented fact is that thousands were involved. We know that the military and especially the judiciary were little affected, but we do not know the impact on other administrative sectors and over time.

53 A perfect example of the change in judicial behavior is a sentence imposed by the Court of Cassation in March 1951. It interpreted the meaning of "cruel tortures" as a circumstance excluding a Fascist criminal from Togliatti's amnesty: "Tortures are especially cruel only if by their atrocity they horrify persons who are not alien to torturing." (Reported in

THE INITIAL PHASE

*Roy Palmer Domenico, "Italian Fascists on Trial, 1943-1948"**

[Efforts of the Badoglio Government 1943-44]

[Marshal Badoglio's] vague plans for a purge before September 8 existed largely on paper. Paranoid fear of neo-Fascist *revanche* rather than faith in democratization prompted Badoglio to consider a "defascistization commission," a purge office in embryo for a bifurcated attack, separate assaults against the high and the low bureaucracy. The campaign against the high bureaucracy was the more important and perplexing of the two. Every upper-level government official, from grade 6 (assistant prefect) and up was to be screened by the relevant minister. Lower-ranking bureaucrats would be vetted by a separate commission working in liaison with the ministries and chaired by the esteemed professor and rector of the University of Naples, Adolfo Omodeo. The chaos of September 8, however, guaranteed that this early idea would never be implemented. [T]he Omodeo defascistization commission ... was dissolved, and its nascent activities were melded into a broader commission under the more important purge measure to come, Decreto legislative luogotenenziale (DLL), July 27, 1944, number 159....

Thus, from the start, the Italian government was presented with a vexing problem: how to treat bureaucrats and government officials who, for twenty years, had been loyal to their Duce. Did their presence in the new government create a dilemma for the Allied cause and for Italy's democratic prospects?... Subsequent ... directives displayed the uncertainty that would continually plague Italy's treatment of Fascists. For example, the two fundamental purge principles in these guidelines were ambiguous and, indeed, contradictory. The first of them stated that, outside of the RSI [the Saló regime], "the Fascist regime ... is decidedly dead in the minds of Italians." The second principle, however, found that "it is indispensable to eradicate every last vestige of Fascism." Further on, Badoglio's circulars defined the political criteria that seemed designed to exclude more people than it did include in a classification of "Fascist."

Realizing that not every Fascist could be purged or prosecuted and that distinctions had to be made, Badoglio's November [1943] notes enumerated four categories in a hierarchy of political crime. But by drawing a line between fascism and more traditional, nonpolitical crime, the marshal appeared to be less interested in prosecuting political figures than in chasing embezzlers, extortionists, and thieves. There was little logic in the

---

Pavone, "La continuita dello stato," pp. 252.) Whereas leniency toward fascists increased, punishment of partisans who had committed illegal acts during the liberation became harsher. See Battaglia, *Allied Military Administration of Italy*, pp. 102-123.

* Excerpted from Roy Palmer Domenico, *Italian Fascists on Trial, 1943-1948* (Chapel Hill: The University of North Carolina Press, 1991), pp. 15, 19-21, 32-34, 41-44, 55-64, 73, 75.

marshal's classifications, which betrayed his hasty, slapdash approach. The first class included those who merely had held the party card but did not use it for illicit gains. These were, "*rara avis*," disillusioned but honest folk. Badoglio would probably have included himself here. The second group included Fascists who not only occupied government positions but also had a hand in the graft or violence that so discredited the regime. "They must be arrested and denounced before the military authorities," Badoglio declared. The third somewhat vague category included street fighters (*squadristi*) and propagandists. The fourth embraced those who did not necessarily take part in politics but who, through illicit methods, obtained the support of the *gerarchi* for protection and favors. Badoglio labeled these last "the most lurid vermin" and demanded that they be discovered and inflexibly prosecuted. He likely emphasized this because the fraud and payoffs of those "lurid vermin" had pushed Italy's, and his, armed forces into a swamp of corruption during the late 1930s. The faulty equipment and false numbers engineered as a result rendered Italy's defenses ineffective in the 1940s.

The prime minister's November circular concluded with cryptic advice: friendships must not get in the way. The purge must be ruthless and total. But friendships and connections, impossible to see on paper, naturally persisted and would always exist in the Italian government, as they do in all governments. Such friendships and connections would contribute to the purge's ruin.[12]

Reaction to Badoglio's instructions immediately indicated that his measures were not as ruthless as envisaged. Within a few days the prefect of Brindisi inquired whether or not those *ex-gerarchi, squadristi,* and *fascisti* who had been stopped by the police should lose their salaries during their absences from office. Badoglio's office replied on December 10 that a suspension was "only a cautionary police measure" that did not call for the loss of a stipend.[13] Furthermore, an unsigned directive to the police stated that the mere possession of a *tessera* [membership card from the Fascist National Party (PNF)] meant nothing, and that the government was not interested in "a sterile persecution of a very extensive part of the substantially healthy middle class." Holding a party card signified only "a guarantee or at least a hope for a peaceful existence."[14] This distinction amounted to virtual absolution for simple membership in the PNF. The Badoglio government, in this early decision, had cleared practically everyone from the political crime of being a Fascist, affirming an important approach toward sanctions....

The most sustained voice within the Allied Commission for concrete defascistization measures came from the American [Chief Administrative Officer], Charles Poletti.... Poletti advocated ... cost-effective methods to identify and punish Fascist culprits. Toward this end he participated with Allied political intelligence and some Italians in the creation of the first

---

12 ACS PCM Gab 1943-44 Salerno 3/4 f. 2.

13 Ibid.

14 Ibid.

Allied framework to identify Fascists, a scientific methodology that took form soon after the initial landings in Sicily and was refined in the following months.

The finished product was the *scheda personale,* which appeared in many incarnations before the final format was agreed upon in mid-1944 and employed in both the AMG [Allied Military Government] and Royal Italy. Throughout the course of the war it served as the basic "Were you a Fascist?" questionnaire and embodied the principles found in subsequent anti-Fascist legislation.

But behind official acceptance, many Italians considered the document as a joke. Just as the Germans would later make a mockery of its cousin, the *Fragebogen,* many lied, fabricated, and generally used the *scheda* to suit their own ends, regarding the document as a monument to silly American notions of scientific precision. The jurist Mario Bracci noted that such a questionnaire was utterly foreign to Italians. In the journal *Il Ponte* he predicted that "Colonel Poletti's *scheda* ... will remain in the museums of Italy as a singular document of historic incomprehension ... and of total ignorance of things Italian."[51]

In its final form, the *scheda* theoretically ascertained, through forty-three categories of questions, one's connection to the Fascist regime. Eventually all Italian government and parastate employees were ordered to fill them out. As if it mattered, a warning at the top of the *scheda* indicated "very severe penalties and fines" for lying. After the inevitable questions of whether or not the person had been enrolled in the PNF, the *scheda* got down to specifics. Was the person a veteran *sansepolcrista, squadrista,* a "Fascist of the First Hour?" Did he or she participate in the March on Rome, or in [other Fascist campaigns]? Did the person hold any party offices or a position in the Balilla, the University Youth, the Fascist Militia, the Duce's bodyguard, the secret police, the political office of the Public Security forces? Was the person a volunteer in Africa or Spain? Did he or she receive any honoraria or participate in political conferences or discourses over the radio?

By charting the framework to identify Fascists, the *scheda* itself added fire of its own to the sanctions debate. It created legal distinctions between two types of Fascists, distinctions based on a person's decision of September 8: those who loyally followed their king south and those who loyally followed their Duce north. Conduct after September 1943 became considerably distinct from what happened during the 1922-43 *ventennio.* Categories 32 to 38 of the *scheda* pertained to Mussolini's Social Republic. If someone professed loyalty to Saló, then (increasingly in Allied eyes, as well as in Badoglio's) he or she was guilty of very serious crimes, specifically treason. The concept here was not original. Rather, the *scheda* accentuated Badoglio's notion of two fascisms that he had included in his

---

[51]Chief of Political Intelligence Section for Chiefs of Staff report, NARS CAD files 319.1 Foreign (1), November 1, 1943, in Coles and Weinberg, *Civil Affairs,* pp. 383-84. See also Bracci, "Come naque l'amnistia," pp. 1090-107. For an account of Germany's equivalent of the *scheda* that rings as cynical as the attitude of the Italians, see Salomon, *Fragebogen, The Questionnaire.*

November circulars: on the one hand was the fascism under which all Italians had lived, the amorphous, all encompassing regime of the PNF;... on the other was the subsequent fascism, that of the Republica Sociale Italiana, the illegal Italy of traitors and collaborationists. This duality elaborated in the *scheda* came to be accepted by both the Italians and the United Nations. It tempered all subsequent debates and government action....

[Marshal Badoglio] announced a new measure to punish Fascists: Royal Legislative Decree (RDL) 29/B of December 29, 1943.[71] Much of it sounded similar to Badoglio's August measures.... RDL 110 of April 13 [1944] created a High Commission for a National Purge of Fascism and entrusted it to the old Socialist Tito Zaniboni. The program was so ineffectual and unpopular, however, that when Zaniboni took charge, he was immediately chastised by his comrades on the Left, and his career was ruined.

Attempts to put teeth into RDL 29/B, undertaken within Badoglio's government, were doomed to failure. The minister of justice, Ettore Casati, one of the most determined voices for true reform, pushed for an enactment to get the ministers involved in the purge and advocated easier suspensions and loss of salaries. Badoglio and his other ministers unanimously condemned the measure. The marshal felt that Casati's suggestions were too harsh. His minister of finance lamented their "excessive rigor," and they were also compared to the Anglo-American measures that had been applied "with disastrous consequences."...

Another jarring indication of doom was the state of the administrative machine at Sforza's disposal. What the high commissioner inherited was a desk with nothing on it; the sanctions program had accomplished practically nothing since December. Only the creation of a small staff for Omodeo's moribund commission on the purge of lower-level bureaucrats served to demonstrate that, indeed, nothing at all had been accomplished. A report on the conditions of this staff indicated the miserable progress that had been made on defascistization almost a full year after the fall of Mussolini. In July 1944 Benvenuto Piovani and Nino Contini, the two secretaries, wrote to Omodeo. The tone of the letter reveals that the chief could not have been very aware of what was happening. The two complained of an absence of every reasonable tool for their job. For example, they and their staff of three did not possess a single copy of defascistization laws or decrees. They requested agents, more staff, and even some form of transportation. Piovani and Contini reminded Rome that the defascistization commission had not really gotten off the ground until May 1944. Without tools, "without the use of even a single pencil, or a sheet of paper," nothing could be accomplished.

Despite these handicaps, the commission was able to perform some investigations. Piovani and Contini listed 182 preliminary "inquests" and 72 other cases that had been sent to higher authorities such as the AMG, Zaniboni, or later on, Sforza. These "inquests" were apparently little more than registrations of simple accusations.

---

[71] Harris, *Allied Administration*, pp. 147-49.

Piovani and Contini wrote that, in AMG areas, a more positive attitude toward sanctions existed and the Allies seriously endeavored to establish purge commissions. In Royal Italy, and more specifically in the area where Omodeo's defascistization commission was theoretically "operating,"... nothing was happening, despite the importance of haste. To be effective, the purge must begin and begin quickly. A delay could spell disaster in the defascistization process. The two warned that, after a lapse of a year or two, the government would never be able to purge someone for his Fascist past.[76]...

[Debate Between the Political Parties]

Sanctions against fascism, particularly and significantly, divided the parties. All CLN factions—mainly the Communists, Socialists, adherents to the "Action" Party, or *azionisti*, Christian Democrats, and Liberals—advanced their own approaches to the problem. Their points of view were tempered by both ideology and experiences during the *ventennio*, and they took the form of a lively journalistic debate which began soon after Rome's liberation. Each party, through its press organ, expressed opinions on the nature and parameters that sanctions should take.[27]

The Communist party position had shifted radically by June 1944.... In June [1943], PCI leader Concetto Marchese confided to Liberal friends that his party would collaborate with the king to rid Italy of Mussolini. But many other Communists resisted the new arrangement and preferred to deride the Royal House, the military, big business, and the entire ruling class.... The issue was settled in March 1944 when the party's leader, Togliatti, returned to Italy from his Moscow exile and enforced the new policy. This astonishing about-face, known as the "Salerno turnaround" (*svolta di Salerno*), guaranteed the adoption of the national front. The PCI endorsed the Badoglio regime and modified its intransigent stand on sanctions.[29]

In April 1944 Togliatti was taken into the government as minister without portfolio.... Applied to sanctions, the *svolta* meant that the PCI would support Badoglio's actions, a far cry from its earlier dicta. Togliatti would go so far that in April 1944 he announced in the party journal that sanctions against fascism meant ferreting out saboteurs and spies, nothing more.[31]

---

76 Piovani and Contini to Omodeo, July 3,1944, ACS PCM 1944-47 10124 1/7 s 3-1 b. 100....

27 The sixth party in the CLN coalition was Bonomi's Labor Democrats. It was hardly a mass party and existed mainly as an association of some southern landowners and old-line northern liberals around the figure of Bonomi. His retirement from politics resulted in the party's demise. For a summary of its stance on sanctions, see Lucio D'Angelo, "I demolaburisti" in Bizzarri, *Epurazione e stampa di partito*, pp. 43-66.

29 Spriano, *Storia del Partito comunista italiano*, pp. 138-77; Roberto Battaglia, *Storia della resistenza italiana*, pp. 250-61; Delzell, "Allied Policy," pp. 40-41; Urban, *Moscow and the Italian Communist Party*, pp. 154-67, 172, 190-200.

31 L'Unità, April 11, 1944, cited in Gambino, *Storia del dopoguerra*, p. 90.

Communists could never, of course, abandon completely their demand of sanctions against Fascists. With the liberation of Rome, *L'Unité* continued to endorse an effective purge.... But anxious not to embarrass or worry any right-wing factions within the government, which had been guaranteed its support, *L'Unité* added that the purge was to be neither a personal nor an anti-Fascist vendetta against the old "*aguzzini*." The party's vision of the all-embracing purge that would cleanse Italy for the new people's democracy had been replaced by one of moderation in the national interest.[32]

Gathered under the temporary banner of the Italian Socialist Party of Proletarian Unity (PSIUP, later PSI), the Socialists surpassed the PCI's original line. Gathered around party leader Pietro Nenni, most among the radical wing would not consider abandoning their harsh sanctionist stance in return for cordial relations with Badoglio. Although even Nenni had flirted with fascism in its early days and had counted himself among Mussolini's oldest, though ersatz, friends, under his leadership the PSIUP became the most powerful force for effective defascistization and for the punishment of the maximum number of Fascists.... In the June 5 *Avanti!*, the PSIUP proclaimed its faith in a purge that spared no important Fascist and declared that no collaborationist should ever receive a position in the free Italian government. The paper predicted that some would try to disguise their pasts and slink back into office. For them the Socialists promised "rigorous punishment."[34]

The PSIUP demanded not only stringent measures but also their application over a broader spectrum of Italian society, beyond the narrow political class. Their first target and the object of their most heated attacks was the crown....

Attitudes of the numerically weak Action party were as vehement as the Socialists'. Primarily a grouping of intellectuals and whitecollar professionals, the Action party was an outgrowth of the fiercely republican left wing of the old anti-Fascist Giustizia e Libertá movement; and its intellectual and moral weight within the Resistance movement and the CLN was much greater than numbers could indicate. The party's views on sanctions were first printed in a clandestine edition of *Italia Libera* in January 1943 and were conceived in much the same terms as those of the Socialists, holding that fascism had not been merely a corruption of society or a dictatorship by a few thugs and criminals. Rather, they concluded, the ruling classes had bankrolled Mussolini's regime and were collectively responsible for the *ventennio*. In order to eradicate fascism and bring democracy to Italy, those culprits must be dealt with severely. The monarchy must be abolished, large capital and industry must be

---

32 On July 9 Togliatti reiterated his support for conservative elements within the CLN coalition. Before an audience at the Teatro Brancaccio he repeated, "here in Rome, capital of the Catholic world, this declaration: that we respect the Catholic faith, the traditional faith of the majority of the Italian people" (Mercuri, "Il primo governo De Gasperi," pp. 145-46).

34 *Avanti!*, June 5-6, 1944.

nationalized, and radical agrarian reform, including the breakup of the great *latifondi*, must be implemented.

The Action party was the only CLN faction to seriously treat the church in its platform. This was a particularly sensitive subject in that relations between the church and the Fascists had run hot and cold over the years, although for the most part it was a symbiotic affair. The *azionisti* considered essential an analysis of the church's role in their new Italy, but even they could not lay much blame on the institution and in the end called rather blandly for separation of the two spheres....

The *azionisti* carried the left banner of the Giustizia e Libertá movement. Its right banner was held by those in the Liberal party who congregated around the overwhelming figure of Benedetto Croce and the organization's mouthpiece, *Risorgimento Liberale*.... Their arguments echoed those of Badoglio, labeling Mussolini's followers as traitors and refusing to categorize fascism as a class phenomenon, as the Socialists and *azionisti* had done, but by emphasizing personal choice in the matter of political alignment. This was reinforced by a quite sincere elaboration of Liberal philosophy. Grounded in the Hegelian tradition, Croce considered the problem as a corruption of the individual spirit. As there were murderers, criminals, and social deviants, so there were Fascists. The upper classes were responsible only insofar as they did not use their moral weight in an all-out battle against Mussolini. But they were not collectively guilty. Certainly there were Fascists in the ruling classes, but Fascists existed in all classes. The prison guard was as guilty as the minister of the interior.

Croce published one of the most famous polemics on this subject in the October 29, 1944, *Giornale di Napoli*. Soon acknowledged as the standard Liberal line, his article "Who Is Fascist?" ("Chi é fascista?") conceptualized Mussolini's regime as an intellectual and moral illness (*morbo intellettuale e morale*) that affected all ranks. Quick to challenge Marxist accusations that, as part of the ruling political structure of the country, middle-class parties like the Liberals were particularly guilty of fascism,... Croce insisted that to look for the roots of fascism meant more than an analysis of Italian class structure. It meant exploring the dark corners of the psyche, something very difficult to do, as Croce admitted. But to put Italy on the mend, one had to purge individual minds and spirits.[39]

Upon the liberation of Rome, Croce's thoughts echoed in the *Risorgimento Liberale* [, which] reiterated in its editorial "Giustizia" that any purge or punishment must be directed at individuals and not at social categories.[40]

The Catholic position was the most distinctive and did not correspond to those of the other parties.[41]... Christian Democracy (DC) postured as the

---

39 Benedetto Croce, "Chi è fascista?," reprinted in Legnani, *L'Italia dal 1943 al 1948*, pp. 48-50.

40 *Risorgimento Liberale*, June 14, 23, 30, 1944.

41 Eliza Bizzarri goes so far as to say that, before July 1944, the Christian Democrats had no policy at all. Bizzarri, *Epurazione e stampa di partito*, pp. 15-22.

champion of all people, rejecting special interests, be they interests of privilege or social revolution. As an avowed "mass party," it labored to maintain and extend its constituent base among the Italian bourgeoisie, made serious claims on the loyalty of the working class, and was undoubtedly the most popular force among peasants, especially in the south, and later, Lombardy and the northeast. It refused to defend or attack social groups in the way that the Socialists attacked the ruling classes and the Liberals in effect defended them. The party never urged or even intimated notions of revenge or overt harshness in punishment. And while the DC could always be suspected of defending its own bourgeois constituency and shielding the church, its religious tradition necessitated that mercy and a resistance to radical measures be incorporated into its stance on sanctions. Christian Democracy could, therefore, urge conciliation and forgiveness in the debate, as virtues unto themselves, and not sound entirely self-serving.[42]

The Christian Democrats' most nagging problem, however, was that the church was heavily compromised by the Fascist regime.... [A] clerical network numbering in the tens of thousands embraced Italy.... Lest that clergy be implicated in punishments, the Catholic party sidestepped this issue. And it was highly successful: a purge of the church was never seriously considered, and, except for a few Saló fanatics, no cleric ever served a prison sentence for his role in the Fascist regime.

Despite its evasions, the DC presented some embryonic opinions on punishment in a series of clandestinely published articles, mostly written by Alcide De Gasperi, in December 1943 and January 1944 editions of its organ, *Il Popolo*.... The most innovative thought here was an allusion to generational guilt for fascism. Christian Democracy claimed to be a union of the young and the old but made little reference to the middle aged. It professed to speak for a continuity between two extreme generations: the Catholics who fought the *squadristi* in the early 1920s and Resistance heroes of the mid-1940s.... Emblematic of Catholic defascistization notions was the call to transform the Via Tasso torture chambers into a "haven of charity" (*un asilo di caritá*), just as a church, St. Agnes in Agony, had been built over the spot where, in antiquity, the Roman soldier "attempted to rape the innocent Roman virgin."[44]

Christian Democrats had also already begun to question the wisdom of past anti-Fascist measures. [They argued] that Poletti's defascistization measures contained the risk of hurting the small, "the weak, next to the criminals," and that universal consensus and cooperation were required to determine responsibility for fascism. The DC maintained, nevertheless, that reform and proper punishment must come from above, not from the people[, and] advised the Romans to put their faith in government justice.[45]

---

[42] Mantelli, "La democrazia cristiana," pp. 253, 254, 257. Among the best histories of the DC in this period are Baget-Bozzo, *Il Partito cristiano al potere*, and Scoppola, *La proposta politica di De Gasperi.*

[44] *Il Quotidiano*, June 21, 1944. See also Legnani, *L'Italia dal 1943 al 1948*, pp. 36-42.

[45] Sandro Mercuri, "I democristiani," in Bizzarri, *Epurazione e stampa di partito*, pp. 245-63.

Another presence in the political fray, although unrepresented in the CLN coalition, was the crown. A monarchist movement formed, nevertheless, and its newspaper, *Italia Nuova,* was among the first to attack the broad sanctions. The newspaper claimed that a purge based on wide-ranging Socialist and *azionista* parameters would create deep fissures in the social rock upon which Italy was built. Any defascistization program should practice special caution since the nation was at war, and tampering with its fragile government could not be afforded. Harsh punishments would harm the government's ability to fight the Nazis and serve the Allied cause. Already, by June 14, before any serious purge had even begun, *Italia Nuova* claimed that fear of one had gripped the state bureaucracy in a paralyzing terror....

[T]he monarchists added another distinction that echoed Liberal and Badoglian arguments: criminalization of selected Fascist political acts. The monarchists adopted the position that a difference existed between wellmeaning card holders and those Fascists who had abused their powers for illicit ends, that being a Fascist per se was no crime, but the abuse of Fascist power was.... But this [position] was tempered with the caveat that summary justice and vendetta would solve nothing. The new government must treat the Fascists with "justice, tolerance, and magnanimity."[47]

Inauguration of the CLN government had pushed the lively debate on defascistization onto the front pages of the popular press. The five major parties could count on their positions being heard in the Council of Ministers and in their journals, while the monarchists could rely on their own press, as well as on the Royal House itself, for publicity. The only agreement between them was on the narrowest of foundations, that is, that someone or some persons should be punished somehow. How this was to develop into a policy was still anyone's guess....

The Allies, officially at least, and the Left parties, however, pressured the Bonomi government [which assumed office in 1944] to construct some sort of Fascist policy. Badoglio's actions had clearly failed and could never be applied to the gigantic Roman bureaucracy. Upon the liberation of the capital, Bonomi would be forced to oversee a program to deal effectively with Fascists in the government.... Badoglio's first attempts, regardless of their motivation and effectiveness, were important if only as precedents. His defascistization left a heritage of narrow visions: timid measures selectively directed, which ignored the extensive presence of fascism in Italian society. A dictatorship of twenty years had not been so successful because a handful of ideologues and bureaucrats in the government made it so.

---

47 [*Italia Nuova,* June 14, 1944.]

THE SECOND PHASE

*Roy Palmer Domenico, "Italian Fascists on Trial, 1943-1948"**

[The New Purge Law: DLL 159]

The Italian government's measure, DLL 159, issued on July 27, 1944, superseded all previous provisions against Fascists. It created the High Commission for Sanctions against Fascism, the government machinery to investigate and punish. The law was divided into five parts or titles. The most significant titles, the first and the fifth, spelled out the parameters of Fascist crime and set up the High Commission.

Article 2 of Title 1 proclaimed the intent of the new decree: "The members of the Fascist Government and the *gerarchi* of Fascism guilty of having annulled constitutional guarantees, destroyed popular liberties, created the Fascist Regime, [and] compromised and betrayed the nation's destiny in the current catastrophe are punished with life imprisonment and, in cases of graver responsibility, with death."

These sanctions, however, as harsh as they appeared on paper, were insufficient to lighten the prosecutors' handicaps. All of the bureaucratic machinery created in the measure did not alter fundamentally the scope of Badoglio's earlier decrees. Definitions remained vague, and Rome seemed to abdicate its responsibility, leaving interpretation up to the jurists and purgers themselves. Who, for example, were to be the objects of prosecution? Who had destroyed popular liberties or had created the Fascist regime? What specific acts had these people committed to establish their guilt? Did someone throw a bomb or beat up a Socialist? Did someone make a political deal? Investigators used the old *scheda personale* to evaluate cases, but that document merely described, rather than created, categories of guilt.

Other sections of Title 1 dealt with Fascist crime, but none sufficiently addressed it. Articles 3, 4, and 8 faulted some for using the regime to further their own careers. Article 8 in particular was the great catchall in that it contained a nebulous provision for "acts of special gravity which, while not in the bounds of crime, [were] considered contrary to the norms of sobriety and political decency." It called for punishments like "temporary interdiction from political office," loss of political rights, or internment in agricultural colonies for up to ten years. Once again, clarification was left up to others.

Only Article 5 of Title 1 established a clear crime for which people could be prosecuted: collaboration with the enemy after September 8—that is, treason against the Royal government. Here was an offense, an obvious violation against the Regno del Sud, that allowed the government to take full measures against Fascists, albeit the neo-Fascists of Mussolini's Social

---

* Excerpted from Roy Palmer Domenico, *Italian Fascists on Trial, 1943-1948* (Chapel Hill: The University of North Carolina Press, 1991), pp. 75-77.

Republic. Article 5 emphasized the ideas drawn from Badoglio's measures and the *scheda personale* that distinguished between the Fascists of the *ventennio* and those of Saló. According to Article 5, anyone who, after September 8, 1943, had committed treason, "delitti contro la fedeltá e la difesa militare dello stato," would be punished according to the Military War Code. Both civilians and soldiers would be prosecuted under this code, but they would be tried respectively in civil and military courts.

But even this prosecution had its limitations. As clear a crime as treason is, Title 1 provided an escape clause: Article 7 noted that the penalties, life imprisonment or death, could be reduced to five years in the event that the accused had "actively, participated" in the struggle against the Germans. It would be a handy tool for many Fascists upon the liberation of the north....

Title 5 of DLL 159 gave the program its teeth—the new High Commission for Sanctions against Fascism. Placed in charge was the high commissioner, of equal rank to top magistrates.[3] With a well-defined office and task, at the end of July the leadership question was finally settled. Count Carlo Sforza, who had agreed to replace Tito Zaniboni shortly after the May 26 decree, would carry on and expand Zaniboni's duties. Adolfo Omodeo also left both his vague defascistization post and his minister's chair to return, as rector, to the University of Naples. Sforza could now clearly and rightfully claim sole directorship of the government's program of anti-Fascist sanctions.

Giuseppe Di Palma, "Italy: Is There a Legacy and is it Fascist?"[*]

Contradictory provisions marked the act. On the one hand, it confirmed the principle of penal retroactivity already introduced under party pressure by the second military-civilian Badoglio government, although retroactivity was implicitly rejected by sanctioning the application of liberal codes which, the drafters of the act claimed, had been illegally discontinued under the Fascist regime. It also embodied sweepingly magniloquent definitions of Fascist crimes committed during the deposed regime and during the regime of the Italian Social Republic in the north, mandating that any and all Fascists could in principle be condemned, irrespective of the posts that they had held. The act circumvented the Allied directive, accepted by the first Badoglio government, of carrying out automatic purges by category (i.e., of removing or imposing sanctions against local and central administrators above a certain rank who had held party or paraparty posts). Instead of mandating purges, the act prescribed liability for vaguely stated but potentially widespread behavior and attitudes. It topped these measures by authorizing the

---

[3] The term "High Commission" reflects the Anglo-American, particularly the British, input into the legislation. It is not typically an Italian title.

[*] Excerpted from Giuseppe Di Palma, "Italy: Is There a Legacy and is it Fascist?" in John H. Herz, ed., *From Dictatorship to Democracy: Coping with the Legacies of Authoritarianism and Totalitarianism,* Copyright © 1982 by John Herz (Greenwood Press, 1982), pp. 119-121, an imprint of Greenwood Publishing Group, Inc. Westport, CT. Reprinted with permission.

appointment of political commissioners who were entrusted with initiating and carrying out a task that, on the basis of the measures to be applied, seemed to be quintessentially political.

On the other hand, Count Sforza's patently unassailable directive to "hit high and forgive below" was incorporated in the act and in subsequent acts and executive interpretations thereof. The provision identified sweeping, extenuating circumstances and punctiliously but never exhaustively listed specific instances warranting exceptions and derogations. Further, daily applications of the act, from sweeping sanctions to sweeping derogations, were entrusted not to the political commissioners, who experienced difficulty in effecting their powers of initiative and who were at times wary of subjecting matters relating to trials to pressures reminiscent of Fascist practices, but to a host of judicial and semijudicial bodies.... A mixed Central Commission was appointed by the prime minister to hear appeals by the concerned party or the high commissioner. The attitudes of the members of these bodies toward most of the cases they judged, especially those involving purges, could have been predicted. Usually composed of justices and officials who were wary of subjecting former colleagues and superiors whom chance had at times placed on the other side of the bench to vague and retroactive legislation, these judicial bodies ended up by asserting—often beyond the bounds of reason—all sorts of extenuating circumstances so as to impose sanctions of a less severe nature.[42]

This approach to defascistization tended to prolong judicial cases, as did the often overlooked fact that the war, the division of the country, and the poor state of communications impeded the convening of the courts and commissions as well as the collection of all admissible evidence.[43] The result did not evoke a feeling of justice painstakenly rendered (Sforza had also called for "swift" justice) but a "growing and diffuse feeling of hypocrisy and simulation."[44] Instead of redounding on the monarchy, which had set the ambiguous defascistization process in motion, the feeling was displaced unto the anti-Fascist parties, especially the left, which had committed a serious miscalculation that affected its fortunes and the legitimacy of the new order.

---

42 The most exhaustive documentation on this point is in Battaglia, *Allied Military Administration of Italy*. See also Algardi, *Processi ai fascisti*; Bevere, "Fascismo e antifascismo."

43 The central commission for purges was not set up until February 1945. Local commissions began to operate one month later.

44 Gambino, *Storia del dopoguerra della liberazione*, p. 75....

Roy Palmer Domenico, "Italian Fascists on Trial, 1943-1948"[*]

[The Commissioners]

Sforza's task was to direct four offices, each concerned with a different type of sanction. One office, or *commissariato aggiunto*, dealt with criminal proceedings, another with a government purge, a third with confiscation of ill-gotten profits, and the last with sequestering Fascist party property. Day-to-day operations were directed by the high commissioner's four assistants, the *commissari aggiunti*. These vice administrators were equal in rank to third-level judges.

Much of the Alto Commissariato was activated in three auxiliary decrees: DLL 198 of September 3, 1944, which launched a High Court to try the biggest Fascist criminals; DLL 238 of October 3, 1944, which clarified personnel details; and DLL 285 of October 23, 1944, which set procedural rules for the High Court and the purge and which first faced the task of extending the purge out of Rome and into the provinces....The high commissioner promised a new, tough program that would severely punish the higher-ups while indulging the lesser functionaries of Mussolini's dictatorship. Attack high and indulge low became the professed modus operandi for sanctions.

Sforza chose his assistant *commissari aggiunti* from the ranks of the CLN parties. DLL 159's Title 5 allowed him to nominate them and present the list to the prime minister for final approval. For his commissioner of sequestered Fascist property, the count chose a personal friend of Bonomi, F. S. Stangone. Stangone had been an anti-Fascist journalist and was a member of the Labor Democrats. The Christian Democrat Mario Cingolani was picked to oversee the office on illegal profits. The two most important commissioners were those for the prosecution of Fascist crimes, Mario Berlinguer, and for the government purge, Mauro Scoccimarro.

An *azionista*, Mario Berlinguer was a wealthy Sardinian landowner and lawyer who had remained in Italy during the *ventennio*. He never cooperated with the Fascists or took out membership in the party. He kept a low political profile but maintained contacts with the anti-Fascist *Giustizia e Libertá* groups abroad and spent a brief period in prison. Berlinguer sincerely held humanitarian values and was esteemed as a decent man by many who met him. On the other hand, Mauro Scoccimarro was unable to keep a low profile during the *ventennio*. Born in Udine in 1894, he was known as a tough, high-ranking member of the Communist party at the time of its dissolution by the Duce in 1926. A protégé of Antonio Gramsci, he represented the PCI in Moscow as well. Along with many comrades Scoccimarro was sentenced in the anti-Communist trials of 1927-28 and spent a decade and a half in Fascist prisons. He was released after the

[*] Excerpted from Roy Palmer Domenico, *Italian Fascists on Trial, 1943-1948* (Chapel Hill: The University of North Carolina Press, 1991), pp. 77, 79, 80-82, 87-89, 90-94, 97-105, 107.

overthrow of Mussolini in July 1943 and resumed his role in the party's directorate.[7]

The backgrounds of the two men, one legalistic and humanitarian, the other combative and a partisan in the class struggle, set the tones for their respective commissions. Both were true in their determination to eradicate fascism, but each went about it in his own way.

Berlinguer's classical, humanistic education was reflected in his aims. Although he was an *azionista* and later a Socialist, his trials never upset the social equilibrium he was anxious to maintain. Berlinguer would not attack the ruling class through the courts, and arguments concerning legal sanctions against Fascists remained within the bounds of liberal juridical propriety.

Where legal scholars might argue loopholes and intent, however, Scoccimarro concerned himself with firing Fascists. He confided to an OSS informant that he was "essentially" happy with the new law and that its real value depended on a "rapid, just, and severe" application. The commissioner predicted an effective purge with "no fear of reactionaries and imperialists."[8] The letter of the law did not much concern Scoccimarro; rather, it was in the spirit of its application. He said as much in his September 8, 1944, circular to the purge staffs.[9] The *commissario aggiunto* would attempt to use DLL 159 as a spearhead in a broader attack, and he found himself in the maelstrom of the first and greatest controversy over sanctions.

[The Administrative Purge]

Many took great interest in Sforza's tasks and feared that the problems faced in DLL 159 would surface most apparently in Scoccimarro's subcommission. It was universally acknowledged that timing was crucial and that it was imperative to strike while the iron was hot. If action did not begin immediately, it never would.... But time proved to be an impassable obstacle against Sforza's and Scoccimarro's efforts. Like most of the world in 1944, Rome was a city in chaos.... Nothing not directly related to the war effort could be swiftly accomplished. The taxing details of provisions, the day-to-day essentials of operating in government, were ever present and exasperating. Dislocation, destruction, and bureaucratic confusion hampered all sorts of operations. Scoccimarro complained to Major Upjohn that many essential records had simply been lost or destroyed and that this severely hindered his work. The High Commission had no

---

7 ...Regarding Cingolani's *commissariato aggiunto* for illegal profits, see Vassalli and Sabatini, *Il collaborazionismo e l'amnistia politica,* and Vassalli, *La confisca dei beni....* For a list of subordinate figures in the adjunct commissions, see Mercuri, *L'Epurazione,* pp. 58-59.

8 "Z" to State Department and OSS, August 1, 1944, NARS RG226 89256.

9 Flores, "L'Epurazione," in Atti del convegno internazionale organizzato a Firenze il 26-28 Marzo 1976 con il concorso della regione Toscana/INSMLI, *L'Italia dalla liberazione alla repubblica,* p. 422.

autos until the spring of 1945, when it received two.[12] An elderly chief prosecutor, De Villa, often took the tram to court....

The problem of personnel was also particularly acute, a potentially dangerous dilemma that forced the High Commission to rely on ex-Fascists to punish other ex-Fascists. There were purgers, lawyers, stenographers, and judges to procure. Judges were particularly needed to staff both the trials and the purge commissions. But they were in very short supply, and their whereabouts were often unknown. After one purge commission waited months for its magistrate to arrive, Sforza received a letter from the judge's wife thanking everyone for the honor but noting that her husband had, unfortunately, been dead for about a year. Consequently, premiums were placed on all jurists, with little or no mention made of their conduct during the Fascist dictatorship. The Alto Commissariato was even forced to search through prisoner-of-war camps and pension records for retired ones.[14]

The High Commission needed policemen but ran into trouble here as well. As with the magistrates, Sforza was forced to rely on established government functionaries in order to enforce sanctions. But the royalist Carabinieri ranked among the least enthusiastic and receptive to the high commissioner's overtures. On September 16 the commanding general of the Carabinieri, Taddeo Orlando, turned down Sforza's request for men. The commissioners would have to make do with what they had.[15]

More serious problems arose from elements in society: the bureaucracy itself and powerful conservatives, who determined to limit or destroy the sanctions program. To fight Sforza and Scoccimarro, government functionaries undertook a typically bureaucratic mode of operation: quiet, institutional maneuvers. This opposition was conducted on a lower level, but it was more immediate and more desperate than was the "traditionalist" opposition that came later, which was more ideological and was played out in the press and between government ministers. When Mauro Scoccimarro launched the purges in the summer of 1944, his efforts were initially hampered by the first group, a stubborn, large, and powerful bureaucracy. Sensing the impending attack from the High Commission, large segments of the state apparatus closed ranks.

Scoccimarro spent much of August and September sending out *schede personali* to all government employees and forming his purge commissions. Each ministry and government agency was to host a three-person panel of which one member was appointed by the minister or head of the office; another was to be a magistrate "of untarnished reputation"; and the third member was to be chosen by Scoccimarro.

The panels reviewed the *schede* to separate the wheat from the chaff. All questionnaires filled out by the top ranks of the civil service, and

---

12 Charles to Eden, April 12, 1945, regarding Upjohn report on "Epuration," PRO FO371 49756 ZM2293.

14 Justice Ministry to PCM Cabinet, November 20, 1944, ACS PCM 1944-46 10124 1/7 f8 s18.1.

15 Taddeo Orlando to Bonomi, September 16, 1944, ACS PCM 1944-46 10124 1/7 f4 s9.

"questionable" ones filled out by some lower-level bureaucrats, were then sent for final decision to a central commission ... and to Scoccimarro.... In practice, a harsh verdict could mean suspension, often on reduced pay and ration cards, or dismissal, usually with pension (one-twelfth normal pay). Loss of political rights often accompanied these judgments. Most punishments meted out by the Alto Commissariato, however, would be *sanzioni minori*, nothing more than letters placed in the person's file....

To keep track of his attempts at an extensive purge of the entire government, Scoccimarro compiled statistics. The figures present a valuable picture of how far the purge had proceeded under its vigorous commissioner. He reported that 112 of the proposed 157 commissions were functioning. These commissions claimed to have examined 28,399 cases "up until two o'clock on 30 November, 1944." Of these, 6,859 had been judged serious enough for higher review; 1,199 of the 6,859 were recommended for suspension, and, the bottom line, 495 state employees had been "disposte," which seems to have been the accepted euphemism for "sacked." At the higher level, the purge of the top grades of the bureaucracy, Count Sforza also reported that of 3,210 decisions, 1,355 were acquitted, 1,316 received minor sanctions, and 539 were purged.[32]... Employees of quasi-governmental organizations such as the *enti pubblici*, agencies in the national interest, comprised much of the 6,859. Scoccimarro listed that 1,705 employees of these organizations, the largest single figure, had been brought up for review. But if he requested that any of these 1,705 be suspended, record was not made of it.

Purge figures also reflect an imbalance between the various ministries. The Interior Ministry, one of the largest government employers, claimed the dubious honor of having the most workers, 1,430, deferred to judgment. Of these, Scoccimarro requested 422 suspensions, 176 of those were listed as *personale civile*, and 246 were personnel of the *pubblica sicurezza* [PS], a national police force.[33] On the bottom line, 86 bureaucrats and 158 PS seem to have been purged at that point. While the Interior figures were among the most drastic found in the Council of Ministers, others were far less severe. The Ministry of Public Works, for example, a traditional job mill, surrendered 304 workers for review. Suspension requests were made for 18 of these but none were purged.

The Treasury and the military services were among the ministries most representative of traditional, conservative Italy. Of 654 reviews in the Liberal Marcello Soleri's Treasury, 10 requests for suspension were made and 5 were complied with. In General Piero Piacentini's Air Force, the figures, which included only civilian bureaucrats and no top military

---

32 On January 5 Sforza reported that 160 purge commissions were operating. Sforza, *Fini e limiti dell'epurazione*, p. 11. The High Commission acknowledged that the ministers themselves had seen fit to suspend employees. No numbers have come down to us regarding these suspensions, although they are probably smaller than those of the Alto Commissariato.

33 The *pubblica sicurezza* has traditionally taken responsibility for the more quotidian police duties in Italy, such as traffic control and investigation of minor crimes. The Carabinieri have a more elitist reputation and handle more serious crimes as well as being a paramilitary organization.

personnel, were 351, 200, and 2. In Admiral Raffaele De Courten's Naval Ministry, the numbers were 152, 17, and 2. The odd agency in this group was the War Ministry, which purged more—54 out of 99 requests—than the others combined. Perhaps the explanation lies in that the minister of war was a civilian, the Milaness Liberal Alessandro Casati, who saw potential in a purge and seems to have favored it more than did his Liberal colleagues. As minister of war he went so far as to suggest a serious sweep of the marshals and generals and recommended to Bonomi that the first two on the purge list be Badoglio and Messe. He also insisted that, since such a sweep required an enormous show of strength and nerve, Bonomi himself chair the commission. This never materialized.[34]

Despite the efforts of the High Commission, the purge was largely confined to Rome and a few other large cities south of the front, like Naples. Out in the provinces, purge commissions were to be composed of a member appointed by Scoccimarro, one by the local prefect, and one by the CLN parties. This was not a hard and fast rule, and some purging seems to have been carried on by prefects or CLN committees on their own.... Counting all of the figures cited in [a January 1946] report, about half—143,781 of 277,701—of all provincial employees were examined. Of those, 13,737 were felt important enough to judge formally. And from that figure about one-tenth, 1,476, were removed.

The Trials

If the purge touched few people, fewer still were affected by the trials against Fascist criminals. DLL 159 and its corollary decrees created the High Court (Alta Corte), within Mario Berlinguer's subcommission to judge those most responsible for the regime and the disaster of the war. Regular lower courts would handle Fascists of lesser rank.

But as with Scoccimarro's purge, Berlinguer's prosecutions were beset with troubles that reflected the general doubt over sanctions. The capstone to the whole program, the High Court, illustrated this problem. As only one court, its scope was necessarily limited and could not possibly have been devised with the idea of punishing all *gerarchi*.... The proceedings, one trial at a time, went slowly and were complicated by the enormous amount of attention focused on them. The early cases, particularly the first one against Pietro Caruso, were presented at the very least as much for public and Allied consumption as they were an effort to rid the Roman bureaucracy of Fascists.

Berlinguer was also plagued by the incessant and never-resolved battle of legal scholars, journalists, and the public on the parameters and limits of guilt. The stated purpose for the High Court, as defined in DLL 159 and auxiliary decrees, was to try key criminals of the *ventennio*, aiming at the pervasive fascism before 1943 and not at the imposed, Vichy-like puppet RSI. As it turned out, however, although military courts were

---

[34] Scoccimarro report, December 5, 1944, ACS Alto Commissariato per le sanzioni contro il fascismo (hereafter ACSF) 1/20; Casati to Bonomi, October 4, 1944, PCM 1944-47 10124 1/7 f36.

designed to process traitors, the trials often concerned RSI personnel and the treasonous crimes committed, not between 1922 and 1943, but after September 8. Beyond the time frame, furthermore, the parameters were still quite narrow: government officials. In both cases the dockets were filled with targets—"strategic" figures closely tied in the public's mind to the regime. Thus, while conservatives may have grumbled about the trials, they did not enlist the same kind of frontal assault against Berlinguer as had been thrown at Scoccimarro. There was no need for such drastic measures. No doubt many may have shuddered at the idea of trials—uncertainty regarding one's own relationship with the Fascists or one's position within the defunct regime could easily determine a stand against too-effective legal sanctions. But not only was most of the traditional "establishment" safely beyond the limited goals of the trial program, it could also rely on a sincere and important faction within Italian society who believed that sanctions were morally questionable.

Many well-intentioned Italians, the *benpensanti*, were simply reluctant to prosecute Fascists. *Ex post facto* application of ill-defined offenses, complicated by the threatened use of the death penalty, were foreign to legal tradition. Before 1943 the most important sanctions in modern Italian history had been conducted by the Fascists during the 1920s. This was not an admirable standard to emulate. In August 1944 a group of eighteen prestigious legal scholars, all of them anti-Fascists, published a manifesto condemning a legal campaign that prosecuted people for violation of laws that had never existed.[38]

The composition of the High Court was announced on August 2. Its president, or chief magistrate, was Ettore Casati, former *primo presidente* of a cassation court and justice minister under Badoglio. He was assisted by eight jurists, mainly lawyers, judges, and officials, such as the minister of industry, commerce, and labor [and] the vice mayor of Rome.... Judge Casati, however, was gravely ill and was replaced before the first trial by one of the eight, a *consigliere* from the cassation courts, Lorenzo Maroni. Maroni was among the few high officials in the sanctions network whose tenure would last for practically the entire life of the institution, in his case the High Court.

Maroni's role also illustrated an important flaw in the program that concerned the magistracy. The chief judge was typical of many who had pursued a career through the *ventennio*, and he found himself in that great gray area between the Fascists and the apolitical population at large. Worse, however, was that Maroni was criticized for hidden ties to the old regime. The right-wing historian Luigi Villari related the story told to him by one of the judge's close relatives that, during the dictatorship, Maroni would "go off the deep end" when someone criticized Mussolini's government in his presence. Later, during one of the High Court trials, the Duce's henchman Cesare Rossi defiantly reminded the assembly that

---

[38] Mercuri, *L'Epurazione*, pp. 72-73. The legal scholars published their manifesto in the political journal *Domenica*.

Maroni had often judged cases during the *ventennio* with a black shirt on underneath his robes.[39]

The first High Court trial was the most important one. The accused were Saló's *questore* of Rome, Pietro Caruso, and his assistant, Roberto Occhetto. Caruso had served the Nazis by rounding up partisans and innocent victims for slaughter. The trial was significant for four reasons. First, a riot broke out during the proceedings and seriously damaged the credibility of the Sforza Commission for Bonomi, the Allies, and much of the press. Second, a dangerous precedent was established by the defense attorneys in their argument that if an accused secretly aided anti-Fascists, playing what was called the "double game," his guilt was partly or even wholly exonerated. Third, the crimes of Caruso and his cohort had no strong connection with the *ventennio*. Nor were they overtly political but were traditional crimes of violence and treason against liberated Italy. Fourth, despite the vile nature of Caruso's crimes, many considered that he was a scapegoat, a victim of Sforza's show trials.

Caruso had been a fringe character in the Fascist hierarchy. He was an early party member from Naples but held no important position before the establishment of the RSI.... In February 1944 he was installed as the police boss of Rome, commanding a blood-thirsty gang of sadists and thugs who tortured and murdered for the Duce and the Germans.... The Ardeatine Caves was the site of his most monstrous crime in March 1944. After a partisan attack on a German unit marching up Via Rasella, Caruso and the Nazis retaliated by rounding up 335 innocent men, women, and children—many of them Jews. The people were transported to the Ardeatine Caves in the hills south of the city near suburban EUR. There they were butchered and the entrances to the caves sealed.

The site of the Caruso trial was the mammoth and garish Palazzo di Giustizia on the Tiber near the Castel Sant'Angelo. On a hot September 18, well over 300 people jammed themselves into a courtroom that was built to accommodate sixty. Some were issued guest passes, but they were joined by Allied observers and journalists, a camera crew, Mario Berlinguer, and a crowd of people, mainly women. Most were the mothers, wives, and sisters of victims of the Ardeatine Caves massacre. These people knew Caruso for the cutthroat that he was.[40]

His horrible crime was no secret, particularly to the loved ones present in the Palazzo di Giustizia. They demanded justice. For security the PS and the Carabinieri allotted 450 guards to the building. But only 320 were present, and most of those were in the "lower reaches of the building." Few, often only two or three, guarded key doors.

The first prosecution witness was the former director of the city's Regina Coeli prison, Donato Carretta.... Carretta was ushered into the chamber, where his appearance ignited the spectators, particularly those connected with the massacre victims, into a fire of rage.

---

39 Villari, *The Liberation of Italy*, pp. 152-53. See also Tamaro, *Due anni di storia*, p. 342. Tamaro labeled Maroni a "hot Fascist." Mercuri, *L'Epurazione*, p. 124 n. 91.

40 [omitted]

There was some question whether the people mistook Carretta for Caruso, but, whatever the case, they immediately attacked him. The assault was led by a woman, Maria Ricottini, whose son had been shot by Germans on May 8.[43] Berlinguer jumped onto a table and implored that the crowd get a hold of themselves, but his pleas were drowned in demands to lynch Carretta. Shouts of "Paris, let's imitate Paris" heard in the courtroom indicate that the crowd was inspired by new radical measures then being taken by the French government against Vichyite collaborators.

With a couple of guards trying to protect him, the ex-jailer was jostled and beaten by the mob. His body was dragged out of the building and down the front stairs. All attempts by the police to get him away failed. The guards implored some Americans to put Carretta in their jeep, but they refused to get involved. Carretta was dragged onto the Ponte Umberto spanning the Tiber, and his body was stretched over tram tracks. An approaching trolley slammed on its brakes and screeched to a halt inches before crushing the ex-warden. The infuriated crowd tore the hapless motorman from his berth and beat him until he broke away and ran for his own life. Still the people had not had enough so they carried the bloodied and motionless Carretta to the side of the bridge and tossed him into the river. They were astonished to see the pathetic figure attempt to stay afloat and make for shore. Some young men, bathers on the bank, then finished the job by pummelling Carretta to death with oars. His body was dragged to Regina Coeli and hung there, feet first, for the Romans to contemplate.

Carretta's death was a tragedy on a high level revealing that a submerged and undirected resentment persisted among the population. The events of September 18 revealed also a government incapable of understanding and powerless in controlling its citizens. The riot represented a broad failure in the sanctions program.

Newspapers across the political spectrum deplored Carretta's death. The prison director was seen at once as a symbol and a victim of Fascist oppression.... Caruso's [eventual] execution left many unanswered questions concerning the propriety of the trials, particularly the extreme punishments. [P]rogress of sanctions left many Italians unsatisfied or unsettled....

On the charge that he had transferred 120 tons of gold behind German lines, [governor of the Bank of Italy Vincenzo] Azzolini was hauled before President Maroni [in the next trial]. Azzolini's defense was based on lack of any motive for collaboration and was bolstered with another cry to prosecute the genuinely guilty and leave the little fish alone. The main defense lawyer emphasized the *ventennio*/RSI dichotomy by insisting that the real criminals were not bureaucrats, like Azzolini, but were the others, mainly generals, who had delivered Italy over to the Germans in September 1943. On the last day of the trial the crowd in the courtroom answered the attorney's pleas to bring the real criminals to justice with a concerted, "They're coming." Maroni added, perhaps with some chagrin,

---

43 [omitted]

that eventually all would answer for their crimes. On October 14 Azzolini was given thirty years....

In Naples a debate took place between Eugenio Reale's "social communist" *La Voce* and the Liberal *Il Giornale*. Reale argued that legal niceties had their place but that Azzolini was "overwhelmingly guilty." The people knew it, they felt the truth deep inside, and Maroni should have forgotten the rules to listen to them. The Liberal journalist Manlio Lupinacci retorted that demagoguery had no place in Italian courts. Should Maroni adopt the social communist recommendation, then trials would resemble the Colosseum, with Emperor Maroni watching for a thumbs-up or thumbs-down signal from the mob. Sanctions had to maintain a sensible and orderly course....

Those hoping for a showdown with the military received their wish in the third trial of the High Court. On December 14 Generals Riccardo Pentimalli and Ettore Del Tetto appeared before the High Court on charges of conspiring to surrender Naples to the Germans.... Socialist and Communist journalists keenly awaited the trial. The unpurged military, thoroughly monarchist and tarnished by a record of collusion with fascism that few could match, would be up for serious scrutiny. [United States] Ambassador Kirk cabled Washington to say that the two officers had already been tried and condemned in the Left press....

The trial of Pentimalli and Del Tetto held even more importance for the Center-Right, which feared that the normally moderate Berlinguer, who requested the arrest, might be overstepping certain bounds.... Pentimalli and Del Tetto ... were simply "good" soldiers.... They were not thugs like Caruso nor even occupants of Fascist sinecures like Azzolini.... [T]hey were soldiers of the king; the prosecutors had crossed over into the non-Fascist Right. It seemed as though Sforza and Berlinguer were on the verge of extending prosecutions beyond the narrowly Fascist political class.... The public minister, Pietro Traina, asked for death, but, on December 23, the two generals received twenty years for abandoning their posts. The other charges were dropped.[59]

The two sentences fueled still more flames of dissatisfaction.... [B]road disagreement persisted over the type of people who should be prosecuted and over the confusing and narrow aims of DLL 159. Much of the press complained once again that the prosecutors were missing the mark. The guiltiest, those at the highest levels, enjoyed their freedom while Pentimalli, Del Tetto, Azzolini, or Occhetto languished in jail.... The Socialist's answer echoed those cries in the Caruso riot to imitate the French and establish more popular courts. Demands for justice represented "one of the strongest positive elements" in liberated France that condemned "without pity [the] miserable collaborators." In Italy, corruption and

---

[59] On April 20, 1945, *Italia Libera* reported that Del Tetto died in prison. Promemoria 44, listed as "Memoria OP 44—Promemoria 1 and 2," was reprinted in Zangrandi, *1943*, pp. 364-72.

persistence of the old ruling classes, so heavily compromised with fascism, were effectively killing all hope of real sanctions.[60]

In December 1944 an officer with the Allied Commission was prompted to investigate the French example for himself and visited anticollaborationist courts in Dijon, Toulon, Marseilles, Lyon, and Paris. He concluded that far more local authority was placed in the French courts than in the Italian ones and that the system there was facilitated by two factors: that all the crimes had been committed in the last four years and that they were sins of collaboration. On the other hand, the Italian problem concerned a native regime of over twenty years with no allegiance to a foreign power. Although the observer felt that the Italian methods were sound, he conceded that the French ones were simpler, speedier, and better.[61]

Indeed, events in Italy contrasted with what was occurring in France, where courts reviewed cases with greater speed and displayed much greater propensity to use the death penalty than their Italian counterparts. Through the end of 1944 and into the next year, executions of Vichy personnel were regularly reported in the Roman press while Caruso, a collaborator, remained the one Fascist who had been sent to the wall. On the other hand, few RSI functionaries, who appeared more like Vichy collaborators than officials from the *ventennio*, had been caught. Most of them were still in the north with Mussolini. When the Saló Republic collapsed at the end of April 1945, a style more evocative of the French would be applied to RSI collaborators. Until then the Italians would continue in their inability to come to terms with the crimes of Mussolini's *ventennio*.

Parallel with Maroni's High Court, legal sanctions against fascism also occupied the lesser courts: the Corti di Assise and the military courts. Italian records are closed or scanty, and little quotidian attention was paid in the press to these trials. Our knowledge is limited to the more notorious cases. A December 28, 1944, article in *Italia Nuova* stated that 257 "political" investigations (*posti istruttoria*) occupied places on dockets in Rome's ordinary courts. Most of these cases regarded offenses specified in DLL 159. Colonel Upjohn's April 1945 report listed 4,398 cases pending in the lower courts.[62]

For the most part, judges for these lesser courts were regular Italian magistrates: either brought out of retirement, taken from prisoner-of-war camps, or continuing at their benches. Virtually all had served fascism, and their links to Sforza and Berlinguer or with the Allies were tenuous at best. There was no apparent coordination of policy among these lower courts, and the verdicts were wildly uneven from judge to judge.... [N]ot all merely

---

60 Pietro Nenni in *Avanti!*, December 23, 1944, reprinted in Nenni, *Il Vento del Nord*, p. 249.

61 Upjohn report on Epuration, summarized in Charles to Eden, April 12, 1945, PRO FO371 49756 ZM2293. Regarding the collaborationist trials in France, see Novick, *The Resistance versus Vichy*, pp. 140-90.

62 Upjohn report on Epuration, summarized in Charles to Eden, April 12, 1945, PRO FO371 49756 ZM2293.

exonerated Fascists or called for light sentences. Some defendants received harsh terms despite minimal roles in the maintenance of the regime. The victims of these punishments hardly or never possessed political or social power. Later on, with the fall of the north, many of them would be low-level policemen or soldiers who had been involved in roundups. In 1944, however, a disproportionately high number of these cases involved women. Their strategic or symbolic role is obvious. The public images of them as either guardians of morality or temptresses made charges of collaboration against them strike responsive chords.... The fascination in trials with women defendants reflected the deep uncertainty that permeated the applications of sanctions against fascism. Unable or unwilling to define guilt, the Italians chose to concentrate both their attacks and their interest on easy symbols such as the bloodthirsty Caruso, the shady Azzolini, or the frivolous immoral lover.

The most important trial against a woman before the liberation concerned one of Mussolini's lesser mistresses, Cornelia Tanzi. She wielded no power during the *ventennio* nor held any office. Her guilt was purely by association; the crime of unwise loves. She was privy to some information about a hidden cache of partisan arms and betrayed it in her boudoir conversation.... The great irony of the Tanzi case was that it coincided perfectly with the Pentimalli and Del Tetto trial, and the verdicts were easily contrasted. From whatever political bent, sentences of twenty years for the generals and thirty for Tanzi were shamefully unjust. The embarrassing comparisons were compounded by the conclusion of yet another trial on the same day as Tanzi's. The *ex-segretario federale* of Naples, Domenico Tilena, received a sentence of six years, eight months. Even the American ambassador felt the Tanzi verdict sufficiently odd to relay back to Washington.

The lopsided sentences were so glaring that the trials were universally condemned....

Mario Berlinguer's High Court trials and those before the ordinary magistrates revealed the same sorts of problems that plagued Mauro Scoccimarro's purges and the Sforza commission in general. Logistics hurt their progress but was not enough to derail them. The inability or reluctance to come to terms with the nature of fascism in society, in its broader, more profound terms, and reliance on the limited notions of the July decree hindered meaningful action. The problems were rendered insurmountable by the amount of opposition, particularly to the purges....

The recalcitrant bureaucracy's opposition to the measures was soon reinforced by objections from traditionally minded members of the higher orders—the crown, the military, capital, and the church—who, in turn, were backed by their political allies—Liberals, monarchists, and factions within the Christian Democracy. This combination of forces would close ranks while protecting their first line of defense: the state employees. Mauro Scoccimarro's controversial purge, which aimed at broad segments of society, although this was still only a threat, continued as the focus of most suspicion and bore the brunt of contravention. Mario Berlinguer's tenure, on the other hand, suffered less than Scoccimarro's. His trials had come to be criticized for their uneven sentences, but by and large they were not considered as assaults on whole parts of society and had escaped the conservatives' wrath.

The Final Phase

*Roy Palmer Domenico, "Italian Fascists on Trial, 1943-1948"**

[The Growing Debate over Defascistization]

As 1944 drew to a close, defascistization had emerged as the hottest issue in domestic Italian politics. Arguments concerning the Sforza Commission, by November, were creating deep divisions in the ruling CLN coalition and forced the ultimate crisis of the first Bonomi Ministry [resulting in the collapse of his government].

Some observers had been monitoring the new and rising confidence on the far Right, those beyond the CLN spectrum, since the black mark and embarrassment of fascism had begun to fade. As early as December 2, 1943, Croce had written, "This morning I thought how practically no one now talks of Mussolini; not even to rant against him," and he feared that soon historians would "set about discovering bright and generous traits in that man."[1] By the following November 29, Corrado Barbaglio in *Avanti!* bemoaned that many Italians were recalling the *ventennio* with some fondness and noted the growth of a "certain nostalgia" for it. Perhaps the old regime was not so bad after all, and a hasty, or even unnecessary, purge would upset the nation's society in the face of a rising Marxist menace that seemed particularly strong in the anti-Fascist resistance.[2]

Ironically, the liberation of Rome and open politics also nurtured fresh doubts over the perilous existence of sanctions. By October 1944 Colonel Poletti had detected a growing popular restlessness in Rome and a more heated political debate over the program. The fight between traditionalist forces, which opposed the High Commission, and the Left, which supported it, could not but alter the goals of defascistization, narrow as they may have been, and transform them into symbols in a highly polarized and partisan struggle. Any semblance of nonpartisan sanctions vanished as the High Commission became a political football in an increasingly embittered atmosphere....

During the late autumn of 1944 all party newspapers affirmed their positions in preparation for what they knew to be the coming battle. The Socialist *Avanti!* toughened the most of all. Pietro Nenni and his followers

---

* Excerpted from Roy Palmer Domenico, *Italian Fascists on Trial, 1943-1948* (Chapel Hill: The University of North Carolina Press, 1991), pp. 107-108, 112-113, 118-123, 141-142, 147-148, 156-157, 161-164, 168, 173-174, 178-182, 187, 190-191, 193, 195, 200-202, 206-208, 212, 214, 215, 218-219.

1 Croce, *Croce, the King, and the Allies*, pp. 43-44.

2 Corrado Barbaglio, "Neofascismo," *Avanti!*, November 29, 1944.

... forecast a critical period for sanctions;... now it was time to give Sforza the tools so that he could finish the job. The High Commission should be strengthened and not muzzled.... Viewing the issue in black-and-white terms,... one was either a Fascist or an anti-Fascist. To oppose sanctions meant to support Mussolini.... Nenni was contributing as much as anyone else to the polarization of Italian society into two camps of Left and Right.[31]

Still hesitant and opportunistic, the Communist stance was quite different from that of the Socialists. Velio Spano, the ideologue editor of the PCI organ,... wrote that the Communists were not out to destroy the careers or lives of everyone who had ever been carried away with fascism. Fears over a bloodthirsty PCI bent on the destruction of Italy through a decapitation of its entire political class were unreasonable anxieties spread by obfuscating conservatives.... Spano's solution oddly reflected what essentially had been Croce's: selective purges and trials of top-level Fascists. That this program had not been successfully promoted, Spano felt, was the problem with sanctions.[32]

During the cabinet crisis the Liberal newspapers had taken the most blatantly antisanctions stance. In fact, more than any other political newspaper, *Risorgimento Liberale* advocated the crisis in order to bring the matter of defascistization to a head.... *Risorgimento Liberale* launched, on November 11, a full attack against the High Commission. Scoccimarro bore the brunt of the assault, contained in the article "The Purge and the Masses." He was accused of the worst sectarianism and of using the purge to increase the power of the Communist party.[33]

The monarchists naturally echoed the Liberals but walked on thinner ice. Monarchists had to be careful how far they attacked sanctions against fascism in that a relentless assault would appear self-serving.... In discussing the cause of the cabinet crisis, the chief monarchist ideologue, Enzo Selvaggi, felt that Sforza's moderating influence at the Alto Commissariato had faded in the face of growing "social communism" and charged that Scoccimarro's Communist vehemence had corrupted any positive aspects that had been found in sanctions against fascism. Scoccimarro had stolen the purge machinery and was using it for his own ends, namely to broaden the parameters and attack the Treasury, the armed forces, and the police, institutions dear to traditional Italy.[34]

The ... Vatican had doubted the purge for quite some time. Not that the church stood squarely against punishment of Fascists; it did not. However, *L'Osservatore Romano* worried that a purge might get out of hand. Much of this criticism was based on moral grounds. In April the Vatican paper urged moderation: "let him who is without sin cast the first

---

[31] *Avanti!*, November 28, 1944, December 9, 1944. Nenni's December 9 editorial is quoted in Gambino, *Storia del dopoguerra*, p. 21, and Nenni, *Il Vento del Nord*, p. 239.

[32] Velio Spano, "Epurazione: problema da risolvere," *L'Unità*, January 3, 1945.

[33] *Risorgimento Liberale*, November 10, 1944.

[34] *Italia Nuova*, January 4, 1945; Enzo Selvaggi, "Dietro la facciata," *Italia Nuova*, November 19, 1944.

stone." On July 4, 1944, the organ of Catholic Action, the very powerful conservative lay organization, called for justice and not vendetta against the Fascists. And by October, the Vatican specifically criticized what it deemed were the purge's excesses.... By the time of the November cabinet crisis the Vatican's clear opposition to Sforza's commission was well known.[35]... Scoccimarro's presence provided the DC with an easy way out. In November *Il Popolo* also worried that the Communist had carried the purge too far and sacrificed justice to further his own ideological ends....

Resolution of the Crisis

Despite his November 26 resignation, Bonomi remained a caretaker in office, determined to kill the Sforza Commission and to form a new ministry.... Bonomi [formed a] new cabinet, revealed on December 12, [that] reflected a clear victory for the traditionalist ruling class and its Center-Right political forces and did not bode well for serious sanctions against fascism....

Bonomi himself restructured the High Commission in January 1945, a reorganization that the dejected and outcast Nenni felt "had all the characteristics of a first-class funeral."[42] The office charged with confiscated profits was conveniently submerged into Soleri's Treasury. Scoccimarro was replaced by the Neapolitan Communist Ruggiero Grieco. The choice of Grieco, one of the most stalwart of party leaders and Togliatti's chief collaborator for many years, was certainly a concession to the PCI, but, perhaps in return, the new man proved more pliant than his predecessor. The office in charge of trials remained under Mario Berlinguer. Bonomi evidently felt that he could be dealt with, while conceding that such an important part of the sanctions could not be eliminated.

Most important, the high commissioner's chair went to Bonomi himself, and the Alto Commissariato became a tightly regulated function of the Council of Ministers....The new complexion of the High Commission revealed the growing pessimism over sanctions and interwove with the reemergence of a non-Fascist political Right. While a call to arms for unrepentant Fascists would still have been suicidal, support for sanctions was no longer a political necessity, and public criticism of the program became increasingly acceptable....

[Liberation and Purge of the North]

[One] effect of peace in Europe was the quick transformation of the nature of the anti-Fascist struggle, from a civil war into a combination of popular violence and sanctions against a defeated enemy.... Mussolini's Social Republic ceased to exist, and blackshirts were rendered largely physically defenseless against vendetta. During the weeks after the liberation, several thousand Fascists died violently at the hands of their

---

[35] Bizzarri, "Mondo cattolica," in Bizzarri, *Epurazione e stampa di partito*, pp. 16, 21, 23, 33.

[42] Mercuri, *1943-1945*, p. 255; Mercuri, *L'Epurazione*, p. 85.

political enemies.... No doubt anti-Fascist retribution was openly endorsed by many. The chorus, however, was far from universal, and the "justice of the piazza" itself was limited largely to left-wing zealots and radical elements within the working class.... [O]nly later would ... the more conservative hand of Rome ... moderate the popular attacks and oversee more formal sanctions against fascism.

Another complication to affect defascistization was the different socioeconomic structure found in the newly liberated area. Actions undertaken in the south could not easily be reapplied to the north. The two were now politically rejoined, but it was not the fusion of two identical halves. Unlike the agricultural south, there existed in the north heavy industrial concentration.... [N]o special measures had yet existed to address issues raised by the north's intense, but largely private, capital concentration. Until the liberation, an attack on the magnates of commerce and industry had remained on the back burner.

...Collusion between money and fascism emerged as an issue difficult to ignore, and the obvious complicity of many industrial and commercial leaders served to force the case for a broadened definition of "Fascist." But an assault on collaborationist capital threatened to cross the crucial line between the political and ruling classes. Thus far, sanctions had been applied to government employees and to very few others, with only spotty effectiveness. Most conservatives within the ruling class had been able to avoid inclusion into the list of sanctions targets. But popular sentiment to purge big capital fit into a vague and larger theme, particularly strong in the Left Resistance, to redistribute wealth in postwar Italy. And these ideals were simply too strong, for that moment, to ignore....

Upon the liberation, a significant impulse for broadened and intensified sanctions came from partisan formations, usually on the political Left.... In June [1945], the leader of the Resistance, Ferruccio Parri, would carry the CLNAI ideals to Rome and replace Ivanoe Bonomi as prime minister. From Parri on down to the rank and file came a fresh impulse to purge and prosecute Fascists....

In the last week of April, the first days of the liberation, loose popular courts were established to judge whatever blackshirts could be dragged before them. CLNAI representatives also attempted to channel anti-Fascist anger into their more structured tribunals, *commissari di giustizia*, where the accused might have some semblance of a trial before they were executed. In effect, there seems to have been little difference in the two. They might be held by citizen's committees or partisans acting on vague orders from higher-ups. No one is sure how many of Mussolini's followers were tried in makeshift popular courts and executed or simply shot on the spot. Justice was often accomplished hurriedly before more rigorous public order could be imposed by regular partisan units or by the Anglo-Americans.... The events of the Duce's death are well known. Shot at Giulino di Mezzegra on the shore of Lake Garda, his body was brought back to Milan. The corpse and those of fourteen companions were hideously beaten, trampled, and spat upon until they were barely recognizable as human beings. Photos of the dead Duce reveal something inhuman: caved-in eyes, twisted, misplaced features. He had no face left. Beaten and blood stained, the bodies were then hanged upside down at a gas station facing the enormous dusty Piazzale Loreto, where the Fascists had publicly executed fifteen partisans some months before.

Undoubtedly most blackshirts who died were never given the benefit of due process and were immediately killed at the hands of the people and partisans. One Allied administrator wrote in June that recriminations were so extensive that "any person tainted with Fascism has been extremely fortunate if he has remained alive ... with the result that not a great deal has been left to do in respect of epuration. The methods have been cruel and summary—perhaps sometimes unjust—but thorough." The chaos, furthermore, rendered complete tallies of the dead impossible....

For many, May 1945 represented a clean finality, a good point to end, or at least to envision an end to, the campaign against fascism. Mussolini's corpse was a tangible symbol of the final terrible end of his revolution. It was a powerful image, and many were impressed by it. A great deal of the tone in the political journals conveyed that feeling of resolution.... Mussolini's execution was applauded as a necessary conclusion to fascism's final act. The demise of the Duce and the rebirth of a new Italy were often described in tones of hope, and sometimes in Christian resurrection.... [O]n April 29 the CLNAI issued a proclamation claiming that the Duce's execution was necessary for Italy to make a clean break, "un taglio netto," with fascism.[43]... The DC called for an end to all the unnecessary violence since now had come the time to forget. "We have the strength to forget! Forget as soon as possible."[44]...

Upon his assumption of power, Parri broadcast on June 22 a radio address to the nation concerning the new situation and the place of sanctions. Some of his stance seemed to soften, his tone more pacific and reminiscent of Croce's suggestion that "civil re-education" was the key to defascistization. He urged the partisans to end their "arbitrary acts of justice [that] compromise us with the Allies and, above all, offend our spirit of justice." "Thugs" was the term he used for those engaged in popular justice against the Fascists, and he urged all partisans to place their trust in Rome and to "cooperate for the defense of law and order which our own revolution secured for us."[59] But regarding sanctions against fascism, Parri still had an agenda. The prime minister appointed new personnel for the Alto Commissariato. He scrapped Bonomi's tight control and relinquished authority to the dreaded Pietro Nenni. Mario Berlinguer remained in charge of the trials, while in July the purge was placed under an *azionista*

---

43 *Avanti!*, May 1, 1945; Pavone, "La continuità dello stato," in Piscitelli, *Italia, 1945-1948*, p. 154; Falaschi, *Gli Ultimi giorni del fascismo*, p. 101.

44 Risorgimento Liberal, April 30, 1945; *Italia Libera*, May 1, 1945; *Il Popolo*, April 30, 1945. The May 1 *Il Quotidiano* urged that Italians become Christians again and that the "heroic beauty" of the liberation not be marred with "repugnant gestures, cruelty, and vendetta." Regarding the DC position, see also Mantelli, "La democrazia cristiana," p. 264.

59 Parri, *Scritti*, p. 143. See also PWB report, June 23, 1945, PRO FO371 49772 3361-695, pp. 272-73.

Piedmontese judge, one of the best legal minds in Italy, Domenico Peretti Griva.

...Despite new legislation, however, Rome's official purge in the north never amounted to much. By the summer of 1945 it appeared that the application of sanctions in the newly liberated areas would be as dismal as it had been in the south. From July 3 to 16 the Alto Commissariato in Rome sent an investigator, Roberto Franceschelli, north to measure the situation firsthand.... Franceschelli found ... that in many areas High Commission panels had yet to be formed, and in other places they were riddled with corruption, such as in Venice, where a Liberal member was caught blackmailing the wife of a detained Fascist. In Milan no one who had weathered the liberation had been suspended. Also, like Rome, the local governments were succumbing to paralysis, with sanctions hanging over their heads.[60]...

Frustrated with Rome, the CLN factory councils, or CLNAS, often acted on their own, and it was within these grass-roots efforts that the most serious purge activity in the north was found.... Looking for authority from Parri and the Allies, the CLNAS were determined to push through effective sanctions and were given a good head start; the Anglo-Americans postponed their effective administration of Milan until the end of May and, to a degree, held aloof for a while even after they took control of the city and other provinces.... This gave the CLNAI the opportunity and authority to establish purge commissions in factories and offices....

The autonomy worked both ways for the commissions. Without the Allies or Rome breathing down their necks, they were able to innovate and occasionally accomplish quite a bit. But like everything else with the purge, these commissions were composed of uneven talent, zealots, and saboteurs. Each large concern and many small ones experienced a purge, but the particulars and results varied in extraordinary degree. An observer from the British consulate in Bern was generally correct when he wrote that some of the big magnates would go into temporary retirement and divest some of their war profits. "But," he continued, "it is not thought that in the long run they will be completely eliminated, as big industry in Northern Italy is so largely tied up with these personalities and their collaborators."[63]...

Along with directors, many lower-level bureaucrats and blue-collar workers were brought before CLNA purge commissions. Two important sets of records, from Milan's Breda and Brown Boveri (TIBB) plants, exist that enable some insight into the proceedings. Regular hearings in both places did not begin until September 1945 and lasted for one or two months. These meetings were generally open to the workers, and as many as two hundred could be present. Sanctions roughly paralleled those called for in DLL 159. The accused from any sector of operations might be exonerated; a letter might be placed in the file; he or she might be suspended with or without

---

[60] Mercuri, *L'Epurazione*, p. 137; Franceschelli report, ACS ACSF 1/20.

[63] Clifford J. Norton to Foreign Office, June 29, 1945, PRO FO371 49777 File 3 1945 p. 29.

pay, or fired. Occasionally some were turned over to the authorities for criminal prosecution....

[The Trials of Saló Regime Collaborators]

Like the purges, post-liberation trials against the Fascists were convoluted affairs. Mario Berlinguer still directed what was left of Lorenzo Maroni's High Court in Rome. One of Bonomi's last acts, DLL 142, April 22, 1945, furthermore, braced the court system for the impending avalanche of collaboration trials by the establishment of the Extraordinary Assize Courts (Corti straordinarie di Assise) for each northern province along with an appellate Court of Cassation (Sezione speciale provvisoria della Corte di Cassazione) in Milan. The Assize Courts also assumed most of the responsibility for judging collaborationists who otherwise would have been prosecuted in the military tribunals. In October, the Extraordinary Assize Courts would cease, and their duties would be entrusted to "special sections" of the ordinary Assize Courts. All of these courts served as the most important vehicles in the punishment of Saló personnel. They consisted of a president assisted by four popular judges. Historian Antonio Repaci has termed them "the only revolutionary aspect of Italian political justice."[88] They were the closest parallels to France's anti-Vichy tribunals. The president was chosen from among a pool of judges by the chief magistrate (Primo presidente) of the Appellate Court (Corte d'Appello) and could not himself come from a rank lower than councillor of that institution. The popular judges were chosen from lists compiled by the provincial CLNs. The first of these Extraordinary Assize Courts was installed on May 4. More Fascists were processed and sentenced in the new Assize Courts than in any others. The records of the guilty verdicts, however, illustrate both uneven punishment and a predominance of severe sentences against minor but visible figures such as policemen.

In keeping with the trend of downplaying the *ventennio* and of emphasizing the crimes of Saló, collaborationists were the explicit targets of DLL 142. The Assize Courts were directed to judge officials of the RSI and not of the 1922-43 *ventennio*. The accused were to be examined according to both the earlier guidelines of DLL 159's Article 5 (collaborationism) and Articles 51, 54, and 58 of the Military War Code. The main crimes delineated were the holding of the following positions in the RSI:

ministers or undersecretaries of state
president or members of the Special Tribunal for the Defense of the State
provincial heads, secretaries, or *commissari federali*
directors of political journals
high officials in blackshirt formations

---

88 [omitted]

Provisions were also made for lower-ranking members of the RSI armed forces who were guilty of exceedingly grave or vicious acts of cruelty.[89] Important *gerarchi* still remained to be tried, and their appearances in the new courts triggered raucous scenes filled with screaming audiences calling for execution....

The ambiguity and dearth of consistency in verdicts revealed a problem that had plagued the trials program since its inception—the lack of a purged judiciary. This obvious dilemma had never been seriously dealt with and reveals one of the most jolting arguments against sanctions: that they could never have been truly effective. Many hearings, even into 1947, were chaired by men who were terrified by sanctions or at least doubted their validity, magistrates who had never been purged and who inevitably had a hand in the end of the program. The problem also surfaced in Germany, where, one observer concluded, 60 percent of Bavarian judges and 76 percent of public prosecutors had been National Socialists. A historian of the French sanctions against Vichy noted a similar problem. In Italy, this problem had plagued the High Commission since its inception. As early as May 1944 General Mason-Mcfarlane had recommended that, in order to procure magistrates, the Italian army's judge advocate general, Francesco Traina, be allowed to comb the prisoner-of-war camps to "see what's available." In a report one month before the liberation, Mario Berlinguer gravely doubted the ability of the judges to appreciate their tasks and lamented the unavoidable reliance on them. "One must always remember," he wrote, "that the *Alta Corte* ... cannot judge more than the fewest number of cases (one can say one in a thousand); all of the others are the exclusive competence of the peripheral magistracy, where ... hearings [*istruttorie*] are stagnating. Sometimes, due to an inability of the magistrates to interpret political norms, they conclude with an acquittal which causes popular unrest."...

Right-wing sympathies among the northern magistrates triggered a number of complaints. The Ligurian CLN's Commission for Justice and the Purge discussed it in a report on the judicial problems of defascistization that was sent to Parri and Nenni. It stressed that the regular magistracy was not able to judge political crimes. "In the North," it said, "there is no need to forget, the regular judiciary ... served [Mussolini's] Republic ... [and its work] should be viewed with suspicion by the people. On the other hand, one might fear that the regular judiciary believing itself suspect will wish to display excessive zeal and would not judge freely."...

Criticism of Sanctions Mounts

Opposition to sanctions from business, the Anglo-Americans, traditionalists, and others intensified through 1945. The two most specific attacks against the program regarded its essence and its application, particularly focusing on first, what many considered a perversion of the

---

89 Carabiniere reports. ACS Interior Ministry 1944-46 f12414 b140. See also ibid., f22208 b209.

nation's legal patrimony in order to punish Mussolini's followers, and second, the conditions of prisons. Both attacks, but particularly the first, were profound in that they represented the thoughts and sensibilities of the educated bourgeoisie. The second argument was unexpected because, had sanctions been properly handled, prison conditions should never have been an issue. Both criticisms of sanctions were couched in certain tones of middle-class gentility and Christian morality that cried out to the rest of Italy, "This defascistization business does not suit us."

The primary arena for these debates was the legal community. The committee of eighteen scholars who attacked *ex post facto* application of laws in August 1944 submitted to *Domenica* the first of many articles that appeared when journals resumed publication at the end of that year and into 1945. The forms taken in these debates depended on the writers, but sanctions were criticized from all sides.

Among the first articles in 1945 were those from Mario Vinciguerra, a Neapolitan follower of Croce and a long-time anti-Fascist.... With its inauguration, Vinciguerra served the Alto Commissariato in various capacities and chaired the purge of journalists. But ... Vinciguerra doubted the wisdom of an administrative purge. Moreover, prosecution of Fascists went out of bounds, he argued; it went beyond the fine traditions of Italian jurisprudence to embrace the blood-stained legacy of the French Terror. Vinciguerra called for simple justice, not the vendetta he feared was taking place. He also commented negatively on the program of confiscation of profits, an indefinable concept that could never be enforced....

Achille Battaglia also spoke for a wide range of well-meaning yet conservative anti-Fascists. A lawyer, he served the cause of antifascism during the 1930s in Rome, in an underground network.... Battaglia was never a friend of fascism, but in a June 1, 1945, article, he doubted the validity of the government's legal campaign. His theme concerned the definition of crime found in DLL 159, that is, the concept of "significant acts" (*atti rilevanti*) that had maintained the Fascist regime for power. Not only was it a vague notion, it ran against legal tradition, a violation of *nullem crimen sine legge*. By sacrificing that principle against retroactivity, DLL 159 trampled on good sense. Here again the notion of civilized behavior and the superiority of Italian Christian culture played a role for influential jurists. Civil rights were treasured goals of ... those who had struggled in the underground. Victory over fascism would be a sham if those rights were ignored in the punishment of old oppressors.[100]

In the summer of 1945, Arturo Carlo Jemolo, arguably Italy's most prestigious jurist and a distinguished historian of the Catholic church, [who] had served as a consultant to the High Commission,... attacked the Alto Commissariato's inability to purge while creating chaos in government. The question was not Fascist guilt; that was obvious. Rather, the nation's moral strength and its competence to face Mussolini's legacy were at stake. He traced a history of sanctions in other places and concluded that it was not the thing that truly civilized people did. The

---

100 Achille Battaglia, "Il Tarlo di una legge."

desire to punish political losers was mean spirited and unbecoming to decent people. As far as creating a new ruling class, Jemolo felt it was impossible. To renovate the government through an attack on the top four grades of the administration would destroy Italy, "and no politician would assume the tremendous responsibility of destroying a nation so far gone in the first place for the sake of justice."[102]

...Symptoms of the declining sanctions program—controversies over the prisons and the continued violence against Fascists—reached a broader spectrum through the popular press. Here were issues unclouded by legalisms such as *nullem crimen sine legge*, issues that aroused emotions and furthered the decline of anti-Fascist sentiment and sanctions....

Comparisons to Sanctions Against Fascists Elsewhere

Axis collapse added other dimensions to the history of sanctions. No longer did the Italian and Vichy French examples stand as the only programs to be studied. The obvious change in the broader European history of defascistization was its application to Germany. The connections and parallels between the two Axis partners were at once strong and tenuous. Both countries lived under Fascist (or National Socialist) regimes firmly entrenched in 1939. On the other hand, a German purge need not have to deal with the dual nature that characterized Italian fascism—Mussolini's 1922-43 *ventennio* and his collaborationist regime of 1943-45. In that sense, Italy could be considered as a bridge between Hitler's and Pétain's states, with aspects of both....

The Anglo-Americans concerned themselves much more with German denazification than they had with Italian defascistization.... One reason for this was that Britain and America considered Germany's position to be more critical than Italy's in the postwar world, and events there were subsequently watched and controlled more carefully. Only in the sensitive areas of Trieste and Venezia Giulia did the Anglo-Americans continue to exercise an important watch. Furthermore, the Nazis' reputation was more insidious. When the legacy of their brutal conquests and occupations combined with the revealed horror of the Holocaust, the Reich had clearly become guilty of some of the most unspeakable crimes in history. In popular perceptions Hitler and his SS murderers embodied evil the way Mussolini and his "clownish" blackshirts never did....

The End of Sanctions

The year 1946 marked the effective conclusion of sanctions against fascism. Three years after the July 1943 coup, an equilibrium returned to Italian politics in the form of a republic guided by an increasingly powerful Christian Democratic party, in the end of the sanctions program itself, and in an amnesty for most Fascists. A constituent Assembly, furthermore,

---

[102] Jemolo, "Le Sanzioni contro il fascismo e la legalità," p. 277. See also V. E. Alfieri, "La Legge contro il fascismo," pp. 682-86.

inaugurated in 1946 and piloted by Carlo Sforza, prepared for a renewal and improvement of the parliamentary system upon which the Fascists had trampled for twenty years. The revolutionary impulses of Resistance and liberation proved short-lived, and the "Wind from the North" was no match for the entrenched traditionalist segments within the ruling class, the state bureaucracy, and politics....

Parri's defeat and [Alcide] De Gasperi's victory in December 1945 ... guaranteed that Rome would recapture the controls and that the traditionalist impulse that had tempered sanctions in the south would return to control them in the north. This was accomplished in two ways: first, the traditionalists and their Center-Right political allies in Rome defused northern defascistization, particularly the factory purges and trials; and second, conservative forces crushed what remained of the anti-Fascist partisan movement and, albeit only partially, its legacy of opposition to the old regime.

Italy's institutional referendum of June 2, 1946, furthermore, which abolished the monarchy, combined with the amnesty for Fascists to affect the last phase of debates. Both convinced many that Italy was finally rid of its Fascist king and, by extension, its Fascist past. They also reinforced the argument that a healthy democracy proved its strength through magnanimity—even exoneration—of Fascists.

The referendum and the amnesty also cast new light on old problems that had plagued sanctions since 1943—the tendency to concentrate punishment on highly visible, or strategic, elements of fascism, and a general reluctance to punish people for *ex post facto* political crimes....

Gradual but determined dismantling of sanctions angered many anti-Fascists who had pinned high hopes on the program as a step toward a new, more progressive and democratic Italy. Many took their resentment to the streets, and among the new prime minister's first tasks was that of grappling with the continued nuisance of leftist popular violence. Disorder also came in different forms in the late 1940s: attacks on southern latifundia, separatism in Sicily, labor trouble, and for our concerns here, popular justice against Fascists.

In its broader sense, opposition to anti-Fascist violence masked a struggle between the new order and the partisan legacy. Armed antifascism was a heritage that proved powerful enough to accentuate political lines well after the end of the war....

Active and thorough sanctions clearly interested Prime Minister Parri, who expressed complete faith in his Socialist high commissioner and, despite the sorry state of the purge, urged him to intensify it. On July 4 he wrote that Nenni should accentuate the Alto Commissariato's political character instead of its juridical side. Parri decided to broaden the attack to include big capital. To implement this he enacted DLL 479 and DLL 702. The former, released on August 9, extended the purge to large private corporations with assets over 5 million lire and aimed at the punishment of important business figures.

The more far reaching of the two measures was the "Nenni Law," DLL 702, November 9, 1945, which scrutinized top administrators in government, in publicly controlled businesses, and in private concerns with government contracts. The law, however, did not categorize the business levels included in the purge. Nenni nevertheless took it upon himself to specify that, regarding the government, all those over the eighth rank were to be examined. Offenses warranting dismissal concerned the RSI exclusively; included were simple enrollment in the Republican Fascist party or service in the Saló Regime. Lower-level employees were also susceptible to the purge, but their crimes needed to be far more serious—"extremely grave Fascist partisanship"—than those of their bosses.[5]

A panel of judges quickly chose 393 figures for investigation; the situation appeared foreboding. But the reality of DLL 702 did not live up to the anxiety it created: all had been specified before.... [T]he notion of punishing the high and indulging the lesser had been a standard since the beginning....

Sanctions had to end.... In December 1945 government officials began seriously to discuss dismantling the Alto Commissariato, and a time limit was placed on Nenni's organization.[20] March 31, 1946, was designated the final day of operations. With his hands full as vice president of the Council of Ministers, Nenni quickly became a transitional lame duck at the High Commission.... To oversee the end of sanctions, on March 31, 1946, a coordinating Office for Sanctions against Fascism was established in the prime minister's State Council. Domenico Carugno headed this agency for the next few years in what essentially became an administrative "mopping up" operation. Real power had shifted to the cabinet. To that body all purge delegations surrendered their files and any more information that was required by the ministries....

During these death throes of sanctions it is ironic that, in accordance with what remained of the Nenni law, one last attempt was made to create a purge commission for private industry. No comprehensive history exists of this committee. Its entire existence, spanning about two years, was marked not by an active implementation of sanctions but by interested groups trying to place their men on the committee.... In the end, however, there is no record of anything at all being accomplished by this committee....

Furthermore, statistics indicate that almost no government purge had been applied since the end of the war. In January and February 1946 Rome reported its sanctions record to the Allies. Of 394,041 employees concerned, 1,580 had been formally dismissed. Of that figure, 728 were in the top seven grades of the bureaucracy; 531 others took early retirements; and 8,803 received *sanzioni minori,* a reprimand note placed in the persons file.... The bottom line figure in the 1946 report, 1,580, represents as many

---

[5] Ibid, October 11, 1945; Vinciguerra, "Sanzioni contro il Fascismo," pp. 907-9; Piscitelli, *Da Parri a De Gasperi*, pp. 78-79.

[20] The official decree that ended the High Commission was DLL 22, February, 8, 1946. The other Commissariati aggiunti had already been phased out by this period. The last to go was the office for the confiscation of Fascist profits, which was merged into the Treasury, (and into obscurity) through the February 8 decree. Criticism and lack of direction determined that *commissariato* would never be effective. It was opposed by the entire business community and by the Allies, who represented British and American commercial interests in Italy....

government bureaucrats as were purged. Few, if any, were dealt with after February 1946, while many more were readmitted to their positions and exonerated.[25]

For sanctions in general, 1946 also completed a process that had begun with a vague idea of punishment and had become a policy to forgive, or at least try to forget—a transition from sanctions to exoneration or a national loss of memory. Not only had the purge been halted and the High Commission begun to dismantle, dismissed Fascists were being rehired.

As early as June 29, 1945, reports from the Allied Commission no longer spoke of firing but rather of merely denying raises to RSI personnel. One circular ordered that "all such officials still in office are entitled to receive only the salary due to them according to the rank they held on 8 September 1943, without any recognition of the promotions in grade given by the Fascist Republican Government."[26]

In Rome, among the first to readmit purged personnel on a significant level was the Treasury's State Accounting Office (*ragioneria dello stato*). The minister ... was Giovanni Persico. As early as August 16, 1945, he wrote to Parri that the *ragioneria dello stato,* "like the rest ... of the other state administrations," was beset with "a grave personnel crisis" and advocated that the accounting office make use of those who followed the Duce north, about 130 "young men of sure value who could be immediately put into service."[27] By mid-September the rehiring had begun.[28]...

Along with the demise of the monarchy, the other factor in the sanctions struggle during 1946 was the amnesty. Based on the lessons of

---

25 British embassy in Rome to Ernst Bevin, April 26, 1946, PRO FO371 60547 ZM 1406. The Allied Commission assembled, during the early months of 1946, a statistical compilation of the purge in grades 1 through 6. Each subcommission of the AC obtained the figures from their corresponding Italian ministries.... A copy of the document was forwarded to the British Foreign Office on April 26, 1946.

Subcommission	Employees		Epuration Proceedings		Appeals		Appeals	
	Number	Investigations	Initiated	Concluded	Lodged	Heard	Dismissed	Retired
Education	7,168	7,099	613	462	165	86	118	26
Legal	3,228	3,077	517	431	129	52	58	55
Local Government	764	764	269	225	102	55	13	15
Public Safety	729	506	249	139	48	16	22	2
Agriculture	813	742	205	160	49	14	22	26
Finance	8,290	4,169	1,267	1,007	367	111	113	23
Industry and Commerce	4,620	2,387	708	591	190	64	130	10
Transportation	3,981	3,981	679	580	192	56	205	479
Communications	442	439	221	202	85	24	33	4
Public Relations	49	49	37	20	16	5	14	0
Totals	30,084	23,213	4,765	3,817	1,343	483	728	640

Regarding Germany, see Herz, "The Fiasco of Denazification in Germany," pp. 590-91.

26 [omitted]

27 Persico to Parri, August 16, 1945. ACS PCM 1944-47 10124 1/7 s87-H. One OSS report claimed that the Treasury had begun to hire some "Fascists and neo-Fascists" at the end of 1944. OSS report, March 17, 1945, NARS RG59 Lot file 2688.

28 Persico to Parri, September 15 and 18, 1945, and "appunto" PCM, n.d., ibid.

history, an amnesty toward the Fascists was inevitable.... Aristotle tells us of an amnesty after the First Peloponnesian War.... During the Renaissance, Machiavelli, cast out of Florence into years of exile, was eventually accorded a minor official position after an amnesty. The magnanimous impulse has perhaps eroded in our age of political animosities, but it persists; and modern civil wars fought between ideological adversaries have still often been resolved with forgiveness. The Restoration after Waterloo, the Third Republic, and the American Reconstruction were all launched in part with amnesties. In Germany, similar measures would also be undertaken toward the Nazis.... The establishment of the Italian Republic in June 1946 was no denial of this tradition.[37]

...Togliatti's amnesty ... allowed the judges to ... invalidate most of the anti-Fascist sentences that had been handed down since the inauguration of judicial sanctions in July 1944.[39] All verdicts of under five years were canceled. Those with longer sentences, furthermore, also received indulgences, since all terms were reduced. Only those with very important Fascist positions and those guilty of particularly brutal crimes were to remain in prison. Death sentences were commuted to life, life was changed to thirty years, all other tenures were reduced one-third, and all financial indemnities were canceled. On June 22, 1946, De Gasperi approved the Togliatti amnesty, and its provisions were put into effect. So prepared for the decree were authorities that some prisoners seemed even to have been released in anticipation of it.[40]...

[I]n the collapsing juridical framework, decisions were being reversed and the amnesty was being applied. The Corti straordinarie di Assise, so functionally and symbolically important for the prosecution of Fascists, had been officially terminated in Parri's DLL 625 of October 5, 1945. Lorenzo Maroni's Alta Corte di Giustizia, created under DLL 159, was also canceled except for the ongoing judgments of senators. The Corti straordinarie were to be replaced by "special sections" of the regular Assize Courts, one for each provincial capital. They were manned by regular magistrates chosen by the president of the Appeals Court and included four "popular judges" picked by the president of the Tribunale from lists compiled by the local CLN. These special sections could rule on crimes specified in earlier legislation, mainly DLL 159 and DLL 142.... Some Corti straordinarie continued to review after the inauguration of DLL 625. The last one functioned in Milan until December 1947.

But whether special or extraordinary courts, there was a pronounced new conservative tenor to all verdicts by the end of 1945....

The new Special Sections were not the only changes described in DLL 625. Equally important to the end of sanctions was the increased reliance on

---

37 Hearder, *Italy in the Age of the Risorgimento*, pp. 236-37. Since the end of World War II, Italy has had twenty-four amnesties. *Corriere della Sera*, March 6, 1986. Herz, "The Fiasco of Denazification in Germany," p. 573.

39 Gambino, *Storia del dopoguerra*, pp. 255-56.

40 Achille Battaglia, *Dieci anni dopo*, pp. 347-48; Vassalli and Sabatini, *Il collaborazionismo e l'amnistia Politics*, pp. 529-31; Canosa, *La Magistratura in Italia*, pp. 138-40; Algardi, *Processi ai fascisti*, pp. 18-19.

the regular cassation courts. After the amnesty, the appellate hearings staged in them resulted in the release of most Fascists who had been sentenced by all other courts....

The End of the Anti-Fascist Threat

...All over the north many gathered to voice their discontent over the course of sanctions, but their demonstrations in 1946 and 1947 tended not to have the intensity of the immediate postwar period. The speakers exclusively represented either the leftist partisan veterans association (ANPI, or Associazione nazionale dei partigiani italiani) or the "Chambers of Labor" (*camere di lavoro*). They varied in place and size: Venice witnessed fifty thousand demand justice against Fascists, two thousand protested in Castel San Giovanni near Bologna, five thousand in Ravenna, and two thousand in Piacenza, where the crowd, mostly workers, demanded a thorough purge of the telephone company, SEPRAL. Calls for severe justice, however, also came to be amalgamated into demands for other left-wing goals—such as cost-of-living reductions, increased food supply, unemployment relief, and land reform—or criticisms of American hegemony and aid....

Suppression of the partisan legacy through police action had already begun by late 1946.... But it was the overwhelming 1948 electoral victory that gave De Gasperi and the DC freedom of action to undertake the final push and to crush northern partisan violence. In the autumn of 1948 DC Interior Minister Mario Scelba directed paramilitary operations against the Emilian insurgents [in the North]. From Bologna, a special 1,500-man assault mobile unit was armed with heavy equipment including grenade launchers and fifty flame throwers. By September 9 over three hundred partisans and workers were arrested in Bologna alone....

Many commentators on the Left regarded these raids as part of a Christian Democratic ploy to distance the Italian people from the partisans and the Resistance heritage.... [P]articipation in the war against fascism and support for sanctions became suspect, anti-Italian, and unpatriotic. *Milano Sera*'s Nicola Giudice claimed as much. "The Government," he wrote, "is attempting to turn around the historic relationship between the partisans and neo-Fascists, transforming the fascists into victims and the partisans into criminals."... Naturally, Christian Democrat ideologues did not view the situation in such terms. The party vice secretary, Paolo Taviani, labeled Emilia "the test of democracy" and hailed the police action....

ASSESSMENT OF THE PURGE

Roy Palmer Domenico, "Italian Fascists on Trial, 1943-1948"***

Controversy and bitterness over sanctions against fascism still plague Italians. The issues of the mid-1940s have been sub-merged but never satisfactorily resolved: neither goals nor accomplishments have been clarified. What was the purpose of defascistization? Did sanctions aim at Fascists or fascism? Why, indeed, were sanctions applied at all? Was blanket forgiveness a more appropriate answer than a brutal purge or a bloodbath?

If eliminating "top Fascists" from office had been the goal, then prosanctionists must have received some satisfaction because the *gerarchi*, whether as political leaders of the *ventennio* or Saló, were out of power by 1946. The regime's highest visible elements were gone. Mussolini, Starace, Farinacci, and the rest of the top *gerarchi* were either dead, in jail, abroad, or in hiding. Of course the official sanctions program had less do with that than did the war and popular violence, but the results were the same.

On the other hand, Italian government sanctions, framed in Carlo Sforza's and Pietro Nenni's dictum of aim high and indulge low, cannot be considered successful. Traditionalist opposition against both the High Commission and the Resistance heritage; the pressures and complications of war; the tendency to blame visible, "strategic" members of the regime; and a general reluctance to chastise killed anti-Fascist punishments. A few carried sanctions further than the government was willing to allow: CLNA factory purges and popular violence in the north were the most important of these attempts. Nevertheless, disturbed by actions taken against its authority and beyond its own criteria for sanctions, Rome successfully defused those alternate campaigns.

In order to evaluate the sanctions program, furthermore, one must consider two fascisms. First, as ideology, party, and regime, what remains of the blackshirt legacy? Between the two world wars, Mussolini used an old state bureaucracy and built on top of it one of his own. Constructing a self-consciously new system, Fascist philosophers and ideologues ... sought to structure a new worldview for their faithful. What, then, became of those who believed and acted on those beliefs?

Second, as a condition of state and society, fascism's definition becomes broader and more difficult. A strong current in Italian society had "accepted" the dictatorship and benefited from it in a myriad of ways. After the war people who had been swimming in that current could state, often quite innocently, that their *tessera* had been taken out merely to preserve their careers or for other conveniences, while other important figures may never have possessed a party card. The High Commission and the rest of the sanctions program hardly addressed this broader picture of fascism in society. How seriously Italian democracy has been threatened by

---

* Excerpted from Roy Palmer Domenico, *Italian Fascists on Trial, 1943-1948* (Chapel Hill: The University of North Carolina Press, 1991), pp. 220-221, 223-224.

these persistent fascist tendencies in the mainstream of national life is a question that has occupied scholars for over forty years.

The lesser problem has been the resurrection of neo-Fascist groups. Organized neofascism came surprisingly soon after the defeat of Hitler. Some blackshirts, usually identified with the RSI rather than with the *ventennio*, staged a few rash acts in late 1945. In October they attempted an astonishingly ill-advised March on Rome to commemorate the twenty-third anniversary of the original one. There were other scattered incidents....

Finally, Mussolini's most die-hard followers opted to constitute themselves as a political party. But legal restrictions against neo-Fascist revival hampered their attempts to reenter the political fray. Among Badoglio's first acts after the July 1943 coup had been to outlaw the PNF. Furthermore, most subsequent anti-Fascist legislation, including the armistice terms, prohibited its resurrection. Despite these formal sanctions, Togliatti's amnesty and the establishment of the republic indicated that Italian society might tolerate public neo-Fascist activity.

The result was not long in coming. Six months after the amnesty, on December 26, 1946, a nucleus of RSI survivors gathered in Rome to found the Movimento Sociale Italiano (MSI), their new Fascist party. As its name implied, the MSI was more the ideological heir of Saló than of the *ventennio*. Its first years were dominated by the "Men of Verona," those who endorsed the socialistic measures employed by Mussolini in his final two years. Early rallies often ended in brawls with Communists, but by October 1947 the Movimento felt respectable enough to participate in the Rome municipal elections. The MSI garnered 25,000 votes, which put three representatives in the city council.... In the national elections of April 1948 the neo-Fascists won slightly under 2 percent of the ballots, enough to elect six deputies and a senator to Parliament.[76]... However, neo-Fascist political activity did not necessarily signal a return of the PNF of Mussolini's *ventennio*. Its appearance in the late 1940s angered many, particularly veterans of the Resistance, but the MSI was then, and still is, little more than a fringe organization that commands about 6 percent of the popular vote.

Giuseppe Di Palma, "Italy: Is There a Legacy and is it Fascist?"[*]

Limits also affected democratic reconstruction. By the end of the constitution-making period, a lot of the prewar organic legislation (penal, civil, police, and local government codes; family law), some of which raised issues of constitutionality, was still on the books.... The Constitutional Court did not begin operating until 1956, the Council of the

---

76 Weinberg, *After Mussolini*, pp. 16-17; Murgia, *Il Vento del Nord*, pp. 312-13; Murgia, *Ritorneremo!*, pp. 87-100; Rosenbaum, *Il Nuovo fascismo*; Ferraresi, "The Radical Right in Postwar Italy," pp. 71-119.

* Excerpted from Giuseppe Di Palma, "Italy: Is There a Legacy and is it Fascist?" in John H. Herz, ed., *From Dictatorship to Democracy: Coping with the Legacies of Authoritarianism and Totalitarianism*, Copyright © 1982 by John Herz (Greenwood Press, 1982), p. 126, an imprint of Greenwood Publishing Group, Inc. Westport, CT. Reprinted with permission.

Judiciary not until 1958. The popular referendum and the regional governments (with the exception of five regions already enjoying the special status of autonomy) became effective between the end of the sixties and the beginning of the seventies. Similarly, civic and social reforms eliminating prewar legislation by judicial and legislative means or responding to constitutional innovations were not enacted until the sixties and the seventies. Compared to developments in West Germany, little if anything was done to resocialize the country by democratizing the great socializing agencies (the schools and the army) and expose the new generations to the study of Fascism. For years civics was not a subject of instruction, and the teaching of history did not go beyond World War I.

*Roy Palmer Domenico, "Italian Fascists on Trial, 1943-1948"**

[T]he other consequence of the failure of sanctions [has been the] persistent fascist tendencies in Italian society and government. The most important case in examining the effect of sanctions, or their failure, is what had been the center of that storm, the state bureaucracy.

Robert Putnam's attitudinal study of British, German, and Italian government functionaries in the early 1970s clearly demonstrated that the last-named were the most antipluralist, antidemocratic, and alienated. Ninety-five percent of Italy's senior civil servants in 1971 had begun their careers before 1943. But Putnam also concluded that time was taking its toll, and, within eight years or so, the aged cohort would retire. Sabino Cassese also noted the weeding-out process in his 1974 work.... By the 1950s, Cassese wrote, old prewar and new postwar bureaucracies stood side by side; and by the 1960s, a great mutation of Italy's governance had begun that would render irrelevant the legacies of Mussolini's regime. Furthermore, despite the antidemocratic sentiments noted in Putnam's study, Italy's bureaucracy, particularly its elders, has generally refrained from political action....

A defense of sanctions points to the absence of dictatorship in Italy after the war. What eventually replaced the regime was a constitutional, republican form of government, characterized by aims largely different from the Duce's. It is inconceivable today that the Italian Republic would launch any type of ideological militarization of society or expansionist foreign policy. Although the bureaucracy had emerged relatively intact after sanctions had ended, the government it served had been significantly altered....

Sanctions against fascism, as studied here, moreover, were not directed at the state's machinery but rather at its members, functionaries, or leaders. And the lack of success against state employees ensured that the program would never be the first assault in a truly revolutionary restructuring of Italian relationships between power, wealth, and class. Those beyond the narrowly defined "state", those who controlled Italy's society and economy in 1948, emerged essentially from the same group who had controlled it in 1939 and in 1921. In their mild, final form, the sanctions

---

* Excerpted from Roy Palmer Domenico, *Italian Fascists on Trial, 1943-1948* (Chapel Hill: The University of North Carolina Press, 1991), pp. 224, 227, 228, 229.

battle ended as a victory of traditionalists in the ruling class over more radical Left forces. A moderate policy of selective punishment won out over aspirations to fit sanctions into a broader plan aimed at a restructured Italian society. The inherently slow and complex methods of a tepid purge and limited trials, whether undertaken consciously or not, was the wrong means to process and try large numbers of people, and it was an indication that few Fascists would languish in prisons....

As postwar Italy's largest and strongest political formation, with the most socially diverse following among the CLN coalition, the Christian Democrats must draw particular mention in the balance sheet on sanctions. Their policies, and ambiguities, were decisive in determining the treatment of fascism and Fascists in the new Italy. The highest rank of the DC leadership was truly anti-Fascist as was much of its electorate; but the party also represented large segments of the middle class, which had bided its time and had fared not too badly during the *ventennio*. Sanctions must have made them uneasy. As a whole, however, Christian Democrats undoubtedly recognized that the threatened Marxist revolution would never succeed and, thus, neither would truly radical sanctions. Christian Democracy was acting from a position of strength, and its consideration of purges and trials were not based on fear. It could afford to approach them with a healthy element of propriety, fairness, and mercy, which were inherent components of its principles....

Italy has faced ... crises and has overcome them; it has become a republic with open politics and a voting public that elects its representatives. It is a troubled republic, to be sure, but it is not a police state. Italy is, in the Western sense, a free country. Institutional leadership still consists of the victorious CLN coalition: Christian Democrats, Communists, Socialists, and the "Lay" parties.

6

SOUTH KOREA

EDITOR'S INTRODUCTION

In 1945, at the end of World War II, Korea was liberated from Japanese rule by Soviet forces in the north and U.S. forces in the southern part of the country. Following United Nations-supervised elections in the south, the Republic of Korea was proclaimed in the U.S. zone on August 18, 1948. Syngman Rhee, who had returned to Korea in 1945 after a forty-year exile, was elected president.

Rhee moved quickly toward authoritarian rule. Between October 1948 and April 1949, for example, over 89,000 individuals were arrested for such crimes as printing articles that were "contrary to the policy of the government" and "having a detrimental influence on the public mind." Tension between north and south—which led to the 1950-53 Korean War—provided a perpetual pretext for the repressive policies. In the late 1950s, as opposition to Rhee grew, so did suppression of free speech and the press. Many writers, newspaper reporters, and publishers were arrested. In 1954, near the end of Rhee's second term in office, he forced a constitutional amendment through the National Assembly to remove the two term limit for president, ensuring his continuation in power.

In March 1960, Rhee mobilized the national police and the army to ensure by force the election of his unpopular vice-president, Yi Kibung. Popular reaction to the election fraud and to general corruption in the government grew. Student demonstrations and riots erupted throughout the country, culminating in the April 19 student uprising in which 142 students were killed by the police and dozens more wounded. The students called for political reform, nullification of the March election, and the removal of the Rhee government. On April 26, Rhee and his cabinet resigned.

Ho Chong led a transitional government from April through July 1960. He exiled Rhee and his wife to Hawaii, arrested many members of the Rhee administration and replaced a number of army generals. On June 15, the National Assembly adopted a series of constitutional amendments which restored the freedoms of speech, press, and association. On July 29, a newly-created bicameral National Assembly was elected. On August 12, this Assembly chose Yun Po-son president and Chang Myon prime minister.

The Chang government was perceived as weak and indecisive, unable to cope with the country's economic and political problems. One major source of dissatisfaction was Chang's policy with respect to those associated with the regime of Syngman Rhee. Premier Chang opposed the adoption of *ex post facto* laws or the curtailment of due process rights in these cases. Nevertheless, in late 1960, the National Assembly adopted retroactive criminal legislation to punish those connected with the March elections or with the wounding and killing of protesters, and those who had amassed wealth through illegal means, affecting more than 40,000 people. As the article which follows describes, Chang was viewed as too harsh toward the old regime by those on the right, too lenient by those on the left, and succeeded in alienating them both.

On May 16, 1961, a relatively small military group led by Major General Park Chung Hee overthrew the Chang government, effectively ending South Korea's "democratic interlude." Park promptly created the Korean Central Intelligence Agency (KCIA), with power to arrest anyone suspected of opposing the junta. Limited press and political liberty was reduced by the close of the decade. By 1972, Park had proclaimed martial law, closed the National Assembly and the universities, suspended political activity, imposed strict press censorship, and pushed through a new constitution which removed his terms limits and provided Park significant control over the new National Assembly. Park issued a series of emergency decrees, making it a crime to criticize the 1972 constitution, conduct student political activity, or provide press coverage of either. Although Park achieved a rapid rate of economic growth, opposition continued to build, particularly from the student community.

In 1979, Park was killed by the director of the KCIA. There followed a brief relaxation of controls, but Chun Doo Hwan, head of the Defense Security Command, soon seized power, suspending the constitution and political activity, closing the universities, imposing censorship, and outlawing any criticism of the government. In May 1980, Chun sent troops to suppress a student demonstration in the city of Kwangju. Approximately 200 students were killed, prompting a general citizen uprising of 50,000 people which was quashed by the army. Chun then announced a "clean-up campaign," purportedly to weed out corruption in government and society. At least 8,000 officials were removed from office throughout the government, the KCIA, and state-owned enterprises and banks. 172 periodicals were closed. A far-reaching reeducation program was launched.

Chun restored some political rights to permit 1985 legislative elections. Opposition continued to mount, reaching a peak in advance of 1987 presidential elections. In June of that year, Chun's chosen successor, former general Roh Tae Woo, publicly agreed to most opposition demands, including direct presidential elections to replace the controlled electoral college, release of political prisoners, and guarantee of various rights. Roh was elected president in December. His administration combined limited democratic reforms with renewed tightening of controls on the basis of the "national security threat" from the north. In the aftermath of legislative hearings and trials addressing the abuses of the Chun regime, the National Assembly adopted a law in July 1990 establishing rates of compensation for victims of the Kwangju massacre.

South Korea continues to address the issues of transitional justice under the presidency of long-time opposition leader Kim Young Sam, elected in 1992. In October 1994, following a lengthy investigation by Seoul District Prosecutor's Office, the government issued its formal finding that Chun and Roh had each engaged in "premeditated military rebellion" in 1979. However, noting that they had also made positive contributions and fearing that a trial would divide and re-polarize the country, the government announced that it would not prosecute the two men.

The articles which follow examine in depth the treatment of the Rhee legacy by the Chang Myon government, followed by a brief account of the handling of the Chun legacy by the government of Roh Tae Woo.

THE DEMOCRATIC INTERLUDE: 1960-61

*Sung-Joo Han, "The Failure of Democracy in South Korea"**

Caught in the Middle: The Chang Myon Government Between the "Revolutionary" and "Anti-Revolutionary" Forces

[In 1960,] there was a considerable discrepancy between the behavior of the Syngman Rhee government and the value system of a significant part of the political public, including the students.... [T]he April uprising could be considered a revolutionary attempt by those with liberal-democratic orientations to destroy the "power-dependent" pro-government forces allied with Syngman Rhee. This is not to say, of course, that the South Korean population could be neatly classified into these two clearly definable categories. Most of the people did not belong to either of them, and even those who could be identified with one or the other category differed among themselves in terms of degree and motivation.

It is clear, however, that many people regarded the political upheaval favorably—both for practical and ideological reasons—while

* Excerpted from Sung-Joo Han, *The Failure of Democracy in South Korea* (University of California Press, 1974), pp. 138-177. Copyright © 1974 The Regents of the University of California.

many others feared that they had more to lose than gain from the changed situation. Generally speaking, the liberal-democratic, anti–Rhee forces included most of the university professors and students, members of the press, and many professional politicians, while the pro-Rhee forces included those in the "police-bureaucratic nexus," the highest layer of the military, and the business community. The Chang Myon government thus represented a coalition of the party politicians (at least a majority of them), intellectuals, students, and the press.[1]

Dissatisfaction of the Anti–Rhee Groups

The record of the Chang government shows that, while it was in office, it systematically and successively alienated various political sectors—first those which could be considered pro-revolution and later the "anti-revolution" groups. Within a relatively short period of time it became apparent that there was little support for the Chang government from any of the major political groups, the only exceptions being the few individuals who were directly connected with it.

First to show dissatisfaction and disenchantment with the Chang government were the liberal intellectuals and university students. Specifically, they were highly critical of the government in dealing with those who had participated in the "undemocratic" actions of the Rhee government and those who had accumulated wealth during its rule by illegal means. This task was initially taken up by the interim government of Ho Chong. However, because of its "unrevolutionary" nature, as already pointed out, little progress had been made on the issue before establishment of the Chang government.

An important source of their dissatisfaction was the failure of the new government to take stern measures against the leaders of the Rhee government and the Liberal Party. Following the inauguration of the Chang government, national attention was focused upon the trials of 48 former officials of the Liberal regime who were accused of being responsible for the April 19th massacre; the Liberal Party's plot to assassinate Chang Myon in 1956; March 1960 election frauds; and political gangsterism under the Rhee regime.[2] While the trials were being conducted, friends and relatives of those who had been wounded during the April uprising disrupted the court proceedings when the defense attorneys requested dismissal of the charges against some of the defendants on the grounds that with the constitutional amendment of June 15, those laws concerning the presidential election of March 15 were no longer applicable and the defendants could not be prosecuted on charges of violating those laws.[3] The lawyers in turn refused to participate in the court proceedings until they could be carried out under orderly and safe conditions or until new laws

---

1 Hahn-Been Lee characterized the Chang government as one supported "by a university-press nexus." See his *Korea: Time, Change, and Administration*, p. 117.

2 Shin-dong-a, December 1964, p. 160.

3 Tong-a Ilbo, September 6, 1960, p. 1.

concerning punishment of the defendants were passed. Since no trials could be held without the presence of defense attorneys, this constituted a critical stumbling block. It also aroused speculation that the defendants would have to be released without a trial in case the lawyers did not return before the end of the six-month period after their arrest.

On its part, the Chang government felt that it could not apply pressure on the courts and attempt to influence the outcome of the trials in the fashion of the Rhee government, largely because of its commitment to liberal democratic principles[4] and "due process." Chang and his close associates rejected the suggestions from many quarters to enact retroactive laws enabling the courts to impose more severe punishment on the political and economic "criminals" than was possible under the existing laws.[5] Such legislation would require an amendment to the constitution, as it specifically prohibited the enactment of retroactive laws.[6]

The situation during this period represented a deadlock between the judiciary, the administration, and the National Assembly (now consisting of two houses, the House of Representatives and the House of Councillors), none of which showed willingness to take the initiative in resolving the difficulty by taking the risk either of angering the demonstrators by defending the existing laws or violating the legalistic norms by means of retroactive legislation. The deadlock was temporarily resolved by the defense lawyers' return to the courts after they had received a promise from the government that it would make every effort to guarantee orderly and safe trials.[7]

Consequently, the defendants were tried solely on the basis of the existing laws, and the outcome of the trials proved highly unsatisfactory to those who considered themselves victims of the Rhee dictatorship and demanded heavy punishment for their past oppressors. The severe discrepancy between the penalties demanded by the prosecution and those given by the court for each of the defendants ... can serve as a measure of the dissatisfaction among the general public aroused by the unexpectedly light sentences.[8]... [O]f the 9 defendants for whom the prosecution demanded the death sentence, none received prison terms of over five years and 4 were released by acquittal or through suspended sentences. Of the other 39 defendants, for whom the prosecution demanded prison terms ranging from eight months to ten years, 16 were released immediately after the trial and all of the others received far lighter sentences than those asked for by the prosecution.

---

[4] In this case the most important principle involved was the separation of powers.

[5] Chang Myon, *Memoirs*, pp. 69-70; also, interview with Mr. Kim Yng-sn, November 4, 1968.

[6] Article 23 Of the Constitution stated: "No person shall be prosecuted for a criminal offense unless such act shall have constituted a crime prescribed by law at the time it was committed, nor be placed in double jeopardy." See *The Constitution of The Republic of Korea*, 1960.

[7] *Kynghyang Shinmun*, September 23, 1960, p. 3.

[8] It should be noted that no sign of dissatisfaction was expressed from any quarters when heavy penalties were demanded by the prosecution in early August.

As soon as the court sentences were made known to the public, protest marches and demonstrations were instigated by relatives and friends of those who had died and been wounded during the April uprising. On October 10, two days after the trials ended, an angry mob of students, including those wounded during the April demonstrations, surged into the National Assembly chamber and occupied the platform, from which they protested the National Assembly's failure to take positive action for achievement of the "revolutionary goals." Startled by the extreme course of action taken by the demonstrators, the National Assembly and the Chang government agreed to push through emergency legislation establishing a revolutionary court to try the former Liberal officials charged with brutalities and election rigging.[9] The demonstrations and protests spread throughout the major cities of the country.

Although the participants in the demonstrations were mostly students wounded in the April uprising and the relatives of those who had been killed, and were thus relatively few in number, they represented the widespread grievances of not only all the students who had participated in the uprising, but also the intellectuals and the press who encouraged such protests by providing moral justification for them. An editorial in *Tong-a Ilbo*, analyzing the contemporary situation, eloquently reflected the views of the liberal democratic intellectuals who were dissatisfied with the Chang Myon government's cautious manner in dealing with former officials of the Rhee regime. The editorial, entitled "The Responsibility for the Fortune of the Revolutionary Trials," is quoted below at length:

> Following the collapse of the Liberal regime with the resignation of Syngman Rhee as President on April 26, we demanded that the existing counter–revolutionary National Assembly be dissolved immediately and that the task of rewriting the Constitution be given to a newly-elected legislature. At that time, we argued that since the dictatorial regime was overthrown, not by the peaceful transfer of power, but through a revolutionary method, the Constitution of the Second Republic had to provide legal guarantees which would enable the achievement of the revolutionary goals. Instead, the existing National Assembly, which was still controlled by the Liberal members who had been elected through government manipulation, was satisfied with the adoption of a cabinet form of government. To have let the existing National Assembly assume the task of rewriting the Constitution was tantamount to leaving the task of carrying out revolutionary goals to the counter-revolutionary elements themselves. Indeed, this counter-revolutionary legislature succeeded in deceiving the nation by merely changing the institutional framework of the government. Thus, it deliberately abandoned the opportunity to make legal provisions for achieving revolutionary tasks. It is a matter of common sense that the revolutionary punishment of the counter-revolutionary pro-Rhee officials is a basic and necessary first step toward the achievement of revolutionary goals. Therefore, the fact that such a punishment was effectively blocked by the revised Constitution means that the revolutionary path was met with a

[9] *New York Times*, October 12, 1960, p. 22.

> serious setback at the outset. Hence, even after the establishment of the Chang Myon cabinet, the public was urging the government at every opportunity to enact special revolutionary laws, only to be told that the culprits could be effectively punished under the existing laws. The existing laws, however, were laws meant to serve in ordinary times, and had not been enacted in anticipation of an emergency situation like the present. Therefore, to say that the culprits should be punished under the existing laws was merely a subterfuge to ignore today's reality, namely revolution.... The supreme task of the Second Republic is the completion of the revolution.... Since all three branches of the government—the legislature, the administration, and the judiciary—have proved themselves incapable of carrying out the first objective of the revolution, their existence cannot be justified any more. For anything that has lost its raison d'être, the quicker its disappearance, the better.[10]

The court sentences of October 8 thus provided an opportunity for the supporters of the April uprising, led by the intellectual community, to rally together and register dissatisfaction over both the Ho Chong and Chang Myon administrations for their "unrevolutionary" attitude toward the pro-Rhee elements.

The court action had at least two serious consequences which had a direct bearing upon the stability of the Second Republic. In the first place, it had the effect of profoundly alienating those political sectors which were responsible for the fall of the Rhee government, and which subsequently constituted the core groups in the coalition which made the creation of the Chang government possible. Second, it forced the National Assembly to take a strong position against the pro–Rhee elements through the enactment of retroactive laws to punish them, with the result of alienating the former supporters of the Rhee regime from the Chang government.

The first consequence—the alienation of the liberal democratic elements—which was evident from the composition of the demonstrators and the general trend of editorials after the judicial "slap on the wrist" given to officials of the Rhee regime, continued to afflict the Democratic administration until its downfall in May 1961.[11] The intellectual sector, whose primary medium of communication with the general public consisted of the newspapers and various journals—the number of which more than doubled in 1960 after the April uprising (from 581 to 1,362)[12]—continued to

---

[10] *Tong-a Ilbo*, October 11, 1960, p. 1.

[11] The following titles of editorials which appeared in the major newspapers in Seoul during this period reflect the disillusionment of the journalistic sector over the development of events: "Are trials for the satisfaction of the judges alone?— *Han'guk Ilbo*; "Less-than-fair revolutionary trials"—*Tong-a Ilbo;* "Unexpected light sentences by senseless judges"—Kynghyang Shinmun; "We urge again speedy legislation for the punishment of the culprits"—*Seoul Shinmun*. All these editorials were highly critical of the judges who passed the light sentences, but more so of the Chang government and the National Assembly for their failure to act before the embarrassing consequences of permitting trials under the "existing laws" become apparent.

[12] *Haptong yn'gam* [Haptong Annual], 1959, p. 1004; also *Han'guk hyngmyong chaep'ansa*, I, 258.

criticize the Chang government in the harshest possible terms. With some truth, a member of that sector was later to state that the "intellectuals should take full responsibility for the fall of the Chang government."[13]

The second consequence—the fact that the National Assembly was forced to take a stronger position against the individuals who had been active in the Liberal regime—had an even more important impact on the Democratic government as far as its survival was concerned. The legislation for retroactive punishment of the former pro-Rhee elements, which was enacted by the National Assembly because of the pressure put upon it by the students, the intellectual–press sector, and a number of rank–and–file members of its own party, had the effect of incapacitating a large number of the police whose support the Chang government needed for its own protection. It also alienated from the Chang government many who held high-status and leadership positions in their localities, because most of those who had actively cooperated with the Rhee government were also individuals who needed a close tie with the government in order to maintain or develop some leadership position in the society.[14]

The irony was that the Chang administration had to take the blame for both the "unrevolutionary" actions of the court and the "revolutionary" actions taken by the legislature. It was evident, as Chang himself made clear later,[15] that the initiative for legislation for retroactive punishment of the pro-Rhee elements was taken not by the Chang administration, but by the National Assembly. However, most of those who later became subject to prosecution under the retroactive laws regarded the Chang administration as having been primarily responsible for the enactment of those laws.[16] According to Ko Chong-hun, when former Liberals met Cho Chae-ch'n, Chang's minister of justice, in prison following the military coup d'état, a few of them accused Cho of having initiated the retroactive laws.[17] The explanation for this paradox was that the public had been so used to the omnipotence of the executive department under the Rhee administration that they found it difficult to accept the fact that the executive department lacked the ability to control the other branches of the government under the Second Republic.

The Enactment of Special Laws to Punish Former Rhee Supporters

Upon facing demonstrations and protests throughout the country following the announcement of the court decision, various branches of the

---

13 Kim Pung-gu, "The Nature and Behavior of Korean Intellectuals," p. 86.

14 This was probably one of the most important reasons for the poor showing of the Democratic candidates in the local elections of December 13. In those elections, in which local leaders had much more influence over the voters than in national elections, the Democratic Party won control of only 2 of the 10 provincial councils. The independents won 216 seats, compared to 195 for the government party and 70 for the opposition New Democratic Party. See *Taehanmin'guk sngsa* [History of Korean Elections], p. 963.

15 Chang Myon, *Memoirs*, p. 69.

16 Yi Chae-hak, "*Memoirs*," in *Sasiri Chnburl kisulhanda*, p. 176.

17 Ko Chng-hun, *Kut'o: Purji mot'han norae* [Songs I Could Not Sing], p. 78.

government responded to the critical situation. On October 10, President Yun Po-sn issued a statement in which he expressed his astonishment at the light sentences conferred upon the defendants and asserted that "the only way to cope with the present crisis is to convene the National Assembly as soon as possible and pass a law which would allow the severe punishment of former government and Liberal Party officials."[18] President Yun then sent letters to the presiding officers of both houses of the National Assembly urging prompt action on the matter. In the meantime, the prosecutor's office declared that it would investigate the possibility of re-arresting those who had been freed by the court by charging them with other offenses.[19] The National Assembly, which had been in recess since October 4, reconvened on October 11 and began to revise the laws dealing with treason, so as to make possible the trial of those persons already released.

However, conspicuously absent in this flurry of activities in many branches of the government was the positive leadership and initiative of Chang himself, who, apparently because of personal opposition to retroactive legislation, refused to take the lead in the move.[20] Although Chang publicly declared that "together with the legislative branch" he would try to "enact a constitutional amendment and subsequently pass extraordinary laws for the punishment of traitors to democracy and those with illegal wealth,"[21] the actual initiative was taken by the old-faction members of the Democratic Party in the National Assembly rather than by the executive branch led by Chang Myon. Both Prime Minister Chang and his justice minister, Cho Chae-ch'n, spent most of their energy criticizing the court, which had failed to accept the validity of the evidence the prosecution had presented in the cases against the former government and Liberal Party officials. Furthermore, in response to a question in the National Assembly, justice Minister Cho failed to take a stand on the issue of retroactive legislation.[22]

In anticipation of a constitutional amendment and special legislation, the National Assembly adopted on October 12 a tentative measure which postponed all future trials of the "traitors of democracy" until enactment of the extraordinary laws; the measure also authorized the re-arrest of those defendants released following the recent trials.[23] The measure received strong support from the members of the old faction.[24] In accordance with this law, an order was issued to re-arrest 8 of those who had been freed on October 8, and all further trials for the remaining defendants, including

[18] *Tong-a Ilbo*, October 10, 1960, evening ed., p. 1, and October 11, p. 1.

[19] *Kynghyang Shinmun*, October 10, 1960, evening ed., p. 3.

[20] Chang Myon, *Memoirs*, p. 69. According to Chang Myon, on November 11, when the Democratic caucus met to decide whether or not to support the retroactive legislation, he declared that he would consider leaving the party if the members of the party insisted on its passage.

[21] *Kynghyang Shinmun*, October 12, 1960, p. 1.

[22] *Miniwn hoeirok*, 37th session, no. 28, pp. 13-15.

[23] *Kynghyang Shinmun*, October 14, 1960, p. 1.

[24] *Miniwn hoeirok*, 37th session, no. 28, pp. 5-12.

Ch'oe In-gyu, the most condemned member of the Rhee supporters, were postponed indefinitely.

The first step toward such legislation was a constitutional revision which would nullify Article 23, prohibiting the prosecution of a person for a criminal offense by *ex post facto* laws.[25] The amendment, which passed both houses of the National Assembly without change by a two-thirds majority, made it possible for the National Assembly to enact special retroactive laws to punish those who had been responsible for the irregularities in the March 15 presidential and vice-presidential elections and for the killing and wounding of the demonstrators protesting those irregularities; to suspend the civil rights of the persons who had committed grave anti-democratic acts by taking advantage of special positions attained before April 26, 1960; and to undertake administrative or criminal actions against persons who had accumulated property by unlawful means during the same period.[26] Furthermore, the National Assembly was also empowered to create a special court and a special prosecuting department in order to deal with these criminal offenses.

On the surface, very few people inside or outside the National Assembly, opposed the constitutional amendment. The editorials in major newspapers all supported the proposal enthusiastically,[27] to say nothing of those who demonstrated for such legislation. The proposal passed the Lower House on November 23, *without* discussion.[28] Undoubtedly most of the representatives voted for the amendment out of necessity rather than conviction. In the voting itself, there were 191 affirmative votes compared to only 1 negative vote, 2 abstentions and 6 invalid votes. However, 33 members failed to show up for the voting, all except 9 of them without justifiable reasons. To most of them, to be absent during the voting was one way of not supporting the constitutional amendment without actively opposing it. Among the 32 representatives who either abstained or cast invalid votes were 9 former Liberal assemblymen, 2 former policemen, 12 Democrats, 2 New Democratic Party members, 1 Socialist Masses Party member, and 6 independents.[29] The fact that those who failed to show up for the crucial voting were mainly Democrats and former Liberal Party members reflected, at least in part, the lukewarm attitude of the Chang government on this particular issue.

Despite the apparent absence of formidable opposition against the constitutional amendment, there were signs of uneasiness, not only among those who would be directly affected by the retroactive laws but also among many lawyers, who feared the adverse long-term consequences of retroactive legislation. Many members of the House of Councillors also

---

[25] *Constitution of the Republic of Korea.*

[26] *Tong-a Ilbo,* January 3, 1960, p. 1.

[27] See editorials in the major papers on October 17, 18, and 19, 1960.

[28] *Miniwn hoeirok,* 37th session, no. 45, pp. 1-3; no. 48, pp. 1-3.

[29] See *ibid.*, no. 48, pp. 2-3; also Chng Yng-mo, *Iback samshipsamin'gwa oshipp'alin* [233 Representatives and 58 Councillors] *passim.*

expressed reluctance to pass the amendment although, when the actual voting took place two days later, the amendment passed the House of Councillors with 44 affirmative votes against 3 negative and 3 invalid votes; 6 were absent.[30] Of the 10 councillors who failed to vote for the constitutional amendment (excluding those who were abroad), 7 were former Liberals, 1 was the former commandant of the Korean Marine Corps, and 1 a reformist. Significantly, 5 former officials of the Rhee government or party voted in favor of the amendment.

From the above discussion, it is clear that there was a considerable degree of resentment toward the proposed constitutional amendment, although those who opposed it were forced to acquiesce to the demands of the "revolutionary" forces because of "public opinion" (most conspicuous through newspaper editorial columns) and agitation favoring such legislation. An almost identical situation prevailed during the enactment of the Special Laws, on which deliberation had already begun in both houses of the National Assembly before passage of the constitutional amendment.

The special legislation, much of which was subsequently adopted by the National Assembly, could be classified into four distinctive segments: (1) laws dealing with individuals who had committed criminal offenses (according to the retroactive laws) in connection with the presidential and vice-presidential elections and were thus subject to relatively severe penalties; (2) laws dealing with the restriction of civil rights (i.e., rights to vote and to hold public offices) of those who had held relatively high positions in certain government and other public organizations such as the Liberal Party, the police department, and the Korean anti-Communist Youth Corps; (3) laws providing for the organization of a Special Court and a Special Prosecution Office to administer the Special Laws; and (4) laws dealing with those who had accumulated wealth by illegal and unjust means. All except those in the last category managed to pass both houses before the end of 1960; enactment of the laws concerning "illegal wealth" had to wait until the middle of April 1961. Table VII-2 shows the major features of the first two Special Laws in their final form.[31]

---

30 At this time, the House of Councillors was composed of 20 members of the Councillors' Friendship Club, 17 New Democratic Party members, 11 Democrats, and 8 independents; about two-thirds of the members of the Friendship Club were either former Liberals or former police officers. Voting on the constitutional amendment scheduled for November 26 had to be postponed because of the absence of 19 out of 56 councillors (including 2 who were abroad), most of whom were members of the Friendship Club. There were a number of reasons why former Liberals had a better chance of getting elected to the upper house (*ch'amiwn*) than to the lower house (*miniwn*) in the July election. The voters were not easily able to identify the candidate's political affiliation because councillors were elected from multi-member districts. And many former Liberals were in a better position in terms of campaign financing, which was particularly helpful in large electoral districts.

31 These laws were almost identical with their original bills.

Table VII-2

MAJOR FEATURES OF THE SPECIAL LAWS OF DECEMBER 31, 1960

Name of the Law	*Law Concerning Punishment of Those Involved in Election Rigging*	*Law Concerning Restriction of Civil Rights of Those Who Committed Anti-Democratic Acts*
Initiator	Committee on Judiciary and Legislation, House of Representatives	Same
Primary Purpose	To punish those who committed illegal acts in connection with the presidential and vice-presidential elections held on March 15, 1960, and those who were responsible for wounding and killing citizens protesting the election frauds. (Article 1)	To restrict the civil rights of those who performed clearly anti-democratic acts by taking advantage of special positions they occupied prior to April 26, 1960. "Anti-democratic acts" are defined as those acts which destroyed various principles of democracy by violating the constitutionally guaranteed basic rights of the citizens. (Articles 1 & 2)
Those Subject to Punishment	1. The president, cabinet members, Liberal presidential aides, directors of the Party, members of the LP election preparation Committee, and central directors of the Korean Youth Corps at the time of the March 15, 1960 elections, who participated in the conspiracy to conduct frauds in the elections or who played a leading role in their implementation. 2. Members of the monetary and currency committee, central directors of the banking organizations, cabinet members, and leading members of the political parties or other social organizations during the same period who supplied funds for use in the elections. 3. Those who are not included in the above categories, but who actively cooperated with the Liberal Party in carrying out fraudulent elections or supplied it with illegal funds. 4. Those who caused the death of others in connection with the elections, or those who killed the citizens protesting the election frauds, or those who ordered the acts described in the following item. 5. Those who committed assault on, wounded, threatened, confined, or arrested citizens protesting the fraudulent elections. (Articles 3, 4, & 5)	1. "Automatic Cases": Those who occupied any one of the following special positions at the time of the March 15, 1960, elections would be *considered* as having committed clearly anti-democratic acts: Liberal Party's presidential and vice-presidential candidates; chairman and vice-chairman of the LP central committee; members of the LP election preparation committee; central directors of the LP; cabinet members; presidential aides; assistants to the House speaker; chiefs of the National Police, provincial police, and local police stations, and their immediate subordinates in charge of intelligence and investigation; the mayor and vice-mayor of Seoul; governors of provinces; district chairmen of the LP; provincial chairmen and vice-chairmen of the LP; director and vice-director of the Korean Anti-Communist Youth Corps; heads of government-owned enterprises; chairman of the National Central Election Commission; and chiefs of major government agencies. (Article 4) 2. "Investigatory Cases": Those who occupied any one of the following positions at the time of the March 15, 1960, elections and who, in the judgement of the Screening Commission to be set up in accordance with the present law, committed clearly anti-democratic acts; members of the central committee of the Liberal Party; local heads of the LP; heads of the social organizations affiliated with the LP; central and local leaders of the Korean Anti-Communist Youth Corps; the prosecutor general and his immediate staff and other prosecutors in charge of intelligence and elections; local prosecution office chiefs;

		Liberal Party chairmen of legislative committees and the floor leaders of the LP in the National Assembly; members of the central and provincial Election Preparation Committee of the LP; central and provincial heads and vice-heads of the General League of Korean Labor Unions; chiefs of the armed forces; commander of the Counter Intelligence Corps; floor leaders and legislative committee chairmen of the LP, the Speaker, vice-speaker, chairman of the steering committee and Secretary General of the National Assembly as of December 24, 1958. (Article 5)
Punishment	Seven-year imprisonment to death penalty for those in categories #1 and #4 of the above; 5- to 15-year imprisonment for those in #2; 1- to 10-year imprisonment for those in #3; 1- to 15-year imprisonment for those in #5. (Articles 3, 4, & 5)	A 7-year suspension of civil rights for those in automatic cases; 5-year suspension of civil rights for those in investigatory cases. "Civil rights" are defined here as rights to vote and to hold public office. (Article 12)
Agencies Responsible for Administration of the Law	Special Court consisting of five separate divisions and a joint division under the Chief Judge, to be elected by the Lower House. Each division other than the joint division is to consist of five judges (one regular judge, one representative of the organizations representing the April revolution, one lawyer, one college professor, and one journalist) to be commissioned by the Chief Judge of the Supreme Court. The joint division will consist of the Chief Judge and all other judges of the Special Court.	A Screening Commission, to consist of the following members to be commissioned by the Chief Judge of the Special Court: one regular judge, one lawyer, one college professor, one representative of the April revolutionary organizations, three representatives of the religious, journalistic and other communities.

A close examination of the two Special Laws indicates that there were important differences between them: one was intended to punish the leading officials of the government and the Liberal Party because of the illegal actions they had committed; the other was intended to punish individuals for the positions they had held. The first law, it appeared, was a reasonable response to public demands for severe punishment of those who had been responsible for the election frauds and police brutality and a logical consequence of the constitutional amendment which made such laws possible. Consequently, there was no audible opposition to its enactment from any quarter. With regard to the second law, however, a great deal of controversy erupted both in and out of the National Assembly. A number of important political groups and individuals expressed their opposition to the bill while it was still being considered.

Those who wished to see the relaxation or removal of the law included, in addition to the individuals who were directly affected by it, a number of leading journalists,[32] a few assemblymen of various political parties, a considerable number of lawyers, and most importantly, the Chang Myon government itself. Although opposition to the law was made on different points and with varying degrees of intensity, its critics generally shared the notion that the bill was difficult to justify from either legal or practical points of view.

It was argued that, from the legal point of view, to *consider* that those who had held certain official positions under the Rhee regime had committed anti-democratic acts and thus to punish them (in the "automatic cases") was against the constitutional guarantee that all citizens should have the right to be tried by judges authorized by law.[33] Furthermore, it was argued that the enactment into law of such a provision was an infringement upon the powers of the judiciary by the National Assembly. For the National Assembly, by specifying the individuals to be punished, regardless of their actual actions, was in effect acting as both legislator and judge.[34]

From the practical point of view, the main consideration was that those who would be directly affected by the law would number more than 1,500 individuals in the "automatic cases" and 40,000 in the "investigatory" cases, and that it would be detrimental for the stability of the new government to seriously alienate these people, as most of them had high social, economic, or government positions. It was also argued that many of them were serving as officials of the new government, and that their removal or the threat of their removal from these public offices would seriously jeopardize the new government's effort to reestablish public order and administrative effectiveness.[35] At the same time, two of Chang's cabinet members, the ministers of finance and foreign affairs, reported after their visit to the United States that other friendly countries had misgivings about the National Assembly's attempt to enact sweeping punitive laws against the former officials of the Rhee government.

Therefore the Democratic Party proposed an amendment to the bill, abolishing the "automatic cases" and drastically reducing the categories of individuals to be included in the "investigatory cases."[36] Premier Chang explained that such an amendment was necessary if the members of the National Assembly did not wish the people to regard the legislation as a purely retaliatory measure against their political enemies and if they wished to prevent the social and political chaos resulting from anxiety and

---

32 See especially the editorials of *Chosn Ilbo*, a prestigious Seoul newspaper noted for its objective editorial policy. Its editorials of November 2, November 19, and November 26 were entitled, respectively, "The undemocratic nature of the bill with so-called 'automatic case' provision," "Problems concerning the bill intended to limit the civil rights of those who committed anti-democratic activities," and "The national interest should have preference over the punishment of antidemocratic elements."

33 Article 22 of the Constitution.

34 *Miniwn hoeirok*, 37th session, no. 49.

35 Chang Myon's speech in the National Assembly made on November 29, 1960 (*Ibid.*, 37th session, no. 53, pp. 6-21.)

36 For the proposal, see *Kynghyang Shinmun*, November 26, 1960, evening ed., p. 1.

fear in numerous public servants and police personnel.[37] Meanwhile, Chang assured the former Liberal members of both houses of the National Assembly that he would do his best to protect their status as members of the National Assembly.[38]

However, those who disagreed with relaxation—i.e., those who insisted on the desirability of a strong law against the former pro-Rhee officials—argued that the revolutionary situation both justified and demanded such a measure. They asserted that suspending the civil rights of those who had actively cooperated with the Rhee regime on the local level was an important way of satisfying the grievances of the "revolutionary groups" and a necessary measure to check the growth of anti-revolutionary forces throughout the nation.[39] Although the various political parties and social groups did not speak with one voice on this issue, those who supported strong retroactive legislation included a majority of the New Democratic Party members and members of the "junior group" of the Democratic Party within the House of Representatives, and most self-styled "revolutionary organizations," numbering approximately forty.[40] A majority of newspapers also supported this strong position.[41]

The New Democratic Party took a stronger position than the Democratic Party against the former Liberal officials because, first, it feared that the lenient measures proposed by the Democratic leadership would help it win the support of local government and police officials; and second, it wished to ingratiate itself with the demonstrators and the general public by posing as strongly "pro-revolution." However, even among the New Democrats, there were many who wished to relax the bill, either by eliminating the "automatic" clause or by reducing the number of those whose civil rights were to be suspended.[42] Although the Democratic Party was more inclined than the New Democratic Party to modify the bill concerning the suspension of civil rights for former pro-Rhee officials, the younger members in both major parties were generally persistent in their opposition to change in the proposed law.

Those who advocated stronger punishment of local law enforcement officers were especially enraged when, in mid-November, former minister

---

37 *Miniwn hoeirok*, 37th session, no. 53, p. 7.

38 *Kynghyang Shinmun*, November 23, 1960.

39 These views were clearly reflected in the speeches of National Assembly members during the period of deliberation. See *Miniwn hoeirok*, 37th session, nos. 50-53.

40 According to an assemblyman, only four of these groups had any type of legitimate claim to represent the "revolutionary forces." (*Miniwn hoeirok*, 37th session, no. 51, p. 3.)

41 In contrast with most other legislative issues, there was no unanimity of opinion among the various newspapers on this particular issue.

42 In a public hearing on this issue held on November 10, a division of opinions occurred among the various groups: Groups opposed to the "automatic clause" included the Association of Newspaper Publishers; the Democratic Party; the Republican Party (led by Kim Chun-yn, who had separated himself from the Democratic Party in 1956 after Chang Myon was nominated for the vice-presidency; and two of five "citizen representatives." Groups supporting the "automatic clause" included the Revolutionary Students Association; the University Professors' Association; the New Democratic Party; the Seoul National University Student Association; the Crippled Students' Friendship Society; and three of five "citizen representatives." *Miniwn hoeirok*, 37th session, no. 51, pp. 4-5.)

of internal affairs Chang Kyong-gn escaped to Japan while on bail for health reasons. Supporters of a strong bill argued that the fact that Chang, who was a faithful supporter of the Rhee regime, was able to escape to Japan despite his criminal status was indicative of and attributable to the presence of numerous anti-democratic, pro-Rhee elements at the lower levels of law enforcement.[43]

Despite a strong feeling against the "automatic" clause and his public stand to this effect, Premier Chang failed to rally his own party's members behind the amendment he supported. In the actual voting, the amendment proposal, which would have eliminated the "automatic cases," received only 60 votes in its favor out of 163 members present.[44] The original (automatic) clause remained in the bill by a vote of 90 affirmative votes out of 164 members present.[45] From the floor discussion itself, it is clear that not all of the 60 members who supported the Democratic Party amendment were Democrats. Among them were members of the independent group who had been closely affiliated with the Liberal regime, and of minor parties such as the Republican Party and the Socialist Mass Party, which objected to the bill as a matter of legal and political principle.[46] This indicates that those Democrats who voted for the Democratic proposal numbered less than 50, dramatizing the ineffectiveness of Chang's leadership within the Democratic Party on a very crucial issue. Other proposals, aimed at mitigating the adverse effect of the law, met similar fates.[47] Finally, when the "unrevolutionary" House of Councillors returned the bill with changes which turned the "automatic cases" into "investigatory cases," the lower house overruled it by an overwhelming vote of 161 to 6. The end product was practically the same as the bill originally proposed by the judicial and legislative committee of the lower house one and a half months earlier.

As shown in the legislative process described above, the bill concerning the suspension of the civil rights of former government and Liberal Party officials passed the National Assembly over a considerable degree of opposition and reluctance on the part of many members-especially the elderly and those who were close to the Chang government. The law (concerning the suspension of civil rights) passed the National Assembly in

---

43 According to Kim To-yn, Chang would frequently provide President Rhee with distorted arguments in cabinet meetings in order to win Rhee's favor. (*Ibid.*, pp. 1-2.) For a brief description of Chang's personal background, see Chapter Two of this book.

44 *Miniwn hoeirok*, 37th session, no. 54, pp. 5-7. The proposal was actually discarded because of failure to receive a majority vote after two attempts.

45 *Ibid.*

46 Yun Kil-chung, one of the three SMP assemblymen, also made it clear that he was opposed to this particular bill. See Yi Chae-hak, "*Memoirs*," p. 177.

47 An amendment proposed by Han Kn-jo, a Democrat and close associate of Chang, which attempted to strike out the "investigatory case" clause from the bill, was defeated by a vote of 10 to 9 on the floor, most of the 224 members present in the chamber not voting. (*Miniwn hoeirok*, 37th session, no. 58, p. 4.) A proposal by Kim Chun-yn, head of the Republican Party, attempting to combine the automatic and investigatory cases into a single category, also failed to pass the House of Representatives, receiving only 6 affirmative votes against 5 opposing votes out of 163 members present (*Ibid.*).

part because of the desire of many assemblymen to eliminate possible competitors (i.e., former Liberals) in their respective districts and to replace the former government and police officers with their own supporters. The desire of the New Democratic Party to support what seemed to be a popular issue at the time and to prevent the Democratic Party from strengthening its position among former officials of the Liberal regime was also an important factor in the passage of the law. However, it seems that the two most important factors were the inability of the Chang government to exert strong pressure on the Democrats to push through its own amendment, and the general passivity and lack of conviction of a majority of the assemblymen, which made it easy for the demonstrators and a few radically oriented legislators to force the National Assembly to pass a "revolutionary" law. This law, providing for the punishment of low-level officials, had the serious effect of immobilizing a number of important personnel in law enforcement agencies and of alienating them from the constitutional order of the Second Republic as well as from the Chang government itself.

Demoralization of the Police

...[T]he Ho Chong government had taken only limited and reluctant steps toward "democratizing" the national police, limiting its actions to the dismissal of a few top-ranking officers and personnel shifts between and within the various provinces.[48] Therefore, the task of a major police overhaul was left to the Democratic government of Chang Myon. Immediately upon assuming power, Chang Myon recognized the need to purge a large number of police officers at all levels who were accused of illegal or brutal actions while serving the Liberal regime, and also to restore police authority, which had been badly damaged as a result of the student uprising, as well as in anticipation of purges within the police department. Police atrocities had constituted one of the most important factors responsible for provoking the April uprising.[49]

During the first few weeks of his administration, Chang placed higher priority on the first task—that of meeting the public demand for a large-scale police purge. Within three months of taking office, the Chang Myon government purged a total of 4,500 police officers who had allegedly cooperated with the Liberal regime in election rigging or who were known to be the objects of public hatred. Table VII-3 shows the number of police officers at different levels who were dismissed by the Chang government during the period between September 1 and November 30, 1960.

In addition, about 80 percent of all police personnel were transferred to different positions—most of them in other localities—during the same period.[50] Among those who were dismissed, a majority consisted of the heads of provincial, county-level, and local police stations and their

48 See Chapter Four.

49 See Kim Sng-t'ae, "Psychology of the April Uprising."

50 *Haptong yn'gam*, 1961, p. 152.

immediate subordinates in charge of investigative work. Although the percentage of those purged was smaller among the lower–ranking officers, the dismissal of many of the middle-level officers (inspectors, lieutenants, and sergeants) made it difficult for the police as a whole to function adequately, especially in the area of investigation. Furthermore, those police officers who had been most valuable to the Liberal Party were also those who were more experienced and capable in a professional sense, and their loss had a great impact upon the effectiveness of the police force throughout the nation.

Table VII-3
DISMISSED POLICE OFFICERS BY RANK
SEPTEMBER 1-NOVEMBER 30, 1960

Rank	Number Dismissed	Total number	Percent Dismissed
National chiefs	18	20	90%
Superintendents	115	160	70
Inspectors	265	500	54
Lieutenants	678	4,000	18
Sergeants	1,276	6,200*	20
Policemen	2,169	22,000*	10
TOTAL	4,521	32,880	14%

Sources: *Haptong yon'gam*, 1961, p. 152; *Tong-a Ilbo*, May 7, 1960 p. 1.
*Estimated number.

The police and other law enforcement agencies, already under–manned in maintaining social order and public security, were further weakened with the passage of the constitutional amendment and the law concerning the suspension of civil rights for former officials of the Liberal regime. For, of the nearly 15,000 individuals affected by the law, more than 2,500, or about one-sixth, were police officers in leadership positions.[51] Of these, there were 7 inspectors, 84 lieutenants, 454 sergeants, and 1,979 Policemen. Of about 600 individuals included in the "automatic" category, about 400 were former National Police officers and detectives who had allegedly intimidated voters and anti-Rhee candidates, terrorized polling places, and assisted in the burning and stuffing of ballot boxes.[52] The seriousness of the situation was such that the intelligence department of the Seoul district prosecutor's office appealed to the National Assembly and the cabinet to exempt a total of 611 police officers working for the department from civil rights suspension, stating that their expulsion from the police

---

[51] *Kynghyang Shinmun*, January 31, 1960, evening ed., p. 3.
[52] *New York Times*, February 1, 1961, p. 17.

force would mean the loss of 74 percent of the police detectives engaged in political (anti-Communist) intelligence activities.[53]

Significantly, the ministers of both home affairs and justice testified in the National Assembly that the loss of many experienced police officers en masse would have serious consequences for the security of the nation.[54] Eventually, however, they could not stop the dismissal of the police officers. The real significance of the problem was that, although the police officers specializing in investigative work here ostensibly engaged in counterespionage missions, they also had the vital task of collecting information concerning any anti-government activities within the country. The loss of these individuals made the protection of the government from its domestic enemies virtually impossible.[55] It was also difficult to expect unreserved loyalty to and cooperation with the new government from the police officers included in the "investigatory" category.

A similar situation prevailed among the officials in other branches of the government. Chang had already dismissed about 5,000 senior officials appointed under the Rhee government in September, and another 12,000 were affected following the passage of the Special Law.[56] There was thus a sharp contrast between the way the police were treated by the Chang government in 1960 and by the American Military Government in Korea following the Japanese defeat in 1945. Under the American Military Government, those who had served in the Japanese police were effectively protected by Cho Pyong-ok, who headed the National Police at that time, and they subsequently played a critical role in protecting and stabilizing the occupation government and later the government of President Syngman Rhee. Now, however, under somewhat similar circumstances, many of those who had served the Liberal regime were made objects of persecution. It would seem that these police officers could easily have transferred their loyalty to the new government if it had shown the willingness and capability to give them protection from those who assailed them for their past service to Rhee. Because of the Chang government's failure in this regard, the National Police not only failed to secure the absolute number of personnel necessary to carry out its task, but was also unable to restore the self-confidence among the police officers which had been lost as a result of the unsuccessful attempt to suppress the violent student uprising.

So long as no politician could provide the needed protection from their critics or justification for effective action for the government, most police officers were unwilling to risk their lives or positions in defense of the new regime. Even before the passing of the Special Law, there were many instances of police incapacitation and unwillingness in dealing with social disorder. The weakness of the police was well shown in a clash between a police-backed group and their opponents which took place in Ch'angnyong,

---

53 *Kynghyang Shinmun*, January 10, 1961, p. 1.

54 *Miniwn hoeirok*, 38th session, no. 14, pp. 19-26.

55 Interview with Kim Yng-sam, October 10, 1969.

56 *New York Times*, September 24, 1960, p. 3; also *Kynghyang Shinmun*, January 31, 1961, evening ed. p. 3.

Kyongsang Nam-do Province, immediately following the July 29 election. In that election, Shin Yong-ju, a former Liberal, and Pak Ki-jng, a Democratic candidate, competed for the National Assembly seat in this district. Both had strong kinship ties among the electorate, but Shin had the implicit backing of the Ch'angnyong police department as a former police officer and Liberal assemblyman. However, there were very strong feelings against his candidacy among the rival kinship groups in the district who accused Shin and his close relatives of having been responsible for the banishment of a number of villagers shortly before the end of the Korean War. It was believed that truckloads of villagers who had been branded as Communists were sent off to an island on the southwestern coast and drowned.[57]

In the midst of the ballot-counting, Shin, who had superior organization and abundant financial resources, led Pak, whose campaign workers charged Shin with election rigging. This resulted in a scuffle between the campaign workers of the two candidates, injuring some 30 people. Subsequently, the villagers and townsmen supporting Pak invaded the polling-stations and burned a number of ballot boxes. Furthermore, they kidnapped candidate Shin and gave him a "people's tribunal" which sentenced him to death. Although Shin's life was saved by visiting students, who urged restraint, a state of complete anarchy reigned during the next few days in the district as the townsmen and villagers captured the district police chief and his wife and publicly ridiculed them. The rioting, which resulted in burning and destruction of the houses of Shin's friends and relatives, as well as the lynching of government officials, ended only after an army contingent was brought in. As a result of the rioting, however, Pak, the Democratic candidate, was declared winner in the Ch'angnyong District by the Central Election Office.

Similar incidents took place in a number of other districts, and in all the cases of violence growing out of the election, the police found themselves completely incapable of dealing with the mobs who demanded the withdrawal of the "anti-revolutionary" candidates.

Members of the police force often refused to face a direct confrontation with the demonstrators, even when their own buildings and superiors were objects of attack by the mobs. Late in September, when some 50 students from Seoul National University stopped all automobiles without "regular" license plates (presumably because they belonged to the "privileged class"), the authorities found it necessary to mobilize a total of 1,500 policemen to free 76 automobiles from the hands of the students.[58] On October 8, when the president of Han Yang University, a former Rhee supporter, sought asylum in a major police station following student protests against his mishandling of school funds, some 500 policemen failed to prevent the students from forcibly taking the college president away from the police building. In mid-November, the home of the president and

---

[57]For detailed description, see *Kynghyang Shinmun*, August 10-12, 1960; also *Han'guk hyngmyong chaep'ansa*, I, 188-189.

[58] *Kynghyang Shinmun*, September 23, 1960, p. 3.

chairman of the board of directors of Yonsei University, an American, was ransacked by some 1,500 students who met with no police resistance; the students were protesting that he had failed to dismiss a number of pro-Rhee professors at the university.[59] In all these cases, the police showed themselves timid and unwilling in confronting the demonstrators.

The effectiveness of the police force was further hindered by the instability in the ministry of home affairs, which was in charge of its operation.... [T]here were three ministers of internal affairs during the first three months of the Chang administration.

One reason for the rapid turnover among internal affairs ministers was the ineffectiveness of the National Police. However, such turnover itself contributed to the weakening of the police force. Only belatedly did the Chang government try to ameliorate the effects of its personnel policy and the Special Law passed by the National Assembly. There were three general lines of action that the government took to achieve this objective. The first was to supplement the existing police force with new recruits at various levels. Thus the new government recruited 2,000 new police officers during its administration in 1960. Of these, 430 were college graduates who, it was hoped, would provide needed new blood for the police department. In addition, about 120 college graduates were recruited as cadre candidates, and were later appointed as sergeants in the police force. In the major personnel reshuffle in late September, 20 new superintendents were appointed from outside the department, while 36 inspectors were promoted to that rank. In all, during the year 1960, 540 police officers were promoted to the rank of lieutenant or above as a result of intra-department reshuffling.

...[M]any of the higher-ranking officers were promoted after establishment of the Chang government. Although such promotions might have served to generate their loyalty toward the new government, they instead brought about internal dissension and demoralization because of the unhappiness of those who were not promoted and of those who came to occupy positions subordinate to new officers recruited from outside the department.[60]

The Chang government also tried to restore the effectiveness of the police by exhortation, and when that failed, by harassment. Police officers were constantly warned against neglect of duty and threatened with dismissal or other punitive measures. Thus, within a few weeks after the establishment of the Chang government, the Seoul police department ordered all members of the police force to work on both Saturdays and Sundays "just like any other weekday." The measure, instead of "restoring alertness" as intended, only served to demoralize and antagonize most of the police officers.[61]

Furthermore, the National Police headquarters warned in repeated declarations that those in charge of operations which failed to deal

---

59 *Tong-a Ilbo*, October 16, 1960, p. 1; also, *Kynghyang Shinmun*, October, 9, 1960, p. 3.

60 *Tong-a Ilbo*, January 15, 1961, p. 4.

61 *Kynghyang Shinmun*, September 18, 1960, evening ed., p. 3.

adequately with "various demonstrations and scandals" would be dismissed. Subsequently, a number of major district police chiefs were told to resign from their respective offices.[62]

Following the overthrow of the Rhee government, street demonstrations became widespread because of the extraordinary success of the April uprising and the docility of the police. Some tended to become violent, and in most cases the police were not able to cope with them.[63] In a similar manner, when the police could not capture two former top police officers who had been sought for punishment under provisions of the Special Law, the head of the Seoul police department declared that all those in charge of the investigation should resign if the former police officers were not captured before the expiration date of the arrest warrant.[64] In order to make sure that the police officers were fully cooperating with the government's effort to maintain public security, special observers were dispatched to various branches of the police.

The government action represented an attempt to rectify deficiencies in police effectiveness through internal, coercive measures. Such measures, instead of improving the effectiveness of the police, served to cause an adverse reaction from the police officers, who became more concerned with the politics of their fate than with their actual work.[65]

Caught between the possibility that he might be noticed by the public in the course of suppressing demonstrations and the possibility of being dismissed for not acting vigorously enough on behalf of "law and order," most police officers chose to take an opportunistic course, acting only under obvious pressure and then only to the extent necessary to satisfy their superiors.[66]

The ineffectual and uncooperative nature of the law enforcement agencies during this period was well described in a special report of the legislative and judicial committee of the Lower House released on March 7, 1961. According to the report, the Special Prosecution Department (which had been established in order to punish the former officials of the Rhee regime) was able to bring indictments in only 31 of the 820 cases which had originally been brought to its attention, and the major reason for the

---

[62] *Ibid.*, March 31, 1961, p. 4.

[63] According to a report made by the military government which overthrew the Chang Myon government, there were more than 1,800 demonstrations, involving some 950,000 participants, between May 1960 and May 1961. Half of the participants were students (*Han'guk hyngmyong chaep'ansa* I, 246). See also Henderson, *Korea: The Politics of the Vortex*, p. 179 and pp. 431-432.

[64] *Kynghyang Shinmun*, February 12, 1961, p. 3.

[65] *Ibid.*, April 5, 1961, p. 3.

[66] The policeman's dilemma during this period was further dramatized when the Revolutionary Court sentenced to death a former national police officer on April 15 on charges of having killed anti-government demonstrators during the April uprising. The sentence, coming in the aftermath of the major demonstrations, served to discourage the police officers from taking vigorous steps to cope with the militant demonstrators. See *New York Times*, April 16, 1961, p. 27.

unusually small number of indictments was the "uncooperative and negative attitude" of the police.[67]

It can be concluded that the Chang government's strenuous effort to restore the morale and effectiveness of the police was largely unsuccessful. The law enforcement agencies remained generally uncooperative with the new government. This situation had two serious consequences. In the first place, it became difficult for the Chang government to obtain necessary information concerning the possible activities of those conspiring against it. Secondly, it helped convince various political sectors in South Korea that a "crisis situation" the Chang government could not cope with was emerging. Rumors suggesting the possibility of a large-scale uprising, either in the cities or in the rural areas, were widespread among the population and the politicians, despite the prime minister's public denials that there was any factual basis for such rumors.[68]

Many were particularly concerned that the students would erupt again on the occasion of the first anniversary of the April uprising. A. M. Rosenthal wrote in the *New York Times*, "Many Koreans and foreigners are awaiting the anniversary of the revolution with considerable nervousness. Their fear is that the revolution created too many expectations that the Chang government, burdened by economic realities, has not been able to meet. They are concerned that the student revolutionaries may go into the streets again."[69] The anxiety and nervousness of observers proved to be not without some substance, as the streets were indeed filled again with demonstrating students in late March and early April.... [T]he anti-government demonstrations, organized largely by the leftist organizations (students and non-students) and reformist parties, provided a timely excuse for those in the military who were plotting to take over power from the Chang government.

The Question of Illegal Wealth

In dealing with those who had accumulated wealth by illegal means during the Rhee regime, the Chang government followed a pattern similar to its treatment of former Liberal officials. Initially the government angered the "pro-revolutionary" elements by its failure to take strong measures against the holders of illegal wealth, but was subsequently forced to propose punitive legislation sufficiently harsh to cause a strong reaction from the business sector.

...[T]he Ho Chong government had not taken positive action concerning illegal wealth during its three-month administration. Ho Chong's interim cabinet had resolved on May 21, 1960, that the matter would be handled only "within the boundaries of existing laws."[70] From among various

---

67 *Kynghyang Shinmun*, March 8, 1961, p. 1.

68 *Ibid.*, February 26, 1961 p. 1.

69 *New York Times*, March 15, 1961, p. 6.

70 *Shin-dong-a*, December 1964, p. 160.

illegal business activities,[71] the Ho Chong government had chosen only violations of tax laws for investigation and punishment. On June 4, the ministry of finance made public a list of individuals who had at least 5 million hwan in unpaid taxes, accumulated during the five years prior to 1960. Included in this list were 71 enterprises represented by 25 individuals. In the meantime, the Ho government requested and received authorization from the National Assembly to establish a Consultative Committee for the Regulation of Tax Violators, which was to consist of representatives from the ministry of finance, ministry of justice and the grand prosecution office. As we noted in earlier chapters, the Consultative Committee took the rather passive step of simply asking the accused enterprises to voluntarily report their illegal business activities during the Rhee regime.[72]

In response to the declaration of the Consultative Committee, the 16 largest corporations in Korea, represented by the 9 wealthiest individuals, reported having evaded a total Of 4.8 billion hwan (equivalent to about $7 million) in taxes. In terms of both the number of individuals admitting their guilt and the amount of delinquent taxes reported, the figures were far lower than expected by either the general public or government authorities. In recognition of this, the Committee ordered a thorough investigation of the amount of tax evasion by leading enterprises. Subsequently the Prosecution Office revealed, after a month-long investigation, that during the five years prior to 1960 more than 9 billion hwan in taxes (about $14 million) had been illegally evaded by 28 enterprises controlled by 12 individuals.[73]

One crucial factor in delaying the punishment of those guilty of large-scale tax evasion was continuing disagreement between the ministry of finance, which advocated relatively mild treatment of the delinquents, and the Prosecution Office, which demanded harsher punishment for them. For example, the ministry of finance, which had retained most of the officials who had close ties with business and who understood the adverse economic consequences of harsh treatment of the large enterprises, argued that those who were guilty of tax evasion should be required to pay only two to three times the amount evaded during the past two years as a penalty (this would be in addition to the total amount evaded during the past five years). On the other hand, the Prosecution Office wished to see them pay as a penalty four to five times the amount evaded during the past two years.[74]

Despite repeated conferences aimed at ironing out their differences, the two governmental branches could not reach agreement on this point, and the issue had to be handed over to the new government.

---

71 See Chapter Four of this book. The illegal activities included: (1) illegal or improper purchase of government property; (2) receiving improper bank loans at rates far lower than the current ones; (3) purchase of government foreign currency (dollars) through preferential treatment; (4) tax evasion, illegal or improper tax exemption, or tax reduction; (5) illegal or improper acquisition of concessions and privileges; (6) acceptance of grafts and bribes.

72 *Han'guk hyngMyong chaep'ansa*, I, 278-279.

73 *Ibid.*, pp. 279-286.

74 *Ibid.*, pp. 283-287.

A still more important and basic reason for the failure of the Ho Chong government to take positive action on this matter was its reluctance to assume the responsibility of attacking the business sector too vigorously. It repeatedly postponed major decisions on the matter, until it could pass the task on to the forthcoming government. However, the Chang Myon government had to work on the basis of two important decisions made by the Ho government regarding this problem. The first was the decision to make any punishment "financial" rather than criminal. Hence the representatives of business enterprises were freed from the possibility of imprisonment for their unlawful business activities during the Rhee administration. Such a decision stemmed from the recognition by both the Ho and Chang governments that the physical punishment of businessmen might cause general panic in the economy. Secondly, owners of the enterprises were encouraged to pay whatever they were supposed to owe to the state in stocks rather than in cash, so that their enterprises would continue to operate and repayment would not have an adverse impact on the national economy.[75]

Immediately after its assumption of power, the Chang government issued notice to those guilty of tax evasion to pay back in fines the taxes evaded during the preceding five years, plus four to five times the evaded amount in fines. In addition, it announced that a second round of investigation was being launched to deal with other business enterprises. In all, notices were sent to 47 corporations represented by 25 individuals who presumably owed the government a total of 19 billion hwan (about $29.3 million). A majority of these enterprises were engaged in such crucial economic activities as manufacturing (especially cement, textile, sugar, chemical goods, and metallic goods), fuel, transportation, insurance, and foreign trade.[76]

Despite the Chang government's relatively prompt action in trying to deal with the issue of illegal wealth, dissatisfaction was voiced inside and outside the National Assembly over the facts that the Chang government was overly generous in repayment terms; that many illegal economic activities other than tax evasion were not being punished; and that tax-delinquent individuals were all treated in a uniform manner, without regard to the different ways in which the illegalities were committed. The old faction of the Democratic Party (later the New Democratic Party) was thus pushing for special legislation to correct these "shortcomings," while the Chang administration insisted that sweeping new legislation was not necessary.

One complicating matter in the resolution of this issue was the widespread belief that the Chang government's soft stand toward illegal wealth was attributable to financial contributions from its holders. The funds were allegedly used in the election campaign for new faction members and in the later parliamentary maneuvering in the contest for the prime

---

75 Interview with Mr. Kim Yng-sn (former minister of finance in the Chang Myon cabinet), November 4, 1968.

76 *Kynghyang Shinmun*, September 1, 1960, p. 1.

ministership. Shortly after the new National Assembly was convened, the old faction alleged that including the months of July and August the major banks in Seoul had provided some 2 billion hwan in loans to individuals accused of having illegally accumulated wealth, and that they suspected that much of the money went to the new faction of the Democratic Party.[77] Subsequently, a special committee created by the House of Councillors to investigate the matter revealed that during the period between July 1 and August 10, a total of 2,002,770,000 hwan had been loaned to eight major corporations, all of which were being accused of having evaded taxation, and that the final destination of the loans could not be determined.[78] There was strong suspicion that the money had indeed been used by the Democratic new faction. Chang Myon wrote later that his faction had indeed received a considerable amount of money from businessmen, including a group of textile industrialists who contributed some 200,000,000 hwan, "in order to forestall the rise of leftist and progressive "groups."[79]

Faced with strong pressure from the students and the press, the Lower House on February 9 passed a bill aimed at punishing those who had accumulated wealth through "impure" means during the Rhee regime. The earlier constitutional amendment had called for such legislation. According to the bill, "special measures" were to be taken against certain individuals who, by taking advantage of their privileged positions, had accumulated wealth during the five years prior to April 3 1960. Thus the bill would have enabled the government to take administrative measures against those who had evaded taxes in excess of 50,000,000 hwan (approximately $80,000), those who had acquired wealth in excess of 30,000,000 hwan (approximately $46,000) through other "impure" practices, and government or party officials who had accumulated more than 15,000,000 hwan (approximately $25,000). "Punishment" ranged from redemption of between 100 percent to 400 percent of the illegally acquired profit.[80] The bill passed the lower house over the opposition of a considerable number of representatives who thought its provisions "too soft."[81]

However, the bill received immediate and intense reaction from the business sector. Through a petition to the National Assembly, public announcements and paid advertisements, the leading business organizations[82] asserted that the bill would "destroy" the fabric and

---

77 *Miniwn hoeirok*, 37th session, no. 7, pp. 1-2.

78 *Han'guk hyngmyong chaep'ansa*, I, 203.

79 Chang Myon, *Memoirs*, p. 84.

80 The text of the bill passed by the Lower House can be found in *Han'guk hyngmyong chaep'ansa* I, 644-651.

81 Most of the representatives who expressed views opposing the bill because of its "softness" were either independents or non-leadership members of the two major parties. It was suggested, although not explicitly stated, that the leadership of the two parties had close connections with the business community, so that they were anxious to pass a watered-down version of the bill. *Miniwn hoeirok*, 38th session, nos. 12-23.

82 They included the Korean Business Consultative Conference, established on January 10, 1961, with a membership of 57 leading businessmen (many of these were included in the original list of those charged with serious tax evasion); the Korean Chamber of Commerce; and the Korean Trade Association. *Kynghyang Shinmun*, March 4, 1961, p. 1.

foundation of the free enterprise system in South Korea through the "nationalization" of private property. Their statement argued:

> If what the Kim Il-song clique in the North fears most is the economic prosperity of the South, and if what it would like to see happen in the South is economic disaster, we can conclude that the present bill concerning the punishment for so-called illegal wealth that has just been passed by the House of Representatives will certainly ensure the success of its scheme. If the bill accomplishes its objectives, it would turn all businessmen into criminals, thereby bringing about economic catastrophe in South Korea....
>
> Therefore, it is difficult to counter the argument that what the present bill is aiming at is a socialist revolution in South Korea. Furthermore, it is no exaggeration to say that the bill would open ways for a "Communization" of the South.[83]

Subsequently, the business groups submitted a separate proposal to both chambers of the National Assembly, which called for construction of an industrial park through mobilization of the entrepreneurial ability and industrial capital of the business enterprises accused of having committed illegal business practices under the Rhee regime.[84]

As in the case of the other laws discussed previously in this chapter, the law concerning illicit wealth was modified in the House of Councillors, limiting the number of persons liable. The final version of the bill, which passed both houses of the National Assembly on April 15, specified that only those who had accumulated substantial amounts of wealth (50 million hwan in the case of tax evasion; 30 million hwan in other activities; 15 million hwan in the case of government or party officials) through illegal means, and who also *voluntarily* gave the Liberal Party 30 million hwan or more in political contributions for the March 1960 elections, would be punished under the law.[85]

This substantially reduced the number of businessmen who were to be affected by the law. However, the Chang government was never forgiven by the business community for its presumed role in the attempt to punish illegal business activities, and they remained suspicious of the Democratic administration's willingness to protect the basic interests of business.[86]

"Purifying" the Military

Let us now turn our attention to the relationship between the military and the Chang government. During the campaign, the Democratic Party made public that it planned to reduce the size of the Korean army by some

---

83 *Ibid.*

84 *Tong-a Ilbo*, March 3, 1961, p. 1.

85 *Han'guk hyngmyong chaep'ansa*, I, 651-659.

86 Interview with Kim Yng-sn. The business community's dissatisfaction with the Chang government was also expressed in connection with the devaluation of the Korean hwan by 100 percent. See "Round Table Talks over Devaluation of the Currency."

100,000 men on assuming power.[87] The same plan was confirmed by Chang Myon himself, after he was elected prime minister, in a speech he made in the National Assembly on August 27, 1960.[88] In accordance with the Democratic administration's "economic development first" policy, it attempted to limit defense spending to within 20 percent of tax revenue, as compared with 30 to 40 percent under the Liberal regime.[89] The reduction in the absolute number of troops was to be compensated for by modernization of equipment and an increase in firepower capacity. The Korean plan thus envisaged a drastic reduction in the defense expenditures provided by the Korean government while maintaining or increasing the level of support from the United States, which, in the period 1954-1960, had supplied about 40 percent of South Korea's military expenses.[90]

However, the reduction plan met with serious opposition not only from high-ranking South Korean army officers, but also from American military and diplomatic officials who feared that troop reduction might bring about much uneasiness and anxiety within the Korean armed forces, basing their opposition on the grounds that the government had not yet produced a plan for the employment of the men to be released.[91] Hence, notwithstanding the government position concerning reduction in the size of the army, both South Korean military leaders and United States officials made their opposition known to the public on numerous occasions.[92] A few weeks later, Gen. Williston B. Palmer, director of military assistance at the Pentagon, expressed his opposition to any sizable reduction in South Korea's 600,000-man army. General Palmer's statement reiterated the views expressed earlier by the Commander of the United States troops in Korea, Gen. Carter B. Magruder.[93]

Faced with opposition both within the Korean army and from United States officials, the Chang government was forced to revise its original plan. Thus on September 3, less than two weeks after assuming office, the Chang government accepted a 50,000-man reduction proposal made by a conference of top-level Korean military officers, including the chiefs of staff of the various services and the minister of defense.[94] This number was further reduced to 30,000 by the middle of October, and by early November the Chang government's minister of defense declared that, after all, South

---

87 For example, Kim Yng-sn, who was considered Chang Myon's top braintrust, expressed this view in his "Essential Elements of the Democratic Party Platform," p. 149.

88 *Miniwn hoeirok*, 36th session, Aug. 27, 1960, p. 4.

89 Kim Yng-sn, *op. cit.*, p. 150.

90 The South Korean side provided most of the expenses necessary for "troop maintenance," which occupied about three-quarters of the total defense budget during the same period. See Chn Pyng-wn, "Kukpangbi" [The Defense Budget: The Cost and the Result of Korean Security].

91 *New York Times*, August 28, 1960, p. 2.

92 For example, the newly appointed Army Chief of Staff declared that he was opposed in principle to the government's plan for troop reduction. According to him, it would seriously affect the combat capability of the South Korean Army. (*Miniwn hoeirok*, 37th session, no. 6, p. 23.)

93 See *New York Times*, September 21, 1960, p. 16.

94 *Kynghyang Shinmun*, September 3, 1960, p. 1.

Korea would continue to maintain a 600,000-man army, although there would be some personnel cuts on a limited scale.[95]

The Chang government's eventual withdrawal of its proposal for the reduction of military size dramatically demonstrated the formidable nature of the pressures from the military and the United States, and the Chang government's inability to withstand them. Like the Ho Chong government, the Chang government was preoccupied with the fear of provoking the top-ranking officers into rebellion against the new government, and took every precaution to avoid it. At the same time, American military leaders, because of their personal ties with top Korean military officers, constantly warned the Chang government against angering the generals. By catering to the pressures from the top military officers and the American military representatives, the Chang government exposed its inability not only to carry out its own reform program in the armed forces, but also to meet the demands of the junior and more radically-minded officers within the Korean army.

The objective of cleaning up the military (*chnggun*), which had become an extremely popular slogan both in and out of the armed forces following the April uprising, was not achieved by the resignation of half a dozen generals, considering the extensive nature of Syngman Rhee's influence in the military and the illegal and corrupt activities of military officers during the Rhee period. The demand for a more thorough purge in the army came, predictably, from the lower-ranking officers who exhibited more ideological, nationalistic, and self–assertive characteristics than their superiors. These junior officers were critical of the senior officers who, by taking advantage of the irresponsible nature of the Syngman Rhee regime, had become involved in a series of scandalous and corrupt practices during the past years.

The junior officers, for example, demanded that many of the senior officers be held responsible for election rigging within the armed forces under the Rhee regime. In the March 1960 election, the senior commanding officers had cooperated with the Liberal candidates, and they often used the official line of command to secure support for Syngman Rhee and Yi Ki-bung. In past elections they had instructed servicemen whom to vote for, used intelligence personnel to spy on the actual voting, and fabricated election results. It was also known that a few of the relatively high-ranking officers had been transferred to less desirable posts because of their association or acquaintance with anti-Rhee politicians.

As early as May 2, 1960, on behalf of some of the junior officers, Maj. Gen. Pak Chng-hi reportedly asked Army Chief of Staff Song Yo-ch'an's to withdraw from active service for his participation in election rigging.[96] On May 8, eight lieutenant colonels, all members of the military academy's class of 1949, were temporarily arrested when they circulated a petition for

---

95 *Tong-a Ilbo*, October 12. 1960, evening ed., p. 1; and *Kynghyang Shinmun*, November 3, 1960, p. 1.

96 *Han'guk kunsa hyngmyongi chnmo* [A Complete Picture of the Korean Military Revolution], p. 63.

an early and thorough purge within the armed forces. Gen. Song Yo-ch'an's subsequent resignation was not sufficient to satisfy the desires of the reform-minded junior officers, who wished to see most of the senior officers depart from the army. As we pointed out earlier, Ho Chong was reluctant to carry out a major personnel change within the armed forces because of his fear of hostile reaction from the high-ranking officers. Therefore, it was the Chang government which was expected to carry out this difficult task.

During the campaign period, the Democratic Party had promised effective cleansing of the armed forces through the elimination of incompetent and corrupt military officers. Upon the Chang government's assumption of power, both of its plans—to reduce the size of the armed forces and to carry out a clean-up operation within them—faced powerful opposition within the Korean armed forces and from the military and diplomatic representatives of the United States government. General Magruder was particularly concerned about the prospect of complete disorganization of the Korean armed forces resulting from a massive personnel change. He repeatedly warned the junior officers of the South Korean army to refrain from accusing their seniors of irregularities committed in the past, and counseled the Korean government to take cautious and gradual steps in pursuing reform within the armed forces.[97] The American opposition to the Chang government's plans for a military reform once resulted in an emotion-laden exchange between an American general and a Korean army chief of staff during the early days of the Chang government. When General Palmer remarked that he was gravely concerned over the fact that capable officers in the Korean armed forces were being forced to resign as a result of pressure from the lower officers, and that those who were still in office were unsettled and anxious because of such pressure, the South Korean army chief of staff publicly denounced the "American interference in South Korea's domestic affairs." Lt. Gen. Ch'oi Kyong-nok had been appointed to the top army post by the Chang government because of his support for the policy of eliminating officers with dishonest records, and because of the respect he received from many junior officers. Ch'oi was especially resentful of the fact that the American general had been approached by a few Korean military leaders during a recent trip to Korea. Ch'oi thus declared: "A few senseless top-ranking officers who worship the powerful have given a false impression to a foreign military leader, and such action cannot be tolerated. They must be expelled from the army."[98] The army chief of staff apparently had in mind Lt. Gen. Ch'oi Yong-hi, chairman of the joint chiefs of staff, who was one of the targets of the junior officers, and on whose invitation General Palmer had visited Korea.[99]

---

97 For example, see *New York Times*, May 27, 1960, p. 9; also October 15, 1960, p. 5.

98 *Kynghyang Shinmun*, September 23, 1960, evening ed., p. 1.

99 *Han'guk kunsa hyngmyongi chnmo*, p. 64.

Immediately after the above exchange took place, 16 junior officers (5 colonels and 11 lieutenant colonels) visited Gen. Ch'oi Yong-hi[100] to demand an explanation for the Palmer statement and ask for his resignation.[101] Subsequently, Gen. Ch'oi Yong-hi issued an emotional statement denouncing those who treat most of the Korean generals "as if they were criminals," and condemning the junior officers who attempted to "overpower" their seniors.[102]

The immediate result of the above incident was the resignation of Ch'oi Yong-hi from active service and the court-martialing of the 16 officers, who were eventually dismissed from the army.[103] In the farewell ceremony for Ch'oi, General Magruder again declared that South Korea faced a "threat of internal disruption," because of "dissension within its armed forces," and urged South Koreans to end disputes in the military forces to maintain "the confidence of her allies and of her own forces," strongly hinting that General Ch'oi was a victim of forced retirement.[104] There was, however, a far more significant consequence of this episode beyond the resignation of the chairman of the joint chiefs of staff. This was the subsequent abandonment by the Chang government of its plans to carry out a vigorous clean-up program in the armed forces.

Following the Palmer-Ch'oi exchange, the Chang government showed itself to be far more concerned with the problem of insubordination and rebelliousness within the army than with corruption among the top officers. Thus, in repeated statements, the successive ministers of defense declared that there would be no major purge within the armed forces and that the highest priority would be given to the prevention of internal dissension and the problem of insubordination.[105] The most explicit sign of the government's policy shift was shown in the appointment on December 5, of Lt. Gen. Chang To-yong to succeed Gen. Ch'oi Kyong-nok as the army chief of staff. General Chang was accused of having been rather opportunistic in his dealings with his superiors, both Koreans and Americans, and of having committed many unprincipled and irregular acts as the commander of the Second South Korean Army (support troops) prior to the April uprising.[106] General Chang had tendered his resignation to the interim government but it was returned by Prime Minister Chang Myon, following his election as chief executive.

When questioned in the National Assembly why General Ch'oi, who had not committed any conspicuous blunders, was prematurely ousted from the position of army chief of staff, Chang's minister of defense explained

---

100 Ch'oi had served as army chief of staff following the resignation of Lt. Gen. Song Yo-ch'an on May 27 and until the establishment of the Chang government.

101 *Han'guk kunsa hyngmyongi chnmo*, pp. 66-67.

102 *Kynghyang Shinmun*, October 5, 1960, p. 1.

103 *Ibid*, October 28, 1960, p. 3. These officers became the core members of those who engineered a military coup d'état on May 16, 1961.

104 *New York Times*, October 15, 1960, p. 5.

105 See press conferences by Minister Kwn Chung-don on January 19, and by Minister Hyn Sk-ho on January 31, 1961. *Kynghyang Shinmun*, January 20, 1961, p. 3, and February 1, p. 3.

106 *Miniwn hoeirok*, 38th session, no. 30, pp. 8-9.

that the change was inevitable "for the strengthening of the line of command in the military and the long-term development of the Korean armed forces," and that the appointment of Chang was strictly in accordance with the regular order of succession within the Army.[107] Although both the Chang government and the ousted General Ch'oi denied that the United States had anything to do with his resignation, major newspapers in Seoul speculated that Ch'oi's failure to serve out the normal two-year term as army chief of staff was attributable to his earlier clash with the United States generals and his outspoken advocacy of all-out reform within the Korean army.[108]

The choice of Chang To-yong as army chief of staff proved to be the undoing of the Chang government, partly because of his failure to command respect among the lower-ranking officers, and partly because of his less-than-absolute loyalty toward the Democratic regime. Upon assuming office, Chang ordered discontinuation of the investigation of the past illegal activities of 20 generals which had been initiated by Gen. Ch'oi Kyong-nok.[109] He also declared that there would be no significant personnel changes in the army, and that all future acts of insubordination and rebelliousness by junior officers would be severely punished.[110] It turned out, however, that his opportunism was responsible for the abandonment of his commitment to establish strict discipline within the army, as the plot of a military coup d'état among the junior officers unfolded.

Three months after his appointment as army chief of staff, when the military coup d'état finally materialized, Chang joined those who engineered the coup and attempted in vain to take over the military junta himself. Although he received reports concerning subversive activities among the younger officers prior to the coup, Chang failed to act to forestall the plot; instead he maintained what could be characterized as a wait-and-see attitude.[111]

In retrospect, it seems that the appointment of Chang To-yong, a man of questionable reliability, to the important position of army chief of staff was one in a series of crucial blunders made by the Chang government in its handling of the armed forces. Furthermore, there was extremely fast turnover in the post of minister of defense—three times during the brief life of the Democratic administration. None of the three who served as defense minister had any experience in defense matters, and they received little

---

107 *Ibid.*, p. 1.

108 See February 17-20 issues of *Tong-a-Ilbo* and *Kynghyang Shinmun*.

109 *Ch'amiwn hoeirok* [House of Councillors Record], 38th session, no. 22, pp. 1-4.

110 *Kynghyang Shinmun*, February 21, 1961, p. 3.

111 See for example, Chang Myon, *Memoirs*, pp. 86-90. Premier Chang later disclosed that he had received reports about the plot about a week before the actual coup, and that Chang To-yng, when asked, flatly denied any knowledge of such developments. On the morning of the coup, General Chang was again contacted by the prime minister about the reported invasion of Seoul by the rebel troops. However, the general failed to mobilize his troops to protect the Democratic government. According to a description of activities the night before the coup by the plotters of the coup themselves, General Chang had been informed about the coup before his conversation with Premier Chang on the morning of May 16th (*Han'guk kunsa hyngmyongi chnmo*, pp. 140-141.)

respect from either the senior officers or the junior officers of the armed forces.[112] The Chang government hoped in vain that the minister of defense could secure his constitutional authority over the generals and colonels as under normal and stable circumstances. Other crucial mistakes made by the Chang government in handling the military included underestimation of the *esprit de corps* and determination of the junior-level officers to carry out their scheme to overthrow the government, and excessive dependence and reliance on the United States in maintaining control over the army and preventing possible rebellion.[113]

Our discussion ... shows that the Chang government systematically alienated various political sectors during its reign without strengthening existing support or gaining new political allies. We have observed that the anti-Rhee, anti-police groups and the junior officers in the armed forces were disillusioned and disenchanted with the Chang administration because of its failure to take positive action against former supporters of the Rhee regime, whose punishment was supposedly mandated by the April uprising. At the same time, the former pro-Rhee elements, including the police, the national bureaucracy, and most local leaders, were turned against the Chang government because of the actions taken by the National Assembly against them, despite the Chang government's reluctance in the matter; they were generally understood as reflecting Chang's policies and the former Liberal officials who were affected by them blamed the Chang government for their punishment.[114] In a political culture in which people were accustomed to strong executive control—for good or bad—it was impossible for the Chang government to avoid the responsibility for this legislation, despite the limited nature of its own power and capability.

In order to meet the enormous demands made upon the Chang government from various sectors of the society during the post-uprising period, a great deal more power was required beyond that normally exerted by a government committed to liberal-democratic principles.

This was the basic dilemma of the Chang government, and Chang proved incapable of resolving the conflicting demands through the display of decisive leadership. Consequently, he presided over the breaking up of the "coalition" which made his ascendence to power possible—the coalition of the liberal students, the intellectual–press nexus, and the conservative party politicians. At the same time, he failed to secure the support of the police, the intelligence agencies, the bureaucracy, and the armed forces....

---

112 House Speaker Kwak Sang-hun complained immediately after the formation of the first Chang cabinet that Hyn Sk-ho, the minister of defense, had no experience in military affairs and that under the circumstances he doubted whether the cabinet could work smoothly. (*New York Times*, August 24, 1960, p. 3.)

113 Interview with Mr. Kim Yng-sn, November 5, 1968.

114 Ko Chng-hun, *Kut'o*, pp. 105-106.

Return to Transition: Dealing with the Chun Legacy Post-1987

*Sung-Joo Han, "The Experiment in Democracy"**

Korea, along with the Philippines, was at the forefront of a democratic revolution in 1987 that has since swept through Eastern Europe and Central and South America, toppling authoritarian governments and redefining the nature and balance of international relations. As the world began to focus on the 1988 Seoul Olympics scheduled for the following year, businesspeople, workers, and housewives joined student radicals in the streets to demand free elections and an end to the authoritarian government led by former general Chun Doo Hwan. After weeks of escalating tension and confrontation in the streets between fire-bomb-wielding protesters and helmet-clad riot police armed with tear gas, the government yielded to the people's demands.

Roh Tae Woo, a former classmate of General Chun's who had been anointed in April as new leader of the Democratic Justice Party (DJP) and successor to the Korean presidency, declared at the height of the confrontation on June 29, 1987, that the next Korean president would be chosen by the people through free elections under a new democratic constitution, thus launching the Korean experiment with democracy.

This pathbreaking venture truly was an experiment. The only previous democratic revolution, led by student protesters who toppled South Korea's first leader, Syngman Rhee, in April of 1960, lasted only a year. The popularly elected successors to Rhee, Prime Minister Chang Myon and President Yun Po Sun, were ousted in a military coup d'etat led by General Park Chung Hee. Park imposed a strict authoritarian regime and ruled until he was assassinated by the director of the Korean Central Intelligence Agency, Kim Chae Kyu, in 1979. After months of political turmoil, General Chun took power the following year and bloodily suppressed a popular uprising at the provincial city of Kwangju to consolidate his control....

Having ratified a new, democratic constitution in October 1987, the people went back to the polls in December for the first election of a president by direct popular vote in 26 years. Over 90 percent of the people participated in the presidential election, which was won by DJP candidate Roh Tae Woo with a plurality of less than 37 percent of the votes cast. Roh won because the vote for the two long-time opposition leaders, Kim Dae Jung of the Party for Peace and Democracy (PPD) and Kim Young Sam of the Reunification Democratic Party (RDP), was split almost evenly. Kim Jong Pil of the New Democratic Republican Party (NDRP), a fourth candidate whose party comprised former leaders in the Park Chung Hee government, did much better than expected, capturing 8 percent of the vote. A divided opposition together received a majority (55 percents) of the votes, yet the DJP, with only a plurality, retained its hold on power....

---

* Excerpted from Sung-Joo Han, "The Experiment in Democracy," in *Korea Briefing, 1990* (Westview Press, 1991), pp. 5-12. Copyright 1991 by The Asia Society.

But the voters handed the DJP an unexpected and serious setback in the April 1988 parliamentary elections. The party failed to secure a majority, winning only 125 seats in the 299-seat National Assembly. Kim Dae Jung's PPD won 71 seats and became the largest opposition party. With Kim Young Sam's RDP and Kim Jong Pil's NDRP securing 59 and 35 seats respectively, the three parties in opposition to the ruling DJP held a substantial majority of the parliamentary seats....

Although significant political changes from authoritarian rule to democratically elected government had occurred during this first year, the successful preparation and hosting of the Olympics became the first priority for politicians and their supporters from both the opposition and the ruling parties.... After the conclusion of the Olympics, the opposition parties went to work by invoking the Legislature's investigative powers. They made it the first order of business to investigate and expose the wrongdoings and scandals of the previous regime, the Fifth Republic of General Chun. From October through December of 1988, the National Assembly held hearings in which the Chun government was accused of wrongdoings including, most notably, the violent suppression of the 1980 Kwangju uprising.

Amid revelations of many serious irregularities by the Chun government, including the financial scandals of his close relatives and the existence under his regime of "democratic reeducation camps" for political prisoners, the nation became preoccupied with the "Chun issue"—that is, what to do with the former president. This put President Roh, a close friend of Chun and his primary political beneficiary, in a difficult situation. In addition, President Roh himself was politically vulnerable to rumors that he had been directly involved in the decision to use force in the Kwangju massacre, which had consolidated Chun's control in 1980. President Roh could neither fully protect Chun nor allow him to be prosecuted. In November, a deal was struck between the Chun and Roh camps of the ruling DJP under which the former apologized in a nationally televised address and left Seoul for a self-imposed exile to Paektamsa, a temple in mountainous northeastern South Korea near the demilitarized zone....

The Politics of Settling Old Scores

As a member of the previous government, President Roh was politically vulnerable if he did not make efforts to punish prior wrongdoings. To Roh's credit, Chun's two brothers were arrested and received prison sentences on charges of extortion and embezzlement. Also, one of Chun's closest aides, Change Se Dong, former chief of the President Security Service and late director of the Agency for National Security Planning, was put on trial and received a ten-month jail-term for abusing power during the Chun period. Nonetheless, many criticized the Roh government for making insufficient efforts to settle the issue of the "irregularities" that occurred during Chun's Fifth Republic.

After many months of debate, opposition demands on the Fifth Republic issue boiled down to the following two items: that former presidents Chun Doo Hwan and Choi Kyu Hah (the president during the interim between Park Chung Hee's assassination and Chun's takeover of power in 1980) testify in the National Assembly about Fifth Republic government scandals as well as the Kwangju incident, resign from all public positions, taking responsibility for the violent suppression of the Kwangju uprising in 1980. Considering the magnitude and complexity of the Fifth Republic irregularities, the opposition parties' demands in effect represented a major concession on their part, reflecting their desire to bury the corruption of the previous government in the past.

However, even with the scaled down demands of the opposition the Roh government could not resolve the issue. One reason was the lack of consensus, indeed the existence of a serious division, within the DJP itself. In particular, Chung Ho Yong and his supporters resisted taking the role of "fall guy" in the political game between Roh and the opposition leaders. Furthermore, Roh was not entirely comfortable with the idea of Chun's testifying in the National Assembly. Inasmuch as Roh was himself a close colleague of Chun when the latter took over power in 1980 and a member of the government inner circle during the Fifth Republic, he had reason to be concerned about the possibility that Chun's testimony, particularly if it was to be given over live telecast, could damage his own image and standing. Much groundwork needed to be done before the opposition demands could be met.

Having set the end of 1989 as the deadline for resolving the issue, Roh and his three political opponents—Kim Dae Jung, Kim Young Sam, and Kim Jong Pil—eventually agreed at the eleventh hour (on December 16th) on a framework for resolving the Fifth Republic issues. An 11-point joint statement by the four leaders contained two key items of agreement: that former president Chun would appear before the National Assembly to answer questions submitted in advance concerning allegations of corruption and abuse of power during his term in office, and that national assemblyman Chung Ho Yong would be forced to give up his legislative seat....

Chung was forced to resign by the force of events that had made him seem to be the only obstacle to the restoration of political stability. Former president Chun agreed to testify, but on the last day of the year so that there would be no drawn-out sessions. In his appearance before the legislature and on nationwide telecast, Chun denied allegations of wrongdoing, and his testimony was interrupted by protesting legislators. However, the ritual of Chun's appearance before the National Assembly made it official that divisive issues from the previous administration were settled and that parties and politicians could concentrate on the real business of politics: maneuvering for advantageous positions in future elections, including the next presidential election scheduled for 1992, and vying for political power.

7

GREECE

EDITOR'S INTRODUCTION

On April 21, 1967, a few weeks before Greek national elections, a group of mid-level military officers seized power from Prime Minister George Papandreou. The junta pledged to hold power temporarily, prevent Communist control of the government, eliminate corruption, and restore Greece to democracy. In reality, Colonel George Papadopoulos, the head of the new military regime, suspended the constitution and Parliament. Hundreds of senior military officers of uncertain loyalty were forcibly retired and several hundred new positions were created for the promotion of others. There was an extensive purge of government offices and the courts. Military "commissioners" were appointed to every university to monitor the curriculum as well as the political views and conduct of all faculty and students; dozens of professors were dismissed. Throughout society, hundreds of organizations were dissolved. Newspapers were censored and several were shut down. The junta banned nearly 800 books, including plays by Sophocles and Shakespeare. It ordered young people to cut their hair and attend the newly-purged church. The junta imprisoned thousands of people for their suspected political views or actions and used torture extensively against these detainees. As Harry Psomiades notes in one of the articles that follows, Colonel Papadopoulos justified this repression by suggesting that "if the patient is not strapped to the table, the surgeon cannot perform a successful operation."

As evidence mounted of the junta's actions, so did international pressure to curtail the abuses. By December 1969, facing expulsion from the Council of Europe as a consequence of its use of torture and related policies, Greece withdrew from the organization.

Papadopoulos began to re-civilianize the government and ease his policies. In 1973, he promised elections and the reinstitution of the constitution the following year. Following the brutal military dispersal of a student protest at the Athens Polytechnic in November 1973, however, when thousands were arrested and many were killed or injured, Papadopoulos reimposed martial law. Brigadier General Demetrios Ioannides, commander of the military police and an original junta member, soon replaced Papadopoulos.

The status and governance of the island of Cyprus, divided between ethnic Turkish and Greek communities, had long been a source of tension between Turkey and Greece. In the midst of increasing economic difficulties, the Ioannides regime sponsored a bloody coup on Cyprus in July 1974, prompting Turkey to land its troops on the island and bringing the two "mother" countries to the brink of war. Faced with likely defeat, the top military leaders ousted Ioannides and negotiations began with politicians for a return to civilian rule. As a result, on July 24, former prime minister Constantine Karamanlis returned from exile in France to become head of a Government of National Unity.

The Karamanlis government quickly implemented a program of "dejuntafication." By one account, he dismissed or replaced over 100,000 people in the military, in government down to the local level, and in state organizations. Some 3,000 files assembled by the military police (ESA) were destroyed. Within six months, criminal proceedings were initiated against more than one hundred former officials for participation in the 1967 coup, the Polytechnic incident, or torture of detainees. The torture trials of the military police gained the most public attention; by December 1976, the Greek government stated that more than 400 such trials had taken place around the country.

In December 1990, the Greek government announced its intention to pardon "for humanitarian reasons" three of the junta's leaders and ten related military officers, who had each served fifteen years of sentences ranging from twenty years to life in prison. A storm of public protest forced the government to drop the plannned release.

A THEORETICAL ANALYSIS

*P. Nikiforos Diamandouros, "Regime Change and the Prospects for Democracy in Greece: 1974-1983"**

[Comparison with other Transitions]

The transition from authoritarian to democratic rule in Portugal, Spain, and Greece in 1974 and 1975 coincided with, and added momentum to, the growing scholarly interest in the nature and internal structure of authoritarian regimes and, especially, in the dynamics of regime change. The obvious and significant differences in the transition patterns followed by each regime-in-crisis offer a rich ground for theoretical and empirical analyses....

The fundamental weakness of the colonels' regime was its failure to consolidate, to institutionalize, and to legitimate itself. A study of the circumstances under which their efforts fell far short of their goal suggests, in broad outline, the qualitative differences distinguishing the Greek from the Portuguese and Spanish experience with authoritarian rule. Instituted at a time when the legitimacy of democratic rule was clearly on the defensive, the Iberian regimes could, during their critical initial phases of consolidation and institutionalization, count the general climate of psychological insecurity and fear, brought about by the international economic crisis, the apparent collapse of the liberal democratic order, and widespread unemployment, to promote social order and discipline. Similarly, the strong wave of protectionism and isolationism fostered by these international conditions further facilitated the consolidation of the authoritarian regimes in Spain and Portugal by providing the protective vacuum within which they could grow relatively free of international pressures, whether economic or political. Finally, distance from the main theaters of war during 1940-45 made it much easier for Franco and Salazar to pursue, more or less unhindered throughout the 1940s and most of the 1950s, policies of political and economic isolation, and of low economic growth designed to avoid the social dislocations and political turbulence caused by the social and political mobilization of sectors excluded from full participation in the political system. Thus, under fairly unusual, if not unique, circumstances, an initially receptive international political climate, an international economic situation conducive to isolationism and protectionism, and a subsequent period of international indifference and neglect combined to provide both regimes with time to consolidate their hold over their respective societies, to institutionalize themselves, and to

* Excerpted from P. Nikiforos Diamandouros, "Regime Change and the Prospects for Democracy in Greece: 1974-1983," in Guillermo O'Donnell, Philippe C. Schmitter and Laurence Whitehead, eds., *Transitions From Authoritarian Rule: Southern Europe* (The Johns Hopkins University Press, 1986), pp. 138, 145-146, 154-164.

gain and maintain a considerable degree of legitimacy among strategic segments of the society.[12]

By contrast, the international climate facing the Greek regime in 1967 could hardly have been more different. In Europe, which was the region with the greatest political, economic, and cultural influence upon Greece, except for the United States, the disrepute into which authoritarian rule had fallen since the days of Fascist experiments; the widespread acceptance of the legitimacy of democratic rule and of pluralist politics; the multiplicity of international organizations committed, with varying degrees of intensity, to the preservation and defense of democratic politics; and the high degree of integration of the international (especially the European) system—certainly by comparison with the situation that prevailed in the 1930s—combined to create a situation marked, above all, by the absence of compartmentalization. There were no interstices where a newly established authoritarian regime could, with minimum external interference and pressure, slowly attempt to cope with the critical problems of regime consolidation, institutionalization, and legitimation.[13]...

[T]he collapse of the Greek authoritarian regime involves, at its very center, an inability to overcome the major difficulties created by the need to accomodate liberalization with social and political mobilization before institutionalization and legitimation had been secured. Given an international climate decidedly hostile to authoritarian rule, and the existence of significant social and political mobilization in the country, the Greek regime, unlike its Iberian counterparts, was unable to benefit from circumstances favorable to its legitimation and institutionalization without liberalization; instead, it was forced to pursue the latter in search of the former, and was unable to avoid conflict between regime and civil society which eventually brought about its demise.

Time, in the form of the longevity of the regime, is also of importance in understanding the different trajectories followed by the three authoritarian regimes as they approached "dissolution." In the Greek case, the existence of a significant degree of social and political mobilization, which had been achieved prior to the regime's coming to power, made institutionalization and legitimation more difficult, and forced the colonels to opt for liberalization before sufficient time had elapsed. In the case of Spain, which embarked upon a policy of rapid economic growth only in the late 1950s, social and political mobilization did not occur until almost thirty years after the installation of the regime; the regime had become institutionalized before it had to face the strains resulting from social and political mobilization. In Portugal, where social and political mobilization had, for all practical purposes, been contained almost to the end, the regime did not have to face a challenge to its strength arising from civil society....

The central role assigned to regime institutionalization ... raises a relevant question. If a chief characteristic distinguishing an authoritarian

---

12 [omitted]
13 [omitted]

regime from a mere dictatorship, as suggested by Linz and most observers, is precisely the presence or absence of institutionalization in the exercise of power, does the failure of the colonels to institutionalize deny the authoritarian nature of their regime? My answer would be that, by its very concern with constitutional formulations that sought to divide state affairs into "national" and "ordinary" so as to ensure the armed forces control over politics in Greece, the colonels' regime had all the characteristics of an incipient authoritarian regime seeking to render itself permanent. According to this analysis, opposition from within civil society and insufficient time prevented it from realizing its aims....

The transition phase of regime change involves a series of critical decisions and delicate political choices designed to cope with the problems relating to regime legitimation and enhancing the chances of its eventual consolidation. More specifically, these measures seek to: (1) ensure the active cooperation of social and political actors crucial to the maintenance of the momentum sustaining the regime-in-genesis; (2) secure the acquiescence of wavering but potentially hostile forces; (3) minimize the probability of regression, breakdown, and relapse to noncompetitive politics posed by calls for a return to the *status quo ante* or for immediate social and economic transformation; and (4) bring about the delegitimation of the predecessor regime among as many of the public as possible.[30]

How open-ended a transition is varies from case to case, because a variety of factors both domestic and international limit the degree of choice available to decision-makers. Thus, in Spain, the strength of the "bunker" and the issue of peripheral nationalisms posed definite and very real limits to the options entertained by the transition managers in that country. Conversely, the weakness of the extreme Right and the ease with which the disintegration of the authoritarian regime was brought about in Greece tended, in the short run, to create the impression of the absence of such limits, thereby facilitating the potential for a rapid radicalization of the situation.

In this context, the Greek case acquires particular interest because of an apparent paradox relating to the impact of the Cyprus crisis on the transition as a whole, but especially on its initial moments. On the one hand, the circumstances under which the crisis was brought about (a Greek-led coup against the government of Archbishop Makarios); its dismal handling; and the subsequent popular reaction to it, which revealed the enormity of the authoritarian regime's ineptitude and led to its immediate collapse and profound delegitimation, all created the possibility for radicalization and for a powerful "popular emergence," to use O'Donnell's and Schmitter's terminology. Indeed, the crowds that filled the streets of Athens and other major cities on 23 July, when the surrender of power to the civilians was being negotiated, pointed in that direction. What rendered radicalization even more likely was the additional fact that the badly

---

[30] For a fuller discussion of these issues, see P. Nikiforos Diamandouros, "Transition to, and Consolidation of, Democratic Politics in Greece, 1974-1983: A Tentative Assessment," in *New Mediterranean Democracies*, ed. Pridham, pp. 50-71.

managed general mobilization, spasmodically announced and carried out by the regime, had brought reserve officers and many civilians from the more radicalized urban centers to the countryside and gave the "popular emergence" a national dimension.[31]

At the same time, however, the very real threat of war which the crisis produced acted as a powerful counterweight, containing radicalizing forces, imposing self-restraint on mass actors, and producing a wave of national solidarity which greatly expanded the new civilian leadership's freedom of movement and effectively neutralized substantive opposition to its handling of the transition. To understand the dynamics of this process and to appreciate the extent of the change that it brought about, it is necessary to look at three contrasting transition strategies: (1) the outgoing regime's preference for a transfer of power; (2) the formulas for surrender of power envisaged by the civilian leadership in the "national council" convened by the moderate elements in the collapsing regime for that purpose; and (3) Karamanlis's own strategy for the democratization of the Greek political system.[32]

[The Transfer of Power]

The outgoing regime's search for a formula that would make possible a transfer of power to a segment of its supporters has to be understood in the context of the internal divisions brought about by the suppression of the Polytechnic uprising in November 1973, the end of Papadopoulos's liberalization experiment, the rise of the *hard-liners* to power under Ioannides and his supporters within the military police and the lower ranks of the army, and the latters' deep involvement in the events that led to the Cyprus crisis and to the brink of war with Turkey. These events, starting on 21 July, the day following the mobilization order, produced a major split within the regime and led to the decision of the Joint Chiefs of Staff to seek a "political solution" out of what was fast threatening to become a major domestic crisis as well. Having gained the support of the regime-appointed president of the Republic, Lieutenant-General Phaedon Ghizikis, the Joint Chiefs, invoking the threat of war, reasserted the hierarchical lines of command within the armed forces and effectively neutralized the power base sustaining Ioannides and the hard-liners. This move signaled the distancing of the armed forces from the disintegrating

---

31 For a discussion of the concept of the "popular emergence," see Guillermo O'Donnell and Philippe C. Schmitter, "Political Life after Authoritarian Rule: Tentative Conclusions about Uncertain Transitions," Volume 4 in this series.

32 Schmitter points out that a "transfer of power" involves handing power over to a segment of the authoritarian regime's moderate supporters; by contrast, in a "surrender of power" the outgoing regime's moderate opponents are the beneficiaries of change. See Philippe C. Schmitter, "Speculations about the Prospective Demise of Authoritarian Regimes and Its Possible Consequences" (Paper presented at the workshop on "Prospects for Democracy: Transitions from Authoritarian Rule," at the Woodrow Wilson Center, September 1980, pp. 9-15, subsequently revised and reprinted as Working Paper of the European University Institute, Florence, Italy, 1984) and Figure 1.

regime and made easier the search for a transfer-of-power formula under their initial aegis.[33]

The Joint Chiefs' next move was to convene a meeting with selected civilian leaders to explore the specific format under which the transfer of power could be effected. Documentary evidence concerning the nature of the transfer of power envisaged by the military is scant. What has come to light, however, suggests that the Joint Chiefs' distinct preference lay in a transfer of power that would ensure the liberalization of the existing political system, leaving, at least initially, significant power in their and their moderate civilian supporters' hands, and containing the forces clamoring for more structural change.... It is within this context and the limited political democratization logic that underpins it that one has to understand the final decision to ... opt ... for Constantine Karamanlis, the charismatic founder and former leader of the National Radical Union (ERE), as the best person to undertake such a difficult task.[35]

Leader of the anti-Communist Right during most of the 1950s, a powerful personality who had dominated Greek politics into the early 1960s and had gone into self-imposed exile in Paris following a clash with the monarchy and defeat in the 1963 elections which first brought the Center Union to power, Karamanlis had remained untarnished by direct involvement in the events that led to the demise of parliamentary politics in 1967. Acceptable to the military on account of his past anti-Communist record, he could also command the support and confidence of the nonroyalist Right and of large segments of the traditional Center, and he was tolerated as the lesser of two evils by monarchists opposed to the military regime. Therefore, he appeared to possess the ideal credentials for the delicate mission of not merely managing the transition crisis but also of presiding over an effort to construct an improved version of the postwar political system capable of coping with the uncertainties generated by political mobilization and radicalization among major segments of the electorate in the previous decade. Simply put, once the dynamic of the situation had made it clear that a mere transfer of power was no longer a viable option, Karamanlis emerged as [the best] candidate ... for carrying out a strategy of surrender of power that envisaged more a restoration of the previous system than an instauration of political democracy in Greece. The Karamanlis solution implied an unspoken decision to deemphasize the role of existing political parties in the transition process and suggested instead a preference for leadership that stood "above parties" and appealed to the "nation" as a whole. This perspective, which Karamanlis shared with those who recalled him and which was in conformity with his charismatic image, was best reflected in the fact that he was initially invested with

---

33 For a discussion of these events in English, see Diamandouros, "Transition and Consolidation," pp. 53-54, as well as Harry J. Psomiades, "Greece: From the Colonels' Rule to Democracy," in *From Dictatorship to Democracy*, ed. John H. Herz, pp. 250-55. In Greek, see Psychares, [The Change], 5-130, and Markezinis, [Reminiscences], pp. 506-540.

35 On the decision to substitute Karamanlis for Kanellopoulos and Mavros, see Psychares, [The Change], pp. 140-43, 147-49, 156-60, 189-91, and 210-12.

sole political power and only subsequently appointed the first members of his government.[36]

What, above all, characterized Karamanlis's strategy during the 116 days between 24 July, when he was sworn into office, and 17 November, when his electoral triumph provided him with popularly derived legitimacy and independence vis-á-vis earlier partners and supporters at the elite level, was his studied attempt to minimize commitments to collective and individual actors, to personalize crisis management, to maximize his freedom of movement, and to create the preconditions for a genuine political democracy in Greece. The last goal, which went far beyond the assumptions and expectations of those who had recalled him, and which envisaged more a new democratic regime than a restoration of some improved version of the postwar political system, constituted Karamanlis's central long-term aim which, though unspoken at the outset, permeated his entire transition strategy and surfaced slowly over time.

[The Legacy Problem: From Gradualism to Stern Punishment]

In pursuit of these goals, Karamanlis adopted a deliberately gradualist course of action in which elements of continuity and change as well as substantive and symbolic acts were judiciously balanced in an effort to attain three distinct short-term objectives: (1) the maintenance, for as long as possible, of the unity of the founding coalition and of the momentum for national solidarity generated by humiliation over Cyprus and exhilaration at the fall of the military; (2) gradual distancing from, and eventual isolation of, the more recalcitrant and unreconstructed elements of the Right, and (3) the need to reassure, and even to placate, that significant part of public opinion and those emerging political forces which clearly favored a radical democratization of the postwar political system and a major change in the rules of the game.[37]...

Karamanlis's gradualism was ... evident in the ... incremental approach adopted in the announcement of changes, and, especially, in the deliberately slow pace at which the government proceeded in dealing with the most sensitive and explosive popular demands: purges of the military, the state bureaucracy, the universities, the security forces, and, above all, the prosecution of the protagonists in the 1967 coup, in the suppression of the Polytechnic uprising, and in the torturing of prisoners during the seven-year authoritarian regime. Here, Karamanlis's attitude seems to have been largely determined by his justified fear of a military reaction in the event

---

36 Karamanlis's handling of the transition and his subsequent behavior, initially as leader of the Right which he tried to modernize, and eventually as head of state, have won him quasi-universal approbation, but his earlier role as the standard bearer of the anti-Communist forces in the 1950s and early 1960s remains much more controversial. To this day, there exists no satisfactory treatment of the life of this complex man, and of the slow evolution of his style of leadership, if not his thought, toward increasingly more liberal and democratic positions. Despite their hagiographical qualities, the best works to date are C. M. Woodhouse, *Karamanlis: Restorer of Greek Democracy* (Oxford: Clarendon Press, 1982), and Maurice Genevoix, *La Grèce de Caramanlis ou la démocratie difficile* (Paris: Plon, 1972).

37 The best source on the 1974 elections is Howard R. Penniman, ed., *Greece at the Polls*.

of a thorough purge, or even of one that was perceived as "excessive" among military and civilian quarters close to the fallen regime.[39]

The gradualist component of Karamanlis's transition strategy included three additional implicit assumptions: first, that these issues should not be directly addressed until after the election, when the legitimacy of the new civilian government would place it in a much better position to face such a delicate enterprise; second, that, before dealing with these intractable issues, measures had to be taken to ensure civilian control of a number of agencies and institutions (police, security services, intelligence agencies, chiefs of staff) whose loyalty would be a crucial precondition for the uneventful handling of these emotion-laden issues; and third, that, in the application phase of the strategy, a line had to be drawn between retiring, and therefore isolating, those officers implicated with the former regime, and prosecuting them for various offenses. This line he carefully observed until after the elections of 17 November.

It is characteristic that the only criminal prosecution proceedings initiated against protagonists of the colonels' regime prior to the elections were the result of a private suit, and did not involve government initiative. Equally significant, the case was not tried until almost nine months later, long after an overwhelming electoral victory had provided Karamanlis with unquestioned legitimacy, with independence vis-á-vis other actors in the transition, and with a crushing parliamentary majority—in excess of two-thirds of all seats. It was only after a foiled coup, in February 1975, that he was given the long-awaited opportunity to move decisively against adherents and sympathizers of the previous regime, and to eliminate a source of major potential resistance to further change without risking serious erosion of his political support.[40]

At this point in the transition, gradualism gave way to a policy of swift, decisive, credible but contained retribution. It was designed to enhance the legitimacy of the new regime, further to delegitimate its discredited predecessor, and, at the same time, to appear equitable, to avoid the potentially negative repercussions from too protracted a public focus on past traumas, and to prevent excesses that might undermine the climate of national solidarity so crucial to the regime's long-term consolidation chances. Thus, in less than six months, the protagonists of the 1967 coup, the leaders of the foiled February 1975 coup, together with the major figures in the suppression of the Polytechnic uprising, and in the torturing of prisoners during the seven-year regime were brought to trial, and received sentences ranging from life imprisonment for the major figures to lesser sentences for others. In line with the government's determination to avoid action of a potentially destabilizing and divisive nature, the death sentence handed down by the courts against the three leaders of the

---

39 On the threat of a military reaction and on Karamanlis's handling of the situation, see the interesting comments by Psomiades, "Greece: From the Colonels' Rule to Democracy," in *From Dictatorship to Democracy*, ed. Herz, pp. 255-58.

40 On the failed coup of February 1975, see Clogg, *A Short History of Modern Greece*, pp. 207-9.

previous regime, George Papadopoulos, Stylianos Pattakos, and Nikolaos Makarezos, was immediately commuted to life imprisonment. The government's announcement of clemency significantly stated that "in the fair state, the work of justice is completed by the final procedure ... which permits the reduction of sentences. In this final phase, a high sense of political responsibility must prevail."[41]

By the end of 1975, therefore, and despite opposition accusations that it had exercised excessive restraint, and that the commutation of the death sentences "smacked of a deal," the new Greek democratic regime had effectively dealt with what John Herz has recently referred to as the "legacy problem" crucial to the definition of a successor democratic regime's self-image, and for the demystification of its predecessor.[42]

[A Strategy for Democratization]

If the conclusion of the various trials marks the natural end of the new government's policy for dealing with the "legacy problem," a series of actions taken early in the transition attests to the significance attached to this issue: the immediate banning of the authoritarian regime's symbols, including the universally loathed "phoenix"; the prohibition of all references to the "revolution" as a term to describe the 1967 coup in school textbooks; the appointment of men with known antijunta and even leftist sentiments in key positions in the sensitive Ministry of Education; the early dismissal of junta appointees from the university system; and numerous official and unofficial utterances concerning the freedom of the press. All these constituted symbolic acts designed to serve the dual goal of demonstrating the new regime's unequivocal condemnation of its predecessor, and, equally important, to signal its determination to proceed with the democratization of the political system, and to work for the consolidation of democratic politics in Greece.

If a judicious mixture of continuity and change and deliberate gradualism in dealing with potentially divisive issues were conspicuous elements in Karamanlis's transition strategy, a less obvious but equally important component focused on the need to maximize the benefits that the circumstances of the surrender of power gave to the Center and Center-Right forces, and consequently to contain the opposition and neutralize the Left. In pursuit of these objectives, Karamanlis exploited the *carte blanche* context of his accession to power, ran an issueless campaign, took advantage of the colorless opposition provided by George Mavros's Center Union, and, above all, opted for elections sooner rather than later. He knew that an early

---

41 See *Facts on File*, 30 August 1975, p. 637 for the quotation. The decision not to proceed with the execution of the three leaders of the 1967 coup was motivated as much by a desire to prevent a possible military reaction as by the determination to avoid the type of profound and traumatic polarization brought about by the execution of six conservative political leaders in the wake of the Greek defeat in Asia Minor in 1922. The so-called execution of the Six remained a haunting and lasting reference point in the interwar and postwar liberal-conservative cleavage in Greek politics.

42 On the legacy problem, see John H. Herz, "Introduction: Method and Boundaries," and "Conclusion," in *From Dictatorship to Democracy*, ed. Herz, pp. 3-11 and 275-91 respectively.

election would allow his potentially more dangerous opposition, the recently surfaced Communist party and the newly formed PASOK, minimal time to mobilize or to articulate an effective electoral platform. It would also make it easier to give the whole event a plebiscitary flavor in which the slogan "Karamanlis or the tanks" would become the dominant theme, ensuring his success, and enabling him to proceed with the implementation of his consolidation strategy.

As noted earlier, this strategy, which went beyond the expectations of the predominantly conservative forces that had engineered his recall, sought to ensure consolidation through a genuine democratization of the political system designed to make it responsive to, and congruent with, the deep structural changes that had occurred in Greece over the previous quarter century. In the course of the transition, Karamanlis carefully sought to pave the way for such an eventuality by pursuing a policy of national reconciliation which put an end to the Civil War divisions perpetuated by the postwar exclusivist state, and by bringing about a radical redistribution of power. The first goal he achieved through the thorough dismantling of the postwar legal and institutional nexus which effectively reserved the benefits of the political system exclusively for the victors in the Civil War, and through a series of actions designed to underscore that a new system open to all Greeks was in the process of being constructed. The second, more troublesome, task entailed the subordination of the military to civilian authority, and the settlement of the nature of the head of state. The latter was decisively settled on 8 December 1974 with an impressive 69.2 percent of the electorate favoring a republic in what by all accounts was the fairest and freest plebiscite in modern Greek history.[43]

The elimination of the monarchy fulfilled a central precondition for genuine democratization. Another central precondition, the subordination of the military to civilian authority, required putting an end to the institutional autonomy that the military had acquired over the previous forty-five years and especially since the Civil War. Though this was more of a long-term proposition, there can be little doubt that the dismal failure of the military's seven-year experiment with direct government, and the humiliation it suffered in the context of the Cyprus crisis, had had an immensely sobering effect and had served greatly to redress the balance between the military and civilian elements in the political system in favor of the latter. Karamanlis's post-1974 policies certainly reinforced that trend and, especially after the elimination of recalcitrant elements in the course of 1975, strengthened the likelihood that the Greek military would henceforth confine its activities to the barracks.[44]

---

[43] See Pararas, [Return to Democracy], pp. 58-59 for the various measures designed to put an end to restrictive legislation and to provide for an open political system.

[44] On the role of the monarchy in Greek politics, see Jean Meynaud, *Les forces politiques*, and his *Rapport sur l'abolition de la démocratie en Grèce. 15 juillet-21 avril 1967* (Montreal: Etudes de Science Politique, 1967). See also Clogg, *A Short History of Modern Greece*, pp. 166-99, and Nicos Mouzelis, "Capitalism and Dictatorship in Post-War Greece," in *Modern Greece*, pp. 115-33. On the Greek military, in general, see the interpretative essays by Mouzelis, "Class Structure and the Role of the Military in Greece: An Interpretation," in *Modern Greece*, pp. 105-14, and Thanos

Thus, less than half a year after the dramatic events that led to the collapse of the authoritarian regime and to the recall of Karamanlis, the basic political and institutional arrangements establishing the first genuine political democracy in Greece had been completed. In the ensuing years, the new political system would evolve smoothly, coping successfully with the reentry of the Left in the political arena; the meteoric rise in the strength of new Left-of-Center forces (PASOK) under Andreas Papandreou; Karamanlis's rise to the presidency of the Republic in 1980 and the orderly election of his successor by the New Democracy party he had founded in 1974; and, as of 1981, with its first and impeccably conducted alternation in governmental incumbency which brought PASOK to power and signaled the end of forty-five years of almost uninterrupted rule by the Greek Right. The smooth operation of the system [since the transition] bears testimony to its legitimacy and institutionalization and serves as a reminder that, whatever its weaknesses, it is by far the most open, inclusive, and democratic regime in modern Greek history.

Looked at in comparative perspective, the Greek case amply bears out O'Donnell's and Schmitter's generalizations regarding successful transitions to political democracy: the dominance of Right-of-Center forces in the transition; the judicious handling of the military, despite the fact that its own mismanagement of the Cyprus crisis had drastically reduced its ability to react effectively; the preference for an inclusive system in which all political forces could legally participate, all tend to confirm the general observations that emerge from the study of transitions.... What is striking about the Greek transition, however, is that it occurred under initial conditions of a grave external crisis and was accomplished smoothly in a short period of time. As I have argued above, the conditions of external crisis paradoxically facilitated the transition to the extent that they tended to act as a powerful restraint against popular mobilization and radicalization, while, at the same time, they enormously enhanced Karamanlis's freedom of movement, providing him with a golden opportunity to determine the pace, timing, and scope of various measures deemed necessary to lay the foundations for a new political system which vastly transcended the expectations of those who recalled him and radically democratized political life in Greece. There can be little doubt that, in the absence of these conditions, Karamanlis's ability to impose his own agenda on the transition would have been quickly and strenuously opposed from a number of quarters: at the very least, the whole process would have been more protracted and the end-result quite different.

Veremis, "Security Considerations and Civil-Military Relations in Post-War Greece," in *Greece in the 1980s*, ed. Richard Clogg (New York: Macmillan, 1983), pp. 173-83, as well as the fine study by Nikolaos A. Stavrou, *Allied Politics and Military Interventions: The Political Role of the Greek Military* (Athens: Papazisis, 1977).

A HISTORICAL ACCOUNT

Harry J. Psomiades, "Greece: From the Colonels' Rule to Democracy"[*]

I. The Regime of the Colonels

On July 23, 1974, the seven-year military dictatorship of George Papadopoulos (1967-1973) and Demetrios Ioannides (1973-1974) came to an abrupt end.[1] When the end came, the short-lived regime of the colonels

---

[*] Excerpted from Harry J. Psomiades, "Greece: From the Colonels' Rule to Democracy," in John H. Herz, ed., *From Dictatorship to Democracy: Coping with the Legacies of Authoritarianism and Totalitarianism*, Copyright © 1982 by John Herz (Greenwood Press, 1982), pp. 251-265, an imprint of Greenwood Publishing Group, Inc. Westport, CT. Reprinted with permission.

[1] The colonels' regime seized power on April 21, 1967, less than a month before scheduled elections and after two years of political turmoil originating in part from a confrontation between young King Constantine and his prime minister, the elder Greek statesman, George Papandreou. The confrontation was over the question of royal prerogatives in military affairs. Following the 1965 resignation of Papandreou, who commanded the loyalty of the largest single bloc in parliament and broad public support, a series of caretaker governments supportive of the king were installed. Their bare majorities consisted of forty-five breakaway or *apostate* members of Papandreou's Center Union party and the conservative opposition parties in parliament. At issue were the removal of the monarchy from politics, civilian political control over the military, and the alleged involvement of Papandreou's son, Andreas, in the *Aspida* (shield) affair, a purported left-wing conspiracy within the army. It was not until December 1966 that Papandreou and Panayiotis Kanellopoulos, the leader of the conservative National Radical Union (ERE), agreed to bring an end to the crisis and hold elections on May 28, 1967. Although the colonels justified the coup on the grounds that it was necessary to save the nation from a government of villains and from an imminent Communist takeover, their primary goal was to prevent the May elections and the possible return to power of George Papandreou. The charge of a likely Communist takeover was completely unfounded.

The coup of middle rank army officers was virtually bloodless and caught the Greek political world and the senior officers of the armed forces completely off balance. The belief that the king and the generals, along with certain political elements, were themselves preparing a coup tended to blunt the significance of the colonels' surprise coup and indeed facilitated it. In the remaining months of 1967, many believed that the junta would moderate its position and would soon institute "a new and purer democracy." The failure of the king's countercoup in December 1967 ended that hope, although the junta continued to speak of its role as a "parenthesis" in Greek history. Colonel George Papadopoulos, the junta strong man, became prime minister and gradually concentrated power in his own person, promising to restore democracy when the Greek people acquired sufficient maturity. The regime became increasingly repressive. Seeking to justify its brutality, Papadopoulos explained that "if the patient is not strapped to the table, the surgeon cannot perform a successful operation." Parliament was abolished, the constitution was suspended, the press was censored, political opponents were arrested, some were tortured, and abuse was heaped on politicians representing all shades of the political spectrum. The military police assumed the major role in maintaining public order. Wholesale purges were carried out in the armed forces (of mostly royalist officers) and in various ministries and state institutions. Consequently, relations with most West European states reflected increasing strain, and Greece withdrew from the Council of Europe rather than face expulsion for torturing prisoners. The EC was so repelled by the junta's actions that it suspended Greece's associate membership. However, EC member states continued to trade with and invest in the colonels' Greece and, along with the United States, refused to expel Greece from NATO.

By 1973 Papadopoulos appeared to have consolidated his power at the expense of his fellow conspirators; civilian technocrats were brought in to replace the military in a number of high government posts. He began to relax the stern rule of his government and promised free elections in 1974, along with the implementation of the regime's 1968 constitution that had replaced that of 1952. Although the regime was clearly unpopular and the bulk of the Greek

had hardly moved from a mere dictatorship to authoritarianism. It had failed to consolidate power, to acquire legitimacy, and to institutionalize the decision-making processes. This was partly the reflection of insufficient time, as the colonels experimented with direction and purpose, and the confutative stance of Greek civil society. Domestic resistance was reinforced by international (West European) antagonism to the subversion of democracies in Europe.

The regime's lack of a coherent and meaningful ideology and the contradictions of the policies that it had chosen confounded its quest for power and legitimacy and ultimately led to its downfall. It sought to impose and perpetuate the ideology of the anticommunist state, an ideology that had long been anachronous in the Greek context, but in arrogating to themselves the right to rule, the colonels estranged themselves from the crown, royalist military officers, and the conservative

---

political world refused to deal with it, relatively little in the way of active organized opposition developed in Greece.

The most serious threat to the regime's stability was an aborted naval mutiny at the end of May 1973 and the defection of the destroyer *Velos* to Italy. Although the mutineers vehemently denied and indeed resented Papadopoulos' charge that King Constantine had conspired in the plot from his exile in Rome, the regime saw fit to blame Constantine for the mutiny and declared him deposed. In June Papadopoulos issued a decree abolishing the monarchy and calling for the establishment of a republic. Accordingly, the 1968 constitution was revised. Until then Greece had remained a monarchy under the military regime, although Constantine steadfastly refused to lend legitimacy to Papadopoulos and his cohorts. In July 1973 Papadopoulos, in a controlled referendum, put himself forward as the sole candidate for a seven-year term as president of the republic and in the following month assumed that office.

Papadopoulos' republic was destined to be short-lived. As he began to moderate his policies and attract a civilian following, tension mounted in the country. In early November crowds attending a memorial service marking the anniversary of George Papandreou's death were fired on by the police. A few days later when students occupied the Athens Polytechnic to protest the rescinding of draft deferments, workers joined in the student general strike, and soon appeals were made to overthrow the dictatorship. Hesitant to use force, Papadopoulos was overruled by his hard-line associates in the military who feared widespread public sympathy for the students unless their action was ended immediately. Troops and tanks were used to evict the students from the Polytechnic in a show of extreme brutality. Scores of students and others were killed, hundreds were wounded, and almost a thousand were arrested. Martial law was reimposed. Although shaken by these events, Papadopoulos reaffirmed his intention of proceeding with national elections.

At this point Papadopoulos was removed from power by the more extreme ideologues led by Brigadier General Demetrios Ioannides, commander of the hated military police (ESA) and an original junta member. For some time they had resented their gradual loss of power under Papadopoulos. They pledged to return the country to the "ideals of the 1967 revolution" and to save it from an "electoral travesty." The constitution was modified, and Lieutenant General Phaedon Ghizikis was installed as a figurehead president along with a civilian government. However, it was clear to all that Ioannides and his military supporters would remain the real power behind the government. The new regime, unable to govern effectively, employed even harsher measures against dissidents. Also, unable to cope with soaring inflation caused in part by the 1973 oil crisis, it sought to deflect a massive discontent at home by instigating a foreign adventure in Cyprus.

Some of the better works on the 1967-1974 dictatorship include P, Clogg and G. Yannopoulos, eds., *Greece Under Military Rule* (New York, 1972); George Katephoris, *I nomothesia tou varvaron* [*The Legislation of the Barbarians*] (Athens, 1975); Chariton Korizis, *To aftarchiko kathestos*, 1967-1974 [*The Authoritarian Regime*, 1967-1974] (Athens, 1975); S. Grigoriades, *Istoria tis diktatorias* [*The History of the Dictatorship*], vols. 2 and 3 (Athens, 1975); Spyros Markezinis, *Anamnesias*, 1972-1974 [*Reminiscences*, 1972-1974] (Athens, 1979); Rodis Roufos, *Inside the Colonels' Greece* (New York, 1972); Constantine Tsoucalas, *The Greek Tragedy* (Harmondsworth, 1969); and Richard Clogg, *A Short History of Greece* (Cambridge, England, 1979), chapter 7.

political leadership of the country. They should have been the regime's natural allies because they had all benefited from such an ideology in the past. But the colonels feared that cooption of these groups would have led to the diminution of the personal power of the military rulers of the regime.

In the early days the regime spoke of itself as a temporary government and by 1968 proclaimed itself to be the necessary expression of a transitional phase of the country's development toward parliamentary democracy. Its commitment to the restoration of democracy, central to its strategy of attaining legitimacy at home and abroad, precluded the full development of a bureaucratic-authoritarian model of government. It brought Papadopoulos into conflict with the expectations of the civil society as well as those of his hard-line colleagues and supporters. For the former, the pace toward democracy was too slow and for the latter too fast. In the end, Papadopoulos found himself in a no-win situation. Closely related to this dilemma was the contradiction inherent in the regime's commitment to rapid economic and social mobilization within severe political and institutional constraints. Indeed, in the past fifty years but particularly since 1952, there has occurred the significant transformation of Greece from a traditional rural to a modernizing urban society. Despite the repressive features of eleven years of uninterrupted right-wing rule (1952-1963), in this period of political stability and effective political leadership consistently high, if distorted, rates of economic growth were achieved, which hastened the middle-class transformation of Greek society. It should not come as a surprise that prior to the 1967 coup, the essence of political tension in Greece centered on the demands of the newly mobilized classes for greater political participation. There was considerable questioning of the legitimacy of the system of political representation. It was in this period of political readjustment that the colonels struck.

The regime attempted to halt and reverse the process of democratization. But at the same time it was committed to rapid economic growth and modernization. These dual and often contradictory goals provided concrete hurdles for the colonels to surmount in stabilizing their regime. Although, until the world energy crisis of 1973, economic growth contributed to the passivity of much of the population toward the dictatorship, it reinforced the increasing level of social frustration that made political discontent inevitable. Limited democracy was unacceptable, and the regime that advocated it found few takers....

II. The Arrival of the Savior

The immediate cause of the regime's loss of nerve and self-liquidation was its ill-conceived military adventure in Cyprus. This mindless act furnished Turkey with an excuse to seize much of the island and created an intolerable situation for the Greek dictatorship. Confronted with the policy alternatives of either accepting a humiliating retreat from Cyprus or ordering a general mobilization and risking a full-scale war with

Turkey, Ioannides chose the second option. He assigned the air force and the navy the task of attacking Turkish positions on Cyprus and ordered the army to prepare for operations on the Thracian frontier with Turkey. Obedience to these decisions would have meant military disaster, with far-reaching political consequences. The senior military officers of the three services decided that a return to civilian rule was opportune and forced the ouster of Ioannides. Faced with a mutiny of his top military commanders, Ioannides reluctantly acceded to their demands that he not oppose their decision to call back the former civilian leaders.[2] The irony of the finale in Athens was that the same military leaders who had supinely acquiesced in the establishment of the junta and then collaborated with it returned the government to the civilians during a military crisis created by the regime.[3] Fearful of military disaster and mindful of the authoritarian regime's failure to institutionalize and legitimate itself in Greek society, the senior officers forswore continued political leadership in order to preserve the military as an institution congenial to them.[4]

The generals' revolt against Ioannides and the decision to return the country to civilian hands took place on Monday, July 22, 1974. Following a weekend of heavy fighting on Cyprus and the landing of Turkish tanks on the island, a precarious cease-fire was arranged; the president of the republic—Phaedon Ghizikis, a former lieutenant general—called for an emergency meeting of Greece's most notable civilian politicians and the senior service chiefs.[5] On July 23, between 1:00 and 2:00 P.M., the politicians arrived at the spacious office of President Ghizikis in the parliament building at Constitution Square and began to discuss with the military

---

2 On the collapse of the junta, see Nikos Kakaounakis, *2650 meronyhta synonmosias* [*The Conspiracy of 2650 Days and Nights*], vol. 2 (Athens, 1976); Solonos Grigoriades, *Istoria tis diktatorias*, and P. Nikiforos Diamandouros, "The 1974 Transition from Authoritarian to Democratic Rule in Greece: Background and Interpretation from a Southern European Perspective," to be published in *Transition from Authoritarianism to Democracy in Southern Europe and Latin America*, under the auspices of the Centro de Investigaciones Sociologicas, Madrid.

3 Laurence Stern, *The Wrong Horse: The Politics of Intervention and the Failure of American Diplomacy* (New York, 1977), p. 129.

4 Keith Legg of the University of Florida reminds us that "at no time was a regime established by military forces in Greece, except by force from within the military institution itself. The military has traditionally chosen the moment of its own withdrawal, or more accurately, the moment when the officers holding the reins of government would be abandoned. Between 1909 and 1935, there were eight important military upheavals in Greece (1909, 1916, 1922, 1923, 1925, 1926, 1933, and 1935) and countless incidents of pressure exerted on the government by individual officers or military cliques." "Before, during and after the revolts rebellious officers used selected politicians in a symbiotic fashion or employed the military to exert pressure on recalcitrant politicians." (S. Victor Papacosma, "Pseudo-History in Recent Writing on the Greek Military," *Slavic Review*, vol. 34, no. 1, March 1975, p. 127.) In previous dictatorships, the responsibilities of political leadership were shared between the army and the politicians. The regime of April 21, 1967, is the sole example in modern Greek history in which the military assumed and maintained political leadership on its own. This explains in part the inability of the regime to legitimate itself in Greek society. For the role of the military, see also George Dertilis, *Koinonikos metaschimatismos kai stratiotiki epemvasi*, 1880-1909 [*Social Transformation and Military Intervention, 1880-1909*] (Athens, 1977); Thanos Veremis, *I epemvasis tou stratou stin Helleniki politikis*, 1916-1936 [*The Intervention of the Army in Greek Politics, 1916-1936*] (Athens, 1977); and George A. Kourvetaris, "The Role of the Military in Greek Politics," *International Review of History and Political Science*, vol. 8, no. 3 (August 1971), pp. 91-111.

5 L. Stern, *The Wrong Horse*, p. 123. S. Grigoriades, *Istoria tis dictatorias*, vol. 3, p. 259.

leaders the transition to civilian rule. Gathered around the table were President Ghizikis, who chaired the meeting; the chief of the armed forces, General Grigorios Bonanos; the chief of the army, Lieutenant General Andreas Galatsanos; the chief of the navy, Vice Admiral Petros Arapakis; and the chief of the air force, Air Marshal Alexander Papanikolaou. The civilians, most of whom had served some time in the junta's jails, were four former premiers: Panayiotis Kanellopoulos, leader of the National Radical Union (ERE) and the last legal prime minister of Greece; George Athanasiades-Novas; Spyros Markezinis; and Stephanos Stephanopoulos. Also present were Center Union party leader George Mavros, former Foreign Minister Evangelos Averoff-Tositas, former Defense Minister Petros Garoufalias, and Xenophon Zolatas, former governor of the Bank of Greece. With the exception of Mavros, the civilians represented the conservative light in the Greek political spectrum.

President Ghizikis reminded the politicians that the country had been without a government for three days and urged them to form a government immediately. Only a civilian coalition of national unity, he pleaded, could avert a national catastrophe and honorably extricate Greece from its intense confrontation with Turkey. Time was of the essence because Turkey was violating the cease-fire agreement with impunity. He insisted that they not leave the room until a government was formed and installed. The politicians were elated but cautious. Where is Ioannides, they asked. Ghizikis replied that the question of Ioannides was no longer relevant. In any case, he added, "he agrees with us and will not create any problems." During the discussions an attempt was made to bind the civilian leaders to a promise not to question the "revolution" of April 21, 1967, not to call immediately for national elections, and to reserve to the military the ministries of Defense, Interior, and Security. However, in the face of strong protest by the politicians, most of whom threatened to walk out, Ghizikis withdrew the conditions.[6]

After two hours of talks, it was agreed that a government should be formed with a wide base of public support and that there were only two figures of sufficient stature to lead Greece out of the chaos of the moment: Panayiotis Kanellopoulos and exiled former premier Constantine Karamanlis. Although the general preference was for Karamanlis, a consensus emerged that the pressure of time excluded Karamanlis from consideration and that a government of Kanellopoulos and Mavros, representing the two major parties prior to the 1967 coup, should be formed immediately. The meeting adjourned at 5:30 P.M. to give Kanellopoulos and Mavros time to discuss in private the formation of a broad coalition government with Kanellopoulos as premier. The meeting was to be resumed at 8:30 P.M., and it was assumed that a government would be sworn in that evening.[7]

---

[6] Nikos Kakaounakis, *The Role of the Military in Greek Politics*, vol. 2, pp. 310-342. S. Grigoriades, *Istoila tis diktatorias*, vol. 3, pp. 274-284.

[7] Ibid., p. 295.

In the meantime, Averoff returned to the conference room after the meeting had adjourned to talk with Arapakis and found the military chiefs talking with Ghizikis. He chose the opportunity to raise again the issue of Karamanlis. He warned the leaders that the domestic and foreign situation of Greece was so threatening that only Karamanlis could handle it "But we discussed it and agreed that we do not have time," replied Ghizikis and Bonanos. "Where are we going to find him and when can he get here?" demanded Ghizikis. Averoff took out his address book and said, "Let's call him and find out." Ghizikis agreed, and a call was made to Karamanlis's residence in Paris. There was no answer. Despite the military's increasing impatience, Averoff telephoned his cousin, George Averoff, in Paris and asked him to find Karamanlis immediately and gave him Ghizikis's telephone number. Within the hour, Karamanlis returned the call, and after speaking with Ghizikis and each of the military chiefs, he agreed to fly to Athens immediately. At 7:00 P.M. Ghizikis called Kanellopoulos to tell him that Karamanlis had agreed to form a government and would be arriving in Athens within a few hours.[8] Athens Radio interrupted the martial music that it had been playing constantly since mobilization was declared the week before to announce that "The armed forces have decided to turn the governing of the country over to a civilian government." Although the announcer did not broadcast the fact that Karamanlis was returning to Greece to form a government, the news of his impending return spread quickly.

Before long thousands of people spilled into the streets of Athens, and waves of humanity converged on Constitution Square, exploding into cheers and chants of hysterical celebration. And thousands more rushed to the Athens Airport to await the "savior" of Greece. It seemed that all the vehicles of the city were rhythmically trumpeting the joyful message on their horns: "Erchete," "Erchete" (He's coming, he's coming). The best description of that night was one of a historic fiesta of joy. It should be noted that there was little evidence of bitterness or revenge. When President Ghizikis and his military aides appeared in front of the Parliament building, the few boos were shouted down by cheers of "all together now."

---

[8] Ibid., pp. 285-286. In June 1963 Karamanlis resigned as prime minister because of the deterioration of his personal relations with King Paul and Queen Frederica and left for Paris. He had been prime minister for eight years, the longest term served by a prime minister in modern Greek history. He returned to contest the November 1963 elections, but after his defeat he departed again, after expressing his disenchantment with Greek political life, for a self-imposed exile in France that lasted for almost eleven years. The official reason given for his resignation in June was his disagreement with the king over the monarch's projected state visit to London. The real reason was disagreement between himself and the palace over the respective powers of the government and the crown. A few months before his resignation, Karamanlis had recommended a revision of the constitution that would substantially restrict the king's privileges, which were extensive, and increase the powers of the executive. The implementation of his recommendations would also have diminished the parliament's prerogatives. For his efforts, he was subjected to attack by the center and left parties as well as by the palace.

After the colonels took power, Karamanlis from Pairs denounced them and made it clear that he would not return to Greece until the soldiers returned to their barracks and ceased to meddle in politics.

At 2:05 A.M. on July 24, Karamanlis arrived at Athens Airport from Paris in a plane that had been placed at his disposal by the president of France. Half a million people voiced their welcome with what seemed like a single voice exploding in a roar. As he rode into Athens, a cavalcade of cars, four abreast and miles long, trailed his limousine. Thousands along the route showered him with flowers. At 4:14 A.M. in the ceremonial hall of the Parliament, Karamanlis was sworn in as premier of Greece by the archbishop of Athens in the presence of the military and civilian leaders. Fifteen minutes later, the first echelon of the cabinet was sworn in; two days later, the cabinet membership was complete. George Mavros was named deputy prime minister and minister of foreign affairs. The Government of National Unity was primarily composed of prominent centrists and conservatives.

III. The Liquidation of the Dictatorship

As soon as the Karamanlis government took office, it initiated a series of decrees aimed at liquidating the disastrous programs of the dictatorship and setting Greece on the road to democracy. It released all political prisoners, and the concentration camp on the island of Gyaros was closed down. Political offenses, except for the crimes of the dictatorship, were amnestied. It restored the freedom of the media and set in motion procedures to restore citizenship to persons who had been disfranchised before and during the dictatorship. It recognized all political parties willing to conform to the democratic process, including the Communist party of Greece (KKE), which had been outlawed since 1947. It pledged a democracy in which all Greeks would have a voice and promised to abrogate every decree violating civil rights. It stripped the Military Police of the functions that had made it a dreaded instrument of the dictatorship and confined it to military duties. All general secretaries of the ministries and all prefects (district commissioners) who held office under the junta were dismissed. Shortly thereafter the proscription was extended to all agencies, organizations, and corporations operating as corporate bodies under public law, including public corporations and state banks. Personnel dismissed or otherwise discriminated against by the dictatorship because of their opposition to the regime were reinstated. In all, 108,000 civil servants and other officials and employees had been dismissed, transferred, or otherwise disciplined by mid-January 1975.

On August 1, 1974, the 1952 constitution was temporarily reinstated, except for the clauses referring to the form of government; the junta had abolished the constitution in 1967 and issued its own document the following year. The delicate issue of the monarchy was placed in abeyance. The government also ordered the removal from all public buildings of the junta's emblem, a phoenix rising from flames, and ordered the revision of school texts, poems, and songs to rid them of their prejunta slant. In time all currency bearing the junta's emblem was withdrawn. However, before the government could proceed with a program of " dejuntafication," it first had to restore civilian control over the armed forces and to bring the Cyprus crisis to a peaceful conclusion.

The junta had not been overthrown by a popular uprising but because of its incompetence by a military leadership that had for the most part supported it and enjoyed its benefits for seven years. The basic command structure of the Greek military and its control over the physical means of coercion remained intact. Indeed, until mid-August the military loomed heavily as a potential arbiter of the actions of the Government of National Unity. The charged atmosphere in the capital was rife with rumors of coups and countercoups. No officers, not even Ioannides, who merely dropped out of sight, had been dismissed or arrested.

On Cyprus the Turks had been blatantly violating the July 22 cease-fire; and Karamanlis dispatched Foreign Minister George Mavros to Geneva for what became the first round of talks (July 25-30) with representatives of Greece, Turkey, and Britain. On July 30 a new cease-fire was agreed to, and a second round of talks at Geneva was convened on August 8 to work out a political settlement with all the parties to the dispute, including Greek-Cypriot and Turkish-Cypriot representatives. The talks broke down on August 14 following a Turkish ultimatum that Greece capitulate to Turkish demands. Within hours the Turkish forces that were marshaled for a second-stage operation proceeded to occupy over a third of the island, driving out about 180,000 Greek Cypriots who became refugees in the Greek-Cypriot controlled south. A new cease-fire line was negotiated on August 16 and continues to be observed by the Turkish army to this day.

The way in which the junta fell and the dangerous confrontation with Turkey over Cyprus initially imposed severe restraints on the task of undoing and neutralizing the machinery of the dictatorship. The popular Greek perception of the Turkish threat helped check public demands for an immediate purge of the armed forces and diverted the attention of the military to external defense after assurances were given that a hasty, major purge of the armed forces would not take place.

The assertion of civilian authority over the military was not a simple task. When Karamanlis assumed the premiership, the military was disorganized and its forces unprepared for war thanks to the purges and neglect of the junta years. Morale was low, and fears of losing job security and of punishment were widespread. Moreover, military elements had not removed themselves from the Athens area and could retake the city at any time. The first clash with military leaders occurred over the dire need for naval officers to man the fleet. In early August Admiral Arapakis obtained approval from Defense Secretary Averoff for the recall of naval officers purged by the junta. However, General Bonanos, the chief of the armed forces, protested vigorously and attempted to block the recall decree by asking General Ghizikis, the president of the republic, not to sign it. After a heated discussion in the Supreme National Defense Council, which had been reconstituted on August 8 and placed under the prime minister, Bonanos was overruled. Eighty naval officers who had been dismissed or pensioned off for opposing the dictatorship were restored to active service; and a review of the service status of officers of the other services who had been dismissed or otherwise prosecuted by the junta was promised.[9]

The major test of civilian control over the military came on August 11, when war with Turkey appeared imminent. On that day Karamanlis invited the four military chiefs to President Ghizikis's office[10] and asked for the removal of all tank units from the Athens region within twenty-four hours. General Bonanos and the chief of the army, General Galatsanos, balked and insisted that these units remain in place for the defense of Athens. The other officers present supported the prime minister who insisted that the units were needed to bolster the army in Thrace. An angry Karamanlis told Bonanos that "Either you take the tanks out of Athens immediately, or the people will decide the issue at Constitution Square."[11] Bonanos then pleaded that he needed more time and that he was fearful that the younger officers would resist the order. Karamanlis warned Bonanos that if he did not remove the tanks, he would have his minister of public order, Solon Ghikas, do the job. In the meantime, gendarmes, led by Ghikas and loyal to Karamanlis, were in the outer office prepared to arrest the insubordinate military and protect the civilian leaders.[12] Bonanos finally promised to obey the order, and the principle of civilian control over the military was reaffirmed.

Screening out subversion from the armed forces and restoring the rule of law and discipline among their ranks were not simple tasks. Although on August 14 Karamanlis eliminated the military option as a solution to the Cyprus problem and ordered a partial demobilization,[13] tension with Turkey remained at a high level and thus restricted his freedom of action in depoliticizing the military. It was argued that any widespread purge of prejunta officers in the face of the perceived external threat would have deleterious consequences for the country's military posture. Nevertheless, with the ceasefire agreement of August 16, Karamanlis moved to tighten his control over the military apparatus without completely alienating the generals. Three days later the Supreme National Defense Council met and decided to replace the armed forces leadership. Generals Bonanos and Galatsanos, until then, respectively, chief of the armed forces and chief of the army, were removed. President Ghizikis signed their retirement orders. They were replaced by Lieutenant General Dionysios Arbouzis (ret.), who was recalled to active duty, promoted to general, and appointed chief of the armed forces, and by Lieutenant General Ioannis Davos, who had been the commander of the powerful Third Army Corps, positioned in Thrace. Davos, an early supporter among the active duty officers of the return of Karamanlis, was appointed chief of the army. Admiral Arapakis and Air

---

9 Stavros P. Psiharis, *I 70 krisimes imeres* [*The 70 Critical Days*] (Athens, 1976), pp. 111-114.

10 Until the November 1974 elections, Karamanlis used his quarters at the Grande Bretagne Hotel as his office.

11 Stavros P. Psiharis, *I 70 Krisimes imeres*, p. 128.

12 Ibid., p. 129.

13 On August 14 the military chiefs, who were told by Karamanlis to prepare for a war against Turkey, informed the premier that they could not successfully resist the second Turkish invasion of Cyprus taking place that day. (Ibid., pp. 16-26.)

Marshal Papanikolaou, who had cooperated fully with the civilian authorities, retained their commands. When they retired in January 1975, they were awarded for their service to the state the titles of honorary chief of the navy and honorary chief of the air force, respectively. On September 21 twenty-nine army officers, three air force officers, and four naval officers who had held key positions under the dictatorship were placed on half pay. Earlier in the month, there were changes in the leadership of the National Police, the Metropolitan Police, the Central Intelligence Service, and the National Security Service. However, only a handful of officers from those forces, namely, some but not all who had acquired notorious reputations for brutal conduct under the dictatorship, were placed on inactive rosters and were given half pay.

The government's cautious policy of removing, retiring, or sequestering key junta militants, which was designed to prevent a sizable revolt, proved disappointing to many of those who had actively opposed the dictatorship. Its policy of isolating and then suspending junta leaders and their accomplices in the military, the security services, and the state bureaucracy and its apparent lack of a sense of urgency in bringing them to the courts of justice served to dampen the government's popularity. In September the slow pace of the government's attempt to formulate a comprehensive plan of punishment for the crimes of the dictatorship prompted a large number of private citizens to initiate legal action against the junta leadership and officials, alleging high treason and/or the torture of political prisoners.[14] To assuage public discontent and to further the consolidation of civilian rule, Karamanlis deemed that the time was ripe for political initiatives.

IV. The Road to Legitimacy

On October 3 Karamanlis announced that parliamentary elections would be held on November 17, less than four months after the collapse of the dictatorship, and would be followed on December 8 by a referendum on the monarchy. The announcement was severely criticized by the opposition parties. They maintained that there was insufficient time for the reorganization of the parties and the mounting of a full-fledged campaign. They also objected on the grounds that the registers to be used for the elections were outdated and that there had not been a thoroughgoing purge of junta appointees from the state apparatus, thus calling into question the possibility of whether a truly free election could be conducted.[15] Although early elections would obviously allow Karamanlis to exploit his immense prestige as the man who restored democracy in Greece, he judged them necessary not only to enable the people to confer legitimacy on the government but also to consolidate civilian rule. Karamanlis argued that only a government with a popular mandate could properly deal with the many crucial problems facing Greece, including the important question of

---

14 S. Grigoriades, vol. 3, pp. 354-355.

15 Richard Clogg, *A Short History of Modern Greece*, p. 203.

"dejuntafication." Moreover, by announcing the referendum on the monarchy, he laid to rest rumors that he would seek the return of the king without the approval of the Greek people.

On the same day, the government promulgated a constituent act stipulating that offenses committed by the dictatorship were not subject to amnesty and that those charged with committing such crimes would be tried by five-judge appellate courts. Karamanlis declared that the determination of individual guilt for the crimes of the dictatorship would be left to the courts that would operate under traditional standards of due process. Concurrent with these announcements, the newspapers printed the decree that stripped former high functionaries of the dictatorship of their pensions. On October 9 martial law was lifted, and two days later criminal prosecution was formally initiated against G. Papadopoulos, D. Ioannides, M. Roufogalis, and twenty-nine army and police officers for their acts in the Athens Polytechnic University uprising of November 1973 in which scores of students were killed or wounded. They were charged with "moral responsibility" for premeditated murder in connection with the incident.[16]

In the meantime, most of the junta leadership and the virulently right-wing officers who provided the foundation of the junta's power remained at large. Only G. Papadopoulos had been placed under house arrest. Nonetheless, the former dictator planned to run for election, and there were rumors that his political ambition went much further. Indeed, a number of his followers from among the junior military ranks approached President Ghizikis and asked for his help in preventing or disrupting the elections. Their plan was to create disturbances and to force the government to call in troops and tanks for riot control. In the process, they would act to delay elections for an indefinite period or perhaps take over the government. Ghizikis admonished them to stay out of politics and to return to their units. He then immediately reported the meeting to the government. As a result of this information and rumors of plots by cashiered military and security officers, security precautions were increased throughout Athens. Additional guards were ordered for prominent politicians of all the parties. The political leaders were advised to devise irregular schedules and to be prepared to go into hiding if antielection disturbances got out of hand.[17]

On October 23 the five ringleaders of the April 1967 coup, G. Papadopoulos, St. Pattakos, N. Makarezos, I. Ladas, and M. Roufogalis were arrested and deported to the Aegean island of Kea. (D. Ioannides could not be found.) They were charged with plotting to undermine the peaceful progress of the elections and engaging in subversive activities.[18] A few days later, they, along with forty-four former officers, were officially

---

16 S. Grigoriades, *Istotia tis diktatorias*, vol. 3, p. 355. N. Kakaounakis, *The Role of the Military in Greek Politics*, vol. 2, pp. 5-45.

17 Stavros P. Psiharis, *I 70 Krisimes imeres*, pp. 152-153, 158-159.

18 *Time Magazine*, October 27, 1974.

charged with high treason and insurrection for their seizure of power in the 1967 coup. Conviction on either charge carried a possible death penalty.[19]

The election passed without a major incident thanks to the precautions taken by Karamanlis and his associates. The military and the security forces, under their new leadership, remained loyal to the civilian government, and the opposition parties of the left while conducting a vigorous campaign, refrained from taking any action that could have provided a pretext for military intervention.

V. Elections

In the parliamentary election of November 17, 1974, Karamanlis's New Democracy (ND) party, which was a somewhat more liberal version of the precoup conservative National Radical Union (ERE) party, received 54 percent of the popular vote and 220 of 300 parliamentary seats....

The overwhelming victory of Karamanlis at the polls did not mean that many Greeks had sanctioned a shift to the right even though the election was a setback for the left. Although the election signaled that the lid would be clamped on the cauldron of political and social change for seven years and that demands for liberal reform would ferment, rise, and spill over the political arena, the Greek people had obviously decided that moderation, stability, and orderly process, instead of rapid change and the possible polarization of society, were particularly desirable in the difficult period of transition from dictatorship to democracy. Domestic and external threats did not permit political experimentation....

VI. Dealing with the Legacy: Purges and Trials

Fortified by a formidable parliamentary majority, Karamanlis hastened the pace of "dejuntafication." In December the government reviewed all cases of officers removed by the junta for political reasons and retired fifty senior officers; a number of others, known as close associates of the junta, were transferred to less central and sensitive posts. The financial dealings of Papadopoulos during the years of his dictatorship were probed, and his wife, Despina, was remanded to jail pending trial on the charge of fraud against the state. It was found that she received a salary from KYP (the Greek Intelligence Service) without performing any known service.

In early January 1975 the parliament unanimously passed a resolution declaring that the seizure of power on April 21, 1967, had been a coup d'etat and not, as its protagonists argued, a revolution creating its own laws. It further resolved that the subsequent crimes of the dictatorship were not subject to statutory limits. Thus parliament cleared the way for the official

---

19 S. Grigoriades, *Istoria tis diktatorias*, vol. 3, p. 354. This action was in part prompted by a lawsuit brought against members of the original junta in September by Alexandres Lykourezos for "conspiring and overthrowing by force the constitutional order by a military coup against the lawful government of the land." The action was subsequently sponsored by the Union of Democratic Lawyers and was expanded to include those who carried out arrests or moved military units in support of the coup.

indictment of the leading conspirators responsible for the seizure of power and other crimes. The task of justice was to deal with the offenses committed under the dictatorship, crimes that fell into four categories: the coup itself, killings during the Athens Polytechnic incident, charges of torture; and the coup in Cyprus. Prosecution on the Cyprus matter was suspended on March 7, 1975, with the concurrence of the opposition in parliament for reasons of national policy and security. On January 14 Ioannides was finally jailed in Korydallos prison in Athens, and on January 20 Papadopoulos and his coconspirators, the " Kea Five," were remanded in custody by court order and transferred to the same prison. Before the end of the month, criminal procedures were initiated against 104 ministers, undersecretaries, and secretariesgeneral who had served the dictatorship. They were formally indicted in March, and a month later about fifty officers and noncommissioned officers of the army and the police forces, who had been accused of torturing political prisoners, were also indicted.[24]

The most serious of several attempted military plots or conspiracies against the government occurred in February 1975. The government initially claimed that the plot was a minor affair, limited to a few prejunta officers concerned with their professional careers as the postjunta military purge began. The Conspiracy of the 39, as the plot was called, was much more serious than the initial government communique had suggested. Those arrested included six general officers and eleven colonels. Ioannides was also implicated. Some of the officers were subsequently cleared of the charge that they had planned to overthrow the government and restore the dictatorship. However, scores of officers were retired from the services following inquiries into the plot and the loyalty of the officer corps to a democratically elected government. On March 16 fourteen major generals, twelve brigadiers, four commodores, and two major generals, as well as eight brigadiers of the air force, were retired. The purge of the armed forces was completed more or less on March 14, when one hundred senior army officers, thirty senior naval officers, and thirty senior air force officers were retired.[25] The purge was also extended to the security forces, leading to the forced retirement of a number of officers and the prosecution of twenty-five officers of the National Police (gendarmerie) and nineteen of the Metropolitan Police.[26]

Although fears were voiced that the government had not yet managed to reestablish civilian control over the armed forces, Karamanlis was apparently in control of the situation. All the plots against the government were discovered and cut short by the military itself, and the series of trials of the junta conspirators and torturers that took place in 1975 proceeded without provoking military intervention. Karamanlis's policy of shielding the officer corps from criticism and his sensitivity to its professional demands and requirements forestalled a possible backlash by officers on

---

24 The Greek Press and Information Service, *Democracy in Greece: The First Year* (Athens, 1975). See also Grigoriades, *Istoria tis diktatorias*, vol. 3, pp. 355-356.

25 *Democracy in Greece: The First Year*, p. 60.

26 Ibid., p. 61.

active duty. The policy of a limited purge of junta principals conducted under regular legal procedures and after public passion had subsided also relieved much of the anxiety of the officer corps. Moreover, the trials, which received widespread radio, television, and press coverage, served to demystify the dictatorship. The trials made possible the exposure of seven years of maladministration, repression, scandals, corruption, and conspiracies and depicted a regime much worse than even the military had imagined. The details of torture, particularly of distinguished senior military officers by subordinates, were most offensive to the professional officer class. The statements and the demeanor of the accused revealed to many their pettiness and their incompetence and destroyed within seconds the military image of the strong man. The trials exposed the "supermen" without their clothes, and what the public and the officer corps saw, they did not like. If we add to this their responsibility for the Cyprus tragedy, we can understand the disillusionment of the officer corps with the military as politicians and its desire to separate itself from the regime of the phoenix and the bayonet.[27]

The trials, which sought to apportion responsibility for the dictatorship, began in July and ended on August 23 with eighteen convictions. Three ringleaders of the April 1967 coup were given death sentences on the count of mutiny and life sentences on the count of high treason. They were Colonels George Papadopoulos and Nicholas Makarezos and Brigadier Stylianos Pattakos. Eight others received ten years for mutiny and life sentences for high treason. They included the strong man of Greece after the overthrow of Papadopoulos in November 1973: Brigadier Demetrios Ioannides, the former regent, General George Zoitakis, the chief of the army at the time of the coup of 1967, Lieutenant General Gregory Spandidakis, and the former head of the Central Intelligence Service (KYP), Major General Michael Roufogalis. Seven others were given lighter jail sentences. Instead of making martyrs of the ringleaders, the government immediately decided to commute the death sentences to life imprisonment. Protesting opposition circles considered the decision a response to pressure exerted by the army. Nevertheless, the permanent incarceration of those most responsible for the crimes of the dictatorship set a precedent in modern Greek history.[28]

The trial that perhaps aroused the most emotion was the first Military Police (ESA) torture trial that took place in Athens in August and September 1975. Trial testimony offered a detailed picture of the junta's

---

[27] Amnesty International, *Torture in Greece: The First Torturers' Trial, 1975* (New York, 1977). Panis Voultepsis and Pericles Rodakis, *I dikes tis Hountas* [*The Trials of the Junta*], Proceedings, vol. I (Athens, 1975). "Impressions from Greece and Cyprus, " a paper presented by Theodore A. Couloumbis at the American University upon his return from observing the trials, October 3, 1975.

[28] S. Grigoriades, *Istoria tis diktatorias*, 356-357. Capital punishment is not in the Greek tradition. The last time it was used for high treason was in 1922, when the revolutionary government of the time set up a commission to determine responsibility for the Asia Minor catastrophe. Eight politicians and military commanders were found guilty of high treason, and six were condemned to death. Their execution cast a long shadow over subsequent political developments in Greece. (Richard Clogg, *A Short History of Modern Greece*, pp. 119-120.)

system of torture and conclusive evidence that torture was practiced in a systematic way in order to perpetuate the junta's control. It dramatized the system's degrading effects on victims and torturers. Like subsequent torture trials, the prosecution of the thirty-two ESA defendants was prompted by the cumulative pressure of civil suits brought by several former prisoners against their torturers in the absence of public prosecutions.

Three former commanders of the junta's most notorious detention center, EAT/ESA—Nicholas Hajizisis, Anastasios Spanos, and Theodore Theofiloyannakos—were sentenced to twenty-three, twenty, and twenty years' imprisonment, respectively. Eight other officers received shorter prison sentences. Three officers were acquitted by a three to two vote. Of the eighteen enlisted men placed on trial, five were found guilty and were given sentences of up to six years. Twelve were found innocent by a vote of three to two; and one had fled the country before trial. In most of the cases the charges on which the men were convicted were abuse of authority and violation of duty. Nearly all the enlisted men denied the charges against them, and nearly all based their defense—as did the accused at Nuernberg—on the simple position that they were required to obey orders.[29] Lesser sentences were given in torture trials held in the remainder of 1975, such as the second ESA trial, the naval torture trial, and the first Athens security police (asfalea) trial. In April 1976 a military appeals court reduced the sentences of several people who had been convicted of crimes. In September and October 1976 the Athens National Police (gendarmerie) trial and the second Athens Security Police trial were held. According to Amnesty International, between one hundred and four hundred torture trials were conducted in Greece.[30]

The other trial that attracted a great deal of public attention was conducted to determine responsibility for the bloody repression at Athens Polytechnic. For their role in the brutal attack on the students, Brigadier Demetrios Ioannides received an additional life sentence and Colonel George Papadopoulos a further twenty-five year sentence. Other defendants received lesser sentences. Finally, those who had served as members of the various civilian governments of the junta were not tried for complicity, although some were defendants in trials alleging corruption.[31]

Some discontent was expressed over inadequate punishment for the crimes committed and over the failure to prosecute some former members of ESA against whom there appeared to be ample evidence of misconduct The procedure of allowing offenders to escape prosecution by "turning state's

---

29 *Torture in Greece: The First Torturers' Trial, 1975*, p. 36. Article 30 of the Greek Military Penal Code punishes with death the refusal to obey an order of the commanding officer.

30 Ibid., p. 75. Because there appears to be no central record of these trials, any list would perforce be incomplete. Moreover, the charges against the defendants in these trials were usually recorded only as assaults of various kinds or as abuses of authority rather than as torture, thus making it even more difficult to compile a central record that distinguishes a "torture trial" from a more ordinary local criminal proceeding.

31 Richard Clogg, *A Short History of Modern Greece*, p. 209.

evidence" was fairly widespread and deeply resented.[32] No compensation was given to the victims of torture, although employees of the state who had been dismissed by the junta were reinstated where possible or had their pensions updated or restored. Some torturers, especially members of the Security Police, were not tried. Others, after being convicted, were set free after paying modest fines or were given suspended sentences. Many Greeks contended that the public authorities should have taken more active roles in bringing the offenders to justice, instead of relying on individual citizens to initiate the majority of the prosecutions. Government initiative would have ensured the fullest possible investigation and prosecution of torturers. Nevertheless, Karamanlis had gone a fair distance in meeting the widespread desire for a public national purge and for the punishment of the worst criminals of the dictatorship.

THE TORTURERS' TRIAL

*Amnesty International, "Torture in Greece: The First Torturers' Trial, 1975"**

The First ESA Trial

At the time of the April 1967 military coup in Greece, the number of political prisoners in Greek prisons was relatively small. Several of these people were long-term prisoners from the days of the Civil War (1946-49), and early in 1967 there was reason to believe that these and other prisoners sentenced under long-standing emergency legislation would be released before the expiry of their sentences. The coup changed this situation drastically, and within a few months there were about 6,000 people held in deportation camps on the Greek islands. During the next half-year this figure dropped considerably, but in late January 1968 there were still 2,777 deportees held without trial in the island detention centres on Yaros and Leros as well as an unknown number of detainees in police stations and prisons throughout the country.

Among these deportees and prisoners were some who were old and infirm, having been arrested on the basis of security files prepared during the Civil War 20 years earlier. Many deportees remained in the island detention camps solely because they refused to sign a "Declaration of

---

32 *Torture in Greece: The First Torturers' Trial, 1975*, p. 59. The deadline introduced by the government for the filing of private lawsuits against torturers (six months for high junta officials and three months for other officials) clearly hampered the course of justice. The government argued that this was necessary in order to provide a sense of urgency in dealing with torturers and in bringing them to justice as quickly as possible. It also argued that speedy trials were necessary because evidence of torture cannot be easily preserved. The fact is, however, that two-thirds of the privately initiated cases against accused torturers were dismissed in the courts on the grounds that the alleged torture victims filed their private lawsuits with the public prosecutors one day too late! (ibid., p. 68).

* Excerpted from Amnesty International, *Torture in Greece: The First Torturers' Trial, 1975* (Amnesty International Publications, 1977), pp. 10-14, 21-22, 36-42, 57-60.

Loyalty" to the government. This declaration required the renunciation of any connection with the Communist Party of Greece (KKE) or "its variously named organisations" and the acknowledgement that, among other things such activities sought "the mutilation and enslavement of the country to the Slavo-Communist camp and the removal of the Greek people from Helleno-Christian ideals".[1]

From the first day of the Junta's rule, torture was an integral part of the state machinery for suppressing opposition. It should be stressed, however, that during the seven years of dictatorship it was used for different purposes at different periods. During the period 1967-71 the purposes of torture were to extract information about resistance activities and to deter the population from political activity. Torture was conducted by trained officers of middle rank from the gendarmerie, the civilian security police (*Asfaleia*), the navy, and the military police (ESA). The policy was to avoid leaving marks, or at least not to allow detainees any contact with the outside until such marks had disappeared. During the period 1971-74, however, the purpose of torture increasingly became intimidation and terrorisation, with the specific aim of destroying the student movement. To a large extent torture was conducted by military police conscripts who were encouraged by their officers to leave marks on the victims. During these years the military police would arrest and detain people almost at random, subject them to ill-treatment and torture and often release them after a relatively short period of time, without ever having brought formal charges against them.

Although torture was used from the beginning of the Junta's rule in April 1967, it was not until November 1967 that reliable reports began to reach the world outside Greece. In response Amnesty International dispatched American lawyer James Becket and British lawyer Anthony Marreco to Greece in late December 1967 to investigate the torture allegations as well as to determine the extent and implementation of a much publicised Christmas amnesty for political prisoners. The beneficence of the amnesty proved almost entirely illusory, and the situation regarding torture confirmed Amnesty International's worst fears. Necessarily restricting themselves to Athens alone, the Amnesty International delegates interviewed 16 released victims of torture and obtained evidence about 32 other cases. Twenty-two methods of torture were documented, including sexual abuse, psychological pressure, electric shock and, most commonly, *falanga* (beating on the soles of the feet), which in almost every case was the initial form of torture. Major Theodores Theofiloyannakos, a defendant at the first ESA trial in 1975, which is the specific subject of this report, was named as a torturer in the January 1968 Amnesty International

---

1 The text of this declaration was analogous to the forced recantations under torture that were extorted 30 years before, during the near-fascist dictatorship of Ioannis Metaxas, 1936-41. It is important to note that although torture was used in Greece before the Junta (specifically, during the Metaxas dictatorship, in the island concentration camps during the 1946-49 Civil War, and within the air force in a particular incident in the early 1950's), it was never an endemic part of Greek political life, as some apologists for the Junta have argued.

report. The report of a second Amnesty International mission, published in April 1968, confirmed the findings of the first.

The two Amnesty International mission reports affected the deliberations concerning the status of Greece within the Council of Europe. The governments of Sweden, Denmark and the Netherlands had already filed applications in September 1967 to the European Commission of Human Rights, charging the Greek regime with violating eight articles of the European Human Rights Convention. This application did not include Article 3, the one prohibiting torture, but after the 1968 Amnesty International reports and other evidence, the sponsors amended their application to include Article 3. A sub-commission then heard the evidence of witnesses, and unlike the Amnesty International mission, the sub-commission was able to gather evidence concerning the police stations outside the capital. This process and the writing of their well-documented, four-volume report lasted until the middle of 1969. In December of that year, after intense diplomatic negotiations and in the face of certain expulsion from the Council of Europe, the Greek government withdrew in order to avoid diplomatic defeat. Subsequent publication of the Commission's report left no doubt that torture and ill-treatment were regular and "officially tolerated" activities inside the Junta's police stations in Athens and throughout the country,[1] but torture continued as usual despite these limited diplomatic efforts....

The severity of Greek torture is further borne out in the specific courtmartial that is the subject of this report. As the first of the so-called "torture trials" in Greece, it deserves attention. In addition, this trial conformed to high legal standards, and after both the prosecution and the defense had been given ample time to argue their cases, the tribunal was able to sort out individual responsibility and to apportion blame for certain of the acts of torture during the Junta years....

Unfortunately, the standards of this first trial were not sustained in later trials. As a consequence, this first trial of some of the military police torturers stands as a better precedent in itself than the whole of the procedure by which some and not other torturers have been brought to trial. Therefore, we have decided to trace the background, development and findings of the first torture trial and to assess its significance and value as a judicial precedent for bringing to justice the violent excesses of oppressive regimes.

The trial began on 7 August 1975, when 14 officers and 18 soldiers of non-commissioned rank were brought before the Athens Permanent Court Martial on charges arising from torture during interrogation. Although all Greek Constitutions since the first in 1822 (including those of 1968 and 1973 promulgated by the Junta) contain general prohibitions against torture, there is no specific prohibition in the Greek Penal Code, which would have to provide the precise implementing law. Therefore, only indirect charges could be preferred against the 32 ESA defendants. These charges were

---

[1] Council of Europe, European Commission of Human Rights, *The Greek Case: Report of the Commission*, 1969.

repeated abuse of authority, violence against a superior officer, unconstitutional detention, ordinary and serious physical injury, repeated insults to a superior, and recurrent moral responsibility for ordinary or serious physical injury. The defendants faced various permutations of these charges, but the only defendant to plead guilty to all charges against him was Sergeant Michail Petrou, a former jailor at the Athens headquarters of ESA who had returned from abroad to face the charges.

The court-martial was conducted according to Military Penal Procedure, which is a combination of the Penal Code and the Military Penal Code. Evidence called on behalf of the prosecution fell into five distinct categories: first, the evidence of retired officers as to their arrest and treatment from 1969 onwards; second, the evidence of students arrested after the Law school demonstrations in early 1973; third, the evidence of naval officers arrested after the unsuccessful naval mutiny in May 1973; fourth, the evidence of students and others arrested after the Athens Polytechnic events in November, 1973; finally, the evidence of former ESA soldiers who described the processes of dehumanisation to which they had been subjected.

Like subsequent torture trials, the prosecution of these 32 ESA defendants was prompted by the cumulative pressure of private civil suits brought by several former prisoners against their torturers in the absence of public prosecutions. The prosecutor of the military court ordered a preliminary investigation which was facilitated by a deposition from Sergeant Petrou. Statements were taken before a military examining magistrate, and several of the accused were remanded in custody. Brigadier Digenopoulos was appointed chairman of the court-martial, with the remainder of the tribunal consisting of three colonels from the army legal branch and two active service officers. The prosecutor, Major Michail Zouvelos, was a member of the army legal service. The defendants were represented by counsel; many of the defendants, however, carried out some cross-examination themselves.

The defendants ... were all members of the Junta's military police (ESA, *Elliniki Stratiotiki Astynomia*) who had served in the Special Interrogation Section in Athens (EAT, *Eidikon Anakritikon Tmima*),[1] at its training centre (KESA, *Kentron Ekpaidevseos Stratiolikis Astynomias*), at its Piraeus section or at the military prison in Boyati. Toward the end of 1968 ESA was endowed with nearly absolute powers of arrest, detention and interrogation. The object of its attention was anyone suspected of being an opponent or potential opponent of the regime—whether civilian or military personnel—in short, anyone, whether communist or conservative democrat, who did not completely support the dictatorship. "Some of the defendants," said the prosecutor in his closing speech at the end of trial, "wanted to present EAT/FSA not as a place of torture but as a national

---

[1] EAT literally translated is the "Special Interrogation Section". However, in colloquial usage EAT meant the place where the special unit operated, namely, ESA's Athens headquarters.

reformatory. Modestly reserving to themselves infallibility of judgement, they have tried to follow in the footsteps of the Holy Inquisition."

Many of the more senior intelligence officers were described in the trial as being guided by a fanatical anti-communism which they worked hard to instill in their command. Indeed, it was to be the defense of almost all the soldier defendants that they were merely obeying orders and were acting in a situation of compulsion and duress.

The first commanding officer of EAT/ESA, not under charge, was Major Petros Koutras. He was succeeded on 25 August 1970 by Major Theodores Theofiloyannakos who had, in fact, exercised control even during Koutras' period of command. It was Theofiloyannakos who built up an efficient system of shadowing, arrests, and interrogation techniques, and who did so with the complete confidence of his patron, Brigadier Ioannidis, the chief inspirer of the system.

Theofiloyannakos was portrayed by the prosecutor as totally indifferent to the physical condition of his prisoners and firmly convinced of the infallibility of his own judgement. He was also a fanatical anti-communist. "I am convinced," said the prosecutor, "that if there had been a catastrophic earthquake, the only person in the whole of Greece to attribute it to the communists would have been Major Theofiloyannakos."

On 28 August 1972, Theofiloyannakos was succeeded by his second-in-command and protégé, Major Nikolaos Hajizisis, who was described at the court-martial as "a violent and most dangerous man". Finally, on 29 August 1973, Major Anastasios Spanos succeeded as the fourth and last commanding officer of the Junta's military police....

The Officers

Of the 14 officers charged at the first ESA trial, 11 were found guilty and three were acquitted. On the whole, the officer defendants were the interrogators who had ordered the torture rather than the men who had actually used the clubs and whips. However, one exception to this general rule relates to the severe bodily injury to (then) Major Moustaklis: according to the soldier defendant Petrou, the torture marks on Moustaklis' face indicated that he was beaten by an officer, because no soldier would have beaten a major in the face.

"How could Greek officers sink to this moral degradation? Who are those responsible?" asked Major Zouvelos the prosecutor, broaching the issues of responsibility for torture and, by implication, of the officer defendants' motives and indoctrination: "Were they born with criminal instincts, or did external factors deform their characters? It is certain, members of the tribunal, that those morally responsible are not in this court. They are those who used the defendants, who inspired in them wrong ideas about our national interest. They are those who, for many years, have given thousands of hours instruction on the fighting of communism without sparing even one hour to the defense of democracy."

In this speech the prosecutor raised questions that the trial did not fully answer. Although the tribunal examined the issue of responsibility with regard to the specific charges against the 32 ESA defendants, it did not pursue the broader questions concerning the political implications of a public authority committing such offences, nor did it expose the facts concerning the whole network of suppression and torture of which ESA was only a part and for which the Junta leaders were ultimately responsible. For example, some prosecution witnesses were reprimanded for mentioning names of those responsible in the leadership who were not tried for establishing the torture system. When interrupted by the chairman on one such occasion, prosecution witness Alexandres Panagoulis objected, saying that at his own trial in 1968, "I was allowed to say the things I want to say now."

Nevertheless, the tribunal was able to apportion blame for individual acts of brutality, and it is important to examine the issue of responsibility within these limits before attempting to analyse the broader issue of the motivations for establishing this particular torture system. Theofiloyannakos accepted responsibility "as officer in command" for the enforced standing and the deprivation of food suffered by some victims, but without acknowledging that this mistreatment amounted to torture. Nor did he accept responsibility for actually giving the orders that led to his soldiers' actions. In fact, it was a tactic of the officers' defense at the trial to appeal for the acquittal of the soldiers, thus appearing as their protectors, while at the same time to disclaim any direct knowledge of brutalities allegedly committed by the soldiers and to deny any responsibility beyond general moral responsibility.

If the officers' strategy was to win their subordinates' silence in court, they were not highly successful. The soldier Alexandres Lavranos said, "We served under them, and now they haven't the courage to take responsibility for what they ordered." "Now I'm in the dock," said soldier Dimitrios Stambolidis bitterly, "and that's because none of those in the front rows [i.e., the officer defendants] will take responsibility and say, 'Yes, Sirs, they were carrying out our instructions.'... Our reward was to be ruined and get a bad name which will stick throughout our lives; to help them carry out their crazy ideas. They ought to have killed themselves. Instead, they try to throw the blame on us."

It was of course in the soldiers' interest to accuse their superiors and to shield themselves behind the position of having to obey orders. By placing officers and soldiers together in the dock at the same trial—a procedure to which some officers took exception—the prosecution prevented each group from shifting blame to the other and thus trying to escape their own individual culpability. One of the most provocative exchanges between an officer defendant and a non-commissioned officer defendant followed an apparent verbal slip by Hajizisis as he was defending himself: "I am accused in regard to things that happened at KESA, and I found out that there is no deposition from the KESA commanding officer. Why should I be accused of things done by [the KESA corporals] Kainich and Demertzidis?" A voice from among the soldier defendants called out, "What *are* you saying?" and Kainich, crimson with wrath, left the courtroom, saying as he went, "I thought I was dealing with men, but it seems they're pampered harem women. I covered them, and now they're putting it all on me. That scum Hajizisis has forgotten when he sent me prisoners to KESA with instructions to beat them to a pulp. Now the coward says he didn't know what went on there." Though Theofiloyannakos tried to calm him and though Hajizisis attempted to make amends the next day by claiming moral responsibility for the soldiers, the result of the exchange was Kainich's supplementary statement to the court in which he named....

The Soldiers

> ...the subordinate ranks were ... conscripted. They were not, as some people have tried to pretend, volunteers. After they had had every trace of individuality and humanity crushed out of them at KESA, after their lowest instincts had been aroused, after they had been threatened, terrorised and misled, they were let out like wild animals from their cages and set on their brothers to tear them to pieces. Most of them, not having the strength to resist, followed their orders. Some adjusted and identified themselves [with the procedures], after which they acted on their own, varying the repetitive monotony by personal initiatives. How can we today, members of the tribunal, go deeply enough into this to find out who are the guilty?—from the prosecutor's closing address.

At the trial it was variously estimated that the number of soldiers at any one time at EAT/ESA ranged from 100 (defendant's estimate) to 2,000 (prosecution witness's estimate). Because of the burning of ESA files at the fall of the Junta regime, exact figures can only be deduced. It appears that the figure was much higher than allowed for by defendants at the trial and probably ranged from 400 to 600 at any one time, while as many as 4,000 conscripts may have served there during the Junta years.[1] Yet only 18 soldiers were placed on trial. Nearly all denied the charges against them, and nearly all based their defense—as did the accused at Nuremberg—on the simple position that they were required to obey orders.

Article 70 of the Greek Military Penal Code punishes with death the refusal to obey an order of a commanding officer. The prosecutor pursued the question of subordinates' responsibility as follows:

> Therefore, what system obtains in Greece? It seems—and the commentators agree—that it is the system of blind obedience. Therefore he who receives an order can question only its formal and not its basic legality.... The law says that the soldier is obliged, when ordered, to carry out any service required of him. Service in the military sense is defined by regulations and the basic decrees and communiqués.

The level of the soldiers' responsibility and the degree of their indoctrination consequently became matters of some importance for the

---

1 This deduction was made meticulously by Maria Daraki-Malle (*I ESATZIDES*, Athens, Kedros ed. 1976, pp 13-15). Her calculation is based on the number of months spent on average at EAT/ESA by conscripts, an analysis of the varying estimates given by the commanding officers on trial and the evidence of soldier prosecution witnesses and defendants.

trial. Michail Sabatakakis, a dentistry student who was arrested for a second time in May 1973, summed up both issues in his evidence as follows: "There were two categories of ESA men. To the first belonged those who obeyed orders so as to survive.... To the second category belonged those who had been specially trained so that fascism had passed into their personalities.... They are not weird monsters but the results of a system of training."

ESA was presented to the trainees as "the most select unit in the Greek army". There seems to have been a triple screening—first to enter KESA, second from KESA to EAT/ESA, and third to become one of the jailors or a member of the Prosecution Section. Even when posted to headquarters, they would have further instruction, including courses given by Antonopoulos for jailors and soldiers in shadowing, methods of disguising and varieties of ill-treatment.

This effort to foster in the soldiers' minds the notion of being a select cadre affected their behaviour, especially if there was some reason to show social resentment toward the prisoner, as was the case with students. An ESA guard at the Piraeus interrogation centre told students as he beat them, "I learned about life the hard way, but you in the University learn nothing." At KESA, Demertzidis forced the student Sabatakakis to kneel before a photograph of Papadopoulos and his book *My Credo*, presumably as an act of intellectual self-abnegation. When a guard at ESA headquarters in Athens struck the textual proof-reader Stavros Stratidakis, who almost lost consciousness, the guard was taken aback and said, "Pardon, friend. I thought you were a student." The unmistakable bullying of prisoners appears to have become acute whenever students were the victims: when Petrou indulged in fisticuffs, he would ask students if he had a big fist, and the victim was supposed to answer, "as big as the Peloponnese".

As with the officers, an Athens posting was obviously attractive to soldiers, and in the case of ESA, it bestowed a certain amount of prestige. ESA soldiers were further not required to wear uniforms, had free entrance to all forms of public entertainment, the use of a car, and guaranteed entrées to employment in the public service on leaving. Hajizisis even claimed that a Greek from Australia had sent him 28,000 drachmas for distribution among the ESA guards.

A fairly consistent picture of the rigours of ESA selection and training emerged from the evidence of former ESA soldiers called as prosecution witnesses. This picture was corroborated rather surprisingly during the trial by one of the defendants, Georgios Kambanas, who had been an ESA corporal and jailor. After making the following statement, Kambanas was put under special protective guard:

> "I was called up in April 1973," said Kambanas. "I was in perfect health and was thrilled at the prospect. Now, two years later, I am in despair. My health is broken and my name is stigmatised. From the moment we arrived at KESA from the Basic Training Centre, the torture began. They snatched us from the army lorries and threw us down like sacks. The beating began and they made us eat the straps

> from our berets.... They beat us with belts and clubs.... The beating never stopped.... They beat us in the lorries, in the lecture halls and during the lessons.... I thought of asking to be transferred from ESA, but I realised that it was as much as my life was worth.... I beat prisoners to save myself.... Living in that atmosphere I got ill, and one Sunday evening I had a haemorrhage. Next day I was taken in the Military Hospital, and they found a patch on my lung. When I was transferred, it was as though I went from night to day. The officers behaved like officers, and the commanding officer was like a father to me. But my health got worse. I cough the whole time and have difficulty in breathing from kicks in the chest at KESA.... Now I'm a physical and mental wreck and disgraced in the eyes of the community."

Vasilios Tzortzatos, a prosecution witness and a former ESA soldier now employed as a waiter, said that KESA training had the effect of turning the trainees into "clockwork soldiers". The beatings continued even when they left KESA and were posted as new guards.

Many ESA men may well have suffered beatings similar to those they themselves later meted out. "It's nothing, Mr. Chairman," said former Corporal Themistoklis Vlochaïtis, a prosecution witness, "to give someone five blows when you've had sixty from your comrades." "I could say," said Ioannis Kontos, a student who served at ESA for two years, "that I've suffered more than some of the prisoners. We were made to forget what we had learned at school and from our parents. They tried to awaken the beast in us.... Sometimes one was ordered to beat in the presence of an officer. If a guard was lenient to a prisoner, he could be in danger. We had to choose between our own lives and that of another. The instinct for self-preservation dominated." Even Michail Petrou, the sergeant who pleaded guilty and on whose deposition the trial was largely based, said: "I beat prisoners, Mr. Chairman. They were my orders and that's what I did. A soldier couldn't do anything else but obey."

The degree of the soldiers' responsibility and the amount to which they acted on their own initiative is a matter for assessment. Many of their victims seemed unable to form a view. "I think," said Ioannis Papadonikolakis, a retired squadron-leader who was arrested in November 1970, "that the guards carried out orders. Perhaps they could react within very restricted limits. I believe that many of their actions were done under the influence of drugs." The lawyer Michail Vardanis also gave evidence that he believed the guards may have been drugged because of their "glazed eyes", but there was nothing to support this view. If it had been the case, then certainly those guards who gave evidence seemed totally unaware of it.

Most of the victims who were called held a surprising amount of sympathy for their former guards, and opinion varied as to their culpability. "In my opinion," said navy Captain Alexandres Papadongonas, currently Minister for the Merchant Marine, who had been arrested in May 1973, "I was dealing with people—I mean the guards and the other soldiers—who had been deprived of their personalities, and I do not know how far they were responsible...." Wing-Commander Anastasios Minis actually sought clemency for the soldiers whom he regarded as "so dehumanised" as to be without responsibility. They had, said Minis, a vocabulary of little more than 130 words, almost all abusive. Ioannis Starakis, a French journalist who had been arrested in August 1969, proposed still another theory. "My long stay at ESA," he said, "gave me a chance to understand how the system worked. I think Theofiloyannakos and Hajizisis tried in every way to involve the ESA men in their guilt. It is the system which compels a new member to commit a crime so as to have a hold over him afterwards. It is a system for creating a new generation of criminals."

Against this, however, was the evidence of the former ESA soldiers, Dionysios Charalambopoulos and Evangelos Manolopoulos, and of Major Ilias Menenakos. Even though Charalambopoulos gave evidence that he had been severely beaten for helping a prisoner and was then transferred, and that another sympathetic guard, known as Papandreopoulos, had completely disappeared, he also testified that the guards did have some initiative with regard to the exact method by which they implemented their orders. Manolopoulos said he was merely threatened for assisting prisoners and that "perhaps" there were ways of not carrying out distasteful orders. Major Menenakos, who had been arrested in January 1974 for failing to carry out an order to attack the Athens Polytechnic students and who was subsequently deported to Yaros, was crossexamined by counsel for some of the soldier defendants on the issue of responsibility:

> *Counsel*: Could a soldier not execute orders?
> *Menenakos*: I think he could.
> *Counsel*: And wouldn't he suffer for it?
> *Menenakos*: I think not. But he would be transferred.
> *Counsel*: But surely a soldier must execute orders?
> *Menenakos*: Certainly—as far as they are legal.
> *Counsel*: Has a soldier the discrimination to judge whether an order is legal or not?
> *Menenakos*: Yes.
> *Prosecutor*: Do not all soldiers know that it is illegal to beat someone?
> *Menenakos*: Of course.

There was also evidence that sometimes soldiers would enter the cells in a drunken condition and begin to torment the prisoners. Ioannis Koronaios, a United States citizen who was arrested in October 1970 after placing a protest bomb in the National Park and stopping passersby to warn them, said: "On the Sunday they warned me that in the evening, drunken soldiers would enter my cell and that I would have trouble. And at midnight they actually came. What I went through in the next hours was a real hell. One who was behind me kicked me wherever he could, and they called out like football umpires 'Goal!', 'Foul!', 'Offside!'. They struck and kicked me. I fell down, they raised me, they struck me again and again I fell."

Publisher Viktor Papazisis, a member of a resistance group who had been arrested on the pretext of a traffic accident, gave evidence of a similar experience. "On Sunday evening, many guards came in and beat me till they drew blood. I remember this because it made an impression on me that they were all drunk. Later, I learned from fellow prisoners that these guards made a round of the cells. They had come from a bar and were discussing whom they should beat. Finally they decided: 'Let's beat Number 7 because he's new'.... Before they transferred me from ESA, I also remember very well how a guard rushed on me when I was in the hands of the gendarmes and beat me in front of them. I think this shows that neither the drunkard who beat me nor that guard could have had a definite order. They simply had power over life and death and did what they liked there. They made no impression of discipline or of an army. It was a swarm of ruffians."

If the evidence of Papazisis and Koronaios is true—and there is no reason to doubt it—then it is a powerful counter to the soldiers' general protestations of being nothing more than an indoctrinated cadre responding only to orders which they dared not disobey. It may be in some cases that they were unaware of the identity of prisoners; for example, when the naval officers were arrested in May 1973, they had their uniforms taken away. It may be that the soldiers became worse when in a group. For example, Andreas Stavroulakis, a senior Electricity Board official who had been arrested on 4 September 1972, said: "Even the worst torturer showed some human instincts when he was alone. It was when he was with others that he became like a wild beast." But unordered beatings and the use of personal initiative by the soldiers cannot be denied.

Certainly several former soldiers who were called as prosecution witnesses spoke of the deep shame that they felt for their association with ESA. Ioannis Kontos, who had served from September 1971 until August 1973, said: "I feel ashamed of having served in ESA. When someone asks me in conversation where I served, I say, 'as a simple infantryman'. Mr. Chairman, who is going to cleanse us of this stain?" Another witness, Vasilios Tzortzatos, spoke in similar terms: "We're stuck with the stain now and we'll never get rid of it. Everyone thinks all ESA men are criminals. In my district, no one speaks to me."

Antonis Georgalas, who had served from February 1969, gave a detailed example: "One day I was told that Theofilyannakos was asking for a sergeant. There was no one else, so I went. I saw a dark girl, whose name I do not know, but I think she worked in Telecommunications. She was at the mercy of a furious Theofiloyannakos, who was hitting her on the soles of her feet with a club. He said: 'Why are you looking at me?' If I had had a pistol, I would have killed myself. I was ashamed not only as a soldier but as a human being."

Dimitrios Staikos, who had been called up in 1971, claimed that he had wounded himself with his service pistol in an effort to get a transfer. But perhaps most emphatic of all was Michail Petrou, the defendant who had pleaded guilty: "I feel it is my duty to state publicly that I take full responsibility for what I did and to apologize to those who suffered in the dungeons of EAT/ ESA. I also want to say that I will not forget what happened in that dreadful place. Publicly, I ask forgiveness.... I want to reveal the truth. The only feeling which prompts me is the need to come clean."

How far such sentiments were a genuine expression of their feelings, and how far they may have been prompted by the national attention that the trial received, is, of course, impossible to say. Many conscripted soldiers, however, came from respectable, middle and working class families throughout the countryside, and there is no doubt that their relatives and friends felt shocked and bitter at what had become of the promising young men they had known. Character witnesses called on behalf of the defendant Alexandros Lavranos provide a convincing example. "We are a poor but decent family,..." said his father, a farmer, "and now I see him in the dock as a torturer. I want to ask the court to examine how a boy who everyone said was 'a diamond' became a torturer. Who morally destroyed my family and my home?" His future father-in-law was equally incredulous: "I can't believe it. He was a good boy and that's why I gave him my daughter."

When Lavranos himself later came to give his defense statement, he reiterated what was becoming the traditional soldier defense:

> I think that in this hurricane of terrorism, violence and fear, I tried to participate as little as possible. I would rather not have participated at all, but it was impossible.... I was caught up in a machine and became a tool without any will of my own to resist. I remember Spanos threatening a soldier that he would ruin his family. The next day the boy began to beat prisoners.... Now all my friends and relations look upon me with suspicion and pity. I can't find work. A friend took me on and, after a few days, he gave me a quiet hint to leave. The ESA discharge certificate is like a leprosy.
> ...I feel the need to tell this respected tribunal and the Greek people that I am a human being like you, like your neighbour's son, like a friend. When I struck, it was not Lavranos' hand, but the hand of Spanos, of Hajizisis....

Assessment

On 12 September, after the closing speeches had been concluded the members of the tribunal retired to consider their verdicts. At 7:15 pm the same day they returned to court. Theodoros Theofiloyannakos was found guilty by unanimous vote and sentenced to 20 years' imprisonment. Nikolaos Hajizisis was found guilty by unanimous vote and sentenced to 23 years' imprisonment. Anastasios Spanos was found guilty by unanimous vote and sentenced to 20 years' imprisonment. Among the others who were convicted was Dr. Dimitrios Kofas, who received a sentence of seven years' imprisonment for violation of duty. Fifteen soldiers, including Alexandros Lavranos, were acquitted, but only one by unanimous verdict. Michail Petrou, who had struck a number of prisoners but whose confession had greatly facilitated the trial, received a sentence of six years' imprisonment—the heaviest given to any soldier defendant—and was visibly overwhelmed at what he considered to be its severity. (See Appendix A [of the Amnesty International report] for the complete list of defendants and a summary of the verdicts and sentences.)

To offer an adequate assessment of the first ESA trial is difficult. It is clearly not possible to weigh the credibility of each witness who testified; besides, in many cases, it must be said that cross-examination was unsatisfactory. In some cases, the allegations and the denials could have been proved either way. One of the defendants, Ioannis Angelis said, for example:

> Students have come and testified that I beat them between 7 and 8 May. But I was on leave then and only returned on the 17th.... After the change of regime, Mr. Vernikos [a prosecution witness] went up to Arachova for skiing. I was in a farm lorry with a friend and we ran into his car. We exchanged names and addresses.... That day he didn't recognise and remember me. Now he comes here and says I beat him.

Although ESA archives (including records of leave from duty) had been burned, thus making Angelis' first point impossible to document or refute, his second point could presumably have been pursued. But evidence was not called either to rebut or to confirm the latter point.

Nevertheless, from the totality of the evidence—even leaving aside the several individual confessions by, for example, Michail Petrou—a portrait emerges of systematic torture by ESA. In many cases the details of methods employed are both specific and corroborative. In some cases, as with Major Moustaklis, the evidence of injury while in detention is indisputable. This systematic procedure of violence and deprivation was applied to a very large number of people who were arrested by ESA; it is a procedure which appears to have varied only in degree.

The main value of the trial lies in the exposure of such practice and in setting the example that torturers, even though protected and sponsored by a political regime, can be brought to trial and punished. The traditional process of detection, trial and sentence is here seen to work with torturers as with other criminals, and this should provide a deterrent. A clear precedent now exists to show that political torture is not a crime of immunity outside the rule of law and condemned only by international declaration. A state's domestic courts can, and should, provide a proper and effective forum for sanction in torture cases.

To what extent can this torture trial be regarded as a model for others and as an ideal precedent? The answer requires examination of two issues: first, the role played by the authorities in initiating the prosecution and the steps taken as a result; second, the manner in which the trial was conducted and its procedural fairness.

The Greek authorities are to be credited with bringing the prosecution, but the decision to prosecute was very largely the direct result of cumulative pressure from private civil suits that had been commenced by several former prisoners against their torturers. In this the government could be criticised. If, on the evidence, there is a case to answer, the decision to prosecute should be exercised solely with regard to that criterion and not to outside pressure or public opinion. On the evidence heard at the trial there was a clear case to answer, and the unfortunate inference is of an initial reluctance on the part of the authorities responsible to prosecute. One prosecution witness, G. Lambiris, said in evidence that he had been distrustful of the prosecutor because "the state had not taken up the issue of punishment on its own initiative".

Under Greek law, torture *per se* is not a crime. The ESA trial was held, therefore, within the limits of the only possible charges. These concerned "insults", "abuse of authority" and "bodily injury", which in Greek law are misdemeanours. It was only because some of the torture victims were officers superior in rank to the defendants that stiff sentences were imposed in the first ESA trial....

There is also the issue of the conduct of the first ESA trial and its procedural fairness. Several criticisms can be made, but, in making them, it is important to stress that this was a court-martial and not a trial in a domestic court criminal court, and that the standards and procedural requirements of a judicial hearing—so far as they are over and above the principles of natural justice—vary from jurisdiction to jurisdiction.

The lack of depth in cross-examination, and the failure to investigate a number of allegations and denials which could have been substantially proved one way or the other, have already been mentioned. Perhaps this is not wholly surprising considering that the trial itself lasted only from 7 August until 12 September during which time well over a hundred witnesses gave evidence. It can be argued that a trial of several months would have allowed a more exhaustive examination of every issue. A desire for speed and efficacy is not necessarily a matter for criticism, however, nor is length necessarily a matter for praise. What is important is that neither the defense nor the prosecution should be curtailed or prejudiced in the presentation of its case, and there is no evidence in this case to suggest that it was.

Less easy to understand is the selection of defendants. Some former members of ESA against whom there appears to have been available evidence simply were not prosecuted, and it seems clear that in return for testifying against their former colleagues, the prosecutor used his discretion in effect to grant them immunity. This procedure of allowing certain witnesses to escape prosecution by "turning state's evidence" prevented the bringing to trial of some who are possibly as guilty as those tried and convicted. With understandable grievance Spanos said in his defense statement that he regarded it as incomprehensible that he should be accused while neither Colonel Koutras (the first commanding officer of ESA) nor Major Bakas (the officer in command at KESA) was charged. Major Spyridon Triantos, a defense witness, and ESA soldiers Ioannis Kostouras and G. Panagopoulos, both prosecution witnesses, disclosed in their evidence that although initially charged they had not been proceeded against. When Evstathios Panagoulis later came to give evidence, he identified Panagopoulos as one who had beaten him up and commented:

> Gentlemen of the tribunal, if Panagopoulos is a prosecution witness, then all the defendants from the third row backwards [i.e., the soldiers] ought to be allowed home. Panagopoulos broke two clubs on my body.

The trial itself received a good measure of both national and international press coverage, and the temptation to turn it into a show trial must have been great. The widespread desire for a public national purge was also fairly apparent. To the credit of all concerned, the trial never degenerated into spectacle. It should be stressed that the overall impression is that the prosecution was fair. The defendants had the offer of representation and the opportunity to cross-examine and state their case. Moreover, if during a prosecution witness's oral evidence his testimony differed from his deposition before the examining magistrates, the prosecutor declined to question him further and placed no reliance on his previous evidence.

Amnesty International welcomes the precedent of the first ESA trial in that it generally met high standards of jurisprudence while apportioning blame for individual acts of physical injury and abuse of authority. Primarily, the trial has established a truth and proved a point: torture *was* practised by the Junta's military police on a systematic scale as a means to enforce authority, and torture *can* be punished by the ordinary criminal process. The first ESA trial was a promising beginning.

8

PORTUGAL

EDITOR'S INTRODUCTION

In 1926, the Portuguese army overthrew an unstable parliamentary government in that country. António de Oliveira Salazar, a respected professor of economics, became Minister of Finance, with authority over expenditures of all government agencies. As the economic situation improved, his political strength grew. By 1932, Salazar became the first civilian prime minister since the coup and proceeded to establish a dictatorship under the banner of the "New State" (*Estado Novo*). This New State was strongly corporativist and purportedly Catholic in its orientation. The educational system, from primary through graduate levels, was required to comport with the official ideology; university professors were purged at various times. The regime instituted a system of repression, censorship, and cultural uniformity. Three groups—conservative, quasi-fascist intellectuals, a small number of family businesses, and a brutal secret police (the PIDE)—comprised the base of power. The PIDE relied on an extensive network of informers which included a voluntary "Portuguese Legion" and public employees who were legally obliged to inform on others or be dismissed. Although a restricted opposition was allowed to challenge the regime in manipulated periodic elections, only one political organization, the National Union (*União Nacional*), was officially permitted. Hundreds of regime opponents were deported to detention centers in the Azores and Cape Verde.

After Salazar's death in 1970, President Américo de Teus Tomás invited Marcello Caetano, an architect of the New State, to become prime minister. Caetano continued many of the repressive policies of his predecessor.

Portugal became enmeshed in a series of unpopular wars against the independence movements in its centuries-old African colonies of Angola, Mozambique, Guinea-Bissau, Cape Verde, and São Tomé and Principe. By 1974, in the midst of a worsening economy and growing domestic and international opposition to these conflicts, the colonial wars absorbed over 45% of the Portuguese national budget. On April 25, 1974, the Portuguese Armed Forces Movement (MFA) removed Tomás and Caetano in a coup d'état and installed a leftist seven-man National Salvation Junta (*Junta de Salvação Nacional* or NSJ) under the presidency of General António de Spínola. Over the next two years, the former colonies gained independence. The MFA played a key role in the new government.

One of the NSJ's first measures was a program to purge the people and institutions of the Salazar regime. Tomás and Caetano were exiled, the PIDE was dissolved and many of its leaders arrested and prosecuted, and the National Union was abolished. Many who had collaborated with the old regime become the subject of electoral prohibitions as well as *saneamentos* (purges) from various fields. In addition, the MFA directed the retirement of sixty generals. A special committee was established to investigate and disclose behavior after the April 1974 coup that was "contrary to the established order."

On September 30, 1974, Spínola was overthrown by the MFA and the Portuguese Democratic Movement, and General Gosta Gomes was installed as president. A second wave of *saneamentos* began, now expanding from a strict definition of collaborator to entail the purge of traditional capitalist sectors as well. This process did not adhere to any clear strategy, often driven by demands from workers' committees and varying from one sector to another.

Ongoing power struggles between leftists and rightists resulted in the successive downfall of five provisional governments between 1974 and late 1975. Following the "hot summer" of 1975, which brought Portugal to the brink of civil war and which culminated in the November suppression of a left-wing coup effort, a more moderate government assumed control. When this sixth government suspended the purge process at the end of 1975, some 20,000 citizens had been affected.

A new legislature was democratically elected in 1976. During the period from 1976 into the early 1980s, a reversal of the *saneamentos* occurred. A law was passed nullifying the 1974-75 purges of citizens for political or ideological reasons. A process of reintegration of purged individuals was most apparent in the economic sector, with incentives to return to Portugal extended to many of the people who had fled the country. Property nationalized following the April 1974 coup was reprivatized.

THE SALAZAR LEGACY

*António Costa Pinto, "The Radical Right in Contemporary Portugal"**

Unlike other regimes of the "Fascist period", Salazar's did not leave to posterity, after its fall, the symbols, organisation, ideology and human support capable of feeding a neo-Fascist party. One component of Francoism was a native Fascism which ultimately acknowledged him as head of the movement. In post-authoritarian Spain a neo-phalangism was possible, though it remained marginal. In Portugal it was impossible to introduce a neo-Fascist practice based on the abolished regime.

Though it shared some features and underwent the influence of Fascism, the EN [Estado Novo or New State] differed from it in a number of basic aspects. Historically, it emerged from a military dictatorship, introduced in 1926 after a coup which abolished a liberal republic. It was not based on a Fascist-type party (which did not exist during the crisis and the downfall of liberalism).[3] The single party of the regime—the National Union [*União Nacional*, UN]—was created in 1930, from above and through a decisive intervention of the state apparatus. The corporative institutions, inspired by Italian Fascism, were tempered by the "Social Catholicism" from which the dictator originated. In practice they were mere appendages of the state machinery, without life of their own or autonomy. Furthermore, the regime—unlike its Fascist counterparts—did not rely on the intense political mobilisation of the population....

The threat represented by the Second Spanish Republic and the start of the Civil War in that neighboring country induced a shift towards Fascism in the [Portuguese] regime. Salazar allowed the formation of the Portuguese Legion [*Legião Portuguesa*, LP], which sent volunteers to fight beside Franco, as well as a paramilitary organisation, Portuguese Youth [*Mocidade Portuguesa*, MP]. Both provided a Fascist political backing to the regime in the second half of the 1930s, but they remained under the strict domination of the state. MP was under the direct rule of the Ministry of Education and the LP was controlled by the army. There was no linkage with the party which was merely an institution of the regime, without any effective powers.[6]

Anticipating a new international situation after the defeat of Fascism, the regime prepared a cover-up operation in 1944. The single party was resurrected to ensure a "certain victory" in the general and presidential elections, in which the opposition was allowed to participate. It took

---

* Excerpted from António Costa Pinto, "The Radical Right in Contemporary Portugal," in Luciano Cheles, Ronnie Ferguson, & Michalina Vaughan, eds., *Neo-Fascism in Europe* (Longman, 1991), pp. 168-170.

3 On some of the failed attempts to set up Fascist parties after the First World War, see A. Costa Pinto, "O Fascismo e a crise da I Republica: Os Nacionalistas Lusitanos, 1923-25", *Penélope*, 3, pp. 43-62.

6 On the origins of the MP, see A. Costa Pinto and N. Ribeiro, *A Acção Escolar Vanguarda*, 1933-34, História e Critica, Lisbon, 1988.

advantage of those brief interludes to denounce the dictatorial nature of the regime, until its fall in 1974.[7]

In the post-war period, the EN came to define itself as an "organic democracy" and endeavoured, without too much difficulty, to conceal the outward signs of its association with Fascism. The paramilitary organisations, the MP in particular, acquired a more "former-student" and "sporting" character. *The Secretariado de Propaganda Nacional* (Secretariat for National Propaganda), entrusted with organising mass demonstrations throughout the 1930s, and led by António Ferro, an intellectual extrovert and admirer of Mussolini, changed name and leader. It acquired a more anodyne image as a promoter of "tourism and information." The LP, downgraded since 1939, when Franco won the Spanish Civil War, vanished from the streets and went into terminal decline.

In the unfavourable international climate of 1945, Salazar was able to secure the survival of his regime. This he owed to his neutrality during the war, to his military concessions to Britain and the United States, and to the rapid onset of the cold war, which gained him recognition of the new international community (Portugal joined the UN and NATO, at the end of the decade.[8]) However, changes at the level of institutions and of decision-making machinery proved very limited. There were no basic changes in 1945, as far as the authoritarian nature of the regime was concerned. It was only when Salazar was replaced by Marcello Caetano, in 1968, that a series of reforms took place, and that part of the political elite associated with the old dictator was removed.

Some of the characteristics which demarcated the EN from European Fascism may account for the fragility of the Portuguese radical right on the eve of the regime's fall.[9] The main one, no doubt, was the minimal autonomy of party institutions in relation to the state. One author rightly concluded that "the truth about the way Portugal was governed from 1930 to 1974 was (that it was) an administrative state".[10] Apart from administration, the little that existed disintegrated over time, if only for lack of functions, as the regime—once established—did not attempt any extensive or intensive political mobilisation. Political militancy was weak and participation in the single party or the paramilitary organisations remained limited since, from the inter-war period, but more explicitly after 1945, the regime promoted depoliticisation. Salazar never sponsored any

---

[7] On the opposition to Salazarism, see D.L. Raby, *Fascism and Resistance in Portugal: Communists, Liberals and Military Dissidents in the Opposition to Salazar, 1941-74*, Manchester University Press, Manchester, 1988.

[8] See A.J. Telo, *Portugal na Segunda Guerra*, Perspectivas e Realidades, Lisbon, 1987.

[9] On authoritarian regimes, see J.J. Linz, 'Totalitarian and Authoritarian Regimes', in F. Greenstein and N. Polsby (eds.), *Handbook of Political Science*, Reading, Mass., 1975, vol. 3, pp. 175-411.

[10] L.S. Graham, 'Portugal: The Bureaucracy of Empire', LADS. *Occasional Papers*, IX, 1973, p. 8.

ideological or mobilising organisation, even when confronted with a colonial war in the early 1960s.[11]

POLITICAL CONTEXT OF THE TRANSITION

Kenneth Maxwell, "Regime Overthrow and the Prospects for Democratic Transition in Portugal"[*]

Liberation by Military Intervention

The immediate origins of the coup of 25 April 1974 lay as much in Africa as in Europe. Portugal had been struggling for over a decade to contain a spreading guerrilla war in its overseas colonies. Violence had erupted first in Angola in 1961, and rapidly spread to Portuguese Guinea in West Africa and then to Mozambique in East Africa. Portugal had possessed the first and oldest of Europe's colonial empires. In 1974 it possessed the last. As other European powers had been obliged to divest themselves of overseas territories during the 1950s and 1960s, Portugal had, with embarrassing tenacity, remained, surviving even the preeminence of Europe itself in world affairs.

The burdens of the African campaigns on a small, poor nation with limited natural resources and severely retarded economic and social infrastructures proved unsustainable. The burden was especially onerous on those called to fight the battle: the Portuguese army. The single most important fact about the Portuguese Revolution is so obvious that its significance is often overlooked. It is that no mass movement brought the old regime down, and that the participation of the clandestine political parties of the Left was negligible. The dictatorship was toppled by the army, not by Communists or anyone else.

The coup d'état of 25 April 1974 was carried out by a small group of junior and middle-rank officers, all of them influenced by their extensive experience in the colonial wars, most of them believing that the military should play a major role in the political process. The action of the Portuguese military and its many factions was a central and unique element in the Portuguese situation. The multitudes that assembled in the streets of Lisbon and Oporto in the hours and weeks that followed the coup made the army's action irreversible. Popular mobilization followed the coup; it did not cause it.

---

[11] For the interpretations of the EN, see M. de Lucena, 'Interpretações do Salazarism: notas de leitura critica. I', *Análise Social*, LXXXIII, 1984, pp. 423-51 and A. Costa Pinto, 'O Salazarismo e o Fascismo Europeuos primeiros debates nas ciências socias', *Salazar e o Salazarismo*, Publicações D. Quixote, Lisbon, 1989, pp. 155-88.

[*] Excerpted from Kenneth Maxwell, "Regime Overthrow and the Prospects for Democratic Transition in Portugal," in Guillermo O'Donnell, Philippe C. Schmitter and Laurence Whitehead, eds., *Transitions from Authoritarian Rule: Southern Europe* (The Johns Hopkins University Press, 1986), pp. 109-112, 115-116, 118, 121-122.

The Armed Forces Movement (MFA) originated in response to professional grievances and concerns with status and privilege.[1] The dissension within the officer corps, however, was a reflection of a much deeper malaise which grew out of the scale, composition, and organization of the Portuguese armed forces, all of which in turn was a consequence of the seemingly endless military commitment in Africa.

Initially, the MFA was composed exclusively of regular captains and majors. Later, some trusted senior officers were incorporated or, more often, kept informed of developments. It was a small, compact group, with strong personal interrelationships, numbering less than 200 out of a middle-rank corps of some 1,600. Members were spread throughout most units, and the MFA was especially strong in Guinea and Mozambique. After 1 December 1973, the organization was held together at the center by a fifteen-man coordinating committee, subdivided into a military committee charged with the detailed planning of the uprising and a political committee which formulated the program for the post-coup situation.

For a determined minority within the army, a protest that originated in professional concerns provided a cover for political objectives. The movement as a whole, however, consisted of men with divergent political views. Their coalescence was the result less of any uniform conspiratorial objective than of a convergence of resentments, loss of a sense of purpose, and emotional and intellectual estrangement from the long colonial wars. Despite conventional wisdom, the work of the young officers had to be liberalizing and liberating. The intransigence of the Portuguese regime and its commitment to the wars made that inevitable. "The Revolution had come from the Left," one officer commented in April 1974; "after fifty years of right-wing dictatorship, where else could it come from?"

It is important to emphasize this point since it serves to demonstrate an important difference between the Portuguese case and the other democratic transitions of the 1970s and 1980s in Europe and Latin America. In every other case a vital element in the process of democratization was the extraction of the military (in most cases a military regime) from power. By contrast, in Portugal it was the military that destroyed a fundamentally nonmilitary authoritarian system. Whereas elsewhere the military saw its institutional interests best served by removing themselves from the political area, in Portugal the military saw their institutional

---

1 On the origins and growth of the MFA, see Douglas Porch, *The Portuguese Armed Forces and the Revolution* (Stanford: Hoover Institution Press, 1977); *Insight on Portugal: The Year of the Captains* (London: André Deutsch, 1975); Denis de Almeida, *Origins e evolução do movimento de Capitaes* (Lisbon: Edições Sociais n.d.); Otelo Saraiva de Carvalho, *Alvorada em April* (Lisbon: Bertrand, 1977); Jacinto Baptista, *Caminhos para uma Revolução* (Lisbon: Bertrand, 1975); Avelino Rodrigues, Cesario Borga, and Mário Cardoso, *O Movimento de Capitães e o 25 de Abril* (Lisbon: Moraes, 1974); George Grayson, "Portugal and the Armed Forces," *Orbis* 19 (Summer 1975): 335-78. Also see Thomas Bruneau, "The Portuguese Coup: Cause and Probable Consequences," *The World Today* 30, no. 7 (July 1974): 277-88; António Rangel Bandeira, "The Portuguese Armed Forces Movement: Historical Antecedents, Professional Demands, and Class Conflicts," *Politics and Society* 6, no. 1 (1976); and Marcio Moreira Alves, *Les Soldats Socialistes du Portugal* (Paris: Gallimard, 1975). Also Philippe C. Schmitter, "Liberation by *Golpe*: Retrospective Thought on the Demise of Authoritarian Rule in Portugal," *Armed Forces and Society* 2, no. 1 (November 1975): 5-33.

future (in fact, the avoidance of outright military defeat in Guinea-Bissau) as being served by a coup....

Reform or Revolution

At first the most characteristic reaction abroad to the successful coup d'état of 25 April 1974 was uncertainty. At home it was euphoria—a springtime of exuberance which gave the revolution its popular identification as the "revolution of flowers" after the red carnations with which the victorious soldiers adorned themselves and their rifles.

Civil society was caught by surprise at the suddenness and rapidity of the young officers' success. During the weeks prior to the coup, the Armed Forces Movement (MFA) had deliberately kept away from the civilian opposition for reasons of security. The clandestine political parties were known to be thoroughly infiltrated by the secret police. Nevertheless, opposition to the dictatorship had always existed and provided almost automatically a cadre of civilian collaborators for the military in the vacuum that had emerged. The old republicans had never accepted the corporate state and its Fascist overtones, for instance, even if their countless platforms of dissent never came close to shaking the formidable apparatus of censorship, repression, and cultural uniformity that Salazar imposed. The Communist party had been the most serious thorn, and had in consequence suffered the most severe repression.

Although no one under seventy had ever voted in anything resembling a free election under the dictatorship, local political organizations called "democratic election commissions" (CDE) did exist throughout Portugal. They were used principally (most recently in 1973) as an opportunity for criticism and debate during the regime's periodic contests for seats in the National Assembly. The electoral system itself was stacked in the regime's favor, and opposition groups regarded the whole affair as a fraud. Nevertheless, the opportunities were used to articulate a forceful critique of the dictatorship's positions. The CDE was comprised of coalitions of "anti-Fascist forces," mainly middle-class liberals, Social Democrats, Catholic radicals, independent Marxists, and the Communists (PCP)....

The program of the Armed Forces Movement which was incorporated into the institutional provisions, providing a framework and timetable for the transition, called for a long period in which a new political system was to be defined. During this time, the new political parties had to find their public, and face preelectoral struggles.[5] Constituent Assembly elections were to take place within one year from 25 April 1974. In another year a parliament and president were to be elected under terms to be drawn up by the Constituent Assembly.

Apart from the Communists, no party possessed a strong organization. In the weeks immediately after the coup, the PCP took full advantage of this organizational advantage to take over key positions, especially in the

---

5 For constitutional amendments following the 25 April coup d'état, see Orlando Neves, ed., *Textos históricos da Revolução*, 3 vols. (Lisbon: Diabril, 1974-76).

trade unions and the municipalities. The Communist-dominated union coordinating organization, Intersindical, became the basis of Portugal's new trade union federation. In trade unions that had formerly been controlled by supporters of the old regime, Communist leaders were quickly elected to replace the old leaders. Also on the initiative of the Communists, new unions were organized for groups whose unionization had been prohibited by the old regime—most particularly public employees and farmworkers. In most of the country's municipalities, new councils were elected by public assemblies, the Communists often taking key positions or securing places for reliable allies.[6]

After April 1974, however, a large part of the population, intensely traditionalist and conservative, found themselves without spokesmen. Temporarily muted by the speed with which the power of the state had evaporated, the conservative rural peasantry and the Catholic community constituted a political constituency of some importance. The principal new political organizations of 1974, therefore, were not those of the Left, most of which existed before the coup and had longstanding relations with one another, but the fledgling parties of the Center and the Right....

Despite the Left's apparently formidable assets in March 1975—control of the administration, unions, army, the media, and the political initiative—the Left's ascendancy proved short-lived. By the end of November 1975 the Left was disunited, weakened, and on the defensive.

Three aspects of those turbulent months help explain this reversal of circumstances. First, the all-important alliance with the military radicals failed. The MFA leadership split into various factions, all ostensibly "on the Left," but each with a different view of tactics and objectives. Simultaneously, discipline collapsed within the armed forces, and it did so more quickly among the "leftist" units than among the centrist or rightist units. Second, the decolonization process, which had helped cement the MFA's internal solidarity, became, after March 1975, a major irritant and divider as the situation in Angola proved increasingly intractable and as outsiders intervened there at will. Third, the economic situation in Portugal became increasingly precarious, allowing outsiders leverage which they had lacked before; during the summer of 1975 the Western governments made it clear to Lisbon that economic assistance would be dependent on political good behavior.

The behavior of the Portuguese Communist party was also an important element in the equation since by late 1974 Communist action had alienated powerful elements of the Portuguese Left which had previously collaborated with the Communists in the anti-Fascist struggle. Most especially and dramatically, the Communists were alienating the rapidly expanding Socialists led by Mário Soares.... The Communists also made several major tactical blunders: they misread the balance of forces within Portugal and hence the power of their enemies; they also misunderstood the psychological impact of some of their actions, throwing potential allies

---

[6] For a good account of Portugal after the coup, see Avelino Rodriguês, Cesario Borga, and Mário Cardoso, *Portugal depois de Abril* (Lisbon: Intervoz, 1976).

into the embrace of their opponents. Finally, the election returns of April 1975 were a startling setback for the Communists and the military radicals, demonstrating graphically that although the Portuguese desired change they wished that change to be brought about by democratic means.

It was the elections that came first. Ironically, much of the foreign press, obsessed with the power of the Communists, dismissed the elections of 1975 as being of minor significance. They were wrong. In reality, the elections were of enormous significance, and their importance was well recognized once the results were in. In one of the highest turnouts ever recorded in a national election (91.7 percent), Soares's Portuguese Socialist party took 37.9 percent of the vote; the Popular Democrats, 26.4 percent; Cunhal's Communists a mere 12.5 percent nationwide, and the PCP's sister party, the Portuguese Democratic Movement (MDP/CDS), a mere 4.1 percent; the conservative CDS got 7.6 percent.[9]

PURGES AND COUNTER-PURGES

António Costa Pinto, "The Radical Right in Contemporary Portugal"*

Some specific features of the transition to democracy, such as the lack of compromise with the old regime's elite and "anti-Fascist" radicalism of 1974-75, deeply affected the overall political realignment of the Portuguese right. For the radical right, this new situation was devastating, [not only] politically and organisationally, but ideologically as well.

In the first two years, while political parties were set up and the new constitution was approved, the radical right was affected by a number of electoral prohibitions, political *saneamento* (purges) and party bans. Hence, any quick reconversion of the elite of Salazarism or—at the outset—of the groups discussed here was impeded.[41]...

In the context of the transition to democracy in Southern Europe in the 1970s, the *saneamento* movement, which started immediately after the coup and developed throughout 1975, was a singularity of the Portuguese

---

[9] For the elections, see especially Nuno Vitorino and Jorge Gaspar, *As Eleições de 25 Abril: Geografia e imagem dos partidos* (Lisbon, Horizonte, 1976); B. Pimlott, "Parties and Voters in the Protuguese Revolution," *Parliamentary Affairs*, Winter 1977. Also see the important analysis by John Hammond in *Contemporary Portugal: The Revolution and Its Antecedents*, ed. Lawrence Graham and Harry Makler (Austin: University of Texas, 1979). For good background analyses of this period, see Avelino Rodrigues, Cesario Borga, and Mário Cardosa, *Portugal: Depois de Abril* (Lisbon, Bertrand, 1976) and Gianfranco Pasquino, *Le Portugal: De la dictature corporatiste à la démocratie socialiste* (Association française de Science politique, Round Table 6-7 May 1977); T. Bruneau, "Portugal: Problems and Prospects in the Creation of a New Regime," *Naval War College Review* 29 (Summer 1976); Jonathan Story, "Portugal's Revolution of Carnations," *International Affairs* 52, no. 3 (July 1976).

* Excerpted from António Costa Pinto, "The Radical Right in Contemporary Portugal," in Luciano Cheles, Ronnie Ferguson, & Michalina Vaughan, eds., *Neo-Fascism in Europe* (Longman, 1991), pp. 175-177, 180-182.

[41] For an introduction to the *saneamentos* (literally 'cleanings out'), the political purges after the fall of the regime, see A. Costa Pinto, 'Revolution and Political Purge in Portugal's Transition to Democracy', in S.U. Larsen (ed.), *Modern Europe after Fascism, 1945-1980s*, Norweigan University Press, Bergen (forthcoming).

case.[44] Although it was ultimately rather limited, as was the whole process of "defascistisation" after the Second World War, it still had significant consequences in that it prevented a rapid readjustment by most of the old regime's political personnel.

The first measures of the National Salvation Junta [*Junta de Salvação Nacional*, JSN], presided over by General Spínola, were directed towards a rapid and straightforward purge programme. The former president of the republic and the prime minister, together with some ministers, were exiled. The paramilitary and the police groups (the political police and the old anti-Communist militia, LP), who attempted resistance, were dissolved and a part of their elite entourage arrested. The single party, the official youth organisation and other institutions from the fascist era were also dissolved. The Armed Forces Movement (*Movimento das Forças Armadas*, MFA), which led the coup, proposed to retire 60 generals, the majority of whom had participated, some time before, in a public demonstration of solidarity with the old regime.[45]

The first legislation on *saneamento* included the demise of the civil service and the loss of political rights of all presidents of the republic, ministers, and national leaders of the single party, and of the LP. At the local level, the clandestine and semi-legal opposition to the old regime—particularly the Portuguese Democratic Movement [*Movimento Democrático Português*, MDP], a front organisation connected with the Communist Party [*Partido Communista Português*, PCP]—occupied the majority of the town councils and expelled their previous leaders. The old corporative unions were occupied by the leaders, the majority of whom were affiliated to the Communist Party. The pressure of left-wing political movements and the effect of "liberation" prevented any action, which could have permitted the survival of the institutions and the national political elite of the dissolved regime, against the initial wish of Spínola.

The first policy declarations of the left-wing parties were, in general, fairly cautious as far as *saneamentos* were concerned. The Socialist Party asked in its first communiqué for "the removal of all those directly involved in the previous government". The Communists also made rather moderate declarations. Nevertheless, the first *saneamentos* occurred in various sectors, and the demands for purges were part of the first workers' strikes. In the Universities of Lisbon and Coimbra, lecturers and staff who had co-operated with the former regime were denied entrance by the students' unions.

---

44 On this subject, see G. O'Donnell and P.C. Schmitter, *Transitions from Authoritarian Rule. Tentative conclusions about uncertain democracies*, The Johns Hopkins University Press, Baltimore and London, 1986.

45 On the coup and the Armed Forces Movement, see O. Saraiva de Carvalho, *Alvorada em Abril*, Bertrand, Lisbon, 1977, and D. de Almeida, *Origem e Evolução do Movimento dos Capitães*, Edições Sociais, Lisbon, 1977; see also P.C. Shmitter, 'Liberation by *Golpe*', *Armed Forces and Society II* (Nov. 1975), pp. 5-33; Douglas Porch, *The Portuguese Armed Forces and The Revolution*, Croom Helm, London, 1977; and, on the military in the twentieth century Portugal, M. Carrilho, *Forças Armadas e mundanças politica em Portugal no século* XX, Imprensa Nacional, Lisbon, 1985.

In response to these spontaneous movements, the provisional government issued the first regulations on civil servant *saneamentos* creating an inter-ministerial re-classification committee in order to bring to justice those who might reveal behaviour "contrary to the established order after 25 April 1974".[46] This committee functioned until 1976 and the legislation was reviewed several times, thus revealing the radicalisation of the political situation. At the beginning of 1975, the legal text itself referred to the previous regime as "Fascist regime" and the behaviour of civil servants before the revolution became subject to *saneamento*.[47]

After Spínola's overthrow, the anti-capitalist thrust of events provoked a second wave of purges. Individual *saneamentos* were encouraged. The nationalisation of the most important firms and the expropriation of the great land-owners were called for. These two groups were considered the supporters of the previous regime by the two main agents of the second part of the process—the PCP and the ultra left-wing groups, which dominated the Portuguese revolution until the end of 1975. Purging and anti-capitalism were strictly connected in the second period.

In February 1975, the official reports on the purge process declared that 12,000 citizens were involved.[48] Between March and November 1975, this figure must have significantly increased, since, by 25 November 1975, when the purge movement was suspended, this number was approximately 20,000, if we consider all types of punishments: from the simple transfer to dismissal from work.

The proponents of the purge process were many and varied. If we exclude the first measures of the JSN immediately following the coup, it was, however, essentially the PCP and the small but influential extreme-left parties which led the movement.

The demands for purges were often led by workers' commissions, independent of the unions and organised according to place of work (the so-called *Comissões de Trabalhadores*), where the PCP had to share control with the extreme-left parties. Most of the "wildcat purges" were implemented by these committees which occasionally escaped the control of the PCP bureaucracy.

In general, the purge movements did not keep to clear strategies and coherent patterns, being extremely diverse from sector to sector. The concept of "collaborator" changed during the period of "exception". In 1974, the first purge movement was based on a strict concept of collaboration, but in 1975, with the burgeoning anti-capitalist wave, a number of traditional attitudes held by industrialists were considered as symbols of the old regime.

The purge deeply affected the top cadres of Salazarism, most of whom went into exile or retreated into political silence without giving much symbolic commitment to the reorganisation of the radical right at the time....

---

[46] See Decree-law No. 277/74 of 25 June 1974, *Diário do Governo*, 1st ser., No. 146, p. 744.

[47] See Decree-law No. 123/75 of 11 March 1974, *Diário do Governo*, 1st ser., No. 59, p. 375.

[48] *O Século*, Lisbon, 27 Feb. 1975.

The end of the revolutionary period and the gradual establishment of democracy from 1976 onwards led to the vanishing of illusions about an extreme-right restoration, and even about the minimum programme on which any such organisation could be based. The return of exiles to Portugal, the growing press activity of those who had been "plundered" in 1974-75, and the search for anti-Communist "military heroes", ended without leaving any trace. Decolonisation, made worse by the inability to mobilize the *retornados*, marked the end of an era in the political culture of the radical right.

The reintegration process of purged individuals went forward between 1976 and the early 1980s. Based upon new legislation, the most rapid measures were taken in the economic sector, where the "wildcat purge" had been strongest. The governments implemented a set of incentive measures aimed at the return of emigrés or purged managers, in a climate of economic crisis and negotiations with the International Monetary Fund. The law declared that the purge of citizens for political or ideological reasons, occurring between 1974 and 1976, was legally non-existent.

Within the civil service, new legislation invited purged people to apply for rehabilitation. The purge committees were dismantled, and a rehabilitation commission was set up, which worked until the 1980s and rehabilitated individuals in the majority of the cases presented. However, in the light of present knowledge it seems that "reintegration" did not mean a return to former positions. For example, in the case of the armed forces, the old elite remained in reserve or retired. Because of complicated administrative processes, it took longer to reintegrate the victims of legal purges.

In the same period an anti-leftist purge developed: militants from the extreme left and the PCP were dismissed from the media, state departments and public enterprises. This was particularly evident in the Ministries of Agriculture and Work, and in the nationalised banks where Communists had exerted a strong presence.

With the renegotiation of the pact between the democratic parties and the inheritors of the MFA, and the disappearance of military tutelage, some leading figures of the old regime returned to Portugal. The President, Tomás (who remained politically silent until his death), and some ministers returned from Brazil, and only Marcello Caetano refused permission to return, and died in Brazil in 1980.

However, these figures were not associated with a possible future revival of the native radical right, and the old ministerial elite of Salazar died in silence. Exceptions prove this rule: only one ex-minister made a political career in the new democracy: Adriano Moreira, former Minister of Overseas Territories, who was deputy and general secretary of the CDS for a short period. Two reformist ministers of Caetano's were brought back into the fold: the Secretary of State for Corporations, who introduced the liberalisation of the unions before the end of the regime, and also the architect of the education reform.

The new political climate of "political reconciliation", which characterised the end of the 1970s, influenced some processes connected with the inheritance of the old regime, e.g., in the case of the members of the ex-political police.

Despite efforts by some military sectors to save the colonial branch of the political police, the entire body was, after brief resistance, totally dismantled. In 1974, in an atmosphere of persecution, those who had not fled spent the two years of the period of exception awaiting trial. Their trials were already organised in accordance with the new political ethos. Consequently, those who had not taken advantage of conditional freedom to emigrate were lightly punished by military courts, which were especially lenient towards those with good military records.

The end of the 1970s, with the gradual withdrawal of the military from the political arena, the consolidation of parliamentary parties, and the settling down of their electorate, ended any chance of political reconversion for some populist military figures, tempted to capitalize on the success of their anti-leftist action in 1975.

CONCLUSION

*Kenneth Maxwell, "Regime Overthrow and the Prospects for Democratic Transition in Portugal"**

The democratic regime inaugurated by the 1976 Constitution ... had two distinct legacies which strongly affected the attitudes of those who had to work within its rules—one legacy came from the reaction against half a century of right-wing dictatorship, but no less important was the legacy that came from the reaction against a traumatic encounter with the authoritarian Left. The politicians of the new regime, especially the Democratic Socialists, Centrists, and Christian Democrats, therefore, had as clear a view of the threat to them represented by the Communists as they did of the threat from the Right....

The essence of the Portuguese dilemma in the 1980s, in fact grows out of the ambiguous result of the struggles of 1975. In Portugal the outcome of the conflict was not clear-cut and remains in many ways unresolved. There were no martyrs such as Allende and no generals like Pinochet. Neither Left nor Right won outright. In fact, a most unlikely hybrid emerged and looked to all intents and purposes like a Western liberal and representative democracy, even if in many respects Portuguese democracy was constrained and hampered by the heritage of a long dictatorship and a tumultuous flirtation with revolution.

The break with the past after 1974 was profound to be sure. But the Portuguese Revolution was half finished. Its propagandists became isolated from the majority of the population and fell out among themselves, and as they squabbled, the tide turned. The counterrevolution

* Excerpted from Kenneth Maxwell, "Regime Overthrow and the Prospects for Democratic Transition in Portugal," in Guillermo O'Donnell, Philippe C. Schmitter and Laurence Whitehead, eds., *Transitions from Authoritarian Rule: Southern Europe* (The Johns Hopkins University Press, 1986), pp. 133, 135.

was only partly successful. The compromise that resulted was thus based on two contradictory views of social and political organizations, each rooted in its own powerful but polarized social base. Both coexisted within the same system only because they possessed neither the power to overthrow it nor the desire to face the bloody consequences of the attempt to seize supremacy, although under changed circumstances the forces of the Right might be just as tempted to make the attempt as the Communists were in 1975.

The political system of Portugal that emerged after 1976, therefore, is based on a truce [between Right and Left], a truce that muted but did not resolve the hostilities. The settlement embodied in the 1976 Constitution is thus paradoxically both remarkably stable and extremely fragile. The contradictions beneath the compromise, however, are part of the explanation for the inability of the constitutional governments to act effectively or to resolve the structural problems that Portugal must solve.

9

SPAIN

EDITOR'S INTRODUCTION

General Francisco Franco emerged victorious from the Spanish Civil War in 1939 and proclaimed "a totalitarian state with the mission to give direction to the people." During his 46-year dictatorship, he concentrated in himself several roles, including prime minister, head of state, chief of the armed forces, and leader of the official political organization, the National Movement. (The National Movement incorporated the key bases of Franco's power: the military, monarchists, the extremist "falange" movement, and the Catholic church.) Franco vowed that competing political parties would never again be permitted. Although a compliant parliament (*Cortes*) still existed, Franco selected a significant portion of its members. A 1947 law declared a restoration of the monarchy, with the future king to be designated by Franco; he announced his choice of Prince Juan Carlos de Borbón y Borbón in 1969—although there was to be no ascension to the throne until after Franco's death.

Franco maintained tight control over Spanish society. In the first years of the regime, those who had supported the defeated republican government during the civil war were eliminated. All publications were censored and all associations and public meetings were made illegal without prior government approval, with the exception of those of the Catholic Church. Divorce was banned and religious education became compulsory in the public schools. Labor unions and strikes were also banned, with workers forced into official state syndicates. Concerned about regional and ethnic separatism, particularly in the Basque, Catalan, and Galician parts of the country, Franco attempted to suppress any expression of ethnic culture or tradition, prohibiting the use of any native language other than

Spanish even in one's home. Various separatist groups, most notably the Basque ETA, took up terrorist activity, and a cycle of violence and counter-violence escalated.

The dictatorship became somewhat milder over time. By the mid-1960s, economic controls were slowly loosened by a group of largely Western-educated technocrats loyal to Franco. Prior censorship was ended, as was legal discrimination against non-Catholic religious groups and beliefs. In 1967, *Cortes* membership and the right to vote were each expanded. By the 1970s, growing separatist violence was accompanied by more active dissent from students, labor, elements within the church, and even from the newly emergent middle class. In response, repression escalated during the final years of the regime. Franco vowed to leave a society which would not easily shed the institutions and approach of his regime—a society which was, in his words, "tied down and well tied down."

In 1973, the ailing Franco named Luis Carrero Blanco prime minister. Carrero Blanco was assassinated a few months later by Basque terrorists and was succeeded by Carlos Arias Navarro. On November 20, 1975, Franco died. Juan Carlos was crowned King two days later. In 1976, the reform-minded Juan Carlos had Arias replaced as prime minister by Adolpho Suárez González, who in turn appointed a more democratically inclined cabinet. The use of native languages was permitted for the first time in nearly forty years. The Public Order Tribunal, which had been a key element in the system of repression, was closed. In 1977, a new bicameral legislature was popularly elected; its membership ranged from conservative Francoists (dubbed the "bunker" for their resistance to any reforms) to Communists to Basque nationalists. On December 29, 1978, a new constitution took effect, declaring Spain to be a parliamentary monarchy and guaranteeing basic rights. Changes were made in the police, including the replacement of a limited number of senior officials.

The demand from the far left for a *ruptura* with the Francoist past failed, however, and the transition proceeded without a radical break. Early reforms to dismantle the Franco regime complied with the existing laws. A substantial portion of Franco's network was absorbed into the new state structures. Although a number of senior political people were dismissed, many Franco appointees retained their positions throughout the government. The "National Movement," for example, was dissolved in 1977 and its property was transferred to the state, but much of the party organization was folded into government ministries. The employees of party-related organizations were converted into civil servants. The same was true of other Franco-era institutions.

In keeping with this non-confrontational approach to the legacy of the former regime, police files from the long Franco era were not used to purge those implicated in the abuses of the regime; these files have remained sealed to the present day. In 1976, Juan Carlos issued a royal amnesty for many convicted of political crimes, excluding those sentenced for acts of terrorism. In 1977, the newly elected parliament approved an amnesty which covered all political crimes previously committed by both government forces and the opposition. Professor Fernando Rodrigo has provided a useful glimpse of the parliamentary debate over this amnesty. A Communist representative stated that "amnesty must be the cornerstone of this policy of national reconciliation. How can we be capable of reconciliation after years of killing each other if we don't have the capacity to forget our past forever?" In advocating an "amnesty of everybody to everybody," another legislator noted that the new parliament forced "together people who have spent many years in jail or exile and people who have been in Government and have caused these years of exile and prison ... because that is the expression of what is happening in our society at large." Prime Minister Suárez summarized the attitude which characterized the Spanish transition as follows: "The question is not to ask people where they are coming from, but where they are going to."

THE GRADUAL TRANSITION

José María Maravall and Julián Santamaría,
*"Political Change in Spain and the Prospects for Democracy"**

This chapter deals with the processes of transition to, and consolidation of, Spanish democracy. In the mid-1970s Spain was still ruled by a repressive and exclusive authoritarian regime which arose from the 1936-39 Civil War. In the early 1980s a constitutional and politically responsible government was established in the country, several elections were celebrated, the protection of human and civil rights was guaranteed, and a competitive political party system existed. In other words, the old authoritarian regime was replaced by a different, democratic one.

Obviously, the new regime could be described as a "fragile" or "difficult" democracy. Furthermore, the presence of certain elements of continuity could give rise to speculation as to whether the change in regime had been complete or not. But there could be no doubt whatsoever that the configuration of political institutions in force in 1980 was not the same as that which had existed in 1974....

Origins, Dimensions, and Scope of the Crisis

The transition from authoritarian rule to democracy took place in Spain not by means of a radical break with the previous regime, or through

* Excerpted from José María Maravall and Julián Santamaría, "Political Change in Spain and the Propects for Democracy," in Guillermo O'Donnell, Philippe C. Schmitter and Laurence Whitehead, eds., *Transitions From Authoritarian Rule: Southern Europe* (The Johns Hopkins University Press, 1986), pp. 71, 73.

a process of self-transformation by the regime itself.[7] It was rather the product of a series of pacts and negotiations in which several political actors were the key protagonists. The Spanish terms *rupture pactada* and *reforma pactada* are expressive of this ambiguity. The former underlines the lack of political continuity between the two regime types and the principles of legitimation that support them, and the latter emphasizes the element of legal continuity through which the change was put into practice, with a high degree of formal respect for the legality of Franco's political system. In any case, both formulas emphasize the significance of agreement, consent, or compromise during the political operation that permitted the substitution of one regime for another.

Edward Malefakis, "Spain and Its Francoist Heritage"[*]

[T]he Spanish process [of transition was] more organic and evolutionary than that of any other examined in this volume. In dealing with the latter regimes, one can begin one's study of the restoration of democracy on the day of the fall of the antecedent regimes without sacrificing much richness of analysis. In Spain, however, the events after November 20, 1975, would be completely incomprehensible if one did not understand what had transpired during the previous two decades. Unlike the situation elsewhere, the past in Spain was not connected to the present solely in an adversary role; a far more complex relationship existed, blending antagonism with parentage. Democracy in Spain was made possible only because it was preceded by a long period of what might loosely be called protodemocratization. This period is therefore as deserving of examination as the one following Franco's death....

José María Maravall and Julián Santamaría, "Political Change in Spain and the Prospects for Democracy"[†]

When the profound economic crisis of the late 1950s demonstrated the exhaustion of the economic model introduced after the Civil War, and the fragility of the grounds on which the regime was based, the existing policies of economic self-sufficiency were replaced by a new development

---

7 Nevertheless some authors have described the Spainish transition as a process of self-transformation. See Guy Hermet, "Esagne: Changemont de la Société, Modernization Autoritaire de la Démocratie Octroyée," *Revue Francaise de Science Politique* 27, nos. 4-5 (1977): 582-600. Simlarly, Gianfranco Pasquino, "La difficlie democrazia in Spagne," *Il Mulino* 27, no. 4 (1981): 595-624. Also, José Casanova, "Modernization and Democratization: Reflections on Spain's Transition to Democracy, Social Research 50, no. 4 (1983): 929-73.

* Excerpted from Edward Malefakis, "Spain and Its Francoist Heritage," in John H. Herz, ed., *From Dictatorship to Democracy: Coping with the Legacies of Authoritarianism and Totalitariansim*, Copyright © 1982 by John Herz (Greenwood Press, 1982), p. 216, an imprint of Greenwood Publishing Group, Inc. Westport, CT. Reprinted with permission.

† Excerpted from José María Maravall and Julián Santamaría, "Political Change in Spain and the Propects for Democracy," in Guillermo O'Donnell, Philippe C. Schmitter and Laurence Whitehead, eds., *Transitions From Authoritarian Rule: Southern Europe* (The Johns Hopkins University Press, 1986), pp. 74-75.

strategy for survival.[8] These policies were directed toward rapid industrialization and modernization of the economy by encouraging the import of foreign capital on a massive scale, persuading unemployed manpower, particularly from the agricultural sector, to emigrate either to the EEC (European Economic Community) nations or to the industrial areas of the country, and financing the overall project with international loans and aid, revenue from the tourist sector, and the emigrant remittances in foreign currency. Indiscriminate protectionism was abandoned; liberalizing measures were adopted; the Spanish economy was opened to competition; and the Spanish market was linked to international markets.

The revised economic strategy produced some spectacular results. Between 1960 and 1970 the industrial sector of the economy grew at an average yearly rate of 15 percent; the gross national product (GNP) and real salaries doubled; and productivity rose by an annual average of 7 percent. This rapid growth made it possible for the regime to preserve the passive consent of large segments of society at a safe level. These unprecedentedly explosive rates of change, however, also had some unintended consequences, which made it much more difficult for the regime to confine other social groups within the conservative patterns that had characterized the previous two decades.

First of all, rapid industrialization imposed more drastic changes upon the occupational and territorial distribution of the population than had been experienced in the first half of the century. For example, by 1950 about half the population was occupied in agriculture—a level unchanged since 1940. By 1970 less than a quarter of the population still remained in that sector. The industrial population rose from less than 25 percent in 1950 to over 37 percent in 1970, and approximately the same occurred in the service sector.

The redistribution of the working population brought with it massive migratory movements from the countryside to urban areas, giving a dramatic boost to the transfer of manpower that had begun in the 1950s. The figures are eloquent enough. In 1950 about 70 percent of Spaniards lived in towns and villages with fewer than 50,000 inhabitants. In 1970, only 55 percent still resided in them. In short, within an extremely brief period a predominantly agrarian and rural society had become a predominantly industrial and urban one, with a solid industrial working class and a renewed middle class on its way to consolidation.

Second, the liberalization and modernization of the economy could not have been achieved without a certain liberalization of industrial relations. Collective bargaining was legalized; a certain flexibility was introduced in the mechanisms of representation within the official syndicates; and penalties for strikers were reduced, although the right to strike was not acknowledged. This liberalization of industrial relations, coupled with the sudden economic expansion, the social mobilization, the imbalanced distribution of the social product, both at regional and at

---

8 Manuel-Jesús González, La Economia Politica del Franquismo (1940-1970)(Madrid: Tecnos, 1979), chap. 3.

individual levels, the rising expectations prompted by the general atmosphere of economic euphoria, led to widespread collective bargaining and a dramatic increase in industrial conflict.

*Edward Malefakis, "Spain and Its Francoist Heritage"**

No longer dependent on the dictatorship vis-á-vis labor relations, the economic elite tended to abandon it ideologically. The benefits that it conferred could be provided equally well by a stable democracy of the European type, and the regime increasingly came to be regarded as an obstacle to further economic growth. Some of its "social fascist" remnants, such as the protection of jobholders against dismissal, made more difficult the rationalization of production; of greater importance, its continuation prevented serious negotiations for Spanish entry into the EEC. The principal avenue for future economic expansion was blocked by the pariah status of an outmoded and no longer particularly useful political system.... By accepting association with Europe as the main, long-term goal of the Spanish economy, the government sharpened the contradictions that undermined it.

José María Maravall and Julián Santamaría, "Political Change in Spain and the Prospects for Democracy"†

Third, these changes in the "economic market" had a clear impact on the "political market," particularly in some working-class enclaves, the universities, and the historically autonomous regions such as Catalonia and the Basque country, where the democratic political organizations of the prewar years had managed to survive or where a number of new political organizations had emerged by the end of the 1950s. In the early 1960s, these organizations began openly to challenge the legitimacy of the regime, both internally and externally.

Edward Malefakis, "Spain and Its Francoist Heritage"‡

Other elite groups also drew away from the regime, although for reasons less directly related to economic change. This was true especially of the church, which responded to the new attitudes of the Spanish population by particularly far-reaching *aggiomamento* during the decade following the death of Pope John XXIII. It was also true in intellectual

---

* Excerpted from Edward Malefakis, "Spain and Its Francoist Heritage," in John H. Herz, ed., *From Dictatorship to Democracy: Coping with the Legacies of Authoritarianism and Totalitariansim*, Copyright © 1982 by John Herz (Greenwood Press, 1982), p. 220, an imprint of Greenwood Publishing Group, Inc. Westport, CT. Reprinted with permission.

† Excerpted from José María Maravall and Julián Santamaría, "Political Change in Spain and the Propects for Democracy," in Guillermo O'Donnell, Philippe C. Schmitter and Laurence Whitehead, eds., *Transitions From Authoritarian Rule: Southern Europe* (The Johns Hopkins University Press, 1986), p. 75.

‡ Excerpted from Edward Malefakis, "Spain and Its Francoist Heritage," in John H. Herz, ed., *From Dictatorship to Democracy: Coping with the Legacies of Authoritarianism and Totalitariansim*, Copyright © 1982 by John Herz (Greenwood Press, 1982), p. 220, an imprint of Greenwood Publishing Group, Inc. Westport, CT. Reprinted with permission.

circles, where greater freedom of expression and the huge expansion of university education permitted the swamping, both quantitative and qualitative, of the small and sterile intellectual establishment that had justified Franco's rule. Enthusiasm for the regime and the belief that it could survive its founder began to evaporate even within the principal organs of the state. Much of the bureaucracy, sectors of the army, many high-level administrators, and some ministers began to operate as autonomous technicians, for whom the particular form of government they served was not important as long as it was stable and effective. A complicated game began to be played in the late sixties by important leaders, such as Manuel Fraga, in which the minimal possible adherence to the regime was maintained while the main thrust of their activities was directed at staking out a strong position in the more liberal political system whose appearance was regarded as imminent.

José María Maravall and Julián Santamaría,
"Political Change in Spain and the Prospects for Democracy"[*]

Finally, and paradoxical as it may seem, the relative success of development policies during the 1960s weakened rather than strengthened the regime's internal cohesion. Franco closed the breach opened between Catholic and Falangist groups in the mid-1950s by simultaneously rejecting both the former's moderately "liberal" projects and the latter's attempts to increase the influence of the authoritarian movement within the state, although the conflict was to remain more or less latent and to resurface repeatedly during the 1960s and 1970s. A new group, the technocrats of the Opus Dei (a semisecret religious society of lay Catholics) entered the political scene as the main protagonists of the new economic policy. Beginning with the economic ministries that they first occupied in 1957, they gradually invaded other areas of government previously reserved for the exclusive influence of the Catholic or Falangist groups. The old coalitional equilibrium was thus broken and tensions among the regime factions increased. What was at stake from the mid-1960s was the hegemony within the coalition. These internal conflicts acquired a new dimension as Franco aged and each faction approached the succession problem with different perspectives and conflicting interests.[10] The disintegration of the coalition became more acute as the working classes grew more politically active and organized, and the democratic opposition began to reorganize itself. Thus, in spite of uninterrupted economic growth and unprecedented prosperity, the period from 1965 to 1975 was characterized by a gradual erosion of the regime's suppressive capabilities,

---

[*] Excerpted from José María Maravall and Julián Santamaría, "Political Change in Spain and the Propects for Democracy," in Guillermo O'Donnell, Philippe C. Schmitter and Laurence Whitehead, eds., *Transitions From Authoritarian Rule: Southern Europe* (The Johns Hopkins University Press, 1986), pp. 76-77.

[10] See Julián Santamaría, "Transición controlada y dificultades de consolidación: el ejemplo español," *Transición a la democracia en el Sur de Europa y América Latina* (Madrid: Centro de Investigaciones Sociológicas [CIS], 1982), pp. 382-85. Raymond Carr and Juan Pablo Fusi, *Spain, Dictatorship to Democracy* (London: George Allen & Unwin, 1979).

a progressive narrowing of its social support, and a continued disintegration of the internal balance and consistency of the ruling coalition. However short a period of time it may seem, three distinct phases can be defined in that process of deterioration and decay.

WEAKENING OF THE REGIME

*José María Maravall and Julián Santamaría, "Political Change in Spain and the Prospects for Democracy"**

The first covers the period from 1965 to 1968. It was marked above all by a qualitative jump in the combativeness of the working-class organizations that had emerged or reemerged at the beginning of the 1960s. If we take the number of working hours lost through strikes as an indication of working-class pressure, these rose from 1.5 million hours in 1966 to 7.8 million in 1970 and then to 14.5 million in 1975. This conflict was widely discussed by the recently liberalized press and it had a serious political impact. But at the same time, and in a more specific way, the working-class movement took on a political dimension. From 1963 to 1967 political demands had made up only 4 percent of all strike demands; after 1967 they escalated to 45 percent.[11]

This first phase was also marked by a more persistent and open conflict than before among the regime's factions. This conflict was linked to opposing views about the economic role of the state and the institutionalization of the regime.... The main issues involved the future of the Falangist movement as an organization and the succession problem. They were the cause of a serious confrontation between the technocrats of the Opus Dei and the bureaucrats of the Falange. The former proposed the dissolution of the movement into a loose, ideological framework, allowing political differentiation among the regime's factions and favoring immediate restoration of the monarchy and even the transfer of power from Franco to Juan Carlos so that the general could preside over the initial years of succession. The Falangists favored the postponement of any decision on this matter until Franco's death and demanded a tighter institutionalization of the movement within the structure of the state. In his memoirs, Manuel Fraga Iribarne located the "beginning of the great confrontations" in this period, more specifically in 1967.

The outcome of the confrontation was a stalemate. The Falangists achieved their goal of strengthening the role of the movement, while the technocrats managed to impose the nomination of Prince Juan Carlos as Franco's successor. The harsh struggle within the regime, however,

---

* Excerpted from José María Maravall and Julián Santamaría, "Political Change in Spain and the Propects for Democracy," in Guillermo O'Donnell, Philippe C. Schmitter and Laurence Whitehead, eds., *Transitions From Authoritarian Rule: Southern Europe* (The Johns Hopkins University Press, 1986), pp. 77-78.

11 On the workers' movement under Francoism, see J.M. Maravall, *Dictatorship and Political Dissent* (London: Tavistock, 1978).

hindered the development of the political "liberalization" inaugurated in 1966 with the Law of the Press. It also prevented the implementation of a strategy intended to divert the working-class movement by reforming trade union legislation, as had been planned. Finally, it made the continued coexistence of opposed factions within the cabinet almost impossible. In the summer of 1969, two cabinet members uncovered the biggest financial scandal in the history of the regime, in which several ministers and officers of the Opus Dei were implicated. Franco dismissed his cabinet in October 1969.

*Edward Malefakis, "Spain and Its Francoist Heritage"**

Against this erosion of commitment, the regime could offer little resistance. Never deeply ideological, the dictatorship had discarded perhaps its most important source of ideological support even before the boom period began by means of the final emasculation of the Falange in 1956-1957. Its backing among monarchists had always been ambivalent, capable at best of producing a marriage of convenience in which passion was lacking on both sides. Because of Spain's unusual history during the nineteenth century, militarism and nationalism had never emerged as viable bases for political legitimization and could certainly not be so constituted by a regime that had neglected military budgets and divested itself of its colonies without struggle. The dictatorship's legitimacy had come to rest entirely on the peace and order that it had restored to Spanish life and on the socioeconomic progress over which it presided. As the former started to be taken for granted and as ever wider sectors of the population and of most elite groups began to believe that the regime was no longer necessary for and might even have become a hindrance to consolidation of the latter, the justification for its continuation evaporated.

The regime could offer no model that exerted nearly so great an attractive force as that emanating from Europeanization. And Europeanization necessarily implied democratization....

The dictatorship could have avoided the impasse into which the dialectical process just outlined had placed it only if it had followed the suicidal course set by the Salazar/Caetano regime in Portugal of denying the reality of Europe and rigidly setting its sights on chimeras of its own invention. Not having done this from the start, such a shift in policy became more costly with each passing year as the distance between the new society and the old political machine that governed over it grew ever greater. The realm of illusion within which the Franco dictatorship sought to console itself was far more limited and less dangerous to future democratization than that of Salazar. Paradoxically, it consisted of the attempt by a regime born in lawlessness that ruled without the restraint of

---

* Excerpted from Edward Malefakis, "Spain and Its Francoist Heritage," in John H. Herz, ed., *From Dictatorship to Democracy: Coping with the Legacies of Authoritarianism and Totalitariansim*, Copyright © 1982 by John Herz (Greenwood Press, 1982), pp. 220-223, an imprint of Greenwood Publishing Group, Inc. Westport, CT. Reprinted with permission.

law for at least the first decade of its existence to create a legal framework that would ensure its survival.

The binding by which Franco, in his celebrated phrase, sought to "fasten, and securely fasten" Spain to his regime for all time was composed solely of formalistic legal arrangements—unreinforced either by societal ties or by genuine institutional reform. There was never a serious effort to win back the church; passive army allegiance was considered sufficient and no one sought to recreate the more intense involvement with the regime that had existed before; the "*contraste de pareceres*," the emergence of tolerated political associations that against all probability, might have transformed the moribund National Movement into an active state party, remained merely an aspiration of unreconstructed Falangists. The regime was too divided, its vigor had drained away, the risks seemed too great and the benefits too improbable for such measures to be taken. All that remained were the legal changes embodied in the Organic Law of the State of 1967, but even these were vitiated because Franco's refusal to step down denied the regime the opportunity to test and strengthen them during a transitional period. Personalistic rule continued, and the shadow it cast stunted the growth of the only arrangements, however inadequate, that the regime had made to ensure its peaceful preservation.

The dialectical processes generated by economic change profoundly affected not only the dictatorship but also its opposition.... The air of unreality that surrounded the endless debates and intricate maneuvers through which Francoism sought to "institutionalize" itself also characterized the even more complicated activities through which the opposition pursued its stated goal of overthrowing the regime. For opposition as for dictatorship, the pertinent changes that were taking place were mostly structural and beyond the control of individual actors.... The repressiveness of the Franco regime, once far greater than that employed by any of the other dictatorships discussed in this volume, against domestic enemies under peacetime conditions had grown very mild indeed. Despite memories of the past brutality, the subliminal recognition that *in extremis* the regime might resort to its original techniques, and the lapses—the 1970 Burgos trials, the harsh prison sentences meted out to *comisiones* leaders in 1974—that occasionally occurred, opposition to Franco had become something of a parlor sport for upper middle class youth whose risks were minimal. The catch phrase that was later jokingly employed—"against Franco, we lived better"—suggests a diminution of bitterness, even an inverted nostalgia, that would have been impossible had the regime remained a hard dictatorship (a *dictadura*) and not become a soft one (a *dictablanda*).

RETURN TO REPRESSION

José María Maravall and Julián Santamaría, "Political Change in Spain and the Prospects for Democracy"*

The second phase runs from 1969 to 1973. It was administered by an Opus Dei "mono-color" government under the leading figure of Admiral Carrero Blanco and was characterized by an increase in repressive policies aimed at undercutting working-class advances and undermining the democratic opposition.

During these years, at least 500 union leaders were arrested (in January and February 1974 alone, 24,818 workers were laid off and 4,379 fired for political activities). Some 2,000 worker representatives lost their jobs and three states of emergency were decreed. The repression was not only intensified, but also extended to other sectors. The university was permanently occupied by the police and a number of professors and students were confined to remote villages in the countryside, arrested, or dismissed from their positions. Opposition groups became a prime target for the police and the Tribunal de Orden Público (a special court for political crimes). In January 1970 alone, this court dictated 100 sentences in trials for "crimes of association and propaganda." The press suffered frequent attacks. Almost 700 sanctions were imposed on it, according to official statistics, between 1968 and April 1972, ranging from fines of 10,000 pesetas to the confiscation of offending newspapers, their temporary or permanent suspension. The sermons of certain priests were censored and the political activities of others led to imprisonment.

Although the intensified repression from 1968 to 1973 succeeded in containing the working-class movement, it was much less effective in controlling the mounting terrorist activities of ETA (Euskadi Ta Askatasuna-Basque Homeland and Freedom) and other groups. Moreover, it led to a spread of the political "contagion" to larger groups of students and university professors, indignant at the indiscriminate and brutal actions of the police and the paralysis of the universities. Repression and censorship also failed to prevent the hardest-hit newspapers from continuing daily to print the vindictive political cartoons that caustically caricatured the regime's unchanging and anachronistic attitude.

The greater internal solidarity within the "mono-color" cabinet, and its blocking of the "liberal" legislation that had been designed in the late 1960s to reestablish the coherence of the dictatorship, narrowed the bases of its social support and proved ineffective in neutralizing the regime's internal conflicts. Even more important, these conflicts were no longer confined to the cabinet. Confrontation set the government against the Falangist movement, while generational and tactical differences surfaced at all levels and in all institutional settings. The Catholic church ...

---

* Excerpted from José María Maravall and Julián Santamaría, "Political Change in Spain and the Propects for Democracy," in Guillermo O'Donnell, Philippe C. Schmitter and Laurence Whitehead, eds., *Transitions From Authoritarian Rule: Southern Europe* (The Johns Hopkins University Press, 1986), pp. 78-80.

finally broke its politically legitimizing ties. This action became publicly explicit when it published a document in 1971 acknowledging its error in taking sides in the Civil War.

The mounting evidence that immobilism and repression were as inadequate as they were ineffective led to a growing discontent within the economic elite, the highest levels of the public administration, and the middle classes. A serious political crisis—especially a collapse—would have resulted in social and economic catastrophe for them. For this reason, informal groups, frequently associated with a newspaper or magazine, arose; they questioned the viability of the system and put forward proposals for democratic reform based on legal continuity. The withdrawal of their support was a clear indication of the deep erosion of the regime's social bases. The survival of the regime was closely linked to the continuance in power of Carrero Blanco as a temporary guarantor of continuity.

His assassination by ETA in 1973 dashed this last hope. As López Rodo, his faithful adviser, put it: "His death meant the end of Franco's regime." From that moment, the regime went into an open crisis. The efforts of Carrero's successor, President Arias Navarro, to reconstruct the social bases of Franco's political system by giving new impulse to the "liberalizing" policies of the previous decade and by preparing the Statute for Political Associations failed dramatically. His strategy of liberalization (*apertura*) exacerbated the opposition of Franco's extremist supporters, the so-called Bunker, but did not attract moderate sectors of the democratic opposition. Nor did it isolate or divide the Left, which reacted by taking advantage of the increased freedom to give a final impulse to its reconstitution as a political force.

The extremists were able to rally Franco's support and succeeded in neutralizing the government's strategy of liberalization. They forced the minister responsible for freeing the press to resign and defeated the president in the debate on the Statute for Political Associations. Their success was seen as a clear indication of the regime's inability to adapt. The expectations generated by the liberalization policies were completely frustrated. Several groups belonging to the so-called civilized right wing emerged with the aim of backing some politically known figure who might lead the country toward an eventual pluralist or semipluralist outcome.

On the Left, by 1973, clandestine workers' organizations were regaining their momentum. Strikes in 1973 increased by 84 percent over 1972, and in 1974 by an additional 62 percent. During these two years Workers' Commissions (CCOO) began to recover from their repression, particularly in Madrid where they had been hardest hit.... [In 1975], the Plataforma de Convergencia Democrática including the Socialists, Social Democrats, Christian Democrats, the Basque Nationalist party, and some other smaller parties was formed. In spite of the fact that the democratic opposition remained divided from that moment, it had become a "credible alternative."

When Franco died in November 1975, the political pillars of the regime were already crumbling. The church had withdrawn its valuable support. The old political factions within the regime were deeply fragmented because of their differing views on a strategy for survival. Large sectors of the new industrial bourgeoisie saw the dictatorship as fully dispensable, considering it a political impediment to Spanish integration into the European Common Market. For their part, large sectors of the middle classes set their hopes on democracy. Most of the surveys conducted during this period demonstrated increasing support for democracy, particularly among the middle classes and educated people.

On the other hand, the regime's values no longer corresponded to those of a largely secularized society.[12] Its institutions lacked all authority and credibility. The regime's authorities were largely discredited because of their inability to counter terrorism effectively or to face the economic challenges, their complicity in brutal repressive practices, or their participation in the financial scandals that had come to light in the last few years, and which extended even to some members of the dictator's immediate family and entourage.

Nevertheless, faced with a divided opposition, and short of financial and organizational resources as well as of a solid social following, the remaining segments of the ruling coalition still retained their monopoly of the repressive apparatus, controlled the largest portion of the ideological apparatus, and could rely on a large part of the civil bureaucracy, as well as on an army recruited during the Civil War that was suspicious of democracy and firmly loyal to Franco's memory. It was this unequal and unstable equilibrium between democratic and antidemocratic elements that initially framed the transitional process in Spain.

THE IMMEDIATE POST-FRANCO PERIOD

*Edward Malefakis, "Spain and Its Francoist Heritage"**

The process of democratic restoration after November 20, 1975,... [l]ike the last years of Franco,... continued to be characterized by much ambiguity, as well as by considerable tension and conflict.

On the one hand, Franco's death brought an immediate and a dramatic shift in the framework of political aspirations. Press censorship, lightly enforced since the early 1970s, practically disappeared, and political parties, although still legally banned, began to organize and agitate openly. The new king, Juan Carlos, finally freed from the silence and impotence into which dependence on Franco had forced him, championed rapid liberalization in word and deed. Many ecclesiastics did the same,

---

12 See Rafael López Pintor and R. Buceta, *Los españoles de los años 70* (Madrid: Tecnos, 1975). Also Rafael López Pintor, *La opinión pública española: del franquismo a la democracia* (Madrid: CIS, 1982).

* Excerpted from Edward Malefakis, "Spain and Its Francoist Heritage," in John H. Herz, ed., *From Dictatorship to Democracy: Coping with the Legacies of Authoritarianism and Totalitariansim*, Copyright © 1982 by John Herz (Greenwood Press, 1982), p. 225, an imprint of Greenwood Publishing Group, Inc. Westport, CT. Reprinted with permission.

especially the church primate, Cardinal Tarançon. The major reformist figures of the preceding decade—Fraga and José Maria Areilza—reentered the cabinet in important posts. Other "establishment" dissidents, such as Antonio Garrigues, were also given ministerial positions.

On the other hand, the cabinet also included unreconstructed Francoists, such as Ramón Solis. It continued to be presided over by Arias Navarro, whose credentials as a reformer were tarnished because of the degree to which loyalty to Franco had caused him to retreat from his February 12, 1974, liberalization program. Above all, the legal arrangements that Franco had made in the late 1960s to ensure the continuity of his regime still bound Juan Carlos.

*José María Maravall and Julián Santamaría, "Political Change in Spain and the Prospects for Democracy"**

In purely legal terms, as Franco once said, "Everything was tied up and well tied up." When Franco died, Prince Juan Carlos was to succeed him as the head of state, with the title of king.... He would be under the tutelary advice of several institutions to which he was expected to be accountable. An example of these was the Consejo del Reino, in which the aristocracy of extremist Franco supporters remained entrenched. Therefore, King Juan Carlos was supposed to have only limited capacities to engineer an overt transformation of the old regime....

It seemed rather doubtful that this newly restored and weak monarchy could gain in strength and legitimacy by linking its fate to that of a decaying and largely delegitimized dictatorship. The examples of Spain in 1931, of Italy in 1946, and, more recently, of Greece in 1974 raised additional doubts on this score.

Within the regime itself, some readily understood that, under such conditions, the monarchy would not have much chance of achieving a solid institutionalization. Some sort of popular legitimation was needed. The plebiscite on the monarch advocated by some parties of the Left was not even considered. The recent experience in Greece was only one of the reasons for discarding that option. Instead, the idea that the institutionalization of the monarch required a democratic transformation gained ground among reformist sectors within the regime.... The king himself expressed a similar view before the Cortes when he accepted the crown in December 1975....

Prime Minister Arias Navarro never accepted the idea of transforming the inherited regime into a pluralist democracy. He reshuffled his cabinet to include some supposedly reformist figures, tried to divide the opposition with a policy of selective repression designed mainly to isolate the leftist parties, cautiously enlarged the margins of tolerance, and promised a project to introduce some type of controlled or limited democracy. His government never got off the ground. The opposition took the initiative

---

* Excerpted from José María Maravall and Julián Santamaría, "Political Change in Spain and the Propects for Democracy," in Guillermo O'Donnell, Philippe C. Schmitter and Laurence Whitehead, eds., *Transitions From Authoritarian Rule: Southern Europe* (The Johns Hopkins University Press, 1986), pp. 80-82.

during the crucial, post-Franco months, putting into practice a most effective strategy of "pressure from below." In the early months of 1976, the workers' movement showed unprecedented strength and combativeness. In 1976, the number of working hours lost through strikes reached 150 million (as compared to 14.5 million in 1975). The struggles and mobilizations were especially intense in the first three months of the year. In that period alone there were 17,731 strikes; whereas, in 1975, the year of the most widespread working-class militancy under Franco, there had been only 3,156.

The worker mobilization was coupled with the fusion of the Junta Democrática and the Plataforma de Convergencia into a single organization, Coordinación Democrática (CD), which expressed the common purpose of all democratic parties to force a transformation in the nature of the regime. CD included liberals, a fraction of the Christian-Democrats, Social Democrats, Socialists, Communists, Maoists, and the illegal trade unions. They resisted the divisive and isolating tactics of the government. Instead, they took advantage of the new margins of tolerance. In response to the persistently repressive actions taken by the government, every arrest of a leader, every abuse or provocation was used as an occasion for joint actions and massive demonstrations. The government responded with a spiral of repression and concessions, with moments of dramatic violence. In order to appease the "Bunker" at the end of April, Arias Navarro finally disclosed his "reformist" project, as well as his firm refusal to negotiate with the opposition.[14]

Only a few weeks later, the king himself confirmed his unease with that program. Before the United States Congress, he made explicit his desire for Spain to move toward a parliamentary democracy. On the other hand, in the Spanish Cortes, the immobile sectors of the "Bunker" struck the government a fatal blow by rejecting a bill that partially facilitated the legalization of some parties.

---

[14] The project was presented in a television address and was never entirely published. As it was known, it proposed a bicameral parliament. One of the chambers would be elected by universal suffrage, while the other would be of the corporatist type. The president of the government would be appointed by the king and selected from a set of three proposed by a council, which was not bound to take into account the electoral results.

The Suárez Approach: Democratization Without Rupture

*José María Maravall and Julián Santamaría, "Political Change in Spain and the Prospects for Democracy"**

Arias Navarro resigned. The main difficulty facing the government formed by Adolfo Suárez at the beginning of July was that of finding a way out of the impasse produced by the previous government. His declaration of program aimed at doing so. In it, he proclaimed the principle of popular sovereignty and his government's intention to work for the "establishment of a democratic political system." He also announced the granting of a political amnesty and he promised to submit to the nation, by way of a referendum, a project of constitutional reform which would include the celebration of general elections before 30 June 1977. The declaration thus fixed the government's objectives and the process intended to carry them out. This "legal" process respected the demands and conditions set by existing institutions and established powers (*poderes de hecho*), in clear opposition to the formula of *ruptura pactada*, advocated by the opposition. Nevertheless, this strategy basically coincided with the opposition's expressed aims and was in open conflict with the aspirations for continuity of important sectors within the regime. Thus, the government recovered the initiative and situated itself in an intermediate position between those in favor of rupture and those in favor of continuity.

The declaration also expressed the government's willingness to start talks with the most important groups in the regime and the opposition; informal contacts were initiated at once. But the cabinet's mediating and conciliatory strategy was, in the first phase, directed toward negotiating with the right wing. The church had already declared its support for the installation of a democratic system in December 1975. During the spring and summer, Suárez obtained the support of the financial aristocracy by assuring them that the reform would not jeopardize the foundations of the capitalist system. In September, with the king's backing, Suárez managed to coax consent out of the top military command by guaranteeing that the authorities within the armed forces and the civil administration would remain untouched, that the established legality would be scrupulously respected in putting the reform in practice, and that the Spanish Communist party would be excluded. The last impediments were the Consejo Nacional del Movimiento (National Council of the Movement), which was supposed to decree the projected Law for Reform into being, and the Cortes, still packed with Franco appointees, which was to approve it before submitting it to referendum.

---

* Excerpted from José María Maravall and Julián Santamaría, "Political Change in Spain and the Propects for Democracy," in Guillermo O'Donnell, Philippe C. Schmitter and Laurence Whitehead, eds., *Transitions From Authoritarian Rule: Southern Europe* (The Johns Hopkins University Press, 1986), pp. 82-84.

Both institutions were already somewhat conditioned in their response by the backing the government had obtained from the established powers and by the relatively favorable public response to the project. However, the government had to offer better guarantees in order to persuade the Francoist "political class" to go along. First, there were guarantees of personal continuity. Of the 500 Procuradores in the Cortes, some 80 reappeared in 1977 as deputies or senators. Detailed information on the composition of the boards of directors of public bodies between 1977 and 1982 is not available, but a study of these would probably be most revealing. Second, the government deleted the preamble to the project, which increased the margins of uncertainty about its final aim.[15] Whether or not the Cortes members would become "constituents" was left to the results of the subsequent election. In addition, certain amendments were admitted to the electoral system outlined in the project, which reinforced the possibilities for the electoral success of the conservative forces. The project was finally approved by the Cortes with 426 votes in favor, 59 against, and 13 abstentions. On 15 December 1976 it was ratified by referendum. The turnout was 78 percent; 94 percent of the voters approved the transition to democracy.

The successful outcome of the referendum considerably strengthened Suárez's position. He could interpret the favorable results as a sign of his own popular backing. The symbolic legitimacy of the democratic opposition groups was seriously damaged when they failed in their attempt to persuade the electorate not to vote. It was in this context that Suárez moved to negotiate with the Left, whose participation in the projected "founding" election was obviously essential. The opposition was represented by a Committee of Nine, ranging from liberal monarchists to Maoists and including Basque and Catalan nationalists. Suárez rapidly agreed to some of their basic demands. Among these were the extension of political amnesty, a proportional electoral law, legalization of the parties extended to cover the PCE (the Spanish Communist party), and the dissolution of the Movimiento (the single party created by Franco) and the Sindicatos Verticales (the state corporatist interest associations for workers and capitalists). The last was, however, the only reform directly affecting the political apparatus and personnel of the Franco regime. Even then, the syndicate bureaucrats were merely recycled into the regular state administration.

*Donald Share, "The Making of Spanish Democracy"**

A ... concession to the democratic opposition was the dismantling of franquist institutions. Since in transitions through transaction members of

---

[15] The uncertainty was so great that only 54 percent of the population thought that the approval of the law would lead to democracy, whereas 53 percent of those who abstained in the referendum thought it would not. See *La reforma política* (Madrid: CIS, 1977), p. 33.

* Excerpted from Donald Share, *The Making of Spanish Democracy*, Copyright © 1986 by Praeger Publishers and the Center for the Study of Democratic Institutions (Praeger Publishers, 1986), pp. 129-130, an imprint of Greenwood Publishing Group, Inc. Westport, CT. Reprinted with permission.

an authoritarian regime control the regime change, these same leaders must dismantle at least some parts of the regime to which they belong. That many leaders would be unwilling or unable to do so, as the case of Arias's presidency so clearly illustrated, seems obvious. Authoritarian institutions may enhance the leadership's ability to control the transition, and are thus surrendered only begrudgingly. Nevertheless, Suárez dismantled some of the most important franquist institutions before the June elections, and this helped to make the break between the authoritarian and democratic regimes less traumatic.

In early January, despite the crisis provoked by political violence, Suárez disbanded the infamous Tribunal of Public Order by decree-law. The tribunal had been established to deal with terrorism, but had effectively prosecuted all forms of opposition. Two other powerful franquist institutions were abolished by the start of the electoral campaign in June 1977: the National Movement and the Syndical Organization. The National Movement was abolished on April 7, when its familiar Falangist standard (the bow and arrows) was removed from its headquarters. Ironically, the fact that the MN was Suárez's own power base made it easier for the president to abolish the vast patronage network. His aides assured many MN officials that they would find government positions after the elections and that there was no danger of future recrimination. Influential National Movement bureaucrats were instrumental in asssuring hesitant MN members that they would be taken care of in the future. By June 2, when Suárez issued a decree law dismantling the powerful Syndical Organization, the Spanish public was already preoccupied with the ongoing electoral campaign. The voices of dissent were drowned out by campaign activity, the likes of which Spaniards had not experienced in over four decades.

*José María Maravall and Julián Santamaría, "Political Change in Spain and the Prospects for Democracy"**

The opposition groups were, in turn, compelled to make some important concessions. The idea of a government including both opposition and reformist groups was abandoned. In the same vein, the opposition groups had to renounce any policy of prosecution and punishment of those politically responsible authorities and officials involved in repressive activities under Francoism. The regionalist parties accepted a postponement of the process of territorial devolution until after the elections. The Left parties were unable to extract more progressive economic policies. They had to withdraw their republicanism and to admit to certain national symbols, as well as to a series of correctives to the proportionality of the electoral system that openly favored the conservative parties.

---

* Excerpted from José María Maravall and Julián Santamaría, "Political Change in Spain and the Propects for Democracy," in Guillermo O'Donnell, Philippe C. Schmitter and Laurence Whitehead, eds., *Transitions From Authoritarian Rule: Southern Europe* (The Johns Hopkins University Press, 1986), p. 84.

That the opposition made more concessions than necessary or showed more moderation than was needed are questions open to discussion. However the heterogeneity of the Committee of Nine made its survival as a "pressure block" unlikely, particularly when some of the moderate conservative groups represented in it were negotiating at the same time for the formation of the union (UCD). The concessions were also conditioned by the persistent threats against democratic reform that hovered over the transitional period, leading to periods of extreme violence and tension, such as the "Black Week" in Madrid (23-28 January 1977) when two students, five Communist lawyers, and five policemen were murdered. Although the pressures from the working-class movement remained intense until the June 1977 elections, they did not entail the mobilization of other sectors of society and were, therefore, insufficient to compel the government to yield to leftist claims. Finally, faced with the pending electoral challenge, the opposition parties had to consider the political and ideological predispositions of their presumed constituencies and not be misled by the views of their more active militants. In fact, popular attitudes were quite moderate. On an ideological scale of 1 to 10, over 40 percent of the population placed itself in the middle (positions 5 and 6). The average position was 5.47. Even the bulk of the working class proved rather moderate in its general political views.

From a different perspective, Suárez had considerable success in subduing the resistance of the continuist "hard-line" groups and in leading the democratic opposition to accept limitations, and the content and procedures of "legal reformism." His success made him the natural leader of a coalition of moderate parties—Liberal, Christian Democrats, populists, and Social Democrats—that he subsequently put together. These groups provided him with some form of democratic legitimacy, while he contributed his personal popularity and authority to make of the resultant UCD (Union of Democratic Center) a political party that was widely accepted and initially viable.

New Elections and a New Constitution

José María Maravall and Julián Santamaría,
"Political Change in Spain and the Prospects for Democracy" *

The second phase of the transition began with the general elections of 15 June 1977. The result of these elections would determine whether the new Cortes would meet as a Constituent Assembly and, if so, whether the new constitution it drafted would be more or less progressive and whether it could count on wider or narrower political support.

---

* Excerpted from José María Maravall and Julián Santamaría, "Political Change in Spain and the Propects for Democracy," in Guillermo O'Donnell, Philippe C. Schmitter and Laurence Whitehead, eds., *Transitions From Authoritarian Rule: Southern Europe* (The Johns Hopkins University Press, 1986), pp. 85-90.

The election ... results confirmed the moderation of the electorate and its desire for democratic change. The insignificant electoral support for the extreme Left (3.1 percent) and Right (0.6 percent) denied both parliamentary representation.... Their prospects for holding back the democratic process were severely deflated. The new Cortes would meet as a Constituent Assembly, which was agreed to at the first session. In the third place, the results established a clear electoral balance between Right and Left. The electorate was divided almost evenly between them. Only about 6 percent of the vote went to the regional parties. Within both Left and Right, the predominance of the centrist formations was clearly established.... The prospect that a constitution would be either imposed by force or impregnated with a marked ideological bias was greatly diminished.

The ... electoral results of 1977 implied an extension and renovation of the strategy of compromise and pact-making.... The first of these major efforts at compromise was aimed at reaching a social pact to face the economic crisis that began in 1973. The final Franco governments had lacked the authority to face it, and the first of the transition governments, concentrating their efforts on the solution of political problems, paid little attention to it. As a result, the deficit in the balance of foreign trade reached a record figure in the summer of 1977, while unemployment rose to 7.5 percent of the active population and inflation was running at a rate of nearly 30 percent. In order to deal with this situation it was necessary to apply a policy of austerity and reform which required the support of all partisan and trade union forces. The agreement took shape in September 1977 and was called the Pact of Moncloa. It was signed by the government, parliamentary parties, and trade unions, giving the government authority to freeze salaries, reduce public spending, restrict credit, and increase fiscal pressure. In exchange, the government promised to carry out a progressive tax reform, to make the social security system more efficient, to reorganize the financial system, and to put into practice a series of urgent political reforms....

The constitutional agreements were the ... most pivotal of the pacts reached at this stage of the transition process. They included, on the one hand, compromises between Left and Right and a set of guarantees conceded to established powers. Briefly, the rightist parties wanted a short constitution, institutionalizing the monarchy and protecting it against any threat of change by means of an extremely rigid procedure of constitutional amendment. They also insisted on explicit recognition of a free market economy and a strong, stable cabinet with clear supremacy over parliament. The leftist parties doubly conditioned their backing to the monarchy: (1) it should be a "parliamentary" monarchy with limited, well-defined powers; and (2) the rigidity of the amendment procedure should be extended to cover all possible revisions of a progressive and detailed bill of rights that was to preface the constitution. They accepted the principle of a market economy in exchange for recognition of the state's powers of economic initiative and its right to intervene in the economy. They accepted the principle of reinforced governmental stability within the framework of a greater equilibrium between government and parliament, in exchange for the insertion of proportionality within the constitution as the basis of any future electoral law.

These constitutional pacts could not overlook the significance of the established powers. Therefore, in addition to the guarantees provided for the existence of a capitalist economy, they recognized the special position of the Catholic church and the armed forces within the Spanish state. Although the constitution consecrated the secular character of the state, it also guaranteed the Catholic church's freedom to teach, to found educational institutions (not only schools), and to receive state subsidies to run them.

The constitution referred to the armed forces in its preliminary title as a symbol of the recognition and importance of their political role. They were charged with ensuring the sovereignty, independence, and territorial integrity of Spain. To this charge was added an explicit role as defenders of the constitutional order. Though the last clause was subject to some ambiguous interpretation, it was clear, in the light of other sections of the constitution, that the armed forces had not been elevated into what Carl Schmitt used to call the "defenders of the Constitution."[17] It rather stressed their submission to the basic law, while their constitutional duty of defending the territorial integrity of Spain helped to calm any possible unrest caused by the institutionalization of the "federal-regional" structure of the state. They were also put under the direct command of the king himself, an arrangement that satisfied some military claims without granting to the armed forces full corporate autonomy. The determination of the military policies and the administration were unequivocally assigned to the national executive.

The constitution was not only elaborated by compromise and consensus. It was passed almost unanimously by the Cortes. Only some of the AP's deputies voted against it, whereas the National Basque party abstained, as a protest against the refusal of the main parties to accept an amendment to the text concerning recognition of the "historical" territorial privileges of the Basque country. The constitution was ratified by a referendum in which 87.8 percent of the voters approved, with a rather considerable 32.3 percent of those eligible abstaining. After the parliamentary and municipal elections in the spring of 1979, the new regime was installed. The composition, organization, and functioning of its basic institutions, as well as the relations among them, conformed to the patterns established by the newly agreed-upon rules of the game. Transition, as we have defined it, was practically at an end. The problem now was consolidation.

Problems of Consolidation

The consolidation of democracy means guaranteeing the necessary conditions for the regime's regular functioning, its autonomy, and its

---

[17] See articles of the Constitution 8, 28, 29, 62, 117, and 149. As for Carl Schmitt, see his "Der Hüter der Verfassuag," *Beiträge zum öffentichen Recht der Gegenwart* 1 (Tubingen, 1931).

reproduction. It requires the institutionalization of the regime's norms and structures, the extension of its legitimacy, and the removal of the obstacles that, in its initial phases, made its establishment difficult.[18] It is a prolonged process, and in some cases may last an entire generation. It is during the initial phases of the new regime, however, that problems are most acute, since these are the moments when democracy is usually most fragile. Its principles and values still have to be converted into norms and practices. Its institutions have not yet been completely developed. The regime may still exhibit a certain lack of coherence, while the incipient democratic legality must continue to coexist with important elements of the authoritarian legality which contradict it. These inconsistencies are likely to occur within certain institutions. Their suppression, the fixing of priorities, and the solution of the basic problems are a logical cause of division within the main political formations and institutions at a time when it is most probable that those sectors sympathizing with the previous regime have not yet totally transferred their loyalties to the new one and have not yet resigned themselves to accepting the change. If, in addition, some of those groups have retained strategic positions within the newly inaugurated regime, the difficulties for consolidation are likely to be greater....

As far as consolidation processes are concerned, the way in which the transition from authoritarian rule was effected had an ambivalent impact for a certain period. The power imbalance from which it arose, together with the symbolic continuity represented by the king, made possible a high degree of material and personal continuity with those groups previously identified with the Franco regime and occupying key positions in its state apparatus, such as the armed forces, the judiciary, the intelligence services, the police, the various national bureaucracies, the municipal and provincial governments. The peaceful and law-abiding nature of the transition did not imply—nor could it ever imply—that the legitimacy of the old regime had been transferred and, thereby, reinforced the new regime since the latter was clearly inspired by contrary values and purposes. It did, however, permit the legitimation of the monarchy to remain beyond dispute. The guarantees offered to the Francoist political class and the established powers resulted in a fragmentary and partial transfer of loyalties from one regime to the other. One sector of the previous ruling group integrated itself with the new regime through the AP and UCD in particular. Another stayed out of the fray, weakened and incapable of causing serious harassment. Only the so-called Bunker maintained a position of open hostility, giving rise to extreme right-wing terrorism and support for several conspiracies aimed at a coup. The case of the armed forces was more complex. It is practically impossible to detect the degree of unity or diversity within their ranks, although it seems in retrospect obvious that the diversity was greater than was popularly thought at the time. Their acceptance of the new regime seems to have been

[18] Otto Kirchheimer, "Confining Conditions and Revolutionary Breakthroughs," *American Political Science Review* 59 (1965): 964-74.

cautious and conditional, limited in any case by their loyalty to the king as commander of the armed forces. The continued monopoly of the military high command by officers appointed during the Civil War aroused suspicion, whether justified or not, about their commitment to democracy. Various incidents demonstrated the persistence of hostile military sectors. Hence, during the early years, the consolidation was overshadowed by a permanent threat of impending coup d'état.

In order to counteract the menace of these factors, a political annex was included in the Moncloa Pacts, in which the government promised to carry out a series of reforms directed at modernizing the military, civil, and legal administrations, and replacing or modifying important parts of previous legislation. The UCD governments were reticent about fulfilling these commitments and the left-wing parties lacked the strength to impose them. The persistence of those elements of continuity constituted a considerable obstacle for the consolidation of the new regime, and was proof of its fragility from 1979 to 1982.

*E. Ramón Arango, "Spain: From Repression to Renewal"**

The civil service, and in particular its extraordinarily prestigious and powerful upper echelons, called *cuerpos,* which are akin to the French *grands corps,* had traditionally been almost above the control of the state. Even Franco made no fundamental changes in either the operation or the recruitment of the cuerpos, perhaps because their personnel was drawn almost exclusively from among the classic ruling elite that accepted Franco's philosophy of governing. These men and women, who often have less than a full commitment to democracy, now run the machinery of the constitutional monarchy just as they ran the machinery of the Francoist dictatorship. There are serious students of Spanish politics who contend that effective democracy will be little more than superficial until the massive power of the cuerpos has been serious reduced.

José María Maravall and Julián Santamaría, "Political Change in Spain and the Prospects for Democracy"†

Otherwise, the comprehensive, inclusive nature of the new regime, together with its strategy of consensus-building among the main political parties during the second phase of the transition, partially counteracted the intrinsic fragility. First, as has been mentioned, it made possible solid parliamentary and popular support for the constitution. Second, the consensual method and practices were highly instrumental for the

* Excerpted from E. Ramón Arango, *Spain: From Repression to Renewal* (Westview Press, 1985), pp. 223-224.

† Excerpted from José María Maravall and Julián Santamaría, "Political Change in Spain and the Propects for Democracy," in Guillermo O'Donnell, Philippe C. Schmitter and Laurence Whitehead, eds., *Transitions From Authoritarian Rule: Southern Europe* (The Johns Hopkins University Press, 1986), pp. 90-93.

reciprocal legitimation of parties and their leaders.[19] Third, the new habits of democratic compromise and negotiation were signs of a new pragmatism, substituting old cultural patterns of intolerance, exclusiveness, and rigidity. Finally, these very facts, together with the common dangers experienced by most parties as a consequence of the double threat represented by terrorism or coup, clearly contributed to setting up both an encompassing network of political communication among parties, leaders, government, and opposition, and to reducing any temptation to resort to a pattern of adversarial politics with the debilitating effects it would have produced during the early stages of consolidation....

The main difficulties were, however, related to the ... territorial reform of state power, the political violence, and the economic crisis.... The [Basque and Catalan] regional problem reemerged with force from the very beginning of the transition.... From 1976 to 1982, ETA wounded 540 people and murdered 345, including among the latter some 30 high-ranking military officers. Terrorism also increased throughout these years. Sixty-eight people were killed in the Basque country in 1977, 70 in 1978, and 130 in 1980. At the same time extreme right-wing violence also increased, particularly after 1978, producing 40 deaths and 128 wounded in the Basque country alone, as well as a long list of assaults and deaths in Madrid and other big cities. This considerable level of violence was mainly connected with nationalism and with the regionalization of the state. It was also connected with the general process of democratization since it reflected in some cases opposition to the reform of certain institutions, including the security forces, and the persistent toleration of an underground rightist plot (*trama negra*) which involved top military officers and former ministers from the Franco period.

Additional difficulties stemmed from the prevailing economic crisis. By the summer of 1977, the figures for unemployment, inflation, and the trade imbalance had grown to previously unknown proportions. In large part, the crisis was a legacy of the Franco regime, whose late governments had been weak and lacking in authority as well as unwilling to face the aftermath of the oil crisis and to enact needed fiscal reform that would have permitted a counteracting budgetary policy.... As in the 1930s, the initiation of democracy coincided with an international economic crisis which badly affected the Spanish economy after a long period of prosperity associated with the outgoing authoritarian regime....

Increased political violence, unchecked by effective government measures, and a sense of disenchantment with the hesitant, erratic, inconclusive, and complex policies related to the regional issues, were also sources of public frustration. In addition, the recourse to "invisible politics" during the constituent period, the growing monopolization of political life by party elites, the reorientation of political conflict toward the parliamentary arena, and the general demobilization that followed the 1977 elections may have proved highly instrumental in reaching and

---

19 Giuseppe Di Palma, "Founding Coalitions in Southern Europe: Legitimacy and Hegemony" *Government and Opposition* 15, no. 2 (Spring 1980): 162-89.

implementing a policy of pacts and compromises, but this strategy also had negative side effects. Party affiliation stagnated or diminished. The rates of electoral abstention increased alarmingly. Political pessimism became rampant from 1979 on. Moreover, these attitudes were not confined to the mass public. Intellectuals and columnists daily voiced their frustration and disenchantment (*desencanto*) with the restrictions imposed by compromised democracy. Antidemocratic groups increased their harassment of the regime. Undoubtedly, this rarified atmosphere favored the attempted [but failed] military coup of 23 February 1981.

CONCLUSION

Edward Malefakis, "Spain and Its Francoist Heritage"[*]

The process of democratic restoration in Spain differed considerably from that of the other countries studied in this volume.[†] Several of the differences are related to the fact that the antecedent dictatorial regime was not abruptly removed from the scene by a single decisive blow. The defeat in war of their predecessors was the obvious catalytic agent in the cluster of new democracies—Austria, France, Germany, Italy, Japan—that emerged after World War II. In Portugal three decades later, a military coup seconded by a mass movement that soon acquired the dimensions of a popular revolution swept the stage relatively clean for the appearance of democracy. In Greece the sudden loss of nerve and the self-liquidation of the colonel's regime created the political vacuum that Karamanlis subsequently filled so successfully. The death of Franco in November 1975 did not produce conditions that approximated a political tabula rasa. Rather than an unexpected event that could not be planned for, Franco's demise was a long anticipated eventuality.

This lack of a sudden, sharp break with the past had at least three significant consequences. First, it meant that leading figures of the antecedent regime would play a greater—indeed, the dominant—part in the shaping of the new political structure. The contrast with Greece and with all the post-World War II successor democracies except for Italy is so obvious that elaboration is unnecessary. In these cases no important officials of the collapsed dictatorships ever again possessed significant power, and even minor figures could reenter politics only covertly after years of ostracism. In Italy and Portugal special nuances of the changeover process gave to important actors of the anciens regimes—Victor Emmanuel, Badoglio, Spinola—some early influence over events. But their involvement proved brief; the shock to the old power structures had been so

---

[*] Excerpted from Edward Malefakis, "Spain and Its Francoist Heritage," in John H. Herz, ed., *From Dictatorship to Democracy: Coping with the Legacies of Authoritarianism and Totalitariansim*, Copyright © 1982 by John Herz (Greenwood Press, 1982), pp. 215-216, an imprint of Greenwood Publishing Group, Inc. Westport, CT. Reprinted with permission.

[†] [Editor's note: The "other countries" referred to are Germany, Italy, Austria, France, Japan, Portugal, and Greece.]

profound as to leave former leaders without any firm base from which to exercise authority. In Spain by contrast, state power remained completely in the hands of persons intimately involved with Francoism. Its legacy was liquidated not by outsiders but by some of the very persons entrusted with its preservation.

Second, the absence of a clean break permitted the much longer coexistence of democratic and undemocratic forms of government in Spain, at least if one counts from the time that self rule was reestablished in the countries affected by the world war. The new constitution did not take effect until December 1978, three years after Franco's death. Local officials appointed or elected under Franco governed Spain's municipalities until March 1979. The army was never systematically purged, continued occasionally to exercise judicial power over civilian critics even during the peak periods of democratic euphoria, and almost brought the democratic experiment to an abrupt end with the coup attempt of February 23, 1981. The former Falangist press, even that sector that has not substantially altered its views, is still subsidized by the state. The police, the judiciary, the bureaucracy, and the educational institutions are still staffed [in 1982] in large part by Franco appointees. Indeed, the only part of the Francoist state structure that was dismantled relatively quickly was the syndical organization, precisely the most moribund of the Francoist institutions.

A third corollary of the absence of a *ruptura*, to use the Spanish term, was that a far wider range of political options remained available in the transition period and that the process of succession was considerably more open-ended than elsewhere. No limits were imposed on this process by victorious military powers, as happened in the countries whose future was decided after 1944 and 1945. There was no Revolutionary Council to supervise the process, as in Portugal. The right did not narrow the possible political parameters by abject surrender, as in Greece. On the contrary, the Spanish right, although leaderless after Franco's death, held many bastions of power and had behind it a solid record of achievement on which to advance its ideological claims.

10

ARGENTINA

EDITOR'S INTRODUCTION

The armed forces seized power in Argentina in a 1976 coup d'etat that deposed President Isabel Peron. The coup was initially welcomed by much of society for ending a chaotic period characterized by widespread political violence and for replacing runaway inflation with apparent economic stability. Behind this veneer of order, however, the military unleashed a vicious campaign that came to be known as the "dirty war" for its brutality and continued it long after the elimination of any armed threat from the left, targetting all "subversives" suspected of opposing the junta's virulently anti-Communist notion of Western Christian civilization. Torture was inflicted on a massive scale. While refusing to acknowledge most arrests and detentions, the armed forces were suspected of causing to disappear and killing an estimated 10-30,000 people. Censorship and manipulation of press propaganda exaggerated the subversive threat while masking or denying governmental repression.

Over time, international condemnation of the human rights abuses of the regime increased from the United Nations, foreign governments, and non-governmental organizations. Opposition also became more vocal within Argentina as a result of economic crises and growing domestic awareness of the abuses. In one prominent example, the "Mothers of the Plaza de Mayo"—mothers of disappeared people demanding information on the whereabouts and fate of their children—held weekly demonstrations in Buenos Aires' main square. Ultimately, the disgrace of military defeat in a 1982 war with Great Britain over the disputed Malvinas/Falklands islands forced the military to prepare for a return to civilian rule.

Following generally free elections, Raul Alfonsin was inaugurated in December 1983 as president. Within his first week in office, Alfonsin appointed a National Commission on Disappeared Persons under the leadership of the distinguished Argentine author, Ernesto Sabato. The Commission's final report, *Nunca Más* ("Never Again"), was widely read in Argentina and abroad and provided powerful documentation of the systematic violation of human rights by the military regime. The "Law of National Pacification," an amnesty which the military granted itself before leaving office, was quickly repealed. The new government undertook prosecution of members of the first three juntas of the dictatorship for violations of human rights and mishandling of the Malvinas War. The military leaders were charged with over 700 separate crimes; five of nine men were convicted and sentenced to prison.

Once the trials of the junta members were completed, the courts turned to charges of human right violations against numerous other military personnel. The armed forces exerted heavy pressure on the government to suspend the trials, and beginning in late 1986, repeatedly rebelled against the Alfonsin government. The government placed a limit on the trials through enactment in December 1986 of the "Full Stop Law," which established a two-month deadline for the filing of all criminal complaints against military officers by victims or their families. Still facing the prospect of numerous trials, junior army officers carried out a major rebellion during Easter week, 1987. Alfonsin met with the rebels and claimed to have resolved the crisis with no concessions, but within a few weeks he proposed to Congress the "Due Obedience Law" which was adopted in June. By creating an irrebuttable presumption that all but the most senior military officers had only committed abuses under orders from their superiors, the law exonerated virtually all military personnel.

Declaring that "permanent reconciliation among all Argentinians ... is the only possible solution for the wounds that still remain to be healed," President Carlos Menem, Alfonsin's successor, granted pardons in 1989 for 39 military officials convicted of or charged with human rights abuses, along with more than 200 other pardons for leftist guerillas, military personnel charged in connection with the Malvinas war, and those convicted for the mutinies under Alfonsin. In December 1990, Menem pardoned the convicted leaders of the junta.

A January 1992 law provided financial compensation to those who were jailed under the military regime, to relatives of political prisoners who had died in custody, and to those who were forced into exile during the 1976-83 period.

The following documents related to transitional justice in Argentina can be found in Volume III of this collection:

- *Nunca Más*—Report of the Argentine National Commission on the Disappeared
- Amnesty Law ("Law of National Pacification")
- Amnesty Nullification
- Trial of Members of the Former Military Junta
- Full Stop Law
- Due Obedience Law
- Supreme Court Decision on the Due Obedience Law
- Presidential Pardons
- Organization of American States, Inter-American Commission on Human Rights—Decisions on Full Stop and Due Obedience Laws
- Indemnification Law

THE END OF THE MILITARY REGIME

Alejandro M. Garro and Henry Dahl, "Legal Accountability for Human Rights Violations in Argentina"[*]

In 1979 the commanding officers of the armed forces claimed victory in the war against subversion,[58] notwithstanding the fact that not a single death penalty was applied as a result of any finding by a military court.[59] The explanation for the manner in which victory had allegedly been achieved rested on the concept of a "dirty war". To characterize this war, the commanding officers alluded to the use of "unconventional methods" to maintain the utmost secrecy concerning information related to the military operations, justifying their actions and their secrecy by claiming that they were consistent with the covert nature of the operations.[60] Subsequent to

[*] Excerpted from Alejandro M. Garro and Henry Dahl, "Legal Accountability for Human Rights Violations in Argentina: One Step Forward and Two Steps Backward," *Human Rights Law Journal*, vol. 8 (1987), pp. 299-301.

[58] *See* App. Court Judg., §§ 45-47....

[59] During the period 1976-1983, military courts in Argentina sentenced only 365 individuals accused of subversive activities. Sábato Commission Report, at 448.

[60] [omitted]

this claim of victory, the number of missing persons decreased considerably.[61]

On September 12, 1979, in the face of mounting national and international pressure concerning the fate of the disappeared, the military government issued a law allowing those who had been reported missing during the previous five years to be declared dead. This law was one of the army's first attempts to efface the effects of its deplorable human rights record through legislation.[62] By 1981 the military were facing demands from all quarters for a clarification of the fate of the "disappeared". Continuing official silence on their fate contrasted sharply with the stream of evidence being published in Argentina and abroad. More importantly, the military government was also facing greater opposition from restless trade unions and political parties. Against this background of popular hostility to the junta's repressive methods, its political isolation, and widespread economic disaster, Argentina suffered a humiliating defeat by Great Britain in the 1982 Falklands-Malvinas War.[63] By 1983, the relative support or peaceful acquiescence which the armed forces had enjoyed after the 1976 coup had vanished. A transitional junta was obliged to declare a return to civilian democracy.[64]

"Final Document" and "Self-Amnesty" Law

The fourth and transitional military junta prepared the way for popular elections in October 1983.[65] Although the armed forces had been relatively united with regard to the issue of the "dirty war" against subversion, they were haunted by the prospect of being held responsible for past human rights abuses when it became clear that military rule would end. Human rights leaders and a substantial sector of the Argentine people increasingly demanded the prosecution of the military commanders.

In order to ensure that military officers would not be prosecuted, the outgoing military government took three steps to avoid accountability for human rights abuses. First, on April 28, 1983, the government published the "Final Document on the War Against Subversion and Terrorism".[66] The

---

61 Sábato Commission Report, at 342.

62 Law No. 22068, September 12, 1979 on "Presumption of Death Because of Disappearance" [1979-C] A.L.J.A. 2845. This law was harshly criticized inside and outside Argentina for failing to raise the fundamental question—whether the disappeared were dead or alive.

63 *See* Mignone, Estlund & Issacharoff, *Dictatorship on Trial: Prosecution of Human Rights Violations in Argentina*, 10 Yale J. Int'l. L. 118, 124 (1984).

64 For a discussion of this difficult transitional period of the military government see Osiel, *The Making of Human Rights Policy in Argentina: The Impact of Ideas and Interests on a Legal Conflict*, 18 Journal of Latin American Studies 135 (1986)....

65 General Leopolda Galtieri was forced to resign as Head of State after the debacle in the Malvinas/Falklands Islands. General Reynaldo Bignone, appointed President on June 22, 1982, led the country during an 18-month transition to civilian rule. For information on the events and political strategies surrounding Raúl Alfonsín's road to victory in the October 1983 popular elections, *see* Schumacher, *Argentina and Democracy*, Foreign Affairs 1070, 1078-1081 (1984); Cox, *Argentina's Democratic Miracle*, The New Republic, March 19, 1984, at 18, 19-22.

66 App. Court Judg., § 46....

document conceded that human rights abuses occurred ("errors were committed as in all wars"), but stated that "the actions of the members of the armed forces in the conduct of the war were in the line of duty". It declared that those "disappeared" who were not in exile or in hiding must be considered dead "for all legal and administrative purposes", but claimed that they met their death in open combat rather than in custody. The military government stressed that there would be no further disclosures about the consequences of the "dirty war".[67] Second, just before handing over power, the military junta enacted the "Law of National Pacification", granting immunity from prosecution to suspected terrorists and every member of the armed forces for crimes committed between May 25, 1973 and June 17, 1982.[68] Third, the government issued a decree (Decree No. 2726/83) ordering the destruction of documents relating to the military repression.

None of these measures decreased popular feeling against the military. On October 29, 1983 the state of siege was suspended and free elections took place. The civilian government of President Alfonsín took over two months later.

THE NATIONAL COMMISSION ON DISAPPEARED PERSONS

Americas Watch, "Truth and Partial Justice in Argentina"[*]

Only a few days into his presidency, Alfonsín electrified the Argentine nation and, indeed, the world, by announcing an impressive series of actions to restore Argentina's adherence to the rule of law and respect for human rights. He ordered the prosecution of former Junta members; proposed increased penalties for torture; signed international human rights treaties; proposed reforms of the military code of justice; and created an investigative commission on forced disappearances. By far the most publicized of those actions was his decision to order the prosecution of Generals Videla, Viola and Galtieri, Admirals Massera, Lambruschini and Anaya, and Air Force Brigadiers Agosti, Graffigna and Lami Dozo, all the members of the first three Juntas, for the crimes they had committed in the context of the "war against subversion." In the same decree, President Alfonsín ordered the prosecution of seven reputed leaders of the Montoneros and the ERP organizations. The strategy was to condemn equally state

---

67 For a discussion of the series of disingenuous explanations giving by the military government regarding the disappearance of thousands of persons listed as missing after their arrest by the security forces, *see* Americas Watch, *The Argentine Military Junta's "Final Document": A Call for Condemnation*, May 20, 1983.

68 Law No. 22924, September 22, 1983, [1983-B] A.L.J.A. 1681. Many political prisoners who had spent years in detention immediately rejected the benefits of the self-amnesty law. *See* Americas Watch, *Trust and Partial Justice in Argentina* (12 August 1987) [hereafter cited as Americas Watch Report].

* Excerpted from Americas Watch, *Truth and Partial Justice in Argentina: An Update* (Human Rights Watch, 1991), pp 13-14, 17-18.

terror and anti–state political violence, an approach that has been frequently labelled in Argentina as "the theory of the two devils."

In addition, President Alfonsín submitted to Congress legislation raising the penalties for torture, and making it a crime to take over the government by force of arms. The crime of organizing a military *coup* would not be subject to a statute of limitations, and its prosecution would take place no matter what actions might be taken by the *de facto* regime to ensure its impunity. Congress acted swiftly and these proposals became law. In a similar manner, Argentina ratified several international human rights instruments, including the U.N. Covenants on Civil and Political Rights and on Economic and Social Rights, and the American Convention on Human Rights. Also, Argentina accepted to be bound, for future cases, by the decisions of the Inter-American Court of Human Rights. Argentina also became a party to the recently drafted U.N. Convention Against Torture.

With respect to the crimes of the past, President Alfonsín submitted to Congress legislation to regulate the prosecutions, including those of Junta members....

President Alfonsín then created a "National Commission on Disappeared Persons" (CONADEP) and appointed ten prominent citizens as members. Six other positions were left open for the House of Deputies and Senate to appoint representatives, though in the end only the House named three members. At its first meeting on December 18, 1983, the Commission chose Ernesto Sabato, a leading Latin American novelist, to chair it. CONADEP was charged with investigating the fate and whereabouts of the disappeared, and with producing a report to the President. It was given means to hire personnel and access to all government facilities, and the security forces were ordered to cooperate with it. It was not given subpoena powers nor the ability to compel testimony, and if it uncovered evidence of the commission of crimes, it was supposed to provide the information to the relevant courts.

From the beginning, the Argentine human rights movement, which had gained great prestige and national and international credibility for its courageous stands against the dictatorship, objected publicly to some aspects of Alfonsín's plan. In the first place, the groups that make up the movements would have preferred a congressional commission of inquiry rather than the Sabato Commission, since with a strong majority backing it, a congressional body would have had extraordinary powers to compel testimony and to obtain access to documents. Nobel Peace Laureate Adolfo Pérez Esquivel declined his appointment to CONADEP for that reason. Nonetheless, with the exception only of the Mothers of Plaza de Mayo, the human rights organizations of Argentina, after making clear their disagreement, then contributed enthusiastically to CONADEP's work. Many prominent human rights leaders and activists joined CONADEP as staffers or advisors. CONADEP also encouraged the formation of provincial investigatory commissions, and invited the Senate and House of Deputies to engage in their own investigations....

The CONADEP hired staff and consultants in the first few weeks of 1984, and almost immediately began receiving testimony from relatives of the disappeared and from survivors of the camps where the disappeared had been held. Human rights organizations based in Buenos Aires had gathered extensive documentation that was turned over to the Commission; the files of the *Centro de Estudios Legales y Sociales* (CELS) and of the *Asamblea Permanente por los Derechos Humanos* (APDH) proved particularly valuable. Relatives of the disappeared went to the offices of CONADEP to repeat their stories. A significant number of families who had never previously made public statements about their disappeared relatives went to CONADEP. In that fashion, the list of 6,500 disappearances gathered during the dictatorship by APDH, grew to 8,960. (CONADEP made it clear that it estimated that there were many more victims of disappearances but their families never came forward with the information.)

CONADEP established branches in several major provincial cities such as Mar del Plata and Córdoba, and staff and commissioners travelled to certain areas to receive testimony. In Tucumán, for example, in the few days of CONADEP presence, the list of the disappeared in that province grew by a factor of four. The estimate by CONADEP, therefore, that many more cases have still gone unreported, is based on the fact that little or no gathering of information has taken place in areas of the country where repression was hard, but the population is poor and isolated. In some cities, CONADEP established a relatively permanent presence in order to continue receiving information from the public. At the same time, Argentine consulates abroad were instructed to request exiles to come forward and to provide information. Some CONADEP commissioners and high officials of the government travelled to Europe and the United States and themselves encouraged exiles to provide testimony. Many Argentines living abroad participated in the process, mostly by returning briefly to Argentina to testify. Testimony was also taken in consulates and embassies in Mexico City, Caracas, Los Angeles, New York, Washington, Paris, Madrid, Barcelona, Geneva and other cities.

In pursuit of leads provided by some witnesses, CONADEP actually inspected certain police and military facilities where concentration camps were said to have operated. Commissioners and staff also visited clandestine cemeteries and areas of public graveyards where unidentified bodies had been buried on orders of local military authorities. These public activities of CONADEP, which were highly publicized in the media, provoked complaints by military authorities, and elicited political pressures on CONADEP to exercise restraint.

Military Opposition

*Amnesty International, "Argentina: The Military Juntas and Human Rights"**

The armed forces and security services were reluctant to cooperate with the commission, refusing to reply to written questions and sometimes refusing to permit inspections of military establishments. Members of CONADEP became a major target of attacks attributed by the authorities to right-wing paramilitary groups linked to the security services. In three cities—Mar del Plata, Cordóba and Rosario—the homes and offices of CONADEP delegates were bombed.

The CONADEP Report

Americas Watch, "Truth and Partial Justice in Argentina"†

On July 4, 1984, CONADEP conducted a two-hour program on television, consisting mostly of testimonies from survivors of concentration camps and of parents and relatives of some of the disappeared. The program was so powerful that the government seriously considered not showing it. In the end, however, President Alfonsín himself authorized it, after a private airing. In the public presentation, however, Minister of Interior Antonio Troccoli joined Ernesto Sabato in introductory and closing statements. Troccoli's words were designed to temper the impact of the program by reminding the viewers of the onslaught of revolutionary violence that had caused the repression. Before the end of the program, nonetheless, President Alfonsín confronted his first insubordination from military quarters, which included rumors of tanks rolling into Buenos Aires. As a result, the President dismissed the Chief of Staff of the Army, General Jorge Arguindeguy.

In September 1984, CONADEP delivered its report to the President. It consisted of 50,000 pages of documentation, and a summary that was later published as a book, by EUDEBA, the publishing arm of the University of Buenos Aires. The book was entitled *Nunca Más* and included a foreword by Ernesto Sabato. It was sold with an annex listing the names of 8,961 *desaparecidos*; the names of those who were seen alive in concentration camps; and a list of 365 clandestine detention centers. The book and the annex became enduring bestsellers in Argentina. Foreign language versions have been published abroad. (In the United States, Farrar, Straus, Giroux published an English-language edition under the title *Nunca Más* in 1986.)

The book describes in detail the methodology of disappearances, using a profusion of examples to illustrate the way the kidnappings took place, the torture to which the unacknowledged prisoners were subjected, the use of clandestine detention centers under the jurisdiction of all three armed

---

* Excerpted from Amnesty International, *Argentina: The Military Juntas and Human Rights Report of the Trial of the Former Junta Members* (Amnesty International Publications, 1987), p. 9.

† Excerpted from Americas Watch, *Truth and Partial Justice in Argentina: An Update* (Human Rights Watch, 1991), pp 18-19.

forces and of various police and security forces, and the methods of extermination. It also describes in some detail the "commitment to impunity" that was an essential part of the method, and discusses the cases of several prominent members of Argentina society who were victims of disappearances. The first chapter ends with a discussion of cases of disappearances of Argentines in which the Argentina armed forces kidnapped their victims across South American borders; and with cases in which the armed forces engaged in theft of property in the course of kidnappings and disappearances.

The second chapter describes the targets, and cases of several categories of victims, including children, pregnant women, teen–agers, whole families, the handicapped, priests, nuns and ministers, conscripted soldiers, journalists, trade union leaders and political activists. We learn, for example, that there were 84 journalists reported as disappeared who were never found (not including some like Jacobo Timerman—publisher of the daily *La Opinion*—who were held as disappeared for some time but who were eventually released). 30.2 percent of all the cases reported to CONADEP were blue-collar workers, and 17.9 percent were white–collar workers. 21 percent were students, but of these, one third also worked. The report quotes from Junta statements of 1977 detailing the plan to operate against workers in factories and workplaces as a way to counter what General Tómas Liendo, then Minister of Labor, called "industrial subversion."

In conclusion, the report discusses the inability of the judiciary to deal with the phenomenon of disappearances, including the ineffectiveness of *habeas corpus*, the targeting of lawyers for disappearances, as well as the harassment of human rights leaders. The Commission registered 107 cases of lawyers who disappeared after their arrest by security forces who remain unaccounted for. In addition, the report lists 196 persons who were seen alive in concentration camps at a time when *habeas corpus* writs on their behalf were being rejected on the grounds that the person "had not been arrested."

The CONADEP Report is a powerful indictment of the repressive policies of the military dictatorship. It establishes that a complex and extensive machinery of state terror was put in place involving abductions, unlimited torture, clandestine imprisonment and murder of defenseless persons. It also demonstrates that the policy could only be carried out with extensive complicity from different sectors and institutions, in exchange for promises of impunity. The CONADEP Report is also significant in that it shows how a democratic government, with the assistance of human rights organizations, can take important steps toward establishing the painful truth about repression which took place just a few years earlier, provided that the political will is available to investigate and report that truth.

THE TRIAL OF THE FORMER JUNTA MEMBERS

*Amnesty International, "Argentina: The Military Juntas and Human Rights"**

When the new government of Argentina decided to bring to trial those it regarded as chiefly responsible for the human rights violations that had occurred during the period of military rule, it was faced with intricate legal problems as well as urgent political pressures. The most important legal problems arose from the provisions of the Argentine Code of Military Justice, Article 108 of which (approved in 1951) specified that military courts had jurisdiction in two distinct types of case: a) those in which a member of the armed forces committed a military offense, that is, an offense defined in the Code of Military Justice, such as insubordination or desertion; and b) those in which a member of the armed forces committed an ordinary offense, that is, an offense defined not in the Military Code but in the Penal Code, while on duty in a place subject to military jurisdiction, such as a barracks, an arsenal, a ship, a base, etc. Since most of the offenses which the government wished to investigate fell into the second category, it was necessary to obtain a change in the law unless such offenses were to be tried exclusively by military rather than civilian courts.

The chief difficulty in the way of changing the law so that the defendants might be tried in a civilian court was the necessity of simultaneously upholding the safeguards established in the Argentine Constitution, especially those defined in Article 18, which states that "no inhabitant of the Nation shall be punished without previous trial founded on a law antedating the act for which he is tried, nor shall he be tried by special commissions, or removed from the jurisdiction of judges appointed by law prior to the commission of the offense with which he is charged". This article provided what is termed the "*juez natural*" or "natural judge" safeguard. The law in force prior to the offenses in question would, of course, have allowed the defendants to be tried solely in a military court.

Understandably, the new democratic government did not wish to open its term of office by introducing laws which appeared to violate constitutional guarantees. At the same time there was a need for rapid decisions to demonstrate the political will of the government to bring to justice those alleged to be guilty of extremely serious crimes. On 27 December 1983 a new law (23.040) was passed, repealing the Law of National Pacification (otherwise known as the Amnesty Law) which had been promulgated by the military government on 23 September of that year. The Amnesty Law was declared null and void on the grounds that it was unconstitutional. At about the same time (on 18 December 1983), the President issued Decree 158, which stated that all members of the first three military juntas in power from 1976 to 1982 should be brought to trial

---

* Excerpted from Amnesty International, *Argentina: The Military Juntas and Human Rights Report of the Trial of the Former Junta Members* (Amnesty International Publications, 1987), pp. 10-13.

before the highest military court, the Supreme Council of the Armed Forces. In issuing this Decree, President Alfonsín was exercising a legal right embodied in Article 179 of the Code of Military Justice, which states that in trials of high-ranking officers (army generals or their equivalents in other forces), the order to initiate legal proceedings must always come from the President of the Nation (who, according to an Article in the Argentine Constitution, is the commander-in-chief of the nation's entire armed forces). But Decree 158 also included a section stipulating that any judgment reached by the military courts could be appealed against in civilian courts, under new legislation that the President intended to submit to Congress. Throughout the subsequent trial of members of the juntas, this section of Decree 158 was objected to as unconstitutional by the defense lawyers on the ground that this law was not in force at the time of the alleged offenses. The defense lawyers attempted to argue that the trial was "political", since it had been initiated by a presidential decision, and that in taking this decision the President had already imputed guilt to the defendants.

The impending legislation referred to in Decree 158 materialized in Law 23.049, passed by the Argentine Congress on 9 February 1984. This law, an important element in the legal framework of the subsequent trial, contained clauses of two different types: those referring to offenses committed after the passing of the law and those referring to offenses committed during the recent repression. Within the first category were two significant alterations to the text of the Code of Military Justice. The first was an article stating that, in future, military jurisdiction would apply only to offenses of an essentially military nature, that is, to offenses specified in the Military Code. It would not be possible, therefore, for future offenses against the Penal Code to be dealt with by a military court, even if the offenses had been committed by military personnel and on military premises. Secondly, the law provided that even in the case of these strictly military offenses, the decision reached by the military court could be appealed against in a civilian court, namely, the Federal Appellate Court within whose area of jurisdiction the alleged offense had been committed. In these two ways, and for future offenses, Law 23.049 sharply limited the scope of military justice.

More relevant, however, to the subsequent trial were those articles of Law 23.049 which referred to past offenses. Of crucial importance was Article 10, which laid down that the Supreme Council of the Armed Forces should, by means of the summary procedure applicable in peacetime, take cognizance of penal offenses committed before the law came into effect, provided that they could be attributed to military and security personnel acting under the orders of the armed forces between 24 March 1976 and 26 September 1983 in any operations allegedly undertaken to repress terrorism. The law also stated that all these cases required the involvement not of a military prosecutor, but of the Public Prosecutor, that is, the representative of the Attorney General's Office, which was part of the general legal system. In this way, respect for the public interest in the prosecution of these offenses was legally assured.

Law 23.049, then, required that all offenses committed during the recent period of repression should be tried, in the first instance, by the Supreme Council of the Armed Forces. However, it also provided a second tier to the judicial procedure. Just as in future all sentences passed by military courts for specifically military offenses could be appealed against in a civilian court, so too the decisions of the Supreme Council concerning past criminal offenses could also be the subject of an appeal, by either the defense or the prosecution, to the appropriate Federal Appellate Court. Law 23.049 defined in detail the requisite mechanisms of such an appeal, as well as stating the acceptable legal grounds (arbitrary omission or incorrect evaluation of relevant evidence). In cases where an appeal resulted in a transfer of jurisdiction from the Supreme Council of the Armed Forces to a Federal Court, the latter would have the procedural status of an appellate court.

There was, however, another possibility of transfer from military to civilian jurisdiction envisaged in Law 23.049—and this, as it happened, was the process which actually occurred. The law stated that after six months from the inception of the proceedings in the Supreme Council, the military court should inform the appropriate Federal Court of the reasons that had prevented the trial from being completed. In the light of this information the Federal Court could either specify a period within which the trial must be concluded or fix a date by which a new report must be submitted. If, however, there was evidence of "unwarranted delay or negligence in the conduct of the trial", the Federal Court would itself "take over the hearing of the case whatever stage the proceedings may have reached". In cases where the Federal Appellate Court assumed jurisdiction over a case handled by the Supreme Council, the Federal Appellate Court has the procedural status of a trial court.

One other provision of Law 23.049 is notable on account of its subsequent repercussions. Article 11 made reference to "due obedience"—that is, it attempted to clarify the circumstances in which a military subordinate could be held responsible for crimes committed in the execution of orders from a military superior. Previously existing Argentine law had been ambiguous on this controversial point. Article 34(5) of the Argentine Penal Code laid down the general principle that persons acting in "due obedience" were not punishable for offenses committed. Article 514 of the Code of Military Justice stated that "when an offense has been committed in the discharge of an order in the course of duty, the superior who gave the order shall be held solely responsible, and the subordinate shall only be held to be an accomplice if he exceeds the order given". However, there was also a tradition in Argentine jurisprudence that a military order should not be obeyed when it clearly involved the commission of a crime, and this tradition was consonant not only with international legal principles but also with Article 674 of the Code of Military Justice itself, which limits the duty to obey "orders received in the line of duty" and even seems to admit that it is possible to disobey them when there is good reason to do so. In an attempt to rationalize these existing provisions, Article 11 of Law 23.049 established the principle that subordinates were not to be held responsible for crimes committed in the execution of orders except when a) they were in a position to exercise discretion; or b) they were aware of the illegality of the order they were carrying out; or c) the order involved the commission of atrocious or aberrant acts. In any of these three cases no subordinate (that is, no serviceman below the rank of commander-in-chief) could seek immunity from prosecution by virtue of the principle of "due obedience". This Article was one of those in Law 23.049 which applied to past offenses.

With the approval of Law 23.049, the immediate legal framework of the trial was completed....

Political Considerations Underlying Military Jurisdiction

*Mignone, Estlund & Issacharoff, "Dictatorship on Trial"**

The decision to route all criminal proceedings through military tribunals rested on a political rather than a jurisprudential calculation by the Alfonsín government.[31] Any evaluation of this strategy must begin with an understanding of what the Argentine experience was *not*. Unlike the much-cited precedent of Nuremburg, any Argentine prosecutions would not have the security of those initiated by a victorious foreign military power standing in judgment over its defeated wartime adversary.[32] The armed forces remained omnipresent after the victory of President Alfonsin.

The legal framework which the new government devised was therefore inextricably linked to the political decision to avoid confronting as an institution the armed forces that had seized power six times since 1930,[33] and whose aggregate tenure had since considerably outweighed that

---

* Excerpted from Emilio Fermin Mignone, Cynthia L. Estlund, & Samuel Issacharoff, "Dictatorship on Trial: Prosecution of Human Rights in Argentina," *Yale Journal of International Law*, vol. 10 (1985), pp. 126-127, 142.

31 Although a few government officials attempted to justify the decision by arguing that the acts would have been subject only to military jurisdiction at the time they were committed, some of the president's closest advisors frankly acknowledge in public and private the political nature of the decision. *See* Foster, *After the Terror*, Mother Jones, Feb./Mar. 1985, at 37 (comments of Presidential advisor Jaime Malamud).

32 Notwithstanding its celebrated rejection of the "following orders" defense, the Nuremberg trials provide only limited guidance for Argentina. In post-war Germany, the balance of power between the accusers and the accused appeared far more conducive to a full investigation and punishment of the atrocities of the state, yet standards of guilt remained ill-defined and few convictions resulted. The difficulties encountered at Nuremberg highlighted "the inadequacy of the prevailing legal system and of current judicial concepts to deal with the facts of administrative massacres organized by the state apparatus." H. Arendt, Eichmann in Jerusalem 294 (1963). Thus, while Nuremberg represents a rare attempt to apply legal norms to punish state terror, its invocation as a legal and historic precedent in the Argentine context must be carefully qualified.

33 The current cycle of military coups began with the overthrow of President Hipólito Yrigoyen in 1930. In 1943, President Ramón S. Castillo was overthrown in a military uprising that included Colonel Juan D. Perón. Perón subsequently became president and was in turn removed from office by a coup in 1955. In 1962, the military again intervened and deposed elected President Arturo Frondizi; another civilian government headed by President Arturo Illia was allowed to take power. Illia was in turn overthrown in 1966 by the first of the "national security" dictatorships under the leadership of General Onganía. *See* J. Ocón, Historia Argentina

of civilians. By vesting original jurisdiction in the military tribunals, the government sought to avoid the military solidarity that might ensue if all military personnel faced trials in civilian courts. Trials in the military tribunals would, according to the government, allow a section of the armed forces to condemn its own, and, in the process of purging itself of the taint of the "dirty war," to repudiate the most culpable officials.[34] In terms of deterrence, criminal sanctions imposed by fellow military officers could, arguably, have a greater impact on future military conspirators than those meted out by civilian courts, the latter being dismissable as "revanchisme."

The government also believed that, as a practical matter, trials before military tribunals offered the best possibility of ending the conspiracy of silence which the institutional loyalty of the armed forces had created. As the National Commission noted, Argentina "distinguished itself from the methods employed in other countries by the total secrecy in which [the repression] was carried out, the detention of persons following their disappearance and the persistent official refusals to recognize the responsibility of the intervening organisms."[35] Testimony on the methods of repression, except for isolated instances, came from the survivors and was necessarily incomplete. A discovery process initiated within the armed forces themselves could arguably help to reveal the source of actual orders and the direct chain of responsibility....

The decision to place in the hands of the military itself the prosecution of human rights abuses was a gamble. The Alfonsín government hoped that the Supreme Council—and the vast majority of the armed forces not directly involved in the human rights violations—would sacrifice a handful of military officers in order to help rebuild the integrity and prestige of the armed forces as an institution with a role in the new constitutional order. This gamble was based on an empirical assessment of the nature of the armed forces as a largely bureaucratic institution flanked by a small fascistic fringe and a small democratic sector.[107] The government believed that a condemnation by the prestigious Supreme Council of the methodology of the repression and its underlying ideology would isolate the fascist elements and push the large bureaucratic center toward alliance with the more democratic forces within the military.

553-66 (1974). Finally, in 1976, the last dictatorship, actually a series of three juntas, took power in a coup led by General Videla.

[34] A leading government official described the armed forces as seventy percent bureaucratic (i.e., inclined to follow the lead of their superiors), fifteen percent fascist, and fifteen percent "democratic" (i.e., in favor of civilian rule). The government's strategy was described as a gamble that it could bolster the pro-civilian wing, rally the majority of the apolitical bureaucracy to its side, and jettison the fascist right-wing. (record of conversation on file with the *Yale Journal of International Law*.)

[35] [Report of the National Commission on the Disappearance of Persons, 16-17 (1984).]

[107] [omitted]

*Amnesty International, "Argentina: The Military Juntas and Human Rights"**

The First Stage of the Trial

The Supreme Council of the Armed Forces

Under Law 23.049 all offenses allegedly committed by military and security personnel between 1976 and 1983 would come for trial in the first instance before the highest military court, the Supreme Council of the Armed Forces. These included the alleged crimes of the former members of the military juntas, who accordingly first came before this nine-man military court. The accused were: from the first junta (March 1976 - March 1981): Lieutenant General Jorge Rafael Videla, President and Army Commander; Admiral Emilio Massera, Navy Commander; and Brigadier Orlando Agosti, Air Force Commander; from the second junta (March 1981 - December 1981): Lieutenant General Roberto Viola, President and Army Commander; Admiral Armando Lambruschini, Navy Commander; and Brigadier Omar Graffigna, Air Force Commander; from the third junta (December 1981 - June 1982): Lieutenant General Leopoldo Galtieri, President and Army Commander; Admiral Jorge Anaya, Navy Commander; and Brigadier Basilio Lami Dozo, Air Force Commander.

In Argentina the granting of jurisdiction in the first instance to the Supreme Council aroused opposition from all eight major human rights organizations, and from CONADEP, which had submitted over 1000 cases of "disappearance" to civilian courts for judicial investigation (these were subsequently passed on to the Supreme Council). Among the objections raised were that the Supreme Council was not strictly part of the Judiciary but of the Executive, since it was accountable to the armed forces, whose Commander-in-Chief was the President; and that its proceedings were not open to the public and were subject to more limitations of access than those of civilian courts. Doubts about the efficacy of military justice were also based on concrete precedents.... During its proceedings against the former members of the juntas, the Supreme Council placed General Videla and Admiral Massera in preventive detention, but allowed the other defendants to remain at liberty.

Transfer to Civilian Jurisdiction

As noted above, the Supreme Council had (by Article 10 of Law 23.049) been given 180 days to complete its proceedings, failing which it would have to explain its reasons for delay. Accordingly, in July 1984 the Supreme Council submitted a report to the Buenos Aires Federal Court of Criminal Appeals whose competence in the case was due to the fact that the accused

---

* Excerpted from Amnesty International, *Argentina: The Military Juntas and Human Rights Report of the Trial of the Former Junta Members* (Amnesty International Publications, 1987), pp. 14-15.

commanders had their headquarters in the capital city. In the Argentine legal system, there are eleven Federal Courts of Appeal throughout the country. The Federal Courts of Criminal Appeals are the courts of highest federal jurisdiction in the application of criminal law, only the Supreme Court being above them on matters of constitutional import. The Buenos Aires Federal Court of Appeals was composed of six judges, none of whom had entered the magistracy as a result of the coming to power of the democratic government although some of them were promoted in the judiciary by the Alfonsín government. These judges were: Jorge Torlasco, Guillermo Ledesma, Andrés D'Alessio, Ricardo Gil Lavedra, Jorge Valerge Aráoz, and the president, León Arslanian.

On receiving the first report from the Supreme Council on the trial of the members of the juntas, the Federal Court considered that the proceedings were advancing too slowly and consequently decided [to set a deadline of October 11, 1984 for completion of the trial.]

Report of the Supreme Council

*Mignone, Estlund & Issacharoff, "Dictatorship on Trial"**

In the midst of the proceedings in these cases, on September 20, the National Commission on the Disappearance of Persons submitted its report to President Alfonsín, further raising expectations for immediate action against the highest ranking military officials. The report's prologue, released to the press that day, declared with unmistakable clarity that the more than nine thousand documented disappearances[92] were the work of a repressive structure coordinated from the highest levels of the armed forces and various police and security forces down to hundreds of individual police precincts and military task forces.[93] The prologue stated that even the worst abuses of human rights constituted an integral part of the repressive methodology for which the armed forces bore institutional responsibility.

In assigning institutional responsibility for human rights abuses to the armed forces, the report discredited the government's attempt to focus responsibility on a handful of commanding officers and notorious individuals. The government's strategy received a severe setback five days later, when the Supreme Council issued a report, in anticipation of the October 11 deadline, declaring its inability and unwillingness to complete proceedings against the junta members.[94] The content of the document left little doubt that the Supreme Council had chosen to close ranks behind its

---

* Excerpted from Emilio Fermin Mignone, Cynthia L. Estlund, & Samuel Issacharoff, "Dictatorship on Trial: Prosecution of Human Rights in Argentina," *Yale Journal of International Law*, vol. 10 (1985), pp. 139-141.

92 [omitted]

93 *See* [Report of the National Commission on Disappeared Persons 7-11 (1984)] (prologue presented publicly on Sept. 20, 1984).

94 La Prensa, Sept. 26, 1984, at 1, col. 1.

colleagues at the risk of an open confrontation with its new constitutional commander-in-chief....

The Supreme Council's provocative declaration contained a number of legal propositions which confirmed the unwillingness of the military tribunal to assess the evidence objectively and issue a verdict free of prejudice. First, the Supreme Council declared that it had reviewed all the orders and decrees issued in the "battle against subversion" and found them wholly unobjectionable; the commanders could be found culpable, if at all, only in failing to exercise adequate supervision over their subordinates in order to prevent possible excesses.[95] The Council expressed great doubt concerning the likelihood of proving such excesses. First, the Council stated that the most typical charge, "illegitimate deprivation of liberty" could only be proved if it were first demonstrated that the alleged victim had not actually engaged in "subversive" activities; it appeared to the Council that most had.[96] The Council's report thus suggested that an individual with "subversive" connections—e.g., membership in a leftist political group—was not entitled to procedural due process rights such as formal arrest, notification of the charges, and a fair trial, but was properly subject to summary "disappearance."

Second, the Supreme Council cast a blanket aspersion on the credibility of all those tainted by charges of subversion. Thus, the Council stated that the specific allegations of torture and detention in clandestine concentration camps were particularly difficult to investigate in light of what it saw as the biased nature of the witnesses. Most such witnesses were themselves once held by the military as "subversives" or were relatives of such "subversives;" therefore, according to the Council, "their credibility [was] only relative."[97] Furthermore, the Council stated that certain consistencies in the testimony of these observers as to the pattern followed upon abduction of an individual and the nature of the torture methods used suggested that the witnesses had previously agreed among themselves on the content of their testimony.[98] The Council thus viewed consistent testimony paralleling that submitted to the National Commission not as a confirmation of the accuracy of such accounts, nor as evidence of a uniform, coordinated methodology of, but as a sign of an anti-military conspiracy utilizing deliberate falsification. Finally, the Council paid tribute to the importance of discipline, hierarchy, and obedience to the orders of superior officers.[99]

The public reacted with dismay to the Council's statement, and the press featured overwhelmingly critical commentary by political leaders, lawyers, human rights activists, and other observers.[100] A group of plaintiff-prosecutors petitioned the Supreme Court to intervene and

---

95 *Id.* at col. 5.

96 *Id.*

97 *Id.*

98 *Id.*

99 *Id.* at 4, col. 3.

100 *See, e.g.*, La Prensa, Sept. 28, 1984, at 5, col. 1.

invalidate Law 23.049 on the basis of the prejudgment manifested in the Council's report. The Council responded by sending a letter to the Defense Minister in November complaining of the criticism and, in essence, requesting his intervention to stop what it regarded as scurrilous attacks in the press.[101] Defense Minister Raul Borras responded with a brief letter explaining that, under the constitutional government, freedom of speech and press prevailed, and that the members of the Council, like all citizens, retained their right to proceed legally against those whose criticism they considered defamatory.[102] Within two weeks, the entire membership of the Supreme Council resigned en masse in protest against what they regarded as disrespectful treatment by the press, the public generally, and the Defense Ministry.[103]

The Trial in Civilian Court

Amnesty International, "Argentina: The Military Juntas and Human Rights"[*]

At this point, and on examination of the trial records, the Federal Court observed that since the imposition of a fixed period for completion the Supreme Council had made no progress whatever in the proceedings. The Court accepted that this amounted to the unwarranted delay envisaged by Article 10 of Law 23.049 and that it would therefore have to assume responsibility for hearing the case as it stood at that moment. In its decision, delivered on 4 October 1984, [t]he Federal Court further decided to involve itself collectively in the trial, with all six of its members sitting together rather than in two chambers with three judges sitting in each, as was the normal procedure when judging lesser offenses.

The Second Stage of the Trial

Appeals to the Supreme Court

Following the transfer of jurisdiction to the Federal Court, the former military commanders were advised to appoint defense counsel. General Videla alone refused to do so, arguing that the trial was unconstitutional and that it removed him from the jurisdiction of his natural judges. The other defendants all appointed defense counsel and, in most cases, a team of defense lawyers. To fulfil the requirements of Argentine law, General Videla was represented by the public counsel of the Buenos Aires Appeals Court.

---

101 La Nación, Nov. 10, 1984, at 4, col. 1.

102 *Id.*

103 La Nación, Nov. 15, 1984, at 1, col. 1.

* Excerpted from Amnesty International, *Argentina: The Military Juntas and Human Rights Report of the Trial of the Former Junta Members* (Amnesty International Publications, 1987), pp. 16-22, 34-35, 39-40, 42-48, 53-54, 71-76, 79-83, 85-86.

The first action taken by the civilian defense lawyers was the filing of special appeals to the Supreme Court on the grounds that Law 23.049 was in violation of the constitutional requirement of due legal process. Their case was that, at the time of the events which had led to the trial, the Code of Military Justice had provided that the only court in which they could be tried (even for offenses against the Penal Code) was the Supreme Council of the Armed Forces. Since a civilian court was now empowered to hear the trial, whether through appeal or removal to a higher court, the Argentine Constitution had been violated, for the civilian court was a "special commission", removing the defendants from their "natural judges".

On 27 December 1984 the Supreme Court rejected the arguments of the defense lawyers and declared Law 23.049 to be constitutional and valid....

Preliminary Developments in the Federal Court

Before the Oral Public Hearings of the Federal Appeals Court got under way, there were a number of developments. After the case had been passed back to the Federal Court, the Public Prosecutor, Dr. Julio Strassera, requested that the defendants again be interrogated with a view to obtaining further testimony on what he now referred to as 711 specific counts of criminal actions which had occurred during the rule of the former juntas. The Court accepted his request, and the defendants were brought from prison to testify in answer to his questions. Though all the defendants claimed that they were being brought to trial illegally, only four—Videla, Massera, Galtieri and Lambruschini—refused to make any further statement. The others agreed to give further testimony and thus the procedure requested by the Prosecutor was completed. On 19 March 1985 Strassera announced that he intended to prosecute the defendants on 711 charges, including murder, illegal detention, torture, rape and robbery.

Next, both prosecution and defense counsel submitted their evidence. The prosecution presented eight portfolios with 35 bundles of dossiers and a 20,000 page report containing 3,000 statements with, in addition, a request for the release of 1,500 official documents.... The Court ... ordered that the trial would begin on 22 April 1985 and would be heard in sessions from Monday to Friday of each week. It also ordered that new systems be introduced to record the documentary evidence and to video-tape the testimonies. It also authorized the parties to cross-examine the witnesses (even though this was not allowed in the Military Code), the better to ensure the right to legal defense, albeit with the restriction that the cross-examination be made only at the end of each witness declaration, for the sake of order. The Court further ordered that the defendants need not appear in person if they did not wish to do so, unless the proceedings required their presence. In this matter the Court was rigorous in applying military criminal legislation, since the Code of Military Justice requires the presence of the defendants only at the moment of stating the charges or the plea, and even that appearance has the sole purpose of enabling them to exercise the right to answer the charges granted them by Article 376 of the Code.

The Federal Court was faced with a number of practical problems in organizing a trial of this nature. Argentine criminal procedure is basically conducted in writing, and hence there was a lack of experience of the organization of oral public hearings. The situation was also affected by the number of defendants, their legal status, the positions they had held, and the large number of defense lawyers, since most of the defendants opted to be defended by teams of lawyers. In addition, there was considerable public and journalistic interest, both in Argentina and internationally, in the conduct and outcome of the trial....

As for public and press access to the court room, rows of seats on the ground floor were reserved for persons attending by special invitation. The invitations (distributed by the clerk to the Court) were issued at the discretion of the Court ... or of the Prosecutor or defense counsel. About 100 members of the general public had access to the upper level of the court room, in apparently uncomfortable conditions. The only requirement for admission was to have obtained a pass the day before from an office set up by the Court for the purpose. Accredited journalists were assigned spaces on each side of the rows of seats occupied by persons attending by special invitation. The main reporting restriction was that television networks were not permitted to make live recordings of the sessions. The Court's reason was lack of space to accommodate them all; for their part, the authorities offered to obtain footage taken by the official television network and distribute this to other networks. Foreign television reporters, however, found that they were offered only pictures with no live soundtrack.

In the course of the trial, one change was made regarding attendance. When Public Prosecutor Strassera came to the end of his final remarks, the public broke into loud applause and some shouting, which provoked strong words from General Viola and a defiant gesture from General Videla. As a result, the presiding judge, Dr. Arslanian, ordered the evacuation of the court room and afterwards the Federal Court ruled that the public would not be admitted to further hearings, though access would continue for journalists and persons attending by special invitation.... Although the Federal Court's decision to exclude ordinary members of the public following the outburst of applause did not mean that the trial lost its public character, the decision was seen as excessively harsh by many in Argentina. The incident had been an exceptional one and had been preceded by good behavior on the part of the public during the weeks in which witnesses had been interrogated, despite the intensely emotional significance that the subject matter undoubtedly possessed for many of those present.

The Oral Public Proceedings in the Second Stage of the Trial

The civilian trial proper, the Oral Public Proceedings, began on 22 April 1985 and concluded with the Court's verdict on 9 December 1985. The following account of the oral proceedings is derived largely from official court records and attempts to summarize the general lines of argument of the defense and the prosecution.... During the course of the oral proceedings more than 800 witnesses were called, the majority by the prosecution. Many of the witnesses were released prisoners who described their imprisonment and torture in secret detention centers in different parts of the country. The prosecution also called a number of foreign experts, such as the North American forensic pathologist, Dr. Clyde Snow, and the Dutch former Director of the Division of Human Rights of the United Nations, Dr. Theo van Boven. The defense called former ministers of the Peronist government, senior military officers and trade union leaders. This stage of the trial lasted several months and the Court allowed ample opportunity to both defense and prosecution for the cross examination of witnesses....

The Prosecution Case

In the course of his long statement, the Public Prosecutor set out to prove that:

a) A criminal plan had been put into effect during the rule of the military juntas to secure the elimination by unlawful means of subversive organizations, which had led to abductions, torture, murder, robbery, kidnapping of children, etc.
b) This criminal plan had been designed and the order to carry it out had been given by the military juntas who occupied the highest levels of state power and also of the military and security apparatus. The criminal plan had been implemented through the normal hierarchy and organizational structures of the military and police forces, and with their collaboration. The operation had covered the whole country and had been carried out by all the security services.
c) Evidence of the existence of this plan arose from the proven facts: the disappearance of persons, the appearance of corpses, denunciations both from within Argentina and from abroad, testimonies of survivors and witnesses, etc., the absence of trials and arrests within the legal framework, and the decline of ultra-right wing clandestine organizations, such as the *Alianza Anticomunista Argentina—Triple-A* (Argentine Anti-communist Alliance), after the coup d'état in March 1976.
d) The members of the juntas could not claim ignorance. All of them were aware of what was happening. Not only did they order that the plan should be carried out, but they took steps to ensure the impunity of those who performed the task: impeding the crime-prevention forces in the performance of their duty, restricting the provision of information to the press, using dissimulation and deceit in their dealings with international organizations and with the Argentine judicial system.
e) In the last resort, they were guilty by omission. But their true role was that of indirect perpetrators or "armchair criminals" ("*autores de escritorio*").

The Public Prosecutor began his exposition by citing practical and technical reasons for his decision to limit himself exclusively to 709 cases, although these certainly did not account for all of what he described as the "horrifying number of victims of what we may call the greatest act of genocide ever recorded in our country's brief history". One of the reasons he cited was the absence in Argentine law of any specific offense which adequately encompassed the criminal acts that had given rise to the proceedings.

Next, the Prosecutor placed in its historical context the problem of what he called "state terrorism", which he understood to mean the criminal exercise of power using clandestine methods of repression, beyond the borders of legality. This historical context demonstrated, according to the Prosecutor, the existence of widespread violent guerrilla activity in Argentina in the period before the military juntas came to power.... He went on to list the main guerrilla operations, such as acts of violence, killings, bombings, abductions and ransom demands, etc....

Having argued that it was not a matter of excesses but of illegal actions ordered by superiors, the Prosecutor addressed the question of criminal liability in the particular case of the person who orders an unlawful action to be carried out but is not himself present at the time or place of the crime, and whose role consists in having issued the general orders from which all the offenses have originated.

The members of a part of the apparatus of State had been ordered to abduct, torture and murder vast numbers of people vaguely defined by their opposition, whether moderate or extreme, to the system of the government in power. These orders, by reason of the operating methods prescribed—secrecy and absolute freedom in setting objectives—implied the acceptance that in that area of activity other crimes, such as robbery, rape, suppression of the legal status of minors, etc., would be committed on a massive scale. For the Prosecutor the question then was how the conduct of the defendants in these offenses could be expressed in legal terms under the Penal Code.

International Practice

The Prosecutor made reference to cases indicative of international practice, notably the Eichmann case, where the defendant had been found guilty in spite of not having been materially involved in any actual offense. Can someone in charge of an organized power apparatus which commits a crime be held responsible for this crime, even if he has not been materially involved in it? This was the question which Dr. Strassera posed at this stage in his argument. The expression "organized power apparatus" is uniformly accepted in criminal legal doctrine and signifies a type of organization directed by a decision-making center. It is at this decision-making center that the choice of whether or not to commit the offenses in question arises. The decision-making center dominates the organization in such a way that any decision to commit a crime results in the crime being committed automatically. For the order to be carried out, there is no need for the decision-making center to know the identity of the actual agent; this is due to the substitutability of the agents. Should any agent fail to carry out his duty, another agent would do so in his stead, since the organization is capable of replacing any part of itself with another part, with the result that the order is finally, inexorably, fulfilled.

In these situations, said the Prosecutor, it was possible to speak of an "armchair criminal" in the sense that the person who brings about the commission of the offense is the person behind the direct agent. Beyond the will of the person actually performing the actions there was a higher will which determined the commission of the offense. The identity of the actual agent was immaterial, since the "armchair criminal" was sure that the order, once issued, would be accomplished. Hence, those who control the organized power apparatus should be considered as indirect perpetrators (*"autores mediatos"*) of the crimes committed by its operatives.

The Prosecutor pointed out that his reasoning was based on the accepted notion of "perpetrator" (*"autor"*) in modern criminal theory, according to which the "perpetrator" is identified with the person who plays the dominant role in the commission of the crime. In confirmation of this view he cited Article 514 of the Argentine Code of Military Justice, which was applicable in the present case. Under this law, those who give orders leading to the commission of an offense must inevitably be considered the perpetrators of the offense.

The Criminal Plan of the Juntas

Having stated that he believed the defendants criminally liable, Dr. Strassera applied himself to demonstrating the existence of the criminal plan to which he had been referring. He claimed that on the overthrow of the constitutional government, the military junta had worked out a new operational strategy whose most notable feature was clandestine action, which explained why the plan was also kept secret and never openly admitted. The evidence submitted was nonetheless sufficient for it to be considered fully proven that the plan had existed and had been systematically carried out. The proof lay in the mass of data contained in the assembled evidence.... Finally, he emphasized the significance of the "Final Document" issued by the junta on 28 April 1983, and the Statute of the same date published in the Official Gazette on 2 May 1983. The single article of this last document read as follows:

> All anti-subversive and anti-terrorist operations under-taken by the armed forces and by the Security, Police and Penitentiary Services under operational control and in fulfillment of Decrees 2770, 2771 and 2772/75 were carried out in accordance with plans approved and supervised by the official high commands of the armed forces and by the military junta from the time it was constituted.

...The Prosecutor then turned his attention to the definition in criminal legal terms of the actions that had been ordered by the defendants, and proceeded to enumerate their offenses.

Firstly, he pointed out, the defendants were responsible for numerous crimes of murder under Article 79 of the Penal Code, with aggravating circumstances under sections 2 and 6 of Article 80 of the Code. That is, the murders were carried out with an aggravating circumstance (*alevosía*[7]) and by two or more persons....

Secondly, the defendants were liable for numerous offenses of illegal detention under Article 141 of the Penal Code, with aggravating circumstances....

The third offense mentioned by the Prosecutor was that of infliction of torture on detainees, under Article 144 of the Argentine Penal Code, according to the text in force at the time the offenses were committed. That text carried lower penalties than the present one, as modified by the Law of October 1984.

Fourthly, there was the offense under Article 140 of the Penal Code of reducing a person to servitude or a similar condition....

The fifth offense was that of concealment, under Article 277, section 6, of the Penal Code, which declares punishable anyone who "fails to communicate to the authorities any information he may have in his possession relating the commission of an offense, when his profession or occupation makes it incumbent on him to do so."

The sixth offense was robbery, under Article 164 of the Penal Code, aggravated by the use of violence (section 1 of Article 166) and by the holding of public office by the perpetrators (Article 266).

The seventh offense referred to by the Prosecutor was falsification of public documents under Article 293 of the Penal Code.

Finally, he also listed the following as being among the offenses committed by the defendants:

- abduction of minors (*sustracción de menores*)...
- abduction with extortion (*secuestro extorsivo*)...
- extortion, under Article 168, which declares punishable anyone who, by means of intimidation, forces somebody to yield possession of objects, money or documents;
- suppression of documents, under Article 294 of the Penal Code, which declares punishable anyone who destroys documents in such a way as to cause injury to others....

Nobody, the Prosecutor continued, could claim that the state should remain supine and passive in situations of grave emergency. On the contrary, it should take strenuous steps to prevent and suppress acts of violence and even, if necessary, introduce special legislation. What it should never do was murder or torture in order to prevent some group from torturing and murdering. The emergency powers that the state might require in a crisis, under the Argentine Constitution and under the

---

[7] *Alevosía*: the aggravating circumstance whereby the perpetrator of a crime against persons is assured that there is no danger to himself in committing the offence, either from the victim or from other causes.

International Covenant on Civil and Political Rights and other international instruments, could never extend to the abolition of the rule of law. It might temporarily suspend the exercise of certain rights to ensure continued enjoyment of the more basic ones. The defendants, however, were responsible for having transformed the Argentine state into a huge criminal organization. State terrorism had produced 15 times the number of victims that the guerrilla war had claimed. This was why, said the Prosecutor, the trial and sentence were important and necessary for a country which had been offended against by the perpetration of atrocious crimes. This trial could enable the Argentine people to recover their self-esteem and their trust in the values on the basis of which they had constituted themselves as a nation. This was why the trial and sentence were also important for the armed forces. It was not they that were on trial, but those who had led them. It was not military honour that was at stake, but actions that were at variance with military honour.

The Argentine people, said the Prosecutor, had tried to bring peace by forgetting the past, and had failed: as was demonstrated by past unsuccessful amnesties. They had sought peace through violence and the extermination of the enemy; and had failed. From this trial and the sentence to be pronounced, peace might follow; based not on forgetting but on remembering; not on violence but on justice. "This is our opportunity, and it may be our last," he said.

On the basis of these arguments, the Prosecutor brought his statement to a close by indicating the offenses which in his judgment had been committed by each of the defendants and by asking for the appropriate sentences.

1. **Jorge Rafael Videla**: responsible for 83 murders; 504 acts of illegal detention; 254 acts of torture; 94 aggravated robberies; 180 falsifications of public documents; 4 illegal expropriations; 23 acts of reduction to servitude; 2 abductions with extortion; 1 act of suppressing documents; 7 abductions of minors; 7 acts of torture followed by death.
   The penalty asked for in respect of these offenses was life imprisonment as prescribed by Article 52 of the Penal Code; that is, imprisonment for an unspecified period.

2. **Emilio Eduardo Massera**: responsible for 83 proven murders; 523 acts of illegal detention; 267 acts of torture; 102 aggravated robberies; 201 falsifications of public documents; 4 illegal expropriations; 23 acts of subjection to servitude; 1 extortion; 2 abductions with extortion; 1 act of suppressing documents; 11 abductions of minors; 7 acts of torture followed by death.
   The same penalty was asked for in respect of these crimes as in the case of Videla.

3. **Orlando Ramón Agosti**: responsible for 83 proven murders; 581 acts of illegal detention; 278 acts of torture; 110 aggravated

robberies; 243 falsifications of public documents; 6 illegal expropriations; 27 acts of reduction to servitude; 1 extortion; 2 abductions with extortion; 11 abductions of minors; 7 acts of torture followed by death.
The same penalty was asked for as in the case of Videla.

4. **Roberto Eduardo Viola**: responsible for 5 proven murders; 152 acts of illegal detention; 49 acts of torture; 17 aggravated robberies; 105 falsifications of public documents; 1 illegal expropriation; 32 acts of reduction to servitude; 1 abduction of minors.
A sentence of life imprisonment[8] was asked for.

5. **Armando Lambruschini**: responsible for 5 proven murders; 117 acts of illegal detention; 35 acts of torture; 8 aggravated robberies; 98 falsifications of public documents; 1 illegal expropriation; 32 acts of reduction to servitude; 1 abduction of minors.
A sentence of life imprisonment was asked for.

6. **Omar Graffigna**: responsible for 34 acts of illegal detention; 15 acts of torture; 67 falsifications of public documents; 1 illegal expropriation; 18 acts of reduction to servitude; 172 acts of fraudulent concealment; 1 abduction of minors.
A sentence of 15 years' imprisonment was asked for.

7. **Leopoldo Fortunato Galtieri**: responsible for 11 acts of illegal detention; 1 act of torture; 17 acts of fraudulent misrepresentations in public documents; 1 illegal expropriation; 8 acts of reduction to servitude; 217 acts of fraudulent concealment.
A sentence of 15 years' imprisonment was asked for.

8. **Jorge Isaac Anaya**: responsible for 1 act of illegal detention; 3 acts of fraudulent misrepresentation in public documents; 1 illegal expropriation; 1 act of reduction to servitude; 217 acts of fraudulent concealment.
A sentence of 12 years' imprisonment was asked for.

9. **Basilio Arturo Lami Dozo**: responsible for 1 act of illegal detention; 1 act of fraudulent misrepresentation in public documents; 1 illegal expropriation; 1 act of reduction to servitude; 217 acts of fraudulent concealment.
A sentence of 10 years' imprisonment was asked for....

---

[8] Life imprisonment (*prisión perpetua*) is normally for a period of 20 years.

On reaching the end of his exposition, the Prosecutor delivered the following words: "Your Honours, I shall renounce any pretensions to originality, by using an expression which is not mine, but which belongs to the Argentine people. Your Honours: Never Again." At this moment there was shouting and applause from the public gallery, which resulted in the evacuation of the courtroom and the ban on free public access to the Court's hearings thereafter.

The Defense Case

...From its beginning all the defense lawyers denied the legal validity of the trial on several grounds. The first was that the offenses being tried were subject to an amnesty by Law 22.924, issued by the junta towards the end of its rule (23 September 1983). According to defense counsel, the legislation passed by the democratic parliament as Law 23.040 on 9 February 1984, declaring Law 22.924 to be null and void, was in effect making the defendants subject to a stricter criminal law *ex post facto*, in violation of the constitutional safeguard of due legal process.

The second basis for impugning the legitimacy of the trial was that it effectively created a "special commission" ("*Comisión especial*"), explicitly prohibited in the Argentine Constitution, to try the offenses, thus removing them from the authority of the Court legally competent to try them at the time they were committed, and was therefore in violation of the constitutional principle of due legal process. It was also argued that the fact that the legal proceedings consisted of a single action without the right of appeal (except to the Supreme Court) effectively deprived the defendants of a due legal process. The defense also questioned the legality of the procedural changes ordered by the Federal Court to make the Code of Military Justice more flexible: in taking this step, the defense maintained, the Federal Court had usurped legislative functions or powers and was consequently in violation of applicable procedural norms, by replacing them with others without the authority to do so.

The final argument of defense counsel against the validity of the trial was that President Alfonsín's Decree No 158/83 to institute legal proceedings against the former members of the junta was null and void. They argued that through this decree the executive was prejudging the issue of criminal liability for the offenses against the defendants, imputing guilt before the trial had begun.

A second line of argument employed by the defense lawyers, relating to the charges themselves, was to deny that the events mentioned in the presidential Decree of December 1983, the evidence for which had been provided by the National Commission on the Disappearance of Persons, had ever taken place. The defense took the view that the events had not occurred, that they could not be considered as self-evident, and that therefore it was up to the prosecution to produce the evidence that the offenses had really taken place and that, if so, they were attributable to the defendants.

In the event of the defendants' actions being proved, the defense was concerned to explain and justify these actions, without prejudice to placing the burden of proof on the prosecution, as it was judicially correct for them to do. In doing this they first invoked the "due obedience" principle by which the defendants, as Commanders-in-Chief of the armed forces, had done no more than carry out the orders given by a constitutional government. This would give them indemnity from prosecution under Article 34, section 5, of the Penal Code.

They further claimed that in the course of the operations which it was necessary to carry out in order to fulfil the mandate given them by the constitutional government, a virtual war was unleashed which they described in terms such as irregular, unpublicized, dirty, and so forth. Wars, the defense maintained, cannot ever be brought under the rule of law, since in the course of an armed conflict it is not possible to be bound by rules, especially in the face of an enemy which operates clandestinely and mounts treacherous attacks on the armed forces.

They did, of course, admit that excesses can always be committed in the course of a war and that this certainly had occurred in the case of the irregular war undertaken by the armed forces in Argentina. They emphatically denied, however, that such excesses had been the consequence of orders from above or of a systematic policy on the part of the Commanders-in-Chief. Thus, they reasoned, there were no legal grounds for holding them responsible for the excesses or offenses, nor was there any proof that they had issued orders for the forces under their command to act illegally....

The defense lawyers' final argument on the matter of excesses was to reiterate their opinion that the persons criminally responsible for the offenses would be those who directly perpetrated the deeds and not the accused.

With regard to the evidence actually produced at the trial, the defense's attitude to testimonial evidence is worth examining. In some cases the defense lawyers decided to call persons to give evidence. Much of their evidence aimed to show that officials of the government which had been deposed by the junta were responsible for instituting the procedures which the junta had subsequently followed; or it attempted to show the democratizing intentions of members of the junta, or their concern to avoid excesses or offenses being committed by the personnel under their command.

Throughout the trial, the defense lawyers had continuously sought to discredit the testimony of the persons called to the witness stand by the Prosecutor. Using their opportunities to cross-examine, they had attempted to cast doubt on the testimony by pointing to the witnesses' political opinions (in the vast majority of cases, these were, of course, opposed to the military juntas), or their family ties with the victims, or even their personal backgrounds. This they did with both Argentine and foreign witnesses....

The defense strategy in relation to the voluminous documentary evidence produced at the trial was basically to assert the inadmissibility of the evidence contained in the files and documents prepared by the

National Commission on Disappeared People, CONADEP. The defense lawyers maintained that the Commission was disqualified from presenting evidence on account of the political inclinations of its members, saying that its only purpose had been to carry out a political manoeuvre for the government.... In denying that the CONADEP records had the status of public documents and in discrediting its members, the defense was seeking to invalidate the mass of evidence which had emerged from the activities of the Commission presided over by Sr. Sábato....

The Verdict of the Court

Before commencing a detailed analysis of the verdict pronounced by the Federal Court of Appeals, some general remarks are in order. The verdict was, of course, the climax of a trial unique in Latin American legal history and was therefore also, in a sense, unprecedented. It was spread over 3,200 pages; of these, 2,000 were devoted to a case-by-case analysis of the 700 cases which were finally submitted and 1,200 contained general legal considerations. The work of drawing up the document went on for 43 days, during which the Court was in permanent session with all six of its members.

Having studied the vast amounts of evidence assembled—the 29,000 pages of trial records, the 7,000 writs of habeas corpus, etc.—the judges considered all the legal points raised in the course of the trial and addressed every argument of the prosecution and the defense. Every incident brought to the attention of the Court was subjected to meticulous scrutiny and, in the light of the documentary and testimonial evidence produced at the trial, pronounced to be proven or not proven. In every case on which the Court made a judgment, the items of evidence that led it to its conclusions were fully specified....

The verdict began by discussing a number of peripheral objections raised by the defense, which were all rejected by the Court. The first had to do with the amnesty declared by Law 22.924 of September 1983, repealed by Law 23.040 (1983) after the re-establishment of democratic institutions. The Court pointed out that it had already had occasion, in October 1983, to deliver a judgment stating that Law 22.924 was null and void, and that law 23.040 was not in breach of any constitutional precept in declaring the total invalidity of Law 22.924. The Court then rejected the alleged nullity of Presidential Decree 158/83,[9] reiterating that this Decree should not be seen as prejudging any issue, but simply as the exercise of a prerogative of the President in his capacity as Commander-in-Chief of the Armed Forces, in fulfillment of an indispensable precondition, laid down by law, for the initiation of proceedings to inquire into offenses allegedly committed by officers holding the rank of general. The Court also put aside any imputation made by the defense as to the validity of Law 23.049, which had modified the Code of Military Justice and on the basis of which the juntas had been brought to trial. It pointed out that the constitutionality of

---

[9] [omitted]

the law had been upheld by the Supreme Court and therefore that the question could not be raised anew.

Finally, the Court rejected the argument that the invocation of Article 502 and subsequent clauses of the Code of Military Justice[10] , as well as the changes ordered by the Court itself to introduce greater flexibility, were in violation of the right of defense and hence rendered the trial invalid.... If the ordinary procedure had been applied, much less latitude would have been allowed, and for the defense lawyers to claim that a system which gave them greater freedom of action was in violation of the right to a fair trial was therefore incomprehensible....

The Court concluded:

> It should only be added that this Court has no other means of deciding the case submitted to its consideration than the application of the rules of law. This is not to deny the gravity of the revolutionary war but to accept that society has reached a stage in its cultural progress where it can make provision for exceptional situations, internal unrest, sedition, even war, in the existing legal ordinances. These circumstances can only be addressed from a legal standpoint, which cannot be ignored by the victors or by the vanquished, even when the goal is the destruction of a malignant enemy. The Commanders are in the dock, not for winning a victory but for the means they adopted in bringing it about. They are not there for putting an end to the scourge of subversion, but for leaving Argentine society deeply wounded by the damage done to the values that are a vital part of its culture, traditions and way of life, the very things that were being fought for.

The Court then stated that to deal with the insurgents ... the constitution provides for powers to declare a state of siege, under Article 23, in the event of disturbances to law and order, and to suspend constitutional guarantees. Even in this case, however, the executive is restricted in its powers and therefore the existence of the state of siege in the period during which the defendants were in office could not justify the actions of which they were accused. The Court also referred to the "state of internal war" provided for in Law 14.072. It examined the legislation contained in the Code of Military Justice, the National Defense Law and the Penal Code, and finally the detailed regulations issued by the armed forces themselves governing their role in operations against irregular forces. It was impermissible, it concluded, for a *de facto* government in whose hands the most wide-ranging powers were concentrated, and which had even arrogated constitutional powers to itself, to find no other means of combatting terrorism than by recourse to clandestine methods and the imposition of a terror of equal ferocity.

The Court analysed the provisions of international law, including ... the Geneva Conventions for the Protection of Victims of War of 12 August 1949.

The provisions of the four conventions that the Court held to be the most important were contained in Article 3, which is common to each of the

---

10 [omitted]

Geneva Conventions. This article provides that in armed conflict not of an international character occurring in the territory of a Contracting Party, each party to the conflict must apply the following provisions: persons taking no active part in the conflict, members of the armed forces who have laid down their arms, and those placed *hors de combat* by sickness, wounds, detention or any other cause, shall in all cases be treated humanely. Acts prohibited at all times in respect of such persons include: violence to life and person, in particular murder of all kinds, mutilation, cruel treatment and torture; also the passing of sentences and the carrying out of executions without previous judgment pronounced by a regularly constituted court, affording all the judicial guarantees which are recognized as indispensable by civilized peoples. Article 3 also states that wounded and sick persons shall be collected and cared for.

The Court noted the need to bear in mind certain conventions on the rules of war, which emphasize that the belligerents do not have an unlimited right to inflict harm on the enemy. It mentioned, as being the most important of these: the Geneva Conventions of August 1864 and July 1906; the St. Petersburg Declaration of 11 December 1868; the Hague Convention of 1899; and the resolutions of the Hague Conference of 1907, stressing this as the most important of its age, having resulted in what are known as the "Hague Regulations." Finally, the Court examined the consensus of authors of public international law that war is a terrible scourge and should be rendered as humane as possible through the application of the humanitarian principles which characterize public international law. In this context of humanizing war, the Court mentioned the pronouncements of the Second Vatican Council on the subject.

The Court considered whether these standards were also valid for a conflict described as a revolutionary war. Having consulted the work of various authors, including Argentine generals who were experts in the field, it reached the conclusion that humanitarian principles were indeed relevant to this type of conflict. This section of the verdict concluded with the words: "Not for homicide, torture, robbery, or illegal detention is there even the suggestion of any justification or immunity from blame in the provisions of statutory or common law, or in the writings of these authors."

The eagerness of the defense to refer to the law in some circumstances and place itself entirely outside it in others, on the grounds that a war was going on in Argentina, had, said the Court, made it necessary to make the detailed study outlined in the previous paragraphs. It had done so to follow the line of argument taken by the defense, but it had to be emphasized that its decision was based exclusively on Argentine law as it stood; this was what had enabled the Court to find that the actions which had led to the trial were against the law.

The Court then recapitulated the offenses deemed to have been proven and considered the question of parties to the crime and criminal liability. "As has been demonstrated during the proceedings, on or near 24 March 1976, the day the armed forces overthrew the constitutional authorities and took over the government, some of the defendants, in their capacity as

Commanders-in-Chief of their respective forces, gave orders to fight terrorist subversion in a way which basically meant:

> a) taking into captivity anyone who might be suspected, on the basis of intelligence information, of having links with subversion;
> b) removing them to places located inside establishments belonging to or controlled by the armed forces;
> c) once there, interrogating and torturing them to obtain as much information as possible about other persons who might be involved;
> d) submitting them to inhuman living conditions to break their morale;
> e) effecting the above in conditions of absolute secrecy; the abductors having to conceal their identity and carry out their operations at night, the victims remaining blindfolded and completely incommunicado, and public officials, relatives and close associates being denied information as to what had befallen the victim and the location of residential establishments;
> f) giving the lower ranks a very free hand in deciding the fate of the prisoner, who might be released, placed at the disposal of the Executive, tried by a military or civilian court, or physically eliminated.
>
> These actions were to be undertaken within existing legislation relating to the war against subversion, but without complying with the rules that forbade this kind of activity.
>
> Another feature of the system was the guarantee of impunity enjoyed by those who undertook the actions, which was achieved by ensuring that the legal crime-prevention agencies would not interfere, by denying and concealing the truth when approached by judges, organizations, relatives and foreign governments, and by faking investigations into the incidents and using state power to convince public opinion at home and abroad that the denunciations were false and were the result of a concerted campaign to discredit the government.
>
> The trial has also shown that the orders resulted in a large number of cases of illegal detention, torture episodes and homicides. The evidence has also shown that in carrying out these actions, subordinates committed other offenses which were not part of their actual orders but can be regarded as being a natural consequence of the system.

The Court asked if the defendants were liable for these misdeeds, even though none of them actually committed any of the offenses in person. It reviewed the usual arguments about principals and accessories, concluding that nowadays the prevailing view is to accept the principle of "*dominio del hecho*" ("control over the act"). It then established that the relevant provision was Article 514 of the Code of Military Justice, which stated: "When an offense is committed in the execution of an order in the course of duty, the superior officer who gave the order shall be solely responsible...." This provision, said the Court, was the direct embodiment of the "*dominio del hecho*" principle.

Next, the Court examined what rules are to be found on this aspect in military criminal law in Germany, Italy, Brazil, Peru and Venezuela, among others, and found that the rule contained in Article 514 embodied a principle explicitly accepted in other military legal systems....

From a legal point of view, the Court said, the degree of liability of the direct perpetrators was not important in determining the liability of the defendants. Whether those who in fact carried out the actions were liable or not, the defendants were at all times in control of these actions and must therefore be held vicariously liable for all the offenses that were committed. The order to implement the illegal system was conveyed through the regular chain of command and was intended to render existing legal ordinances to be ineffective, insofar as they forbade the newly established procedures; otherwise, the previously existing regulations continued to be fully operative. The whole military apparatus continued to function normally, and only the "method" of combat changed.

The guarantee of immunity from punishment was also part of the plan. The ordinary crime-prevention mechanisms were prevented from intervening, and the strategy was adopted of denying that anything untoward had occurred in the face of all manner of protests, giving false replies to judicial requests, and preventing information from being published in the press.

> The defendants were in control of the acts because they controlled the organization that produced them. The incidents that these proceedings are concerned with are not the consequence of the erratic, isolated decisions of the individuals who carried them out, but the tactics which the Commanders-in-Chief of the armed forces conveyed to their men.... The defendants not only commanded their own forces but also the security forces, including the crime-prevention agencies.

If a subordinate had attempted to disobey an order, said the Court, he would automatically have been replaced by someone who would have carried it out. The plan could never have been frustrated by the will of a single direct agent, since they were no more than small cogs in a gigantic machine.

> The fact that the defendants were not aware of the individual incidents or the identity of the victims is of no consequence.... The Commanders at all times had it in their power to prevent the offenses that were being committed from taking place. All they had to do was order that the system be discontinued. Convincing proof of this is afforded by the fact that when they thought it necessary they suddenly put a stop to the irregular operations, announcing publicly that the war was over. After that there were no more abductions, torture, or 'disappearances'.

The Court then proceeded to determine specific responsibility in respect of the charges proven against each defendant, and to rule out their liability in respect of other charges. Before examining each situation, the Court reiterated its view that responsibility derived from having been in command of a branch of the armed forces and not from having been a member of the military junta.

> It has been reasonably established that the orders in question did not originate from the body known as the military junta, but that each defendant was in effective and exclusive command of his

> respective force, and hence the Prosecution's contention that they are liable for offenses perpetrated by the subordinates of others is rejected....

In the last section of the verdict, the Court expounded its reasoning in assessing the penalties to be imposed on the five defendants, dealing with each case individually. These explanations had a common introduction which may be quoted in full:

> The offenses in this case not only include some of the gravest charges provided for in legal ordinances, but were carried out indiscriminately and in a particularly despicable manner, namely, by secretly making use of the apparatus of the state. This form of activity encouraged the impunity and implied that the harm done to the victims would also be inflicted on relatives and close associates who had nothing to do with the activities of which the victims were accused; it also did serious damage to the legal system and the institutions it had set up. This damage was also suffered by the armed forces who were in the position of having to obey the orders given by the defendants even though they were made illegal by the very legislation from which their authority was derived.
>
> Without wishing to reduce the very real gravity of the offenses that were committed, it should be pointed out that they occurred as a reaction against the criminal attacks which Argentine society and the state had been suffering at the hands of terrorist organizations. These attacks both undermined confidence in the ability of the forces of law to maintain order and uphold the rights of the individual, and gave rise to a feeling of anxiety and insecurity in the absence of which these offenses would never have taken place....

The Court ... sentenced Videla to the maximum penalty of life imprisonment (*reclusión perpetua*).[14] It also absolutely disqualified him in perpetuity from holding public office.... [Eduardo Massera was sentenced] to *prisión perpetua* instead of *reclusión perpetua*. Massera too, was absolutely disqualified in perpetuity from holding public office.... [The Court] sentenced Agosti to four years and six months' imprisonment, and absolute disqualification in perpetuity from holding public office.

In view of the the number and severity of the offenses committed by Roberto Eduardo Viola, the Court sentenced him to 17 years' imprisonment and absolute disqualification in perpetuity from holding public office.... Lambruschini was ... sentenced to eight years' imprisonment, and to absolute disqualification in perpetuity from holding public office.

The Court then examined the additional penalties ("*penas accesorias*") to be imposed on the defendants. They were all required to pay the costs of the proceedings and were, in addition, definitively stripped of their rank, discharged from the armed forces and deprived of all entitlements from the state in respect of services rendered (pensions, decorations)....

---

14 The difference between *reclusión* and *prisión* is as follows: in the past, the penalty of *reclusión* was more dishonourable and was accompanied by forced labour. As Argentine criminal law changed, the humiliating aspect of *reclusión* was dropped. At present the difference is that the person sentenced to *reclusión* faces a harsher régime than the ordinary prisoner, being permanently confined to his cell in a maximum security institution. For the ordinary prisoner, conditions are more relaxed.

Appeals from the Federal Court to the Supreme Court

...In the case of the five military commanders convicted by the Federal Court, writs of error were duly lodged by counsel on the grounds that their sentences were arbitrary and that the charges were unsubstantiated and that the liability of the defendants was not proven. On 24 December 1985 the Prosecutor also filed an appeal against the acquittal of some of the defendants, on the ground that the Court had overlooked evidence. The Prosecution maintained that the Federal Court, by attributing differing degrees of liability to members of one and the same junta, had acted in an arbitrary manner. The Prosecution maintained that all the members of each junta should have been considered equally accountable for the crimes which had been committed, and should have been subjected, therefore, to the same penalties.

A number of similar writs were also filed on behalf of individual injured parties, such as the parents of a seventeen-year-old boy, Pablo Fernández Meijide, who had been abducted in 1976. The parents called upon the Supreme Court to impose life sentences on all nine military commanders. Such appeals were *prima facie* admissible as Law 23.049 had granted the victims and their families the right to initiate criminal proceedings and to appeal against the verdict.

The Federal Court allowed all the appeals to proceed and on 30 December 1986 the Supreme Court delivered its ruling, which basically confirmed the verdict of the Federal Court. The Supreme Court rejected the defendants' claim that the trial was unconstitutional and the sentence arbitrary, and it similarly rejected extraordinary appeals from the parents of disappeared persons. However, in two cases the sentences were slightly reduced... The Supreme Court also modified the verdict of the Federal Court by designating the defendants necessary participants in rather than indirect perpetrators of criminal acts. While this change did not affect the penalties imposed, the Supreme Court thereby emphasized the individual responsibility of the commanders for the human rights violations which had occurred under their rule.

> In conclusion, in so far as the accused issued secret oral illegal orders to combat terrorism, and in so far as they also provided the direct perpetrators with the necessary means for carrying out these orders—by assuring them that having committed these crimes they would not be pursued nor would they have to answer for them, and by guaranteeing their impunity—the necessary cooperation of the accused in the commission of the deed is on a par with the contribution of the other participants....

[D]espite its political implications, this was not a "political" trial but a criminal action undertaken to inquire into violations of Argentine penal law. The accused were not on trial for having organized a coup d'état, overthrown the Constitution, or deposed the legitimate authorities. Nor were they on trial to answer for the way they had exercised power, politically speaking, during their period of government. They were on trial to answer before a criminal court for their possible involvement in illegal acts allegedly committed during the period of anti-terrorist struggle. They stood accused in their capacities as commanders of the armed forces and as members of the military juntas which had governed Argentina at the time. Furthermore, they were tried for offenses defined by the laws in force throughout their period of office. They were not tried under criminal laws introduced after the alleged offenses, nor were they charged under norms created for doctrinal or jurisprudential reasons or under international legal concepts such as genocide or war crimes. They were tried for possible offenses under the Argentine Penal Code, which remained in force throughout the period that they were in charge of the government.

In the opinion of Amnesty International's observers, the conduct of the trial by the judges left little room for criticism. Each judge, when acting as Chairman, was strictly impartial in his dealings with both prosecution and defense, fully upholding freedom of expression while insisting on relevance to the point at issue. Both the Prosecution and the counsel for defense were given great latitude in calling as many witnesses, foreign or Argentine, as they deemed necessary; and the Court made arrangements in every case for the witnesses to be summoned at the hearings.... In general, the criteria for admitting cross-examination were ample and generous. All the indications are that these criteria were maintained throughout the 78 days during which evidence was heard. During this time 833 witnesses were examined, resulting in a total of 487 hours of testimony.

The Court was no less generous in the criteria it applied to the admission of documentary evidence. All manner of documents, files, reports, certificates, etc. were admitted as evidence, including 7,000 writs of habeas corpus filed during the period the military juntas were in power, 4,000 diplomatic protests received by the Argentine government in the same period, and a large number of records of judicial proceedings resulting from incidents such as the discovery of corpses. The main body of the trial records contained a total of 29,700 pages, plus 12,000 pages of transcriptions of the public hearings.

There is no doubt that the right of the accused to legal defense was properly upheld at the trial....

From the many issues at stake in the trial, two points of principle have emerged as important: the concept of collective responsibility and the claim of "due obedience". As described earlier in this report, the Prosecution's case was that the defendants were collectively responsible for the planned and systematic crimes committed by the military and security forces during the period when the defendants were at the summit of state power. The Prosecution maintained that the apparatus of repression could not have functioned on such a scale without the sanction of the military juntas. The Court, however, rejected the thesis that the juntas as a whole should be held liable for the offenses, and instead assigned differing degrees of responsibility to the Commanders-in-Chief of the different services. There had, it emerged, been an enormous disparity between the Army and Air Force in the number and gravity of offenses committed by each. The Court may have feared that if it decided to punish General

Videla and Brigadier Agosti equally, it might give credibility to allegations that the trial was politically motivated, or it may have feared that such a decision might lead to a successful appeal to the Supreme Court on the grounds of arbitrariness. But undoubtedly, too, the Court was guided by the basic principle in criminal law that liability and the corresponding sentence must be assessed individually and not collectively. Collective entities cannot stand trial, only individual persons, and this poses major difficulties in cases of offenses planned or perpetrated by groups....

LIMITATIONS ON FURTHER PROSECUTIONS

*Alejandro M. Garro and Henry Dahl, "Legal Accountability for Human Rights Violations in Argentina"**

The Directives of the Minister of Defense

...On April 24, 1986, the Minister of Defense issued a set of directives for the General Prosecutor before the Supreme Council of the Armed Forces. Some of those directives were aimed at speeding up the trials; others were widely understood as being designed to bar the military prosecutor from bringing charges against those who had committed atrocities.[216] The General Prosecutor was instructed to assimilate outstanding cases into already existing trials, grouping the defendants according to the army corps to which they belonged. He was also requested to make use of the evidence produced at the trial of the former commanders to simplify the prosecutions, following as closely as possible the method for grouping the evidence used by the Federal Court of Appeals in the case of the former commanders.

Those instructions had the ostensible purpose of expediting the numerous military proceedings pending against subordinate officers. However, a closer reading of those directives discloses the Government's intention to encourage the General Prosecutor to dismiss as many cases as possible.[217] Thus the General Prosecutor was instructed to request the acquittal of the defendants or the dropping of cases related to charges for which the commanders had been acquitted. This instruction cannot be reconciled with the fact that the acquittal of the former commanders was

---

* Excerpted from Alejandro M. Garro and Henry Dahl, "Legal Accountability for Human Rights Violations in Argentina: One Step Forward and Two Steps Backward," *Human Rights Law Journal*, vol. 8 (1987), pp. 333-337.

216 La Prensa, April 26, 1986, p. 1; La Nación, May 4, 1986, p. 9; El Periodista de Buenos Aires, No. 86, p.3-4, May 2-8, 1986.

217 *See* A. M. Garro, *Las instrucciones del Ministro de Defensa al Fiscal General de las Fuerzas Armadas: "Punto final" o aceleración de procesos?*, Revista el Derecho ... No. 6553, August 21, 1986; H. Verbitsky, Civiles y Militares 162-163 (1987).

linked to their responsibility as commanders-in-chief and for criminal acts committed while performing such functions....[218]

Under art. 11 of Law No. 23049 the defense of due obedience could not be claimed: (a) when the subordinate officer was in a position to exercise discretion; or (b) when it could be proved that the subordinate officer was aware of the illegality of the order; or (c) when the crime involved the execution of atrocious or aberrant acts.[219] According to the instructions, however, the General Prosecutor was directed to request the acquittal of a subordinate officer unless it was clear that he went beyond the orders or had exceeded the "global orders" or criminal plan implemented by the former commanders-in-chief. The instructions of the Ministry of Defense raised considerable controversy because they made it extremely difficult for a plea of due obedience to be rejected. Judge Jorge E. Torlasco, one of the judges of the Federal Appeals Court, resigned after the publication of the directives issued by the Minister of Defense. Two other judges, León C. Arslanián and Jorge A. Valerga Aráoz, tendered their resignation but agreed to stay only after President Alfonsín assured them that there had been no intention to undermine the judgment of the Appeals Court.[220]

[A Deadline for New Cases: The Law of "Full Stop"]

A few months after the issuance of the instructions, the pressures on the Government to limit the prosecutions increased. The second major setback to the Government's initial human rights policy was the passing of Law No. 23492 on December 24, 1986, which later became known as the "full stop" (*punto final*) law. Before submitting the bill to Congress, President Alfonsín announced his intention of proposing legislation to curtail the prosecution of military officers in order to extinguish the "interminable suspicion" hanging over the military. Alfonsín denied that his actions were prompted by military pressure. Instead, he argued that it was time for the armed forces to take part in rebuilding a democratic society. The President emphasized that it was now time for Argentina to break free of its bitter past, which he said was a shared burden.[221] Human rights organizations opposed the legislation, arguing that the bringing of charges should be allowed to continue for as long as evidence could be amassed and the statute of limitations was not exceeded. Many leaders of the radical party also expressed disagreement. Nevertheless, the President's lobbying efforts were successful.[222] In spite of the protests of a significant segment of

---

218 *See* App. Court Judg., § 69....

219 *See* art. 11, Law No. 23049....

220 [omitted]

221 New York Times [hereafter referred to as N.Y.T.], December 28, 1986, p. 4.

222 [omitted]

Argentine society,[223] Congress passed Law No. 23492, severely limiting the time available to bring military and law enforcement officers to trial.[224]

The full stop law attempted to curb the initiation of new prosecutions and the further prosecution of pending cases. The law established a 60-day deadline from the date of its promulgation for lodging formal charges and issuing summonses for crimes "related to the establishment of violent methods of political action" [*delitos vinculados a la instauración de formas violentas de acción política*] which were committed before December 10, 1983.[225] The Supreme Council of the Armed Forces was given 48 hours to pass on information about every case pending to the competent federal appeals court. The appeals courts could then decide whether to press charges by summoning the defendants within the 60 day period.[226] The crimes of kidnapping and concealment of minors were excluded from the law of full stop.[227]

Considering the slow pace of the administration of criminal justice in Argentina, and the obvious difficulties in gathering evidence at the time the full stop law was enacted, Government officials involved in the drafting of the statute considered unlikely that many more military officials would be tried other than those who had already been taken to court.[228] But, the result of the full stop law was a flurry of last minute filings by prosecutors, human rights groups and relatives of victims. By shifting the burden to the courts to permit accused murderers and torturers to escape prosecution, the law backfired on the Government.[229] Many federal appeals courts decided to remain open during January, traditionally the summer vacation season for the Argentine judiciary. During that period federal courts of appeals took over most cases pending before the Supreme Council of the Armed Forces, worked to expedite the process of indictment, and received new cases. After the passing of the midnight deadline of February 22, 1987, more than 300 summonses had been issued by eight federal appeals courts around the country against military officers, at least

---

223 *Silent Majority Opposed to Full Stop?*, Buenos Aires Herald..., December 14, 1986, p. 3. *Incidentes con Madres de Plaza de Mayo*, La Nacion, December 29, 1986, at p. 5; *Protesta de ex detenidos frente al Parlamento*, La Nacion, December 29, 1986, at p. 5.

224 Law No. 23492, promulgated on December 23, 1986.... Judge Guillermo Ledesma, the presiding judge of the Federal Appeals Court which handed down the judgement against the former commanders, resigned shortly after President Alfonsín proposed the "full stop" law. El Informador Publico, December 19, 1986, p. 21.

225 Under the broad terms of the law, formal charges against members of leftist guerilla groups accused of criminal activity also had to be brought within 60 days.

226 *See* Victor A. Guerrero Leconte, *Pero, qué es el procesamiento*, El Informador Público, December 19, 1986, p. 21. The deadline for issuing summonses was extended to allow 60 days from the time a particular court took jurisdiction over the case, so that the time taken by jurisdictional disputes between military and federal courts were not counted. Law No. 23492, Art. 4.

227 Law No. 23492, Art. 5.

228 *See* Americas Watch Report, *supra* note 68, at 66. ("By all accounts, the government expected that by February 22, 1987, when the 60 days were to expire, only some 30 to 40 members of the armed forces, mostly in retirement, would continue to face charges.").

229 Americas Watch Report, *supra* note 68, at 66.

30 of whom were army and navy officers in active service.[230] The passage of the full stop law did not significantly improve relations between the Government and the armed forces, costing the President a significant loss of credibility for the adamant way in which he forced its acceptance on his own party.[231]

The Directives of the Procurator General

On February 3, 1987, the Procurator General of the Nation issued a set of directives to federal prosecutors before the federal appeals courts on how to proceed in human rights cases.[232] The directives were issued, once again, for the ostensible purpose of "speeding up the trials" against military officers. To this end, federal prosecutors were urged to stick to those cases of human rights violations which had been proven in the trial against the former commanders, concentrating on those charges on which the defendants were most likely to be convicted. Prosecutors were also urged to concentrate on those who were in charge of illegal anti-terrorist operations, who actually committed atrocities, and those believed responsible for the kidnapping of minors. Federal prosecutors were reminded that, according to the Supreme Court decision of December 30, 1980, the statute of limitations for those crimes should run as of the time of the accused serviceman's last contact with the victim.

On the subject of "due obedience", the directives repeated almost word for word those issued by the Ministry of Defense to the military prosecutor in April of 1986.[233] The federal prosecutors largely agreed with the instructions, claiming that they did not alter the legal framework of the prosecutions. However, human rights groups interpreted those instructions as a renewal of Government pressure to limit the prosecutions against military officers.[234]

[The Defense of "Following Orders:" The Law of "Due Obedience"]

By March 1987, a total of fifty-one military and police officers had been arrested in connection with human rights cases. Twelve had been sentenced while only five convictions, those of the former commanders, were ratified by the Supreme Court. The large number of cases still pending[235] gave rise to anger within the armed forces, with resulting

---

230 N.Y.T., February 24, 1987, at A-3.

231 Americas Watch Report, *supra* note 68, at 67.

232 The directives were issued in compliance with a presidential decree. Decree No. 92 of January 22, 1987. [1987-A] A.L.J.A. 356-357. The complete text of the directives was published in La Prensa, February 4, 1987, p. 1.

233 [omitted]

234 *Instrucciones a los Fiscales Federates: Consagrar la Impunidad*, El Periodista, No. 125, January 30 - February 5, 1987, p. 6.

235 The information on the court filings was not gathered in one place, but the number of pending cases before the Easter weekend uprising was estimated at anywhere from 200 to 450. About one-third were thought to be active-duty officers and the remainder retired officers,

pressure on the Government. Amid an atmosphere of growing tension and assertiveness within the armed forces, a military crisis of major proportions exploded when an army officer refused to appear before the Federal Appeals Court of Córdoba. Major Ernesto Guillermo Barreiro sought refuge in his army unit, whose chief announced that he would not deliver Barreiro to the court. The incident was followed by a series of rebellions in army units during Easter of 1987, led by middle-ranking officers opposed to the continuation of the trials....[236]

*Kathryn Lee Crawford, "Due Obedience and the Rights of Victims: Argentina's Transition to Democracy"**

...On Easter Sunday, after a dramatic visit with the rebels, Alfonsin announced that the rebellion had been put down.[47] From the balcony of the Government House in Buenos Aires, Alfonsin told the 80,000 gathered that democracy was not negotiable. Nearly one month after this speech, despite public antipathy toward the military revolt, the government proposed Law No. 23521, the law of due obedience.[48]...

The due obedience law creates a conclusive presumption that low- and middle-ranking officers, as well as most officers of higher rank, acted under superior orders and duress and therefore may not be prosecuted for human rights abuses. The law is based upon the justificatory doctrine of due obedience, or the "following orders" defense found in Article 514 of the Code of Military Justice and in Article 34 of the Argentine Criminal Code (*Codigo Penal*).[49]

---

police or former civilian operatives. *Argentina Considering Steps to Appease the Military,* N.Y.T., April 23, 1987, at p. A-3.

236 N.Y.T. April 18, 1987, p. 1.

* Excerpted from Kathryn Lee Crawford, "Due Obedience and the Rights of Victims: Argentina's Transition to Democracy," *Human Rights Quarterly,* vol. 12 (1990), pp. 26-40, 44-46, 48-50.

47 As soon as the uprising began, a federal judge initiated criminal proceedings against the participants' "rebellion." At a meeting with government officials, the leader of the rebellion, Colonel Rico, insisted on immunity for everyone but himself. The government proposed the case as "mutiny," a lesser offense with exclusive military court jurisdiction. The Argentine Penal Code (*Codigo Penal*) defines "rebellion" as an "attempt to overthrow the government or to influence its decisions." Colonel Rico was arrested and confined to the officer's club of an army unit. On 25 May, Argentina's national holiday, dozens of officers sang the national anthem at his window. *Americas Watch Report* [*Truth and Partial Justice in Argentina* 68, 79 (August 1987) [hereinafter *Americas Watch Report*]]. Critics say the lack of clear structural reform of the military by the government is related to the revolt.

48 After the *Semana Santa* rebellion, Alfonsin had stated on 16 May in his speech to the Legislative Assembly that there would be no concessions or any pressure to limit the equal submission of all citizens—with or without uniform—to the dictates of the law. 3 Madres de la Plaza de Mayo 2-3 (May 1987). In addition to the proposal of the law of due obedience, the commander-in-chief of the armed forces, General Hector Rios Erenu, was dismissed, and other generals were retired, some for supporting the rebels and others for not being able to control them. *Americas Watch Report, supra* note [47], at 68. (Thousands of Argentines in Buenos Aires and other cities took to the streets in support of Alfonsin; 50,000 of them surrounded the military compound at Campo de Mayo that Colonel Rico and his companions were holding.) [Washington Office on Latin America12 *Latin American Update* 2 (May/June, 1987)].

49 Decree No. 158 (15 Dec. 1983). Decree No. 158 was based on Article 514 of the CMJ, Law No. 14029, which states: "When a crime has been committed through the execution of an order of service, the superior who has given it will be the only party responsible, [and] the

Article I of the due obedience law states that all officers subordinate to chiefs of security areas, chiefs of security forces, or chiefs of security subareas (such as the police chief of Buenos Aires) are innocent because they were following orders.[50] The presumption of due obedience forbids the court from considering evidence that would show the defendants were not acting under duress or that they had an opportunity to consider the illegality of the orders.[51] This presumption departed from Article 11 of Law No. 23049, which had required the defendant to show he mistakenly believed the orders were legitimate. Law No. 23049 created a rebuttable presumption of due obedience; the presumption could be overcome by evidence that the orders were manifestly illegal, and the defense was not allowed for aberrant or atrocious crimes.[52] Under the new law, the courts could not review any evidence to determine if the officer knew or should have known he was acting on illegal orders. The due obedience law's presumption of innocence covers all crimes mentioned in Article 10 of Law No. 23049—those committed by the military between 24 March 1976 and September 1982 in operations with the alleged "motive to combat terrorism."[53]

The irrebuttable presumption of following orders in Article 1 applies also to superior-ranking officials who did not have "decisionmaking capacity" (*capacidad decisoria*) or who did not participate in the "formulation of the orders" (*elaboracion de ordenes*) to commit the illegal acts. The law creates a presumption that these officials operated under coercion or duress since they were subordinate to a superior authority. They are presumed not to have had the ability to oppose the orders or investigate their legitimacy.[54]

Under Article 2 of the law, the due obedience defense is not available in cases of rape, theft, and the kidnapping of minors and falsification of their civil status, the crime by which children of the *desaparecidos* were assigned false identities and given to other families.[55] The law's

---

inferior will only be considered an accomplice when he has been excessive in the fulfillment of said order." *Compare* arts. 34(5) and 248 *with* art. 514 of the CMJ. (In the civilian *Codigo Penal*, Article 34(5) contains a general due obedience doctrine that subordinates shall not be prosecuted for following orders. However Article 248, which applies to the civilian public official (*funcionario publico*), expressly excludes the subordinate who follows illegitimate orders (and he cannot invoke the justification in Article 34(5))....

50 Alfonsin submitted the law to benefit everyone under the rank of colonel. But the joint chiefs of staff demanded that the presumption be extended to higher ranks, including some generals. In the final adoption of the law, the Senate (*Camara de Senadores*) and the House of Representatives (*Camara de Diputados*) followed the demands of the chiefs. *Americas Watch Report, supra* note [47], at 70.

51 *Cf.* [Supreme Court of Argentina, 22 June 1987, "Causa No. 547 incoada en virtud del Decreto No. 280/84 del Poder Ejecutivo Nacional," 1987-D Revista La Ley [hereinafter L.L.] 220 [hereinafter Constitutionality of the due obedience law]] (Petracchi, concurring, Bacque, dissenting). Justices Petracchi and Bacque point out that the justificatory doctrine has never been allowed when it has been found that the subordinates had the opportunity to decide that the orders were manifestly illegal, therefore exempting them from the duty to obey.

52 [omitted]

53 Law No. 23521, art. 1.

54 *Id.*

55 [omitted]

presumption of innocence does cover torture, murder, arbitrary arrest, and misrepresentation.[56]

Article 3 states that the presumption of due obedience will automatically be applied by the courts in any pending cases. Article 4 establishes that those officers whom the former law of *Punto Final* did not exempt would not be subject to arraignment (*acusacion*) if they fell under Article I of the due obedience law. The due obedience law virtually nullifies all the frantic work months earlier by *querellantes* and prosecutors to file complaints before the *Punto Final* deadline. Article 5 establishes that any lower court application of this law (*recurso ordinario de apelacion*) may be appealed to the Supreme Court.[57]

Procedural History of the Camps Case

Before the due obedience law was passed, the Federal Court of Appeals (Criminal Division) for the District of Buenos Aires decided the case of two former police chiefs, Ramon Juan Alberto Camps and Ovidio Pablo Riccheri, along with four lower-ranking officers. Like the prosecutions of the *junta* leaders, the case against Camps and Riccheri began 18 January 1984, when it was submitted to summary trial (*juicio sumario*) before the Supreme Council of the Armed Forces by way of presidential decree.[58] The federal appeals court in Buenos Aires took cognizance of the case in 1985 by way of Article 10 of Law No. 23049 just as it had assumed jurisdiction over the prosecution of the *junta* leaders when the military court unduly delayed the proceedings.[59] The appeals court received new evidence, including testimony from approximately ninety-five victims of the abuses perpetrated by the defendants, and found the defendants guilty of various crimes including torture, kidnapping, and murder.[60] The court sentenced Camps to twenty-five years in prison as the perpetrator (*autor responsable*) of seventy-three counts of torture of civilians,[61] and it sentenced Riccheri to fourteen years imprisonment as perpetrator of twenty counts of torture. In the same case, the court found Miguel Osvaldo Etchecolatz, the chief inspector of the police for the Province of Buenos Aires, guilty of ninety-one counts of torture and sentenced him to twenty-three years imprisonment. Two others, Jorge Antonio Berges,

---

56 *Americas Watch Report, supra* note [47], at 90.

57 Article 5 allows the Supreme Court to review issues such as whether officers of higher ranks, not listed in Article 1, had decisionmaking capacity. The control of the constitutionality of the law proceeded through *recurso extraordinario. See infra* notes 62-64 and accompanying text.

58 Decree No. 280/84 (Jan. 1984) ordered the prosecution of the higher-ranking military officers Ramon Juan Alberto Camps, Ovidio Pablo Riccheri, Miguel Osvaldo Etchecolatz, Jorge Antonio Berges, Norberto Cozzani, and Luis Hector Vides and Alberto Rousse. *See* Federal Appeals Court, Judgment of the Camps case, (2 Dec. 1986) [hereinafter Appeals Court Judgment, Camps case], court copy; *see also* Constitutionality of the due obedience law, *supra* note [51], at 185.

59 *See Cuestion de competencia originaria a raiz del decreto 280-84,* 1986-A L.L. 624 (1985).

60 [omitted]

61 [omitted]

a medical officer, and Corporal Norberto Cozzani, were convicted as coperpetrators of two and four counts of torture, respectively.

On 22 June 1987, the Supreme Court received this joint case from the federal appeals court by way of a writ of error (*recurso extraordinario*)....

The most important issue before the court was the question presented in a writ proposed by one of the attorneys for the *querellantes*. The writ challenged the application of Law No. 23521, the new due obedience law, which had been passed while the Supreme Court was considering the appeals.[69] Under Article 3 of the new law, the conclusive presumption of due obedience could be applied in any pending cases. The *querellantes'* writ alleged that the law violated rights to a republican form of government, equal protection, and due process.[70] The law had also been challenged in the lower court on the grounds that it unduly encroached upon the constitutional sphere of the judicial branch and that it violated the principle of separation of powers, but the lower court rejected this argument.[71] Although the Supreme Court denied the victims standing to challenge the due obedience law,[72] the court agreed to review the appeals court's denial of the writ. The court based jurisdiction on Article 5 of the law, which provides for review of erroneous application of the law by the lower courts, and on the writ of *recurso extraordinario*, which allows the court to examine the constitutionality of a law.[73]

The Supreme Court's Holding

The majority ruled that the due obedience law was constitutional and went on to apply the conclusive presumption to the defendants' case. The court acquitted Etchecolatz, Berges, and Cozzani, who fell within the lower ranks described in Article 1, and ordered their immediate release.[74] The court reduced the sentences of Camps and Riccheri as "necessary accomplices" (*cooperador necesario*).[75] The court found that Camps and Riccheri, who held the highest rank in the police force, were not subject to the irrebuttable presumption created by Article 1. However, neither officer was found to be a "direct" or "immediate" perpetrator (*autor inmediato*) of the crimes for which he was convicted, although the two men had effective control over security forces and controlled detention centers where alleged

---

69 Constitutionality of the due obedience law, *supra* note [51], at 258 (Bacque, dissenting). Justice Bacque argues as well that the due obedience law was to apply only to cases pending at the time of enactment, while Camps had been convicted by the court of appeals *before* the due obedience law was enacted.

70 Specifically, the writ cited Articles 1, 14, 16, 18, 33, 67, 95, 100, and 101 of the national constitution. Constitutionality of the due obedience law, *supra* note [51], at 195.

71 *Id.*

72 *See infra* notes 123-143 and accompanying text.

73 Constitutionality of the due obedience law, *supra* note [51], at 195-96.

74 As a result of the holding, approximately 182 officers were released in cases pending in federal appeals courts. [Garro & Dahl, *Legal Accountability For Human Rights Violations in Argentina: One Step Forward and Two Steps Backward*, 8 Human Rights L.J. 283, 340 [hereinafter Garro & Dahl, *Legal Accountability*]].

75 [omitted]

subversives were held captive and tortured.[76] The court found that they merely received orders from the commander of the First Division of the Army and passed them on to the General Bureau of Investigations.

Etchecolatz, an officer of superior rank in the police force, fell under the second paragraph of Article 1, which stipulates that a defendant can be convicted only if he had some decisionmaking capacity or participated in the formulation of illicit orders.[77] The court reasoned that since the crimes for which Etchecolatz was convicted had occurred in "restricted areas" (*areas restringuidas*) in which only military personnel were allowed, and since he was subordinate to the chief of police, who was in turn under the authority of the military, Etchecolatz did not have decisionmaking capacity and therefore was immune under Law No. 23521.[78] Although he may have known about the torture taking place in the units under his control, he did nothing more than to follow and pass on orders received from superiors.[79]

The Majority Arguments of the Court

The majority opinion of Chief Justice Jose Severo Caballero and Associate Justice Augusto Cesar Belluscio addressed two main challenges to the law of due obedience presented in the writs: the argument that the law violates the doctrine of the separation of powers, and the argument that it violates the equal protection clause (Article 16) of the Argentine constitution. The opinions of Justice Carlos S. Fayt, who concurred, and Justice Enrique S. Petracchi, who dissented in part, addressed the issue of the due obedience law as a constitutional amnesty under Article 67(1 7), the "necessary and proper" clause of the constitution.[80] The lone dissenter, Justice Jorge A. Bacque disagreed that the due obedience law could pass constitutional muster as an amnesty law.

The majority first addressed the separation of powers challenge. It stated that Congress had great latitude within its legislative sphere to amend the criminal law. Exercising its prerogative to enact the Criminal Code under Article 67(11) of the constitution, Congress is entitled to rule that certain criminal acts are exempt from punishment.[81] The legislative branch has the constitutional discretion to amend the law and consider which acts are to be crimes and which are to be punished. The court analogized the due obedience law's conclusive presumption to certain other legal presumptions created by the legislature.[82]

---

76 [omitted]

77 [omitted]

78 [omitted]

79 [omitted]

80 Article 67(28) of the constitution reads:

> The Congress shall establish lower courts to the Supreme Court; create and authorize positions, determine their functions; give salaries, decree honors, and grant general amnesties.

81 Constitutionality of the due obedience law, *supra* note [51], at 196.

82 *Id.* For example, Articles 185, 232, 279 of the *Codigo Penal.*

The majority placed two conditions on this congressional power. First, Congress may not pass a law that deprives a person of a right protected by other laws in force prior to passing the new law. Beneficiaries of a former law have a fundamental right deserving of constitutional protection.[83] Second, policy objectives must be pursued by "reasonable" means. "Reasonable" is interpreted by the court to mean proportional to the ends sought and compatible with individual rights protected by the constitution.[84]

The judiciary, on the other hand, has the constitutional function of assisting the legislative and the executive in the application of the law. The court cannot obstruct Congress when Congress is pursuing legitimate policy objectives,[85] nor is it for the court to judge the merit or opportuneness of the decisions of the other branches.[86]

Justice Petracchi, concurring, and Justice Bacque, dissenting, disagreed with the majority that the due obedience law did not violate the constitution's principle of separation of powers. They argued that the legislative branch promulgates general rules of law that are applied to future events, while the judiciary ascertains whether past events submitted to its judgment are subject to the laws to be applied in a particular case. The power to decide facts and declare applicable laws is reserved to the judiciary.[87] Justice Petracchi and Justice Bacque went on to state that the due obedience law prevented judges from deciding whether the circumstances described in the law actually occurred. The law created a conclusive presumption that officers were acting under duress, had no way of knowing whether the orders were illegal, and did not go beyond the scope of the orders.[88] The justices argued that such rebuttable presumptions about facts involving proof of guilt or innocence are inadmissible in the area of criminal law.[89]

Justice Bacque also mentioned that the decision of the majority is contrary to "fundamental law" because it establishes an unconstitutional interpretation of due obedience: A subordinate can be legally obliged to follow an order to kill or torture for political reasons.[90] Justice Petracchi

---

83 Constitutionality of the due obedience law, *supra* note [51], at 196.

84 *Id.* at 197.

85 *Id.*

86 *Id.* at 196-97.

87 *Id.* at 228-29 (Petracchi, concurring); 238-42 (Bacque, dissenting)....

88 Constitutionality of the due obedience law, *supra* note [51], at 229 (Petracchi, concurring), 240 (Bacque, dissenting).

89 Determinations of guilt or innocence through the judicial process are the core of the constitutional right to due process. The separation-of-powers doctrine limits congressional power to make such determinations. Independent judicial fact-finding is generally seen as mandatory today only insofar as it is implied by constitutional rights of due process. *See* Tribe, *American Constitutional Law* 15 (1978). The issue of the legislative encroachment on the judicial sphere is broad and complex, including topics such as the delegation doctrine, legislative control of jurisdiction, and the doctrine of judicial deference among others. *See e.g.*, Note, *Eroding the Separation of Powers: Congressional Encroachment on Federal Judiciary Power*, 53 Brooklyn L. Rev. 669 (1987).

90 Bacque gave three reasons why such an interpretation is unconstitutional: (1) it is a legislative usurpation of judicial function; (2) it is an arbitrary sentence (*sentencia arbitraria*)

closely followed Justice Bacque's analysis of the separation of powers issue. Petracchi advocated a strict separation of powers as the most important means to preserve democracy and the rights of the individual guaranteed in the Constitution. He cited *McCulloch v. Maryland*,[91] which stands for the principle that the power of the legislature to enact any laws it deems necessary and proper is limited by the letter and spirit of the constitution.[92]

The majority, in its consideration of the equal protection issue, held that the due obedience law does not violate the constitution's guarantee of equal treatment under the law because the legislature is entitled to treat different situations differently. The equal protection guarantee can only be violated when there is unfair or invidious discrimination of those in like situations.[93] The right to equal protection simply prohibits Congress from enacting laws that show hostility toward particular individuals or groups of people.[94] It does not prohibit laws benefitting a group of people by specifying military status as the criterion for determining whether certain acts are to be punished.

Justice Bacque in his dissent argued vehemently that the due obedience law was unconstitutional, because among other reasons, it was based on a personal quality of those favored by it—their military rank—instead of being based on the nature of the act.[95]

Reactions of Human Rights Organizations

Human rights attorneys argued that the due obedience law violated the constitution's guarantee to equality under the law.[96] Well-known attorney activists such as Emilio Mignone, director of Argentina's largest human rights organization, claimed that the due obedience law aggravated the ethical conscience of the nation and compromised the credibility and respectability of the judiciary by benefitting those who tortured and murdered defenseless people.[97] Another human rights group,

---

because the facts in each case have not been considered; and (3) Congress could not make such a law to cover future acts, of torture. Constitutionality of the due obedience law, *supra* note [51], at 239-40 (Bacque, dissenting); *see also* Sancinetti, *supra* note 87, at 137-38.

91 17 U.S. 316 (1819).

92 Justice Petracchi argued that the preclusion of judges from the fact-finding process in a criminal trial also violates Article 18 of the constitution, which guarantees the right to obtain a judicial pronouncement of guilt. *See* Constitutionality of the due obedience law, *supra* note [51], at 230-31 (Petracchi, concurring).

93 *Id.* at 196.

94 *Id.* at 196, 203 (Fayt, concurring).

95 *Id.* at 242-43 (Bacque, dissenting).

96 *Americas Watch Report, supra* note [47], at 94.

97 E. Mignone, 3 *Centro de Estudios Legales y Sociales*, No. 9, (1987). Mignone states that "[n]o obedience is due when orders are clearly criminal and illegal, such as torturing and assassinating persons." N.Y. Times, 2 June 1987, at 27, col. 1. Ernesto Sabato, Argentine author and politician and leader of the government's investigation commission, CONADEP, stated that although subordinates must naturally obey orders of superiors, every human act is submitted to supreme ethical principles. *See 2 Derechos Humanos: Revista de la APDH* 12 (1987).

the Mothers of the Plaza de Mayo, winner of the 1984 Nobel Peace Prize, called the law a "judicial parody."[98]

Arguments the Majority Did Not Address: Amnesty

Although the majority opinion of Chief Justice Caballero and Justice Belluscio did not refer to the due obedience law as an amnesty, both Justice Fayt and Justice Petracchi, in separate opinions, justified the law as a constitutional amnesty under Article 67(17) of the constitution. After expounding upon the "serious flaws of this law," Petracchi found the due obedience law nevertheless justified by the particular political context in which it was enacted.[99]

The portion of Petracchi's opinion in which he dissents from the majority ruling is marred by an apparent inconsistency. He first found that the due obedience law violated a series of constitutional principles, including the distinction between political offenses and ordinary offenses connected to political motives (*delitos comunes conexos*).[100] This distinction had been consistently followed in previous denials of amnesty for those who had committed barbarous crimes. The "heinousness of the criminal offense," he stated, has always been taken into account by Congress while enacting amnesty laws.[101] He cited Supreme Court precedent that granting indiscriminate pardons for atrocious and inhuman crimes that had no connection to the political motives alleged by the perpetrator "borders with arbitrariness in the exercise of legislative powers."[102] However, twenty paragraphs later, Petracchi found the due obedience law to be a legitimate amnesty by the legislature.[103] Despite Article 18 of the constitution, which outlaws torture or lashing,[104] the legislature is not prohibited from enacting a law that blocks the criminal

---

98 3 Madres de la Plaza de Mayo 2-3, 4-5 (June 1987); *see generally* 3 Madres de la Plaza de Mayo.

99 Constitutionality of the due obedience law, *supra* note [51], at 232 (Petracchi, concurring). Justice Petracchi analyzed the constitutional propriety of the due obedience justification by resorting to historical legal principles in American, German, and Argentine law, canon law, military law, and liberal common law principles. He concluded that the due obedience justification in the case at bar violated the "general legal conscience," because the orders to torture and commit other atrocities given by the superior officers were "patently illegal," not within the sphere of their authority, or within the sphere of competence of the subordinate officers. *Id.* at 224. It seems odd that Petracchi went into elaborate interpretations of historical use of the due obedience doctrine under Article 514 of the CMJ, finding that the law violated the doctrine requiring that orders not be manifestly illegal, and then concluded that the law was a constitutional amnesty, extinguishing judgement of the illegality of the acts amnestied.

100 *Id.* at 221 (Petracchi, concurring).

101 *Id.*

102 *Id.* at 259-60 (citing 254 Fallos 315). Justice Bacque also makes the argument that the constitutional history of Argentina has not allowed amnesties for "atrocious" crimes.

103 *Id.* at 232 (Petracchi, concurring).

104 Article 18 of the constitution states in pertinent part: "The death penalty in political cases, all forms of torture, and flogging remain abolished forever."

prosecutions of those acts "in order to safeguard peaceful coexistence in the country."[105]

For whatever reason, Petracchi falls in line with the majority in upholding the due obedience law; but his opinion points to more than mere "formal flaws" in the law.[106] In particular, his doubts about the legality of an amnesty for torture and other "heinous" crimes is consonant with many well-established legal and political arguments against the use of a general amnesty for military abuses.[107]

Justice Bacque and other commentators met Petracchi's conclusion with two crucial arguments: (1) the due obedience law technically is not an amnesty, and (2) no amnesty could be granted under the constitution for the acts in question.[108] First, the law is not an amnesty because the acts that it addresses are no longer considered crimes but are legally justified within the limits of the due obedience doctrine. The law merely has the effect of an amnesty by precluding a criminal penalty.[109] Justice Bacque argued that the law cannot be an amnesty because it not only extinguishes the criminal cause of action but also affects civil actions against the defendant, while a genuine amnesty would have no effect on civil actions.[110]

Second, even if the law were an amnesty, Bacque disagreed with Petracchi's view that, in some circumstances, an amnesty can be granted for the crime of torture.[111] Bacque gives two reasons why the law could not be construed as a constitutional amnesty for the crimes in question. First, a settled legal tradition recognizes that the primary goal of an amnesty is to cover only political crimes or common crimes reasonably connected (*relacion atendible*) to the alleged political purpose the crimes were meant to advance. Consequently, it has always been understood that no political objectives may justify atrocious or aberrant crimes, and no amnesty may be applied to them.[112] Second, the ethical principle embodied in Article 18 of

---

105 Constitutionality of the due obedience law, *supra* note [51], at 232 (Petracchi, concurring). *Cf.* Birdle v. Perovich, 274 U.S. 480, 486 (1927) (obiter dictum of Justice Holmes: "a pardon in our days is not a private act of grace from an individual happening to possess power. It is part of the constitutional scheme. When granted, it is the determination of the ultimate authority that the public welfare will be better served by inflicting less than what the judgment fixed.").

106 Justice Petracchi notes that although the Supreme Court is bound to support the legislative responsibility to preserve "social peace and the reconciliation of the Argentine people within a democratic system,... this amnesty does not necessarily amount to a first step towards a lasting peace where stable institutions and harmonious coexistence can take root." Constitutionality of the due obedience law, *supra* note [51], at 233-34.

107 *See e.g.*, Perez Guilhou, *Los jueces de facto: amnistia politica* (1983).

108 *See* Sancinetti, Derechos Humanos en Argentina Post-Dictatorial 141. (1988)

109 *Id.* at 142-43.

110 Justice Bacque illuminated the problem for the plaintiff-prosecutor victims in potential civil actions against the military officers. Constitutionality of the due obedience law, *supra* note [51], at 242. Any eventual civil defendant who was merely following superior orders may automatically be considered a subordinate.

111 *Id.*

112 *See* Perez Guilhou, *supra* note 107, at 58-59.

the constitution, outlawing torture, presents an insurmountable obstacle for the constitutionality of the law.[113]

The majority opinion not only ignored the constitutional arguments for and against the due obedience law as an amnesty but also neglected to address the international law implications of an amnesty for the crime of torture.[114] Neither Argentina nor any nation-state may implement an amnesty for crimes that are violations of international law.[115] In international proceedings, the pardon of a criminal can implicate a state's responsibility for a "denial of justice...."[116]

Petracchi at least mentioned the UN Convention Against Torture and Other Cruel, Inhuman and Degrading Treatment or Punishment.[118] However, he reasoned that the amnesty did not legitimize or justify the crimes of torture committed by the accused but merely "cut off the criminal sanctions attached to specific acts that took place in the past," and therefore was justified as a "general" amnesty...."[119]

The court denied standing to sue to two *querellante* parties who presented writs challenging the application of the due obedience law in *Camps*.[120] The court reasoned that the victims, although parties to the case, did not have a direct personal interest in the outcome of the case since they had not suffered any concrete loss (*agravio concrete*). The court stated that the victim parties were not the "targets" of the alleged discrimination created by the due obedience law, and they did not represent the third parties that may be affected.[121] The court reasoned that the law only affected the officers invoking the defense.

Victims of human rights abuses have the right to prosecute and be compensated for abuses, and they have the right to be protected from state sanctioned torture. These rights are secured under the Argentine civil statutory scheme of the *querella*, the Argentine constitution, and international law.... In denying the *querellas* standing to bring their

---

113 [omitted]

114 Torture by the state of its citizens violates the "law of nations"—customary and positive international law. Filartiga v. Pena-Irala, 630 F.2d 876, 878-80, 882 (2d Cir. 1980).

115 Paust, *Contragate and the Invalidity of Pardons for Violations of international Law*, 10 Houston J. Int. L. 51, 54 n.10. *See e.g.*, United States v. La Jeune Eugenie, 26 F. Cas. 832, 846 (C.C.D. Mass. 1822) (no. 15,551) (regarding "an offence against the universal law of society ... no nation can rightfully permit its subjects to carry it on, or exempt them.").

116 Paust, *supra* note 115, at 55 n.15 (citing In re James, 4 Rev. Int'l Arb. Awards 82, 87) ("especially so if the Government has permitted the guilty parties to escape or has remitted the punishment by granting either pardon or amnesty").

118 Constitutionality of the due obedience law, *supra* note [51], at 221 (Petracchi, concurring) (citing UN Convention Against Torture and Other Cruel, Inhuman and Degrading Treatment or Punishment, U.N. Doc. A/RES/39/46 (1984), 39 GAOR Supp. (No. 51) at 197 (*adopted* 10 Dec. 1984, *entered into force* 26 June 1987) [hereinafter Convention Against Torture]).

119 Constitutionality of the due obedience law, *supra* note [51], at 232.

120 The victims, Stella Maris Ageitos and Norma Susana Maratea challenged the constitutionality of Law No. 23521 through a writ of *recurso extraordinario* allowed under Law No. 48 of the Civil Code for anyone alleging a violation of their constitutional rights. *See supra* notes 62-64 and accompanying text; Interview with Luis G. Moreno Ocampo, Fiscal de la Camara Nacional de Apelaciones en Lo Criminal y Correccional Federal, 30 Sept. 1988.

121 Constitutionality of the due obedience law, *supra* note [51], at 195 (citing 25 Fallos 255, 262 Fallos 86, 263 Fallos 545).

claims, the court did little more than nod in the direction of its own precedent upholding the rights of victims and victim parties. And by upholding the due obedience law, the court sanctioned the law's extinguishing of all rights of the victims to prosecute and thus secure protection from torture and other human rights abuses in the future....

Article 18 of the Argentine constitution guarantees due process and judicial review (*defense en juicio*) to citizens whose constitutional rights have been violated. Victims of crime have a protected interest under the Argentine *querellante* statutory scheme in which the victims of crimes, or their representatives, are entitled to initiate and prosecute criminal complaints.[123] Victims who are directly injured by the criminal acts of another[124] may join the state prosecutor or file a criminal complaint alone and may participate in the proceedings by bringing evidence, requesting criminal sanctions, and receiving compensation.[125] Also, anyone who is indirectly injured by the crime, such as a family member who was financially dependant on a *desaparecido*, can join in the prosecution.[126] By allowing victims and parties to prosecute criminal actions and receive compensation, the *querellante* system combines civil and criminal actions into one proceeding....[127]

---

123 *See Codigo de Procedimiento en Materia Penal* (Federal Code of Criminal Procedure), arts. 170-76. This "plaintiff-prosecutor" (*querellante*) system originated during the time when criminal law in Argentina was primarily a way of providing private retribution, permitting victims and their relatives the chance to pursue criminal prosecutions for human rights abuses in which the state was implicated. Argentine criminal procedure allows victims of crimes or their representatives to initiate and prosecute criminal complaints (*querellas*) depending on what is required by the *Codigo Penal* to prosecute the crime. Article 71 of the *Codigo Penal* distinguishes criminal offenses between (1) *acciones dependientes de instancia privada* (such as rape, sexual offenses, and negligent assault and battery) and (2) *acciones privadas* (such as adultery, defamation, unlawful competition, etc.). The *delito de accion privada* can be prosecuted only by a *querella* which requires that the victim request and/or join the prosecution. (*See* arts. 72, 73, *Codigo Penal*) All crimes which do not fall under the two mentioned categories are *delitos de accion publica* which must be prosecuted *ex oficio*. Torture, murder, and all other human rights abuses fall under this category. But in the *delitos de accion publica* the victim may join the prosecutor as *querellante*. *See* G. R. Navarro, *La Querella: El proceso penal ante la justicia nacional y bonarense con intervencion del particular damnificado* 299-323 (1986); [Mignone, Estlund & Issacharoff, *Dictatorship On Trial: Prosecution of Human Rights Violations in Argentina*, 10 Yale J. Int'l. L. 118, 123 n.17 (1984) [hereinafter Mignone, *Dictatorship On Trial*]].

124 Victims who were directly injured are referred to as *querellante-conyuntos*. Navarro, *supra* note 123, at 299-301.

125 *Id.* Articles 1077 and 1079 of the Argentine Civil Code (*Codigo Civil*) provide that every penal offense gives rise to an obligation to repair damages resulting directly or indirectly therefrom. The Penal Code in Article 29 provides for restitution and damages for the victim. The victim has the burden of showing direct injury by a preponderance of the evidence, as opposed to the "beyond a reasonable doubt" standard used to determine guilt in criminal proceeding. Merryman & Clark, *Comparative Law: Western European and Latin American Legal Systems* 736 (1978).

126 This type of *querellante* is referred to as a *particular damnificado*. Many times the *particular damnificado* is also the *querellante-conyunto*. Navarro, *supra* note 123, at 109, 303.

127 The ability of the victim to secure damages in these private criminal prosecutions makes the *querellantes* functionally similar to an American civil action under 42 U.S.C. § 1983. Mignone, *Dictatorship On Trial, supra* note [123], at 123 n.17. During the last months of the military government and the first months of civilian rule, many relatives of the disappeared demanded the prosecution of military officers in criminal courts. *See* [Garro & Dahl, Introductory Note, Argentina: *National Appeals Court (Criminal Division) Judgment on Human*

In its holding, the Supreme Court failed to consider that Argentina, by enacting the due obedience law, violated its duty under principles of customary and conventional international law to: (1) provide judicial recourse and remedy for victims of military crimes, especially torture; and (2) protect potential victims from crimes by the state.[150] As a state party to the American Convention on Human Rights[151] and the UN Convention Against Torture,[152] Argentina has a duty to punish military officers for human rights abuses.

Although Argentina was not a state party to either the American Convention or the Convention Against Torture during the repression,... the Argentine government and Supreme Court were bound by the conventions at the time they enacted and upheld the due obedience law. The American Convention and the Convention Against Torture recognize certain preexisting legal obligations in international law and establish requirements for states, not for the particular individuals who abuse human rights.[153] The state parties' obligations include the obligations to prohibit acts that were already punishable and nonexculpatory in the law of the state party as well as in the international community, such as torture. The rights to life and freedom from torture were in place in Article 18 of the Argentine constitution.[154]

It is a universally accepted norm of international law that torture and other cruel and inhuman treatment by the state are violations of fundamental human rights. In *Filartiga v. Pena-Irala*,[155] the US Court of Appeals concluded that official torture violates the law of nations and established that there is a universal customary international law, made part of US federal common law in civil actions brought by aliens.[156] Regardless of the nationality of the parties, the court recognized a claim based on the law of nations,[157] which prohibits official acts of torture.[158] The court stated that various international treaties and accords "make it clear that international law confers fundamental rights upon all people vis-a-vis their own governments. While the ultimate scope of those rights will be subject to continuing refinement and elaboration, we hold that the

---

Rights Violations by Former Military Leaders, 26 *International Legal Materials* 317, [3]22 (March 1987) [hereinafter Garro & Dahl, Note, *Appeals Court Judgment*.]].

150 [omitted]

151 [omitted]

152 Convention Against Torture, *supra* note 118.

153 Sancinetti, *supra* note 87, at 129.

154 Existing constitutional and criminal law rules in national legal systems are weighty evidence of the existence of an international law rule against torture. N.Y. Times, 2 June 1987, at 27, col. 1.

155 630 F.2d 876 (2d Cir. 1980).

156 See Christenson, *The Use of Human Rights Norms to Inform Constitutional Law Interpretation*, 4 Houston J. of Int'l L. 39 (1981); Blum & Steinhardt, *Federal Jurisdiction over International Human Rights Claims: The Alien Tort Claims Act after Filartiga v. Pena-Irala*, 22 Harv. Int'l L.J. 53 (1981).

157 The court stated explicitly that the plaintiffs relied upon treaties and other international instruments as evidence of an emerging norm of customary international law, rather than independent sources of law under which a claim could arise. 630 F.2d at 880 n.7.

158 *Id.* at 881-85.

right to be free from torture is now among them."[159] Finally, the law of nations is part of US federal common law by way of the constitution.[160]

The Argentine executive's proposal and implementation of the law, the legislature's approval, and the judiciary's acceptance and application of the law violated numerous principles embodied in positive sources of international law that provide express legal rights for victims. The rights include the right to judicial process, the right to judicial remedy, and the right to be protected from torture by the government.[161] The due obedience law violates all of these rights.

Article 25 of the American Convention on Human Rights, to which Argentina was a party when the due obedience law was passed, establishes the right to judicial process and judicial protection for people who have been deprived of life or humane treatment.... As a member state in the American Convention, Argentina is bound by Article 25 to provide a judicial forum and judicial remedy for the victims whose rights have been violated....

The principle that victims of state-sponsored torture must have effective judicial recourse and remedy has also been codified in the Convention Against Torture.[172] Argentina technically was not bound by the Convention Against Torture at the time the due obedience law was passed, since the Convention had not entered into force. But Argentina was bound by the principles of customary international law embodied in the positive law of the Convention....[173] Article 13 of the Convention provides in pertinent

---

159 *Id.* at 882.

160 *Id.* at 886.

161 UN Charter, art. 55, 59 Stat. 103 (1945); Universal Declaration of Human Rights, G.A. Res. 217A (111), U.N. Doc. A/810 art. 5 (1948); Declaration on the Protection of All Persons from Being Subjected to Torture and Other Cruel, Inhuman or Degrading Treatment, G.A. Res. 3452, 30 U.N. GAOR Supp. (No. 34) at 91, U.N. Doc. A/1034 (1975); European Convention for the Protection of Human Rights and Fundamental Freedoms, 213 U.N.T.S. 222, art. 3 (1968).

172 The powers and responsibilities imposed on individual governments to ensure the enforcement of the principles established under the Convention Against Torture are set forth in Articles 5 and 7. Article 5 outlines a system of universal jurisdiction based on the place of torture, the nationality of the offender, the presence of the offender in the territory of a state party, and the nationality of the victim. Under Article 5, state parties are required to take any measures necessary to establish jurisdiction over persons accused of offenses condemned in Article 4. In Article 7, state parties are also obligated to prosecute any person accused of torture over whom they have jurisdiction. In the event a state either cannot or will not try an offender in its own courts, the state is then obligated under Article 7 to extradite the individual to another state party for prosecution.
Boulesbaa, *An Analysis of the 1984 Draft Convention Against Torture and Other Cruel, Inhuman or Degrading Treatment or Punishment*, 4 Dickinson Int. L. Ann. 185, 191-92 (1986).

173 Justice Petracchi, in his concurrence, argued that Argentine Law No. 23338 approved the UN Convention Against Torture. According to a report filed with the Supreme Court, the Convention was signed and ratified by the president with the consent of the Senate on 2 Sept. 1986, and the instrument of ratification was deposited at the United Nations headquarters on 24 Sept. 1986. Petracchi admitted that the Convention had not yet become a part of Argentine law because only nineteen ratifications of the provinces had been received to date, and twenty ratifications were needed for the convention to enter into force. (The Convention entered into force on 26 June 1987.) He noted, however, that Argentina was responsible for the Convention's principles according to Article 18 of the Vienna Convention on the Law of Treaties of 23 May 1969, which states in pertinent part:

part: "Each State Party shall ensure that any individual who alleges he has been subjected to torture in any territory under its jurisdiction has the right to complain to and to have his case promptly and impartially examined by its competent authorities." This provision, like Article 25 of the American Convention, establishes a right to judicial recourse for anyone whose rights have been violated by a state official....

The balance of legal arguments concerning the due obedience law, based on principles of separation of powers, equal protection, congressional amnesty powers, and due process for victims, weighs against the law's constitutionality. This points to the conclusion that the court justified its decision on political grounds. Indeed, Justice Fayt admitted in his concurring opinion that the court was not deciding this case "divorced from the realities of the present time, no matter how bitter the reality."[177] Justice Fayt felt compelled to uphold the law in light of the serious political circumstances prompting the enactment of the law, which he described as "the virtual collapse of the constitutional system...."[178]

[**Editor's note:** Shortly before this article went to press, Argentine President Carlos Saul Menem issued a pardon covering approximately 280 members of the security forces who still faced trial for human rights abuses and for mismanaging the war with the United Kingdom over the Falklands/Malvinas Islands. The pardons included senior generals and other high-ranking officers.]

COMPENSATION

Emilio F. Mignone, "The Experience of Argentina"[*]

Since 1983, some ex-prisoners who had been detained for political reasons during the period between 1976 and 1983 (they were taken prisoner on the orders of the National Executive and convicted by military tribunals), obtained judgments from civil courts in which the State was ordered to compensate for the damage and injury suffered. Among them was Carlos Saúl Menem himself—before reaching the country's highest office—

> A State is obliged to refrain from acts which would defeat the object and purpose of a treaty when: (a) it has signed the treaty or has exchanged instruments constituting acceptance or approval, until it shall have made its intention clear not to become a party to the treaty; or (b) it has expressed its consent to be bound by the treaty, pending the entry into force of the treaty and provided that such entry into force is not unduly delayed.

Constitutionality of the due obedience law, *supra* note [51], at 221 (Petracchi, concurring).

177 Constitutionality of the due obedience law, *supra* note [51], at 204 (Fayt, concurring).

178 *Id.*

* Excerpted from Emilio F. Mignone, "The Experience of Argentina," in Theo van Boven, Cees Flinterman, Fred Grünfeld, & Ingrid Westendorp, eds., *Seminar on the Right to Restitution, Compensation and Rehabilitation for Victims of Gross Violations of Human Rights and Fundamental Freedoms* (Netherlands Institute of Human Rights, 1992), pp. 127-129.

for having been detained on the orders of the Executive in this period of time.

Later on, two legal norms have clarified, facilitated, and, to some extent, placed limits on this situation. The first is decree number 70, signed by President Menem on 10 January 1991, which provided that persons who, at the time that the state of siege was in force, had been placed at the disposal of the National Executive, would be eligible to receive indemnification from the State,—the calculation of which was laid down in the norm—, *provided that they had started proceedings for damage and injury prior to 10 December 1985.* In some way the decree was a restriction: a) it bound benefits to that date: and b) it set a figure lower than that normally fixed by the courts, but it guaranteed receipt. In reality, very few persons benefitted under the decree.

Act no. 24.043, approved by Congress and promulgated by the Executive on 23 December 1991, has a wider scope. It provides for an indemnification from the State, payable in six installments, to persons who, at the time that the state of siege was in force, were placed at the disposal of the National Executive or, who, as civilians, suffered detention by virtue of acts of military tribunals, providing that they did not receive any indemnification by virtue of a judgment. The indemnification amounts to one thirtieth of the monthly remuneration assigned to the highest category on the wage scale for civilian personnel employed in the national public administration, for each day in detention. *It is an administrative procedure and it is executed under the Human Rights Office of the Ministry of the Interior—with the cooperation of the human rights organizations—and it requires, indeed, renunciation of any other type of compensation or judgment.*

The foregoing account makes clear that, although legal measures have been adopted in Argentina intended to compensate for damage and injuries suffered by unlawfully detained persons, this does not apply to the victims (or their relatives) of the most grave of the crimes committed by the régime of the armed forces: the abduction and forced disappearance of persons and the torture suffered by them.

This situation is due to the following three reasons: a) to this day, the Armed Forces have refused to acknowledge these abductions and the constitutional régime has neither been capable nor powerful enough to demand disclosure of the fate of the persons detained/disappeared (on whom, no doubt, documents are—or were—kept by the intelligence service of the armed forces); b) the difficulty of proving the responsibility of State agents for the abductions, given the clandestine system employed by the Armed Forces government; c) little or no interest on the part of the relatives of the persons detained/disappeared in obtaining pecuniary compensation, which they consider a mockery or a way of buying their silence. The parents and relatives of the persons detained/disappeared demand information regarding their fate, not money. Regrettably, nothing has been achieved in that respect.

POST SCRIPT: A RETROSPECTIVE BY FORMER PRESIDENT ALFONSÍN

*Raúl Alfonsín, "'Never Again' in Argentina"**

During my years as president, Argentina went through a phase of its transition toward democracy that posed tremendous challenges to our society and its leaders. It is not easy to build democracy in a setting where political culture and civic habits have been degraded by authoritarianism. Nor is it easy to build democracy in the midst of a deep economic crisis exacerbated by the need to repay a huge foreign debt that the old dictatorial regime had contracted and irresponsibly misspent.

In our society, the building of democracy could not be viewed simply as a process of restoration; it was essentially a process of creating new institutions and implementing new routines, new habits, and new ways for people to live together. It was a matter not of reconstructing a system that was functioning well until it was interrupted by authoritarianism, but of establishing new foundations for an authentic democratic system, something that we had never fully achieved.

There was a tradition in Argentina that after each dictatorship, the crimes and abuses committed by the authoritarian government would go unpunished. My administration, moved by an urgent ethical imperative, for the first time opened the judicial channels so that the extreme violations of human rights perpetrated by both revolutionary terrorism and state terrorism could be investigated and judged by an independent judicial body. Thus the impunity of the powerful would come to an end.

We created a commission of distinguished personalities to investigate the fate of the "disappeared"; after an arduous effort, it enlightened the public about the tragedy that had occurred. We also annulled the amnesty law imposed under the military dictatorship, and put in place a juridical regime that would respect the constitutional guarantees of due process, the right to a fair trial, and the principle of legality while making possible the conviction of those most responsible for these atrocious crimes.

Our intention was not so much to punish as to prevent: to ensure that what had happened could not happen in the future, to guarantee that never again would an Argentinean be taken from his home at night to be tortured or assassinated by agents of the state.

As we repeatedly explained, our principal objective was not to obtain retribution for every wrong but to help prevent the recurrence of similar wrongs in the future by internalizing in the collective conscience the idea that no group, however powerful it might be, is beyond the law.

This objective required that we take into account the necessity of assuring the loyalty of the armed forces to the democratic system, since the preservation of democracy is the main shield for the protection of human rights. Therefore, a careful distinction needed to be made between the

---

* Reprinted from Raúl Alfonsín, "'Never Again' in Argentina," *Journal of Democracy*, vol. 4, no. 1 (1993), pp. 15-19.

legitimate and open struggle against terrorism and such practices as the torture and clandestine murder of human beings, which are universally recognized as illegitimate.

To be sure, the pursuit of this objective—supported by the vast majority of our people—was opposed by those who saw one side in the struggle between revolutionary terrorism and state terrorism as the transgressor and the other as a group of idealists that at most had committed some excusable excesses. These partisans either demanded punishment for each and every member of the group that they had a priori condemned, or else called for casting a cloak of absolute oblivion over these events, as had often been done both in Argentina and elsewhere.

In implementing judicial proceedings, a series of juridical and practical obstacles had to be overcome. Moreover, prudence required that three important limits be observed: a limit on the public unrest provoked by the judicial investigations and proceedings; a limit on the time period of the trials; and a limit on the categories of persons considered responsible for criminal behavior. That is why even during our electoral campaign we made distinctions among those who planned the actions and gave the orders that set in motion the repressive state apparatus; those who committed excesses in carrying out their orders; and those who in a climate of error and compulsion had decision-making power but limited themselves to carrying out the orders that they received.

In order to make possible a discreet and efficient investigation of the entire state of affairs, we established the National Commission on Disappeared Persons. It was composed, for the most part, of prestigious and politically independent citizens, and was presided over by the distinguished writer Ernesto Sábato, perhaps the most respected intellectual in our country. As originally conceived, the commission would also have included some congressmen, but the opposition parties, especially the Peronists, objected.

The extraordinary work accomplished by this commission of patriots is well known. It interviewed thousands of witnesses and visited sites throughout the country. Its final report, published under the title *Nunca Más* and translated into several languages, had a significant international impact. The work of this commission provided irrefutable testimony of the magnitude of the tragedy and helped to keep much of the tension that followed within the channels of the law.

Principles of Punishment

Our search for truth and justice with respect to the crimes of the past was based upon the following premises:

1. The violence that stained Argentina with blood during the 1970s was initiated by the terrorism of the left. Animated by an elitist view of social transformation, these leftists did not hesitate to commit terrible crimes in pursuit of an insane agenda.

2. Armed combat against this terrorism of the left, employing a degree of force proportional to the threat, was morally and juridically justified; kidnapping, torture, and clandestine assassinations clearly were not. In no case is there justification for resorting to terrorist methods to combat terrorism, for that ultimately defeats the principles that are supposedly being defended.

3. The most atrocious acts committed by both types of terrorism had to be judged by an independent judicial body, and those found guilty had to be punished. This would help ensure that never again would groups with access to firearms think that they were above the law and able to decide with impunity whether their fellow citizens would live or die.

4. Given that the pursuit of justice relied only on the strength of society's moral convictions, our objective had to be carried out without risking the stability of Argentina's democratic institutions, which are the best guarantee against the recurrence of similar episodes. This required limiting both the time period of the trials and the number of those held responsible.

It is clear, then, that all our initiatives aimed both at setting in motion and at limiting the trials and the assignment of responsibility were determined by the stated objectives—namely, preventing any repetition of the atrocious episodes of the previous decade without at the same time endangering the stability of the institutional framework that provides the best barrier against that threat.

It is worth bearing in mind that in addressing the problems generated by the violation of human rights, there are theoretically only three policies that can be adopted:

1. Total forgetfulness, either through an amnesty law or through simple inaction. This is the policy that has almost always been followed, especially in the countries of Latin America.

2. The prosecution of everyone who is in any way implicated. This has never been done, since it is both practically and juridically impossible.

3. The condemnation of paradigmatic violations, with the purpose of demonstrating that there is no impunity and preventing the repetition of such violations in the future.

This last course is the one that we followed in complete accordance with our pledges during the electoral campaigns. We can affirm that nowhere else in the world—neither in America, nor Europe, nor Africa, nor Asia—has any country committed itself to such a policy as strongly as Argentina did at that time.

Those who criticize our decision to place limits on the trials and eventual sentences of those responsible hold a completely retributive conception of punishment. According to this conception, it is a moral duty to punish every transgression; if this is not done, an injustice is committed that cannot be compensated for by any other social benefit.

By contrast, for those of us who find such a conception of punishment difficult both to justify from a rational point of view and to render compatible with the principles of social morality, punishments are morally justified only if and when they are effective in preventing society from suffering greater harm.

Our common sense seems to support both positions: that a voluntarily committed criminal act is deserving of punishment, and that the social consequences of applying this punishment must be considered. It would be irrational to impose a punishment when the consequences of doing so, far from preventing future crimes, might cause greater social harm than that caused by the crime itself or by the absence of punishment. It would be unjust, however, to seek merely to avoid future crimes without taking into account, when applying the penalty, whether the person who committed the misdeed deserves to be punished.

When these general considerations are applied to the case of Argentina, the moral legitimacy of measures such as the Punto Final or Obedencia Debida laws will ultimately depend on whether their consequences are socially beneficial.

The social consequences of such policies are not easy to weigh. Among the beneficial effects of punitive measures are the deterrence of future crimes, the clarification of the facts through the judicial process, the consequent social condemnation of past abuses, and the promotion of a wider awareness that all individuals, without distinction, are subject to the rule of law.

The harmful effects of a punitive policy include the fostering of hostile attitudes toward certain social groups, especially the military. This in turn provokes these groups to isolate themselves from the rest of society, creating a serious threat to the preservation of the democratic system.

In the final analysis, punishment is one instrument, but not the sole or even the most important one, for forming the collective moral conscience.

The revelation of the truth through impartial judicial proceedings and the resulting public condemnation serve just as well as the imposition of punishment to impress upon the public mind the kinds of behavior that society is unwilling to accept. Of course, it is also necessary that penal laws be regarded as legitimate, and there seems to be no other source of legitimacy than that which emerges from democratic discussion and decision making, which ensure impartiality and fair consideration of all competing interests and opinions.

There is no better guarantee for the protection of human rights than an individual and collective moral conscience rooted in the defense of human dignity. National laws and international efforts, especially when they help to develop this moral conscience, are valuable instruments for protecting human rights, but they cannot replace moral conscience as the ultimate guarantor of such rights.

11

URUGUAY

EDITOR'S INTRODUCTION

By 1971, the Uruguayan revolutionary group Movement for National Liberation, better known as the *Tupamaros*, had grown both in number of adherents and in the frequency of their recourse to violence. To combat this revolutionary threat, the armed forces took over the police role in fighting the *Tupamaros* and the government temporarily suspended many civil liberties. In 1973, the armed forces declared that the *Tupamaros* had been destroyed, but nevertheless forced President Juan Maria Bordaberry to dissolve the parliament. This marked the effective beginning of military rule, which was formalized in June 1976, when Bordaberry was deposed and a military-dominated Council of the Nation seized power.

By the late 1970s, Uruguay was reported to have the world's highest ratio of political prisoners to population, with one out of every 500 citizens in prison for political reasons and one in fifty detained for interrogation. Thousands were detained for months without charges; hundreds were killed or disappeared. Organized labor and the press were often attacked. All faculty and curricula, from primary school through university, were closely monitored and forced to adhere to the regime's ideology. Every adult was investigated and graded on their level of "democratic faith;" this ideological screening resulted in the firing of 30,000 civil servants. Censorship was enforced. The use of torture was extensive.

In a 1980 plebiscite, the population rejected a draft constitution which would have institutionalized the role of the armed forces in national government. The military then initiated talks with some of the major Uruguayan political parties on the terms for a transition to civilian government. The culmination of those talks was the Naval Club Pact, signed in August 1984, providing for presidential and congressional elections in November followed by inaugurations on March 1, 1985. The parties to the Pact were also reported to have agreed that the new government would not initiate prosecutions of security personnel for human rights violations which had occurred under the military regime, but neither would it block the efforts of private citizens to bring such cases before the civilian courts.

The newly elected president, Julio Maria Sanguinetti, moved swiftly to free political prisoners held by the military without trial. Within his first week in office, he created a national commission to facilitate repatriation of Uruguayans in exile. On the same day, March 8, 1985, a Law of National Pacification was enacted, granting an amnesty to most remaining political prisoners, but specifically excluding members of the security forces accused of human rights violations. This law also provided for restitution of property and funds to those covered by the amnesty.

When the civilian courts began efforts to try military and police officers accused of abuses, the military pressed to end such trials. In December 1986, the Law Nullifying the State's Claim to Punish Certain Crimes ("*Ley de Caducidad*") was passed, effectively freeing nearly all military personnel from the threat of prosecution. The Law also required that the Executive investigate all disappearance claims that had been filed in the courts and report the results to the plaintiffs. Controversy over the *Ley de Caducidad* resulted in a hotly contested 1989 national referendum to repeal it; 58% of Uruguayans voted to retain the law. In a 1992 decision, however, the Inter-American Commission on Human Rights determined that the law violated Uruguay's obligations under the American Convention on Human Rights.

When the Sanguinetti government did not initiate an official investigation or accounting of the abuses which had occurred, a private human rights group, *Servicio Paz y Justicia* (SERPAJ) undertook such an inquiry. Excerpts from its report, *Uruguay Nunca Más*, which took its lead from the similarly titled Brazilian and Argentinian reports described in this volume and which played a significant role in Uruguay's treatment of the legacy of military rule, appear at the end of this chapter.

The following documents related to transitional justice in Uruguay can be found in Volume III of this collection:

- Law Nullifying the State's Claim to Punish Certain Crimes ("*Ley de Caducidad de la Pretensión Púntiva del Estado*")
- Letter from President Sanguinetti to Amnesty International Regarding the *Ley de Caducidad*

- Organization of American States, Inter-American Commission on Human Rights—Decision on the *Ley de Caducidad*
- Amnesty Law and Implementing Decree
- Decree Establishing the National Commission for Repatriation

THE CONTROVERSY OVER AMNESTY FOR PAST HUMAN RIGHTS VIOLATIONS

*Americas Watch, "Challenging Impunity: The Ley De Caducidad and the Referendum Campaign in Uruguay"**

Transition to Civilian Rule: The Naval Club Pact

Following the rejection of the military government's draft constitution in the November 1980 plebiscite, the armed forces entered into protracted discussions with representatives of the country's political parties over the terms for transition to civilian government. On August 3, 1984 the armed forces signed an agreement, popularly known as the Naval Club Pact, with the Colorado Party, the partially reconstituted left-of-center Frente Amplio (Broad Front) coalition of parties and the Unión Cívica (Civic Union), a small conservative party, which called for Presidential and congressional elections on November 25, 1984 and the inauguration of the civilian government on March 1, 1985. It was widely known, though never publicly confirmed, that the parties to the Pact agreed that the Executive branch of the future elected government would not itself prosecute members of the security forces for human rights violations, although it would not interfere with the adjudication of such cases by civilian courts. The National or Blanco party (whose principal leader, former Senator Wilson Fereira Aldunate, was detained by the military and "proscribed" from an political activity) publicly rejected the Pact, as it was committed to prosecuting human rights violations. The Pact was also opposed by the Frente Amplio, whose Presidential candidate was also proscribed.

* Excerpted from Americas Watch, *Challenging Impunity: The Ley De Caducidad and the Referendum Campaign in Uruguay* (Americas Watch Committee, 1989), pp. 11-21. [Editor's note: The footnotes in the following selection have been renumbered for the purposes of clarity.]

During the election campaign, the four leading presidential candidates, including Colorado candidate Julio María Sanguinetti, publicly committed themselves to bring to justice those responsible for human rights violations during the military regime. With Ferreira and other proscribed politicians out of the race, Sanguinetti won the election. The country's military, not defeated in war like their Argentine counterparts, withdrew from government with their unity intact and with an army strongman, General Hugo Medina, as the new government's defense minister. It would soon become clear that the armed forces, notwithstanding the Naval Club Pact, were determined to escape responsibility for their past actions.

Attempts at Judicial Resolution

The Sanguinetti government moved swiftly to restore democratic institutions and to promote national reconciliation. It reinstated the 1967 constitution, reestablished the independence of the civilian judiciary, reinstated with back pay thousands of civil servants fired by the military, and legalized trade unions, political parties and other groups banned by the military government, including the ecumenical human rights organization *Servicio Paz y Justicia* or SERPAJ (Peace and Justice Service). In addition, it pardoned all persons awaiting trial by military courts, including Wilson Ferreira, and got overwhelming legislative approval of the *Ley de Pacificación Nacional* (Law of National Pacification). This law freed all but 65 of the country's remaining 800 political prisoners,[1] but contained a provision expressly excluding from the amnesty military and police personnel responsible for human rights abuses during the period of *ex post facto* military government (June 27, 1973-March 1, 1985). Unlike those freed from prison, they had not been exposed to any punishment or public documentation and condemnation of their acts. In April, President Sanguinetti sent Alberto Zumarán, a National Party presidential candidate, and Luís Hierro Gambardella, a Colorado politician, to a session of the UN Human Rights Commission where they acknowledged the veracity of complaints detailing gross human rights violations under the military dictatorship, and pledged on behalf of the new elected government to clarify events and to bring the perpetrators of these abuses to justice. (Uruguay's permanent delegation to the UN made a similar pledge exactly one year later to the Human Rights Committee, which oversees state compliance with the Covenant on Civil and Political Rights and receives individual complaints under that instrument's Optional Protocol.) Shortly after Sanguinetti's inaugural, attorneys representing victims of human rights violations and relatives of "disappeared" persons presented evidence to civilian courts which opened legal proceedings in some forty cases involving, eventually, 180 military and police personnel. These cases

---

1 While all prisoners held for politically motivated offenses were freed in March 1985, the law did not apply to those prisoners convicted by the military courts for murder. But, in recognition of the harsh penal regime they had endured, the law provided that each day in prison counted for three days of their sentence if found guilty by the civilian court on review. As a result, persons sentenced to 30 years, but who had served 10 years or more remained free.

progressed slowly in part because Defense Minister Medina ordered these officers not to appear personally before the civilian courts and to communicate with them only in writing. Proceedings were virtually halted in August 1985 when military courts challenged the civilian court's assertion of jurisdiction over all armed forces personnel. The dispute was submitted for resolution to the civilian Supreme Court whose decision was expected in late 1985. That decision was greatly delayed, however, and in the intervening period, the Executive sought to redefine the issue.

The Search for a Political Solution

Despite his government's pledges, President Sanguinetti did an about-face in mid-1986 and began seeking a political solution in the Parliament to the issue of the military's accountability for past abuses. To win legislative approval for a government initiative, he needed support from opposition legislators since his ruling Colorado Party, while numerically the largest, did not have a majority in either chamber of Parliament. The fact that most opposition party members were on record against an unconditional amnesty for the military made Sanguinetti's task particularly difficult and politically sensitive. In June 1986 he tested the political waters by introducing in the Senate a draft law providing an amnesty to the combined security forces for most crimes, but not for grave crimes whose perpetrators would be tried by military, not civilian courts. The bill predictably faltered without opposition support.

Apparently under increasing pressure from the military, Sanguinetti then introduced in the Senate on August 6, 1986 another but more sweeping draft amnesty. This bill would have provided unconditional amnesty to the security forces for all crimes committed during anti-subversive operations between January 1, 1962 and March 1, 1985 and would have terminated ongoing legal actions. The two opposition parties, the Blancos and the Frente Amplio, defeated the measure by 16 votes on September 29. The Senate then provisionally approved a substitute amnesty bill, sponsored by the Blancos, known as Defensa de la Democracia y los Derechos Humanos (Defense of Democracy and Human Rights). This measure limited trials to only the "gravest" human rights abuses, such as murder, rape, disappearances and serious woundings, provided that such cases had been filed with the civilian courts before September 22, 1986. Another provision, however, expressly nullified the exercise of the State's prosecutorial powers for "lesser" offenses, including torture. During the Senate debate on the measure, the armed forces reportedly advised leaders of the National Party that they would not tolerate any inquiry by civilian or military courts into the armed forces' actions during "the war against subversion." The Colorados, who supported a full amnesty, and the Broad Front, which unsuccessfully attempted to amend the bill, defeated the Blanco substitute bill in a Senate vote. This legislative impasse paved the way for high-level talks between the leaders of the Colorado and Blanco parties. Coincidentally, after nearly sixteen months of deliberation, the Supreme Court in November 1986 upheld the civilian courts' claim to jurisdiction in two key cases, implicating members of the Uruguayan military in disappearances. The decision cleared the way for these cases to proceed in the civilian courts, and it was expected that the Supreme Court would rule similarly in the remaining cases.

Shortly thereafter, on December 1, President Sanguinetti made public a statement issued by seventeen retired generals who had held top command positions during the military regime, in which they acknowledged and assumed full responsibility for human rights abuses committed by their subordinates during the antisubversive campaign and indicated that such excesses would not be repeated. Sanguinetti declared that the statement deserved "a response of equal grandeur of spirit."[2] By this time, Sanguinetti knew that several military and police officers who were scheduled to appear before the civilian courts on December 23 would fail to do so, on direct orders from his defense minister. The President was now in a race against the clock to win legislative approval of an amnesty law before the December 23 deadline in order to avert what he publicly called an "imminent institutional crisis." Sanguinetti convinced National Party leader Wilson Ferreira to drop his opposition to such a law and, on December 22, just hours before the officers' scheduled court appearances, a majority of Colorado and Blanco legislators in both chambers of the Parliament passed Law No. 15,848, sponsored by the Blancos, by a vote of 81 to 46. The law was opposed by 1 out of 54 Colorados and 16 of 44 Blancos, as well as by all Frente Amplio and Unión Cívica legislators.

[Law Nullifying the State's Claims to Punish Certain Crimes]

The text of Law No. 15,848, *Ley de Caducidad de la Pretensión Púntiva del Estado* (Law Nullifying the State's Claim to Punish Certain Crimes) reads as follows:

> Article 1. It is recognized that, as a consequence of the logic of the events stemming from the agreement between the political parties and the Armed Forces signed in August, 1984, and in order to complete the transition to full constitutional order, the State relinquishes the exercise of penal actions with respect to crimes committed until March 1, 1985, by military and police officials either for political reasons or in fulfillment of their functions and in obeying orders from superiors during the *ex post facto* period.
>
> Article 2. The above article does not cover:
>
> a) judicial proceedings in which indictments have been issued at the time this law goes into effect;
>
> b) crimes that may have been committed for personal economic gain or to benefit a third party.

---

2 *See* Amnesty International, "Reply from Uruguayan government to AI's letter on investigation into past human rights abuses," AI Index: AMR 52/03/86; Distr: SC/CD (12-8-86).

> Article 3. For the purposes contemplated in the above articles, the court in pending cases will request the Executive branch to submit, within a period of thirty days of receiving such request, an opinion as to whether or not it considers the case to fall within the scope of Article 1 of this law.
>
> If the Executive branch considers the law to be applicable, the court will dismiss the case. If, on the other hand, the Executive branch does not consider the case to fall under this law, the court will order judicial proceedings to continue.
>
> From the time this law is promulgated until the date the court receives a response from the Executive branch, all pretrial proceedings in cases described in the first paragraph of this article will be suspended.
>
> Article 4. Notwithstanding the above, the court will remit to the Executive branch all testimony offered until the date this law is approved, regarding persons allegedly detained in military or police operations who later disappeared, including minors allegedly kidnapped in similar circumstances.
>
> The Executive branch will immediately order the investigation of such incidents.
>
> Within a 120-day period from the date of receipt of the judicial communication of the denunciation, the Executive branch will inform the plaintiffs of the results of these investigations and place at their disposal all information gathered. (*Unofficial translation*).

The *Ley de caducudad* terminated the State's power to prosecute and punish military and police personnel responsible for human rights violations during the period of military rule. The law's framers purposefully omitted any reference to or use of the word "amnesty" because, as previously noted, several draft amnesty laws had already been rejected, and under Uruguayan law a defeated measure could not be reconsidered in the same parliamentary session.

The *Ley de caducudad* also empowered the Executive to order dismissal of judicial proceedings already before the courts (except those in which indictments had been issued), including proceedings that involved disappearances, if they were committed by military or police personnel "for political reasons or in fulfillment of their functions and in obeying orders from superiors during the *ex post facto* period." The law did not cover cases in which indictments had already been issued, but this mattered little, in that no person was known to have been indicted before the law's passage.

Under the law, the Executive was mandated to conduct investigations into disappearance cases and to inform the relatives of the victims of the results of the investigations.

The *Ley de caducudad* did not end the State's power to punish three kinds of crimes:

1. Crimes committed "for personal economic gain" (Article 3). Critics of the law note that if a member of the military or police, acting on orders, "disappeared" a person and also stole the victim's car, he could not be prosecuted for the "disappearance" but could be tried for car theft.

2. Crimes committed before the period of *ex post facto* military government, i.e., prior to June 27, 1973. This date is particularly significant since it was during 1972—when the military was fighting the Tupamaros and the parliament proclaimed "a state of internal war" and enacted the Use of State Security and Public Order—that human rights groups and intergovernmental bodies began receiving hundreds of complaints alleging murder, torture, arbitrary arrests and denials of fair trial guarantees by government agents. According to Amnesty International there were, as of December 22, 1986, about twenty cases under investigation in the civilian courts implicating military and police personnel for torture and ill treatment occurring before June 27, 1973.[3] The present status of these cases is unclear for legal and political reasons. But, as Amnesty International has reported, the civilian judge in the case of the "disappeared" victim Roberto Julio Gomensoro Josmán sought a ruling from the government which ordered the case dismissed under Article 3 of the *Ley de caducudad* although the victim disappeared on March 12, 1973, before the period of military rule began.[4]

3. Crimes committed by members of the military high command before and/or during the *ex post facto* military regime. Article 1 of the *Ley de caducudad* by implication excludes these officials since it expressly applies only to crimes committed by "military and police officials" acting "in fulfillment of their functions and in obeying orders from superiors...." Attorneys at the Instituto de Estudios Legales y Sociales del Uruguay (IELSUR, Uruguayan Institute of Legal and Social Studies) told Americas Watch that since 1985 it had filed complaints in civilian courts on behalf of victims and their families against nine former officers in the high command, including retired General Hugo Chiappe Posse, a former commander of the army. No indictments have ensued, and the cases have apparently been stalled.[5]

Challenges to the Law's Constitutionality

Shortly after enactment of the *Ley de caducudad*, attorneys representing victims and relatives, as well as the civilian judges presiding over cases under investigation, filed writs with the Supreme Court attacking the law as unconstitutional. They, together with most of

---

[3] Amnesty International, "Uruguay Official Investigations Fail to Establish the Fate of the 'Disappeared'," AI INDEX AMR 52/01/88 (June 1988) at p. 7.

[4] *Ibid.*

[5] Amnesty International reports that the case against Posse involves accusations of four deaths in custody, rape of a woman prisoner, and 23 cases of torture against prisoners between May 1972 and May 1973. On February 1, 1988 this case "was filed away (*archivado*) due to confusion as to which judge or judges had jurisdiction over the case. IELSUR has contested this decision in a communication to the judge. However, the case has not progressed." *Ibid*, at p. 8.

Uruguay's noted constitutional law scholars,[6] argued that the only constitutionally sanctioned mechanism for the State's desisting from punishing crimes was limited to an actual amnesty or pardon and that Article 3 of the law, granting the Executive branch sole and conclusive authority to terminate judicial proceedings was an impermissible encroachment on powers exclusively vested in the Judicial branch. The Supreme Court on May 2, 1988 upheld the law's constitutionality by a three-to-two vote. The majority found that, despite omission of the term "amnesty" in the text, the legislative intent was to confer an "authentic amnesty" on the security forces.

Application of the Law to "Disappearance" Cases

Cases seeking to clarify the fate of the "disappeared" were among the first to be filed after President Sanguinetti's inaugural.[7] At the time of the amnesty law's enactment, civilian courts were investigating the involvement of security forces in the "disappearances" of six persons, Fernando Miranda Pérez, Félix Sebastián Ortíz Piazoli, Omar Antonio Paitta Cardoza, Eduardo Pérez Pérez, Amelia Sanjurjo Casal and Roberto Julio Gomensoro Josmán. In May 1987, the Sanguinetti government reportedly ordered the courts to dismiss all six cases, on the grounds that they involved crimes committed by the security forces for political reasons or in carrying out orders.

Although Article 4 of the *Ley de caducudad* obligated the Executive to launch an administrative investigation into these cases and to report the results to the victims' relatives, it did not establish the mechanism for or procedures governing the investigation. These matters were left to the discretion of the Executive. President Sanguinetti, later in May 1987, delegated his authority to his Defense Minister, Hugo Medina, who assigned the task to a military prosecutor, Colonel José Sambucetti. This appointment was widely criticized and particularly outraged the relatives of the disappeared and their lawyers at IELSUR.[8] They charged that Sambucetti, as an active duty officer and Medina's subordinate, lacked the independence to conduct an impartial inquiry into wrongdoing by other

---

6 See Horacio Casinelli Muñóz, "Es Inconstitucional, Pero no Impide Investigaciones," *Brecha*, Año 2, No. 62 (Dec. 26, 1986) at p. 10.

7 A parliamentary Commission on the Situation of "Disappeared" People and its Causes reported in November 1986 that 164 Uruguayans, including eight children, had "disappeared" between 1973 and 1982. Thirty-two were disappeared after arrest in Uruguay, 127 after being abducted in Argentina, as well as three in Chile and two in Paraguay under similar circumstances. The Commission said it had evidence implicating Uruguayan security forces in these crimes. It concluded that "all of the adults died as a result of the brutal treatment to which they were submitted, or were directly executed." The Commission's conclusion that all the "disappeared" were dead amounted to a presumption, since it did not make specific evidentiary findings in each case and lacked the power to subpoena records or compel testimony from the armed forces. Amnesty International, *Amnesty International Report 1986*, London, 1986, pp. 202 and 203.

8 See IELSUR, "Acciones Legales Contra la Impunidad del Terrorismo del Estado," in *Revista del IELSUR 1*, Montevideo, 1987, at pp. 10-11.

members of the military, and, therefore, they refused to cooperate with him.

[Criticisms of Investigations]

In all six cases he investigated, Col. Sambucetti concluded that the evidence did not substantiate allegations of security forces' involvement. Amnesty International, which obtained official documents detailing Sambucetti's findings and conclusions, has severely criticized all six investigations: "The government's use of the December 1986 law seems to amount to disregard for the international legal requirement to establish the fate of the `disappeared' and bring those responsible to justice."[9]

Sambucetti's investigation into the disappearance of Eduardo Pérez Pérez, for example, reveals the conflict between military resistance to exposure and the government's stated interest in learning the truth. This is the only case in which Col. Sambucetti called a military officer to give testimony. The primary suspect in this case was an army officer in the First Artillery unit, a Col. José Nino Gavazzo Pereira also implicated in the abductions of Uruguayans in Argentina in 1976,[10] and in numerous cases of torture. Eduardo Pérez Pérez disappeared, according to his relatives, on May 5 or 6, 1974, and was later seen and his voice heard in three military detention centers during that month. The only witness willing to present testimony on this case stated that while in custody in the First Artillery unit barracks in May 1974, he heard Pérez's voice and later was told by other prisoners that Pérez had died. The armed forces denied to Col. Sambucetti that Pérez had been detained. When Sambucetti interviewed Gavazzo on this case, he was told that the only circumstance in which Gavazzo would reveal information was by order of his military superiors.[11] Yet in Sambucetti's report there is no record of his having sought such an order from the army's Commander-in-Chief. It appears he accepted at face value Gavazzo's claim to official secrecy, even though the government had given Sambucetti responsibility to find out the facts. On this basis, Sambucetti concluded that there was no evidence of armed forces involvement in Pérez's disappearance.

The military prosecutor's conclusions that there was insufficient evidence to establish the culpability of security forces in these disappearances patently contradict what the government affirmed to the civilian courts when it had the cases dismissed, i.e., that they did involve crimes committed by the security forces. Attorneys for the relatives of the "disappeared" maintain, in light of Sambucetti's investigations, that all six cases should now be returned to the civilian courts without application

---

9 Amnesty International, "Uruguay: Official Investigations Fail to Establish the Fate of the 'Disappeared'" *supra*.

10 An Argentina court has twice requested the Sanguinetti government to extradite Gavazzo for his role in these abductions. To date, Uruguay has not honored the Argentine court's request.

11 A military judge does not have sufficient authority to oblige a witness to reveal classified information.

of the *Ley de caducudad.*[12] The Directorate of the Uruguayan Bar Association has effectively endorsed their position.[13]

SETTLING ACCOUNTS

*Lawrence Weschler, "A Miracle, A Universe: Settling Accounts with Torturers"**

One of the more appalling accounts of torture which I encountered during my stay in Uruguay came in the form of a written narrative, the testimony of Miguel Angel Estrella, the world-famous Argentine pianist, who was arrested as he was preparing to leave Uruguay, following a brief stay, in December, 1978. (An ardent Peronist back in Argentina, he had never engaged in any political violence and had undertaken no political activity whatsoever while in Uruguay.) During his first week of imprisonment, his torturers focused with particular relish on his hands. "They were like sadists," Estrelia recalled in a subsequent book. "They applied electricity under my nails, without stopping, and later they hanged me from my arms. After two days of torture I hurt all over, and had no sensation whatsoever left in my hands. I touched things and didn't feel anything. They kept making like they were going to chop off my hands. The last time they even had an electric saw going. They'd pull on my finger and ask, 'Which is the finger you use most in playing the piano?' I didn't say anything, I was praying, and one of them says, 'Is it maybe the thumb?' They pulled on the fingers and made like they were going to slice them off with the electric saw. They said, 'We're going to cut off your hands, one finger at a time, and then we're going to kill you, just like with Victor Jara.'" (Jara, the great Chilean folk singer and guitarist, indeed had each of his fingers smashed, before he was killed, in Santiago in the days after Pinochet's coup in 1973.)

I asked Dr. Mandressi whether, being a plastic surgeon, he got many former torture victims as patients nowadays.

"No," he said. "You have to understand that these guys were specialists—the main torturers. They were highly trained in methods of exacting the maximum pain without leaving any significant physical traces—and, for that matter, without killing the victim in the process. There were relatively few deaths under torture in Uruguay. This was because there were usually doctors in attendance at the sessions."

---

12 See *Revista del IELSUR supra* at pp. 11-12.

13 In a press release dated April 4, 1988, the Directorate stated that if the investigations into the disappearances of Félix Ortíz, Omar Paita and Fernando Miranda exonerate the security forces of responsibility, then the cases should be restored to the competent criminal court for further proceedings since the Ley de Caducidad was inapplicable.

* Excerpted from *A Miracle, A Universe: Settling Accounts with Torturers* by Lawrence Weschler. Copyright © 1990 by Lawrence Weschler. Reprined by permission of Pantheon Books, a division of Random House, Inc. and Sterling Lord Literistic, Inc., pp. 126-128, 161-169, 175-179, 182-191, 211-212, 231-232, 235-236.

[The Doctors]

This remarkable assertion—that doctors regularly supervised torture sessions in Uruguayan military prisons—was one I heard again and again in Montevideo, in the accounts of both victims and subsequent researchers. According to the most authoritative random survey so far made of former political prisoners, fully 70 percent claimed that doctors had attended their torture sessions.

In the wake of Uruguay's return to democracy, the country's revitalized Medical Association, under the directorship of Dr. Gregorio Martirena, has been the single most active professional organization seeking to document allegations of complicity by its members with the dictatorship and seeking professional sanctions against members whenever such allegations can be proved. Dr. Martirena informed me that as of September, 1986, cases were pending against eighty *médicos militares*. These were variously accused of direct participation in torture (monitoring vital signs of victims so as either to suspend or reinitiate the sessions, and in particular ferreting out those victims who they determined were exaggerating their physical distress), of sharing with the military authorities medical files which ought to have been kept confidential, of prescribing inappropriate psychotropic drugs at inappropriate dosages, of falsifying medical records in cases of problematic autopsies, and so forth.[20]

I asked Dr. Martirena how such systemic abuses could have developed. He explained that up through 1975, doctors working for the military had retained their civilian status, but that at that point they'd all been militarized. More than 100 doctors had refused to submit to such conscription, and many of those were themselves arrested and fed into the repressive apparatus. In fact, some of the worst cases currently bedeviling the Medical Association involve doctors' allegations of having been tortured by other doctors. In 1973, there had been only 300 doctors working with the military, but by 1985 there were between 800 and 1,000, out of a total of 6,000 in the entire country. Some of the behavior evinced by these doctors could be ascribed to the constraints of military discipline, some to true belief (many of the doctors who remained with the military after 1973 were devout acolytes of the doctrine of national security), but much of it

---

20 Consider, for instance, the following testimony which an architectural student named Alvaro Jaume subsequently delivered to Amnesty International regarding his ordeal in a Uruguayan torture center.

"I was thoroughly examined by a doctor. He asked me about my family, any chronic or present illnesses, and about any parts of my body which might be delicate because of previous sickness. I thought that giving that information might reduce the torture. Hours later I realized the real reason for the doctor's interest. I heard his voice—unmistakably—saying: 'That's OK, you can carry on.' I felt angry and impotent. Here was an individual trained by society to save lives, dedicating himself to inflicting pain. Mostly I was angry with myself for being so naive as to believe that a doctor who worked in such a place could possess a trace of humanity. These doctors are saving lives, but in a perverse way. The aim of torture is thwarted if the victim cannot support the interminable ordeal. The doctor is needed to prevent you from dying for your convictions." (Quoted in "They Condone Torture," by César Chelala in *World Health*, the journal of the World Health Organization, April, 1989.)

involved considerations of professional ambition and financial reward (military doctors earned between twice and four times as much as their civilian counterparts).

I asked Dr. Martirena how the various cases against the military doctors were going, and he explained that most were still under way, that procedures were painstakingly designed to ensure due process, and that thus far only a few cases had resulted in determinations of guilt, which in turn entailed foreclosing the possibility of any future employment at institutions where the Medical Association held sway. However, in all of these cases, military officials had taken the guilty parties under their protection, assuring them of continued employment at inflated salaries in military hospitals; and the civilian officials who now presumably outranked these military "subordinates" in the newly reinstituted constitutional democratic order had either felt incapable of or uninterested in enforcing any further sanctions....

[Reintegration of Victims]

The country's economy staggers along, and meanwhile the victims of the repression try to fit back in. Sanguinetti's government offered help by way of a decree stipulating that all former public employees who had been unjustly stripped of their jobs by the military regime, whether through imprisonment, blacklist, or exile, could return to them. This was, of course, a blessing for many (so far, more than 9,000 have taken the government up on its offer), but many others were in the position of my traveling companion Alfredo Peña. "I'm having a terrible time finding a job," he told me.... "After all, my life was cut off at the age of twenty, and now, twelve years later, I'm just thrown back in. The people who were already established can resume their lives, perhaps, but I hadn't even started mine. Most jobs require experience, and I don't have any. The jobs that don't require experience are for young people—and the employers of young people don't want to waste their time with someone like me. And, anyway, I *am* awkward. I have had none of the experiences of my peers on the outside. In many ways, I feel I'm still twenty: I live with my family—I couldn't possible afford an apartment of my own. I identify with twenty-year-olds, but they're different, too. It's a kind of limbo. In Argentina, the authorities disappeared people. In Uruguay, they disappeared people's lives."...

"You get different sorts of response from different people," Louise Popkin told me. "Some tell you, 'I'm a total mess, God do I need therapy.' Some say, 'You can't go through an experience like that and not be marked, I was marked, but I take responsibility for it and I try to go on.' Some say, 'What a marvelous experience prison turned out to be'—they launch into some long political speech and end up insisting that they're fine, they're just fine. Of course, they're in the worst trouble of all."

"The prison experience is a bit like an ironworks," Marcelo Vignar, the psychoanalyst, told me, drawing on his experiences in treating victims of repression. "With a human being, as with iron, beating can either strengthen or break. Some people are deepened by the experience, others...." He shook his head, and mentioned a man I'd met a few days earlier. "He, for instance, has been made lesser, narrower. You should have known him before. He was expansive, delightable, brilliant. Now he's foreshortened, brittle."

Some returning prisoners were having children—and in a hurry. One of the ways they'd tormented the women at Punta de Rieles was with the prospect of ending up childless. Prison psychiatrists kept assuring the young prisoners that they wouldn't be released till well past menopause. In some cases they proved right, but other prisoners just made it....

For all the hopes embodied by new children, many returning prisoners faced their biggest challenge in learning how to parent kids who'd grown up in their absence. "It takes thirteen years of preparation in the best of circumstances to learn how to be ready to parent a teenager," one therapist told me. "Here you have parents who've been away the entire time, who arrive on the scene confused, disoriented, and debilitated in all sorts of ways, and suddenly you expect them to deal with teenage kids! The situation is compounded by the years of idealization that have gone on both sides—parents for whom the growing child on the outside was the thin, pure reed around which they organized their entire psychological survival; children who nurtured an almost fairytale conception of their absent parent's virtue and prowess and heroism. And now the parent is back, trying to regulate the volume on the record player. You see it over and over again, the kids finally shouting, 'Who are you to order me around? Where were you all those years when I needed you?' The parents crumpling when faced with the dissonance of this new reality in which *they're* being cast as the arbitrary disciplinarians. Families shattering under the strain. There are hundreds of divorces. You see these people who spent over a decade yearning to be with their families—and then they can't be with their families. You see them walking around the city, all alone."

You do see a lot of zombies walking along the streets of Montevideo. I asked Louise Popkin whether she assumed they were all veterans of Libertad [prison]. "Oh no, "she said, "because I don't assume that prison was necessarily the worst experience. You had people in prison, you had people in exile, you had people in inxile—and all three of those experiences, in their different ways, created zombies."

Therapists who've been working with the survivors of Uruguay's repression often comment on the ways in which the three groups—those out of prison, those back from exile, and those who'd stayed and cowered—seemed to inhabit three different universes, each imagining they'd suffered more than the others, or that the others' suffering was somehow less real. They all talked past each other, further contributing to the general social fragmentation that was another legacy of the generals. "All of us were affected," a young therapist named Damian Schroeder commented. "That's why we try to avoid setting up therapy groups exclusively for torture victims, or relatives of disappeared persons, or returned exiles. That would just exacerbate the fragmentation, when what we desperately need are vehicles for reintegration." He explained that he preferred to work with groups that included, say, a veteran of Libertad, the grown child of a disappeared father, a returned exile, and a soul-wracked inxile. But, he went on, such groups were at best reaching only a minuscule proportion of the population; many were still too shell-shocked to seek help; and anyway, there were far too few resources and far too little money to help even those who were reaching out.

Marcelo Vignar, for his part, pointed out that therapy—individual or group—could only do so much, that finally the problems facing Uruguay in its reintegration were political. They'd been contracted as a community, and sooner or later they were going to have to be addressed as a community as well.

[The Question of Amnesty]

Perhaps the biggest problem that Uruguay faced in the latter half of 1986, and certainly the one most roiling the political waters, was the question of what to do with the former torturers. This problem has confounded each of the Latin-American countries in turn as one by one they have attempted to navigate the passage back from national-security dictatorship to some sort of constitutional democracy. And, as the participants at that Aspen Institute conference on the punishment or pardon of state crimes noted, the question here is not simply one of justice—what to do with particular individuals who can be shown to have participated to varying degrees in various sorts of tortures—but also one of truth, of how to document what really went on during the previous period and how to assimilate and honor that knowledge.*

Such issues of truth and justice, meanwhile, have to be addressed within the context of the ongoing existence of social sectors that themselves participated, to varying degrees, in the repression. In Argentina, the process was somewhat facilitated by the fact that the military there abandoned power in abject defeat; for at least several months, the new civilian government in Buenos Aires found it possible to pursue both truth, through *Nunca Más*, and a modicum of justice, through public trials of leading members of the junta and other senior offenders. In time, the Argentine military regrouped and began to mount an increasingly stiff resistance to the civilian incursions, and the situation has grown more and more complex.

In Brazil, the process was finessed, in part owing to the fact that the military there managed to leave gradually, so that when the final transition to democracy occurred, the worst human-rights violations were a full fifteen years in the past. Besides, the worst violence had all along been aimed at a comparatively small sector of society. The transition was accomplished within the context of a consensus—subscribed to, for the most part, by both the ruling elites and the middle class (the only two groups with any real clout at the time)—that there would be no need for

---

* [Editor's note: The conference referred to, "State Crimes: Punishment or Pardon," was organized by the Aspen Institute in November 1988. Excerpts from the conference report are reprinted in Volume One of the present collection.]

exhaustive trials or, for that matter, for any trials. The interests of truth were nevertheless fortuitously served by the remarkable efforts of the secret team that, working under the auspices of the archbishop of Sáo Paulo, produced the best-selling volume *Brasil: Nunca Mais*.

Uruguay's situation had none of these facilitating characteristics. The military there had left power largely of its own volition, and certainly unbowed, while gross human-rights violations were occurring right up to the moment of its leave-taking—violations that affected a much wider proportion of the country's citizenry. The size of the country inevitably presented particular difficulties during the Uruguayan transition. Almost half of the population lived in the capital, and, even so, Montevideo was not a large city. When the exiled widow of the assassinated legislator Gutiérrez Ruiz reclaimed her family home following the return to democracy, it turned out that José Nino Gavazzo, allegedly one of the most notorious torturers, was living in a house just down the street; each morning, she faced the prospect of having to see him. Pérez Aguirre, for his part, had already twice encountered his torturer on the street. Such chance meetings were fairly common, and they happened even more often in the small towns of the interior.

It's not at all clear what, or whether, arrangements regarding all this were agreed upon during the negotiations at the Club Naval. For a while, Sanguinetti maintained in interviews that the subject hadn't even come up. At one point, he told William Montalbano, of the *Los Angeles Times*, "The question of amnesty for the military was not discussed in the negotiations, just as no one said that the jailed prisoners would be turned loose the day after an elected government took office. It was an intelligent omission. We were seeking ways to remove obstacles, not to create them. You can't make a peace treaty discussing the origins of the war."

Nevertheless, when that first amnesty was promulgated, within days of Sanguinetti's inauguration, violators of human rights were expressly excluded from its provisions. More recently, Sanguinetti's people have admitted that during the negotiations the future President assured General Medina that the executive branch would not itself launch any prosecutions of violators, though it would not stand in the way of private citizens' bringing claims through the normal judicial channels. Some observers feel that in fact there were also guarantees as to what would eventually be done about such judicial actions, but Sanguinetti emphatically denies this.

Very early in the new administration, Uruguayans began lodging complaints against specific individuals, alleging torture, kidnapping, disappearance, extortion, rape, murder, and other violations, and the judiciary undertook a deliberate and painstaking consideration of these claims. Presently, thirty-eight cases, involving almost 400 accusations against 180 officials (torturers, psychologists, doctors, supervising officers, and others), were wending their way through the courts. The military initially refused to allow any of its members to honor subpoenas to appear before civilian courts, on the ground that they could be tried only by juries of their peers—that is, before military courts. This issue sidetracked developments for almost a year while the question made its way up to the

Supreme Court. The closer that court's decision loomed, however, and the clearer the indications that the court would decide in favor of civil jurisdiction, the more agitated the military became and the fiercer its demands for a speedy resolution of the entire situation.

In September, 1986, President Sanguinetti's Colorados proposed a blanket amnesty for the military. "Originally, I personally wanted some trials and a partial amnesty," he subsequently told Montalbano. "But once a general amnesty was declared for one side it became almost indispensable for the other." This sort of logic became the object of heated protest. For one thing, many victims of the worst repression had been ordinary citizens going about their ordinary lives; they had never belonged to any "side" of any putative "war." Furthermore, how could there be any basis for the Claim of virtual equivalence between the situation of prisoners who had spent five or ten or more years undergoing continuous physical or psychological torments and the situation of those who had been administering the torments and had never suffered even the slightest inconvenience as a result? The Colorado Party's initiative was easily defeated by a coalition of Blanco and Frente legislators.

As the Supreme Court now began assigning civil jurisdiction in one case after another, nineteen retired Uruguayan generals issued a statement proclaiming the "irreversible solidarity" of the armed forces and declaring that no soldier would ever be required to honor the subpoena of a civilian court. "Armies cannot be tried after the fact for winning wars," the generals asserted, and then, in an eerie variation on the old Tupamaro slogan, "Either we are all responsible or no one is responsible."

In reply to this assertion, Pérez Aguirre declared that, on the contrary, not everyone in the military was guilty and that indeed it was only through the just application of the law that the innocence of the great majority of its members could be firmly established. But the Blancos, in particular, were growing increasingly nervous about the prospect of widespread and blatant military disobedience. Alberto Zumarán, a Blanco Party lieutenant, who had been Wilson Ferreira's stand-in during the 1984 Presidential election, warned, "The threat is not of a coup but of something worse: a sector of society that remains defiantly outside the law—a kind of permanent *ex post facto* coup." The Blancos proposed an amnesty of their own, covering everything but the most egregious cases. That, however, was too little for the Colorados, who were holding out for a blanket amnesty, and too much for the Frente, who were outraged because under this formula wholesale torture would not be considered an "egregious crime." On October 17, 1986, the Blancos' initiative, too, went down to defeat.

The military was growing more and more adamant in its refusal to allow itself to be judged in civilian courts, and at the same time the debate among civilians was intensifying. Sanguinetti asked rhetorically, "What is more just—to consolidate the peace of a country where human rights are guaranteed today or to seek retroactive justice that could compromise that peace?" It was becoming a question of how the future development of democracy could best be secured: by cautiously refraining from its full exercise at this delicate juncture or, rather, by boldly insisting upon it.

"Democracy isn't just freedom of opinion, the right to hold elections, and so forth," one exasperated judge told me. "It's the rule of law. Without equal application of the law, democracy is dead. The government is acting like a husband whose wife is cheating on him. He knows it, everybody knows it, but he goes on insisting that everything is fine and praying every day that he isn't going to be forced to confront the truth, because then he'd have to do something about it." Eduardo Galeano offered a different analogy in an interview he gave *Report on the Americas*, the bimonthly magazine of the North American Congress on Latin America: "On the part of the government and some important sectors of the population, there is a belief that democracy is a fragile old lady in a wheelchair. If she moves too much she will collapse, and—if you speak too loudly she will have a heart attack. So democracy is something that shouldn't be touched. These ideas are actually the enemies of democracy because true democracy must move forward, deepen, and develop."

Most Uruguayans had taken to lumping the various amnesty proposals under the term *impunidad*—"impunity." One Colorado Party leader told me that he didn't much like that term—that he'd rather characterize the process as "searching for peace." The search for peace, however, was hardly proving peaceful: debate was growing shriller. The Colorados were now tending to classify all the former prisoners as Tupamaros and to maintain that the opposition to the amnesty was principally a tiresome Tupamaro vendetta. Antonio Marchesano, Sanguinetti's Interior Minister, was even quoted at one point as justifying amnesty for rape, provided "it was intended to instill fear" in the prisoners.

Public opinion, however, seemed to be holding fast. Uruguayans were, if anything, more viscerally anti-militarist than ever. A major poll released in October showed 72 percent still in favor of punishing those convicted of human-rights violations (68 percent among the Colorado Party rank and file) and only 11 percent opposed....

[The *Ley de caducudad* was adopted in December 1986.] So there it was, a *punto final*—"period, full stop"—as everyone now took to saying, borrowing a phrase from the roiling debates in neighboring Argentina, where the Argentine military's officers were now demanding a swift end to all the human rights trials.... Sanguinetti, for his part, now adopted an identical rhetoric: a year and a half of controversy was enough, it was time to move on, it was time for a *punto final*. "I don't have eyes in the back of my head," he declared. "I have eyes only for the future."

"But how can one even consider a *punto final?*" one of Sanguinetti's opponents had said to me at the time. "How can you have a period, end of paragraph, end of story, without any preceding paragraph, let alone any preceding story? Here in Uruguay, we've had no commission of inquiry, no officially sanctioned truthtelling. We've had no trials, no verdicts. All we have now is this period, hovering there in the middle of a blank page. It's unreal."...

[The Referendum to Rescind the Amnesty Law]

Indeed, the period wasn't holding, it wasn't staying put. Late in February, 1987, a coalition of former torture victims, relatives of "disappeared" individuals, human-rights activists, anti-*impunidad* politicians, labor leaders, professionals, and other citizens inaugurated a campaign to overturn the *impunidad* law. As their vehicle, they would seek to use the referendum provision in Uruguay's constitutions—something that had never been done before. "Our current constitution," Luis Pérez Aguirre, at SERPAJ, explained to me, "was based on the Swiss constitution, and we copied the referendum provision from the Swiss. However, our politicians endeavored to make the procedure much more arduous, by requiring the petition signatures of 25 percent of the total number of people who had voted in the immediately prior election. In Switzerland, for instance, with its population of over 6 million, you need only 50,000 signatures on a qualifying petition. Here, with less than half that population, we are required to get over ten times as many signatures—more than 555,000! That's roughly the same number of total signatures you'd need to collect to qualify a referendum in Italy, only there you'd be able to draw from a total population of 57 million people."...

Without the generals ever actually saying so, the subtext of many of their well-publicized commentaries was, "Fine, go ahead, sign the petition, that's the list we'll be using next time we come into power." The fact that they were registering any attitude, of course, went against the spirit of the new democratic order, in which they were supposed to remain absolutely subordinate to civilian control. Yet all they had to do was express misgivings about the course of the democracy and the unacceptable resurgence of "the treasonous left", and people felt a fresh waft of the terror that had so characterized the military's earlier tenure. People didn't need to be reminded about that system whereby the military had categorized almost everyone in the country as politically acceptable, suspect, or pariah. People knew that the archives upon which those categories were based were still being maintained. They knew that the fact of someone's signing a petition, say, against the United States invasion of the Dominican Republic in 1965, back in the days of the Great Democratic Exception, had come up ten years later, during the tortures and the summary trials, and that on the basis of little else such a person had received a prison sentence of five years, ten years, or more. And yet, knowing all this, they were signing. By May 26, 1987, the commission had reported 438,000 signatures.

However, the tide now turned abruptly. In neighboring Argentina, during the Easter holiday a few weeks earlier, a small number of officers and soldiers had rebelled, under the leadership of a renegade colonel named Aldo Rico, and virtually none of the rest of the military seemed willing to move against them. Following the passage of Argentina's *punto final* law, in December, scores of prosecutions had been lodged at the last possible moment, and Colonel Rico wanted all of them quashed forthwith. Alfonsín called on the civilians, and hundreds of thousands of them rallied in defense of their reclaimed democracy. After a helicopter visit by Alfonsín to Rico's headquarters, the mutinous colonel and his men relented. There was a brief period of euphoria. Over in Uruguay, where signature-gathering had stalled, there was a sudden upsurge of activity.

But in the ensuing weeks it gradually became clear that democracy's victory in Argentina had been problematic at best. Alfonsín soon fired the chief of staff of the armed forces, whose ouster had been one of Rico's principle demands, and although Alfonsín continued to oppose a full amnesty, which had been another of Rico's demands, he now moved quickly to propose a so-called due obedience law, which he managed to force through the Argentine Congress on June 5, 1987; this had the effect of voiding most of the remaining prosecutions of lower-ranking officers, who in many cases had been the actual torturers. In Uruguay, Sanguinetti used these developments to attack the petition campaign. Did Uruguayans really want to jeopardize the peace they had so precariously achieved? Was a Uruguayan Rico what they were asking for? New signatures became sparser and sparser. By October, the campaign had leveled out at 520,000 signatures.

Up to this point, the Pro-Referendum Commission had made a near-fetish of preserving the security of its completed petitions. People were being assured that their signatures would be kept secret, no one's business but that of the Electoral Court, which was charged with verifying the signatures and supervising any subsequent referendum (with the actual petitions presumably to be destroyed immediately thereafter). But now a Colorado observer, a deputy named Rubén Díaz, pronounced that once the petitions were turned over to the Court they should all be reviewed by the police, supposedly in order to weed out any known criminals or subversives. In reality, it was clear, the intent of his proposal was to intimidate would-be signers, and it seemed to be working. There was an immediate outcry from pro-referendum forces, and the proposal was temporarily shelved, but there was no guarantee of how the Electoral Court might eventually rule on it. Many of the activists on the commission began to abandon hope. Late in October, however, the commission launched a final offensive, mailing out 200,000 flyers. In response, it received enough signatures to go over the 555,701 goal, though it still continued to campaign, hoping to build up an adequate reserve. Finally, on the eve of Christmas, 1987, the Pro-Referendum Commission submitted petitions containing 634,702 signatures to the Electoral Court for verification....

It was against this backdrop that I returned to Montevideo, in August of 1988. On my previous trip, I had spoken mainly with victims of the country's systematic human-rights violations. This time, I wanted to make a point of talking with some of the proponents of the amnesty law—particularly some of the leaders of the Colorado Party—because I sensed that they, too, had a case to make.

With Senator Manuel Flores Silva, for example. A handsome man in his late thirties, Flores Silva is a journalist and a professor, the scion of an important political dynasty, and the head of one of the more centrist factions of the Colorado Party. He had voted in favor of the amnesty—to the surprise of some, because during the transition of the early eighties he'd been a close collaborator of people like Pérez Aguirre, at SERPAJ, and a frequent, and very articulate, proponent of human rights.

"The problem of amnesty cannot be understood out of the context of the whole situation of our country," he said one afternoon when I visited him in his Senate offices. "Uruguay lived through a transition from authoritarian rule which was not at all typical. We didn't have the benefit of the classic situation in which the dictatorship suffers an external defeat, like Argentina in the Malvinas or the Greek generals in Cyprus, and therefore has to step down. We didn't have the other classic way out, either, in which the dictatorship loses as a result of an internal war, as happened in Nicaragua with the downfall of Somoza. Our way was to mobilize civil society and gradually encircle the regime until it accepted the transition. That was accomplished through a series of steps—the votes in 1980 and 1982 and 1984, for example—all of which were imperfect, which is to say they were not completely democratic. But each step made it possible to advance, and we achieved two things that no one else has achieved: democracy-which, for instance, Chile still hasn't—and a peaceful transition, without any deaths along the way.

"In all this the Club Naval pact was of key importance. It didn't speak explicitly, or even implicitly, about what would happen with regard to the past, but the military had a right to assume that a peaceful transition would entail a peaceful working out of the past. Now, if you were living in a dictatorship and I offered you elections in three months and democracy in six months, and you said you wouldn't accept such an arrangement until the dictators agreed in advance to go to prison that would obviously be a wrong strategy. Naturally, two years later someone will say that this problem should have been included explicitly in the initial agreement—and this is understandable in theory. But we got rid of the dictatorship in reality.

"The trouble is that by mid-1986 we were falling back into the logic of extremes. Ironically, dictatorships freeze things, and, coming out of ours, we almost seemed to be back in 1972 and 1973—the same hatreds and polarizations all over again, leading toward an identical impasse and an identical probable outcome. We had to find a way out of that trap. It was very important, because it hasn't been shown anywhere that there is a law according to which dictatorships automatically fall. Sometimes they don't fall. For us to present an amnesty project, therefore, was not a matter of doing the necessary dirty work. It was a matter of making a moral decision to give priority to the possibility of a future of agreement over a past of division. We are consolidating democracy, which is the only guarantee of human rights."

I asked him what he could say to the victims of the abuses.

"We made a moral decision," he replied. "I didn't say it was an easy one. These abuses must never happen again. I can do nothing to change the fact that we lived under Fascism. What I can do is prevent it from happening again. Listen, as far as I'm concerned they should all have gone to prison. There should never have been any dictatorship, never any coup.

I'm in favor of the Tupamaros' never having existed. But we did have Tupamaros, and war, and the logic of war, and Fascism—that's what happens in war, that's why you shouldn't start shooting in the first place—and my job is to give my son a country where we will again have civil government and democracy. That takes time, and peace."

Next I spoke with Vice President Enrique Tarigo, another hero of the transition, the lawyer who'd founded Opinar and then gone on to articulate, in a most courageous and convincing fashion, the "no" position during the 1980 televised debate regarding the military's proposed national-security constitution. Sanguinetti had subsequently chosen him as his running mate in part to capitalize on the honorable reputation he'd garnered on that occasion. In March 1985, Tarigo, like Flores Silva, had favored an amnesty that explicitly excluded the military from its provisions. But like Flores Silva, he too had changed his mind.

"In March, 1985, when we took over, we didn't think we should amnesty the military," Tarigo explained to me. Tarigo is a large, jowly man, reminiscent in his physical presence of the late Chicago Mayor Richard J. Daley. "We thought the justice system would be able to act independently and process the accused as individuals. But the system needs quiet as a context in which to work. You can't conceive of a judge having to rule on a case with the multitudes screaming at him. With the question of the military, the subject unfortunately became polarized. I think the leftists—the Communists and others—intentionally politicized it, publicizing photos, accusing individuals of crimes, spreading rumors with no evidence. The trials hadn't even begun and the military stood convicted. Now, there *were* crimes—you can't argue with that: twenty or thirty people were disappeared, and 'disappeared' is of course a euphemism. But the responsibility is difficult to establish, many were involved, it's all diffuse. And to have trials under those conditions would have involved the entire Army. A good part of the left was looking for exactly that, to put the entire Army on trial."

I pointed out that some of those I'd spoken with before, who'd opposed the amnesty, had insisted, on the contrary, that the entire Army was not to blame, only certain individuals, and that by isolating the guilty ones and removing them, the rest of the armed forces would be affirmed in their innocence. "But the thing is," Tarigo explained, "to secure convictions against, say, fifty military people, we would have had to have at least five hundred officers parading through the courts—as accused, as suspects, as accomplices, or, at any rate, as witnesses. It would have taken anywhere from four to eight years, because that's how long a penal process does take. If we had been able to plug all the information into a computer and get out all the verdicts on the same day—well, then maybe things could have been different. But, as it was, half the officers were going to be involved in one way or another. And I don't think any state can withstand having its armed forces destroyed in such a fashion."

I asked him what role he felt the armed forces should play in a small country like Uruguay. "We will have to deal with that. I believe the military should have less weight in the national budget. We have a military organized as if for the First World War, with a huge infantry, which makes no sense. But this is a subject which can be discussed only in tranquility."

I asked him whether he felt it would ever be possible to discuss such subjects when the current civilian government was still, in the opinion of many, under the military's domination. "I deny that we're living under the thumb of the military," Tarigo replied. "With the '86 law, we've given the military the tranquil knowledge that their past won't be revived, but the military in turn has assumed the responsibility of being subordinate. This is how we build democracy. As with all things in life, when a problem has been solved, it's better to let it be."

I quoted the Zbigniew Herbert line regarding the way "ignorance about those who have disappeared undermines the reality of the world." A democracy can have many components and attributes, I said, but didn't it at least have to be "real," in Herbert's sense? Could any democracy be built on a foundation of "undermined reality"?

"Of course it can," Tarigo countered vigorously. "We can do it perfectly well, as others have—Spain, for instance. When Franco died, a new page was turned, because everybody realized that to go back and review events of forty years earlier would be to provoke a whole new civil war. Life continues, life is made up of things that are not pretty, that are not the subject of a beautiful poem. And the function of a government is not to write poetry but to build a real future. In response to your poet, I would cite the political theorist Max Weber who distinguished between individual ethics and the ethics of those in positions of responsibility. I understand the point of view of the victim's family, but in the ethic of governance one has to weigh, for example, the question of justice for twenty or thirty individuals versus the possibility of losing democracy again in this country. This is what we had to do, and this is what we did."

[Views of President Sanguinetti]

Then I went to visit President Sanguinetti in his executive offices, which were in Libertad, the sleek, modern building that the military dictators had originally built for their Defense Ministry, and from which Sanguinetti had evicted them as one of his first Presidential acts. The building's interior, I found, was imposingly self-important—in fact, neo-Fascist—particularly the door at the end of a long hall which led to the President's inner sanctum. Actually, the door *was* the end of the long hall: the entire wooden wall—floor to ceiling, side to side—pivoted portentously on a gleaming brass axis to admit visitors. But once I was inside the office and in the presence of Sanguinetti himself such observations tended to fade from consciousness, for the President was a genuinely commanding presence—tall, self-confident, firmly planted. Various observers of the Southern Cone (journalists, diplomats, academics) had told me that of the region's three civilian Presidents who had wrested power from their military counterparts within months of each other during the mid-eighties—José Sarney, in Brazil, Alfonsín in Argentina, and Sanguinetti in

Uruguay—Sanguinetti was far and away the most competent, the one with the greatest gift for politics and the finest feel for the job. Nothing in the hour I spent with him gave me reason to doubt that assessment.

At one point in our conversation, when I asked him to characterize the generals' dominion during their tenure, he replied, "They were omnipotent. They could do whatever they wanted. They overpowered everything else. We fought a lot against that dictatorship, a lot more than those speaking out now." He paused, and then added quietly, "But that's not important." That answer would no doubt have annoyed many of "those speaking out now," people who continued to criticize Sanguinetti for the way he sat out much of the dictatorship, declining to take a more active and public role in the opposition. But I'm sure he was being sincere: he is precisely the sort of person who would believe that only the crunch negotiation—*mano a mano*, leader squared off against leader, as he and General Medina were squared off during the secret talks at the Club Naval—could have had any serious relevance to the process that culminated in the military's withdrawal. All the acts of civil disobedience—the increasing grassroots activism, the hunger strikes, the women in their backyards at first furtively and then ever more boldly banging pots and pans in protest—had been simply so much background noise.

At any rate, I began by asking Sanguinetti why the military had been explicitly excluded from the March, 1985, amnesty, only to be granted what amounted to amnesty in the law of December, 1986. What had happened in between?

"The perspective changed," he said. "The reason that the amnesty for the terrorists and the political prisoners, as they're generically called, didn't include the military was that at the time it didn't seem that denunciation of their crimes would become so important. There might be a few accusations, but it wasn't going to be a big deal. Then things began to grow—accusations, confrontations, bigger confrontations."

Were the leaders unaware of the extent of the problem, I asked, or, rather, did they just think that there weren't going to be so many outright accusations?

"No. People pretty much knew what had happened. But such a generous amnesty in favor of the terrorists, it was thought, would serve to calm the society. Things looked different at the time from the way they look now."

So then what happened?

"Great numbers of accusations began rolling in, and we proposed an amnesty. Why? For many reasons. First, few of the accusations were going to lead anywhere—there wasn't enough evidence. It was going to disturb society, and there would simply be a lot of confrontation. Second, it was a question of moral equivalency: we felt that if we were going to have a settling of accounts for the left and the terrorists the military should be amnestied, too. A lot of those involved in violent left-wing groups had never been in jail at all. To begin the arithmetic of judging levels of responsibility, we would have been faced with complications of such magnitude that we thought it best to amnesty everybody—the left and the military. Third, it was necessary to have a climate of stability so as to consolidate democracy. Having lived through such turbulence for so many years, we felt we needed a more peaceful situation. If the country was going to insist on maintaining the old conflicts from before the coup, it was unlikely that we'd ever be able to consolidate democracy. And, finally, for historical reasons. Traditionally, after all great conflicts in a country the solution has been an amnesty for both sides."

Regarding this notion of moral equivalency, what percentage of those in prison was he classifying as terrorists? Weren't there many prisoners who were not even Tupamaros?

"Most were guerrillas—most of the long-term ones."

Wasn't that one of the outstanding questions? Shouldn't there have been at least a truth-telling phase, in which such facts could have been established, once and for all?

"We could have had a moral trial, an investigation followed by an amnesty. But that situation had all the problems and none of the advantages. To open that discussion would have been to preserve old wounds. One can always make mistakes, but, looking over the last four years, I'm convinced that I'm right. The experience of Argentina confirms it: the trials there were not permitted to continue—only the top generals were punished, and not those directly responsible for all the assassinations."

But in both Argentina and Brazil there have been truth-telling phases, either officially sanctioned or based on official documents. One knows how many prisoners were "terrorists" and how many were not. There has been nothing like that in Uruguay.

"That's why Uruguay is stable. The bottom line is that either we're going to look to the future or to the past."

Did he think it possible to have an honest disagreement on this subject—for example, that other people might feel that without attending to the past the future would be built on a faulty base?

"Obviously, on all these matters one can have other perspectives. But, while we were all responsible for what happened, those who carried out the violence on the right and the left were the most responsible. The majority of the country has rights, too, and the great majority don't want violence and do want their rights guaranteed, so they can exercise them today. And it's hard to have a balance when this sort of discussion is going on between minorities. However, more and more are coming to our view: the great majority want democracy and stability. The country still has to grow. During the last three years of the military government, Uruguay's GNP fell 17 percent; in our first three years, it rose 13 percent. Unemployment has gone from 15 percent to 8 percent. All of that is possible only because of political stability."

Was it really such a marginal minority who disagreed with his position? Close to 25 percent of the country's voting population had signed the petition.

"That's an argument in favor of my position. We've gone down a totally legal road. If there should ever be an actual vote, I'm convinced that it would come out seventy to thirty in favor of retaining the amnesty, and that would end the debate."

But if the referendum should be held and should pass—and, remember, this is an electorate that has surprised people before—what would happen?

"To begin with, you're talking science fiction. I have no doubt that the amnesty law would be upheld. But, if not, a period of very strong judicial and political conflict would begin. The country would suffer a lot. Most people understand this. That is why I'm so certain."

Before the December law was passed, soldiers had refused to answer subpoenas and attend trials. If in the wake of the referendum a new dispensation required that they do so, would they?

"I'm sure we'd have serious problems, and I don't want to make predictions. I think you should realize that the people in favor of the referendum are not people known for their defense of democracy. Prior to the coup, they were not defending democracy."

All 25 percent?

"No, no, no, but the Tupamaros, who are the ones in the vanguard. Some surely believe this is the better option, but the people who have all the money to buy up radio stations are Tupamaros." (Since June the Tupamaros had been leasing seventeen hours a day of airtime from an established radio station to present their own mix of news, interviews, and cultural programming; they were covering their expenses through the sale of advertising.)

What of the woman whose nineteen-day-old son was kidnapped? He was now twelve years old. For her, a legal process might reveal something and ease her future anguish. Weren't we talking here about the future and not the past? What could he say to *that* person, or to the widows of Deputy Héctor Gutiérrez Ruiz and Senator Zelmar Michelini?

"I have a great pain for them in my heart and understand their attitude. But what I'm really concerned about is its not happening again. That's why there can be two ways of thinking that are equally honest—their way, which is that the only means of overcoming the problem of the military is to have trials, and our way, which is that the only means is a pardon. The question is, Who can guarantee the future? I'm convinced that we will, this way, and they can't offer the same security."

Once again, I cited the Herbert poem, this time quoting a longer passage:

And yet in these matters
accuracy is essential
we must not be wrong
even by a single one

we are despite everything
the guardians of our brothers

ignorance about those who have disappeared
undermines the reality of the world.

I asked Sanguinetti whether he thought it possible to found a secure democracy on the basis of a sort of willed mass ignorance.

"That's not the basis of democracy," he replied. "The basis of democracy is the people's conviction that it's the best system and that everyone can expect to exercise his rights. The former terrorists now have their radios and newspapers, they shout insults at me at the top of their lungs. That's the basis of democracy—that everyone has a place under the sun. As for your poet—Ernest Renan, the great nineteenth-century French historian, who was very influential here in the Southern Cone, once said, "*Las naciones son plebiscitos todos los días. Y se hacen en base de grandes recuerdos y grandes olvidos*"—"Nations are a plebiscite every day, and they are constructed on the basis of great rememberings and great forgettings." If the French were still thinking about the Night of St. Bartholomew, they'd be slaughtering each other to this day.

"This is a political, and not a moral, decision. It has to be resolved politically because it's a political conflict. Uruguay didn't fall apart by chance, and it's not going to be reconstructed by chance, either."...

[Conclusion of the Referendum Campaign]

Luis González, the premier political pollster in Uruguay, is stone deaf. It's curious that this master of the art of political soundings (the French word for polls is actually *sondages*), this man with his ear to the ground of his country, cannot actually hear a thing. But he can lipread marvelously, fluently, in both Spanish and English (he was trained at Yale), and though his speech is vaguely slurred, it's hearty, expansive, and eminently understandable. The only scary part is when he insists on conversing while driving. To keep up your own end of such conversations is simply to risk death. It was, at any rate, on one such drive that Luis González laid out for me the results of the latest polling that his organization, Equipos, had done on the question of any eventual referendum vote. "When you study the data, three main points emerge," González said. "Everybody knows that there were huge violations of human rights. Most people think that the military men responsible for those violations should be held accountable in some manner. Yet most people have the idea that it won't be easy, or even possible, to hold them to account. People are generally not as worried about any imminent coup as they were in the early days of the transition—except when you bring up this question of the referendum. Then the anxiety level rises sharply. The figures are very clear and remarkably steady. Early in 1987, we predicted the number of people who would be willing to sign the petition, and we got the numbers almost exactly right. Now we're predicting that if there is ever an election, at most 40 percent and probably a bit less (right now, it's about 35 percent), will vote to overturn the *impunidad* statute. It's not that people approve of *impunidad*—they emphatically don't—but that they just don't see any alternative."

Waiting till we'd come to a red light, I asked González if he himself felt that it would be healthy for the country, in the long run, to ignore its history.

"That's not the right question," he replied. "It assumes that you have a single wrong actor, and that this devil is the military. But that isn't fair. We know that it was guilty of terrible violations, but why restrict the blame for those to the military? From 1971 on, certainly, the military had a clear mandate from the politicians—it had been ordered to impose order on the country, and nobody was bothering to tell it how. The politicians brought the military in. But if we acknowledge that huge problem, where does that put us? Perhaps it's better just to start again from scratch." He paused. "You know," he said, sighing, "what was instrumental in the earliest building of democracy in Uruguay—when the country was emerging from that series of fratricidal wars between bands of Colorados and Blancos at the turn of the century—was that there would be, as people said, 'no winners and no losers.' Perhaps such an approach can be instrumental again in the current reconsolidation of democracy. I don't know."

I met a lot of people in Uruguay who had not signed the petition—often, especially in the case of public employees, out of fear for their jobs or their pension—but who said that in the event of a referendum they would vote to overthrow the *impunidad* law. I also met several who said that though they had signed the petition, they intended to vote against the referendum. "From an ethical point of view, it was important to sign," one woman explained to me, "but politically it's not the right time."

When, I asked her, would it be the right time?

"There will never be a right time," she replied sadly. "It's all just too risky."

Over and over during my stay in Montevideo, I encountered this distinction between the ethical and the political. With that young woman, the two were held in a kind of self-consciously dynamic equilibrium. But more often one side predominated, almost to the exclusion of the other. People who saw the issue as essentially a political one—that is, susceptible to negotiation, concession, compromise, the interplay of power centers on the field—considered discussion of its ethical component a frivolous self-indulgence. Conversely, those who saw the issue as an ethical one—a matter of absolute principle, by definition nonnegotiable—were appalled by what they considered the spineless opportunism of the so-called pragmatists....

During its last few weeks, the campaign leading up to the election recapitulated all the major themes of the preceding years' debates. To simplify matters, it was decided that the ballot for the eventual plebiscite would be color-coded: those desiring to overturn the amnesty would be invited to put a green ballot in their secret envelope, while those desiring to reaffirm the law would insert a yellow ballot. The yellow (or "gold", as its proponents preferred to characterize it) side continued to enjoy the fervent endorsement of the major media and most of the leaders of the two principle parties. Its backers argued that only through a yellow vote could the continuity of a democratic future be assured. By contrast, were green to win, as President Sanguinetti said, "I can't promise anything; it would be like entering a blind alley." In the days just before the election, General Medina simply warned, "The pacification, the future's calm, and the army's dignity will be at stake on April 16"—whereupon he made a great show of going off into the interior to consult with some of the prior regime's retired generals. One of those generals, addressing a military rally in Montevideo on the eve of the election, baldly asserted that the Uruguayan military would never tolerate being insulted or separated from power.

The green side's supporters, for their part, urged voters not to succumb to this fear campaign; once again they tried to argue that the only true guarantee of democracy's future would be a sense of justice regarding the past. However, they continued to have problems getting this message across. The Pro-Referendum Commission, for example, bought time on all three television stations for the Friday before the vote. The ad, which they delivered for broadcast that morning, was a simple one: Sara Méndez recounting the story of her nineteen-day-old son's kidnapping and explaining how only through a repeal of the impunidad statute could she ever stand a chance of seeing him again. None of the television stations would air the commercial. When lawyers for the Pro-Referendum Commission demanded an explanation, they were told that the decision to ban the ad had been made "at the highest possible level."...

(The next morning, the final tally would show 53 percent had voted yellow, as against 41 percent green, with 6 percent of the ballots either spoiled or blank.)...

Pérez Aguirre was ... unbowed. "The entire referendum movement has provided a very strong boost for our work on behalf of the human-rights cause. The debate was very important and useful: the whole scene was affected in a very intense way. The fact that in a tiny country like ours, 800,000 defied the fear and misinformation to vote green, that's enormously heartening. And in any case, there are further options still open to us." He went on to suggest that lawyers for some of the victims and their families were already preparing to bring test cases before the Inter-American Court for Human Rights.... Meanwhile, he continued, just a few weeks before the election, SERPAJ issued a major compendium of documentation, the product of over three years' work, on the abuses of human rights during the military dictatorship. Patterned after its Argentine and Brazilian forebears, it was entitled *Uruguay: Nunca Más*; and though it could neither boast an official imprimatur nor claim to be based on the prior regime's own documentation, it still featured the results of an extraordinarily thorough survey of a large random sampling of former prisoners, conducted for SERPAJ by the universally respected Equipos firm and focusing on such issues as types of torture, conditions of imprisonment, the presence of doctors during torture, and so forth.

When I reached Marcelo Vignar, the psychoanalyst who two years earlier had expressed for me his serious misgivings regarding the country's psychopolitical health (in the meantime he'd abandoned Paris, returning to Montevideo for good), I found him, like Galeano and Pérez Aguirre, surprisingly upbeat. "Two years ago," he said, "the authorities were desperately trying to make it seem as if nothing had happened—torture and disappearances and so forth had all been merely marginal, unimportant occurrences, one no longer needed to think about them—and it looked like they were going to succeed in doing so. But all the work of the past two years forced people to think—*everybody*.

The campaign allowed an inscription of all that history into the collective memory, even if, in the end, that inscription couldn't be translated into action." He was quiet for a moment. "Of course, the victims themselves this week are subdued and sad and drained. But even with them.... As one of my patients commented, 'For once, *they* were the ones who had to be afraid: for the first time, even if just for a few months, we had them trembling that justice might come yet. At least that was satisfying.'"

REVIEW OF THE *LEY DE CADUCIDAD* BY THE INTER-AMERICAN COMMISSION ON HUMAN RIGHTS

*Robert K. Goldman, "Amnesty Laws and International Law"**

The Inter-American Commission on Human Rights was the first inter-governmental body to squarely address this contentious question. It recently found that Uruguay's 1986 amnesty law (*Ley de Caducidad*) violated basic provisions of the American Convention of Human Rights and of the American Declaration of the Rights and Duties of Man.[1]

The Position of the Petitioners

The Theory of Complaints

The Commission's action decided eight consolidated cases, with multiple victims, which were jointly filed by the Institute of Legal and Social Studies of Uruguay and Americas Watch shortly after the Uruguayan Parliament, under pressure from the military, passed the *Ley de Caducidad* on 22 December 1986. This law terminated the State's power to prosecute and punish military and police personnel responsible for human rights violations committed during the period of *ex post facto* military rule (June 1973 to March 1985). The application of this law resulted in the

---

* Excerpted from Robert K. Goldman, "Amnesty Laws and International Law," in International Commission of Jurists, *Justice Not Impunity*, from the International Meeting on Impunity of Perpetrators of Gross Human Rights Violations, November 2-5, 1992, Geneva (International Commission of Jurists, 1993), pp. 210-221.

[1] Report N°29/92 (Cases 10.029, 10.036, 10.145, 10.305, 10.372, 10.373, 10.374 and 10.375) Uruguay, OEA/Ser.L./V.II.82, doc. 25, dated 2 Oct. 1992.

In Report N°28/92 (Cases 10.147, 10.181, 10.240, 10.262, 10.309 and 10.311) OEA/Ser.L/V/II.82, also dated 2 Oct.1992, the Commission found that Argentina's "Due Obedience" and "Final Stop" laws violated the American Convention on Human Rights and the American Declaration of the Rights and Duties of Man. While factually dissimilar from the Uruguayan cases, the Commission disposed of challenges to these Argentine measures applying essentially the same legal reasoning as in the Uruguayan cases.

dismissal of 40 criminal cases in civilian courts, initiated by attorneys for victims of human rights abuses or their relatives against approximately 180 military personnel. Uruguay's Supreme Court upheld the law's constitutionality on 2 May 1988. The law won narrow approval by Uruguay's electorate in a national referendum on 16 April 1989.

All eight cases before the Commission involved violations by State agents of certain "preferred" human rights, *inter alia*, the right to life, the right to humane treatment and the implicit freedom from forced disappearance. The complaints were not based directly on violations of these rights—all of which had occurred before Uruguay ratified the American Convention—but rather on the effect of the amnesty law, which was enacted after Uruguay's ratification of that instrument.

Specifically, the petitioners' fundamental claim was that the *Ley de Caducidad*—by terminating judicial investigation of these past abuses and dismissing proceedings against their perpetrators—denied petitioners their rights to judicial recourse and remedies in violation of articles 8.1 and 25 of the American Convention and in relation to Article 1.1 thereof.

The Misapplication of Amnesty

During three lengthy oral arguments before the Commission, petitioners freely conceded that every government has the prerogative to amnesty or pardon certain criminal offences or offenders under its domestic law. But petitioners claimed that when the effects of such a measure deprive victims of such offences of judicial protection guaranteed by an international instrument to which that State is a party, then the matter could no longer be regarded as purely domestic in nature or beyond the scrutiny of competent international bodies. Petitioners also asserted that the *Ley de Caducidad* was a morally and legally perverse application of the concept of amnesty.

In this connection petitioners noted that, conceptually, amnesty abolishes or forgets the particular offence. It normally applies to crimes against the sovereignty of the nation, i.e., political offences. Petitioners argued that, properly viewed, this concept should not apply to the *Ley de Caducidad* and similar measure that forgive agents of the State who have grossly violated the human rights of citizens. The State's right to abolish or forget the crimes of those who have infracted its sovereignty, by rebellion or other means, flows from the role of the State as the victim. Thus, the State may find that its interests, such as national reconciliation, are best served by an amnesty. However, petitioners contended that the State should not have the prerogative to abolish or forget its own crimes or those of its agents committed against its citizens. If the right to abolish or forget such crimes exists, then it belongs only to the victims themselves.

The American Convention's Superiority

The petitioners also argued that even if the *Ley de Caducidad* could deny them judicial remedies, as a purely domestic legal matter, it could neither deprive petitioners of their remedies under the American Convention nor relieve Uruguay of its duty to fulfill its obligations thereunder. Petitioners contended that, by denying them access to local legal redress, Uruguay had rendered illusory its basic obligation to respect, ensure and remedy violations of Convention-based rights and in effect had interposed its domestic law as a bar to compliance with the Convention.

Petitioners noted that, on the international level, it is well established that a State's international obligations are superior to any obligations it may have under its domestic law. Thus, a State cannot invoke its own contrary domestic law as an excuse for non-compliance with international law. With regard to international agreements, this principle is codified in Article 27 of the Vienna Convention on the Law of Treaties, which states in pertinent part: "A party may not invoke the provisions of its internal law as justification for its failure to perform a treaty...."

Accordingly, notwithstanding its failure to give internal legal effect to a provision of the American Convention, Uruguay remained bound by that treaty and was responsible for its violation. This principle has been repeatedly invoked and affirmed in decisions of the Permanent Court of International Justice and of the International Court of Justice, as well as those of other international tribunals.[2]

Petitioners also cited another related and basic principle of international treaty law directly binding on Uruguay: the customary law doctrine of *pacta sunt servanda*, embodied in Article 26 of the Vienna Convention. It states: "every international agreement in force is binding upon the parties to it and must be performed by them in good faith." This principle implicitly reinforces the doctrine that a State's treaty obligations are unaffected by changes, whether by legislation or referendum, in its domestic law.

Governmental Succession to Treaty Obligations

Similarly, petitioners pointed out that a change in government, by whatever means (since the identity of a State remains the same), does not alter the binding nature of the State's international legal obligations. Thus, the Sanguinetti and Lacalle administrations were internationally responsible for unredressed violations of the American Convention, attributable to the *ex post facto* military regime. The Inter-American Court of Human Rights applied this principle specifically to State-sponsored human rights violations in the Velásquez Rodríguez case: in a landmark decision on 29 July 1988 it found Honduras responsible for the disappearance of Manfredo Velásquez. The Court said in this regard:

---

[2] For example, in its 1930 advisory opinion in the Greco-Bulgarian Communities case the Permanent Court of International Justice stated: "It is a generally accepted principle of international law that in relations between powers who are contracting parties to a treaty, the provisions of municipal law cannot prevail over those of the treaty." The Permanent Court has also ruled that this same principle applies even when a state invokes its constitution "with a view to evading obligations incumbent upon it under international law or treaties in force".

> [a]ccording to the principle of continuity of the State in international law, responsibility exists both independently of changes in government over a period of time and continuously from the time of the act which created responsibility to the time when the act is declared illegal. The foregoing is also valid in the area of human rights although, from an ethical or political point of view, the attitude of the new government may be much more respectful of those rights than that of the government in power when the violations occurred (para. 184).

The State's Obligations

During these oral arguments, the petitioners particularly emphasized the authoritative interpretation by the Inter-American Court of Convention Article 1.1 in the Velásquez case to support their claim that Uruguay was obliged to investigate and prosecute perpetrators of State-sponsored human rights violations.[3]

In its opinion, the Court declared that Article 1.1 "constitutes the generic basis of the protection of rights recognized by the Convention" (para. 163). The Court indicated that the obligation to "respect" rights recognized in the Convention is founded on the notion that "the exercise of public authority has some limits which derive from the fact that human rights are inherent attributes of human dignity which are, therefore, superior to the State" (para. 165). It interpreted far more broadly the State's other obligation under Article 1.1 " to ensure the free and full exercise" of these rights. The Court stated that this "obligation implies the duty of the States parties to organize the governmental apparatus and, in general, all the structures through which public power is exercised, so that they are capable of judicially ensuring the free and full enjoyment of human rights" (para. 166).

The Court stated that whenever a State organ, agent or public entity, violates a right protected by the Convention, the State is internationally responsible, not only for the violation of the infringed right, but also for a violation of its duty, under Article 1.1, to respect and to ensure that right. Significantly, the Court found that as a consequence of their dual obligations under Article 1.1, States "must prevent, investigate and punish any violation of the rights recognized by the Convention and, moreover, if possible attempt to restore the right violated and provide compensation as warranted for damages resulting from the violation of human rights" (para. 166). The Court also noted that compliance with Article 1.1 necessarily requires that government to investigate each and every violation of a protected right. Failure to investigate or an investigation not undertaken in "a serious manner" and "as a mere formality preordained to be ineffective," resulting in the violation going unpunished and the victim

---

[3] The States parties to this Convention undertake to respect the rights and freedoms recognized herein and to ensure to all persons subject to their jurisdiction the free and full exercise of those rights and freedoms, without any discrimination for reasons of race, colour, sex, language, religion, political or other opinion, national or social origin, economic status, birth or any other social condition.

uncompensated, violated the duty "to ensure" the full and free exercise of the affected right (paras. 176 & 177).

Petitioners argued that since the *Ley de Caducidad* terminated criminal investigations, it clearly violated Article 1.1. They also contended, from a policy perspective, that the prosecution of perpetrators "ensures" the protection of human rights by preventing or deterring future violations by the actor(s) or others. Moreover, such prosecution symbolically represents a clear break with the legacy of the past and helps restore public confidence in democratic institutions.

The Position of the Government of Uruguay

The Law's Contextual Setting

The Uruguay Government's basic arguments, some of which were oral, were summarized and explained in its written response to the Commission's preliminary report.[4]

The government criticized the Commission for having ignored the "democratic juridical-political" context, the "domestic legitimacy" and the "higher ethical ends" of the *Ley de Caducidad*. Specifically, it asserted that the amnesty question "should be viewed in the political context of reconciliation, as part of a legislative programme for national pacification that covered all actors involved in past human rights violations" (Commission Official Report, Para. 22). It emphasized that the law was enacted with the requisite parliamentary majority and had been the subject of a national referendum expressing "the will of the Uruguayan people to close a painful chapter in their history in order to put an end, as is their sovereign right, to division among Uruguayans" (Official Report, para. 22). As such, the government continued, the law "is not subject to international condemnation". In addition, the government pointedly declared that it "cannot accept the Commission's finding that while the domestic legitimacy of the law is not within the Commission's purview, the legal effects denounced by petitioners are".

Lawful Restrictions

The government contended that the *Ley de Caducidad* violated neither the American Convention nor any other international engagement, but was instead a legitimate exercise of the State's basic rights to grant clemency and to place lawful restrictions on rights. It argued that Conventions Articles 8.1 and 25.1 must be interpreted in light of Convention articles 30 and 32, which permit States to restrict the enjoyment and exercise of Convention-based rights "when such restrictions are the product of laws enacted for reasons of general interest or when those rights are limited by the rights of others, by the security of all and by the just

---

4 Uruguay, which has accepted the jurisdiction of the Inter-American Court, had 90 days upon receipt of the Commission's report to submit these complaints to the Court but declined to do so.

demands of the general welfare in a democratic society" (Official Report, para. 23). Furthermore, the government contended that Convention Article 4.6, as well as Articles 6.4 and 14.6 of the International Covenant on Civil and Political Rights, granted Uruguay the requisite authority to enact the disputed law.

Articles Disputed

The government averred that the fair trial guarantees in Conventions Article 8.1 refer to "the rights of the accused in a criminal action" (Official Report, § 24). While asserting that "private parties are not the owners of a criminal action", and that Uruguayan procedural law does not recognize an individual right to bring a criminal complaint independently of a case brought by the public prosecutor, the government conceded that private interests are allowed to "intervene" in "exceptional cases" (Official Report, para. 24). It claimed that such an individual right is "not protected by international human rights law".

The government asserted that it had not violated Article 25.1 of the Convention whose purpose, it argued, was intended to "redress the injured rights and, if not, secure reparation for the damage suffered" (Official Report, para. 25). It further stated that "since, in the cases being denounced, it is impossible to redress rights injured during the *de facto* regime, all that remains is the right to damages, which the [ley] has in no way impaired".

The Ley's Intentions

The government claimed that the *Ley de caducudad* did not violate Article 1.1 as interpreted by the Court in the Velásquez case. Noting that the duty to investigate and the question of an amnesty law "must be analyzed as a whole", the government noted that the *ley's* intention was in furtherance of the common good because "investigating facts that occurred in the past could rekindle the animosity between persons and groups", thus obstructing reconciliation and the strengthening of democratic institutions. While acknowledging that the legal system should make available to interested parties the procedural means to establish the truth, the government, nonetheless, argues that, for those same reasons, the State may choose "not to make available to the interested party the means necessary for a formal and official inquiry into the facts in a court of law" (Official Report, para. 26).

The Commission's Opinion and Conclusions

Competence to Examine the Ley's Effects

Before addressing the merits of the cases, the Commission first rejected Uruguay's claim that it was not empowered to decide whether the *Ley de Caducidad* was compatible with the American Convention. While admitting that it lacked jurisdiction to pass on the domestic legality or constitutionality of national laws, the Commission stated that "application of the Convention and examination of the legal effects of a legislative measure, either judicial or of any other nature, insofar as it has effects incompatible with the rights and guarantees embodied in the Convention ... are within the Commission's competence" (Official Report, para. 31). The Commission affirmed that its competence arises from the Convention which, *inter alia,* vests it with jurisdiction respecting matters relating to the fulfilment of the commitments made by States parties to the Convention (Article 33) and to receive and take action on petitions pursuant to its authority under that instrument (Articles 41, 44 and 51). It also noted that contracting States are obliged by Convention Article 2 to adopt "such legislative or other measures as may be necessary to give effect to those rights and freedoms". Thus, it concluded, "a fortiori, a country cannot by internal legislation evade its international obligations" (Official Report, para. 32).

Violation of Fair Trial Guarantees

The Commission noted that by sanctioning and applying the *Ley de Caducidad,* Uruguay had not only, by design, dismissed all criminal proceedings against perpetrators of past human rights abuses, but also, had not undertaken any official investigation to establish the truth about these past events. It pointedly cited its own "general position on the subject" as stated in its 1985-86 *Annum* Report:

> [o]ne of the few matters that the Commission feels obliged to give its opinion in this regard is the need to investigate the human rights violation committed prior to the establishment of the democratic government. Every society has the inalienable right to know the truth about past events, as well as the motive and circumstances in which aberrant crimes came to be committed, in order to prevent a repetition of such acts in the future. Moreover, the family members of the victims are entitled to information as to what happened to their relatives. Such access to the truth presupposes freedom of speech, which of course should be exercised responsibly; the establishment of investigating committees whose membership and authority must be determined in accordance with the internal legislation of each country, or the provision of the necessary resources so that the judiciary itself may undertake whatever investigations may be necessary (Official Report, para. 37).

The Commission also indicated that it had "to weigh the nature and gravity" of events to which the *ley* applied, such as forced disappearances and abduction of minors, stating that "the social imperative of their clarification and investigation cannot be equated with that of mere common crime" (Official Report, para. 38).

The Commission indicated that the *Ley de Caducidad* "had various effects and adversely affected any numbers of parties on legal interests. Specifically, the victims' next of kin or parties injured by human rights violations have been denied their right to legal redress, to an impartial and exhaustive judicial investigation that clarifies the facts, ascertains those responsible and imposes the corresponding criminal punishment" (Official Report, para. 39)

It then addressed the merits of the petitioners' essential claim that the disputed measure, as applied, violated their rights to a fair trial and judicial protection guaranteed in Convention Articles 8.1 and 25.1, respectively. Article 8.1 provides in pertinent part: "Every person has the right to a hearing with due guarantees [by a competent tribunal] ... in the substantiation of any accusation of a criminal nature made against him or for the determination of his rights and obligations of a cure, labour, fiscal or any other nature."

The Commission rejected Uruguay's contention that Article 8.1 only applies to the rights of criminal defendants. In concluded that Uruguay, by enacting and applying the *Ley de Caducidad* after it had ratifies the Convention, had deliberately prevented petitioners from exercising rights "upheld" in Article 8.1 and, accordingly, had violated the Convention. For the same reasons, the Commission found that Uruguay had violated the petitioners' right to judicial protection stipulated in Article 25.1 of the Convention.[5]

A Violation of Obligation

The Commission also concluded that the *Ley de caducudad,* which prevented investigation of past human rights abuses, violated Uruguay's duty under Article 1.1 "to ensure" petitioners the free and full exercise of these Convention-based rights. Predictably, it found the Inter-American Court's authoritative interpretation of Article 1.1 in the Velásquez case to be controlling on the issue of investigation in these cases. The Commission cited with approval the following passages, among others, from Velásquez:

> [i]f the State apparatus acts in such a way that the violation goes unpunished and the victim's full enjoyment of such rights is not restored as soon as possible, the State has failed to comply with its duty to ensure the free and full exercise of those rights to the persons within its jurisdiction. As for the obligation to investigate, the Court noted that an investigation must have an objective and be assumed by the Sate as its own legal duty, not as a step taken by private interests that depends upon the initiative of the victim or his family or upon their offer of proof, without an effective search for the truth by the government (Official Report, para. 50).

Commission's Recommendations to Uruguay

Based on its conclusion that the *Ley de Caducidad* was incompatible with the American Convention, and violated Articles 1.1, 8.1 and 25.1, as well as Article XVIII of the American Declaration of the Rights and Duties

---

[5] Article 25.1 states: "Everyone has the right to simple and prompt recourse, or any other effective recourse, to a competent court or tribunal for protection against acts that violate his fundamental rights recognized by the constitution or laws of the State concerned or by this Convention, even though such violation may have been committed by persons acting in the course of their official duties."

of Man, the Commission recommended to the Uruguayan Government that it pay just compensation to the applicant victims or their rightful claimants for its violations of these rights. It also recommended that the government adopt "the measures necessary to clarify the facts and identify those responsible for the human rights violations that occurred during the *de facto* period" (Official Report, para. 54).

NUNCA MÁS REPORT ON HUMAN RIGHTS VIOLATIONS

Servicio Paz y Justicia, "Uruguay Nunca Más: Human Rights Violations, 1972-1985"*

Preface

When we committed ourselves to this investigation, we also undertook a commitment to the people of Uruguay. Our motives, which were many and urgent and are therefore difficult to state, must be the same as those that moved our neighbors in Argentina and Brazil to publish similar books. These motives are eloquently expressed in a phrase that now belongs to all those who endured and suffered under state terrorism and the so-called Doctrine of National Security. The phrase, *Nunca Más*, concluded the memorable opinion given by Attorney General Julio César Strassera on Wednesday, September 18, 1985, at 3:25 in the afternoon at the trial of Argentinean commanders accused of human rights abuses. Strassera said, "Your Honors, I expressly want to renounce any pretension to originality in closing this examination. I want to use a phrase that is not mine because it belongs to your people. Your Honors, *Nunca Más*!"

Argentineans and Brazilians both saw the need to write and publish a report that would make *Nunca Más* sound loud and clear in their countries. In Argentina, the investigations were carried out with government support; in Brazil they were carried out with the support of the church. But in Uruguay neither the government nor the church provided a *Nunca Más* report. A few individual researchers attempted to do so, but they were overcome by the difficulty of the task and were unable to complete it. As a result, SERPAJ (*Servicio Paz y Justicia*, Peace and Justice Service) of Uruguay took on the job.

In addition to honoring the basic claim of justice owed to the victims, those of us who wrote and edited *Uruguay Nunca Más* felt an obligation to do everything possible to prevent the events from happening again. But first we had to learn the magnitude of the catastrophe by penetrating the period from 1972 to 1985, when Uruguayan society was continually subjected to lies, isolation, silence, and fear. Only with difficulty did we come to

---

* Excerpted from Servicio Paz y Justicia, *Uruguay Nuca Más: Human Rights Violations, 1972-1985*, translated by Elizabeth Hampsten (Temple University Press, 1989), pp. vii-xii, 315-318, 321-324.

realize how deeply the dictatorship had affected the whole body of society, what it meant to have spent years living as collective *encapuchados*, as if with the torturer's hood over our heads, in silence. We pretended to be ignorant, a strategy some found necessary for survival, for salvaging the salvageable.

It was not that we did not know the "things" that were happening. Some censored information got through, more or less, by word of mouth, though it sometimes confused fact with rumor. But certainly the population at large was not learning the truth or realizing the real dimensions of the ecosocial disaster that the dictatorship was bringing about. Because Uruguayans never fully understood what was happening, it has been easy to minimize and lie about the crimes that were committed. The gravity of the attack on liberties, on civil and political rights, on personal dignity is so poorly understood by the majority of the population that our lack of knowledge and critical understanding place us at risk of having the disaster repeated.

As Strassera aptly said, "We have a responsibility to found a peace based not on forgetfulness but on remembrance, not on violence but on justice. This is our chance; it may be the last." We too are convinced of that and so apparently was the Uruguayan military when, in their campaign against subversion, they quoted George Santayana: "Those who do not remember their past are condemned to repeat it." But remembering the past means knowing it accurately; in no other way will people learn their lessons. One does not investigate and judge the past only to condemn and punish but rather to learn.

On February 5, 1983, at 10:15 at night, Klaus Barbie was imprisoned in the fort at Montluc in Lyon, France, accused of crimes against humanity. Soon afterward a historic trial began, in spite of the forty years that had elapsed since the crimes of which he was accused. Like the Nüremberg trials of Nazi war criminals, this book concentrates on accusations and repudiations, not on the evasive actions by which some officers sought, with impunity, to hide their crimes and their identities. Nüremberg entered the annals of history as an occasion when the international community and the collective consciousness of nations agreed to judge serious war crimes and establish legal, political, and moral principles that would prevent the Nazi madness from being repeated or guilty persons from acting again with impunity. We know that Nüremberg affected only a few, yet its effect on the conscience and the memories of nations was exemplary.

That is what we want to accomplish in this book. Nobel Peace Prize winner Elie Wiesel, one of 105 witnesses at trial of the "butcher of Lyon," wrote to his lawyer that year: "'Are you looking for fire?' asked a great Hassidic rabbi. 'Look in the ashes.' It is what you are doing from the beginning of this process; it is what we have tried to do since the Liberation. In spite of everything, we have searched in the ashes for a truth to affirm human dignity, which does not exist if it is not in the memory. Thanks to this process, survivors find a justification for their survival. Their testimony counts, their memory will be part of the collective memory. It is clear that no one can bring the dead back to life. But thanks to the words pronounced there, the accused cannot again kill the dead." If we look at instances of war, state terrorism, genocide, and other atrocities, there have been few times when it was possible to bring the guilty to justice, and many of these cases ended in sentences that were ridiculous in relation to the magnitude and gravity of the crimes. The "true judgment" has always been a moral one and has been the heritage of nations and of history.

The "war" in Uruguay produced nothing so spectacular as the bombing of Government House by Pinochet in Chile or the genocide committed by the military juntas in Argentina when thousands disappeared. But in Uruguay it was carried out with unprecedented sophistication; it was a hushed, progressive repression measured out in doses until it gained absolute control over the entire population. Our country was occupied by our own army, and we Uruguayans were made impotent and defenseless before an uncontrolled despotic will. Even humanitarian acts and expressions of solidarity became targets for accusations of subversion. Helping a torture victim or finding relief for a relative of a political prisoner or a relative of someone who had disappeared could be called "assistance by association to commit a crime." This was our "war"; a war in which the armed forces admit to having lost their "points of reference"; an undocumented war, without clear enemies; a war in which acts of service, the defense of national security, and patriotism were confused with immorality, a breakdown in ethics, and crime. The "dirty war" turned into common criminality, guaranteeing a national security system that no one had elected. And the business worked well: The actors performed with impunity.

How can this social-ecological disaster be measured? The open sores, the infection left in the social body of the Uruguayan people can be healed only by a truthful diagnosis. That is the other principle that guides us here.

There is the matter of the law that is allowing criminals and rapists to have acted with no fear of punishment when they denied any number of elementary rights in the name of national security. Techniques of state terrorism were employed to disorient and dominate the country; torture, forced disappearances, and imprisonment for ideological reasons were all crimes the perpetrators knew had to be carried out with impunity if they were to succeed at all. This ability to act with impunity, with official absolution from consequences, strikes most painfully at the situation of the disappeared. The disappeared are considered nonbeings. The Doctrine of National Security does not recognize them as human, let alone as criminals. In all democratic societies criminals reserve the right to be prosecuted and tried, to be acknowledged as prisoners and to know their sentence; regardless of the offense, they remain persons. But the disappeared suffer an extreme transformation, for they have been denied that aspect of the human condition that locates them in place and time. Their families live in the shadows, harassed by doubts and fantasies, in permanent torment, unable to file a claim in court or even to bury their dead. This shadow in the soul that constitutes the disappeared goes beyond family members and touches all society.

Unless we commit ourselves to revealing the truth, to seeing that justice is carried out, and demonstrate that acting with impunity no longer has any place on the national scene, our Uruguay will be committing political suicide. That is simply how things are, because if we continue with the notion that the Mengeles and Barbies who roam our streets cannot be found or be brought to justice, we are asserting that terrorist action in the name of the state is acceptable, that we can never know what happened or who the guilty were. In the end, justice will never touch them, and we will be left with a mockery forever.

To demand truth and justice is not to desire vengeful revisionism. It is a mistake to suppose that removing the specter of the ability to act with impunity, which covers our future like a sticky hood, and replacing it with the rule of law promises political upheaval. As Einstein said, "A sad time, ours. Easier to take apart the atom than a prejudice." Allowing acts to have been performed with impunity keeps us from recovering essential things that were lost in the dark years, and this impediment is causing severe psychosocial disturbances in Uruguay. Before a suffering for which we find no meaning, the anguished question Why? remains unanswered, and especially among the young, it is causing an entire generation to live with an ahistorical sense of its own identity. Identity means asking such questions as Who are we? Where did we come from? Where are we going? To give more or less definite answers, you need a social and political geography, a known history; you need to know what happened and why, what went on in a historical period, how events were resisted or submitted to, how rights were abused, how passage out of a dark period was achieved, and how the future will be. To rescue that history is to learn a lesson, to come to certain conclusions, and to look without shame at the future.

Some say that dwelling on past events opens up old wounds, but we have to ask, When were those wounds closed? They remain open; the only way to close them is to achieve true national reconciliation based on truth and justice about what happened. And the mere passage of time will not be enough to heal the infection from which Uruguay is suffering, for the pain remains on the national conscience as long as we do not treat it properly. To close wounds and be reconciled is not to forget. Forgetting is a sign of weakness and fear of the future; remembering is a sign of courage. It would be regrettable, an unsupportable loss of dignity, to know that we had turned into a fainthearted people, cowed by threats from a few military commanders to leave criminals unpunished and force ourselves into forgetfulness. Moreover, we cannot tolerate the confusion of mind that, pretending to place a *punto final* on the events we are reporting here, announces an amnesty proclamation that names criminals and innocents in the same category. Under such a shameful abandonment of justice, peace becomes no more than an unattainable vision.

Readers will have to decide for themselves what this report is really about. We ourselves can better say what it is not. It is not a scientific analysis of political, economic, cultural, ideological, and military elements of a given period; nor is it a contemporary history. *Nunca Más* is not simply a narration of testimonials, bitter indictments, or bad memories, although it is true that these pages contain irrepressible demands for dignity and justice as well as complaints against outrages that are made sometimes calmly and sometimes bitterly. As authors and editors, we have tried as far as possible to exclude opinion and allow the force of testimony to speak directly to readers, so that they may come to their own conclusions. We have also tried to provide all possible assurance of the information's accuracy and authenticity. All survey data are available to interested scholars. We do not intend that this report be read as a moral treatise. If the violation of ethical principles is more graphically described in some cases than in others, that does not mean that we value one right more than another or care more about preserving life than about liberty or social and economic rights. Our single aim is to bring to light what has been clouded over by silence, for if those of us who survived do not give voice to those who have been silenced, we ourselves become accomplices in that silence.

This book may give the impression that despite a few uplifting testimonials to endurance and courage, everything was a nightmare, as indeed it very likely was. What is important is that readers learn how much there is to do. It must never happen again. What René Maheu said at UNESCO in Paris in April 1968, in celebration of the twentieth anniversary of the Universal Declaration of Human Rights, remains true today: "As great as the forces have been, and progress achieved, as heroic as have been innumerable sacrifices, the price of human freedom has not yet been paid by mankind, nor even defined at its just value. The immemorial work continues, at this very moment."...

Epilogue

We pretend to no conclusions; instead, we provide data and statistics—information that speaks for itself and allows readers to come to their own conclusions. The facts do not only speak, they call out in the midst of an intolerable silence that is being imposed on the immediate past. Silence has become a cornerstone—placed in the past by the dictatorship and in the present by those who believe that it can assure a peaceful future. But the facts, the victims, are there; they speak or call out to us. There is no future in pretending to be deaf to what they are saying.

We do not understand those who claim that time, a natural process without normative value, will have a diluting effect on the horror and the assault on human rights narrated here. We have written these pages so that others may know that what we all thought was impossible indeed was possible. So as not to forget. We have written in homage to all the authentic democrats who resisted, fought, and suffered before totalitarianism.

These dramatic encounters were not the result of human accident, of aberration, or of the unexpected. As we argue repeatedly in these pages, what happened was planned; the result of calculated policies. Furthermore, we cannot accept the judgment that to speak of the Doctrine of National Security and State Terrorism is to state the "opinions" of the authors of this report, any more than the suffering imposed on the social body of Uruguay is an abstraction. That corporate entity is made up of men, women, and children of flesh and bone. We do not want to place the final period, to distance ourselves from these facts, without a word that might somehow recapitulate the experience. We must meditate on the unsuppressible crime that must not ever be forgotten, so that *nunca más* holds us in its clutches.

As a first meditation, faced with the nature of what happened, it is not easy to know whom to hold accountable, whom to punish. With whom should we begin? Do we accuse those simple and honest citizens who were silent in the presence of crimes? The sadistic torturers? The president who justified events for reasons of the state? The general or colonel who understood it all as "the logic of war"? It took many years for us to realize the enormous dimensions of the catastrophe. We have come to that realization appalled, as though after a disproportionately vicious crime or as if it were the day after a great disgrace, watching the effects and size of the catastrophe being measured even as we are taking our distance from them. Because the lasting consequences do not appear at first sight; they grow with time and do not stop; they expand like the waves of the sea, always increasing.

We Uruguayans analyzed here feel ourselves carriers of a heavy and inexpressible secret that separates us from our children. How can we tell them the truth? How can we explain what happened? How can we explain to new generations that a policy made children disappear? How can we explain that all morality was canceled in order to overpower a society for certain ends? These pages are intended to answer these weighty questions. Only by transcribing the truth in these crowded sheets can we unburden ourselves of the sentence truth lays down. At the conclusion of our investigation, we were convinced that it had been absolutely necessary. Some critics have persisted in asking whether it was really useful to turn over that sad, painful, inglorious past, to reopen national wounds only badly healed. Would it not have been wiser and more prudent to leave behind in obscurity all that happened to us?

With apparent "realism" and goodwill, they wish to forget, for the sake of peace. Many Uruguayans think that way. Especially those who did not resist the dictatorship would rather forget as quickly as possible. But in that act of forgetting, there is loss as well. What is forgotten is the country's individuality, its spirit, its genuine traditions, those subtle actions that make us Uruguayans and not something else. And now some want to forget because at the time they did not act to avoid what happened, thinking its alternative would be a worse disgrace. As if there could be a worse disgrace than to make a lie of the law, of civil rights, of justice and morality. The truth is that when an action denies the essence of the human being as human being, any scheme to absolve it in the name of some higher morality contradicts that morality. To forget past crimes becomes a new crime against human nature.

This *nunca más* is a shining and compassionate turn to face misery and pain, to turn toward the grief and despair of so many defenseless persons. As the years go by, we have to gather together those painful shadows that, unable to find repose, seek shelter in our memory. Will we have to forget; will we have to close forever those eyes that begged us, appalled, for a minimum of justice? No. Truth and justice is what they claim, and to write this account has been a contribution to that cause. Our act of writing has tried to press to the limits the arrogant power that death imposes on us. As Odiseo Elytis has said, "I write so that death does not have the last word." We are writing not to exercise a vain revenge against a cowed enemy but to turn over to new generations a past that many of our contemporaries have refused to narrate. And we are writing because what the tortured said was so difficult to believe, and this was exactly what the torturers had planned when they invented a system of human destruction that went so far beyond ordinary barbarity it was bound to encounter incredulity. Also, we are writing because the younger generation knows almost nothing of that time when our history appeared to go mad and left the known world to inhabit for a time the reality of hell.

Without the data, the statistics, the facts, and the testimonies reported here, it would not be easy to know the degree of ignominy humanity is able to descend to when it recognizes no moral law. In recording these testimonies, we have tried to stand guard against a return to the kind of horror that hammers people into despair and hate. And it must not be said that such a return is impossible or that history does not repeat itself. History does repeat itself, ever since Cain. We should never doubt the anodyne and banal form, ridiculous at times, that the ground prepares for a return to those histories. It would not be hard to begin again, little by little, another attempt to disgrace, with fear and psychological violence, to dominate, to get a police state going again—a persecution that has the eyes of Cain. To bring disgrace by means of contempt is not that hard; the offense against what is left of a victim's dignity comes easily when elemental ethical limits are erased.

What we have been through not only has remained in a hidden corner of memory but has integrated itself into the persona of Uruguayans. It is part of their being forever. We should have the courage not to hide that experience in our collective subconscious but to recollect it so that we do not fall again into the trap. Let our youth be alert.

Let them never sacrifice their conscience and their memory on the altar of petty interests, whether of party, ideology, or conformism. Let them conserve the profound idea of Right and Justice that they received from the founders of our nation and that comes from the Universal Declaration of Human Rights....

Methodology

The Genesis of Uruguay Nunca Más

For a long time there was little real awareness in Uruguay of the human rights violations that had taken place during the so-called anti-subversive struggle. During the years of military dictatorship, it was practically impossible to get word out about the crimes being committed. Iron censorship, the widespread atomization of social organizations, and the profound fear that made it more prudent to keep silent than risk suffering the same atrocities one was trying to denounce were causes enough for such lack of public awareness. Only abroad was it possible to disseminate information about what was really going on in Uruguay, and even there it was difficult to open the eyes of the international community to the outrages.

Eventually, in the last stages of the dictatorship and, of course, once the democratic period had begun, the truth of what had happened during those years began to unfold, but information was incomplete and scattered, predominantly appearing in daily and weekly newspapers. These media, despite their courage in having been the first to take up human rights issues—some even during the military period—usually were the news organs of political parties and therefore did not reach all sectors of the population. But what undoubtedly most impeded the spread of information was the unwillingness of radio and television stations, the media of widest circulation, to devote air time to human rights issues. Most of the information about human rights violations was hurriedly issued in the first months of democratic government, after which a curious relapse occurred. While the media purported to allocate space about the events of 1972-1985 in almost every program or newspaper edition, in fact what they were reporting was the progress of those interminable negotiations among political parties that concluded with the approval of the *Ley de Caducidad* ("Law of Immunity"). As a result, even though the print and air media were saying little about the violations themselves, the public was suffering from an information overdose. The media claimed to be publicizing news about human rights, when actually, they were only publicizing the same political comings and goings that had kept the abuses from being recognized in the first place.

Even so, no seeming lack of information can hide the fact that most Uruguayans were never totally unaware that the armed forces had committed serious human rights violations. As time went on, the magnitude of the crimes caused the conviction to spread spontaneously; it was impossible not to know. What people did lack was full and exact knowledge, a reasonably accurate perception of the tragedy that Uruguayan society underwent.

Hence the cardinal inspiration for this work—the desire to nurture collective memory. We began with the realization that when pain is too agonizing, a person tries to erase it from conscious awareness; to survive, one's psychological defenses have to deny the trauma's existence. In a like manner the social body attempts to dilute the memory of wounds, the more so when no judicial recourse has been provided that might hasten healing. (In Uruguay torturers and those who ordered torture have legal immunity, and the disappeared, by law, for the most part may not be discovered.) Furthermore, in Uruguay, some people advocate forgetfulness in order to justify the crimes; their arguments begin by minimizing the wrongs and conclude by denying them altogether. If that active silencing succeeds, the day may come when even the existence of the atrocities will be the subject of controversy, and it will have to be proven that they ever occurred.

Threats like those against collective memory drove SERPAJ to realize the need for documenting in order to inform, to make sure that what had happened would not be forgotten or, considering the awfulness of the experience, its lessons lost. What caused brutality to such a high degree? Trying to learn its causes is a beginning toward avoiding repetition. As the investigation progressed, several people expressed the hope that the information they were giving might be a help for the future; our response was that there was no guarantee but that we too hoped that the investigation would increase respect for human rights. Uruguayans have the right and the duty to know what happened because a clear memory, we are convinced, can more easily control the pain and lead to recuperation from the lacerating effects. Forgetfulness always is deceptive, not to mention impossible; as we have suggested, groups no more than individuals are able to overcome traumatic experiences while denying their existence—denial only makes their repetition more likely. Thus we believe that the best way to avoid another dictatorship is to keep fresh the memory of its effects.

These, then, are reasons, in addition to those mentioned in the Preface, that SERPAJ took up an investigation it hoped might fill, even partially, the holes we mentioned.... The two principal sources for this investigation have been testimonials on file in SERPAJ, and the survey, "The Long Imprisonment in Uruguay: The Prisoners' Version," carried out by Equipos Consultores Asociados at the behest of SERPAJ. In addition, we have used two principal documentary sources: published testimonies of ex-prisoners about their prison experiences, and published articles and documents—reports to intergovernmental agencies such as the United Nations, the Organization of American States—as well as articles appearing in the Uruguayan and foreign press. Obviously a limitation of these very rich sources is our not being able to know how representative they are. One assumes that only persons affected negatively by prolonged prison life would want to make their experiences known, while those with more positive memories would be less willing to speak with the same intensity. That was why it seemed necessary to make a systematic investigation (the survey) that would look at the problem from a quantifiable perspective in order to complement other available data.

The Contents of Uruguay Nunca Más

This book is intended for the general reader, not for social scientists, even though we rely to a certain extent on statistical data and bibliographical sources. We have tried to seem as little partisan as possible: Our purpose is to present facts as we find them, not emotional arguments, so that while there are pages that may well move readers, we have wanted to avoid the slippery ground of sensationalism and horror. We have tried to leave out the researchers' personal impressions, even though we have not always succeeded, for there are some human events that in their wretchedness remain indescribable.

The book does not include a list of names of those responsible for the aberrations described. In cases where they were known, names are printed. But it was not possible for SERPAJ to carry out the research to establish the identity of all those responsible, since we lack the resources to carry out the minimal steps necessary to seek out probable evidence. Nor does data from the "The Long Imprisonment" survey include the names of those implicated in the repression documented there. We agreed with Equipos Consultores Asociados of Montevideo, which carried out the survey between March and June of 1987, according to topics of inquiry proposed by SERPAJ, that identities would not be revealed of anyone interviewed or anyone who had participated in any form in the arrest and eventual mistreatment or torture—to guard against the survey's being used for reasons other than sociological study. *Uruguay Nunca Más* has as its purpose to discover how the machinery of terror worked, but it has not been able in most cases to find out who was running it. Whenever someone is identified, it is always because of eyewitness testimony.

We want also to reject any claim that this work is "of and for" those who agree with the political views of persons persecuted by the Uruguayan dictatorship. That said, we cannot deny feeling committed to those whose rights were violated during those years. Numerous chapters we think demonstrate that the victims of that aggression did not belong to a category separate from the rest of us Uruguayans. Their abuse wounded all of us. Therefore, it is impossible for us not to identify with the victims, though ours is no more than a commitment to their human condition as victims, precisely the same as what the tyrants had in mind in their wide concept of the enemy. The French philosopher Vladimir Jankélévitch has said appropriately: "Racist crimes are an attack on humans as humans, not against a person as this or that individual, as communist, freemason, an ideological adversary. No! The racist takes aim at the core humanity of all persons."

Survey Population

The study on which this book is based includes all persons of both sexes prosecuted by the Military Justice System between April 14, 1972, and March 1985, those who were incarcerated in Libertad and Punta de Rieles prisons, and some persons held in other places. Gender was included strictly proportional to the distribution of the universe, and for place of residence, differentiations were made between Montevideo and the interior, but without proportional criteria. The sample was designed with a margin of error of plus or minus 5.5 percent in 95 percent of the sample. For the sample of people in the interior, five representative cities were chosen: Paysandú, Bella Unión, Rocha, San José, and Juan Lacaze....

The survey was carried out by fourteen interviewers under the supervision of two field workers in direct contact with one of the members of Equipos. The reaction of those interviewed was very good, the level of support and information generally presented without reticence, the relationship established with interviewers friendly. There were few refusals: twenty-one in Montevideo and three in Paysandú, or 7.1 percent, a figure considered normal and not producing bias in the results. Refusals were substituted from a list that took into account the principal characteristics of the sampling.

12

BRAZIL

EDITOR'S INTRODUCTION

When the Brazilian armed forces overthrew President João Goulart on April 1, 1964, they were reacting against both the threatened implementation of a leftist agenda by the president and decades of political instability under civilian and military-backed regimes. For the next twenty-one years, the Brazilian military ruled their country while pledging an eventual return to civilian rule. The military allowed local, state, and national legislatures to continue to operate during almost the entire period, but denied these bodies almost any autonomy. The junta granted itself the power to rule by decree and severely limited political participation, frequently changing laws regulating political party activity, to exclude all but the most moderate politicians.

The systematic use of torture by the security forces was widespread, although the number of dead and disappeared—approximately 300 from the time of the 1964 coup to the end of the 1970s—was much smaller in Brazil than in less-populated neighboring Argentina. Many Brazilians, however, numbering in the tens of thousands, were forced into exile, arrested for political reasons, or expelled from their jobs or schools. The most brutal years of military rule were 1968-1974. Although the regime concurrently achieved a period of sustained rapid economic growth known as the "Brazilian miracle," disparities in distribution of wealth also expanded throughout this period.

The limited political activity still open to mainstream politicians fostered cooperation between the civilian and military elites. Prodded in part by increasing economic difficulties, the military regime relied on these political alliances to manage a gradual political opening, or *abertura*, beginning in 1974. A slow renewal of various freedoms was accompanied by periodic regressions, including the return of the use of torture and the perpetration of violence against members of the opposition. Election results made possible by the gradual opening of the political process consistently demonstrated the military's lack of popularity .

Throughout this process of *abertura,* the regime sought to ensure continued heavy military influence in the Brazilian government and the avoidance of any accountability for human rights violations by security forces during their rule. In 1979, shortly after his presidential inauguration, General João Figuiredo put forward an amnesty bill which was adopted in August. The amnesty covered all those who were imprisoned or exiled since 1961, except those who had committed certain violent crimes, and restored to many politicians their rights of political participation. Importantly, the amnesty also covered all "connected crimes," understood to mean all human rights abuses committed by members of the security forces. The amnesty drew a number of exiles back to Brazil and significantly expanded the political process. The military was determined, however, that the new openness would not extend to an examination of its own past abuses. Thus, when one magazine published an account of military torture camps, the government moved to close it down; a second publication was seized when it printed a list of accused torturers.

In the early 1980s, Brazil entered a severe economic recession. With the 1982 legislative elections, opposition parties for the first time controlled a majority of the lower house of Congress. On January 15, 1985, Tancredo Neves was chosen by the electoral college as the first civilian president in over twenty years. Neves was reported to have negotiated a pact with the military leadership conceding that there would be no official inquiry into allegations of human rights abuses during military rule. On the eve of his inauguration, however, Neves fell gravely ill and, upon his death, vice president José Sarney was sworn in as president. The armed forces maintained a heavy influence in government.

In keeping with the character of this negotiated and managed transition, the new civilian government did not attempt to confront the legacy of abuses during the period of military rule. Instead, the most significant effort to do so was a project carried out under the aegis of the Catholic Church and released in 1985 as *Brasil: Nunca Mais* (Brazil: Never Again) and published in English as *Torture in Brazil: A Report by the Archdiocese of São Paolo.* Based on documents from the military's own courts, this report analyzed the nature of the regime and its violations of human rights. In its first ten weeks, more than 100,000 copies of the original Brazilian edition were sold in the country. The introduction to the report is included at the end of this chapter.

The following document related to transitional justice in Brazil can be found in Volume III of this collection:

- 1988 Constitution—Transitional Provisions

AN ANALYTICAL FRAMEWORK

Guillermo O'Donnell, "Challenges to Democratization in Brazil"*

The process of democratization which occured in many Latin American countries—Brazil, Argentina, Peru, Ecuador, and the Dominican Republic—actually consists of two transitions. The first is the removal of the previous authoritarian regime and the installation of a democratic government. The second, at least as challenging and lengthy as the first, is the consolidation of democracy: the foundation of a continuing and stable democratic regime. Unless such a regime becomes an accepted fact of a country's political, economic, social, and cultural life, the country is in danger of backsliding into authoritarianism, either through the "quick death" of a conventional military coup or through the "slow death" of a gradual erosion of democratic practice.

Among these nascent Latin American democracies, Brazil is in many ways an atypical case. The transition away from authoritarianism was unusually protracted and was, at least until the late stages, carefully managed by the military government. Moreover, that government had enjoyed relative economic success and, compared to other Latin American dictatorships, was only moderately repressive. Thus the new democratic government in Brazil has inherited less economic chaos and social strife, and has a less alienated military, than some of its neighbor countries.

According to most studies of democratic transitions, a country that, like Brazil (and Ecuador and Spain, to cite two other examples), experienced greater economic prosperity and less repression under authoritarianism is more likely to succeed in the transition from democratic government to democratic regime. But I have come to doubt this conventional wisdom: the apparent advantages of Brazil and countries with similar experiences may in fact turn out to be obstacles. Because the authoritarian regime in Brazil

---

* Excerpted from Guillermo O'Donnell, "Challenges to Democratization in Brazil," *World Policy Journal*, vol. V, no. 2 (Spring 1988), pp. 281-290, 292, 298-300.

had greater relative success, both economic and political, than those in other Latin countries, actors left over from that period have retained significant power and influence in the current Brazilian government. As a result of their continued presence, Brazil is particularly vulnerable to the "slow death" style of regression. The advances of the past few years could be undone: there might be a closing of the space available for the exercise of civilian authority and the observance of constitutional liberalism. In this case, Brazil would be left with a civilian government controlled by military and authoritarian elements—what I have elsewhere called a "*democradura*."[1]

Authoritarian Regimes and Transitions

To understand the different forces pressuring the nascent Latin democracies, we must understand the varieties of authoritarianism from which they emerged. Within the "family" of bureaucratic-authoritarian regimes, we can distinguish two basic types.[2] The more extreme type, economically destructive and highly repressive, has been found in Argentina, Uruguay, Bolivia at certain times, and continues today in Chile. These countries have been marked by acute recessions, deindustrialization, and loss of jobs. Although many in the business and middle class support the introduction of these regimes, they usually soon discover that the economic policies of the authoritarian regime cause serious harm to them as well. In terms of repression, these regimes border on out-and-out state terrorism. Many individuals suffer untold physical horrors, and few feel entirely safe: insecurity and fear grip much of the population, including many who had supported the regime's establishment.[3]

With some exceptions, such as Uruguay, the conflicts inherent in these regimes tend to erupt, causing the governments to collapse.[4] This process is abetted by the opposition, which is generally massive even if it has remained muzzled during periods of repression. In some cases, these regimes bring about their own downfalls by trying to alleviate their problems through some sort of military adventure—as Argentina did in the Falklands-Malvinas and the Greek colonels' regime did in Cyprus.

After these regimes collapse, there is a transition period during which the authoritarian rulers negotiate continuously with the opposition. The rulers, however, cannot control either the agenda or the outcome of the negotiations; for example, they generally fail to impose upon the future

---

1 "*Democradura*" is a composite of the Spanish words for democracy and dictatorship—*democracia* and *dictadura*. See Guillermo O'Donnell and Philippe Schmitter, and Laurence Whitehead, eds., *Transitions from Authoritarian Rule: Prospects for Democracy*, Vol. 4 (Baltimore: The Johns Hopkins University Press, 1986).

2 See Guillermo O'Donnell, *El Estado Burocrático-Autoritario: Argentina 1966-1973* (*The Bureaucratic-Authoritarian State: Argentina 1966-1973*) (Buenos Aires: Editora de Belgrano, 1982).

3 With regard to the 1978-82 period in Argentina, I have explored these questions in Guillermo O'Donnell, *Contrapontos Autoritarismo e Democratização* (São Paulo: Ediciões Vértice, 1986) and in "Democracia en la Argentina: Micro y Macro," forthcoming in *Lua Nova*.

4 O'Donnell and Schmitter (fn. 1).

civilian government an extensive institutionalized role for the armed forces. The democratic actors, on the other hand, gain power during this period. Foremost among their tasks is to identify who belongs to their own camp and who remains on the authoritarian side. Typically, this is done through a democratizing agreement or covenant (sometimes explicit, but usually implicit) that establishes the democratizing strategy and sets the terms of political competition—including an understanding as to which actors are to be excluded from participation.

In transitions from the other, less extreme type of authoritarian regime, events tend to proceed quite differently. In this case, the regime has had relative economic success and, though it employs repression, does so less systematically and extensively than in the cases outlined above. I should hasten to add that this is only a comparative judgment; I am not disregarding, in Brazil's case, the economic crisis of the authoritarian regime's last years, the extremely lopsided income distribution accompanying the country's impressive economic growth, or the harsh repression that prevailed, especially between 1969 and 1971. But that repression was less massive, continuous, and systematic than in the other cases, and it had much less impact on the bourgeoisie and middle sectors' sense of personal safety. Moreover, despite inequitable income distribution, the rapid economic growth achieved by this second group of countries contrasts sharply with the economic contraction and deindustrialization suffered by the first group. And, as was true in Brazil, the transition away from authoritarian rule in these less extreme cases tends to be more tightly controlled by the departing regime than in cases like Argentina.

Both these types of countries—the Argentinas and the Brazils, if you will—face a number of serious obstacles as they make the transition from democratic government to a more broadly based and deeply entrenched democratic regime. These obstacles include the continued presence, sometimes in influential positions, of obstinately authoritarian actors; the neutral or apathetic attitudes of many other political actors toward the democratic government; and the persistence, at many social and political levels, of distinctly authoritarian patterns of domination. Compounding these difficulties is the fact that democratically inclined people—those who know and practice the rules of political democracy—constitute only a minority of the population. If political democracy is to be consolidated, democratic practice needs to spread throughout society, creating a rich fabric of democratic institutions and authorities. Thus a paradox of this second transition is that a minority of democratic actors must advance the country toward the consolidation of a political regime based on the principle of majority rule.

When things are put in this light, there seems to be little cause for optimism. Nevertheless, the democratic actors have some things in their favor. First, the majority of the population is anti-authoritarian: though they may not know or understand the principles of political democracy, they do not want to return to the authoritarian or military regime they recently had to endure. Second, democratic discourses currently enjoy wide prestige and, conversely, openly authoritarian political messages carry little appeal. This is a new development for Latin America, and an extremely important one.

In order to consolidate these advantages, the democratic actors must work to build representative institutions—institutions that can effectively indicate between the various interests within society. Fair or "clean" and competitive elections should generate the major arenas for decisions on national issues. Moreover, special attention must be paid to the task of establishing a democratic majority. To start, the democratic actors must neutralize the unconditionally authoritarian actors, either by isolating them politically (particularly for the armed forces) by finding them institutional roles that hinder their ability to thwart the regime's survival. Among the "neutral" segment of the population, the challenge to democratic actors is to promote preferences (or at least practices) that are not inconsistent with the functioning of democracy. The democratic actors should use the anti-authoritarian majority as the support base for the democratic consolidation process, hoping in the medium term to swell the ranks of those truly committed to democracy.

Clearly, politicians—those whose personal vocation consists of seeking election to important governmental posts—are crucial to the process of democratic consolidation. Perhaps even more than the fate of the first transition, or the fate of an already consolidated democracy, the fate of the second transition depends on the caliber of the democratic political leadership—those who believe in and understand the significance of the institutionalized practice of political democracy. But these democratic actors face certain constraints. Though personal conviction and pragmatic concern for their own roles give them an interest in preserving and consolidating the democratic process, they are subject to the prevailing rules of the political game. In general, they must adapt to, or at least not depart excessively from, the style of politics that predominates among their peers. Accordingly, the larger political atmosphere in which they find themselves plays a critical role in determining the effectiveness of their work.

That larger political atmosphere depends in part on the authoritarian regime that preceded the democratic government. In the case of a transition from the more extreme type of regime, the new democracy faces the formidable problems arising from a devastated economy and the deep political and psychological wounds left by severe repression. On the positive side, the old regime's economic destructiveness does generally mean that the rulers and principals of the authoritarian government, including the armed forces, are widely held in disrepute. In consequence, the new democratic government is not heavily militarized. The armed forces occupy a diminished institutional role: they lose much of the civilian state apparatus they had conquered during the authoritarian period, and are not usually given the power to decide or veto policies except those referring specifically to themselves. The new democratic governments, then, have a relatively wide margin of freedom to act without direct pressure or vetoes by the military.

These governments do, however, find their maneuvering room restricted by the economic and social crisis left over from the preceding authoritarian regime. Moreover, there is a negative side to the new governments' greater freedom vis-à-vis the armed forces and the interests they represent: the armed forces, demoted and politically isolated, tend to be hostile to the government and alienated from civilian power. As a result, these democracies are subject to the threat of "quick death" through military coups.

The situation of the second type of democracies—those making the transition from less repressive, more economically successful authoritarian regimes—is quite different. Because those regimes experienced periods of strong economic growth, a good part of the bourgeoisie and the middle sectors may be viewed as the products, almost the offspring, of the authoritarian regime. Although many in those sectors go over to the opposition during the transition from authoritarianism,[5] they harbor a more positive memory of the authoritarian regime than they would if that regime had been highly repressive and economically destructive. Moreover, the authoritarian regime's economic successes tend to mitigate the unpopularity of the armed forces that backed it.

A further difference is that the transitions away from these less extreme authoritarian governments do not occur through collapse; rather, they are brought about through a series of agreements or covenants.[6] The rulers of these regimes retain a high degree of control over the transition's timetable and agenda, successfully imposing a large number of their views on the opposition. Furthermore, when the authoritarian regime is based mainly upon the military, the armed forces' considerable bargaining power often enables them to obtain firm guarantees that there will be no investigation of their past actions under authoritarianism and that they will be given a broad participatory role in the new civilian government.

Brazil is an extreme case in these respects.[7] The transition from authoritarianism took about 12 years and was, until its final phases, closely controlled by the regime. In fact, there is widespread speculation that Tancredo Neves, the relatively conservative opposition politician who was chosen as president during the indirect election conducted by the Electoral College, concluded a crucial agreement with the armed forces, assuring them that there would be no "revision of the past" and guaranteeing them an extensive role in the government he was about to form. It is known that another covenant was arrived at with some of the leading civilian figures of the authoritarian regime, who had by then

---

[5] On the limitations and ambivalences of this opposition, see Sebastião Velasco e Cruz, *Os Empresários e o Regime: A Campanha contra a Estatização*, doctoral thesis, University of São Paulo, 1984; and Fernando Henrique Cardoso, "The Entrepreneurs and the Transition Process: The Case of Brazil," in O'Donnell, Schmitter, and Whitehead, Vol.2 (fn. 1).

[6] See Donald Share and Scott Mainwaring, "Transitions through Transaction: Democratization in Brazil and Spain," in Wayne Selcher, ed., *Political Liberalization in Brazil: Dynamics, Dilemmas and Future Prospects* (Boulder, CO: Westview Press, 1986).

[7] Alfred Stepan, *Os Militares: da Abertura a Nova República* (Rio de Janeiro: Editoria Paz e Terra, 1986).

become dissidents. These covenants helped forestall the danger of a coup, but they also gave those "notables" of the authoritarian regime a disproportionate amount of bargaining power, and helped some of them gain important positions in the new government.

A great question remains unanswered: whether the Brazilian opposition could have called the bluff of the armed forces and of the notables of the authoritarian regime by pressing for direct elections rather than allowing the president to be selected by the Electoral College. But the fact is that the opposition leadership, including Neves, preferred to avoid the (certainly serious) risks of further encouraging the mass mobilizations that would have been necessary to force general, unconstrained elections. Thus the Brazilian transition was channeled through what was virtually an all-for-all agreement. The result has been a set of conditions that operate as severe constraints on the second transition now under way.

The Paradoxes of Success

Most analyses of transitions from authoritarian regimes assume that the second type of case described above—of which Brazil is a prime example—would more likely succeed in consolidating democracy than would the first. According to this view, the combination of a devastated economy, a society rent by repression and violence, and a military hostile to the new government is highly unfavorable to the consolidation—and mere survival—of the fledgling democracy. In the case of transitions from less extreme authoritarianism, however, the growth of productive forces that occurred during the previous regime offers better possibilities for governing the economy and alleviating at least the most urgent social problems. Consolidation of democracy also seems more feasible if past repression has been milder, directed at a limited range of targets; if the personnel of the authoritarian regime have conducted negotiations and reached understandings with the new democratic leaders; and if the armed forces are less alienated from the new government. In these cases, the new democracies seem to have a better chance of governing the economy and of avoiding violent breakdowns.

In Brazil's case, an additional advantage has been seen in the fact that the authoritarian regime did not eliminate the national, state, and municipal legislatures (though it significantly curtailed their roles) and that political parties, even if created by the regime itself, were allowed continued existence. In cases of more abrupt discontinuity, these institutions have to be practically "reinvented" by a political class lacking recent experience in democratic practice and institutions. Brazil, then, would seem to be at an advantage, since it already had in place an institutional framework through which to manage the many conflicts and uncertainties of the transition.

I would argue, however, that these assumptions need to be reconsidered. I am not, of course, going to make a 180-degree turn and argue that countries in the second group—which, like Brazil, are making a transition from a less extreme type of authoritarianism—face the greatest difficulties in consolidating and even keeping alive their nascent democracies. The aftermath of extreme repression and economic destruction in the first group of countries is too severe to allow for this simplistic conclusion. But I believe that the process of democratic consolidation in Brazil faces serious difficulties, and that these are in many ways the results of the relative economic success and only moderate repressiveness of the previous bureaucratic-authoritarian regime.[8]

To begin with, let us recall that the "quick death" by military coup to which countries in the first group are liable is not the only possible way in which a democratization process might be terminated. There is another possibility, whose outcome would not be much different: a "slow death," resulting from a gradual constriction of civilian authority till it is little more than a facade for highly repressive, military-based power. This deterioration would be driven by worsening economic and social crises, the accompanying sense of the civilian government's powerlessness, and a growing perception of threats to the basic interests of the bourgeoisie and middle sectors. In Brazil, where the armed forces and the conservative politicians previously tied to the authoritarian regime are deeply entrenched in the present government, such a situation would result in successive authoritarian repressions until the country had what would be tempting to call a civilian government with military sovereignty. That this scenario is a possibility in Brazil is suggested by a number of recent developments, such as the use of harshly repressive tactics to put down some "disorders" (that is, strikes) and the establishment of various informal mechanisms to censor the mass media.

The apparent advantages of the type of experience Brazil has undergone present difficulties in other areas as well. In situations as complex and precarious as these second transitions, often there are a number of hurdles, limitations, and economic and social crises that tend to diminish the popular support and enthusiasm for democracy. To counteract this disenchantment, and to encourage democratic practices and attitudes, the democratic actors can draw on the anti-authoritarianism that is present in a significant part of the population. This anti-authoritarianism tends to be stronger in transitions from highly destructive, repressive regimes: although many people may be disillusioned with the democratic government, it would take a longer period of social and economic crisis for them to yield to a generalized apathy about that government's survival. Consider, for example, Argentina's massive civilian reaction against the April 1987 military revolt.

But in cases like Brazil, there exist important sectors that are less staunchly negative toward the past authoritarian regime than in cases where the regime was highly destructive and repressive. Thus the ranks of the authoritarian actors may be more readily swelled by individuals who originally supported the introduction of the democratic government. People

---

[8] See Anita Isaacs, *Dancing with the People: The Politics of Military Rule in Ecuador, 1972-1979*, doctoral thesis, Oxford University, 1986. This work originally drew my attention to the paradoxes or trade-offs that may arise in such cases as Brazil.

in all countries going through this kind of transition tend to criticize the governments they currently live under; it is significant, though, that in Argentina and Uruguay these criticisms are not so often accompanied by nostalgic references to the authoritarian past as they are in Brazil.

This tendency may be particularly strong within the bourgeoisie and the middle sectors. As I have pointed out, these classes, though at times in conflict with the authoritarian regime, in many cases benefit from it enormously. Consequently, in such countries as Brazil, these classes' initial neutrality may more easily be turned into support for, or at least passive consent to, an authoritarian regression. Since they remember the past authoritarian regime as having positive as well as negative aspects, they are likely to imagine a future return to authoritarianism in similar terms and hence as potentially favorable to them. This type of thinking may be at the root of the ambivalent and unsteady support that democratic actors today receive in Brazil.

Another difficulty lies in the carry-over of the civilian "notables" from the authoritarian regime. In transitions from highly repressive, destructive regimes (or from regimes that have embarked their countries on catastrophic wars), this problem does not arise, as politicians that supported the authoritarian period are left out of the democratization process, either because they are legally prohibited, because they are deeply discredited, or because they lack electoral experience and constituencies. But in the Brazilian case, many government personnel and leading political figures have survived from the authoritarian regime and now have important roles in the present government.

By contrast, consider the experience of politicians under highly repressive regimes. Such regimes tend to exclude most politicians from the political game, and in fact subject many of them to exile, imprisonment, or death. Accordingly, after a transition toward democracies, these politicians will fear that any authoritarian regression would expose them to the same type of mistreatment. They will therefore feel that they have their backs against the wall—that they can continue performing their roles only if the democratic process continues. It is not, then, necessary that all these actors be true democrats; it is enough that they believe that the exercise of their role depends on continued democratization. This enlightened self-interest provides an important element of unity around the democratizing agreements or pacts.

In a case such as Brazil, on the other hand, politicians may have experienced some coercion under authoritarianism, but were in general treated fairly benevolently. If, despite subordination to the authoritarian executive, important institutions continued to function—the national, state, and municipal legislatures, as well as many clientelistic practices in the state apparatus—then a large part of the political class under authoritarianism was able to continue the political activities it had engaged in previously. In Brazil, this was indeed the situation; it led to a perpetuation of the style of politics that, with only brief and partial interludes, had always predominated in this country.

As a result of this continuity, presently there is in Brazil tremendous difficulty in defining who, within the political class, are the truly democratic actors. There are many politicians who do not seem to feel they have their backs against the wall: on the contrary, they may imagine that—as happened during the preceding period—an authoritarian regression would not destroy their role or fundamentally alter the way they conduct their political lives. For the moment, everyone may be talking about democracy, because of various mixtures of personal conviction and opportunism. But how does one distinguish the truly democratic actors from those whose preference for democracy is, at most, lukewarm? Who are the legitimate parties to a democratizing agreement of covenant, and who are the parties that agreement should exclude?

A high degree of institutional carry-over from the bureaucratic-authoritarian regime may prove to be a serious obstacle to the consolidation of democracy. In Brazil, this has to do specifically with the persistence, as mentioned above, of the same predominate old style of politics. Essentially, this is a style based on patronage and clientelism, typical of an oligarchic republic in a primarily agrarian society, in which capitalist relations are relatively undeveloped and the lower classes are unorganized and unmobilized....

In the three years since Brazil made its first transition away from authoritarianism, the style of politics I have outlined—related to what Max Weber termed "patrimonialism"[11]—has continued to dominate Brazilian politics. Patrimonialist politicians have often formed powerful alliances with politicians who are unabashedly (if, today, not too explicitly) authoritarian, whereas democratic politicians, who might have been expected to take more definitive stands, have generally not been outspoken in their criticisms of Brazil's traditional political style. This reticence is understandable: because these democratic politicians do not yet form a critical mass, or because there has not arisen from their ranks a leader capable of creating that mass or compensating for its absence, they must play by the established rules in order to remain in the game. If their goal is to gain elective office so as to modify the system from within, they must calculate that challenging or threatening the established political style would make it hard for them to get elected, or even nominated by their parties. Unfortunately, however, the perpetuation of politics as usual, and the tendency of Brazilian officials to wield authority in a patrimonialist rather than a republican manner, not only tarnishes the image of given political parties and leaders, but also seriously harms the authority of democratic political institutions in general. Such a trend poses severe dangers to the democratization process....

---

[11] Max Weber, *Economy and Society*, ed. Guenther Roth and Claus Wittich (Berkeley, CA: University of California Press, 1979). See also Simon Schwartzman, *Bases do Autoritarismo Brasileiro*, second edition (Rio de Janeiro: Editora Campus, 1982). Expanding upon Weber's analysis, Schwartzman develops an interesting general interpretation of Brazil in terms of the category of neopatrimonialism. Though I disagree with various aspects of that interpretation, I believe that many of the topics he addresses are fundamental to understanding current problems in a way that more fashionable approaches do not.

It would be tempting to speculate, as some analysts do, that the high degree of social and political continuity in Brazil might in fact produce a stability that would help democracy's chances rather than hurting them. Even though the military has made some disturbing statements, there is no acute and immediate fear of a coup. Yet this does not mean that a democratic regime has been established, or is even in the making. The armed forces retain a strong, direct presence in the state apparatus and in the government; their role has not been institutionalized in such a way as to distance them from or subordinate them to the civilian government. In any event, the present configuration of political actors will, if maintained, at best perpetuate a highly elitist political democracy, preserving the patrilmonialist style that distorts Brazil's complex economy and society, fostering a biased pattern of growth and distribution, and, in more or less disguised ways, proving repressive for a large part of the population. This raises the question of whether Brazil would increase its liability to a sudden, violent authoritarian regression if it attempted more than very slow and gradual advances from the present situation. For my part, I believe that Brazil's present path may in fact pose the greater danger. If the country fails to democratize and modernize its social and political relations to a reasonable extent, democracy is likely to die a slow death.

One fundamental problem—an offshoot of the way Brazil's transition from authoritarianism was managed—is that the political actors capable of carrying out democratization have not been sufficiently differentiated. The political actors who can and should be parties to the democratizing agreement and those whose political defeat is a necessary condition for the consolidation of democracy are confusingly mixed in the same parties and governments, from local governments all the way up to the national executive. This is not a problem in other Latin American countries, where, because of ideological conviction or because the transition from authoritarianism was more traumatic and polarizing than Brazil's, the task of identifying who should and who should not be party to the democratizing covenant was fairly clear. These countries develop coalitions of "some against others": the political and ideological victory of democratization gives the democratic political actors the authority and ability to politically isolate authoritarian or nondemocratic political actors.

But in Brazil's transition, what has emerged is a coalition of "everyone with everyone" (or, rather, "everyone with almost everyone," since the alliance has recurrently excluded the Workers' Party and the Democratic Labor Party). From the ensuing political confusion there have emerged, at all levels of government, complex combinations of democratic-republican actors with actors who are patrimonialist or authoritarian (though not, for the moment, openly so). What matters is not so much ideological orientation, party affiliation, or personal history, but adherence to democratic-republican institutions and practices and, in Brazil's case, a commitment to modernizing and democratizing social relations. The failure of significant numbers of Brazilian political actors to make this commitment, and the confusion of political alignments that makes it difficult to defeat those nondemocratic actors in elections—these factors pose what I see as the greatest challenge for the future of democracy in Brazil.

BRASIL: NUNCA MAIS—THE CLANDESTINE REPORT ON HUMAN RIGHTS VIOLATIONS

Lawrence Weschler, "A Miracle, A Universe: Settling Accounts with Torturers"[*]

In March, 1979, the wary, gradual, fitful process of military liberalization, which had been underway for several years during the Presidency of General Ernesto Geisel, entered a new phase with the inauguration of Geisel's chosen successor, General Joáo Baptista Figueiredo. (It was at this point that the *distensão* began turning into the *abertura*). The institutionalized practice of torture against opponents of the military had been on the wane for some time, but military officials were concerned about an eventual investigation into and retribution for their earlier human-rights abuses. In fact, the prospects for any further liberalization were momentarily frozen, pending the resolution of these concerns. Against this backdrop, President Figueiredo, as one of his first initiatives, promulgated a plan for a so-called mutual amnesty. For several years, there had been a rising cry on the part of civil society, led by Cardinal Arns and his associates, among others, for a complete amnesty of those accused of political crimes—both exiles and prisoners. Figueiredo now acceded, in part, to these demands (there were several conspicuous loopholes in his initiative), but he coupled this gesture with another, offered in a sudden spirit of ostentatious magnanimity: a blanket amnesty for any state security agents who might otherwise someday become liable to charges arising from their human rights violations. Indeed, his edict was drafted in such a way as to foreclose even the possibility of any future official investigations into the behavior of the security forces between 1964 and 1979. Bygones were to be bygones: the book was closed. The *abertura* could proceed.

For the regime's thousands of victims and their families and friends, however, closing the book wasn't going to be so easy. Furthermore, for Jaime Wright, Cardinal Arns, and several of their colleagues, allowing the book to remain closed would prevent any future understanding of what had happened in Brazil between 1964 and 1979 and what its happening had meant—an understanding without which, they feared, the country would forever be liable to a harrowing reversion. It was during this period that Wright and a very small group of his colleagues hit upon a daring plan.

"To understand what we set out to do in 1979, you have to understand something about the unusual nature of the military dictatorship in Brazil,"

---

[*] Excerpted from *A Miracle, a Universe: Settling Accounts with Torturers* by Lawrence Weschler. Copyright © 1990 by Lawrence Weschler. Reprined by permission of Pantheon Books, a division of Random House, Inc. and Sterling Lord Literistic, Inc., pp. 14-18, 73-75.

Wright told me. "The Brazilian generals, you see, were technocrats. They were intent on doing things by the book, on following the forms, even if the results were often cruel and perverse. For example, they were obsessed with keeping complete records as they went along. They never expected anyone to delve into those records—certainly not in any systematic fashion. They never imagined they'd be held accountable to anyone. But the forms, the technicalities, required complete and well-ordered records, so they kept them. Now, in the early stages of an internee's *processo*—that's the Portuguese word for a military court proceeding—the authorities often had recourse to torture. This was partly because they were eager to extract as much information as quickly as possible so they would be able to make further arrests before the prisoner's friends and comrades could learn of his arrest and cover their tracks. But it was also an almost traditional reflex, going back to the days of slavery and the Inquisition. A confession was extracted through torture, and its truthfulness was conclusively affirmed when the victim signed the written version of his statement. About a third of the *processos* eventually came to semi-public trial before one of twelve five-judge military tribunals operating throughout the country. (The other two-thirds never made it that far). At that point, the prisoner or his lawyers sometimes denounced the supposed confession as having been obtained under duress. It's amazing, when you think about the risks involved—after all, these prisoners could expect to be given back over to their jailers following the trial—that anybody ever chose to make such a denunciation. But, from what they've been able to ascertain, about 25 percent of the prisoners did. Anyway, in such cases the judges would dutifully listen as the defendants described their tortures; the judges would then summarize these accounts and order the court reporters to enter the summaries into the record. And then the tribunals would hand down their decisions. Once in a while—admittedly, very rarely—they'd actually find the defendant innocent. But it didn't really matter, because either way the losing side would appeal the case to the Supreme Military Court in Brasília, which would almost invariably find the defendant guilty after all. In the process, though—and this became very important for us—all the transcripts and files of all the cases were transferred from the various provincial tribunals back to Brasília, where they were carefully catalogued and stockpiled in the archives of the Supreme Military Court.

"It therefore occurred to us, back in 1979, that the regime's own records would include detailed sworn testimony regarding the use of torture throughout the period of military rule—if we could only get at them."

The 1979 amnesty law ironically provided Wright and his colleagues with a pretext, because lawyers were now being permitted access to the archives, though only on a piecemeal basis, as they prepared amnesty petitions on behalf of their still imprisoned or exiled clients. Lawyers were allowed to take out individual files for twenty-four-hour periods, after which they had to return them. Wright and his colleagues quickly realized that under this pretext they might be able to photocopy a sampling—perhaps even a significant sampling—of the Supreme Military

Court's own records, thereby laying the groundwork for an unimpeachable study on the subject of torture in Brazil....

By the beginning of 1980, the secret collaborators had hired their first staff members and rented a little suite in a nondescript office building in Brasília. "No sign on the door," Wright recalled, "and, inside, just three leased photocopy machines. We had twelve lawyers working with us who on a seemingly random basis began systematically checking out files from the archive. Our staff put in ten-hour days, seven days a week, copying page after page. The lawyers would then return the originals, as required, thus allaying any suspicion. There were 707 cases in all in that section of the archives, involving over 7,000 defendants. You could check out a whole case at a time, and I remember one time a lawyer arrived with a case consisting of more then two dozen volumes, weighing over eighty kilos. We'd initially hoped to be able to photocopy a scientific sampling of the cases in the archive—we certainly didn't expect to be able to continue on such a basis without being discovered for long. We were transporting the photocopies out of Brasília almost immediately, storing them in São Paulo and already starting to process them there. We just resolved to keep photocopying until we were somehow forced to stop. Eventually, we'd copied half of the archive—way more than we ever expected—and then, one day, after three years of photocopying, we realized, to our astonishment, that we'd managed to copy *every single file* in their entire holdings—over a million pages! We had duplicated the entire universe of documents in the archive....

"The book had less of an impact than one might have expected," Elio Gaspari commented when I interviewed him at his *Veja* offices.

I asked him whether he thought that *Brasil: Nunca Mais* was a book more bought than read.

"No," he said. "It is a book both bought and read—avidly read. No, that's not my point. Rather, it's a question of who has been reading it. People in this country over age forty bought few copies. Either they already knew all about the torture and didn't want or need to hear more, or they didn't know and didn't want to know. Furthermore—and this is fundamental—the book came out after the compromise of the elites had been sealed. The transition from military rule in 1985 was consummated only because the civilian elites in this country—personified by the politicians—had in effect already signalled to the generals that they would not delve into the past and would honor the amnesty. There was to be, in effect, a giant coverup—for the sake of the future, they all assured themselves. The appearance of the book was a definite snag in that coverup, but it didn't fundamentally alter the spirit of the politics which had initially sustained it. I think, however, that the compromise was possible for many reasons besides its obvious expediency. For one thing, here in Brazil, although there had been much torture, there hadn't been nearly as many disappearances or outright murders as there were in Argentina, for example. For another, what torture there had been was, for the most part, over a decade past—unlike the situation in Uruguay, for instance, where the military were torturing people right up to their abdication, in 1985.

The per-capita extent of torture, for that matter, was much, much lower in Brazil than it was in Uruguay. And, perhaps most important, here in Brazil, as opposed to both Uruguay and Argentina, the military itself had played a substantial role in gradually reining in the tortures over the years since 1975—admittedly, more out of concern over the breakdown in internal discipline than out of concern for the human rights of the regime's opponents. Beyond that, large sectors of the civilian elite had at least tacitly supported the military during much of its tenure, and these people were only too happy to move on beyond such a past. At any rate, the compromise was achieved, and it now held, despite the book's publication."

"Where the book truly had an impact," Alfred Stepan told me was with the young, the generation that came of age in the early seventies, for whom a whole swath of history had been suppressed as part of the repression. It seems that those were the people who bought the book in such huge numbers and made it such a cultural presence. Brazil, for all its inequalities, is in many ways a consensual society—there's a great tendency to let things pass. *Brasil: Nunca Mais* worked against that tendency, so that even if its immediate political impact was relatively limited, it had a deep impact on how people, and especially the young, came to think about the recent past."

Cardinal Arns has commented that frequently on his pastoral tours through the country strangers come up to him, beaming with pride, and report, "I'm in your book—that's me on page such-and-such." They seem in some small but important way mended by the mention.

Around the time I was in São Paulo, in late 1986, one of the main characters on the country's most popular prime-time television soap opera, "Rodo de Fogo" (Wheel of Fire), began carrying a copy of *Brasil: Nunca Mais* tucked prominently under her arm. Everyone I spoke with was eagerly anticipating the episode that was going to air shortly before Christmas, when—or so the tabloids were all proclaiming—this character was actually going to confront her former torturer.

Throughout the county, the compromise of the elites notwithstanding, grassroots organization calling themselves *Tortura Nunca Mais* began to form, addressing themselves not only to the bedeviling legacy of past political torture but also to the scandalous problem of continuing torture and mistreatment of common criminals. I was told that most precinct houses in Brazil still have electric-shock machines and that many have parrot's perches that can be set up or struck down virtually at a moment's notice. The wildly disproportionate distribution of wealth in Brazilian society, a perennial reality aggravated by twenty years of military repression, has recently led to a sharp increase in petty crime, such as theft and pickpocketing, which, in turn, has led an anxious upper middle class to range itself increasingly behind the arbitrary and often brutal authority of the police forces. The year 1985 saw more than 550 killings by police in metropolitan São Paulo alone—an astonishing rate of well over one per day. Some victims died as they were being arrested, others from beatings routinely administered in the vans on the way to the precinct houses, others from torture administered there. In almost every instance, death was publicly attributed to the prisoner's resistance or effort at escape—just as the occasional deaths of political prisoners under military rule had been. In recent months, perhaps partly as a result of the sensation caused by *Brasil: Nunca Mais*, the Brazilian press has shown growing interest in such stories, although the middle class remains much less perturbed by arbitrary violence directed against poor people than by political violence directed against middle class students and professionals. Cardinal Arns, for his part, has been one of the leaders trying to prick the public conscience in regard to the poor.[9]

Nor was *Brasil: Nunca Mais* wholly without tangible political impact. Partly as a result of the ground swell of public awareness and revulsion which its revelations engendered, President Sarney felt compelled, on September 23, 1985, to sign the United Nations Convention Against Torture.

EXCERPTS FROM THE REPORT

Joan Dassin, Editor, "Torture in Brazil: A Report by the Archdiocese of São Paulo"[*]

Introduction to the Brazilian Edition

Brazil is today experiencing a new page of hope in its history. With the election of the civilian Tancredo Neves to the presidency in January 1985 and the installation of his successor, José Sarney, following Neves' death just months later, twenty-one years of military rule have been overcome. The nation is dreaming of plans for reconstruction. Laws are beginning to be rethought. Those now in power have promised important policy changes to vast crowds gathered in public squares.

These same people, in earlier times, journeyed from hope to hope through similar new political beginnings that did not last very long. Years of greater tolerance of dissenting opinions and greater concern for social problems gave way, even before 1964 (the year of Brazil's most recent

---

[9] For more on the current treatment of nonpolitical prisoners in Brazilian jails, see two recent reports from Americas Watch: *Police Abuse in Brazil: Summary Executions in São Paulo and Rio de Janeiro* (December, 1987), and *Prison Conditions in Brazil* (April, 1989). The latter report details one particularly gruesome incident that occurred on Carnival night, February 5, 1989, when, allegedly retaliating for an attempted rebellion, police in the 42nd Police District in São Paulo forced fifty-one naked prisoners into an unventilated isolation cell measuring five by ten feet. By the time the cell's heavy iron doors were reopened an hour later, eighteen of the men had suffocated to death. The international furor over this incident eventually resulted in the closing of the São Paulo DEIC facility, one of the notorious prisons and formerly one of the military's most dreaded torture centers.

[*] Excerpted from Joan Dassin, ed., *Torture in Brazil: A Report by the Archdiocese of São Paulo*, translated by Jaime Wright (Archdiocese of São Paulo, 1986), pp. 3-9.

military coup), to fresh periods of intransigence, persecution, and even contempt for the demands of the marginalized.

This cannot now be repeated. The hope that is being born again today cannot be another transitory one. Decisions must be made and courageous measures taken to encourage the consolidation of democratic society. We must labor, tirelessly and constantly, to remove the vestiges of authoritarianism and to build a state based on the rule of law. That state must not only be firm in its foundations but also receptive to criticism. People must be allowed to participate, dissent, and challenge, and the cry of the poor, the cry of all the people, must be heard. Toward this end, we must learn the lessons that our recent past, our own history provides.

This book is the report on an investigation in the field of human rights. It is an unprecedented examination of the political repression that was directed against thousands of Brazilians considered by the military to be adversaries of the military regime that took power in April 1964. It is also an analysis of the resistance to that regime.

In March 1979, General Joáo Baptista de Figueiredo was inaugurated as Brazil's president. He promised to broaden the political freedoms initiated during the previous administration of General Ernesto Geiset and to introduce democracy. A few months later, the research project "*Brasil: Nunca Mais*" ("Brazil: Never Again") began. Discretion and secrecy were essential to the success of the project. A small number of specialists dedicated themselves, for a period of more than five years, to produce the comprehensive study summarized in this book.

The "Brazil: Never Again" Project

Everywhere in the world, the issue of political repression is almost always brought to public notice by the denunciations of victims or by reports written by organizations dedicated to the defense of human rights. Whether emotional or well balanced, these testimonies help reveal a hidden history. But at times they are accused of tendentiousness because they come from victims who are often politically motivated.

The "Brazil: Never Again" (BNM) research project was able to resolve this problem by studying the repression carried out by the military regime through the very documents produced by the authorities performing the controversial task. This was done by bringing together the official legal proceedings of practically all political cases tried in Brazilian military courts between April 1964 and March 1979, especially those that reached the Supreme Military Court.

By fixing 15 March 1979, the date of Figueiredo's inauguration, as the end of the period to be investigated, those responsible for the research project assured that the work could proceed with a degree of historical detachment from the political repression being studied.

In numerous ways, copies of the complete proceedings of 707 political trials and dozens of incomplete proceedings were obtained, amounting in total to more than one million pages. These pages were immediately microfilmed in duplicate so that one copy could be kept in safety outside

Brazil. The BNM team studied these records for more than five years, producing a report (Project A) of approximately 7,000 pages. Copies of a limited edition of Project A will be distributed to universities, libraries, documentation centers, and organizations dedicated to the defense of human rights in Brazil and abroad. Project A is a full account of what this book contains in summary form.

There were numerous difficulties as well as substantial risks for those involved in the BNM project. On the one hand, the traumatic period from 1964-79—marked by routine torture, deaths, and disappearances—was still very much alive in people's minds, causing fear and making precautions necessary. There was never certainty that the project could be finished or that it would ever be possible to publish it.

On 30 April 1981, for instance, when the BNM project was well under way, a failed bomb attack on a Rio de Janeiro theater indicated that the repressive organizations studied in the project were still active. In the incident, two military police officers were injured, one of them fatally, when the bomb they were transporting exploded. It was widely assumed that the police bomb was intended for the thousands of young people attending a May Day celebration. In view of the fact that the repressive forces were still capable of attempting such crimes, those involved in the BNM project went through some alarming moments.

There was also the pressure of time. The investigation was necessarily slow, given the difficulty in bringing together the documentary sources and the necessity that each page of hundreds of military court proceedings be studied carefully. Nevertheless, there was a real urgency to complete the task before a change in the political situation could put an end to the study or before a "convenient" fire in government offices could destroy valuable documents. In 1945, at the end of Getúlio Vargas' authoritarian New State (*Estado Novo*), such a fire in Rio de Janeiro destroyed the documents of the political police headed by Felinto Müller.

That is why the BNM project was always racing against the clock. The publication of its results is therefore an encouraging victory over all those risks and difficulties.

Some further explanation is in order regarding our sources.

Why were official military court proceedings chosen as the basic documentary source? In his book *Surveiller et punir* (Surveillance and Punishment), the French thinker Michel Foucault demonstrates that it is possible to reconstruct a good portion of the history of a certain period through the penal proceedings kept in the archives of the judiciary of any given country. The real nature of the state is recorded there in the form of court sentences involving torture or the quartering of bodies in public and in rules for the surveillance of prisoners and for corporal and psychological punishment. We thought that if in Brazil we could reconstruct the history of torture, murders of political prisoners, police persecutions, and biased trials—using the government's own official documentation—then we would have irrefutable evidence that these practices were officially authorized.

It could be argued that, by dispensing with statements by the victims themselves and working instead with documents produced by the authorities of the military government, the BNM project would be doomed to confirming only a small proportion of the human rights violations committed during that period. The documentary sources could be compared to objects from which the agents of repression had removed the "fingerprints" of crimes committed during the investigation. There was, on the other hand, a compensation: whatever official documentation could be produced regarding judicial irregularities, illegal acts, unjust measures, and reports of torture and deaths would constitute incontrovertible conclusive evidence. In other words, confirmation that the facts of torture were presented before a military court, confirmed by witnesses, and even recorded officially by medical examiners, without resulting in any steps to eliminate such practices or to make their perpetrators criminally responsible, is as much of a direct challenge to government authorities as is the denunciation that a victim of torture makes before a human rights organization.

The challenge was thus accepted to work with the basic information contained only in military court proceedings. Only occasionally did the BNM project use complementary sources. These are cited in the endnotes.

[Overview]

It is no simple task to produce an easily readable summary of thousands of pages containing the conclusions of an extended research project. It would be like trying to make a 28-minute TV program out of a 10-hour epic series.

Project A, the complete report on which this book is based, begins by describing the development of political institutions in Brazil between 1964 and 1979, starting with the origins of the military regime and ending with the building up of the repressive apparatus on the foundation of the Doctrine of National Security, the principal ideology of the regime.

Next, the methodology of the research project is explained, with military court proceedings classified according to the type of defendant charged (e.g., belonging to a particular leftist organization, social sector, etc.). An explanation regarding the collection of data, is also provided. In brief, it notes that two questionnaires were used to compile the information, which was then stored and processed on computers. Special computer programs were written for the project. The programs and the data generated, as well as microfilms of the actual documents, are stored safely outside of Brazil. In addition, a separate collection of 10,000 political documents appended to the military court proceedings also forms part of the project documentation. This entire archive will be of great value for future research into the Brazilian labor movement, the student struggle, and the history of clandestine leftist organizations, among other topics.

The third part of Project A is a detailed discussion of the results of research in the juridical field, through a comparison of what the laws—including those promulgated by the military regime—were intended to do and the actual practices of judicial inquests and proceedings. The dubious legitimacy of various national security laws and other legal codes decreed by the military regime is also discussed, followed by a study of the way these laws were routinely ignored in all cases where there was irregular treatment of persons being investigated.

In the fourth section there is a harrowing sequence of transcriptions of testimonies describing tortures, totaling approximately 2,700 typed pages. These denunciations, made in military courts, contain the names of torturers, torture centers, murdered political prisoners, the "disappeared," and countless other infamies. A list of all torturers named in military proceedings is provided, together with lists of all authorities connected with police and judicial acts of repression, as well as of all persons named as defendants or indicted.

The last section sets out the main conclusions that can be drawn from the study.

How was it possible to compress this vast amount of information into this book? A form had to be devised that could communicate the essence of those results without repeating the ungainly structure of a report or distressing readers with endless descriptions of the agonies of torture. Of course, it was not possible to extract a light or reassuring report from Project A. Only a strong and challenging book could emerge from a story of horrors.

In the following chapters, we have alternated the shocking denunciations with analytical passages that show the origins of the repressive apparatus, its structure, the uses of torture in the course of interrogation, and the collaboration of the judicial authorities in these abuses. In this fashion we have attempted to avoid the tedium of endless descriptions as well as the error of talking about those tortures and crimes as if they were unrelated to the political system installed in Brazil in 1964....

The objective of the research project "Brazil: Never Again," from its inception in August 1979 to its conclusion in March 1985, was to turn the wish expressed in its title into a reality, that is, to ensure that the violence, the infamy, the injustice, and the persecution of Brazil's recent past should never again be repeated.

It is not the intention of the BNM project to prepare evidence to be presented at a Brazilian Nuremberg trial. The project was not motivated by revenge. In their quest for justice, the Brazilian people have never been moved by such sentiments. What is intended is a work that will have an impact by revealing to the conscience of the nation, through the light shed by these denunciations, the dark reality of the political repression that grew unchecked after 1964. We thus observe the Gospel precept that counsels us to know the truth as a precondition for liberation ("You will know the truth, and the truth will make you free," John 8:32).

It is a happy coincidence that the results of this research project should be published at a time of national hope, when authoritarianism is being overcome, when new laws for the country are being promulgated, and when there is a new possibility of convening a constituent assembly to strengthen democratic institutions.

It is our hope that all who participate in that national debate will take note of the contents of this book, so that measures may be taken in order that these years of persecution and hatred may never again be repeated.

It is our hope that all who read this book will make a sacred vow to commit themselves to struggle ceaselessly to sweep from the face of the earth the practice of torture and eliminate from humanity the source of torture, of whatever type, for whatever offense, for whatever reason.

It is in this spirit that the project "Brazil: Never Again" was undertaken.

13

CHILE

EDITOR'S INTRODUCTION

In 1973, Chile was in turmoil. Under the government of leftist president Salvador Allende, political polarization and popular violence were on the rise and inflation reached 500 percent. On September 11, General Augusto Pinochet Ugarte, head of the army, led a coup d'état in which Allende and many of his supporters died. The coup and its aftermath were especially violent, with security forces responsible for the death or disappearance of 1,200 people by the end of the year. The Congress was dissolved, all political activity banned, and censorship was imposed.

Espousing a virulent anti-Communism and a goal of economic reform, the Pinochet regime brutally repressed any suspected opposition or subversion. The intelligence service DINA and its successor, the CNI, led this effort, as thousands were subjected to searches, harassment, torture, killings, disappearances, and exile. The judiciary remained in place, but the court system—and particularly the Supreme Court—did not seriously examine claims of human rights abuses. By 1978, an amnesty law barred prosecution of those who committed these abuses from the time of the coup through early that year—the period of the worst violations.

Protests against Pinochet's rule and policies grew in the 1980s. In response, Pinochet declared a state of seige in August 1983. 18,000 troops took to the streets and promptly arrested 1,200 people. In 1986, a demonstration and subsequent assassination attempt on Pinochet brought a new declaration of a state of seige and the arrest of 15,000 people. The ongoing and large-scale abuse of human rights drew international condemnation and isolation of Chile.

The trend towards the restoration of democratic government which swept through Latin America in the 1980s increased pressure for a limited political opening in Chile. In January 1987, prompted in part by the forthcoming visit to Chile of Pope John Paul II, the state of seige was lifted. Two months later, non-Marxist political parties were permitted to register. Notwithstanding these positive developments, the security forces maintained a significant degree of political repression.

In 1988, confident that Chilean society would not oppose him, Pinochet consented to a plebiscite allowing the population to vote for or against his continued rule. A peaceful political campaign resulted in a "No" victory, paving the way for general elections in 1989. Christian Democrat Patricio Aylwin won the presidency and assumed office in March 1990.

Using the phrase coined by Francisco Franco in Spain, General Pinochet had vowed to leave office with Chile "tied and tied well." In designing an approach to deal with the abuses of the past, President Aylwin was constrained by the facts that the 1980 constitution preserved military influence and autonomy, General Pinochet was to remain Commander-in-Chief of the Army through 1997, most of the judiciary was named by Pinochet, and the Senate was weighted with military supporters, including nine senators hand-picked by the former dictator.

Following the example of the new democracy in neighboring Argentina, Aylwin appointed a National Commission on Truth and Reconciliation. The politically diverse commission, which included a former member of Pinochet's cabinet, was given nine months to investigate and report on the human rights violations of the previous period and to make recommendations for reparations and prevention of future abuses. Its final report, presented in February 1991, was over two thousand pages long. In accepting the commission's report, Aylwin issued a nationally televised apology to the nation on behalf of the government. An extensive reparations program was created, as recommended by the commission.

Conflicts over the legacy of the Pinochet regime continue to confront Chilean society. As the commission and the Congress examined human rights abuses and corruption under the military regime, General Pinochet bluntly warned the new government not to "touch a single hair of a single soldier" nor ignore the 1978 amnesty law lest he repeat the events of September 1973. The Aylwin government suggested that the disappearance of political prisoners was an ongoing crime until their death could be verified—putting the investigation and prosecution of this crime beyond the scope of the amnesty. In December 1990 and again in May 1993, Pinochet put the army on alert, with troops in battle-readiness mode, to signal the seriousness of this threat. In response to the second alert, in August 1993, Aylwin proposed legislation to (1) guarantee anonymity to military defendants and witnesses in pending court cases involving past abuses and (2) make permanent the 1978 amnesty. Strong opposition from human rights groups and relatives of the victims threatened to split his governing coalition, obliging Aylwin to withdraw the proposal the following month.

As of early 1994, more than twenty people had been convicted for human rights abuses committed after 1978; these cases are under appeal.

The following documents related to transitional justice in Chile can be found in Volume III of this collection:

- Decree Establishing the National Commission on Truth and Reconciliation
- Report of the National Commission on Truth and Reconciliation
- Statement of President Aylwin on the Report of the National Commission on Truth and Reconciliation
- Law Creating the National Corporation for Reparation and Reconciliation

THE POLITICAL SETTING FOR THE TRANSITION

*Jorge Correa S., "Dealing with Past Human Rights Violations: The Chilean Case After Dictatorship"**

[A. Overview]

There can be no doubt ... that political conditions limit a government that succeeds a dictatorship as to the kind of policies it can follow when dealing with past human rights violations. The goals, from a normative standpoint may be exactly the same, yet, the actual possibilities of achieving them and the best strategies to do so may be very different. A new government that had a military victory over those who had participated in gross human rights violations (like Nicaragua) is very different from an elected government that had to collaborate for a long time with the very same guerrillas that were responsible for past human rights violations in order to continue to fight a common enemy (like El Salvador). In the Nicaraguan example, there are no political restrictions, and the only dangers that the new authorities face are probably the excesses that one can commit when trying the cases in the courts. In the El Salvador example, however, attempting to keep the army and the police within the

* Excerpted from Jorge Correa S., "Dealing with Past Human Rights Violations: The Chilean Case After Dictatorship," Volume 67, Issue 5 *The Notre Dame Law Review* (1992) 1457-1464. Reprinted with permission. © by *Notre Dame Law Review*, University of Notre Dame. The publisher bears responsibility for any errors which have occurred in reprinting or editing.

boundaries of civilian rule and forcing them to respect human rights are the only things that can be done.

Between these two extremes are cases like Greece and Argentina where the armed forces left power after a moral collapse, both because of internal political discontent and because they had lost an external war. Uruguay illustrates a negotiated transition after the armed forces suffered a political defeat; and, of course, less could be achieved in the Uruguayan case than in the Argentinean one.[5] Time is also a very important factor. It is of course a very different situation when the democratic authorities gain power shortly after the massive violations of human rights have been committed, than the case, like Spain, where there is a totally new generation in the most influential positions.

In the Chilean situation, the political constraints were great, and the newly elected government thought that it did not have enough power to bring about punishment. Therefore, acknowledgement became its policy. It thought that a full disclosure of an official truth would help to achieve the three moral objectives that the government perceived as its basic and unavoidable obligations: (1) to do as much as it could to build a solid and preventive barrier against future human rights violations; (2) to compensate, as much as possible, the survivors that had been most severely damaged; and (3) to bring about reconciliation....

B. A Plebiscite Where the Ruling Junta Loses (Though Not Everything)

In the case of the Chilean transition, it was not so much the threat of another coup that made it difficult for the new government to impose sanctions, but rather the way it achieved power and the expectations it created. The opposition to the military regime had been active and mobilized in the early 1980's, but it could not overthrow the authoritarian government. Neither the peaceful strategy of civil disobedience nor the most violent acts, ranging from street riots to attempts to kill General Pinochet, were successful enough to overthrow the regime.[6] Nevertheless, in order to stay in power, the authoritarian regime had to allow some civil liberties, and that liberalization made the final difference. After the democratic political parties failed to remove Pinochet by other means, they viewed the 1988 plebiscite as the only opportunity to beat the military rulers. Yet, the price they had to pay was high, and the democratic coalition could not eat the sweet without tasting the bitter.

In order to compete in that plebiscite, the democratic political parties had to accept the Constitution of 1980, and they had to promise that they would only change it according to its own rules.[7] This Constitution

---

5 *Supra* notes 3-4.

6 REPORT, *supra* note 1, at 665-709. For a good source of information about the political atmosphere of those years, see ASCANIO CAVALLO, HISTORIA OCULTA DEL REGIMEN MILITAR (Antarctica ed., 1989).

7 The decision to accept the constitutional order as a given was highly contested among the democratic political parties for a long [time]. The discussion took place first in the Christian Democratic party, where Aylwin's group made this an important point. This decision was even

established the calling of the plebiscite and regulated what should happen after the plebiscite. In order to win the plebiscite, the democratic forces had to be prudent. A large part of the population feared that the return of democracy could bring disorder and chaos, threatening the peace and economic progress that the country was experiencing. Because their vote could be decisive, the democratic parties had to promise full respect for the Pinochet institutional framework and that they would only change that framework through its own mechanisms.

The democratic political forces had to inaugurate a new political rhetoric that was not as confrontational. As a result, the human rights issue was strongly presented as a demand to encourage pacification and depolarization rather than as a demand for punishment.[8] The slogans chosen for the campaign in the plebiscite offer a good example: "Chile, happiness is already on its way" or "Without fear, without hatred, vote no." Another one of those slogans stated, "You only need a pencil to beat Pinochet."

As a result, the democratic forces not only won the plebiscite, but their new strategies were the key factor to victory and left indelible marks in the characteristics of the Chilean transition to democracy and the period of consolidation. From the moment of Pinochet's defeat in the plebiscite, the acceptance of the rules and the institutional scheme that had been created by the armed forces began to work to the advantage of the democratic parties. The Constitution stipulated that a general election was to be held in one year, and there was no doubt that the same forces that had defeated Pinochet could defeat any other person that would be seen as his candidate. Moreover, from the night after the plebiscite of October 1988, the possibility that the army could break its own rules and try to avoid future elections was the only real threat to the transition to democracy. So, surprisingly enough, it was the democratic groups who were caring about the maintenance of the Constitution enacted by the ruling junta and its scheduled plan to recover democracy.

Of course, there were broad and well structured provisions in that constitutional and legal scheme that were designed to ensure that the new democratic forces would not make radical changes to the Constitution. The democratic parties could not take only one part of those rules, decide to play according to Pinochet's constitutional scheme, and then try to change the Constitution according to their own rules. Yet, between the plebiscite and the presidential election, negotiations were held for the first time to repeal some of the most important of those authoritarian devices embodied in the Constitution. Unfortunately, only a limited number of agreements was reached. They were approved by another plebiscite with 87.7% of

---

more contested among the Socialists. Only the Communists resisted entering the political process through this means and were left outside the political coalition that fought together in the plebiscite and the subsequent presidential election.

[8] For a general description of this campaign, see EUGENIO TRIONI, LA INVISIBLE VICTORIA (Sur ed., 1990).

popular support.[9] The rest of the well-designed authoritarian structure remained.

C. The Issue of Human Rights During the Presidential Campaign

The discussion of human rights was very important during the Presidential campaign that followed Pinochet's defeat in the plebiscite. The democratic forces had Aylwin as a candidate, while the political right and the forces that had supported the military regime backed a civilian, the former Secretary of the Treasury Department, Hacienda. Chilean long-standing tradition is one in which the candidates are to put forward a program. The coalition giving support to Aylwin had great difficulty agreeing on how to deal with past human rights violations. The language of the final text of the program may express the difficulty in achieving agreement:

> The democratic Government will put forth its best efforts in order to establish the truth in the cases of violations of human fights that have occurred since September of 1973. It will also procure the trial according to the actual penal law, of the human rights violations that represent atrocious crimes against life, liberty and personal integrity....[10]

The program continued, "Cases are to be tried in civilian courts, which should act in accordance with the principle of due process of law, and with full respect of the procedural guarantees of victims and those held responsible."[11] Having in mind the Argentinean case and its problems with the *Ley de Punto Final*,[12] there was a promise to establish a special and limited period to present the cases to the court. Finally, some very careful words were devoted in the program to the amnesty law of 1978:

> Due to its very legal nature and true meaning, the amnesty decree-law of 1978 has not and cannot become an impediment for the disclosure of the truth, the investigation of the facts and the establishment of criminal responsibilities in cases of crimes against human rights, as are the detention of people followed by disappearance, crimes against the right to life and grave physical and psychological wounds. The democratic government will

---

9 The plebiscite was held on July 30, 1989. An overwhelming majority (87.7%) of the population approved the proposal for reforming the Constitution.

10 PROGRAMA DE GOBIERNO, CONCERTACIÓN DE PARTIDOS POR LA DEMOCRACIA (1989) (translation by the author of this Article).

11 *Id.*

12 The Argentinean *Ley de Punto Final* was enacted on December 24, 1986, after major manifestations of discontent made by the military. It aimed at limiting the cases of past human rights violations that would be presented to the courts by limiting the time in which they could be presented. A large number of cases were brought to the courts during the established period. However, far from calming the discontent in the armed forces, the cases augmented it. *See* Zalaquett, *supra* note 3, at 55; Acuña *supra* note 4, at 43.

> continue the program to promote the derogation or nullification of the amnesty law.[13]

The promise was not to repeal the amnesty law, but to make efforts to achieve that result.

Notwithstanding the careful wording of the program, it quickly came under forceful attack. Both the political right and the armed forces spoke out. Although the active officers of the armed forces refrained from making open statements on electoral issues during the presidential campaign, the Commander in Chief of the Air Force decided to speak. He was considered to be a key actor in support of liberalization and a very strong supporter of civilian rule. He had kept his soldiers away from the secret police and fired most of the men that were highly compromised in human rights violations. He was also the first to publicly recognize the defeat of Pinochet the night after the plebiscite (a very crucial moment where the government was not publishing the results and thus creating a tense climate).[14] This same general, very shortly after the program was presented, publicly said that repealing the amnesty law ran against the compromise the democratic parties had made to respect the institutional scheme. He further asserted that this represented a threat to the whole process of transition to democracy. Pinochet, of course, did not use very elegant words to say the same thing—announcing that if one of his men was touched, the rule of law would end. The democratic forces defended their program during the campaign. They frequently repeated that they would not risk a peaceful transition to democracy, that all they had promised in their program was to make efforts to repeal the law, and that obviously, those efforts had their natural limits in the very stability of the political process.

D. The Final Political Conditions

After the presidential and congressional election in 1989, it became clear that changing the Constitution and the laws of the previous regime would not be easy. Although the new government held a majority in the Lower Chamber, it did not control the Senate, where nine of the forty-six members were not elected, but rather, were designated to ensure a conservative, majority coalition. Therefore, the new government had to compromise with at least one of the right-wing political parties every time it proposed a legislative or constitutional change.

The newly elected authorities had accepted the institutional framework that included other strong protection mechanisms that were impossible to overcome. Among the many was a self-amnesty law passed in

---

13 PROGRAMA DE GOBIERNO, *supra* note 10.

14 Some versions argued that the results of the ballot-box were not given by the government in order to provoke street riots by the people that had voted no, and thus to regain political control by authoritarian methods. This version was denied by government officials. The weekly magazines covered this development the week after the plebiscite. *See generally* HOY, Oct. 1988; ANALYSIS Oct. 1988; QUE PASA Oct. 1988; APSI, Oct. 1988.

1978. The new government could not repeal or invalidate this law because it lacked the legislative majority to do so. A second inhibiting factor was the ideological sympathies of the judiciary. The Supreme Court applied the broadest interpretation possible to the amnesty law, making it difficult even to investigate the truth. The Court also had demonstrated a weak commitment to investigate and punish the cases that occurred after 1978. Because Pinochet had intervened in the judicial nominations only in accordance with the 1925 constitutional framework, the new authorities could not just replace the judges.

So Aylwin's problem was not an easy one. On the one hand, he had a moral obligation to disclose the truth and punish human rights violators. On the other, he could only achieve the final results he desired by breaking the very rules that had brought him into power.

Aylwin addressed the issue of past human rights violations in his opening speech the day he became President.[15] Until that point, he had not defined a precise policy beyond its main principles. In his speech, he called for a compromise between the virtues of morality and prudence, stating clearly that a full disclosure of the truth was indispensable. His choice seemed to be judicial trials followed by pardon.[16] This strategy presented an enormous problem: the courts clearly would not follow that path and would continue to interpret the amnesty law as broadly as possible.

The Argentinean experience was close enough in time and distance to illustrate to Aylwin that even in much more favorable conditions maximalist policies had to be compromised (*e.g.*, Alfonsin had to abandon some of his goals in the midst of open and violent military resistance).[17] In Chile, a threat to the authority of the civilian president was very dangerous because the unity of the armed forces is a long standing tradition, and nothing showed that it had weakened. The political intervention of the military after the presidential election would have meant nothing but a coup.

The Uruguayan experience also influenced Aylwin. In Uruguay, the democratic forces had also started their transition to democracy with a plebiscite called and lost by the military rulers. Unlike the Chilean case, however, Uruguay had no amnesty law. When the cases were brought to the civilian courts, the officers openly resisted testifying, claiming that military courts had proper jurisdiction. The Supreme Court ruled that the civilian courts had jurisdiction. Shortly thereafter, the newly elected parliament passed an amnesty law. After that, twenty-five percent of the citizens signed petitions demanding a plebiscite in order to repeal the amnesty law. However, the plebiscite upheld the amnesty law. More than eight years passed between the first and the last of the aforementioned

---

15 The inaugural speech was made at the National Public Stadium, March 12, 1990, and published in all newspapers the next day. *See* Patricio Aylwin, Inaugural Speech (Mar. 12, 1990) (transcript available at the Secretaria de Cultura y Prensa, Ministerio Secretaria General de Gobierno).

16 *Id.*

17 See *supra* note 4 for a general description of this situation in Argentina.

plebiscites.[18] The Uruguayan experience taught many Chileans to do quickly whatever had to be done.

In this environment of political restrictions, Chile's new democratic government believed that its basic moral obligations of prevention, compensation for the victims, and reconciliation could be met through an official disclosure of the truth. Accordingly, the Government created the Commission for Truth and Reconciliation....

Within its first month in office, the government started private conversations in order to establish a commission that would investigate and disclose the truth regarding human rights violations. It soon became clear that the forces of the right, now in the opposition but controlling the Senate, would not follow such a strategy. During the electoral campaign, the opposition had claimed that remembering old wounds and divisions would not benefit Chilean society. They had also argued that only the courts could properly conduct such investigations. Nevertheless, some voices among the coalition supporting the new government argued in favor of an investigative commission of the House of Deputies.

Aylwin decided to create the Commission by presidential decree. He personally tried to integrate people from the right into the Commission. Although no member of the right-wing parties joined, some important and well-reputed, conservatives accepted. Aylwin drafted the plan and discussed it with those who accepted. On April 24, 1990, the creation of the Commission was announced, less than two months after the new government had taken office.[19]

The National Commission on Truth and Reconciliation

*David Weissbrodt and Paul W. Fraser, "Book Review: Report of the Chilean National Commission on Truth and Reconciliation"**

"Only on the basis of the truth," stated the Commission's founding decree, "will it be possible to satisfy the basic demands of justice and create the indispensable conditions for achieving an effective national reconciliation."[3] The name of the new Commission in itself was cause for concern among human rights groups, particularly among groups of relatives

---

18 *See* Zalaquett, *supra* note 3.

19 The announcement of the Commission was made in a solemn and public act on the night Aylwins' speech had been published in all the newspapers. An official version has been edited by the Secretaría de Communicación y Culture, Ministerio Secretaría de General del Gobierno.

* Excerpted from David Weissbrodt and Paul W. Fraser, "Book Review: Report of the Chilean National Commission on Truth and Reconciliation," *Human Rights Quarterly*, vol. 14, no. 4 (November 1992), pp. 601-622 (as amended by author).

3 Preambular Paragraph No. 2 of Supreme Decree No. 355 (April 25, 1990), *in* 1 *National Commission on Truth and Reconciliation, Report* at vii (1991) (*Informe de la Comisión Nacional de Verdad y Reconciliación*).

of the disappeared.[4] How could such a commission, created with the purpose of "national reconciliation," be expected to develop an accurate historical record of conditions during the Pinochet period and fulfill the demands of truth and justice about human rights abuses.[5]

Nongovernmental human rights organizations and international organizations, such as the United Nations (UN) and the Organization of American States (OAS), painstakingly monitored the human rights violations in Chile under Pinochet.[6] The human rights organizations, surviving victims, and relatives of victims insisted upon a thorough investigation by the Commission. Among the most frequent demands of relatives' groups were establishing the whereabouts of all "disappeared detainees," the prosecution of the military and security personnel implicated in human rights violations, compensation for relatives of victims, and the creation of a permanent center for investigating disappearances.

President Aylwin's aims in establishing the Commission were a thorough truth-telling, the pursuit of "justice insofar as possible" and, most importantly, national reconciliation.[7] In the interest of national coexistence, President Aylwin sought repentance by the perpetrators as well as their forgiveness by the victims.[8] Aylwin's goals were manifested in his selection of commissioners, in the mandate given the Commission, in the way the Rettig Commission was different from commissions in other countries, in the methodology the Commission employed to produce its report, and in the overall content of the 1350-page Rettig Report....

---

4 Meeting with members of FEDEFAM (Latin American Federation of Associations for Relatives of Disappeared Detainees) and its Chilean affiliate, the *Agrupación* of Relatives of Disappeared Detainees, Caracas, April 1990.

5 *Id.*

6 NGOs like Chile's Catholic Church Vicariate of Solidarity and the Chilean National *Agrupación* (or "Solidarity Group") of Relatives of Disappeared Detainees labored resolutely and under severe risk throughout the Pinochet years to document and press for an end to the human rights abuses. The human rights situation in Chile also captured the attention of many international NGOs, such as Amnesty International, Americas Watch, and the International League for Human Rights. In addition, the UN and OAS took concerted action for the protection of human rights in Chile, In 1975, the UN Commission on Human Rights established an Ad Hoc Working Group on Chile, which was subsequently replaced in 1979 by a Special Rapporteur for Chile. These fact-finders undertook investigative visits to Chile and presented annual reports to the UN Commission on Human Rights and the General Assembly. The Inter-American Commission on Human Rights of the OAS also vigorously monitored Chile, issuing reports on Chile in 1974, 1976, 1977, and 1985.

7 Americas Watch, *Human Rights and the "Politics of Agreements": Chile During President Aylwin's First Year* 4-5, 17 (1991). Along with survivors and relatives of victims, senior Chilean government officials stated repeatedly that reconciliation was not possible without both truth and justice. President Aylwin has clarified, however, that he actually expected *justicia en lo posible* (justice insofar as possible). This limit did not satisfy victims, for whom the Chilean justice system had not provided any remedy for past violations and had often seemed to have been an adversary. *Id.* at 5.

8 *Id.* at 4.

Selection of Commissioners

As President Aylwin formulated his approach to the legacy of the Pinochet period, he was undoubtedly well aware of the obstacles he faced in obtaining a clarification from the Chilean military about past violations. Most notably, General Pinochet remained as Commander-in-Chief of the Army. Aylwin also could study the difficulties experienced by other recent transitions to democracy throughout Latin America and elsewhere, and the problems they faced in dealing with past human rights abuses. President Aylwin knew if he pressed too hard, he would risk a confrontation with the military, further instability, and perhaps even another military coup. Aylwin was determined to formulate an approach based upon consensus and to avoid the shortcomings of other countries in dealing with past human rights violations.

From the outset, Aylwin was careful not to appoint a commission with an apparent political bias. Headed by the lawyer and former Senator Raúl Rettig, the Commission was composed of respected human rights figures—three commissioners had held posts in or were associated with the Pinochet government; another was a personal friend of Aylwin; and the others had various nongovernmental links and political affiliations.[9] Two commissioners were exiles under Pinochet. Chair Rettig, a distinguished lawyer known for his allegiance to the old tradition of the Radical Party in Chile, had served as his country's Ambassador to Brazil under President Salvador Allende. By appointing a Commission which was more-or-less evenly divided in political terms, Aylwin communicated his desire that the Commission's work should be done in good faith; that the matter was too important to be pursued in partisan terms.[10]

Aylwin's selections earned immediate credibility for the Rettig Commission to consider the human rights issue in Chile. The Commission, laboring intensely with a tight nine-month deadline imposed by its founding decree, submitted its report to President Aylwin in February 1991.[11] The fact that all eight commissioners signed the final report, no

---

[9] Members appointed to the National Commission on Truth and Reconciliation were: Raúl Rettig Guissen, president; Jaime Castillo Velasco; José Luis Cea Egaña; Mónica Jiménez de la Jara; Ricardo Martin Díaz; Laura Novoa Vásquez; Gonzalo Vial Correa; and José Zalaquett Daher. Mr. Vial was Pinochet's Minister of Education in the late-1970s. Mr. Martin founded a government-sponsored human rights commission. Later Pinochet appointed him a Senator as Pinochet prepared to leave office. Mr. Cea is a conservative constitutional law professor who studied in the United States. The remaining commissioners were politically closer to the Aylwin government. Mr. Castillo is a respected jurist who founded the Chilean Human Rights Commission in exile and subsequently returned to Chile in 1983. Castillo is a Christian Democrat who served as minister of Justice in the administration of President Eduardo Frei. Ms. Jimenez, also a Christian Democrat, headed PARTICIPA, an organization encouraging voter registration prior to the 1988 Chilean plebiscite. Mr. Novoa Vásquez, a lawyer and respected public servant, is a personal friend of President Aylwin. Mr. Zalaquett is a well-known human rights lawyer and former Chair of the International Executive Committee of Amnesty International. Zalaquett had been arrested without charges in the mid-1970s, and Pinochet ordered his exile.

[10] Washington Office on Latin America, *Human Rights: Truth and Reconciliation in Chile* 8 (Issues in Human Rights No. 2, 1991) [hereinafter WOLA].

[11] The University of Notre Dame Press has received a grant from the Ford Foundation to translate and publish an English version of the report which is scheduled for release in Fall 1993.

small accomplishment for the Aylwin administration, provided the broadest possible endorsement of the report.[12]...

Mandate

The Rettig Commission's mandate was four-fold.[73] First, following Zalaquett's recommended approach,* the Commission was to describe how the repressive system worked—how the events came to pass, how the secret police operated and how the judiciary, the press, and the church reacted. Second, the Commission was to account for every dead and disappeared person. Third, the Rettig Commission was asked to propose measures of reparation. Fourth, President Aylwin asked the Commission to propose measures of prevention.

The Rettig Commission was limited to considering "grave acts" which consisted of only the most flagrant human rights abuses. "Grave violations" were defined in the founding decree as "situations of disappeared detainees, executed persons, and those tortured to death, in which the moral responsibility of the State appears to be engaged through acts of its agents or persons in its service, as well as kidnappings and attempts on peoples' lives committed by individuals under political pretexts."[74]

This directive dramatically limited the scope of the Commission's mandate. As a result, the Commission was not authorized to consider cases of torture which did not result in death for the victim, attacks which caused only wounds to the victims, or cases of arbitrary arrest, detention, or exile. Consideration of such abuses would have increased the Commission's universe of cases many-fold.

---

[12] In contrast, the Rettig Commission's counterpart in Argentina, the Sabato Commission ... did not represent as broad a political spectrum. The Sabato Commission's original ten members were chosen for their international and national prestige, consistent defense of human rights, and representation of different walks of life. National Commission on the Disappearance of Persons, *Nunca Máis* 428 (1986). The Alfonsín government then invited both Chambers in the Argentine Congress to send three representatives to join the Commission. Only the Chamber of Deputics complied, adding three Radical Party members to the Commission. *Id.* Many human rights organizations in Argentina preferred an inquiry by a congressional committee. *See José Zalaquett, Confronting Human Rights Violations Committed by Former Governments: Principles Applicable and Political Constraints, in State Crimes: Punishment or Pardon* 23, 54 (A. Henkin ed., 1989).

[73] In its founding decree, the Rettig Commission was mandated to:

a) establish the most complete picture possible about the grave acts referenced, their antecedents and circumstances;

b) gather background material which permits the individualization of victims and establishment of their fate and whereabouts;

c) recommend measures of reparation and restoration which allow for justice; and

d) recommend legal and administrative measures which, in its judgment, should be adopted to impede or prevent the commission of acts referred to in this article.

Supreme Decree No. 355, *supra* note 3, at Art. 1 (translation of the authors).

* [Editor's note: The approach referred to is that presented by José Zalaquett in "Confronting Human Rights Violations Committed by Former Governments: Principles Applicable and Political Constraints," in *State Crimes: Punishment or Pardon* (The Aspen Institute, 1989). The Zallaquet article is reprinted in Volume One of the present collection.]

[74] *Id.*

The Aylwin government's rationale for limiting the Commission's mandate, in addition to selecting a more manageable number of cases, was that the military government never denied the facts of exile and imprisonment, but they did deny that people were killed and disappeared—among the gravest forms of human rights violations. Indicating that it would have been impossible to document every torture case, the Commission did choose to deal with torture as a phenomenon rather than individually in the Report.[75]

President Aylwin appointed the Rettig Commission by presidential decree, which does not allow for subpoena powers to compel testimony from witnesses; only a congressional mandate could have created such a commission. Some believed Aylwin should have attempted to create such a commission and have Congress vote on the proposal. Such a proposal would have undoubtedly failed or been extremely limited, but the positions of all members of Congress on the issue would have been publicly recorded.

Aylwin did not choose this confrontational and potentially divisive path. The founding decree explicitly stated that the Commission could not assume the role of a court of justice, nor could it determine the responsibility of individuals for acts committed. Hence, the decree generally limited the Commission to an information-gathering role.

Content

Because of the efforts of the OAS, the UN, and nongovernmental organizations, the world generally knew about the truth regarding human rights violations during the Pinochet period. The critical purpose of the Rettig Commission was to produce the officially sanctioned version of the truth, to translate knowledge to acknowledgement.[76] Well over half of the Rettig Commission Report is devoted to a systematic and thorough description of the repression of the Pinochet years.[77]

The history is divided into three distinct periods: (1) the period just after the military coup from September to December 1973, when the majority of the human rights violations occurred; (2) the period of 1974 through August 1977, when the intelligence service known as the DINA (*Dirección de Inteligencia Nacional*) was the principal instrument of political repression; and (3) the period of August 1977 to March 1990 when the CNI (*Central Nacional de Informaciones*) succeeded the DINA as the primary means of state repression, until the election of Aylwin. In addition to describing the system of repression and attributing institutional

---

75 WOLA, *supra* note 10, at 8 (quoting Zalaquett).

76 Weschler, *supra* note 25, at 4. Professor Thomas Nagel drew this distinction between "knowledge" and "acknowledgement" at the Aspen Institute conference to which José Zalaquett presented his paper in 1988.

77 Interestingly, the most heated discussion following the Report's publication focussed not on a dispute of the facts of the human rights violations, but on the historical interpretation of the Pinochet period. Americas watch, *supra* note 7, at 33. Among the Chilean Army's objections to the report was the contention that an internal war did exist in 1973, the alleged bias of some of commissioners, and the Report's lack of "historical validity." *Id.*

responsibility for human rights violations at each stage, the first volume provides a chronological listing of individual human rights violations under Pinochet. This day-by-day and week-by-week chronology covers violations from all regions of Chile.

The Rettig Commission chose to report on victims of armed opposition groups as well as victims of governmental human rights violations. Hence, in addition to the 2,115 individuals described in the report as having been subjected to human rights violations, largely at the hands of the DINA and the CNI, there were 164 "victims of political violence." Included in this category were: killings of uniformed personnel following the 11 September 1973 military coup; shootings of civilians by police or security personnel during peaceful political protest; assassinations of government agents attributed to leftist groups, such as the *Frente Patriótico Manuel Rodríguez;* and the killing of civilians by terrorists, which became more common as violent opposition to Pinochet grew in the 1980s. These victims were recounted to provide a rough balance in the Rettig Commission Report. The Rettig Commission also indicates that there were 642 cases where they could not reach a final conclusion due to insufficient evidence or time constraints.[78]

The size and sophistication of the Rettig Commission's "official truth" are impressive. The Report, in addition to serving as the official truth, also functions as an ethical and educational document aimed at promoting national reconciliation and preventing future human rights abuses.

Americas Watch, "Human Rights and the 'Politics of Agreements:' Chile during President Aylwin's First Year"[*]

Findings

The report is a massive document, more than 2,000 pages long. It is also a richly detailed document, often moving and, despite its subject matter, written to be readable. In one sense, the entire contents of the report constitute its findings, for the decision to include a case or a historical detail in the report confers a certain judgment on its importance and veracity. Thus, it is meaningful that, in describing the context in which the coup took place, the essay on "Historical Framework" in Part II includes material on factors internal to Chile and factors external, such as U.S. covert intervention; that it begins with the situation facing the country in 1973 and not before, as the Right had demanded; and that the essay is careful to clarify that all political actors played a role in a polarization that invited extreme "solutions." The report answers questions about famous cases, such as the circumstances of Salvador Allende's death—the Commission became convinced that the former President took his own life,

---

[78] National Commission on Truth and Reconciliation, *supra* note 3, at 787.

[*] Excerpted from Americas Watch, *Human Rights and the "Politics of Agreements:" Chile during President Aylwin's First Year* (Human Rights Watch, 1991), pp. 21-25.

rather than surrender—and devastates some of the military regime's central justifications for its repressive policy, such as the concept that, in September 1973, the country faced an "internal war."[32]

The Commission's emphasis on certain aspects of responsibility for abuses served to direct national attention, for example to the role played by the Judiciary and the special importance of the DINA as a repressive entity. Of the Judiciary, almost more than the armed forces as institutions, the report presents harsh judgments. It notes, for example, "the feeling of sympathy that the majority of the members of the Supreme Court showed for the new regime,"[33] and describes the conduct of the courts unsparingly:

> During the period which concerns us, the Judicial Power did not react with sufficient energy when faced with human rights violations....
>
> The Judicial Power was the only one of the three Powers of State that continued functioning without being intervened or dissolved.... Interest in maintaining a structure or an image of legality, on the new military authorities' part, made them especially careful with members of the judiciary.... This would have permitted the Judicial Power to assume a more resolute attitude in defense of the human rights that were being violated. However, and although jurisdictional activities continued functioning normally in almost all areas of national concern whose conflicts arrived at the courts, in the area of human rights violated by agents of authority in a magnitude unknown before, jurisdictional oversight was notoriously insufficient....
>
> The attitude adopted during the military regime by the Judicial Power produced, to an important and involuntary extent, an aggravation of the process of systematic violations of human rights, both in the short term—in not lending protection to detainees in denounced cases—and insofar as it offered repressive agents an increasing certainty of impunity for their criminal actions, whatever form of aggression might be employed....
>
> The Courts, in spite of not being able to ignore the existence of centers like the National Stadium, the Chile Stadium, the Air Force War Academy, [and DINA centers] Villa Grimaldi, José Domingo Cañas 1367, Londres 38 and many other places in Santiago and provinces—including, in the early period, centers belonging to military institutions—where detainee were kept and where torture was common practice, did nothing to remedy this illegality, nor to denounce it, despite continuous complaints formulated in writs of habeas corpus.[34]

Of DINA, the report describes it as an organization

> whose functioning was *secret and above the law;*... its internal organization, composition, resources, personnel and actions escaped not only public knowledge but also the control of any legality. Even more, DINA was effectively protected from any control, not only that which the Judicial Power might have exercised, but also that of the other aspects of the Executive Power, of high officials of the Armed Forces and including of the Governing Junta; in effect, although formally the DINA was subordinate to the Junta, in

---

32 [omitted]

33 Volume I, Part II, Chapter I, B.1

34 Volume I, Chapter IV, A and B.l.(b.3)

> practice it was responsible only to the President of the Governing Junta, later President of the Republic.[35]

At its peak, the DINA employed thousands of persons ranging from DINA agents as such—civilians as well as military and police personnel—to paid advisors, collaborators and contacts in government institutions and the press. It also maintained contact with the secret services of neighboring dictatorships and foreign terrorist groups.

In all structural descriptions of DINA, the report makes clear that the organization reported to the President of the Junta and Commander in Chief of the Army and was the principal agent in a "patten of previous planning and central coordination which reveal, in combination, a will to exterminate certain categories of persons: those considered to be politically highly dangerous."[36]

It is also unsparing in its description of what DINA did to the "disappeared." The Commission "reached moral conviction that so-called 'disappearance' was not that [but rather] a detention accompanied or followed by measures of concealment and official denials; detention during which, in general, tortures were applied; and of which there is a moral certainty that it concluded in the victim's assassination and the disposal of his remains in such a way as not to permit them to be found."[37]

Similarly, the report explores the phenomenon of torture at length in its discussion of the 1974-77 period, including descriptions of the secret interrogation centers of DINA and the types of torture in which each center specialized. Methods described include the *parrilla* (electricity applied while prisoner tied to metal bed; literally, "the grill"); prolonged suspension of the victim by wrists or knees; the *submarino* (repeated submersion of head in liquid, generally mixed with feces or urine, until moment of near suffocation); beatings; psychological torture; breaking of bones of aggravation of existing wounds by, for example, driving a vehicle over the victim's limbs; rape and other sexual abuse, which in some interrogation centers was practiced regularly.[38]

In its description of the final period, late 1977 to March 1990, the report focuses partially on defining circumstances of "political violence," whether police abuse at anti-government demonstrations (shootings leading to death) or confrontations between armed leftists and security forces where death resulted. The State agents in situations of political violence were generally police; the armed individuals belonged principally to three groups, the preexisting *Movimiento de Izquierda Revolucionaria* (MIR), the *Frente Patriótico Manuel Rodríguez* (FPMR) with links to the Communist Party, and, later, the *Movimiento Lautaro*. Each of these groups has undergone splits and variations of tactic over time.

---

35 Volume I, Part III, Chapter II, A.l.(b.l.). Emphasis in the original.

36 Volume I, Part III, Chapter II, A.l.(a)

37 Volume I, Part I, Chapter II, A.2.(a)

38 Volume I, Part III, Chapter II, A.1. (e.2.)

During the period studied in this portion of the Rettig report, there also were continuing human rights violations. The report defines some actions by the extreme–left as human rights violations, but the bulk of human rights abuses was carried out by the State, principally CNI, the security police that replaced DINA. The false "clash" with leftists was one scenario for murder; there were also cases of detention–disappearance and of kidnapping followed by mutilation and execution. Torture was often a prelude to the execution of members of armed groups. Terrorist actions committed by leftist opponents of the regime that the report defines as human rights violations included assassinations of government agents and the indiscriminate killing of bystanders or accidental victims.

Much of the report is devoted to case descriptions, the accumulated bulk of which—each case with its details of occupation, age, civil status, home town, number of children—constitutes the basic message of the Commission's endeavor. These are individuals with private histories and families, whose absence, and the way they were removed from life, has traumatized the society. The majority of victims were humble people, and young; the largest category of victim was workers and campesinos, and more than 60% were younger than 30 years of age. Nearly 95% were men, and 46% had no known party affiliation.[39]

The statistics emerging from the Commission's work are necessarily conservative, given the shortness of the period it was given to carry out its task, the selectiveness of its mandate, and its inability to compel cooperation from the armed and security services. Here are not counted the tens of thousands who were either forced formally into exile or fled the country under harassment; the further tens of thousands detained in massive sweeps, right after the coup and in the later years of the regime; those who were tortured but survived. The wounded are not represented; only the dead, of both "sides," and the disappeared, who are presumed dead....

Half (1,068 cases, or 50.2%) of the persons whose deaths are deemed human rights violations in the Commission's report were those killed by agents of the State or persons in their service. These were victims sentenced to death by *consejos de guerra* in the months following the coup, shot while supposedly trying to escape imprisonment at that time, killed during the protests that became frequent after May 1983, or—the most numerous—"other executions and deaths from torture."[41] A further 45.2% (957 cases) are also attributed to State agents; these are the disappeared detainee of whose fate the Commission considered it had substantial evidence. Individuals acting on political pretexts—that is, leftist armed groups—are held responsible for 90 deaths, or 4.3% of deaths qualified as human rights violations.

---

39 Appendix II, "*Estadísticas*."

41 The report's Appendix II lists 59 dead due to *consejos de guerra*, 93 killed during protests, 101 whom the former authorities claimed to have killed because they tried to escape, and 815 in the final category; total 1,068.

Finally, there are 164 cases considered "victims of political violence," a category which contains both victims of State policy and victims of violent opposition to the regime. Thus, uniformed personnel killed in 1973, during the coup and immediately after, are in this category. The Commission considered, meanwhile, that a person shot by police or security agents during a peaceful political protest or during an armed confrontation was a victim of political violence.

*David Weissbrodt and Paul W. Fraser, "Book Review: Report of the Chilean National Commission on Truth and Reconciliation"**

The Rettig Commission served effectively as an official opportunity for victims and their relatives to testify about their suffering and loss.[79] For many years their efforts to complain were met with disdain, mockery, and lies. The Rettig Commission received them gently and offered them a seat and coffee; the Chilean flag was there on the desk and the Commission's stationary read "Presidency of the Republic." The victims and their relatives could allow themselves some measure of relief.[80]

The Rettig Commission devotes the last fifty pages of the primary, substantive volume of its Report to four short chapters entitled: "Proposals for Reparation," "Prevention of Human Rights Violations," "Other Recommendations," and "Truth and Reconciliation." The reparation proposals include both symbolic measures for restoring of the good name of victims, such as monuments identifying each victims, as well as legal measures, such as a monetary compensation and health benefits to relatives of victims. To permit persons with disappeared relatives to collect monetary reparations, the Rettig Commission proposed a procedure for declaring the victim "presumed to be dead."[81]

A subsequent law, which the Chilean Congress adopted in February 1992, granted compensation to families of victims recorded in the Rettig Commission Report and created a National Corporation of Reparations and Reconciliation to clarify the cases in which the Rettig Commission was unable to reach a decision as well as an additional hundred cases presented after the expiration of the Commission's mandate.[82] Chilean relatives

---

* Excerpted from David Weissbrodt and Paul W. Fraser, "Book Review: Report of the Chilean National Commission on Truth and Reconciliation," *Human Rights Quarterly*, vol. 14, no. 4 (November 1992), pp. 601-622 (as amended by author).

79 [Washington Office on Latin America, *Human Rights: Truth and Reconciliation in Chile* 9 (Issues in Human Rights No. 2, 1991) [hereinafter WOLA].]

80 *Id.*

81 *National Commission on Truth and Reconciliation, supra* note 3, at 826.

82 *Senate Approves Compensation to Victims of Human Rights Violations*, El Mercurio, Jan. 24, 1992, at 1. An estimated 7,000 relatives of victims will benefit from the reparations law. Beneficiary families were entitled to receive approximately 140,000 pesos (US $380) per month to be divided in fixed percentages among the spouse, parents, and children, in addition to health benefits. *Reparations Law to Take Effect Soon*, El Mercurio, Feb. 4, 1992, at 1. *See* Cecilia Medina Quiroqa, *The Experience of Chile*, in Seminar on the Rights to Retribution, Compensation and Rehabilitation for Victims of Gross violations of Human Rights and Fundamental Freedoms 101, 109 (The Van Buren *et al*, eds., 1992).

cautioned that the reparations and the declarations of presumed death should not prevent efforts to locate disappeared relatives.[83]

The Report's recommendations concerning preventive measures include ratification of international human rights treaties; modifying Chile's national laws to conform with international human rights standards; assuring the independence of the judiciary; fostering a society where the Armed Forces, police, and security forces operate in a manner which respects human rights; and creating a permanent office of "Ombudsman" to protect citizens from future human rights abuses. The concluding essay on "Truth and Reconciliation" emphasizes the Rettig Commission's goal of providing the fundamental truth about events in Chile, which the nation had to assimilate and then use to explore avenues for reconciliation.

The second volume of the Rettig Commission Report is devoted to a comprehensive alphabetical listing of the 2,279 victims identified by the Commission. Each entry lists the date and location of the person's death or disappearance; brief personal information, such as age, profession, and political party or trade union affiliations; and a short description of the circumstances of the victim's experiences.[84]

Following the Report's release, President Aylwin indicated that the Rettig Commission had transmitted relevant information to the courts and called upon the judiciary to carry out "extensive investigations" for which "the current Amnesty Law cannot be an obstacle." The amnesty law, which President Aylwin mentioned, was passed in 1978, and although it was intended to prevent prosecutions for human rights violation before 1978, the courts have invoked it to block even preliminary investigations into cases.[85]

Methodology

The Rettig Commission, like the Sabato Commission in Argentina, made great efforts to gather information and receive testimony on human rights abuses. Each commission consisted of over sixty staff members. The Rettig Commission even used six social workers to minister to the needs of the victims and their families. The commissions made themselves very

---

[83] *Human Rights Reparations Meaningless Without Justice*, El Mercurio, Jan. 22, 1992.

[84] A typical entry reads:

> SARA DE LOURDES DONOSO PALACIOS
> Disappeared Detainee. Santiago, July 1975.
>
> Sara Donoso, 25 years of age, single, student of nursing at the University of Chile and worked in a consulting office subordinate to the Ministry of Health. She was an activist in the Socialist Party, where she carried out tasks associated with its Central Directorate. She was detained on July 15, 1975, at her workplace by agents of the *Dirección de Inteligencia Nacional* (DINA). Since that date the whereabouts of Sara Donoso are unknown.

2 *National Commission on Truth and Reconciliation, Report* 129 (1991) (translation of the authors).

[85] Amnesty International, *Chile: Report of Governmental Human Rights Commission Made Public*, Weekly Update, Mar. 14, 1991, at 11 (AI Index: AMR 22/WU 01/91).

accessible to victims, relatives of victims, and human rights organizations; members of both commissions travelled extensively to gather testimony.[86] The Rettig Commission received information from over 4,000 complainants and a few members of the Chilean military who wished to relieve their conscience about human rights violations, as well as from witnesses from abroad.[87]

In addition to individual testimony, the Rettig Commission relied upon many other sources to pursue its mandate.[88] The *Vicaría de la Solidaridad* provided impressive files on most cases. Amnesty International supplied all its relevant information as did the International Committee of the Red Cross, which only transmits information to governments or governmental institutions. The Rettig Commission also had access to official data, such as autopsy reports, travel certificates, and judicial transcripts of any past investigations of cases.[89]

With respect to the reparation and prevention aspects of its mandate, the Rettig Commission consulted widely among international human rights organizations and Chilean political parties, churches, and unions. The Commission sent a questionnaire to these groups and received 150 responses. The questionnaire asked for advice about providing symbolic and legal reparation and about implementing reforms of the judiciary, police, and other institutions in order to prevent future human rights abuses. The questionnaire also solicited suggestions on means of promoting a culture of human rights and preventing a recurrence of violations over the long term.[90]

While the Rettig Commission, like the Sabato Commission, faithfully reached the essential truth about what happened, an important element is conspicuously absent from their respective reports. Both reports avoided explicit findings of individual responsibility. The Rettig Commission report determined the responsibility of certain military units and other institutions without mentioning the names of officers or perpetrators. Both the Sabato and Rettig Commissions left it to the courts to determine responsibility. The Legal Department of the Sabato Commission prepared files on individual cases for the courts. The Rettig Commission sent to the courts all information it gathered regarding individual responsibility. The Commission did not make public such findings, because doing so would have been improper. A commission appointed by the Executive (Aylwin) cannot pass judgment about individual responsibilities, which is reserved to the courts. A person publicly implicated by the Commission would potentially have their reputation tainted without due process. The Commission's communications to the courts have resulted in a number of important indictments and

---

86 Nunca Más, *supra* note 17, at 431; WOLA, *supra* note 10, at 9.

87 Speech by José Zalaquett, October 15, 1991, at Hastings College of Law, San Francisco, California.

88 WOLA, *supra* note 10, at 8.

89 *Id.*

90 *Id.* at 9.

prosecutions through which the public has been made aware of the names of people implicated in those crimes.[91]

Assessing the Impact of the Rettig Commission Report

The greatest contributions of the Rettig Commission are in establishing the "official truth" with which few argued[92] and in providing an officially sanctioned forum to which victims and relatives could give their testimony. The Rettig Commission reconstructed the collective memory of the Chilean people and produced a broadly endorsed, authoritative version of the history of Chile during the Pinochet period.

To its credit, the Rettig Commission managed to keep its primary focus on the victims. In the preparation of the report, the Commission gathered an enormous number of testimonies from witnesses and constantly solicited input from the relatives of victims. The meticulous chronology of individual violations and the enormous alphabetical listing of victims contained in volume two of the Report are tributes to the fallen.

The Rettig Commission Report's official truth was not satisfactory to everyone. Some argue that it is not possible to achieve an authoritative version of the facts without the authority to compel testimony from military officials and without revealing the names of the individual perpetrators of human rights violations.

The drawback of vesting such commissions of inquiry with greater investigative authority is the confusion which results when criminal prosecutions of individual perpetrators are subsequently launched. As was demonstrated in the Iran-Contra investigation and resulting trial of Colonel Oliver North, a broader investigative mandate for a commission may impair any subsequent criminal prosecution.[93]

If governments cannot provide such commissions with the power to compel testimony, future inquiries might consider the alternative of providing incentives for some members of the military to cooperate more fully with the process of justice, offering less or no punishment in exchange for testimony. Less punishment might include public censure, demotion, or payment of damages rather than prison sentences. The testimony of some officers may help to obtain more direct evidence of the worst violations.

The Rettig Commission might also have taken a stronger stance in favor of the revocation of the 1978 Amnesty Law, which constitutes a major obstacle to prosecution and even investigation of a large number of cases. President Aylwin made only a rather weak request that the judiciary not

---

91 J. Zalaquett, letter of 3 October 1992 (on file with authors).

92 While there was heated discussion about the historical interpretation of the Report, no one really disputed the facts—except for Gen. Manuel Contreras, the former head of the DINA, who denied everything. WOLA, *supra* note 10, at 11.

93 *United States v. North*, 910 F.2d 843, 872 (D.C. Cir. 1990) (testimony of several witnesses prejudicially influenced by exposure to defendant's compelled testimony before Congressional committee; conviction reversed), *rev'd in other respects* 920 F.2d 940 (D.C. Cir. 1990); *United States v. Poindexter*, 951 F.2d 369, 375, 388 (D.C. Cir. 1991) (same).

interpret the 1978 Amnesty Law to block investigations of the cases that the Commission submitted to the courts.

The Rettig Commission's goal of eliciting repentance from the perpetrators of the human rights violations has met with little success. Very few military personnel presented information or testimony to the Rettig Commission prior to the Report's release. Public attention and discussion was insufficient regarding the Rettig Commission's key objectives of justice, forgiveness, and repentance.

The impact of the public release of the Rettig Commission Report in March 1991 was dampened by the 1 April 1991 assassination of right-wing Senator Jaime Guzmán.[94] [Following] that killing, public attention turned to concerns about left-wing violence.... For a time, public events overtook the Rettig Commission Report. The Report was widely circulated, however, and there was wide national debate about it among diverse social organizations.

The Rettig Commission Report represents an important step in the evolution of commissions of inquiry about past human rights violations. Governments in other regions, such as Central and Eastern Europe, as well as South Africa, can learn from the experience of Chile in investigating violations committed by previous officials. Inquiry commissions in countries which have experienced political transitions could successfully model their work on the principles and practices of the Rettig Commission, and depending upon the specific political constraints, modify their approach to achieve the desired truth, justice, and reconciliation.

Americas Watch, "Human Rights and the 'Politics of Agreements:' Chile during President Aylwin's First Year"[*]

Public reaction to the report is difficult to gauge in that it occupied the nation's attention for so short a time. One limited indication, however, is a poll released on March 7, based on a universe of 300 Santiago residents of various ages and social strata. According to this poll, President Aylwin's March 4 speech was seen as "positive" by 91%, although 69% believed that the report "does not contain the whole truth of what happened." Eighty percent of respondents favored continuing judicial investigations of the cases forwarded to the courts by the Rettig Commission, while 15% did not. And 70% did not consider the report a definitive solution to the problem of human rights violations.[48] Another poll, released a month later and highlighted in the Sunday edition of the conservative *El Mercurio*, asked the question, "In your view, does the Rettig report contribute to

---

[94] WOLA, *supra* note 10, at 11.

[*] Excerpted from Americas Watch, *Human Rights and the "Politics of Agreements:" Chile during President Aylwin's First Year* (Human Rights Watch, 1991), pp. 30-33.

[48] Telephone poll conducted by *Base de Información, Comunicación y Análisis* (BASICA), reported in *La Epoca*, March 8, 1991. On a related matter, 71 % believed the armed forces bore a great responsibility for human rights violations, while 17.7% believed their responsibility was minor.

reconciliation?" and obtained quite even responses: 42.5% answered yes, 39.5% said no.[49]

One immediate effect of the report was to bolster the credibility of legal cases before the courts. The Commission forwarded information on some 230 victims to the civilian courts with requests that existing cases be reopened on the basis of the new data or, in some instances, that cases be initiated for the first time. A list of the cases forwarded was leaked to the press; it included the names of witnesses to the detentions of the victims, a summary of each case, its court of jurisdiction, date of detention and date of death if known.[50] At this writing, it is unclear what the legal future of those cases may be. However, another important result of the Commission's work—public criticism of the Supreme Court—may end by improving somewhat the chances for investigation.

President Aylwin, in presenting and commenting upon the Commission's findings, was emphatic in criticism of the Judiciary, and in particular of the Supreme Court.... The Supreme Court, at first offended and defensive, waited several weeks before responding to a formal request from the President that it support the reopening or initiation of legal cases as recommended by the Rettig Commission. In April the Court acted favorably, instructing lower courts to reopen cases forwarded by the Rettig Commission, including cases previously closed by virtue of the 1978 amnesty law. This gesture does not indicate that the Court will change its position fundamentally, but it does permit fresh examination of evidence in new political conditions.

The Commission's recommendations were generally well received, but the first to be given legislative form became extremely controversial. A special interministerial committee, created to follow up on reparatory measures, produced a proposal to declare the disappeared presumed dead, to create a National Corporation for Reconciliation (the State-sponsored foundation recommended in the Rettig report), to fix a pension for the survivors, and other related matters. The Relatives of Disappeared Detainees objected that a declaration of presumed death would suggest that disappearance cases were somehow "resolved" and remove incentive for the State to locate remains, pursue the truth about the victims' circumstances of death and seek justice.... They considered the Corporation as proposed inadequate, because it would have no authority to investigate the whereabouts of the disappeared and locate their remains, but only to advise relatives in these tasks....

---

[49] Bestland poll reported in "*El Test del Pruner Año,*" *El Mercurio*, April 14, 1990.

[50] *Las Ultimas Noticias*, March 4, 1991. Prominent among the witnesses are two former agents of the repression, Andrés Valenzuela—an Air Force intelligence officer who participated in the *Comando Conjunto*, a squad linked primarily to the Air Force and specializing in disappearances from late 1975 to late 1976—and Luz Arce Sandoval, a torture victim who became, and remained for several years, a collaborator of DINA, denouncing former friends and allegedly participating in their interrogations under torture. Valenzuela came forward in 1985, sharing information which enabled an investigating judge to indict 40 military and civilians for a group disappearance (See Section III, "Cerda case."); Arce testified to the Rettig Commission. Both now live abroad, Arce's testimony too found its way into the press in March 1991, and caused a considerable impact.

The government's proposal would have declared all male children of disappeared detainees exempt from military service. The relatives objected to this, and their reasons reveal much about an experience of marginalization that the Rettig Commission understood and the government then proceeded to oversimplify. The relatives did not wish, one more time, to be marked off as a special group, excluded from patriotic duty and thus somehow lesser patriots, lesser citizens than other Chileans. They did not wish their children to be pointed at as exceptions any more. In small towns all over Chile, military service carries a certain status; and the military institution is, generally, distinguished from Pinochet. What the relatives proposed, rather, was that the Corporation to be created have, as one of its functions, to make representations to the armed forces in those cases in which, because of extreme trauma, the son of a disappeared person is not in condition to perform military service. They wished, for a change, to have options....

The reactions of the guilty parties, however, took longer to emerge. While Air Force commander Gen. Fernando Matthei readily accepted the report's findings, he personally had not been implicated in human rights abuses, and his service—whose command he assumed in 1978, after the most widespread abuses were over—had not been implicated in the gravest human rights violations of the later years. Likewise, the relatively mild reaction of Carabinero commander Gen. Rodolfo Stange came as no surprise; Stange, like Matthei, was neither an original member of the junta nor personally tainted. The Army and Navy waited and let supporters speak for them, however, in an atmosphere of increasing tension, until on March 27, more than three weeks after the report was released, both Gen. Pinochet and Adm. Martinez Busch explained their positions to a meeting of the National Security Council and later in more detail publicly. Both criticized the report as inaccurate and unjust, Pinochet in the more strident terms.

Stating the Army's "fundamental disagreement" with the report, Pinochet called its findings:

> personal and precarious convictions [which] have been transformed into condemnatory sentences against many persons, outside due process, opening the way to their discredit before public opinion and exposing them to terrorist vengeance.
>
> The Army of Chile solemnly declares that it will not accept being placed as if on trial before the citizenry [*en el banquillo de los acusados*] for having saved the freedom and sovereignty of the homeland at the insistence of the civilian population. Even less will it tolerate this when, among those who attempt to elevate themselves through moral judgments of other men, are those who were principally responsible for the tragedy experienced [by the nation] in their capacity as senior leaders of the Popular Unity [Allende's coalition].[51]

---

51 Portions of text reprinted in *El Mercurio*, March 28, 1991.

Among the Army's nine objections to the report was the contention that an internal war did exist in 1973; another was the alleged bias of some Commission members; a third was the report's alleged lack of "historical validity." According to the Army, the regime completed its mission, "reestablishing social peace and democracy and returning political leadership to civilians, in a country free and reconciled."[52]

Nor did the Army ignore the report's call for national determination that *nunca más*, never again, should such crimes occur in Chile. Pinochet responded to this with a somewhat contemptuous threat:

> For an important part of the nation, which understood the task of the llth of September of 1973, the true "*nunca más*" must come, before anything else, from those who, with their different ideological experiments, brought the country to an unavoidable reaction of legitimate defense before the open illegitimacy which had been produced. It is necessary that *nunca más* does anyone [*sic*] propose to initiate in Chile an experiment of the nature and scope of the Popular Unity. In such circumstances, it will be impossible to prevent the experience that legitimate use of force—by its nature—stimulates or makes difficult to avoid.[53]

As defiant as these statements were, they did not include denials of any specific crimes. Also, it was understood that they would be the armed forces' last criticisms of the report, that the subject was closed.

---

52 *Ibid.*

53 Quoted in María Irene Soto, "*El 'pronunciamiento' de las Fuerzas Armadas*," *Hoy* magazine, No. 715, April 1-7, 1991, p. 8.

TWO VIEWS FROM THE COMMISSION

Perspective of Jorge Correa S.

[Editor's note: In the selection which follows, Professor Jorge Correa, who served as secretary and chief of staff of the Chilean National Commission on Truth and Reconciliation, provides a unique perspective on the goals, philosophy and accomplishments of the Commission.]

*Jorge Correa S., "Dealing with Past Human Rights Violations: The Chilean Case After Dictatorship"**

What Kind of Truth

1. Universal or General

The decree that created the Commission,[20] after stating that the moral consciousness of the nation required the truth about past human rights violations, established that the truth about individual cases would not alone allow a general appreciation of what had happened. Accordingly, the Commission attempted to realize the following goals: (1) obtain an account of methods, policies, and excuses for human rights violations; (2) procure a history of the reactions of the different relevant sectors of society; and (3) attempt to explain the causes of such violations and their consequences for the victims, their relatives, and society. The Commission thought that these goals would provide a beneficial exercise for the sanity of social conscience and that the public exposure of the truth would have a special cathartic effect. Judicial investigation of particular cases clearly would not achieve these goals.[21]

The final report of the Commission tries to state all these characteristics. It tries to explain the political, legal, and judicial conditions that made the violation of human rights possible.[22] For each period studied, one can read the organization, the methods of acting, and the impunity of the violators of human rights.[23] Special attention is paid to torture. A description of the reactions of the most relevant social,

---

* Excerpted from Jorge Correa S., "Dealing with Past Human Rights Violations: The Chilean Case After Dictatorship," Volume 67, Issue 5 *The Notre Dame Law Review* (1992) 1464-1485. Reprinted with permission. © by *Notre Dame Law Review*, University of Notre Dame. The publisher bears responsibility for any errors which have occurred in reprinting or editing.

20 Ministry of the Interior Decree No. 355, *Diario Oficial* (May 9, 1990). *See also* REPORT, *supra* note 1, at 7-10.

21 For a general analysis of the judicial behavior during the authoritarian years, see REPORT *supra* note 1, at 95-104. *See also* Jorge Correa, *Formación de Jueces para la Democracia*, in FILOSOFIA DEL DERECHO Y DEMOCRACIA EN IBERO-AMÉRICA 34-35 (Agustín Squella ed., 1992); Hugo Fruhling, Justicia y Violacion de Derechos Humanos en Chile (1987) (unpublished paper on file with author).

22 REPORT, *supra* note 1, at 33-104.

23 *Id.* at 107-764.

political, and moral forces inside and outside the country is also stated for every period.[24] Finally, the report, in one of its most moving chapters, describes the suffering and the expectations of the victim's relatives, using their own words and statements.[25]

2. *The Individual Case by Case Story*

The Commission's aim was not only to achieve a general truth, but also to reach the truth concerning individual cases. There are two reasons for this. First, the only way to convincingly infer or explain a general truth, as previously described, is through the actual, individual cases of human rights violations. Second, because there were no real possibilities of judicial investigation in many of the cases,[26] some minimal justice had to be done in individual cases. Because authorities had neglected past violations, the relatives of those victims needed some kind of official recognition. As one of them said to us, "They told me that he had been freed. Now we find him in the tomb, with his eyes blindfolded and his hands bound."[27] Another said, "I want to cry out to the world, and with pride, that my father died because of his ideals. I want society to finally understand that the sons and daughters of those they killed are not dangerous people."[28] As these words demonstrate, the individual truth was important to reestablishing the dignity of the victims and their relatives.[29]

Of course, one of the most important goals of the Commission was to disclose the truth about the missing people. As one of the members of the Commission stated concerning disappearance: This kind of human rights violation is "a method of repression which, by its very nature, rests on secrecy and perpetuates its pernicious effects as long as truth remains hidden."[30] A mother of one missing person told us that after more than fifteen years, she still keeps the door of the house open during every holiday so that her disappeared son can come in. As a sister of another victim told us, "On every windy night my mother thought that it was him coming back. She would walk up, open the door, and cry."[31]

In order to achieve this individual truth, the Commission called the relatives of those persons who had been killed or were missing to present their cases and asked anyone with relevant information on any case to

---

24 *Id.* at 441-48, 606-15, 745-64.

25 *Id.* at 766-85.

26 Since the report was delivered, the courts have made significant advances in the investigation of a very few but highly symbolic cases. For example, Manuel Contreras, the former chief of the secret police, was tried for the assassination of Orlando Letelier in Washington D.C. in September 1976.

27 REPORT, *supra* note 1, at 781.

28 *Id.* at 785.

29 The recovery of the dignity of the victims was one of the established goals the Commission had to achieve. *See* Ministry of the Interior Decree No. 355, *supra* note 20.

30 Zalaquett, *supra* note 3, at 30.

31 REPORT, *supra* note 1, at 770.

testify. Special requests were sent to the groups that had done human rights work in the past and to those who were named as being responsible for past human rights violations.[32]

The final report includes the individual history of each of the 2,279 cases in which a moral conviction was achieved, meaning that a human rights violation had resulted in a death or disappearance after detention. The report also briefly states the reasons for such a conviction so that readers will be able to form their own opinion. In 641 cases, the Commission could not definitively conclude that a human rights violation had actually occurred, and another special commission is now being created to decide such cases.[33] As explained later, another 508 cases presented to the Commission were outside of its jurisdiction.

The series of explanations that the report establishes for distinguishing among cases may interest human rights scholars.[34] Probably the most important is the line drawn between those who died as victims of political violence and those who were victims of human rights violations. In the first group are those who were killed in the midst of the few combats that followed the military takeover and lasted only a few hours. Also considered as victims of political violence instead of human rights violations are those persons killed in the episodic armed conflicts between the police and the armed groups of the left. The report gives other conceptual considerations to explain the criteria applied to those who committed suicide while in prison. The principles used in other cases are more difficult to categorize.

The Commission largely failed to know and disclose the actual destiny of the missing people. In some thousand cases, the members of the Commission did arrive at the moral conviction that a person was missing and that either state officials were responsible for the initial arrest, or there was enough indirect evidence to point to state involvement.[35] Nevertheless, there was not enough collaboration on the part of former human rights violators to find out exactly when and how the missing people were killed and where their remains could be found. People that had played minor roles in the early months of the repression by the military regime did disclose some of that information either to us or other human rights groups. After that initial period, however, only a small number of highly trained and loyal men and women were involved in killing operations. Their methods also became much more sophisticated, both as to the secrecy of the ways of arresting the victim and to the way of disposing of the bodies of those killed.[36] As a result, much less is known about this period. Actually, only a couple of those involved with the secret police decided to testify before the Commission. Sending this information

---

32 For a complete description of the methods of the Commission, see *id.* at 3-13.

33 DIARIO OFICIAL § 19.123 (Feb. 8, 1992) (creating this new Commission called Comisión Nacional de Reparación y Reconciliación).

34 REPORT, *supra* note 1, at 27-30.

35 *Id.* at 107-763.

36 *Id.* at 478-84.

to the courts was difficult because we knew that the secrecy of those testimonies could no longer be guaranteed. Because some of the testimonies we received were given to us under the condition of secrecy, we had to protect them while still sending the relevant information so that the court could find and excavate the bodies.

Yet, most of the cases of missing people have not been resolved, leaving an open wound in Chilean society. A special new commission is now being created in the country to continue with that work,[37] a mission that the Catholic Church, through the Vicaria de la Solidaridad, is continuing to develop.

3. *Authoritative Truth that Could No Longer be Contested*

The Commission certainly was not the first group in Chile to investigate or report human rights violations. A wide range of such reports had already been published, both by national and international organizations.[38] Moreover, the work of the Commission would have been much more difficult, if not impossible, if the documents and files of human rights groups had not been made available to us (especially the ones of the Vicaria de la Solidaridad, an organization created by the churches and sustained by the Catholic Church).[39] The Commission did not take these reports for granted. In many cases, the Commission could add more information to the reports by extracting data from public records to which the Commission had legal access. In other cases, the data of the Vicaria was a very useful starting point for our own investigations.

The Church had already published part of its information, and some journalists had published books with many of the most relevant cases. Those publications had already become long-standing best sellers.[40] Legal and illegal copies were sold at bookstores, newsstands, and on the streets in all the cities and towns throughout the country. In this respect the Chilean transition was quite unique.

There are several reasons why a country should need a special commission to search for a truth that was quite widespread. First, none of

---

37 DIARIO OFICIAL, *supra* note 33.

38 Among the most internationally known reports about human rights in Chile is *Report on Human Rights in Chile*, INTER-AM. C.H.R. (Sept. 1985) (photocopy of original Spanish version on file with the author).

The United Nations published many reports during the Chilean dictatorship. Especially important were the reports published from 1979-1989, which where elaborated upon by the special rapporteur.

In its annual report, Amnesty International analyzed Chile in several instances. For information about the human rights violations during the dictatorship, see reports of 1979-1989, published both in English and Spanish.

39 The Vicaría de la Solidaridad and its predecessor organization, the Comité de Cooperación para la Paz en Chile, have documented tens of thousands of cases of violations of human rights in Chile. This organization presented its cases to the courts and had the most complete files on the subject. Most of them were made available to the Commission.

40 The most prominent example is probably PATRICIA VERDUGO, LOS ZARPAZOS DEL PUMA (America Cesoc ed., 1989). Another big best-seller was EUGENIO AHUMADA, CHILE LA MEMORIA PROHIBIDA (Pehuen ed., 1989).

the previous reports had tried a comprehensive coverage of the entire period in its generalities, and none had tried to cover all the individual cases. I have argued the importance of both. Second, and more importantly, all the previous disclosures were highly contested, even the ones deriving from the Church or from international forums. One has to remember that for a long time, and certainly for the time during which the massive violations of human rights were committed, the regime had absolute control over the press. So, for a long time, the killing and kidnapping of political dissidents was reported as being an invention of the Communist Party and its satellite groups who simply could not accept the fact that they had lost their power in Chile after their democratic experiment had finished in total chaos. Even the President of the Supreme Court advanced this explanation when referring to the writs of habeas corpus that were presented to the courts.[41] The propaganda of the regime could prove that some Communists were working at the Catholic Church's Vicaria de la Solidaridad, so they made the argument that the organization had been infiltrated and was dominated by the Communists.[42] Additionally, the regime attempted to discredit the stories of human rights violations that human rights groups were publishing by producing untrue stories about millions of people killed by the military regime and its secret police.

Aylwin, therefore, needed to appoint people to the Commission that the whole country would trust. He needed moral figures that could be trusted from the right to the left and especially by the relatives of the victims. Finding men and women that had taken a brave stand in defense of human rights and that had personally suffered for taking such a position so that the left and the human rights groups could trust them was not difficult. The problem was to find people on the right side of the political spectrum, especially after the right-wing parties had denied their collaboration. Aylwin made personal efforts in this. Finally, some

---

41 According to article 5 of the CIVIL CODE the Chief Justice of the Supreme Court has to give an opening speech at the beginning of each year. In 1975 the Chief Justice of the supreme stated:

> Chile, which is not a land of barbarians, as it is often said abroad, either by bad chileans or by foreigners has made diligent efforts to comply strictly with these rights. As to torture and other atrocities, I can say that here there are no walls where executions are committed and no Berlin wall, and any information in that sense is due to a political media compromised with ideas that have not and will not prosper in our country.

DIARIO OFICIAL (Mar. 14, 1975) (translation by author of this Article). Then, the Chief Justice discounted the fact that there were people missing in Chile, and went on to say that:

> [T]he Appellate Court in Santiago and the Supreme Court had both been pestered in their work by the numerous habeas corpus presented to them, on the pretexts of arrests ordered by the Executive. This has disrupted the work of the Courts, interfering with their duty to occupy themselves on the urgent matters of their jurisdiction.

Id.

42 REPORT, *supra* note 1, at 608. (Pinochet sent a letter dated November 11, 1975, to the Archbishop of Santiago, Cardinal Silva Henriquez, requesting the dissolution of the Comite Pro Paz and arguing it was an instrument for the Marxists).

well-reputed, conservative scholars accepted, including a former member of the Supreme Court and a former secretary of State of the Pinochet government.

The problem then became that of split votes. A dissenting opinion could deprive the report of all its value, or, even worse, two reports was a possible outcome. Fortunately, all the members became highly involved in the investigation of the cases. They personally heard many testimonies and checked the evidence. The final outcome was reached unanimously, and there is not a single dissenting opinion in the report.[43]

The report has not been recognized as the truth by the armed forces or the Supreme Court. Each branch of the armed forces answered the report separately and in quite different terms. The army, in a solemn act with Pinochet speaking, denied the truth of the Commission, arguing that it was partial (because not enough attention was paid to the state of war in the country), that it was unilateral (because it only considered the victim's version), and that it was biased (as an attack on the armed forces and their patriotic contribution to peace and order).[44] Yet, not one single case or fact was contested as being untrue. The critics could only single out some of the more general interpretations or recommendations established in the report. The facts remain uncontested, a point that the government strongly argued in response to the army's statement. As I will argue later, a positive recognition by the critics of the report would have been of enormous importance.

4. *An Official Truth*

An effort for an authoritative truth needed an official commission. It also was important that the commission be a state entity because of the political significance it represented. It was the same state that had violated human rights in the past and was now hearing the cases and gathering the information. This state role was especially important for the relatives of the victims. Although they have had access to nongovernmental organizations and international commissions and had received their support and comfort, the relatives pointed out that those were not official entities. As one relative said, "I don't want to have secret consultations any more."[45] The Chilean flag was at the entrance of our building and on top of every desk where a testimony was given. The same flag that was used so many times by the propaganda of the military was being recovered. It was a first reparation to their long standing feeling of

---

43 Not all the cases were solved unanimously. The differences were not important enough for the members to state them in the report.

44 The army, in its final declaration, stated its fundamental disagreement with the report of the Commission and denied its historical and legal value. *See* EL MERCURIO, Mar, 28, 1991. The navy said that the situation in Chile during the coup was that of a virtual civil war and denies the value of the report because of its procedures, saying that the Commission recognized that not all gave their version of what had happened. *Id*. For an answer of the police, see EL MERCURIO Mar. 29, 1991.

45 REPORT *supra* note 1, at 785.

marginality. "We feel like exiles in our own land,"[46] were the words used by one of them to express this common feeling.

5. Publicly Exposed

For all this effort to have some meaning, it was indispensable that the report be made public. Only one single copy of the report was released to the President, who read it during his summer vacations in 1991. He made the entire report public on March 4, 1991. It was fully published in a newspaper the very next day.[47] Many new reprints were made and sold in the streets during the next several months. Finally, a three volume book appeared in the bookstores. A private group of politicians, scholars, and people related to cultural activities edited a short summary of the report in order to make a public campaign for its acknowledgement and discussion. That very short summary was translated into English[48] and French. The Center for Civil and Human Rights at the Notre Dame Law School is currently translating the full report into English.

The collected records and data have been kept secret to this day. The Commission for Reconciliation, an institution recently established by law, will dispose of them.

Whether the Commission should have published the names of the individuals that had actually committed the violations of rights was a publicly discussed issue. The Commission understood that it could not do so. As a special entity different from a court, it was clear from the beginning that it lacked the authority to try the violators, a right that only the preestablished courts could perform.[49] Because a full trial with due guarantees was not conducted in every case, the Commission understood that it could not disclose names. Instead, the Commission stated in every conviction that public officials had intervened, and their membership is frequently identified as if they were part of a branch of the armed forces or of the secret police. The Commission also published the places where people were killed or tortured, but the names of violators were not publicly disclosed.[50]

6. Quick and, Thus, Limited

The official truth could not be delayed for too long, or both its importance and impact would have been severely diminished. The Commission was given six months to deliver its report, with a possible extension of three more months, which it used. In such a time period it

---

46 *Id.* at 780.

47 DIARIO LA NACION, Mar. 5, 1991.

48 CHILEAN HUMAN RIGHTS COMMISSION, TO BELIEVE IN CHILE (Jean Becker trans., 1992).

49 Decree No. 355 clearly states that it should not perform judicial functions. *See supra* note 17; *see also* CHILE CONST. art. 19, no. 3 (1980) (guaranteeing that nobody can be tried by special commissions, but only by courts created by law).

50 For a more complete explanation, see REPORT, *supra* note 1, at 28-30.

would have been impossible to issue a statement that addressed all the cases of human rights violations that had occurred in the country during seventeen years of military government. It would have been impossible, not only because of the number of cases, but it also would have been difficult to distinguish what should have been counted as a human rights violation. The President decided that the Commission should only investigate the cases resulting in the death or the disappearance of the victim, and those cases where the Commission concluded that the state was morally responsible because of the involvement of a public official or a person working for the government. The President also decided to include one other type of case: those killed for political reasons. This meant that the Commission also had to report the actions of the guerrilla and liberation movements responsible for someone's death.[51] This was criticized by some human rights scholars, who argued that considering political crimes not committed by the state as human rights violations on the same level as the others was a great mistake because it deprived the notion of violation of human rights of its force. The Commission was careful in saying that cases could not be compared and that they were different in many ways.[52] I would certainly argue today that it was politically important to include those cases.

In choosing only to investigate and disclose the truth about the people killed or missing, the government not only selected the most dramatic situations, but in so doing it also chose to focus on the truth that was more clearly denied by the human rights violators. Others, like exiles, restrictions on the press, and violations on socioeconomic rights, were not denied but excused as justified under the emergency conditions. Torture was also denied. Only because of time constraints could it be considered legitimate to leave the individual cases of torture aside. The report made an effort to generally describe the practice of torture and illustrated its explanations with some examples.[53] The report of the Commission only incidentally refers to those who lost their jobs for political reasons, suffered major physical or psychological injuries, had to go to exile, or were kept in prisons for long time without charges.

WHY THE TRUTH?

I will consider now the importance of publicly disclosing an official truth, and its impact on the goals of prevention, compensation, and reconciliation, the three issues considered by the democratic government as the basic moral obligations that it could not compromise. I will start by focusing on prevention and its relation to penal sanctions.

---

[51] *Id*. at 432-441, 602-06, 665-701.

[52] *Id*. at 17-19.

[53] For the concept of torture used by the Commission, see *id*. at 25. For a description of the practices of torture during the different periods, see *id*. at 111-14, 478-83, 651-53.

A. Truth and Prevention: Truth as a Lesser Alternative of Punishment

It is commonly accepted by legal doctrine that the goal of penal sanctions are retributive and preventive. The first is highly contested as a desirable end in society, while the second is generally accepted.

1. *Retribution*

The retributive function of penal sanctions is illustrated by the classic examples of Kant, in which he argues that criminals should even be punished by a society living on an island that decides to dissolve itself.[54] According to this theory, penal sanctions have a moral, autonomous, and obligatory character. When applying this theory to militarily imposed human rights violations, however, major problems arise. According to this theory, all wrongdoers should be punished. This would severely restrict the theory of due obedience to superior orders. This is not to claim that the theory is wrong or morally illegitimate. Yet, it illustrates the difficulties of fully complying with Kant's theory when there are political restrictions.[55] Moreover, even if one is not dealing with human rights violations during transitions to democracy, one would have to recognize that in any given system, only a minority of the crimes committed are actually punished by the state.

The only way that an outcome can be consistent with the goals that the retributive theory assigns to penal sanctions is obviously through judicial application of prison sentences. One cannot meet them through other ways, and the Chilean results could not be justified in these terms.

2. *Prevention*

Utilitarian arguments justifying criminal sanctions have normally considered its preventive character. This preventive character may be achieved because of the following: First, the society protects itself from the wrongdoers by keeping them in jail; second, it avoids future criminal actions committed by the wrongdoer through the threat that the actual sanction poses to him or her; third, it may rehabilitate the criminal through some kind of specialized treatment; fourth, potential, future wrongdoers may be persuaded not to act considering the costs they can be obliged to pay by way of the penal sanctions; and fifth, the criminal sanction reinforces the desired values in the general community.[56]

---

54 IMANUEL KANT, DIE METAPHYSIK DER SITTEN (F. Nicolovious Koenisberg ed., 1797).

55 An interesting analysis of this topic related to the Argentinean situation can be found in Luis Moreno Ocampo, Justicia y Derechos Humanos Balance y Futuro, C.E.D.E.S (1991) (unpublished paper, on file with author).

56 H.L.A. HART, PUNISHMENT AND RESPONSIBILITY (1968); JOSÉ ANTÓN ONECA, LA PREVENCIÓN GENERAL Y LA PREVENCIÓN ESPECIAL EN LA TEORÍA DE LA PENA (1945); SANTIAGO MIR PUIG, DERECHO PENAL, PARTE GENERAL (1984). For a more recent discussion about the role of criminal punishment in Latin America, see EUGENIO RAÚL ZAFFARONI, EN BUSCA DE LAS PENAS PERDIDAS (1989).

It can be argued that any of the first three reasons be convincing in dealing with human rights violations committed by a military regime. They are all reasons directed at preventing future crimes by the actual criminals that have already committed them. I will not argue that those who committed the human rights violations in Chile, and especially those who planned and directed them, have no personal responsibility in doing so. Yet, I would argue that if one accepts preventing criminals from future criminal actions as the goal of criminal punishment, then, sending human rights violators to a jail is not a very effective device. I think it is generally accepted that these people cannot be rehabilitated through special treatments. Their commitment to crime is largely due to ideological fanaticism. Nor is it convincing that their future criminal action would be dissuaded by their actual imprisonment. Except for very few cases, they will violate human rights again only if they recover political power. And under such conditions human rights violations would again be granted impunity. The preventive theory in this area is related not so much with the past wrongdoers, but with the conditions that made it possible. The two other arguments of the preventive theory are directed towards those conditions.

The last two reasons justifying the preventive theory of punishment—persuading potential criminals not to act and reinforcing the positive values in society—are, from my own perspective, the most important goals a democratic government must achieve when dealing with past human rights violations. I am convinced that one of the most important moral obligations of a government conducting a transition to democracy is to prevent future human rights violations. In order to do that, social repudiation of past human rights violations is of great importance. It sends a message to potential violators that the society grants no legitimacy to their actions and that it is willing to punish them.

The second reason, social reinforcement of the doctrine and the values of human rights, is probably the most effective way to prevent future violations. A culture that views such actions as highly illegitimate makes it less probable that any political actor in need of popular support would be tempted to violate them. If my argument is correct, then the most important justification for punishing human rights violators during a transition to a democracy is that the criminal sanction best expresses society's moral repudiation of the human rights violations. Punishment appears then as a means and not as an end in itself.

I would certainly argue that the criminal sanction is the best means, the best way to express and reinforce social repudiation. Full disclosure of the truth may be considered a second best option because it demonstrates the moral repudiation of the violations and helps society remember the facts.

But perhaps I passed too quickly through the issue of rehabilitating the criminal. There is a related problem in human rights violations, and it is of maximal importance. I refer to the task of destroying the organization that was built up for violating human rights. In the Chilean case, that organization was highly institutionalized and was transformed into a department of the army that today performs intelligence functions. Many, though not all, of the officers that were involved in human rights violations are now retired.

If one compares the situation of Chile with that of Argentina, some paradoxes exit. The Argentineans made an attempt to punish the human rights violators. Military intervention threatening democracy was successful enough to restrict punishment only to the most important political figures, who were afterwards pardoned. One could conclude that such a situation of partial justice was not unlike the Chilean situation by referring to the previously discussed goals of general prevention. But a great difference can be seen in the changes that the democratic rulers could make in the armed forces. As a faction of the Argentinean armed forces struggled violently in support of their former leaders, Alfonsin backed the loyal officers who were able to beat and retire the most radical officers. But, in order to gain such loyalty from the moderate militaries, the government had to guarantee them that its punishing policies would be restricted. Through such concessions, the government cleaned the army of its most dangerous people.[57]

Other means are especially relevant in this effort to prevent human rights violations, and the Commission addressed some of them: the approval of international covenants of human rights, the reinforcement of the internal legal system, and others. Two seemed especially important in the Chilean situation. The first was the reinforcement of the Chilean judiciary in its capacity to protect human rights. The report of the Commission extensively analyzes this fact.[58] Shortly after announcing the report, the President stated that many judges had lacked moral courage in dealing with human rights cases. The Supreme Court reacted very strongly to both the Commission's analysis and the President's statement.[59] A public discussion on the role of the judiciary followed, and a compromise is now being achieved among the political parties. Some changes will be made in the judicial structure to reinforce its accountability to the people and its modernization, while still protecting its independence.

Another preventive issue that the report addresses is the need to reinforce the values of human rights in the culture of the country. Some measures are now being undertaken to introduce the topic of human rights in the curriculum of elementary schools.[60]

---

57 *See* Acuña, *supra* note 4.

58 REPORT, *supra* note 1, at 843-52.

59 The Supreme Court strongly criticized the report stating that the Commission went beyond its mandate, that it unjustly criticized the role of the courts, and states that the judges went as far as the law permitted them in the protection of human rights. A complete version of the answer was published in EL MERCURIO, May 16, 1992.

60 There is a bill that has been enacted by the Education Department (Ministerio de Educacion), that must be approved by the Superior Council of Education (Consejo Superior de Educacion), called "Bill of Fundamental Objectives and Minimal Contents for the Elementary and High School Education." This bill establishes some minimal requisites that all schools must fulfill. Among other things, this bill requires that students be taught the importance of human rights.

B. Truth as a Starting Point for Reparation

As prevention of future human rights violations is a very important moral obligation in the type of situations on which I am focusing, another inescapable one is the need to compensate, to the extent that it is possible, the suffering of the people most severely affected. To comply with this obligation, the truth seems indispensable.

To be sure, full compensation for the suffering of the victims and their relatives is impossible, but that does not eliminate the obligation to do whatever is possible. It is also true that compensation should come directly from the wrongdoer. Although too long to argue, I would make the case that in situations of past human rights violations, an obligation arises for the state and for all of society to involve itself in that reparative process.

It became clear early to the members of the Commission that a full disclosure of the truth had enormous links with the beginning of a reparative process and in the way we came to understand it. The report frequently insists that a meaningful reparative process must express a recognition of the truth, both by the state and society. "The reparative process presupposes the courage to face the truth and to bring about justice: requires the generosity to recognize the responsibilities and the attitudes of pardon in order to achieve reconciliation."[61] It is the recognition of the truth that produces the three basic components of the compensatory process upon which the Commission focused. These components include the following: First, the disclosure of the truth and the end of secrecy as reparation; second, expressions signaling the recognition of the dignity of the victims and the pain of their relatives; and third, efforts to increase the quality of life of the relatives of the victims.

1. Truth as One of the Most Important Components of the Reparative Process

The suffering of the relatives of those killed and missing is the pain that anybody suffers when losing a beloved, yet it is much more. Among those considerations, violence and secrecy are of great relevance. As one relative stated:

> My mother died a year ago, and I told myself that she was finally at rest. My father died when I was young and I told myself that was going to make me mature and responsible. Concerning the unjust and inexplicable death of my husband, I can find no meaning.[62]

Another said, "I had to explain to my five year old son that as human beings destroyed the lives of the flowers and the animals, sometimes human beings killed human beings."[63] If those words, spoken to us by the relatives themselves may explain the extra suffering of violent crimes, the

---

[61] REPORT, *supra* note 1, at 824.

[62] *Id.* at 767.

[63] *Id.*

following may express the extra suffering because of secrecy: "I have been looking all around the world. I have lost all I have because of the false information that was given to us, all false. I need to rest and die peacefully. That is why I need to know what happened to my son."[64] As another stated, "Even if nothing else can be done, even if it may seem of no use, I need to know why they killed him, what happened, what was he doing, or how did they discover him. Anything that would bring my mind to rest."[65] Secrecy affects not only the people who need to know the truth about what happened, but it is also frustrates the need for social recognition. Other statements made by the relatives may explain this need. As one relative stated:

> I was taken prisoner in the same truck as my husband. His parents came to believe that I had denounced him. I could not enter into their house during seventeen years. I was left alone, hated by those who had killed him and scorned by those who loved him. What happened in this country that people can believe that a woman in love is capable of turning in her husband?[66]

The truth is especially indispensable in the reparative process of the relatives of those missing:

> Until recently we were expecting to find him alive. Today we are looking for his bones. This will never end ... this long nightmare, from which I don't know any more if I can awake because I forgot normal life... I need to know what happened to him.... Every time I eat good food, I ask myself if he is not hungry.[67]

As I said before, although some progress was made by the Commission, it was, to a large extent, incapable of finding this truth about the missing people.

2. *Recognition of the Dignity of the Victim and of Relatives' Claims*

Not only did the relatives have to suffer the loss and the secrecy, but they also had to suffer a long campaign where their relatives were treated as the worst criminals in the world. A newspaper tabloid entitled, "They killed themselves like rats do,"[68] explained that some people were killed by their comrades after there had been an armed struggle between factions of the extreme left. This version was then discovered to be a covert action of the Chilean secret police to explain the deaths of people they had previously arrested.[69] Again, some relatives said, "In the first meeting we

---

64 *Id.* at 771.
65 *Id.*
66 *Id.* at 777.
67 *Id.* at 771.
68 *Id.* at 482-84, 610.
69 *Id.*

had with the governor he told us that our husbands were criminals."[70] Still another relative stated, "The newspapers said that they were terrorists. With that, everybody justified their murders."[71] This propaganda affected all the population, especially the children: "In the school I was told, 'your father was killed because he was a politician.' We were called the small terrorists."[72] As one person stated, "This was like the plague, both relatives and friends turned their backs on us."[73]

Following the general proposals of the Commission, some, though few, symbolic acts have taken place both to remember the dignity of the victims and to keep the social memory of the facts.[74] The President made a solemn declaration of the dignity of the victims when he presented the report. Congress followed with similar acts. Artists have been working on symbols in the cemetery and in other places. Public parks have been proposed. A national symbol, like the impressive one that the United States has built to keep alive the memory of the Vietnam war and its casualties, is still lacking.

Not only a recognition of the facts and the victims is needed, the relatives also need the social recognition that the battle they have fought for many years was not a campaign of marxism but the expression of their deeper sentiments. For many years, they were told lies and the official version was not that they were fighting for truth and punishment, but that they were trying to subvert the political order. The country has also benefitted from recognizing the enormous signs of life, solidarity, and compassion that can be gained from examining the victims' organizations and movement.

3. *Compensating for the Quality of Life*

The Commission also recommended that measures be taken to compensate the relatives of the victims.[75] First, the Commission recognized that there were many unresolved legal problems for the families of those missing that the ordinary legislation could not adequately resolve. Second, the Commission proposed that the state freely provide physical and psychological treatment. As to the psychological effects on the families, much literature has been written, and I am no specialist in that field. One of the psychological effects that most impressed me while working in the Commission was the guilt that many spouses felt. There were no accepted norms of how to live in such situations. Some spouses felt that they had dedicated themselves "too much" to finding out about their spouses and felt guilty because they had abandoned their children who were also suffering.

---

70 *Id.* at 780.

71 *Id.*

72 *Id.*

73 *Id.*

74 Some actions have been taken to build a monument in the main graveyard of Santiago, in honor of all those who died as victims of human rights violations during the dictatorship.

75 REPORT, *supra* note 1, at 827-35.

On the other hand, spouses had moved away from their communities soon after their husband or wife had disappeared and had dedicated themselves to raising their children. These spouses were often viewed by themselves and their children as traitors of the memory of their spouses because they could have dedicated more time on behalf of the organization or trying to find their relatives.

Another component of reparation that the Commission proposed was to grant scholarships to the sons and daughters of the victims. The legislature recently approved such a measure. Finally, the Commission proposed that the state provide a pension for the relatives of those considered victims. A law was finally approved in February, 1992, granting state pensions to the parents, spouses, and young sons and daughters of those considered victims by the report.[76]

Although these social expressions of recognition have generally been accepted and welcomed by the relatives, they insist that justice should be achieved and that the truth about those missing is absolutely indispensable in bringing about reconciliation.[77]

C. Truth and Reconciliation

I will now turn my attention to a final and very important point. It focuses on the issue of reconciliation. The Commission was not only an entity created to disclose the truth, but it was also created to bring about reconciliation. Reconciliation was an extremely important moral goal of the transitional government.

The relation between truth and reconciliation is evident. I will only focus now on two components, or possible meanings of the word reconciliation. One is depolarization, and the other deals with the problematic issue of reconciling the people with their history.

1. Reconciliation as De-Polarization

One of the biggest problems that frequently faces a government during a period of transition to democracy is the one of a polarized society. To bring about peace is then a necessary goal of the new democratic government.

After the creation of the Commission, the military and the political right publicly stated their fears that the truth would open old wounds from the past that the country had successfully overcome, and that it was going to create again (and now artificially) a division among the Chileans. The government insisted that the truth was a moral obligation and that the old wounds were not healed but merely bandaged. Analogies to the situation of gangrene were frequently made.

---

76 DIARIO OFICIAL § 19.123 (1992).

77 *See* Sola Sierra, Speech as President of the Association of Relatives of the Disappeared Detainees (Jan. 1992).

Relatives and human rights groups recognized that the creation of the Commission was a good decision, a step in the right direction, though they claimed that justice was also necessary. They probably understood that the government could do no more at that moment, and their demands for more forceful steps were frozen. Viewing it from a political perspective, the creation of the Commission produced an important result. It postponed for a year a discussion that was viewed as highly dangerous for the stabilization of democracy. The democratic government had time to prove and reinforce its authority before facing one of its most difficult topics. Finally, the issue of the creation of the Commission dissolved itself in a way that will be analyzed later.

The truth brought some relief and moral compensation for the relatives of the victims. While insisting that it is not enough, they have frequently recognized the work and report of the Commission as being of enormous value. The relatives' strongest criticism of the Commission is, of course, the old, largely unanswered question of where are the missing?

If justice cannot be achieved, what else can be done? When delivering the report, President Aylwin, in a solemn and emotional moment of his speech, said with a broken voice, "That is why I endeavor, as the President of the Republic, to assume the representation of all the nation in order to, in its name, acknowledge accountability to the relatives of the victims."[78] He continued to "solemnly request the armed forces and all those who could have participated in the excesses committed, to make gestures of recognition of the suffering caused and to collaborate in diminishing it."[79] His statements were widely commented upon and they were followed by some similar words from leaders of the right-wing parties. The President's speech was a major sign of reconciliation.

The second request was not followed. Full recognition of the truth by the armed forces and some gestures to demonstrate this on their part would have made an enormous change in the situation and could have transformed a situation of impunity into a situation of pardon. As a mother of a victim once said, "I want to pardon; just tell me, whom should I pardon?" Even from a religious perspective, pardon requires the acknowledgement by and repentance of the wrongdoer. Armies, however, except when they are beaten, do not excuse themselves. The reaction of the Chilean armed forces, and especially the reaction of the army was not, unfortunately, an exception.

2. *Reconciling People with Their History: Accepting the Truth*

Finally, one can give another meaning to the word reconciliation. Men and women not only need to reconcile with each other, but they also need to reconcile themselves as a people. They need to reconcile their own history as a nation. History is their mirror and, in order to reconcile themselves, they first need to recognize themselves in that mirror.

---

78 EL MERCURIO, Mar. 5, 1991 (translated by the author of this Article).

79 *Id.*

The Chilean situation is difficult in this area. We like to see ourselves as a highly civilized nation. It is part of our national myth to call ourselves the "Englishmen of Latin America." We take pride in our history of democratic stability, and we used to love to make comparisons with other Latin-American countries that had a worse record than ours. Our national anthem names Chile as the asylum against oppression. Violence, torture, and massive human rights violations were reserved for those "banana republics," as we used to call them with arrogance.

Soon after the delivery of the report, politicians started discussing responsibilities for the crisis of the democratic government. Some talk addressed the issue of who was responsible for human rights violations. But the discussion about how Chileans involved themselves in sophisticated methods of torture, or how Chileans could hate each other so much that such massive and gross human rights violations could take place were never seriously addressed. Chileans could not handle facing for too long the worst part of our collective history, except at the superficial, political level. The introductory chapters of the report were widely discussed, but an explanation of the facts described there was never seriously attempted.

Perhaps it is too early to expect such a collective reaction. The time for the artists and the psychiatrists' explanations will come. Perhaps the report came too late. The country had already known about the horrors by rumors and partial stories when nothing or very little could have been done and when the only way to stay alive was to continue minding your own business, while acknowledging that something was happening to somebody else.

A month after the report was made public and the media and public opinion had focused widely upon it, somebody killed one of the most influential young leaders of the right, Senator Jaime Guzman. Attention shifted from the "past" to the dangers of the future. Political violence and delinquency became the new issues. As one politician said, the report of the Commission was buried with Jaime Guzman. Yet, the report remains as a testimony of horror.

To be sure, not wanting to face and discuss the issue any more is not a frivolous reaction. It comes from a people who can no longer suffer from the stories of horror that they have finally come to believe. Yet, the question remains whether the country has looked at these horrors enough to build a sufficiently strong cultural barrier against the possibility of that happening again.

Perspective of José Zalaquett

[Editor's note: In the excerpt which follows, José Zalaquett, a Chilean lawyer and human rights activist who served as one of the eight members of the National Commission on Truth and Reconciliation, provides an additional perspective on the manner in which Chile has addressed the issue of transitional justice. An article presenting Zalaquett's general views on how countries deal with this issue appears in Volume One of the present collection.]

*José Zalaquett, "Balancing Ethical Imperatives and Political Constraints: The Dilemma of New Democracies Confronting Past Human Rights Violations"**

With the inauguration of President Aylwin in March of 1990, Chile became the last of the Southern Cone countries ruled by similarly minded military dictatorships to achieve a restoration of democratic government. This dubious privilege afforded Chilean politicians the possibility of learning from the example of Chile's neighbors as well as from the world events of the late 1980s. Though it is too early to determine whether those lessons were put to the best use, the Chilean government has certainly tried to be guided by the ethics of responsibility, so far with promising results.

Unlike Argentina, the transition to democracy in Chile took place after the new government negotiated rules of the game with a united, undefeated military that continued to enjoy considerable, albeit minority, political support. Despite this difference, the Argentinean case was telling for Chileans. It proved the importance of a systematic effort to reveal the truth. It also showed the extent to which a government can lose authority when it raises expectations it cannot fulfill.

Uruguay also provided an example for Chile in that the transition there was made under conditions similar to those present in Chile. But in Uruguay the government took too cautious an approach, avoiding not only trials for past state crimes but also any significant official disclosure about past violations. Citizens' opposition to this approach led to a nationwide campaign to collect signatures. The campaign succeeded in fulfilling the constitutional prerequisites for a plebiscite on whether to keep or repeal the legislation that granted impunity. The majority ultimately voted to keep it, but the issue was very divisive and distracted the nation's attention during the crucial first period of democratic restoration.

Taking these lessons into account, the Aylwin government decided to follow a course it could sustain. It adopted the guiding principle that reparation and prevention must be the overall objectives of the policies regarding past human rights violations. Righting a wrong and resolving not

---

* Excerpted from José Zalaquett, "Balancing Ethical Imperatives and Political Constraints: The Dilemma of New Democracies Confronting Past Human Rights Violations," *Hastings Law Journal*, vol. 43, no. 6 (1992), pp. 1432-1433, 1435-1438.

to do it again is, at its core, the same philosophy that underpins Judeo-Christian beliefs about atonement, penance, forgiveness, and reconciliation.

At a societal level, the equivalent of penance is criminal justice. Yet the Chilean government's assessment of the situation led it to conclude that priority ought to be given to disclosure of the truth. This disclosure was deemed an inescapable imperative. Justice would not be foregone, but pursued to the extent possible given the existing political restraints. Forms of justice other than prosecuting the crimes of the past, such as vindicating the victims and compensating their families, could be achieved more fully. The underlying assumption, which I share, was that if Chile gave truth and justice equal priority, the result might well have been that neither could be achieved. Fearing that official efforts to establish the truth would be the first step toward widespread prosecutions, the military would have determinedly opposed such efforts.

Truth was considered an absolute, unrenounceable value for many reasons. To provide for measures of reparation and prevention, it must be clearly known what should be repaired and prevented. Further, society cannot simply black out a chapter of its history; it cannot deny the facts of its past, however differently these may be interpreted. Inevitably, the void would be filled with lies or with conflicting, confusing versions of the past. A nation's unity depends on a shared identity, which in turn depends largely on a shared memory. The truth also brings a measure of healthy social catharsis and helps to prevent the past from reoccurring.

Bringing the facts to light is also, to some extent, a form of punishment, albeit mild, in that it provokes social censure against the perpetrators or the institutions or groups to which they belonged. Although the truth cannot in itself dispense justice, it does put an end to many a continued injustice. It does not bring the dead back to life, but it brings them out from silence. For the families of the "disappeared," the truth about their fate would mean the end to an anguishing, endless search.

For the truth to achieve these purposes, it must be established as solemnly and officially as possible and in a manner that is widely recognized as objective and rigorous. It must cover all the relevant facts about which there is doubt, dispute, or public disbelief. It must also expose all antecedents and circumstances that are necessary to understand why and how the past came to happen.

To establish the truth, President Aylwin appointed the National Commission for Truth and Reconciliation, a panel of eight people from across the political spectrum. Apart from guaranteeing widespread credibility, the even number of members sent a signal, which did not escape political observers, that no precautions were being taken to secure a majority vote in case of divided opinions, that the exercise was done in good faith, and that the matter was too important to be treated in a partisan manner....

The report of the Commission for Truth and Reconciliation was published and widely disseminated and discussed in Chile. Congress [adopted] a bill to provide reparations for the victims' families and to put into effect many of the commission's other recommendations.[5] Controversy about the report, including rebuttals by General Pinochet and by the head of the navy, centered mainly on its historical interpretations and other contextual references. None of the report's findings about individual victims has been refuted. Across the political spectrum, those findings were explicitly recognized as the truth.

The report had self-imposed limits. It did not name individual culprits. But it did declare whether the victimizer in a given case had been an agent of the state or a member of an opposition group. It also identified the military branch and unit or the political group responsible for the crime, but referred to the courts of law all specific evidence pointing to the criminal responsibility of particular individuals. Naming culprits through an official commission appointed by the executive, which did not have subpoena powers and could not conduct trials, would have been analogous to publicly indicting individuals without due process. The commission declared that the "disappeared" were dead, but because of its lack of subpoena powers it could provide specific information about the remains of the "disappeared" in only a minority of cases. The commission proposed that an agency be created to assist the relatives of the "disappeared" in their search.[6]

The overall policy of the Chilean government has other limitations. Prosecutions have been drastically curtailed by an amnesty law passed by the military regime in 1978 that effectively decreed impunity for human rights violations committed from 1973, the time of the coup d'etat, to 1978. This was the worst period, when repression was under the control of DINA, the regime's feared secret police which systematically practiced "disappearances." The Supreme Court has upheld the validity of this illegitimate amnesty. One major crime, however, was exempted from the amnesty: the assassination of Orlando Letelier, a former Chilean ambassador to the United States, and his colleague Ronni Moffitt, a United States citizen, in the streets of Washington, D.C. in September 1976, when a bomb placed under Letelier's car was activated....

The Chilean tribunals are also conducting investigations of crimes committed after the time period covered by the 1978 amnesty law. However, in most cases evidence is difficult to obtain without cooperation by the armed forces and the police.

Legal restrictions have also prevented the government from releasing all the prisoners who are being tried or have been found guilty of murder or other politically motivated crimes committed during the military regime. These prisoners have not received fair trials and most, if not all, were subjected to torture during the investigations. They have also been detained for years. The president pardoned many, but his powers in this respect are limited. While the Aylwin government does not have the votes needed to pass legislation without compromises, Congress did approve legislation

---

5 This bill ... was published on February 8, 1992 as Law No. 19,123 in Chile's Diano Oficial [Official Gazette].

6 Law No. 19,123, *supra* note 5, created this agency.

that contributed to the release of many others. By now a large majority of them are out of prison. However, nineteen months after the restoration of democracy in Chile, about eighty still remain in prison.

In an imperfect way, Chile has been earnestly searching for the most feasible course of action to heal the wounds of the past. With the benefit of hindsight, some things could have been done differently. Perhaps others may avoid our mistakes. However, this responsible approach has also produced important salutary results.

In concluding, allow me to offer some very personal recollections and reflections. I had the privilege of serving as one of the members of the Commission for Truth and Reconciliation. I traveled through Chile. I heard hundreds of cases. The contact with so many families of victims convinced me of the paramount importance and cathartic power of seeking to establish the truth. It was a very personal experience to ask what happened to the victims' families, and not just what happened to the victims. The families had refused to allow the previous government authorities to see them cry as they searched for their loved ones. But now they were being received with respect and offered a seat and a cup of coffee. The Chilean flag was on the desk as befits an official commission. They often broke down, because now they could allow themselves that measure of relief. At first, we did not realize that the very process of seeking the truth was thus also a patient process of cleansing wounds, one by one.

The relatives of the victims showed great generosity. Of course, many of them asked for justice. Hardly anyone, however, showed a desire for vengeance. Most of them stressed that in the end, what really mattered to them was that the truth be revealed, that the memory of their loved ones not be denigrated or forgotten, and that such things never happen again.

For me, as for many of my friends and colleagues in the human rights movement in Chile, an eighteen-year period is coming to a close. It began the moment we started to organize the defense of human rights in Chile after the coup d'etat of September 1973, and has continued through our present efforts to overcome this dark chapter in our country's history. During this period the human rights movement has grown strong. Major changes have occurred in Chile and in the world. We have learned from them.

Of the many lessons learned, I will refer to one. Back in the hazardous days of late 1973, all of my friends and colleagues in the human rights movement had to face danger on a daily basis. None of them ever claimed to have been endowed with innate bravery. They realized that courage was just another name for learning how to live with your fears. Eighteen years later, we all have come to realize that under changed circumstances, a less striking form of courage is called for. It is the courage to forgo easy righteousness, to learn how to live with real-life restrictions, but to seek nevertheless to advance one's most cherished values day by day to the extent possible. Relentlessly. Responsibly.

PROBLEMS OF PROSECUTION

*Americas Watch, "Human Rights and the 'Politics of Agreements:' Chile during President Aylwin's First Year"**

The issue of jurisdiction affects accountability in cases of past human rights abuse. Military court jurisdiction was expanded by the Pinochet regime to cover most criminal acts committed by uniformed personnel. Article 5(3) of the Code of Military Justice defines military jurisdiction as covering

> proceedings for common crimes committed by military personnel during time of war, being in the field, in an act of military service or occasioned by such service, in the barracks, camps, bivouacs, forts, military works, stores, offices, premises, foundries, workshops, factories, parks, academies, schools, vessels, arsenals, lighthouses and other military or police establishments or premises of the armed forces.[67]

When the armed forces wish to contest civilian jurisdiction, the Military Prosecutor General argues that the crime involves military personnel and took place in military or police quarters of some kind.... In the Aylwin government's first year, as in the years of the dictatorship, human rights cases continued to pass to military jurisdiction once military personnel were indicted—or once it was alleged that those responsible for the crime were members of the military; that is, the Supreme Court continued to approve military demands for the transfer of human rights cases, and often it was not even necessary to have reached the stage of formal indictment. For example, after the Pisagua grave was uncovered in June 1990, victims' relatives launched a criminal case for illegal burial.[69] In August, just two months after the 19 corpses had been unearthed, and before key military figures had been questioned and all remains identified, the Military Prosecutor General demanded jurisdiction. Though no one had been indicted as yet, the military argued that the location of the grave suggested army involvement in the events being investigated; Pisagua, as an army camp, fell within the scope of the relevant law. The Supreme Court accepted this argument, as it had so regularly in the past, and almost immediately after transferral, a military judge closed the case....

---

* Excerpted from Americas Watch, *Human Rights and the "Politics of Agreements:" Chile during President Aylwin's First Year* (Human Rights Watch, 1991), pp. 40-44, 50-52.

67 In 1984, Law No. 18,342, which amended the Code of Military Justice, the State Security Law and the Arms Control Law, expanded military jurisdiction to include the phrase "military or police premises." The law then defined such premises as "any duly delimited space, vehicle, vessel or aircraft in which a military or police authority performs his specific functions." *See Ibid.*, p. 182.

69 ...The relatives focused their case on the burials because earlier cases, seeking to investigate the executions themselves, had already been closed by virtue of the 1978 amnesty, described below.

The 1978 Amnesty Law

For the first eight and a half years of the military regime, legislation was enacted by decree of the Government Junta. Thus, the amnesty that became law on April 18, 1978 was a decree-law. It covered criminal acts—implicitly including disappearances, extrajudicial executions and torture—committed by uniformed agents between the date of the coup and March 10, 1978. Decree Law 2,191 reads, in pertinent part, as follows:

> The Government Junta has agreed to dictate the following:
>
> Article 1: that an amnesty be extended to all persons who, as principals or accessories, have committed criminal offenses during the period of state of siege, between 11 September 1973 and 10 March 1978, unless they are currently on trial or have been convicted.

Article 2 applies the amnesty also to those convicted by military tribunals before March 10, 1978. By including this provision the military could appear to be benefiting both sides equally, and the regime accordingly released several hundred persons imprisoned without trial. Article 3 lists common–crime exceptions to the amnesty's application, not including homicide, kidnapping or assault, and Article 4 makes a special exception of anyone involved in the assassination of former Defense Minister Orlando Letelier.[72]

The Supreme Court's current posture on the amnesty law dates from 1986. A case involving the disappearance of 13 Communist leaders was being investigated thoroughly by the Appeals Court judge assigned to it, and in August 1986, that judge, Carlos Cerda Fernández, indicted 38 retired and active-duty military officers and two civilian collaborators. When a group of the accused contested the indictment, the Appeals Court ruled that, under the 1978 amnesty, they were relieved of criminal liability even before being found guilty. A month later the Supreme Court—which earlier had supported Cerda's investigation—ordered it closed in accordance with the Appeals Court ruling. Since then, the Supreme Court has permitted the military courts to apply the amnesty to close cases prior to full investigation. Typically, execution and disappearance cases from the years before 1978, which are the vast majority of human rights cases before the courts, have been closed without indictments by the *Corte Marcial* by virtue of the amnesty, and the Supreme Court has rejected *recursos de queja* that challenge the *Corte Marcial's* position. In a few cases, the Supreme Court has explicitly ratified the amnesty's preindictment application....

---

72 [omitted]

Government Position on the Amnesty Law

In its 1989 campaign document, "Platform of Government," the multiparty coalition led by Patricio Aylwin committed itself, once in power, to "seek the repeal or annulment of the Decree Law on amnesty." The [coalition] pledged that the amnesty law "will not be able to impede the establishment of the truth, the investigation of the facts and the determination of penal responsibilities and consequent sanctions in cases of crimes against human rights, such as detentions followed by disappearances, crimes against life and the gravest physical or psychological damage."[82]

In practice, given the makeup of Congress, the government has been able only to establish a generic truth. The permanence of the amnesty law is taken as a matter of fact, because the legislative leverage of the Right makes annulment a close call in the Senate—and because legislators fear confrontation with the armed forces. Proposals to annul or limit the law have not prospered even in the Chamber of Deputies.

At various moments, there has been discussion of the government's becoming a party to human rights cases subject to amnesty, like the cases arising from the discoveries of clandestine mass graves in 1990, but to date the government has decided against this. Nor did the Truth and Reconciliation Commission confront the amnesty law head on. Despite the fact that such a law is manifestly illegitimate under international instruments to which the Rettig report makes reference, and despite the report's insistence that the law not be used to impede investigation, the Commission did not go so far as to suggest annulling the amnesty as one of its reparatory recommendations.

President Aylwin, in presenting the Rettig report to the nation on March 4, 1991, challenged the Supreme Court to change its position on applying the amnesty:

> Today, I have sent the Supreme Court a message to which I have attached the text of the Report and I ask that ... they instruct the relevant courts to activate with greatest expediency the cases which are pending on human rights violations and those which must be heard as a result of the information that the Truth and Reconciliation Commission has forwarded to them; informing it [the Supreme Court] that in my view, the amnesty in force, which the Government respects, cannot be an obstacle to the realization of a judicial investigation and the determination of responsibilities, especially in the cases of disappeared persons.[83]

This gesture was popular: a poll released in late March, gauging public perceptions after the Rettig report, showed that 72% of respondents felt the judiciary had performed poorly during the military regime, and that 57% believed that the judiciary bore major responsibility for past human

---

82 Quoted in Americas Watch, *Chile in Transition, op. cit.*, p. 82. Translation from the original document by Americas Watch.

83 Full text of speech reprinted in *El Mercurio*, March 5, 1991.

rights violations.[84] Aylwin's critique was also consistent with the government's insistence that the courts be the final arbiter in human rights cases. And the President went farther than many observers expected him to go, defining the issues not on the basis of expediency or prudence but on the basis of principle.

At this writing, the full Supreme Court has not yet considered an amnestied case since the President's speech. It has answered the President's message, however, with an instruction to the lower courts to pursue the cases forwarded to them, reopening those which have been closed. There are indications that lower-court judges are taking advantage of this permission to pursue investigations more aggressively than in the past.

THE REPARATIONS PROGRAM

Cecilia Medina Quiroga, "The Experience of Chile"[*]

The [report of the Retting] Commission states that under "redress" (*reparación*) it understands a set of measures to express the acknowledgement of the state's responsibility in the events described in its Report.[11] Because of the peculiar nature of the damages brought about by the violations, the Commission correctly envisages three categories of reparation: one is a symbolic reparation to vindicate the victims;[12] a second one is legal and administrative measures to solve several problems of that nature (such as the legal status of wives or husbands of the disappeared, inheritance, legal representation for minors); and the third is financial reparation, under which social benefits are envisaged, health care (particularly psychological assistance), and financial support for education. A measure that stands on its own as a reflection of the dramatic events in Chile is to exempt from mandatory conscription the sons of the victims of the human rights violations investigated in the Report, in order to spare them further suffering....

---

[84] Poll by Centro de Estudios de la Realidad Contemporeanea (CERC), released March 25, 1991, as reported in *La Epoca*, March 26, 1991. As to who bore important responsibility for human rights violations, the largest group, 76%, answered DINA; the Army came next with 75.3%; and Pinochet next with 71.5%; the judiciary was fourth, followed by the other armed and police services and the ultra–left.

[*] Excerpted from Cecilia Medina Quiroga, "The Experience of Chile," in Theo van Boven, Cees Flinterman, Fred Grünfeld and Ingrid Westendorp, eds., *Seminar on the Right to Restitution, Compensation and Rehabilitation for Victims of Gross Violations of Human Rights and Fundamental Freedoms* (Netherlands Institute of Human Rights, 1992), pp. 108-111.

[11] *Ibidem*, p. 823.

[12] With respect to symbolic reparation, the Commission suggests various forms to publicly restore the dignity of the victims, such as a monument or a park, and also the promotion of human rights by organizing campaigns or giving due importance to December 10, turning it into the National Day for Human Rights. It also recommends that the state, by an act of Congress or a proper law solemnly restores the dignity of the victims, who had been accused of crimes without ever having had the opportunity of defending themselves.

The National Corporation for Reparation and Reconciliation

1. Following the Report of the National Commission for Truth and Reconciliation, the Government introduced a new bill to Congress establishing various provisions to implement the measures recommended by the Commission, among which, the creation of a new organ to continue its work. The bill was approved by Congress and was promulgated by the Government on 31 January, 1991, becoming Law No. 19.123, published in the Official Gazette of 8 February, 1992. Article 1 of the law establishes a National Corporation for Reparation and Reconciliation as a temporary[15] decentralized state organ, under the supervision of the Ministry of Interior, whose task will be the coordination, execution and promotion of all necessary actions to carry out the recommendations made in the Report of the National Commission for Truth and Reconciliation (Article 1). The Corporation will have a small staff and will be financed by the state and by donations made by national or foreign entities (Articles 11 and 14).

2. Two specific tasks of the Corporation seem crucial for achieving reconciliation, since they constitute the very minimum which the relatives of the victims are willing to accept, and are, in my opinion, an essential part of the state's obligation to redress past violations. One is that the Corporation is directed to promote and contribute to actions leading to the discovery of the whereabouts of those who disappeared after arrest and of those whose bodies have not been found, although they have been legally recognized as dead (Article 2.2). The second is the investigation of the cases in which the Commission was not able to affirm that there were victims of human rights violations and of new cases not handled by the Commission or on which it did not make any pronouncement (Article 2.4). The Government and Congress seem to have understood the importance of this type of reparation, since Article 6 of the law declares that this right is an inalienable right of the relatives of the victims as well as of Chilean society. Following the trend started with the Commission, Article 4 of the law sets forth that the corporation may not pronounce on the responsibility of individuals in connection with the crime it investigates, but has to send all the information to the ordinary courts, adding that the activities of the Corporation have to be carried out confidentially. The law sets forth a 90-day term counted from the moment the respective Regulations are published in the Official Gazette for people to request the investigation of new cases (Article 2.4).

3. With regard to reparation, the law does not spell out all the suggestions made by the Commission, concentrating in setting forth in detail only financial reparation. Other measures are left to the Corporation's initiative, as the aim of the Corporation is to coordinate, execute and

---

15 The corporation is supposed to be dissolved after 24 months, or before if its tasks are fulfilled. It is possible to further its existence for 12 more months (Article 16).

promote the necessary actions to carry out the recommendations in the Commission's Report (Art. 1).[16]

Financial Reparation

Cecilia Medina Quiroga, "The Experience of Chile"[*]

The Commission recommended the state to compensate relatives of victims, considering that the patrimonial and psychological effects of having looked for the victims for so many years had to be redressed with money and other types of financial support.[17] It suggested that this support should be discussed with the beneficiaries, since they knew better than anyone which were their most urgent needs and which was the best way to meet them; it also pleaded for a quick and efficient solution, since problems had accumulated for many years and were an obstacle to the families' reincorporation into Chilean society. Finally the Commission acknowledged that many of the individuals who were killed or disappeared might have given cause for social benefits which their relatives had never received or had received only partially. The [complexity that would have been required by an individualized approach] spoke against this sort of solution for the relatives of the victims and, consequently, the Commission deemed it convenient to grant an equal compensation to all beneficiaries without regard to their different social, economic and cultural circumstances. Furthermore, the Commission recommended to make of the compensation not a circumstantial but a permanent redress, that is to say, that the compensation ensure a process aimed a improving the quality of their lives and at giving them more dignity....

Following the Report's recommendations, the law sets forth the details of the compensation that the state is to grant these individuals.

The law considers that all victims identified as such in the Report of the National Commission for Truth and Reconciliation and those declared as victims by the Corporation itself will give cause for financial reparation (Articles 17 and 18). Entitled to request the reparation are the following relatives of the victims: surviving spouse; mother, or father in the mother's absence; and children under 25 years of age or handicapped children of any age (Article 20). The law established the proportion in which concurring petitioners will enjoy the financial reparation (Article 20).... Children, except those handicapped, will have a right to the monthly pension until they reach 25 years of age. For the rest of the beneficiaries, the pension is for life (Article 22).

---

16 The only measure set forth in the law is a provision to exempt the children of the victims from mandatory military service (Article 32).

* Excerpted from Cecilia Medina Quiroga, "The Experience of Chile," in Theo van Boven, Cees Flinterman, Fred Grünfeld and Ingrid Westendorp, eds., *Seminar on the Right to Restitution, Compensation and Rehabilitation for Victims of Gross Violations of Human Rights and Fundamental Freedoms* (Netherlands Institute of Human Rights, 1992), pp. 111-112.

17 *Informe Rettig, supra* note 2, pp. 828.

*Alejandro González, "Treatment of Victims and of their Families: Rehabilitation, Reparation and Medical Treatment"**

With respect to annuities, the law fixed a monthly compensation to the families of victims, of up to Ch$ 140,000 (roughly US$ 370) to be periodically adjusted according to the general norms of readjustment of social security benefits, and was distributed in the following way:

—40% to the surviving spouse (Ch$ 56,000 = roughly 150 US$);

—30% to the mother of the victim, or in her absence to the father
(Ch$ 42,000 = roughly 110 US$);

—15% to the mother or the father of any natural children of the person in question (Ch$ 21,000 = roughly 55 US$);

—15% to each child of the person in question up to 25 years of age but without limit of age if incapacitated (Ch$ 21,000 = roughly 55 US$). If there is more than one child, all and each one will receive 15% unless this exceeds the global amount of compensation.

If one or more of these beneficiaries does not exist, or dies, or voluntarily forgoes the compensation, his or her quota will devolve to that of the remaining beneficiaries, *pro rata* of their rights. If only one single beneficiary exists or is found, monthly compensation will be Ch$ 100,000 (roughly 263 US$).

Although the law was promulgated on 8 February 1992, compensation to the beneficiaries of those causes qualified by the National Commission for Truth and Reconciliation were drawn with retroactive effect from 1 July 1991. To the beneficiaries of causes designated in the future by the National Corporation for Reparation and Reconciliation, compensations will be drawn from the date when the Superior Council of the Corporation accords the relevant verdict.

In addition, the designated beneficiaries collect one [lump sum] compensatory allowance equivalent to 12 months of their rightful annuity.

Neither the annuity nor the compensatory allowance is subject to a rebatement or to any [taxes] and the allowance is not considered as income for any legal purpose....

---

* Excerpted from Alejandro González, "Treatment of Victims and of their Families: Rehabilitation, Reparation and Medical Treatment," in *International Commission of Jurists, Justice Not Impunity*, from the International Meeting on Impunity of Perpetrators of Gross Human Rights Violations, November 2-5, 1992, Geneva (International Commission of Jurists, 1993), pp. 330-332.

Finally, the annuities are compatible with any other, of whatever nature, enjoyed by or which could agree with the respective beneficiary, and with any other social security benefit fixed by the law.

Up until September [1992], monthly annuities were collected by 4,505 beneficiaries with respect to victims who did not survive human rights violations or political violence, accredited by the National Commission for Truth and Reconciliation with the following parenthood:

—children of victims less than 25 years of age or any age and incapacitated:	1,867(41.44%)
—spouses of spouses by common law (fathers or mothers of natural or illegitimate children):	1,300(28.86%)
—mothers or fathers of victims:	1,338(29.70%)

The figure for annuity beneficiaries just quoted should increase with the families of victims already designated by the Commission for Truth and Reconciliation whose recognition of the right to annuities is in progress and with those of persons designated in the future by the National Corporation for Reparation and Reconciliation as victims of human rights violations or political violence. It is estimated that the final figure of beneficiaries of these compensations will come to about 8,000 people.

The fiscal outlay for this cause for the year 1992 will amount to 8,200 million pesos (some 22 million US$).

Health Benefits

*Cecilia Medina Quiroga, "The Experience of Chile"**

Special attention is given to health and educational benefits, as recommended by the Commission. As to health benefits, the law grants the right to receive free medical assistance from all institutions of the National System for Health Services, and allows the Health Ministry to set up a special form of assistance for parents, children and [siblings] of the victims (Article 28). Actually, the Government did not wait for the law to be approved to start this type of special assistance.

---

* Excerpted from Cecilia Medina Quiroga, "The Experience of Chile," in Theo van Boven, Cees Flinterman, Fred Grünfeld and Ingrid Westendorp, eds., *Seminar on the Right to Restitution, Compensation and Rehabilitation for Victims of Gross Violations of Human Rights and Fundamental Freedoms* (Netherlands Institute of Human Rights, 1992), p. 113.

*Alejandro González, "Treatment of Victims and of their Families: Rehabilitation, Reparation and Medical Treatment"**

[A]nticipating the promulgation of the law, in 1991 the Ministry of Health established the Programme of Reparation and Integral Health Care,... which covered those affected by human rights violations for general medical care, social services, health check-ups, individual and family psychological attention, consultations with specialists and laboratory tests, all free except when the beneficiaries count on some other security system, in which case they must use the latter.

Up until the present, this Programme has established eleven multiprofessional teams in different cities of the country, from Iquique in the north to Punta Arenas in the south, offering general medical and mental health care. By June of the current year (1992), the number of patients who had been brought to its specialized and systematic attention reached 5,007, to whom should be added those the Programme teams have directed to the Service of Health for immediate care.

The cover[age] given by this Programme is significantly greater than that of the [compensation or education reparations], inasmuch as its benefits are extended to the relatives of detainees who disappeared and politicians who were executed, to families in which one member had lived through a traumatic situation of detention and torture, and to exiles who had returned.

Educational Benefits

Cecilia Medina Quiroga, "The Experience of Chile"†

With regard to education, and due to the fact that many of the victims' children are currently adults who were minors when their father or mother was killed or disappeared, the law grants the benefits to people up to 35 years of age (Article 29). The benefits consist of a scholarship to pay for registration fees and tuition fees (Article 30), plus a monthly subsidy to help them pay for their daily expenses (Article 31). Here again, the Government ... started to grant benefits without awaiting the approval of the law. Since mid-1991, the Ministry of Education is paying university fees and scholarships to children of the disappeared and of those executed during the Pinochet regime, using mechanisms which were already in operation, such as the President of the Republic scholarships.

---

* Excerpted from Alejandro González, "Treatment of Victims and of their Families: Rehabilitation, Reparation and Medical Treatment," in *International Commission of Jurists, Justice Not Impunity*, from the International Meeting on Impunity of Perpetrators of Gross Human Rights Violations, November 2-5, 1992, Geneva (International Commission of Jurists, 1993), p. 333.

† Excerpted from Cecilia Medina Quiroga, "The Experience of Chile," in Theo van Boven, Cees Flinterman, Fred Grünfeld and Ingrid Westendorp, eds., *Seminar on the Right to Restitution, Compensation and Rehabilitation for Victims of Gross Violations of Human Rights and Fundamental Freedoms* (Netherlands Institute of Human Rights, 1992), p. 113.

*Alejandro González, "Treatment of Victims and of their Families: Rehabilitation, Reparation and Medical Treatment"**

In the first six months of the school year (March-August), monthly subsidies were paid off to 782 students at different levels of education, with a fiscal layout of Ch$ 87,218,794 and an estimated annual cost for this benefit reaching to 150 million pesos (roughly 400,000 US$).

As to the payment of matriculation and tariff to students of higher education, in 1992 it had benefited approximately 560 students, with an annual cost of around 215.5 million pesos (575,000) US$).

Reparation for Remaining Political Prisoners

Cecilia Medina Quiroga, "The Experience of Chile"†

1. Although the violation of due process, torture and arbitrary arrest was not included as a "serious human rights violation" in the Supreme Decree which created the National Commission for Truth and Reconciliation, the Government felt that political prisoners who had suffered these violations had to be helped in some way. When President Aylwin took office, there were around 400 political prisoners, and many more defendants who had been released on bail. As a first measure, the Government decided to press for an amendment of Article 9 of the 1980 Constitution, which forbade amnesties, pardons and release on bail for those who were ... charged under the Law on Terrorism. Its effort succeeded and Law 19.055 of 1 April, 1991 amended the pertinent constitutional provision allowing the President of the Republic to grant pardons and amnesties in this type of crime. The President has used this power whenever conditions made it possible.

2. A second action was the introduction by the Government of three bills to amend several laws in order to better guarantee human rights.[18] The issue of political prisoners was particularly addressed in transitional provisions in Law 19.047, the first of which directs the military judges and military courts to transfer many of the trials [of political prisoners] under their consideration to ordinary criminal courts (Articles 1 and 2). Around 2000 dossiers have already been transferred, either to criminal judges or to

---

* Excerpted from Alejandro González, "Treatment of Victims and of their Families: Rehabilitation, Reparation and Medical Treatment," in *International Commission of Jurists, Justice Not Impunity*, from the International Meeting on Impunity of Perpetrators of Gross Human Rights Violations, November 2-5, 1992, Geneva (International Commission of Jurists, 1993), p. 334.

† Excerpted from Cecilia Medina Quiroga, "The Experience of Chile," in Theo van Boven, Cees Flinterman, Fred Grünfeld and Ingrid Westendorp, eds., *Seminar on the Right to Restitution, Compensation and Rehabilitation for Victims of Gross Violations of Human Rights and Fundamental Freedoms* (Netherlands Institute of Human Rights, 1992), pp. 113-115.

18 The bills were passed by Congress becoming Law No. 19.027, of 24 January 1991 which modifies Law 18.314 on Terrorism; Law 19.029 of 23 January 1991, which suppresses the death penalty in several crimes; and Law 19.047, of 14 February 1991, modifying Law 12.927 on State Security, the Code of Military Justice, Law 17.798 on Arms Control, the Penal Code, and the Code of Criminal Procedure.

a member of the Court of Appeals. Another provision sets forth that the defendants may request from the ordinary judges handling these trials admission of a new declaration about their participation in the events which prompted the trials, enabling the judges to ponder the new declaration in accordance [with] the provisions established for ordinary crimes, leaving thus some procedural room to the judges not to take into account the first confession, if they come to the conclusion that it was given under duress (Article 3). The law also allows the judge to open a new period to receive evidence (Article 4), seeing that most of the trials were carried out without regard to due process. It is encouraging to see that part of the political opposition was willing to go along with these governmental proposals. This in itself is an acknowledgement that gross violations of several human rights were perpetrated by the military judges and courts.

3. The reduction of some penalties, the redefinition of some crimes and the possibility for a defendant to be released on bail—all as a result of the laws enacted at the proposal of the Government—have had a very positive impact on political prisoners. There are at the moment only around 50 of them, with pending trials. Once a judgment has been passed, they may be eligible for a presidential pardon.

In this same direction, the Ministry of Justice has started, with financial help from abroad, a program to reincorporate former political prisoners into Chilean society.

14

UGANDA

Editor's Introduction

Following Uganda's independence from Great Britain in 1962, its first prime minister was Dr. Milton Obote, leader of the Uganda People's Congress party. Obote soon began to centralize power in himself. In 1966, he suspended the constitution and ordered his close aide and army commander, Colonel Idi Amin, to attack the secessionist kingdom of Buganda. Hundreds were killed. This marked the beginning of an increased militarization of power in Uganda, the deterioration of the rule of law, and gross human rights violations. Obote dismissed the president and vice president and imprisoned several senior ministers. Thousands of people were detained without trial.

In 1971, Amin overthrew Obote and oppression worsened. Government critics and members of any independent groups were targetted for attack. Mass detentions, routine torture, killings and disappearances were commonly carried out by government forces. Ethnic and religious divisions were exacerbated. As one example of the brutality of the regime, the military, which was characterized by a significant lack of discipline, massacred tens of thousands of the Acholi and Langi peoples. In 1972, Amin expelled all 100,000 Asians living in Uganda and confiscated their property. Anarchy reigned in much of the country. Resistance movements attempting to overthrow the government also contributed to human rights abuses.

Invading Tanzanian troops ousted Amin in 1979. After three brief governments, Obote returned to power in 1980. Rebellion and repression continued. In the Luwero Triangle area, an armed insurgency brought massive military retaliation. Tens of thousands of people were reportedly killed, and half a million were displaced. As had been the case under Amin, the use of torture was extensive. Commander Tito Okello seized power from Obote in 1985. The army of the National Resistance Movement (NRM) overthrew Okello on January 26, 1986 and its leader, Yoweri Museveni, became president. Museveni pledged that the government was transitional, and would only be in existence for four years. (In 1989, Museveni extended the government for another five years.)

When the NRM came to power in 1986, it stated a policy of a commitment to the rule of law and the protection of human rights. The theme of a break with the past was frequently repeated. Many political prisoners were freed and indiscriminate killing and torture ceased. The NRM instituted a policy of integrating the soldiers of the defeated regime's armed forces into its own National Revolutionary Army.

In May 1986, the NRM appointed a Commission of Inquiry into Violations of Human Rights to investigate "all aspects of violation of human rights, breaches of the rule of law and excessive abuses of power, committed against persons in Uganda by the regimes in government, their servants, agents or agencies" from independence in 1962 until the entry of the NRM government in 1986. Through August 1991, the Commission investigated over 550 complaints. As of the date of this writing, the Commission has not yet released its report.

The following document related to transitional justice in Uganda can be found in Volume III of this collection:

- Legal Notice Creating the Commission of Inquiry into Violations of Human Rights

Commission of Inquiry into Violations of Human Rights

*Justice Arthur H. Oder, Chairman, Commission of Inquiry into Violations of Human Rights, "The Role of the Commission of Inquiry into Violations of Human Rights Promotion in Uganda"**

1. Background and Reasons for the Commission

The commission was set up by the Minister of Justice/Attorney General in the National Resistance Movement Government by Legal Notice No. 5 of 1986, published on 16 May 1986. The background and reasons for doing so are contained in the Legal Notice and in his address to the Commissioners by the then-Minister of Justice/Attorney General Mr. J.N. Mulenga when they were sworn in on 13 June 1986.... Briefly, an inquiry by a commission such as the present was felt necessary because for nearly two decades the people of Uganda had experienced various forms of violation of human rights, breaches of the rule of law, and excessive abuse of power, in contravention of articles of the constitutions of 1962 and 1967 guaranteeing fundamental rights and freedoms and international conventions to which Uganda is a State party; for example the United Nations Universal Declaration of Human Rights of 1948. For many years, Uganda's name was synonymous with unlawful killings, disappearances, torture, excesses by the security forces and agents, destruction and looting of property, expulsions of population groups, etc. In order to prescribe solutions for prevention of reoccurrence of the past in this regard, it was felt necessary to dig into the relevant history to find out [exactly what] happened, why, when they happened, who were the perpetrators and victims of the violations, etc.

2. Terms of Reference

As stated in the Legal Notice the terms of reference are both in terms of the period to be covered by the inquiry (about 23 years and 3 months), the variety of human rights violation to be investigated and the recommendations to be made in the eventual report. The period in question is between 9 October 1962 and 25 January 1986. The task is to inquire into all aspects of violation of human rights generally and more particularly into the ten categories of violations enumerated by the Legal Notice and to recommend to the Government possible ways of preventing the reoccurrence of such violations. Complaints of violations subsequent to the period under the inquiry fall within the jurisdiction of the Inspector General of Government, created by Statute in 1987. The Commission is a temporary body with a specific mandate. After writing and presenting its report to the Appointing Authority it will have accomplished its task and will come to

---

* Excerpted from Justice Arthur H. Oder, *The Role of the Commission of Inquiry into Violations of Human Rights Promotion in Uganda* (August 1991), pp. 1-9.

an end. The instrument appointing it did not set a time limit. It was enjoined to carry out the investigation and make a report as expeditiously as possible. On commencing their work, the Commissioners expected to complete the task within 2 1/2 or at most 3 years. But logistical problems and insecurity in the North and North Eastern parts of the country rendered the target unattainable. The exercise of hearing evidence is virtually complete and the task of report writing will soon commence. We have been asked so many times when the report will be presented that we now tend to shy away from giving any specific date....

3. Composition and Set-Up

(a) Members

The Commission consists of six members. The members are: Mr. Justice Arthur H. Oder, a Judge of the Supreme Court of Uganda; Mr. John Kawanga, a lawyer in private practice at the time of his appointment and now a member of the National Resistance Council; Dr. Jack Luyombya, a Medical Consultant and member of the National Resistance Council; Dr. Edward Khiddu-Makubuya, an Associate Professor of Law in Makerere University and a member of the Constitutional Commission since the appointment of that Commission; Mr. John Nagenda, a tea-farmer, businessman and a writer; and Mrs. Joan Kakwenzire, a lecturer in history in Makerere University.

(b) Secretariat

The Secretariat, headed by an administrative officer responsible for the records, document and other papers, and for administration and finances of the Commission.*

(c) Legal Counsel

The Commission functions as a judicial commission and consequently is assisted by a Legal Counsel who assembles and adduces evidence before [the Commission].† Any person wishing or summoned to appear as a witness before the Commission is entitled to Legal Counsel and to cross examine any witness who has given evidence adversely affecting him.

---

* [Editor's note: During the course of remarks she made at a November 1992 conference, Commission member Joan Kakwenzire stated that the secretariat was staffed by approximately 26 people.]

† [Editor's note: Commissioner Kakwenzire noted that this department of the Commission consists of a senior counsel and four staff attorneys.]

(d) Investigation Team

Headed by a Police Officer of the rank of Superintendent, the team consists of Police C.I.D. Special Branch Officers and an N.R.A. Officer.* Complaints of human rights violation are initially made to, and subsequently investigated ... by the team. The team also identifies potential witnesses, collects documentary, photographic and other evidence for production before the Commission. It does not arrest persons who have been implicated by evidence given before the Commission. It is the duty of the Police C.I.D. to make such arrests for purposes of prosecution, as further discussed later in this paper.

4. Modus Operandi and What Has Been Achieved So Far

(a) Investigation of Complaints

When the Commission was still receiving evidence from victims of human rights violations, complaints came from such victims or their relatives, from whom statements were then recorded by the investigation team either at the Secretariat or up-country to which the team often went to carry out investigations or follow up information. The team has investigated 577 complaints all over Uganda out of the 1478 received.

(b) Itineraries of Hearing of Evidence

The Commission's first Session of hearing evidence from the public was held in Kampala on 11 December 1986. Thereafter, the Commission sat and heard witnesses in all thirty three Districts of Uganda except four, namely, Soroti, Kumi, Moroto and Kotido. The main cause of the Commission's failure to visit those areas was insecurity, which is now very much improved. The method by which the Commission gathered evidence made it unsafe to hold Sessions in these areas while insecurity lasted. Consequently a few witnesses who could travel to Kampala were identified and did so, and gave their testimony here.†...

In areas which the Commission visited the procedure was that complaints or cases of human rights violation were first investigated and categories of violations identified. the Legal Counsel then selected from each category samples of cases for testimony before the Commission. A program of itineraries in given areas were then prepared. The length of time for hearing sessions in any area was determined by availability of funds—depending on distances from which witnesses traveled by public transport or were fetched in the Commission's motor vehicles and other factors. The Commission's trip to an area was preceded by publicity on the radio in English Language and vernacular. The investigators and

---

* [Editor's note: Commissioner Kakwenzire noted that the Investigation Department began with a staff of 22 people.]

† [Editor's note: The Commission was eventually able to hold hearings in these four remaining districts.]

administrative staff also preceded the Commission to make suitable arrangements on the ground. District Administrators and Resistance Councils of different levels were invariably involved in the arrangements and often assisted in giving publicity to the Commission's programs and mobilizing local people to respond by giving evidence or attending to see and listen while others gave their testimony.*

(c) Criteria for Calling Witnesses

Persons who responded by coming forward to be heard as witnesses were so numerous that it was impossible to hear all of them. Consequently only witnesses of samples of cases from categories of human rights violations were selected to testify. Categories handled included killings of groups, families or individuals; torture by burning, by gadgets and other methods; persecution on grounds of religion, tribe, race and politics; sexual assaults and other abuses; destruction and looting of property; and detention without due process of law, etc.

(d) Testimony in Person, by Affidavits or Answers to Questionnaires

Witnesses identified to testify were summoned either because they had volunteered to do so or had been implicated by a previous witness. Formal evidence was and is still given in public on oath or affirmation; where necessary a witness may testify in camera. 535 witnesses have so far given formal evidence, the majority doing so in public. Only about 20 or so have given evidence partly in public, partly in camera for reasons which vary from fear of personal safety to the necessity to comply with the official Secrets Act, 1964. Fears of personal safety have come mostly from witnesses who feel that persons implicated are still at large and may harm them or their relatives. Only very occasionally have such fears arisen on the grounds that persons implicated are holders of office now. For practical

---

* [Editor's note: During her November 1992 remarks, Commissioner Kakwenzire described the process as follows:

> Prior to taking a trip to a particular District , a team of investigators is dispatched ahead of time, to identify cases and witnesses, take statements and do the sampling of all categories of violations of human rights. They then bring back several cases, out of which the Legal Department selects representative cases for the Commission to hear.
>
> For example, in Kampala District, the Investigation Department opened 237 files with several witnesses, but only 45 have been heard by the Commission. The rest will be in our appendix as unheard cases. The same goes for other Districts....
>
> Evidence is also collected on questionnaires from the hundreds of witnesses for whom it is impossible to open files. That information is very useful for the final report. So far the whole country has been completed. Volumes and volumes of transcribed proceedings of the Commission have been produced and more are still being produced. These will constitute a verbatim report.

Excerpted from report given by Commissioner Joan Kakwenzire at a conference organized by the International Commission of Jurists, November 2-5, 1992, Geneva, p. 4.]

reasons some evidence is given on affidavits or as answers to the Commission's questionnaires because it is impossible to hear everybody formally or because of distance or residence outside Uganda.

(e) Record of Evidence

Formal evidence is recorded verbatim on tape and transcribed in cyclostyled form. 6361 pages of formal evidence have now been transcribed and about one-fifth of that number is still on tapes, a state of affairs caused by logistical and manpower problems, which are being gradually solved. While information gathering by the questionnaires have been extensively used, few witnesses have given evidence on affidavits. It was originally expected that the former Ugandan Asians resident abroad where they went after the 1972 expulsion would take advantage of this procedure, but none of them has done so. Despite publicity in London and other countries where they are known to be residents, they have not shown interest in the Commission. In fact only one Ugandan Asian has so far testified to it, in Kampala. The reasons for this can only be a matter of speculation. It may well be that the persecution of this category suffered under Amin is now a dim memory in the past, not worth bothering about anymore, except their everlasting interest in their property or compensation in lieu. There is currently a clamor for return of such property to their owners or for compensation, a matter which many Ugandans are not very happy about.

(f) Public Response

The ordinary people have been very enthusiastic and keen. They have come forward and testified in large numbers. This has been in contrast to the rather poor response from the more educated and elite sections of the population. Such apparent reluctance to give evidence or their views on the part of this section is attributable to many reasons: for example apathy in public affirs; unwillingness to attract publicity; uncertainty of the end results of the Commission's work and eventual report; restrictions of the Commission's terms of reference to what some people regard as history, to the exclusion of current alleged violations; failure by the relevant authorities to prosecute persons who have been implicated by evidence given to the Commission; a feeling that raking the past would not serve any useful purpose, etc. The Commission's views about these various reasons for lack of enthusiasm to give evidence is that they are not justified; and that more good would be done [for] the cause of human rights and the future of this Country by speaking out on what happened and suggesting solutions for the future than by keeping quiet. This view has been consistently expressed both at home and abroad wherever members of the Commission have met Ugandans in other countries. When, however, the Commission announced that general hearing of evidence would close,... a sizable number of elites and opinion leaders responded and expressed interests in giving testimony. This was an opportunity we could not miss. Consequently we now hold three sessions a week to hear them....

(g) Discussions and Exchange of Views on Uganda with International Groups and Individuals

Members of the Commission collectively or individually have had useful discussions and exchanged views on human rights with diplomats of many countries accredited to Uganda, and many international organizations concerned with human rights issues....

Impact of the Commission

Although the Commission has not yet fully completed its work and presented its report to the Appointing Authority, its role on human rights issues has already had a great impact on the people of Uganda:

(a) Demonstrations of Government Seriousness

The appointment and work of the Commission has demonstrated the resolve of the Ugandan Government to promote and protect human rights.

(b) Educational Encouragement

(i) The exercise has made the people of Uganda become more aware of their human rights and encouraged them to speak up for them.

(ii) Afforded the victims of human rights abuse the opportunity to accuse the perpetrators openly and to speak out their feelings whether they want compensation or not.

(iii) Served as a warning to people in authority now or in the future to refrain from abuse of human rights or of authority of their office.

(iv) Indicated the factors which should be considered in formulation and implementation of human rights policies by the present and future governments, for instance with regard to prosecution of offenders and compensation for victims.

(v) Given more publicity both locally and abroad to the nature and extent of atrocities committed against the people of Uganda by governments for many years and has hopefully strengthened the collective and individual will of Ugandans to resist and prevent such occurrence in the future.

(vi) Since human rights are no loner regarded as internal matters of States, the exercise has afforded the members of the Commission and other Ugandans a forum for cross-fertilization of ideas on human rights issues for the mutual benefit of all concerned.

(vii) Has demonstrated the difficulties involved in prosecution of past human rights abuse and that it is imperative to prosecute offenders as promptly as possible after the

> occurrence of human rights violation. The Commission not being a tribunal having powers to try human rights offenders it has had to refer such cases to the Police C.I.D. for prosecution. But it is disappointing that out of over 50 cases so referred, very few have been prosecuted. Reasons for this are many, varying from unwillingness on the part of some police personnel to prosecute to lack of logistics by the C.I.D. and inability of the police to cope with the work-load in their hands. Recently the Commission discussed this matter with the Hon. 3rd Deputy Prime Minister [and] Minister of Justice/Attorney General, who is the Commission's appointing authority, with a view to improving the situation.

(c) Necessity for a Permanent Human Rights Commission

The exercise has demonstrated that there may be a need for a permanent Human Rights Commission with sufficient constitutional or statutory independence, powers and resources equal to its task. [T]his is an idea which the present Commission has in view with specific recommendations which it intends to give to the appointing authority.... [T]he Commission's proposals to the Uganda Constitutional Commission on issues of Human Rights are nearly complete and will be presented soon.

Conclusion

The appointment and work of the Uganda Commission of Inquiry into Violation of Human Rights has ushered concern for fundamental human rights and freedoms [into] the [center] of the arena of conduct of public affairs in this country. More than ever before, persons in authority and ordinary Ugandans are now alive to the necessity to respect, protect and promote human rights, and to adhere to the rule of law and constitutional governance. From the ruins and ashes of human rights history some good will emerge. I have no doubt that Uganda will never be the same again insofar as issues of fundamental rights and freedoms are concerned. It is the duty of every Ugandan to make the maximum contribution in this regard and leave the country better than he/she found it.

Comments by Four Members of the Commission of Inquiry

*Justice Arthur H. Oder, Chairman, Commission of Inquiry into Violations of Human Rights, February 14-17, 1990**

The Commission can only perform [its] task if it receives information or complaints from those who have been directly or indirectly affected as victims of human rights violations and views from those who wish to see a change for the better. But before information and views can flow to the Commission, its own message must first reach the public. For this, the Commission is and has been dependent on the media and its personnel in several ways:

Publicity: At its inception, the Commission issued—through the radio, the television and newspapers—public announcements explaining its terms of reference and methods of its work. Newspapers have unfailingly since the Commission started its formal hearing of evidence given a wide coverage of evidence and witnesses before the Commission. Two dailies and one weekly in particular have followed the Commission everywhere around the country sending back to their readers detailed reports of evidence of atrocities suffered by the victims or their relatives. Though we have at times disagreed with them about the accuracy and the degree of objectivity of their reporting, we have no doubt that the end result of their reporting has been ... positive....

Regular radio and TV programs for the last two or so years about the work of the Commission have increased the interest of the public in the Commission and their awareness on matters of human rights in general. Wide publicity by the newspapers and other media has educated the public and increased their awareness in this regard and it is hoped that it will strengthen people's resolve to resist violation of their rights in the future.

There are, however, some shortcomings to which I must allude.... First of all, the limitation [of] access. In Uganda as in most Third World countries, newspapers have limited circulations confined mostly to urban areas where only about ten percent of the population lives. Illiteracy also limits the use of newspapers, few of which are in vernacular languages, the majority of them being in the English language, which only the educated people understand. In Uganda, the TV [also] has a limited application. It is therefore the radio which is the most accessible, but even there, lack of cheap reliable radio sets and constant supply of battery cells—since electricity is not generally available—put this media beyond the reach of many villagers....

Then the other drawback is the risk.... Journalists in Third World countries have to be very courageous professional workers; a journalist interested in the promotion of human rights has to be even more courageous

* Excerpted from remarks by Justice Arthur H. Oder at a seminar organized by the Commission, February 14-17, 1990, seminar transcript, pp. 3-5, 187-192.

and must be prepared to suffer detention or worse for reporting on aspects of human rights violations which governments consider subversive or seditious....

Publicity: At its inception, the Commission issued to all 33 District Administrators copies of the Legal Notice and Circulars explaining to them and the public the purpose and the work of the Commission. Since then, officials of the Commission in addition to the investigators have visited District headquarters and held discussions with Resistance Councils. Publicity has also been done by announcements on the radio and television. A regular TV programme of the Commission's sessions of hearing evidence has done a great deal to inform only the urban population about the Commission and its work. Newspaper publicity has had equally little impact in rural areas because the newspapers circulate only in a few large urban centers....

Support and encouragement from the Ugandan Government: The Commission has so far carried out its work without ... hindrance from the Government or Government officials. There has been no interference in all the Commission does and how it does its work; it has had complete independence. On the contrary, both His Excellency the President, the current Minister of Justice/Attorney General ... and his predecessor ... have given the Commission all possible assistance and encouragement. The President even appeared ... before the Commission to explain ... what he knew in his capacity as the Minister of Defense at the time [of a particular incident.] He also exchanged with the Commission views about human rights and the rule of law.

Problems encountered by the Commission:... From its inception, the Commission encountered very serious logistical and financial problems which hindered its work. The earliest problems were lack of office accomodation and transport. Work started in a borrowed conference room of the Ministry of Justice until a year later when the Commission secretariat was housed in the Post and Telecommunications Building.... It is now accomodated inadequately in Uganda House. Only one motor vehicle was available at the beginning, but due to tireless efforts of the Minister of Justice/Attorney General, the Solicitor General, and the Commissioners, nine vehicles were at the service of the Commission by the end of 1987. Two of the vehicles came through the generosity of the Ford Foundation. The next problem was lack of recording equipment and shortage of stationery. Recording machines which the Commission at first borrowed from the National Assembly were soon required for [a different government entity]. The method of recording the Commission's proceedings consumed a lot of stationery of which the normal supply through the Government was grossly inadequate.

Grants received from the Ford Foundation, the Austrian Government, the Federal Republic of Germany, and DANIDA subsequently the situation in these areas. The Commission now has efficient recording equipment and the supply of stationery is sufficient to clear the backlog of untranscribed evidence still on tape. DANIDA has also offered to provide materials and some funds [for] the cost of printing the expected report of the Commission. For the various forms of assistance mentioned above, sincere gratitude must be expressed to the governments and donor agencies concerned. Apart from the external grants referred to, the bulk of the funding of the Commission comes from the Treasury. In view of the many demands competing for the Government's financial resources, the condition of permanent inadequacy of funds is something which will continue to bedevil the Commission's work to the end.

Failure to prosecute persons implicated: After it was realized that completion of the Commission's work will take longer than was originally envisaged, the Commission's mandate was modified to enable it to recommend for prosecution persons implicated in the course of inquiry. This step was considered necessary to encourage public interest in the work of the Commission. Prosecution will also be evidence of the Government's resolve to bring perpetrators to book and demonstrate that efforts to accuse them were not in vain.... Consequently, where it appears that an offense known to the law had been committed, the Commission's investigators will pass a copy of the investigated docket to the police—CID. Disappointingly, few prosecutions of cases passed on to them have so far been commenced [or] completed. This is not because of lack of evidence or because culprits are few but because of the serious logistical and manpower problems in the CID which the Government is endeavoring to ameliorate. Out of about fifty cases referred to the CID in the last two years, fourteen cases are still in court pending prosecution....

On security: due to insecurity from rebel activities from north and northeastern parts of the country, the Commission's work of investigation and inquiry has not yet been done at all in some of these areas.... This has been one of the main causes prolonging the Commission's work for a period beyond what was originally envisaged. Problems related to insecurity have also adversely affected the interest of the people from these areas in the work and the purpose of the Commission.

*John Nagenda, Member, Commission of Inquiry into Violations of Human Rights, February 14-17, 1990**

[The CID were very slow in following up cases referred for possible prosecution.] I thought this was actually a great problem because in the end you felt that people lost the urge to come forward since, especially from the villages, if they came forward and reported and gave us evidence on what had happened and we didn't follow it up, they were very much exposed. I remember well the case of somebody in Mubende who had been mutilated by having his testicles crushed by people that he named.... The people he mentioned live where he lives and to this day nothing has been done to them, and I feel very much for that particular gentleman....

Chairman Oder, I think perhaps you were being kind in glossing over some of the problems we have had with our administration.... [T]he poor

* Excerpted from remarks by John Nagenda at a seminar organized by the Commission, February 14-17, 1990, seminar transcript, pp. 195-198.

quality of manpower afforded to this Commission has really been a hindrance to us and we might as well say it. We have wondered often and with reason whether we were actually being given ... this deadwood to hinder our work. It is something, I think, which will come out in the report. We have been singularly unlucky in that direction....

Hopefully, our people will come away from the experience of this Commission better able to face the future. Whether the people responsible for these harrowing misdeeds are,... as I hope they will be, brought to justice and punished severely for what they did,... it is not in our hands to really decide.... [But] forever, where the reports of our Commission are digested by this and future generations, the people concerned will be known and I hope their names will go down in history the way they deserve—in mud and worse.

John Kawanga, Member, Commission of Inquiry into Violations of Human Rights, February 14-17, 1990[*]

Very simple people have come up to this Commission to tell us what terrible things happened to them. They have given evidence at the risk of ... their life or that of their relatives and friends who have come to support them, but somehow the machinery of the Government, and particularly the CID, has not been able to come to the rescue of these people. In some cases, the ... problems are logistical, but in some cases, they are not.... Perhaps at this late juncture, I might as well ask ... the new director of CID ... [to] take all the necessary steps to ensure that these cases get heard as soon as possible. We shouldn't take another year; let these cases be heard and completed.

...I want to comment on what [Chairman Oder] has called ... in the case of elites the lack of public response.... [I]t is a reflection, a very sad reflection, on the history of this country: the elite tend to let things pass by, play it safe, [not] get involved.... So many terrible things have happened because of this attitude.... This country will suffer because the elite continues to bury its head in the sand whenever a crisis occurs; the reasons [Chairman Oder] has given are valid, but at the end of the day, they are the very ones which actually tend to lead to further violations of human rights.... [When a violation occurred some people thought] "Let that one go; he is not my friend." But then this thing has continued and continued and it has eventually caught us all in this mess. We always feel that if it is not near me,... it can go on.... I think the elites should find time to know that even what does not concern you today may concern you tomorrow and you should take a concerted action to prevent this happening again.

---

[*] Excerpted from remarks by John Kawanga at a seminar organized by the Commission, February 14-17, 1990, seminar transcript, pp. 198-200.

Justice Arthur H. Oder, Chairman, Commission of Inquiry into Violations of Human Rights, February 14-17, 1990*

[T]raining of our security forces should include ... humanitarian law.... [In the case of the] police, the CID, the intelligence organizations, the army, and so on,... not only humanitarian law, but also procedural law ... and rights of the individual ... should be included in their training.... I think we shall go evern further: not only security forces, but also students in schools right from the early stages in primary schools, secondary schools, university.... [T]he reason why people in this country have submitted to their rights being violated, folding their arms, watching things going on, is that perhaps they did not know that they [have] rights ... which ... they should stand up to protect.

Joan Kakwenzire, "Problems of Implementing Human Rights in Uganda"†

Restoration of respect for human rights was the principal aim of the National Resistance Movement (NRM) struggle launched in 1981. The Ten-Point Program on which NRM came into power highlights in detail the violations of human rights committed by past regimes, and resolves in principle to end them. It was precisely because of that promise that the NRM got popular support in the Southern parts of Uganda, where violations of human rights had reached monstrous proportions by 1980.[1] When the NRM finally took over state power in 1986, it moved quickly to ratify a number of human rights treaties and to introduce new domestic safe-guards against human rights violations, thus indicating its commitment to the rule of law. The NRM administration, therefore, set for itself very high standards in as far as protection of human rights is concerned. This was an unprecedented posture in the history of post-colonial Uganda.

Ugandans braced themselves for peace, and indeed the change in January 1986 was a dramatic one. Political prisoners were temporarily freed, arbitrary political harassment stopped, and so did looting, killing, and torture of innocent civilians by the army, at least in the Southern parts of the country. Even in Northern parts, the National Resistance Army (NRA), temporarily received welcome as it pursued the ousted Uganda National Liberation Army (UNLA).

By August 1986, however, the hope was shattered by insurgency in the North and North East leading, unfortunately, to significant human rights abuses, similar to those already being investigated by the on-going Commission of Inquiry into Violations of Human Rights set up in 1986. [2]...

---

* Excerpted from remarks by Justice Arthur H. Oder at a seminar organized by the Commission, February 14-17, 1990, seminar transcript, p. 214.

† Excerpted from Joan Kakwenzire, Member of the Commission of Inquiry into Violations of Human Rights, *Problems of Implementing Human Rights in Uganda*, unpublished paper, presented at the Commission seminar, February 17, 1990, pp. 18-32.

1 See NRM's Ten Point Programme, by Yoweri Kaguta Museveni.

2 (a) See Amnesty International Report on Uganda 1986-1986.

In spite of these set-backs, however, the NRM is seen as pursuing a human rights policy that would, given peace and economic prosperity, safeguard people's human rights. The policy, however, is dogged by a host of problems, as this paper will strive to show....

One of the safeguards introduced by the NRM administration is the institution of Resistance Committee[s] (RCs).

The Ten-Point Program explains the role of RCs as follows: the local RCs are to deal with their respective local affairs, provided they operate within the established laws of the country. The Committees are empowered to discipline and punish law-breakers in cooperation with the chiefs and police. They take part in discussing local projects with government officials, and, in addition, they are the political forums for discussing relevant issues concerning the whole country.

Above all, these committees constitute the forums through which ordinary people discuss cases of corruption and abuse of office by public servants of all categories and rank. In this regard, the Resistance Committees are the channel of communication between the rank and file on the one hand and the top on the other. Last but not least, they participate in screening candidates who apply to join important security institutions such as the army, police, and prisons. They also participate in screening applicants for passports, businesses, etc. The idea here is to check undesirable people finding their way through corruption into positions where they can destabilize the country.[3]

The second safeguard was the setting up of the Commission of Inquiry into Violations of Human Rights, (CIVHR) in May 1986.... This Commission was charged with a duty to inquire into all aspects of violations of human rights, breaches of rule of law, and excessive abuse of power committed against persons in Uganda by regimes in government, their servants, agents, and agencies during the period from October 9, 1962, to January 26, 1986, as well as possible ways of preventing the reoccurrence of such violations, and in particular those that are specified in Legal Notice No. 5.

The NRM government and members of the Commission regard this inquiry as a necessary post-mortem of the ills of our society with a view to finding a permanent cure. Ordinary people have warmly welcomed this inquiry, regarding it as an indication of the government's commitment to punishing violators, and re-establishing the rule of law.

The public was given to understand by the then-Minister of Justice, Joseph Mulenga, that "in commissioning the inquiry, government intended first, to facilitate the assembling of evidence through which those responsible for the crimes and atrocities committed against the people of this country and against humanity in general can be identified and brought

---

(b) Uganda Human Rights Activists Reports on Human Rights from 1986-1989.

3 See NRM's Ten-Point Programme under 'Democracy'.

to book." A responsible government, he emphasized, cannot turn a blind eye to the perpetrators of such tragedy.[4]

One hopes that, in the future, if government lives up to its word, and past violators are punished, then potential violators may be deterred from committing further atrocities, knowing that sooner or later, they may be called upon to account for their crimes.

By the Commission's terms of reference, government also expects us to probe into the systems and machineries of state that facilitated the violation of human rights and the cover up of the same, and the protection of the perpetrators from the supposed long arm of the law, with a view to identifying the loopholes and abnormalities in them.

Joseph Mulenga further promised that the NRM government would not treat our Commission and its findings in the same way Amin and Obote treated the analogous Commissions of Inquiry they themselves had set up.

He cited the example of a Commission of Inquiry on missing persons instituted by Idi Amin in the 1970s—whose findings proved useless—and that of Obote into the disappearance of Dr. Ibanda—whose findings have never been communicated to the public.

He assured the country that the NRM government is committed to the restoration of the rule of law as a prerequisite not only for the enjoyment of human rights, but also for economic and social advancement of Ugandans. Our recommendations, he assured us, "will receive maximum government attention with a view to taking action and, where applicable, necessary implementation."[5]

These and other safeguards, like the [Inspector General of Government] (IGG) that deals with current and re-current violations of human rights, the Pubic Accounts Committee that grapples with corruption, the Military Tribunal that deals with army indiscipline, etc., have no doubt made an impact, but they are far from solving the problem of violations of citizens' rights. Occasional reports of abuse of power appear in local newspapers and occasionally in international media, and Ugandans voice discontent at what they consider a repeat of past violations, albeit in a different and less prevalent manner.

There have also been periodic reports from Amnesty International, Uganda Human Rights Activists, the U.S. Committee for Refugees, etc., which highlight violations of a nature almost similar to what Ugandans have seen in the past, especially in the zones which remain insecure.

Equally significant, is the apparent lack of quick follow-ups on the part of authorities on the findings of the Human Rights Commission, contrary to what was originally intended.

Originally, after it was realized that completion of the Commission's work would take longer than had originally been envisaged, the Commission's mandate was modified to enable it to recommend for prosecution persons implicated in the course of the inquiry. This step was

---

[4] See Minister of Justice's speech at the opening ceremony of the Commission of Inquiry into Violations of Human Rights.

[5] Ibid.

considered necessary to encourage public interest in the work of the Commission, and to show the government's resolve to restore the rule of law. By committing to court past perpetrators of crime, the government hoped it would deter potential criminals in the future.

So far, few prosecutions have been carried out, and the public is genuinely dismayed, but there have been recent improvements.

The Commission initially pressed both the Ministry of Justice and the Criminal Investigation Division for action, demanding to know why cases it recommended for prosecution were not attended to, but no satisfactory answer was given. The problem [is one] of implementing human rights standards in a poor country like Uganda. Suffice to say at this juncture that the legacy of abuse of power is still apparent in Uganda today. However, within the last six months, the new CID Director has brought about marked improvement....

The NRM Government at the time it appointed the Commission, in May 1986, did not probably envisage the northern problem as it eventually turned out, and neither did it envisage the dilemma it was going to face when it comes to implementation of our recommendations about past violations of human rights.

I suspected there would be a dilemma, because of the broad-based government, the amnesty bill, and the integration of fighting forces into one national Army in spite of their past violations, and the legacy of abuse of human rights for over a century....

Larger-scale human rights violations have occurred in context of acute political, social and ethnic polarization, armed conflict, and breakdown of the rule of law and the institutions of society. A human rights policy, therefore, on past violations of human rights is influenced by existing constraints (military, political, social, and economic), and by the need to achieve pacification, national unity, and to build or restore the rule of law and functioning institutions.

The NRM government faces the challenge of reconciling justice, peace, and stability in the whole country, a consideration which, in my view, has made them ignore, and I hope temporarily, speedy prosecutions of people implicated in our inquiry. Some of those people are already holding big posts in government, the Army and Police, much to the dismay of the majority of our population.

In some forums, it has been charged that the NRM administration is not as concerned about justice as it is concerned about its own survival; in other forums, its dilemma is appreciated.

Sympathizers of the Government argue that there is no single formula for preventing re-occurrence of violations of human rights. Each must be decided by taking into account all particulars of a given situation and seeking to harmonize short-term needs with long-term objectives.

One way of preventing re-occurrence is indeed the prosecution of violators no matter who they are. The penalty, it is generally believed, has a preventive function. It is believed that the penalty fulfills both a general preventive function on society at large, and on the individual criminal.

On the other hand, clemency, be it in the form of an amnesty bill, pardons, or reduction of sentences, may also serve a preventive objective. This seems to be the case in Uganda, because, I suspect, the Government sees it as necessary to bring about peace and national unity, and to give support to its term of office.

After all, the more people you arrest, the more you send to the bush to fight you.

In this case, it may reasonably be assumed that national pacification and unity will in the long-run achieve more than insisting on punishment and risking political instability.

Personally, I do not like the latter argument. I believe the people can ... isolate individual criminals, and criminals must in accordance with natural law be brought to book. Short of this, I do not see how the government can hope to re-establish the rule of law.

I also believe that government should have the obligation of treating physically and psychologically the victims of atrocities of war, and help to rehabilitate them.

Many have come to the Commission expecting sympathy, only to be reminded of the government bill that dispensed with compensation for crimes committed by past regimes. It breaks my heart to tell someone who both arms were chopped off, or a student who became paralyzed after torture, that there is nothing Government can do.

*John Nagenda, "The Human Rights Commission"**

You could sit up night and day for years and relate the horror stories visited upon this country, some of which we have heard in our four years of collecting evidence, and there is no joy in cataloguing them one by one. But retell them we must if we are to come anywhere near to understanding the kind of systematic barbaric depravity and cruelty unleashed on our nation.

At River Rwizi in Mbarara, sixty old people were massacred by their neighbours and thrown into the river. Those who fished them out in some cases found mothers with their babies still strapped to their backs, both cut to death with pangas.

At another river, Matte, in Luwero District, a lorryful of half starved prisoners from Mityana was led into the bush and all were casually knifed to death. Of course the Luwero Triangle was the main dying ground, with hundreds of thousands killed, and none who saw them will easily forget the piles of skulls there, at Nakaseke, at Kaya's Farm.

At Ombache Mission in West Nile we visited the place of the massacre of ordinary men, women and children who had sought sanctuary from marauding forces intent on revenge on "Amin's people."

And then there were the more personalised stories. In the Nile Mansions which doubled as a top State Hotel as well as a torture centre, we

* Reprinted from John Nagenda, "The Human Rights Commission," in *Uganda 1986-1991: An Illustrated Review* (Fountain Publishers, 1991), pp. 29-32.

heard of people paraded naked through the lobby where others were relaxing with drinks; of prisoners in their dozens kept in the upstairs rooms and balconies for months on end. Was this some kind of warped humourist's idea of sharing the luxurious hotel with the ordinary people of Uganda? Many did not survive the experience.

A man on his deathbed from tortures undergone at Nile Mansions and other places told us of a girl he had seen in the offices of one of the more powerful figures in the Obote II regime. She was undressed and sat above a muchomo charcoal stove. Meantime they started cutting off her breasts and then, when she started to die, they removed a red hot poker from the muchomo and thrust it to her body.

We saw two boys who had been ordered by an army detach in Luwero to eat each other's nose and chew well before swallowing!

A young woman who had been at the trouble at Namugongo when holy places sacred to Christians and Moslems had been ransacked by army personnel and people killed, detailed how she had been made to lie on a lorry with a broken leg upon which a soldier had placed a spare wheel and sat on it! When he saw her cry with pain and asked her what was the matter she said, because she was afraid of him, that it was the wind that brought the water to her eyes!

Distressing as it was, it was more than matched by the callousness of least one high official of the church who made no representations to government on the Namugongo incident, although it is fair to add that some other churchmen came out with great force.

What has the Commission done in all this?

The Commission of Inquiry into Violation of Human Rights was set up in 1986 by the Government of Uganda, through the appointing authority of the Minister of Justice and Attorney General. It was the second such body in the world, after Argentina and followed by, among others, Chile and Philippines.

Its Chairman is Judge of the Supreme Court, Arthur Oder, and the Commissioners are Dr. Jack Luyombya, Medical Doctor and Historical Member of the National Resistance Council, Mr. John Kawanga, lawyer and now Deputy Minister of Transport and Communication, Mrs. Joan Kakwenzire, History Lecturer at Makerere University, Dr. Kiddu Makubuya, Associate Professor of Law at Makerere (he is also now on the Constitutional commission) and Mr. John Nagenda, farmer, businessman and writer. Legal Counsel to the Commission is Mr. Edward Sekandi and the Head of the Investigative team is Supt. (Mrs) Mawa. The Acting Secretary is Mr. Okello.

The Legal Notice that set up the Commission spells out in some detail what our function is. Briefly, we are to find out what happened, when, how, why and by whom and where possible to bring the guilty to book. And also we have to recommend ways and means so that these atrocities never happen again. This last is a tall order indeed!

I readily confess that while all the aims are crucial, I have a particular affinity to the one about punishment; few people with proper knowledge of what has happened in our country would wish the violators to get off scot free. Thus it is with constant and growing regret that I know that many of these are still freely infesting our environment. This is due to a number of factors, including logistical ones with the CID and so on, but it can be scant comfort to those who have suffered so hideously, who have been maimed and mutilated both physically and mentally, to come face to face with the very tormenters they have bravely exposed before us.

Myself, I believe there should always be special measures for special needs and that on this occasion Special Tribunals would have been set up in order to cleanse out society and bring catharsis to those who have suffered so overwhelmingly. But I am also aware that this suggestion would offend many, and not all of them lawyers, indeed some of them my own colleagues on the commission.

As it is all one can do in this regard is to apologise to the boy who was put in a sack and set on fire, that the woman who is said to have done it has still not been charged with the offence, more than two years on. Also to the man whose testicles burst with the heavy weights put on them and who named the people he said were responsible. Three years later I know he comes face to face with them in his usual day to day existence; I hope the time is not far off when he will not.

In fact I am sometimes accosted by people who hold that our commission is worse than useless because it unnecessarily exposes our witness to new dangers without doing anything practical for them. We are keenly aware of this. But we stand our ground and say that at least we try to make the truth public and that it will be on parade in our Report for generations to come. Those who had perpetrated the atrocities are being exposed and the suffering had not been wholly in vain. Indeed we have had many encounters both with total strangers and people we know who have loudly praised the Commission's work on this score. They say that at least their people did not perish without trace.

Also people have remarked that this or that notorious figure who rode roughshod over people and systems has been much reduced by publicly being brought to account. I say Amen to that.

But yet others say that we should let bygones be bygones, that in any case skeletons hide in each cupboard. They say, don't open old scars; you can't bring the dead back to life. They ask, where do you stop? I can see these arguments but I am passionately against them. My answer is that you cannot face the future confidently without unravelling the past—deal with the past to fashion a better future.

And I am warmed by the sentiment voiced again and again: Now everyone knows that whatever you may do today you are likely to be called to account for it in the future, perhaps by an inquiry like ours. Yes, indeed. In fact one of our witnesses said that our own Commission was bound to come up before another one, charge with not having a single Moslem on ours. "To say nothing of those over six and a half foot tall!" I added.

Others are just plain tired of us, charging that we should have reported long ago and returned to the obscurity from which we were plucked.

How we all wish we could! But the truth is that we have had a number of hiccups not of our own making, and mostly to do with cash. Until this July we were drawing Shs. 400 per sitting, and Shs. 250 for lunch when we sat. But even these minuscule were not always available, so that we had to adjourn again and again.

Other problems have been logistical, including areas we could not visit because of disturbances. But we have covered 31 districts on the spot and only Soroti, Kumi and Karamoja remain.

After that we shall embark on the draining work of preparing our report. This will be in two forms: the report itself submitted to Government and a verbatim compilation of all our work, including sworn statements and affidavits. This latter might well come to thirty thousand pages.

And after that? Will some of the ghosts be exorcised? We hope so. Our brief was to cover the years between Independence in December 1962 and the coming of the NRM government on 26 January 1986. The Inspector General of Government takes over from that date but everyone knows he is not enough and there is a distinct possibility of a permanent Human Rights Commission, with perhaps branches in every region. Our President has made it known that he is in favour of such a commission.

And Human Rights would be a subject for study from the earliest classes and should be discussed at every RC in the country regularly.

We hope we were a reasonable start.

15

CZECHOSLOVAKIA

EDITOR'S INTRODUCTION

Communists forced the resignation of a coalition government and seized power in Czechoslovakia in February 1948. Following the Soviet model, they imposed a system of government in which the party controlled the state. Forced labor became routine as the economy and agriculture were nationalized. The secret police—the StB—monitored citizens at home and at work; arbitrary arrests were common, particularly of dissidents. Religion, culture, the media, and foreign travel were all tightly restricted. During the early 1950s, the Communist Party was purged of "bourgeois nationalists." From 1948-1956, over 100,000 political prisoners were sent to prisons or labor camps, and thousands were killed by government forces.

In the late 1950s, Czechoslovakian authorities resisted pressure to modify their system in accordance with the Soviet thaw under Nikita Kruschev. By the 1960s, however, a reform movement spread across the country, prompted in part by a worsening economy and by political trends outside Czechoslovakia. New economic programs were discussed, and some of those previously purged were rehabilitated. In January 1968, after Communist Party chief Antonin Novotny tried unsuccessfully to quell the reform movement, he was replaced by Alexander Dubcek, ushering in a period known as the "Prague Spring." Dubcek lifted censorship and promised a series of democratic and economic reforms. On August 20, however, the Prague Spring came to an abrupt end when Soviet, East German, Hungarian, Polish, and Bulgarian troops invaded and occupied Czechoslovakia. Dubcek was removed in April 1969 and replaced by Gustav Husak, who promptly instituted a program of "normalization" to return Czechoslovakian politics and society to the pre-reform period.

In the late 1980s, democratic openings in the USSR and parts of Eastern and Central Europe stimulated activity in Czechoslovakia, facilitated once again by a deteriorating economy. New independent groups pressed for a wide range of reforms in demonstrations throughout the country. On November 17, 1989, police brutality during a student march galvanized the masses and prompted a nine-day peaceful demonstration in Prague's Wenceslas Square. By November 25, the crowd in the square swelled to 750,000 people. A two-hour general workers strike followed on November 27. By the end of December, this "Velvet Revolution" (so-called for its peaceful character) forced the resignation of Husak and the end of the Communist regime. Vaclav Havel—playwright, dissident leader, and co-founder of the country's preeminent human rights group—was appointed president. Arbitrary arrests, searches and seizures ceased. New laws guaranteed due process of law and freedom of speech, expression, association, and the press. Political crimes were abolished.

The new government moved quickly to confront the Communist regime's legacy of injustice. President Havel granted amnesty to over 20,000 prisoners. Momentum grew to expose the more than 100,000 individuals identified in StB files as collaborators or informants, culminating in the October 4, 1991 "Law on Lustration." This measure barred from a wide range of elected and appointed state positions and quasi-state positions, until January 30, 1996, all those included in a list of activities under the Communist regime and all those identified as "conscious collaborators" in the StB records. The law received significant international and domestic criticism. In November 1992, Czechoslovakia's Constitutional Court struck down those provisions in the lustration law dealing with "conscious collaborators," leaving the rest of the law in effect.

In 1990, Czechoslovakia changed its name to the Czech and Slovak Federal Republic (CSFR). On January 1, 1993, the CSFR officially split into two countries: the Czech Republic and Slovakia. Lustration proceeded with greater vigor in the former. By August 1993, 210,000 people had been screened. Over 10,000 were identified as collaborators; of 70 people who challenged these findings in the courts, 65 were successful. The army was also screened to identify former "political officers." On July 9, 1993, the parliament of the Czech Republic adopted a "Law on the Illegality of the Communist Regime," suspending the statute of limitations for crimes committed from 1948 to 1989 which had not been prosecuted for political reasons—removing a major obstacle to the prosecution of former communist officials. The Constitutional Court rejected challenges to the law.

In Slovakia, the government of Prime Minister Vladimir Meciar opposed lustration and, in January 1994, petitioned the Constitutional Court to overturn the law. The Court rejected this petition in May, and Meciar's successor, Jozef Moravcik, announced his intention to continue the screening process. The CSFR dissolution treaty left the StB files under Czech control, with Slovakia-related records to be transferred over a 25-year period; the new government arranged the timely transfer of files relevant to lustration.

Laws were enacted to provide for rehabilitation of political prisoners and restitution of property confiscated by the Communists. By April 1994,

Czech Prime Minister Vaclav Klaus reported that 218,000 applications had been processed; 70,000 people had been granted compensation totalling more than $90 million. After much debate, Slovakia ultimately provided for the return of confiscated church property in October 1993; the issue remained unresolved in the Czech Republic. Redress of past Communist injustices also prompted demands from those whose rights were violated by the government prior to the February 1948 Communist takeover. A May 1994 Czech law provided for restitution of Jewish property confiscated during the Nazi period. However, the question of compensation—or even apology—to Sudetan Germans and Hungarians who were expelled and whose property was confiscated in the 1945-47 period continues to be highly controversial. In May 1994, arguing that uncertainty of ownership caused by ongoing restitution programs was impeding the privatization process, Klaus and parliament chairman Milan Uhde urged that these programs be ended. "The extent of wrongdoings and crimes which had been committed against property, human rights and lives is much higher than any law could have tackled," stated Uhde. "But this does not mean that we ... should engage in a lifetime search for definitive and absolute justice."

The following documents related to transitional justice in Czechoslovakia can be found in Volume III of this collection:

- Report of the Parliamentary Commission on StB Collaborators in Parliament
- Screening ("Lustration") Law
- International Labour Organisation Decision on the Screening law
- Memorandum on the Applicability of International Agreements to the Screening Law
- Constitutional Court Decision on the Screening Law
- Law on the Mitigation of the Consequences of Certain Property Losses ("Small Restitution Law")
- Law on Extrajudicial Rehabilitation ("Large Restitution Law")
- Act on the Illegality of the Communist Regime and Resistance to It
- Constitutional Court Decision on the Act on the Illegality of the Communist Regime

An Interview with President Václav Havel

Adam Michnik & Václav Havel,
*"Confronting the Past: Justice or Revenge?"**

[Editor's note: Adam Michnik was a leader of the Polish opposition to communist rule, both as a writer and as a prominent advisor to Solidarity. Today he is a historian and an editor-in-chief of the Warsaw daily newspaper Gazeta Wyborcza. *Václav Havel, a noted playwright and essayist who helped lead the Czechoslovak opposition to Communist rule, was elected president of the Czech and Slovak Federative Republic in December 1989 and served in that capacity until his resignation in July 1992. The text below is excerpted from a longer dialogue that appeared in* Gazeta Wyborcza *on 30 November 1991. It was translated from the Polish by Magdalena Potocka....]*

Michnik: What do you think is happening and will happen to all that is called the *ancien régime*: both its people and its institutions?

Havel: I think this constitutes a great problem for the entire postcommunist world. We are all in this together—those who directly, to a greater or lesser degree, created this regime, those who accepted it in silence, and also all of us who subconsciously became accustomed to it. There remain vast, centralized, and monopolistic state enterprises, filled with administrators and bureaucrats from the previous era. This is one source of the great problems and troubles with which the postcommunist world must struggle. It is not the only problem, but it is one of the most serious.

I refer not only to a struggle with the particular institutions and people related to the old regime or its representatives, but above all, to a struggle with the habits of normal, average citizens. It is true that they hated the totalitarian regime, yet they spent all their lives under that regime and they unintentionally became accustomed to it. They became accustomed to the fact that an omnipotent state stood above them, a state that could do everything, that took care of everything, and that was responsible for everything. They learned to expect a paternal attitude from the state, and it is not possible to get rid of that habit in one day. All the bad habits that were systematically ingrained in people over many years could not disappear all of a sudden. It is a powerful and troublesome heritage, and a source of problems that the postcommunist world must resolve.

Michnik: There are two symbolic names for two different ways of thinking about what our attitude should be toward communists or people of the old

---

* Excerpted from Adam Michnik and Václav Havel, "Confronting the Past: Justice or Revenge?" *Journal of Democracy*, vol. 4, no.1 (January 1993), pp. 20-27.

regime. One is polemically called in Poland the "policy of the thick line" (*polityka grubej kreski*). [Former prime minister] Tadeusz Mazowiecki used this term in his first speech. He meant that a thick line should be drawn between the present and the past, and that competence and loyalty toward the new government should be the only criteria for evaluating public officials. He was then accused of wanting, by means of the policy of the thick line, to protect communists, criminals, thieves, and the like.

The other way originated in the Czech and Slovak Federative Republic (CSFR), and is symbolized by the term "lustration" [verification or screening]. These are two opposite ways of thinking about those issues. What do you think about the philosophy offered by Mazowiecki and the one offered by the supporters of lustration?

Havel: This presents the next serious problem. One must somehow manage to steer between Scylla and Charybdis. I think that both concepts, in their extreme form, are faulty. The history of our country shows that every time we took the approach of thinking that we should not be interested in whatever happened in the past—that it was not important—the consequences were always severe. It meant that we did not remove an ulcer that was poisoning the whole system. The ulcer kept festering and producing new toxins. I think that the need to cut out this ulcer, to administer justice, is clearly justified and natural.

At the same time, in my opinion, one should not leave the door open to unlawful revenge and hunt people down, because that would be only another version of what we had gotten rid of. This kind of approach also has a broad tradition in our country. I can remember all those postwar avengers after the Second World War—usually the most energetic ones were themselves the most guilty. I think that a call to reveal the names of all those who in some way were in contact with the police—no matter when or why—is very dangerous. It is a bomb that could go off at any moment and ruin the social climate. It could reintroduce elements of fanaticism, lawlessness, and injustice.

It is important to find the right balance, the right approach, one that would be humane and civilized, but would not try to escape from the past. We have to try to face our own past, to name it, to draw conclusions from it, and to bring it before the bar of justice. Yet we must do this honestly, and with caution, generosity, and imagination. There should be a place for forgiveness wherever there is confession of guilt and repentance.

Therefore I am for a humane approach and not new persecutions and an atmosphere of fear. It is enough that people were afraid of the secret police for 40 years. They should not be afraid that someone will reveal something about them in 15 years' time. Many people do not even know whether, by accident, they might not have stepped into something. Therefore I approached our lustration bill with caution and publicly suggested that the parliament should amend it....

I have to make a factual remark. The bill is indeed commonly called a lustration bill, but it really has a broader scope and refers not only to lustration. This term refers to checking whether anyone was listed as a collaborator in the files of the Ministry of the Interior; yet the bill also prevents people who in the past 40 years were members of the Workers' Militia, the communist Verification Committees of 1948 and 1968, or party committees from the county level up from holding certain positions for five years. There is one exception, however—the bill does not refer to party officials from the period between 1 January 1968 and 1 May 1969....

On the whole, I think that the bill is very harsh and unjust. If someone was a member of the Workers' Militia for one day, 30 years ago, today he is barred from holding certain positions. This also includes Workers' Militiamen who in 1968 defended the extraordinary Party Congress at Vysocany against the Soviet occupation army. I am not saying that there is a majority of such people. Certainly there are only a few, but from the moral point of view even if only one innocent man were to suffer because of that bill, I would still think it was bad. Thus normally such a rule of collective guilt and responsibility is not applied, and it is only the individual deeds of every person that are subject to judgment.

The amendment that I proposed to the Federal Assembly provides for the right of appeal to an independent court, which would have the right to pronounce people capable of holding certain positions according to the specific circumstances of the individual case. For example, if a person later fought for human rights, the court would have the power to declare that this contribution was greater than the guilt of having belonged to something sometime in the past. This would also cover persons who were forced to cooperate with the regime or who were ordered to cooperate by underground organizations—it is possible to imagine such cases during the 1950's.

Michnik: There is one more problem. I have heard that one Dlovak political leader, Jan Carnogursky, has accused another, Vladimir Meciar, of cooperating with the secret police, and that Meciar has accused Carnogursky of the same thing. The only competent arbiter in such an argument would be a secret police official. It seems that things are becoming absurd if secret police colonels are to give out morality certificates.

Havel: Yes, that is true. I also drew the parliament's attention to this point. It is absurd that the absolute and ultimate criterion for a person's suitability for performing certain functions in a democratic state should come from the internal files of the secret police....

Michnik: You have said that there must be a way to steer between Scylla and Charybdis. Where, in your opinion, is the point where the quest for justice ends and the quest for revenge begins?

Havel: Such a limit could be defined only by something intangible, certain human qualities like feelings, taste, understanding, wisdom, something that is not easily expressed in legal norms. If we followed our human side, maybe we would be able to find that border [between justice and revenge]. It is a very pressing problem, and such borders are difficult to find. Our lustration bill is the proof of it—it is flawed even though it was the result of two years of study and discussion. It is an example of how difficult it is to define this borderline in legal terms—and yet it must be defined in such terms, because a severe law is better than no law at all. Without a law, anyone could "verify" anyone else and shame him publicly.

Michnik: You mentioned in one of your interviews that you could sense how people begin fearing the past. Recently I was in Germany and talked to our friends there from the dissident years. They all talked about the Stasi [the East German secret police]. I had a feeling that they were obsessed by the subject. They said that Stasi activities could be compared to an "Auschwitz of the soul." They added that the whole problem should be considered from the victims' point of view. If someone had been hurt by the Stasi, he has the right to seek justice, in the sense that he has the right to know who hurt him. This means that he has the right to look into his files and see who denounced him.

On the other hand, I recently spoke with a Spanish writer, Jorge Semprun, and asked him: "How did you handle that in Spain?" (where there was a dictatorship, police who tortured people, informers, and so on). He answered: "If you want to live a normal life, you must forget. Otherwise those wild snakes freed from their box will poison public life for years to come."

A German writer, Jürgen Fuchs, said something else again: "Listen, Adam, I am not bloodthirsty, I write poetry, but I would not be able to live with that. If we do not solve this problem in a definite way, it will haunt us as Nazism did. We did not denazify ourselves, and this has weighed on us for many years."

What does a Czech writer, who at the same time is the president of his country, think about that?

Havel: I want to say that my private opinion on this issue differs slightly from that one that I have and must have as president. As president, I must take society and its will into consideration.

My personal attitude can best be illustrated by the following example. Shortly after I had been elected president, I was given a list of all my friends who had written denunciations of me. The same day I not only lost this piece of paper, but also forgot whose names were on it. That simply means that I personally am inclined to let this matter rest. I have a considerable distance toward all this because I have come to know the machinery [of the police state] and how it can destroy people. I wrote plays and essays about this, and I managed to resolve that problem for myself. Therefore, I have no need to punish anyone for having acted badly.

Yet as president, I must bear in mind that society needs some public action in this regard because otherwise it would feel that the revolution remains unfinished. There are people whose own lives and whose families have been destroyed by the regime, who spent their entire youth in concentration camps, and who will not be easily reconciled to all that—

especially since many of those who had persecuted than are much better off than their victims.

This sharpens people's emotions. Our society has a great need to face that past, to get rid of the people who had terrorized the nation and conspicuously violated human rights, to remove them from the positions that they are still holding. As I mentioned before, it is probably a historic necessity to look back on one's own past without any blinders on, and to give it a precise name. Therefore, as president, I cannot neglect these issues, as I did that piece of paper listing my "own" informers.

Michnik: ...When I was still in prison, I promised myself two things: First, that I would never belong to any violent organization that would give me orders for struggling against communism; and second, that I would never take revenge on anyone.

On the other hand, I kept repeating to myself a certain stanza from a poem by Zbigniew Herbert, who wrote: "And do not forgive, because it is not within your power to forgive in the name of those who were betrayed at dawn."

I think that we are condemned to such a dialectic. We can only offer absolution on our own behalf; to offer absolution on behalf of others is not within our power. We can try to convince people to forgive, but if they want justice, they have the right to demand it.

Havel: This is exactly the dilemma that I have just spoken about. My official position does not allow me to behave the way I would as a private person. I have no need for revenge. But as a state official, I have no right to pronounce an act of grace for everyone.

Michnik: Earlier in our conversation you used a term that slightly alarms me—you spoke about an unfinished revolution. What does it mean exactly? When do you think that the revolution will be over?

Havel: It is difficult to say. This revolution will not simply end one day, and there is no indicator which would tell us that it has just ended. The revolution is a certain process that unfolds, then slows down, and finally comes to an end. Only when new generations enter political life shall we be able to say that it is all behind us. In some sense, this revolution is indeed unfinished. Let us recall, for example, that our revolutionary program included a market economy—yet 95 percent of property is still state-owned. The same situation holds with respect to the legal system—95 percent of our laws and regulations date back to the communist period. The political system presents a similar case. Only with time will new people appear to replace the present state officials. For now, everything remains in flux.

Still, I agree with you that it is difficult to say: the revolution now has finished. But there is always going to be a certain symbolic moment—for example, when the biggest steel plant becomes privatized.

Michnik: ...It seems to me that the demonstrations which forced the totalitarian power to give in constituted a revolution. And later on, what journalists called the Velvet Revolution chose the path of a legal state.

There is a theory in our countries, however, that this approach was wrong, that we should not have chosen the path of law; instead, communism should have been destroyed once and for all by applying revolutionary methods rather than lawful ones. Revolution always means discriminating against both political enemies and people of the old regime—but law means equality within the regime. Either the law is equal for everyone or it does not exist at all.

I am afraid that it is still possible for certain categories of people to be outside the protection of the law (for example, former communists), as was the case in Russia after the Bolshevik Revolution, when the kulaks and the bourgeoisie were outside the protection of the law. In asking what an "unfinished revolution" means, I know what I am afraid of—that this process may lead to its next phase. We know from history many examples of revolutions that began by struggling for freedom and then ended in despotism—from Cromwell through Napoleon and up through Khomeini.

Many years ago Semprun, whom I mentioned before, wrote a screenplay for a film by Alain Resnais entitled *The War is Over*. In the film, the Spanish Civil War had just ended, and war tactics and methods were no longer necessary. When you speak of an "unfinished revolution," I begin to think that there may be people who will say: look, even Havel—a humanist, writer, and philosopher, a good man—says that this revolution must be continued.

Thus are we still continuing the revolution, or do we say that the war is over? There are communists, but do they have the same right to live as other people do? If they committed crimes and there is evidence to prove that, they will be punished as criminals. But if not, they cannot be discriminate against just because some years ago they belonged to a communist party.

Havel: I think that the essence of these changes—if you prefer, we do not have to call them revolutionary—lies in introducing law instead of lawlessness, and not in introducing new lawlessness. The only problem is that social pressures have been caused by the old lawlessness, whose impact is still felt. For example, try to picture the case of one of my friends, Standa Milota, who was persecuted for 20 years and could not work; today he has a pension of one thousand Czech crowns because he could not be promoted and therefore his salary was always low. Meanwhile, the person who persecuted him and prevented him, from having a normal job today has a pension of five thousand Czech crowns, a house, and many other goods. People observe such cases and say that it is true that the "top" officials have changed, censorship has been lifted, and newspapers may publish whatever they want, but the real, material, everyday wrongs and results of the old lawlessness have remained unchanged.

This is exactly what many people rebel against. They are different from the few political extremists because they are driven not by revenge but by justice and a need for both moral and material satisfaction. This has nothing to do with any kind of jacobinism or "permanent revolution." It is important to finish the process of repairing the public damage. At least that is the way I regard it. If I hear of any instances of revenge or fanaticism, however, I react strongly against them.

THE NATURE OF THE TRANSITION

*Michael Kraus, "Settling Accounts: Postcommunist Czechoslovakia"**

Since the new democracies in East and Central Europe confront similar legacies of the past, one would expect similar approaches to the issue of settling accounts. But this, in fact, has not been the case. In contrast to Czechoslovakia, where the adoption of the lustration law epitomizes the widespread demands for political justice, neither Hungary nor Poland have had to contend with the same outcry demanding "debolshevization." Notable differences have emerged also in other areas of coming to terms with the past. These differences stem from a number of factors, to which the nature of the transition may well hold the key.

In his recent study, Samuel Huntington ... argues that the process of democratization can be seen in terms of the interplay between governing and opposition groups along a continuum that produces three types of transition: transformation, when the elites took the initiative to bring about democracy; replacement, when the initiative rested with the opposition; and transplacement, when democratization came about through joint action on the part of both government and opposition.[4] While each specific case of transition combined elements of two or more, each transition "more clearly approximated one type of process than others."[5]

Transitions in one-party Leninist systems, according to Huntington, fell into all three categories. Hungary and Bulgaria were transformations; Poland and Czechoslovakia transplacements; and East Germany a case of replacement. In typical cases of transformation, like Spain, Brazil or Hungary, the regime liberalization is a "liberalization from above," in which the regime reformers lead and where the regime is stronger than the opposition. In transplacement transitions, such as Korea, Poland or Czechoslovakia, "the dominant groups in both government and opposition recognized that they were incapable of unilaterally determining the nature

* Excerpted from Michael Kraus, *Settling Accounts: Postcommunist Czechoslovakia*, revised version of paper delivered at 1992 Annual Meeting of the American Political Science Association, The Palmer House Hilton, September 3-6, 1992.

4 *The Third Wave*, esp. ch. 3. [Editor's note: Excerpts from *The Third Wave* appear in Volume One of this collection.] For another, though parallel, approach to transitions, see Yossi Shain and Juan Linz, "The Role of Interim Governments," *Journal of Democracy* 3 (January 1992): pp. 73-89.

5 Huntington, *The Third Wave*, p. 115.

of the future political system in their society."[6] The transplacement "dialectic" of protest and repression eventually leads both sides to recognize the virtues of negotiations, opening the doors to a negotiated agreement. Thus transplacements "required some rough equality of strength between government and opposition as well as uncertainty on each side as to who would prevail in a major test of strength."[7] By contrast, replacements, such as those in the Philippines, Romania, or East Germany, occurred in the absence of reformers within the regime, where the opposition gains strength at the expense of the government, until the latter collapses or is overthrown.[8]

The mode of transition has implications for the likely pattern of punishment and prosecution of the human rights abuses on the part of the old regime. Whereas in transformations, "former officials of the authoritarian regime were almost never punished; in replacements they almost always were."[9] Nearly all authoritarian regimes that underwent transformation to democracy provided an amnesty for the officers of the regime, or for the opposition, or both. In transplacements, the issue was typically subject to joint negotiations. Replaced authoritarians, by contrast, consistently tended to be targeted for prosecution and punishment.

In light of the foregoing generalizations, it is instructive to reassess the nature of the Czechoslovak transition. Revisiting Prague in November 1989, Timothy Garton Ash, caught in the euphoria of the revolution, confided to Vaclav Havel: "In Poland it took ten years, in Hungary ten months, in East Germany ten weeks: perhaps in Czechoslovakia it will take ten days!"[10] Ash was right: it took more or less ten days in Prague, and the snowballing effect of the rapidly disintegrating world of communism played a major role in undercutting whatever resolve the Communist leadership had left in it. The events that begun with a student demonstration on November 17, culminated in a general strike of November 27, when millions across Czechoslovakia joined hands to walk out on the government. Acting under mounting pressure, the authorities caved in to virtually all conditions presented in a series of negotiations with the leaders of the opposition.

The available record of those negotiations reveals that the Civic Forum, headed by Havel, was in the position to stipulate the measures that had to be taken by the government, including the abolition of the constitutionally sanctioned "leading role" of the party (on November 29), and President Gustav Husak's resignation (on December 10). Breaking the state monopoly on the mass media, especially the television, the opposition was able to dictate the tempo of these changes, issuing deadlines that had to be met, lest the (remarkably disciplined) street crowds get out of control. Similarly, the opposition dictated which

---

[6] *Ibid*,. p. 152.

[7] *Ibid*,. p. 153.

[8] *Ibid*,. p. 142.

[9] *Ibid*,. p. 161.

[10] *The Magic Lantern* (N.Y.: Random House, 1990) p. 78.

personalities were acceptable for cabinet posts, as well as the numbers of non-party representatives. When the Communist prime minister, Ladislav Adamec, presented his first cabinet on December 3, it was deemed unacceptable by the Civic Forum; while Adamec chose to resign in protest against the Civic Forum demands, his successor, Marian Calfa accepted the same demands in composing the new cabinet, in which the party had a minority representation, and which included a new deputy prime minister in charge of security, who had just been freed from prison. In short, the outcome of the negotiations reflected almost wholly the preferences of the opposition.[11]

That the opposition negotiated with a mortally wounded partner was a key factor in the ultimate triumph of the Civic Forum. The Communist Party, facing an upheaval within the ranks of its 1.7 million members, many of whom supported the demand that the Party's monopoly rule be ended, was in a state of complete disarray. As Judy Batt aptly put it, the Party "had been weakened to the point of dependence on the opposition to avert its complete obliteration and to protect it from uncontrolled acts of retribution by the population."[12]... Because it resisted reforms on the Hungarian or Polish model to the bitter end, the Communist leadership in Prague was in an exceptionally weak position to stem the tide of protest that swept all East European capitals. To sum up, the pattern of the velvet revolution fits better Huntington's model of replacement (or ruptura, to use Linz's classification), a transition characterized by a collapse of the old regime. In this sense, Czechoslovakia's exit from Leninism had more in common with the transition in East Germany than with Poland or Hungary.... Huntington's framework helps us to understand why in postcommunist Czechoslovakia, in contrast to Poland or Hungary, the voices demanding justice and retribution grew loud and clear after November 1989.

THE PROCESS OF PURGING: "LUSTRATION"

Introduction

*Jiri Pehe, "Parliament Passes Controversial Law on Vetting Officials"**

In a step that some Czechoslovak politicians hailed as the most important defeat of communism since the "velvet" revolution of late 1989 and that others criticized as a possible violation of Czechoslovakia's

---

11 The key sessions were recorded, transcribed, and published. See Vladimir Hanzel, *Zrychleny tep dejin: Realne drama o deseti jednanich* (Prague: OK Centrum, 1991). Evidently, some negotiations took place outside the recorded sessions (interviews in Prague, July 1993.)

12 *East Central Europe From Reform to Transformation* (N.Y.: Council on Foreign Relations Press, 1991) p. 40. In fact the possibility of "uncontrolled acts of retribution by the population" against the Communists was implied in the negotiations by the Civic Forum.

* Reprinted from Jiri Pehe, "Parliament Passes Controversial Law on Vetting Officials," *Report on Eastern Europe*, vol. 2, no. 43 (October 25, 1991), pp. 4-5.

international human rights commitments, the Czechoslovak Federal Assembly approved a law on October 4 that provides for the systematic screening of officials in certain government agencies and offices and the subsequent dismissal of those among them who are found to have worked either for the communist regime's State Security (secret police) or to have been high-level communist officials. The law, which is valid through January 30, 1996, could affect hundreds of thousands of people....

The Initial Screening Attempts

The screening of various categories of officials and politicians for possible ties with the former secret police started in early 1990.[1] Prior to the general elections held on June 8 and 9, 1990, almost all political parties had asked that their candidates be vetted, but they were not required to withdraw candidates found to have had links with the communist secret police. In the spring of that year, the Federal Assembly and the Czech and Slovak National Councils agreed that all members of the provisional federal and republican governments (which were set up after the revolution and which remained in place until the elections) should be screened so that the electoral campaign would not be disrupted by revelations and mutual accusations by rival political parties and candidates. The vetting was implemented by the federal Ministry of Internal Affairs, which was the only institution at that time with legal access to the relevant documents. But the fact that many people still on the ministry's staff had also worked for the former secret police cast considerable doubt on the validity of the screening process.

There were several scandals during this period involving politicians who were not government officials and who were accused of having collaborated with the former secret police. These prompted some politicians to call for firmer regulations on the vetting of officials. However, the federal and the republican parliaments could not agree on how comprehensive the screening should be or what kind of guidelines to employ. In the fall of 1990 the Czech National Council asked the Czech Electoral Commission to order all parties registered in the forthcoming local elections to screen their candidates. Instead, however, the commission merely recommended they do so. As a result, the screen was not uniform, since some parties followed the recommendation and others ignored it....

Lawrence Weschler, "The Velvet Purge: The Trials of Jan Kavan" [*]

The trouble was, the StB [the Communist secret police] hadn't just disappeared; it had persisted, like a bad dream from which the country was having a terrible time trying to awaken. People started looking back at those miraculous days of November of 1989, when what had started as a

---

[1] For a detailed treatment of the earlier screening efforts, see Jan Obrman, "Laying the Ghosts of the Past," *Report on Eastern Europe*, no. 24, June 14, 1991.

[*] Excerpted from *The New Yorker*, vol. 68, no. 35, (Oct. 19, 1992), p. 68. Reprinted by permission; © 1992 Lawrence Weschler. Originally in *The New Yorker*.

simple student demonstration managed, within weeks, to upend an entire era of totalitarian domination, and a worm of suspicion began to eat at the core of their cherished common memory: How could it all have happened so effortlessly, almost as if it had all been planned? Maybe it had all been planned. It *had* to have been planned. The StB itself—rumors were now running rampant—must surely have orchestrated the whole thing.... Not only had the StB staged those seminal events, people were now saying, but it had also succeeded in loading the new Parliament with its former agents and informants—people who were either organizationally or ideologically committed to following the ongoing secret edicts of its hidden High Command, or else people who could be blackmailed into doing so. The new Parliament went through a sudden crisis of legitimacy, and, as a result, on January 18, 1991, an overwhelming majority passed a resolution empowering [a special fifteen-member parliamentary commission known as] the November 17th Commission to vet the entire body [as well as all employees of the Prime Minister's office and the Office of the Federal Assembly]; that is, to delve into the sealed files and registries of the StB and to identify any former agents or informers who were now members of [these bodies]. Such individuals were to be confronted privately with the charges against them and allowed quietly to resign or else within fifteen days be subject to public denunciation. [Member of Parliament Jan] Kavan may have had some mild civil-liberties reservations about the resolution, but, on the other hand, as he said at the time, "I didn't want to sit in the same room with people who were guilty of denouncing my friends."

Jiri Pehe, "Parliament Passes Controversial Law on Vetting Officials"[*]

All parties represented in the parliament had one or more representatives on the commission. On March 22, 1991, a spokesman for the commission informed the parliament that it had identified 10 deputies—all of whom had chosen not to resign after the commission had informed them of its findings—as former collaborators with or agents of the secret police. Two days later, the commission informed the Federal Assembly that two more deputies had been identified as former collaborators with the secret police. The Federal Assembly passed a resolution calling on the accused deputies to step down. Thus far, however, none of them has complied, since the federal electoral law contains no provision for the recall of deputies.

The commission further identified 33 collaborators among the employees of the Office of the Prime Minister and 25 collaborators among the employees of the Office of the Federal Assembly. According to the commission's spokesman, 14 federal ministers and deputy ministers had been identified as agents or collaborators. Apparently, 13 of these were deputy ministers, since the only official with full ministerial rank to step down amid accusations of having collaborated with the former secret police

---

[*] Reprinted from Jiri Pehe, "Parliament Passes Controversial Law on Vetting Officials," *Report on Eastern Europe*, vol. 2, no. 43 (October 25, 1991), p 5.

thus far was former Deputy Prime Minister Vaclav Vales. In connection with the parliamentary commission's screenings, in the spring of 1991 President Vaclav Havel asked the Ministry of Internal Affairs to screen the members of his staff; the results were not made public, however.

Some screenings were also conducted at the republican level. On January 18, 1991, the Czech National Council adopted a resolution calling for an investigation into the past activities of its deputies, members of the Czech government, employees of the Offices of the Prime Minister and of the National Council, and republican prosecutors and judges. One month later the Czech National Council approved a set of strict criteria for identifying informers. The criteria included establishing whether the person listed in the secret police files had known that he had been meeting with agents; whether he had met with agents repeatedly and secretly; and whether he had actually carried out the tasks he had been asked to perform by the secret police.

On May 23, 1991, the Slovak National Council adopted a similar resolution demanding that all deputies of the Slovak National Council, ministers, deputy ministers, judges, employees of the Offices of the Prime Minister and of the Slovak National Council, and the managers of Slovak Radio and Television should be screened for possible links with the former secret police. A proposal for the adoption of a separate law regulating screening procedures was rejected.

*Lawrence Weschler, "The Velvet Purge: The Trials of Jan Kavan"**

[Pressures for Further Action]

Being lustrated, as various observers have noted, is every bit as painful as it sounds. The word "lustration" derives from the Latin *lustratio,* which means purification by sacrifice. Czechoslovakia's 1991 lustration law, which established the basic ground rules for the country's political-purification rituals, derived from the Czech public's rapidly evolving attitude toward the country's immediate past. On New Year's Day of 1990, shortly after becoming Czechoslovakia's President, Vaclav Havel gave an address in which he spoke of a "decayed moral environment" as being one of the country's principal legacies from its Communist past, but he was careful not to assign blame too narrowly. In a passage that in many ways epitomized the velvetness of the Velvet Revolution he noted, "When I talk about a decayed moral environment ... I mean all of us, because all of us became accustomed to the totalitarian system, accepted it as an unalterable fact, and thereby kept it running.... None of us is merely a victim of it, because all of us helped to create it together.... We cannot lay all the blame on those who ruled us before, not only because this would not be true but also because it could detract from the responsibility each of us now faces—the responsibility to act on our own initiative, freely, sensibly, and quickly."

---

* Excerpted from *The New Yorker*, vol. 68, no. 35, (Oct. 19, 1992), pp. 78-79. Reprinted by permission; © 1992 Lawrence Weschler. Originally in *The New Yorker.*

This attitude, at once expansive, forward-looking, and scrupulously lucid, typified much of the thinking at the top of the new government, including such veteran oppositionists as the Czech Premier Petr Pithart, and the foreign minister, Jiri Dienstbier. As had happened earlier in Poland, a decision was made that there would be no easy scapegoats. In part (again as in Poland), this decision grew out of the very way in which the final transfer of power had been effected—through negotiations, without violence. One just didn't turn around and arrest the very people whose hands one had been shaking on occasions of high solemnity only a few weeks earlier. In the Czech case, however, the forbearance was taken to such an extreme that for the first six months of the new order the StB was left largely to its own devices; it is partly for that reason that so many of the key files were subsequently found to be missing. And that forbearance was in turn partly responsible for aggravating the growing public feeling that the entire transition must have been one big fix.

During any extended period of totalitarian governance, terrible things happen to good people and wonderful things happen to bad ones. And during any transition from such a period of unjust governance a principal challenge is that both those legacies must be addressed. One problem with Havel's magnanimous initial position was that it addressed neither. There were many people—and not just dissidents—who had suffered grievously under the previous regime, and many other people who had inflicted much of that suffering. As upset as Czechs were by the continuing plight of the victims, they were even more galled by the seemingly blithe impunity being lavished upon the perpetrators. Unpunished, these earlier winners were quickly turning their advantages of position to more purely financial advantage, and thus setting themselves up to emerge as the new winners.

*Michael Kraus, "Settling Accounts: Postcommunist Czechoslovakia"**

The end of the party's monopoly rule did much to expose, but not enough to destroy, the underlying structure of corporatist interests. The interlocking bureaucratic interests linking state bureaucrats and state managers had been "tied into the structure of the communist party power itself."[38] Auctioning state property to the highest bidder also brought the nomenklatura into public eye. Its privileged lifestyle as the "new class" under the old regime was a measure of hypocrisy; its return as the triumphant nouveaux riches under the new regime formed an assault on the public's sense of social justice....

In the debate leading up to the adoption of the October 1991 lustration law, which banned party officials (but not the party rank and file) from top positions in the state sector, a key argument centered around the privileges of the nomenklatura. The proponents of the law argued that

---

* Excerpted from Michael Kraus, *Settling Accounts: Postcommunist Czechoslovakia*, revised version of paper delivered at 1992 Annual Meeting of the American Political Science Association, The Palmer House Hilton, September 3-6, 1992.

38 Batt, *East Central Europe from Reform to Transformation*, p. 76.

owing to the continued presence of the old structures, it is the ordinary citizen who suffers political discrimination. Equal opportunity, they argued, demanded that party functionaries, former agents of the security, and their secret collaborators, be temporarily, i.e., for a period of five years, removed from leading posts, so as to gradually eliminate the long-standing discriminatory measures against the non-party masses.

*Lawrence Weschler, "The Velvet Purge: The Trials of Jan Kavan"**

As months passed, the calls for a more thoroughgoing housecleaning became increasingly insistent, and as those calls began to be answered by ad-hoc improvisations, differing radically from one region or ministry or industry to another, pressure grew for the central government to arrive at some unified policy on the matter.

Right-wing parliamentarians, in particular, were clamoring for a bill that would simply prohibit all former Communists above a certain level, all military officers above a certain rank, and all security agents and their collaborators from holding any positions of authority—fairly broadly defined—within the state. While Havel and his allies now acknowledged the validity of some of the thinking behind that impulse, they nevertheless objected to its basic premise of collective guilt—the theory that individuals ought to be punished for mere membership in a group, regardless of personal culpability for the evils perpetrated by that group. A draft bill that the government presented to Parliament in early September of 1991 required that whatever purging eventually took place be limited to those members of other previously delineated categories who could themselves be shown to have participated in "suppressing human rights," with the burden of proof falling on the government, and the accused guaranteed a certain minimal due process and right of appeal. The rightist parliamentarians objected that such a standard would have the opposite effect of insulating most of the malefactors, since it would be virtually impossible to prove any given individual's participation in suppressing human rights.

The Lustration Law

Jiri Pehe, "Parliament Passes Controversial Law on Vetting Officials"†

In early September [1991] the federal government submitted a draft law to the parliament. The bill arrived in the midst of a controversy caused when some rightist parties, reacting to the attempted coup the previous month in the USSR, demanded the "de-Bolshevization" of public life and

---

* Excerpted from *The New Yorker*, vol. 68, no. 35, (Oct. 19, 1992), p 79. Reprinted by permission; © 1992 Lawrence Weschler. Originally in *The New Yorker*.

† Reprinted from Jiri Pehe, "Parliament Passes Controversial Law on Vetting Officials," *Report on Eastern Europe*, vol. 2, no. 43 (October 25, 1991), pp. 5-9.

insisted that former high-level communist officials be forced to leave their current government and parliamentary posts. They also demanded that the names of all former agents of and collaborators with the secret police be made public. On September 5, some federal lawmakers even called for outlawing the communist party.[2] The proposals caused a furor among left-of-center politicians, who considered them an attempt to launch a witch-hunt.

The government's draft law did take into account some of the concerns of the right-of-center politicians, inasmuch as it banned former communist officials from holding government positions. Despite this concession, the right-of-center politicians almost immediately attacked the bill as being too liberal because of a provision stating that in order to ban someone from holding a senior-level government post, he had to be identified as a secret police agent, a secret police collaborator, or a former communist official who had participated in "suppressing human rights between February 25, 1948, and November 17, 1989." Some right-wing deputies said the provision would actually protect former agents, collaborators, and communist officials, since in most cases it would be virtually impossible to prove that someone had violated human rights. Instead, they argued that mere membership in some of the agencies that had constituted the backbone of the communist system of oppression should be reason enough for forbidding certain categories of people from holding senior positions in the new democratic government.[3]

During the debate on the bill, the right-of-center deputies proposed a number of amendments.... The parliament approved most of the amendments. Predictably, all 41 deputies of the right-of-center Civic Democratic Party, headed by [then] Finance Minster Vaclav Klaus, voted for the law; all the deputies of the communist party as well as the Movement for a Democratic Slovakia voted against it. In the end, the vote of the 300-strong bicameral Federal Assembly was 148 to 21, with 22 abstentions; 29 deputies boycotted the vote in protest, and the rest were absent.[4]

People and Posts Affected

Under the law, former agents of or collaborators with the secret police and communist officials will be barred [through January 1996] from holding positions in the state administration at both the federal and the republican levels; the Czechoslovak Army (the rank of colonel and higher); the federal Security and Information Service (the federal intelligence agency); the federal police; the Office of the President; the Office of the Federal Assembly; the Office of the Czech National Council; the Office of the Slovak National Council; the offices of the federal, Czech, and Slovak governments; the offices of the federal and republican Constitutional

---

2 See AP, September 5, 1991; and CTK, September 6, 1991.

3 CTK, September 17, 1991.

4 AP, October 4, 1991.

Courts; the offices of the federal republican Supreme Courts; and the Presidium of the Czechoslovak Academy of Sciences. The law also applies to top positions in Czechoslovak, Czech, and Slovak Radio and Television, as well as in the Czechoslovak Press Agency. Finally, the ban applies to top management positions in enterprises and banks owned by the state, to top academic positions at colleges and universities, and to judges and prosecutors.[5]

More specifically, the government posts listed above are not open to people who between February 25, 1948, and November 17, 1989, were members of the State Security; registered with the secret police as agents; the owners and the occupants of the "conspiration apartments" used by the secret police; informers and evaluators for the secret police; knowing collaborators with the secret police; Secretaries of the Communist Party of Czechoslovakia at the district level or higher; political officers in the Corps of National Security; members of the People's Militia (the party's private army); and members of action committees of the National Front after February 25, 1948, or of committees that conducted party and other purges in 1948 and after August 21, 1968. Also banned from the government positions specified in the law are former students (or fellows for more than three months) of Felix E. Derzinski College in Moscow for members of the State Security Service; at the College of the Ministry of Internal Affairs of the USSR for the police; or the Higher Political School at the Ministry of Internal Affairs in the USSR.

The people whom the law describes as "knowingly collaborating with the secret police" are those who were registered with the secret police as "trustees" or "candidates for secret cooperation." To be considered as such, however, it must be proved that these people knew they were in contact with a member of the secret police, were giving him information, or performing tasks for him.

In a special section, the law lists the categories of people who cannot be employed by the Ministry of Internal Affairs, the Federal Security and Information Service, the federal police, and the police protecting Prague Castle (the so-called Castle Police, meaning the special police units guarding the residence of the President). Under the law, people are prohibited from occupying senior posts in these government bodies who between February 25, 1948, and November 17, 1989, were members of the State Security Service's counterintelligence department; heads of departments and divisions in the State Security Service; students at one of the aforementioned three secret police and regular police training centers in the Soviet Union; or communist officials.

The law provides for some exceptions. First, those party officials who rose to power during the Prague Spring (between January 1, 1968, and May 1, 1969) will not be affected by the ban. Second, the federal Minister of Internal Affairs, the Director of the Federal Security and Information Service, and the Minister of Defense may pardon some of the people

---

[5] For the full text of the law, see CSTK, October 9, 1991.

affected by the law should their dismissal threaten "an important security concern of the state."

The Screening Process

The people listed above who have been or are to be appointed to a senior government post are required to submit to the head of the state agency, enterprise, or institution where they are working or will work a certified statement affirming that they did not work for the former State Security Service.

The certified statements are to be issued by the Ministry of Internal Affairs upon the request of the official (or prospective official) or of his employer. The employee must submit the certified statement to his employer within 30 days of its receipt. If this is not done, the employer may request a copy of the certified statement from the ministry. This provision is obviously meant to protect those people who, after having received the certified statement affirming that they worked in some capacity for the former secret police, decide to resign from their posts voluntarily. In such cases, an employer is not entitled to receive a copy of the document.

All those holding or applying for the positions listed in the law must also submit a personal affidavit that they were not communist party officials at the district level or above, members of the People's Militia, or students at one of the three Soviet police schools. In addition, the law stipulates that all those who apply for one of the senior government posts listed must submit an affidavit stating that they have never worked for a foreign intelligence service.

Under the new law, a citizen over the age of 18 may request that the federal Ministry of Internal Affairs certify that he or she was not a police informer or agent. Such a certificate will be given only to the citizen who has requested it.

Redress

The federal Ministry of Internal Affairs will set up a special commission soon whose members will be appointed by the Federal Assembly, the Czech and the Slovak National Councils, the federal, the Czech, and the Slovak Ministries of Internal Affairs, the Ministry of Defense, and the Federal Security and Information Service. The commission, serving as a body to which citizens affected by the law can appeal in the first instance, will examine the backgrounds of certain people, in the special cases specified under the law, using information submitted by the Internal Affairs Ministry, the testimony of witnesses, and the oral and written testimony and documentation submitted by the examinee.

The commission will investigate upon request cases of government officials who claim that the Ministry of Internal Affairs wrongly certified that they were "knowing collaborators" of the secret police. (People certified to be former secret police agents, holders of "conspiration" apartments, and informers will not be allowed to take their cases to the commission.) The commission will also examine the background of anyone who submitted an affidavit the truthfulness of which is questioned by that person's employer or by another citizen. If someone asks the commission to examine the past of another person, because he doubts the truthfulness of the information contained in that person's affidavit, he must first deposit 1,000 koruny with the commission. Should the commission conclude that the affidavit stated the truth, the money will not be returned. The commission must rule on such cases within 60 days of the start of its investigation.

Witnesses and experts who provide the commission with false statements may be punished by a prison term of up to three years. Publishing any information contained in the commission's ruling is permitted only with the consent of the person whose case is under examination.

If someone is certified as having worked for the former secret police, having been a communist official, a member of the People's Militia, or a student at one of the police schools in Moscow, his employer will terminate his employment or will transfer him to a less important position not specified by the law within 15 days of receiving such information. The employer must also terminate or transfer the employee within 15 days if the employee has refused to submit the required affidavit.

Citizens seeking redress may ask the appropriate civil court to examine the findings of the commission. They must appeal the commission's ruling within two months of the date of the ruling. Also, those who have been dismissed by their employer on the basis of the aforementioned certified statement from the Internal Affairs Ministry, in which the claims are later found to be unsubstantiated, may ask a civil court to reinstate them in their positions.

As the interpretation of the law would suggest, not all officials will be able to seek redress. The apparent reason for the distinction made between those who may and may not seek redress is that the names of former agents, holders of "conspiration apartments," and informers (most of whom signed a cooperation agreement with the secret police) are all registered in the files of the Internal Affairs Ministry. The authorities evidently believe that there is little doubt that these people did indeed work for the secret police.

Who Will Be Affected?

It is estimated that as many as 140,000 people were secret police informers under the communist regime. The dreaded secret police itself had tens of thousands of agents. The People's Militia also had tens of thousands of members. Between 1948 and 1989, thousands and perhaps tens of thousands of people worked as party officials at the district level or higher. Obviously, the majority of these people will not be directly affected by the law, as they currently do not hold any of the senior government posts listed in the law and are not likely to aspire to any of these positions in the next five years. Moreover, those recruited by the secret police to be informers or collaborators are for the most part average citizens who have neither held, nor are qualified to hold, the government posts listed in the law....

Reactions

Reactions to the law's passage were mixed. Right-of-center politicians insisted that the law was a necessary step toward "the purification of public life" in Czechoslovakia.[6]... Former Minister of Internal Affairs Richard Sacher, who himself was in charge of the first round of vetting in 1990, argued that the law "proves not the strength but the weakness of the regime."[8]

Left-of-center parties criticized the law and suggested that the parliament did not realize its possible consequences.... Zdenek Mlynar, who was a [Communist Party] secretary in 1968 and was expelled following the Soviet-led invasion of Czechoslovakia in 1968[,] argued that, in banning entire categories of people from holding certain positions only because they had held certain jobs in the past, the law violated internationally recognized human rights. He asked Havel to reject the law by not ratifying it.[9]...

Assessment

The law on the vetting of officials provides a legal framework for a process that has caused much controversy. President Havel had repeatedly asked the Federal Assembly to pass such a law, since earlier screenings had been based on nothing more than resolutions. Havel had, however, stressed that the law should be "good and just." In this context, the new law is likely to raise a number of questions. Havel had himself said that, in his opinion, the law went far beyond the government's original intent, which was reflected in the draft law submitted initially to the parliament. He added that he would probably ratify the law but might at the same time ask that it be amended. But he would not, he said, "choose to oppose the bill by means of a symbolic gesture but [would] use other methods instead."[11] On October 17 Havel ratified the law but, as he had suggested he might do, proposed a number of amendments, which he said he hoped the parliament would act to implement soon. More than anything else, Havel stressed that the law should give all those affected by the ban the possibility to appeal the decision in a court. He also underscored that the case and the possible guilt of each person should be assessed individually. Parliamentary chairman Dubcek refused to ratify the law; deputy

---

6 For various reactions, see CSTK, October 4, 1991.

8 AP, October 4, 1991.

9 CSTK, October 6, 1991.

11 AP and CSTK, October 13, 1991.

chairman Rudolf Battek did so in his stead, in accordance with the federal constitution.[12]

The chief flaw of the new legislation is that it is partially based on a presumption of guilt rather than of innocence: that is, the burden is on people in certain government positions to prove they did *not* work for the secret police or were *not* communist officials. Moreover, by barring entire categories of people, such as former communist officials, from holding certain positions, the law espouses the principle of collective guilt. Impractical as it might have been, the government's original draft sought to avoid enshrining that principle by stipulating the necessity of proving a particular official's participation in the suppression of human rights under the communist regime. Finally, the law does not distinguish between various degrees of guilt. Former secret police officials will be treated no more severely than people who were coerced into collaborating with or informing for the secret police.

Another contentious issue, which is not strictly related to the law itself but rather to the entire screening process, is the reliability of the Interior Ministry's files. Although responsible officials have repeatedly claimed that the files are reliable and that the former secret police had in place an elaborate system of cross-checking, some deputies and other politicians have publicly voiced their doubts about the reliability of the files. It is known that some of the files were destroyed by the secret police shortly after the revolution; and some former secret police members have testified that they "invented" informers by recording in their files the names of people who had never officially agreed to collaborate with the secret police.[13]

Paulina Bren, "Lustration in the Czech and Slovak Republics"[*]

The Independent Appeals Commission

An Independent Appeals Commission—as allowed for in the lustration law—came into being in February 1992, when its members were named. Although the commission was to have had fifteen permanent members it never achieved this number.[5] Because the members continued to hold their

---

[12] AP, October 22, 1991.

[13] See Obrman, "Laying the Ghosts..."; and *Newsweek*, October 6, 1991. See also a copy of a letter sent by Miloslav Tomicek, a former secret police agent, to the Office of the Federal Assembly on March 22, 1991, in which Tomicek revealed that he falsely recorded in the police files the name of Jaromir Gabas, one of the Federal Assembly's deputies accused of having collaborated with the secret police (available from the RFE/RL Research Institute in Munich).

[*] Excerpted from Paulina Bren, "Lustration in the Czech and Slovak Republics," *RFE/RL Research Report*, vol. 2, no. 29 (July, 16 1993), pp. 18-19.

[5] The Federal Assembly appointed the commission's chairman, Jaroslav Basta, as well as his deputy and one other member; the Czech and Slovak National Councils each named three members: the Federal Ministry of Internal Affairs named two; each republic's minister of internal affairs named one; and the federal defense minister and the director of the Federal Security and Information Service each chose a member.

regular jobs, it was often difficult to find the time for the growing caseload; reportedly they met on average two-and-a-half days a week.[6]

In hearing appeals from people who claimed to have been wrongly accused of being conscious collaborators, the commission could request materials from the federal Ministries of Internal Affairs and Defense and the Federal Security and Information Service (FBIS). They were entitled to call witnesses and at this juncture the accused was given the right to see his file. Upon completion of the investigation, the commission judged whether the accused had indeed been a conscious collaborator according to the criteria specified in the lustration law. If the commission found someone guilty, he could then turn to the district court for an appeals hearing.[7]

Questions and controversy began almost at the outset of the commission's existence. Much of the problem was due to the fact that the lustration law had never clearly outlined the exact mandate of the appeals commission. Quite soon it discovered that the overwhelming majority of its caseload was made up of individuals who had been accused of being candidates for secret collaboration, or what (from the wording of the law) became known as "Category C." A candidate for collaboration was usually someone whose name had been entered into the StB's files after having been brought in for a "talk." A common scenario, as described by the commission's chairman, Jaroslav Basta, on the basis of his experience in hearing many such cases, would involve a Czechoslovak citizen who had a relative resident in the West or had some contact with the West. That person would then be called in for a "talk," usually held at the Office of Passports and Visas. These "talks" persisted, but when the individual was finally asked directly to collaborate with the police, he refused. From then on the person's name remained in the register as a potential candidate for collaboration.

Given these experiences, Basta, a former dissident and trained archaeologist, identified the commission's mandate in a markedly different way from that of most other members of the commission. He argued that approximately 70,000 people had been registered in the StB files as candidates for collaboration; by October 1992, 4,000 of these had requested lustration (presumably because it was being carried out at their workplace) and 3,000 of these had appealed their case. The commission had only been able to rule on 600 of them: and of these 600, only fifteen individuals had been ruled to be conscious collaborators with the StB.[8] Citing these statistics. Basta questioned the very inclusion of "Category C" in the lustration law. He said that he believed that it had only been included for reasons of political expediency and had been hastily balanced out by the clause allowing for an appeals commission that in effect would take on the laborious task of determining individual guilt: something that the lustration law as a whole failed to do. Consequently, he interpreted

---

[6] Author's interview with Jaroslav Basta on 1 December 1992.

[7] Jaroslav Basta, "Lustration Process in the CSFR—Genesis of the Problem" (unpublished conference paper, issued November 1992 in Budapest).

[8] *Ibid.*

the commission's primary aim as that of proving that "Category C" should never have formed part of the law in the first place. Other members of the commission, however, did not share Basta's criticism of the lustration law.

The debate brought into question the trustworthiness of the StB files themselves. Basta claimed that in his three years of experience with the StB files[9] he had found that if someone named as a candidate for collaboration had agreed to work with the state security agencies then his file had been changed to the category of agent. But Petr Folk, another member of the commission, argued that some candidates were not shifted to the category of agent "only because they [the StB] forgot to do so. Or they were so active ... that a file change was unnecessary."[10] Arguing along similar lines. Jan Vidim, a deputy for the Civic Democratic Party pointed out that there were enormous differences between local StB offices, and this included their methods of registering individuals: in some districts a candidate for collaboration might never have spoken with an StB officer, while in other districts the category of candidate was equivalent to that of agent.[11] Evidently the problem remained, however, that even those people defending the actual inclusion of "Category C" in the lustration law inevitably had to accept the untrustworthiness of the former StB files as a systematic network of evidence, thereby bringing the whole lustration debate full circle.

The ability of the commission to function independently, without being influenced by public opinion and media reaction, came into question over the infamous Jan Kavan case.

---

[9] In 1990 Basta was a member of the Citizen's Screening Commission, which screened former members of the StB and the Ministry of Internal Affairs. Following that, he went on to the Office for the Protection of the Constitution and Democracy, where he worked in a number of capacities, becoming deputy director in the fall of 1991.

[10] *Respekt*, 30 October 1991, p. 8.

[11] *Ibid.*, 21 September 1992, p. 5.

Problems of Implementation: The Jan Kavan Case

*Lawrence Weschler, "The Velvet Purge: The Trials of Jan Kavan"**

[Editor's note: Jan Kavan was a Czech student leader during the Prague Spring of 1968. Subsequent to that, from a base in London, he was a prominent member of the Czech democratic opposition movement, founding the Palach Press Agency and publishing many of the movement's documents. In late 1989, Kavan returned to Prague; following the downfall of the communist government, he was elected as a member of the new parliament. In the selection which follows, Lawrence Weschler describes the lustration law in the context of its application to Kavan.]

[O]n February 22, 1991, Kavan himself was summoned to the commission's offices. Four of the panel's members were seated stiffly behind an oblong desk, and one of them—Stanislav Devaty, a man for whom Kavan had organized several emergency campaigns throughout the eighties, and whom Kavan regarded as a friend—informed him that his name had shown up in the files, along with a code name (Kato) and a sheaf of incriminating evidence, and that he was therefore being given fifteen days in which to resign.

...[T]he file allegedly documented the circumstances of his initial recruitment ... in January of 1969, when Kavan had been detained on charges of currency violation as he was attempting to leave the country to continue a year's program of study at Oxford. Kavan had already been travelling in and out of Czechoslovakia for a couple of years by 1969, and everyone acknowledges that up till then, at least, he had been one of the radical-student opposition's most effective spokesmen abroad, both before and after the Warsaw Pact's August, 1968, invasion and crackdown, working in venues as diverse as London, Paris, Chicago, Berkeley, Budapest, and Dubrovnik. But on that January day he had been caught; his money, and even more important, his passport had been confiscated, and his Oxford education suddenly appeared to be in jeopardy.

According to the file, Devaty now asserted, it was on this occasion that he was first approached by an StB agent. This man, named Stanislav Patejdl (code name Pavlasek), apparently offered to grease the wheels for him—to free his passport and allow him to return to England—in exchange for his future cooperation and collaboration. Panic-stricken, Kavan had agreed to this bargain (or so it was alleged) and almost immediately after his return to Britain had dutifully reported to Patejdl's man at the London Embassy—the education attaché, Frantisek Zajicek (code name Zachystal). Over the next year, he had reported often (over forty meetings were listed) and thoroughly, providing detailed information on both his student contacts and the opposition's principal British allies....

---

* Excerpted from *The New Yorker*, vol. 68, no. 35, (Oct. 19, 1992), pp. 68-72, 80-86, 92-94. Reprinted by permission; © 1992 Lawrence Weschler. Originally in *The New Yorker*.

The commission had apparently assumed that when Kavan was confronted with the charges he would simply fold and slink away. When he refused to do so, the commission was thrown into consternation. For a month, in high secrecy and with increasing urgency, the commission's members and Kavan and his trusted allies struggled over how to proceed. By March 16th, the day of Kavan's wedding, it looked as if the commission had decided not to denounce him after all. On March 18th, he was at last allowed to examine selected portions of the file—sixty pages out of five hundred—on the condition that he leave the door ajar and not make any copies. On March 21st, the commission debated the case until well past midnight; it finally decided, by vote of six to five (with four members absent), to denounce Kavan.

The next day, Kavan's name was the fifth one on a list of ten names of unmasked agents read out to the Parliament by the commission's spokesman, Petr Toman. A few minutes later, Kavan approached the speaker's stand to deliver a speech, which was being broadcast live to a nationwide television audience. "I do fervently hope that at least some of you will be able to listen in good faith to what I have to say," he began—at which point thirty-five M.P.s stalked out of the chamber. He then continued, "I am not being condemned to eight weeks' or eight years' imprisonment but am being branded a secret-police collaborator for the rest of my life."...

[Kavan later explained,] "As for Zajicek, his was a name I did remember. You see, I was the leading officer then living in Britain of the S.V.S., the Union of University Students of Bohemia and Moravia—the association hadn't yet been disbanded—and, as such, I naturally had all sorts of official dealings with the Embassy's education attaché, intervening in matters like the visa extensions for my fellow-students and constituents who happened to be stranded in Britain at the time.... [O]ur conversations occasionally ranged a bit afield, though I never disclosed any secrets or any information damaging to anyone else. How was I supposed to know he was recording everything I said for transmittal back to the StB, sometimes with considerable embellishment?"

Kavan declared that he wasn't expecting anyone to credit his protestations of innocence on the basis of his word alone. All he wanted, he said, was some sort of due process, a forum in which he could prove his innocence by calling witnesses and cross-examining his accusers. He said he was trying to get the entire file released to the public, on condition that the release be accompanied by his own point-by-point commentary. But the authorities were pleading the sacrosanct confidentiality of the files—all the while allowing out-of-context leaks of their own that were sometimes quite damaging. (All three hundred members of Parliament had now been granted free access to the entire file.) As his only apparent legal recourse, Kavan had launched a defamation suit in Prague Civil Court against the Interior Ministry, but the case had bogged down in the chaotic post-Communist judicial system....

"This whole StB de-Communization business is now becoming terribly politicized," Kavan told me. He was pale and trembling as he talked."...

It's an awful situation, and there are good people, some of them old friends of mine, who feel that the only way to break the logjam is to expose the longstanding ties of many ... politicians, say, with the StB—for many of them do have such histories....

"And here I am desperately claiming that the process behind such exposures is seriously flawed. So these good people come up to me, with great circumspection, and say. 'Listen, we realize that there has been some terrible mistake in your personal case, but can't you just let it be, can't you just quietly take the fall, *for the greater good of the country?*' And for me the terrible thing in such suggestions is that those were precisely the kinds of arguments that his interrogators tried to use on my father during his incarceration—how, yes, he'd obviously been a dedicated Communist, but how he should still sign this confession, *for the greater good of the Party.* And I just won't have it!"...

[G]rasping the extent of the StB's penetration of Czech society requires an understanding of how the StB operated. In part thanks to the dramas of Vaclav Havel himself, people in the West are fairly familiar with the classic totalitarian quandary of whether or not to sign the petition—the decent, if somewhat weak, man faced with the terrible dilemma of whether to risk his livelihood and his family's well-being by finally taking a principled stand in opposition to some particular state travesty. The tattered page before him, his trembling hand: To sign or not to sign? But we are perhaps not as aware of another sort of signing drama—this first one's eerie obverse—that was continually occurring inside Czechoslovakia, as in the other Communist countries, all through those years. For the secret police there demanded more than mere conformity; they craved collusion. They would set their sights on a given individual, and through artful blends of threat and seduction, of extortion and bribery, they would endeavor to get that person to cross over to their side, to join their ranks. And this dance always culminated—for theirs was a bureaucratic culture par excellence—in the proffering of a form, a mere sheet of paper, and the request for a signature. A pact with the devil, and again the same barbed question: To sign or not to sign? Sometimes all that was being asked for was that signature; sometimes, more would be required. Sometimes, that signature connoted the commitment to do considerably more, sometimes nothing more than solemnly to promise never to speak to anyone else of these dark contacts (an odd agreement, that: "Sign here your confirmation that we never met"). The StB agents were under considerable pressure continually to expand their web of complicity, to recruit more informers, to collect more signatures. They got bonuses: three more signatures, a television set! Sometimes, as is now known, they fabricated signatures, although not people: the people were real, the signatures were faked. ("We're not talking Kafka here," as one observer noted. "This was Gogol, or Graham Greene: 'Our man in Prague.'") All the signatures gravitated toward the center and got entered into the registry, a master list, which also included the names of mere subjects of investigation, or even of established enemies of the state. Sometimes it was easy to tell the difference, but often it was not.

At any rate, this mastery registry became the focal point for the lustration process as it related to the security services. The drama of signing would now be turned inside out—into a drama of naming. According to the new law, every state employee or applicant for state employment above a certain defined level would be required to have himself lustrated; that is, his name would be submitted to a panel at the Interior Ministry, and the panel would consult the register and, within sixty days, issue a certificate declaring the person "StB positive" or "StB negative." If the applicant turned up negative, he would present that certificate to his superior and retain his job. If he came out positive, the best thing for him to do would be to resign quietly.

As the lustration campaign began to kick into high gear, it aroused concern among several international monitoring organizations, ranging from the International Labor Organization, in Geneva, to Helsinki Watch, in New York. Serious questions were raised about the principle of collective guilt, the reliability of the StB registry, the failure to distinguish between levels of culpability within that registry, the lack of due-process safeguards (including a misplaced burden of proof and a too limited right of appeal), and the imminent likelihood that the campaign would break out of its current high-governmental context.

...I made a point of visiting [Jaroslav Basta, chairman of the independent commission charged with implementing the lustration law] at his office when I went to Prague.... Basta is a relatively young man—roughly Kavan's age. He had known and worked with Kavan when both were student radicals. Basta was an archeologist by training, but after being arrested, in 1970, for "subversive activities" and serving a subsequent two-and-a-half year sentence in prison he had been blocked from pursuing his chosen profession—officially, at least. He had been consigned to work in construction thereafter, yet he nevertheless managed to pursue his real vocation in his spare time, composing dozens of highly regarded papers on the prehistory of Western Bohemia. In our conversation he acknowledged that many of the skills he had honed in those studies were of considerable value in his current work, which consisted of sifting through reams of ambiguous data in search of plausible accounts of the prehistory of various fairly or unfairly accused individuals, and our talk turned to the archeology of collaboration.

"I feel I've seen it all by this time," Basta said, with a deep sigh. One of the first signers of Charter 77, Basta was one of the first delegates that the Civic Forum finally posted to the Interior Ministry and he had held various positions there and in its successors. "I've scoured hundreds of files," he went on. "There were so many different kinds of collaboration and reasons for collaborating. Some people informed for the StB out of ideological conviction—though, actually, surprisingly few. With some, the motivation was petty jealously or small-time revenge. Some were just born informers; in many ways, those were the worst—the twisted ones. Some collaborated for material gain, or to advance their careers—so as to be able to travel abroad for instance—or not to have their careers dashed. There were some who were blackmailed into collaborating: the StB was regularly on the lookout for people's weaknesses, and it would exploit every lapse, every vulnerability. I've heard horrible stories. Some people were put under terrible pressure while serving jail sentences for various political crimes—or, threatened with jail, they were unable to withstand that pressure—and signed on. Some did it out of love—so as not to blight a child's education, or so as to be able finally to visit a family member stranded abroad. Some who signed went on to do terrible damage to the lives of their neighbors or co-workers. Others signed and did virtually nothing, offering no information of any import whatever. Still others signed and almost immediately thought better of it; racked by guilt, they may have collaborated for a few weeks and never again. Some of those then joined—or rejoined—the dissident movement and subsequently put in years of solid, important work."

And was that his job, I interjected—to sort out all those gradations and evaluate all those mitigating factors?

"Oh, no," he replied. "The great majority of those people I can't help at all. The law makes no provision for any such mitigating circumstances. If you ever signed—if you're listed in the registry under Category A or B, which means that your signature is one file—that's it: You're StB positive, and there's no appeal. You're lustrated. No, our commission is empowered under the law to handle only the appeals of people in the borderline so-called Category C, which is a very narrow category—maybe only two thousand cases. We can examine the entire files of those people, subpoena witnesses and enforce testimony under oath, and then render a binding verdict. When it comes to those people, we do have the authority to clear their names. But everybody else...." He shrugged, paused, and went on, "I've considered this law for a long time, and I have to tell you I don't think much either of it or of the people who initiated it."

There were all kinds of arguments both in favor of and opposed to lustration, some more convincing than others, but it seemed to me that the real sources of the passion swirling around the issue ran deeper than mere argumentation. This was particularly evident, I came to feel, with regard to two types of support that the campaign was garnering.

The first involved former dissident activists who were vehement proponents of lustration. They were a small minority. In general, you could almost take it as a rule: go through Amnesty International's old Czechoslovak files, and you'd find that the more severely persecuted an oppositionist had been under the old regime, the less adamant he was likely to be today about lustration. Nevertheless, its enthusiastic advocates did include some distinguished longtime oppositionists, and I had a lengthy conversation with one of these: Pavel Bratinka, a leading Catholic radical free marketeer, who had become one of the guiding lights of the relatively small but remarkably dynamic new O.D.A. (Civic Democratic Alliance) political party. At one point in our discussion, I brought up a couple of Basta's examples—people who had been blackmailed into signing, or those who had signed out of love, out of a wish to be able to visit a daughter abroad, say—and I asked Bratinka whether he felt that such cases might not rate some special dispensation.

His lips curling with disgust, he said, "If they were blackmailable before, who's to say they wouldn't be blackmailable again? The people have a right to protect themselves from those who enslaved them; of course such people should be lustrated. The point is that these acts of cowardice of theirs had consequences. There were people who didn't sign, who retained their dignity and didn't get to go see their daughter. If a man admits that he was nothing but a weakling—and that is what his having signed those papers proves—why shouldn't people have the right to know he was a weakling? And why should society have to endure the continued presence of such weaklings in positions of authority? I am a solid-state physicist, but for eight years, because I refused to sign, I was forced to work as a street-cleaner and a stoker. Everybody could earn a living honestly during those years in this country. And those who failed to showed a bizarre lack of moral conscience. Why should they be spared the publication of that truth now?"...

The self-righteously vindictive theme, however, amounted to only a trickle in the pro-lustration flood, perhaps because only a small number of lustration's supporters had any claim to feelings of self-righteous purity. For the fact is—and this was a key part of the Czech reality and, indeed, the principal source of lustration's main tributary of support—that hardly anybody in Czechoslovakia ever did actively oppose the regime. Unlike the situation in Poland, for example, where millions took an active role in the 1980-81 Solidarity movement—the movement that both prefigured and provoked the collapse of Communism—the post-1968 opposition in Czechoslovakia was never able to claim more than a few thousand active members....

"That silence was what mattered, not any individual bastards," Jan Urban, a journalist, who was one of the bravest and most dynamic opposition activists during the eighties, told me. "And all the current noise surrounding lustration is simply a way of keeping silent about that silence."...

Jaroslav Basta told me during our conversation, "You may have noticed how the countries having the most trouble with issues of the lustration sort are those where the transition was the most abrupt—Czechoslovakia and East Germany, for example, as opposed to Poland and Hungary. I see this as a delayed reaction to the way we did away with Communism. People found that if they just went into the streets en masse for a few days, jangling their key rings, the whole regime would crumble—and after a few weeks of merriment they began asking themselves, somewhat sheepishly, 'Well, why didn't we do it sooner if it was all so easy?' And they answered themselves, 'Because we were afraid.' But of what? The thought that there may have been nothing to be afraid of would be very unpleasant to accept. That's why it became better to speak of this demonic, omnipresent StB apparatus, with its treacherous agents everywhere who held us all down and now needed to be revealed and expunged—better that than admitting the truth, which was one's own lack of courage."

Zdenek Kavan, Jan's brother, [suggested "]It is those who never lifted a finger to oppose the old regime who are pushing for these purges, demanding the publication of all those lists. The nice thing about a list is that if you're not on it you can consider yourself pure."...

And matters were even more perverse: it wasn't just who got to purify himself; there was also the question "At whose expense?" Though the lustration law cited various categories of lustratable offenders—officials of the Communist Party above a certain rank, members of the People's Militia, informers on the StB registry, and so forth—it was principally the informers on the StB registry who most seemed to capture the public imagination and to provoke the greatest ire. And this was no accident.

Jana Frankova, a well-connected interpreter, told me "The terrible thing is that those most likely to arouse the notice of the StB in the first place and hence to get dragged in for questioning—whether or not they subsequently succumbed to its pressures or seductions and thus ended up being placed, rightly or wrongly, on the registry list—were those who had been showing their opposition to the regime in some active way. With a few exceptions, one can see in retrospect how that was the organizing principle behind all those lists."... [I]t was former activists—and in significant numbers—who were likely to be making appearances on that list, right alongside the authentically reprehensible.

"People now realize that it was possible to live differently, not just in silence," commented Jirina Siklova, the sociologist who put in many years as Kavan's key interior contact.... People hate themselves and project that hate upon the StB or onto the dissidents. And whenever it becomes possible to imagine that the StB and the dissidents were somehow collaborating all along—well, that's enormously satisfying to people. 'See?' they can tell themselves. 'The dissident movement *was* completely infiltrated and controlled by the StB, just the way I always figured!'" (A few days later, I heard a variant of this formulation from the mouths of organizers of the Anti-Communist Alliance, an extremist wing of the purifying crusade. "The other day, there was a Charter 77 reunion," one of them told me. "Jesus, I've never seen so many StB agents in one place." He paused, and then added confidentially, "You know, we have evidence that fully one-third of the Charter 77 members were StB agents.") "See?" Siklova continued her encapsulation of the majority temper. "I was *right* not to get involved in their silly games. The *smart* thing to do was to keep quiet."...

The lustration law's defenders regularly pointed to its rigorous provisions delimiting applicability and guaranteeing confidentiality. Many [complained of the perception that] the lists were just floating about free, so that people were liable to be sacked from just about any job on their account, [noting that] the law was quite specific about which positions were to be affected and about how the procedures followed in establishing any particular individual's liability under the law were to be cloaked in absolute confidentiality. What could be more civilized? Why all the fuss?

The trouble was that, whether or not this was how the law was supposed to work, or had even started out working, by the time I got to Prague late this past spring the practice of lustration was breaking wildly out of its contours. The law stipulated which positions *had* to be lustrated but didn't preclude lustration for other positions, either governmental or private; and overzealous public officials quickly overreached. When the education minister was asked about the propriety of having head cooks at schools lustrated—a move that had recently been required—he said "This is not exactly in harmony with the law, but it answers pressure from the public."

As long as somebody was being officially lustrated, at least the confidentiality of any eventual determination was still being assured. However, the master list itself soon began leaking in sporadic batches, along with choice unprocessed files. At first, the leaks seemed maddeningly random. As I was visiting Peter Brod, an exceptionally knowledgeable researcher for Radio Free Europe/Radio Liberty, at his office one afternoon, his fax machine started clattering away, spewing out, without any covering letter, a numbered and alphabetized list of names, birth dates, alleged code names, file numbers, and current professions—five pages, with a hundred and seventy-seven names. Brod was singularly unfazed. "Oh, that?" he said. "That happens all the time these days—anonymous lists of supposed StB operatives coming in unsolicited, over the transom. Notice that it's not even identified as such. It's simply a list of names—with no source identified, either. An everyday occurrence. We don't broadcast or publish such lists ourselves, but others do. Who's to say whether it's an authentic list, and, even if it is, what having one's name on the list signifies? But the city is swarming with such things."

Susan Greenberg, the *Guardian*'s correspondent, told me how difficult it was to be a journalist in such an atmosphere. "If you come along and try to make distinctions, then you are part of the conspiracy," she said. "Stefan Bacinsky, the former head of the F.B.I.S"—the Federal Security Information Service, one of the replacements of the old StB and a principle keeper of the master list—"recently declared that criticism of the F.B.I.S. was part of a conspiracy to discredit Czechoslovakia. People here don't know how to argue. Everything is framed in Manichaean terms and immediately gets personal. This, of course, is one of the persistent legacies of the Communist style. I can understand their desire to come to terms with the past, but what I don't like is how the minute you try to defend a principle, you get accused of taking sides. More and more, people have stopped putting up any argument about observance of the lustration law, for fear of being labelled."

And things were about to get significantly worse. With the official start of the parliamentary-election campaign a few days off, Stefan Bacinsky suddenly let it be known that the F.B.I.S., apparently without any authorization or directive, had gone off and compiled a list of several hundred journalists known to have been StB informants. Actually, what he had done was simply to run the membership list of the newly reconstituted Journalists Syndicate through a computer already containing the celebrated master list—a process that resulted in a new list of purported journalist-StB agents. The results were utterly shocking, he declared, and constituted a serious imminent threat to national security, because of the evident potential for widespread disinformation or blackmail. (He offered no specific instances of either disinformation or blackmail.) He wasn't about to release the list himself—he wasn't empowered to, he explained primly—but he did let it be known that he had given copies to the Prime Minister and to the chairman of Parliament. Furious debates ensued, with right-wing parliamentarians, in particular, demanding immediate publication of the list, on the ground that those listed posed grave threats to the nation's well-being, especially on the eve of such a crucial electoral campaign. Parliamentary leaders eventually decided to distribute the list to all parliamentarians, for information purposes only, and only on the condition that they all swore to keep its contents a secret. "Well, that does it," Jan Urban told me when he heard the news. "You watch. Within twenty-four hours, the entire list will have been published."

And, indeed, within twenty-four hours it was—by the right-wing daily *Telegraf*, whose deputy editor, the respected journalist Jindrich Hoda, was himself on the list. Wasting no time, *Telegraf* summarily fired him.

I had a chance to talk with Hoda a few days later, and he still looked shell-shocked. He said he doubted whether he'd ever be able to get similar employment. He explained to me that he had indeed been courted by the StB over a period of several years, several years ago. He had then been working at *Lidove Demokracie*; in fact, he had put in twenty-five years there, fifteen as head of the foreign desk. *Lidove Demokracie* was the daily of the long-standing, Catholic-based People's Party, which continued to print during the Communist regime, and, as such, it was allowed slightly more independence than most of the mainstream Communist journals. For that reason, however, it became a particular target of StB concern and penetration, and so StB agents would approach him fairly regularly and insist that he come out with them for a few drinks, just to talk things over informally. Scared—yet a bit bemused as well by their sheer oafishness—he would go. "But I always paid for my own drinks," he said. "And sometimes even for theirs. I know that sounds bad, but what if I'd let *them* pay for *my* drinks? That, too, would have sounded bad. That's the kind of knot they were able to tie you into." The agents weren't after any information about his co-workers, he said. Instead, they were trying to recruit him as a foreign courier in their international division: if he would just agree to deliver the odd occasional envelope or package to the assigned mail drop, they would arrange for him to get a passport. In all those years as foreign editor, he had never been allowed to travel abroad. He said he regularly declined the offer. "And then, one time, they suddenly took out a sheet of paper and pressed me to sign," he recalled. "All at once, things turned very serious, and I became terrified. But I refused. I swear on the lives of my children that I never signed anything. I never informed. And the best proof is that I never did get to travel abroad. What I wish I could do is demand that my file be opened. Then everybody could see there's no signed oath, it's all a lie. The trouble is, this is a private proceeding—I was fired by a private company—so I have no standing; the records are confidential. My life has been stripped from me, and I have virtually no recourse."...

On one of my last days in Prague, I visited the Interior Ministry headquarters.... [T]he deputy minister, Jan Ruml, indicated that he would be willing to see me. Ruml—the son of the veteran dissident Jiri Ruml, who had chaired the November 17th Commission—was himself a veteran oppositionist. In fact, he had been a key link in Kavan's secret distribution network....

I asked him what it had been like when he first arrived in this office. "It was terrible," he said. "This was April of 1990—up to then, for the first six months of the Velvet Revolution, the old StB had continued to have pretty much free run of the place, and you could still feel the ruling spirit. In fact, most of the old people were still here. And it was my first task to dissolve the StB as an organization. During the past two and a half years, we've released eight thousand of the old employees."

This means that he had been one of the people who uncovered, collected, and secured the surviving StB registries and files. That, too, he said, had been an excruciating experience—repeatedly coming upon the names of trusted old friends in the various registries. "It was always the same," Ruml recalled. "I would confront them privately, and invariably they'd deny it. I'd dig deeper into the files, pulling up their personal records, and there you'd find all the evidence—the signed documents, the receipts, and so forth—and I'd confront them again, and they'd break down crying, admitting it, offering up their various excuses. It was all very painful...."

What about Kavan?

"Kavan was a person who for a long period, especially before 1981, helped us very much in keeping up contact with the world outside—both the world of exile and the world of our potential international sympathizers. At the same time, he was a very contradictory person."

...[A]s far as this top security official was concerned—a man who, after all, had had open access to all the files and data involved—the case against Kavan largely boiled down to the question of his behavior during 1969 and 1970. "And, having carefully reviewed the files, I've made a determination that Kavan must have known that he was dealing with an StB agent in 1969-70, during those contacts with the Embassy's education officer," Ruml concluded. "I don't think he would have continued much longer, no matter what—as you know, the education officer was himself recalled to Prague by late summer of 1970—and maybe he just imagined himself to be playing some kind of game, thinking he could outsmart or manipulate them, or something. I've seen hundreds of cases like that. In fact, that's maybe the most frequent motive."

And ought that to be cause enough for lustration?

"He was labelled a person who knew he was collaborating with the StB," Ruml declared, stiffening noticeably. "I myself would not have been terribly concerned about this, especially in Kavan's case. According to the file, he did not offer them any substantive information, or anything that could have harmed others. But the November 17th Commission came to the conclusion that he collaborated knowingly, and if he says he did not, then he's lying, and *that's* why he shouldn't be in Parliament." Ruml seemed very pleased with that formulation.

But, I persisted, if all he was doing was playing games....

"I believe that those who knowingly collaborated, even if they did nothing harmful, even if they were just playing games, should be lustrated. It's difficult for you in the States to understand this—you didn't live for forty years under Communist rule. This regime destroyed all of us; we have all been to a greater or lesser extent tainted—even those of us in the opposition. We are attempting some kind of moral cleanup here, to clean the society of those who morally compromised themselves. And one of the criteria we're using is that people not have knowingly collaborated with the StB—it's as simple as that. Kavan did, and if he says he didn't then he's lying; and, furthermore, by taking his case internationally, the way he's doing, he's undermining the reputation of the country, and that's another reason he deserves to be lustrated."...

On my last evening in Prague, I was talking with Helena Klimova, a psychotherapist, in her consulting office.... I asked Klimova what she thought of the lustration process.... "Its initial motivation was a healthy one, it seems to me, this need for a sense of justice," she replied. "Only, we missed the opportunity for real justice, and lustration now serves as a kind of facsimile. At the very outset, you see, there was this consensus: we wanted justice, but we didn't want to be like them. What we really wanted to hear from the Communists was an expression of sorrow or contrition, some kind of confession, after which we'd have been prepared to forgive. We wanted to forgive, I think. But the forgiveness came too soon. There was anxiety at the very top, among people like Havel and Czech Premier Pithart and Foreign Minister Dienstbier. They stopped various attempts at wholesale purges: *we weren't going to be like them*. And then the Communists stopped confessing before they even started. Instead, they became all puffed up with their success—their economic success, for example. They were shameless, and people got angry, and that's when the cry for punishment began to be heard."

The room was darkening. I could hardly see her anymore in the gloom.

"What happened then is comparable to obsessive neurotic behavior in individuals," she went on. "Such patterns usually start when a person has an aim that for some reason can't be reached, and instead you get a series of ersatz fulfillments of that aim, as in bulimia, for instance. In our case, we binge on these lists, ever larger lists—only, they are hollow, because what can you say about these supposed master lists of informers? Isn't the whole point that the masters of the list aren't on the master list? It's all phony. The impulse isn't phony. It's quite authentic, it needs to be addressed. But the execution in this instance is empty, the justice is ersatz."

COMPENSATION AND RESTITUTION IN CZECHOSLOVAKIA

Background

*Michael Kraus, "Settling Accounts: Postcommunist Czechoslovakia"**

The creation of a strong private sector has come to be seen by most pro-democracy forces as "a political guarantee of the death of the old order, in that removing the center's ownership claims upon society's resources prevents it from exerting excessive control over socioeconomic processes that characterized the old system."[13] Moreover, building a private sector where there was virtually none is surely crucial for the development of a viable middle class that many students of democracies see as a prerequisite to democratic political order.[14] Furthermore, some political groups view privatization as a form of redistributive justice, whereby property rights and property as such are transferred from undeserving claimants to deserving ones.[15]

Owing to successive waves of nationalization, the Czechoslovak economy by the end of the 1980s was one of the most centralized and "socialized," i.e., state-controlled, economies in the Communist world. Unlike Poland, where private landownership was preserved under communism, Czechoslovakia's land was fully collectivized in the 1950s and the 1960s. In contrast to Hungary or East Germany, where small retail enterprises were tolerated, the private sector in Czechoslovakia, with the exception of the black market, was virtually extinguished. On the eve of the velvet revolution of 1989, nearly 100 percent of Czechoslovakia's economy was in the public sector.[16] That is also why the new government regarded privatization as one of the highest priorities.

In April 1990, the Federal Assembly passed a series of laws dealing with the economy. They gave the citizens the right to establish their own businesses and placed private, cooperative and state property on an equal status. But the growth of private business activity was agonizingly slow, at least in part, because the new laws contained loopholes that opened the doors to bureaucratic abuse, especially in the entrenched lower echelons of the former nomenklatura.[17]...

---

* Excerpted from Michael Kraus, *Settling Accounts: Postcommunist Czechoslovakia*, revised version of paper delivered at 1992 Annual Meeting of the American Political Science Association, The Palmer House Hilton, September 3-6, 1992.

13 Ben Slay and John Tedstrom, "Privatization in the Postcommunist Economies," *Privatization: A Special Report*, RFE/RL, (Munich: Radio Free Europe/ Radio Liberty Research Report, (hereafter cited as RFE) 24 April, 1992, p. 1.

14 See, for example, Barrington Moore, *Social Origins of Dictatorship and Democracy* (Boston: Beacon Press, 1967) esp. pp. 413-32.

15 Slay and Tedstrom, op. cit., p. 1, 3.

16 *Czechoslovakia: Transition to a Market Economy*, (Washington DC: The World Bank, 1991) p. 2.

17 Jiri Pehe, "The Instability of Transition, *RFE*, January 1991, p. 15.

What particularly infuriated many activists in 1990 was the party's continued hold on the top managerial positions in most of the large state enterprises. In June, the Civic Forum in the district of Hodonin in southern Moravia published a document listing the leading managers in the district. It showed that out of 205 managers, 130 were Communists and that virtually all key managerial positions in the district remained in party hands. In response to the Hodonin complaint, on July 1, Petr Pithart, the Czech Prime Minister (a former leading dissident and one of the founders of the Civic Forum) came out against such tactics, lest they fuel demands for "a purge."[19] He warned of the danger of applying the principle of "collective guilt" against all Communists on the grounds that this was the very principle that the party had used as an instrument of policy against the so-called "class enemies." Pithart argued that a distinction must be made between "decent experts," who had been (or still were) party members, yet who had demonstrated their competence, and those Communists who had indeed behaved like "members of a Mafia." While the latter should be kept in check, concluded Pithart, it would be wrong, "to hunt down" Communist managers and thereby to revive the Communist practice of awarding jobs according to political criteria.

Instead of persuading his fellow activists, Pithart's able defense of skills and expertise as the relevant criteria for managerial leadership prompted a widespread debate in July and August 1990. And the Hodonin "manifesto" not only received much backing, but the same problems were said to exist in other communities. Many Civic Forum organizations now lined up against the Czech Prime Minister. Thanks to their tradition of Party discipline, his critics charged, the Communists continue to maintain a tight grip on economic power and on promotions throughout the country. Because top managerial posts, as a rule, required many years of experience, which only the party loyalists could obtain and because the party had historically promoted only its own kind, only Communists today were in the privileged position, they argued.

Pithart's critics also claimed that yesterday's Communist bureaucrats, who had turned in their party cards, continued to sabotage the efforts of the new private entrepreneurs to set up their business. Worst of all, the most adept of the "mafia" took advantage of the new laws to transform the most profitable parts of the state enterprises they ran into joint-stock companies, in which they become the controlling share-holders. Thus, now as before the revolution, Pithart's critics thundered, it is the non-Communists who are being discriminated.

---

19 My account here is based on Jiri Pehe, "The Controversy over Communist Managers," *RFE*, Vol. 1, September 7, 1990, pp. 6-10, and Petr Janyska, "Druha revoluce," *Respekt*, no. 24, 22-28 August 1990.

*Alexander H. Platt, Imtiaz T. Ladak, Alan J. Goodman, Matthew R. Nicely, "Compensating Former Political Prisoners: An Overview of Developments in Central and Eastern Europe"**

The following is a chronological list of the pertinent legislation passed by the Czechoslovak Federal Assembly since early 1990:

a. April 23, 1990: Law on [Judicial Rehabilitation] (Law No. 119/1990) passed to allow Czechoslovak citizens who were imprisoned for political reasons to request that the court verdict against them be declared null and void and to demand financial compensation from the state.[11]

b. May 1990: Penal code amended to abolish a number of "political crimes" and to abolish the death penalty.[12]

c. Fall 1990: Restitution Law and "Small" Privatization Law passed.[13]

d. December 6, 1990: The Federal Government announced it would provide emergency compensation payments for entitled persons who were waiting for the conclusion of the bureaucratic procedures set out by Law No. 119/1990.

e. January 30, 1991: Law No. 47/1991 passed to modify and amend the Law on [Judicial Rehabilitation].[14]

f. February 21, 1991: Law on Extrajudicial Rehabilitation passed, which returns to its previous owners all property confiscated by the Communists and provides for the rehabilitation and compensation of victims of political persecution, other than those who were convicted of a "political crime".[15]

g. February 27, 1991: "Large" privatization law passed to regulate the transfer of state-owned companies to private owners.[16]

---

* Reprinted from Alexander H. Platt et al., Akin, Gump, Strauss, Hauer, & Feld, *Compensating Former Political Prisoners: An Overview of Developments in Central and Eastern Europe*, unpublished paper, August 14, 1992, pp. 5-6.

[11] Zakon c.119/1990 Sb....

[12] Jiri Pehe, *Toward the Rule of Law*, RFE/RL Res. Rep., July 3, 1992, at 11.

[13] Jan Orbman, *Two Landmark Bills on Privatization Approved*, RFE/RL Rep. on E. Eur., March 14, 1991, at 12.

[14] Zakon c.47/1991 Sb....

[15] [omitted]

[16] Orbman, *supra* note 13.

April 1990 Law on Judicial Rehabilitation

Michael Kraus, "Settling Accounts: Postcommunist Czechoslovakia" *

The Confederation of Czechoslovak Political Prisoners, born in December 1989, was the largest group representing the interests of the victims of communist injustice. Pressing for a law on the rehabilitation of political prisoners, it took an active part in the preparation of the Law on Judicial Rehabilitation, which was enacted on April 23, 1990 [Law No. 119/1990]. The law sets out to "correct the injustices against people who were unjustly sentenced" between February 25, 1948, the date of the Communist seizure of power, and December 31, 1989.[26]

Jan Obrman, "Rehabilitating Political Victims" †

The new law differentiates between two kinds of rehabilitations. Many "political crimes" under the communist regime were abolished *ex lege* after November 1989, and the sentences handed down for these crimes thus became null and void. Those convicted of such acts have consequently been automatically rehabilitated. No retrials are necessary in these cases, which include all convictions on charges of high treason, espionage, sabotage, illegal emigration, illegal gathering, insult of public officials, and some 60 other offenses that were frequently used either to eliminate any sign of opposition to the communist regime or to harass individual activists. According to some sources, about 90% of what the communist authorities considered political crimes will be eliminated by this process.[2]

The second kind of rehabilitation will require a new investigation into the circumstances of the individual trials. Those affected must apply for review of their cases within two years. Those who were sentenced under laws that have since been abolished but who were charged with using violence or propagating fascism or similar goals may be rehabilitated only after a new trial. If such people are exonerated, all the legal costs for the retrials will be covered by the state.

Law No. 119/1990 also deals with compensation and the adjustment of pensions, both questions that could have been addressed with the help of the existing civil code. The law provides guidelines for redressing fines and legal costs victims were forced to pay, as well as for loss of earnings and damage to health resulting from incarceration. These streamlined provisions were apparently designed to prevent complicated and time-consuming litigation based on the civil code in each individual case. The law does not rule out the possibility of requesting more than the

---

* Excerpted from Michael Kraus, *Settling Accounts: Postcommunist Czechoslovakia*, revised version of paper delivered at 1992 Annual Meeting of the American Political Science Association, The Palmer House Hilton, September 3-6, 1992.

[26] Jan Obrman, "Rehabilitating Political Victims," RFE, December 14, 1990, pp. 5-8.

† Excerpted from Jan Obrman, "Rehabilitating Political Victims," *Report on Eastern Europe*, vol. 1, no. 50 (1990), pp. 5-6.

[2] *Pol* no. 3, September 1, 1990, p. 2.

maximum amount stipulated in the law if the victim believes that the compensation offered is too low....

Virtually all state institutions ... issued their own instructions concerning the rehabilitation of former employees who were dismissed for political reasons. For example, schools and universities have rehabilitated professors, teachers, and students who lost their positions or had to terminate their studies because of their political or religious beliefs. This form of professional and educational rehabilitation has resulted in the return of many former state employees—including diplomats, military officers (who have been given back their previous ranks or even promoted), scientists, and others—to their former professions. Many former students who were not permitted to complete their studies can now continue and, without excessive bureaucratic problems, earn their degrees. This process will also affect the pensions of those who were discriminated against. If they have already reached pensionable age, they may apply for readjustment of their retirement benefits to the Ministry of Labor and Social Affairs....

Estimates of the number of individuals who will be affected by these different forms of rehabilitation are not precise and often contradict one another. The first official estimates said that about 100,000 individuals would be affected by the Law on [Judicial] Rehabilitation in the Czech Republic alone.[4] This figure was soon modified, however, and in April officials were saying that the rehabilitation would affect between 200,000 and 220,000 people in the Czech Republic and about 64,000 in Slovakia.[5] But even these revised figures might be too low, some observers have pointed out. It is still not clear exactly how many people were imprisoned for political reasons between 1948 and 1989, either with or without trial. A document presented by the Confederation of Czechoslovak Political Prisoners[6] said that 200 people were officially executed following political trials, an estimated 8,000 to 10,000 died as a result of forced labor, were tortured to death, or were shot during an escape attempt; and 48,000 were held in forced-labor camps (in addition to those held in prisons). These figures have, to some extent, been confirmed by official statements.[7]

More than 50% of all cases of legal rehabilitation are said to involve people sentenced *in absentia* for "illegally leaving the republic" or attempting to do so,[8] although once again, many details are still not

---

4 *Ibid.*, March 12, 1990, 5:10 p.m.

5 *Narodna Obroda*, August 29, 1990.

6 [omitted]

7 Former Czechoslovak Prosecutor General Tibor Boehm said in April that 178 people had been executed for political reasons and that "several thousand" had been tortured to death in prison (see Radio Czechoslovakia, April 20, 1990, 6:00 p.m.).

8 *Vecerni Praha*, August 17, 1990, p. 2. See also Radio Czechoslovakia, April 3, 1990, 11:15 a.m. These figures are equally unreliable. According to another source, about 400,000 Czechs and Slovaks emigrated between 1948 and 1989 (*Hospodarske Noviny*, October 5, 1990, p. 8), and the vast majority of them were sentenced for "illegally leaving the republic." At a recent press conference, Deputy Prime Minister Pavel Rychetsky estimated that as many as 800,000 Czechoslovak citizens emigrated after 1948 (see *Svobodne Slovo*, November 21, 1990. p. 1). The

available. Emigrés who were sentenced for "illegally leaving the republic" will be rehabilitated, but only those who can prove that they were in fact forced to emigrate can ask for redress.

Alexander H. Platt, Imtiaz T. Ladak, Alan J. Goodman, Matthew R. Nicely, "Compensating Former Political Prisoners: An Overview of Developments in Central and Eastern Europe"[*]

For both categories of persecuted persons described above, special judges must review each individual's case to determine whether he or she does in fact qualify for rehabilitation and compensation. Since the majority of the persecutions took place 30 to 40 years ago, many of the former prisoners are elderly and in need of immediate aid. The Government's stated policy is to give priority to rehabilitating those who were persecuted in the 1940s and 1950s. In reality, however, the process is not working quickly enough.[24] On December 6, 1990, the government announced that it would provide emergency compensation payments equalling about $330 per person while the recipients wait for the normal bureaucratic procedures to be concluded.[25]

Jan Obrman, "Rehabilitating Political Victims"[†]

Under the Law on [Judicial Rehabilitation], the victims are granted 2,500 koruny [$100] for each month they spent in a prison or a labor camp, as compensation for loss of earnings. If the losses are deemed to have been higher than that amount, appeals for higher compensation may be addressed to the appropriate commissions of the republican Ministries of Justice. Sums of up to 30,000 koruny must be handed out as lump-sum cash payments, while larger amounts will be repaid in installments in 10 years or less. But there are no provisions for adjustment to the expected inflation rate, and some victims fear that they will actually lose some, if not most, of their compensation.

Those who were rehabilitated can also ask for financial compensation for damage to their health, legal fees incurred at the initial trials, and fines they were ordered to pay. Immediate relatives (widows and children) of those who were executed or who died in prisons and labor camps can apply compensation for loss of financial support. As an alternative to a lump-sum cash compensation, the law offers 15 to 20 koruny for each month spent in a prison or a labor camp, in addition to the deceased's monthly pension, which under the law may not be more than 3,800 koruny a month.

---

number of those who must be rehabilitated will therefore far exceed the approximately 280,000 listed in official statements.

[*] Reprinted from Alexander H. Platt et al., Akin, Gump, Strauss, Hauer, & Feld, *Compensating Former Political Prisoners: An Overview of Developments in Central and Eastern Europe,* unpublished paper, August 14, 1992, pp. 7.

[24] [Jan Orbman, *Two Landmark Bills on Privatization Approved,* RFE/RL Rep. on E. Eur., March 14, 1991], at 6.

[25] N.Y. Times, [Dec. 7, 1990, at A12].

[†] Excerpted from Jan Obrman, "Rehabilitating Political Victims," *Report on Eastern Europe,* vol. 1, no. 50 (1990), pp. 6-7.

Michael Kraus, "Settling Accounts: Postcommunist Czechoslovakia"*

According to the official statistices, between July 1990 and December 1992, over 36 thousand rehabilitated individuals were indemnified in the amount of nearly two billion crowns [$80 million].[29]

But the Law on Judicial Rehabilitation did not actually address the far greater number of victims, who suffered for their political or religious convictions, without going to court. The Confederation has estimated that some 1.5 to 2 million Czechoslovak citizens had been punished in one way or another for political crimes under the previous regime. The total includes individuals who were imprisoned without trial, dismissed from their jobs, forced to move out of their homes, students expelled from universities for their beliefs, individuals coerced to give up their property to the successive waves of nationalization, farmers whose land was confiscated, as well as family relatives of political prisoners who experienced job or housing discrimination. To the extent that such wrongs involved property issues, the notion of restitution gradually emerged as the guiding principle.

[Restitution of Property]

Originally, the new government in Prague did not contemplate to redress the forced collectivization of land and nationalization of private property by way of restitution. Though the interim government was fully in favor of privatization, it did not view reprivatization, or restitution, as economically sound policy. Given the confusion over property rights and claims, restitution seemed costly and inefficient. The determination as to whether or not given property would be eligible for reprivatization or available for privatization seemed like a compelling deterrent against restitution for most government economists.[30]

What changed the nature of the debate was the demand from former political prisoners for rehabilitation. Since their punishment often included confiscation of property by the state, it was logical that their rehabilitation must include some form of compensation, if not the restoration of their property. Since many members of the clergy were victimized by the old regime, the issue of church property came into the fore. In the early 1950s, the Catholic Church was decimated, with many priests and nuns landing in prisons. The church property, which included over eight hundred churches, parishes and monasteries, as well as six percent of all agricultural land, was confiscated without any pretense to legality. The June 1990 Law on Regulation of Property Relations of Religious Orders and Congregations attempted to redress the injustice and it became the first property restitution law of postcommunist

* Excerpted from Michael Kraus, *Settling Accounts: Postcommunist Czechoslovakia*, revised version of paper delivered at 1992 Annual Meeting of the American Political Science Association, The Palmer House Hilton, September 3-6, 1992.

[29] *Rude pravo*, 20 January 1993. Since other cases are still pending in courts, these are not definitive statistics.

[30] This and the following two paragraph's observations are based on *The Different Paths of Privatization*, Working Papers, (Prague: Federal Ministry of Economy, 1991).

Czechoslovakia. It returned some 74 properties, setting aside another 176 properties for a later consideration, while the church gave up the right to claim the remaining 550 on account of their poor condition or destruction. (In fact, the attendant complications with the facilities housed on the church property, including hospitals, schools, etc., have resulted in the repeated postponements, and no new legislation concerning the full restitution was enacted before Czechoslovakia's dissolution.)

On October 2, 1990, the Federal Assembly passed the Restitution Law on Relieving the Consequences of Some Property Injustice, covering some 70,000 small businesses and apartment houses nationalized by the state between 1955 and 1961. [Former owners were required to file their claims within six months of the law's enactment.] The October 1990 law established the principle of physical restitution of property, whenever feasible. The same principle was applied in February 1991, when the Federal Assembly approved the Extrajudicial Rehabilitation Law, returning nationalised property from the period after the February 1948 communist takeover through 1955. Because many industrial enterprises had been nationalised by the Benes government already in the 1945-48 years, the property involved in the February 1991 act amounted to only about 10 percent of all state-owned property, and its estimated worth to over $10.0 billion.[31]

In addition, in May and December 1991, Land Restitution Laws were adopted, giving the original owners the right to recapture the land that the state collectivized into cooperative farms in the 1950s. In contrast to Poland, Communist Czechoslovakia collectivized agriculture and forestry in their entirety. Organized into about 1900 collective and state farms, the agricultural sector in 1989 employed around 650,000 employees.[32] That is also why the potential impact of land restitution is far-reaching. Though the new laws do not rule out the retention of the collective farms, the latter will in effect become tenants of the restituted owners. Each farm established a transformation council to supervise the redivision of farms on the basis of weighted voting, depending on the size of the original property.

The passage of these laws was preceded and accompanied by a wide ranging debate that inevitably focused public attention on the human rights violations of the previous regime. Each provision of the law had its defenders and critics. In the first place, some, like Finance Minister Vaclav Klaus, argued against restitution in principle, on the grounds that economic considerations render reprivatization inferior to other forms of privatization. Instead, he proposed financial compensation for those whose property rights had been infringed upon. Klaus also argued on moral

---

[31] *The Financial Times*, April 16, 1991. For a full account of the debate surrounding these laws, see Jiri Pehe, "The First Weeks of 1991: Problems Solved, Difficulties Ahead," *RFE*, vol. 2, no. 10, March 8, 1991; and Jan Obrman, "Two Landmark Bills on Privatization Approved," Ibid., No. 11, March 15, 1991.

[32] See Martin Kupka, "Transformation of Ownership in Czechoslovakia," *Eastern European Economics*, Fall 1992, p. 37; somewhat different data appear in Josef Burger,"Politics of Restitution in Czechoslovakia," *East European Quarterly*, XXVI, No. 4, January 1993, p. 494.

grounds against the view that restitution can be an instrument of full justice: "A lawmaker cannot change history, uncover and rectify all past injustice. The events that once happened and that influenced property relations and the lives of many people cannot be erased from life with a stroke of a pen, without causing further, new injustice ... We cannot ... rectify old wrongs at the expense of present and future generations, who should not be held accountable for past wrongs."[33]

The second set of issues centered around the form of restitution. Here, Klaus's argument for financial restitution in the form of vouchers as less costly than physical restitution lost out. Financial restitution would be used only when the nationalized property, for one reason or another, could not be returned. The third set of questions concerned the time span to which the remedy of injustice would apply. Two periods of time were under consideration in the ensuing debate: the years since February 25, 1948, when the Communist established their monopoly of power; and the preceding period between May 1945 and February 1948, when a large scale nationalization (with compensation) of heavy industry, banks, and transportation occurred under a democratically elected government, though, as some argued, under an intimidating Communist influence. Eventually, the lawmakers rejected the proposals advocating restitution from the pre-communist era of nationalization, embracing the date of February 25, 1948 as the cut off point instead. The parliamentarians rejected the May 1945 proposal because most feared it would open the potentially explosive issue of property restitution to the Sudeten Germans. Following the decision sanctioned by the Great Powers at the Potsdam Conference in 1945, nearly 3 million Sudeten Germans were expelled from Czechoslovakia during 1945-48, and their property was expropriated in lieu of German reparations to Prague for war damages.

Much controversy ensued on the question of who was eligible to receive restituted property. For the time being, it was decided that the restitution would apply only to individuals, and not to institutions or political parties, thus also excluding the churches. The government intended to address the church property separately. The entitled persons included the original owners, designated heirs, or relatives. Significantly, none of the restitution laws applied to the emigres, unless they chose to adopt the Czechoslovak citizenship and resettle permanently in the country. The main arguments justifying these provisions were based on the view that the state lacked the resources to satisfy property claims of as many as 500,000 claimants from abroad, and that to try to do so would hopelessly bottleneck the court system and paralyze the privatization process in general. Though reconsidered on several occasions by the parliament, the exclusion of the emigres was not reversed, thereby antagonizing important segments of the Czech and Slovak communities in the process. Even though the legislators repeatedly promised to enact a separate financial restitution measure

---

33 This quote comes from Klaus's letter to Olga Jonas of the World Bank, 21 June 1991, in which he defended the exclusion of emigres from restitution. I am indebted to her for making it available.

concerning the exiles, none was adopted to date. Nor could other classes of claims for property restitution, such as losses incurred in ownership of stocks and bonds in commercial companies, be satisfied.

February 1991 Law on Extrajudicial Rehabilitation

*Alexander H. Platt, Imtiaz T. Ladak, Alan J. Goodman, Matthew R. Nicely, "Compensating Former Political Prisoners: An Overview of Developments in Central and Eastern Europe"**

This law applies to Czechoslovak citizens who were not convicted and sentenced by a court but were otherwise harmed by discrimination for political or social reasons. The law provides for the rehabilitation and compensation of persons dismissed from their jobs, imprisoned without trial, or forced by a court to sell their property or "donate" it to the state. The law provides for the return of almost all private property nationalized or confiscated after the Communist takeover in 1948, or for financial compensation where the actual return of the property is not possible.[30]...

The first two Articles of the law provide redress for the results of property and other injustices that occurred because of political persecution or human rights violations. Victims of such violations may be compensated through the return of property, financial compensation, the revocation of certain directives, and possibly the adjustment of social security payments. Political persecution is defined as "[t]he persecution of a person (A) directly connected to the person's democratically motivated political and social activities and civic position or, (B) as a result of his or her membership of a specific social, religious, property-owning or other group or social strata."[32]

After setting out the rules governing restitution of property, the law focuses on redress for victims of political persecution by stating that:

- Compensation for unjust imprisonment exceeding three months, counting time both before and after sentencing, is governed by the Law on Legal Rehabilitations and the amendments provided in Law No. 47/1991.
- Decisions to send people to forced labor camps are abolished and labor camp victims shall be compensated for time spent there, except in cases where it can clearly be seen that the individual was guilty of property-related criminal activity.
- Students who were expelled from school as a result of political persecution shall be offered educational rehabilitation.

---

* Reprinted from Alexander H. Platt et al., Akin, Gump, Strauss, Hauer, & Feld, *Compensating Former Political Prisoners: An Overview of Developments in Central and Eastern Europe,* unpublished paper, August 14, 1992, pp. 8-10.

30 [Jan Orbman, *Two Landmark Bills on Privatization Approved*, RFE/RL Rep. on E. Eur., March 14, 1991, at 12].

32 Czechoslovak Law on Extrajudicial Rehabilitation, Art. 2, para. 2.

- The legal acts or decisions that led to the unjust termination of an employee as the result of political persecution or general violations of recognized human rights and freedoms are hereby invalid.

Upon request of an employee, an employer is required to issue a statement to the effect that the termination was unjust and invalid. The invalidity of the termination does not, however, entitle the employee to have his or her job returned or to receive back pay from the employer. The employee does have the right to *request* the return of his or her job, and, in cases in which the employee is still qualified *and* it is possible for the employer to take on an additional employee, then the employer is obligated to rehire that employee. The same rights apply to professional soldiers and members of armed corps who were improperly dismissed.

Pension issues are discussed in Article 24, which states that, for the purposes of calculating entitlements for pension disbursements, full credit is given for the time between the date of the individual's invalid termination and the date he or she becomes eligible for old age, partial, or full disability pension. Time spent in auxiliary technical battalions (forced labor groups) of the military counts twice for pension purposes.[33] When calculating pension entitlements, the figure for average monthly earnings is to be based on the total earnings of the year prior to the unjust termination of employment. Finally, victims who have already begun to draw their pensions shall have them readjusted in accordance with this law.

Michael Neff, "Eastern Europe's Policy of Restitution and Property in the 1990's"[*]

[The Return of Property]

[The Law on Extrajudicial Rehabilitation][69] ... called for the return of all real estate that had been illegally seized by the Communists between 1948 and 1989.[70] The law provided for either a return of land to former owners or to their heirs, or for government compensation in the form of bonds or adjustment of social security payments.[71]

Currently, in implementing these forms of compensation, Czechoslovakia's procedure requires the "entitled person" to initiate a

---

[33] During the communist regime, approximately 30,000 members of the Czechoslovak Army were forced to serve in the labor units referred to as Auxiliary Technical Battalions (ATB). An amendment to the Law on Extrajudicial Rehabilitation provides that Kcsl5 (approximately $0.60) will be added to pensions for every month a person spent in an ATB. Widows, children or parents of servicemen who died in the ATB units will receive a one-time payment of Kcs100,000 (approximately $3,700). Brit. Broad. Corp., Summary of World Broadcasts, May 21, 1992.

[*] Excerpted from Michael Neff, "Eastern Europe's Policy of Restitution of Property in the 1990's," *Dickinson Journal of International Law*, vol. 10, no. 2 (Winter 1992), pp. 368-370.

[69] Law on Extrajudicial Rehabilitation, Czech Statute (Feb. 22, 1991).

[70] See *Media, Land, Enterprise Bills Passed*, Facts on File: World News Digest, March 28, 1991, at 225.

[71] *Id.*

claim directly to the "obligated person" for the return of property.[72] The entitled person must be a physical person, rather than a corporation or business, a citizen of Czechoslovakia, and a permanent resident of Czechoslovakia.[73] In case of the death of the entitled person his heir must also be a Czech citizen.[74] The property was to be surrendered to the entitled person in the condition it is in on the day the request is received.[75] The entitled person may demand a monetary reward if the property has deteriorated to the point of being non-usable.[76]

Claimants are required to file within six months of the announcement of the law on February 21, 1991.[77] The obligated person, normally the state or a municipality, is to relinquish the deed to the original owners who file a claim.[78] In addition, the obligated person is to enter into a contract with the entitled person and surrender the item to that person within thirty days.[79]

When a dispute arises, the entitled person has one year to submit his claim to court.[80] For situations in which property cannot be returned in kind, approximately $750 million of Czechoslovakian currency has been allocated for cash compensation to the original owners or their heirs, and the balance of compensation will be paid in government-issued bonds.[81]

If the property has been developed in the interim, the land will not be surrendered.[82] If the real estate has appreciated in value, an agreement in which the entitled person remits the difference in value must be formulated so as to prevent unjust enrichment.[83] Normally, the property has seriously depreciated in value over the forty years. State ownership destroys the individual's incentive to take conscientious care of the property.

In addition to the state being an obligated person, a person who had acquired property or the right to use property from the state within the definition of Article 6 of [the Law on] Extrajudicial Rehabilitation, is also an obligated person. Article 6 describes the instances in which an entity acquired property in an illegal manner. For example, lands "donated" under duress, sold under duress, and confiscated without compensation, are all acquired illegally.[84] In each instance, the entitled person may reclaim his property....

---

72 *See* Czech Law, *supra* note 69. *See* art. 3, The Entitled Person, and art. 4, The Obligated Person.

73 *Id.*, art. 3, §1.

74 *Id.*, art. 3, §2.

75 *Id.*, art. 7, §1.

76 *Id.*, art. 7, §3; *See also* art. 13.Pechota, *Privatization and foreign investment in Czechoslovakia: the legal dimension*, 24 Vand J. Transnat'l 305-24 (1991).

77 *Id.*, art. 5, §2.

78 *Id.*, art. 5, §1.

79 *Id.*, art. 5, §3.

80 *Id.*, art. 5, §4.

81 *Id.*, art. 8, §5; *See also* art. 13.

82 *Id.*, art. 8, §3.

83 *Id.*, art. 7, §4.

84 *Id.*, art. 6, §1 (a-k).

Comprehensive restitution is seen as essential by government because it demonstrates that Czechoslovakia is serious about upholding property ownership rights. However, in implementing the restitution procedures, the fact that Czechoslovakia is a relatively poor country is one main consideration to complete restitution as quickly as possible so that remaining land could be sold to investors. The income gathered from foreign investors will help speed economic growth.

In fact, the Czech government decided that restitution claims will take priority over the privatization process. As a result, prior to privatizing a parcel of property, the management of a business must examine the records of the registry of deeds to determine whether there was a private owner prior to 1948. If a private owner did exist, the action to privatize should be deferred until the six months expires.[86] No notice to the owner is required; therefore, after six months, privatization can begin.[87]

Vojtech Cepl, "A Note on the Restitution of Property in Post-Communist Czechoslovakia"[*]

[Controversies, Problems, and Limitations]

Closer examination of the points raised in the debates on this bill affords us an opportunity to highlight some of the problems the government faced in its attempt to break with the communist legacy and to consider the degree to which its restitution policy contributed to its overall goal of achieving a rapid transition to a market economy in which the private sector would play a crucial role.

The first controversial issue raised by this Law on Extra-judicial Rehabilitation was the question of how far back in time restitution should go. The original government draft proposed a cut-off date of 25 February 1948, the date of the communist seizure of power. However, nationalization had also taken place earlier than that, during the post-war Benes government between 1945 and 1948, and during debates on the bill, voices were raised advocating restitution also of property nationalized during that period. In some cases that involved property which had been confiscated from people shown to have been 'collaborators and traitors' during the Nazi occupation. In others, it involved property targeted by presidential decrees which had authorized the nationalization of all factories and enterprises employing more than 50 people. Although owners affected by these decrees were to have been compensated for their property, no compensation was in fact paid for those businesses which were nationalized after 1948. As a result, when the law on large-scale restitution was debated in parliament, there was pressure to extend its provisions back in time to 1945.

---

86 *Id.*, at 312.

87 *Id.*

* Excerpted from Vojtech Cepl, "A Note on the Restitution of Property in Post-Communist Czechoslovakia," *Journal of Communist Studies*, vol. 7, no. 3 (1991), pp. 368-375.

There were, however, a number of reasons for resisting that pressure. Inclusion of property nationalized in the period immediately after the Second World War within the provisions of the restitution law would have been politically unacceptable and would have set a bad legal precedent. Some of the property confiscated at that time had been acquired through the Nazis' policy of Aryanization of Jewish property or for other reasons connected with the war—and the people who had obtained their property in that way should not be entitled to restitution. It would also have opened up the question of compensating the more than three million Sudeten Germans who had been expelled from Czechoslovakia after the war and, while it is true that their expulsion had been carried out in a very cruel and harsh way, allowing the Sudeten Germans to claim compensation for their confiscated property would have started a never-ending cycle of claims and counterclaims, including the question of responsibility for the war, which could never be resolved.

A further reason for not including acts of confiscation that had taken place before 1948 was the question of political legitimacy. Those acts of nationalization which had taken place between 1945 and 1948 were carried out by a legitimate government, on the basis of presidential decrees and in accordance with the 1920 Czechoslovak constitution. If those decrees were reversed, it would open the door to a practice whereby any government could simply declare all acts of an earlier government invalid ... and a government acting in this way would cause chaos.

A second area of controversy concerned who should be eligible to claim restitution. From the outset it had been decided that only individuals, and not corporate bodies, should benefit from these enactments. That left open the issue of whether the right to restitution should be restricted to individuals who had actually lost property or whether it should be extended to their heirs and even the heirs of their heirs. In the end, the original restrictive proposals were transformed into a more extensive policy which, in the case of intestacy, went beyond traditional practice in Czechoslovakia in the area of inheritance law. Whereas, in cases of intestacy, the Civil Code does not allow rights of inheritance to pass beyond relatives more distant than a brother or sister, in this instance the provisions allowed claims from more remote family members, including not only nephews and nieces of an original owner but even grand-nephews and grand-nieces.

That departure from traditional practice may be seen to reflect the views of those in parliament who saw the restoration of property, to their original owners (or their heirs) as a method of achieving a degree of privatization easily and quickly and who saw this widening of the inheritance law as a means of giving back as much property as possible to as wide a group of people as possible. That policy, however, had the disadvantage that the larger the group of people who could claim property, the more difficult the process of restitution might become for social and technical reasons. Conflicts could arise between relatives which would have to be adjudicated by the courts. That would be a nightmare because the court system in Czechoslovakia is very weak, the number of judges is very small and, irrespective of their quality and moral calibre, they are already overburdened. Furthermore, as its designation as a law on 'extra-judicial rehabilitation' implies, the restitution act was intended to obviate litigation in this area.

This brings us to the third area of controversy: that of the method and process by which restitution was to be carried out. The law specified that a person with a claim was to contact the state enterprise or state official who currently owned the property and ask for its return. The latter was then bound to reply within 30 days and thereafter the property would be registered in the new owner's name at a notary's office. A time limit of six months was set for the lodging of claims, a provision that was considered necessary to prevent delays in other aspects of the privatization programme. The public sale of a state-owned business, for example, could be held up if there was any possibility that it might be subject to claims under the restitution laws.

When it came to deciding how best to achieve restitution, three basic options presented themselves. First, the property confiscated could be returned in its original form—'natural' restitution. Second, claimants could be offered financial restitution, in the form of monetary compensation rather than the property itself. Third, people qualifying for restitution could be awarded vouchers or coupons to exchange for shares in enterprises that were to be privatized under the law on large-scale privatization, mentioned earlier.

This particular issue created great controversy in parliament. Whereas the original government plan had proposed financial restitution, the majority of deputies, especially those on the right wing, expressed tremendous enthusiasm for 'natural' restitution, and their view prevailed. The legislation that was passed specified that 'natural' restitution should be made whenever possible....

The parliamentary debates made it clear that ... 'natural' restitution was favoured for a variety of reasons. Among them were its apparent simplicity, the emotional satisfaction it would bring to those who would receive the actual property that had been confiscated and also doubts about the future value of the Czechoslovak crown. In addition, there were fears that state property offered for sale rather than distributed on the basis of 'natural' restitution would fall into the hands of a new class of private owners largely recruited from former 'apparatchiks' who, unlike the average citizen, had sufficient money to buy businesses offered for privatization in that way. However random the group of heirs who would inherit property under the restitution provisions, and however distant their links with the original owner, that was seen as better than giving it to the communists....

Yet another issue raised in the restitution debates involved the kind of property that would be subject to the restitution law. The original intention (which was subsequently approved) envisaged only immovable residential property, commercial buildings and the land on which they stood.[3] The debates on this subject elicited similar arguments to those on restitution in general and it was clear that those who had advocated the distribution of nationalized property to as many people as possible wanted to go further than the government in this area by including movable property in the legislation.

That, however, would have been extremely problematic. For example, if a claimant was heir to a doctor whose X-ray machine had been confiscated, a butcher who had lost the tools of his trade or a farmer who had lost his livestock, how could that claimant first prove the fact of the confiscation and then establish the value of what had been confiscated perhaps 40 years after the event? Since evidence of the loss would be difficult and in many cases impossible to obtain, many people with rightful claims would fail to establish them. This would contravene the principle of equality under the law, the idea that people in similar situations should be treated similarly by the courts.

Those who advocated making restitution for movable as well as immovable property were willing to accept inconsistent results in which some claims would succeed and other, similar ones fail. They compared the situation to natural disasters in which lucky people manage to escape unscathed while others, not so lucky, suffer serious injury. Fortunately, they failed to win the day and a situation was avoided where a legal system which it is within the legislators' power to ensure is consistent and fair would have been burdened with a provision that would inevitably have been capricious in its application....

Yet another controversial issue that arose during parliamentary discussion of restitution was the eligibility of emigrants. Leaving aside former residents of the Sudetenland, between 500,000 and 600,000 former Czechoslovak citizens live abroad, in most cases people who went into exile for political reasons. Since most left the country illegally, they were punished in part through forfeiture of all their property—indeed even emigrants who had gone abroad legally were forced to surrender their property. Moreover, since a large number of those who emigrated came from the wealthiest strata of society, a large amount of property was at stake.

The government however proposed—and parliament eventually agreed—that property should only be returned to those emigrants who came back to Czechoslovakia and reclaimed Czechoslovak citizenship. The main reason for this decision was fear that according restitution rights to all emigrants would lead to a flight of large amounts of capital from with serious consequences for the economy. On top of that, if restitution had been extended to foreign nationals, it would have opened the way to claims not only by former residents of the Sudetenland but also by Austrian and German aristocrats, many of whom had collaborated with the Nazis and had lost vast tracts of land in Southern Bohemia....

---

3 Agricultural and unimproved land was the subject of separate legislation that had not completed its passage through parliament at the time this article was completed.

Some of course saw restitution as a means to achieving justice for the victims of the communist regime, but that was an unrealistic aspiration. Justice is best served by reexamining the past and determining who and what were responsible for the injustices committed by that regime. It should not be allowed to confuse the issue at the heart of the restitution programme—transforming the system of ownership. Even if all property that had been nationalized without compensation were returned to its original owners or their heirs, justice would still not be achieved.... Restitution ... cannot achieve justice retroactively. It may partially redress certain egregious wrongs but it will never give people back what was destroyed over a period of 41 years. It cannot restore lost careers, opportunities, health and lives. Rather than attempting to use the restitution programme to redress the wrongs of the past, the opportunity should have been taken to look forward and to structure the programme in a way that would best facilitate the societal transformations that are essential to a prosperous future.

Jan Obrman, "Rehabilitating Political Victims"[*]

The costs of extrajudicial exculpation will be even higher [than judicial rehabilitation], because this process affects more people and involves confiscated property and real estate. Czechoslovak Deputy Prime Minister Pavel Rychetsky has said that he expects the total costs (not including higher pensions) to amount to about 21 billion koruny ($840,000,000).[15] According to Rychetsky, this amount is inadequate, and sufficient compensation would cost over 100 billion koruny. Again, compensation will be paid in a lump sum for payments of 30,000 koruny or less, and the rest will be repaid in installments in 10 years or less. Victims of communist persecution must apply for redress within six months of rehabilitation....

The rehabilitation proceedings are complicated by a number of practical and financial problems. Since the "velvet revolution," the Czechoslovak judicial system has developed a backlog of cases owing to the current state of confusion in the legal system, which has been completely overhauled through new laws, constitutional changes, and a purge of many high-ranking judges. One serious complication confronting the authorities is that records of the initial trials are difficult to locate. Another problem is that many of those who were automatically rehabilitated are living abroad and often cannot even be notified of their new status.

A far more pressing problem, however, is the lack of qualified judges. The Czech Republic alone is said to be short of at least 330 judges. After November 1989, some 100 judges were dismissed and another 120 left their positions voluntarily.[16] Only 115 new judges have since been appointed to

---

* Excerpted from Jan Obrman, "Rehabilitating Political Victims," *Report on Eastern Europe*, vol. 1, no. 50 (1990), p 7.

15 *Ibid.*, November 20, 1990, 3:20 p.m.

16 *Ibid.*, June 26, 1990. 11:40 a.m.

replace them. Moreover, assigning judges to rehabilitation cases[17] has created considerable backlogs in earlier proceedings.

Only a few of the judges who were dismissed during the notorious "normalization" period have agreed to return to their positions, and various administrative hurdles slow down the appointment of new judges.[18] Most lawyers and law students are not interested in becoming judges because the salaries are low; in fact, many lawyers earn more than judges.... The social status of judges is rather poor, and the working conditions are unsatisfactory. This situation is not likely to improve soon.... The newly established rehabilitation commissions of the Ministries of Justice in both republics are also said to be overburdened, with little chance for improvement in the near future.

Financing the rehabilitation process will probably be the most difficult task.... Officials have repeatedly made clear that compensation for past injustices is a moral issue and an important step toward national reconciliation. For this reason, they say, financial problems must not be allowed to slow down the process, and certainly not to prevent it. Many observers agree that the costs may turn out to be much higher than originally expected, and it is obvious that Czechoslovakia will hardly be able to finance the rehabilitations immediately from its shrinking budget. Some politicians have demanded that all the communist party's assets, which have been confiscated, be used to fund the rehabilitation procedures. But the value is not sufficient to cover the entire cost of rehabilitation. Moreover, the bulk of the party's assets consists of buildings and real estate, which cannot readily be converted into cash; in any case, legislators are still debating how to dispose of these assets.

Although the process of rehabilitation is complicated, time-consuming, and, above all, very expensive there is general agreement that it is an important step toward settling the nation's accounts with its communist history. For this reason, rehabilitation is likely to remain a priority for Czechoslovakia's new decision makers, regardless of the cost.

Michael Kraus, "Settling Accounts: Postcommunist Czechoslovakia"[*]

Despite the foregoing limitations, the rehabilitation and restitution laws that were enacted provide for a complex legal mechanism of rectifying the wrongs committed under the Communist regime. Motivated by ethical considerations, the new laws mark a significant chapter in the process of establishing the rule of law in postcommunist Czechoslovakia. Moreover, they establish the most ambitious and far reaching property restitution program in East and Central Europe. As such, they have set the tone of the debate and influenced the substance of other such projects in the

---

[17] Radio Prague, September 27, 1990, 6:30 p.m.

[18] *Vecerni Praha*, August 17, 1990, p. 2.

[*] Excerpted from Michael Kraus, *Settling Accounts: Postcommunist Czechoslovakia*, revised version of paper delivered at 1992 Annual Meeting of the American Political Science Association, The Palmer House Hilton, September 3-6, 1992.

neighboring countries.[34] Finally, Prague's restitution policies proved to be a more effective means of moving assests from state to private hands than could have been expected. While the private sector was virtually non-existent in 1989, by 1991, owing largely to reprivatization, it accounted for 8.3% of GNP.[35]

1993 Law on the Illegality of the Communist Regime

Jan Obrman, "Czech Parliament Declares Former Communist Regime Illegal"[*]

On 9 July [1993] the Czech parliament adopted the Law on the Illegitimacy of and Resistance to the Communist Regime. This slightly modified version of a draft proposed by deputies of the governing coalition was approved by 129 members of the 200-strong parliament; thirty-four voted against it (all the deputies of the Communist Party of Bohemia and Moravia and one independent deputy), and three members of the Liberal and Social Union (LSU) abstained.[1]...

In fact, only very few party and state officials have so far been prosecuted for their actions under communism, and even fewer have been sentenced. (Among the few was former Chairman of the CPCS [Communist Party of Czechoslovakia] Municipal Council of Prague Miroslav Stepan, who spent several months in prison for ordering that student demonstrations in 1988 be crushed.) Representatives of the government coalition complained that many of the most outrageous crimes, particularly those committed in the 1950s, would go unpunished because of the statute of limitations, which was still based on the laws of the previous regime. It was also argued that certain victims could not be compensated on the basis of the rehabilitation laws—particularly those who had been tortured and the relations of those who had been killed without having been convicted of a crime, as compensation was paid only to those who been legally tried and sentenced to terms in prisons or concentration camps.[3] Equally important was the demand, voiced by many former political prisoners, that the "third resistance" be granted legal recognition; they argued that people who had actively resisted the communist regime, including those who had used violence, should be granted the same status as veterans of the Habsburg and Nazi resistance movements. In May 1993 some 100 deputies of

---

[34] For an assessment of the regional progress toward the establishment of the rule of law, see "Toward the Rule of Law," *RFE*, vol. 1, no. 27, 3 July 1992

[35] Progress towards the development of private ownership in Eastern Europe," *Oxford Analytica*, July 13, 1992.

[*] Excerpted from Jan Obrman, "Czech Parliament Declares Former Communist Regime Illegal," *RFE/RL Research Report*, vol. 2, no. 32 (August 13, 1993), pp. 6-10.

[1] Czech Television, 9 July 1993.

[3] *Telegraf*, 11 May 1993.

the ruling coalition issued a draft law that was intended to address these matters. Despite media coverage, the draft attracted only limited public interest. In fact, according to some reports, only some 30% of the Czech population considered such a law important.[4]

The Law

The law on the illegitimacy of the communist regime is concise and strongly declarative. In fact, it is more of a proclamation than a piece of practical legislation and is therefore likely to be more significant for its moral implications than its impact on the way the communist past is dealt with. It states that

> the CPCS, its leadership, and its members are responsible for the manner in which our country was administered in the years 1948 to 1989; [they are responsible] for the systematic destruction of the traditional values of European civilization; for the intentional violation of human rights and freedoms; for the moral and economic decay that was accompanied by judicial crimes and terror against those who held views differing [from those of the state]; for the replacement of a functioning market economy by a command economy [and] by the destruction of traditional principles of ownership; for the abuse of education, science, and culture for political and ideological goals; [and] for the destruction of the environment.

Article 1 of the law describes the repressive means employed by the communist regime. It mentions, among others, murder, torture, all forms of persecution, "association with a foreign power," and reliance on "the occupation forces of a foreign power." Article 2 declares that because of all the crimes committed, "the CPCS and other groups based on its ideology were criminal, illegitimate, and abhorrent organizations." Articles 3 and 4 deal with anticommunist resistance. The law characterizes as legitimate, just, morally justified, and honorable the actions of all individuals and groups who, "on the basis of political, moral, or religious convictions with democratic roots," resisted the regime at home or abroad.

The only provisions of the law that will have an impact are the lifting of the statute of limitations for "crimes committed between 25 February 1948 and December 1989 in cases in which, for political reasons, culprits were not sentenced or victims were not acquitted"; the law's rather vague appeal to the Czech government to "redress some of the injustices committed against the opponents of the communist regime"; and, third, the broadening of the postcommunist rehabilitation laws to include those who were not rehabilitated on the basis of previous rehabilitation laws. In practical terms, this last provision will mean that those who were denied rehabilitation or granted only partial rehabilitation because they had been involved in acts of violence against party or state officials may now be fully or partially rehabilitated "if it can be proved that their activities

---

4 *Mlada Fronta Dnes*, 2 June 1993.

were carried out with the aim of protecting basic human and civil rights and freedoms."

Even these provisions of the law are not, however, expected to result in any sweeping changes. The concern voiced by leftist deputies in the parliament that all former and present members of the CPCS could, at least theoretically, be prosecuted was rejected by some of the law's initiators. Justice Minister Jiri Novak stressed soon after the voting that the new law would not initiate a wave of "mass purges"; he added, however, that those "who committed crimes in the name of communist ideas have every reason to be concerned." The minister also claimed that "some people" would have to stand trial.[5] The deputy Marek Benda of the Christian Democratic Party made it clear that only actual criminals who had committed crimes in the name of the communist ideology could be prosecuted; regular members and even leaders of the CPCS who had not committed any felonies could not be punished.[6] Jiri Setina, the prosecutor-general, said that the law would make it possible to prosecute some of "the most serious crimes, such as murder, that could not be prosecuted before." He added, however, that he expected "few trials" and that the main result of the law would be "moral satisfaction" for the victims.[7]

According to some reports, a maximum of 2,000 people could be affected by the law; but as most of the cases date back to the 1950s, it is likely that a lack of evidence will prevent the majority of them from being brought to trial.[8] A military prosecutor pointed out, moreover, that even obvious crimes could go unpunished. He said that the former secret police often selected victims not because of their ideology but on account of their possessions. He gave the example of a former Czechoslovak officer who was detained and beaten to death in prison, allegedly for espionage. The real reason for the murder, however, was his Western car and a considerable amount of valuables, which were distributed among high-ranking secret police officers after his death. The prosecutor explained that the policemen responsible could be prosecuted only if they declared that they had killed the man for engaging in espionage. This is because the law can be applied only to politically or ideologically motivated crimes; other crimes still fall under the statute of limitations.[9]

As for the controversial Articles 1 through 4, which describe the crimes committed between 1948 and 1989 and declare the CPCS a "criminal organization," it is evident that they are of a purely declarative nature and will not have any practical consequences. This means that neither regular CPCS members nor the vast majority of high-ranking CPCS officials will be prosecuted.

The law praises those who opposed the communist regime, but it is questionable whether this praise will have major practical consequences.

---

[5] Czech Television, 9 July 1993.

[6] *Rude pravo*, 15 July 1993.

[7] *Ibid.*, 13 July 1993.

[8] *Die Presse*, 17 July 1993.

[9] *Lidove noviny*, 15 July 1993.

The rehabilitation process will probably be extended to include more people than before, particularly some of those who were involved in acts of violence. But the appeal to the government to compensate some victims of communist persecution may turn out to have little effect. Moreover, one provision of the initial draft, which demanded the return of property to those who had been forced to sell it to the authorities against their will, was voted down. There seems to have been concern that further court cases dealing with restitution might complicate and prolong the privatization process.

Interestingly, one potentially important consequence of the law has hardly been mentioned at all in the media. Although the new legislation does not outlaw the communist party and although there do not seem to be plans to do so, the law on the illegitimacy of that party could serve as a legal basis for its liquidation in the future. German laws obviously served as a model in this respect. While the legislation outlawing both the National Socialist German Workers' Party and the propagation of Nazi ideology did not prevent the formation of neo-Nazi groups, it has been used repeatedly as a justification for banning them. A Czech parliamentary deputy indicated that something very similar could happen in the Czech Republic.[10]

Reactions

While most parties and organizations expressed satisfaction with the law, representatives of the communist party, as expected, were less enthusiastic. Jaroslav Ortman, the chairman of the parliamentary Left Bloc (in which the communist party is the dominant group), declared that the law would initiate a period of legal insecurity and revenge and that it was incompatible with the principles of a democratic state based on the rule of law. The Communist Party of Bohemia and Moravia sent letters to the Council of Europe, Amnesty International, the Socialist International, and a number of other international organizations complaining about the law, which they claim is discriminatory and based on the principle of collective guilt. In addition, the Communists have announced that they will demand that the Czech Constitutional Court assess the law's compliance with the human rights provisions of the Czech Constitution.

Some representatives of parties that voted in favor of the law were also skeptical about its impact. Industry and Trade Minister Vladimir Dlouhy, for example, who himself was a CPCS member until December 1989 (he later joined the Civic Democratic Alliance), declared that the law "measures all former CPCS members by the same standards" and could be used for a "wholesale purge." At the same time, he stressed that he was satisfied with the fact that those who favored the law's adoption "can now concentrate fully on solving problems that are crucial for our future."[11] Transport Minister Jan Strasky, a former Communist who is now a member of

---

[10] *Telegraf*, 25 May 1993.

[11] Czech Radio, 12 July 1993.

the Civic Democratic Party, said that he had no problem voting for the legislation, as it "is not at variance with any other valid laws or human rights provisions."[12]

Other groups and individual politicians drew different conclusions. The Green Party, which is a member of the LSU, demanded an immediate purge of all administration officials "who withdrew their CPCS membership only after 17 November 1989."[13] Party representatives pointed out at a press conference that if the intention of the new law were "to deal with the past," it was rather strange that a number of those who voted for it or even participated in its drafting had been active Communists before the "velvet revolution." For this reason, they said, Dlouhy and Strasky (the latter, in fact, left the party in 1969) should either step down or be fired. Most Czech citizens, however, apparently have little problem with the communist pasts of either Dlouhy or Strasky: both politicians have consistently been ranked among the most popular politicians in the Czech Republic.

Other left-wing politicians maintained that it was not necessary or even advisable to adopt a law morally condemning communist rule; they argued that this amounted to an effort to impose legislative control over the thinking of individuals and prescribe how they should evaluate Czechoslovak history.[14] Another popular argument has been the claim that while the CPCS behaved like a totalitarian organization for a certain period, especially in the late 1940s and 1950s, it also proved open to democratic elements during the Prague Spring. Many social democratic deputies (who voted for the law) seem to have changed their minds later; according to some reports, more than half of them declared that they were opposed to it.[15] At a press conference a few days after the law had been adopted, individual deputies complained that "the retroactive provisions on the lifting of the statute of [imitations" might be incompatible with the Charter of Fundamental Rights and Liberties, which is part of the Czech Constitution.[16] This argument was dismissed by other politicians. Representatives of the Civic Democratic Alliance maintained that the lifting of the statute of limitations had to be permissible; if it were not, they pointed out, an absurd situation would arise in which tyrants and dictators could ensure that they would evade retribution forever. It was therefore crucial to demonstrate that those who committed crimes, regardless of their position or the political circumstances, would eventually be held responsible for them and would not be able to escape justice by introducing statutes of limitations specifically for their own crimes.[17]

---

12 *Mlada Fronta Dnes*, 12 July 1993.

13 CTK, 14 June 1993.

14 *Rude pravo*, 17 July 1993.

15 *Die Presse*, 17 July 1993.

16 CTK, 13 July 1993.

17 *Ibid.*, 14 July 1993.

Czech President Havel signed the new law on 22 July [1993]. Explaining his decision, Havel said that he had reached the conclusion that the law was without judicial flaws and did not contradict the Czech Charter of Fundamental Rights and Liberties. The new legislation was important, he added, because "through this law, the freely elected parliament is telling all victims of communism that society values them and that they deserve respect.', Havel also said that today, in retrospect, he would not sign the [1991 lustration] law, because that law was "imperfect."[18]

It is not yet certain what impact the new law will have. It is, however, clear—as Havel himself stressed—that with the adoption of the law, an important chapter in the post-1989 (and, more generally, the postwar) history of the Czech Republic has been closed. After a period of public debates on how to deal with the communist past, this law constitutes a decisive attempt not only to deal with the past but also to make it possible to shed some of the past's burdens in dealing with the future.

---

18 *Ibid.*, 22 July 1993.

16

GERMANY (AFTER COMMUNISM)

EDITOR'S INTRODUCTION

At the end of World War II, Britain, France, the United States, and the USSR each administered a separate zone of defeated Germany, with the stated goal of demilitarizing and denazifying the four sectors and then reunifying them into a democratic state. With the rapid onset of the Cold War, cooperation between the four occupation forces crumbled. The U.S., Britain, and France merged their three zones and, in May 1949, created the Federal Republic of Germany. Five months later, the German Democratic Republic (GDR or East Germany) was proclaimed in the Soviet zone.

As head of the East German Communist party—officially called the Socialist Union Party or SED—Walter Ulbricht quickly became leader of the new state. A strict adherent of the Soviet party line, he stated that the political arrangement in the GDR "must look democratic but we must have complete control." The SED moved aggressively to centralize power and nationalize industry, adopting Stalinist policies and tactics. Religion and culture were repressed, civil liberties were denied, and objectors were swiftly punished. Censorship of the press and arts and tight controls on foreign publications reduced public exposure to noncommunist ideas.

After Joseph Stalin's death in 1953, a series of strikes and protests erupted around the country, with thousands of demonstrators calling for economic reform, de-Stalinization, the withdrawal of Soviet troops from East Germany, and the removal of Ulbricht. When the collapse of the SED government seemed inevitable, Soviet military forces crushed the revolt. Unlike his counterparts in other Soviet Bloc countries, Ulbricht resisted the pressure to ease repression and initiate economic reforms to match the Soviet thaw under Nikita Kruschev. Ulbricht's ally and successor as SED chairman and prime minister in 1971, Erich Honecker, continued this orthodox approach. During the 1980s, he would similarly resist the reform policies of Soviet Premier Mikhail Gorbachev.

Embarrassed by the flow of refugees into West Germany, in 1961, the GDR government constructed the Berlin Wall to physically separate East from West Berlin. This 102.4 mile wall of concrete blocks and steel became the symbol of division between the East and West political blocs. East Germans could not travel freely, and border guards were instructed to shoot on sight those attempting to escape across the border, resulting in an estimated 200 killings from 1961 to 1989.

Throughout the period of communist rule, the Ministry of Interior and the Ministry of State Security—the "Stasi"—directed the most pervasive secret police network in Eastern and Central Europe. The Stasi persecuted dissidents, conducted arbitrary arrests and torture, and enforced the policies of the regime. Beyond its 100,000 official employees, the Stasi managed an estimated additional 200,000 collaborators who agreed to provide information on their fellow citizens.

Beginning in May 1989, over 120,000 East Germans fled to the West, primarily via Hungary. By the autumn, massive demonstrations called for political and economic reform and unification of the two Germanys. Honecker was replaced in October 1989 by Egon Krenz. Krenz' limited easing of restrictions, including freer travel, did not keep pace with the growing public demand for systemic change and reunification. Within weeks, he was replaced by Hans Modrow, who immediately began "Round Table" discussions between opposition groups and the government. On November 9, he opened the Berlin Wall's Brandenburg Gate—symbolizing the collapse of the East/West division. On March 18, 1990, democratic elections installed a coalition government dominated by pro-unification parties and headed by Lothar de Maiziére. Germany was soon reunified, on October 3, 1990.

The most volatile issue following the downfall of the Communist regime involved the handling of 125 miles of files which the Stasi had maintained on one-third of the East German population. On January 2, 1992, the "Stasi Records Act" opened the files for public inspection, enabling anyone to obtain the contents of his or her Stasi file, including the names of collaborators who had informed on the individual. By early 1994, the commission overseeing the files received some two million applications for information. The law also allows background checks on government employees. As a result, thousands of public employees were dismissed because of incriminating evidence contained in their Stasi files.

Following unification, several border guards were tried and convicted of manslaughter for having shot fleeing East Germans. A trial also began of Erich Honecker, but was dismissed in January 1993 because of the ill health of the defendant and witnesses. In March 1992, a parliamentary commission was created to examine all aspects of repression employed by the old regime, in order to gather information for the prosecution of former officials and to provide history with an account of Communist rule.

The following documents related to transitional justice in Germany after Communism can be found in Volume III of this collection:

- Law Creating the Commission of Inquiry on "Working through the History of the SED Dictatorship"
- Act Concerning the Records of the State Security Service of the Former German Democratic Republic ("Stasi Records Act")
- Brochure of the Federal Commissioner for the Stasi Records
- Trial of Border Guards
- Compensation Acts

OVERVIEW

*Commission on Security and Cooperation in Europe, "Human Rights and Democratization in Unified Germany"**

[I]f de-communization in most East-Central European countries has been the domain of home-grown democratic forces confronting their former oppressors, in Germany, to some degree, it is West Germany putting the East on trial—West German laws, West German courts, West German standards, East German defendants. Not surprisingly, some eastern Germans find the process unsatisfying, all the more so as the system has largely failed to prosecute the leaders of the corrupt and immoral East German regime.

Moreover, as the courts and as society struggle to assess the complicity and guilt of East Germans who cooperated with the communist regime, uncomfortable questions have been raised regarding the role of the West German government during the period of detente. GDR President Erich Honecker had been warmly received by Chancellor Kohl in 1987, at a time when the repressive policies of the East German regime were clearly known; one could argue that the policies of detente led West German authorities to work with their East German counterparts in the same pragmatic way that

* Excerpted from Commission on Security and Cooperation in Europe, *Human Rights and Democratization in Unified Germany* (September 1993), 11-18.

the average East German had worked with the Stasi or the Communist Party. Can one make a moral distinction between the calculated, political actions of the West German authorities, and those of the ordinary East German who wanted his or her children to have a decent future? These kinds of ambiguities make the delivery of justice, and the respect for the rule of law, a terribly complicated endeavor.

Secret Police Files

The dismantling of the dreaded state security police, the Stasi, was one of the primary goals of the opposition movement in East Germany. In the period following the collapse of the Honecker regime, grassroots movements sprang up across the country to prevent the Stasi's voluminous files from being altered or destroyed while a national committee was formed to deal with the issue on a broader scale. The files filled 125 miles of shelves, chronicling in elaborate detail the activities of some six million East German citizens. They promised to reveal countless painful stories of betrayal, and threatened in so doing to weaken the fabric of an already traumatized society. In fact, during the brief tenure of East Germany's only freely-elected government, exposure of secrets contained in the Stasi files ravaged the careers of several prominent East German officials, including, ironically, a number of senior Interior Ministry officials who had been charged with dismantling the organization. Equally stunning was the revelation that Lothar de Maiziere, East Germany's first and last non-communist Prime Minister, had been a Stasi informer from 1981-89. Following unification, the question of what to do with the files and the incriminating information they contained was prominent on the agenda.

On November 15, 1991, the united, federal German parliament approved a law permitting citizens to see their files. As Hans Joachim Gauck, the Protestant clergyman and activist who became custodian of the Stasi archive, explained,

> If Parliament had rejected the law granting people access to their files, I would have left this job....That would have been a way of telling people from eastern Germany that we were too immature to handle these truths, that the Government would make this decision for us. That is not the right message to give people who are getting their first taste of democracy after living under dictatorship continuously since 1933.[4]

The law stipulated, however, that journalists could be penalized for using information from the files they received from unofficial sources. Representatives of the German media protested this move, claiming the restrictions were unconstitutional. On the one side, government authorities alleged that the Stasi files were by definition unreliable, and that the government was obliged to protect citizens from the personal and professional devastation that could result from publication of false

---

[4] *The New York Times Magazine*, "East Germans Face Their Accusers," Stephen Kinsler, April 12, 1992, p. 52.

information. On the other, spokespersons like Ingrid Koeppe, an eastern German activist, maintained that only through full public access could Germany "work through its past."[5]

Mr. Gauck's Berlin-based federal agency and its 14 regional offices across the former East Germany began accepting applications from Germans who wished to see their Stasi files on January 2, 1992, the day the relevant law took effect. The law also empowered government agencies to request background checks on their employees. According to a New York Times article written one year later, "These checks have resulted in the dismissal of thousands of judges, police officers, schoolteachers and other public employees in eastern Germany who once informed for the Stasi."[6]

Beyond these purges, however, there are few policy measures the government has pursued to deal with past Stasi abuses. The legal system is unable to provide remedies to victims of Stasi activities; as scholar Thomas R. Rochon has pointed out, "A firm legal basis for prosecuting Stasi activities has also been hard to find. Unlike the genocidal policies of the Nazi regime, the claim cannot be made that telling the secret police about the activities of a friend, neighbor, or colleague is a violation of international law." West German law made it punishable for East German agents to spy on West or East German citizens, but the five-year West German statute of limitations renders prosecution under these terms near impossible. As a consequence, the government has been obliged to prosecute officials of the former regime for transgressions of East German law, rather than questioning the morality of those laws in the first place.[7]

It cannot be denied that the opening of the Stasi files has had deep and agonizing effects on eastern German society. From well-respected dissident Vera Wollenberger, who learned with horror that her own husband had betrayed her, to Gerhard Riege, a member of the Bonn parliament who hanged himself after it was reported that he had been a Stasi informer, countless lives have been profoundly affected. Some eastern Germans bitterly allege that they have become victims of a zealous western German witch-hunt, masquerading as healthy self-purification, whose ultimate intent is to promote feelings of inadequacy and mistrust among eastern Germans and to remove them from positions of power and authority.

A high-profile example that helps to explain such feelings is the case of Manfred Stolpe, member of the Social Democrats (SPD) and Minister-President of the state of Brandenburg. Stolpe, the only easterner and only SPD member to be elected as minister-president of one of the five new Laender, was perhaps the most promising individual to emerge in eastern public life after unification. A senior lay official in the Protestant Church in the former GDR, he had helped gain the release of many individuals from prison and had actively assisted many East German citizens to leave the

---

5 *The Washington Post*, "Bonn Closing Books, Opening Controversy," November 13, 1991.

6 *The New York Times*, "Germans Anguish Over Police Files, " February 20, 1992.

7 Thomas R. Ronchon, "The Wall Within: Germans Cope With Unification," *German Unification, Problems and Prospects*, Gaines Post, Jr., Editor (The Keck Center for International and Strategic Studies, Claremont, CA: 1992), pp. 32-35.

country. These opposition credentials were tarnished, however, when Stolpe confessed in January 1992 to several decades of regular and extensive contacts with the Stasi—though he claimed he had never been an informer. Despite support from fellow church officials and most of the political spectrum in the former GDR, he was immediately condemned by the Christian Social Union, and later the Green Party, a partner in his own governing coalition, which called for his resignation.

In April 1992, the Gauck commission produced a report which concluded that Stolpe had been an important Stasi informer on the church for many years. A special commission in the state legislature in Brandenburg was established to investigate the allegations. Through the storm, Stolpe has tenaciously clung to his post, maintaining that one had to work with the Stasi in order to work against them, and that those who did not live under the East German system can not properly understand the compromises it demanded. According to press reports, polls show that he is still admired by his constituents and that he is likely to win re-election [in 1994].

While the Stasi files have largely been viewed as an eastern albatross, recent revelations have made life uncomfortable for western politicians and public figures as well. In July 1993, Bernd Schmidbauer, coordinator of intelligence agencies for Chancellor Kohl, announced that a list was going to be handed over to prosecutors containing the names of some 2,000 western Germans alleged to have spied for the Stasi. With important elections just around the corner, accusations have flown that the files are being leaked to the press for political purposes. Chancellor Kohl, however, has denied this charge, issuing a statement that any Stasi material containing allegations about West Germans who spied for the GDR will be "dealt with solely in accordance with the law."[8]

Cases like these, with their manifold ambiguities, may have contributed to the results of a recent poll, which indicated that two-thirds of Germans, including 65 percent of eastern Germans, support the idea of an amnesty for Stasi informers.[9] And yet, closing the files, or providing a blanket amnesty, may ultimately prove unsatisfying for a population which suffered at the hands of the secret police and its lackeys for so many years. The true delivery of justice, in this context, is elusive.

Trials of Communism: Erich Honecker vs. Berlin Border Guards

Indeed, important attempts to deliver justice have been stymied or suspended more than once. In March 1991, to the surprise and fury of many, former President Erich Honecker escaped to the then-Soviet Union—ignoring a warrant for his arrest on charges of ordering border guards to shoot East Germans trying to escape to the West. After a long and complicated set of negotiations among the Germans, the Russians, and the

---

[8] *Sueddeutsche Zeitung*, "Kohl: 'No Party Policy Deals' With Stasi Files," August 11, 1993 (as translated in FBIS, August 12, 1993, p. 15); *The Washington Post*, "Cold War Spy Files Roil German Politics," August 12, 1993.

[9] *Reuters*, "Germans Want Amnesty for Stasi Spies, Survey Says," August 11, 1993.

Chileans (in whose Moscow Embassy Honecker had eventually sought refuge), Honecker was brought back to Germany for trial in July 1992.

Meanwhile, a related set of prosecutions had been undertaken at the other end of the chain of command. In June 1991, four former East German border guards were arrested in the shooting of the last East Germans who tried to flee before the Berlin Wall collapsed. The trial awakened painful memories of the period after World War II, when the issue of responsibility for following the orders of an immoral regime was equally pertinent. It also aroused passionate arguments on both sides, from those who believed that the state had an obligation to hold East German criminals responsible, no matter where they fell in the hierarchy, to those who suspected the government was trying to make scapegoats out of "the little people because it is incapable of punishing the big guys."[10]

On January 20, 1992, Judge Theodor Seidel pronounced 27-year old former border guard Ingo Heinrich guilty of manslaughter and sentenced him to three and a half years in prison. Andreas Kuhnpast, also 27, was given a two year suspended sentence for attempted manslaughter, while two other defendants were acquitted. The ruling set a major precedent, as it established for the first time that West German criminal law and basic human rights norms and standards could be applied to events that took place under East German law. At the time of the conviction, press reports indicated that prosecutors were preparing charges against more than 300 other guards.

Erich Honecker's forced return to Germany in July 1992 reactivated his own prosecution, on 49 counts of manslaughter and 25 counts of attempted manslaughter related to the deaths of East Germans who were trying to flee to the West. Berlin authorities based the charges on three grounds: that Mr. Honecker had exceeded his powers under East German law; that he broke international laws, including the U.N. Convention on civil rights; and that he violated basic human rights. His trial, along with five other high-ranking Communist Party officials (Willi Stoph, 78, former Prime Minister; Erich Mielke, 74, longtime chief of the Stasi; Heinz Kessler, 72, a former Defense Minister; Fritz Streletz, 66, Kessler's former deputy; Hans Albrecht, 72, Communist Party chief in a border district where several would-be refugees were killed) was set to begin in the fall.

The legal, political, and moral complexities, however, were apparent. First of all, Honecker and his cohorts could not be punished for the manifold injustices that characterized East German society, but only for individual violations of the law. Despite the charges against him, there was no hard evidence to prove that Honecker had issued a shoot-to-kill order along the border. Second was the question of legal frameworks. According to the German Unification Treaty, criminal offenses committed in the GDR could only be prosecuted if they were also punishable under GDR law. In its conviction of the border guards, Judge Seidel had ruled—and the Supreme Court later upheld—that the deadly use of firearms by the border guards contravened the universal human right to life and freedom of movement and was therefore illegal, even under GDR law. The same legal bridge needed to

---

10 *The Washington Post*, "On Trial for Death at Berlin Wall," September 10, 1991.

be established for the Honecker trial. Also complicating the process was the memory, played up in the press, of Honecker being received with honors in 1987 by the same authorities that now sought to brand him a murderer. Given these factors, some wondered whether the trial was merely a sop for the public's desire for revenge.

The trial opened on November 12, 1992, with the six former officials specifically charged in the deaths of 13 East Germans killed as they tried to escape to West Germany. It had to be immediately postponed, however, due to the absence of defendant Willi Stoph, who had suffered a heart attack. At the end of the second session, Mr. Honecker, himself terminally ill with cancer, reported weakness and had to be taken to a hospital. The judge eventually decided to drop both Mr. Stoph and Mr. Mielke, who had cardiac ailments, from the trial. By January 1993, it appeared that Mr. Honecker too would be relieved from the trial, and on January 12, the Berlin Constitutional Court dropped the manslaughter charges and lifted the arrest order, paving the way for Mr. Honecker to spend the end of his life with his wife and daughter in Chile. Thus what might have been Germany's most significant court case since the Nuremberg trials was concluded prematurely and without resolution....

Restitution of Property

One of the most contentious issues in east-west German relations since 1989 has been compensation for property confiscated under the totalitarian regime. Before the deadline closed on December 31, 1992, hundreds of thousands of claims for property lost before 1945 or after 1949 had been filed with the central land registry, each one requiring weeks or months to process. Working through the tremendous backlog has been delayed still further by a fire at the registry in April 1993, which is estimated to have destroyed thousands of pre-war records.

The German unification treaty specifies that property claims in the east are to be resolved under the principle "return instead of compensation." This principle does not apply to commercial properties, whose former owners can claim only monetary compensation, but rather to former homeowners. This has meant, in effect, that eastern German residents of single-family houses have themselves borne much of the cost of compensation—suddenly threatened with eviction as former homeowners and their descendants file claims for the return of their property.

The social downside of the "return instead of compensation" principle was tragically brought to light in the spring of 1992, when two eastern Germans whose homes had been reclaimed hung themselves in desperation and protest. Critics allege that the restitution of property seized by the post-war communist dictatorship is not uniformly justified, and that the claimants in many cases are descendants of the original owners and have never actually lived in the properties in question. Press reports suggest that the intent of such claimants is often to renovate and resell the houses, rather than to live in them.

Issues of property restitution are additionally complicated by a series of claims in the former GDR and East Berlin for Jewish property which was confiscated by the Nazis.... Many cases of compensation and restitution, which have hindered business development and property sales in East Berlin, and have actually forced people from their residences, are linked to the Nazi past as well as to the GDR past. In an atmosphere of tension and east-west difference within Germany, these issues inflame the situation. They are presently the subject of proposed legislation in the Bundestag, which promises to be controversial.

The delay in resolving ownership questions has placed not only a psychological burden on eastern Germans, who fear loss of their homes, but also a drag on investment and development in the east. Privatization was so hampered by competing claims on ownership that a new law was passed in early 1992 allowing investors to take precedence over the claims of former owners if they could prove that they would secure or create jobs or improve competitiveness better than the former owner....

Screening the Civil Service[14]

The unification treaty established the legal employment relationship between the Federal Republic of Germany and civil servants of the former GDR, including provisions by which former GDR civil servants could be deemed unfit for employment by the unified German civil service. Based on these regulations, a system of review was established in each of the states of the former GDR. Extensive questionnaires were prepared to obtain information about civil servants, including employment history, political memberships and positions, Stasi-related activities, and personal information. All civil servants were required to complete a questionnaire. The questionnaires were submitted to local personnel review commissions, which in some cases, conducted a private "hearing" of the person under review. After the hearing, the commission usually made a recommendation to the appropriate ministry and then informed the candidate of the decision.

Helsinki Watch, which monitored the de-communization process in Germany in 1992, concluded that the process of reviewing the political and professional integrity of civil servants often surpassed the bounds of what could be considered proper inquiry. The Human Rights Watch World Report for 1993 noted:

> Many employees have been dismissed without ever having been accused of any specific misconduct. Instead, most have been found unsuitable for continued employment in the civil service simply because they held political party or government positions under the previous system. No serious effort has been made to provide evidence that an individual carried out his or her duties in a manner that was repressive, unethical or criminal in nature. Instead, the assumption has been made that any employee who

---

14 The Commission is grateful to Holly Cartner, Staff Counsel to Helsinki Watch, for significant background assistance on this and other aspects of the de-communization process in Germany.

held his position over an extended period of time must have satisfied Party dictates and these dictates were inherently abusive.[15]

TREATMENT OF THE SECRET POLICE FILES

Perspective of the Federal Commissioner for the Stasi Files

Joachim Gauck, "Dealing with a Stasi Past"[*]

In the autumn of 1989, following a period of crippling depression, after years of remaining silent, a great number of men and women began to protest against a fossilized dictatorship no longer able to persuade its citizens that it was doing its job—taking care of people's welfare. The lavish celebrations laid on by the evil old men at the top for the fortieth anniversary of the German Democratic Republic (GDR) was, in the beginning, accompanied only by small-scale protest from splinter opposition groups. However, the hard line taken by the state authorities against these protesters resulted in a sudden wave of solidarity, particularly evident within the churches. Civil movements were formed, and the Social Democratic Party (SPD) was refounded in an East German vicarage. The protest, initially heard at church services and similar Protestant gatherings, soon emerged from the churches and spilled out onto the streets.

The courageous protesters of Leipzig were symbolic of the rebirth of citizenship. It was a heady period for all who for decades had been forced to keep their heads down. The weekly demonstrations, in towns large and small, and the catalog of demands for human and personal rights and for radical political change became more and more determined. These protests culminated eventually in growing demands for German reunification; not because the Easterners had suddenly become nationalists, but because in this manner they were most clearly able to express their desire to turn away from socialism.

The street protests in my home town of Rostock were fairly typical: they were regularly held in front of the local State Security Service (Stasi) offices. There we were able to do away with long discussions about ideology. By simply pointing at the edifice, so to speak, we were able to present the real character of the "socialist" system for popular judgment. The decision was clear—the Stasi and tank socialism were on the way out. The Stasi, the prime instrument of oppression, was to be the first victim. "Put the Stasi men to work in the factories" was the rallying cry of the protesting masses. After that, the demonstrations were directed against the Party's branch offices. The protesters outside the Stasi buildings were especially determined, word having gone around that enormous numbers of documents were being

---

15 *Human Rights Watch World Report 1993: Events of 1992*, Volume II, Human Rights Watch (New York: December 1992), p. 220.

* Excerpted from Joachim Gauck, "Dealing with a Stasi Past," reprinted by permission of *Dædalus*, Journal of the American Academy of Arts and Sciences, from the issue entitled, "Germany in Transition," Winter 1994, Volume 123, Number 1, pp. 277-280.

destroyed. The revolutionaries knew how important it was to save this data, the old regime's hold over its former subjects. It was expected that political use of these materials would one day be made.

In early December 1989, a decision was made to occupy the Stasi regional centers. Unfortunately, the main office in Berlin-Lichtenberg was not reached until January 15, 1990, which gave the Stasi officers six weeks longer than elsewhere to destroy vital material. Thousands of paper sacks full of shredded or damaged dossiers testified to the zeal of those fearful of the typewritten evidence of their activities. All over the GDR civil committees were formed to supervise the winding-up of the secret police, to guard documents, and, where possible, to collate the files they found. Many of these groups produced pamplets on Stasi activities, edited Stasi materials, and from time to time informed the press that someone seemingly destined for high political office had worked closely with the MfS (the official short form for the Stasi).

Following the first free elections in the post communist GDR (in March 1990), the parliament, the *Volkskammer*, decided at a very early stage that all MPs should be vetted to see whether they figured in Stasi records as *Inoffizielle Mitarbeiter* (IM, undercover collaborators). A special parliamentary committee was set up for this purpose. Later, another committee was formed, and the author of this article (at that time an MP representing the civil movement called "Bündnis 90") was elected to be its chairman. This body's task was to supervise the breakup of the MfS, which took place on the orders of the Minister of the Interior. The committee also influenced legislation; it presented a draft bill that became law in August 1990 that fixed the methods for dealing with the Stasi legacy. This law took up many of the themes of the 1990 civil protests; its main thrust was to allow former Stasi documents to be used for "political, judicial, and historical reckoning with the past." Each citizen was to be allowed to examine his or her own file to discover if and how the Stasi had acted. The East German parliament's intention was to return the former rulers' instrument of knowledge to those it had ruled and oppressed. "Political reckoning with the past" (*politische Aufarbeitung*) meant, among other things, the right to vet MPs and all elected bodies, as well as public employees, to see if they previously worked for the MfS, either as Inoffizielle Mitarbeiter or even as *Hauptamtliche* (full-time collaborators). Where the vetting process revealed such collaboration, the MP or public servant was to be dismissed from his post.

Why did the East Germans decide to embark upon this process in 1989? It was not a quest for vengeance; there was no majority in the *Volkskammer* for such vindictive action. On the contrary, the MPs recognized the following problem: In East Germany, from 1933 onwards (i.e., the start of the Nazi dictatorship), the entire public administration, government, and parliament had been largely comprised of people who, to a greater or lesser extent, had collaborated with the antidemocratic rulers. They included judges, lawyers, police, teachers, university professors, and other representatives of the federal and regional legislature and executive offices. If, after more than fifty-five years of Nazi and Communist dictatorship, citizens were to trust elected officials under the new democratic system, it was important that those officials be trustworthy. The intention was not to remove former Communists (members of the Socialist Unity Party, SED) from all posts, but rather to respond to the East German people's minimal demand that persons who had conspired with the regime, unbeknown to their fellow citizens, should be deemed unsuitable for public positions of trust.

Following the establishment of a democratic state in East Germany, only a few full-time state employees attempted to reenter public service; those without such a handicap, on the other hand, applied in large numbers for posts, including major political jobs. The screening process was never designed to deprive individuals of employment; former high officials were allowed to work in business and the professionals, as a doctor or an artist, for example, but not in the service of the democratic state. The Stasi files were to be used for "judicial reckoning with the past" in order to facilitate prosecution where crimes had been committed, but also to vindicate those who had been wrongly accused. Finally, there was historical justification for this legislation. With the aid of the files, historians would be able to portray the actual processes of domination and organization, demonstrating the interplay between the ruling party and its instruments of surveillance and oppression.

The bill passed by the *Volkskammer* in August 1990, which contained these three essential features, was welcomed by the overwhelming majority of the public, regardless of political affiliation. For many MPs the decision to make a clean breast of their country's dark past was linked to a desire to do so in an open, self-critical way, very different from the situation following the end of World War II. This time, collaboration, failure, and guilt would not be suppressed; it would be acknowledged, faced up to.

*Joachim Gauck, "Address to the Conference on Data Protection and Stasi Documents: Push the Issues Aside or Overcome Them?"**

People managed to find a broad parliamentary majority of delegates of all fractions for an arrangement that gave force of law to the following:

First: The ruling knowledge of the former power apparatus will not be protected, but rather it will be transferred over to the formerly oppressed. Concerned parties will obtain extensive access to the files that were compiled on them.

Second: The files should be used for extensive measures of rehabilitation and criminal proceedings as well. The young democracy of the free GDR could not imagine clearing up the past any other way than to extensively use the means of criminal law to proceed against broken laws. A gross historical error, as it turns out.

Third: The elements of verification of the employees as official or unofficial employees became the component of a law. It was decisive for this ... to verify a fairly large group of people who had associated with the State Security as official or unofficial employees and had gained an illegitimate

---

* Excerpted and translated from remarks by Joachim Gauck, in Winfred Hassemer and Karl Starzacher, eds., *Data Protection and Stasi Documents: Push the Issues Aside or Overcome Them?* (Nomos Publishing House, 1993)(*Data Protection Forum*, vol. 1), pp. 20-23.

advantage over the rest of the population. In addition, the delegates had to consider the fact that unlike the true power holders in the SED leadership, who everyone knew, citizens did not know the unofficial activity of State Security employees, and thus were victims in this regard with no protection or defense from the rulers. They were practically defenseless....

The removal of an illegitimate advantage and the absolute necessity to equip the new structures of democracy with personnel deserving of trust guided the actions of the delegates. This is why one can see a touch of the term "political clearing up" in the element of verifications....

Not only the transfer of knowledge, but also the use of formerly protected knowledge to produce trust and renewal was important for the delegates.

In addition to this element of political clearing up by actions of verification, there is, of course, also the fourth element of political and historical clearing up in the sense of transfer of knowledge. Democrats of all political camps foresaw that in times of economic or political pressure, there will be a tendency toward nostalgic reversal. There are plenty of examples for this in the history of the German people, not only in this century but also in the 19th century. We knew early on that a GDR nostalgia would occur. I was already horrified by this before it occurred, knowing that it would occur one day.

In times when the forming of myths can become dangerous because it can start political movement, it is especially important to secure knowledge as an element of processes of change and in the forming of political opinion and to allow knowledge to be disseminated. This is why in 1990 it was also the struggle of the delegates of the lower house to reveal the knowledge hidden in the files, to be able to use it against the forming of legends and in particular to be able to prove the responsibility of the leaders of the political oligarchy of the former SED for the terror against the people. It was not enough for us to be politically convinced and to know that the SED bore this responsibility, because we had experienced it. We also wanted to inform future generations through knowledge that can be read, studied and learned....

These elements have become components of the State Security Document Act of the German Federal Parliament, in a somewhat complicated way. Originally, the Federal Government had agreed with the [last East German] government in the unification treaty that the file affair should be closed out of precaution. The reason given for this was that the danger for domestic peace would be too great otherwise.

In its initial phase in this form, the unification treaty triggered the decisive protest of the entire GDR parliament, in such a way that a clause was added to the unification treaty containing an agreement that in the legislative framework to be laid down in the future by the Federal Parliament, these principles of the lower house act ... should be applicable. The democrats of the lower house were able to agree with this contractual arrangement in the additional clause of the unification treaty. Despite some murmuring in the civil rights scene, the unification treaty found agreement on this point.

The German Federal Parliament made a very careful decision ... to allow justice to grow, not only transporting it according to plan from a zone where democracy had been organized for 40 years, but rather bringing the legal principles of functioning democracy together with the historical requirements of an alienated, legally crooked government. In the process, one had to dispense with applying the thirty year protection period of the [West German] Federal Archive Act for personal data. A conscious decision was made not to apply the benefits of Data Law, to which an innocent citizen of the Republic is entitled, to the former perpetrators and helpers of the MfS. This was a political decision that was prepared by intensive forming of opinion cutting through fractional boundaries. A systematic transfer of valid legal standards for a problem that didn't even occur in the West would not have promoted the further development of justice and democracy, but rather would have hindered it....

Joachim Gauck, "Dealing with a Stasi Past"[*]

The German Bundestag complied with this declaration in 1991 in the "Act concerning the [Records] of the State Security Service of the Former German Democratic Republic" ("*Stasiunterlagengesetz*"), which came into effect at the end of that year. Since 1992, a surprisingly large number of individuals and institutions have made use of their legal options.

The Federal Commissioner for Documents of the State Security Service of the former GDR (my official title) and the body that bears the same name began work on German Unity Day. The Commission is specifically enjoined to work towards the above named objectives, but also to facilitate the press's constitutionally regulated access to the Stasi files (excluding only those relating to victims). It has more than three thousand staff members, divided between the main office in Berlin and fourteen branches in the five East German federal states. The need for such a high level of manpower is dictated by the enormity of the archives (almost 120 miles of shelves) and the number of applications for access to the files. More than 1.85 million requests for access have been made, over 650,000 by private citizens wishing to see their own files.

The Commission's main activities consist of providing data for the public service, preserving and arranging the archive. In 1989—1990, the data was in total disarray; the archivists' main task was to create a reliable archive, reconstructing dossiers completely or partially destroyed. Since the electronic data bases had been wiped out on the orders of the Modrow transitional government, the archive section has the urgent task of sorting, reconstructing, and completing the card-indexes, the principal means for linking names to files. Another principal objective, likely to gain significance in the coming years, is provided by the education and research department, where requests from historians and press research applications are processed. This department's task is to inform the public about Stasi

[*] Excerpted from Joachim Gauck, "Dealing with a Stasi Past," reprinted by permission of *Dædalus*, Journal of the American Academy of Arts and Sciences, from the issue entitled, "Germany in Transition," Winter 1994, Volume 123, Number 1, pp. 280-284.

structure and methods of operation by publishing books aimed both at laymen and experts, by holding seminars on the Stasi, and by organizing exhibitions held in Berlin and in the new federal states.

* * *

There has been for some time now a feeling of unease about this digging up of the past. It is less marked in East German public opinion, and rather more conspicuous in certain media dominated by the "old West." This unease is clearly caused by many factors. Some individuals are simply averse to the media treatment of the issue. For a long time, the public was bombarded with reports about the Stasi. In many cases, particularly where political, cultural, religious, or sports personalities were reported as having been *Inoffizielle Mitarbeiter* (IM), there was, especially in the tabloid press, over generalized and sensationalist treatment. This, along with over saturation, caused public frustration and confusion. It is important for readers in the West to realize that the East German secret service had many different methods for recruiting and guiding IM.

As a rule, the IM undertook to collaborate with the MfS by means of a written and oral statement. But, in the case of a small group of intellectuals and churchmen, the Stasi's rules allowed for a more circumspect recruiting method. "Confidential talks" were arranged which, after a time, were held in secret ("adhering to the rules of conspiracy," as the MfS termed it) by agreement between the two parties. This agreement was typical for the initiation of an IM dossier of this special type. Persons recruited in this way often did not know the term "IM," received no money or presents, apart from birthday gifts, did not intend to betray anyone, and continue today to reject vehemently the charge of collaboration uncovered by the examination of the files. They consider themselves untainted by their past, choosing to forget that they fully accepted long-term contact with a Stasi officer, kept the relationship secret, acquiesced in a role rejected by others in comparable positions in the East. They fail to see also that the Stasi, very naturally, pursued its own interests in processing the data gleaned from the IM, that such information was used, regardless of the supplier's motives, to support the regime's hold over its subjects.

While such collaboration must be distinguished in the public mind from real treachery and espionage, in many cases sensationalist witch-hunting reports (never based on the work of the Federal Government Commission) precluded such a distinction being made. It contributed to the frustration expressed by many. Apart from the special problem of media coverage, there are, of course, other political objections to the German method of dealing openly with the past. Let us consider, for example, the interests of those removed from public posts who understandably protest such action. In the universities, to cite a single instance, some of the IM would prefer that the public regard the special treatment they received as a result of their collaboration with MfS as quite irrelevant. They often do not grasp the fact that they are quite correctly being compared with their East German colleagues who did not allow themselves to be drawn into working with the

Stasi. Many seek support at home and abroad, claiming that West German attempts to dominate the East following on reunification cost them their jobs. This sort of argument needs to be approached with extreme caution. While West German "neocolonialism" does take place from time to time, the investigation of public servants for Stasi collaboration is a result of pressure from the East German democracy movement, legalized by two German parliaments, and cannot be explained as a Machiavellian scheme by the old Federal Republic....

The attempt to deal with the Stasi past reflects the wish, at least partially, to bridge the gap that existed in the former GDR between "us" and "them," the people and the elite. The majority of the oppressed and spied-upon population had a legitimate interest in publicizing the Stasi files. They hoped that the new knowledge would have consequences. The minority, the collaborators, were to be disadvantages, a justifiable result, given the advantages they had enjoyed in the past.

In united Germany, the (Western) majority is not sufficiently aware of this discrepancy; it is very apparent to all in the East.... We find it difficult to comprehend fully the history of individuals who have had different experiences of suffering and alienation. Many East Germans today have great difficulties in explaining their very different experiences of suffering and alienation. Many East Germans today have great difficulties in explaining their very different past lives to West German countrymen. The gap is too wide, the burdens borne over long decades are too unequal. And if it turns out that their Eastern neighbors were indeed oppressed and discriminated against, many Westerners draw back, wishing to protect themselves from the suffering of others. They cannot begin to grasp the magnitude of what was experienced under a totalitarian system....

It is perhaps normal that not everyone is able to understand the emancipatory approach we politicians in the East use in order to rake over the ashes of the recent past. Some accuse those who refuse to forget of being vengeful. They fail to see that there is a need to remember the times and those who restricted our right to freedom and personal expression, not least because these inalienable rights need to be defended now and in the future. The present-day dissension need not be seen as precluding reconciliation and inner stability. We will be in a position to forgive and forget only if we are given enough time and the right to heal our wounds, to calm our anger, and, yes, to curb our hatred. Reconciliation with such a past can only be achieved not simply through grief, but also through discussion and dialogue.

If this fact was not evident to all Germans after the fall of Nazism, we ought to welcome the changed situation that now makes it possible. However, any foreign reader who thinks that our way of coming to terms with the past is too strict and too organized must realize a simple truth: only in such a distinctively German way can a dictatorship set up on the German model be destroyed.

*"The Clean Up Bureau" (Interview with Joachim Gauck)**

I believe the law is absolutely correct. Thanks to this law, we are not walking in a fog; we can eliminate the doubts and restore faith in democracy to the segment of society that had come to think this country could not be democratically ruled. Those who, like Lothar de Maziere, claimed that opening the files would result in public unrest, the settling of old scores, and even murders have been proven wrong. Of course some conflicts have arisen, but they were to be expected. Just imagine what would have happened if the files had been kept secret: not only would it have been impossible to create a climate of trust, but the files could have been used to threaten and blackmail people. The road we have taken is difficult and painful, but in my opinion it is the only road open to us.

Further Consideration of the Files Dilemma

Pawel Müller, "The Gauck Commission"†

[The Federal Commission for the Stasi Files] has recovered over 6 million personal files from the Stasi. At first, the commission was directed to grant information on the perpetrators and victims of Stasi repression to government agencies and other public institutions. When an agency inquired into the past of one of its employees, Gauck's commission would determine whether the person in question had collaborated with the Stasi. If the person in question had in fact collaborated, the commission put together a comprehensive report on his activities: when the collaboration began, whether he received money or other forms of compensation, whether he was coerced into collaboration, and whether he broke off contact with the Stasi. The great majority of requests have come from such institutions as the police, schools, and local or national administrative bodies. These institutions can make such requests without the permission of the individuals under review, who have no more than the right to be told that they are undergoing this procedure. Job applicants, however, must agree to the procedure beforehand. Representatives to the new eastern provincial councils also must agree to this procedure before they begin their service.

The authorities in Saxony, for example, plan to dismiss several thousand teachers. Stefani Rehm, Saxony's education minister, expressed the prevailing view when she told a journalist from *Der Spiegel*, "We face the task of screening our teachers to find out whether they collaborated with the Stasi. We start from the presumption that there were one or two informers in every school. There are 2,000 schools in Saxony, so there are at least 3,000 teachers who collaborated with the Stasi. These people consciously supported the communist regime; they did more than was necessary.... So I

---

* Excerpted from "The Clean-Up Bureau," *Uncaptive Minds*, vol. V, no. 2(20) (Summer 1992), p. 128.

† Excerpted from Pawel Müller, "The Gauck Commission," *Uncaptive Minds*, vol. V, no. 1(19) (Spring 1992), pp. 96-98. The article originally appeared in the January-February issue of the Polish bi-monthly *Przeglad Polityczny*.

think it's right that now we are carefully checking these people and parting company with them. The only thing that worries me is that in the countryside, this process is being deliberately blocked. We know of cases where school superintendents have protected their friends and colleagues. Furthermore, people undergoing verification portray one another as innocent."

From the beginning of 1992, all those on whom the Stasi kept files have had the right to see those files. The first to see their files were activists from the human rights movement. Their findings have confirmed Joachim Gauck's worst fears. He had warned people to carefully weigh the consequences of seeing their own files; to consider the possible impact of their findings on their family or social life. Moreover, he cautioned that "there are some people whose names are not only among the dossiers of the collaborators, but also among those of the victims."

It's too difficult at the moment to make a full assessment of the social and political dimensions of the opening of the Stasi files. Willibald Böck, interior minister of Thuringia, told a journalist that "opening the archives has helped us to come to terms with the past because it sheds light upon the mechanisms of the communist system. We should not, however, pass facile moral judgements. Heroes and martyrs were not in abundance, but those who were neither one nor the other were not necessarily scoundrels, cheats, or informers. It is possible that the perpetrators of evil were also its victims."

*Professor Dr. Spiro Simitis, Address to Conference on "Data Protection and Stasi Documents: Push the Issues Aside or Overcome Them?"**

[Several problems have] been showing up ever more clearly in public dealing with the State Security documents....

[T]he only thing that counts is that something is in the files and not who said what or what is the personal background and under what institutional conditions an item was recorded. The more freely this development progresses, the more clearly the burden of proof is reversed. In other words, someone referring to the files does not have to prove that someone behaved as is shown in the files. Rather it is incumbent upon the incriminated party to prove his innocence. Nothing has to be proven about him anymore; he can only deny things. It is suddenly forgotten which organization is making the given statements and how it worked, i.e. that these are documents that are, mildly put, dubious from the perspective of the constitutional state. What's worse, those who use every opportunity to designate the State Security as a criminal organization are constantly prepared to base their judgments on these statements. It is almost as if an assumption of the infallibility of the State Security has replaced the presumption of innocence. People also forget that no one, except for insiders, can seriously claim to have a reliable overview of the files. The files exist, but no one followed them up from beginning to end. Even the Federal Commissioner for the State Security

---

* Excerpted and translated from remarks by Professor Dr. Spiros Simitis, in Winfred Hassemer and Karl Starzacher, eds., *Data Protection and Stasi Documents: Push the Issues Aside or Overcome Them?* (Nomos Publishing House, 1993)(*Data Protection Forum*, vol. 1), pp. 39-42.

documents is only groping slowly along, can easily run into surprises and has never denied this. No matter how cautiously he expresses himself, and how much he still uses every opportunity to stress the limits of his knowledge, any restriction he makes is easily pushed aside.

[A]s the readiness to simply accept the contents of the files increases, the pressure increases from individual authorities, such as prosecutor's offices, on the Federal Commissioner to provide any documents they wish according to a procedure they determine. But a certain principle, already mentioned and clearly laid down by the law, is increasingly neglected in the process: The files are not freely accessible information sources to be used at will. The prosecutors' offices therefore have no more right than any other office to decide how access to the files should be organized and what individual documents must be handed out. Certainly, quite a few courts, starting with the Supreme Court and down to the individual labor courts have meanwhile showed clear doubts as to the value of the files as evidence. The public discussion does not seem too impressed by this, and the demand for equally privileged access to the files is still quite matter-of-fact.

[Finally,] the discussion on the State Security documents was highly personalized right from the start, but it increasingly runs the risk of only occurring in this form from now on. The significance of the documents for a precise reconstruction of the micro-structure of the State Security and its macropolitical concepts and ambitions or for an equally precise analysis of the very different beginnings of its entanglement with the state and party apparatus and with the various societal institutions and organizations is gradually being eclipsed by the interest in individuals selected more and more by their political and social prominence. For example, what role the "unofficial employees" actually played, how they were recruited in detail, where they were deployed and what means they used seems much less important than the fact that X or Y was an unofficial or even an official employee. But if the discussion on the State Security documents is really to help clear up the experiences of the past decades, then it must not continue to be so exclusively person-related. Rather it is important to avoid taking personal behavior out of the political context.... This will undeniably lead to a selective public stigmatization that not only deforms information but sooner or later substantially reduces responsibility through the intentional personalization. It is therefore very important to obtain as much clarity as possible on the method of operation and the effect of organizations such as the State Security.... The law is clear: The tasks of the Federal Commissioner are not limited to the duty to help the victims find out about the data stored on them, to better understand their fate and, in the cases provided for by law, to provide information on the basis of the documents in his possession or to hand out individual concrete documents. Rather, he is just as obligated to break through the personal context and, to show its organizational-structural elements and its political and social context for the sake of a proper and consequent clearing up of the activities of the State Security.

The Pain of Reading One's Own File

*Hanna Hartwig, "The Shock of the Past"**

The first to see their files are activists of the democratic opposition, harassed and jailed not so long ago. They can look through their dossiers in a small reading room, in other words, relive the last ten or twenty years of their lives, but this time from the Stasi's point of view. When did those problems begin at work? What happened to the letters that never reached their destinations? How did the interrogators know so many details? The answers to these questions are hidden in thick stacks of files: reports filed by informers, transcriptions of secretly recorded conversations, copies of letters, photographs, operational plans.

Among the first to be invited to the bureau was a married couple, Gerd and Ulrike Poppe. Gerd is currently a representative of Alliance '90 in the Bundestag, the federal parliament. He used to work as a physicist—until his opposition activities landed him in jail. After his release, he worked as a stoker for seven years.... The Poppes found reports signed with the pseudonym "Franz." Franz knew a lot about them; he must have been someone close to the family. Who could it have been? The Poppes and their relatives ponder the question, they ask an old family friend—but no one knows. The answer comes the second day in the reading room. A report was filed about one of the Poppes' trips, and Ulrike remembers that there was only one other person with them in the train compartment that day: the old family friend they had spoken to the day before. It was he who was Franz.

Another discovery: a plan that had been methodically formulated by some ambitious Stasi lieutenant was among the documents in the Poppes' dossier. The plan was a step-by-step blueprint for destroying their marriage. It didn't overlook the couple's young children.

"If all this energy had been devoted to conducting a dialogue with society, what a fantastic country this could have been!" sighs another opposition activist, the painter Bärbel Bohley. She is examining her file to find out whether the lawyer who once defended her was honest....

Vera Wollenberger, also a deputy to the Bundestag, did not want to believe what she was reading in the stacks of dusty files. She wanted to think it was just some intrigue against her. But as she read further, the truth became undeniable. An informer using the name "Donald" who had been filing reports on her for ten years was none other than her husband, Knud. "How could someone who is a splendid, loving husband write such reports? How could someone be capable of this? I am not able to understand it." Vera Wollenberger is shattered. She is thinking about divorce, about selling the house and moving to a small apartment in Bonn with her children. How will she ever be able to explain to them what their father did?

Vera's husband assures her that, although he had been a Stasi informer since he was very young, he didn't marry the young dissident because he

---

* Excerpted from Hanna Hartwig, "The Shock of the Past," *Uncaptive Minds*, vol. V, no. 1(19) (Spring 1992), pp. 99-101, 103-104. This article orginally appeared in the February 27-March 5 issue of the Polish weekly *Spotkania*.

had been ordered to do so. Not at all. They simply contacted him again at some point. Knud tells her that when the authorities decided to expel her from the country, he managed to dissuade them. He portrays himself as a man who went into the service of the enemy in order to convey the opposition's arguments and way of thinking, to force the authorities to initiate a dialogue with society.

Saxony's internal affairs minister, Hans Eggert, spent an entire day in the Stasi's Dresden branch. He had eight thick volumes of documents to look through, 2,900 pages altogether. The dossier included transcribed recordings of his sermons (Eggert was a pastor) in which he condemned the regime, and reports submitted by collaborators. "I am shocked by what I read. The friends who were coerced into informing should have a frank talk with me. I will sue the other informers." The pastor has one in mind in particular. The informer once spent his vacation at the Eggerts' house in the mountains. As the files reveal, the man wrote down all the conversations he heard, the names of other guests and the license plate numbers of their cars, and even sketched a floor plan of the Eggerts' house. As a result of the reports filed by the vacationer-informer, the Stasi initiated a harassment campaign against the pastor. His doctors were questioned, his phone was bugged, his mail was read.

When the Eggerts went on vacation by themselves, the security police kept an eye on them the whole time. The Stasi branch at the seaside town that was their destination was alerted, and agents were waiting for them when they arrived at the local campground. The result of their efforts is labeled "photo documentation of E.'s stay at the nudist beach." The only thing Eggert couldn't find in the files is evidence that dysentery-causing bacteria were planted in his food during that trip. It may sound a bit paranoic, but it's a fact that Eggert was the only one at the entire campground who contracted dysentery.

Will the informers be punished? Probably not: according to the unification treaty, citizens of the former German Democratic Republic can only be punished for crimes that were punishable under the East German legal code. So the informers aren't afraid of the law—but they do fear being unmasked and ostracized....

Dissidents from the former East Germany are finding out that they made a mistake when they spoke confidentially with lawyers—many of whom were well known and recommended by friends. Everything they said almost immediately showed up on the desk of a Stasi officer. Doctors couldn't be trusted either. Katia Havemann—widow of the famous oppositionist, doctor, and philosopher Robert Havemann—was shocked to find that even the doctor who cared for her husband until his death had been an informer. "That doctor enjoyed our complete trust. Yet he passed on every detail, immediately." The files included reports of the doctor's private conversations with the Havemanns together with the results of medical tests and assessments of the patient's health....

Other doctors didn't stop at writing reports. There was no lack of psychiatrists who were willing to serve the security apparatus. They gladly accepted cases of patients suffering from "delusions," such as the delusion that there are better systems than socialism.

When Eggert began to suffer from depression, one of his friends recommended a doctor who "could be relied upon." Apparently, the Stasi had the same opinion of the psychiatrist. The doctor, on Stasi orders, put Eggert in a psychiatric clinic and told him that he had no chance of a full recovery. He also stuffed his patient full of psychotropic drugs. Political dissidents in the Soviet Union had once been subjected to this "therapy," which was calculated to deprive them of energy and destroy their will. The doctor warned Eggert's family that he must save his strength, avoid stress and emotional situations, and take large doses of the drugs that had been prescribed for him. Fortunately, the pastor threw out his copious supply of pills as soon as he left the clinic, and he snapped out of his depression. He was luckier than other patients, some of whom—after making a careless joke or critical comment—were locked away for years and really did lose their sanity.

The literary community of the former GDR was—in the words of opposition poet and songwriter Wolf Biermann—"a blooming garden of the Stasi." This garden contained every sort of writer, including subtle poets and sensitive aesthetes who rebelled against the system. These people—such as Sascha Anderson, a poet and a member of the critical circle of writers from the Prenzlauer Berg district of Berlin—were admired by their Western colleagues for their ethos and their courage. But since the Stasi files were opened, it has been found that Anderson wrote not only lyrical verses, but also summaries of his friends' discussions....

West Germans, who fear an avalanche of lawsuits, are warning of the possibility that people will be punished solely on the basis of Stasi files, which could have been tampered with. They also point out that the files—even if they weren't falsified—don't include information on why their subjects agreed to collaborate with the Stasi. Did someone inform to further his career, or because he was hounded by the secret police until he broke down?

East Germans are not so concerned with the legal and moral complications. They simply want to know the truth, no matter what the cost. As Rainer Eppelmann, a minister in the last government of the GDR and currently a deputy to the Bundestag, said, "After reading your file, you are wiser but also poorer." It's true—those who read their files lose many friends, their idealistic memories of resisting totalitarianism, their faith in the loyalty and honesty of bosses, neighbors, even family members.

Those who support opening up the Stasi archives believe that people need to know the truth—the whole truth, no matter how painful it is. Doing so, in their opinion, will not only touch off a wave of lawsuits and perhaps even acts of revenge. More importantly, once the initial disillusionment and bitterness pass, a feeling of relief and catharsis will follow. Perhaps they are right. But will it happen during the lifetime of this generation?

THE DEBATE WITHIN THE GERMAN CHURCH COMMUNITY

*John P. Burgess, "Coming to Terms with the East German Past"**

Last summer, I traveled to East Berlin and East Germany, the culmination of a series of trips reaching over more than a decade. In 1979 I was a tourist paying my first visit. In 1984-1985, I had studied at an East Berlin seminary of the Evangelical Church, the country's major religious body, and in 1987 and 1989 I spent several weeks visiting friends made then, many of whom, in the meantime, had become pastors and members of church-related "alternative groups." They were helping to build the opposition movement that eventually challenged the Communist state. I had again visited the country the very week the Wall fell. And now, this time on a grant to research the contributions of the East German church to democratization, I would again be living at the seminary, many of whose instructors and graduates continue to play leading roles in shaping the future of East Germany. During my visit, I would learn of the difficult challenges and adjustments that unification has brought. But I would be even more struck by the difficult legacy of the past. The 1989 revolution (what East Germans call "*die Wende*," i.e., the turning point) has begun to bring into the open what many would rather bury: complicity in the Communist past, connections with the state security forces, and failures of intellectual integrity and moral courage. The church, which played a significant role in supporting and steering the revolution, finds itself caught in a classic theological dilemma: love or justice. Coming to terms with the past seems to require both forgiveness and accountability, both forgetting and remembering. In practice, however, they easily become contradictions that defy resolution, both personally and socially....

Before World War II, students at Berlin's Kirchliche Hochschule (Church Seminary), a child of the German Confessing Church, used to live and take their first two years of classes—Hebrew, Greek, and Latin—at the Sprachenkonvikt ("language house"). With the division of the city, the Sprachenkonvikt found itself in the eastern sector; after the construction of the Wall, students could no longer go back and forth between it and the Kirchliche Hochschule. The Sprachenkonvikt soon became a full-fledged, five-year seminary, one of only three in all of East Germany.... [T]he Konvikt, as it is now known, continues to exist as a "theology house" with dormitory and study rooms....

Over the past two years, East Germans have experienced incredible change. Many are exhausted. They have ridden an emotional roller coaster of hope and depression. First came the emigration "mania" that took tens of thousands of East Germans to the West by way of Hungary, and later Czechoslovakia, even before the Wall fell. Those who remained felt abandoned and saddened. Then, as if in response, came the mass

---

* Excerpted from John P. Burgess, "Coming to Terms with the East German Past," *First Things*, issue 21 (March 1992), pp. 27-35.

demonstrations that eventually toppled the government. People suddenly felt elated and empowered. They proudly declared that they had achieved the first successful democratic revolution in German history. But days of disagreement and confusion soon followed. Some people wanted an independent East Germany that would embody a "democratic socialism," while others called for quick unification with the West. The weekly Monday demonstrations sometimes deteriorated into shouting matches between different groups with different political agendas.

In the end, unification won out—and more quickly than even its most vocal advocates had ever anticipated. It has brought stability but also left many East Germans unsure of how well they will survive in the free market. It is not so much a question of material but emotional and psychological well-being, of self-confidence and identity. East Germans have always compared themselves to West Germans; with unification, they still feel like poorer cousins, unsure if they have any positive, significant contribution to make to a new Germany. The Trabant is cute, but it is no car for the future.

Under these circumstances, people also have a hard time thinking about the social-political reality that they have just recently left behind. Yet if studying history makes any sense, East Germans will eventually want to learn from their own. While unification has brought more than enough challenges and adjustments to occupy them for the time being, difficult questions about the past will continue to haunt the East German psyche as a whole, just as the Nazi past continues to haunt the German psyche. Indeed, coming to terms with the Communist past may be the most critical challenge before all the fledgling democracies in Eastern Europe. Social and political renewal seems to depend on open, honest confession of the crimes and mistakes of the past. Yet this very effort threatens to pit individuals and groups against one another in settling old scores.

Some of the questions are already clear. How was Communism possible? How did it once establish itself as a seemingly unalterable fact, only to crumble so quickly in the end? How could people have lived in fear of it so long? How could they have failed to resist it sooner?

The attempt to find answers has, as one might expect, a one-word German equivalent: *Vergangenheitsbewaltigung*, literally, "mastery of the past." This word, more than any other, is presently unleashing vigorous public discussion in East Germany. The debate is perhaps fiercest in the Evangelical Church. Church leaders have been at the forefront of the nation's conscience, calling people to examine their own complicity in the Communist past. But the church itself is also deeply divided over the best way to come to terms with its own past.

Some East Bloc intellectuals would argue that everyone shares complicity in the Communist past. In *The Power of the Powerless*, Vaclav Havel, while still a dissident in the country that he has since come to head, suggested that the seductions of a modern, consumerist society made Communism possible. When people have no sense of responsibility to a larger, transcendent reality, when they live only for themselves and their material well-being, they lead "demoralized" lives. They are prey to dictatorships that promise to fulfill their needs through rational, scientific-technological organization.

The theme of an underlying spiritual, intellectual, and moral malaise has also characterized the social-political analyses of those East German theologians most committed to democratization. A book receiving considerable attention during my stay was Hans-Joachim Maaz's *Der Gefuhlsstau* (roughly translated, Jammed-Up Feelings). Maaz, an East German psychotherapist who has worked in a church-run psychiatric center and treated pastors, argues that the entire nation has internalized repressive, authoritarian social structures. Even after the fall of the Wall, only an "inner democratization" and "psychic revolution" can fully free people.

I spent one afternoon asking Richard Schroder, the Konvikt's professor of philosophy, his view of the Communist past. Schroder told me that Communism could thrive only in a society in which people had relinquished their capacity for "critical thinking." He pointed to the impoverished status of philosophy under Communism. In East Germany, nearly every professional philosopher was trained and paid by the state. There was no independent study of "philosophy," only the ideologically defined discipline called "Marxist-Leninist philosophy." To the end, censorship of philosophical publications remained tightly regulated, in contrast to some of the leeway offered novelists and poets.

Schroder, originally trained as a pastor in the Evangelical Church, had to educate himself when the church asked him to teach philosophy. Like others, he found in the church a "free space" for his work. At the seminary, he could teach essentially what he wanted: the philosophical tradition, with its great questions of meaning and morality. To him, it is no accident that the Konvikt produced a disproportionate number of the leaders in the opposition movement and new political order. Schroder himself won a reputation for critical, independent thinking and found a brief but significant career in politics after the Wall fell, serving in the East German parliament as head of the Social Democratic faction.

A balding man with large, strong hands (like many East Germans, he had taught himself various mechanical and technical skills because professionals were always in short supply), Schroder told me that the present situation is not unlike that at the end of World War II. Fascism and Communism were clearly different phenomena. Hitler had enthusiastic support; the East German Communist party lacked any charisma. Yet, in both cases, a kind of mass amnesia fell over the land. After the war, one could find no Nazis. Today, few admit to having believed even a small part of the Communist dream; even fewer can speak self-critically about the past.

The problem, Schroder would keep telling me, is that no state survives without a broad, public consensus. Yet, most East Germans do not want to talk about the ways in which they implicitly or explicitly supported the Communist state.

[Repressing the Past]

I found that this unwillingness, perhaps even inability to discuss and analyze the past took two forms. The first was what several East German friends called *Sprachlosigkeit*, literally, "speechlessness." Many people simply did not question their past involvements in state-sponsored organizations and activities. They did not ask themselves if they had done the right thing by participating, for example, in the *Jugendweihe* (the Communist youth dedication ceremony that had effectively replaced confirmation as a rite of passage). They did not examine the ways in which they had once lived in fear of the state and practiced forms of self-censorship that restricted them perhaps more than the state itself. They did not speak of the meaningless elections in which they had contributed to 99.99 percent majorities, or of the May Day gatherings in which they unenthusiastically but faithfully repeated the slogans of worker solidarity and international Communism.

This *Sprachlosigkeit* even extended to their former fears of, and encounters with, the state security forces (the *Staatssicherheitsdienst*, the so-called "Stasi"). Nearly every East German had once experienced the Stasi as a force of mythic proportions, capable of knowing and controlling everyone and everything. For many years, it had successfully permeated people's spirits to the point of paralyzing their desire for change. Not surprisingly, the self-organized, mass demonstrations that helped people overcome this paralysis finally led them to the Stasi buildings themselves—at first just to march by them quietly and cautiously, later to enter and occupy them. Yet few people today are able to analyze the ways in which the Stasi actually worked or to make sense of their own irrational fears of it. Even the novelists and poets, once the ones who dared to say a little more than the state normally allowed, have grown quiet, seemingly disillusioned and disoriented, and few of those people who actually suffered Stasi harassment and imprisonment have come forward to demand rehabilitation and restitution.

One result of *Sprachlosigkeit* has been that West Germans, who never had any experience of the Stasi, even assumed the rather arrogant and ludicrous posture of trying to tell East Germans what to think about it. Because so few other East Germans are addressing the issue, Schroder has found himself writing and speaking about his own encounters with the Stasi, and in a recent interview with *Der Spiegel* he called on the West German media, instead of spreading myths and inaccuracies, to consider what East Germans could teach them.

The second way in which I found East Germans repressing the past was by scapegoating others. A whole people had been duped. Now it vented its ire against the Politburo, or the party, or the Stasi.... The media in both Germanys make headlines with exposés of the crimes of the once privileged and powerful; unfortunately, they offer little insight into the larger problem: the "demoralization" that infected an entire people.

The revolution gave people a voice. They demanded to be treated as responsible, mature citizens. Yet they also sought recourse in the kind of self-righteous anger against their former leaders that provided a convenient diversion from the problem of their own complicity in the Communist past.

The church has sought to counter this *Sprachlosigkeit* and scapegoating. I spent one afternoon with Ehrhart Neubert, an East Berlin pastor who had helped found *Demokratischer Aufbruch* (Democratic Awakening), one of the first opposition groups to go public in 1989. Neubert, a sociologist of religion, has written extensively on the religious character of the alternative groups that began to appear in the church in the early 1980s. While these groups did not practice a traditional religious piety, the church offered them a space in which they could meet freely and speak openly. Though sometimes subject to state surveillance and harassment, they managed to develop a critical potential that helped spark the revolution. Neubert believes that the church can now offer a similar "free space" for groups seeking reconciliation between the victimizers and victims of the past.

Neubert, a thin, wiry man in his mid-forties, has himself helped to form such a group in East Berlin's Bartholomaus Church, located in an area of high-rise apartment blocks not far from Alexanderplatz, the center of East Berlin. The congregation quietly posted signs and issued invitations. People who in forty years had never set foot in a church building suddenly appeared. Meeting monthly, the group resembles an [Alcoholics Anonymous]-style support group. Participants enjoy a degree of confidentiality; they never identify themselves by name. Yet they have discovered a level of trust that enables them to speak quite openly about their individual pasts. Former agents of the Stasi sit next to former members of alternative groups. The agents hear the pain of those whom they once harassed. The alternative group members come to know the agents as real flesh-and-blood people, not simply as a dark, evil force.

Such meetings have been repeated throughout East Germany, though on an extremely small scale. Siegfried Kasparick in Osterburg has been active in promoting local school reform. He recently helped organize a meeting between the town's high school teachers and some of their former students. It was an opportunity for the young people to express their anger at the rigid, ideological indoctrination that characterized so much of the East German educational system. Several teachers were visibly shaken; others offered apologies.

Many pastors throughout the country have also had the experience of people seeking to make confession to them and receive forgiveness. One pastor told me of a former party official who had come to him in tears. The anxieties, lies, and pressures that had ruled his life under the Communist regime had nearly destroyed him. With unification, he too wanted to make a new beginning. Another pastor, who had been active in the opposition movement, told me how he had discovered that the Stasi had once directed his mechanics to tamper with his automobile. Though they still could not bring themselves to speak about the incident, their attitude was clearly remorseful.

Yet the church itself suffers from *Sprachlosigkeit* and the temptation to scapegoat those of its leaders who had worked with the Communist authorities. Despite its significant role in the revolution, broad segments of the church had once helped support the Communist order They too were part of that public consensus of which Schroder speaks. Schroder has argued that the slogan "church in socialism," which the church adopted to express its commitment to ministry in East Germany, too easily became its way of accepting the Communist state as an established fact. The church largely bracketed the question of the state's legitimacy, rejecting the atheistic element of official ideology but mostly failing to question whether the state had properly interpreted Marx and Lenin, or whether Marx and Lenin themselves had a true understanding of the human condition....

Given the charged public atmosphere of scapegoating, however, it is not surprising that people are reluctant to talk about their past. Some church leaders have argued that their first task is to create an atmosphere in which people will feel freer to examine themselves. They would ask those calling for "mastery of the past" to begin with themselves and to have patience with others, rather than making them lose face. But some pastors believe that people will only examine themselves if someone else first exposes and confronts them. Bringing the truth into light may actually free people to come to terms with a past they would rather repress.

This dilemma raises profound questions. Can people be forced to admit to their complicity in the past? If confession occurs under compulsion, can it be genuine? Will people freely own their past if left to themselves? When does confession belong in the public realm, when does it best remain private?

[Stasi Informants and Stasi Files]

Nowhere do these questions assume more intensity and difficulty than in regard to the files left by the Stasi. In the months after the fall of the Wall, members of the opposition movement slowly became aware that the Stasi had begun to destroy documents. In Leipzig, Dresden, Rostock, and finally East Berlin itself, "citizens committees" decided to occupy and secure Stasi buildings. They believed that the Stasi past had to be preserved, analyzed, and understood.

Over the next weeks, the government, at that time composed of both Communist and opposition forces, debated what to do. Because the political situation appeared increasingly volatile, opposition leaders agreed to help destroy computer tapes that had complete directories and listings of information in the files. They sensed the power in their hands, and they feared it. They wanted to hinder the Stasi from manipulating individuals on whom it had collected information. They wanted to protect the public sphere from poisonous accusations, denunciations, mistrust, and intimidation. Moreover, they feared that the West German security police might attempt to steal information to blackmail individuals for its own purposes.

But the files themselves stretch to more than 180 kilometers. Some church leaders, such as East Berlin's Bishop Gottfried Forck, who had taken courageous stands against the Communist state, suggested that these files be sealed in concrete or destroyed. Others, such as members of *Demokratie Jetzt* (Democracy Now), another of the first opposition groups to go public, insisted that individuals had a right to examine their files.

To try to make sense of this debate, I spoke with David Gill, a young Konvikt student who helped occupy and secure the Stasi headquarters in East Berlin. When the new East German parliament, elected in March 1990, formed a committee to deal with the Stasi question, a member of the committee, a fellow Konvikt student, managed to get Gill appointed secretary. The chairman of the committee, Joachim Gauck, a pastor from Rostock, eventually became head of a government agency to organize, catalogue, and research the files. With unification, this agency—the so-called Gauck-Behorde (Gauck-authorities)—became accountable to the German Bundestag, and Gauck appointed Gill to manage the East Berlin branch.

In early 1990, Gill himself had believed in destroying the files. Unification, however, has brought a political stability that puts the matter in a different light. Now, argues Gill, it is possible, indeed essential, to use the files to help the nation come to terms with its past.

Several hundred thousand East Germans (no one knows the exact number) worked officially or unofficially for the Stasi. They spied and reported on millions of their fellow citizens. They violated the basic trust upon which a free and just society depends. Few broke the law—even fewer will ever come to trial—but their abuse of the public trust constitutes ground for denying them positions of leadership in a new democracy.

The law provides for public institutions to request information from the files. As part of the process of rebuilding themselves and regaining the public trust, city councils, local legislatures, public universities, and government agencies can request the assistance of the Gauck-Behorde. The essential criterion is whether or not [an employee or job applicant] worked for the Stasi. All public officials must declare any Stasi connections. If they deny having them and the Gauck-authorities find evidence to the contrary, they can lose their position....

The church, too, has the right to have the Gauck authorities examine the files of its pastors and leaders. Whether or not to do so has generated passionate debate. In East Berlin, the debate began with a simple request from the Konvikt. Faculty members voted to have their files examined. They were in fact fairly confident that none of them had Stasi connections. They were, however, anticipating the merger with the university and knew that they would eventually have to rebuild the reputation of its theological department, which over the years had largely accommodated itself to the state.

The Berlin-Brandenburg Synod, which oversees the Konvikt, refused their request, arguing that it would establish a precedent that the synod was not ready to honor. The synod has thus far resisted examining pastors, except in cases involving clear evidence. In an open letter to churches, Propst Furian, an official in the Berlin-Brandenburg church headquarters, asked members to consider the special character of the Christian community. Church members are "brothers and sisters." They begin from trust, not suspicion. A general examination could only undermine the church's life and witness.

I had an opportunity to discuss these matters with Ruth Misselwitz, an East Berlin pastor. I had first gotten to know Misselwitz through her husband, who had studied at the Konvikt at the same time as I. Both had been very active in the opposition movement and suffered considerable Stasi harassment. Ruth Misselwitz was now a member of the synodical commission charged with developing a position on the Stasi issue. I asked her how was it possible that some of those who during the revolution had called for "living in truth" (to borrow Havel's phrase) now did not want to deal with the truth about the past. She told me that the commission had struggled to find a solution. Especially important had been conversations with former Stasi officials. Many of them, she said, had sought to do their job with integrity. They had seen themselves contributing to the good of society. With the rise of Gorbachev, they themselves had hoped for changes in East Germany. They had been the first to know that the old system was no longer working, and they had tried, to no avail, to encourage state leaders to institute change.

This process of "demythologizing" the Stasi also extended to the question of so-called "*inoffizielle Mitarbeiter*" (unofficial colleagues, i. e., informants). Through her work, Misselwitz had become aware of the psychological pressures that had been brought to bear on them. There were stories of the Stasi recruiting orphans and social misfits, offering them the acceptance, approval, and love they had never known elsewhere. For others, work with the Stasi represented a necessary concession. Perhaps a person had committed a political offense many years earlier. The Stasi agreed not to destroy his career if he would become an informant.

In any case, it appeared that many, if not all, the members of the Stasi, official and unofficial, were themselves "victims." Since they no longer posed a threat to society, the church could now celebrate the new beginning that the revolution represented and reach out with love and compassion to those who had gotten entangled in the Stasi web. The church's task was to find ways to show concern and offer care. Confronting people with their past would only put them in a defensive position, not free them to come to terms with it. Instead, the Synod had offered to work in confidentiality with any pastors who came forward of themselves.

Commission members were also concerned that the Stasi files were misleading. Agents and informants had sometimes been rewarded simply for producing information; its accuracy was not always established. Moreover, in the weeks between the fall of the Wall and the occupation of the Stasi buildings, the Stasi had had time not only to destroy but to falsify documents as well.

Schroder too helped make me aware of the complexity of the problem. Some church leaders had been regularly questioned by the Stasi; they might appear in the files, but that did not make them informants. Others had tried to make good use of their contacts with the Stasi, seeking to protect individuals against whom the Stasi had suspicions or to make the Stasi aware of public discontent with state policies.

Others, however, have found arguments against using the files unpersuasive. The Synod of Mecklenberg, in contrast to Berlin-Brandenburg, has voted to have its pastors examined. The rationale is that the church cannot rest on its laurels. It can keep the public trust that it won in the revolution only if it shows itself as ready as other public institutions to examine its complicity in the Communist past. Of all public figures, pastors in particular must be accountable to a higher standard. Waiting for informants to come forward of their own accord is like asking alcoholics to admit they have a problem: very few will ever do so, unless exposed and confronted.

I asked David Gill about the accuracy of the files. He argued that the Stasi, true to its reputation, had operated with great care and precision. The files themselves distinguish between rumor and fact. He felt confident, moreover, that little information had been lost. Documents often existed in several copies in several places; missing information could often be reconstructed from other sources. As to the question of falsification, Gill contended that the Stasi had not had time to destroy all the documents; it certainly had not bothered to change individual files.

Moreover, the files alone could help establish the degree to which an individual had actually cooperated with the Stasi. Undoubtedly there were cases of victimization. Undoubtedly there were also cases of pastors using their contacts to the church's benefit. To Gill, the most crucial question was whether or not a person had signed a statement pledging voluntary and secret participation.

Some pastors in Berlin-Brandenburg told me that church leaders had their own reasons for not wanting files examined: they did not want people to know just how much the Stasi had successfully infiltrated every layer of the church bureaucracy, especially in East Berlin. These church leaders also feared that a population tempted to scapegoat might not appreciate the complexity of the Stasi issue....

To help me think through these issues, I visited Harald Wagner, a pastor whom I had first met in 1985. Wagner had a fascinating story. He had once been a top East German athlete, nearly Olympic quality. In the early 1980s, he became involved in a group that distributed banned political and philosophical literature. He was arrested and imprisoned for nearly a year. The state tried, as it often did with political prisoners, to shove him and his family off to the West. But Wagner and his wife, despite their bitter experiences and deep discouragement, insisted on staying in East Germany. Out of a deep sense of faith, they continued to commit themselves to seeking peaceful social and political change. Wagner had eventually come to play a leading role in the opposition movement, helping to lead public protests and found *Demokratischer Aufbruch*....

Like many others in the church, Wagner has sought to respond to his experience of the Stasi with thoughtfulness, not revenge. Unlike some of his fellow pastors, however, he sees responsible use of the Stasi files as an essential component of corporate and personal renewal. Asking people to confront their past, says Wagner, can itself be an act of love. Justice and love need not contradict each other. The victimizer's act of remorse can meet the victim's act of forgiveness. Confrontation does not—in fact must not—exclude compassion....

Other real-life examples confronted me with similar questions and tensions. I knew a pastor who had spent several years in psychotherapy.

During the chaotic days of December 1989, he had gotten hold of a copy of his Stasi files. To his horror, he discovered that his therapist had regularly delivered information to the Stasi, which hoped to have him committed to a psychiatric hospital. He confronted the woman, but she completely denied her involvement. His files further revealed that a fellow pastor had also been an informant. Now he pondered whether or not to confront him: would confrontation only result again in denial, making both justice and love irrelevant?

In other cases, the past seemed to take care of itself. I think of Wolf Krotke, director of the newly merged theological department of East Berlin's Humboldt University. Over the years, Krotke has won a fine reputation in both Germanies for his sensitive interpretation of Barth and Bonhoeffer. Students have admired him not only for his penetrating analyses of church and society, but also for his open spirit—he has always been a rock of support. I have known Krotke ever since I first attended Konvikt. I had even helped teach him English out of an American theological text, Stanley Hauerwas' *The Peaceable Kingdom*. His apartment was in Konvikt, and I had often sat in his cool, dark office. He had never talked much of his personal past. I only knew from students that he had been imprisoned in the late 1950s: as a university student, he had composed a poem mocking Walter Ulbricht and other East German Communists of that era.

Now Krotke himself broached the subject with me. With the political changes, a number of people had encouraged him to apply for rehabilitation. He seemed to struggle to know what to do. All that was so long ago, he said. He had come to terms with it. He had no need to have his justice. Opening the case would only open old wounds. Again, I was left only with questions and tensions: was I viewing liberation or repression, healing or hurting? Could the past sometimes better be left alone, no longer a matter of either love or justice?

A fourth life story moved me most deeply of all. One afternoon, a pastor who had been active in the opposition movement told me of getting his files through a member of a citizens committee, prior to the government reestablishing control over the Stasi buildings. The files were extensive, documenting how the Stasi had bugged his home and prepared, but never executed, his arrest. What shook him most deeply was the discovery that his best friend had been an informant. He had known this man for ten years. Not only had they come to speak openly about politics, but their families had vacationed together every summer; they had shared birthday celebrations; they had hoped and dreamed together about a new kind of society, more free and just.

The shock had gone deep into his bones. To this day, his wife could not forgive the man or his wife, who had been aware of his involvement; she could not even bring herself to talk to them. The pastor himself had spoken twice to the man, by telephone. The first time the man denied everything. The pastor persisted, insisting there be honesty and openness. The second time the man completely broke down, condemning himself and sounding suicidal. The pastor was so concerned that he found himself backing off, suggesting that the friendship was perhaps not completely lost.

Through other mutual friends, the pastor has put more details together. Ten years ago, the man and his wife had attempted to adopt a baby. Everything was in order until the very day they were to receive the child. Suddenly, their request was denied, without explanation. For weeks, the man met with doctors and officials, trying to determine the problem. He got nowhere. [Eventually, s]omething clicked in the man's head. He went to the Stasi and offered to work for them if they would allow the adoption. They denied any involvement but agreed to check into the matter. They added that the decision whether or not to work for them was fully his. He signed a statement. A few days later, he and his wife had the child.

The German Bundestag has decided to give every East German the right to examine his files, if they indeed exist. People will be able to learn who informed on them; personal information about third parties will be blacked out. The debate that has erupted in the church is finally a debate for an entire society. Some argue that opening the files will result in acts of hatred and vengeance. It will destroy friendships; it will undermine all efforts at a desperately needed social reconciliation. Others argue that the only way to healing is through an open, however painful, coming to terms with the truth of the past. They add that to date there have been no acts of violence against known Stasi agents and informers; they do not anticipate any in the future. (Moreover, the law forbids publication of one's files.)

As in all these questions, the church finds itself on both sides. It has no other choice. Without confession, there can be no forgiveness; it may be just as true, however, that without forgiveness, there will never be confession.

Richard von Weizsacker, the West German president, once remarked, in reference to the Nazi past, that there is no such thing as *Vergangenheitsbewaltigung*; we never "master the past," for the past, for good or bad, always remains with us.

PROBLEMS OF PROSECUTION

*Kif Augustine Adams, "What Is Just?: The Rule of Law and Natural Law in the Trials of Former East German Border Guards"**

Introduction

Legal philosophers have long debated the purpose, meaning and nature of law. These jurisprudential debates are often abstract and theoretical. Currently, however, the world is experiencing significant political and legal upheavals which provide practical opportunities to examine the nature of law and the manner in which law organizes society. The transition from communism to democracy and capitalism in Eastern and Central Europe, as

* Excerpted from Kif Augustine Adams, "What Is Just?: The Rule of Law and Natural Law in the Trials of Former East German Border Guards," *Stanford Journal of International Law*, vol. 29 (1993), pp. 272-275, 280, 287-289, 291-314.

well as in the former Soviet Union, underscores the fundamental interdependence of society, law, and morality. The injustices of the old regimes, exemplified by the power of the East German state security force, haunt the new societies. Given these injustices,[2] the questions of law and justice in the new legal systems are particularly acute.

...The rule of law is directed towards fairness and individual freedom, but its principles may conflict with what people perceive as just punishment for those in a previous regime whose actions violated the rule of law. Although law is meant to further justice, law and justice are often not the same.

Few aspects of the Eastern European transition have captured the poignancy, ambivalence, and sheer pain of a massive societal reorganization according to law as the recent trials of East German border guards. These guards stood at the border between East Germany and West Germany, along the Berlin Wall; they were charged with the duty of defending the socialist system against internal and external attack. They now stand trial in a united Germany for killing those who attempted to leave what was supposed to be a socialist utopia. In the context of these trials, the questions that the ordinary citizen asked above are complicated by societal questions. How can a united Germany provide justice for those harmed by the communist regime in East Germany without repeating the injustices of that regime? Does a present commitment to the rule of law preclude punishment of those who had no commitment to the rule of law in the past? Resolution of these questions will influence German society and its perceptions of law, justice, and morality far into the future. A fair outcome will help to provide the basis for a coherent and stable Germany.

The complex issues of how a society in transition uses law and a commitment to the rule of law to reorganize itself are the focus of this paper....

The Rule of Law

Law is a means of organizing society according to rules. The rule of law does not condone mere legality, but is rather "a rule concerning what the law ought to be, a meta-legal doctrine."[5] In other words, the rule of law provides the framework, the over-arching principles, for organizing a system of laws. According to F.A. Hayek, under the rule of law, laws must be general and abstract, prospective, known and certain, and equally applicable to all individuals.[6] In addition, law-making and law-enforcing powers should be

---

2 *See* Alex Kozinski, *The Dark Lessons of Utopia*, 58 U. CHI. L. REV. 575 (1991); Wiktor Osiatynski, *Revolutions in Eastern Europe*, 58 U. CHI. L. REV. 823 (1991); *Former Premier Should Face Tribunal of State, Sejm Resolves*, PAP PRESS WIRE, Oct. 12, 1991, *available in* LEXIS, Nexis Library, Wires File (detailing the Polish Congress's decision to try the former premier for corrupt acts committed under communism); Leszek Maza, *Czecho-Slovakia: Crisis in the Courts*, THE WARSAW VOICE, Nov. 17, 1991, *available in* LEXIS, Nexis Library, Wires File (outlining the difficulty of dealing with collaborators of the former State Security Service).

5 FREIDRICH A. HAYEK, THE CONSTITUTION OF LIBERTY 206 (1971).

6 *Id.* at 208-09.

separated.[7]... This paper uses the term rule of law to describe the meta-legal principles of certainty, publicity, prospectivity, generality, and separation of powers. The value of using the rule of law as a framework is in its method of organizing society to promote individual freedom by making reasonably clear to individuals the legal consequences of their actions....

The Rule of Law and the Trials of Former East German Border Guards

United Germany today faces many of the same questions of law and justice it faced after World War II. The Federal Republic of Germany does not face the same criticism of victor's justice as the Allies did at Nuremberg, because East Germany voluntarily acceded to the Federal Republic of Germany. Nevertheless, the answers to questions of law and justice are all the more important, because law and justice will be among the principles that unite a long-divided German society. The internal cohesion and stability of Germany depend to a large degree on the perceived fairness of unification....

Municipal Law

The voluntary German reunification process provides a benchmark for determining what law should apply in the trials of the border guards. The Treaty between the Federal Republic of Germany and the German Democratic Republic on the Establishment of German Unity ("Unification Treaty") guided the legal transition from two Germanies to one. Article I provided that on October 3 1990, the Lander of East Germany would become Lander of the Federal Republic of Germany in accordance with article 23 of the FRG's Basic Law and the GDR's Lander Establishment Act.[69] On that date, the Basic Law came into effect in the parts of united Germany where it had previously not been in force. While extending the federal law of the FRG into the territory of the former GDR,[70] the drafters of the treaty recognized the immense practical difficulties of integrating two distinct legal systems and detailed a list of exceptions and modifications in Annex I.[71] Thus, the Unification Treaty provided for the continuing validity of much of GDR law.[72]

In addition, the Criminal Code of the FRG provides the foundation for arguing that GDR law should continue to govern crimes committed before unification: "The punishment and its incidental consequences are determined pursuant to the law in force at the time of the act."[73] Furthermore, "[a]n act

---

[7] *Id.* at 210.

[69] *See* Treaty between the Federal Republic of Germany and the German Democratic Republic on the Establishment of German Unity, Aug. 31, 1990, F.R.G.-G.D.R., art. 1 [hereinafter Unification Treaty], *reprinted in* 30 I.L.M., 457, 464 (1991).

[70] *See id.* art. 8, 30 I.L.M. 469.

[71-72] [omitted]

[73] STRAFGESETZBUCH [Penal Code] [StGB] § 2 (F.R.G.) [hereinafter StGB FRG], *reprinted in* 1 GERMAN CRIMINAL LAW: THE CRIMINAL CODE AND THE NARCOTICS LAW 19 (Gerold Harist & Otto A. Schmidt trans., 1989). Friederich-Christian Schroeder opines that GDR law should

can be punished only if the punishability was provided by law before the act was committed."[74] These provisions were part of the FRG's Criminal Code before transition and reflect a long-term commitment on the part of the FRG to the rule of law.

The Law of the German Democratic Republic

...Under the Penal Code of the GDR, an unlawful frontier crossing was a criminal act,[88] which the border guard, as a member of the socialist society, had a duty to prevent—particularly since an illegal border crossing could be seen as maligning the sovereignty of the GDR.[89] It was likewise criminal to resist government measures "by the use of force or threat of force or any other major disadvantage" when an official was engaged "in the dutiful carrying out of public duties entrusted to him for the safeguarding of law and order."[90] Continuing to cross the border after being told to stop could be viewed as resisting government measures designed for safeguarding law and order, although it is hard to see how running away from a border guard with a machine gun could create a "major disadvantage" to the guard. Nonetheless, as a whole, the GDR's Penal Code sanctioned attempts to prevent illegal border crossings.

The Penal Code does, nonetheless, condemn killing. It defines murder as deliberately killing another person;[91] homicide as deliberately killing another person with some mitigating circumstances;[92] and negligent homicide as death that results from "a reckless disregard of provisions for the protection of human life and health or if the offender has violated his duties regarding special care for his fellow human beings to a particularly irresponsible extent."[93] On the other hand, the Code exonerates anyone who "wards off a present illegal attack against ... the socialist state and social order in a manner commensurate with the nature of the attack;" such an individual "acts in the interests of socialist society and its legality, and thus does not commit any punishable act."[94] The fact that no East German border guard was tried by an East German court for murder, homicide, or negligent

apply only where current FRG sanctions are harsher than GDR sanctions. Friedrich-Christian Schroeder, *The Rise and Fall of the Criminal Law of the German Democratic Republic*, 2 CRIM. L.F. 217, 231 (1991).

74 StGB FRG, *supra* note 73, § l.

88 *See id.* art. 213.

89 "The struggle against any criminal offence, particularly against any criminal violations of peace and the sovereignty of the German Democratic Republic and the Workers' and Farmers' State is the common cause of socialist society, its state and all its citizens." *Id.* art. l. The Constitution of the GDR also confirmed this commitment: "It is the joint concern of socialist society, its state and all citizens to combat and prevent crime and other violations of law." VERF, [DIE VERASSUNG DER DDR [constitution] [VERF] art. 8, § 1 (G.D.R.), *reprinted in* 1968 LAW & LEGIS. IN THE GDR 89, 90], art. 90.

90 StGB GDR, [Strafgesetzbuch [Penal Code][StGB], as amended on Dec. 19, 1974, Apr. 7, 1977, June 28, 1979 (G.D.R.)], art. 212.

91 *Id.* art. 112.

92 *Id.* art. 113.

93 *Id.* art. 114.

94 *Id.* art. 17.

homicide, implies that according to the official East German understanding of the law, shooting at individuals crossing the border was commensurate with warding off attacks on the socialist state.

In fact, a newspaper recently reported...: "Guards were constantly fed information and rumors that well-armed groups were planning to crash the frontier and would not hesitate to kill any soldier who tried to stop them."[95] Given this type of information, a soldier may have thought that shooting to kill was a response commensurate with the nature of the attack, even if in fact it were not. Under the Code, when an individual "oversteps the limits" of a response commensurate with the nature of the attack, a court is free to disregard penal measures "if the person who acts has logically been placed into a state of high emotion and therefore exceeded the limits of legitimate defence."[96] Although this language seems directed at immediate causes of high emotion or provocation rather than long term indoctrination, a former border guard could argue under GDR law that even if shooting at escapees was an excessive response, a court should forego punishment because of the high emotional state a border guard maintained as a result of his indoctrination. Also, deliberately shooting at individuals crossing the border does not appear to be the kind of deliberate killing that legally constituted murder in East Germany, particularly given the shoot-to-kill order from the leaders of the government.

Whether the shoot-to-kill order itself was an illegal order under East German law is another question.[97] Socialist legality offered some protection to East German citizens, but socialist legality is not a commitment to the rule of law, where certainty, generality, prospectivity and publicity are paramount. In 1954, Hilde Benjamin, a Minister of Justice for the GDR, provided a revealing insight into how socialist nations viewed legality: "Socialist legality is the dialectic unity of strict adherence to the laws and partiality in their application. "[98] The Constitution of the GDR expresses that partiality as a commitment to the socialist society.[99] Similarly, "[i]t is the meaning of socialism and thus of our country to do everything for the benefit of Man, for the happiness of the people, for the interests of the working class

---

[95] Tyler Marshall, *Berlin Test Case: Can Border Guards Be Punished for Shootings at Wall?*, L. A. TIMES, Sept. 3, 1991 at A14.

[96] StGB GDR, *supra* note [90], art. 17(2).

[97] Erich Honecker, the former leader of East Germany, is widely believed to have given the shoot-to-kill order. He was charged with 49 counts of manslaughter and 25 counts of attempted manslaughter in connection with that order, but charges were dropped after Berlin's Constitutional Court found that "it violates respect for human rights to keep in jail an accused person who is suffering from an incurable illness." Honecker is suffering from liver cancer. Marc Fisher, *Berlin Court Drops Case Against Honecker*, WASH. POST, Jan. 13, 1993, at A16; *see Honecker Charged in Berlin as Wife Heads for Chile*, AGENCE FRANCE PRESSE, July 30, 1992, *available in* LEXIS, Nexis Library, Wires File.

[98] Friederich-Christian Schroeder, *Human Rights in Criminal Proceedings and in the Enforcement of Prison Sentences*, *in* BEFORE REFORMS: HUMAN RIGHTS IN THE WARSAW PACT STATES, 1971-1988, [Georg Brunner, *Freedom of Movement*, *in* BEFORE REFORMS IN THE WARSAW PACT STATES 1971-1988, at 221 (Georg Brunner et al. eds., 1990), at 403, 415.

[99] *See* VERF, *supra* note [89], arts. 86, 87, 90, 97.

and all working persons."[100] The criminal law of the GDR was expressly designed to further that socialist purpose. The shoot-to- kill order could be seen as an order designed to fulfill socialist purposes and therefore legal.

The Law of the Federal Republic of Germany

Some argument can be made for applying the FRG's Criminal Code in the border guard trials, although the Unification Treaty seems to preclude this possibility. While the Criminal Code of the FRG provides that an act cannot be punished if no law prohibited the act at the time it was committed and that the law in force at the time of the act governs punishment,[101] the Criminal Code provides for applicability of FRG law to acts committed abroad in a few limited cases: "German criminal law applies to other acts committed abroad if the act is punishable at the place of the act ... and if the perpetrator ... became a German after the act.[102] Deliberate killing was clearly punishable in the East German system. The deliberate shooting of persons crossing the border may have been illegal under the East German regime and therefore punishable even if never actually prosecuted. The perpetrators of the act became citizens of the FRG at unification and therefore could be subject to criminal prosecution under this provision.

Like the criminal code of the GDR, the FRG's Criminal Code provides punishment for murder,[103] manslaughter,[104] and less severe cases of manslaughter,[105] which could provide legal bases for convicting the border guards if FRG law is found to apply to these cases.

Natural Law

Natural law derives standards for moral conduct from the inherent nature of mankind. What that nature is and how rules are derived from it is the subject of millennia-old debate.[106] Natural law does not provide a criminal code as such; the morality of the shootings rather than their legality would be the focus of prosecution under natural law. The argument that the guards were obeying the positive law of the GDR would be no defense to the fact that they killed individuals who were merely trying to exercise their natural right to leave the country. The role natural law played in the actual

---

100 Central Committee Report to the 8th Congress of the Socialist Unity Party (SED) 5 (Berlin 1971), *cited in* Rudolf Herrmann, *GDR Criminal Procedure Law Governed by Socialist Principles*, LAW & LEGIS. IN THE GDR, 25, 26.

101 See StGB FRG, *supra* note 73, §§ 1, 2.

102 *Id.* § 7.

103 ...*Id.* §211.

104 ...*Id.* §212.

105 ...*Id.* § 213.

106 For a historical survey of natural law, see generally FRANCIS H. ETEROVICH, APPROACHES TO NATURAL LAW FROM PLATO TO KANT (1972). For examples of the current debate, see generally CHARLES COVELL, THE DEFENCE OF NATURAL LAW (1992); CHARLES COVELL, NATURAL LAW THEORY: CONTEMPORARY ESSAYS (Robert P. George ed., 1992).

trial of four East German border guards will be discussed more fully below.[107]...

Decisions in the East German Border Guard Trial

Although investigators in united Germany continue to research the facts surrounding the hundreds of shooting incidents that occurred along the Berlin Wall from 1961 to 1989,[108] a number of prosecutions have already taken place.[109] The reasoning of the judges in the first two trials provides a revealing insight into the tensions underlying the guards' trials.

In the first trial, four guards were charged with manslaughter under East German law for the February 1989 shooting death of Christian Gueffroy as he attempted to cross the "death strip" between East and West Berlin.[110] Judge Theodor Seidel, Chief Judge of the Berlin Regional Court, acquitted defendants Mike Schmidt and Peter Schmett, who "did not kill and did not

---

107 *See infra* text accompanying notes 134-141.

108 *See, e.g., East German Sentry Accused of Shooting West Berliner*, REUTER LIBR. REP., Oct. 13, 1992, *available in* LEXIS, Nexis Library, Wires File.; "Six-year Term for East German Border Guard," Agence France Presse, Dec. 9, 1992, available in Lexis, Nexis Library Wires File.

109 This paper discusses only the first two trials in detail. In the third trial, the Berlin District Court acquitted four former guards accused of shooting and seriously injuring Bernd Sievert as he attempted to escape East Germany near Checkpoint Charlie in 1971. The court cited insufficient evidence in declining to convict the men of attempted manslaughter. The guards also argued that they shot only to wound, despite the fact that they fired 47 shots. *See Four East German Guards Freed in '71 Wounding of Escapee*, N.Y. TIMES, June 23, 1992, at All; *Third Berlin Wall Trial Ends in Acquittals*, REUTER LIBR. REP., June 22, 1992, *available in* LEXIS, Nexis Library, Wires File.

In the fourth trial, the court gave Steffen Scholz a suspended sentence for killing Silvio Proksch in 1983. The judge did not believe that Scholz had aimed only at Proksch's legs as he attempted to escape because seven shots were fired so rapidly that steady aim would have been impossible. The court nonetheless called both men, escapee and guard, "victims of the division of Germany." *Former Berlin Wall Guard Given Suspended Sentence*, REUTER LIBR. REP., July 3, 1992, *available in* LEXIS, Nexis Library, Wires File.

Klaus Kretzschrnar, the defendant in the fifth trial, admitted shooting an escapee, but expressed regret. Finding that military duty did not demand the use of deadly force to secure the border, the court convicted him of manslaughter, but gave him a suspended sentence, explaining: "Soldiers functioned as human beings according to their political education." *Ex-border Guard Convicted of Berlin Wall Shooting*, REUTER LIBR. REP., Oct. 28, 1992, *available in* LEXIS, Nexis Library, Wires File.

In the sixth trial, prosecutors charged Rolf-Dieter Heinrich with murder rather than manslaughter. The court convicted Heinrich of "groundless" manslaughter and sentenced him to six years in prison. The court found that Heinrich shot an additional nine to fifteen bullets into an escapee after he had surrendered. *Six-year Sentence is Longest yet in Wall-shooting Trials*, ASSOCIATED PRESS, Dec. 9, 1992, *available in* LEXIS, Nexis Library, Wires File; *Six-year Term for East German Border Guard*, *supra* note 108.

Two former guards are charged with manslaughter in the seventh trial. They riddled Michael Bittner with bullets after he shouted, *Please let me go." Seventh Trial of East German Border Guards Starts*, REUTER LIBR. REP., Feb. l, 1993, *available in* LEXIS, Nexis Library, Wires File.

Attempted manslaughter charges were dropped against Karl-Heinz Becker in the eighth trial when the judge ruled there was insufficient evidence to show that Becker intended to kill two escapees when he fired warning shots that did not hit anyone. *Border Guard from Famous Photos is Acquitted of Attempted Murder*, ASSOCIATED PRESS, Feb. 18, 1993, *available in* LEXIS, Nexis Library, Wires File; *East German Border Guard Acquitted*, REUTER LIBR. REP., Feb. 18, 1993, *available in* LEXIS, Nexis Library, Wires File.

110 Stephen Kinzer, *Two East German Guards Convicted of Killing Man as He Fled to West*, N.Y. TIMES, Jan. 21, 1992, at Al (quoting Judge Seidel).

intend to kill."[111] Although Mike Schmidt gave the order to shoot, his order was to shoot to apprehend but not to kill.[112] Peter Schmett fired a pistol but apparently aimed low, in an attempt to wound rather than to kill Gueffroy and a friend as they attempted to cross the Wall.[113] Judge Seidel convicted Andreas Kühnpast of attempted manslaughter because he fired directly at the two men, but gave him a suspended two year sentence.[114] Ingo Heinrich, the guard who fired the fatal shots, was convicted of manslaughter and sentenced to three and a half years in prison.[115]

Judge Seidel held that shooting to kill was authorized under East German law.[116] Nonetheless, he concluded, the order infringed a higher moral law.[117] Although the defendants were "at the end of a long chain of responsibility," they violated "a basic human right" by shooting at someone whose only crime was trying to emigrate.[118] Judge Seidel applied natural law when he argued that "not everything that is legal is right: There is a central area of justice, which no law can encroach upon. The legal maxim, 'whoever flees will be shot to death' deserves no obedience."[119] Consequently, "[a]t the end of the 20th century, no one has the right to ignore his conscience when it comes to killing people on behalf of the power structure. "[120] Heinrich "did not just fire bad shots randomly. It was an aimed shot tantamount to an execution."[121]

Judge Seidel did not directly address the prosecution's principal assertion that the secret shoot-to-kill order was in violation of the Helsinki Accords and Geneva Convention, both of which East Germany accepted, nor did he address the issue that citizens, including soldiers such as the border guards, are responsible for obeying the international laws to which their country subscribes.[122] The court rejected the defense argument of superior orders as well as the argument that it was absurd to try people under West German legal procedures and the substantive laws of the East German communist regime.[123]

In the second trial, the court convicted Uwe Hapke and Udo Walther of manslaughter in the December 1, 1984 death of Michael-Horst Schmidt.[124]

---

111 *Id.*

112 *See* William A. Henry III, *The Price of Obedience; Should East German Border Guards have Followed the Law and Their Orders or Listened to Their Conscience?*, TIME, Feb. 3. 1992, at 36.

113 Tyler Marshall, *Wall Guards Convicted in Berlin Death*, L.A. TIMES, Jan. 21, 1992, at Al.

114 See Charles A. Radin, *East German Border Guard is Jailed*, BOSTON GLOBE, Jan. 21, 1992, at l; Robert Tilley, *Trial Reopens Bitter Divide of Berlin Wall; Calls to put Honecker in the Dock*, THE SUNDAY TELEGRAPH (London), Nov. 10, 1991, at 22.

115 *See* Kinzer, *supra* note 110.

116 *See* Adrian Bridge. *Suspended Sentences for Border Guards*, THE INDEPENDENT (London), Feb. 6, 1992, at 10.

117 *See id.*

118 Kinzer, *supra* note 110, at A2.

119 Radin, *supra* note 114, at 1.

120 Kinzer, *supra* note 110, at A2.

121 Marshall, *supra* note 113, at AI.

122 *See* Radin, *supra* note 114, at 4.

123 *See id.*

124 *World News*, STAR TRIBUNE (Minneapolis), Feb. 6, 1992, at 4A.

Hapke was sentenced to twenty-one months in prison and Walther to eighteen months in prison, but Judge Ingeborg Tepperwein of the Berlin Superior Court suspended both sentences.[125]

Judge Tepperwein found that East German law did not require the border guards to shoot-to-kill single, unarmed escapees.[126] Uwe Hapke and Udo Walther did not have to shoot Schmidt because he posed no risk to border security, thus failing to meet the criterion for use of deadly force under communist law. "This unarmed refugee was obviously no such threat. Even if he had been, the mildest [response] should have been used, and that would have been shots at his feet. Beyond that, it should have been possible for them to refuse duty at the border or to shoot over someone's head."[127] "They would not have had to be heroes in order to avoid shooting Schmidt."[128] Nevertheless, the blame lay "not with the border guards but with those who promulgated the laws and orders."[129] Tepperwein suspended the sentences to take account of the defendants' remorse and the system in which they grew up, where unquestioning conformity was rewarded and individual conscience discouraged and often punished.[130] "It was very hard in East Germany to swim against the stream. The defendants were at the bottom of a pyramid."[131]

The differences in the rulings of Judge Seidel and Judge Tepperwein provide insight into the difficulties of justly trying the former border guards. Judge Seidel believes that East German law allowed the shoot-to-kill order; Judge Tepperwein does not. Because East Germany and its legal institutions have ceased to exist and because no East German court ever tried a guard for shooting-to-kill at the border, there is no authoritative East German source to which courts can currently look to decide this question. Judge Seidel applies natural law while Judge Tepperwein looks only at the positive law. Legal consistency is particularly difficult when judges understand the applicable law so differently. Justice in these trials is not only a matter of treating like cases alike, but also about resolving injustices of the old regime. Judge Tepperwein's sentences have generally been regarded as just,[132] while Judge Seidel's condemnation of Ingo Heinrich has not.[133]...

From a rule of law viewpoint,... Judge Seidel's application of natural law is much more interesting and problematic than Judge Tepperwein's reasoning.

---

125 *See* Bridge, *supra* note 116, at 10.

126 See Mark Heinrich, *Two Border Guards Convicted of Berlin Wall Killing*, REUTER LIBR. REP., Feb. 5, 1992, *available in* LEXIS, Nexis Library, Wires File.

127 *Id.*

128 Robin Gedye, *Berlin Wall Guards Who Killed Fugitive Go Free*, DAILY TELEGRAPH (London), Feb. 6, 1992, at 9.

129 *Id.*

130 *See* Heinrich, *supra* note 126.

131 *Id.*

132 *See, e.g., Conviction of Wall Border Guards*, THE WEEK IN GERMANY, Jan. 24, 1992 (presenting German press criticisms of Judge Seidel's sentencing.

133 *See e.g., Verdict in Second Wall Border Guards Case*, THE WEEK IN GERMANY, Feb. 7, 1992 (providing excerpts of press reports supportive of Judge Tepperwein's judgments); David Margolick, *"Just Following Orders": Nuremberg, Now Berlin*, N.Y. TIMES, Jan. 26, 1992, § 4, at 6.

In applying natural law, Judge Seidel worked within a well-established West German legal tradition. Article 20 of the Basic Law states that "[l]egislation shall be subject to the constitutional order; the executive and the judiciary shall be bound by law and justice."[134] Ernst von Hippel argues that this language singles out the judiciary as "protectors of the higher legal orders against the rules of mere positive law."[135] In the Princess Soraya case, the Federal Constitutional Court explained the meaning of article 20:

> The judge is traditionally bound by the law. This is an inherent element of the principle of separation of powers, and thus of the rule of law. Article 20 of our Constitution, however, has somewhat changed the traditional formulation by providing that the judge is bound by "law and justice." The generally prevailing view implies the rejection of a narrow reliance upon [formally] enacted laws. The formulation in article 20 keeps us aware of the fact that although "law and justice" are generally coextensive, they may not always be so. Justice is not identical with the aggregate of the written laws. Under certain circumstances, law can exist beyond the positive norms which the state enacts—law which has its source in the constitutional legal order as a meaningful, all-embracing system, and which functions as a corrective of the written norms.... Where th[e written law fails] the judge's decision fills the existing gaps by using common sense and "general concepts of justice established by the community."[136]

The Court's language in this case appears to ground justice in the positive law of the Basic Law; justice is defined by the constitutional order, but that constitutional order is itself the result of judicial interpretation according to supra-positivist norms.[137] Commenting on the Southwest case,[138] Justice Gerhard Leibholz of the Federal Constitutional Court said:

> The Court holds that each constitutional clause is in a definite relationship with all other clauses, and that together they form an entity.... The Court even goes so far as to acknowledge the existence of a higher law that transcends positive law and to which it is necessary to hold responsible both the legislature and the constituent power.[139]

When the Court defines the supra-positivist norms as principles informing the constitutional order, or as concepts of justice established by the community, it appeals to notions of natural law, to the higher law which transcends positive law. Although one can argue that notions of natural law informed the constitutions of the former East German Lander,[140] the socialist

---

134 GG, [Grundgesetz [GG] art. 20 (F.R.G.)], art. 20.

135 Ernst von Hippel, *The Role of Natural Law in the Legal Decisions of the German Federal Republic*, NAT. L.F., Vol. 4, pp. 106, 111 (1959).

136 KOMMERS, [DONALD P. KOMMERS, THE CONSTITUTIONAL JURISPRUDENCE OF THE FEDERAL REPUBLIC OF GERMANY 59 (1989)], at 132-33 (citing 34 BVerfGE 269 (1973)).

137 *See id.* at 54....

138 *See id.* at 71 (citing 1 BVerfGE 14 (1951)).

139 *Id.* at 52-53.

140 See Gottfried Dietze, *Natural Law in the Modern European Constitutions*, NAT. L.F., Vol. 1, pp. 73, 79-83 (1956)....

tradition of law is essentially one of positivism.[141] It is exactly that positivism to which natural law and Judge Seidel object.

Positivism and Natural Law in Post-World War II Germany

The conflict between positivism and natural law is not new to either German jurisprudence or the German conscience. The current commitment to natural law expressed in the Basic Law and in decisions of the Federal Constitutional Court came about, at least in part, as a result of the excesses of positivism during the Third Reich. German courts in the immediate post-World War II era often looked to natural law to remedy the injustices of the Third Reich. Judge Seidel adheres to that tradition in applying natural law to condemn the actions of the former border guards in East Germany.

Gustav Radbruch, an eminent German legal philosopher whose experience with the Third Reich converted him from positivism to natural law, explained the dangers of positivism and a judge's duty to declare positive laws invalid when they conflict with natural law:

> For the soldier an order is an order; for the jurist, the law is the law. But the soldier's duty to obey an order is at an end if he knows that the order will result in a crime. But the jurist, since the last natural law men in his profession died off a hundred years or so ago, has known no such exception and no such excuse for the citizen's not submitting to the law. The law is valid simply because it is the law; and it is law if it has the power to assert itself under ordinary conditions. Such an attitude towards the law and its validity [i.e., positivism] rendered both lawyers and people impotent in the face of even the most capricious, criminal, or cruel of laws. Ultimately, this view that only where there is power is there law [Recht] is nothing but an affirmation that might makes right [Recht]. [Actually] law [Recht] is the quest for Justice ... if certain laws [Gesetze] deliberately deny this quest for justice (for example, by arbitrarily granting or denying men their human rights) they are null and void; the people are not to obey them, and jurist must find the courage to brand them unlawful [ihnen den Rechtscharakter absprechen]. [142]

Various cases from the post-World War II era demonstrate how seriously judges took this charge. Courts used natural law to demonstrate that the Third Reich relied on the "rule of unjust law" rather than on a true rule of law.[143] On August 12, 1947, the Frankfurt Appellate Court (Oberlandesgericht) heard the case against physicians who had been involved in "experimental killings." The physicians claimed that they had not broken the law (Rechtswidrigkeit) because the laws of the Third Reich sanctioned their actions. The court disagreed:

> Such a way of thinking would not do justice to the true character of the National Socialist "law." Law must be defined as an

---

141 *See, e.g.*, HENRY W. EHERMANN, COMPARATIVE LEGAL CULTURES 27 (1976); MARY ANN GLENDON ET. AL., COMPARATIVE LEGAL TRADITIONS 705 (1985).

142 GUSTAV RADBRUCH, RECHTSPHILOSOPHISCHE BESINNUNG [REAPPRAISAL OF LEGAL PHILOSOPHY], *cited in* von Hippel, *supra* note 135, at 110.

143 Von Hippel, *supra* note 135, at 111.

> ordinance or precept devised in the service of justice [citing Radbruch]. Whenever the conflict between an enacted law and true justice reaches unendurable proportions, the enacted law must yield to justice, and be considered a "lawless law [unrichtiges Recht]." An accused may not justify his conduct by appealing to an existing law if this law offended against certain self-evident precepts of the natural law.[144]

...Towards the end of World War II, Hitler issued the Katastrophen-order, which directed members of the armed forces to shoot deserters without benefit of trial. In a Federal Court case decided on July 12, 1951, [t]he court ruled that the Katastrophen-order had not been law even under the requirements of the Nazi regime.... [T]he court ruled that even if the Katastrophen-order had met the requirements of legislative law in the Third Reich, it still was not valid because it violated natural law:

> Even if the Katastrophen-order had been promulgated in due form it could not have become law [Recht]. For the positive legislative act is intrinsically limited. It loses all obligatory power if it violates the generally recognized principles of international law or natural law [Naturrecht], or if the contradiction between positive law and justice reaches such an intolerable degree that the law, as unrichtiges Recht, must give way to justice.... Thus the Katastrophen-order is null and void; it is no rule of law; obedience to it is against the law [Recht]. The claim of the defendant that he could not know this and that he acted according to the order of his superior is unacceptable. He must be held to know that no legal system permits a soldier to escape responsibility for an infamous crime by relying on the order of a superior, if the later's orders are in stark contradiction to human morality and the laws of all civilized nations, whatever differences in positive law might exist among them.[155]

Positivism and Natural Law in United Germany

Similarities to Application of Natural Law in Post-World War II Germany

Judge Seidel's application of natural law to condemn positivism in East Germany echoes the use of natural law to condemn Nazi Germany. In fact, Honecker's shoot-to-kill order is eerily reminiscent of Hitler's Katastrophen-order, where soldiers were also instructed to shoot people without the benefit of trial. Under a natural law theory, the shoot-to-kill order should be subject to the same condemnation as the Katastrophen-order. First, the existence of the shoot-to-kill order was not widely known until after the fall of communism, so it is doubtful that the order was promulgated according to the required procedures for law of the German Democratic Republic. Second, even had the shoot-to-kill order been properly formulated, it could not have been enforced as law, "for the positive legislative act is intrinsically

---

[144] Judgment of Aug. 12, 1947, 2 SUDDEUTSCHE JURISTEN ZEITSCHRIFT [SJZ] 521 (F.R.G.), *cited in id.*

[155] Rommen, Heinrich Rommen, [*Natural Law in Decisions of the Federal Supreme Court and of the Constitutional Courts in Germany*, 4 NAT. L.F. 1, 14 (1959)], at 11.

limited;"[157] positive law becomes null and void when it contradicts justice to an intolerable degree.

The shooting of individuals attempting to cross the border to West Germany was commonly viewed in West Germany as an unjust and immoral act. Even defense counsel for Ingo Heinrich admitted that the shootings were "naturally an injustice."[158] At least one court in West Germany derived the right to freedom of movement from natural law.[159] The right to emigrate is also recognized as a basic human right in the Convention on Civil and Political Rights.[160] From a natural law standpoint, the shoot-to-kill order was null and void as a violation of the principles of justice and basic human rights.

Nevertheless, following the reasoning of the Federal Court in the Katastrophen case, the communist form of government itself must be considered legal. From a practical point of view, it is hard to discount the forty-year existence of a sovereign state active in international trade and politics. The communist government of East Germany was competent to enact legally valid laws and decrees; moreover, the Unification Treaty recognizes East German law generally as valid law, and in fact provides for the continued efficacy of many East German laws.[161] Further, united Germany has not denounced socialist law in its entirety, as the Allies did with respect to Nazi law.[162] Even in a system governed by the rule of unjust law, only specific laws 'are considered null and void.

Even without the complications of transition, an individual may find it extremely difficult to determine which laws are void and which require adherence. The dilemma is particularly acute if, as in united Germany, the suspect legal system engendered a morality incompatible with the West German understanding of natural law.... As defendant Uwe Hapke said to Judge Tepperwein when he argued that he was a product of his Stalinist upbringing, "You didn't grow up in the GDR."[165] Truly, Hapke grew up with a different set of moral beliefs.

In retrospect, it is easy to say that East German border guards should have known that shooting individuals attempting to cross the border violated natural law; however, the socialist system and the training of border

---

157 Judgment of July 12, *supra* note 154.

158 Marshall, *supra* note 113, at Al.

159 *See* Judgment of Oct. 20, 1947, 2 MONATSCHRIFT FUR DUETSCHES RECHT [MDR] 153, *cited in* Von Hippel, *supra* note 135, at 113.

160 *See* [International Covenent on Civil and Political Rights, art. 12(2), U.N. GAOR, 21st Sess., Supp. No. 16, at 52, 54, U.N. Doc. A/6316 (1966)].

161 *See* Unification Treaty, *supra* note 69, art. 9, 30 I.L.M. 470; Annexes I & II, *in* FEDERAL LAW GAZETTE OF THE F.R.G., *supra* note 71. The Unification Treaty provides for the continued validity of East German court decisions; however, under certain circumstances, individuals convicted of criminal conduct in the former East Germany can seek the quashing of their conviction. Unification Treaty, *supra* note 69, art. 18, 30 I.L.M. 475.

162 *See, e.g.*, Control Council Act No. 1, Repealing of Nazi Laws, Berlin, Sept. 20, 1945, *Official Gazette of the Control Council for Germany*, No. 1, at 6, *reprinted in* I THE FEDERAL REPUBLIC OF GERMANY AND THE GERMAN DEMOCRATIC REPUBLIC IN INTERNATIONAL RELATIONS 51 (Gunther Doeker & Jens A. Bruckner eds., 1979).

165 *Two East Border Guards Convicted In Germany*, WASH. TIMES, Feb. 6, 1992, at A2.

guards fostered a distinct morality. In the first trial, the judges' questioning of defendant Mike Schmidt was designed to show that the guards had some inkling of Western morality, but instead demonstrated how insulated an East German could be from that morality:

> Question: "Weren't there others who chose to oppose the communist system?"
> Answer: "I didn't know about any.
> Question: "Weren't there churches in East Germany?"
> Answer: "I never went."
> Question: "Weren't there other children in school who refused to attend military training?"
> Answer: "Possibly, but if you refused, you got two years in prison."
> Question: "Didn't you know that in West Germany there were great anger and sadness about the border shootings?"
> Answer: "No."
> Question: "Didn't you listen to Western Radio?"
> Answer: "Never."
> Question: "What did you think about the automatic firing devices installed along the border?"
> Answer: "I thought they were a good thing to protect our security."[166]

Mike Schmidt did not participate in the activities or the institutions that would have taught him Western opinion and moral views concerning the shoot-to-kill order.

The East German border guards were rewarded for their special tasks. They earned eighty per cent more money than regular soldiers.[167] Ingo Heinrich, Andreas Kuhnpast, Mike Schmidt, and Peter Schmett each earned "three days extra vacation, a buffet dinner, $85 bonuses" and medals for "defending" the border on the night they killed Christian Gueffroy.[168] The border guards' behavior was also reinforced through intimidation—secret police monitored guards' conversations and threatened guards with prison terms for expressing reservations about shooting.[169]

The East German system rewarded border guards for practicing a morality distinct from a Christian morality—it sanctioned and encouraged killing. This is not to say that even border guards bought into that morality completely. Andreas Kuhnpast initially refused to sign the guard's oath promising to use weapons if necessary to defend the border. When the guards were feted for their deeds he said, "I wasn't in the mood for celebrating. I felt like throwing the money and the medals away."[170] Yet, within the East German system, "We were soldiers—conscripts—who had to obey orders or face military prison."[171] In applying natural law based in a Christian tradition, united Germany is requiring acute legal vision from

---

166 Marc Fisher, *On Trial for Death at Berlin Wall*, WASH. POST, Sept. 10, 1991, at A21.

167 *See id.*

168 Tamara Jones, *East German Guards on Trial: Can Justice Scale the Wall?*, L.A. TIMES, Sept. 17, 1991, at Al.

169 *See* Fisher, *supra* note 166.

170 Tilley, *supra* note 114, at 22.

171 *See* Jones, *supra* note 168.

border guards whose moral sight was trained on a fundamentally different socialist goal. As Andreas Kuhnpast poignantly explained at trial, "We had our own laws, and we could not know others would one day apply."[172]...

Conclusion

Of itself and through the principles of the rule of law, positive law makes a strong claim to be the final arbiter of an individual's legal responsibility and a nation's legal structure. The rule of law says very little about the content of laws as it sets a framework for a legal system. Natural law likewise makes a strong claim to an individual's legal responsibility. However, natural law looks primarily to substantive justice by focusing on a law's content. When a positive law advocates immorality or injustice, natural law requires a higher moral standard. Justice requires moral responsibility which cannot be excused through compliance with immoral positive laws.

It is precisely here where natural law and the rule of law come into conflict. The rule of law demands that law only be applied prospectively, yet positive law may be inadequate to meet the demands of natural law. Natural law demands application of the moral law, even if it is retroactive. Natural law attempts to escape the retroactivity difficulty by imputing to the condemned individual the knowledge that his action was indeed wrong even if sanctioned by positive law.

Positive law organizes at the level of the community. The rule of law gives the sovereign the responsibility of identifying law. Natural law is often derived from a perceived consensus of fundamental human morals and values, but as applied in the East German border guards' trials and in cases condemning Nazi actions, it is very much a morality of individual conscience. The individual, despite the dictates of the community around him, should know that his actions were wrong. The individual, rather than the sovereign or the community through its positive laws, identifies what is legally obligatory.

The Federal Republic of Germany has a strong commitment to both natural law and the rule of law as organizing principles of its society. Although the Unification Treaty represents a societal commitment to how legal transition should take place, the structure of the Basic Law empowers individual judges, like Judge Seidel, to answer not only questions of law but also broader questions of justice for individuals like Ingo Heinrich, Andreas Kuhnpast, Mike Schmidt, Peter Schmett, Uwe Hapke, and Udo Walther. Like the International Military Tribunal, Judge Seidel is in a position to determine what that justice is because his side won in the struggle for unification. Judge Seidel's application of natural law to the former border guards is subject to the same question asked of Nuremberg: Is it anything more than victor's justice? Although East Germany voluntarily acceded to the Federal Republic of Germany, that accession was not clearly an acceptance of the natural law tradition of West Germany....

---

172 *Id.*

When a settled legal system exists, natural law can inform the content of the positive law; there need not be a conflict between the requirements of the rule of law and the requirements of natural law. However, when a society is in transition, as is German society where two very different legal and moral systems have combined, the conflict between natural law and rule of law is thrown into high relief. Unlike Judge Seidel, who emphasizes the precedence of natural law and exacerbates the tensions of transition, Judge Tepperwein resolves the conflict between natural law and positive law by stressing the moral element within the positive law. She accounts for the duress of the communist system by suspending the guards' sentences, but she does not hesitate to condemn their actions. Her reasoning, an analysis of East German law and the moral climate in which the border guards lived, is a better approach, one that will in the long run foster an increased respect for both law and justice within united Germany.

COMPENSATION AND RESTITUTION

David Southern, "Restitution or Compensation: The Property Question" [*]

The Unification Treaty of 31 August 1990 between the German Federal Republic (west Germany) and the German Democratic Republic (east Germany) provided that property in east Germany which had been taken from former owners wrongly or against inadequate compensation should be restored to those former owners. This is the principle of 'natural restitution', that is reconveyance of the property itself rather than financial compensation. Restitution has become a key issue in the economic reconstruction of east Germany. This article examines the role of the open property question in the overall process of German unification....

Restitution Before Compensation

The logical starting point is Article 41 of the Unification Treaty, which enshrines the principle "restitution before compensation". Article 41(1) stated that the Joint Declaration of the two governments on 15 June 1990 on the open property question was incorporated into the Treaty as Annex III. Article 41(2) provided for the overreaching of restitution claims by investment needs, where special legislation provided for this. Article 41(3) said that the FRG would not issue any legislation in contradiction of the principles of the Joint Declaration.[4] Article 45(1) incorporated various appendices and schedules into the Treaty.

---

[*] Excerpted from David Southern, "Restitution or Compensation: The Property Question," *German Politics*, vol. 2, no. 3 (December 1993), pp. 436, 438-439, 442-446.

[4] This ban on subsequent inconsistent legislation constitutes a so-called "Coburg" proviso: *Entscheidungen des Bundesverfassungsgerichts* (BVerfGE) Vol. 22, p. 221. The treaties and associated legislation are conveniently printed in *Die Verträge zur Einheit Deutschlands* (Munich: Beck Text, 1991). For a general survey of the restitution question, see Fieberg and Reichenbach, "Zum Problem der offenen Vermögensfragen", *NJW* 44 (1991), pp. 321-8.

Annex III (the Joint Declaration) enumerated the "touchstones" (*Eckwerte*) on which the governments had agreed:

1. Seizures of property which had taken place in the period of the Soviet occupation (8 May 1945-1 October 1949) were not to be reversed.[5]
2. Confiscated or compulsorily purchased land is in principle to be restored to former owners or their heirs, but subject to certain exceptions:
   (a) where buildings had been substantially altered, used for public or business purposes;
   (b) where the property had been *bona fide* acquired by individuals;
   (c) where the person entitled to restitution opted for compensation.

This lapidary statement of "touchstones" was expanded in two substantial laws, which formed part of Annex III to the Treaty, namely:

1. The Law on Special Investments ("Investments Law"); and
2. The Law on the Open Property Question ("Property Law").

In para. 1(1) of the Property Law the various categories were enumerated in which restitution could be claimed. At the request of the US government restitution was extended to Nazi victims who had lost land or buildings in the period 30 January 1933 to 8 May 1945. While para. 1 dealt with land and buildings, para. 6 applied to undertakings, which remained substantially similar to undertakings at the time of their compulsory purchase by east German authorities. Para. 17 protected the rights of existing tenants. The law provided for the establishment of a network of local and Land offices for the registration and adjudication of property claims.

Under paras. 3(3) No. 1 and 15(2) of the Property Law the person with the right of disposal of the property was not entitled to sell, transfer or lease it if a restitution claim had been registered. This threatened to paralyse many dealings in land. Accordingly, the Investments Law provided for the overreaching claims to restitution where an applicant proved a "special investment purpose" in relation to land or a building. A "special investment purpose" meant, in the original version of para. 1(1) of the Investment Law:

1. the safeguarding or creation of jobs;
2. the provision of housing;
3. the improvement of infrastructure.

The balance struck between restitution and investment rapidly proved unduly favourable to restitution, and—as we shall see—amending legislation

---

5 The reason for this exclusion was originally stated to be that the Soviet Union had made it a condition of their agreement to unification. There is now doubt whether this was in fact the case, and the issue will be re-examined by the Federal Constitutional Court.

was subsequently introduced, which significantly strengthened the investment priority.[6]...

The Decision in Favour of Restitution

In the rush to unification, there was little space to reflect on the practical, legal, economic and moral problems of restitution. The broad assumption was that, once the layer of social ownership was removed, the former owners would magically reappear. There were, indeed, in west Germany many former owners of land in east Germany whose claims were vocal and difficult to deny. In the case of those who had fled east Germany, their property had been taken into state administration and sold on, for example by way of long leasehold for negligible rent but with full obligation on the landlord to repair (see above). Where people had received permission to leave east Germany, a term of that permission could be the sale of the property on dictated terms. Jewish claims were historically sensitive.

It was thought that Article 14 of the Basic law, guaranteeing the rights of private property, made it constitutionally impossible to ignore or override claims in such cases. This consideration may have been exaggerated, for Article 14 is subject to what is called a *Gesetzesvorbehalt*, that is the content of the basic right is inherently limited and is defined and expressed in statute.[14]

These considerations were reinforced by free-market ideologists, who believe that the restoration and protection of private ownership was a necessary and even a sufficient condition for the establishment of a free market economy. These voices were particularly strong in the FDP, which liked to cast itself as the ideological conscience of the government coalition, and Klaus Kinkel, the FDP justice minister at the time, threatened resignation if restitution was not included in the unification settlement. In particular, Kinkel maintained that the cost of financial compensation would be prohibitive. He quoted a figure of DM one billion—an inconsiderable sum in the light of the true costs of unification.

Powerful countervailing considerations were overlooked. Restitution not merely prolonged but substantially increased uncertainty over property rights. This was a material obstacle to investment. A significant proportion of the financial gain of unification—the broad uplift in east German property values—was to be enjoyed by a limited class of individuals outside east Germany, who in many cases had reconciled themselves to their losses or were simply unaware of them, while all the costs were to be borne by the community at large. Finally, within east Germany many people had been occupying for upwards of 40 years houses which they regarded as their own.[15]...

---

6 Fieberg and Reichenbach, "Offene Vermögensfragen und Investitionen in den neuen Bundesädern", *NJW* 45 (1992), pp. 1977-85.

14 Peter Häberle, *Die Wesenshaltgarantie des Artikels 19 Abs. 2, Grundgesetz* (Heidelberg: Müller, 1973), pp. 55-8; H. Maurer, "Die Eigentumsregelung im Einigungsvertrag", *Juristische Zeitschrift* 47 (1992), pp. 183-91.

15 This problem could have been resolved by a transitional phase of imposed leasing (*Erbpacht*).

Compensation Before Restitution

It soon became apparent that the unification legislation would paralyse the property market, and the investment priority needed urgent strengthening.

The Investment Acceleration Law of 22 March 1991 inserted a new para. 3a into the Investment Law, creating a super priority procedure. Where a public authority or the Treuhand had the right to dispose of property, and an investor before 31 December 1992 put forward a scheme which fulfilled a special investment purpose an investment priority authorisation certificate could be issued, thus enabling the land to be sold to the investor. The right to restitution would be overreached and converted into a right to compensation.[17] There are considerable problems with investment proposals by former owners which were sometimes ignored by the local administration.

The Investment Priority Law of 14 July 1992 further strengthened the priority procedure for investors, in the conflict between investors and restitution claimants. All restitution claims had to be made by 31 December 1992. The priority procedure for investors was extended to 31 December 1995. The concept of "special investment purpose"—as the instrument for clearing a path through restitution claims—was expanded. The public authority holding the land has the power of granting the investment priority certificate. Paras. 18-20 introduce a public auction procedure for the disposal of land to investors.[18] The deadline of 31 December 1992 obliged potential claimants to execute some fast footwork, and a rush of claims were registered just before the cut-off date. Where no restitution claims have been registered by 31 December 1992, the land becomes the property of the public authority having possession.

The great gap in the restitution legislation is the compensation law, which has been promised for two years. It is proposed that compensation is to be based upon 1.3 times the 1935 rateable value (*Einheitswert*), up to a maximum of DM250,000, and subject to tapering where the payment exceeds DM100,000. The compensation fund is to be financed by a levy of 30-50 percent of the market value of reconveyed property. No sums will be payable before 1 January 1996, and compensation will be payable in cases where restitution is excluded, for example confiscations by the Soviet occupation authorities or by local communist committees.[19]

---

17 "Gesetz zur Beseitigung von Hemmnissen bei der Privatisierung von Unternehmen und zur Förderung von Investitionen", 22 March 1991, *Bundesgesetzblatt (BGBl)* I (1991), p. 766.

18 "Gesetz über den Vorrang für Investitionen bei Rückübertragungsansprüchen nach dem Vermögensgesetz," 14 July 1992, *BGBl*, 1992.

19 W. Leisner, "Die Höhe der Enteigungsentschadigung", NJW 45 (1992), pp. 1409-15; *FAZ* 12 Feb. 1992, 27 June 1992.

Restitution in Practice

The cut-off date of 31 December 1992 has enabled a balance sheet of restitution claims to be drawn up: 1.1 million claims have been registered comprising over two million separate claims to over half the land area of the former GDR. In short, outside agricultural property, there is very little property in the new Länder which does not have a restitution claim registered against it, often multiple claims. All but 30,500 claims relate to land and buildings. By December 1992 some ten per cent of claims for land and buildings had been resolved (about 200,000).[20] Charged with the task of sorting out the competing claims of owners, former owners, former former owners, putative and pretended owners is an apparatus of one Federal, six Land and 216 local Offices for the Open Property Question. Appeal from the decision of these offices is to be made to administrative courts—not the civil courts; in many fields it is uncertain to which set of courts appeal lies.[21] The whole process is expected to take between ten and 30 years.[22]

The area where the most energetic assault on the problems has been undertaken, and the area which is the most dynamic economically of the new Länder, is Saxony and in particular Leipzig. The decision to accord priority to resolving legal and property questions stems from Minister-President Kurt Biedenkopf. In the centre of Leipzig, 23,000 restitution claims have been registered. Investment priority decisions have been taken in some 400 cases. The process is, however, painfully slow and Chief Burgermeister Lehmann-Grubbe, has complained: "These legal claims of old proprietors block the entire economic development. An application of reconveyance ... is sufficient to put all investment plans on ice." Large projects have gone ahead, because the Treuhand has been willing both to sanction developments and to indemnify the investor against past liabilities in respect of the land and future claims.[23]...

Restitution is undoubtedly a problem in the economic reconstruction of eastern Germany. How far it is an unnecessary problem, a self-inflicted wound, it is now idle to speculate.... What can be said is that restitution is now as an issue under control, and is unfolding in a reasonably orderly manner.

---

20 *FAZ*, 1 Oct. 1992.

21 H.H. Marcus, "Restructuring the Economy of East Germany and the Legal Implications of the Treuhandanstalt System", Gresham College Lecture, 23 Oct. 1991.

22 H.-J. Schäfer, "Wir brauchen wohl zehn Jahre", *Juristisches Wochenblatt*, 26 Aug. 1991; H.G. Strohm, "Beratungspraxis zu Ost-Immobilien nach dem Zweiten Vermögensrechtsänderungsgesetz", *NJW* 45 (1992), pp. 2849-57.

23 *Der Spiegel* Vol. 27 (1992), p. 129; *FAZ* 5 May 1992; *Financial Times* 23 Oct. 1992; S. Heitmann, "Justizpraktische und justizpolitische Probleme der Deutschen Einheit: eine Zwischenbilanz für den Freistaat Sachsen", *NJW* 45 (1992), pp. 2177-85.

17

HUNGARY

EDITOR'S INTRODUCTION

Soviet troops occupied Hungary at the end of World War II. Beginning in 1945 with a coalition government, the Communist Party, led by Matyas Rakosi, gradually took over key ministries. By 1947, with Soviet support, they gained complete control of the country. Rakosi purged the judiciary, civil service, and military. He also suppressed the church, his main source of ideological opposition. The State Security Department (AVO) enforced Communist rule at all levels and became Rakosi's tool of force and terror.

Rakosi concentrated absolute power in himself. After Stalin's death in 1953, however, the new Soviet leadership under Nikita Khrushchev urged him to divest some control. As a result, Imre Nagy became prime minister in July 1953. He instituted the "New Course," a liberal reform program which included the release of political prisoners, reduction of AVO power, and abolition of concentration camps. While Nagy's reforms met with broad popular support, he lacked the support of Moscow and Hungarian hard-line communists. A power struggle ensued. In 1955, Nagy was ousted from office and the Party. Rakosi was reinstated, but was unable to reestablish control. At Khrushchev's behest, he was replaced by Erno Gero in July 1956.

In October 1956, emboldened by Khrushchev's renunciation of Stalinism and the taste of reform under Nagy, Hungarian students staged a peaceful mass march in Budapest. When the police fired into the crowd, however, popular reaction turned the march into a revolution. The army joined the revolutionaries and Gero was ousted. Nagy returned to power and instituted a new series of reforms. He also renounced the Warsaw Pact and petitioned the United Nations to be considered a neutral country. On November 4, 1956, Soviet tanks invaded Hungary to reinstate hard-line communist control. Nagy fled, but was caught and executed in 1958. With Soviet support, Janos Kadar was installed as the new ruler of Hungary.

Kadar purged the Party of Nagy's followers, realigned Hungarian foreign policy with Moscow, and restored internal repression. Many participants in the 1956 revolution, including minors, were executed. By the 1960s, however, Kadar began to relax some controls. He freed political prisoners, closed several labor camps, curbed the AVO, opened Hungary to the West, and permitted a liberal travel policy. Repression did not disappear, but Kadar's theme of "those who are not against us are with us" meant that, so long as its citizens were not openly rebellious, Hungary would tolerate less state interference and greater freedom of expression than other Soviet bloc countries. With his "New Economic Mechanism," Kadar in 1968 introduced many aspects of a market economy into Hungary.

In May 1988, harsh economic conditions led to Kadar's downfall. He was replaced as prime minister by Karoly Grosz, who was replaced six months later by Miklos Nemeth. Demands grew for economic and political reform. Pro-democracy organizations, trade unions, and some fifty new political parties were formed. The Communist Party changed its name to the Hungarian Socialist Party (HSP). Freedoms of assembly, speech, press, and expression expanded, guaranteed by a new 1989 constitution. Hungary also opened its border with Austria, thus dismantling the first section of the Iron Curtain. 1990 saw the first free elections in Hungary in more than 40 years. The HSP was defeated, winning only 10 percent of the seats in Parliament. Three reformist parties formed a coalition government with Jozsef Antall as prime minister and Arpad Goncz as president. Antall died in December 1993 and was succeeded by Peter Boross.

After the democratic transition or 1989-90, calls for prosecution focused on crimes committed in crushing the 1956 revolution. Since the 20-year statute of limitations had expired, a 1991 law attempted to restart the statute for selected crimes committed 1944-1990 which had not been prosecuted for political reasons. The Constitutional Court struck down this move as contrary to the rule of law. However, in October 1993, the Court upheld a revised version which cast the 1956 acts as war crimes and crimes against humanity—for which the statute of limitations was waived under Hungary's international law obligations.

A restitution program was established for land illegally confiscated by the communist regime. Laws were also enacted to void convictions of political prisoners and to compensate victims of unlawful detention and the families of those who were executed. By mid-1992, nearly one million people—some 10 percent of the population—had applied for compensation.

In March 1994, Parliament adopted a law requiring the screening of an estimated 10-12,000 officials—ranging from members of parliament to heads of insurance agencies and newspaper editors—to verify whether they had served as informers for the former secret police.

High unemployment and inflation during the transition to a capitalist economy produced widespread voter discontent, and parliamentary elections in May 1994 returned the former Communists to power. HSP leader Gyula Horn became prime minister.

The following documents related to transitional justice in Hungary can be found in Volume III of this collection:

- Law on Background Checks to be Conducted on Individuals Holding Certain Important Positions
- Constitutional Court Decision on the Statute of Limitations
- Compensation Laws
- Law Voiding Certain Convictions 1963-1989

PROSECUTION OF COMMUNIST CRIMES: THE DEBATE OVER THE STATUTE OF LIMITATIONS

*Judith Pataki, "Dealing with Hungarian Communists' Crimes"**

On 4 November 1991 the Hungarian parliament passed a law suspending the statute of limitations for all crimes of murder, treason, and aggravated assault leading to the victim's death committed during the past forty-five years that for political reasons had not been prosecuted....

Practically all former communist countries are grappling with the same problem: can justice be done now for crimes committed under the former party dictatorship? In the case of most crimes, the time limit for prosecution has expired, many key witnesses have died, and the accused are elderly. Bringing the cases to trial could be a complicated process and in some instances justice could become a hostage of politics, as was the case before the postcommunist political changes.

However, although there are legitimate reasons for not holding such trials, there are also valid arguments for doing so. In Hungary some injustices inflicted under communism, in particular those leading to economic losses, could be partially made up for by the compensation law passed [by the post-communist parliament]; but little has been done about crimes of a political nature committed by former communist officials, often resulting in death. In many cases the relatives of the people executed under the communist regime are still waiting for the names of those responsible to be revealed. Many of the offenses committed by former communist officials

* Excerpted from Judith Pataki, "Dealing with Hungarian Communists' Crimes," *RFE/RL Research Report*, vol. 1, no. 9 (February 28, 1992), pp. 21-24.

would have been crimes not only from today's perspective; they were already so at the time they were committed, as they contravened even the laws passed by the Communists. However, the political circumstances of the time did not allow the victims to ask for an investigation or trial.

Although it was against the law, a number of minors were executed for their involvement in the 1956 revolution. Janos Kadar's regime stopped this practice only as a result of international pressure. A number of people were tortured during interrogation and died as a result of their beatings. It was specific officials who were responsible for ordering the shooting into defenseless crowds in Mosonmagyarovar, Salgotarjan, and other towns during and after the revolution, although their identity is often not known.

The Zetenyi-Takacs Law

The critics of the fact that many perpetrators of politically motivated crimes under the communist regime are living unpunished in Hungary today have been pushing for the adoption of a law that would make it possible to prosecute such people. Despite warnings by some politicians and legal experts that such a measure might be impractical for legal, political, and moral reasons, on 4 November 1989 the Hungarian parliament passed a law designed to deal on a limited scale with past injustices. It was approved by a large majority: 197 in favor, fifty against, and seventy-four abstentions.[1] It had been introduced by Peter Takacs and Zsolt Zetenyi, two deputies of the Hungarian-Democratic Forum (HDF), Hungary's governing party.

The bill, which was very brief and to the point, called for the suspension of the statute of limitations for cases of treason, premeditated murder, and aggravated assault leading to death that had been committed between 21 December 1944 (the day the first Hungarian parliament following the era of Admiral Miklos von Horthy convened in Debrecen) and 2 May 1990 (when the first freely elected postcommunist parliament met) where for political reasons prosecutions had not previously been possible.[2] Most of the crimes were committed by individuals involved in suppressing the 1956 uprising. The bill also stated that, where applicable, lighter sentences than normal could be passed. Obviously the chief aim was not to punish the criminals but to unmask them.

Strong Emotional Reactions

Reactions both for and against the proposed legislation were very strong. The bill's advocates argued that its intention was to call to account only a few hundred individuals at most and that it would therefore hardly set off a witch-hunt, as claimed by its critics. They also argued that the bill called only for the prosecution of those who had been involved in the worst crimes and that it gave the courts a free hand to limit the punishment

---

1 *The Independent*, 11 November 1991.

2 Reuters (Budapest), 4 November 1991.

imposed.[3] But, however restricted in scope, it was clear that this would be the first law adopted by a former communist country that would result in criminal proceedings against former communist officials. Although some countries, including Czechoslovakia, had adopted measures aimed at punishing former Communists and secret police collaborators, these measures had not resulted in criminal proceedings.

The debates surrounding the bill were often emotional and distorted the facts; and they continued even after it had become law. The chairman of the Hungarian Socialist Party (HSP—the Communists' successor), Gyula Horn, claimed a few days after the law had been passed that more than 10,000 people had already been reported to the police for high treason, disloyalty to the country, and homicide committed in defense of communism.[4] He expressed the fear that former minor communist officials would face prosecution. Horn's claims contradicted statements by Andras Galszecsy, minister without portfolio in charge of domestic security, who told a Hungarian newspaper at the beginning of December that not a single person had been reported as a result of the new law.[5] Although Horn was not able to substantiate his comments, Galszecsy's argument was not totally convincing either.

Prior to the adoption of the law many newspapers and opposition party leaders had expressed the fear that it would lead to political hysteria and a vengeful witch-hunt.[6] While such fears were understandable to a degree, they clearly did not reflect the new political climate that had come about in Hungary since 1989; the two years or so under Jozsef Antall's government had been characterized by a lack of revenge-seeking. Many former communist party members were reelected as mayors or hold responsible positions in such bodies as banks, hospitals, and schools. Other party officials who opposed the country's return to democracy opted to live in seclusion. However, despite this notable lack of politically motivated retribution, critics of the bill were afraid that it might trigger it off.

Although the passage of the law was surrounded by emotional debates among experts and politicians, the public in general seems to have been more concerned with the economic activities of the former *nomenklatura* than the crimes of the Stalinist era. Many communist party officials took advantage of their positions to accumulate wealth both legally and illegally, and a number have found ways of investing this wealth in the private economy; this angers those whose incomes have never been high and who are losing their economic security as a result of high inflation. There has been some concern in Hungary that the application of the Zetenyi-Takacs law might prompt people disillusioned with the economic practices of the former *nomenklatura* to demand that further measures be taken against those members of the former communist elite who, in the eyes

---

3 *Nepszabadsag*, 16 November 1991.

4 AFP (Budapest), 17 November 1991; and *Maguar Hirlap*, 9 November 1991.

5 *Maguar Hirlap*, 3 December 1991.

6 *Weekly Bulletin* (MTI), 29 November 1991.

of the public, acquired their current wealth illegally. One reason why many leading members of the opposition Alliance of Free Democrats (AFD) were against the law was anxiety that people might demand moves against former Communists in other areas.[7]...

Political Concern

A great many issues raised in connection with the law were of a political nature. One important consideration for those deputies voting against the law was the fact that it broke the promises the political opposition had made to the reform Communists during the roundtable discussions in the summer of 1989. The AFT politician Imre Mecs, himself sentenced to death for his role in the 1956 revolution, said that "the peaceful transition was helped by the reform Communists from inside [the party]. These are the facts. For this reason, too, it is not ethical that the Zetenyi-Takacs law came into being."[9] Mecs also expressed concern over the basic principles of the law and the precedent it set. Former Chairman of the HSP Rezso Nyers claimed that the "gentleman's agreement" had been broken.[10] Some people, however, reject such arguments, claiming that the opposition side was self-appointed and sat down to talk with the Communists without the consent of the people.

It is not clear whether the law has actually broken any gentleman's agreements or not, since the measure is certainly not intended to punish the reform Communists who engaged in the dialogue. (Indeed, those former officials who would not be liable for trial would in effect receive an indirect amnesty, as Zetenyi himself suggested.) The law is aimed mainly against those former government and party officials who bear the heaviest responsibility for the crimes it outlines. But even if found guilty, none would be sentenced to death, since the Constitutional Court has ruled capital punishment to be unconstitutional.

Arguments in favor of the law have repeatedly been expressed by Imre Konya. Himself a lawyer, Konya was concerned about the fact that the victims of Communists' crimes were still living alongside torturers and murderers. (The same has been said about the members of the freely elected parliament.) In Konya's opinion, this distorted the concept of right and wrong. He objected to the repeated claims by opposition party leaders that the whole of society had collaborated with the communist regime to a certain degree in order to live a better life. Such reasoning, according to Konya, implied that the whole nation was guilty. He believed the trials were necessary precisely because there was a vast difference between the average citizen who might have become a communist party member in order to keep his job and the people involved in torturing or killing defenseless individuals. For Konya, it was not the nation that was guilty, only

---

[7] Hungarian Television 1, 26 November 1991, 10:45 p.m.

[9] *Nepszava*, 18 November 1991.

[10] *Ibid.*, 8 November 1991.

particular individuals.[11] On another occasion Konya said that the HDF should seek justice, although it was not sure that the majority of people wanted this.[12] The local elections in the fall of 1990, Konya argued, showed that the population was divided over this issue.

Indeed, not only the population but the parties themselves are divided over the matter. The AFD stated in its election program that it would not initiate or support moves to call anyone to account for his former political activities, nor would it support the extension of the statute of limitations for any offenses.[13] But the party was inconsistent. Some of its election campaign material stated that the AFD would support such a calling to account should it be elected.

The HDF, on the other hand, projected a different image. The party's constituent meeting had been addressed by State Secretary Imre Pozsgay, a member of the Politburo of the Hungarian Socialist Workers' Party, and the HDF was even criticized for being too friendly with the reform Communists. The HDF's election slogan portrayed the party as "the quiet force"; retribution was not a major issue for it during the election campaign or after it. Only as neighboring countries started to deal with the matter, and probably as a result of pressure from the victims of communist crimes, did it start to play a major role in HDF policies.

During the election campaign another parliamentary party, the Alliance of Young Democrats (AYD), stressed the importance of a clean past; previously, in a speech at the reburial of former Prime Minister Imre Nagy in June 1989, its leader, Viktor Orban, had openly attacked some reform Communists for their past conduct. However, when it came to the vote on the Zetenyi-Takacs bill, the alliance voted against it) according to Orban, on legal rather than political grounds). The AYD, though, was not the only part to shift its stand in this way: most HDF deputies voted in favor of the bill while many AFD representatives abstained, including Mecs and another opponent of the bill, Ivan Peto.

Legal Considerations

The Criminal Code set the statute of limitations for murder at twenty years, for high treason at fifteen years, and for aggravated assault causing death at eight years. In order to carry out the law, these restrictions must be lifted retroactively. Those who oppose the law say that this could destabilize the legal system as a whole.[14] Those in favor of the law claim that in fact the statute of limitations is not being extended or abolished; it is merely being applied differently in exceptional circumstances. They argue that in the previous forty-five years it was impossible to start proceedings against individuals for these crimes because the political

---

11 "Debates about Justice," *Kritika*, January 1992, pp. 11-12.

12 *Magyar Hirlap*, 9 September 1991.

13 *A Szabad Demokratak Programtervezete* [The Program Proposal of the AFD] (Budapest: 1989).

14 "The Old Law of the People and the Legal State," *Beszelo*, January 1992, pp. 10-12.

situation did not allow it; thus, the statute in effect lay dormant and the clock could not start ticking until 2 May 1990, the date from which the above-mentioned time limits now apply. West Germany used the same argument when it sought to lift the statute of limitations for the crimes against humanity committed under the Nazi period.

Many legal experts have serious reservations about the section of the law calling for prosecution for high treason. The definition of treason is subject to broad interpretation. The example of the late party leader Janos Kadar can be used to demonstrate how difficult it may be to charge any former official with treason. Many claim that Kadar could be considered a traitor, because he betrayed the legitimate government in November 1956 and called on a foreign government for "help." The constitution of the time, however, defined the social order of the country in terms of socialism; and Kadar claimed then that he could no longer support Nagy's government because Nagy had gone too far: in other words, Kadar claimed that it was not he but Nagy who had violated Hungary's constitutional order. Moreover, calling for outside intervention was not part of the legal definition of treason in 1956. The situation is different today; a law passed in 1989 (No. 25, Article 7, Section 1) states that anyone who calls for the help of foreign troops or invited them into the country can be sentenced to a term of imprisonment ranging from ten years to life. Many argue, however, that even without this provision, those who turned to the Soviet Union for "help" would count as traitors under any definition of this concept in effect since 1930.

Some legal experts fear that certain provisions of the law may contravene those of international agreements signed by Hungary, such as the right to speedy trial. Because of this and other legal considerations, when the law was sent to President Arpad Goncz for his signature in November 1991 he referred it instead to the Constitutional Court.

Decision of the Constitutional Court Overturning the Law

*Peter Paczolay, "Judicial Review of Compensation Law in Hungary"**

A unanimous Court (nine of the ten judges participated in the decision) declared the law unconstitutional. The Court explained that the [Zetenyi-Takacs] Law runs counter to the current penal law provision defining the applicable statute of limitations as the one in effect at the time that the crime was committed. The lifting of the statute of limitations is unconstitutional because it would create *ex post facto* legislation. The Court also reasoned that the fact that certain crimes remained unpunished for political reasons does not create a constitutional justification for discrimination. An additional reason for holding the law unconstitutional was the inclusion of treason among these crimes, because the definition of treason has changed several times during the past decades: for example,

* Excerpted from Peter Paczolay, "Judicial Review of Compensation Law in Hungary," *Michigan Journal of International Law*, vol. 13, no. 3 (Summer 1992), pp. 828-829.

political changes can qualify the official politics of a State afterwards as treason.

The Court stated that the change of regime in Hungary was based on legal continuity; according to this reasoning, all legal regulations must correspond to the new Constitution, and all exceptions are unconstitutional. A change of regime in the legal sense means nothing more than that laws have to be coordinated with the Constitution based on the rule of law. As the change was based on the principles of legality and legal continuity, there is no difference between the laws enacted before and after the Constitution. The new Constitution is the only standard for judicial review.[49]

Roundtable on the Court's Ruling

Stephen J. Schulhofer, Michel Rosenfeld, Ruti Teitel, and Roger Errera, "Dilemmas of Justice"[*]

[Editor's note: The University of Chicago-based East European Constitutional Review asked four scholars to give their reactions to the ruling by the Hungarian Constitutional Court in which it overturned the November 1991 law. Their responses follow.]

Stephen J. Schulhofer
Professor of Law
U. of Chicago Law School

How can a state dedicated to the rule of law come to terms with the lawlessness of a prior government, without in the process infringing on its own commitment to legality and impartiality? The dilemma is heightened in Hungary and other Eastern European countries by a tradition of short periods of limitation for criminal prosecution, including a fifteen-year statute of limitations for homicide. In this setting, the Hungarian Constitutional Court concluded, efforts to vindicate the rule of law are largely blocked by the rule of law itself. The decision suggests the likelihood of continuing struggle, in Hungary and elsewhere, over the propriety of retrospective justice and over the means available for pursuing it. The opinion indicates the possibility for the Constitutional Court to adopt a vigorously independent role, characterized by an expansive constitutionalism (what Americans might call an activist conception of "substantive due process"), reliance on transnational norms, and concern with legislative rather than only executive abuses of power.

---

49 Judgment of Mar. 5, 1992, Alkománybiróság [Constitutional Court] No. 11/1992(III.5)AB, Magyar Közlöny No. 23/1992 (Hung.) (unofficial translation on file with the *Michigan Journal of International Law*).

* Reprinted from Stephen J. Schulhofer, Michel Rosenfeld, Ruti Teitel, and Roger Errera, "Dilemmas of Justice," *East European Constitutional Review*, vol. 1, no. 2 (Summer 1992), pp. 17-19.

The Spirit of Constitutionalism

The Hungarian legislature's effort to extend the statute of limitations originated in its desire to bring to justice those who had participated in abuses under the prior regime, in particular those involved in the brutal repression that followed the abortive 1956 revolution. The law provided that the statute of limitations for offenses of treason, voluntary manslaughter and infliction of bodily harm resulting in death committed between December 21, 1944 and May 2, 1990, would begin running anew on May 2, 1990, "provided that the state's foregoing of its claim to punish [had been] based on political reasons." The law thus reopened offenses on which the statute of limitations had run and extended the statute of limitations for crimes on which the statute had not yet run.

The Hungarian Constitution prohibits punishment for "an action that at the time when it was committed was not a criminal offense under Hungarian law" [§57(4)]. But this provision would not, by its terms, expressly bar retrospective changes in the statute of limitations. Accordingly, the lion's share of the Hungarian Court's opinion is devoted to two broader constitutional linchpins, the declarations that Hungary is a "state under the rule of law" [§2(1)], and that Hungary recognizes the inviolable fundamental human rights of man." From these premises, the Court deduced constitutional requirements of "security of the law," and "protection of rights previously conferred." Law must be "clear, unambiguous, [its] impact predictable and [its] consequences foreseeable." In a striking passage, the Court stated, "The constitutionality of penal laws [is] not to be evaluated merely by reference to the criminal law guarantees expressly detailed in the Constitution.... Thus, there is no specific provision of the Constitution prohibiting the imposition of strict liability in criminal cases, and yet the right to human dignity dictates that *mens rea* be a constitutional requirement for holding a person criminally liable."

Three features of the Court's opinion seem especially significant for future developments. First, the Court took an expansive "substantive due process" approach to what otherwise might have become unenforceable constitutional exhortations. Second, in doing so, the Court drew upon prevailing international norms, making express reference to its comparative study of the constitutions of other states. Third, the Court showed no trace of the view, common in many of the Eastern European states, that the executive poses the principal threat to human rights and that a democratic legislature need not be feared. On the contrary, the Court stressed that duly enacted legislation may also violate fundamental rights, even rights that have no explicit basis in constitutional text. In combination these features of the Court's approach promise intensive security (drawing in part on American and European precedents) for the statutory law of crimes and criminal procedure, as well as for the details of police investigatory practice. If the Hungarian Court remains on its present course, the Constitution's guarantees of "fundamental human rights" [§8(1)], "human dignity" [§54(1)], "the inviolability of domicile" [§59(1)], and "the protection of private secrets" [§59(1)] seem destined to enjoy an active jurisprudential future.

Retrospective Justice in America

American law largely obviates the need for the sort of legislation that provoked these constitutional questions in Hungary. Under federal law and the law of most states, no period of limitations is prescribed for murder and treason prosecutions. Some states also dispense with any period of limitation for voluntary manslaughter cases (e.g., Pennsylvania) or even for all homicide prosecutions (e.g., Illinois). Though offenses such as fraud or embezzlement normally carry short periods of limitation (three to five years), exceptions are typically made for offenses by public officials, whose position might inhibit prompt prosecution. In California, there is no period of limitations for the offense of embezzling public funds. In New York, Pennsylvania and Illinois, the statute of limitations for charges involving misconduct by a public official is tolled for the period that the official remains in office.

Under American constitutional doctrine, any attempt to extend an expired statute of limitations is deemed an impermissible *ex post facto* law. Yet the American cases uniformly hold (contrary to the decision of the Hungarian Court) that the statute can be validly extended, with respect to offenses already committed, if the statutory limitation period has not run. The Hungarian Court considered such an extension to be a breach of a solemn commitment—the sovereign's promise, made at the time of the offense, as to the applicable limitation period. The American view considers such commitments enforceable only in cases of *justifiable* reliance. Once the limitation period has run, there is a vested interest in repose, on which an offender is entitled to rely. But a wrongdoer cannot reasonably claim a right to rely on stated limitation periods in planning his criminal activities, so extensions enacted before the limitation period expires can fairly be applied to offenses committed beforehand.

Justifiable reliance is not the only interest protected by the *ex post facto* prohibition, however. More fundamental is the requirement of governmental impartiality—that law should be a distillation of general principles suitable for future application, not simply an ad hoc response to individuals and past events. The *ex post facto* prohibition on post-offense increases in applicable punishment surely makes sense from this perspective, though it is hard to defend in terms of justifiable reliance. Likewise, post-offense extensions in the statute of limitations seem to offend the impartiality principle even when the statute has not yet run. The Hungarian decision on this point thus seems more faithful to the core values of the *ex post facto* prohibition than is the more permissive American case law.

However satisfying this result may appear as a matter of legal theory, it remains awkward in the context of present-day Eastern European politics, where rule-of-law protection is claimed for quasi-official conduct under regimes that systematically violated the rule of law. Hungary and other states in the region are likely to confront continuing pressure to settle accounts with those responsible for the abuses of the past. The Hungarian Court's stringent disapproval of *ex post facto* legislation gives priority to claims of continuity and regularity at the expense of demands for substantive justice, as might be expected in a nation anxious to embrace Western liberal traditions and to bury its legacy of result-oriented socialist conceptions of justice. Nonetheless, the decision points to three problems in the effort to reconcile rule-of-law principles with desires for retribution and corrective justice in Eastern Europe.

One question concerns the status or property rights "vested" under unjust or unlawful decrees of a prior regime. In American understanding, the *ex post facto* principles protect property and contract rights from uncompensated takings. Yet the reasoning of the Hungarian Court suggests that a broad "rule-of-law" principle might not be similarly limited.

A second question concerns continued or future employment, especially in official positions, by those who may have been associated in abuses of the past. Disqualification from office on the basis of time-barred misconduct could conceivably be precluded by the same "rule-of-law" principle. The American distinction between punitive and remedial sanctions could be helpful in preserving some room for corrective justice here. Yet disqualification can sometimes have a significant punitive element, as American cases following the Civil War made clear.

Third, one wonders whether there remains any room for criminal prosecution of even the most egregious atrocities of the Communist era. The Hungarian Court's opinion gave no hint that a more narrowly drawn statute might pass muster, and it even criticized as vague and contradictory those clauses of the statute that were designed to limit its reach. A still narrower statute might therefore suffer the same fate. Yet, a prosecution for violation of internationally recognized human rights ordinarily should escape the *ex post facto* objection, as Article 7(2) of the European Human Rights Convention makes clear. The Hungarian Court's unwillingness to pursue a more limited and nuanced analysis of such issues suggests that a powerful aversion to stirring up the past may have been as important as abstract legal analysis in producing the Court's results.

The underlying problem, therefore, is one of determining not only the permissible techniques for retributive justice but, more fundamentally, the place of retribution in the effort to rebuild the economies and legal institutions of the region on liberal, rule-of-law principles. Will efforts to punish past abuses only end by diverting needed energies and, paradoxically, undermining public confidence in governmental respect for the rule of law? Or does some formal exposure and condemnation of past offenses remain an important part of the effort to prevent their repetition?

Michael Rosenfeld
Professor of Law
Cardozo Law School

Establishing the proper balance between political justice and constitutionalism has proven particularly difficult in the context of the recent East and Central European transitions to democracy. Underlying this difficulty is the clash between the clamor for redress in relation to the past abuses and atrocities under oppressive socialist regimes and the apparent dependence of constitutionalism on unbending adherence to the rule of law. Political justice becomes a constitutional issue primarily through consideration of retroactivity laws, thus lending great importance to the Hungarian constitutional court's recent invalidation of that country's retroactivity laws relating to criminal prosecutions for murder and treason. The Hungarian court's action is highly commendable and will hopefully be emulated throughout the region; it also affords an opportunity for further reflection on the problematic relationship between political justice and constitutionalism.

One should not dismiss political justice as being ultimately reducible to revenge or to the whim of those in power. Political justice has a legitimate place in a comprehensive scheme of justice meant for a society with a past marked by a wide gap between moral and legal norms. Indeed, comprehensive justice must be both forward-and-backward-looking as it must address genuine issues of compensation and retribution as well as those of distribution. Moreover, when reliance on established legal norms is insufficient to effectuate the requisite dictates of compensatory and retributive justice, recourse to political justice could well be justified.

Notwithstanding its potential for legitimacy, political justice remains antagonistic to constitutionalism's commitment to the rule of law. In the case of constitutions enacted after violent rupture with the past, the demands of political justice might be reconciled with those of constitutionalism by confining the operation of political justice to the revolutionary period separating the *ancien regime* from the new constitutional order. Even where that is not possible, accommodation could still be achieved, in cases where the *ancien regime* altogether failed to criminalize reprehensible conduct, through appeal to unwritten law or through incorporation of legal norms embodied in international covenants.

When it comes to Hungary and to most of the remaining East and Central European democracies, however, there appears to be no justification for relying on either of these two alternative ways of reconciling political justice and constitutionalism. Focusing on Hungary in particular, the transition to constitutionalism was achieved without revolutionary rupture while the type of reprehensible conduct sought to be punished through enactment of the retroactivity law was fully subject to criminal sanction under the socialist regime. Under these circumstances, the call for political justice must derive its justification from the socialist state's failure to prosecute certain criminal offenders for "political reasons." This, in turn, leads to the following paradox: past injustices and the flouting of the rule of law may be redressed through application of a retroactivity law, but since the determination of what constitutes a "political reason" itself depends on political criteria, use of retroactivity law seems bound to undermine adherence to the rule of law. In the abstract there seems to be no way out of this paradox. Given the historical socialist disregard for the rule of law, however, the Hungarian constitutional court's decision and its commitment to the rule of law as an independent constitutional value seem eminently wise.

Invalidation of retroactivity laws does not entail abandoning the aims of comprehensive justice. It merely forecloses using criminal law to achieve the objectives of political justice.

Ruti Teitel
Professor of Law
New York Law School

The question before Hungary's constitutional court is important to the transitions taking place now in East and Central Europe, but it is also one which has long fascinated legal scholars. What are the rule-of-law constraints on the retroactive application of criminal justice?

In its decision on the November 1991 Law Concerning the Prosecutability of Offenses Committed Between December 21, 1944 and May 2, 1990, Hungary's constitutional court held that tampering with the statutes of limitations for treason and homicide was unconstitutional and offensive to principles of rule of law: "Legal certainty based on objective and formal principles takes precedence over justice which is partial and subjective at all times."

To what extent was the constitutional court's decision to invalidate the legislation required by rule of law principles? Below I suggest that principles of rule of law may well justify upholding that part of the challenged legislation which revives the statute of limitations for homicide; and I offer a basis for distinguishing the tamperings as to treason and homicide, particularly homicide committed against civilians on political grounds.

The rule-of-law principle the challenged legislation was held to offend is that of *nulla poena sine lege*. This principle against retroactivity in the operation of criminal justice requires that as a matter of fairness persons ought not to be held accountable for offenses not known to be unlawful at the time they were committed. The relevant question becomes whether the prosecutable acts would have been offenses and unlawful at the time of their occurrence.

According to the above principle, the revivals of the statute of limitations for treason and homicide in the challenged legislation arguably are distinguishable. As to the treason offense, the reimposition of the statute of limitations today presents a tampering of a substantive nature. A post-Communist understanding of treason is utterly different from the understanding of treason during the prior regime. In 1956, at the time of the treasonous acts in question, persons committing the acts would not have known of their criminal nature. As to this offense, therefore, the revival of the statute of limitations constitutes substantive retroactive legislation.

Concerning the offense of homicide, in distinction, the revival of the statute of limitations does not present the substantive creation of criminal liability for a new offense; homicide was unlawful in 1956. As to homicide, the proposed legislation is arguably jurisdictional in nature, and would not contravene the principle against retroactive criminal justice.

A similar analysis was applied in constitutional review of World War II-related prosecutions. Substantive retroactive legislation has been distinguished from that which is jurisdictional. Under this standard, the proposed homicide provisions would be understood to confer jurisdiction today on Hungary's courts with respect to acts that were unlawful at the time they were committed. With respect to the category of offense, though the proposed legislation still implies a tampering of a jurisdictional nature, it is compatible with the principle rule of law.

An important justification for the jurisdictional tampering is that the homicide acts that are the subject of the challenged legislation fall within a category of grave criminal offenses, crimes against humanity. Protection of the rule of law also implies adherence to fundamental international law norms such as the principle of the imprescriptibility of crimes against humanity. The failure to refer to any national or international precedents on this question is a glaring omission in the Hungarian constitutional court's opinion.

Notwithstanding the above, the challenged legislation may still suffer from a constitutional defect in its selective retroactivity. The principle against retroactive criminal legislation tells us something about the community we properly hold criminally accountable. If the proposed legislation is applied retroactively—and selectively—its selective enforcement raises problems of bill of attainder and equal protection. There would be additional problems which I have not addressed concerning the law's enforcement, for example, the availability of defenses such as due obedience.

The balance struck by the Hungarian constitutional court whereby rule-of-law interests against jurisdictional tamperings override the competing interest in adherence to the principle of the imprescriptibility of crimes against humanity in the long run will not afford legal certainty. The question before the court involved competing principles of criminal justice, and as such will no doubt continue to haunt the region.

Roger Errera
Member, Conseil d'état
Paris, France

I regard this as a decision of a very high legal standard. The legal concepts it applies are essential: rule of law; legal certainty; non-retroactivity of criminal law; *nullum crimem, nullum poena sine lege*; prohibition of vaguely worded statutes, especially in the field of criminal law; equality before the law. There is little doubt that the decision will, in time, be influential in the other Central and Eastern European countries.

How and when, we cannot know at this moment; it will take some time for the decision to be fully translated and known in the other countries. Other factors might be: the scope of the jurisdiction of the new constitutional courts; the kind of statutes that will be referred to them (e.g. the Czechoslovak *lustrace* law); and, most important, the quality of the judges sitting in the courts and the general political context.

In due time, law professors, lawyers, members of parliaments, judges and politicians will not be able to ignore the Hungarian decision. The comments devoted to it in Western Europe and North American law journals will no doubt find their way to Central and Eastern European readers.

Any Western European reader of the decision cannot fail to recognize in it familiar notions. The content of the concept of legal certainty, for example, owes much to the case law of the European Commission and Court of Human Rights construing the words "prescribed by law," which figure in paragraphs of many articles of the European Human Rights Convention. To a French reader at least, the notions of necessity and proportionality of penalties evoke the corresponding clause of the 1789 Declaration of the Rights of Man and Citizen. It is more difficult to find parallels from countries where there is no statute of limitations (see, e.g., the English War Crimes Act of 1991.)

Such a decision will be read with special attention and interest by people from countries which, between 1940 and 1944, were under both Nazi occupation and a collaborationist regime. France is one of them. Two remarks may be in order here: the first is that, immediately after the war, the criminal trials that took place against French citizens were based on such pre-war statutes as those applying to treason, "*intelligences avec l'ennemi*" (acting in conjunction with an enemy power), or murder. Second, in 1964 crimes against humanity, within the meaning of Article 6(c) of the IMT Charter annexed to the 1945 London Agreement, were declared to be outside the reach of the statute of limitations ("*imprescriptibles par nature*"). This was consistent both with what we know of the *travaux preparatoires* of the London Agreement and with Article 7 of the European Convention on Human Rights. While Article 7(1) prohibits retroactivity in criminal law, Art. 7(2) states: "This Article shall not prejudice the trial and punishment of any person of any act or omission which, at the time when it was committed, was criminal according to the general principles of law recognized by civilized nations."

According to the committee of experts that drafted the Convention, Article 7(1) does not relate to statutes which, during the very exceptional circumstances that followed World War II, were adopted in order to punish perpetrators of war crimes, acts of treason and collaboration with the enemy, and does not aim at the legal or moral condemnation of such statutes. It is on this basis that the prosecution of Barbie, Touvier and Bousquet have taken place recently in France.

Since the Hungarian decision does not mention crimes against humanity and indeed had no need to do so, a question arises. Would its absolute prohibition of retroactive criminal law in the form of a direct or indirect modification of the statute of limitations still be valid if, Hungary having ratified the Convention, the question of the prosecution of crimes against humanity were to be raised?

Finally, the Court states wisely: "The Constitutional Court cannot ignore history, for it has itself an historical task to accomplish.... It is aware that its decisions are conditioned by history." Indeed, while judges are not historians and should avoid the temptation to become historians, they cannot ignore history. This applies to all courts in all countries: the past will not be forgotten and cannot be ignored. Even if one approves both the reasoning and the substance of the Court's decision, as I do, there may be in the future situations in which facts, circumstances or characters relating to these years will reappear, even before a court of law. What the courts will then say about the acts, the victims and the perpetrators will be vital. Memory is the ultimate form of justice.

A Different Approach to the Statute of Limitations: The 1993 Law

[Editor's note: In March 1993, the Hungarian Parliament adopted a Law on "Procedures Concerning Certain Crimes Committed During the 1956 Revolution." President Arpad Goncz submitted the Act for pre-promulgation review to the Constitutional Court. In an October 1993 decision summarized in the following selection, the Court upheld the main part of the law.]

*Krisztina Morvai, "Retroactive Justice based on International Law: A Recent Decision by the Hungarian Constitutional Court"**

After the shock caused by the failure of the first attempt the groups favoring "historical justice" began to consider new options for achieving their original aim of prosecuting Communist offenders. The last draft changed the strategy and used international law (as opposed to domestic law) as the means for doing justice. In order to avoid vagueness, the draft also made clear that it had the events of 1956 specifically in mind.

The law was based on these multi-national treaties: the Geneva Conventions Relative to the Treatment of Civilians in the Time of War and Relative to the Treatment of Prisoners of War of 1949 and the New York Convention on the Non-Applicability of Statutory Limitations to War Crimes and Crimes Against Humanity of 1968 [to each of which Hungary is a party]....

Although their titles do not indicate it clearly, the Geneva Conventions were meant to be applied in any case of armed conflict and not

* Excerpted from Krisztina Morvai, "Retroactive Justice based on International Law: A Recent Decision by the Hungarian Constitutional Court," *East European Constitutional Review*, vol. 2, no. 4/vol. 3, no. 1 (Fall 1993/Winter 1994), pp. 33-34.

just in declared wars between states. According to the common articles of the conventions: "violence to life and person" and several other forms of wrongdoing are prohibited also "in the case of armed conflict not of an international character."

The Geneva documents did not include any provisions concerning limitations on the prosecution of these offenses. Nevertheless, several states made laws concerning this point and retroactively declared the absence of limitation on what have been understood as "Nuremberg crimes."

The [New York] Convention regulated the issue of limitation, declaring that "no statutory limitation shall apply to several categories of war crimes and crimes against humanity irrespective of the date of their commission."...

The [1993 Hungarian law on] retroactive justice combined the provisions of the Geneva Conventions and the New York Convention and thereby interpreted the most brutal episodes of the 1956 Revolution as war crimes and/or crimes against humanity.... The ... law was upheld on the basis of the interpretation of Article 7 of the constitution: "The legal system of Hungary shall respect the universally accepted rules of international law, and shall ensure furthermore, the accord between the obligations assumed under international and domestic law." The decision emphasized that the act in fact ensured the enforcement of "universally accepted rules of international law," part of which are the humanitarian principles expressed in the Geneva Convention. Although those "universally accepted principles" do not include the absence of a statute of limitation covering war crimes and crimes against humanity, Hungary undertook the obligation to prosecute those crimes retroactively by ratifying the New York [Covention].

SCREENING LEGISLATION

*Edith Oltay, "Hungary's Screening Law"**

On 9 March [1994], two months before the national elections, the Hungarian Parliament passed a law, by a vote of 177 to twelve with fifty abstentions, that provides for the screening of leading politicians and state officials for possible ties with the former domestic intelligence service. The law is likely to be the last attempt by Hungary's first democratically elected government following the collapse of communism to come to terms with some of the murkiest aspects of the country's recent past.[1]

---

* Excerpted from Edith Oltay, "Hungary's Screening Law," *RFE/RL Research Report*, vol. 3, no. 15 (April 15, 1994), pp. 13-15.

1 *Magyar Hirlap*, 9 March 1994.

Previous Attempts to Deal With the Past

Proposals for calling former Communists to account, for launching a so-called "decommunization" process, and for undertaking a "political spring cleaning" featured prominently in the government program of the late Prime Minister Jozsef Antall. Following the 1990 elections, the government initially regarded the list of informers as classified information and saw to it that files containing documents on the activities of secret agents were placed in archives. It is widely assumed that only the minister of internal affairs and the prime minister had access to the files. While the government had occasionally used the files to exert pressure on its political opponents, it was able to prevent the names of informers from leaking out. More recently, the government drew up guidelines intended to determine the fate of the files and began drafting a law on the screening of leading politicians and state officials. Not unexpectedly, the wisdom of opening the file to the public or using them as a source of information was questions by, among others, members of the cabinet. Others raised the issue of how reliable the files were, especially after it became known that at least some of the files had been destroyed in 1989 on the orders of Ferenc Pallagi, the then chief of Department 3/3, which was an agency of the domestic intelligence service that monitored dissidents.[2]

At the same time, the identity of former informers and the number that held seats in the democratically elected parliament continued to preoccupy the public. Many commentators stressed the urgency of cleansing Hungary's leading institutions of Communists and urged that a screening law be adopted as soon as possible. A First Draft of the law was in fact submitted to the parliament as early as 1990 by the opposition Alliance of Free Democrats (AFD).[3]...

The Screening Process

Under the screening law, Department 3/3 agents; members of the so-called law-and-order squads, which assisted the Soviet troops in quelling the revolution in 1956 and the last pockets of resistance in 1957; and former members of the Hungarian fascist Arrow Cross Party may not hold senior public positions. The law seeks to solve the moral dilemma of punishing the informers and not those who used the information by labeling state and political leaders who used information provided by the intelligence service as "previously convicted," meaning that they have criminal records.[6]

The law, which is to take effect on 1 July, provides for the creation by the end of June of at least two panels consisting of three professional judges each. It will be the panels' task to examine the secret files for the names of those to whom the law applies. The judges are to receive their mandate directly from the parliament, and their nomination is to be approved by

---

2 *Nepszava*, 22 March 1993; and *Heti Vilaggazdasag*, 19 March 1994.

3 *Magyar Hirlap*, 19 June 1992 and 19 June 1994.

6 *Heti Vilaggarzdasag*, 19 March 1994.

the parliament's National Security Committee and by the president of the Supreme Court. Judges who under the communist regime participated in trials based on trumped-up charges cannot be appointed to the panels. Top politicians and officials who voluntarily leave office between 1 July 1994 and 30 June 2000, the period during which the panels are to carry out their investigations, will be able to request that the results of their screening process are made public in order to protect themselves against allegations that they are registered as informers.[7]

Thirty years after the screening process ends—that is, on 1 July 2030—the lists of agents and other documents related to the screening will be made available to the public. Information about public officials screened between 1994 and 2000 will be accessible to the public thirty years after the panel's ruling. There has apparently been widespread resistance among deputies to making the files accessible earlier or to their publication. A proposal by the AFD deputy and former dissident Ferenc Koszeg that called for the publication of parts of the list encountered such widespread opposition in various parliamentary committees that he withdrew it. Moreover, the majority of deputies rejected proposals that individuals be allowed to consult their own files on the grounds that the Justice Ministry could not cope with the avalanche of applications that would ensue.[8]

The panels will seek evidence that the person under scrutiny signed a statement agreeing to work for the domestic intelligence service and also delivered reports. They will give a verdict of guilty if, in the absence of a signature or reports, it can be documented that the person received money or obtained favors. Once it has been proved that someone was involved in the activities specified, the person will be asked to take the consequences and resign within thirty days on the grounds that he is not fit to carry out the duties associated with an important public post. If he refuses to resign within fifteen days of the expiration of the deadline, his name will be made public in the official newspaper *Magyar Kozlony* and by the official news agency MTI. No other punishment is envisaged. The screening process is likely to be slow, however, since many former informers are expected to appeal the panels' ruling and their names cannot be made public until a legally binding court decision has been made. Government officials estimate that the first stage of the screening process could take up to two years.[9]

Posts to Be Screened

Many of the numerous amendments proposed by deputies were incorporated into the law; as a result, the categories of posts subject to screening grew considerably in number. The law stipulates that the holders of twenty-five categories of posts must be screened; this means that between 10,000 and 12,000 people will be under scrutiny—almost double the number

---

7 *Uj Magyarorszag*, 23 March 1994.

8 *Heti Vilaggazdasag*, 19 March 1994.

9 *Magyar Nemzet*, 9 March 1994; and *Uj Magyarorszag*, 23 March 1994.

envisaged in the AFD's draft and some 2,000—4,000 more than in the government's first draft. The parliament rejected an amendment proposed by HDF deputy Gabor Roszik that would have raised the number of those to be screened to some 28,000 by including local government deputies. It also rejected an amendment by Roszik and Zoltan Deme, a deputy from the radical populist Hungarian Justice and Life Party (HJLP), whereby Church leaders could have been screened if 20% of all active priests had voted in favor of such action.[10]

The list of those to be screened begins with parliamentary deputies and officials elected by the parliament who are obliged to take an oath. Included in this category are the president, the chairman and members of the Constitutional Court, the chairman of the Supreme Court, and the prosecutor-general. Next on the list are members of the government, ministerial department heads, ambassadors, and state secretaries and their deputies. The list also includes the chairman and deputy chairman of the Hungarian National Bank, as well as the chairmen of other banks, financial institutions, insurance companies, and firms in which state ownership exceeds 50%. Among the less important positions to be vetted are mayors of major cities and towns, top military and police personnel, decisions makers in the media (editors, editors in chief, and executives of publications with a circulation of more than 30,000), judges and prosecutors, and the heads of educational institutions (with the exception of those that are predominantly private).

In particular, critics have objected to the provision that executives of private newspapers and journals are to be screened and that the circulation threshold was set at 30,000 instead of 50,000, as envisaged in the government's October 1993 draft. The AFD criticized this provision for what it regarded as discrimination against the press; and it was for this reason that most AFD deputies abstained from voting on the bill. The other liberal party, the Alliance of Young Democrats, however, voted for the draft law. The government argued that the editors, editors in chief, and executives of major newspapers were able to shape public opinion and could not be excluded from the screening process. There was a consensus among the coalition parties that the press subjected the government to excessive criticism, while giving favorable coverage to the opposition parties.[11]

Consequences

The Hungarian public will apparently have to wait until 2030 to find out how many agents, secret service officers, and law-and-order squad members were represented in Hungary's first democratically elected parliament following the collapse of communism. Observers have speculated that deputies waited until the end of their term to adopt a screening law in order to exclude themselves from the screening process. Since the law will apply only to the new parliament and government that

---

10 *Heti Vilaggazdasag*, 19 March 1994.

11 *Magyar Nemzet*, 9 March 1994; and *Magyar Narancs*, 17 March 1994.

emerge from the May elections, many compromised deputies will be able to leave politics without having caused a scandal. Justice Minister Istvan Balsai admitted that if screening had taken place earlier and included current deputies "it would probably have disrupted the functioning of the parliament."[12]

Meanwhile, only HFLP leader and parliamentary deputy Istvan Csurka has admitted that he once signed a statement agreeing to collaborate with the domestic intelligence service. Csurka's revelation came under pressure from Prime Minister Antall, who had sought to discredit him. Nevertheless, Csurka denied having harmed anyone or having delivered reports and was thus able to survive politically. He also claimed that some 10% of the deputies either had been informers or had benefited from information provided by informers. Antall also hinted that Jozsef Torgyan, the chairman of the Independent Smallholder's and Civic Party, had been an informer, a charge Torgyan denies.[13]

According to critics of the law, the government was motivated not by legal or moral considerations but by a desire to damage its major political rival, the Hungarian Socialist Party (HSP), the former reform Communists, headed by Gyula Horn. The HSP is currently leading in opinion polls, and Horn is among the ten most popular politicians in the country. Horn himself was a target of the screening law, since he had served in the law-and-order squad in 1956. Since Horn's membership in this body had been public knowledge for some years, the law is not likely to hurt him, although it may serve as a reminder to the public of his party's origins. The HSP was the only parliamentary party to vote against the bill. Party representatives denied that they had rejected the bill because they believed it was directed at the HSP. They argued that the list was not reliable and that the investigation of some 10,000 people would cause social tension.[14]

Other critics of the law expressed fears that the screening process would mark the beginning of a political purge and that public suspicions of politicians would be revived.[15] They asked whether it was right to subject former informers to what they considered the grave consequences of making their names public for acts that had not violated the laws of the communist regime. Some observers argued that the judge's participation in the screening process was irreconcilable with their profession, since their rulings would not be based on evidence presented in the courts and there would be neither a prosecutor nor a defendant arguing his case. Some judges also expressed reservations, saying that colleagues who accepted such a task would be susceptible to manipulation.[16]

---

12 *Nepszabadsag*, 28 March 1994.

13 *Magyar Nemzet*, 16 June 1993.

14 *Nepszabadsag*, 2 April 1994.

15 See the interview with former AFD politician and philosopher Janos Kis in *Magyar Narancs*, 18 November 1993.

16 *Magyar Hirlap*, 25 February 1993.

Another question raised by critics is whether the law will be able to fulfill its objective of "decommunization" and provide a fair screening process that embraces all former agents. Political State Secretary in the Ministry of Internal Affairs Fabian Jozsa admitted that in some cases there was no longer any evidence that the informer had worked for the domestic intelligence service. It is thus likely that at least some former informers and some of those who used the information they provided will slip through the legal net.

On the whole, however, it would appear that the benefits of the law outweigh its drawbacks. The purging of former agents from high-ranking state positions is necessary not only because of moral consideration but also because those occupying such positions are susceptible to blackmail. The law will also deter many compromised deputies and political leaders from running in the May 1994 elections and is likely to contribute toward Hungary's coming to terms with its past.[17]

THE QUESTION OF COMPENSATION: LAND RESTITUTION

Compensation Proposals Before the Constitutional Court

Peter Paczolay, "Judicial Review of Compensation Law in Hungary"[*]

In 1989, Hungary and other East European nations entered a new period in history. They began the transition to democracy and free markets, a transition that is proving to be a very difficult, complex, and unprecedented task. The twentieth century has seen other European countries, such as Germany, Italy, and Spain, evolve from dictatorial political regimes into democratic societies, but in Eastern Europe this transition will be different. In Eastern Europe, former socialist countries must reorganize state-owned and centralized economies. Economic changes, contrary to the view held by Richard Epstein,[1] will provide new and interesting experiences.

One of the most important issues raised by this complex economic and legal transition is the question of property rights. This question encompasses the reformulation of property rights in the Civil Code, land reform, and privatization, as well as compensation for nationalization and injustices under the Communist regime. It is extremely important that all former socialist countries begin to address these pertinent problems. In most East European countries, these complex questions have been addressed through legislation. Hungary is the only country, however, where the legislative acts have passed the scrutiny of judicial review. This article

---

[17] *Magyar Nemzet*, 9 March 1994.

[*] Excerpted from Peter Paczolay, "Judicial Review of Compensation Law in Hungary," *Michigan Journal of International Law*, vol. 13, no. 3 (Summer 1992), pp. 806-831.

[1] Richard A. Epstein, *All Quiet on the Eastern Front*, 58 U. Chi, L. Rev. 555, 557 (1991).

analyzes the Hungarian Constitutional Court's decisions regarding a specific problem of property rights, namely the Compensation Law. It does not attempt to examine the details of broad subjects such as property rights or privatization.

The Role of the Constitutional Court in the Legal Transition

The Hungarian transition to democracy is peculiar in that the Constitutional Court is playing an important role in the revision of the entire legal system.... In the summer of 1989, the independence of the Constitutional Court became a central issue in negotiations among political groups. The issue was discussed extensively during the Opposition Round Table talks.... The opposition submitted two basic proposals. The first was that every citizen should have the right to challenge the constitutionality of the legal norms before the Constitutional Court. The second was that the Court should also review the constitutionality of legislative acts.... Communist Party experts argued against acceptance of the opposition's proposals, but the head of the government's delegation ignored the warnings. Thus, the opposition easily managed to realize its goals concerning the expansive role of judicial review.

Act No. 32 creating the Constitutional Court was enacted in October 1989, and soon after Parliament elected the first five members of the Court. On January 1, 1990 the Constitutional Court commenced its functions.[3] Five additional members were elected by the new, freely-elected Parliament in mid-1990.

The jurisdiction and power of the Court, even by international comparison, is very broad. For instance, the Court can review the constitutionality of legal drafts before their legislative enactment and has the right to review both legislative acts and sublegislative norms, declaring them null and void in case of unconstitutionality. The Court also gives advisory opinions at the request of high State officers. In the first two years of operation, the Court proved its powerful role in the new political system by delivering a series of very important decisions that pertained to capital punishment, the interpretation of human dignity, equal protection, tax issues, the compensation acts, presidential powers, abortion, and lifting the statute of limitations for political crimes.

Meanwhile, the *actio popularis* (the right for all citizens to seek assistance from the Constitutional Court) resulted in a flood of requests on the part of citizens, which in turn created a tremendous overload for the Court. Nonetheless, judicial review essentially functioned well in Hungary, despite the lack of tradition and experience in that field. The Court's

---

[3] The jurisdiction and the functions of the Constitutional Court are regulated in section 32/A of the Hungarian constitution and in Act No. 32 of 1989 on the Constitutional Court. A Magyar Köztársaság Alkotmánya [Constitution] ch. IV, § 32/A (Hung.) *translated in* 7 Albert P. Blaustein & Gisbert H. Flanz, Constitutions of the Countries of the World 13 (1990); 1989 évi XXXII törvény az Alkotmánybiróságról [Law XXXII on the Constitutional Court], Oct. 30, 1989, Magyar Közlöny No. 77/1989, at 1283 (Hung.)(unofficial translation on file with the *Michigan Journal of International Law*).

property rights decisions, in particular, provide insight into the basic characteristics and problems of judicial review in Hungary.

Property Rights Under Socialism and the Problem of Confiscation

Hungary's stormy history created a very complicated legacy for the new regime. Citizens were embittered over the offenses they endured under Communism, and they expressed a need for justice. In order to fulfill these expectations, the new government had to compensate people for the illegalities of the previous political regimes.

Confiscations for political reasons go back as far as 1939, when the so-called "Second Jewish Law" violated the property rights of Jewish citizens. After the "liberation" of 1945, long overdue steps were taken to solve the agrarian problem. Unfortunately, the land reform was mixed with political revenge. On March 18, 1945, the Provisional Government issued a decree abolishing the great estates and transferring the land either to peasant families or to State and communal property. This land reform has been accurately described as "one of the most radical redistributions of land carried out anywhere after World War II."[4] The land of war criminals, members of fascist organizations, and "traitors of the fatherland" was simply confiscated, and the land of others was taken without paying the compensation required by law. In addition, under the terms of the Potsdam Agreement, approximately 240,000 of Hungary's ethnic Germans were expelled to Germany. Nationalization programs also began in 1945, greatly affecting various industrial, real estate, and retail-trade systems.

The inevitable "seizure of power" by the Communists occurred in 1948. On August 20, 1949 the socialist constitution of Hungary was promulgated, declaring the priority of public property.[5] The emerging dictatorship continued to confiscate the property of the "class enemies." Specifically, property rights were regulated in detail by the Civil Code, enacted in 1959. This Code reaffirmed the priority of public property, listing in conformity with Article 6 of the Constitution that resources such as minerals, forests, water, mines, means of transportation, banks, and postal services are exclusively State or public property. Likewise, many provisions clearly favored State or public property (i.e., the property of cooperatives or so-called social organizations).

The two forms of socialized ownership were State ownership and group (mainly cooperative) ownership. To justify State ownership, a rationale was advanced that it "is linked with workers who do not own the enterprise but, as citizens, have a share in the social ownership of the

---

[4] I.T. Berend & G. Rankl, Hungary: A Century of Economic Development 185 (1974).

[5] Art. 4(1) of the 1949 text of the Constitution provides: "In the Hungarian People's Republic the bulk of the means of production is owned, as public property, by the state, by public bodies or by co-operative organizations." A Magyar Köztársaság Alkotmánya [Constitution] of 1949, art. 4(1) (Hung.) *translated* in Constitution of the Hungarian People's Republic 4 (1949).

totality of the means of production."[6] State or public property, in the terminology of socialist law called "social ownership," was protected by Civil and Criminal Codes as the highest category in the hierarchy of ownership.

The economic reforms initiated in 1968 under the name of the "New Economic Mechanism" also affected property rights, but the hierarchy of ownership remained the same. The reforms changed the management of state property, as the regulations gave more and more rights to the managers of state-owned enterprises to make and carry out their own decisions. Also, after 1984, employees had a considerable voice in the basic "strategic" decisions of enterprises, as more than seventy percent of the enterprises were led by self-managed councils.

In 1989, the fundamental change in the political system cleared the way for a complex transformation. In the process of redefining the role of the State, the area of property rights has also undergone gradual yet fundamental changes. The basic revision of the Constitution was promulgated on October 23, 1989. It contains the basic principles of property rights. These important provisions are:

- the Property Rights Clause—Art. 13. (1) "The Republic of Hungary shall guarantee the right to property;"
- the Equal Protection Of Property Clause—Art. 9. (1) "The Republic of Hungary is a market economy where public and private ownership shall enjoy equal rights and equal protection;"
- the Takings Clause—Art. 13. (2) "Property may be expropriated only exceptionally and out of public interest, in cases and in the manner determined by an Act, with full, unconditional and immediate compensation."

On the basis of these constitutional provisions, the legislature was obligated to review entire branches of the legal system in order to abolish the hierarchy of ownership and restrictions on private activities. By 1991, the chapter on property rights of the Civil Code was completely rewritten.[7] These legal reforms, however, have created only the framework for a real market economy based on private ownership; to have true private property, privatization of the state sector must occur.

Privatization and Historical Justice

In Hungary, various economic reforms were directed at state enterprises to encourage self-management and to drive them toward a market economy. The modest success of this reform program urged the Communist government to hasten the pace of the reforms. The Economic Associations

---

[6] Gyula Eörsi, Comparative Civil (Private) Law 307 (1979).

[7] 1991 évi XVI törvény [Act XIV of 1991 (on the Amendment of the Civil Code)], Apr. 30, 1991, *available* in LEXIS, Europe Library, Eeleg File (1991 U.S. Dep't of Commerce—NTIS translation). For the full English text of the pre-amendment Civil Code, see 1991 Hatályos Magyar Jogszabályok [Hungarian Rules of Law in Force] Nos. 21-24 (Oct. 15 — Nov. 15, 1990).

Act (passed in October 1988) provided for the privatization of state-owned enterprises by converting them into joint-stock companies and allowing them to issue shares which are sold to individuals. This step led to spontaneous privatization and made it possible for managers to take over firms. Even today, Hungary is the only country that does not curtail the practice of spontaneous privatization by managers or outside investors, yet clearly rejects privatization through mass distribution of shares to citizens.[8]

In several East European countries, the issue of privatization, which is in itself a very difficult and complicated task, is directly related to the question of compensation for past injustices. Different solutions pertaining to the procedures and ranges of compensation have been offered. One clearly defined approach would be to grant no compensation at all, whereas the opposite solution would be an in-kind return of expropriated goods. An intermediate solution requiring limited compensation in the form of vouchers, however, is the one most likely to be followed.

Other East European countries also have attempted to deal with the compensation issue. In the former East Germany, more than one million property restitution claims have been filed by private individuals. The Polish government is presently seeking a resolution for the compensation of expropriated former owners. Czechoslovakia's legislators enacted two statutes dealing with the restitution of expropriated property. First, the Restitution Law, passed on October 2, 1990, provides for the reprivatization of some 70,000 smaller businesses and properties nationalized by the Communists between 1955 and 1961. A second statute, the Law on Extrajudicial Rehabilitation, was passed on February 21, 1991; it makes restitution possible in the form of in-kind return of property for individuals only (thus excluding political parties and churches). It covers only property confiscated from February 25, 1948 to January 1, 1990. Financial compensation in the form of either cash payments or vouchers will be made in exceptional cases when considerable improvements to property were made and the former owners are not able to pay their expenses.[9] On February 18, 1992, the Czech legislature approved an amendment to the law on the regulation of ownership relations to land and other agricultural property, which waived the upper limit of 250 hectares for the restitution of plots. Under this amendment, aristocratic classes such as the Lobkovic, Kinski, and Schwarzenberg families can claim back large forest areas.

In Hungary, the Independent Smallholders Party raised the issue of reprivatization when it had essentially no other issue to advance during the electoral campaign in the spring of 1990. After the election the Smallholders became the third largest party in Hungary; they not only participated in the coalition government, but also succeeded in forcing it to

---

[8] On the different methods of privatization of state enterprises, see Alan H. Gelb & Cheryl W. Grey, The Transformation of Economies in Central and Eastern Europe 39-40 (World Bank Policy and Research Series No. 17, 1991).

[9] Jan Obrman, *Two Landmark Bills on Privatization Approved*, RFE/RL Report on Eastern Europe, Mar. 15, 1991, at 12.

draft a bill on the reprivatization of agricultural land. (The original political program of the largest party, the Hungarian Democratic Forum, had not even mentioned reprivatization.) In order to clear up the situation, in 1990 the prime minister, József Antall, asked the Constitutional Court for an advisory opinion on the constitutionality of the reprivatization.

Compensation Case I—An Advisory Opinion

The prime minister asked the court whether it constitutes discrimination according to Article 70/A of the Constitution for compensation procedures to provide for certain people's former property to be reprivatized (i.e. returned in kind), while other people's property would not be returned to them. The petition explained the compensation policy of the Government:[10] it considered privatization to be the basic goal of the transformation of the ownership system. The general principle of privatization was to sell state property to new owners in exchange for payment, while giving former owners, whose property was expropriated during the Communist regime, partial compensation. The settlement of land ownership would have been an exception to these principles.

The first question raised in the Government's petition was whether it constitutes discrimination among the former owners if the kind of property (the basic distinction being between land and other kinds of property) determines whether the property was given back. The second question raised by the prime minister was whether it is constitutional to take land from the cooperatives without expropriation proceedings and compensation. According to the plans of the Government, those lands in the possession of cooperatives which were not acquired in a "normal" legal manner determined by the Civil Code would serve without any compensation as the basis for reprivatization.

Act No. 32 of 1989 makes it possible to ask the Constitutional Court for advisory opinions. The Court is obliged to interpret the provisions of the Constitution relating to the requests of certain institutions (the Parliament or the cabinet) and high State officers (e.g., the President of the Republic or the Chief Justice of the Supreme Court). The advisory opinion is one of those decisions that may, and usually does, involve the judiciary in political questions. It is also dangerous because of the general nature of precedent. The same questions may come to the Court again regarding specific situations, and then the judges are bounded by their previous decisions. The Justices of the United States Supreme Court rejected the idea of advising the other branches on general questions as early as in 1793.[11] The advisory opinion had an unfortunate history in West Germany, and that jurisdiction of the West German Constitutional Court was abolished in 1956. The fact that some constitutional courts may be asked for advisory

---

10 I use the word "Government" in this Article in the sense commonly used in parliamentary systems: it refers to the prime minister and the cabinet ministers.

11 Correspondence between Secretary of State Thomas Jefferson and Chief Justice John Jay and the Associate Justices (July 18 – Aug. 8, 1793), *in* Paul M. Bator et al., Hart and Wechsler's The Federal Courts and the Federal System, at 65-67 (3d ed. 1988).

opinions clearly reveals that European constitutional courts are not solely judicial organs, but often have extrajudicial and even political tasks.

Such tasks confronted the Hungarian Constitutional Court when it was required to issue an advisory opinion in response to the prime minister's petition. Later, the firm language of the advisory opinion created difficulties for the Court when the Compensation Law was challenged again, and the issue came back to the Court. In another case, the Constitutional Court narrowed its jurisdiction in this controversial area and successfully resisted an effort to become involved in the affairs of the legislature. There, the finance minister asked the Constitutional Court to interpret several provisions of the Constitution with regard to the drafting of a law raising mortgage interest rates. The petition also presented three different versions of the draft. The Court pointed out the dangers of a broad interpretation of its power to give advisory opinions, stating that this might easily lead to a situation where the competent legislative organs would request "constitutional interpretation" from the Constitutional Court before the drafting of acts or even before making administrative decisions. "This would inevitably result in that the Constitutional Court assumes the responsibility of the legislative and even of the executive branch, and this would create a sort of government by the Constitutional Court."[12] This would contradict the constitutional principle of the separation of powers.

Equal Protection and Reverse Discrimination

The first question raised in the government's petition was whether it constitutes discrimination among former owners if the kind of property determines whether the property was given back. The Court analyzed this question under the General Equal Protection Clause of the Constitution.[13] According to this clause, the Republic of Hungary shall ensure for all persons in its territory human and civil rights without discrimination on account of race, color, sex, language, religion, political or other views, national or social origins, ownership of assets, birth, or any other grounds. The Constitutional Court also took into consideration both the Property Rights Clause and the Equal Protection Of Property Clause.

This was not the first case in which the Court faced the problem of equal protection. As early as April 1990, in its decision No. 9/1990 (IV.25),[14] the Court had outlined its interpretation of the Equal Protection Clause regarding the constitutionality of reverse discrimination.[15] Interestingly enough, a majority of Hungarian citizens prefer a strictly

---

[12] Judgment of Dec. 18, 1990, Alkotmánybiróság [Constitutional Court] No. 31/1990(XII.18)AB, Magyar Közlöny No. 128/1990 (Hung.) (unofficial translation on file with the *Michigan Journal of International Law*).

[13] A Magyar Köztársaság Alkotmánya [Constitution], *supra* note 3, ch. XII, § 70/A.

[14] Judgment of Apr. 25, 1990, Alkotmánybiróság [Constitutional Court] No. 9/1990(IV.25)AB, Magyar Közlöny No. 36/1990 (Hung.).

[15] But, as Chief Justice Sólymon skeptically remarked, the politicians are not likely to have known about this decision in a rather insignificant case. László Sólyom, *The First Year of the Constitutional Court*, 33 Acta Iuridica Hungarica (forthcoming 1992).

formal interpretation of the Equal Protection Clause. They have a perception of equality as the formally equal distribution of benefits and burdens. They consider it unconstitutional if somebody is in a better position than they are. This concept is a result of the continuous propaganda of the value of equality under the socialist regime.

In this earlier reverse discrimination case, the petitioner challenged the constitutionality of a provision of the Income Tax Law that granted special tax benefits to families with at least three children or to single parents with two children. The Court rejected the claim, arguing that "the ban on discrimination does not mean that any discrimination, including even discrimination intended to achieve a greater social equality, is forbidden."[16] Moreover, the Constitution itself allows the positive or reverse discrimination aimed at eliminating inequalities of opportunity.[17]

In addition, the Court gave a broader interpretation to the Equal Protection Clause. Equal protection in this broader sense means the "equal right to human dignity." Although human dignity is one of the most flexible and vague concepts of constitutional law, the Constitution lays down an inherent right to human dignity.[18] The drafters must have borrowed this concept from the German Basic Law.[19] The Court, by referring to the "equal right to human dignity," set up a procedural scrutiny for equal protection. "The ban on discrimination means that all people must be treated as equal (as persons with equal dignity) by law. That means that the fundamental right to human dignity shall be determined with the same respect and prudence, and with the same degree of consideration of individual interests."[20] Thus, the Court transformed the requirement for equality into the requirement that all persons be treated with equal dignity.

The language of the Court's argument is clearly related to Ronald Dworkin's explanation of affirmative action cases.[21] Dworkin differentiates between two different sorts of rights. The first is the right to equal treatment, which is the right to an equal distribution of some opportunity or resource or burden. The second is the right to treatment as an equal, which is the right to be treated with the same respect as anyone else, not the right to receive the same distribution of some burden or

---

16 Decision No. 9/1990, *supra* note 14.

17 *See* A Magyar Köztársaság Alkotmánya [Constitution], *supra* note 3 at ch. XII, § 70/A.

18 *Id.* § 54(1).

19 Article 1(a) of the Grundgesetz (Basic Law) says: "The dignity of man is inviolable. To respect and protect it shall be the duty of all state authority." GG art. 1(1). For the interpretation of this provision by the German Federal Constitutional Court, see Donald P. Kommers, The Constitutional Jurisprudence of the Federal Republic of Germany 305-65 (1989).

20 Decision No. 9/1990, *supra* note 14.

21 The procedure of the Constitutional Court is that the President of the Court assigns the case to one of the judges who prepares the draft of the decision. Then the draft is circulated and the judges are asked to make their written comments on it. Finally, the session of the Court discusses the draft. Hence the final text of the decision is mostly the result of a common effort. Nevertheless, the judge preparing the draft usually has a decisive impact on the final text. Therefore, since 1991, at the end of the decisions it is noted who delivered the opinion of the Court. In the present case this was not noted yet, but the draft was written by Chief Justice László Sólyom, and he also elaborated the theory of "the right to equal personal dignity."

benefit.[22] The Court combined the right to be treated with the same respect and the concept of human dignity, thus transforming Dworkin's conception into the right to equal dignity.

Actually, the scrutiny of treatment as an equal is a sort of final limit on reverse discrimination. Otherwise, reverse discrimination is acceptable. "If a social purpose not in conflict with the Constitution, or a constitutional right may only be achieved if equality in the narrower sense is not met, then such a positive discrimination shall not be declared unconstitutional."[23] This means that the achievement of an important social goal or the realization of a fundamental right justifies reverse discrimination which obviously hurts the principle of equality in the narrower sense of the (quantitatively) equal distribution of assets and choices.

In responding to the first question of the prime minister in Compensation Case I, the Court examined how the privatization program of the Government could fit the scrutiny of treatment as an equal. The Court found that the program does not give any justification for the preferred position of former land-owners and, in general, reflects conceptual uncertainty concerning the relationship among privatization, reprivatization, and partial compensation. Therefore, the Court tried to clarify the meaning of these terms. In the interpretation of the Court, *privatization* involves the assignment of state property to private ownership, whereas *reprivatization* is the return of assets formerly possessed by private persons but presently in the possession of the State. The Government used the term *compensation* in a special sense: the sole legal basis for the partial compensation was fairness. The "fairness argument" became crucially important to the further history of compensation.

The very definite language of the decision underlined the principle that the former owners have no constitutional or subjective right to compensation, and the State has no obligation to compensate them. Compensation is a gratuitous act of the State, based exclusively on its sovereign decision. This argument of the Court had two far-reaching political effects: it gave the Government a free hand to determine the measure of the compensation and, to the great disappointment of the former owners, diminished their claim to a sort of morally justified right with no legally binding force. Thus, the decision upset the Smallholders, but gave the prime minister protection against the Smallholders' claims and pressure.

The Court then examined whether the discrimination among former owners and non-owners is in conformity with the Constitution. The argument followed the line designated by the above-mentioned former decision, namely applying the right to equal dignity test. "The constitutionality of the discrimination depends on whether the discrimination between owners and non-owners is realized in a procedure where the interests of former

---

22 Ronald Dworkin, Taking Rights Seriously 227 (1978).

23 Decision No. 9/1990, *supra* note 14.

owners and non-owners have been weighed with the same degree of prudence and impartiality.[24] The justification for discrimination within the group of former owners would be the purpose of achieving a more complete social equality, for the Constitution permits the positive discrimination only in order to promote the attainment of equality.

The ruling of the Court pointed out that there are at least two instances of unconstitutional discrimination in the Government's program: first, the discrimination among the former owners and non-owners in the process of privatization, and second, the discrimination among the former owners according to the type of the property. The position of the Constitutional Court was that "in this particular case differentiating on the basis of the type of the property becomes discrimination against persons since it relates to the acquisition of property."[25] The Court concluded its interpretation of Article 70/A of the Constitution by stating that "it is a discrimination against persons if certain persons' former property is reprivatized, while other persons' property is not returned to their possession, therefore, the Constitutional Court proclaimed this discrimination unconstitutional."[26]

The Takings Clause and Neutral Principles

The second question raised by the Government's position is whether it is constitutional to take land from the cooperatives without expropriation proceedings and compensation. The Takings Clause of the Hungarian Constitution is very firm: it permits expropriation only subject to very rigorous conditions, and it requires full, unconditional, and immediate compensation. The unusually stark language of this provision must be a reaction to the unlawful expropriations during the socialist era. The spirit of the problem was whether the Court should apply these very strict provisions to the cooperatives. The Court took the position that the Constitution must apply to all cases and to all persons, implicitly endeavoring to set up neutral constitutional principles in the interpretation. Neutrality in this sense means that the constitutional principles and provisions apply equally to everybody, and the past does not justify discrimination or other violations of the Constitution.

This implicit position of the Court provoked sharp criticism from some political groups, mainly from those that suffered severe injustices under the Communist regime. The critics even questioned the very legitimacy of the Constitutional Court; some stated that judicial review is not a necessary element of a constitutional State or of the rule of law. According to these critics, the Court acts contrary to the popular will expressed by the parliamentary majority. In the second question raised by the Government's

---

24 Judgment of Oct. 4, 1990, Alkotmánybiróság [Constitutional Court] No. 21/1900(X.4)AB, Magyar Közlöny No. 98/1990 (Hung.) (unofficial translation on file with the *Michigan Journal of International Law*).

25 *Id.*

26 *Id.*

petition, the real issue was the reprivatization of land owned by agricultural cooperatives without expropriation and compensation procedures. This was a delicate issue because these cooperatives were formed not voluntarily but by using coercive measures against peasants and smallholders. This coercion also was used in the incorporation of private land into the cooperatives. The standpoint of the former smallholders was that these properties were stolen, and, therefore, the protection of property rights should not apply to them.

The Court, after some hesitation, took a formal, normativist position. It considered the Constitution as a strict norm which should be enforced under any circumstances, where past injustices would not influence the present position of the constitutional institutions. The test of the cooperatives' constitutionality is voluntary association, irrespective of the history of their formation. Under Hungarian law, the only organ competent to decide whether a cooperative exists on the basis of voluntary or involuntary association is the general meeting of the members of the cooperative. The legal rules effective at the time of the decision allowed for both the closing down of a cooperative upon the decision of the general meeting and the departure of a member, but did not allow the distribution of the cooperative's property. Recently, however, the regulation has changed: the new regulation on the cooperatives makes it possible for the members of the agricultural cooperatives to leave the cooperative, and the cooperative must assign them their proportion of property.[27]

The Court's formal argument concluded with the strict protection of the cooperatives' property. In the Court's interpretation, the Property Rights Clause of the Constitution means that "the Republic of Hungary guarantees the right to property including the right of agricultural cooperatives to the arable land they own."[28] The taking of property from cooperatives without immediate, unconditional, and full compensation violates the Takings Clause of the Constitution, and is therefore unconstitutional, according to the ruling of the Court.

The ruling of the Court was formal and normative in terms of constitutionality, and it formulated the Court's policy on the strict observation of the rule of law. In contrast to such decisions of the Court, the acts of the legislature are the result of freely raised political arguments and concurring interests. If the Court accepted the same arguments, and made decisions in a similar way, arbitrarily taking into consideration the different principles, policies and interests, it would become a second legislative chamber. The role of judicial review, however, is not political deliberation but the control of constitutionality. Therefore, the Constitutional Court must adhere to objective standards[29] in the

---

27 1992 évi I törvény a szövetkezetekrol [Act No. I on the Cooperatives], Jan. 20, 1992, Magyar Közlöny No. 6/1992, at 73 (Hung.); 1992 évi II törvény a szövetkezetekrol szóló 1991 évi I törvény hatálybalépésérol és az átmeneti szabályokról [Act No. II on the Transitory Provisions Regarding The Law On Cooperatives], Jan. 20, 1992, Magyar Közlöny No. 6/1992, at 86 (Hung.).

28 Decision No. 21/1990, *supra* note 24.

29 *See generally* Kent Greenawalt, Law and Objectivity (1992) (discussing the question of objectivity in the domain of law).

interpretation of the Constitution. Accordingly, the Court in Compensation Case I, and in other cases as well, properly made efforts to define objective standards and follow those neutral principles.[30]

Compensation Case II—Self-Restraint or Activism?

During the ongoing discussion on the draft of the Compensation Bill, fifty-two parliamentary representatives (all members of the largest opposition party, the Free Democrats) proposed that the Constitutional Court review the constitutionality of some provisions of the bill. The resulting decision of the Court consists of two sharply different parts. The first part deals with the nature of preventive norm control and rejects the request to review the provisions of a bill which had not been decided yet by the Parliament. But the Court, contradicting its position in the first part of the reasoning, adds a second part. This second part enters into the discussion of the challenged provisions and gives guidelines to the legislature. Thus, the decision illustrates the Court's wavering between reasonable self-restraint and activism.

In order to analyze this case, it is necessary to understand the procedural peculiarities of judicial review in Hungary. The jurisdiction of the Constitutional Court includes both preventive and repressive norm control. Repressive norm control is the constitutional review of enacted laws; this is the most frequent and important jurisdiction of the Constitutional Court. It gives the Court the right to adjudicate the constitutionality of laws passed by Parliament. This is the most significant check on the supremacy of Parliament. This authority is further strengthened by the possibility that *anybody* can initiate the repressive norm control of parliamentary acts.

Preventive norm control, on the other hand, means the constitutional review of laws before their enactment. The Law of the Constitutional Court specifies the norms that are subject to preventive control. These are:

- bills,
- enacted but not yet promulgated statutes,
- Standing Orders of the Parliament, and
- international treaties.

The review of these special norms can be initiated by the following government authorities:

- the Parliament, any one of its standing committees, or fifty Members of Parliament,
- the President of the Republic, and
- the Government (in the narrower sense of the Executive Branch's Cabinet of Ministers)....

30 *See generally Toward Neutral Principles of Constitutional Law*, in Herbert Wechsler, Principles, Politics and Fundamental Law 3-48 (1961)(defining "neutral principles").

The shortcomings of the entire concept of preventive norm control came to light when the first demand for such control arrived at the Court in April, 1991. The Court, practicing considerable self-restraint, rejected the claim.[32] It investigated the nature of preventive norm control from a comparative perspective. The Court pointed out that it may make sense to review the constitutionality of a bill which is already disputed during the legislative procedure, because preventive norm control may prevent the annulment of an already-promulgated legal rule which has been put into practice. Furthermore, this type of procedure protects the prestige of the legislature. In countries where there is preventive norm control, the review is most often formal; that is, it is aimed exclusively at examining the constitutionality of the legislative procedure.

The Court quoted the text of foreign constitutions permitting the exercise of preventive norm control....

The Hungarian regulation does not constrain the Court's jurisdiction to the final text of the bill, but makes review possible at any stage of the legislative process. The Court declared that adjudicating the constitutionality of some provisions of a bill, the text of which is not definitive, could possibly mean involving the Constitutional Court in the everyday legislative process. The Constitutional Court is not an advisory organ of Parliament; its task is to judge the result of the legislative work. Therefore, the actual regulation of the preventive norm control of bills is incompatible with the principle of separation of powers.

The Court essentially refused to exercise its jurisdiction and thus, by implication, declared some provisions of the Act on the Constitutional Court as conflicting with a fundamental principle of the Constitution, namely the principle of separation of powers. Thus, after restricting its power to give advisory opinions, the Court also curtailed its power in another critical area. Both Compensation Cases corrected the inconsistent concept inherent in the Act on the Constitutional Court. These decisions, however, do not mean that the Court definitely took the road of self-restraint, though some commentators maintain that the Court became more sensitive because of the scholarly and political attacks on the legitimacy of judicial review in a representative democracy.[33] Rather, what the Court really did was to eliminate unreasonable or absurd duties.

In Compensation Case II, the Court did not stop at rejecting the possibility of preventive norm control. The justices supposed that the public would consider such cursory treatment to be escaping the issue. Therefore, they outlined a controversial opinion on the questions at stake (they called it the "theoretical stance of the Court"). In the abstract language describing this theoretical stance, the Court loosened the strictness of the scrutiny set up in Compensation Case I. The Court pointed out that the legislature has

---

[32] Judgment of Apr. 20, 1991, Alkotmánybiróság [Constitutional Court] No. 16/1991(IV.20)AB (Hung.).

[33] *See* Ethan Klingsberg, *Hungary: The Constitutional Politics of Compensation*, 2 Soviet & E. Eur. L. 1, 2 (Parker School Bulletin, Columbia University, June 1991).

excessive freedom in making distinctions in the details. They stressed the jurisdiction of Parliament and the government in deciding the concrete method and measure of the compensation. They also stressed the difference between the projects of the Government that had been adjudicated in Compensation Case I and the proposal admitted to Parliament. The Court recognized that the proposed bill abandoned the idea of reprivatizing land and intended instead to remedy through a unified "partial property compensation" the "unjust" damages caused in private property by the enumerated legal rules within the given period of time. The general justification of the bill emphasized that the State acted solely out of moral obligation, and that the extent of compensation may not be full.

The permissive language of the ruling could be considered an example of self-restraint, suggesting that within the broad limits of constitutionality it is the responsibility of the legislature and not the Constitutional Court to deal with political questions. Nevertheless, merely entering into the evaluation of the challenged proposal contradicted the first part of the ruling. Under the circumstances, the statement that the legislature must decide the question meant that the majoritarian standpoint would prevail, and the proposal of the Government would become law. Finally, the reasoning approving the proposal led the Court to disregard certain elements of the first decision.

Compensation Case III

Finally, in April 1991 the Compensation Law was passed by Parliament and was sent to President Arpád Göncz for signature. As mentioned above, the President of the Republic has the right to ask the Constitutional Court, before signing a law just passed by the legislature, to review the constitutionality of its provisions. This was the first time that the President exercised this right. His move was in harmony with the Court's position that review of constitutionality is possible only when the final text of the law is approved by the legislature. The President formulated six concrete questions; furthermore, he asked in general for the review of the entire Compensation Act. In answering the six questions, the Court upheld the provisions of the law in three cases, while in the other three cases it declared them unconstitutional.

The first question the Court answered referred to the entire concept of the Compensation Act as defined in the first Article of that Act. This article entitled all those natural persons to partial compensation (indemnification) whose property was violated as a result of enforcing legal provisions after June 8, 1949. (The compensation for the confiscation of church property was defined by Law No. 33 of 1991 passed by the Parliament on July 10, 1991.) The preamble of the Compensation Act also referred to the scope of the law by setting up a double purpose: first, the remedy for damages caused unjustly by the past regime, and second, the settlement of property questions.

The Court, after summing up its previous ruling on the subject, introduced a new element into the reasoning, stressing the extraordinary conditions and characteristics of the moment in which private property would be restored. Therefore, it upheld the constitutionality of the Compensation Law because it imposed a moral obligation to compensate the former owners. The key word in the Court's opinion was "novation" or "renewal." Actually, this novation has little to do with novation in the traditional legal sense of the word ("[s]ubstitution of a new contract, debt, or obligation for an existing one, between the same or different parties"[34]). Here, the emphasis is on the point that the new regime has no legal obligation to compensate the former owners, only a moral one. Therefore, the new legal obligation, defined in the Compensation Law creates an independent source of obligation. "The system of novation excludes the references to older legal titles. Since the novation is constitutionally permissible, there is no reason to review further, whether there were or could be claims for reprivatization in the scope of the effected proper damages".[35]

This gives the State great discretion in deciding on the method and measure of the compensation. It is interesting how this controversial linguistic invention tries to harmonize the special character of the transition with the concept of legal continuity. Because of all the extraordinary circumstances and considerations, the Constitutional Court considered the novation of the obligation and its fulfillment by partial compensation to be constitutional. This allowed the State free play, limited only by certain minor constitutional conditions. As put by the Court: "The novation may not violate any constitutional rights or principles."[36] Therefore, the government, even when acting on the grounds of this specific novation, has the obligation to act in such a way that "no affected party is put into a disadvantageous position."[37] This required, in other words, the application of the Equal Protection Clause to the present case.

Under this analysis, the Court held the Compensation Law to be constitutional. "The Act creates a uniform legal basis for compensation claims for those affected under the Act." According to the ruling of the Constitutional Court, the provision that violated the principle of equality was the one which arbitrarily set the starting date of the compensation at June 8, 1949. The Court investigated the entire process of compensation, reviewing both its content and its timing. The Court suggested as a possible remedy for the unconstitutional arbitrariness "that the Compensation Act determines those legal rules, whose application before June 8, 1949 caused the same type of damages as the ones compensated by the present Act, and indicates the final deadline, within which an Act of Parliament on the compensation related to those shall be drafted."[38]

---

[34] Black's Law Dictionary 1064 (6th ed. 1990).

[35] Judgment of July 3, 1991, Alkotmánybiróság [Constitutional Court] No. 28/1991(IV.3)AB, Magyar Közlöny No. 59/1991 (Hung.) (unofficial translation on file with the *Michigan Journal of International Law*).

[36] *Id.*

[37] *Id.*

[38] *Id.*

The Court also rejected another provision of the Act by referring to equal protection. Under the Act, the extent of a claimant's compensation depends upon whether the entitled person claims arable land as compensation or requests only the issuance of a compensation voucher. According to the general rules, the extent of the compensation is equal to 100 percent up to a damage of 200,000 Forint. If, however, the basis for compensation is land, and the person entitled to compensation requires this in the form of arable land, the extent of the compensation is equal to 100 percent up to the value of 1000 gold-crown. The multiplier of the damages in the case of arable land is 1000 Forint per gold-crown; therefore, the maximum compensation, 1 million forints, is five times more for those who formerly owned land. (Gold-crown, a currency used in the Austro-Hungarian Monarchy, is still the measuring unit of arable land in the Hungarian land records, and it reflects the net income of the land.) The government justified the differentiation with the additional costs and burdens pertaining to the land compared to other goods.

In addressing this issue, the Court made a very interesting and controversial analysis. It did not approach the question on purely theoretical constitutional grounds, but it tried to unravel the social impact of this provision. It attempted to determine whether the justification for the discrimination prescribed by the government was backed by sociological facts. It analyzed the data provided by the Land and Cartographic Office, and it came to the surprising conclusion that:

> if there were no distinction between the arable land and other property assets, about 94.2% of the former land-owners would have been in the 100% compensation. The benefits of the digression limit of 1000 gold-crowns are enjoyed only by 1.5% of the land. Only 6% of the land is affected by the determination of a separate digression limit. For at least 94% of the former land-owners the differing digression limit is indifferent; therefore, for the majority of the land proprietors the extra burdens mentioned in the reasoning are not counterbalanced by the benefits provided by the differing extent of compensation. With regard to them those reasons are not valid, and because of the lack of any other justification, the Constitutional Court declares the difference existing between the 1000 gold-crown and 200,000 Ft value limit as arbitrary and contrary to Article 70/A [Equal Protection Clause] of the Constitution.[39]

The Court approved the provisions, ensuring that the Compensation Law provided for claims to compensation by the entitled descendants and the spouse of a deceased person. The Court also approved another provision of the Compensation Law. While the language of Compensation Case I was explicit in protecting the property rights of cooperatives, Compensation Case II expressed a shift in the Court's standpoint. Compensation Case III made possible, to a certain extent, the compensation of the former land-owners by distributing the lands of the cooperatives. This approved the constitutionality of the Government's plan that compelled the agricultural

---

[39] *Id.*

cooperatives to set aside a certain part of their lands for the purposes of compensation.

The reasoning of the Court correctly justified this decision, but it did not really harmonize with the firmness of Compensation Case I.[40] The main line of argument was that there is a compelling interest in limiting the cooperatives' property rights, namely the transformation of the property of the cooperatives. "This double task is a part of the unique historical situation, in which the change in ownership as a task determined by the Constitution takes place, and in which the consequences of a former, opposite change of regime in property relations which is classified today as unconstitutional has to be settled."[41] As the cooperatives acquired their land property mostly from the State, there is no obstacle to compel them to distribute a part of it for compensation vouchers. It seems that the Court reevaluated its position toward the cooperatives that had been overly protective of their property in Compensation Case I.

In Compensation Case III, the *amicus curiae* brief of a law professor (András Sajó) and a study prepared by two leaders of the Alliance of the Free Democrats (János Kis and Mátyás Eörsi) alluded to the firm position of the Court in the compensation case. It was not by chance that the only dissenting opinion in Compensation Case III was written by Justice Imre Vörös, who considerably influenced the drafting of that part of the reasoning in Compensation Case I which deals with the protection of the cooperatives' property. (He did not take part in the decision of Compensation Case II.) His dissenting opinion considered both the entire concept of compensation and the particular provisions unconstitutional. He firmly stated that it is the State, rather than the cooperatives, that has to take responsibility for the damages.

The final text of the compensation law was approved by Parliament on June 26, 1991. President Göncz signed the amended version of the law, and it took effect on August 10, 1991. The legislature fully observed the rulings of the Court. A new provision was inserted in Article 1 requiring that a second law be passed no later than November 30, 1991, to compensate for the illegal confiscation of property between May 1, 1939 and June 8, 1948.[42] Under the new provisions the amount of land to be sold to holders of compensation vouchers cannot exceed fifty percent of the cooperatives' holdings. (About fifty percent of the cooperatives' land is owned by the cooperatives themselves; the other half is owned by the state or by the members.) This rule prevails even when the claims of the former owners exceed this percentage.[43]...

---

40 For a thorough evaluation of the compensation cases, put into the broad theoretical context, see Ethan Klingsberg, *Judicial Review and Hungary's Transition from Communism to Democracy: the Constitutional Court, the Continuity of Law, and the Redefinition of Property Rights*, 1992 B.Y.U. L. Rev. 41.

41 *Id.*

42 Actually, this second compensation law was passed by the legislature in April 1992.

43 Karoly Okolicsanyi, *Compensation Law Finally Approved*, RFE/RL Report on Eastern Europe, Sept. 6, 1991, at 22.

Conclusion: Law and Politics

There is much concern about the political role of judicial review. The fundamental claim is that judges and courts must stay away from politics; they should only interpret the law. But as far as judicial review gives the judiciary the power to invalidate ordinary legislation, and legislation is obviously not only a legal act but also the outcome of highly political debates, judicial review is necessarily involved in and linked to politics....

The history of the Compensation Case reveals that the Constitutional Court attempted to translate highly political questions into legal ones and give them correct legal answers. That history also illustrates the limited possibility of such efforts. These cases created a complicated task for the court because too many different interests and rationales were involved in them. Different and often conflicting issues were linked together in the complex task that the Compensation Law tried to solve.

A fundamental consideration was the economic rationality of the transition to a market economy and to a property system in which private ownership prevails. Another major issue was the moral approach to past injustices: how the State could compensate those whose property rights were gravely violated by the Communist regime. Compensation thus became the subject of a sharp political debate that divided both the society and the political parties. It is also an important part of the transformation of the legal system. Finally, in Hungary, where legislation has to face judicial review by an extremely powerful Constitutional Court, the issue also became an important constitutional question. The Court clearly strived to solve the extraordinary complex question solely on the ground of constitutionality.

The challenge to balance so many different considerations resulted in certain indeterminations and inconsistencies in the consecutive rulings. The first of these problems was whether the Constitutional Court should take an active part in the transition of the entire legal system or limit itself to the role of a final watchdog of constitutionality. The Court, led by its President, László Sólyom, took up an activist stand, not only curtailing and invalidating the unconstitutional acts of the legislation but also developing a concept of constitutional compensation as a guideline for the legislation. Both the first and second compensation cases served that aim, and only the third case can be considered judicial review in the proper sense. But even in the third decision, the Court outlined a possible remedy for the unconstitutional provisions. Though not expressly mentioned, the Court must have been led to this activism by a peculiar historical responsibility for the democratic transition....

Despite the difficulties of the issue and the inconsistencies of the three rulings, the Constitutional Court, after all, successfully faced the complex problems of compensation. As far as it was possible, the Court avoided the political pitfalls, and the rulings were correctly justified by legal arguments. The Court elaborated an important constitutional standard for the adjudication of equal protection and reverse discrimination. The compensation cases helped this young Court to develop a coherent philosophy on the supremacy of constitutionalism that helped it solve other hard cases (such as the statute of limitations case). In the future, the Court must further develop a comprehensive view of constitutionalism and interpretation.

The Compensation Law

Michael Neff, "Eastern Europe's Policy of Restitution of Property in the 1990's"[*]

On June 26, 1991, Hungary joined the growing number of countries offering restitution for property that was illegally seized by Communist countries.[113] However, Hungary's system is quite different from Germany or Czechoslovakia's because it makes no returns of property and offers no money back. Instead, Hungary offers indemnification vouchers that are paid on a fixed percentage basis depending upon the value of the confiscated property.[114]

The law declares a right to be compensated for property taken after May 1, 1939. However, the current law only considers property taken after June 8, 1949. A later law will address how the earlier property owners will be compensated.[115]

Although over 1.5 million people were expected to be eligible[116] for indemnification, only 53,821 claims have been made.[117] A total of 20 billion forints will be issued through vouchers for indemnification purposes.[118] The vouchers will be traded on the Budapest stock exchange as state securities in the first quarter of 1992.[119] The certificates have been available since the end of November 1991.[120]

The estimated value of the state property to be privatized is 1,800 billion forints. When the property is privatized, the local governments will share 300 billion forints and the social security system will receive 100 billion forints. The state budget will have 1,400 billion forints to service

---

[*] Excerpted from Michael Neff, "Eastern Europe's Policy of Restitution of Property in the 1990's," *Dickinson Journal of International Law*, vol. 10, no. 2 (Winter 1992), pp. 373-376.

[113] Hungarian Law No. 25 (1991) (hereinafter Hungarian Law) Proposal to settle ownership conditions for the partial indemnification of damages caused by the state in the property of citizens. It was adopted by the National Assembly at its June 26, 1991 Session, *Id.* at 21. (legislative intent).

[114] *Id.* §4 (2).

[115] *Id.* §1 (3).

[116] *Parliamentary debate on restitution in Hungary*, MTI Hungarian News Agency (Feb. 5, 1991) (LEXIS, Nexis library, Omni file).

[117] *Compensation certificate to be issued soon*, MTI Hungarian News Agency (Oct. 10, 1991) (LEXIS, Nexis library, Omni file).

[118] *Id.*

[119] *Id.*

[120] *Id.*

state debt. However, any amount returned during restitution would increase state debt.[121]

In order to avoid disputes over damage calculations, a fixed rate applies. Only those people whose property was worth less than 200,000 forints (approximately $2,700) will be granted full restitutional value. Since the budget does not allow full value reimbursement for every applicant, a regressive index of repayment has been established. For property valued from 200,001 to 300,000 forints, restitution is 200,000F plus 50% of the amount over and above 200,000F. For property worth 300,000-500,000 forints restitution is 250,000F plus 30% of amount over and above 300,000F. For any amount over 500,000 forints, the owner receives 310,000F plus 10% of any amount over and above 500,000F.[122] Additionally, the owner is entitled to seek restitution for all property under the same claim; however, the maximum amount returnable is 5,000,000F (approximately $70,000).[123] Included within these evaluations is the value of movable property that related to the land at the time of taking.[124]

These vouchers are issued by the office having jurisdiction over the land and are guaranteed by the state.[125] They can be used to purchase pieces of property; to buy stock and business shares sold in the course of privatizing state property; and for the acquisition of arable land property.[126] In addition, the holder of the voucher may use it as a method of payment for state-owned housing units;[127] for collateral on small business loans;[128] or for annuity payments for the entitled person's life.[129]

The following people are eligible to indemnification:[130] any present Hungarian citizens; former Hungarian citizens who had suffered damages; and non-Hungarian citizens who in a manner akin to carrying on their livelihood, resided in Hungary as of December 31, 1990.[131] The law also applies to descendants of owners or to former owners surviving spouses. However, property taken from a former owner before his death cannot be inherited through a will. Thus, the claim itself does not pass through inheritance. The reasoning is that allowing this would unfairly expand restitution.[132]

If recommended by the State Property Agency (SPA), the government may suspend purchases made by indemnification vouchers for a period not

---

121 *Parliamentary debate*, MTI Hungarian News (Feb. 5, 1991) (LEXIS, Nexis library, Omni file).

122 Hungarian Law. *supra* note 112, §4 (2).

123 *Id.* §4 (3).

124 *Id.* at 24 (legislative intent).

125 *Id.* at 23 (legislative intent).

126 *Id.* §7 (1).

127 *Id.* §7 (2).

128 *Id.* §7 (3).

129 *Id.* §7 (4).

130 *Id.* at 23 (legislative intent).

131 *Id.* §2 (1).

132 *Id.* at 23 (legislative intent).

to exceed six months per year.[133] This would be accomplished by freezing the use of bonds owned by a portion of the holders as identified by their bond serial numbers. The law permits this to be done only for the first five years of the process; subsequently, the vouchers can be used without restriction. This provision was enacted to ensure an adequate cash and property flow for the government during the privatization process. This is very important because the property subject to privatization serves as collateral for indemnification vouchers.[134] The government does not want too many vouchers pursuing too little land. It is feared that if the certificates are issued faster than the pace of privatization, the papers would quickly lose their value due to inflation.[135]

Although the vouchers may not be totally liquid during the first five years, the government has granted interest to be paid on the vouchers at a 3/4 percentage rate of the current central bank rate. Interest accrues at the inception of the law and continues through the first three years of the law. The relatively low rate was intended to encourage the holders to quickly make use of their vouchers.[136]

The person entitled to indemnification does hold pre-purchases rights when his former property is to be sold. Exceptions would include rental housing units owned by a local government, property belonging to a corporation, or the sale of a corporation that owned property by the SPA.[137] This prepurchase right granted to the former owner is the least powerful of that in any of the countries offering restitution. However, the stated intent of this law is partial indemnification, not reprivatization.[138] The fewer the privileges granted, the quicker the process will continue.

Karoly Okolicsanyi, "Compensation Law Finally Approved"[*]

Under the first version of the law, former landowners could exchange their property bonds for their original land. In the second version, however, land owned by the agricultural cooperatives will be auctioned off to the highest bidder, regardless of whether he or she is the former owner of the land. Both local residents who receive compensation bonds and present members of the cooperatives can participate in the bidding.[6] The insertion of the clause on land auctions in the second version was in response to another concern of the Constitutional Court: the court reasoned that to return land to its former owners while barring the similar restitution of

---

133 *Id.*

134 *Id.* §8 (1).

135 *Id.* at 26 (legislative intent).

136 *Parliamentary debate*, MTI Hungarian News Agency, (Feb. 5, 1991) LEXIS, Nexis library, Omni file).

137 Hungarian Law. *supra* note 113, at 25 (legislative intent).

138 *Id.* §9.

* Excerpted from Karoly Okolicsanyi, "Compensation Law Finally Approved," *Report on Eastern Europe*, vol. 2, no. 36 (September 6, 1991), p. 23.

6 *Vilaggazdasag*, June 19, 1991.

other types of property to former owners or their descendants was discriminatory.

Nevertheless, thanks to the last-minute lobbying efforts of the Independent Smallholders' Party, the main force behind the compensation law, former landowners still came away with the more favorable compensation terms. Former landowners who commit themselves to keeping the land under cultivation for at least five years will be compensated for 100% of the value of their land, not to exceed 200,000 forint ($2,700). In addition, an "agricultural production support" grant of up to 800,000 forint is provided. Thus, former landowners who agree to cultivate their land for the next five years will, in fact, have up to 1,000,000 forint ($13,500) with which to bid for their former land. (All cooperatives that still possess land once belonging to these owners are required to hold such an auction.[7])

Michael Neff, "Eastern Europe's Policy of Restitution of Property in the 1990's"[*]

Persons entitled to compensation may submit petitions in writing for indemnification within ninety days from the effective date of this law.[139] This time period is the shortest one seen. Legislative intent suggests it was done to speed the process and to prevent legal uncertainty.[140] However, it seems that the time period might not be long enough to enable interested parties to become aware of restitution. Therefore, the legislative intent provides that one acting without fault may apply after the deadline.[141]

The county office where the petition is filed has a deadline of six months from receipt of the petition to make a decision. Documents that verify entitlement should be included with the application.[142] Should the original application be submitted incorrectly, an extension of time would be granted to refile.[143] This deadline can be extended once for a period of no longer than three months.[144] Special rules apply for arable land because of its limited supply and special income potential; therefore, arable land must be sold at auction to entitled persons.[145]

The county office decides whether the petition for restitution should be granted; its decisions are appealable to the national damage claims office. The law provides for judicial review of final decisions rendered by the national office through courts which are empowered to review and change decisions in full.[146]

---

[7] *Heti Vilaggazdasag*, July 7, 1991.

[*] Excerpted from Michael Neff, "Eastern Europe's Policy of Restitution of Property in the 1990's," *Dickinson Journal of International Law*, vol. 10, no. 2 (Winter 1992), p. 376.

[139] *Id.* at 27 (legislative intent).

[140] *Id.* §11 (1).

[141] *Id.* at 28 (legislative intent).

[142] *Id.* at 12, §12 (legislative intent).

[143] *Id.* § 12 (2).

[144] *Id.* § 12 (3), §13.

[145] *See id.* §12-30, *See also id.* at 22 (legislative intent) *See also* Robinson, *Year of record crops—Agriculture*, The Financial Times, Oct. 30, 1991.

[146] Hungarian Law, *supra* note 113, at 28 (legislative intent).

*Karoly Okolicsanyi, "Compensation Law Finally Approved"**

The [law] stipulates that the amount of land to be sold at auctions to holders of compensation bonds cannot exceed 50% of the cooperatives' holdings, even if the claims by former owners exceed this percentage.[9] On average, 20% of the agricultural cooperative's land is state-owned; 30% is owned by individual cooperative members; and only about 50% is owned by the cooperatives themselves. This means that only about 25% of a cooperative's land can be offered for sale at auctions. To provide the land auctions with enough land to meet the claimants' demands, state-owned land will also be put up for sale. Finally, workers in cooperatives who did not "bring in" any land will receive 30,000 forint in bonds; administrative employees will receive 20,000 forint in bonds.[10]...

Anyone who had his property confiscated by the Communists will be able to submit a claim between August 10 and November 8, 1991, to the National Compensation Offices, which will have six months to rule on the case. To facilitate the implementation of the law, the government issued an executive decree that established the precise procedures for land auctions, guidelines for deciding which former owners are entitled to which properties, and so on.[11] A number of legal, perhaps even constitutional, issues may still have to be sorted out.

The Law and the Agricultural Cooperatives

There is some speculation as to whether the new law will bring about the demise of the agricultural cooperatives. Estimates put the number of applicants for compensation at up to 1,500,000 for land and another 60,000 for apartments and other assets.[12] Some claim, however, that the descendants of former owners will not be interested in partial compensation and that there will be no major labor movement back to agriculture, despite the fact that the compensation law gives people willing to cultivate the land some distinct advantages (such as the 800,000-forint "agricultural production support" grant). An Agriculture Ministry study estimated that if all compensation claims were transformed into land purchases, 400,000 hectares would be needed to satisfy all the claims;[13] this is just over 10% of the land now cultivated by the agricultural cooperatives. Thus, compensation claims will not mean the end of cooperatives, although in theory if the claims were numerous enough many of them might cease to exist.

In the end, however, unresolved questions (determining the value of property at the time it was confiscated, calculating its current worth, and

---

* Excerpted from Karoly Okolicsanyi, "Compensation Law Finally Approved," *Report on Eastern Europe*, vol. 2, no. 36 (September 6, 1991), pp. 23-24.

9 *Magyar Hirlap*, June 25, 1991.

10 *Ibid.*

11 *Heti Vilaggazdasag*, August 3, 1991.

12 *Nepszabadsag*, June 13, 1991.

13 *Vilaggazdasag*, August 8, 1991.

ascertaining the number of direct descendants, for example) mean that it is impossible to predict with any degree of accuracy how the situation will eventually turn out. It could be that the number of claimants will be significantly higher than estimated and the land claims considerably greater than for the 400,000 hectares assumed. Moreover, if the prospective bidders for private land decided to join forces to keep prices down, they could end up buying more land than expected. Given all these possibilities, an attempt to predict whether the agricultural cooperatives will survive on a large scale is premature....

Supply and Demand

Because of legal uncertainties and complex valuation problems, it is also difficult to forecast the number of compensation bonds that will be issued. This is not surprising, since many claims are for property confiscated as long ago as 43 years. The Hungarian authorities will have difficulty in finding sufficient privatization possibilities and purchasable land to match the supply of new bonds, which are a form of money. It is, however, very important for them to do so, since compensation bonds for which no property is available for purchase will lose their value. Hungarians who lost their property and who expect to receive at least partial compensation would then receive little or nothing. Aware of this danger, the lawmakers included a proviso in the compensation law allowing the government to suspend for up to six months every year the exchange of compensation bonds for property. In addition, the State Property Agency may decide to raise its current 10% limit on the acceptance of bonds to pay for privatized property.[14] Moreover, the matching of compensation bonds with properties available for sale should be greatly facilitated by the Hungarian stock exchange, which, because it can trade in property bonds, will serve as a secondary source of purchasable property.

Assessment

Many aspects and implications of the compensation law are still unclear, including the effect of land privatization on agricultural production, the amount of inflationary pressure that will ensue from the issuance of the compensation bonds, and to what extent the law's implementation will increase the government's budget deficit. Even so, the law, which is based on remote but legal inheritance rights, does address the grievances of private property owners who lost their land or other property through nationalization or forced agricultural collection. And while it provides only partial, symbolic compensation, if properly implemented it will create a substantial number of small property owners who could serve as catalysts in accelerating the pace of privatization and private production, reforms that Hungary badly needs.

---

14 *Magyar Kozlony*, no. 77, July 11, 1991.

Other Forms of Compensation and Rehabilitation

*Alexander H. Platt, Imtiaz T. Ladak, Alan J. Goodman, Matthew R. Nicely, "Compensating Former Political Prisoners: An Overview of Developments in Central and Eastern Europe"**

1. Voiding of Convictions

On February 19, 1992, the Hungarian Parliament unanimously adopted Law No. 11 voiding convictions for crimes committed against the state and political order between April 5, 1963 and October 15, 1989. Among the convictions invalidated by the new law are the following: conspiracy, insurrection, or incitement against the state or another socialist state; offending an authority or an official person; offending the community; incitement against a law or action by the authorities; abuse of the right to associate with others; rebellion; provoking insubordination; attempts to cross illegally to the West; refusal to return to Hungary from visits abroad; and other convictions related to, and adjudicated jointly with, those enumerated above.[40]

In the preamble to the law, the National Assembly stated that many sentences handed down during Communist rule had violated the constitution in effect at the time and that it was therefore appropriate to provide political, moral, and legal compensation to those convicted.[41]

2. Financial Compensation

[a. Law No. 32: Compensation for Unlawful Deprivation of Life or Liberty]

In addition to the law invalidating prior convictions of political prisoners, the Hungarian National Assembly also adopted on May 12, 1992, Law No. 32 providing financial compensation to those persons (or the families of those who died as a result of their sentence) who for political reasons were unlawfully deprived of life or liberty between March 11, 1939, and October 23, 1989.[42]

For persons still alive who were imprisoned, interned, deported, or sentenced to do forced labor for the Hungarian or Soviet authorities, this law grants a one-time payment in the amount of 11,000 forints for each month the person was unlawfully deprived of liberty. Where such persons have since died, the law entitles their spouse to 5,500 forints for each

* Excerpted from Alexander H. Platt et al., Akin Gump, Srauss, Hauer, & Feld, *Compensating Former Political Prisoners: An Overview of Developments in Central and Eastern Europe*, unpublished paper, August 14, 1992, pp. 12-15.

40 Law No. 11, *Magyar Kozlony*, no. 24, 9 March 1992, pp. 979-980....

41 *Id.*

42 Law No. 32, *Magyar Kozlony*, no. 56, 2 June 1992. To date, both Hungarian and English translations of this law have not been available for review.

month the person spent in captivity.[43] Persons are eligible for this payment regardless of whether they live in Hungary. However those still living in Hungary may elect to draw an annuity instead of receiving the lump sum payment.[44]

For families of those persons who lost their lives as a result of unlawful sentences handed down by Hungarian courts (including capital punishment or other sentences in which intent to cause death can be imputed), the law grants a one-time payment to the family of the person in the amount of one million forints.[45] Surviving spouses, parents, and descendants are eligible for this payment. However, a surviving spouse will receive 50 percent of the payment and all other family members must split the remaining 500,000 forints. If no family members are still living except for the person's siblings, then the siblings are entitled to a payment under this law, but only in the amount of 500,000 forints (if there is more than one sibling, then they must divide this amount among themselves). Again, persons are eligible for payment under this provision regardless of whether they live in Hungary.

[b. Executive Decree No. 93-1990: Increasing Pensions for Former Political Prisoners]

Prior to passage of Law No. 32, an executive decree was signed in 1990 which extends an increase in the monthly pension for those persons who were subject to unlawful deprivation of liberty during Communist rule between 1938 and 1989. This remains in effect despite the new legislation. The rationale for the decree is that if these persons were not unlawfully deprived of their liberty, they would have been working.

According to a Hungarian diplomat, this decree provides for an increase in an eligible person's pension of 500 forints per month for the first year spent in captivity, 250 forints per month for the second through fifth years spent in captivity, and 300 forints per month for each year spent in captivity over five years.

c. Pending Legislation

In addition to the measures already in place, the National Assembly is also considering a law that would compensate those persons (or their families) who were victims of crimes which the state did not prosecute for political reasons. This legislation is pending [as of August 1992].

---

43 The criteria for "spouse" under this provision of the law are that they must have been the person's spouse at the time of the unlawful deprivation of liberty, and also at the time of death.

The exchange rate at the time of this writing is approximately 76 forints per U.S. dollar. Hence, this law provides nearly U.S.$145 (or half that for the spouse) for every month the person was unlawfully deprived of liberty.

44 The law contains provisions setting forth a formula that takes age and other factors into account if a person elects to receive an annuity instead of a flat sum.

45 Based on the present exchange rate, this would amount to about U.S.$13,158.

18

BULGARIA

EDITOR'S INTRODUCTION

Bulgaria was aligned with Nazi Germany through most of World War II. In September 1944, as Soviet forces occupied Bulgaria, a partisan coalition known as the Fatherland Front seized power. The Communist Party soon dominated the coalition, aided by the continuing Soviet occupation. Controlling the interior and judicial ministries, the Communists used a system of terror to eliminate all opposition. On the premise of punishing fascists and war criminals, they created a people's militia and a network of people's courts which conducted the most extensive purge per capita of any country in the region. Official accounts recorded 2,730 people sentenced to death and 1,305 to life imprisonment by April 1945; unofficial estimates put the total in the tens of thousands. By December 1947, when a new constitution declared Bulgaria a "people's republic," the Communists had consolidated their control. In 1949, Vulko Chervenkov became minister president. Known as "the Stalin of Bulgaria" for his emulation of the Soviet dictator, Chervenkov collectivized nearly all agriculture, instituted Soviet-style five-year plans, reduced Western influence, and purged 100,000 members of the Communist Party, sending many to labor camps.

In 1954, Todor Zhivkov was named leader of the Bulgarian Communist Party (BCP) and became a protégé of the new Soviet leader, Nikita Kruschev. In 1956, following on Kruschev's denunciation of Stalin, Zhivkov launched a similar attack on Chervenkov, leading to the latter's ouster. By 1962, Zhivkov purged the BCP of all opposition and became premier. In line with Krushchev's thaw, Zhivkov instituted the "New Course," allowing an initial decrease in the brutality of the repression and a relaxation of cultural controls. Zhivkov improved economic and living standards while consolidating efforts at collectivization and nationalization. The economy continued to improve until beginning a marked decline in the 1980s.

This initial relaxation did not characterize the regime. The party and the political police ruled with impunity. Freedoms of speech, press, assembly, and religion were tightly restricted. Dissenters were sent to labor camps or execution following summary trials. Torture and beatings were common in prisons. Ethnic minorities suffered discrimination. From 1984-1989, Zhivkov conducted a campaign of forced assimiliation against the ethnic Turks who comprised 10% of the population, forcing them to adopt Bulgarian names and barring them from using the Turkish language or practicing their religious customs or culture. Acts of resistance were harshly suppressed, culminating in the exodus of some 350,000 Turks to Turkey.

Coupled with the faltering Bulgarian economy, Mikhail Gorbachev's democratic reforms in the USSR had a strong impact. Throughout more than forty years of communist rule in Central and Eastern Europe, Bulgaria had remained the most loyal adherent of Soviet wishes. Having long stressed this allegiance to Moscow, Zhivkov obligingly announced a reform program in 1987, although he still demonstrated little interest in real change. Calls for political reform and openness became widespread as new independent groups appeared and quickly gained popularity. On November 10, 1989, members of the BCP ousted Zhivkov and arrested him on charges of corruption and abuse of power. The new government, headed by Petar Mladenov, announced a program of economic, political, and legal reform.

The name of the BCP was changed to the Bulgarian Socialist Party (BSP); several newly-formed parties joined in an anti-Communist coalition known as the Union of Democratic Forces (UDF). In the June 1990 elections, the BSP won a narrow majority in the new Grand National Assembly, but Mladenov was soon forced to resign after evidence emerged that he had ordered the use of tanks to put down a pro-democracy demonstration. The Assembly elected UDF leader Zheliu Zhelev as president. The UDF won a majority of seats in the parliamentary elections of October 13, 1991 and Zhelev was popularly elected president in January 1992.

Many called for a reckoning with former Communist officials. To permit the prosecution to reach earlier Communist offenses, the existing 20-year statute of limitations was revised retroactively to 35 years for certain categories of crimes. A number of former officials, ranging from Todor Zhivkov to prison guards, were prosecuted for past abuses.

Although the UDF advocated broad public access to the files of the former secret police and their use in screening, a January 1993 Penal Code amendment closed the files on national security grounds and imposed criminal penalties for dissemination of information from the files. After striking down two screening laws adopted by parliament as unconstitutional, in 1993 the Constitutional Court upheld a third purge law.

A 1990 amnesty for political prisoners was followed by a 1991 law providing for their compensation and rehabilitation. The 1991 "Land Tenure Act" provided for restitution of property seized by the state; by October 1993, over 30 percent of the land subject to restitution had been restored.

The following documents related to transitional justice in Bulgaria can be found in Volume III of this collection:

- Law on Banks and Credit Activity
- Constitutional Court Decision on Law on Banks and Credit Activity
- Law for Additional Requirements of Some Additional Requirements for the Members of the Executive Bodies of Scientific Organizations and the Higher Certifying Commission ("Panev Law")
- Constitutional Court Decision on the Panev Law
- Law on Political and Civil Rehabilitation of Oppressed Persons
- Law on Amnesty and Restoration of Confiscated Property and Implementing Regulations

OVERVIEW

*Commission on Security and Cooperation in Europe, "Human Rights and Democratization in Bulgaria"**

Trials of communist-era officials are but one component of Bulgaria's attempts to wrestle with and overcome the legacy of its communist past, in what is commonly referred to as decommunization. As in other East-Central European states, it was the policies of the ruling Communist Party that were responsible for the egregious human rights violations, not to speak of economic and environmental ruin. Recognizing its own bankruptcy, the Bulgarian Communist Party in 1990 changed its name to the Bulgarian Socialist Party [BSP], and in 1991 even accepted responsibility for the country's economic woes. Soon after the fall of Zhivkov, decommunization measures such as the depoliticization of the police and military, the firing of many Interior Ministry officials, and the dismantling of Communist Party cells at workplaces took place.

In fall 1991, the BSP was accused of massive misappropriation of funds from the state between 1944 and 1990, and most of its financial assets were

* Excerpted from Commission on Security and Cooperation in Europe, *Human Rights and Democratization in Bulgaria* (September 1993), p. 20.

frozen by the Bulgarian Supreme Court. On the other hand, attempts to formally ban the BSP obviously have been unsuccessful. For example, on March 11, 1993, the Supreme Court ruled against a lawsuit calling for the BSP to be declared illegal.

*Józef Darski, "Police Agents in the Transition Period"**

In August 1990, the communist-dominated parliament set up a verification commission [of collaborators with the secret police] and appointed Georgi Tambuyev to be its head. But in December of that year, when the commission recommended publicizing the names of deputies who had been secret collaborators, parliament nixed the idea. In any case, the commission probably didn't even have access to all the relevant files, since the communist minister of internal affairs put at their disposal only what he thought they should see: files of former secret collaborators of the sixth department of the ministry, but not of current collaborators of the new Bureau for the Protection of the Constitution. (In the latter case, the committee was only supplied with personal statistics and the date of recruitment.)

Back in February 1990, the minister of internal affairs liquidated the sixth department together with local divisions of the political police. The most senior functionaries were asked to retire; the rest, however, were offered the opportunity to carry out "tasks arising from the new conception of the rebuilding of the Ministry of Internal Affairs"—that is, employment in the Bureau for the Protection of the Constitution. At that time, some of the collaborators ceased their work for the interior ministry, and their files were given to the parliamentary commission. But many of the collaborators—including all of those in parliament—were reassigned to the first, second, and third departments, thereby avoiding verification. According to the interior ministry official who passed the files to the commission, the list of secret collaborators of the other departments who were deputies at the time included 80 names—20% of the deputies in parliament....

Despite the pressure applied by the interior ministry on Tambuyev "to lock up or destroy the dossiers of the political police" in the interest "of social peace," the commission proceeded with its work. Only the commission's leaders—Tambuyev, Deputy Chairman Rumen Danov, and Stamboliski—had access to the files that were given to the commission. Yet when Tambuyev prepared a draft of a report on the commission's work that included confidential information taken from the files, the information somehow wound up in the hands of the post-communist publication *Fax*, which published a list of 32 names in its April 22, 1991 issue. As it turned out, one of the commission's members, Tsanko Tsankov, was a collaborator who had been transferred from the sixth to the second department.

---

* Excerpted from Józef Darski, "Police Agents in the Transition Period," *Uncaptive Minds*, vol. IV, no. 4(18) (Winter 1991-92), pp. 19-21.

The first list of collaborators in parliament supplied by the interior ministry included 25 names. Eleven seemed questionable, because torture and other forms of coercion had been used to force them to collaborate....

In the end, the communist-dominated parliament decided not to make the commission's report public and sealed the files of secret collaborators for 30 years. Some of the deputies even proposed burning the dossiers. Only part of the opposition was against these measures.

*Helsinki Watch, "Decommunization in Bulgaria"**

On October 13, 1991, the Union of Democratic Forces won 110 seats to 106 for the Bulgarian Socialist Party (BSP) in the parliamentary elections, and thereby became the first government without socialist members to be elected in Bulgaria since World War II. Following the UDF's electoral victory, many of its members intensified their calls for purging the government, as well as many other social, educational, and economic institutions of former communists.

The UDF, which had been the umbrella organization for all major opposition factions in Bulgaria following the events of 1989, had split in July 1991. The precipitating event was disagreement over the passage of a new constitution. However, the divisions between the members who today make up the UDF, and those members who ultimately left the UDF, also include disagreement over the speed and extent of any decommunization program.

Certain elements of the UDF (known as the "Dark Blue") associated with former Prime Minister Filip Dimitrov, strongly favored a rigorous decommunization program, as well as a rapid transition to the free market. The "Light Blue" faction within the UDF (who left the party) favored a less radical approach to decommunization. Those members of the UDF (the "Dark Blue") who, in coalition with the Turkish Movement for Rights and Freedoms, controlled the parliament after the elections of October 1991 were significantly more anti-communist and were advocates for a thorough decommunization plan.

President Zhelev, who ran on the UDF ticket and was elected directly with 54 percent of the vote, has since split with the UDF and, in general, opposes lustration laws....

---

* Excerpted from Helsinki Watch, *Decommunization in Bulgaria*, vol. 5, issue 14 (August 1993), p. 3.

Purge Laws

Helsinki Watch, "Decommunization in Bulgaria"[*]

Draft Lustration Laws

During 1992, several lustration bills were drafted by UDF deputies and submitted to the parliament for consideration. A bill for "Overcoming the Consequences of Communist Rule" ... was introduced by UDF deputies Verzhiniya Velcheva, Vassil Gotsev and Alexander Pramatarski on February 10, 1992.

The proposed bill would ban from public office for five years certain categories of persons who had held leadership positions between September 9, 1944, and January 1, 1990. These positions included, among others, members of the Politburo of the Central Committee of the Bulgarian Communist Party; chairs and deputy chairs of the State Council and of the National Assembly (parliament); prime ministers and vice-premiers; first secretaries and secretaries of district and regional committees of the BCP; chairs of the Central Council of the Bulgarian Trade Unions; and first secretaries and secretaries of the Central Committee of the Dimitrov's Communist Youth League (DCYL)....

Shortly thereafter, on February 14, 1992, the "Law on Decommunization in the Sphere of Government" ... was introduced by Sasho Stoyanov, Alexander Karadimov and another 20 UDF deputies. This bill, known as the "hard" bill, would expand the list of those categories of banned individuals to include lower level Communist Party officials such as "secretaries of local Communist Party organizations, employees who were members of the `nomenclature' of the Central or District Committees of the BCP, lecturers at the Academy of the BCP, and associates of the former State Security."[8]...

Two other lustration bills were submitted to the parliament for consideration during 1992. The "Public Servants Act" would also ban certain categories of persons similar to those listed above from holding public office. Finally, the "Law on Democratization" was introduced by deputy Tosho Pejkov on September 9, 1992....

None of the four bills discussed above have reached a vote in the National Assembly. After the Constitutional Court ruled, in July 1992, that two lustration provisions were unconstitutional (see discussion below), there was some reluctance to submit further laws to constitutional scrutiny.

---

[*] Excerpted from Helsinki Watch, *Decommunization in Bulgaria*, vol. 5, issue 14 (August 1993), pp. 4-15.

[8] "Human Rights in Bulgaria After the October 1991 Elections," Bulgarian Helsinki Committee, (October 13, 1992), p. 8.

The Banking and Pension Laws

In addition to the draft lustration legislation discussed above, the National Assembly included lustration provisions in several substantive pieces of legislation. Two such laws, the Transitional and Concluding Provisions of the Law for Banks and Credit ("Banking Law") and the Amendments to the Pension Law ("Pension Law") were adopted by the National Assembly during 1992. On March 4, 1992, the National Assembly adopted the Transitional and Concluding Provisions of the Law for Banks and Credit which provides, in Article 9,

> No persons can be elected to executive positions or hired on the basis of Article 7, if in the last fifteen years they have been elected in the central, regional, county, city, or municipal governing bodies of the Bulgarian Communist Party, the Comsomol, the Fatherland Front, the Union of Active Participants in the Struggle against Fascism and Capitalism, the Bulgarian Trade Unions, and the Bulgarian Agrarian Union, or who have been appointed to a full-time executive position in the Central Committee of the Bulgarian Communist Party, as well as employees, paid and unpaid collaborators of the State Security. This limitation will be in [force] for five years.[9]

Forty-nine members of the National Assembly submitted a petition to Bulgaria's Constitutional Court challenging the law on the basis of Article 6(2) of the constitution which states that

> All citizens shall be equal before the law. There shall be no privileges or restrictions of rights on the grounds of ... opinion, political affiliation....[10]

The petition also challenged the Banking Law as a violation of international human rights documents which are considered part of Bulgaria's domestic legislation.[11]

Similarly, on June 12, 1992, the National Assembly added a "lustration" provision to the "Amendments to the Pension Law." Article 10(a) states:

> Under this law, the period during which a person has worked at a paid managerial post in the organs and party organizations of the Bulgarian Communist Party, the Fatherland Front, the Dimitrov Young Communist League and the Union of Active Fighters against Fascism and Capitalism is not considered years of employment [for purposes of determination of retirement benefits].[12]

---

[9] Transitional and Concluding Provisions of the Law for Banks and Credit, Article 9, *Official Gazette*, (Issue 25, 1992).

[10] Bulgarian Constitution, Article 6(2).

[11] See the Bulgarian Constitution, Article 5(4), which states: "Any international instruments which have been ratified by the constitutionally established procedure, promulgated and come into force with respect to the Republic of Bulgaria, shall be considered part of the domestic legislation of the country. They shall supersede any domestic legislation stipulating otherwise."

[12] Amendments to the Pension Law, Article 10(a), *Official Gazette*, (Issue 52, 1992).

The constitutionality of Article 10(a) of the Pension Law was immediately challenged before the Constitutional Court on the initiative of President Zhelev.

The Constitutional Court's Decisions

The lustration provisions of both the Banking Law and the Pension Law were considered by the Constitutional Court during July 1992. In Decision Number 8 of July 27, the Constitutional Court held that Article 9 of the Banking Law was unconstitutional. The court based its decision on the equal protection provisions of the Bulgarian Constitution (Article 6), as well as on Article 48(3) of the Constitution which guarantees each citizen the right "to choose his occupation and place of work." What is more, the court also held that Article 9 violated

> the International Covenant on Civil and Political Rights, the International Covenant on Economic, Social and Cultural Rights, and the International Labor Organization Convention No. 111 concerning discrimination in the field of labor and the professions, as well as the Vienna Convention on the Right of Contracts, which have been ratified by the constitutionally-established procedure, promulgated and come into force and are considered part of the domestic legislation of the country and hence supersede any domestic legislation stipulating otherwise.[13]

Similarly, on July 29, the Constitutional Court issued its decision regarding the constitutionality of Article 10(a) of the Pension Law. In Decision Number 11, the court held that Article 10 was unconstitutional in that it violated the constitutionally guaranteed right to social security.[14] The court concluded that the provision

> deals with persons who were incorporated in pension security. By the force of Article 10(a) of the Pensions Act, these persons will be denied, completely or partially, of the years of employment needed for retirement. What we have here is a restricted or completely violated right to social security, which is incorporated in Article 51 (1) of the Constitution. This is one of the basic rights of the citizens of the Republic of Bulgaria and neither its revocation nor restriction is stipulated by the Constitution....

[The Panev Law: Another Attempt at Lustration Legislation]

After the Constitutional Court struck down the Banking and Pension Laws' lustration provisions, the drafters of other lustration bills temporarily delayed further attempts to introduce lustration legislation. However, on December 9, 1992, the Law for Temporary Introduction of Additional Requirements for Members of the Executive Bodies of the Scientific Organizations and the Higher Certifying Commission (referred

---

13 [omitted]

14 The Constitution of the Republic of Bulgaria, Article 51(1) states that: "Citizens shall have the right to social security and welfare aid."

to as the "Panev Law" after its drafter), which had passed on first reading in mid-July, was adopted by the National Assembly....

Article 3 of the Law states, among other things, that [through 1997] only those individuals may hold positions in the executive bodies of scientific organizations and the Higher Certifying Commission who can show that they:

> 1) have not been members or candidate members of the Political Bureau or the Secretariat, or of the Central Committee of the former Bulgarian Communist Party (BCP);
>
> 2) have not been secretaries or members of regional, city, community, county or district committees of the BCP;
>
> 3) did not hold positions before November 10, 1989 which were directly accountable to either the Political Bureau or the Secretariat of the Central Committee of the BCP...;
>
> 4) have not been on the staff or voluntary collaborators of the State Security or the Security and Guard Departments;
>
> 5) have not compromised themselves through participation and involvement in the "revival process";[15]
>
> 6) have not been on the teaching and research staff of the Academy for Social Sciences and Social Management and its branches...;
>
> 7) have not taught History of the Communist Party of the Soviet Union, History of the Bulgarian Communist Party, Marxist-Leninist Philosophy, Political Economy, Scientific Communism or Party Building;
>
> 8) have not been political officers or deputy commanding political officers and have not held positions in the political headquarters of the Armed Forces;
>
> 9) have not been secretaries or members of party committees of the Bulgarian Communist Party in the higher schools and academies, have not been secretaries of the Party organizations of the Bulgarian Communist Party in the faculties, scientific institutes and other scientific organizations, have not been members of personnel commissions under the party committees of the higher schools, academies or other scientific organizations.

The Law requires all persons working in the executive bodies of scientific organizations and the Higher Certifying Commission to provide written statements regarding their prior employment and party activities. The refusal to provide such a statement is regarded as an "admission that the person does not meet the requirements for membership" in these organizations....

Although President Zhelev had consistently opposed lustration measures, he failed to use his authority to return the Panev Law to the parliament for reconsideration. Zhelev signed the bill into law [and] joined a petition challenging the law before the Constitutional Court....

---

15 The "revival process" occurred in Bulgaria between 1984 and 1989. During this time, ethnic Turks and Roma (Gypsies) were imprisoned, forcibly resettled, forced to adopt Bulgarian names, and restricted in many other ways, in an effort to forcibly assimilate them.

[The Constitutional Court's Decision on the Panev Law]

The Panev Law was challenged by 102 members of the National Assembly. Their petition to the Constitutional Court ... argued that the law violated the constitutional right to equal protection (Article 6(2)), to hold opinions without persecution or interference (Article 38), to freely choose an occupation and place of work (Article 48(3)), to academic autonomy for higher educational establishments (Article 53(4)), and to have labor guaranteed and protected by law.

On February 19, 1993, the Constitutional Court issued a six to five decision[16] holding that the Panev Law does not violate the Bulgarian Constitution.... The court stated:

> It is a groundless claim that the requirements are aimed at the political opinion and political affiliations of these persons.... The law is disinterested in past and present political opinion and political affiliation; it takes into consideration only the professionalism of those who will participate in the realization of the national policy in science administration and development. That is why the criterion for membership in administrative boards is the scientific commitment of the person, but not the activities, which has served political and ideological party purposes.[17]

...By defining the provisions of the law as merely "additional requirements", the court avoids the constitutional issues. The court concludes that the Panev Law violates neither the Bulgarian Constitution nor international human rights documents because these do not restrict the state's right to impose additional professional requirements. For example, the court states:

> With the introduction of additional requirements to the members of the administrative boards in the scientific organizations and the Higher Certifying Commission, the civil rights protected by the listed international agreements are not violated. As far as these requirements might be considered as a restriction on the basis of professionalism, this kind of restriction is admissible.

The court also rejected the argument that the law interferes with academic autonomy, stating:

> The law only requires that the members of administrative boards should be scientists with high professional qualities, who have not deviated from scientific work by being engaged in organizational or ideological party work. The law is also applicable to persons from the scientific communities who have combined party activity and administrative functions while taking part in scientific councils, commissions in the administration of scientific organizations and their branches.

---

16 The Constitutional Court's ruling is, technically, a non-decision, although its effect is to uphold the Panev Law. For the Court to have held the Panev Law unconstitutional, seven justices would have had to vote against the law. (There are twelve justices on the Constitutional Court. One justice was absent for the decision in this case.)

17 [omitted]

The court has created a fiction in its reading of the law. The law does not set future professional standards, but establishes a penalty for prior membership and/or activities. To the extent that it deals with the holding of certain positions within the Communist Party and other organizations, it is a violation of the right to free association and expression that are guaranteed in the Bulgarian Constitution and international documents. To the extent that the law deals with prior behavior of individuals, it imposes a penalty that is retroactive in nature. With the possible exception of some conduct that might be included within the extremely vague phrase "participation and involvement in the "revival process," it is clear that none of the conduct covered by the Panev Law was prohibited by Bulgarian or international law.

Finally, to the extent that the court views certain conduct or the holding of certain positions as indicative of a lack of professional competence, each individual covered by the law should be presumed innocent and should have the opportunity to present evidence of that innocence to an independent body. The law, however, provides no such procedural protections.

The Constitutional Court's decision came as a surprise to many who have been monitoring the lustration process in Bulgaria. The court's own decision in the Banking Law case seems to be in direct conflict with its ruling on the Panev Law.... Most of those interviewed by Helsinki Watch considered the law and the court's decision to be motivated by political considerations, and to have little to do with efforts to improve the professional qualifications of those in elected positions within academia.... Boris K. Rolev, professor in the Geography Institute of the Academy of Sciences, stated:

> I don't deny that there were people who became scientists because of their Communist Party membership, and I agree that there should be strict scientific criteria for members of Scientific Councils, but the law does not provide these standards.... The Panev Law is similar to a law in 1945 that kicked out qualified persons with bourgeois backgrounds. In both instances, it is a case of collective guilt without any evaluation of professional qualities....

Implementation of the Panev Law

The implementation of the Panev Law has increasingly affected the atmosphere in Bulgaria's institutions of higher education.... The Panev Law has had a direct impact on the ability of academic bodies to determine by means of secret elections who their leaders will be. Certain categories of individuals who are enumerated in the law cannot be considered for these elected positions....

Many of those interviewed by Helsinki Watch also pointed out that those considered most abusive and compromised by their political pasts had, in fact, already been voted out of the governing bodies of the university prior to the Panev Law. To take away the power of the electing bodies to choose those colleagues which they consider best able to govern the university is a direct interference by the government in the academic autonomy of the university.

The law has created chaos and confusion in the governing bodies of the university. Several faculties initially refused to implement the Panev Law. However, most of these faculties ultimately called new elections for the governing boards out of fear that their institutes might be detrimentally affected during the current process of restructuring academic institutions. Only one department, the History Department at Sofia University, has not called a new election of the dean or faculty council. Other faculties have not been able to elect faculty councils with the prescribed minimum number of members because there were not enough members who could, or would, sign a declaration under the law. In such cases, members outside the respective faculty were required to sit on the faculty board to establish a legal governing body. As one professor stated, "It is questionable whether any of the recently elected faculty councils were elected in compliance with regulations regarding higher education."

The Panev Law has also created severe tensions among colleagues within the university faculties. Reports estimate that the Law has already "led to the removal of several thousand formerly communist-affiliated academic staff from managerial positions."[18]... Dr. Sredkova told Helsinki Watch:

> During the last three years, the communication between faculty members has been very good. It has not been influenced by political developments as it was prior to November 1989. After the 1990 elections, we were very free to choose our leaders within the university, and we appreciate what it means to be free to choose. Before, the Communist Party told us who could hold leading positions, now someone else tells us. In both cases, it is an interference with academic freedom.

Many other faculty members spoke of their fear that academic freedom remains in jeopardy in Bulgaria....

The law is most detrimental in that it denies individuals the right to a fair and individual evaluation of their professional qualifications and moral integrity. Dr. Todorova stated:

> The categories of the law do not allow for a review of the factors that caused certain individuals to take certain party positions, or teach certain courses in the university. It also ignores the important and positive role that some Communist Party members played in the democratization process. Although most members of the Philosophy Department were in the Communist Party, it has always had a reputation as a free-thinking faculty and was a place of democratic attitudes prior to November 1989. Some of the members of the faculty were among the bravest—they dared to oppose the Communist Party, and now they suffer because of the law. The main impact of the law has been to treat all individuals as collectively guilty.

---

[18] Kjell Engelbrekt, "Bulgaria's Communists: Coming or Going?" *RFE/RL Research Report*, Vol. 2, No. 21, May 21, 1993, p. 40.

Although the Constitutional Court argued that the Panev Law only deals with professional standards, in fact, the law establishes categories of people that are defined as unprofessional without any effort to evaluate their qualifications. Inherent in the law is the presumption that all who, for example, taught Marxism-Leninism were unprofessional. The Court makes the assumption that anyone who combined advocacy work for the Communist Party of Bulgaria with his or her scientific work could not have been a good scientist. Such persons have, therefore, forfeited the right to be elected to the executive bodies and High Certifying Commission of scientific departments....

Although there have been recent initiatives in the Bulgarian National Assembly to introduce amendments to the Panev Law or to pass a law that would significantly reduce the impact of the law, these initiatives have made little progress....

*Commission on Security and Cooperation in Europe, "Human Rights and Democratization in Bulgaria"**

UDF parliamentarians have accused the new majority in parliament (which includes the BSP, ethnic-Turkish MRF and some former UDF parliamentarians) of blocking the passage of decommunization laws....

As the ex-communist BSP is still a commanding force on the Bulgarian political scene, there are worries of "recommunization," especially among the opposition UDF. Despite the BSP's continuing, and even growing, influence, it is unlikely that Bulgaria will witness the reestablishment of communism. In response to persistent UDF criticism, President Zhelev has given assurances that recommunization in Bulgaria is out of the question. At the same time, however, he has opposed lustration legislation.

A January 1993 parliamentary decision to prohibit the divulging of secret police files could impede decommunization efforts. This decision effectively overturns some of the decommunization efforts of the UDF-Dimitrov government. According to a penal code amendment, individuals spreading information related to the activities of the secret police can be sentenced to three years in jail, and in the case of an official or if the information is spread by mass media, up to six years.

* Excerpted from Commission on Security and Cooperation in Europe, *Human Rights and Democratization in Bulgaria* (September 1993), p. 21.

PROSECUTION OF PAST ABUSES

The First Trial of Former President Zhivkov

Kjell Engelbrekt and Duncan M. Perry,
"The Conviction of Bulgaria's Former Leader"[*]

In September [1992,] Todor Hristov Zhivkov was given the dubious honor of being the first former communist leader in Eastern Europe to be tried in a court of law, found guilty, and punished. Following an eighteen-month trial, on 4 September Zhivkov was found guilty of embezzlement and sentenced to seven years' imprisonment. The Sofia court convicted the eighty-one-year-old former chief of the Bulgarian Communist party (BCP) and head of state of having given cars, apartments, and other valuable items to his family and closest aides either free of charge or at token prices. Zhivkov, who governed Bulgaria for thirty-five of the forty-six years or so of communist rule, claims that he has been made a scapegoat and is appealing the decision.

The Turning of the Tide

Zhivkov fell from power on 10 November 1989 in a coup orchestrated by his associates in the Politburo and BCP Central Committee. A political pragmatist, even toward the end of his rule he had made efforts to adapt to a rapidly changing situation. After Mikhail Gorbachev had taken power in the Soviet Union in 1985, *glasnost* and *perestroika* were proclaimed in Bulgaria as well, although they were little in evidence. Zhivkov's chief problem was that because of his long rule he had no one to blame for the country's problems; and he feared that if the media were granted greater freedom, he would be subject to criticism, which might undermine his position. During the last four years of his rule, Zhivkov tried to balance the interests of the Soviet Union, on whose political and economic support Bulgaria remained dependent, against those of himself and his chief subordinates.

But Zhivkov was not, of course, able to alter the course of events in other East European countries. Beginning in 1987, Bulgarian dissident actions—inspired by developments in other communist states—gradually got out of control.[1] Also, owing to his forced assimilation campaign against ethnic Turks, which was conducted between 1984 and 1989 and resulted in the country's international isolation, Zhivkov had become a real liability

---

[*] Kjell Engelbrekt and Duncan M. Perry, "The Conviction of Bulgaria's Former Leader," *RFE/RL Research Report*, vol. 1, no. 42 (October 23, 1992), pp. 6-8.

[1] The groups destined to become most influential during the critical phase of democratic transition from 1988 to 1990—the Discussion Club for the Defense of *Glasnost* and *Perestroika*, the Independent Association for the Defense of Human Rights, and the Independent Confederation of Labor Unions *Podkrepa*—were founded during this period. Their stated goals were to "assist" the government in establishing greater freedom of the press, improving its human rights record, and finding a solution to pressing environmental problems. Several members of these groups were arrested but not tried; some were exiled internally.

for the BCP. In the fall of 1989 the government, which continued to alternate force with tolerance, came under increasing criticism. In connection with an international ecological conference in Sofia in October 1989, sponsored by the Conference on Security and Cooperation in Europe, for the first time Bulgarians turned out on the streets to demonstrate, and international pressure on the government mounted. Only one month later Zhivkov was forced from office in what appears to have been a palace coup of Petar Mladenov, the former longtime minister of foreign affairs, and several of his associates. Mladenov subsequently replaced Zhivkov as head of state, a post he held until anticommunist demonstrations in the summer of 1990 forced his resignation.

Zhivkov Powerless

Almost immediately after his fall, Zhivkov found himself isolated within the BCP. Almost all his former supporters and comrades-in-arms chose to abandon him. He became ill in 1990; at the same time, charges of malfeasance were brought against him. It was rumored that he would reveal all and implicate a large number of former communist leaders in illegal and unethical practices; no such revelations were made, however. Continuing to deny any wrongdoing, Zhivkov demanded immunity from prosecution by virtue of having been head of state.

Only weeks after his removal from office the public began to clamor for Zhivkov to be tried for the wrongdoings that Bulgarian society had suffered during the communist era. Bulgaria's new rulers quickly decided to imprison Zhivkov. Preparations for a trial began after the former president had been arrested on 18 January 1990, but as it became clear that the process would be drawn out seemingly indefinitely, popular enthusiasm for prosecuting Zhivkov gradually diminished. When in 1990 and 1991 the governments dominated by the Bulgarian Socialist Party (BSP, the successor to the BCP) did little to press the issue of Zhivkov's trial, legislators and other politicians associated with the Union of Democratic Forces (UDF), the umbrella coalition now in government, demanded that Zhivkov be brought to justice.

A Controversial Trial

The trial, which opened on 25 February 1991 and produced 110 volumes and 216,000 pages of evidence, lasted eighteen months. On several occasions the proceedings had to be postponed owing to Zhivkov's poor health. The defense consistently pleaded not guilty, contending that the accusations of embezzlement were based on "political and moral" grounds, on which, it argued, a head of state could not be convicted. In addition, Zhivkov's lawyers objected to the charge of abuse of office between 1962 and 1989, arguing that this had become a crime only after an amendment had been made to the relevant Bulgarian legislation in 1986.[2]

---

[2] See, for instance, *Die Tageszeitung*, 5 September 1992.

Many observers have criticized the fact that Zhivkov was tried for embezzlement and not for more serious crimes. In particular, it has been said that the former communist leader ought to stand trial as the instigator of the forced assimilation campaign against ethnic Turks. However, the prosecution decided, probably for a number of reasons, to begin by examining accusations of embezzlement and corruption. One of its first tasks was to try to substantiate allegations that Zhivkov had diverted millions of US dollars to personal Swiss bank accounts. When these allegations could not be verified (and today it is generally thought that they were unfounded), the prosecution began probing into a number of less spectacular claims of corruption where, it believed, it would be on more secure ground.[3]

At the same time, the prosecutors may have thought that embezzlement charges were less likely to stir up a political controversy. In 1990 and 1991—when the criminal investigation was under way—there was still widespread popular support for Zhivkov's anti-Turkish policies, as evidenced by the wave of nationalist demonstrations in January 1990. Thus, the authorities may have decided to avoid provoking further ethnic tension. Moreover, the time was probably not ripe for a trial that would have included a political evaluation of the Zhivkov era. As long as a BSP-dominated government remained in power, former communist officials could deny the prosecution access to vital documentation.

Today, nationalism is a less potent political force and Zhivkov's fate is of less concern to the public. Zhivkov now faces the prospect of being tried for at least four other offenses....

The Sentence

Although Prosecutor Krasimir Zhekov had demanded ten years' imprisonment, Zhivkov was sentenced to seven for having misappropriated 21.5 million leva ($24 million at the rate of exchange then). By a vote of four to three of the judges, the court found he had "exceeded his rights and powers" as a state official by reselling at token prices sixty-seven cars and by distributing seventy-two apartments and public funds among his closest aides and members of his family. Zhivkov was also ordered to repay the money he had embezzled. In the same trial his loyal ally Milko Balev, whom Zhivkov had granted the rare privilege of serving simultaneously as secretary of the Central Committee and member of the Politburo, was sentenced to two years in prison for violating foreign currency regulations.[5]

Still, Zhivkov was found not guilty on the charge of embezzling an additional 26.5 million leva. The court considered that this had not been proved, especially since no document signed by Zhivkov himself had been produced. Somewhat surprisingly, it also ruled that the former communist leader did not have to serve his sentence in a regular jail but could remain under house arrest in his granddaughter's villa in a Sofia suburb.

---

[3] See Kjell Engelbrekt, "Bulgaria's Communist Legacy: Settling Old Scores," *RFE/RL Research Report*, no. 28, 10 July 1992.

[5] BTA, 4 September 1992.

Zhivkov's immediate reaction was that the verdict had been fabricated and was "directed against the Bulgarian people." He argued that he had been selected as a scapegoat, denouncing the trial as a political farce. Prosecutor Zhekov, for his part, said that the sentence was too light and that he would appeal to a higher court.[6]

Other Criminal Cases

Helsinki Watch, "Decommunization in Bulgaria"[*]

In addition to having been convicted on corruption charges, Zhivkov and several other former officials currently face criminal charges for their involvement in giving aid to communist governments. On July 22, 1992, Zhivkov was indicted for having used public funds to provide communist governments such as Cuba, the People's Democratic Republic of Yemen, Nicaragua, Mozambique and Afghanistan with military and economic assistance that contributed to the economic disaster in Bulgaria. Ivan Tatarchev, Prosecutor General of Bulgaria, estimates that credits were given to these countries in the amount of 264 million dollars and 56 million rubles. In addition, 63 million dollars, 50,000 Deutschmarks, and 120,000 tons of crude oil were given in aid or forgiven credits.[19] Similar charges have also been brought against [21 other former state and Communist Party officials, including] former prime ministers Grisha Filipov, Georgi Atanasov, and Andrei Lukanov, as well as two former secretaries of the Bulgarian Communist Party, Emil Khristov and Stoyan Milchaylov.

Upon a request from the Chief Prosecutor's Office, the National Assembly stripped Andrei Lukanov, former prime minister and member of parliament for the BSP, of his parliamentary immunity on July 7, 1992. Two days later, on July 9, he was arrested and charged with having misappropriated state funds. As discussed above, Lukanov is being prosecuted for decisions by the Council of Ministers under the government of Georgi Atanasov, of which Lukanov was acting Vice-Chairman, to grant aid to certain socialist countries.

Lawyers for Lukanov, as well as for the other defendants in the case, argue that the conduct for which they are charged resulted in no personal gain for the defendants and, therefore, did not violate Bulgarian law. They also insisted that "the Government unlawfully singled out Lukanov and several others for what were ostensibly collective policy decisions taken by a former government."[20] The Government, however, denies such charges and asserts that there is evidence to show that each defendant charged has individual criminal guilt.

---

[6] *The Independent*, 5 September 1992.

[*] Excerpted from Helsinki Watch, *Decommunization in Bulgaria*, vol. 5, issue 14 (August 1993), pp. 15-16.

[19] "Prosecutor to Arrest, Try Former BCP Leaders," FBIS-EEU-92-127, July 1, 1992, p. 10.

[20] U.S. State Department Country Report on Bulgaria, (1992), p. 731.

Helsinki Watch [and a number of other international observers expressed] concern about the prosecution of Lukanov. Helsinki Watch stated:

> Helsinki Watch is concerned that the Penal Code may never have been intended to prohibit what appear to be routine government decisions regarding the distribution of aid and that the language of the code may not give Bulgarian citizens sufficient notice of the conduct being prohibited. Helsinki Watch urges you to take every measure to ensure that the prosecution of former government officials is not motivated by political considerations and to prosecute officials only for acts that were clearly prohibited at the time they were committed.

Kjell Engelbrekt and Duncan M. Perry, "The Conviction of Bulgaria's Former Leader"[*]

In July [1992] the Constitutional Court rejected a request by fifty-one BSP deputies that the decision to lift Lukanov's parliamentary immunity be reversed. The court ruled that the decision did not violate the constitution and argued that it was not competent to judge whether Lukanov's alleged crime was serious enough to warrant such a measure.[10] Lukanov himself pledged innocence in a series of articles in the BSP daily, *Duma*, as well as in an open letter to Catherine Lalumiere, secretary-general of the Council of Europe.[11] He ... received support from the International Parliamentary Union, which on 12 September [1992] included Bulgaria among countries that [were] considered to have recently violated the rights of parliamentary deputies.[12]

Helsinki Watch, "Decommunization in Bulgaria"[†]

On December 30, 1992, Lukanov was released from prison after the National Assembly voted, on December 29, to rescind the Government's authority to arrest him....

Many observers criticized the prosecutor general's office for having focused on economic abuses while ignoring grave human rights abuses committed by Zhivkov and his colleagues during communist rule. Some observers speculated that prosecutors may have concentrated on the less controversial economic charges first, as opposed to such crimes as the brutal assimilation campaign against Bulgaria's minorities, because of the political climate in Bulgaria. "In 1990 and 1991—when the criminal

---

[*] Kjell Engelbrekt and Duncan M. Perry, "The Conviction of Bulgaria's Former Leader," *RFE/RL Research Report*, vol. 1, no. 42 (October 23, 1992), p. 8.

[10] *Darzhaven vestnik*, no. 64, 7 August 1992.

[11] *Duma*, 3 August 1992.

[12] Reuters (Stockholm), 12 September 1992. The International Parliamentary Union denounced the detention and treatment of Lukanov (a parliamentary deputy since 1976), saying that his arrest could not be justified on the grounds of having granted aid to developing countries in his capacity as prime minister).

[†] Excerpted from Helsinki Watch, *Decommunization in Bulgaria*, vol. 5, issue 14 (August 1993), p. 17.

investigation was under way—there was still widespread popular support for Zhivkov's anti-Turkish policies.... Moreover, the time was probably not ripe for a trial that would have included a political evaluation of the Zhivkov era. As long as a BSP-dominated government remained in power, former communist officials could deny the prosecution access to vital documentation."[23]

After the electoral victory of the UDF in October 1991, however, the political climate became more conducive to prosecution of Zhivkov and his associates for more serious human rights abuses committed during communist rule. At the current time, observers estimate that the number of officials under investigation for past abuses is between 50 and 60.[24]

Commission on Security and Cooperation in Europe, "Human Rights and Democratization in Bulgaria"[*]

In October 1992, Bulgaria's last communist Prime Minister, Georgi Atanasov, was sentenced to 10 years imprisonment, and former Economics Minister Stoyan Ovcharov to 9 years, for embezzlement of state funds during the late 1980's. Not unexpectedly, these and other convicted former officials have charged that the trials were unfair and politically motivated, although most observers agree that due process in these trials has been observed.

Other former officials—former Deputy Premier Grigor Stoichkov and former Deputy Health Minister Lyubomir Shindarov—were convicted in 1991 to three and two year prison terms respectively for withholding information about the aftereffects of the Chernobyl nuclear accident.

Helsinki Watch, "Decommunization in Bulgaria"[†]

Zhivkov faces charges related to his involvement in the assimilation campaign of Bulgaria's ethnic and religious minorities during the mid-1980s. In June, Zhivkov was charged with having incited racial hatred and having violated the Convention on the Elimination of All Forms of Racial Discrimination for having initiated the sometimes brutal campaign to "Bulgarianize" Turks, Pomaks and Gypsies. Petar Mladenov, ex-President and former Minister of Foreign Affairs, is also charged with crimes related to the assimilation campaign. This trial has not yet begun.

In June [1993], Zhivkov was also indicted for having set up two labor camps ... where 147 people died during 1959-62 due to brutal mistreatment. Former Minister of the Interior Mircho Spasov and four senior camp officials—Petar Gogov, Nikola Gazdov, and Tsvyatko Goranov—together

---

[23] Kjell Engelbrekt and Duncan M. Perry, "The Conviction of Bulgaria's Former Leader," *REF/RL Research Report*, (Vol. 1, No. 42, October 23, 1992), p. 7.

[24] *Ibid.*, p. 9. Also, Helsinki Watch interview with United States Ambassador to Bulgaria Kenneth Hill, June 1992, Sofia.

[*] Excerpted from Commission on Security and Cooperation in Europe, *Human Rights and Democratization in Bulgaria* (September 1993), p. 18.

[†] Excerpted from Helsinki Watch, *Decommunization in Bulgaria*, vol. 5, issue 14 (August 1993), pp. 17-18.

with Yuliyana Razhgeva of Skravena camp—[were] indicted for murder for their treatment of inmates in these camps.[25]...

Commission on Security and Cooperation in Europe, "Human Rights and Democratization in Bulgaria"[*]

In a June 1993 trial of [the] four former Bulgarian labor camp guards, the country's Prosecutor-General Ivan Tatarchev demanded the death sentence, given the extreme cruelty practiced at the 1959-1962 Lovtech camp. The defense objected to the trial on the grounds that Bulgaria's 20-year statute of limitations had expired. These objections were rejected by Tatarchev who maintained that Bulgaria did not have a normal legislative system at the time and that there should be no statute of limitations "for such crimes against humanity."...[†]

Five former State Security officials are also on trial in Ruse for applying unnecessary force and detaining ethnic Turks in an improvised labor camp in 1989. According to Radio Free Europe, it is the first time civil servants are being prosecuted for their actions during the forcible assimilation campaign.[2] ...

In August 1993,... Lukanov was formally charged for his role in donating hard currency, arms and other assistance to communist organizations abroad.

In January 1993, the parliament voted to strip former BSP leader Alexander Lilov of his parliamentary immunity. Lilov, a former leader of the Bulgarian Communist Party, also faces charges similar to those against Lukanov. The BSP strongly protested the parliament's actions as being politically motivated.

These efforts to hold former officials responsible for past misdeeds should be seen as part of the overall democratization of Bulgaria, according to a [Radio Free Europe] report on Bulgaria's communist legacy.

> As a result of this process, people may learn more about aspects of their common past that previously were concealed; those who eventually rewrite Bulgaria's postwar history may be given invaluable material; and in the long run, a contribution may be made to the restoration of respect for the law and moral values.[3]

Others, however, view these trials as politically motivated attempts to seek revenge, rather than efforts to ensure that justice is done. Given the politically charged atmosphere in Bulgaria today, even the most sensitive handling of these cases will probably provoke criticism.

---

[25] RFE/RL Vol. 1, No. 28, July 10, 1992, p. 7.

[*] Excerpted from Commission on Security and Cooperation in Europe, *Human Rights and Democratization in Bulgaria* (September 1993), pp. 18-20.

[†] [Editor's note: The trial was postponed in July 1993 because of the death of one of the defendants. The trial of the other three labor camp guards resumed on June 7, 1994.]

[2] RFE-RL, *Daily Report*, August 4, 1993.

[3] Kjell Engelbrekt, "Bulgaria's Communist Legacy: Settling Old Scores," *RFE/RL Research Report*, July 10, 1992.

Some apprehension has been expressed with respect to a draft law that would provide amnesty for several thousand criminal defendants who had been convicted by People's Courts during 1944-45. While many of these people were imprisoned for political reasons, others were convicted for genuine war related crimes. In April 1992, the European parliament issued a resolution urging the government to withdraw this bill because of its blanket coverage.

AMNESTY AND COMPENSATION

*Alexander H. Platt, Imtiaz T. Ladak, Alan J. Goodman, Matthew R. Nicely, "Compensating Former Political Prisoners: An Overview of Developments in Central and Eastern Europe"**

In December 1990, the Government of Bulgaria proclaimed an official amnesty for former political prisoners.[56] According to Amnesty International's 1992 annual report, Bulgaria had released all its political prisoners by January 1991.

A number of former political prisoners have created an organization called "Union of the Repressed" to work on behalf of the victims' interests. According to Mr. Krismir Kostov, Press Attache at the Bulgarian Embassy in Washington, a parliamentary declaration in 1990 proposed financial compensation for them, but a group representing former "repressed" persons refused to accept it, saying that monetary compensation could not make up for what they had suffered and lost.

According to Mariana Katzarova, a Bulgarian journalist working at the Freedom House in New York, the *majority* of former political prisoners in Bulgaria are not willing to accept financial compensation from the government because, in their view, money cannot possibly make up for what they lost. Despite this resistance from the potential recipients of aid, the government in Bulgaria has proceeded to pass several pieces of legislation that attempt to compensate political victims of the Communist regime....

On January 15, 1990, the Bulgarian National Assembly enacted legislation to rehabilitate, or restore the good name of, opposition figures killed, imprisoned or exiled by the Communist regime in Bulgaria during the 1940s, '50s and '60s.[57]

The National Assembly has passed two other laws that pertain to former political prisoners and other victims of the Communist regime: (1) a law enacted on January 19, 1990, that deals in part with amnesty for

* Excerpted from Alexander H. Platt et al., Akin, Gump, Strauss, Hauer, & Feld, *Compensating Former Political Prisoners: An Overview of Developments in Central and Eastern Europe*, unpublished paper, August 14, 1992, pp. 21-23.

56 Amnesty International Report 1992, at 74.

57 Facts on File World News Dig., Jan. 19, 1990, at 34. We have been unable to obtain English translations of relevant Bulgarian legislation. Thus, the following analysis is based on secondary source material and lengthy conversations with experts familiar with Bulgarian legal developments.

political crimes and lifting of certain criminal penalties; and (2) a law enacted on January 4, 1991, that concerns amnesty and the return of confiscated property. The latter law grants a general amnesty to individuals who were convicted of "political" crimes prior to November 10, 1989. It also mandates the return of property that was seized following their convictions.[58]

According to Stephan Kyutchukov, a Bulgarian lawyer at the Center for the Study of Democracy in Sofia, the National Assembly has passed several laws to provide monetary assistance to those who were convicted and imprisoned, or simply accused and imprisoned, for crimes "invented" by the Communist regime. He said that the new laws entitle former prisoners to damages for pecuniary losses, for pain and suffering, and for loss of consortium. The laws also provide restitution of property or financial compensation for property seized by the Communists. Regulations to implement these laws have also been passed. An extremely important question produced by the legislation is how to prove one's status as a former political prisoner to become eligible for compensation, in the absence of comprehensive prison records. According to Mr. Kyutchukov, testimony by one's former fellow prisoners should be an acceptable form of proof.[59]

[A] 1991 law entitled "Political and Civil Rehabilitation of Repressed Persons"[60] ... contains the following provisions:

- Individuals persecuted for political reasons between 1942 and 1989 are declared to be politically and civilly rehabilitated;
- Rehabilitated individuals have a right to a one-time monetary recovery for non-property and property-related damages;
- Time that politically repressed persons spent in prisons, labor camps, detention areas, or in forced relocation areas is counted as "service time" for pension purposes.[61]

---

58 Telephone interview with Ivan Sipkov, a specialist in Bulgarian law in the European Law Division of the Library of Congress Law Library (July 20, 1992)....

59 Telephone interview with Stephan Kyutchukov, a lawyer at the Center for the Study of Democracy in Sofia, Bulgaria (July 16, 1992)....

60 Telephone interview with George Peichenov of the Consular Section of the Bulgarian Embassy in Washington, D.C. (July 16, 1992)....

61 This information is from an unofficial annotation of the Act on Political and Civil Rehabilitation of Repressed Individuals, provided by Mitroslav Sevlievski, National Secretary of the Bulgarian Association for Fair Elections and Civil Rights, in Sofia, Bulgaria.

Land Restitution

*Deyan Kiuranov, "Assessment of the Public Debate on the Legal Remedies for the Reinstatement of Former Owners and the Realization of Liability for Damages Inflicted by the Totalitarian Regime"**

As the restoration of rights in immovable property to former owners and their heirs presents and will be presenting the greatest difficulties, the methods in which owners were deprived of these rights in the past will be summarized below.

1. Most immovable property was nationalized under three laws: the 1946 Confiscation of Speculatively and Illegally Acquired Property Act (CSIAP), the 1947 Nationalization of Private Industrial and Mining Enterprises Act (NPIMEA), and the 1948 Expropriation of Large-size Urban Realty Act (ELURA).

The package of these three acts provided the legal mechanisms to dismantle the existing economic system and create a centralized economy. History deals with the effect of all three laws under the blanket heading of "nationalization."

Under the 1946 CSIAP, all movable and immovable property, moneys, shares of stock, etc. acquired by speculation or in any illegal manner since January 1, 1935 were subject to State confiscation.... The law defined as "speculation" any activity by a natural or legal person which could be proven beyond reasonable doubt to have excessively increased his property holdings through profit, commission charges, fees, incomes or the like, obtained while the country was in difficult circumstances. For the purposes of the same law, the following was considered as acquired in illegal manner: (a) property obtained by public office holders (including members of parliament), by natural or legal persons in connection with a crime or malfeasance, or through direct or indirect abuse of authority for pecuniary advantage; (b) property obtained in any form whatsoever for or in connection with anti-popular activity. Any enhancement of the property holdings of natural or legal persons, which they could not prove to be justified by normal income from the bona fide exercise of a trade or use of their own property or capital or, in the case of public office holders, from their earned income, qualified as acquired by speculation or in illegal manner. Confiscation extended to the heirs and the legatees of persons coming within the provisions of the law, as well as to third parties who had acquired without payment property from owners subject to confiscation.... A characteristic feature of this law was its retroactive effect, as well as the surprisingly wide range of persons who came within its provisions.

Under the 1947 NPMIEA, all private industrial and mining enterprises were nationalized and converted into state property, with the exception of

---

* Excerpted from Deyan Kiuranov, *Assessment of the Public Debate on the Legal Remedies for the Reinstatement of Former Owners and the Realization of Liability for Damages Inflicted by the Totalitarian Regime*, unpublished paper (Center for the Study of Constitutionalism in Eastern Europe, 1991), pp. 1-7, 9-10, 12-14, 16-20, 22-25.

cooperative and craft enterprises and printing establishments owned by public organizations. The owners of the nationalized projects were paid compensation with interest-bearing government bonds. The following were disqualified from compensation: (a) those who served or collaborated with the German state, its army or units during the last World War, or with the Italian fascist state, army and units until their surrender to the United Nations; (b) those who served or collaborated with the Bulgarian fascist police, gendarmerie or army, and those who operated against the fighters against fascism and their organizations between March 1, 1941 and the end of 1944; (c) foreign agents and spies and those implicated in activities aimed at the restoration of the fascist dictatorship from September 9, 1944 until the entry of the law into force. Under this law, nationalization was applied universally, without consideration for the owners' past conduct which only mattered with respect to compensation. Just as characteristically, Parliament voted this act with immediate effect at a time when the parliamentary opposition was already eliminated.

For the purposes of the 1948 ELURA, large-size urban realty meant immovable property within the town plan limits, owned by private persons or partnerships, which was not intended to meet the owners' housing needs, to derive essential extra income or to satisfy direct economic requirements, but rather was used to obtain income in the form of rent on capital invested in that property. Such realty was subject to expropriation and nationalization. The State further expropriated real estates (built-up or otherwise), owned by members of the same family and located within the built-up city limits, in excess of the one or two real properties permitted by law. Under that law, the following were exempt from expropriation: rural immovable property; immovable property of working people, obtained or built to meet their housing needs or to secure an extra income for the support of their families; one residential real estate or shop premises per family; premises used for self-employed labour.

2. A number of immovable properties were nationalized by confiscation imposed as punishment in criminal cases, especially after the crack-down on the opposition after 1946, as well as when political and economic emigrants were deprived of Bulgarian citizenship.

3. A large amount of property was nationalized under the effective laws "for state and public purposes" and the owners were compensated.

4. One feature of Bulgarian law was the actual nationalization of agricultural land. It started with the mass cooperativization of land owners who volunteered or were forced to contribute their lands to the cooperative farms, a process which was more or less completed by 1958. Owners nominally retained their right in the property, but various statutory acts gradually eliminated all their powers to possess, use and dispose of the land. In practice, agricultural land became state-owned after 1975, as its nominal owners were unable to withdraw their plots from the cooperatives, to receive rent, to sell or devise them, to cultivate them personally, etc. and their heirs were unable to inherit them.

Using the above methods of nationalization, the totalitarian regime virtually created an all-embracing state property system, limiting citizens' ownership rights to housing and weekend houses, small means of production and movable property.... Because of all these real and legal changes in the components of property, which evolved over a considerable period of time, the practical implementation of private property restitution is bound to run into considerable difficulties....

Restoration of Ownership Rights in Agricultural Land

...Having considered eight formally introduced bills, the Grand National Assembly (GNA) passed the Agricultural Land Tenure Act (ALTA), published in the *Official Gazette* No. 17 of 1991....

The effective provision is contained in Article 10(1) and (6) of the ALTA. According to it:

- Former owners of agricultural land given over to cooperative and state farms will have their rights to this land automatically and unconditionally reinstated by the statute itself. The question of state farms was not raised in the considered bills, and was obviously included because of situations where land originally contributed to cooperative farms was later nationalized. The final version dropped the requirement that the rights of owners who retain their legal relations of cooperative farm ownership be restored as an undivided legal interest. Restitution in the form of actual plots came to the fore, and this issue of membership in cooperatives was left to the discretion of the former owners after they repossessed their land.
- Persons who transferred their land gratuitously to cooperative farms or the state will have their property rights restored on their request rather than by the statute itself. The law respects those persons' free expression of will to cede their land without compensation....

According to Article 10(2) of the Act, agricultural land nationalized under the repealed Article 12 of the Citizens' Property Act will be restored to its owners after they return the compensation they have received for the nationalization. The general approach was taken in Article 10(3) of the Act, according to which all wrongfully expropriated agricultural land shall revert to its owners. The Agricultural Land Tenure Act By-laws, adopted by Council of Ministers Decree No. 74 of April 25, 1991, do not specify the cases in which agricultural land will qualify as wrongfully expropriated, obviously leaving these judgements to the restitution authorities when they consider the applications on a case by case basis....

The most controversial point [was] the type of agricultural land subject to restitution. [The proposals put forward by two parliamentary factions had provided] that the land given in restitution should be of the same type, size and grade as the land contributed to cooperative farms or nationalized. Debate focused on whether the land must be of the same type, i.e., whether the restored land should be functionally equivalent to the cooperativized or nationalized land: fields, lawns, vineyards, orchards, etc.

ALTA drops the requirement that restored land should be of identical type. According to Article 10(7), agricultural land will be restored to its former owners in its original size and grade within the land use area of the same population center after the distribution and consolidation of the plots. Under Article 17, the municipal land commissions must organize the drawing up of a plan for such land distribution within one year of ALTA's entry into force; among other things, the plan should determine the land from which the restored plots will be formed....

Size of Agricultural Land Subject to Restitution

...Under Article 6 of the Agricultural Land Tenure Act, a household may not own more than 20 hectares of agricultural land in the intensive farming areas designated by the National Land Board and more than 30 hectares in the rest of the country. The regulation is general and applies to private ownership of agricultural land irrespective of the manner of acquisition....

Compensation

...In all cases, compensation is permitted only as a subsidiary form of restitution. Compensation may be either pecuniary or in kind (depending on the grounds) rather than in bonds.... According to ALTA, compensation is due for:

(a) restored agricultural land nationalized under the repealed Article 12 of the Citizens' Property Act—when building rights or rights of use on it have been created for the benefit of third parties (Article 10(2));
(b) land nationalized under Article 8(2) and (3) of the 1946 Land Ownership Act, whose owners have not been paid compensation under Article 14 ff. of the same act; rightful claimants in this case may be compensated by land from the land stock or money, according to their choice (Article 10(5));
(c) cooperativized or nationalized agricultural land which has diminished since its cooperativization or nationalization (Article 15(2));
(d) land which has been transferred to research institutes, research and industrial plants and educational establishments, or to seed-production or stud farms and game farms for the discharge of their research and production functions, or has been incorporated into reserves created under the Nature Conservation Act, into other protected wildlife areas of national and international importance, or which contains inseparable subsurface or surface archaeological sites and cultural monuments, if the rights of owners of such land could not be restored or have been partially restored; in these cases, too, the owners are either paid the pecuniary equivalent of the land or are allocated equivalent land from the state or municipal land stock in the

same area or the neigbouring land-use area or, by their consent, in another land-use area. (Article 24(2-4))....

Agricultural Land Restitution: General Assessment

...The inalienability of agricultural land for a term of three years after restitution (Article 18 of ALTA) follows the general spirit of the act which seeks to make sure that land should be used for farming purposes only and to deter speculation in land; the terms are much more liberal than the parallel restrictions on the property rights of landless citizens and small land-owners whose newly acquired land is inalienable for ten years after its acquisition (Article 20 (2)) and, moreover, may not be rented or leased out within five years of acquisition (Clause 6 of the Transitional and Final Provisions).

The following general conclusions can be drawn from the legal regulation of agricultural land restitution:

First, the restitution of agricultural land is an exceedingly difficult process. The difficulties arise from the position of the holders of property rights (most are heirs who have lost an actual link with the land after urban migration) and from the object of restitution itself. Many experts believe these difficulties will impede farm production for some time and will raise a number of legal problems which may take years to solve.

Secondly, this legal framework is not so much restitution as it is land reform, the idea of which is to help farming develop along private property lines. This conclusion is borne out by the ALTA provisions concerning the acquisition of land by landless citizens and small land owners (Articles 20-23), the restoration of property within limits of 30 or, respectively, 20 hectares (Article 6), the restrictions on land restitution and use by Bulgarians resident abroad (Article 11 (8)), etc....

Restoration of Ownership Rights in Immovable Property Confiscated Under Effective Sentences or at Deprivation of Bulgarian Citizenship...

(a) The title of the enacted statute [to deal with this category of restituion is the] Amnesty and Restoration of Confiscated Property Act (ARCPA)[3], which makes it sufficiently comprehensive to cover subject matter concerning the deprivation of Bulgarian citizenship.

(b) The Act erases the criminal character of actions criminalized as political offences as part of the crackdown on the proponents of opposition ideas after September 9, 1944 and treated in the 1945 Statutory Ordinance on the Defence of People's Rule, the Penal Law effective until March 13, 1951 and the Penal Law, amended as Penal Code, effective between 1951 and 1968. The Act provides for the restoration of property confiscated in connection with acts covered by this amnesty (Article 3 of ARCPA), as Article 2 of ARCPA also grants amnesty for certain acts criminalized under the effective Penal Code

---

[3] *Official Gazette* No. 1 of 1991.

merely by discharge from criminal liability and the effects of conviction, which does not entitle the persons receiving amnesty to restoration of confiscated property.

(c) Under Article 6 of ARCPA, the restoration of property rights extends to property confiscated in connection with certain crimes which were covered by various amnesty acts between 1964 and 1989. In most general terms, these acts cover criminal liability incurred for border trespassing, defection and acts of relatively little social harm.

(d) Under the terms of Article 5 of ARCPA, persons deprived of Bulgarian citizenship will have their confiscated property restored when their citizenship is reinstated (Article 7 of ARCPA).

(e) Under Article 5(1) of ARCPA, confiscated immovable property is restored to its owners or their heirs by law only if before the entry into force of ARCPA, the property was in the possession of the state or of a state or municipal company in which the State has at least 51 per cent holding. According to Article 5(2) of ARCPA, if these conditions cannot be met or the property has been destroyed, demolished or reorganized, the rightful claimants are compensated by another equivalent property or by money. The principle that compensation is subsidiary clearly applies here, too.

Restoration of Ownership Rights in Immovable Property Expropriated for "State and Public Purposes"

Under a variety of laws passed since September 9, 1944, private persons' immovable property could be expropriated for "state and public purposes" with compensation. With total planning and an ideology in which "state and public interests" took unquestionable precedence over personal interests, this legal instrument was used for a mass-scale nationalization of immovable property. People were practically denied a legal remedy against the actions of the authorities who conceptualized "state and public" interests in loose and often arbitrary terms.

With a view to checking this process of virtual nationalization, which all political forces acknowledge as wrong, discussions were held and legislative action taken back in 1990.

In June 1990 the Ninth National Assembly amended the Regional and Urban Planning Act and the Ownership Act which were most often invoked in the expropriation of private persons' property. The amendments severely restricted the grounds for expropriation, enhanced the inviolability of immovable property ownership and established full judicial control over administrative actions of expropriation. By these acts Parliament halted indiscriminate expropriation and actually reversed this wrong policy of the totalitarian regime.

In some cases of unfair nationalization through expropriation, it became possible to restore some of the nationalized property.

In the one such instance of restitution known so far, property expropriated for the purposes of public recreation and tourism was returned to its former owners in the municipalities of Varna and Dolen Chiflik. The following restitution procedure was followed:

Council of Ministers Ordinance No. 15 of July 24, 1991 rescinded the 1973 Council of Ministers Ordinance which effected the expropriation, i.e., eliminated the legal grounds for the expropriation by an equipotent statutory act.

Property is restored in the condition in which it exists at the time the ordinance enters into force.

Property is restored to former owners on the condition that they refund the compensation and pay for improvements and plantings carried out after expropriation.

Property built up with solid structures after expropriation or made available for the uses of national defence, for which the owners have been compensated by another immovable property, may not be restored.

Judging by this act of restitution, the only one so far, other former owners will also be presumably reinstated to their rights in the future, observing the principle of real protection of state interests and the interests of third parties who have made considerable bona fide improvements on the property.

19

ALBANIA

EDITOR'S INTRODUCTION

Italy invaded and occupied Albania in 1939, driving the country's leader, King Zog I, into exile. Nazi Germany replaced Italy as the occupation force following the latter's surrender in World War II. By November 1944, concurrent with the withdrawal of German forces, the Albanian Communist Party (called the Albanian Party of Labor or APL) had defeated the other resistance forces and gained control of the country. Enver Hoxha, the Party secretary-general, became the leader and dictator of Albania—a position he retained for the next four decades.

Under Hoxha, Albania became the most repressive regime in the region and one of the most tightly closed societies in the world. The security police, the Sigurimi, fiercely enforced Hoxha's repressive policies and maintained the APL's power. Political opponents and those attempting to exercise freedoms of speech, press, or association were arrested, often beaten, and sent to prisons with harsh conditions and forced labor. All segments of society, including the party hierarchy, the intellectual community, and the military, were subject to periodic purges resulting in job dismissals, imprisonment, and executions. The courts were completely controlled by the APL. The death sentence was imposed for "propaganda against the state" and for attempts to leave the country. The government arrested the families of escapees to deter future attempts. In 1967, Albania proclaimed itself the first atheist state, constitutionally prohibited religious activity, and moved to eliminate all traces of religion in the country. Over time, Albania became not only the most repressive country in Europe, but also the most impoverished.

Following Hoxha's death in 1985, he was replaced by his chosen successor, Ramiz Alia. In 1990, responding to the collapse of Communist regimes in the region and the resulting rise in domestic ferment, the APL initiated limited efforts to decentralize the economy, restore religious freedom and the right to travel, and revise the penal code and electoral laws. In July 1990, after a mass demonstration took place in the capital city of Tirana, 4,700 people flooded into European embassies seeking asylum. Soon thereafter, they were allowed to leave the country. The formation of independent political parties was permitted. Hoxha's policy of international isolationism was abandoned.

Intimidation and the use of deadly force by the Sigurimi flawed legislative elections in March 1991. Despite these barriers, opposition parties gained one-third of the seats in the People's Assembly. The APL formed a government under Prime Minister Fatos Nano and the People's Assembly elected Alia president. In June, a general labor strike forced the resignation of Nano. A coalition Government of National Stability, led by Ylli Bufi, was formed. The Communists (now renamed the Socialist Party) only received half of the cabinet seats.

Although major human rights violations continued, significant reforms were now undertaken. On April 30, 1991, a "Law on Major Constitutional Provisions" was enacted, guaranteeing the protection of internationally recognized human rights and the right of citizens to free elections. Progress was also made in the areas of freedom of speech, press, religion, and travel. In June 1991, all political prisoners were freed. In December, the opposition parties withdrew from the coalition to protest the Socialist Party's blocking of further reform, forcing Bufi to resign. Alia appointed Vilson Ahmeti to form an interim government until new elections in 1992.

The situation prior to the 1992 elections was one of rampant crime, a lack of resources, soaring inflation, and 50% unemployment. The elections, generally considered to be fair, took place on March 22, 1992. The Democratic Party won nearly two-thirds of the seats in the legislature. Alia resigned and Parliament elected Dr. Sali Berisha president. Aleksandr Meksi became prime minister, and a coalition government of four parties was formed. The new government restored relative order to the country.

In the aftermath of Communist rule, the issues of transitional justice were addressed in a variety of ways. In April 1993, the People's Assembly adopted a law on the restitution of, and compensation for, properties expropriated by the Communist regime. In May 1993, the newly established Constitutional Court struck down a law designed to screen and de-license lawyers who had various party affiliations or who had collaborated with the former secret police.

From 1992-1994, efforts to bring to account those associated with the abuses of the Communist regime resulted in the filing of charges against more than seventy former officials and elites. General Prosecutor Maksim Haxhia was dismissed from office following complaints by members of Parliament that he was not pursuing former Communist officials with sufficient fervor. Nexmijhe Hoxha, wife of the dictator, was sentenced to

11 years in prison for misuse of state funds. A border guard was sentenced to 10 years for the killing of people trying to leave the country. One former prime minister was arrested in connection with missing bank funds, and a second was sentenced to 12 years for embezzlement of foreign humanitarian aid. In a mass trial scheduled to begin in May 1994, ten former top officials—including the last Communist president, Ramiz Alia, former prime minister Adil Carcani, three former interior ministers, a former Supreme Court chairman, and a former attorney general—were indicted in connection with the misappropriation of state property, the deportation over time of thousands of Albanians, the 1951 execution without trial of 22 persons, the 1967 banning of religious activity, and the enforcement of the policy of border killings.

The following document related to transitional justice in Albania can be found in Volume III of this collection:

- Law on Former Victims of Persecution

THE INITIAL TRANSITION

Commission on Security and Cooperation in Europe, "Human Rights and Democratization in Albania"*

The immediate post-election period was marked by exhilaration, which was characterized not by protest and violence like the year before but by the celebrations of crowds exuberant over the end of the communist era in Albania. The Socialist Party made no effort to provoke confrontation or violence that could have put the election result in jeopardy. Democratic Party leader Sali Berisha addressed a large victory rally at Skenderbeg Square in the center of Tirana, where he set a positive tone by stressing that Albania had neither the time nor the inclination to seek revenge for past wrongs.

Efforts were quickly undertaken to get the new Assembly into session to form a new government. Ramiz Alia formally resigned as President on April 4, and the Assembly, convening the same day and chaired by former

* Excerpted from Commission on Security and Cooperation in Europe, *Human Rights and Democratization in Albania* (January 1994), pp. 5, 7, 11.

political prisoner Pjeter Arbnori, quickly chose Sali Berisha to become Albania's new President. Berisha asked Democratic Party member Aleksander Meksi to form a new government. Meksi announced the members of the government, which was then approved by the Assembly on April 19, 1992....

Still, there were challenges. The Socialists continually attacked the new government, playing on popular fears of chaos and further deprivation associated with radical reform. Local elections on July 26, 1992, when viewed nationwide by party, placed the Socialists less than two percentage points behind the Democratic Party. The Socialists also won a plurality of the seats contested, revealing that their following on the local level in rural areas remained fairly strong despite the dramatic changes that had otherwise taken place. As the first year came to a close, the Socialists intensified their criticisms, calling for the Meksi government to resign and new elections to be held.

In addition, there was turmoil within the Democratic Party ranks. From its formation, the party had been as much a mass movement in opposition to communism as it had been a political party. Now in power, the diverse political spectrum it had united for the common goal of breaking the communist hold began to fracture. Gramoz Pashko and Sali Berisha, who together co-founded the Democratic Party, split from each other, with Pashko taking a small segment of the Democratic Party's left wing with him. Meanwhile, within the bulk of the Democratic Party that remained with Berisha, right-wing forces increased their own pressure, supporting, for example, pre-communist landowners seeking to reclaim their former property.

With the Socialists still a threat, and the Democratic Party itself moving to the right, it was not surprising that Albania's second year of democratic transition [was not] as smooth and moderate a journey as the first. While a few select cabinet changes in April 1993 were viewed as placating the Socialists and perhaps the right, Albanian politics soon moved into the realm of acrimony and confrontation.... [T]he Socialists were increasingly the subjects of legal action for alleged corruption and other crimes committed during the communist era, not only during the Stalinist period but the more recent transition as well....

Efforts also began to undo the damage done to individuals by the decades of harsh and unjust communist rule, to the extent such damage could be undone. In January 1993, for example, the Assembly widened the range of people considered to have been victims of the communist regime as stated in the Law on Innocence, Amnesty and Rehabilitation of Former Political Prisoners and the Persecuted. In July 1993, the Assembly passed additional legislation on the status of these people, categorizing them in a way that would determine how much they would be compensated for the harm done to them.[7]

---

[7] Congressional Research Service, Library of Congress, *Parliamentary Development: An Overview of Assistance in Eastern Europe and the Former Soviet Union*, no. 6, May 1993, and no. 7, October 1993.

Prosecution of the Former Communist Leadership

Commission on Security and Cooperation in Europe, "Human Rights and Democratization in Albania"*

Falling within the framework of the rule of law is the treatment of communist officials accused of a variety of crimes, ranging from corruption in public office to genocide against the general population. In practically every formerly communist country seeking to overcome the legacy of totalitarian rule, the question of legal action against former communist officials and, indeed, against the communist party itself, have been greatly and often hotly debated. Options have ranged from efforts simply to put the past aside and start anew, to witch hunts for informers and prosecution of senior and junior officials, to outlawing the communist party, like fascist parties in many countries, on grounds that it poses too serious a threat to be tolerated.

Albania has been no exception in having this debate, and the course chosen was to permit the communist party previously in power—formerly the Party of Labor but now called the Socialist Party—to continue to function just like any other political party in the country. On the issue of personal responsibility of the communist leadership, however, the severity of the communist regime in the past has engendered significant support for prosecuting the members of this leadership. While this is more than understandable, especially from the large number of people who were either political prisoners themselves or relatives of those who perished at communist hands, two questions remain. First, communist controls over Albanian society were so pervasive and the country, as a practical matter, so small that few of the educated, urban intellectuals—who were, in fact, the leaders of the opposition now in power—did not have some relationship with the regime. Efforts to prosecute individual communist leaders could therefore lead to evidence of "compromised" democrats. Second, it is unclear whether such efforts are undertaken in a "rule-of-law" context or whether they are, in fact, encouraged by current political leaders as a means to consolidate their own power and distract the population from current problems. Ismail Kadare, the country's leading writer and himself a controversial figure, expressed concern in regard to the latter point—although he avoided specific mention about whom he was addressing—soon after his return from 18 months of voluntary exile in May 1992:

> Communism in Albania is finished. No one should be afraid of it or should hope that it will return. What bothers me ... [is] that anti-communism is being practiced in a communist style, that is, in the same style, in the same class-struggle fashion, according to Lenin's shameful dictum "ours" [the communists] and "the others" [the

---

* Excerpted from Commission on Security and Cooperation in Europe, *Human Rights and Democratization in Albania* (January 1994), pp. 13-15.

> overthrown classes] in reverse. These are Bolshevik habits that must be uprooted.[13]

The first step in the action taken against the communist elite took place during the year of transition, while the communists were formally still in power but after they held a congress in which they changed their name and rejected their Stalinist past. In May 1991, the most prominent families were told to vacate the villas in downtown Tirana reserved for them. In July 1991, Democratic Party representatives indicated a desire to bring communist officials to trial for misusing state funds. Given the abject poverty in Albania, revelations of the extravagance of the Hoxha family's lifestyle—which included the possession of 25 refrigerators, 28 color television sets and 19 telephones[14] and the use of $1 million for foreign health care by the elite over a ten-year period[15]—infuriated the population. That same month, the opposition in the Assembly unsuccessfully attempted to have communist property confiscated, amid rumors of illegal business dealing. In August, legal proceedings were underway against 28 elite families. Then, in September, the first former officials were arrested, former Party of Labor Politburo member Manush Myftiu and Kino Buxheli, who was in charge of supply for the nomenklatura. In December 1991, the widow of Enver Hoxha, Nexhmije, was placed under house arrest along with some others for corruption, and the parliamentary immunity of former Prime Minister Adil Carcani and others was taken away so that they could also be placed under arrest. Nexhmije Hoxha was found guilty of abusing funds in January 1992 and sentenced to nine years of imprisonment, increased by two years when she sought to appeal the sentence.

In September 1992, former President and Party of Labor leader Ramiz Alia was placed under house arrest, an act which he protested was "purely political."[16] So far, however, those arrested were almost exclusively affiliated with abuses of power during the pre-1990 period, when the communist regime was still in its Stalinist stages. The arrest of Alia indicated that those who might have redeemed themselves somewhat by allowing Albania, albeit grudgingly, to move in a pluralistic direction were no less vulnerable as a result. Prosecuting communist officials, however, came to a new point of controversy with the removal of parliamentary immunity and arrest two days later of Fatos Nano, the new leader of the Socialist Party, in July 1993. Nano, who was known as a reform-minded economist and was not among the communist leadership before 1990, was charged with misuse of office and corruption linked with the provision of humanitarian aid from Italy. His arrest came right in the midst of the controversy in the Assembly over the country's constitution, and led to speculation that it was taken because of Socialist attacks on the

---

[13] *Rilindja Demokratike*, May 20, 1992, as quoted in: Louis Zanga, "Albania's Leading Writer Returns Home," *RFE/RL Research Report*, vol. 1, no. 28, July 10, 1992.

[14] *Radio Free Europe/Radio Liberty Daily Report*, no. 127, July 8, 1991.

[15] *RFE/RL Daily Report*, no. 135, July 18, 1991.

[16] *RFE/RL Daily Report*, no. 176, September 14, 1992.

Democratic Party's agenda and boycott of the Assembly. On August 10, 1993, the Constitutional Court nevertheless rejected a request to have the arrest declared unconstitutional.

Coinciding with the Nano arrest was the arrest of other prominent former communist officials, in particular senior officials from the Foreign and Trade Ministries. In addition, Ramiz Alia was formally arrested and incarcerated on the same corruption charges, with speculation that he might stand trial for genocide as well. Several representatives of the pro-Socialist media were briefly detained at about the same time. Arrests continued into September, and former Prime Minister Vilson Ahmeti received a two year sentence in that month for misusing his office. In October, others were arrested for their role in violating human rights in the 1980s, bringing the total number of communist officials arrested to about 40. In December 1993, ten senior communist officials who had been arrested earlier for misuse of state funds for luxuries were sentenced to prison terms ranging from five to ten years, and ordered to pay back the equivalent of 60,000 U.S. dollars. Foreign and domestic press were prohibited from reporting on the trial on grounds of protecting "public order, national security, morality and the privacy of the accused." Amnesty International expressed concern that the press ban set a dangerous precedent for future trials and possibly undermined the right of the accused to a fair trial in Albania.[17]

What had been largely seen as a generally legitimate effort to bring former communist officials to justice was increasinlgy viewed as having highly political overtones, which Democratic Party representatives steadfastly denied. Soon after the Nano arrest, tens of thousands of supporters took to the streets in protest. As they chanted against the government, which they called a dictatorship, there were reports of clashes with Democratic Party supporters and some arrests. While the Socialists threatened to lengthen their boycott of the Assembly and broaden it to include local officials as well, by late August they had returned to their parliamentary duties.

Constitutional Court Decision on the First Lustration Law

Kathleen Imholz, "A Landmark Constitutional Court Decision in Albania"[*]

On May 21, 1993, the year-old Albanian Constitutional Court held Albania's first "lustration law" unconstitutional and struck it down in its

---

[17] Amnesty International, *Urgent Action Appeal f*or Muho Asllani Bekteshi, Foto Cami, Hajredin Celiku, Vangjel Cerrava, Lenka Cuko, Llambi Gegprifti, Qirjako Mihali, Pali Miska and Prokp Murra, December 16, 1993.

[*] Reprinted from Kathleenm Imholz, "A Landmark Constitutional Court Decision in Albania," *East European Constitutional Review*, vol. 2, no. 3 (Summer 1993), pp. 23-25.

entirety. It is the farthest-reaching judicial decision on this issue to date in any of the de-Communizing countries of East and Central Europe.

Lustration laws, as retributive or "purge" laws directed against Communist-era leaders or collaborators have come to be known, have been enacted in several countries of the region and discussed in all or almost all of them. While the impetus for this kind of law is understandable, the laws and their implementation have generally fallen far short of customary norms of due process.

One would not expect rigorous analysis of the emotion laden issues underlying these laws from a judicial system that has only just been organized, and judges who are unused to independence. That an analytical decision relying not only on local constitutional principles but also on various international covenants should come from Albania, whose Communist regime was the region's most isolationist and brutal, is particularly impressive.

The Overturned Law

While a considerable amount of informal "lustration" has been taking place in Albania, it was not until [1993] that parliament passed a law providing for the removal of persons from specific positions on the basis of their actions in the past.

Law No. 7666 of January 26, 1993 was directed solely at "advocates" or private lawyers. Article 1 provided for the creation of a commission for the reevaluation of licenses to practice law issued up to the effective date of the law. The Minister of Justice was named to head this commission and to propose the remainder of its membership, subject to the approval of the Supreme Council of Justice.

Article 3 contained the heart of the law. It provided for the addition of a new article to the existing law on advocacy, with the following content:

> Article 12/a: There shall not be licensed to work as advocates [private lawyers]:
>
> a) Former officers of State Security and collaborators with it.
>
> b) Former members of the Committees of the Labor Party of Albania as well as their employees in the central office, districts and regions; former directors of state organs in the center and the districts (ministers, vice-ministers, directors of divisions as well as chairmen, vice-chairmen and secretaries of executive committees in the districts and regions).
>
> c) Former employees of prisons and internment camps.
>
> d) Those who have finished the Faculty of Justice on the basis of higher education in the special party school as well as the former chairmen of personnel offices at all levels.

e) Those who have taken part as investigator, prosecutor or judge in special or staged political trials, as well as those who have performed high management functions in the central organs of justice.

f) Those who have used physical or psychological force during investigations or other acts, as well as those who have taken part in border killings.

Article 4 of the law provided for the possibility of appeal to the Supreme Council of Justice against a decision taken under Article 3, and Article 5 provided that persons affected by the law would be prohibited from practicing law for five years. Articles 4 and 5, however, did not purport to amend the existing advocacy law; they stood on their own footing.

On April 20, a meeting of the commission took place at which a decision was reached summarily to revoke the licenses of 47 lawyers. There was no indication as to which of the prescribed categories the disbarred lawyers fit into, nor were any of them present at the meeting that decided their fate or otherwise given a hearing.

On April 30, the Parliamentary Group of the Socialist Party (the largest minority party in the current parliament, successor to the Party of Labor) brought a complaint to the Constitutional Court, alleging that this law was unconstitutional.

The Constitutional and Legal Background

In the past two and a half years, several constitutional drafting commissions in Albania have produced a number of different drafts of a document to replace the 1976 Communist constitution. After the first pluralist elections of March 31, 1991, the Party of Labor (Communist Party) held enough seats in parliament to pass a draft, but a compromise led instead to the adoption on April 29, 1991, of Law No. 7491 "On major constitutional provisions." This transitional law repealed the 1976 constitution and was intended to be replaced by a full constitution by early 1992.

In parliamentary elections held in March 1992, the Democratic Party won almost two thirds of the seats. As of September 1993, while the constitution is the subject of much debate, a new one has not yet been enacted, and the Law on Major Constitutional Provisions remains in force. However, a number of amendments and new chapters have been added, which have fleshed it out substantially. These include a chapter reorganizing the judicial system and establishing a Constitutional Court for the first time in Albania, a chapter on local government, and most recently an extensive chapter on fundamental human rights and freedoms.

Constitutional Law No. 7561, which reorganized the judicial system of Albania in 1992, merits some attention. It sought to establish an independent judiciary, containing much hortatory language to that end. In Article 15, it established a "Supreme Council of Justice," headed by the

President of the Republic and consisting of the Chairman of the Court of Cassation (the renamed Supreme Court of the country), the Minister of Justice, the General Prosecutor, and nine other jurists "recognized for their ability" and elected for a five-year term jointly by the Court of Cassation and the General Prosecutor. The Supreme Council "is the sole authority that decides on the nomination, removal and general discipline of judges of the first level, appellate judges, and also prosecutors." The article that follows (Article 16) turns to the private practice of law and states that "[a]dvocacy shall be conducted as a free profession. The activity of advocacy shall be regulated by separate law. The duty of advocates is to give their clients necessary juridical assistance and counsel according to law and the norms of professional ethics."

Law No. 7561 also established Albania's first Constitutional Court, consisting of nine members, five to be elected by the People's Assembly and four by the president. While the initial terms are staggered, eventually each constitutional judge is to have a twelve-year term, without the right of re-election. The judges had been selected by the end of May 1992, and the Court's first decision was dated July 13, 1992.

Finally, the Constitutional Court's decision overturning the de-licensing law cannot be understood outside the context of Albania's law on advocacy. The private practice of law was not recognized in Albania for over two decades. In May 1990, Law No. 7382 was passed by the People's Assembly. It provided that colleges of advocates would be set up in all of the districts of Albania, and that citizens who had higher juridical education and at least three years' experience would be accepted as members. For the first time since the 1960s, it became legal for an "advocate" to take part in the defense of criminal cases and the representation of the participants in civil cases. Fees were to be under the control of the Ministry of Justice, however.

By the middle of 1991, it had become apparent that a more flexible structure was needed for private lawyers. On December 18, 1991, a completely new advocacy law was passed. The colleges were abolished; advocates were permitted to practice as individuals or in partnerships or collectives and to determine their own fees by agreement with their clients, subject to maxima set by the Ministry of Justice. A Supervisory Council consisting of an official from the Ministry of Justice and six lawyers elected by a general meeting of lawyers was created to oversee the activities of the profession.

The Supervisory Council is to be "independent in the exercise of its activity," and has the competency to grant licenses for the exercise of the profession of advocate "when a jurist fulfills the conditions set out in this law." The conditions are completion of higher juridical education, moral and professional criteria, and proof of not having been convicted of a serious crime. The Supervisory Council has the power to discipline lawyers for false licensing documentation, the commission of unlicensed acts and unlawful interference with state organs, exceeding the maximum fees, and certain record-keeping failures; the maximum punishment is the suspension of an advocate's license for five years.

The Ruling of the Constitutional Court

The Constitutional Court found Articles 1, 3 and 4 of Law No. 7666 unconstitutional for a variety of reasons (only in part for the reasons put forward by the complainant). Their first observation was that the creation of the reevaluation commission in the Ministry of Justice was contrary to Article 16 of the constitutional law on the judicial system, which states that "[a]dvocacy shall be practiced as a free profession." The Court added that advocacy is "consequently self-administered." The Court then quoted at length from the 1991 advocacy law on the powers and duties of the Supervisory Council, noting that the Council's mistakes in granting licenses may be corrected only by the general meeting of lawyers, which is their highest organ, and not by a "reevaluation" commission with a state character.

The Court's second argument was addressed to the fact that under Article 3 of Law No. 7666 (listing categories of persons who may not be licensed to practice law) the sole criterion for licensing is the advocate's performance at some time of one of a variety of functions under the party-state, regardless of whether he meets all the criteria of the advocacy law. "The elimination of the democratic criterion of individual valuation" of the advocate's qualities is in conflict with the new charter of fundamental human rights and freedoms, said the Court, in particular Article 28, the right-to-work clause, and with the same principle in the International Covenant on Economic, Social and Cultural Rights which Albania ratified in 1991.

Further, observed the Court, subparagraph (f) in the list of categories deals with the commission of serious crimes, and "there is the recognized juridical concept that only a competent court may, by its final decision, declare guilty a person whom it has judged for the commission of a crime." (While the existing advocacy law makes conviction of a serious crime a ground for withholding a license, the determination that the crime was committed is not made by the Supervisory Council; it follows from the judicial act of punishment).

Thus, concluded the Court, Article 3 of Law No. 7666 infringes both the separation of powers mandated by Article 3 of the Law on Major Constitutional Provisions as originally passed in 1991, and the presumption of innocence contained in the new charter of fundamental human rights and also sanctioned in the International Covenant on Civil and Political Rights.

The Court's third argument was that Articles 1 and 4 of Law No. 7666, which give the Supreme Council of Justice the exclusive competency to approve the composition of the reevaluation commission and to hear appeals of its decisions, are unconstitutional because the Supreme Council of Justice is, under the constitutional law that created it, the sole authority for naming, removing and disciplining officers of the judicial power (judges and prosecutors). These competencies, said the Court, may not also be extended to private lawyers, who are "professionally free and are not magistrates." This argument, also raised by the complainant, seems somewhat weaker than the first two, but is not necessary to the result in any event.

Finally the Court noted that the Document on the Human Dimension approved in 1990 by the Conference on European Security and Cooperation sets out that "[t]he independence of lawyers is to be recognized and protected, especially insofar as concerns their inclusion in this profession," and Albania is a member of CSCE. In addition, the law on major constitutional provisions states that the Republic of Albania "guarantees the basic rights and freedoms of individuals ... accepted in international documents."

The Court rejected the claim of the Parliamentary Group of the Socialist Party that only a criminal court may take away a lawyer's right to practice his profession, stating that the Supervisory Council is permitted to do that after verifying violations in the performance of duty.

Albania is confronted with a staggering number of problems, like the other countries of the region. If anything, Albania's problems are even more severe, both because of the nature of the Communist regime there and the drastic economic situation of the country, which has been Europe's poorest for many years, dating back to well before Communism.

One of these problems is the perception, and the reality, that people who violated basic human rights under the Communist regime have not been punished but, on the contrary, are still to be found in positions of importance and influence. To analyze and praise this decision of the Constitutional Court is not to deny that the problem exists, or that it is a serious one....

It is an impressive first step, although the decision is not without weaknesses. For example, there is no mention of the need for individual hearings and the opportunity to call witnesses and present rebuttal evidence. If all or most of the proscribed categories are merely reintroduced into the advocacy law for the Supervisory Council to use in its own licensing decisions, the Council may also be under pressure for summary licensings. Perhaps the Court's reference to the "democratic criterion of individual valuation" in connection with the Supervisory Council's application of its licensing criteria will be elaborated in a future decision. Still, guidelines in this decision would have been helpful, and might have obviated a future challenge.

This is not to take away from the courageous decision of the Albanian Constitutional Court, a landmark in an area that will remain troubling and sensitive throughout the entire region for some time. One can hope this decision will be the first step in these countries toward finding a fair balance between individual human rights and the strongly felt desire that those who violated human rights under prior regimes receive due punishment.

20

RUSSIA

EDITOR'S INTRODUCTION

The Bolshevik Revolution of 1917 ended centuries of Czarist rule in Russia. The leader of the revolution, Vladimir Lenin, stated that, "[w]e have never rejected terror on principle, nor can we do so. Terror is a form of military operation that may be usefully applied, or may even be essential in certain moments of the battle...." On December 20, 1917, the Bolsheviks created the Cheka, which executed tens of thousands during the ensuing period known as the Red Terror. A constituent assembly was seated following Russia's first free election, but Lenin dissolved the body after one session. The Constitution of 1924 officially established the Union of Soviet Socialist Republics (USSR). No political faction was permitted other than the Communist Party. The single party completely controlled all organs of the state, creating a model which many countries falling under Soviet influence would be obliged to replicate in later years.

During the 1920s, the Communists created other institutions such as the OGPU to continue the purge of the former ruling classes and crush any opposition. Following Lenin's death in 1924, Joseph Stalin consolidated his power as a brutal dictator and retained absolute power for the next thirty years. At the height of brutality in 1937-38, an estimated 8-12 million people were deported or interned in prisons and labor camps; an additional 7 million were executed between 1935 and 1945. After World War II, the Ministry for Internal Affairs (MVD) and Committee for State Security (KGB) maintained the system of internal espionage and repression. In the late 1950s and early 1960s, a "thaw" under Nikita Kruschev resulted in a limited relaxation of repression, with greater freedom of culture and expression. Nonetheless, although Russia and the USSR never returned to the terror of the Stalin era, they remained closed and harshly repressive societies.

A new sense of openness and change accompanied Mikhail Gorbachev's rise to power in 1985. Gradually, political repression and censorship were relaxed in the context of Gorbachev's twin policies of *perestroika* (economic reconstruction) and *glasnost* (openness). Momentum for reform advanced more rapidly than intended by the regime, accompanied throughout much of the USSR by growing manifestations of nationalism. Between November 1988 and October 1990, all fifteen republics of the Soviet Union declared their sovereignty. Russia did so on June 11, 1990. Boris Yeltsin was democratically elected president of Russia in June 1991.

On August 19, 1991, the day before the signing of a new union treaty to transfer significant political and economic power from the central authorities to the republics, a group of senior Communist Party, military, and KGB officials staged a coup d'état to regain control of the Soviet Union. The coup failed—consolidating the strength of Yeltsin and others and hastening the final disintegration of the USSR—and its twelve leaders were charged with treason. By year's end, the Soviet Union was formally abolished.

Following the failed coup, Yeltsin issued a series of three decrees banning the Communist Party and ordering confiscation of its assets. These decrees were challenged before Russia's newly established constitutional court in a high-profile case that explored the nature of the Communist Party and its relation to the state. Over 130 expert witnesses offered testimony, including a spectacular array of prominent former dissidents and Soviet officials. In November 1992, the court issued a compromise ruling, upholding the ban on the national party while enabling local branches to re-establish themselves and seek return of their property.

The trial of the leaders of the August 1991 coup began on April 14, 1993. It was repeatedly delayed or postponed, however, over the next ten months.

On September 20, 1993, after a long struggle with an increasingly confrontational and conservative parliament which included many old Communists, Yeltsin dissolved the legislature. The Parliament responded by impeaching Yeltsin and electing Vice President Aleksandr Rutskoi as president. Many legislators barricaded themselves inside the Parliament building and called for general insurrection against the Yeltsin government. On October 3, armed anti-Yeltsin forces seized the Moscow mayor's office and a broadcast center. Yeltsin introduced a state of emergency. On October 4, military forces stormed the Parliament building and took it over after a fierce firefight. Those remaining in the Parliament were arrested.

On February 23, 1994, a newly convened Russian parliament proclaimed an amnesty for all those involved in both the October 1991 coup attempt and the events of October 1993.

Already during the Gorbachev era, many victims of Stalinism had been rehabilitated by the government, and a private organization, Memorial, was founded in 1987 to focus on documenting and commemorating these victims. In October 1991, a law was enacted on the "Rehabilitation of

Victims of Political Repression" since 1917, administered by a presidentially-appointed commission. A December 1992 amendment to the law extended its coverage to victims of state abuse elsewhere in the former USSR, beyond the borders of Russia.

Efforts to use secret police files in order to screen and purge those affiliated with the former regime—prominent in many of the former Soviet bloc countries discussed in the present volume—have not been mirrored in Russia. The new government began the process of reviewing and releasing classified documents of the Communist Party and the KGB. By September 1992, more than 600,000 files on victims of illegal repression had reportedly been transferred to state archives from those of the KGB. Two years later, however, a Yeltsin decree on review of archival documents and their possible declassification was still limited to those documents created before 1964. Some members of parliament have called for restrictions on former Communist officials. The following article examines the debate over a draft screening law to address this issue.

The following documents related to transitional justice in Russia can be found in Volume III of this collection:

- Decrees Banning the Communist Party
- Constitutional Court Decision on the Banning of the Communist Party
- Law on Rehabilitation of Victims of Political Repression
- Statute on the Commission on Rehabilitation of Victims of Political Repression

THE TRIAL OF THE COMMUNIST PARTY

Robert Sharlet, "The Russian Constitutional Court: The First Term" *

Background to the Case

The CPSU case arose out of the cauldron of events surrounding the abortive coup of 1991. Not long before the coup, the then recently elected President of Russia had begun a legal campaign against the Russian Communist Party (RCP) (Sharlet, 1992, pp.112-13). Party officials were threatening law suits when the furor was soon eclipsed by the coup, Yel'tsin's successful defiance, and his immediate legal counterattack against the CPSU and the RCP. On August 23rd and 25th, Yel'tsin issued decrees suspending both parties and taking their property into safekeeping pending a judicial investigation into their complicity in the coup (*Ukaz*, 1991a & 1991b).

In those heady days, little was made of the fact that Yel'tsin's decrees exceeded presidential authority under the RSFSR Constitution, preempted prevailing law, and usurped judicial functions. Events rushed on and a few months later, as the Soviet Union was coming apart, Yel'tsin issued his November 6th decree converting the suspensions into a ban and formally nationalizing the parties' buildings and bank accounts. The three decrees taken together formed the basis of the CPSU case in the amended petition submitted to the Constitutional Court by the Ivashko-Kuptsov group of deputies on February 7, 1992. In its final amended version, the deputies' petition asked the Court to review the constitutionality of Yel'tsin's August decrees as well as his November edict.[48] ...

To play the new game of judicial constitutional politics, the adversaries to the CPSU case understood that their political differences had to be presented in legal form. To blunt the conflict and defuse some of its inherent tension, [Chief Justice Valeriy] Zor'kin and the Court attempted to cloak the entire proceeding in the juridical garb of procedure. Initially, the Court was successful and the public, preoccupied with more pressing economic concerns, soon lost interest in what seemed an arcane debate over the near and distant Soviet past. However, unexpectedly, the hearings dragged on, becoming more unruly, and spilling out of the narrow juridical channels into open political waters.

By the end of the trial, a buffeted Court and its helmsman Zor'kin found themselves drifting in the churning surf of transitional politics. What began as a judicial enterprise became months later a test of institutional survival skills. Throughout the uncertain navigation, the Court was faced with what appeared to be a zero-sum choice: find for the Communist side and the law, or decide in favor of the President and

---

* Excerpted from Robert Sharlet, "The Russian Constitutional Court: The First Term," *Post-Soviet Affairs*, vol. 9, no. 1 (1993), pp. 16-31.

[48] See the full title of the amended February, 1992 petition in *Nezavisimaya gazeta*, December 1, 1992, p.1.

political expediency. Without a doubt, the CPSU case had further blurred the divide between law and politics.

President Yel'tsin chose the day before the 74th anniversary of the Bolshevik Revolution in November 1991 to issue his third and final decree on the communist system, probably assuming that he was driving the final nail into the coffin of a dead power structure (*Ukaz*, 1991c). Yet less than two weeks later, the corpse in the form of the Russian Communist Party (RCP) was alive and appealing to the new Russian Constitutional Court to review the legality of the decision banning it and nationalizing its property.[50] While the CPSU case as we know it did not begin to crystallize until six weeks later, when representatives of both the all-union and the Russian parties joined forces in a common petition,[51] the broad outline of the Communist challenge to Yel'tsin was clear from the initial RCP appeal....

Defining the Stakes: Backstage Maneuvering

The Court had accepted the original CPSU petition in late December, but now appeared to be in no hurry to deliberate such a politically charged issue pitting the recent Soviet past against the current Russian present. In an interview two weeks later, the Chief Justice merely allowed that the case was being "intensively studied" and would probably be examined in the first half of 1992 (*Pravda*, February 21, 1992, p.2). Exercising its discretionary prerogative, the Court instead took up other cases involving ongoing legislative-executive disputes, a particularly acute center-periphery conflict, and a couple of individual rights violations. Most of these cases were relatively well defined and concerned clearly justiciable issues. Presumably, by adjudicating them first, Chief Justice Zor'kin hoped to build up the Court's judicial capital before it plunged into the overtly political CPSU case. However, nothing in the preceding cases prepared the Court for the sprawling, diffuse, long-winded and impassioned CPSU case, which would encompass testimony from 62 witnesses and experts in the course of 52 sessions. The case consumed the rest of the year, running a little more than six months from the first hearing on May 26th to December 16, 1992, the day the full decision was published (*Izvestiya*, November 30, 1992, p.1).

What was going on backstage in Russian political circles as the CPSU petition awaited its day in court? No doubt Zor'kin and the Court took into

---

[50] The RCP "appeal" to the RCC concerning Yel'tsin's November 6th decree, was signed by eight RCP secretaries and published in the conservative paper *Sovetskaya Rossiya*, November 16, 1991, p.1. The first signature was that of Valentin Kuptsov, First Secretary of the banned RCP. The public appeal was in the nature of a general political statement and did not include specific legal arguments.

[51] The submission to the RCC of the formal legal petition challenging the constitutionality of Yel'tsin's November 6th decree, took place on December 27, 1991. The petition was filed by 37 Russian People's Deputies, led by Deputy Vladimir Ivashko, Deputy General Secretary of the banned CPSU, and Deputy Kuptsov of the RCP. The tightly argued petition contained a close analysis of the decree in question, several laws, and the Russian Constitution (see *Khodataystvo*, 1992a).

consideration the factor of time, to allow the emotional fallout from the abrupt disintegration of the USSR to subside, and to give the Russian leadership a chance to get its economic reform program underway before having to divert energy and attention to the defense of the 1991 decrees.[53] Within reform circles, a question probably discussed was how to fend off the unwanted challenge to its legally shaky decrees. It was well understood that the politically defeated old guard saw in the Court an opportunity for a second chance, this time presumably on a more level juridical playing field....

[O]n May 12,... the respected constitutional specialist, Deputy Oleg Rumyantsev, filed with the Court a counterpetition concerning the CPSU case.[55] Rumyantsev's petition, which he amended on May 22nd, asked the Court to verify the constitutionality of the CPSU and the RCP, arguing correctly that this fundamental issue had not been addressed in any of Yel'tsin's three decrees at issue (*Khodataystvo*, 1992b). Then on May 25, on the very eve of the opening hearing in the CPSU case, yet another counterpetition was filed with the Court, this one from a group of liberal People's Deputies including Rumyantsev (*Khodataystvo*, 1992c). The two counterpetitions being predictably similar, the Court in closed session that very day decided to merge them into a combined suit which came to be known as the "Rumyantsev petition."...

[The Court] decided to join the CPSU and Rumyantsev petitions and make of them a single case (*Nezavisimaya gazeta*, December 1, 1992, p.1).... Although the Rumyantsev petition did not preempt the CPSU challenge to Yel'tsin, Rumyantsev had succeeded in imposing an unanticipated burden of proof on the CPSU, thus throwing the Party, which had initiated the case as the plaintiff, onto the defensive in the counterpetition. The Presidential legal team, led by Yel'tsin counselor Sergey Shakhray, was now augmented by the well known lawyer Andrey Makarov representing Petitioner Rumyantsev and colleagues. In view of this turn of events in the case and the need for both sides to review strategy anew, the Court recessed until July 7, six weeks hence.

The "Trial of the Century" in Overview

The CPSU hearing opened amidst high expectation of a dramatic legal confrontation which would yield a decisive outcome, probably within several days to a week.[57] The VIP box was full, the press section overflowing, and the spectator gallery packed. Those who could not get into the courtroom, including the correspondent for *Pravda*, had to watch on

---

[53] Indeed, in a February, 1992 interview, Zor'kin took an unabashedly pro-liberal position, asserting that if conservatives gained control of the parliament, "dreams about any changes for the better will be ruined at the root" (*Kuranty*, February 25, 1992, p.4).

[55] The timing and sequence of the countervailing petitions was discussed by the principal organizers of the CPSU petition in a statement criticizing the RCC's procedural decisions on the petitions (see *Sovetskaya Rossiya*, June 12, 1992, p.3).

[57] For instance, Deputy Roy Medvedev predicted the trial might run from five to ten days, or possibly longer (see Goryachev, 1992a).

television monitors. No one at the time envisioned that the proceedings would go on for weeks and months, the press least of all. Indeed, as the trial ran on, the story lost its novelty and media attention waned. Both the structure of the lengthy process, and the procedures for managing its complexities, tended to emerge on an ad hoc basis, frequently on the basis of sidebar consultations between Chief Justice Zor'kin and the lead counsel for the two parties (Thorson, 1992, p.4). The Court had not yet (and still at this writing has not) produced its official Regulations governing the conduct of hearings, so from time to time the Chief Justice would announce improvisations which became "court procedure." In retrospect, the structure of the trial which did emerge, punctuated by several long recesses, included: initial presentations and testimony by witnesses, both followed by cross-examination; introduction of documentary evidence; presentation of expert opinion; and, throughout the proceedings as the need arose, questions put by the bench as well as the summoning of additional witnesses and documents by the Court to clarify issues before it.

Both sides, of course, hoped and expected to win and spared no effort to "try" their cases in the press, as well as use media interviews to project confidence or cast doubt on the opponent's latest move. The President and his representatives often seemed brashly confident of the outcome, while the CPSU spokesmen appeared more tentative about ultimately prevailing, having been thrown offstride by the inclusion of the Rumyantsev petition in the case.[58] Although one of the dissenters from the CPSU case verdict would later label the merging of the two petitions "juridical nonsense," the large margin by which the merger had been voted had discouraged the CPSU defense team. Possibly, the government's more confident public posture was dictated by the fact that Yel'tsin had to win, while the CPSU had nothing further to lose (*Nezavisimaya gazeta*, December 1, 1992, p.1; and December 2, 1992, p.2).

The contending parties saw the issues at stake in starkly different terms. To fully understand these differences, it is necessary to disentangle the real from the nominal aspects of the case at each defense table. Nominally, the government "played" the CPSU case as an opportunity to ensure the momentum of the economic reforms and continue the development of the Russian governmental system. Actually, the more basic issue at stake, in their eyes, was the legitimacy of post-communist Russia and the need to maintain civil peace during the turbulent transition period.[59]

---

[58] During a phone-in program the week before the July hearings opened, Yel'tsin, while conceding that some procedural "inconsistencies" might be found in his decrees, nonetheless asserted that the RCC would not rule them unconstitutional. He concluded that "The Communist Party in the form in which it existed until August, 1991 is doomed" (*Komsomol'skaya pravda*, July 3, 1992, p.2).

[59] Less charitably, former USSR President Mikhail Gorbachev, a critic of the CPSU proceeding in its entirety, argued that the real purpose of the trial was to put Soviet "history in the dock" by way of making the Soviet system a "scapegoat" for the chaos and disarray caused by Yel'tsin's policies. Interestingly, the radical reformer and Yel'tsin adviser, Gennadiy Burbulis, did not disagree with this evaluation, merely making the same point in a more euphemized, diplomatic way (*Komsomol'skaya pravda*, September, 29, 1992, p.2; Ruvinskiy, 1992a).

The CPSU spokesmen histrionically tried to claim that nothing less than the "fate of democracy" and its flipside, the danger of totalitarianism or "fascism in Russia," was at stake in the proceedings.[60] In reality, their goal was the restoration of the shattered status quo before August 1991 or, minimally, the legal rehabilitation of the RCP and the recovery of its property. On the latter issue, the Party was prepared to leave its hotels and resorts in public hands if it could just reclaim its printing plants and publishing houses.[61]

For the Constitutional Court, the CPSU case presented opportunities, but also posed dangers. The proceedings afforded the Court a highly visible occasion to establish itself among elite and public alike as the indispensable "third branch" of government in the emerging separation of powers doctrine in Russia. The Court had already carved out a niche for itself as an impartial mediator of disputes between the other branches but, [with one exception,] its other cases were more technical and garnered less media coverage....

At the same time, the CPSU case was replete with dangers for the Court as a still very new and novel institution in Russia. The case represented a classic "political question" that the Court was supposed to avoid. It was a constitutionally untidy case, since the State's charter was in flux between Yel'tsin's August and November decrees.[63] Then too, there was the possibility that Zor'kin the jurist might not yet be a sufficiently experienced court politician to control the powerful political professionals who would come before the Court, not to mention the unforeseen extramural aspects of the case which might arise. Finally, it was soon evident to court-watchers that the justices were not of a single mind on the case; hence, the shape and composition of the final outcome was unpredictable (*Nezavisimaya gazeta*, December 1, 1992, p.1).

At the outset, Chief Justice Zor'kin tried to project for the Court an image of judicial neutrality, asserting that the proceedings were neither a political trial nor a "show trial," and that the CPSU was not on trial. For Zor'kin, it was a juridical undertaking in which "political expediency" had no legitimate place.[64] Nonetheless, the CPSU team, some journalists, certain critics and even friends of the Court publicly disputed the official image. Burbulis, for instance, described the trial as more of a historical examination "than a juridical one." Feofanov, a pro-Court journalist, added that the proceedings had "acquired a clearly moral overtone." Other commentators labeled the hearings in a variety of pejorative ways, including a political diversion, a political farce, the equivalent of "a

---

[60] See *Komsomol'skaya pravda*, July 9, 1992, p.3; "Lawyers Comments" (1992); and "Slovo" (1992), an appeal by six lawyers which includes the reference to "fascism."

[61] Again, Gorbachev took a more critical view (this time of the CPSU), insisting that the Party had set out to destabilize the transition process by "exploiting the social situation and tension" in Russia (*Komsomol'skaya pravda*, October 7, 1992, p.3; "CPSU Spokesman," 1992).

[63] The RCC's final verdict in the CPSU case was based on two versions of the 1978 RSFSR Constitution, one that was in effect after May 24, 1991 and the other after November 1, 1991 (see *Postanovleniye*, 1992g).

[64] For Zor'kin, the phrase, "law not expediency," became like a mantra which he repeated over and over again in interviews (see, e.g. Krasnov, 1992a).

[Communist] Party Control Committee," a political trial, a political show trial and, at the conclusion, a failed "Nuremburg trial." Gorbachev's early prediction that the CPSU case "may turn out to be compromising for the Constitutional Court" was beginning to look prescient (Yermakova, 1992d; *Izvestiya*, August 4, 1992, p.2; and October 13, 1992, p.2; *Sovetskaya Rossiya*, December 3, 1992, p.2; Gorbachev, 1992).

Pro and Con: Political Combat in the Legal Arena

Thinly disguised in juridical language, the courtroom attack on and defense of Yel'tsin's decrees revolved around three questions: (1) Was the CPSU/RCP involved in the August coup? (2) What kind of organization was the CPSU/RCP? and (3) Did Yel'tsin's decrees have a basis in the Constitution and laws of the RSFSR? Along the way, the issue raised by the Rumyantsev petition was partially subsumed in the second question, and directly addressed in the final question.

The coup and allegations of CPSU complicity had been the catalyst for the Yel'tsin decrees, but the CPSU defense team countered that no judicial evidence had been forthcoming and no trial had been held. Further, the coup leaders had not even been tried, nor was there any indication of local Party organizations, other than the Moscow and Orenburg Party committees, being involved in the coup.[65] In rebuttal, the Presidential side made several points: (1) all of the arrested conspirators awaiting trial had been members of CPSU executive bodies; (2) on the first day of the coup, August 19, the CPSU Secretariat had sent coded telegrams to all local Party committees, urging their support for the coup; and (3) a post-coup investigation by a committee of the Russian Supreme Soviet had established Party complicity.[66]

The gulf between the two sides' perceptions widened even more on the question of the nature of the CPSU/RCP. CPSU witnesses testified that the all-union Party had been in the process of internal reform, and was already implementing the revised Party hegemony clause of the USSR Constitution (Art. 6) by carrying out a division of Party and state structures.[67] In addition, they argued that the reforming CPSU had been "the midwife of democracy in Russia" (*Izvestiya*, July 9, 1992, p.3). As for the RCP, which was established in early 1991, defenders argued that it was a "normal," parliamentary party and, according to a former First Secretary, that the RCP was independent of and even opposed on certain issues to the CPSU.[68]

---

[65] CPSU representatives had surveyed 78 Russian Federation procurators, asking whether they had evidence of RCP committees' involvement in the August coup. Seventy-six of 78 replied in the negative (*Rossiyskaya gazeta*, July 14, 1992, p.1).

[66] On the coded telegram, see Krasnov (1992b). The Russian Supreme Soviet inquiry was referred to in Yel'tsin's November 6th decree (*Ukaz*, 1992c).

[67] Roy Medvedev testified that the CPSU's restructuring "was in progress, but ... was cut short" by the post-coup decrees (*Rossiyskaya gazeta*, July 23, 1992, p.2). Former Politburo-member Yegor Ligachev made the point on the division of structures (see "Ligachev," 1992).

[68] On the claim of the RCP's normalcy and independence, see, respectively, A. Melnikov in Yermakova (1992c), and I. Polozkov in Krasulin (1992).

The government responded that the CPSU was unreformable, that it had remained a continuation of the Party of 1917 and 1937, and that, in fact, the CPSU had never even been a political party.[69] To support the thesis of Yel'tsin's November decree, Makarov argued cogently that the CPSU had been a "state structure" throughout Soviet history. He pointed out that, even after the party's legal status as a political monopoly had been abrogated in March 1990, the Politburo still made decisions on military aid to the Afghan government, ordered the creation of the elite "Alpha" commando unit within the KGB, directed State funds to foreign communist parties, and made *nomenklatura* appointments to public posts.[70] Other assessments of the CPSU called it a "state party," a "party state," and a "criminal association."[71] In reply to the claims made for the RCP, the government answered that it was a creature of the CPSU, that it was in fact ideologically to the right of the parent body, and that it had been primarily set up as a "bridgehead" for returning to the pre-perestroyka administrative-command system (see "Court Hears Witnesses," 1992; Yermakova 1992g).

In the exchanges on the Party, the question of its property was derivative. The CPSU team insisted that the property had been acquired legally and with Party dues. The Presidential representatives brought forth evidence that in some years the dues were insufficient to cover operating costs, and State funds had been transferred to the Party. In addition, they asserted that all CPSU facilities were actually State property; therefore, the decrees merely restored to the State its property ("Shakhray Remarks," 1992). In the course of these cross-arguments, two images of the CPSU's role in Soviet history were presented, both of which were accurate: the Party of industrialization, victory in WW II, and the achievements of Soviet science; and the CPSU of the purges, the Katyn massacre, and the suppression of dissent.[72]

Given the government's "'trump card,"' its significant advantage in controlling the State archives and the CPSU's secret documents, the Yel'tsin side had the stronger case on the first two issues: the nature of the CPSU and its role in the August 1991 coup. However, on the final question of

---

[69] Former Politburo member Alexander Yakovlev made the "unreformable" point in Zherebenkov (1992), while Attorney Makarov argued CPSU continuity from 1917-91 in Yermakova (1992a).

[70] In order to cope with the more than 40 volumes of archival material introduced by the Presidential side, the RCC ruled procedurally on July 10 that only evidence from the period after the revision of Article Six (March 1990) would be admissible on the question of whether the CPSU had become a normal political party (see Thorson, 1992, p.4). On Attorney Makarov's post-Article Six evidence, see Ruvinskiy (1992c).

[71] See *Rossiyskaya gazeta*, August 4, 1992, p.2, and *Izvestiya*, July 13, 1992, p.3. In his testimony for the CPSU side, Medvedev challenged the government's thesis that the CPSU was a "state structure," retorting that it was instead "a suprastate structure" which "stood even higher than the state" (Goryachev, 1992a).

[72] On the fate of two Soviet generals purged in 1947 for private comments on the misery of the masses, see *Izvestiya*, July 16, 1992, p.7. The relevance of the Katyn massacre of Polish officers in 1940 was argued on the grounds that since Gorbachev had suppressed the documents, the CPSU had not actually changed after March, 1990. On the Katyn documents, see Tolz (1992). On the CPSU's repression policy, the government called former political prisoners, Father Gleb Yakunin and People's Deputy Sergey Kovalev, among others, to testify.

the lawfulness of the President's decrees, the contest was much more evenly balanced. As Vadim Bakatin noted, the three decrees were "juridically vulnerable." If they had not been, there would have been no trial (*Komsomol'skaya pravda*, August 7, 1992, p.1; "Bakatin," 1992).

The CPSU opened by attacking the Rumyantsev petition on the procedural ground that the Court did not have jurisdiction over the constitutionality of the Party since the Court's statute had not yet been amended accordingly. Furthermore, the petition violated the law's prohibition against the Court taking up "political questions"; therefore, they argued, the two petitions were wrongly joined into a single case ("Slovo," 1992). Rumyantsev's attorney, Makarov, replied that the April amendment to the Constitution gave the Court sufficient jurisdiction, that the amendment also legitimized the issue as justiciable, and, since Yel'tsin's decree had not dealt with the constitutional question, it was therefore appropriate for the Court to merge the two petitions (*Khodataystvo*, 1992b).

The CPSU lawyers launched a powerful legal assault on the Yel'tsin decrees themselves. The decrees were claimed to have been unconstitutional for three main reasons: they violated the "division of prerogatives" within the executive branch; infringed the constitutional principle of the separation of powers; and usurped both the legislative and judicial spheres of government (*Sovetskaya Rossiya*, July 9, 1992, p.3). In responding, the Yel'tsin team had to skirt the awkward constitutional issues and rely on a political declaration, several technical points of law and a Stalin-era edict. While acknowledging "some legal rough spots," Shakhray nonetheless maintained the President's course of action had been "right and lawful" (Goryachev, 1992b).

The government's rebuttal went as follows:

(1) The Russian Declaration of Sovereignty of 1990 had superseded all Soviet laws not formally adopted by the republic's legislature.

(2) By August 1991, the Russian Supreme Soviet had not adopted the new USSR law on public associations; therefore, that law was not valid on Russian territory.

(3) Although the CPSU had registered under the USSR law, at the time of the coup there were still uncorrected defects in its registration documents; hence, the process of legally registering the CPSU had not been completed.

(4) The RCP had not registered under the association law at the time Yel'tsin issued his August decrees; therefore, the RCP did not enjoy legal status.

(5) The only relevant law in force on Russian territory in mid-1991 was a 1932 Stalinist decree permitting the executive to ban political and social organizations and seize their property without reference to judicial process. Thus, Yel'tsin's decrees were lawful.[73]

---

[73] The 1932 decree was subsequently revoked by the Russian Supreme Soviet in December, 1991 (Thorson, 1992, p.3). On the conflicting legal interpretations of the decree in

Questions about the legality of Yel'tsin's decrees were put to dozens of legal experts who were either called to testify or asked to present their opinions in writing. But if the Court hoped to find guidance in that direction, it did so in vain. The experts divided about equally on the question of the constitutionality of Yel'tsin's decrees, leaving the 13 judges to fare for themselves in sorting out the conflicting and frequently asymmetrical arguments of the adversaries. To a CPSU attorney, the case was simply a matter of "presidential arbitrariness and legal barbarism," while to a government strategist, victory would be attained by continuing to use "the language of legal argumentation and moral political accusation." There was truth in both positions, but if to the reader it appears that the statements talked past each other, that too is correct. The CPSU was using law to try to redress political defeat, while the Yel'tsin government had no choice but to blend politics and law to mask its legal shortcomings (*Izvestiya*, July 9, 1992, p.3; Yermakova 1992g).

The Trial as Political Theater

The case progressively deteriorated into scenes of farce, melodrama and pure theater, with the justices, the Russian public, and even, at points, the world at large as audience. Elements of political spectacle were introduced already at the beginning of the main proceedings in July. Supporters of the CPSU picketed the courthouse. Delegates from one of the rump communist parties petitioned the Court to file an *amicus curiae* brief on behalf of the CPSU. Neither the Court nor the CPSU team would hear of it. During opening arguments, a CPSU "defender" of the Constitution got carried away and called for the armed overthrow of the Yel'tsin government (*Kuranty*, July 8, 1992, p.1; Ruvinskiy, 1992b; Krasnov, 1992a).

During the proceedings, an extraordinary parade of witnesses marched across the judicial stage, from former political prisoner Vladimir Bukovskiy (who quipped that it was his first time in a Moscow courtroom as a witness rather than a defendant), to Professor Richard Pipes of Harvard, and former Politburo member Alexander Yakovlev (Yermakova, 1992f), all of whom testified on behalf of the government. Prominent witnesses for the CPSU included Roy Medvedev, former Prime Minister Nikolay Ryzhkov, Gorbachev's erstwhile conservative opponent Yegor Ligachev, and a well known Soviet cosmonaut.

In the midst of the trial, the chief lawyer for the government was in an automobile accident, which quickly became a well imagined assassination attempt.[74] The CPSU case also had its links to the

---

the trial, see *Rossiyskaya gazeta*, July 8, 1992, p.1, and Bogolyubov's speech in *Sovetskaya Rossiya*, July 9, 1992, p.3.

[74] In mid-July, Shakhray's official car was struck at high speed by a hit-and-run driver. Moscow police almost immediately declared the accident a premeditated crime, while Shakhray's press secretary pronounced it an attempted assassination. Meanwhile, Shakhray's CPSU adversaries in Court quickly disclaimed any responsibility. Several days later, a sheepish barber shop manager turned himself in, explaining that he had been driving while intoxicated and became scared when he realized he had hit a presidential limousine. See several radio and television announcements under "Shakhray's accident" (1992).

forthcoming trial of the August 1991 coup leaders. The Procurator-General was a regular visitor to the VIP box, as he sought possible interconnections and gained a full view of how a grand trial could go awry. On the other side of the aisle, lawyers for two of the coup conspirators were part of the CPSU's legal team, while the daughter of then prisoner Anatoliy Lukyanov, a law professor at Moscow State University, served as a consultant.[75]

Passions inevitably burst forth during the proceedings, with Zor'kin doing his best to hold down the exchange of insults. Representatives from both sides were disciplined by the Court, including a fine for contempt.[76] On the subject of money, the CPSU had none (its property had been confiscated), so as an indigent litigant, it was funded by the government. A bit later in the proceedings, Yel'tsin bestowed on the justices a substantial pay raise, nominally to deal with raging inflation, which was deemed poorly timed even by his own lawyers. In a more mundane matter, some of the Court's guards were caught "renting" out cars from the RCC motor pool for private gain (*Kuranty*, August 15, 1992, p.4; *Komsomol'skaya pravda*, September 16, 1992, p.1).

Hyperbole and histrionics were never far removed from the trial. When the zealous government side tried to flood the proceedings with hundreds of secret documents, the Court characterized most of them as "totally irrelevant" from a legal point of view. Name calling went on in the press; a right-wing newspaper compared Shakhray and Zor'kin to Vyshinskiy and Ulrikh of the purge trials. In court, both sides tried to pull on the heart strings and arouse indignation, with incantations to Party-inspired valor in World War II set against the sealed zinc coffins brought home from the now disfavored war in Afghanistan. From time to time, there were touches of the absurd in the courtroom drama: it was claimed that the KGB had bugged Yel'tsin's sauna and Raisa Gorbachev's hairdresser's phone ("Court," 1992a; *Pravda*, July 9, 1992, p.2; *Rossiyskaya gazeta*, July 11, 1992, p.1; *Pravda*, August 1, 1992, p.2; *San Diego Union-Tribune*, July 29, 1992, p.A-16). Finally, when Gorbachev refused to testify, the CPSU side used his colleague Yakovlev as a surrogate whipping boy, grilling him mercilessly as an apostate of communism.

The Gorbachev-Zor'kin-Yel'tsin triangle converted the still relatively sedate courtroom theater into an outdoor pageant, attracting headlines throughout the world. Early on, the Court had rejected the CPSU's request to call Yel'tsin and had decided not to call Gorbachev. Later, the Court reversed itself and called Gorbachev as a witness.[77]

---

[75] The lawyers for the coup conspirators were Y. Ivanov, who represents V. Kryuchkov, former KGB chairman, and A. Kligman, who represents Kryuchkov's former deputy, V. Grushko, who will be tried separately due to ill health. In addition, Professor Elena Lukyanova, daughter of the former chairman of the USSR Supreme Soviet, served as an expert for the CPSU side.

[76] In September, Makarov, representing Rumyantsev, was fined 100 rubles for contempt of court (see "Constitutional Court," 1992b).

[77] Gorbachev had met privately with Chief Justice Zor'kin in the spring, before the trial opened, and indicated his unwillingness to either represent the CPSU in court or appear as a

Gorbachev steadfastly refused to appear, first respectfully and then raucously. He feared becoming a pawn and a scapegoat in what he regarded as a political confrontation and a show trial. Furious at this defiance, Zor'kin's public remarks on Gorbachev became increasingly strident and intemperate for a jurist. Then Yel'tsin entered the fray, with a decree that blocked Gorbachev from travelling abroad until he answered the summons. Gorbachev responded with criticism of Yel'tsin's leadership and declared himself a "*refusenik*." As the fracas escalated, journalists and public figures took sides, but Gorbachev held his position, announcing that not even handcuffs could compel him to give testimony.[78]

As Russia lurched into the fall of 1992, sinking ever deeper into political and economic crisis, zealots on Yel'tsin's staff added to the sound and fury now enveloping the CPSU case. Calling Gorbachev's foundation "a second Zurich, a Bolshevist center," the tax inspectors were dispatched and the police called in to lock the former President out of his office ("Poltoranin," 1992). Between Gorbachev's ensuing curbside press conferences, his charges that Zor'kin had violated judicial ethics with his caustic comments, and his demands for equal television time to reply, the politician had outmaneuvered the jurist, leaving in shambles the gravity and decorum of the trial. Defeated, Zor'kin withdrew the summons and, not long after in mid-November, the Constitutional Court held its last session on the CPSU case with no end clearly in sight.[79]

Conclusion: The Verdict as Politics, Law and History

Just a few weeks after its final public session, the Court announced its decision in the CPSU case. The verdict was less interesting for what it said than for its timing, the way it was arrived at, and its implications for the players in the long drama.The timing was exquisite—the day before the opening of the Seventh Congress of People's Deputies on December 1, 1992. Two things were thus achieved: the case was concluded before the President entered political battle with the rebellious parliament; and the news of the Congress would foreclose extended press discussion of the decision and how it reflected on the Court....

Internal evidence of the final deliberations ... indicates that no consensus or strong majority existed. Although the final tally was 11-2 in favor of the verdict, a number of procedural votes required on various parts of the verdict were won by only a one or two vote margin (*Nezavisimaya gazeta*, December 1, 1992, p.1)....

---

witness. Initially, the RCC had concurred with his wishes. For Gorbachev's position and his perceptive analysis of the overall CPSU case, see his long interview in *Komsomol'skaya pravda*, October 7, 1992, p.3.

[78] For some of the verbal volleys between Zor'kin and Gorbachev, see Barry (1993).

[79] For a sampling of American press coverage of the fracas, see *USA Today*, October 9, 1992, p.4A; *The New York Times*, October 9, 1992, p.A3; *Washington Post*, October 9, 1992, p. A29.

The actual decision was solomonic, a compromise which gave each side something.[80] None of Yel'tsin's decrees was declared either fully constitutional or unconstitutional. Borrowing from the briefs presented earlier, the Court found for Yel'tsin on the lawfulness of banning the central executive agencies of the CPSU/RCP, but for the Party both on the right to reestablish the local branches of the RCP and on some aspects of the property issue. Given the effective collapse of the CPSU in the fall of 1991, the Rumyantsev petition was declared moot; that part of the case was closed without decision.

In a withering dissent, Justice Luchin argued that President Yel'tsin had exceeded his competence in issuing the three decrees, and that the Court had wrongly joined the two petitions into a combined case (*Pravda*, December 3, 1992, p.1). In essence, he castigated the majority's verdict as a decision based on political "expediency rather than ... law," made by a Court acting as "politicians" rather than jurists.[81]

What are the implications of the verdict for all involved? In brief, the decision could be classified as good politics (it saved face for Yel'tsin at a critical moment), dubious law (political expediency was the driving force, though dressed in legal garb), and inconclusive history (the verdict on the CPSU's involvement in the coup will have to await the forthcoming coup trial).[82]

If we look more closely at the participants in the long drawn-out case, all emerged from the fray weakened, despite their efforts to save face. The Russian Communist Party may now organize from the bottom up, and can turn to the courts to regain some of its property. However, despite proclamations that communism is again on the rise, there is little likelihood that the five to six rump communist groups will come together under a common flag in the foreseeable future.[83] In addition, the RCP will probably face long, expensive, and complicated court battles to recover lost property. Finally, the communist movement has been seriously tarnished in the public mind by the extensive disclosures from secret archives during the trial, especially on the Brezhnev period for the suppression of dissent, and on the Gorbachev period for the handling of Chernobyl.[84]

Yel'tsin and the Presidency saved face but lost prestige. His decrees from the highwater mark of his incumbency were found defective, and, were it not for some juridical sleight of hand by the Court, they might have

---

[80] See *Postanovleniye* (1992g) and the analysis of the verdict in Barry (1993). For a commentary which reported reactions of both parties to the case, see Latsis (1992).

[81] *Nezavisimaya gazeta*, December 2, 1992, p.2. Compare with Zor'kin's appraisal: "The judges were guided only by law and conscience," *Izvestiya*, December 1, 1992, p.2.

[82] In December, 1992, all of the remaining leaders under arrest since the collapse of the 1991 coup were released from jail pending a trial scheduled for April 14, 1992.

[83] A *Nezavisimaya gazeta* reporter wrote on May 26, 1992 (p.1) that there are six communist parties "along the pink-red spectrum." Roy Medvedev has recently described five of these parties. Neither he nor the reporter, however, held out much hope for communist unity in the foreseeable future. See Weir (1993).

[84] For example, a most shocking disclosure from the Gorbachev era was the Politburo's 1986 decision to put on sale, with minimum precautions, meat contaminated in the Chernobyl zone (see *Literaturnaya gazeta*, No. 35, August 26, 1992, p.11).

been declared unconstitutional as well. The great economic difficulties of the first transition year had already cost Yel'tsin much of his accrued political capital, which was now further diminished by the compromise he had to settle for in the CPSU case. Moreover, the RCP was not relegated to history as he had expected, nor was the communist past buried as he had hoped, especially with the coup conspirators, now out on bail, writing books and giving interviews on the August events.

Finally, the Constitutional Court itself, having survived the CPSU trial, strengthened its position as the third branch in the separation of powers. The impassioned conflict between past and present was resolved, although not to anyone's complete satisfaction. The costs were considerable, however. The Court emerged from the case battered, riddled by division and increasingly politicized.

In retrospect, the Court in the Communist Party case served as a mirror reflecting the disorderly, conflict-ridden politics of the transition period in Russia. The resolution of the case did effectively defuse a potentially ominous dispute, and thereby contributed to political stability and social peace, but at the expense of the Court building its moral authority as a judicial institution dispensing dispassionate justice.

References*

"Bakatin Describes CPSU Control Over KGB," INTERFAX, in Foreign Broadcast Information Service, *Daily Report—Supplement: Central Eurasia* (hereafter, *FBIS-Sov-S*), 7-8, October 23, 1992.

"Court Hears Witnesses Speak on Coup Plot," Ostankino Television Network, *FBIS-Sov-S*, 9, July 31, 1992.

"Court Reviews 'Adequate Legal Basis' for Case," INTERFAX, *FBIS-Sov-S*, 14-15, July 17, 1992a.

Gorbachev, M.S., "Further on Interview," ITAR-TASS, *FBIS-Sov-S*, 16, July 17, 1992.

Goryachev, S., "Shakhray Reviews Year Since Coup Attempt," Moscow Central Television, *FBIS-Sov*, 18-21, August 25, 1992.

"Khodataystvo o priznanii nekonstitutsionnosti KPSS i KP RSFSR i podtverzhdenii v etoy svyazi konstitutsionnosti Ukazov Prezidenta RSFSR ... (Petition on the Recognition of the Unconstitutionality of the CPSU and the RSFSR Communist Party and Confirmation, in this Connection, of the Constitutionality of the RSFSR Presidential Decrees...)," *Konstitutsionnyy vestnik*, 13:226-37, 1992b.

"Khodataystvo o proverke konstitutsionnosti CPSU i KP RSFSR, 25 maya 1992 goda (On the Verification of the Constitutionality of the CPSU and the RSFSR Communist Party, May 25, 1992)," *Konstitutsionnyy vestnik*, 13:237-42, 1992c.

Krasnov, A., "Stepanov Draws Warning from Court's Zor'kin," Radio Rossii, *FBIS-Sov-S*, 6-7, July 10, 1992a.

"Poltoranin Says Gorbachev Foundation Not Fulfilling Tasks," INTERFAX, *FBIS-Sov-S*, 20, October 23, 1992.

Ruvinskiy, A., "Court Proceedings on Decrees on CPSU Resumes," Mayak Radio Network, *FBIS-Sov-S*, 8, July 10, 1992b.

"Shakhray Remarks," INTERFAX, *FBIS-Sov-S*, 10, July 10, 1992.

Sharlet, Robert, *Soviet Constitutional Crisis*. Armonk, NY: M.E. Sharpe, 1992.

"Slovo dlya zashchity (Appeal for the Defense)," *Pravda*, 1, July 4, 1992.

Thorson, Carla, "The Fate of the Communist Party in Russia," *Radio Liberty Report on the USSR*, 1, 37:1-6, September 18, 1992.

"Ukaz Prezidenta RSFSR o priostanovlenii deyatel'nosti Kommunisticheskoy partii RSFSR, 23 avgusta 1991 goda (Decree of the RSFSR President on Suspending the Activity of the RSFSR Communist Party, August 23, 1991)," Vedomosti RSFSR, No. 35, Item 1149, 1991a."Ukaz

* [Editor's note: Only those sources referenced in the present excerpt are listed.]

Prezidenta RSFSR ob imushchestve KPSS i Kommunisticheskoy partii RSFSR, 25 avgusta 1991 goda (Decree of the RSFSR President on the Property of the CPSU and the RSFSR Communist Party, August 25, 1991)," *Vedomosti* RSFSR, No. 35, Item 1164, 1991b.

"Ukaz Prezidenta RSFSR o deyatel'nosti KPSS i KP RSFSR, 6 noyabrya 1991 goda (Decree of the President of the RSFSR on the Activity of the CPSU and the RSFSR CP, November 6, 1991)," *Vedomosti* RSFSR, No. 45, Item 1537, 1991c.

Yermakova, L., "Burbulis Comments on Court Hearings," ITAR-TASS, *FBIS-Sov-S*, 3, July 31, 1992d.

Yermakova, L., "Bukovskiy Appears as Witness at Court Hearing," ITAR-TASS, *FBIS-Sov-S*, 1, August 13, 1992f.

Yermakova, L., "Burbulis on Legality of Decrees Banning CPSU," ITAR-TASS, *FBIS-Sov-S*, 7-8, August 13, 1992g.

THE LAW ON REHABILITATION

Alexander H. Platt, Imtiaz T. Ladak, Alan J. Goodman, Matthew R. Nicely, "Compensating Former Political Prisoners: An Overview of Developments in Central and Eastern Europe"*

In November 1991, the Russian Soviet Federated Socialist Republic (RSFSR) Supreme Soviet passed a law regarding compensation for former political prisoners.[49] The purpose of the Law Rehabilitating Victims of Repression ("Rehabilitation Law") is to rehabilitate by restoring the victims' civil rights and by providing compensation for moral and material harm. The Commission of the RSFSR Supreme Soviet on Rehabilitation will monitor the implementation of this law.

A. Definitions and Scope of the Law

The Rehabilitation Law defines "political repression" as "various measures of coercion taken by the state out of political motives" which deprive or restrict the rights and freedoms of individuals. Politically motivated deprivation of life or freedom, forced treatment in psychiatric institutions, expulsion from the country and deprivation of citizenship, resettlement from customary place of residence, exile, banishment, deportation, and compulsory labor are all examples of political repression.

The Rehabilitation Law applies to all individuals, regardless of citizenship, who have been victims of political repression in the RSFSR since the end of 1917. The law compensates victims who, for political reasons, were convicted of a crime, subjected to criminal repression by institutions performing judicial functions, administratively subjected to exile, banishment, deportation, forced labor, and other restrictions of rights and freedoms, and forced to receive treatment in psychiatric institutions.

The Rehabilitation Law does not address individuals justly punished by the courts or nonjudicial organs for the following crimes: 1) treason; 2)

---

* Excerpted from Alexander H. Platt et al., Akin, Gump, Strauss, Hauer, & Feld, *Compensating Former Political Prisoners: An Overview of Developments in Central and Eastern Europe*, unpublished paper, August 14, 1992, pp. 16-20.

49 [omitted]

terrorism; 3) commission of violent acts and aiding traitors during the "Great Patriotic War;" 4) organization of gangs; and 5) commission of war crimes and crimes against law and order.

However, the law compensates all individuals punished for the following crimes, regardless of whether there was justification for the conviction: 1) anti-Soviet propaganda; 2) dissemination of rumors maligning the Soviet state; 3) violation of laws separating church and state; and 4) encroachment on the rights of citizens while pretending to perform religious ceremonies.

B. Procedure for Rehabilitation

The internal affairs department and the "procuracy organs"[50] will be responsible for rehabilitating victims of political repression. The internal affairs department will rehabilitate individuals who, for political reasons, were administratively subjected to exile, banishment, deportation, forced labor or other restrictions of rights and freedoms ("administrative repression"). The procuracy agencies will rehabilitate the remaining victims of political repression.

On application from interested individuals or public organizations, the internal affairs department will check all materials on the victims of administrative repression to determine whether they qualify for rehabilitation. In the absence of documentary evidence, one can judicially prove political repression on the basis of testimony. The internal affairs department must issue certificates of rehabilitation to individuals who qualify for rehabilitation. Those who receive a negative determination can appeal in court.

The procuracy organs will check all files and materials on the remaining victims (persons other than those of administrative repression) to determine whether they qualify for rehabilitation. Interestingly, it seems that the procuracy agencies must establish and verify all cases against individuals subject to rehabilitation regardless of whether an application is filed. Article 8 of the Rehabilitation law provides:

> Procuracy organs ... establish and verify all cases involving decisions of courts and nonjudicial organs that have not been revoked before the introduction of the present law against individuals subject to rehabilitation....

An individual who receives a negative determination from the procuracy organs can petition for reconsideration. The procuracy agencies will thereafter send the case to a court with proper jurisdiction.[51] If the

---

[50] The term "procuracy organs" and "procuracy agencies" refer to agencies of the Prosecutor's Office.

[51] Article 9 provides that, in the case of convicts, the court which made the last judicial decision will have jurisdiction over the reconsideration of the case. For civilians subjected to nonjudicial repressive measures, the supreme court of the autonomous republics will have jurisdiction. Finally, for military service personnel subjected to nonjudicial repressive measures, the military tribunal will have jurisdiction.

court determines that the individual was unjustifiably subjected to political repression, the applicant receives a certificate of rehabilitation. The procuracy organs and interested parties or social organizations can appeal the decision of the court.

C. Benefits and Privileges of Rehabilitation

The Rehabilitation Law creates two categories of repression: 1) repressive measures in the form of deprivation of freedom ("First Category"); and 2) repression in the form of deprivation of freedom, banishment and exile or forced treatment in psychiatric institutions ("Second Category").

All rehabilitated political victims are entitled to the following benefits and privileges: 1) the right to free legal consultation concerning rehabilitation; 2) the right to regain sociopolitical and civil rights and military and special titles 3) the right to reside in the areas where they lived before forced resettlement;[52] 4) the right to citizenship in the RSFSR for those who resided in the RSFSR and were stripped of their citizenship; and 5) the right to review materials and evidence against them in their convictions.

Rehabilitated individuals subjected to repressive measures in the form of deprivation of freedom are eligible for monetary compensation. Rehabilitated victims must have certificates of rehabilitation before they can receive this payment. The monetary compensation is 180 rubles ($103.50) for each month of incarceration, but cannot exceed 25,000 rubles ($14,373.60).[53] The government can make compensation payments as a one-time payment or in installments (at least one-third of the overall amount in the first three months, and the rest within the first three years, as prescribed by the RSFSR Council of Ministers).

Rehabilitated individuals subjected to deprivation of freedom, banishment, exile, or forced treatment in psychiatric institutions have priority in the receipt of housing if they lost their residence because of the repression or if they are in need of improved housing conditions. Workers who live in rural areas and belong to this category of rehabilitated individuals have the right to receive interest-free loans and priority in construction materials for building houses.

Disabled victims or pensioners who belong to this Second Category of rehabilitated individuals also have the following rights: 1) priority in sanitorium-health resort treatment and recreation; 2) extra medical treatment and a fifty percent reduction in the cost of medication; 3) free travel on all urban transportation, except taxis; 4) a free round-trip ticket on rail transportation every year; 5) a fifty percent reduction in costs of housing and municipal services; 6) priority in phone installation; 7)

---

52 This right also extends to family members and relatives who lived with the victims.

53 The U.S. dollar equivalent is based on the November 1991 exchange rate of $1 = 1.7393 rubles. The present exchange rate is not available. According to a statement by the International Association of Former Soviet Political Prisoners and Victims of the Communist Regimes (IASPPV), 180 rubles is presently equivalent to less than $1.

priority admission to boarding houses for the elderly and disabled; 8) free manufacture and repair of dentures; and 9) preferential treatment in obtaining food and industrial goods.

PURGING: THE DEBATE OVER A PROPOSED LAW

Victor Yasmann, "Legislation on Screening and State Security in Russia"[*]

A number of postcommunist countries, including Poland, the former Czechoslovakia, Lithuania, Latvia, and Estonia, have passed or are contemplating the passage of legislation that would bar former high-ranking communist party and state security officials from holding public office and from occupying positions in the educational and legal fields. Czechoslovakia and Poland were the first to pass such laws (in October 1991 and September 1992, respectively) and to label what was in essence a process of decommunization "lustration," a term based on the Latin word lustratio, a Roman pagan ritual of purification performed to avert evil.[1] On 9 July 1993 similar but more stringent legislation was approved by the Czech National Council.[2] In Lithuania and the other Baltic States the screening procedure was aimed mainly at parliamentary deputies. In [1993] the Russian parliament and President Boris Yeltsin have also begun grappling with the problem of lustration.[3]

Galina Starovoitova, a former adviser to President Yeltsin and currently a leader of Democratic Russia, presented a draft screening law at the second of four international conferences on the KGB.[4] The conference, held in Moscow from 29 to 31 May 1993, was sponsored by Democratic Russia, the International Foundation Glasnost, the International Freedom Foundation, and West and East European nongovernmental and human rights organizations. The basic concept of the law was also outlined in Moskovskie novosti.[5]

---

[*] Reprinted from Victor Yasmann, "Legislation on Screening and State Security in Russia," *RFE/RL Research Report*, vol. 2, no. 32 (1993), pp. 11-16.

[1] For a brief outline of lustration legislation, see *Moskovskie novosti*, no. 5, 1993; and *Izvestiya*, 9 June 1993. See also *Rossiiskaya gazeta*, 21 July 1992, and 10 February and 4 June 1993; *Izvestiya*, 30 March and 4 April 1993; *Novoe vremya nos.* 24 and 42, 1992; and *Problemy Vostochnoi Europy* nos. 37-38, 1993. See also Paulina Bren, "Lustration in the Czech and Slovak Republics," *RFE/RL Research Report*, no. 29, 16 July 1993.

[2] *Rude pravo*, 10 July 1993.

[3] The laws and presidential edicts adopted thus far reflect the tug-of-war between the president and the parliament that has been the main political drama of the past year. The parliament has passed more than a dozen new laws, drafted with the help of the Russian Ministry of Security, that appear to be aimed at shielding the past—including the pasts of the legislators—from public view, ostensibly for reasons of "collective repentance" and the protection of intelligence sources and methods. The president, for his part, has issued an edict making access to documentary evidence of totalitarian measures a discretionary power of the President's Office.

[4] The author participated in the conference as member of the organizing committee.

[5] *Moskovskie novosti*, no. 5,1993.

The proposed legislation would impose temporary restrictions on the political and professional activities of the following categories of former officials of the Communist Party of the Soviet Union (CPSU), the KGB, and KGB collaborators:

- Secretaries and members of the federal and republican committees of the CPSU;
- Secretaries of raion, oblast, and city party organizations;
- Full-time (*osvobozhdennye*) officials of the territorial and industrial organizations of the CPSU; the law would apply to those officials still in office at the time of the disbandment of the CPSU (6 November 1991) and also to those who had earlier held such positions for ten years or longer;
- Regular officers and reservists of the KGB Fifth Main Administration for Ideological Counterintelligence, whose responsibilities included political surveillance and taking repressive measures;
- KGB collaborators (secret informers) working for the Fifth Main Administration who had signed a cooperation agreement with the state security organs.

In introducing her proposal, Starovoitova stressed that it was "much milder" than corresponding legislation in Eastern Europe and the Baltic States. She also pointed out the differences between it and the denazification laws in postwar Germany and the *Berufsverbot*[6] legislation adopted by the Federal Republic of Germany in 1956, whose purpose was to prevent members of the officially prohibited German Communist Party from practicing certain professions. According to Starovoitova, her draft law is modeled on postwar Japanese legislation, which was intended to stimulate democratic institutions, not to punish war criminals.

Under the proposed legislation, people falling into the categories outlined above would be barred temporarily from being appointed or indirectly elected to positions of responsibility in government, from the raion and city to the national level. They would also be excluded from all positions in the educational and legal fields and from senior administrative and editorial posts in radio, television, and the press. Starovoitova emphasized, however, that all other professions and positions, including posts in the private and state economic sectors, would be open to them and that all their other rights, including the rights to vote and to travel, would be safeguarded. She proposed that the ban be lifted after ten years. Exempted from the ban would be former KGB agents and informants who had worked for other KGB administrations, such as those involved in foreign intelligence, eavesdropping, postal control, and surveillance.

As noted above, the draft is designed to encourage democratic institutions; therefore, it specifically exempts from the ban anyone directly

[6] A German word meaning a ban on certain professions.

elected to a position. In effect, no one who is directly elected, regardless of his past, is barred from holding office under the draft. Thus there would be no restrictions on, for example, former candidate member of the CPSU Politburo Yeltsin or any publicly identified former official of the KGB Fifth Main Administration who was voted into office in free and democratic elections.[7]

Draft Law Triggers Debate

In the lively debate that promptly followed the announcement of Democratic Russia's draft screening law, almost all major political groups (except the proposal's promulgators) found reasons to oppose it. Communists and hard-liners said that the law would completely paralyze Russia's intelligence community. State Security officials and intelligence veterans were concerned about the draft law's impact on civil rights, claiming that it could divide Russian society and unleash witch-hunts. Some prominent liberal critics questioned whether the law was necessary and whether the current regime, with all its holdovers from the past, had the moral authority to implement such legislation.

The newspaper *Pravda* and the weekly magazine *Glasnost*, both communist-aligned, accused the drafters of the proposed legislation and the organizers of the international conference on the KGB of being agents of influence of "Western secret services."[8] The nationalist *Sovetskaya Rossiya* of 30 May 1993 claimed that there was a concerted effort to disarm the Russian intelligence and secret services." The intelligence community, past and present, focused its criticism on the provisions of the draft law imposing restrictions on KGB veterans. Aleksei Kandaurov, the chief public relations officer for the Russian Ministry of Security, said that the adoption of the proposal could result in discrimination against former KGB officers solely on the basis of their official job descriptions, without there being any proof that they had acted improperly. His other argument was that screening the Ministry of Security's agents might undermine the ministry's cooperation with Western security services.[9] The KGB dissidents" Oleg Kalugin and Vladimir Rubanov, both retired KGB generals, did not object in principle to the law but argued that it would provoke an unnecessary backlash from the KGB and its political supporters.[10]

Former political prisoner Sergei Kovalev, chairman of the Supreme Soviet Committee for Human Rights, said that the draft screening law was unacceptable and potentially dangerous, because the screening process

---

7 Ironically, this means that in theory a former KGB officer could become president of Russia in the fall 1994 elections but would be prohibited from teaching in a kindergarten in Magadan or running trash collection services in Ekaterinburg until 2003.

8 *Pravda*, 30 May 1993; and Glasnost, no. 21, 1993.

9 Kandaurov's presentation to the conference and an interview with him on Ostankino Television, 11 June 1993.

10 Radio Rossiya, 30 May 1993; and Ostankino Television, 11 June 1993.

might divide Russian society into "the clean and the unclean."[11] He also commented that the draft law's proponents were trying in vain to define "the concrete qualities of totalitarianism." More germane, he said, was the concept of "national guilt, because every one of us, without exception, is guilty for what happened to us." Kovalev also argued that existing laws could be used to punish "unjust judges, investigators who falsify evidence, and former communist officials who committed misdeeds." Finally, he noted that barring unfit people from responsible positions required no law: Don't appoint and don't elect those you don't trust," he remarked. Vladimir Nadein, a senior editor of *Izvestiya*, noted that Eastern Europe's experience with lustration had had "horrible consequences" involving personal vendettas.[12] He also said that the potential for falsification "in the depths of the State Security" opened the door for injustice, since a former agent could present false evidence to prove his innocence or to accuse innocent people of having been agents. In practice, he added, the law would target rank-and-file agents and party officials while the senior ranks would "laugh it off." The movers and shakers of the former regime," he said, "have already become capitalists, and against them there are no sanctions [in the proposed legislation]." Aleksandr Tsypko, a political scientist, protested that Democratic Russia and representatives of the present government were being hypocritical in passing judgment on the former CPSU apparatus.[13] "Why should the leaders and ideologists of Democratic Russia, many of whom openly stated their commitment to Marxism and their respect for the Lenist guard, have the right to teach in the new, anticommunist Russia, whereas someone who once worked for the Agricultural Department of the CPSU, for example, would be denied that right?"[14]

One of the few to support the proposed legislation publicly was a former political prisoner, Boris Vail, who currently resides in Copenhagen. Refuting in a written statement the claim that the proposed screening law would infringe civil rights, Vail cited a German case concerning communist teachers that had been brought before the European Court for Human Rights in Strasbourg. The court had ruled that Germany had not contravened the European Convention on Human Rights in barring Communists from the teaching profession. He also took issue with Kovalev's statement that it was easy to bar unfit people from appointed or elected office. Especially in the case of appointments, Vail argued, some sort of shield was needed to prevent an unfit candidate from obtaining a post. The appointment process did not, he said, legitimize the candidate in the same way that a democratic election did.[15]

---

[11] *Moskovskie novosti*, no. 8, 1993.

[12] *Izvestiya*, 9 June 1993.

[13] *Moskovskie novosti*, no. 8, 1993.

[14] *Ibid.*

[15] *Ibid.*

KGB Documents Shed Light on Draft Law

The proposed draft screening law precisely defines the categories of people who would be subject to sanctions. But it will require much effort and research to identify such people and to determine how many in fact would be affected by the law.

Nomenklatura lists were a closely guarded secret under the Communists. After the collapse of the Soviet Union, however, a number of such lists were used as evidence in the hearings on Yeltsin's ban on the communist party and the constitutionality of the CPSU. The last nomenklatura list was approved on 7 August 1991, on the eve of the attempted coup; it named 7,000 top government, state, military, and KGB officials.[16] The *nomenklatura* lists provide important information about people in the top ranks of the KGB, whose appointments were subject to special procedures. All senior KGB administrative officers were *nomenklatura* of the Politburo, a designation that meant that their appointments required the approval of the Politburo and the CPSU general secretary. KGB officers with the rank of major general or higher who did not hold administrative positions had to be approved by the CPSU Central Committee; that is, they were *nomenklatura* of the CPSU Central Committee.

The lists will make the identification of members of the Fifth Main Administration's top ranks straightforward. Starovoitova's proposal, however, covers the entire administration, many of whose staffers did not belong to the *nomenklatura*; identifying all the agents and informants will be far from easy. There is no accepted estimate of the number of full-time, career KGB officers in the Filth Main Administration or of the huge pool of informants and other collaborators who would be subject to the proposed law's sanctions. Identifying career KGB officers poses less of a problem than identifying the agents and collaborators under their control, however. As government employees, the former had lengthy written records (payroll and pension information, promotions, and so on), which was not the case with the informants and other collaborators; their identities and activities were among the most closely guarded secrets of the former regime and still remain a closed book. Nevertheless, the publication of a number of top secret KGB documents has shed some light on KGB recruitment policies and groups of collaborators who would be subject to sanctions.

According to the 1983 Statute on the System of Agents and Trusted Persons of the Soviet KGB,[17] there were four main categories of KGB collaborators: agents (*agenty*), residents (*rezidenty*), keepers of safe houses or meeting places (*soderzhateli yavochnykh ili konspirativnykh kvartir*), and trustees (*doverennye litsa*). When the Politburo of the CPSU moved to reinstitute party control over the secret police after the death of Stalin,

---

[16] See *Vedomosti Sezda Narodnykh Deputatov i Verkhovnogo Soveta Rossiiskoi Federatsii*, no. 11, 1993, p. 672.

[17] The top secret statute was approved by the CPSU Central Commitee and the KGB Collegium and put into effect by Directive No. 00140 of the chairman of the Soviet KGB on 4 July 1983.

the execution of Lavrentii Beria was only part of the strategy. More significant was a measure adopted in 1954 forbidding the KGB to monitor or recruit as a collaborator any high-ranking member of the *nomenklatura*. Off limits were secretaries of party and Komsomol organizations, officials of the party apparatus, political officers of the Soviet armed forces, people's deputies, and trade union officials. The 1983 statute, which was amended in 1988, retained these recruitment and monitoring restrictions.[18] There were, however, no restrictions on the recruitment of rank-and-file CPSU members or anyone not belonging to the party. The statute also provided guidelines for cases in which low-ranking collaborators were eventually promoted to the inner circle of positions that were off limits to KGB recruiters: a KGB collaborator promoted by the CPSU to the *nomenklatura* ranks had to cut off working contacts with the KGB, except those maintained through officially approved party security channels.

Within the CPSU apparatus, covert activities similar to the KGB's conspiration, behind-the-scenes manipulation of events, disinformation, and the like also went on, but they were managed by the CPSU Central Committee Department of organizational Party Work and General Department rather than by the KGB. (The General Department was responsible for CPSU personnel and security.) These details became widely known when the Russian Constitutional Court handed down its verdict on the constitutionality of the CPSU on 30 November 1992. The verdict contained a blunt statement on what "democratic centralism" in fact meant: "The evidence in the case attests to the fact that, in the vast majority of matters, the leading bodies and top leaders of the CPSU engaged in covert activities that were kept from rank-and-file party members and often from senior party officials as well."[19]

In keeping with the division of covert activities between the party and the KGB, the latter concentrated on recruiting (non-*nomenklatura*) socially active and prominent members of the former Soviet establishment. Not surprisingly, the main target of the Fifth Main Administration, whose job it was to focus on ideological counterintelligence, was the Soviet intelligentsia. During public hearings on the KGB in Moscow in October 1992 and May 1993, numerous witnesses gave testimony on how the KGB had advanced its collaborators in the media, Church and academic circles, political parties, and public organizations.[20] In addition, in a number of articles former KGB officers defended and even praised their agents in the intelligentsia. For example, the former chief of the Bashkir KGB, Major General Vladimir Podelyakin, wrote in 1990: It is worth saying a few words to distinguish between our helpers and the stereotypical idea of the stool pigeon [*stukach*]. I must say frankly that we deeply respected those who provided us with their help. From my years of work in organs of the

---

[18] *Vestnik KGB SSSR*, no. 135, 1989, pp. 3-17. (*Vestnik* KGB SSSR was a top secret KGB in-house publication, disseminated only among KGB staffers.)

[19] *Vedomosti Sezda Narodnykh Deputatov i Verkhovnogo Soveta Rossiiskoi Federatsii*, no. 11, 1993, p. 671.

[20] "Yesterday, Today, and Tomorrow," report to the conference on the KGB; and *Pravozashchitnyi vestnik*, nos. 8 and 9, 1993.

KGB, I can remember in this group academicians, scientists, writers, and journalists. I am ready to bow to them: They are decent, honest, and conscientious people.[21]

To illustrate how effective the KGB's secret informers could be, Yurii Shchekochikhin, an investigative journalist, published a story about an engineer from Kazan, Leonid Vasilev, who in 1983 wrote several letters in support of Academician Andrei Salkharov, who at that time was in internal exile in Gorky.[22] Vasiiev addressed his letters to several scientific and cultural institutions and newspapers in order to mobilize the intelligentsia in defense of Sakharov. Although Vasilev signed different names to his letters, the KGB easily discovered his identity. In December 1983 he was arrested and sentenced to two years in a labor camp for anti-Soviet slander." It was later revealed that both the Soviet KGB and the Tatarstan KGB had received more than fifty reports from their secret informers about "anti-Soviet letters". The list of secret informers published by Shchekochikhin included the vice president of the Tatarstan division of the USSR Academy of Sciences, three professors, the director of a theater museum, and the head of a department at the daily *Izvestiya*. This case illustrates that the reality—specially in the 1980 sometimes belies the argument that KGB collaborators were coerced into cooperating and thus should be considered "victims" of the system and exempt from punishment. The documents presented by Shchekochikhin show that all the KGB collaborators who informed on Vasilev did so voluntarily, without pressure or intimidation from the KGB. The draft screening law's sanctions would presumably apply to those who helped send Vasilev to labor camp.

Legal Obstacles to Lustration

While the draft screening law was being quietly debated in Democratic Russia circles prior to being made public in May 1993, some laws on state security were passed that would complicate its implementation. A number of laws adopted over the past year make it a criminal offense to identify KGB collaborators. One, the law on Operative and Detective Activity, bans the exposure of witting agents of the KGB (Article 16).[23] Similarly, the Law on Federal Security Organs of the Russian Federation protects the covert status of persons cooperating with "state security organs" (Article 17).[24] Another piece of legislation, the Law on Foreign Intelligence, states that information about persons "confidentially cooperating" with the Russian Foreign Intelligence Service is a state secret accessible only to authorized officers of the service (Article 19).[25] Thus,

---

21 As cited in Yurii Vlasov, *Kto pravit bal?* [Who Calls the Tune?] (Moscow: Kedr, 1993), pp. 60-61.

22 Yurii Shchekochikhin in *Literaturnaya gazeta*, no. 22, 1990.

23 *Rossiiskaya gazeta*, 29 April 1992.

24 *Ibid.*, 12 August 1992.

25 *Ibid.*, 11 August 1992.

both *dejure* and *ex post facto*, the KGB's successors have inherited the security service's informants without serious discussion by lawmakers or the public. Former KGB and present Ministry of Security officers usually justify concealing a collaborator's identity by saying that no secret service in the world would reveal the names of its agents. They cite legislation in the United States, Canada, France, and Germany that bans the disclosure of the identities of secret informers.[26] Thus, if the screening law is to be passed, the parliament will have to write disclosure requirements applying specifically to the KGB Fifth Main Administration. To give the measure teeth, a disclosure would have to be made even if a former member of the administration or a former collaborator was working for another (still operative) branch of the security service. Otherwise, a simple transfer would provide a loophole.

The fate of lustration is also linked to the current political struggle between Yeltsin's administration and the legislature.... In view of the present internal struggle in the Russian parliament, it is unrealistic to expect that the proposed screening legislation will be adopted, particularly as it would bar from office members of the *nomenklatura* who were elected to the parliament on the list submitted by the communist party. The recent legislation on security issues suggests an attempt to shield from disclosure past misdeeds committed under communism. The best hope for the passage of the draft screening law lies in a political realignment favoring the reformers in the parliament.

---

[26] The former KGB is, however, very different from Western secret and security services. With all their shortcomings, Western security agencies never engaged in terror and repression to the extent that the KGB did. For example, even at the height of the Cold War, the US Federal Bureau of Investigation did not interfere in the daily lives of most US citizens; the USSR KGB and its satellite organizations in Eastern Europe, however, organized all-encompassing political surveillance of their citizens. In the Soviet Union, virtually every adult was put under pressure by the KGB on at least one occasion. One reason why the KGB was so omnipresent was its armada of secret informers. It should also be remembered that neither US nor French society has a legacy of totalitarianism to overcome.

21

LITHUANIA

EDITOR'S INTRODUCTION

After more than one hundred years of Russian rule, Lithuania achieved independence following World War I. Sovereignty proved short-lived, however. In August 1939, Germany and the Soviet Union signed the Molotov-Ribbentrop Nonaggression Pact, a secret protocol which assigned Lithuania and its Baltic neighbors to the Soviet sphere of influence. Without fear of German reprisal, the Soviet army occupied Lithuania on June 15, 1940. Staged elections installed a subservient Communist-dominated parliament which promptly petitioned for incorporation of Lithuania into the USSR; Moscow declared Lithuania a constituent republic on August 3, 1940. During this period, the Soviets deported more than 35,000 Lithuanians to Siberia and executed some 5,000.

Germany attacked the USSR in June 1941 and occupied Lithuania. By October 1944, Soviet forces recaptured Lithuania. Nearly 80,000 Lithuanians fled to the West and another 60,000 were sent to Siberia. A harsh program of Sovietization and Russification included the dissolution of all noncommunist organizations, cultural, religious and linguistic repression, and the swift punishment of any opposition. To accomplish the forced collectivization of agriculture, 60,000 more Lithuanians were deported to Siberia and northern Russia during March 24-27, 1949.

The thaw which followed Stalin's death in 1953 brought a reduction of political terror. Repression of Lithuanian culture and language was somewhat relaxed. During much of the subsequent period of Soviet rule, Lithuania was able to maintain a higher standard of living relative to other Soviet republics. Nevertheless, persecution of Lithuanian nationalists, the Catholic Church, and human rights advocates continued along with severe restrictions on freedoms of speech, press, and assembly. Directed from Moscow, the Communist Party controlled all activity including that of the judiciary. Soviet troops maintained a significant presence in Lithuania, and the KGB and police enforced repressive rule.

In the late 1980s, as a period of reform and liberalization unfolded under Soviet leader Mikhail Gorbachev, a renewed sense of nationalism gained strength in Lithuania, displayed in public demonstrations and in the mass media. In 1988, the formation of independent political groups was permitted. Most prominent among them was the Lithuanian Movement for Support of Perestroika, Sajudis, which called for autonomy from the Soviet Union. Vytautas Landsbergis was elected its president.

On May 19, 1989, the parliament (Supreme Council) declared Lithuanian sovereignty and the supremacy of Lithuanian law over Soviet law. On August 23, two million people formed a 370-mile chain from the capital, Vilnius, to the Latvian and Estonian capitals in a call for Baltic independence. In December, a multiparty political system was adopted and the Lithuanian Communist Party split from its Soviet parent. In February 1990, in relatively free elections for parliament, Sajudis won an overwhelming majority. Shortly thereafter, Landsbergis was elected head of state and Kazimiera Prunskiene of Sajudis was elected prime minister.

On March 11, 1990, Lithuania declared its independence. The Soviets responded by seizing Communist Party buildings in Vilnius and cutting off shipments of oil, gas, and other raw materials. In exchange for Soviet-Lithuanian talks and a lifting of this economic embargo, the Supreme Council temporarily suspended the declaration of independence. The resulting talks made little progress. Instead, from January 11-13, 1991, Soviet troops seized the Press House in Vilnius, Defense Department buildings in several other cities, and the Lithuanian television station and tower. Fourteen Lithuanians were killed at the tower; hundreds were injured. Tensions continued between Moscow and Vilnius.

Following the failed August 1991 coup attempt against the Soviet leadership, Soviet power structures began to falter. Much of the international community granted diplomatic recognition to independent Lithuania, Latvia, and Estonia. Finally, on September 6, 1991, the Soviet Union formally recognized the independence of the three Baltic states.

After independence, concern over previous collaboration by Lithuanian officials with the Soviet secret police became a highly charged political issue. On November 12, 1991, the government decreed that former KGB employees and informers could not hold local or national government posts for five years. Those holding such positions were required to resign by the end of the year. A December 1991 law created a parliamentary commission (known as the Gajauskas Commission for its chairman) to investigate collaboration with the KGB by elected representatives. Among those accused by the Commission were former Prime Minister Prunskiene and Deputy Vergilijus Cepaitis, a close associate of Landsbergis and an advocate of decommunization.

In advance of the October 1992 parliamentary elections, all candidates were required to declare whether they had ever been connected with the

KGB, other state security services, or the Communist Party. In November, the Supreme Court overruled a post-election effort to withhold parliamentary credentials from the newly elected legislators pending their investigation by the Gajauskas Commission for KGB ties.

Screening of collaborators was complicated by the KGB's earlier removal of much of its Lithuanian files to Russia. Following extensive negotiations with Russia, return of these files began in 1992. One shipment alone, a small portion of the total files, consisted of 2,400 boxes containing 31,241 screening files and 11,558 interrogation files. In November 1992, parliament declared the KGB files to be part of the Lithuanian "national heritage," barring their destruction or removal from the country. In 1993, partly on the basis of these records, the government issued warrants for the arrest of several individuals allegedly responsible for the January 1991 Vilnius crackdown.

A 1991 decree ordered that property of the Lithuanian Communist Party and affiliated organizations be confiscated. By mid-1992, the government had filed more than eighty lawsuits for the return of such property. A 1991 law on property restitution enabled former owners or their heirs to petition for rehabilitation of property nationalized during Communist rule. Based on the nature of the property involved, claimants would receive the actual property, a property of equivalent value, or financial compensation.

Concurrent with these efforts, the political pendulum swung away from full-scale decommunization. Having achieved their common goal of Lithuanian independence, the various factions within Sajudis began to splinter. A deteriorating economy under the Sajudis-led government also reduced public confidence in the party. As a result, the Lithuanian Democratic Labour Party (LDLP)—successor to the now-banned Communist Party—won the parliamentary election of October 25, 1992 by a large margin. LDLP leader Algirdas Brazauskas was elected chairman of the Supreme Council, replacing Landsbergis. On February 14, 1993, Brazauskas was elected president of Lithuania.

The following documents related to transitional justice in Lithuania can be found in Volume III of this collection:

- Decree Banning KGB Employees and Informers from Government Positions
- Law on the Verification of Mandates of Those Deputies Accused of Consciously Collaborating with Special Services of Other States
- Law and Implementing Resolution on the Restoration of Property

THE PURGE OF SECURITY AGENTS AND COLLABORATORS

Józef Darski, "Police Agents In The Transition Period"[*]

On November 12, [1991,] the Lithuanian government declared that:

> Former KGB employees and informers will not be permitted, for a period of five years, to hold ministerial positions in the government of the Republic of Lithuania, directorships of departments and other state services and inspectorates, and managerial positions in the basic units of the ministerial structure and in local and regional government.
>
> Former KGB employees and informers who currently hold the positions mentioned above must resign by January 1, 1992.
>
> ...those who are collaborating with the structures of the KGB should be informed that such activity will henceforth be regarded as a state crime, and that they will be punished in accordance with the law.

The government did show mercy: it offered an amnesty for all former KGB collaborators who reported to the police. But those who failed to do so are to be deprived of their positions and have their names made public.

The KGB archives in Vilnius [had] been plundered; the files in provincial KGB branches, however, [were] put under safekeeping and remain largely intact. The parliamentary commission appointed to investigate the matter believes that it will be possible to reconstruct the lost lists of collaborators on the basis of the documentation of criminal cases against members of the political opposition, since these files contain information provided by informers.

Józef Darski, "Decommunization: The Case of Lithuania"[†]

[The Law and Procedures]

On December 17, 1991, the Supreme Council (Seimas) passed legislation to "verify the mandates of deputies suspected of conscious collaboration with the security services of other states." The legislation was based on the premise that voters had the right to know whether a candidate for parliament or local council had collaborated with the KGB or other Soviet intelligence, military or police services. The Seimas did not, however, pass a proposed overall decommunization bill.

---

[*] Excerpted from Józef Darski, "Police Agents In The Transition Period," *Uncaptive Minds*, vol. IV, no. 4(18) (Winter 1991-92), pp. 27-28.

[†] Excerpted from Józef Darski, "Decommunization: The Case of Lithuania," *Uncaptive Minds*, vol. VI, no. 1 (Winter-Spring 1993), pp. 78-81.

Under the adopted procedures, a parliamentary commission had the power to question elected representatives to parliament and to local and regional councils who were accused of collaboration with the KGB or other services. An accused representative was allowed to review any evidence against him and to explain his actions to the parliamentary commission. After evaluating the evidence, the commission informed the accused of its conclusions. If the representative accepted the commission's conclusion, the commission passed on its findings to the parliament or to the relevant regional or local council. If the representative objected to the commission's conclusions, the case was passed to the Supreme Court, in the case of a parliamentary deputy, or to the relevant regional court in the case of a local or regional council member. The court had the power to affirm or reject a parliamentary commission's findings of collaboration.

Upon notice of the commission's or the court's findings, the relevant elected body was obligated to call for a recall election in the given representative's district, to be held within thirty days of formal notice, with that electoral seat's mandate suspended until the election. The ballot required the following statement: "Having learned of Deputy [X's] collaboration with the KGB [or other branch of the security services], I vote to affirm/to annul his mandate." A representative's reaffirmation would require at least half of the registered voters deciding in his favor. (Thus, not voting is a vote against). At any stage in the process, of course, the deputy can choose to resign.

"Collaboration" is defined as any act of collaboration following [the Soviet invasion of Lithuania on] June 15, 1940, or employment in the security services, or serving these services in other ways as evidenced by lists of collaborators of the security services, or by appearing in documents that prove a given individual had worked for the security services or had consciously and systematically supplied the security services with information on at least two occasions.

On February 28, 1992, the Seimas broadened the jurisdiction of the Temporary Commission of the Supreme Council to investigate collaboration with the KGB and other services in Lithuania and to expand the scope of inquiry to include parliamentary members of each party and caucus.

The commission, commonly known by the name of its chairman, Balys Gajauskas, was established after the Lithuanian government took control of the KGB headquarters in Vilnius following the August 1991 coup attempt. It began work in February 1992 and has investigated several members of parliament.

[Major Cases]

The first major case erupted when the Gajauskas Commission established that Deputy Vergilijus Cepaitis—one of President Landsbergis' closest associates—had collaborated with the KGB. Notified of the commission's finding, the Supreme Council ordered that an election be held in Cepaitis's district. Only 11% of the eligible citizens voted, and a majority of those voting annulled his parliamentary mandate. Cepaitis, proclaiming innocence of wrongdoing, claimed that information he gave the KGB had not caused any harm. He nonetheless lost his seat in parliament and, in late May, his position as chairman of the Independence Party.

On May 12, the Gajauskas Commission declared that Deputy Jakubas Minkevicius had worked for the security services during the Second World War. Initially, Minkevicius claimed that he had merely served in the army, a fact the voters in his district were aware of. The Gajauskas Commission demonstrated, however, that Minkevicius had served in the NKVD, the predecessor of the KGB, and that even after the war he had participated in the "struggle against banditry," that is, the suppression of the Lithuanian partisan movement. The commission also found a document signed by Minkevicius ordering the arrest and execution of an individual suspected of helping the partisans. The Supreme Council, by a vote of eighty nine to ten, confirmed the findings, and Minkevicius resigned, foregoing any electoral challenge.

The Gajauskas Commission also found that Vladimir Berezov, the number two man in the Lithuanian Democratic Labor Party (LDLP), the reformed communist party, had been a collaborator. Berezov claimed he served only as a translator during his employment with the KGB, 1948-49. But most people had not been aware of Berezov's employment with the KGB in any capacity. His case went to the Supreme Court on July 8, 1992.

The most notorious case followed. On July 23, Eduardas Vilkas, one of the founders of the Liberal party grouping that had allied itself with the communists against Landsbergis, and the former Prime Minister Kazimiera Prunskiene both came before parliament to defend themselves against the temporary commission's charges of collaboration. Prunskiene denied any collaboration despite clear evidence presented by the Commission, which included her original declaration of cooperation and "work notebooks" on her activities, both of which were found within the security services' files. The declaration, signed in 1980, had already been published in the newspaper *Amzius* on April 30, 1992. On May 8, *Lietvos Aidas* published official reports by the head of the Lithuanian branch of the KGB, General A.S. Caplinas, sent to the head of the all-Soviet KGB, Vladimir Kryuchkov, in which he describes Prunskiene's efforts to keep Lithuania in the Soviet Union. Upon Prunskiene's appeal, the Supreme Court reviewed her case and, on September 17, 1992, confirmed that she had been a collaborator of the KGB.

[KGB Files and Agents]

While the KGB had taken the files on its collaborators and other material to Moscow, it left behind the files on the individuals it had investigated. The file of a person under investigation would also include the name of the informer or informers who had provided information. The KGB also left behind copies of the reports prepared for its director, Vladimir Kryuchkov, and its highly detailed "work notebooks." Painstaking study of these documents disclosed the network of informers and agents active in Lithuania. The *Lietuvos Aidas* published these documents in a section called "The Spider's Web." Readers could easily identify agents and informers, who thought that all documents compromising them must have been taken to Moscow. According to P. Varanauskas, a member of Gajauskas Commission, many people came to confess their collaboration to the commission, hoping to avoid blackmail. (*Lietuvos Aidas* has agreed to refrain from publishing information that compromises those volunteering such confessions.)

In the spring of 1992, *Lietvos Aidas* published a series of reports based on KGB records from 1988 to 1991 on the activities of an agent code-named "Kliugeris." According to documents in the Gajauskas Commission's possession, this agent last met with members of the security services a month before the August 1991 coup attempt. At the time, he was serving Prime Minister Prunskiene as an advisor on foreign affairs and he later became a leader of the LDLP. Kliugeris was recommending to the KGB and its agents in the West that it withdraw support form Prunskiene and stop promoting her in the West because her influence and power in Lithuania were declining. Kliugeris was also active in the European Parliament in Strasbourg, where he formed the Baltic Group and tried to delay diplomatic recognition of independent Lithuania. (The documents show that resolutions the Baltic Group proposed to the European Parliament were first cleared with the KGB). From the records, Kliugeris has been identified as Algis Klimaitis. A Lithuanian born in Hamburg, Klimaitis became involved in opposition activities during the 1980s. After his connection with the KGB was discovered, he was arrested by the Lithuanian authorities, making Lithuania the only country that has dared to bring KGB agents to justice. KGB agents who signed declarations stating that they will not work against Lithuania and who resigned from the KGB before March 11, 1991 are not being pursued by the authorities.

The Gajauskas Commission is preparing a report on its work for the newly elected parliament, in which the names will be revealed of all deputies who are still collaborating with the KGB.

In the wake of these revelations, the Lithuanian parliament decided also to bar all KGB collaborators from high government or elected positions. On July 8, 1992, parliament passed a law governing candidates for elective offices, requiring all candidates to declare whether they knowingly collaborated with the security services of other states. Any elected representative discovered to have lied will be removed from office. The Gajauskas Commission has the responsibility of confirming the loyalty of candidates and of disclosing the names of elected officials who had been collaborators. Unfortunately, in May, the Supreme Council rejected a fuller decommunization law that would have barred a much broader category of collaborators with the secret services and the communist party, as well as their employees and appointed functionaries, from service in sensitive government or state economic posts and, more importantly, any of Lithuania's newly formed armed forces or police services.

AUTHOR INDEX

Volume I: General Considerations

Contents

Volume III: Laws, Rulings, and Reports

Contents

United States Institute of Peace

The United States Institute of Peace is an independent, nonpartisan federal institution established by Congress to promote research, education, and training on the peaceful resolution of international conflicts. Established in 1984, the Institute meets its congressional mandate through an array of programs, including research grants, fellowships, professional training programs, conferences and workshops, library services, publications, and other educational activities. The Institute's Board of Directors is appointed by the President of the United States and confirmed by the Senate.